KT-169-193

INTRODUCTION

A Tour of the World **Chapter 1**
A Tour of the Book **Chapter 2**

THE CORE

The Short Run (IS-LM)

The Goods Market **Chapter 3**
Financial Markets **Chapter 4**
Goods and Financial Markets: The *IS-LM* Model **Chapter 5**

The Medium Run (AS-AD)

The Labor Market **Chapter 6**
Putting All Markets Together: The *AS-AD* Model **Chapter 7**
The Natural Rate of Unemployment and The Phillips Curve **Chapter 8**
Inflation, Activity, and Nominal Money Growth **Chapter 9**

The Long Run

The Facts of Growth **Chapter 10**
Saving, Capital Accumulation, and Output **Chapter 11**
Technological Progress and Growth **Chapter 12**
Technological Progress, Wages, and Unemployment **Chapter 13**

EXTENSIONS

EXPECTATIONS

Expectations: The Basic Tools **Chapter 14**
Financial Markets and Expectations **Chapter 15**
Expectations, Consumption, and Investment **Chapter 16**
Expectations, Output, and Policy **Chapter 17**

THE OPEN ECONOMY

Openness in Goods and Financial Markets **Chapter 18**
The Goods Market in an Open Economy **Chapter 19**
Output, the Interest Rate, and the Exchange Rate **Chapter 20**
Exchange Rate Regimes **Chapter 21**

PATHOLOGIES

Slumps and Depressions **Chapter 22**
High Inflation **Chapter 23**

BACK TO POLICY

Should Policy Makers Be Restrained? **Chapter 24**
Monetary Policy: A Summing Up **Chapter 25**
Fiscal Policy: A Summing Up **Chapter 26**

EPILOGUE

The Story of Macroeconomics **Chapter 27**

To the Student:

If your textbook did not come bundled with the *"Active Graphs CD-ROM to Accompany MACRO-ECONOMICS, 3/e,"* you may order it for purchase separately through your bookstore using this ISBN: 0-13-100501-4. The CD-ROM contains 44 Active Graphs which correspond to important figures in the text. With each graph, you can change certain variables and see the effects on the equilibrium.

ACTIVE GRAPH (AG)	FIGURE NUMBER AND PAGE NUMBER	TITLE
AG1	Review	Curves, which way do they shift?
AG2	Review	Adjacent or stacked graphs
AG3	Chapter 2 Appendix	Real vs. Nominal GDP
AG4	3-2, 3-3, page 54	The determination of equilibrium output
AG5	Page 55	Introduction to econometrics
AG6	4-2, 4-3, 4-4, pages 73, 74, 76	Interest rate determination in the money market
AG7	5-3, page 91	IS curve
AG8	5-4, page 92	Shifts of the IS curve
AG9	5-6, page 95	LM curve
AG10	5-7, page 95	Shifts of the LM curve
AG11	5-9, page 98	IS/LM: effects of a tax increase
AG12	5-10, page 101	IS/LM: effects of monetary expansion
AG13	Page 102	IS/LM: Clinton-Greenspan mix and policy coordination
AG14	5-11, page 105	IS/LM and dynamic effects of monetary contraction
AG15	6-6, page 125	The wage and price setting relations
AG16	6-7, page 127	The natural rate of unemployment
AG17	7-3, page 140	The derivation of aggregate demand
AG18	7-6, page 143	Equilibrium output and prices in the short run and long run
AG19	7-7, 7-8, pages 145, 146	The dynamic effects of monetary expansion on output, interest rates, and prices
AG20	7-9, 7-10, pages 150, 151	The dynamic effects of a decrease in the budget deficit on output, interest rates, and prices
AG21	7-11, 7-12, pages 153, 154	The dynamic effects of an increase in the price of oil
AG22	8-3, page 165	Phillips curve graph with expectations
AG23	10-5, page 214	Production function and sources of growth
AG24	11-2, page 224	Capital and output dynamics
AG25	11-3, page 227	The effects of different savings rates
AG26	12-2, page 246	Dynamics of capital and output per effective worker
AG27	13-2, page 270	The effect of an increase in productivity on output in the short run
AG28	13-4, page 273	The effect of productivity growth on the natural rate of unemployment
AG29	14-5, page 301	The short run effect of an increase in money growth with expectations
AG30	14-5, page 301	The medium run effect of an increase in money growth
AG31	15-3, 15-4, page 318	The U.S. economy from November 1, 2000 to June 1, 2001
AG32	15-7, 15-8, pages 323, 324	The stock market response to expansionary monetary policy and increases in consumption spending
AG33	17-3, 17-4, pages 361, 362	The new IS/LM with expectations: monetary expansion
AG34	17-5, page 365	The new IS/LM with expectations: deficit reduction
AG35	19-3, page 401	Equilibrium output and net exports: increase government spending
AG36	19-4, page 402	Equilibrium output and net exports: increase foreign demand
AG37	19-5, page 407	Reducing the trade deficit without changing output
AG38	20-3, page 424	The IS/LM model in the open economy: government spending
AG39	20-4, page 425	The IS/LM model in the open economy: monetary contraction
AG40	20-5, page 430	The effects of a fiscal expansion under fixed exchange rates
AG41	21-1, 21-2, page 441	AS-AD in an open economy: adjustment to potential output with and without a devaluation
AG42	22-5, page 470	IS/LM: Effects of a Monetary Expansion in the presence of a Liquidity Trap
AG43	22-7, page 472	The Great Depression and the IS/LM
AG44	Page 544	The practice of monetary policy: a model of the reserve market

Macroeconomics

Third Edition

Prentice Hall Series in Economics

Adams/Brock, *The Structure of American Industry,* Tenth Edition
Blanchard, *Macroeconomics,* Third Edition
Blau/Ferber/Winkler, *The Economics of Women, Men, and Work,* Fourth Edition
Boardman/Greenberg/Vining/Weimer, *Cost Benefit Analysis: Concepts and Practice,* Second Edition
Bogart, *The Economics of Cities and Suburbs*
Case/Fair, *Principles of Economics,* Sixth Edition
Case/Fair, *Principles of Macroeconomics,* Sixth Edition
Case/Fair, *Principles of Microeconomics,* Sixth Edition
Caves, *American Industry: Structure, Conduct, Performance,* Seventh Edition
Colander/Gamber, *Macroeconomics*
Collinge/Ayers, *Economics by Design: Principles and Issues,* Second Edition
Eaton/Eaton/Allen, *Microeconomics,* Fifth Edition
DiPasquale/Wheaton, *Urban Economics and Real Estate Markets*
Folland/Goodman/Stano, *Economics of Health and Health Care,* Third Edition
Fort, *Sports Economics*
Froyen, *Macroeconomics: Theories and Policies,* Seventh Edition
Greene, *Econometric Analysis,* Fifth Edition
Heilbroner/Milberg, *The Making of Economic Society,* Eleventh Edition
Hess, *Using Mathematics in Economic Analysis*
Heyne/Boettke/Prychitko, *The Economic Way of Thinking,* Tenth Edition
Keat/Young, *Managerial Economics,* Fourth Edition
Lynn, *Economic Development: Theory and Practice for a Divided World*
Mathis/Koscianski, *Microeconomic Theory: An Integrated Approach*
Milgrom/Roberts, *Economics, Organization, and Management*
O'Sullivan/Sheffrin, *Economics: Principles and Tools,* Third Edition
O'Sullivan/Sheffrin, *Macroeconomics: Principles and Tools,* Third Edition
O'Sullivan/Sheffrin, *Microeconomics: Principles and Tools,* Third Edition
O'Sullivan/Sheffrin, *Survey of Economics: Principles and Tools*
Petersen/Lewis, *Managerial Economics,* Fifth Edition
Pindyck/Rubinfeld, *Microeconomics,* Fifth Edition
Reynolds/Masters/Moser, *Labor Economics and Labor Relations,* Eleventh Edition
Roberts, *The Choice: A Fable of Free Trade and Protectionism,* Revised
Schiller, *The Economics of Poverty and Discrimination,* Eighth Edition
Weidenbaum, *Business and Government in the Global Marketplace,* Sixth Edition

Macroeconomics

Third Edition

Olivier Blanchard
Massachusetts Institute of Technology

Pearson Education International

Credits and acknowledgments borrowed from other sources and reproduced, with permission, in this textbook appear on appropriate page within text.

Executive Editor: Rod Banister
Editor-in-Chief: P. J. Boardman
Senior Development Editor: Mike Elia
Managing Editor: Gladys Soto
Assistant Editor: Marie McHale
Editorial Assistant: Lisa Amato
Project Manager, Media: Victoria Anderson
Executive Marketing Manager: Kathleen McLellan
Marketing Assistant: Christopher Bath
Managing Editor (Production): Cynthia Regan
Production Editor: Michael Reynolds
Production Assistant: Dianne Falcone
Permissions Supervisor: Suzanne Grappi
Associate Director, Manufacturing: Vinnie Scelta
Art Director: Kevin Kall
Interior Design: Karen Quigley
Cover Design: Kevin Kall
Cover Illustration/Photo: Artville
Manager, Print Production: Christy Mahon
Print production Liaison: Ashley Scattergood
Composition: Progressive Information Technologies
Full-Service Project Management: Progressive Publishing Alternatives
Printer/Binder: Courier/Kendallville

Pearson Education LTD.
Pearson Education Australia PTY, Limited
Pearson Education Singapore, Pte. Ltd
Pearson Education North Asia Ltd
Pearson Education, Canada, Ltd
Pearson Educación de Mexico, S.A. de C.V.
Pearson Education–Japan
Pearson Education Malaysia, Pte. Ltd
Pearson Education Upper Saddle River, New Jersey

10 9 8 7 6
ISBN 0-13-110301-6

A Noelle

About the Author

Olivier Blanchard is the Class of 1941 Professor of Economics at MIT. He is also Chairman of the Department of Economics at MIT. He did his undergraduate work in France, and received a Ph.D. in economics from MIT in 1977. He taught at Harvard from 1977 to 1982, and has taught at MIT since 1983. He has frequently received the award for best teacher in the department of economics.

He has done research on many macroeconomic issues, from the effects of fiscal policy, to the role of expectations, to price rigidities, to speculative bubbles, to unemployment in Western Europe, and more recently transition in Eastern Europe. He has done work for many governments and many international organizations, including the *World Bank*, the *IMF*, the *OECD*, the *EU Commission*, and the *EBRD*. He has published over 150 articles and edited or written over 15 books, including *Lectures on Macroeconomics* with Stanley Fischer.

He is a research associate of the National Bureau of Economic Research, a fellow and a council member of the Econometric Society, a member of the American Academy of Arts and Sciences, and a past Vice President of the American Economic Association. He is also a member of the French Council of Economic Advisers.

He lives in Cambridge, with his wife, Noelle. He has three daughters, Marie, Serena, and Giulia.

Brief Contents

Contents

Boxes

Preface

I had two main goals in writing this book:

- To make close contact with current macroeconomic events.

  What makes macroeconomics exciting is the light it sheds on what is happening around the world, from the introduction of the Euro in Western Europe, to the current U.S. recession, to the Japanese slump, to the economic and political crisis in Argentina. These events—and many more—are described in the book, not in footnotes, but in the text or in detailed boxes. Each box shows how you can use what you have learned to get an understanding of these events. My belief is that these boxes not only convey the "life" of macroeconomics, but also reinforce the lessons from the models, making them more concrete and easier to grasp.

- To provide an integrated view of macroeconomics.

  The book is built on one underlying model, a model that concentrates on the implications of equilibrium conditions in three sets of markets: the goods market, the financial markets, and the labor market. Depending on the issue at hand, the parts of the model relevant to the issue are developed in more detail while the other parts are simplified or lurk in the background. But the underlying model is always the same. This way, you will see macroeconomics as a coherent whole, not a collection of models. And you will be able to make sense not only of past macroeconomic events, but also of those that unfold in the future.

Changes

The response to the first two editions, in the United States and around the world, has shown that there is a large demand for such an approach. At the same time, feedback from instructors and from students has led to a number of important changes since the first edition.

- The main change from the first to the second edition was in the architecture of the book. I reorganized the book into two parts: A core, and a set of three major extensions.

  The core focused on the behavior of the economy in the short run, the medium run, and the long run.

  The three extensions focused on the role of expectations, on the implications of openness, and on pathologies—times of very high inflation, or times of very high unemployment.

  The response to this new organization in the second edition has been very positive, and I have kept it in this third edition, with only a few minor changes: I have eliminated one chapter on pathologies, allocating some of its content to other chapters. Two chapters are largely new: Chapter 22 examines the economic slump in Japan. Chapter 21 focuses on the implications of different exchange rate regimes.

- The main focus of revisions for this third edition has been on simplification.

  The truth: Macroeconomics is hard. It is hard because it is about understanding what economists call "general equilibrium." In thinking about what happens to the economy, you must keep in mind all at the same time, what happens in the labor market, what happens in the goods market, and what happens in financial markets. One way of writing a macroeconomics text is to hide these complexities, taking different "convenient" approaches when looking at different topics. This way makes for a textbook which may be easy to read, not a textbook you can use to understand events other than the events you read about in the text. As you may suspect, this is not the route I have taken. And so, because I did not want to take these intellectual shortcuts, I have had to work hard to make the arguments as simple as they could be.

  In the second edition, I introduced margin notes running in parallel to the text. These notes serve many purposes: to emphasize an important point, to help you follow a derivation, to relate an argument to an earlier one, to summarize a series of steps, to give a related fact, or to tell a related anecdote. My hope was that these notes would make reading the book and learning from it much easier. The reaction has been extremely positive, and you will find margin notes again in this third edition.

To simplify further, I prepared for this third edition by putting together a team of students and giving them a simple mandate: Look at each argument in the book; tell me if it feels hard or confusing; tell me how it could be presented more simply. Their work has led to a nearly complete rewrite of the book. The architecture of the book is the same. But the book is very different in the small, that is, in the way things are discussed, explained, and illustrated. The arguments are, I believe, simpler and easier to grasp.

Organization

The book is organized around two central parts: A core, and a set of three major extensions. An introduction precedes the core. The set of extensions is followed by a review of the role of policy. The book ends with an epilogue. A flowchart on the front end paper makes it easy to see how the chapters are organized, and fit the book's overall structure.

- Chapters 1 and 2 introduce the basic facts and issues of macroeconomics. Chapter 1 offers a tour of the world, from the United States, to Europe, to Japan. Some instructors will prefer to cover it later, perhaps after Chapter 2, which introduces basic concepts, articulates the notions of short run, medium run, and long run, and gives a quick tour of the book.

  While Chapter 2 gives the basics of national income accounting, I have put a detailed treatment of national income accounts to Appendix 1 at the end of the book. This decreases the burden on the beginning reader, and allows for a more thorough treatment in the appendix.

- Chapters 3 to 13 constitute the **core**.

  Chapters 3 to 5 focus on the **short run**. These three chapters characterize equilibrium in the goods market and in the financial markets, and they derive the basic model used to study short-run movements in output, the *IS-LM* model.

  Chapters 6 to 9 focus on the **medium run**. Chapter 6 focuses on equilibrium in the labor market and introduces the notion of the natural rate of unemployment. Chapters 7 to 9 develop a model based on aggregate demand and aggregate supply, and show how that model can be used to understand movements in activity and movements in inflation, both in the short and in the medium run.

  Chapters 10 to 13 focus on the **long run**. Chapter 10 describes the facts, showing the evolution of output across countries and over long periods of time. Chapters 11 and 12 develop a model of growth, focusing on the determinants of capital accumulation and technological progress and the role of each in growth. Chapter 13, which is optional, focuses on the effects of technological progress not only in the long run, but also in the short run and in the medium run. This topic is typically not covered in textbooks but is important. And the chapter shows how one can integrate the short run, the medium run, and the long run—an example of the payoff of an integrated approach to macroeconomics.

- Chapters 14 to 24 cover the three major **extensions**.

  Chapters 14 to 17 focus on the role of **expectations** in the short run and in the medium run. Expectations play a major role in most economic decisions, and, by implication, play a major role in the determination of output.

  Chapters 18 to 21 focus on the implications of the **openness** of modern economies. Chapter 21, which is largely new, focuses on the implications of different exchange rate regimes, from flexible exchange rates, to fixed exchange rates, to currency boards, to dollarization.

  Chapters 22 and 23 focus on **pathologies**, times when (macroeconomic) things go very wrong. Chapter 22 looks at depressions and slumps. Much of the chapter, from the discussion of the dangers of deflation and the liquidity trap to the analysis of Japan's economic slump, is new. Chapter 23 looks at episodes of hyperinflation.

- Chapters 24 to 26 return to macroeconomic **policy**. While most of the first 23 chapters constantly discuss macroeconomic policy in one form or another, the purpose of Chapters 24 to 26 is to tie the threads together. Chapter 24 looks at the role and the limits of macroeconomic policy in general. Chapters 25 and 26 review monetary policy and fiscal policy. Much of Chapter 26 is devoted to recent developments in monetary policy, from inflation targeting to interest rate rules. Some instructors may want to use parts of these chapters earlier. For example, it is easy to move forward the discussion of the government budget constraint in Chapter 26.

- Chapter 27 serves as an **epilogue**; it puts macroeconomics in historical perspective, showing the evolution of macroeconomics in the last 60 years and discussing current directions of research.

Alternative Course Outlines

Within the book's broad organization, there is plenty of opportunity for alternative course organizations. I have made the chapters shorter than is standard in textbooks, and, in my experience, most chapters can be covered in an hour and a half. A few (Chapters 5 and 7 for example) may require two lectures to sink in.

- Short courses (15 lectures or less)

  A short course can be organized around the two introductory chapters and the core. Leaving aside Chapters 9 and 13 gives a total of 11 lectures. Informal presentations of one or two of the extensions, based for example on Chapter 17 for expectations (which can be taught as a stand alone) and on Chapter 18 for the open economy, can then follow, for a total of 13 lectures.

  A short course may leave out the study of growth (the long run). In this case, the course can be organized around the introductory chapters, and Chapters 3 to 8 in the core; this gives a total of 8 lectures, leaving enough time to cover, for example, Chapter 17 on expectations, Chapters 18 to 20 on the open economy, and Chapter 22 on depressions and slumps, for a total of 13 lectures.

- Longer courses (20 to 25 lectures)

  A full semester course gives more than enough time to cover the core, plus at least two extensions, and the review of policy.

  The extensions assume knowledge of the core, but are otherwise mostly self contained. Given the choice, the order in which they are best taught is probably the order in which they are presented in the book. Starting with the study of the role of expectations is useful, for example, in understanding the interest parity condition and the nature of exchange rate crises.

  One of the choices facing instructors is likely to be whether to teach growth (the long run) or not. If growth is taught, there may not be enough time to cover all three extensions and have a thorough discussion of policy. In this case, it may be best to leave out the study of pathologies. If growth is not taught, there should be time to cover most of the other topics in the book.

Features

I have made sure never to present a theoretical result without relating it to the real world. In addition to discussions of facts in the text itself, I have written a large number of **Focus** boxes, which discuss particular macroeconomic events or facts, from the United States or from around the world.

I have tried to recreate some of the student-teacher interactions that take place in the classroom by the use of **Margin notes** running parallel to the text. The margin notes create a dialogue with the reader, to smooth the more difficult passages, and to give a deeper understanding of the concepts and the results derived along the way.

For students who want to explore macroeconomics further, I have introduced the following two features:

- **Short appendices** to some chapters, which expand on a point made within the chapter.
- **Further readings** section at the end of each chapter, indicating where to find more information, including a number of key Internet addresses.

Each chapter ends with three ways of making sure that the material in the chapter has been digested:

- A **summary** of the chapter's main points.
- A list of **key terms**.
- A series of **end-of-chapter exercises**; some easy, some harder; some requiring access to the Internet, some requiring the use of a spreadsheet program. More challenging exercises, web based or otherwise, are indicated by an asterisk.

A list of symbols on the back endpapers makes it easy to recall the meaning of the symbols used in the text.

The Teaching and Learning Package

The book comes with a number of supplements to help both students and instructors.

For Instructors

- **Instructor's Manual**. Written by Mark Moore, of the University of California-Irvine, the Instructor's manual discusses pedagogical choices, alternative ways of presenting the material, and ways of reinforcing students' understanding. For each chapter in the book, the manual has 7 sections: (I) a motivating question; (II) why the answer matters; (III) key tools, concepts, and assumptions; (IV) summary; (V) pedagogy; (VI) extensions, and (VII) observations and additional exercises. The Instructor's Manual also includes the answers to all end-of-chapter questions and exercises. The Instructor's Manual is available for download at **http://www.prenhall.com/blanchard**.

- **Test Item File**. Written by David Findlay, of Colby College, the test bank is completely revised with an all new set of short-answer, analytical questions.
- **New TestGen-EQ Software**. The print Test Bank is designed for use with the TestGen-EQ test generating software. This computerized package allows instructors to custom design, save, and generate classroom tests. The test program permits instructors to edit, add, or delete questions from the test bank; edit existing graphics and create new graphics; analyze test results; and organize a database of tests and student results. This new software allows for greater flexibility and ease of use. It provides many options for organizing and displaying tests, along with a search and sort feature. The software can prepare twenty-five versions of a single test.
- **Transparency Masters**. A complete set of transparency masters for all figures in the text can be downloaded from **http://www.prenhall.com/blanchard**. Contact your Prentice Hall representative for a password.

For Students

- **Study Guide**. David Findlay, of Colby College, has once again done an outstanding job of writing a student-friendly study guide. Each chapter begins with a presentation of objectives and review. It is organized in the form of a tutorial, covering the important points of the chapter, with learning tips along the way. The tutorial is followed by quick self-test questions, review problems, and multiple-choice questions. Solutions are provided for all study guide problems.
- **Active Graph CD-ROM**. This interactive student tool contains a series of active graphs created specifically for this text and corresponding to the most important figures in the book. Each graph allows the student to change the value of some variable and see the effects in the movement of the graphs. Experience indicates that using graphs in this way considerably strengthens the students' intuition and understanding of the mechanisms at work.

For Both Instructors and Students

- **Companion Web site (http://www.prenhall.com/blanchard)**. The Companion Web site is a content-rich, multidisciplinary Web site with Internet exercises, activities, and resources related specifically to the third edition of *Macroeconomics*. It includes the following features:

  The Online Study Guide, prepared by David Black of the University of Toledo, offers students another opportunity to sharpen their problem-solving skills and to assess their understanding of the text material. The Online Study Guide now contains two levels of quizzes with a total of 20 questions per chapter. The Online Study Guide grades each question submitted by the student, provides immediate feedback for correct and incorrect answers, and allows students to e-mail results to up to four email addresses.

  Current Events Articles and Exercises, related to topics in each chapter, are fully supported by group activities, critical-thinking exercises, and discussion questions. These articles, from current news publications to economics-related publications, help show students the relevance of economics in today's world.

  Internet Exercises—New Internet resources are added every two weeks by a team of economics professors to provide both the student and the instructor with the most current, up-to-date resources available.

  Syllabus Manager—For the instructor, the Companion Web site offers resources such as the answers to Current Events and Internet exercises, and a *Faculty Lounge* area including teaching resources and faculty chat rooms.

  Downloadable Supplements—From the Companion Web site, instructors can also download supplements and lecture aids. Instructors should contact their Prentice Hall sales representative to get the necessary username and password to access the faculty resources. The supplements include the following:

- **The PowerPoint Presentation**—This lecture presentation tool, prepared by Fernando and Yvonn Quijano, offers outlines and summaries of important text material, key equations, terms, tables and graphs. Many important graphs "build" upon themselves so that students may see the step-by-step process involved in these economics activities. This tool will allow instructors to make full-color, professional-looking presentations and custom handouts to be provided to their students.
- The Instructor's Manual
- Transparency Masters

Online Course Offerings

- **WebCT**. Developed by educators, WebCT provides faculty with easy-to-use Internet tools to create online courses. Prentice Hall provides the content and enhanced features to help instructors create a complete online course. For more information, please visit our Web site, located at **www.prenhall.com/webct**.
- **Blackboard**. Easy to use, Blackboard's single template and tools make it easy to create, manage, and use online course materials. Instructors can create online courses using the Blackboard tools, which include design, communication, testing, and course management tools. For more information, please visit our Web site located at **www.prenhall.com/blackboard**.
- **CourseCompass**. This customizable, interactive online course management tool powered by Blackboard provides the most intuitive teaching and learning environment available. Instructor's can communicate with students, distribute course material, and access student progress online. For further information, please visit our Web site located at **www.prenhall.com/coursecompass**.

Subscription Options

- **The Wall Street Journal Print and Interactive Editions Subscription**. Prentice Hall has formed a strategic alliance with *The Wall Street Journal*, the most respected and trusted daily source for information on business and economics. For schools that adopt a special package containing the book and subscription supplement, professors will receive a complimentary one year personal subscription and students will receive a 10-week subscription to *The Wall Street Journal* print edition and *The Wall Street Journal* interactive edition. As well, professors will receive a weekly subject-specific Wall Street Journal educators' lesson plans.
- **The Financial Times Subscription**. We are pleased to announce a special partnership with *The Financial Times*. For schools that adopt a special package containing the book and subscription supplement, instructors will receive a complimentary one-year personal subscription and students will receive a 15-week print subscription. Please contact your Prentice Hall representative for details and ordering information.
- **Economist.com Subscription**. Through a special arrangement with Economist.com, upon adoption of a book and subscription supplement package, professors will receive a six-month subscription and students will get a 12-week subscription to the online version. Please contact your Prentice Hall representative for further details and ordering information.

Acknowledgments and Thanks

This book owes much to many.

I thank Adam Ashcraft, Peter Berger, Peter Benczur, Efe Cakarel, Harry Gakidis, David Hwang, Kevin Nazemi, Stacy Tevlin, Gaurav Tewari, Corissa Thompson, John Simon, and Jeromin Zettelmeyer for their research assistance. I thank the generations of students in 14.02 at MIT who have freely shared their reactions to the book over the years.

I have benefited from comments from many colleagues and friends. Among them are John Abell, Roland Benabou, Samuel Bentolila and Juan Jimeno (who have adapted the book in a Spanish edition), François Blanchard, Roger Brinner, Ricardo Caballero, Martina Copelman, Ludwig Chincarini, Daniel Cohen (who has adapted the book for a French edition), Larry Christiano, Bud Collier, Andres Conesa, Peter Diamond, Martin Eichenbaum, Gary Fethke, David Findlay, Francesco Giavazzi (who has adapted the book for an Italian edition), Yannis Ioannides, David Johnson, P.N. Junankar, Paul Krugman, Peter Montiel, Bill Nordhaus, Angelo Melino (who has adapted the book for a Canadian edition), Tom Michl, Athanasios Orphanides, Daniel Pirez Enri (who has adapted the book for a Latin American edition), Jim Poterba, Ronald Schettkat, Watanabe Shinichi (who has adapted the book for a Japanese edition), Changyong Rhee, Julio Rotemberg, Robert Solow, Andre Watteyne, and Michael Woodford. I have also benefited from often stimulating suggestions from my daughters, Serena, Giulia, and Marie; I did not however follow all of them.

I have benefited from comments from many readers, reviewers, and class testers. Among them:

- John Abell, Randolph-Macon Womans' College
- Carol Adams, Cabrillo College
- Terence Alexander, Iowa State University
- Robert Archibald, College of William & Mary
- Stephen Baker, Capital University
- Charles Bean, London School of Economics and Political Science
- Dr. David C. Black, University of Toledo
- Scott Bloom, North Dakota State University
- Pim Borren, University of Canterbury, New Zealand
- Henry Chappell, University of South Carolina
- Maria Crummett, University of Tampa
- Brad DeLong, UC Berkeley
- Wouter Denhaan, UC San Diego
- F. Trenery Dolbear, Brandeis University
- John Edgren, Eastern Michigan University
- J. Peter Federer, Clark University
- Rendigs Fels, Vanderbilt University
- Yee-Tien Fu, National Cheng-Chi University, Taiwan
- Marc Fox, Brooklyn College
- Randy Grant, Linfield College
- Reza Hamzaee, Missouri Western State College
- Thomas Havrilesky, Duke University
- John Holland, Monmouth College
- Ralph Husby, University of Illinois, Urbana-Champaign
- Fred Joutz, George Washington University
- Miles Kimball, University of Michigan
- Paul King, Denison University
- Ng Beoy Kui, Nanyang Technical University, Singapore
- Leonard Lardaro, University of Rhode Island
- Hsien-Feng Lee, National Taiwan University
- Frank Lichtenberg, Columbia University
- Mark Lieberman, Princeton University
- Mathias Lutz, University of Sussex
- Bernard Malamud, University of Nevada, Las Vegas
- Rose Milbourne, University of New South Wales
- W. Douglas Morgan, University of California, Santa Barbara
- Jack Osman, San Francisco State University
- Allen Parkman, University of New Mexico
- Gavin Peebles, National University of Singapore
- Jack Richards, Portland State University
- Kehar Sangha, Old Dominion University
- Peter Sephton, University of New Brunswick
- Ruth Shen, San Francisco State University
- Kwanho Shin, University of Kansas
- Carol Scotese, Virginia Commonwealth University
- David Sollars, Auburn University
- Abdul Turay, Radford University
- Frederick Tyler, Fordham University
- Doug Waldo, University of Florida
- Susheng Wang, Hong Kong University
- Mark Wheeler, Western Michigan University
- Mark Wohar, University of Nebraska, Omaha
- Michael Woodford, Princeton University
- Ip Wing Yu, University of Hong Kong
- Chi-Wa Yuen, Hong Kong University of Science and Technology
- Ky H. Yuhn, Florida Atlantic University.

They have helped me beyond the call of duty, and each has made a difference to the book.

I have many people to thank at Prentice Hall, from Stephen Dietrich for convincing me to write this book in the first place, to Rod Banister, the executive editor for Economics, to P.J. Boardman, the editor-in-chief, to Gladys Soto, the managing editor, to Marie McHale, the assistant editor, to Lisa Amato, the editorial assistant, to Victoria Anderson, the media project manager, to Kathleen McLellan, the marketing manager, to Chris Bath, the marketing assistant, and to Michael Reynolds, the production editor.

I want to single out both Steve Rigolosi, the outstanding editor for the first edition, and Michael Elia, the equally outstanding editor to the second and third editions. Steve forced me to clarify. Michael has forced me to simplify. Together, they have made all the difference to the process and to the book. I thank both of them deeply.

At MIT, I continue to thank John Arditi for his absolute reliability.

At home, I continue to thank Noelle for preserving my sanity.

Olivier Blanchard
Cambridge, MIT
February 2002

Introduction

The first two chapters of this book introduce you to the issues and the approach of macroeconomics.

Chapter 1

Chapter 1 takes you on a macroeconomic tour of the world, from the slowdown in the United States after the long expansion of the 1990s, to the introduction of a common currency in Western Europe, to the economic slump in Japan.

Chapter 2

Chapter 2 takes you on a tour of the book. It defines the three central variables of macroeconomics: output, unemployment, and inflation. It then introduces the three concepts around which the book is organized, the short run, the medium run, and the long run.

A Tour of the World

What is macroeconomics? The best way to answer is not to give you a formal definition, but rather to take you on an economic tour of the world, to describe both the main economic evolutions and the issues that keep macroeconomists and macroeconomic policy makers awake at night.

At the time of this writing (the start of 2002), they are indeed sleeping poorly. In the United States, the long economic expansion that began in the early 1990s has given way to an economic slowdown. In Europe, economic growth has also declined, while unemployment is still very high. And the Japanese economy seems stuck in an economic slump, which has now lasted for close to a decade.

This chapter looks at what is happening in these three parts of the world:

- Section 1-1 looks at the United States.
- Section 1-2 looks at Europe.
- Section 1-3 looks at Japan.

Read the chapter as you would read an article in a newspaper. Do not worry about the exact meaning of the words, or about understanding all the arguments in detail: The words will be defined, and the arguments will be developed in later chapters. Regard it as background, intended to introduce you to the issues of macroeconomics. If you enjoy reading this chapter, you will probably enjoy reading this book. Indeed, once you have finished the book, return to this chapter; see where you stand on the issues, and judge how much progress you have made in your study of macroeconomics. ■

Figure 1-1

The United States, 2000

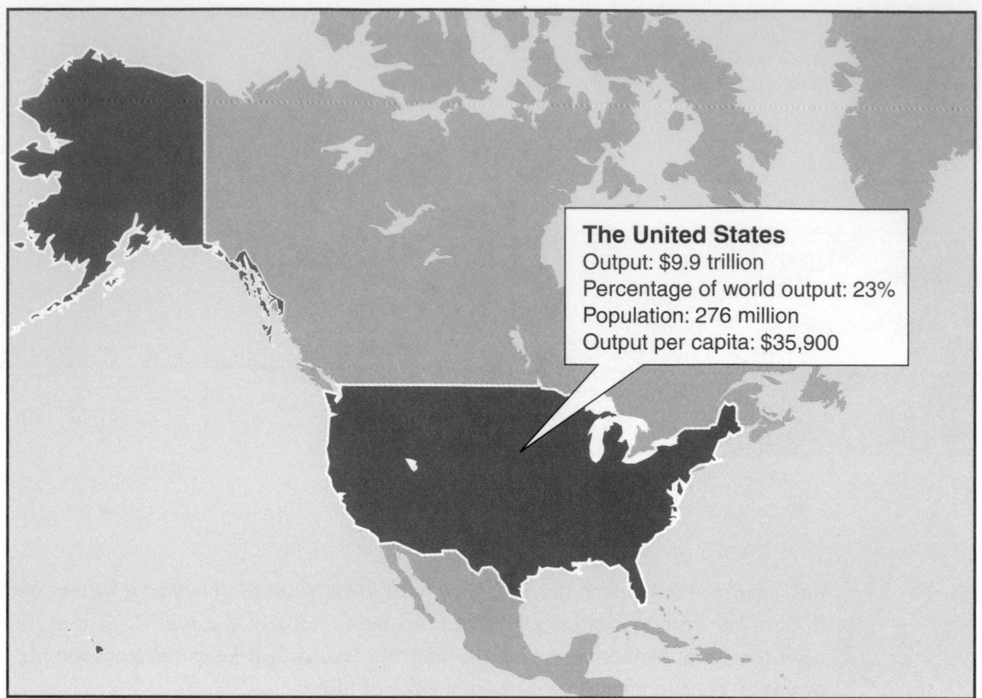

1-1 The United States

When macroeconomists study an economy, they first look at three variables:

- *Output*—the level of production of the economy as a whole—and its rate of growth
- The *unemployment rate*—the proportion of workers in the economy who are not employed and are looking for a job
- The *inflation rate*—the rate at which the average price of the goods in the economy is increasing over time

The basic numbers for the U.S. economy are given in Table 1-1. To put the current numbers in perspective, the first column gives you the average value of the rate of growth of output, the unemployment rate, and the inflation rate in the United States for the period 1960 to 2000. The second column gives you the same three numbers, but for the period 1992 to 2000. The last three columns give you the numbers for 2000,

Table 1-1 Growth, Unemployment, and Inflation in the United States, 1960–2002 (in percent)

	1960–2000 (average)	1992–2000 (average)	2000	2001	2002 (forecast)
Output growth rate	3.5	3.7	4.1	1.1	0.7
Unemployment rate	6.1	5.4	4.0	4.8	6.2
Inflation rate	5.1	1.7	2.3	2.1	1.2

Output growth rate: annual rate of growth of output. Unemployment rate: average over the year. Inflation rate: annual rate of change of the price level.

Source: OECD Economic Outlook, December 2001.

2001, and 2002. Despite the fact that this is written at the start of 2002, the numbers for 2001 are still projections: It takes some time to get the information needed to construct output and inflation numbers, and the final numbers will not be published until the middle of 2002. The numbers for 2002 are forecasts, made at the end of 2001.

Start with the column giving the numbers for the period 1992–2000. From an economic point of view, that period was one of the best in recent memory:

- Output growth was positive for nine years in a row, making the period the longest U.S. economic *expansion* since the end of World War II. In 2000, the last year of the expansion, output growth was 4.1%, a growth rate substantially higher than the average growth rate since 1960.
- Sustained growth in output was associated with a steady increase in employment, and a steady decrease in the unemployment rate. In 2000, the unemployment rate stood at 4%, more than 2% below the average unemployment rate since 1960, and the lowest unemployment rate in three decades.
- Although low unemployment is typically associated with increasing inflation, the inflation rate remained low throughout the period. In 2000, the inflation rate was only 2.3%, nearly 3% below the average inflation rate since 1960.

In short, the economic performance of the United States from 1992 to 2000 was impressive: high output growth, low unemployment, and low inflation. But that was then—this is now. As the last two columns in Table 1-1 indicate, 2001 has turned out to be much less bright:

- Output growth for 2001 is projected to be 1.1%, a full 3% below the growth rate for 2000. Preliminary numbers suggest that output growth was actually negative in the third quarter of 2001, and close to zero in the fourth quarter. Economists disagree as to whether this should be called a *recession*. Some point out that the traditional definition of a recession is at least two consecutive quarters of negative growth, and this was not the case in 2001. Others argue that output growth has been so low since the middle of 2001 that this qualifies as a recession. Whether we call the slowdown a recession or not, there is little question that the U. S. economy did poorly in 2001.
- Lower output growth has led to lower employment growth, and the unemployment rate has started increasing, from 4% in 2000 to 4.8% for 2001.

The forecasts for 2002 are not much better. Output growth is forecast to be positive but very low. The unemployment rate is forecast to increase to 6.2%, roughly back to its average value over the last 40 years.

And so, macroeconomists worry mainly about two sets of issues:

- The first concerns the current slowdown. What triggered it? Couldn't we have used monetary and fiscal policy more aggressively to avoid it? How long will it last?
- The second issue concerns the more distant future: Looking beyond the current slowdown to the next decade or two, can the United States hope to replicate the high rates of output growth that characterized the end of the 1990s? Has the United States entered a *New Economy*, an economy in which fast technological progress will lead to higher output growth than in the past?

Let me discuss both issues in turn.

The Current Slowdown

The first signs that the long economic expansion that began in 1992 might be coming to an end became visible just after the November 2000 presidential elections.

Investment spending by firms, which had grown very fast during the expansion, started declining. By the middle of 2001, this decline in investment spending became strong enough to lead to a decline in the overall demand for goods and a decline in output; the United States economy entered a recession. The events of September 11, 2001 made a bad situation worse. Uncertain about the future, consumers cut their spending. The combination of lower consumption spending and lower investment spending further decreased demand, and in turn further decreased output.

As it became clear that the U.S. economy was slowing down, both monetary and fiscal policy were used, first to try to avoid a recession, and then, when it appeared that a recession may have started, to hasten the recovery:

- In early 2001, Alan Greenspan, the chairman of the *Federal Reserve Board* (the U.S. central bank, informally known as the Fed), indicated that he was worried about an economic slowdown, and that the Fed stood ready to use monetary policy to counteract this slowdown. And throughout 2001, as news came that the slowdown was indeed on the way, the Fed steadily decreased the *federal funds rate*, the interest rate it controls most closely. Figure 1-2 shows the evolution of the federal funds rate from June 2000 to December 2001. Note how, after remaining flat throughout the second half of 2000, the federal funds rate was decreased from 6.5% in January 2001 to less than 2% in December 2001.
- In 2000, the federal government budget surplus—the excess of federal government revenues over federal government spending—had been equal to 2.5% of U.S. output, the highest budget surplus (as a percentage of output) in more than four decades. It is therefore not surprising that one of the issues dominating the 2000 presidential campaign was what the government should do in light of this budget surplus. Should it continue to run a surplus, and continue to decrease its debt? Or should it instead cut taxes, decreasing the surplus?

  When the Bush administration came to power in 2001, increasing evidence of a slowdown and the risk of a recession added a new dimension to the debate, and provided a new argument in favor of tax cuts. Tax cuts, the argument went, were urgently needed: By increasing the after-tax income of consumers, they would

Figure 1-2

The Federal Funds Rate, June 2000 to December 2001 Weekly Average

In an attempt to counteract the economic slowdown, the Fed aggressively decreased the federal funds rate throughout 2001.

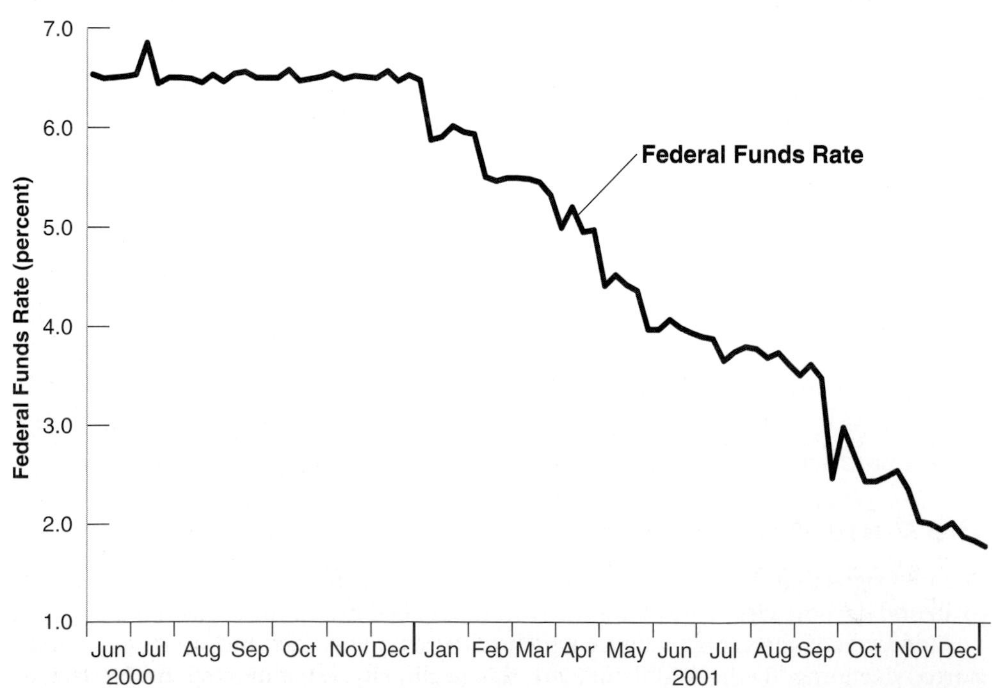

lead to higher consumer spending, and thus decrease the risk of a recession. A tax bill was passed in the spring of 2001, and starting in the summer of 2001, U.S. taxpayers received tax refunds of about $300 per taxpayer.

With these two strong policy responses on the part of U.S. policy makers, why was growth so low in 2001? The answer: Because fiscal policy and monetary policy are coarse policy instruments. The size of their effects is uncertain: How firms and consumers react to a change in either policy depends not only on what the Fed and the government do today, but on what they are expected to do in the future. The effects of policy also take time: It takes more than a year for lower interest rates to have their full effect on spending and output. By the time Alan Greenspan started cutting interest rates in early 2001, it was already too late for monetary policy to have much effect on what happened in 2001.

The question now is how long the slowdown will last. As you can see from Table 1-1, the forecast is for positive but still low output growth in 2002. Forecasters believe that both the decrease in the federal funds rate and the sharp decrease in taxes in 2001 should be enough to avoid negative output growth in 2002. At the same time, they believe that it will take some time for investment and consumption demand to recover, and so they do not expect a sharp recovery in 2002.

Has the United States Entered a New Economy?

With the long expansion of the 1990s and the rapid development of the high-tech sector of the economy came the claim that the United States had entered a *New Economy*, where the future was bright and old economic rules no longer applied. With the slowdown, talk of a New Economy has been temporarily stilled. But, sooner or later, the question will surely come back: What about the New Economy?

Just as the valuation of some of the dot-com Internet companies trading on the *Nasdaq* (the stock market, where shares of most high-tech companies are traded), many of the New Economy claims had no basis in fact. One claim, however—that the U.S. economy has entered a period of faster technological progress and therefore we can expect higher growth in the future than in the past—is more plausible and worth examining.

The way to examine this claim is to take a long view, and plot the rate of growth of *output per worker* since 1950 in the United States. (Output per worker is also called *productivity*; the rate of growth of output per worker is called the rate of productivity growth.) This is done in Figure 1-3. A look at the figure suggests two conclusions:

- Although growth rates vary a lot from year to year, it appears that starting at some point in the 1970s, there was a decrease in the average rate of growth of output per worker. The average growth rate for the period 1950 to 1973 (represented by the dashed horizontal line from 1950 to 1973 in the graph) was 2.5%. The average growth rate for the period 1974 to 1995 (represented by the dashed horizontal line from 1974 to 1995) was only 1%.
- In the recent past, however, the average rate of growth of output per worker appears to have increased again. The average growth rate for the period 1996 to 2000 (represented by the dashed horizontal line from 1996 to 2000) has been 2.6%, thus roughly equal to the pre-1973 average. This recent increase in growth rate per worker is the fact that has been emphasized by the New Economy proponents.

A difference in the average growth rate of output per worker of 1.5% per year may not seem like much—but it is! Think about it in this way: If the average growth rate of

FIGURE 1-3

Rate of Growth of Output per Worker in the United States Since 1950

The average rate of growth of output per worker decreased in the mid-1970s. It appears to have increased again since the mid-1990s.

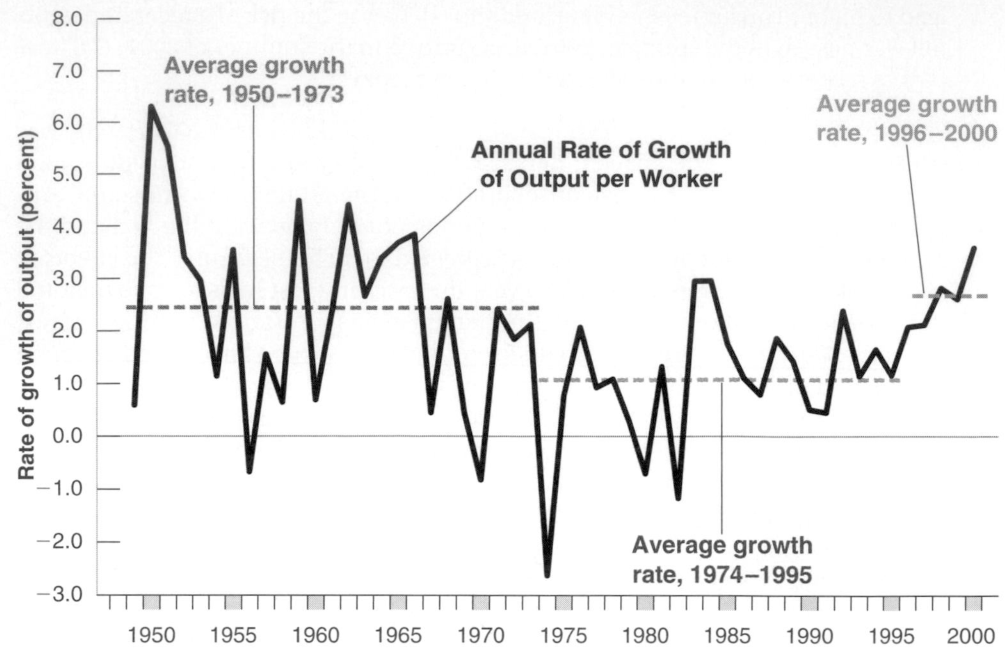

If the growth rate of output per worker had been 1.5% higher from 1974 to 1995 (for 22 years), the level of output per worker would have been $(1.015)^{22} - 1 = 39\%$ higher than it actually was in 1995.

output per worker had remained the same after 1973 as it had been from 1950 to 1973, then output per worker in 1995 would have been 39% higher than it turned out to be. Other things equal, the same would have been true of output per capita, what economists call the *standard of living*: The U.S. standard of living would have been 39% higher—a substantial difference. By the same argument, the higher rate of growth of output per worker since 1996 implies, if it continues, a much higher standard living in the future than if the U.S. economy returned to the low average growth rate observed from 1974 to 1995.

Per capita **means per person. (In Latin,** ***capita*** **means head.)**

Can we be confident that growth of output per worker will continue in the future at the same high rate as it did in the second half of the 1990s? Figure 1-3 suggests the answer: Not really. The rate of growth of output per worker fluctuates a lot from year to year. The high growth rates of the late 1990s may indicate the beginning of a period of higher productivity growth. But they may also be just a series of lucky years, not to be repeated in the future. In other words, the underlying trend may have increased, but it is too early to be sure.

This discussion may remind you of the controversies about global warming. The world temperature varies a lot from year to year. We need to observe many unusually warm years to be confident we are indeed seeing a trend toward global warming.

1-2 The European Union

In 1957, six European countries—Belgium, France, Germany, Italy, Luxembourg, and the Netherlands—decided to form a common European market—an economic zone where people and goods could move freely. Since then, nine more countries—Austria, Denmark, Finland, Greece, Ireland, Portugal, Spain, Sweden, and the United Kingdom—have joined. This union is now known as the **European Union**, or EU. (Until a few years ago, the official name was the *European Community* or EC. You may encounter either name.) Not only has the number of members increased, but the ties among them have tightened. Together, they form a formidable economic power: As Figure 1-4 shows, their combined output is close to the output of the United States, and many of them have a standard of living—a level of output per capita—close to that of the United States.

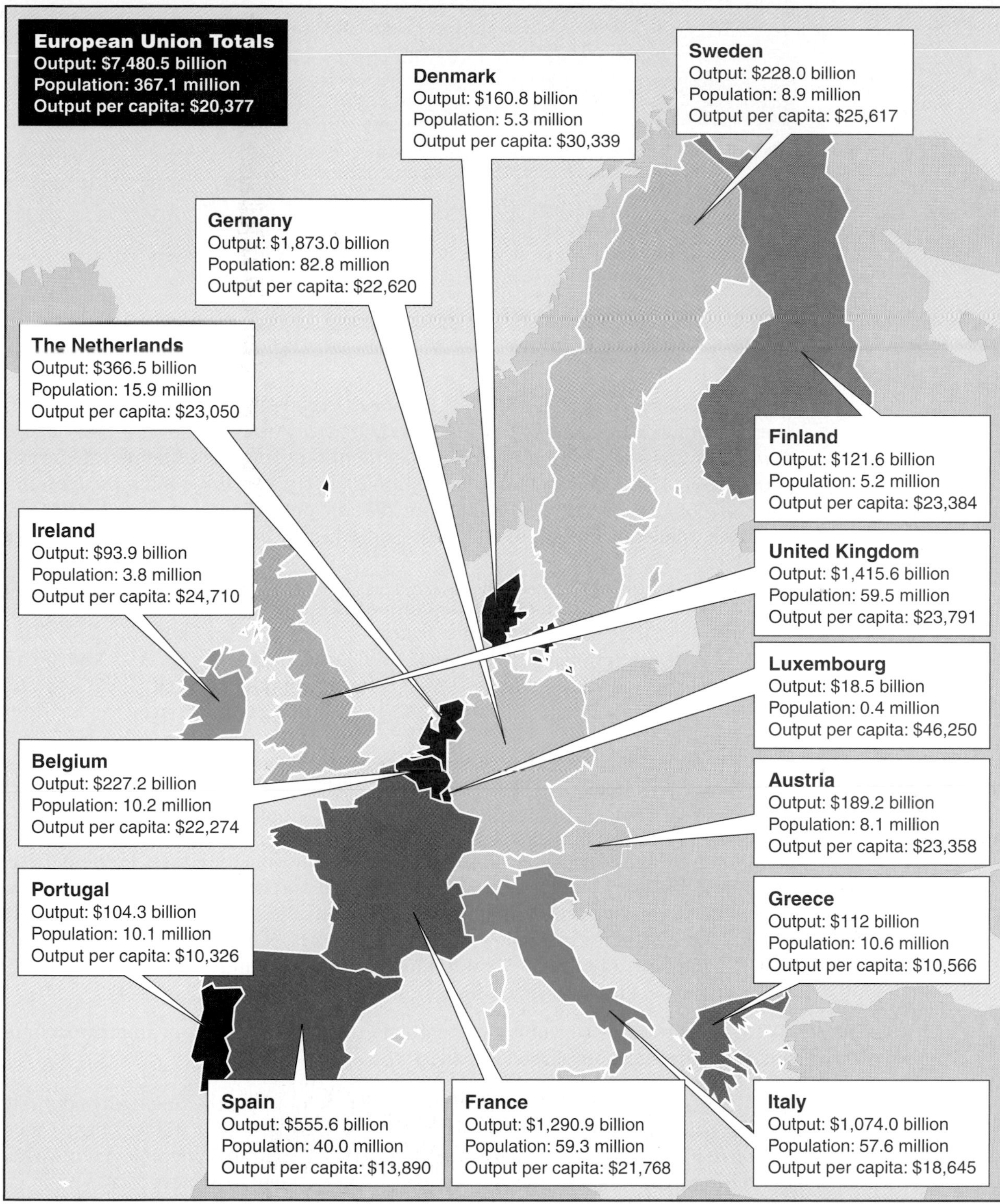

Figure 1-4

The European Union, 2000

Source: *GDP:* OECD, *March 2001;* Population: International Data Base, *Bureau of the Census, 2001. Output is GDP in domestic currency in 2000, converted in dollars at the average exchange rate for 2000.*

Table 1-2 Growth, Unemployment, and Inflation in the European Union, 1960–2002 (in percent)

	1960–2000 (average)	1992–2000 (average)	2000	2001	2002 (forecast)
Output growth rate	3.1	2.1	3.3	1.7	1.5
Unemployment rate	6.5	9.9	8.1	7.8	8.1
Inflation rate	5.6	1.7	1.5	2.5	2.2

Output growth rate: annual rate of growth of output. Unemployment rate: average over the year. Inflation rate: annual rate of change of the price level.

Source: OECD Economic Outlook, December 2001.

The economic performance of the European Union is shown in Table 1-2. The format of the table is the same as Table 1-1: The first two columns give the average value of the rate of growth of output, the unemployment rate, and the inflation rate for the period 1960 to 2000, and for the period 1992 to 2000. The next three columns give numbers for 2000, 2001, and 2002. Numbers for 2001 are projections. Numbers for 2002 are forecasts, made at the end of 2001. You should draw two main conclusions from the table:

- The economic performance of the European Union in the last decade was far less impressive than that of the United States.

  Average output growth from 1992 to 2000 was only 2.1%. This was 1.6% below the average growth rate in the United States during the same period. It was also 1% below the average growth rate in the European Union over the last four decades.

  Low output growth was accompanied by persistent high unemployment. The average unemployment rate from 1992 to 2000 was 9.9%. In 2000, the unemployment rate was 8.1%, more than twice the U.S. unemployment rate.

- While the European Union has so far avoided a recession, the current economic situation looks grim. Output growth was low in 2001 and is forecast to be even lower in 2002. As a result of low output growth, unemployment is expected to remain high. The forecast for the unemployment rate in 2002 is 8.1%, the same rate as in 2000.

  The only good news is on the inflation front. Inflation has been low for a decade, and the forecasts are for continuing low inflation.

At this time, two sets of issues dominate the agenda of European macroeconomists and macroeconomic policy makers:

- The first is, not surprisingly, high unemployment. While the unemployment rate has come down from its peak, reached in the mid-1990s, it is still very high. Can it be reduced further, say, all the way down to the U.S. rate of unemployment? What reforms and what macroeconomic policies are needed to achieve this?
- The second issue is associated with the introduction of a common currency. Twelve of the fifteen E.U. member countries have now adopted a common currency, the *Euro*. What macroeconomic changes will this bring? How should macroeconomic policy be conducted in this new environment?

Let me discuss both issues in turn.

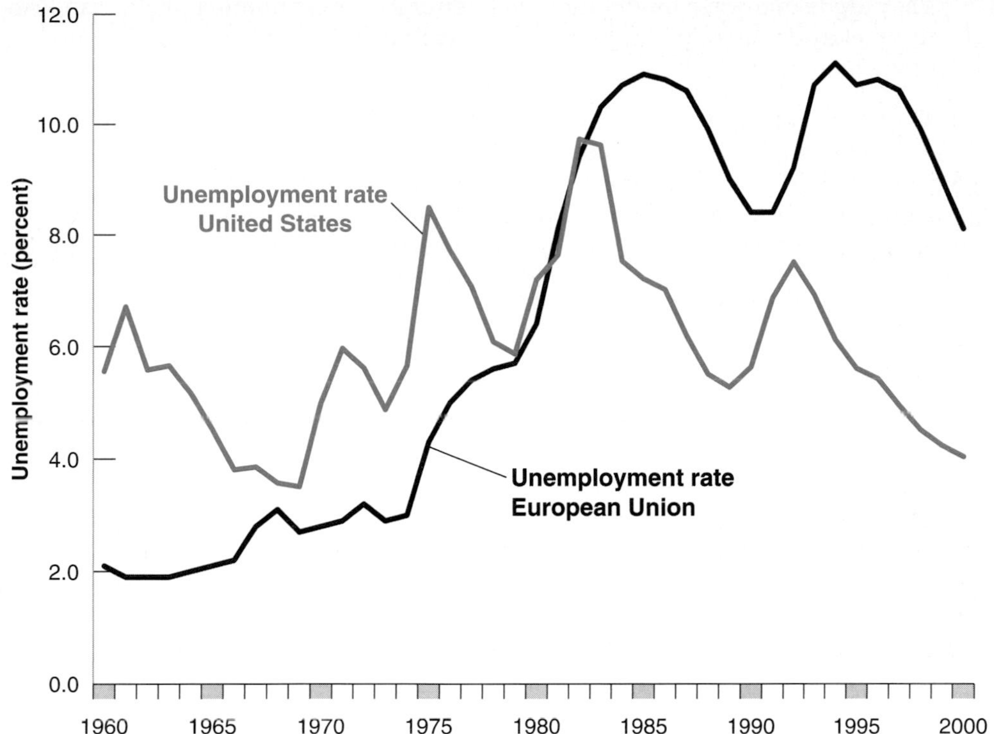

Figure 1-5

Unemployment Rates: Europe Versus the United States; 1960–2000

The European unemployment rate has gone from being much lower than that of the United States to being much higher.

How Can European Unemployment Be Reduced?

High unemployment is not a European tradition. Figure 1-5, which plots the evolution of unemployment rates in the European Union and in the United States since 1960, shows how low the European unemployment rate was in the 1960s. At that time, the talk in the United States was about the European *unemployment miracle*; U.S. macroeconomists went to Europe in the hope of discovering the secrets of that miracle. By the late 1970s, the miracle vanished. Since the early 1980s, the unemployment rate in Europe has been much higher than the unemployment rate in the United States. Despite a decline in the late 1990s, it still stands at roughly twice the U.S. level.

Despite a large amount of research, there is no agreement on the causes of high European unemployment:

- Some economists point to what they call *labor market rigidities.* Europe, they argue, suffers from too high a level of unemployment benefits, too high a minimum wage, and too high a level of worker protection. They say all these rigidities lead to high unemployment. The solution, they conclude, is to remove these rigidities, to make European labor markets more like the U.S. labor market. When this is done, they argue, the European economies will soar, and unemployment will decrease.
- Other economists point out that many of these "rigidities" were already in existence in the 1960s, when European unemployment was very low. They point to other factors instead, a wage explosion in the 1970s, which increased labor costs and led firms to decrease employment. They point to inadequate macroeconomic policies, in particular to high interest rates in the 1980s and 1990s.

They argue that wage moderation and better macroeconomic policies can lead to a steady decrease in unemployment, without the need for dramatic reforms of the labor market.

Most economists stand somewhere in between. They believe that a sustained decrease in unemployment will require a combination of some labor market reforms, wage moderation, and appropriate macroeconomic policies. This leaves open many questions: What specific labor market reforms should be implemented? How can wage moderation best be achieved? Finding the answers to these questions is one of the tasks facing European macroeconomists and policy makers today.

What Will the Euro Do for Europe?

In 1999, the European Union started the process of replacing individual national currencies with one common currency, the *Euro*. Only 11 of the 15 EU countries participated at the start; they were joined in 2001 by Greece. For the time being, the three remaining members of the EU, Denmark, Sweden, and the United Kingdom, have not joined, but they may do so in the future.

What to call the group of countries that have adopted the Euro is not settled. "Euro zone" sounds technocratic. "Euroland" reminds some of Disneyland. "Euro area" seems to be gaining favor, and this is the expression I use in this book.

The transition took place in steps. On January 1, 1999, each of the 11 countries fixed the value of one unit of its currency to the Euro. For example, a Euro was set equal to 6.56 French francs, 166 Spanish pesetas, and so on. From 1999 to 2002, some prices were quoted both in national currency units and in Euros, but the Euro was not yet used as currency. This happened on January 1, 2002, when Euro notes and coins started circulating together with national currencies. Early in 2002, national currencies were removed from circulation. The Euro is now the only currency, and the 12 countries of the Euro area are a *common currency* area, similar to the 50 states of the United States.

What will the Euro do for Europe?

- Supporters of the Euro point first to its enormous symbolic importance. In light of the many past wars between European countries, what better proof that the page has definitely been turned than the adoption of a common currency? They also point to the economic advantages of having a common currency: no more changes in the relative price of currencies for European firms to worry about, no more need to change currency when traveling between Euro countries. Together with the removal of other obstacles to trade between European countries that has taken place since 1957, the Euro will contribute, they argue, to the creation of a formidable economic power, perhaps the largest economic power in the world. There is little question that the move to the Euro is one of the main economic events of the start of the twenty-first century.
- Others worry that the symbolism of the Euro may carry economic costs. They point out that a common currency means a common monetary policy, and that means the same interest rate across the Euro countries. What if, they argue, one country plunges into recession while another is in the middle of an economic boom? The first country needs lower interest rates to increase spending and output; the second country needs higher interest rates to slow down its economy. If interest rates have to be the same in both countries, what will happen? Isn't there the risk that the country in recession may remain there for a long time, or that the country with the booming economy may not be able to slow it down?

Throughout the 1990s, the question was: Should Europe adopt the Euro? That question is now moot: The Euro is here, and it is here to stay. So far, no member country has had to face a severe recession, so the system has not been really tested. The full costs and benefits of the Euro remain to be assessed.

Table 1-3 Growth, Unemployment, and Inflation in Japan, 1960–2002 (in percent)

	1960–2000 (average)	1992–2000 (average)	2000	2001	2002 (forecast)
Output growth rate	5.5	1.2	1.5	−0.7	−1.0
Unemployment rate	2.0	3.0	4.7	5.0	5.5
Inflation rate	4.5	−0.1	−1.6	−1.6	−1.4

Output growth rate: annual rate of growth of output. Unemployment rate: average over the year. Inflation rate: annual rate of change of the price level.

Source: OECD Economic Outlook, December 2001.

1-3 Japan

Forty years ago, Japan might not have been included in our economic tour. Its output per capita was low compared to the United States or Europe. Things are very different today. As the first column of Table 1-3 indicates, Japan's average annual output growth rate since 1960 has been 5.5%. This is more than 2% higher than the U.S. average annual output growth rate over the same period. As you can see from Figure 1-6, Japan's output per capita is now *higher* than U.S. output per capita.

This is the good news. The bad news can be seen in the remaining columns. Japan's economic performance over the last decade has been nothing short of dismal:

- The average annual rate of growth of output from 1992 to 2000 was only 1.2%. This is 4% below the average growth rate since 1960. The projection is for negative growth in 2001, and the forecast is for negative growth in 2002. This long period of low and sometimes negative growth is known as the *Japanese slump*.
- As a result of this slump, the unemployment rate, which used to be very low in Japan, has steadily increased. It is projected to reach 5.0% in 2001, and 5.5% in 2002. By U.S. and even more so by EU standards, this would still seem to be a very low unemployment rate. But for Japan, this is the highest unemployment rate ever.

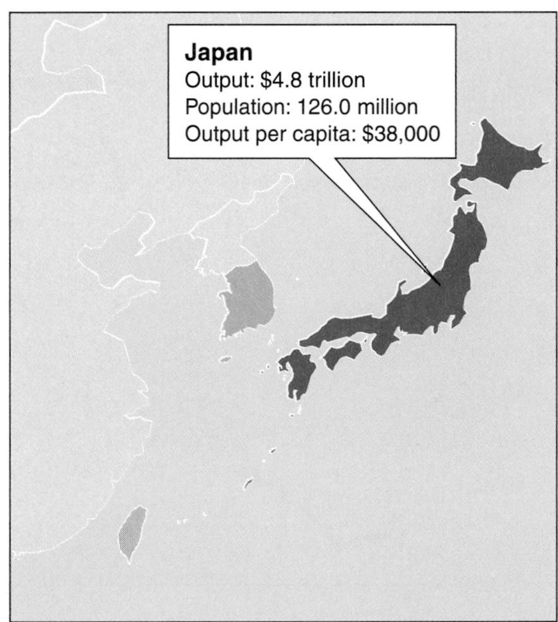

Figure 1-6

Japan, 2000

- As a result of high unemployment, the inflation rate has decreased and turned negative. In other words, Japan is experiencing *deflation*—a decrease in the average price of goods over time. You might conclude that if inflation is bad news, deflation must be good news. But, as we shall see later in this book, the evidence is that deflation—as opposed to low inflation—is actually dangerous, so, even here, the news is not good.

Given this description of where Japan stands, you can guess the two main issues confronting Japanese macroeconomists at this point:

- What went wrong? How could an economy that had done so well for so long go through such a long period of low growth?
- How can Japan recover? Does it need structural reforms, and if so, which ones? What should be the role of macroeconomic policy?

Let me take both questions in turn.

What Happened to Japan in the 1990s?

Just as there was talk of a "European unemployment miracle," so there was talk of a "Japanese growth miracle." It would seem that being labeled a miracle is a mixed blessing: In both cases, the miracles came to an abrupt end.

Until the early 1990s, the main question on macroeconomists' minds was: Why is Japan doing so well? What explains its sustained high growth rate? Is it its high saving rate and the rapid accumulation of capital such a high saving rate generates? Is it its high level of education, which allows it to adapt foreign technologies and achieve a high rate of technological progress? Is it the internal organization of Japanese firms, which leads them to become steadily more efficient over time?

Now the central questions are radically different: Why has Japan done so poorly for more than a decade? What broke and how can it be fixed?

Most economists believe that the trigger for the slump of the 1990s can be found in the striking movements in Japanese stock prices from the mid-1980s to the early 1990s. Figure 1-7 shows the behavior of the *Nikkei* index—an index of stock prices in

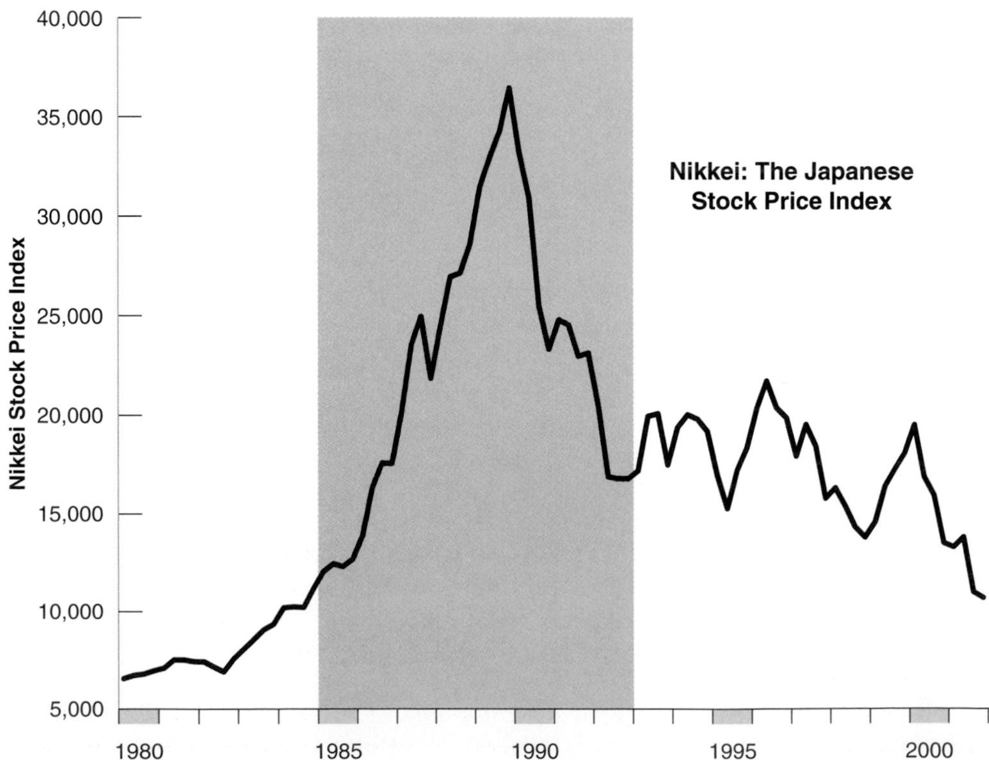

Figure 1-7

The Japanese Stock Market Index, 1980–2000

The large increase in the index in the second half of the 1980s was followed by an equally sharp decline in the early 1990s.

the Japanese stock market—since 1980. From 1985 to 1989, the Nikkei increased from about 13,000 to 35,000; in other words, the average price of a share in the Japanese stock market nearly tripled in less than four years. This sharp increase was followed in the early 1990s by an equally sharp decrease: In less than two years, from 1990 to 1992, the Nikkei fell from 35,000 to 16,000! Since then, the Nikkei has further decreased, although by less. At the end of 2001, it stood at 11,000.

Why did the Nikkei go up, and then down so much and so quickly? In general, stock prices can move for one of two reasons:

- One is what economists call *fundamentals*: For example, anticipations of higher profits in the future lead financial investors to pay more for shares today, so stock prices increase.
- The other is *speculative bubbles*, or *fads*, where investors buy stocks at high prices, hoping to resell them at higher prices in the future, whether or not justified by fundamentals.

Most observers interpret the rise and fall of the Nikkei as a speculative bubble, an excessive increase in stock prices in the 1980s, followed by a sharp decline and a return to reality in the early 1990s. They point to parallel movements in the prices of other assets, such as land or housing: Real estate prices increased in line with the Nikkei, and since 1990 have declined even more than stock prices. They argue that the result of the stock market boom was a boom in demand and in output in the late 1980s, and that the result of the stock market fall was a sharp drop in demand and output in the 1990s.

Does this remind you of what has happened to the Nasdaq (the U.S. stock market where shares of many high-tech companies are traded)? The Nasdaq has decreased from 5,000 at its peak in early 2000 to around 2,000 at the end of 2001. However, the broader U.S. stock market indexes, such as the Dow Jones or the Standard and Poor's index, have fallen by much less.

How Can Japan Recover?

How can Japan return to higher growth?

- In an effort to increase demand, the Japanese central bank has decreased interest rates to very low levels: Interest rates in Japan have remained under 1% since the mid-1990s and are now roughly equal to zero. Clearly, monetary policy cannot decrease them further.
- The government has also used fiscal policy to increase demand. It has increased spending on public works, and cut taxes to stimulate spending by consumers and firms. Both increased spending and lower taxes have led to large budget deficits. So far, however, neither monetary nor fiscal policy has been enough to take Japan out of its slump.

This has led a number of economists to conclude that the problem cannot be solved by macroeconomic policies alone, and that the Japanese economy will not grow fast again before several structural problems are recognized and solved. They point to a long list of problems with the Japanese economy, from a very inefficient retail distribution system, to political corruption. The problem with this line of argument is that all these problems were largely present when the Japanese economy was growing fast. One problem, however—the state of the banking system—has clearly gotten worse and may well be important.

With the sharp decline in growth in the 1990s, many firms which had taken out bank loans found themselves unable to repay them. Rather than writing off these loans, many banks have preferred to hide their losses by lending more to precisely those borrowers who cannot repay previous loans. Meanwhile, firms with viable projects cannot borrow. Without a healthy banking system, some economists argue, it will be difficult for Japan to return to steady growth.

Even if this is the right diagnosis, the solution will be painful. Returning the banking system to good health requires forcing many borrowers, and probably many banks who have portfolios of bad loans, into bankruptcy. Not surprisingly, no Japanese government has so far found the political courage to do so.

Given the lack of room for using monetary policy, and given the economic and political difficulties associated with cleaning up the banking system, it is difficult to predict when and how growth will resume in Japan. The Japanese slump may well be the toughest problem confronting macroeconomists today.

1-4 Looking Ahead

This concludes our world tour. There are many other regions of the world we could have looked at:

- Central and Eastern Europe, where most countries shifted from central planning to a market system in the early 1990s. This shift was characterized, in most countries, by a sharp decline in output at the start of transition. Only later did output growth become positive; in some countries, output is still below its pre-transition level.
- Latin America, which went from very high to low inflation in the 1990s. Some countries, such as Chile, appear to be in good economic shape. Some, such as

FOCUS: Gathering Macro Data

Where do the data we have examined in this chapter come from? Suppose we wanted to find the number for inflation in Germany over the past five years. Forty years ago, the answer would have been to learn German, find a library with German publications, find the page where inflation numbers were given, write them down, and plot them by hand on a clean sheet of paper. Today, improvements in the collection of data, the development of computers and electronic databases, and access to the Internet make the task much easier.

International organizations now collect data for many countries. For the richest countries, the most useful source is the **Organization for Economic Cooperation and Development (OECD)** based in Paris. You can think of the OECD as an economic club for rich countries. The complete list of member countries includes Australia, Austria, Belgium, Canada, the Czech Republic, Denmark, Finland, France, Germany, Greece, Hungary, Iceland, Italy, Japan, Korea, Luxembourg, Mexico, the Netherlands, New Zealand, Norway, Poland, Portugal, the Slovak Republic, Spain, Sweden, Switzerland, Turkey, the United Kingdom, and the United States. Together, these countries account for about 70% of world output. The *OECD Economic Outlook*, which is published twice yearly, gives basic data on inflation, unemployment, and other major variables for member countries, as well as an assessment of their recent macroeconomic performance. The data, often going back to 1960, are available on diskettes; they are on most macroeconomists' hard drives.

For those countries that are not members of the OECD, information is available from other international organizations. The main world economic organization is the **International Monetary Fund (IMF)**. The IMF publishes the monthly *International Financial Statistics (IFS)*, which contains basic macroeconomic information for all IMF members. It also publishes the annual World Economic Outlook, an assessment of macroeconomic developments in various parts of the world. Although their language is sometimes stilted, both the World Economic outlook and the OECD Economic Outlook are precious sources of information.

Because these publications sometimes do not contain sufficient details, you may need to turn to specific country publications. Major countries now produce remarkably clear statistical publications, often with an English translation available. In the United States, an extremely good resource is the *Economic Report of the President*, prepared by the Council of Economic Advisers and published annually. This report has two parts. The first is an assessment of current U.S. events and policy and is often a good read. The second is a set of data for nearly all relevant U.S. macroeconomic variables, usually for the entire post–World War II period.

A longer list of data sources, both for the United States and for the rest of the world, as well as how to access data sources through the Internet, is given in the appendix to this chapter.

Argentina, are struggling. At the time of this writing, Argentina is in crisis. Output growth is negative, and the country appears unable to pay its foreign debt.

- Africa, where some countries may be starting to grow after decades of economic stagnation.
- Southeast Asia, where many countries experienced a sharp decline in output in the late 1990s—the Asian crisis—but appear to be recovering quickly.

But there is a limit to how much you can absorb in this first chapter. Think about the questions to which you have been exposed already:

- What determines expansions and recessions? Why did the United States have such a long expansion in the 1990s? Can monetary policy and fiscal policy prevent a recession? How will the Euro affect monetary policy in Europe?
- What are the interactions between the stock market and economic activity? Can the poor performance of Japan in the 1990s be attributed to the sharp decline in the Japanese stock market in the early 1990s?
- Why is inflation so much lower in the 1990s than in previous decades? What is so bad about high inflation? What is so bad about the deflation which we are now observing in Japan?
- Why is unemployment so low in the United States? Why is it so high in Europe? How could the Japanese unemployment rate be so low for so many years?
- Why do growth rates differ so much across countries, even over long periods of time? Why did Japan grow so much faster than the United States and Europe for so long? Why did growth of output per worker decrease in the mid-1970s in the United States? Has the United States entered a New Economy, where growth will be much higher in the future?

The purpose of this book is to give you a way of thinking about these questions. As we develop the tools you need, I shall show you how to use them, by returning to these questions and showing the answers they suggest.

Key Terms

- European Union (EU), 8
- Organization for Economic Cooperation and Development (OECD), 16
- International Monetary Fund (IMF), 16

Questions and Problems

Quick Check

1. Using the information in this chapter, label each of the following statements true, false, *or* uncertain. *Explain briefly.*

a. Recently, inflation has been below its historical average in the United States, the European Union, and Japan.

b. In the 1960s and early 1970s, the United States had a higher rate of unemployment than Europe, but today it has a much lower rate of unemployment.

c. The rate of growth of output per worker in the United States has decreased since 1973.

d. The collapse of the Japanese stock market in the early 1990s was followed by a sharp drop in Japanese output.

e. The European "unemployment miracle" refers to the extremely low rate of unemployment that Europe has been enjoying since the 1980s.

f. Japanese fiscal policy is responsible for Japan's economic slump.

2. Using the information from Tables 1-1, 1-2, and 1-3, compute the average annual growth rate of output for the period 2001–2002 (use the projected growth rate for 2001, the forecast growth rate for 2002) for each of the following regions: the United States, the European Union, and Japan.

a. For each of the three regions, compare the average rate of output growth for 2001–2002 computed above with the average rate over 1960–2000. In particular, how do the recent experiences of each of these regions compare to their respective long-run averages?

b. Do you expect the average growth rate for the next 10 years to be closer to the average growth rate for 1960–2000 or to the average growth rate for 2001–2002? Explain your answer.

3. Politicians often tell only one side of the story. Consider each of the statements made about economic issues below, and comment on whether there is another side to the story.

a. There is no such thing as too low a rate of unemployment. Unemployment is bad. The lower it is, the better.

b. There has been no slowdown in growth since the mid-1970s, just a slowdown in the ability of economists to measure output correctly.

c. There is a simple solution to the problem of high European unemployment: Reduce labor market rigidities.

d. The slump in Japan is caused by poor regulation of the financial system.

e. What can be wrong about joining forces and adopting a common currency? The Euro is obviously good for Europe.

Dig Deeper

4. In 2001, the United States entered a recession, following a large decrease in the stock market. This is very similar to what happened to Japan in the early 1990s. Do you think that the United States will suffer a decade of stagnation, much like Japan in the 1990s?

5. The New Economy and growth

The average annual growth rate of output per worker in the United States rose from 1% during the period 1974–1995 to 2.6% for the years 1996–2000. This has led to talk of a New Economy and of sustained higher growth in the future than in the past.

a. Suppose output per worker grows at 1% a year. What will output per worker be—relative to today's level—in 10 years? 20 years? 50 years?

b. Suppose output per worker grows instead at 2.6% a year. What will output per worker be—relative to today's level—in 10 years? 20 years? 50 years?

c. If the United States has really entered a New Economy, and the average annual growth rate of output per worker has increased from 1% a year to 2.6%, how much higher will the U.S. standard of living be in 10 years? 20 years? 50 years?—relative to what it would have been had the United States remained in the Old Economy?

d. Can we be sure the United States has really entered a New Economy, with a permanently higher growth rate? Why, or why not?

6. When will China catch up with the United States?

In 2000, U.S. output was $9.9 trillion. China's output was $1.1 trillion.

Suppose that from now on, the output of China grows at an annual rate of 8% per year (roughly what it has done during the past decade), while the output of the United States grows at an annual rate of 3% per year. How many years will it take for China to have a level of output equal to that of the United States?

Explore Further

7. This question looks at the recessions of the last 40 years. To do so, first obtain quarterly data on U.S. output growth for the period 1960–2002 from the Web site **www.bea.gov/bea/dn/gdpchg.xls.** *Look at the data series for the percentage change in quarterly gross domestic product (GDP) in chained (1996) dollars. Using the standard definition of recessions as two or more consecutive quarters of negative growth, answer the following questions:*

a. How many recessions has the U.S. economy undergone since 1970?

b. How many quarters has each recession lasted?

c. In terms of length and magnitude, which two recessions have been the most severe?

At the time of this writing, there is some uncertainty whether the slowdown in 2001 and 2002 should be called a recession. The question is whether, when the final numbers for GDP are put together and published, they will show the U.S. economy has had at least two quarters of negative growth. When you read this book, the final numbers will be out, and so you will be able to answer the question:

d. Did the U.S. economy undergo two consecutive quarters of negative growth in 2001–2002?

8. From problem 7, write down the quarters during which the U.S. economy has experienced negative output growth since 1970. Now look at the behavior of the unemployment rate. Go to **www.bls.gov/data/webapps/legacy/cpsatab5.htm**, *and download the series for the unemployment rate, monthly, since 1970.*

a. Look at each recession since 1970. What was the unemployment rate in the first month of the first quarter of negative growth? What was the unemployment rate in the last month of the last quarter of negative growth? By how much did it increase?

b. Which recession has the largest increase in the rate of unemployment? For comparison, by how much did the unemployment rate increase from January 2001 to January 2002?

We invite you to visit the Blanchard page on the Prentice Hall Web site at:
www.prenhall.com/blanchard
for this chapter's World Wide Web exercises

Further Readings

This book has a Web page (**www.prenhall.com/bookbind/pubbooks/blanchard/**), which is updated regularly. For each chapter, the page offers discussions of current events, and includes relevant articles and Internet links. You can also use the page to make comments on the book, and have discussions with other readers.

The best way to follow current economic events and issues is to read *The Economist*, a weekly magazine published in England. The articles in *The Economist* are well informed, well written, witty, and opinionated. Make sure to read it regularly. (This book comes with a 12-week subscription to the Web version of *The Economist*. Take advantage of this!)

Appendix: Where to Find the Numbers?

The purpose of this appendix is to help you find the numbers you are looking for, be it inflation in Malaysia last quarter, or consumption in the United States in 1959, or youth unemployment in Ireland in the 1980s.

For a Quick Look at Current Numbers

- The best source for the most recent numbers on output, unemployment, inflation, exchange rates, interest rates, and stock prices for a large number of countries is the last four pages of *The Economist*, published each week (Internet address: **www.economist.com**). This Web site contains both information available free to anyone and information available only to subscribers, as do most of the Web sites listed here. The 12-week subscription to the Web version of *The Economist*, which comes with this book, gives you access to all numbers and to all articles.
- There exist several Web pages that collect and analyze recent data. One such site is **www.geoinvestor.com**, which provides access and links to data from many countries.

For More Detail About the U.S. Economy

- For a detailed presentation of the most recent numbers, look at the *Survey of Current Business*, published monthly by the U.S. Department of Commerce, Bureau of Economic Analysis (Internet address: **www.bea.gov**). A user's guide to the statistics published by the Bureau of Economic Analysis is given in the Survey of Current Business, April 1996. It tells you what data are available, in what form, and at what price.
- Once a year, the *Economic Report of the President*, written by the Council of Economic Advisers and published by the U.S. Government Printing Office in Washington, D.C., gives a description of current evolutions, as well as numbers for most major macroeconomic variables, often going back to the 1950s (the report and the statistical tables can be found at **www.access.gpo.gov/eop/**).
- The authoritative source for statistics going back as far in time as data have been collected is *Historical Statistics of the United States, Colonial Times to 1970*, Parts 1 and 2, published by the U.S. Department of Commerce, Bureau of the Census.
- The standard reference for national income accounts is *National Income and Product Accounts of the United States*. Volume 1, 1929–1958, and Volume 2, 1959–1994, published by the U.S. Department of Commerce, Bureau of Economic Analysis (Internet address: **www.bea.gov**).
- For data on just about everything, including economic data, a precious source is the *Statistical Abstract of the United States*, published annually by the U.S. Department of Commerce, Bureau of the Census (Internet address: **www.census.gov/statab/www/**).

Numbers for Other Countries

The OECD, located in Paris, publishes three useful publications. The OECD includes most of the rich countries in the world. (The list was given earlier in this chapter.) (Internet address: **www.oecd.org**)

- The first is the *OECD Economic Outlook*, published twice a year. In addition to discussing current macroeconomic issues, it includes data for many macroeconomic variables. The data typically go back to the 1970s, and are reported consistently, both across time and across countries.
- The second is the *OECD Employment Outlook*, published annually. It focuses more specifically on labor-market issues and numbers.
- Occasionally, the OECD puts together current and past data, and publishes the OECD Historical Statistics. At this point in time, the most recent is *Historical Statistics, 1960–1993*, published in 1995.

The main strength of the publications of the International Monetary Fund (IMF, located in Washington, D.C.) is that they cover most of the countries of the world (Internet address: **www.imf.org**).

The IMF issues four particularly useful publications:

- The *International Financial Statistics* (IFS), published monthly. It has data for member countries, usually going back a few years, mostly on financial variables, but also on some aggregate variables (such as GDP, employment, and inflation).

- The *International Financial Statistics Yearbook*, published annually. It has the same coverage of countries and variables as the IFS, but gives annual data going back up to 30 years.
- The *Government Finance Statistics Yearbook*, published annually, which gives data on the budget of each country, typically going back 10 years. (Because of delays in the construction of the numbers, data for the most recent years are often unavailable.)
- The *World Economic Outlook*, published twice a year, describes major evolutions in the world and in specific member countries.

For long-term historical statistics for several countries, a precious data source is Angus Maddison's *Monitoring the World Economy, 1820–1992*, Development Centre Studies, OECD, Paris, 1995. This study gives data going back to 1820 for 56 countries. An even longer and broader source is *The World Economy. A Millenial Perspective*, Development Studies, OECD, 2001, also by Angus Maddison.

Finally, if you still have not found what you were looking for, here are two useful sites:

- The Macroeconomics Resources site of the Harvard Business School (**www.hbs.edu/units/bgie/internet/**) assesses the quality of—and provides links with—a large number of other potentially useful Web sites.
- A site maintained by Bill Goffe at SUNY (**www.rfe.org**) lists not only data sources but sources for economic information in general, from working papers, to jokes, to jobs in economics, and so on.

A Tour of the Book

The words *output, unemployment*, and *inflation* appear daily in newspapers and on the evening news. So, when I used them in Chapter 1, you were familiar with them. At least you knew roughly what I was talking about. We now need to define them precisely and this is what I do in the first two sections of this chapter.

Section 2-1 focuses on aggregate output, and shows how we can look at aggregate output both from the production side and from the income side.

Section 2-2 looks at the unemployment rate and at the inflation rate.

Then, in Section 2-3, I take you on a tour of the book. In that tour, I introduce the three central concepts around which the book is organized:

- The *short run*: what happens to the economy from year to year.
- The *medium run*: what happens to the economy over a decade or so.
- The *long run*: what happens to the economy over a half century or more.

Building on these three concepts, I end the chapter with a road map to the rest of the book. ■

2-1 Aggregate Output

Two economists, Simon Kuznets, from Harvard University, and Richard Stone, from Oxford University, were given the Nobel Prize for their contributions to the development of the national income and product accounts—a gigantic intellectual and empirical achievement.

Economists studying economic activity in the nineteenth century or during the Great Depression had no measure of aggregate activity (*aggregate* is the word macroeconomists use for *total*) on which to rely. They had to put together bits and pieces of information, such as the shipments of iron ore, or sales at some department stores, to try to infer what was happening to the economy as a whole.

It was not until the end of World War II that **national income and product accounts** (or national income accounts, for short) were put together. Measures of aggregate output have been published on a regular basis in the United States since October 1947. (You will find measures of aggregate output for earlier times, but these have been constructed retrospectively.)

Like any accounting system, the national income accounts first define concepts, and then construct measures corresponding to these concepts. You need only to look at statistics from countries that have not yet developed such accounts to realize how crucial are such precision and consistency. Without them, numbers that should add up do not; trying to understand what is going on often feels like trying to balance someone else's checkbook. I shall not burden you with the details of national income accounting here. But, because you will occasionally need to know the definition of a variable and how variables relate to each other, Appendix 1 at the end of the book gives you the basic accounting framework used in the United States (and, with minor variations, in most other countries) today. You will find it useful whenever you want to look at economic data on your own.

You may come across another term, **gross national product**, or **GNP**. There is a subtle difference between "domestic" and "national," and thus between GDP and GNP. We examine the distinction in Chapter 18 (also in Appendix 1 at the end of the book). For now, ignore it.

GDP: Production, and Income

The measure of **aggregate output** in the national income accounts is **gross domestic product**, or **GDP**, for short. To understand how GDP is constructed, it is best to work with a simple example. Consider an economy composed of just two firms:

- Firm 1 produces steel, employing workers and using machines to produce the steel. It sells the steel for $100 to Firm 2, which produces cars. Firm 1 then pays its workers $80, leaving $20 in profit to the firm.
- Firm 2 buys the steel and uses it, together with workers and machines, to produce cars. Revenues from car sales are $210. Of the $210, $100 goes to pay for steel and $70 goes to workers in the firm, leaving $40 in profit to the firm.

Not only workers and machines are required for steel production, but so are electricity, iron ore, etc. We ignore these to keep this example simple.

We can summarize this information in a table:

Steel Company (Firm 1)			Car Company (Firm 2)		
Revenues from sales		$100	Revenues from sales		$210
Expenses		$80	Expenses		$170
Wages	$80		Wages	$70	
			Steel purchases	$100	
Profit		$20	Profit		$40

There are then three ways of defining GDP in this economy, all equivalent:

1. **GDP Is the Value of the Final Goods and Services Produced in the Economy During a Given Period.**
The important word here is **final**. To see why, ask yourself: Should GDP be constructed as the sum of the values of all production in the economy—the sum of $100 from the production of steel plus $210 from the production of cars, so $310? Or should GDP be constructed as the value of the production of final goods, here cars, equal to $210?

Some thought suggests that the right answer must be \$210. Why? Because steel is an **intermediate good**, a good used up in the production of the final good, cars, and thus should not be counted in GDP—the value of *final* output. We can look at this example in another way: Suppose the two firms merged, so that the sale of steel took place inside the new firm and was no longer recorded. The accounts of the new firm would be given by the following table:

An intermediate good is a good used in the production of another good. Some goods can be both final goods and intermediate goods. Potatoes sold directly to consumers are final goods. Potatoes used to produce potato chips are intermediate goods. Can you think of other examples?

Steel and Car Company	
Revenues from sales	\$210
Expenses (wages)	\$150
Profit	\$60

All we would see would be one firm selling cars for \$210, paying workers \$80 + \$70 = \$150, and making \$20 + \$40 = \$60 in profits. The \$210 measure would remain unchanged—as it should.

This first definition suggests one way to construct GDP: by recording and adding up the production of final goods—and this is roughly the way actual GDP numbers are put together. But it also suggests a second way of thinking about and constructing GDP:

2. **GDP Is the Sum of Value Added in the Economy During a Given Period.**
The term **value added** means exactly what it suggests. The value added by a firm in the production process is defined as the value of its production minus the value of the intermediate goods it uses in production.

In our two-firms example, the steel company does not use intermediate goods. Its value added is simply equal to the value of the steel it produces, \$100. The car company, however, uses steel as an intermediate good. Thus, value added by the car company is equal to the value of the cars it produces minus the value of the steel it uses in production, \$210 − \$100 = \$110. Total value added in the economy, or GDP, equals \$100 + \$110 = \$210. (Note that aggregate value added would remain the same if the steel and car firms merged and became a single firm. In this case, we would not observe intermediate goods at all—as steel would be produced and then used to produce cars within the single firm—and the value added in the single firm would simply be equal to the value of cars, \$210.)

This definition gives us a second way of thinking about GDP. Put together, the two definitions imply that the value of final goods and services—the first definition of GDP—can also be thought of as the sum of the value added by all the firms in the economy—the second definition of GDP.

3. **GDP Is the Sum of Incomes in the Economy During a Given Period.**
So far, we have looked at GDP from the *production side*. The other way of looking at GDP is from the *income side*. Think about the revenues left to a firm after it has paid for its intermediate goods:

- Some of the revenues are collected by the government in the form of taxes on sales—such taxes are called *indirect taxes.*
- Some of the revenues go to pay workers—this component is called *labor income.*
- The rest goes to the firm—that component is called *capital income* or *profit income.*

In short, looking at it from the income side, value added is the sum of indirect taxes, labor income, and capital income.

Return to our example. Indirect taxes equal zero. Of the \$100 of value added by the steel manufacturer, \$80 goes to workers (labor income) and the remaining

Table 2-1 The Composition of GDP by Type of Income, 1960 and 2000

(in percent)	1960	2000
Labor income	66	65
Capital income	26	28
Indirect taxes	8	7

Source: Survey of Current Business, December 2001.

$20 goes to the firm (capital income). Of the $110 of value added by the car manufacturer, $70 goes to labor income and $40 to capital income. For the economy as a whole, value added is $210 ($100 + $110), of which $150 ($80 + $70) goes to labor income and $60 ($20 + $40) goes to capital income.

In our example, labor income accounts for 71% of GDP, capital income for 29%, indirect taxes for 0%. Table 2-1 shows the breakdown of value added among the different types of income in the United States in 1960 and 2000. The table shows that, except for indirect taxes (zero in our example), the proportions we have been using in our example are roughly the same proportions as for the U.S. economy. Labor income accounts for 65% of U.S. GDP. Capital income accounts for 28%. Indirect taxes account for the remaining 7%. The proportions have not changed much since 1960.

Two lessons to remember:
1. GDP is the measure of aggregate output, which we can think of from the production side (aggregate production), or the income side (aggregate income).
2. Aggregate production and aggregate income are always equal.

To summarize: You can think about aggregate output—*GDP*—in three different but equivalent ways.

- From the *production side*: GDP equals the value of the final goods and services produced in the economy during a given period.
- Also from the *production side*: GDP is the sum of value added in the economy during a given period.
- From the *income side*: GDP is the sum of incomes in the economy during a given period.

Nominal and Real GDP

In 2000, U.S. GDP was $9,872 billion, compared to $526 billion in 1960. Was U.S. output really 19 times higher in 2000 than in 1960? Obviously not: Much of the increase reflected an increase in prices rather than an increase in quantities produced. This leads to the distinction between nominal GDP and real GDP.

Warning! People often use "nominal" to denote small amounts. Economists use nominal for variables expressed in current prices. And they surely do not refer to small amounts: The numbers typically run in the billions or trillions of dollars.

Nominal GDP is the sum of the quantities of final goods produced times their current price. This definition makes clear that nominal GDP increases over time for two reasons:

- First, the production of most goods increases over time.
- Second, the prices of most goods also increase over time.

If our intention is to measure production and its change over time, we need to eliminate the effect of increasing prices on our measure of GDP. That's why **real GDP** is constructed as the sum of the quantities of final goods times *constant* (rather than *current*) prices.

If the economy produced only one final good, say, a particular car model, constructing real GDP would be easy: We would use the price of the car in a given year, and then use it to multiply the quantity of cars produced in each year.

A simple example will help: Consider an economy that produces only cars—and to avoid issues we shall tackle later, assume the same model is produced every year.

Suppose the number and the price of cars in three successive years are given by:

Year	Quantity of Cars	Price of Cars	Nominal GDP
1995	10	$20,000	$200,000
1996	12	$24,000	$288,000
1997	13	$26,000	$338,000

Nominal GDP, which is equal to the quantity of cars times their price, goes up from $200,000 in 1995 to $288,000 in 1996—a 44% increase—and from $288,000 in 1996 to $338,000 in 1997—a 16% increase.

- To construct real GDP, we need to multiply the number of cars in each year by a *common* price. Suppose we use the price of a car in 1996 as the common price. This approach gives us, in effect, *real GDP in 1996 dollars.*
- Using this approach, real GDP in 1995 (in 1996 dollars) equals 10 cars × $24,000 per car = $240,000. Real GDP in 1996 (in 1996 dollars) equals 12 cars × $24,000 per car = $288,000, the same as nominal GDP in 1996. Real GDP in 1997 (in 1996 dollars) is equal to 13 × $24,000 = $312,000. So real GDP goes up from $240,000 in 1995 to $288,000 in 1996—a 20% increase—and from $288,000 in 1996 to $312,000 in 1997—an 8% increase.
- How different would our results have been if we had decided to construct real GDP using the price of a car in, say, 1997 rather than 1996? Obviously, the level of real GDP in each year would be different (because the prices are not the same in 1997 as in 1996); but its rate of change from year to year would be the same as above.

To be sure, compute real GDP in 1997 prices, and compute the rate of growth from 1995 to 1996, and from 1996 to 1997.

The problem in constructing real GDP in practice is that there is obviously more than one final good. Real GDP must be defined as a weighted average of the output of all final goods, and this brings us to what the weights should be.

The *relative prices* of the goods would appear to be the natural weights. If one good costs twice as much per unit as another, then that good should count for twice as much as the other in the construction of real output. But this raises the question: What if, as is typically the case, relative prices change over time? Should we choose the relative prices in a given year as weights, or should we change the weights over time? More discussion of these issues, and of the way real GDP is constructed in the United States, is left to the appendix to this chapter. Here, what you should know is that the measure of real GDP in the U.S. national income accounts is called **real GDP in chained (1996) dollars**. ("1996" because, as in our example above, 1996 is the year when, by construction, real GDP is equal to nominal GDP). It uses weights that reflect relative prices and that change over time. It is a measure of the output of the U.S. economy, and its evolution shows how U.S. output has increased over time.

Figure 2-1 plots the evolution of both nominal GDP and real GDP since 1960. By construction, the two are equal in 1996. Figure 2-1 shows that real GDP in 2000 was 4 times its level in 1960—a considerable increase, but clearly much less than the 19-fold increase in nominal GDP over the same period. The difference between the two results comes from the increase in prices over the period.

Suppose real GDP was measured in 2000 dollars rather than 1996 dollars. Where would the nominal GDP and real GDP lines on the graph intersect?

The terms *nominal GDP* and *real GDP* each have many synonyms, and you are likely to encounter them in your readings:

- Nominal GDP is also called **dollar GDP** or **GDP in current dollars**.
- Real GDP is also called **GDP in terms of goods**, **GDP in constant dollars**, **GDP adjusted for inflation**, or **GDP in 1996 dollars**—if the year in which real GDP is set equal to nominal GDP is 1996, as is the case in the United States at this time.

Figure 2-1

Nominal and Real U.S. GDP, 1960–2000

From 1960 to 2000, nominal GDP increased by a factor of 19. Real GDP increased by a factor of 4.

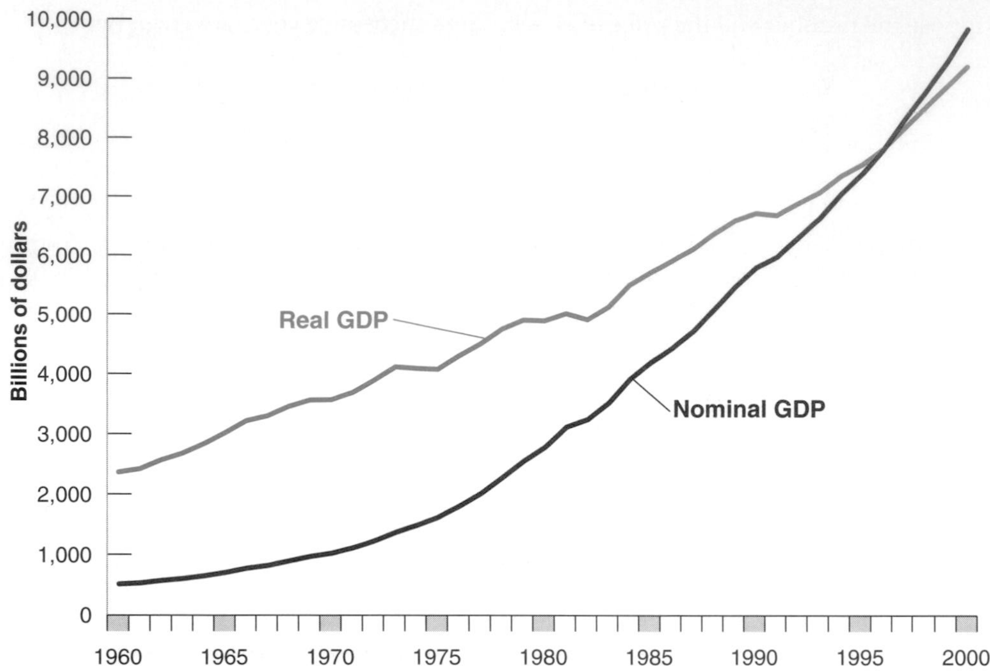

This concludes your introduction to the main macroeconomic variable, GDP. In the chapters that follow, unless indicated otherwise,

- GDP will refer to *real GDP* and Y_t will denote *real GDP in year t.*
- Nominal GDP, and variables measured in current dollars, will be denoted by a dollar sign in front—for example, $\$Y_t$ for nominal GDP in year *t*.

Similarly, **GDP growth** in year *t* will refer to the rate of change of *real GDP* in year *t*. GDP growth equals $(Y_t - Y_{t-1})/Y_{t-1}$. Periods of positive GDP growth are called **expansions**. Periods of negative GDP growth are called **recessions**. There is no official definition of what constitutes a recession, but to avoid calling just one quarter of negative growth a recession, macroeconomists usually refer to a "recession" only if the economy undergoes at least two consecutive quarters of negative growth. The U.S. recession of 1990 to 1991, for example, was characterized by three consecutive quarters of negative growth, the last two quarters of 1990 and the first quarter of 1991. At the time of this writing, whether the U.S. economy had a recession in 2001 is unclear. According to the preliminary numbers, growth was negative only during the third quarter of 2001. If these numbers are confirmed, then, at least according to the usual definition of recessions, the U.S. economy did not have a recession in 2001, just a strong slowdown.

2-2 The Other Major Macroeconomic Variables

Because it is a measure of aggregate activity, GDP is obviously the most important macroeconomic variable. But two other variables, unemployment and inflation, tell us about other important aspects of how an economy is performing.

The Unemployment Rate

To think about the unemployment rate, start with the definition of the labor force: The **labor force** is the sum of those employed and those unemployed:

$$\begin{array}{ccccc} L & = & N & + & U \\ \text{labor force} & = & \text{employed} & + & \text{unemployed} \end{array}$$

Real GDP, Technological Progress, and the Price of Computers

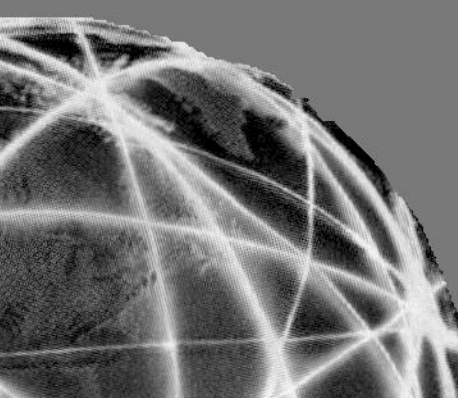

FOCUS

A tough problem in computing real GDP is how to deal with changes in quality of existing goods. One of the most difficult cases is computers. It would clearly be absurd to assume that a personal computer produced in 2001 is the same good as a computer produced in 1981 (the year in which the IBM PC was introduced): The same price clearly buys much more computing in 2001 than it bought in 1981. But how much more? Does a 2001 computer provide 10 times, 100 times, or 1,000 times the computing services of a 1981 computer? How should we take into account the improvements in internal speed, the size of the RAM or of the hard disk, the fact that computers can access the Internet, and so on?

The approach used by economists to adjust for these improvements is to look at the market for computers and how it values computers with different characteristics in a given year. Example: Suppose the evidence from prices of different models on the market show that people are willing to pay 10% more for a computer with a speed of 1,000 megahertz rather than 600 megahertz. (The first edition of this book, published in 1996, compared two computers, with speeds of 50 and 16 megaherz, respectively . . . a good indication of technological progress.) Suppose all new computers this year have a speed of 1,000 megahertz compared with a speed of 600 megahertz for new computers last year. And suppose the dollar price of new computers this year is the same as the dollar price of new computers last year. Then, economists in charge of computing the adjusted price of computers will assume that new computers are in fact 10% cheaper than last year.

This approach, which treats goods as providing a collection of characteristics—here speed, memory, and so on—each with an implicit price, is called **hedonic pricing** ("hedone" means pleasure in Greek). It is used by the Department of Commerce, which constructs estimates of real GDP, to estimate changes in the price of complex and fast changing goods, such as automobiles and computers. Using this approach, the Department of Commerce estimates that, for a given price, the quality of new computers has increased on average by 15% a year since 1981. Put another way, a typical personal computer in 2001 delivers $1.15^{21} = 19$ times the computing services a typical personal computer delivered in 1981.

Not only do computers deliver more services, they have become cheaper as well: Their dollar price has declined by about 10% a year since 1981. Putting this together with the information in the previous paragraph, this implies that their quality-adjusted price has fallen at an average rate of 15% + 10% = 25% per year. Put another way, a dollar spent on a computer today buys $1.25^{21} = 108$ times more computing services than a dollar spent on a computer in 1981.

The **unemployment rate** is then defined as the ratio of the number of people who are unemployed to the number of people in the labor force:

$$u = \frac{U}{L}$$

unemployment rate = unemployed/labor force

Determining whether somebody is employed is straightforward. But how do we assess whether somebody is unemployed or just not looking for work?

Until the 1940s in the United States, and until more recently in most other countries, the number of people registered at unemployment offices was the only available source of data on unemployment, and only those workers who were registered in unemployment offices were counted as unemployed. This system led to a poor measure of unemployment. How many of the truly unemployed actually registered at the unemployment offices varied both across countries and across time. Those who had no incentive to register—for example, those who had exhausted their unemployment benefits—were unlikely to take the time to come to the unemployment office, so they were not counted. Countries with less generous benefit systems were likely to have fewer unemployed registering, and therefore smaller measured unemployment rates.

Today, most rich countries rely on large surveys of households to compute the unemployment rate. In the United States, this survey is called the **Current Population Survey (CPS)**. It relies on interviews of 60,000 households every month. The survey classifies a person as employed if he or she has a job at the time of the interview; it classifies a person as unemployed if he or she does not have a job *and has been looking* *for work in the last four weeks*. Most other countries use a similar definition of unemployment. In the United States, estimates based on the CPS survey show that, during 2000, on average 135.2 million people were employed, and 5.7 million people were unemployed, so the unemployment rate was 5.7/(135.2 + 5.7) = 4.0%.

Note, only those *looking for work* are counted as unemployed; those not working and not looking for work are counted as **not in the labor force**. When unemployment is high, some of those without jobs give up looking for work and therefore are no longer counted as unemployed. These people are known as **discouraged workers**. An extreme example: If all workers without a job gave up looking for work, the unemployment rate would equal zero. This would make the unemployment rate a very poor indicator of what is happening in the labor market. The example is too extreme; in practice, when the economy slows down, we typically observe both an increase in unemployment and an increase in the number of people who drop out of the labor force. Equivalently, a higher unemployment rate is typically associated with a lower **participation rate**, defined as the ratio of the labor force to the total population of working age.

At the start of economic reform in Eastern Europe in the early 1990s, unemployment increased dramatically. But equally dramatic was the fall in the participation rate. In Poland in 1990, 70% of the decrease in employment was reflected in early retirements—by people dropping out of the labor force rather than becoming unemployed.

Why do macroeconomists care about unemployment? For two reasons:

- The unemployment rate gives them an indication of whether an economy is operating above or below its normal level of activity.
- Unemployment has important social consequences.

Let me discuss both reasons in turn.

Unemployment and Output

In most countries, there is a clear relation between the change in unemployment and GDP growth. This relation is known as **Okun's law**, after the economist Arthur Okun, who first identified and interpreted it in the 1960s. It is plotted in Figure 2-2 for the

Figure 2-2

Change in the Unemployment Rate versus GDP growth, United States, 1960–2000

High output growth is typically associated with a decrease in the unemployment rate. Low output growth is typically associated with an increase in the unemployment rate.

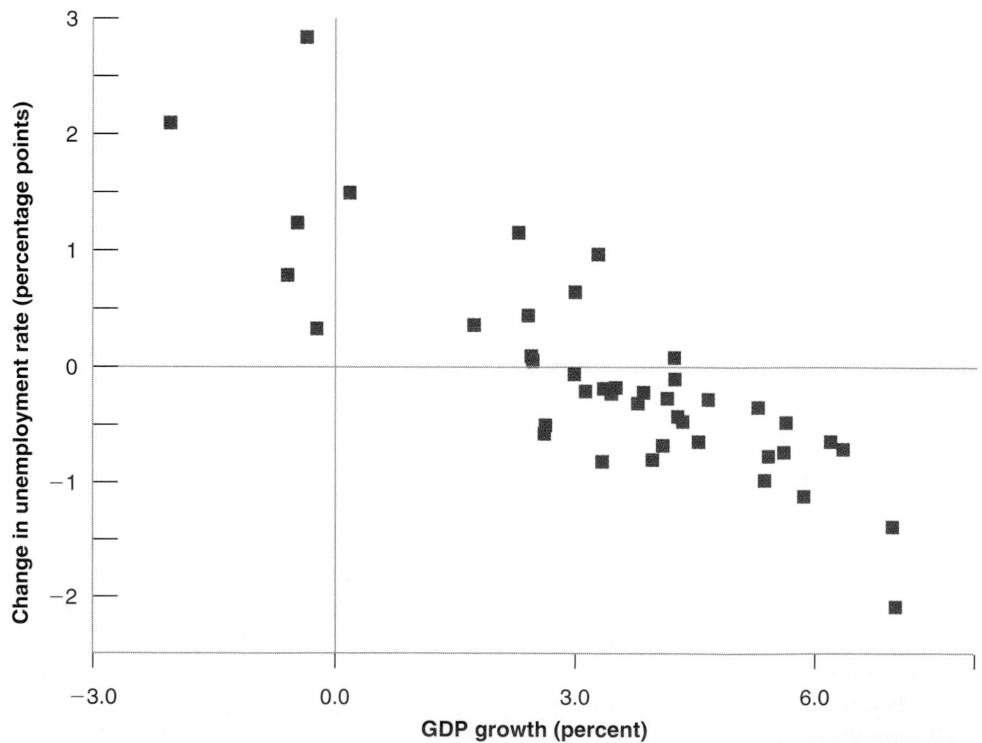

United States since 1960. Each point in the figure shows the growth rate of GDP and the change in the unemployment rate for a given year. (Figures such as Figure 2-2, which plot one variable against another over time, are called **scatter diagrams**.) The figure shows that:

- High output growth is typically associated with a decrease in the unemployment rate,
- Low output growth is typically associated with an increase in the unemployment rate.

This makes sense: High output growth leads to high employment growth, as firms hire more workers to produce more output. High employment growth leads to a decrease in unemployment. And the opposite holds when output growth is low. This relation has a simple but important implication: If the current unemployment rate is too high [what constitutes *too high* or *too low* will be the topic of many chapters later in this book; we can leave this discussion until then], higher output growth is needed to reduce it. If the unemployment rate is too low, then lower output growth is needed to increase it. If the unemployment rate is about right, then output growth should be able to maintain roughly constant unemployment. The unemployment rate therefore provides macroeconomists with a signal of where the economy stands and what growth rate is desirable.

Okun's law:
High output growth ⇒ unemployment rate ↓
Low output growth ⇒ unemployment rate ↑

From Figure 2-2, what is the rate of growth of output associated with no change or nearly no change in the unemployment rate?

Returning to our description of the state of the U.S. economy from Chapter 1: At the end of 2000, many economists worried that the prevailing unemployment rate, about 4%, was actually *too low*. A very low unemployment rate, they argued, might actually be bad for the economy, leading to labor shortages for firms, and to increasing inflation (more on this coming next). So, while they did not advocate creating a recession, they favored lower (but positive) output growth for some time, so as to allow the unemployment rate to increase to a somewhat higher level. It turns out that they got more than they had asked for: a recession, rather than a slowdown.

Social Implications of Unemployment

Macroeconomists also care about unemployment because of its direct effects on the welfare of the unemployed. Although unemployment benefits are greater today than they were during the Great Depression, unemployment is still often associated with financial and psychological suffering. How much depends on the nature of the unemployment. One image of the unemployed is that of a stagnant pool, of people remaining unemployed for long periods of time. As you shall see later in this book, this image does not reflect what happens in the United States. In the United States each month, many people become unemployed, and many of the unemployed (on average, 25–30% of them) find jobs. But, even in the United States, some groups (often the young, the ethnic minorities, and the unskilled) suffer disproportionately from unemployment, remaining chronically unemployed and being most vulnerable to becoming unemployed when the unemployment rate increases.

Things are quite different in Europe. There, the unemployed typically remain unemployed for a long time, and the image of a stagnant pool is much more appropriate.

The Inflation Rate

Inflation is a sustained rise in the general level of prices—the **price level**. The **inflation rate** is the rate at which the price level increases. (Symmetrically, **deflation** is a sustained decline in the price level. It corresponds to a negative inflation rate.)

Deflation is rare, but it happens. We saw in Chapter 1 that inflation was negative in both 2000 and 2001 in Japan.

The practical issue is how to define the price level. Macroeconomists typically look at two measures of the price level, at two *price indexes*: the GDP deflator and the consumer price index.

Did Spain Really Have a 24% Unemployment Rate in 1994?

FOCUS

In 1994, the official unemployment rate in Spain reached 24%. (It has decreased since then, but still stands above 10%.) This was roughly the same unemployment rate as in the United States in 1933, the worst year of the Great Depression. Yet Spain in 1994 looked nothing like the United States in 1933: There were few homeless, and most cities looked prosperous. Can we really believe that nearly one-fourth of the Spanish labor force was looking for work?

To answer this, we must first examine how the Spanish unemployment number is put together. Much as in the United States, it comes from a large survey of 60,000 households. People are classified as unemployed if they indicate that they are not working but are seeking work.

Can we be sure that people tell the truth? No. Although there is no obvious incentive to lie—answers to the survey are confidential and are not used to determine whether people are eligible for unemployment benefits—those who are working in the underground economy may prefer to play it safe and report that they are unemployed instead.

The size of the **underground economy**—that part of economic activity that is not measured in official statistics, either because the activity is illegal, or because firms and workers would rather not report it and thus not pay taxes—is an old issue in Spain. And because of that, we actually know more about the underground economy in Spain than in many other countries: In 1985, the Spanish government tried to find out more and organized a detailed survey of 60,000 individuals. To try to elicit the truth from those interviewed, the questionnaire asked interviewees for an extremely precise account of the use of their time, making it more difficult to misreport. The answers were interesting. The underground economy in Spain—defined as the number of people working without declaring it to the social security administration—accounted for 10–15% of employment. But it was composed mostly of people who already had a job and were taking a second or even a third job. The best estimate from the survey was that only about 15% of the unemployed were in fact working. This implied that the unemployment rate, which was officially 21% at the time, was in fact closer to 18%, still a very high number. In short, the Spanish underground economy is significant, but it just is not the case that most of the Spanish unemployed work in the underground economy.

How do the unemployed survive? Do they survive because unemployment benefits are unusually generous in Spain? No. Except for very generous unemployment systems in two regions, Andalusia and Extremadura—which turn out to have even higher unemployment than the rest of the country—unemployment benefits are roughly similar to unemployment benefits in other OECD countries. Benefits are typically 70% of the wage for the first six months, 60% thereafter. They are paid for a period of 4 to 24 months, depending on how long people have worked before becoming unemployed. The 30% of the unemployed who have been unemployed for more than two years do not receive unemployment benefits.

So how do they survive? A key to the answer lies with the Spanish family structure. The unemployment rate is highest among the young: In 1994, it was close to 50% for those between 16 and 19, and was around 40% for those between 20 and 24. The young typically stay at home until their late 20s, and have increasingly done so as unemployment has increased. Looking at households rather than at individuals, the proportion of households where nobody was employed in 1994 was less than 10%; the proportion of households that received neither wage income nor unemployment benefits was around 3%. In short, the family structure, and transfers from the rest of the family, is what allows many of the unemployed to survive.

The GDP Deflator

If we see nominal GDP increase faster than real GDP, the difference must come from an increase in prices. This remark motivates the definition of the GDP deflator. The **GDP deflator** in year t, P_t, is defined as the ratio of nominal GDP to real GDP in year t:

$$P_t = \frac{\text{nominal GDP}_t}{\text{Real GDP}_t} = \frac{\$Y_t}{Y_t}$$

Note that, in the year in which, by construction, real GDP is equal to nominal GDP (1996 at this point in the United States), this definition implies that the price level is equal to 1. This is worth emphasizing: The GDP deflator is what is called an **index**

number. Its level is chosen arbitrarily—here it is equal to 1 in 1996—and has no economic interpretation. But its rate of change, $(P_t - P_{t-1})/P_{t-1}$, has a clear economic interpretation: It gives the rate at which the general level of prices increases over time—the rate of inflation.

Index numbers are often set equal to 100 (in the base year) rather than to 1. If you look at the *Economic Report of the President* (see Chapter 1) you will see that the GDP deflator, reported in Table B3, is equal to 100 for 1996 (the base year), to 101.9 in 1997, and so on.

One advantage to defining the price level as the GDP deflator is that it implies that a simple relation holds between *nominal GDP, real GDP*, and the *GDP deflator*. To see this, reorganize the previous equation to get:

$$\$Y_t = P_t Y_t$$

Nominal GDP is equal to the GDP deflator times real GDP.

Compute the GDP deflator and the associated rate of inflation from 1995 to 1996 and from 1996 to 1997 in our car example in Section 2-1, when real GDP is constructed using the 1996 price of cars as the common price.

The Consumer Price Index

The GDP deflator gives the average price of output—the final goods *produced* in the economy. But consumers care about the average price of consumption—the goods they *consume*. The two prices need not be the same: The set of goods produced in the economy is not the same as the set of goods purchased by consumers, for two reasons:

- Some of the goods in GDP are sold not to consumers but to firms (machine tools, for example), to the government, or to foreigners.
- And some of the goods bought by consumers are not produced domestically, but rather imported from abroad.

To measure the average price of consumption, or, equivalently, the **cost of living**, macroeconomists look at another index, the **consumer price index**, or **CPI**. The CPI has been in existence since 1917, and is published monthly (in contrast, numbers for GDP and the GDP deflator are constructed and published only quarterly).

Do not confuse the CPI with the PPI, or *producer price index*, which is an index of prices of domestically produced goods in manufacturing, mining, agriculture, fishing, forestry, and electric utility industries.

The CPI gives the cost in dollars of a specific list of goods and services over time. The list, which is based on a detailed study of consumer spending, attempts to represent the consumption basket of a typical urban consumer. The list used to be updated roughly only once every ten years; starting in 2002, it will be updated every two years.

Each month, Bureau of Labor Statistics (BLS) employees visit stores to find out what has happened to the price of the goods on the list; prices are collected in 85 cities, from about 22,000 retail stores, car dealerships, gas stations, hospitals, and so on. These prices are then used to construct the consumer price index.

Like the GDP deflator (the price level associated with aggregate output, GDP), the CPI is an index. It is set equal to 1 in the period chosen as the base period and so its level has no particular significance. The current base period is 1982 to 1984, so the average for the period 1982 to 1984 is equal to 1. In 2000, the CPI was 1.71; thus, it cost 71% more in dollars to purchase the same consumption basket than it did in 1982–1984.

Like the GDP deflator, the CPI is typically set to 100 rather than to 1 in the base period.

You may wonder how the rate of inflation differs depending on whether the GDP deflator or the CPI is used to measure it. The answer is given in Figure 2-3, which plots the two inflation rates since 1960 for the United States. The figure yields two conclusions:

- The CPI and the GDP deflator move together most of the time. In most years, the two inflation rates differ by less than 1%.
- But there are clear exceptions. In both 1974 and 1979 to 1980, the increase in the CPI was significantly larger than the increase in the GDP deflator. The reason is not hard to find.

  Recall that the GDP deflator is the price of goods produced in the United States, whereas the CPI is the price of goods consumed in the United States. That means when the price of imported goods increases relative to the price of goods produced in the United States, the CPI increases faster than the GDP deflator. This

Figure 2-3

Inflation Rate, Using the CPI and the GDP Deflator, 1960–2000.

The inflation rates, computed using either the CPI or the GDP deflator, are largely similar.

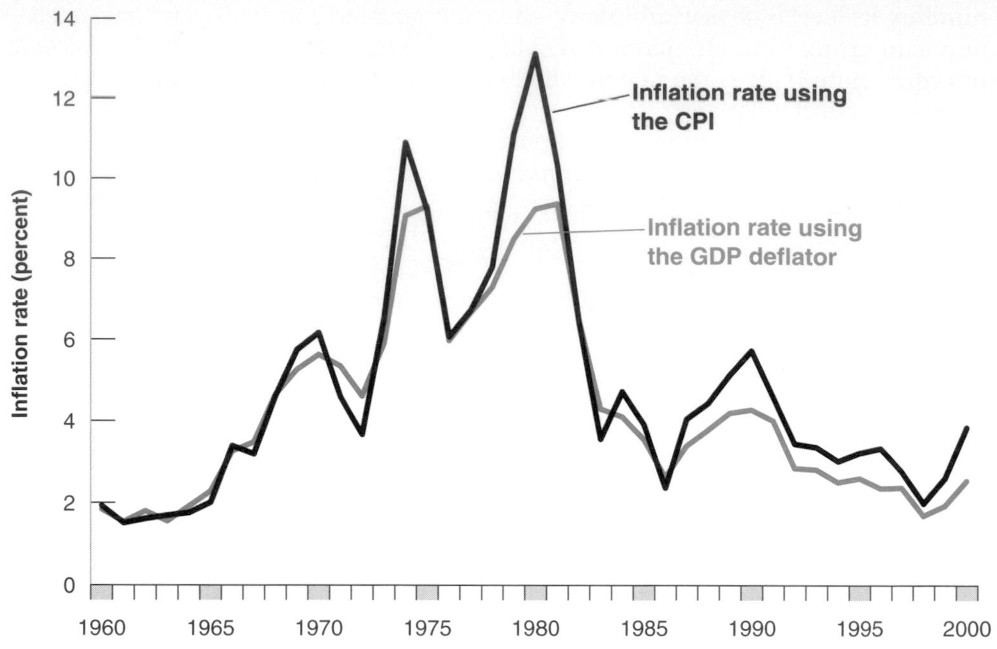

is precisely what happened in both 1974 and 1979 to 1980. In each case, the price of oil doubled. And although the United States is a producer of oil, it produces much less than it consumes: It was and still is a major oil importer. Thus, in each case, there was a large increase in the CPI compared to the GDP deflator.

The same mechanism was at work, but on a smaller scale, in 2000. The reason was the same: a large increase in the relative price of oil.

In what follows, I shall typically assume that the two indexes move together so I do not need to distinguish between them. I shall simply talk about *the price level* and denote it by P_t, without indicating whether I have the CPI or the GDP deflator in mind.

Inflation and Unemployment

Is there a relation between inflation and activity? Or does inflation have a life of its own? The answer: There is an important relation between unemployment and inflation, but it is far from mechanical—the relation has changed over time, and varies across countries.

The relation between unemployment and inflation in the United States since 1970 is shown in Figure 2-4. The figure plots the *change in* the inflation rate (using the CPI)—that is, the inflation rate this year minus the inflation rate last year—on the vertical axis, the unemployment rate on the horizontal axis. Each point in the figure gives the combination of unemployment rates and changes in inflation rates in a given year.

Figure 2-4 shows a negative relation between the unemployment rate and the change in inflation:

- When the unemployment rate is low, inflation tends to increase.
- When the unemployment rate is high, inflation tends to decrease.

The Phillips curve:

Low unemployment $\Rightarrow$ inflation $\uparrow$

High unemployment $\Rightarrow$ inflation $\downarrow$

This negative relation is called the Phillips relation, and the curve that fits the set of points best is called the **Phillips curve**. It is named for the economist A. W. Phillips, who, in the 1950s, was the first to document the relation between unemployment and inflation. Where this relation comes from, why it has changed over time, and what it implies, will be the focus of many later chapters. But, continuing our earlier discussion of the current U.S. unemployment rate, you can already see one implication: A very low unemployment rate is likely to lead to an increase in inflation.

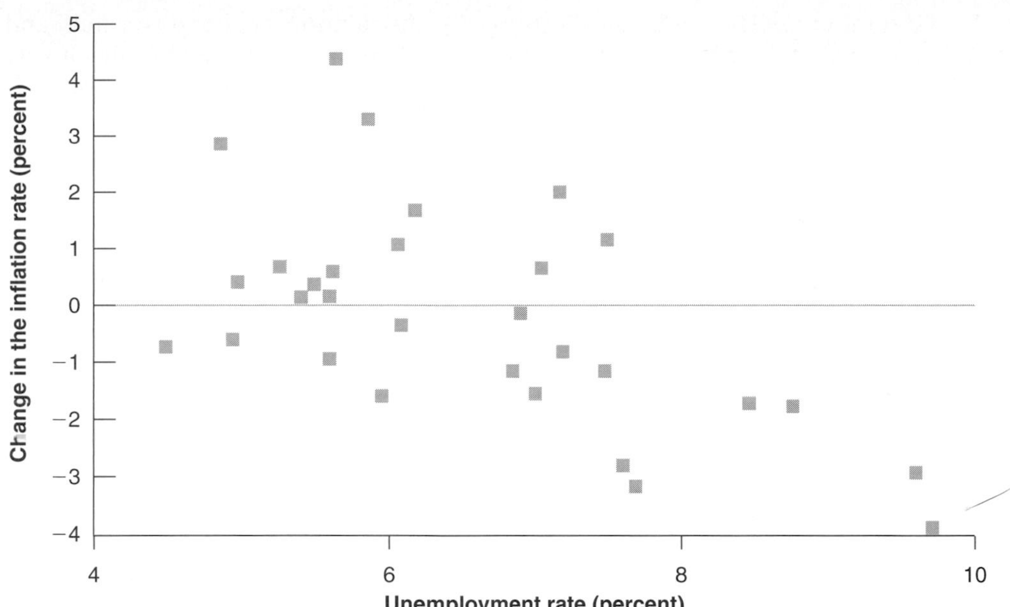

Figure 2-4

Change in the U.S. Inflation Rate Versus the U.S. Unemployment Rate, 1970–2000

When the unemployment rate is low, inflation tends to increase. When the unemployment rate is high, inflation tends to decrease.

Why Do Economists Care About Inflation?

If a higher inflation rate meant just a faster proportional increase in all prices and wages—a case called *pure inflation*—inflation would be only a minor inconvenience. Relative prices would not be affected by inflation.

Take, for example, the workers' *real wage*—the wage measured in terms of goods rather than in dollars. In the economy with 10% inflation, prices would increase by 10% a year. But so would wages—and real wages would remain the same. Inflation would not be entirely irrelevant; people would have to keep track of the increase in prices and wages when making decisions. But this would be a small burden, hardly justifying making control of the inflation rate one of the major goals of macroeconomic policy.

This ignores the changes in real wages that would occur even if there were no inflation. A more accurate statement is that under pure inflation, the rate of inflation would have no effect on the evolution of real wages.

So, why do economists care about inflation? Precisely because there is no such thing as pure inflation:

- During periods of inflation, not all prices and wages rise proportionately. Because they don't, inflation affects income distribution. For example, retirees in many countries receive payments that do not keep up with the price level, so they lose in relation to other groups when inflation is high. This is not the case in the United States, where Social Security benefits automatically rise with the CPI, protecting retirees from inflation. But during the very high inflation that took place in Russia in the 1990s, retirement pensions did not keep up with inflation, and many retirees were pushed to near starvation.
- Inflation leads to other distortions. Variations in relative prices also lead to more uncertainty, making it harder for firms to make decisions about the future, such as investment decisions. Some prices, which are fixed by law or by regulation, lag behind the others, leading to changes in relative prices. Taxation interacts with inflation to create more distortions. If tax brackets are not adjusted for inflation, for example, people move into higher and higher tax brackets as their nominal income increases, even if their real income remains the same.

This is known as *bracket creep*. In the United States, the tax brackets are now adjusted automatically for inflation: If inflation is 5%, all tax brackets also go up by 5%—in other words, there is no bracket creep.

To summarize: High inflation affects income distribution, creates distortions, and increases uncertainty. How important these problems are, and whether they justify trying to achieve and maintain, say, zero inflation, are much debated questions. We shall take them up later in this book.

2-3 A Road Map

Having defined the main variables, let's now turn to the central question of macroeconomics. What determines the level of aggregate output?

- Reading newspapers suggests a first answer: Movements in output come from movements in the demand for goods. You probably have read news stories that begin, "Production and sales of automobiles were higher last month, apparently due to a surge in consumer confidence, which drove consumers to showrooms in record numbers." Such explanations point to the role of demand in determining aggregate output, as well as to factors ranging from consumer confidence to tax rates to interest rates.
- But, surely, no amount of Indian consumers rushing to Indian showrooms can increase India's output to the level of output in the United States. This remark suggests a second answer: What matters for aggregate output is the supply side, how much the economy can produce. This depends on how advanced the technology of the country is, how much capital it is using, the size and the skills of its labor force. These factors, not consumer confidence, must be the fundamental determinants of the level of output.
- The previous argument can be pushed one step further: Neither technology, nor capital, nor skills are given. The technological sophistication of a country depends on its ability to innovate and introduce new technologies. The size of its capital stock depends on how much people save. The skills of workers depend on the quality of the education system. Other factors may also be important. If firms are to operate efficiently, they need a clear system of laws under which to operate, and an honest government to enforce them.

  This suggests a third answer: The true determinants of output are factors such as the education system, the saving rate, and the quality of government. It is there that we must look if we want to understand what determines the level of output.

Which of the three answers is right? Answer: All three. But each applies over a different time frame:

- In the **short run**, say, a few years, the first answer is the right one. Year-to-year movements in output are primarily driven by movements in demand. Changes in demand, which can arise from changes in consumer confidence or from any other source, can lead to a decrease in output (a recession), or an increase in output (an expansion).
- In the **medium run**, say, a decade, the second answer is the right one. Over the medium run, the economy tends to return to the level of output determined by supply factors: the capital stock, the level of technology, and the size of the labor force. And, over a decade or so, these factors do not move so much that it is a mistake to take them as given.
- In the **long run**, say, a half century or more, the third answer is the right one. To understand why Japan grew so much faster than the United States for the 40 years following World War II, we must explain why both capital and the level of technology increased so much faster in Japan than in the United States. We must look at factors such as the education system, the saving rate, and the role of the government.

This way of thinking about the determinants of output underlies macroeconomics, and it underlies the organization of this book.

A Tour of the Book

The book is organized in three parts: a core; three extensions; and, finally, an in-depth look at the role of macroeconomic policy. This organization is shown in Figure 2-5. Let me describe it in more detail.

The Core

The core is composed of three parts—the short run, the medium run, and the long run.

- Chapters 3 to 5 look at the determination of output in the short run.

  The focus is on the determination of the demand for goods. To focus on the role of demand, we assume that firms are willing to supply any quantity at a given price; in other words, we ignore supply constraints.

  Chapter 3 looks at the goods market. Chapter 4 focuses on financial markets. Chapter 5 puts goods and financial markets together.

  The resulting framework is known as the *IS-LM* model. Developed in the late 1930s, the *IS-LM* model still provides a simple way of thinking about the determination of output in the short run, and it remains a basic building block of

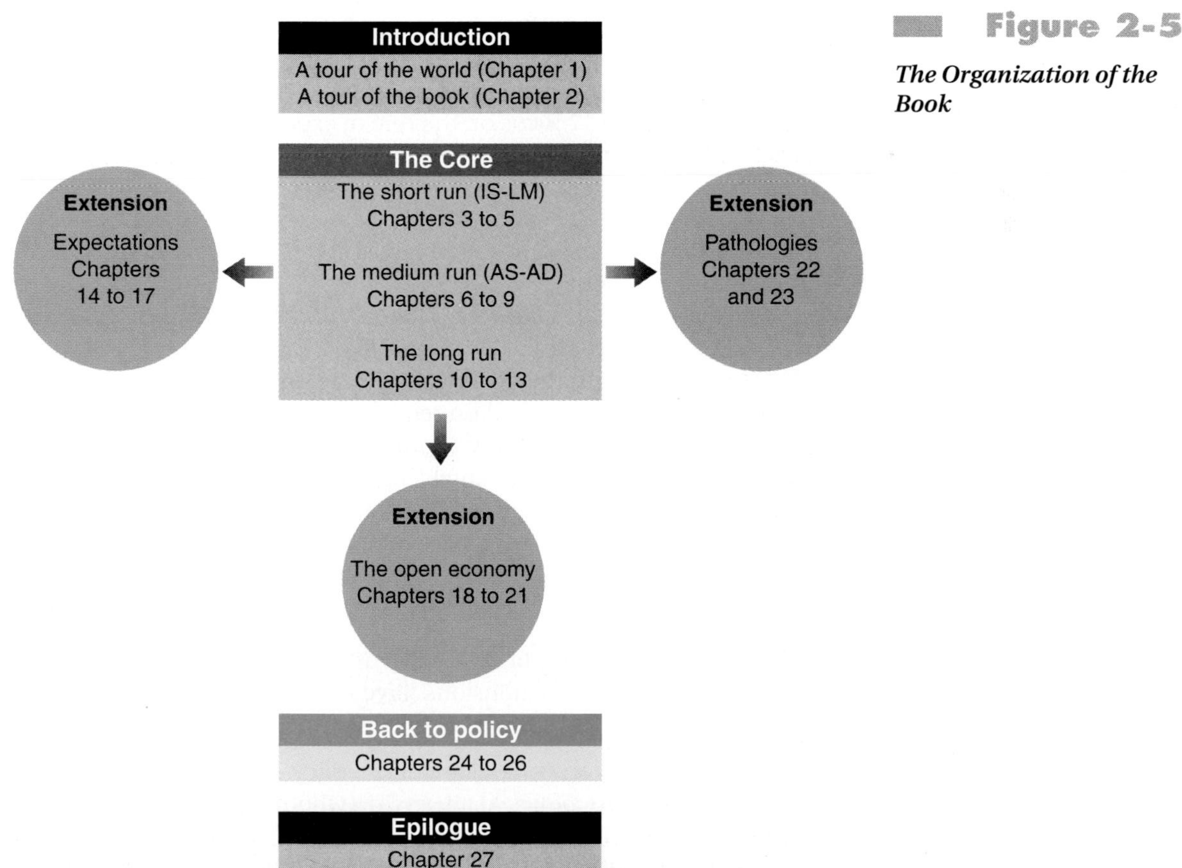

Figure 2-5

The Organization of the Book

macroeconomics. It also allows for a first pass at studying the role of fiscal policy and monetary policy in affecting output.

- Chapters 6 to 9 develop the supply side, and look at the determination of output in the medium run.

  Chapter 6 introduces the labor market. Chapter 7 puts together goods, financial, and labor markets, and shows you how to think about the determination of output both in the short run and in the medium run. The model developed in Chapter 7 is called the aggregate supply–aggregate demand *AS-AD* model of output. Chapters 8 and 9 then show how the *AS-AD* model can be used to think about many issues, from the relation between output and inflation, to the role of monetary and fiscal policy both in the short run and in the medium run.
- Chapters 10 to 13 focus on the long run.

  Chapter 10 introduces the relevant facts, and looks at the growth of output both across countries and across long periods of time. Chapters 11 and 12 then discuss the role and the determinants of both capital accumulation and technological progress in growth. Chapter 13 looks at the interaction between technological progress, wages, and unemployment.

Extensions

The core chapters give you a way of thinking about the determination of output (and unemployment and inflation) over the short, medium, and long run. However, they leave out several elements, which are explored in three extensions.

- The core chapters largely ignore the role of *expectations*. But expectations play an essential role in macroeconomics. Nearly all the economic decisions people and firms make—whether to buy bonds or whether to buy stocks, whether or not to buy a machine—depend on their expectations of future profits, of future interest rates, and so on. Fiscal and monetary policy affect activity not only through their direct effects, but also through their effect on expectations.

  Chapters 14 to 17 focus on the role of expectations, and their implications for fiscal and monetary policy.
- The core chapters treat the economy as *closed*, ignoring its interactions with the rest of the world. But economies are increasingly *open*, trading with other countries both in goods and in financial assets. As a result, countries are more and more interdependent.

  The nature of this interdependence and the implications for fiscal and monetary policy are the topics of Chapters 18 to 21.
- The core chapters on the short run and the medium run focus on fluctuations in output—on expansions, and on recessions. Sometimes, however, the word "fluctuations" does not accurately capture what is happening. Something goes very wrong: Inflation reaches extremely high rates. Or, as was the case during the Great Depression, unemployment remains very high for a very long time. Or, as is Japan today, a country goes through a prolonged economic slump.

  These *pathologies* are the topics of Chapters 22 and 23.

Back to Policy

Monetary policy and fiscal policy are discussed in nearly every chapter of this book. But, once the core and the extensions have been covered, it is useful to go back, put things together, and assess the role of policy.

- Chapter 24 focuses on general issues of policy, such as whether macroeconomists know enough to use policy at all, and on whether policy makers can be trusted to do what is right.
- Chapters 25 and 26 then assess the role of monetary and fiscal policy.

Epilogue

Macroeconomics is not a fixed body of knowledge. It evolves over time. The final chapter, Chapter 27, looks at the recent history of macroeconomics and how macroeconomists have come to believe what they believe today. From the outside, macroeconomics often looks like a field divided between schools—Keynesians, monetarists, new classicals, supply-siders, and so on—hurling arguments at each other. The actual process of research is more orderly and more productive than this image suggests. I identify what I see as the main differences among macroeconomists, and the set of propositions that define the core of macroeconomics today.

Summary

- We can think of GDP, the measure of aggregate activity, in three equivalent ways: (1) GDP is the value of the final goods and services produced in the economy during a given period; (2) GDP is the sum of value added in the economy during a given period; and (3) GDP is the sum of incomes in the economy during a given period.
- Nominal GDP is the sum of the quantities of final goods produced times their current price. This implies that changes in nominal GDP reflect both changes in quantities and changes in prices. Real GDP is a measure of output. Changes in real GDP reflect changes in quantities only.
- The labor force is the sum of those employed and those unemployed. The unemployment rate is the ratio of the number of people unemployed to the number of people in the labor force. Somebody is classified as unemployed if he or she does not have a job and has been looking for work in the last four weeks.
- The empirical relation between GDP growth and the change in the unemployment rate is called Okun's law. The relation shows that high output growth is associated with a decrease in the unemployment rate, and low output growth is associated with an increase in the unemployment rate.
- Inflation is a rise in the general level of prices—the price level. The inflation rate is the rate at which the price level increases. Macroeconomists look at two measures of the price level. The first is the GDP deflator, which gives the average price of the goods produced in the economy. The second is the consumer price index (CPI), which gives the average price of goods consumed in the economy.
- The empirical relation between the inflation rate and the unemployment rate is called the Phillips curve. This relation has changed over time, and also varies across countries. In the United States today, it takes the following form: When the unemployment rate is low, inflation tends to increase. When the unemployment rate is high, inflation tends to decrease.
- Inflation leads to changes in income distribution. It also leads to distortions and increased uncertainty.
- Macroeconomists distinguish between the short run (a few years), the medium run (a decade), and the long run (a half century or more). They think of output as being determined by demand in the short run, by the level of technology, the capital stock, and the labor force in the medium run, and by factors such as education, research, saving, and the quality of government in the long run.

Key Terms

- national income and product accounts, 22
- aggregate output, 22
- gross domestic product, or GDP, 22
- gross national product, or GNP, 22
- final good, 22
- intermediate good, 23
- value added, 23
- nominal GDP, 24
- real GDP, 24
- real GDP in chained (1996) dollars, 25
- dollar GDP, GDP in current dollars, 25
- GDP in terms of goods, GDP in constant dollars, GDP adjusted for inflation, GDP in 1996 dollars, 25
- GDP growth, expansions, recessions, 26
- labor force, 26
- hedonic pricing, 27
- unemployment rate, 27
- Current Population Survey (CPS), 27
- not in the labor force, 28
- discouraged workers, 28
- participation rate, 28
- Okun's law, 28
- scatter diagrams, 29
- price level, 29
- inflation, deflation, 29
- inflation rate, 29

- underground economy, 30
- GDP deflator, 30
- index number, 30
- cost of living, 31
- consumer price index (CPI), 31
- Phillips curve, 32
- short run, medium run, and long run, 34

Questions and Problems

Quick Check

1. Using the information in this chapter, label each of the following statements true, false, *or* uncertain. *Explain briefly.*

a. The share of labor income in GDP is much smaller than the share of capital income.

b. U.S. GDP was 19 times higher in 2001 than it was in 1960.

c. If a high unemployment rate discourages workers from looking for work, the unemployment rate can be a poor indicator of labor market conditions. To assess the situation, one must also look at the participation rate.

d. A reduction in the rate of unemployment requires high output growth.

e. If the Japanese CPI is currently at 108 and the U.S. CPI is at 104, then the Japanese rate of inflation is higher than the U.S. rate of inflation.

f. The rate of inflation computed using the CPI is a better index of inflation than the rate of inflation computed using the GDP deflator.

2. Suppose you are measuring annual U.S. GDP by adding up the final value of all goods and services produced in the economy. Determine the effect of each of the following transactions on GDP:

a. You buy $100 worth of fish from a fisherman, which you cook and eat at home.

b. A seafood restaurant buys $100 worth of fish from a fisherman.

c. Delta Airlines buys a new jet from Boeing for $200 million.

d. The Greek national airline buys a new jet from Boeing for $200 million.

e. Delta Airlines sells one of its jets to John Travolta for $100 million.

3. During a given year, the following activities occur:

i. A silver mining company pays its workers $200,000 to mine 75 pounds of silver. The silver is then sold to a jewelry manufacturer for $300,000.

ii. The jewelry manufacturer pays its workers $250,000 to make silver necklaces, which it sells directly to consumers for $1,000,000.

a. Using the "production of final goods" approach, what is GDP in this economy?

b. What is the value added at each stage of production? Using the "value added" approach, what is GDP?

c. What are the total wages and profits earned? Using the income approach, what is GDP?

4. An economy produces three goods: cars, computers, and oranges. Quantities and prices per unit for years 2001 and 2002 are as follows:

	2001		*2002*	
	Quantity	**Price**	**Quantity**	**Price**
Cars	10	$2,000	12	$3,000
Computers	4	$1,000	6	$500
Oranges	1000	$1	1000	$1

a. What is nominal GDP in 2001 and in 2002? By what percentage does nominal GDP change from 2001 to 2002?

b. Using the prices for 2001 as the set of common prices, what is real GDP in 2001 and in 2002? By what percentage does real GDP change from 2001 to 2002?

c. Using the prices for 2002 as the set of common prices, what is real GDP in 2001 and in 2002? By what percentage does real GDP change from 2001 to 2002?

d. Why are the two output growth rates constructed in (b) and (c) different? Which one is correct? Explain your answer.

5. Use the data from problem 4 to answer the following:

a. Suppose we use the prices for 2001 as the set of common prices to compute real GDP in 2001 and in 2002. Compute the GDP deflator for 2001 and for 2002, and the rate of inflation from 2001 to 2002.

b. Suppose we use the prices for 2002 as the set of common prices to compute real GDP in 2001 and in 2002. Compute the GDP deflator for 2001 and for 2002, and the rate of inflation from 2001 to 2002.

c. Why are the two rates of inflation different? Which one is correct? Explain your answer.

6. Use the economy described in problem 4.

a. Construct real GDP for years 2001 and 2002 by using the average price of each good over the two years.

b. By what percentage does real GDP change from 2001 to 2002?

c. What is the GDP deflator in 2001 and 2002? What is the rate of inflation from 2001 to 2002, using the GDP deflator?

d. Is this an attractive solution to the problems pointed out in problems 4 and 5 (i.e., two different growth rates, and two different inflation rates, depending on what set of prices was used)? (The answer is yes, and is the basis for the construction of chained-type deflators. See the appendix to Chapter 2 for more discussion.)

Dig Deeper

7. Hedonic pricing

As the first Focus box of Chapter 2 explains, it is hard to measure the true increase in prices of goods whose characteristics change over time. Hedonic pricing offers a method of computing the quality-adjusted increase in prices.

a. Consider the case of a routine medical checkup. Name some reasons why you may want to use hedonic pricing to measure the change in the price of this service.

Now consider the case of a medical checkup for a pregnant woman. Suppose that the year a new ultrasound method is introduced, the price of this checkup increases by 20%, and all doctors adopt the ultrasound simultaneously.

b. What information do you need in order to determine the quality-adjusted increase in pregnancy checkups?
c. Is that information available? Explain. What can you say about the quality-adjusted price increase of pregnancy checkups?

8. Measured and true GDP

Suppose that instead of cooking dinner for an hour, you decide to work an extra hour, earning an additional $12. You then take out some Chinese food, which costs you $10.

a. By how much does measured GDP increase?
b. Should true GDP increase by more or less? Explain.

Explore Further

9. To answer this question, you will need monthly data on U.S. unemployment rates and annual data on U.S. real GDP growth rates. The former can be retrieved from the Web page of the Bureau of Labor Statistics, **www. stats.bls.gov/** *(look for "Labor Force Statistics from the CPS," "most requested series"). The latter can be retrieved from the Web page of the Bureau of Economic Analysis (look under "GDP and Related Data"),* **www.bea.doc.gov/**. *However, you should feel free to use any data source you wish (see the appendix to Chapter 1).*

Examine Figure 2-2. Imagine or draw a straight line joining the data point corresponding to the largest positive change in the unemployment rate and the data point corresponding to the largest negative change in the unemployment rate.

a. Write down the equation corresponding to this line. What is (roughly) the intercept of the line? What is (roughly) the slope of the line?
b. Using the answer to (a), derive the growth rate of GDP such that the unemployment rate stays roughly constant.
c. From the data on GDP growth, find a year during which the GDP growth rate was roughly equal to the growth rate you got as an answer to (b). What happened to the unemployment rate during that year?
d. Suppose that U.S. policy makers want to reduce the unemployment rate by one percentage point in one year. Using the answer to (a), derive the growth rate needed to achieve this reduction in the unemployment rate.

We invite you to visit the Blanchard page on the Prentice Hall Web site at:
www.prenhall.com/blanchard
for this chapter's World Wide Web exercises

Further Readings

If you want to know more about the definition and the construction of the many economic indicators that are regularly reported on the news—from the help-wanted index to the retail sales index—two easy-to-read references are

The Guide to Economic Indicators, by Norman Frumkin, third edition, M. E. Sharpe, New York, 2000.

The Economist Guide to Economic Indicators, by the staff of the *Economist*, Wiley and Sons, New York, 1998.

In 1995, the U.S. Senate set up a commission to study the construction of the CPI, and to make recommendations about potential changes. That commission concluded that the rate of inflation computed using the CPI was on average about 1% too high. If this conclusion is correct, this implies in particular that real wages (nominal wages divided by the CPI) have grown at 1% more a year than is currently reported. For more on the conclusions of the commission, and some of the exchanges that followed, read *Consumer Prices, The Consumer Price Index*, and *The Cost of Living*, by Michael Boskin et al, *Journal of Economic Perspectives*, Volume 12, number 1, Winter 1998, 3–26.

For a short history of the construction of the National Income Accounts, read *GDP: One of the Great Inventions of the 20th Century*, Survey of Current Business, January 2000, 1–9. (Internet address: **www.bea.gov/bea/articles/beawide/2000/0100od.pdf**)

For why it is hard to measure the price level and output correctly, read "Viagra and the Wealth of Nations" by Paul Krugman, 1998 (Internet address: **web.mit.edu/krugman/www/viagra.html**). (Paul Krugman, an economist at Princeton University, regularly writes columns for a number of newspapers and magazines. Many of the columns are available on the Internet; they are insightful and fun to read.)

Appendix: The Construction of Real GDP, and Chain-Type Indexes

The example I used in the chapter had only one final good—cars—so constructing real GDP was easy. But how do we construct real GDP when there is more than one final good? This is what this appendix is about.

All that is needed to make the relevant points about the construction of real GDP in an economy with many final goods is to look at an economy where there are just two final goods. What we do for two goods works just as well for millions of goods.

So, suppose that an economy produces two final goods, say, cars and potatoes:

- In year 0, it produces 100,000 pounds of potatoes, at a price of $1 a pound, and 10 cars that sell for $10,000 a car.
- In year 1, it produces and sells 100,000 pounds of potatoes at a price of $1.20 a pound, and 11 cars at $10,000 a car.
- Nominal GDP in year 0 is therefore equal to $200,000. Nominal GDP in year 1 is equal to $230,000.

This information is summarized in the following table.

Nominal GDP in Year 0 and in Year 1

		Year 0	
	Quantity	**$ Price**	**$ Value**
Potatoes	100,000	1	100,000
Cars	10	10,000	100,000
Nominal GDP			200,000
		Year 1	
	Quantity	**$ Price**	**$ Value**
Potatoes	100,000	1.20	120,000
Cars	11	10,000	110,000
Nominal GDP			230,000

The increase in nominal GDP from year 0 to year 1 is equal to $30,000/$200,000 = 15%. But what is the increase in real GDP? The basic idea in constructing real GDP is to evaluate quantities in both years using the *same set of prices.*

Suppose we choose, for example, the prices of year 0; year 0 is then called the **base year**. The computation is then as follows:

- Real GDP in year 0 is the sum of the quantity in year 0 times the price in year 0, for both goods: (100,000 × $1) + (10 × $10,000) = $200,000.
- Real GDP in year 1 is the sum of the quantity in year 1 time the price in year 0, for both goods: (100,000 × $1) + (11 × $10,000) = $210,000.
- The rate of change of real GDP from year 0 to year 1 is ($210,000 − $200,000)/$200,000, or 5%.

This answer raises however an important issue: Instead of using year 0 as the base year, we could have used year 1, or any other year. If, for example, we had used year 1 as the base year, then:

- Real GDP in year 0 would be equal to (100,000 × $1.2 + 10 × $10,000) = $220,000.
- Real GDP in year 1 would be equal to (100,000 × $1.2 + 11 × $10,000) = $230,000.
- The rate of change of real GDP from year 0 to year 1 would be equal to $10,000/$220,000, or 4.5%.

The answer using year 1 as the base year would therefore be different from the answer using year 0 as the base year. So, if the choice of the base year affects the constructed rate of change of output, what base year should one choose?

Until the mid-1990s in the United States—and still in most countries today—the practice was to choose a base year and change it infrequently, say, every five years or so. For example, in the United States, 1987 was the base year used from December 1991 to December 1995. That is, measures of real GDP published, for example, in 1994 for both 1994 and for all earlier years were constructed using 1987 prices. In December 1995, national income accounts shifted to 1992 as a base year; measures of real GDP for all earlier years were recalculated using 1992 prices.

This practice was logically unappealing. Every time the base year was changed, and a new set of prices was used, all past real GDP numbers—and all past rates of change of real GDP—were recomputed: History was, in effect, rewritten every five years! Starting in December 1995, the U.S. Bureau of Economic Analysis (BEA)—the government office that produces the GDP numbers—shifted to a new method, which does not suffer from this problem.

The method requires three steps:

- The rate of change of real GDP from each year to the next is computed using as the common set of prices the average of the prices for the two years.

  For example, the rate of change of GDP from 1998 to 1999 is computed by

  1. constructing real GDP for 1998 and real GDP for 1999 using as the common set of prices the average of the prices for 1998 and 1999, and
  2. computing the rate of change of real GDP from 1998 to 1999 (this is actually a slightly simplified description of what the BEA does; but it is close enough, and much easier to understand).
- An index for the level of real GDP is then constructed by *linking*—or *chaining*—the constructed rates of change for each year.

  The index is set equal to 1 in some arbitrary year. As this is written (2002), the arbitrary year is 1996. Given that the constructed rate of growth from 1996 to 1997 by the Bureau of Economic Analysis is 4.4%, the index for 1997 equals (1 + 4.4%) = 1.044.

The index for 1998 is obtained by multiplying the index for 1997 by the rate of growth from 1997 to 1998, and so on. (You will find the value of this index—multiplied by 100—in the second column of Table B3 in the *Economic Report of the President.* Check that it is 100 in 1996 and 104.4 in 1997, and so on.)

- Finally, this index is multiplied by nominal GDP in 1996 to give *real GDP in chained (1996) dollars.*

As the index is 1 in 1996, this implies that real GDP in 1996 equals nominal GDP in 1996.

Chained refers to the chaining of rates of change described above. The year in parentheses—*(1996)*—refers to the year where, by construction, real GDP is equal to nominal GDP. (You will find the value of real GDP in chained (1996) dollars in the first column of Table B2 of the *Economic Report of the President.*)

This index is more complicated to construct than the indexes used before 1995. But it is clearly better conceptually: The prices used to evaluate real GDP in two adjacent years are the right prices, namely, the average prices for those two years. And, because the rate of growth from one year to the next is constructed using the prices in those two years rather than the set of prices in an arbitrary base year, history will not be rewritten every five years or so—as it used to be when, under the previous method for constructing real GDP, the base year was changed.

Key Terms

- **base year, 40**

The Short Run

In the short run, demand determines output. Many factors affect demand, from consumer confidence, to fiscal and monetary policy.

Chapter 3

Chapter 3 looks at equilibrium in the goods market and the determination of output. It focuses on the interaction between demand, production, and income. It shows how fiscal policy affects output.

Chapter 4

Chapter 4 looks at equilibrium in financial markets and the determination of the interest rate. It shows how monetary policy affects the interest rate.

Chapter 5

Chapter 5 looks at the goods market and financial markets together. It shows what determines output and the interest rate in the short run. It looks at the role of fiscal and monetary policy. The model developed in Chapter 5 is called the *IS-LM* model and is one of the workhorses of macroeconomics.

The Goods Market

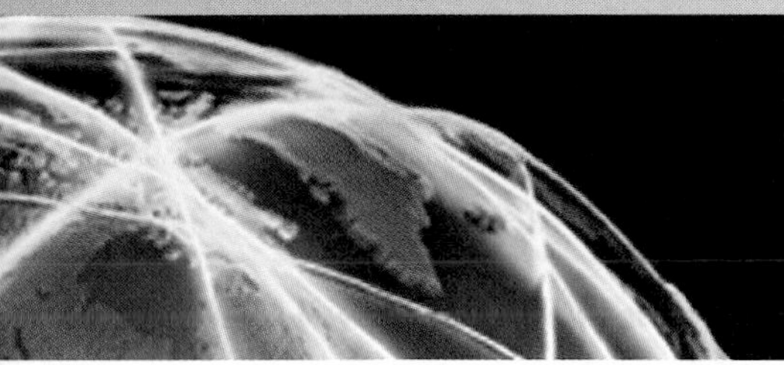

When economists think about year-to-year movements in economic activity, they focus on the interactions between *production, income,* and *demand:*

- Changes in the demand for goods lead to changes in production.
- Changes in production lead to changes in income.
- And changes in income lead to changes in the demand for goods.

Nothing makes the point better than this cartoon:

9/24/91

This chapter looks at these interactions and their implications.

- Section 3-1 looks at the composition of GDP, and the different sources of the demand for goods.
- Section 3-2 looks at the determinants of the demand for goods.
- Section 3-3 shows how equilibrium output is determined by the condition that the production of goods must be equal to the demand for goods.
- Section 3-4 gives an alternative way of thinking about the equilibrium, based on the equality of investment and saving.
- Section 3-5 takes a first pass at the effects of fiscal policy on equilibrium output. ■

3-1 The Composition of GDP

The purchase of a machine by a firm, the decision to go to a restaurant by a consumer, the purchase of combat airplanes by the federal government—these are clearly very different decisions and depend on different factors. So, if we want to understand what determines the demand for goods, it makes sense to decompose aggregate output (GDP) from the point of view of the different goods being produced, and from the point of view of the different buyers for these goods.

***Output* and *production* are synonymous. There is no rule for using one or the other. Use the one that sounds better.**

The decomposition of GDP typically used by macroeconomists is given in Table 3-1. (A more detailed version, with more formal definitions, is given in Appendix 1 at the end of the book.)

- First comes **consumption** (which I shall denote by the letter C when I use algebra throughout this book). These are the goods and services purchased by consumers, ranging from food to airline tickets, to vacations, to new cars, and so on. Consumption is by far the largest component of GDP. In 2001, it accounted for 69% of GDP.

TABLE 3-1 The Composition of U.S. GDP, 2001

		Billions of Dollars		Percent of GDP	
	GDP (Y)	10,208		100	
1.	Consumption (C)	7,064		69	
2.	Investment (I)	1,692		17	
	Nonresidential		1,246		12
	Residential		446		5
3.	Government spending (G)	1,839		18	
4.	Net exports	−329		−3	
	Exports (X)		1,051		11
	Imports (IM)		−1,380		−14
5.	Inventory investment	−58		−1	

Source: *Survey of Current Business*, April 2002, Table 1-1.

- Second comes **investment**, (I), sometimes called **fixed investment** to distinguish it from inventory investment (which we shall discuss shortly). Investment is the sum of **nonresidential investment**, the purchase by firms of new plants or new machines (from turbines to computers), and **residential investment**, the purchase by people of new houses or apartments.

  Nonresidential investment and residential investment, and the decisions behind them, have more in common than might first appear. Firms buy machines or plants to be able to produce output in the future. People buy houses or apartments to get *housing services* in the future. In both cases, the decision to buy depends on the services these goods will yield in the future; so it makes sense to treat them together. Together, nonresidential and residential investment accounted for 17% of GDP in 2001.

Warning! To most people, *investment* refers to the purchase of assets, such as gold or shares of General Motors. Economists use *investment* to refer to the purchase of *new capital goods,* such as (new) machines, (new) buildings, or (new) houses. When economists refer to the purchase of gold, or shares of General Motors, or other financial assets, they use the term *financial investment.*

- Third comes **government spending**, (G). This represents the purchases of goods and services by the federal, state, and local governments. The goods range from airplanes to office equipment. The services include services provided by government employees: In effect, the national income accounts treat the government as buying the services provided by government employees—and then providing these services to the public, free of charge.

  Note that G does not include **government transfers**, such as Medicare or Social Security payments, nor interest payments on the government debt. Although these are clearly government expenditures, they are not purchases of goods and services. That is why the number for government spending on goods and services in Table 3-1, 17% of GDP, is smaller than the number for total government spending including transfers and interest payments. That number, in 2001, was 29% of GDP.
- The sum of lines 1, 2, and 3 gives the purchases of goods and services by U.S. consumers, U.S. firms, and the U.S. government. To get to the purchases of U.S. goods and services, two more steps are needed:

  First, we must subtract **imports** (IM), the purchases of foreign goods and services by U.S. consumers, U.S. firms, and the U.S. government.

  Second, we must add **exports** (X), the purchases of U.S. goods and services by foreigners.

  The difference between exports and imports, ($X - IM$), is called **net exports**, or the **trade balance**. If exports exceed imports, a country is said to run a **trade surplus**. If exports are less than imports, the country is said to run a **trade deficit**. In 2001, U.S. exports accounted for 11% of GDP. U.S. imports were equal to 14% of GDP, so the United States was running a trade deficit equal to 3% of GDP.

Exports − imports ≡ net exports ≡ trade balance

Exports > imports ⇔ trade surplus

Exports < imports ⇔ trade deficit

- So far, we have looked at various sources of purchases (equivalently, sales) of U.S. goods and services in 2001. To get to U.S. production in 2001, we need one last step:

  In any given year, production and sales need not be equal. Some of the goods produced in a given year are not sold in that year, but sold in later years. And some of the goods sold in a given year may have been produced in an earlier year. The difference between goods produced and goods sold in a given year—equivalently, the difference between production and sales—is called **inventory investment**. If production exceeds sales, firms accumulate inventories: Inventory investment is positive. If production is less than sales, firms decrease inventories: Inventory investment is negative.

  Inventory investment is typically small—positive in some years, negative in others. In 2001, inventory investment was negative, and equal to −1% of GDP. Put another way, production was lower than sales by an amount equal to 1% of GDP.

Make sure you understand each of these three equivalent ways of stating the relation between production, sales, and inventory investment:

Production − sales = inventory investment

Production = sales + inventory investment

Inventory investment = production − sales

We now have what we need to develop our first model of output determination.

3-2 The Demand for Goods

Denote the total demand for goods by *Z*. Using the decomposition of GDP we saw in Section 3-1, we can write *Z* as

$$Z \equiv C + I + G + X - IM$$

This equation is an **identity** (which is why it is written using the symbol "≡" rather than an equal sign). It *defines* *Z* as the sum of consumption, plus investment, plus government spending, plus exports, minus imports.

We now need to think about the determinants of *Z*. To simplify our task, let's first make a number of simplifications:

A model nearly always starts with the word *Assume* (or *Suppose*). This is an indication that reality is about to be simplified to focus on the issue at hand.

- Assume that all firms produce the same good, which can be used by consumers for consumption, by firms for investment, or by the government. With this (big) simplification, we need to look at only one market—the market for "the" good—and think about what determines supply and demand in that market.
- Assume that firms are willing to supply any amount of the good at a given price, *P*. This assumption allows us to focus on the role of demand in the determination of output. As we shall see later in the book, this assumption is valid only in the short run. When we move to the study of the medium run (starting in Chapter 6), we shall need to give it up. But for the moment, the assumption will simplify our life.
- Assume that the economy is *closed*, that it does not trade with the rest of the world: Both exports and imports are zero. This assumption clearly goes against the facts: Modern economies trade with the rest of the world. Later on (starting in Chapter 18), we shall abandon this assumption and look at what happens when the economy is open. But, for the moment, this assumption will also simplify our life: We shall not have to think about what determines exports and imports.

Under the assumption that the economy is closed, $X = IM = 0$, so the demand for goods *Z* is simply the sum of consumption, investment, and government spending:

$$Z \equiv C + I + G$$

Let's now discuss each of these three components in turn.

Consumption (*C*)

Consumption decisions depend on many factors. But the main one is surely income, or, more precisely, **disposable income**, the income that remains once consumers have received transfers from the government and paid their taxes. When their disposable income goes up, people buy more goods; when it goes down, they buy fewer goods.

Let *C* denote consumption, and Y_D denote disposable income. We can then write

$$C = C(\underset{(+)}{Y_D}) \tag{3.1}$$

This is a formal way of stating that consumption, *C*, is a function of disposable income, Y_D. The function $C(Y_D)$ is called the **consumption function**. The positive sign below Y_D reflects the fact that when disposable income increases, so does consumption. Economists call such an equation a **behavioral equation**, to indicate that the equation captures some aspect of behavior—in this case, the behavior of consumers.

I shall use functions in this book as a way of representing relations between variables. What you need to know about functions—which is very little—is described in

Appendix 2 at the end of this book. This appendix develops the mathematics you need to use this book. Do not worry: I shall always describe a function in words when I introduce it for the first time.

It is often useful to be more specific about the form of the function. Here is such a case. It is reasonable to assume that the relation between consumption and disposable income is given by

$$C = c_0 + c_1 Y_D \qquad (3.2)$$

In words: It is reasonable to assume that the function is a **linear relation**. The relation between consumption and disposable income is then characterized by two **parameters**, c_0 and c_1:

- The parameter c_1 is called the **propensity to consume**. (It is also called the *marginal propensity to consume*. I shall drop "marginal" for simplicity.) It gives the effect of an additional dollar of disposable income on consumption. If c_1 is equal to 0.6, then an additional dollar of disposable income increases consumption by $\$1 \times 0.6 = 60$ cents.

  A natural restriction on c_1 is that it be positive: An increase in disposable income is likely to lead to an increase in consumption. Another natural restriction is that c_1 be less than 1: People are likely to consume only part of any increase in disposable income, and to save the rest.
- The parameter c_0 has a simple interpretation. It is what people would consume if their disposable income in the current year were equal to zero: If Y_D equals zero in equation (3.2), $C = c_0$.

  A natural restriction is that, if current income is equal to zero, consumption is still positive: People still need to eat! This implies that c_0 is positive. How can people have positive consumption if their income is equal to zero? Answer: They dissave. They consume either by selling some of their assets, or by borrowing.

The relation between consumption and disposable income implied by equation (3.2) is drawn in Figure 3-1. Because it is a linear relation, it is represented by a straight line. Its intercept with the vertical axis is c_0; its slope is c_1. Because c_1 is less than 1, the slope of the line is less than 1: Equivalently, the line is flatter than a 45-degree line. (A refresher on graphs, slopes, and intercepts is also given in Appendix 2.)

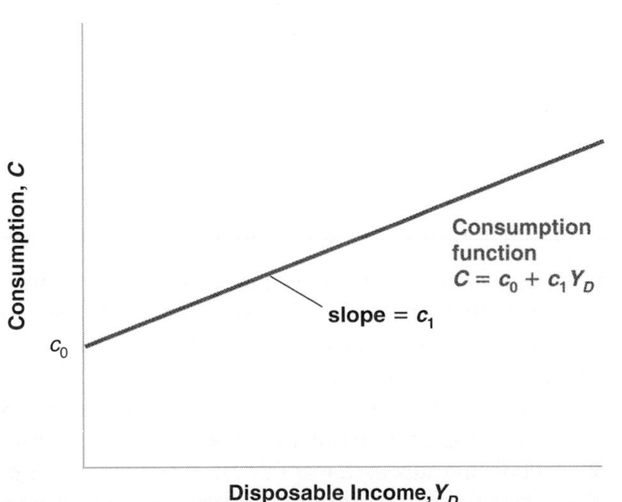

Figure 3-1

Consumption and Disposable Income

Consumption increases with disposable income, but less than one for one.

Next we need to define disposable income, Y_D. Disposable income is given by

$$Y_D \equiv Y - T$$

where Y is income and T is taxes paid minus government transfers received by consumers. For short, I shall refer to T simply as taxes—but remember that it is equal to taxes minus transfers. Note that the equation is an identity, indicated by the symbol ≡.

In the United States, the two major taxes paid by individuals are income taxes and Social Security contributions. The main sources of government transfers are Social Security benefits, Medicare (health care for retirees), and Medicaid (health care for the poor). In 2001, taxes paid by individuals were $1,306 billion; transfers to individuals were $1,148 billion.

Replacing Y_D in equation (3.2) gives

$$C = c_0 + c_1 (Y - T) \tag{3.3}$$

Equation (3.3) tells us that consumption, C, is a function of income, Y, and taxes, T. Higher income increases consumption, although less than one for one. Higher taxes decrease consumption, also less than one for one.

Investment (I)

Models have two types of variables. Some variables depend on other variables in the model, and are therefore explained within the model. Such variables are called **endogenous**. This was the case for consumption above. Other variables are not explained within the model but are instead taken as given. Such variables are called **exogenous**. This is how we shall treat investment here. We shall take investment as given, and write

$$I = \bar{I} \tag{3.4}$$

Putting a bar over investment is a simple typographical way to remind us that we take investment as given.

Endogenous variables: explained within the model
Exogenous variables: taken as given

We take investment as given to keep our model simple. But the assumption is not innocuous. It implies that, when we look later at the effects of changes in production, we shall be assuming that investment does not respond to changes in production. It is not hard to see that this implication may be a bad description of reality: Firms that experience an increase in production may decide that they need more machines, and increase their investment. We leave this mechanism out of the model for the moment; we shall introduce a more realistic treatment of investment in Chapter 5.

Government Spending (G)

The third component of demand in our model is government spending, G. Together with taxes, T, G describes **fiscal policy**—the choice of taxes and spending by the government. Just as we just did for investment, we shall take G and T as exogenous. But the reason why we assume G and T are exogenous is different from the reason we assumed investment is exogenous. It is based on two arguments:

Recall: Taxes stand for taxes minus government transfers.

- First, governments do not behave with the same regularity as consumers or firms, so there is no reliable rule we could write for G or T corresponding to the rule we wrote, for example, for consumption. (The argument is not fully convincing: Even if governments do not follow simple behavioral rules as consumers do, a good part of their behavior is predictable. We shall look at these issues later, in particular in Chapters 24 to 26, but we leave them aside until then.)
- Second, and more important, one of the tasks of macroeconomists is to think about the implications of alternative spending and tax decisions. We want to be

able to say, "If the government were to choose these values for G and T, this is what would happen." The approach in this book will typically treat G and T as variables chosen by the government, and not try to explain them within the model.

◀ Because we shall (nearly always) take G and T as exogenous, I shall not use a bar to denote their value. This will keep the notation lighter.

3-3 The Determination of Equilibrium Output

Let's collect and put together the pieces we have introduced so far.

Assuming that exports and imports are both zero, the demand for goods is the sum of consumption, investment, and government spending:

$$Z \equiv C + I + G$$

Replacing C and I from equations (3.3) and (3.4), we get

$$Z = c_0 + c_1(Y - T) + \bar{I} + G \tag{3.5}$$

The demand for goods, Z, depends on income, Y, taxes, T, investment, $\bar{I}$, and government spending, G.

Let's now turn to **equilibrium** in the goods market, and the relation between production and demand. If firms hold inventories, then production need not be equal to demand: For example, firms can respond to an increase in demand by drawing inventories, by having negative inventory investment. They can respond to a decrease in demand by continuing to produce and accumulate inventories, by having positive inventory investment. It will be helpful to ignore this complication here, and to start by assuming that firms do not hold inventories. In this case, inventory investment is always equal to zero, and **equilibrium in the goods market** requires that production, Y, be equal to the demand for goods, Z:

Think of an economy that produces only haircuts. There cannot be inventories of haircuts—how can there be haircuts produced, but not sold? Equilibrium requires production of haircuts be equal to demand for haircuts. We shall come back later to what happens when firms can hold inventories, so production need not be ◀ equal to demand.

$$Y = Z \tag{3.6}$$

This equation is called an **equilibrium condition**. Models include three types of equations: identities, behavioral equations, and equilibrium conditions. You now have seen examples of each: The equation defining disposable income is an identity, the consumption function is a behavioral equation, and the condition that production equals demand is an equilibrium condition.

◀ Three types of equations:
Identities
Behavioral equations
Equilibrium conditions

Replacing demand Z in equation (3.6) by its expression from equation (3.5) gives

$$Y = c_0 + c_1(Y - T) + \bar{I} + G \tag{3.7}$$

Equation (3.7) represents algebraically what we stated informally at the beginning of this chapter:

In equilibrium, production, Y (the left side of the equation), is equal to demand (the right side). Demand in turn depends on income, Y, which is itself equal to production.

Relate this statement to the cartoon at the start of the chapter. ◀

Note that we are using the same symbol, Y, for production and income. This is no accident! As you saw in Chapter 2, we can look at GDP either from the production side or from the income side. Production and income are identically equal.

Having constructed a model, we can solve it to look at what determines the level of output, how output changes in response to, say, a change in government spending. Solving a model means not only solving it algebraically but also understanding why the results are what they are. In this book, solving a model will also mean characterizing the results using graphs—sometimes skipping the algebra altogether—and describing the results and the mechanisms in words. Macroeconomists always use these three tools:

1. Algebra to make sure that the logic is correct.
2. Graphs to build the intuition.
3. Words to explain the results.

Make it a habit to do the same.

Using Algebra

Rewrite the equilibrium equation (3.7):

$$Y = c_0 + c_1 Y - c_1 T + \bar{I} + G$$

Move $c_1 Y$ to the left side and reorganize the right side:

$$(1 - c_1) Y = c_0 + \bar{I} + G - c_1 T$$

Divide both sides by $(1 - c_1)$:

$$Y = \frac{1}{1 - c_1}[c_0 + \bar{I} + G - c_1 T] \qquad (3.8)$$

Equation (3.8) characterizes equilibrium output, the level of output such that production equals demand. Let's look at both terms on the right, beginning with the second term.

Autonomous **means independent—in this case, independent of output.**

- The term $[c_0 + \bar{I} + G - c_1 T]$ is that part of the demand for goods that does not depend on output. For this reason, it is called **autonomous spending**.

  Can we be sure that autonomous spending is positive? We cannot, but it is very likely to be. The first two terms in brackets, c_0 and $\bar{I}$, are positive. What about the last two, $G - c_1 T$? Suppose the government is running a **balanced budget**—taxes equal government spending. If $T = G$, and the propensity to consume (c_1) is less than one (as we have assumed), then $(G - c_1 T)$ is positive and so is autonomous spending. Only if the government ran a very large budget surplus—if taxes were much larger than government spending—could autonomous spending be negative. We can safely ignore that case here.

If $T = G$, then $(G - c_1 T) = (G - T) + (1 - c_1)T = (1 - c_1)\,T > 0$.

- Turn to the first term, $1/(1 - c_1)$. Because the propensity to consume (c_1) is between zero and one, $1/(1 - c_1)$ is a number greater than one. For this reason, this number, which multiplies autonomous spending, is called the **multiplier**. The closer c_1 is to one, the larger the multiplier.

  What does the multiplier imply? Suppose that, for a given level of income, consumers decide to consume more. More precisely, assume that c_0 in equation (3.3) increases by \$1 billion. Equation (3.8) tells us that output will increase by more than \$1 billion. For example, if c_1 equals 0.6, the multiplier equals $1/(1 - 0.6) = 2.5$, so that output increases by 2.5×1 billion = \$2.5 billion.

  We have looked at an increase in consumption, but equation (3.8) makes clear that any change in autonomous spending—from a change in investment, to a change in government spending, to a change in taxes—will have the same qualitative effect: It will change output by more than its direct effect on autonomous spending.

Where does the multiplier effect come from? Looking back at equation (3.7) gives the clue: An increase in c_0 increases demand. The increase in demand then leads to an increase in production and income. But the increase in income further increases consumption, which further increases demand, and so on. The best way to strengthen this intuition is to represent the equilibrium using a graph. Let us now do that.

Using a Graph

Let's characterize the equilibrium graphically.

- First, plot production as a function of income.

  In Figure 3-2, measure production on the vertical axis. Measure income on the horizontal axis. Plotting production as a function of income is straightforward: Recall that production and income are always equal. Thus, the relation between them is the 45-degree line, the line with a slope equal to 1.

- Second, plot demand as a function of income.

  The relation between demand and income is given by equation (3.5). Let's rewrite it here for convenience, regrouping the terms for autonomous spending together in the term in parentheses:

$$Z = (c_0 + \bar{I} + G - c_1 T) + c_1 Y \tag{3.9}$$

Demand depends on autonomous spending, and on income—through its effect on consumption. The relation between demand and income is drawn as ZZ in the graph. The intercept with the vertical axis—the value of demand when income is equal to zero—equals autonomous spending. The slope of the line is the propensity to consume, c_1: When income increases by 1, demand increases by c_1. Under the restriction that c_1 is positive but less than 1, the line is upward sloping but with slope less than 1.

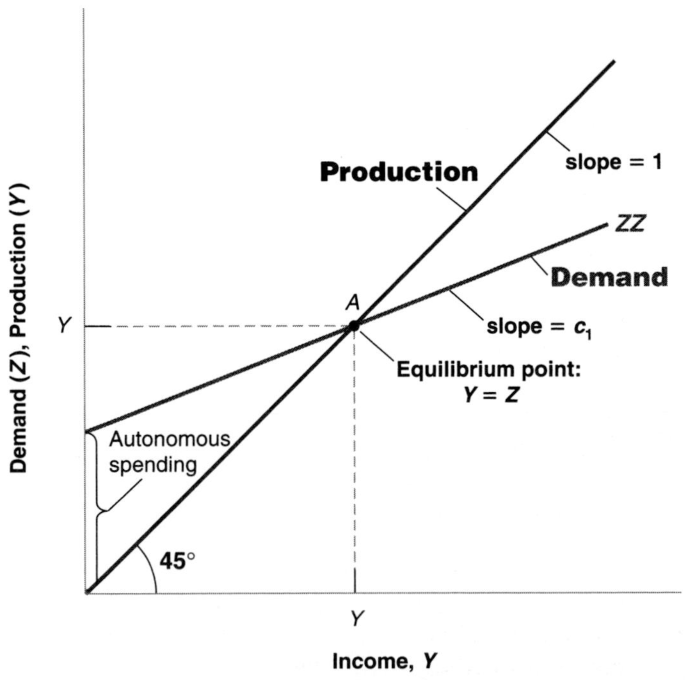

Figure 3-2

Equilibrium in the Goods Market

Equilibrium output is determined by the condition that production be equal to demand.

■ In equilibrium, production equals demand.

Thus, equilibrium output, Y, is given by the intersection of the 45-degree line and the demand relation, at point A. To the left of A, demand exceeds production; to the right of A, production exceeds demand. Only at A are demand and production equal.

Now, suppose that c_0 increases by \$1 billion. At the initial level of income (the level of income associated with point A), consumers increase their consumption by \$1 billion. What happens then is shown in Figure 3-3, which builds on Figure 3-2.

Equation (3.9) tells us that for any value of income, demand is higher by \$1 billion. Before the increase in c_0, the relation between demand and income was given by the line ZZ. After the increase in c_0 by \$1 billion, the relation between demand and income is given by the line ZZ', which is parallel to ZZ but higher by \$1 billion. In other words, the demand relation shifts up by \$1 billion. The new equilibrium is at the intersection of the 45-degree line and the new demand relation, at point A'.

Equilibrium output increases from Y to Y'. The increase in output, $(Y' - Y)$, which we can measure either on the horizontal or the vertical axis, is larger than the initial increase in consumption of \$1 billion. This is the multiplier effect.

The distance between Y and Y' on the vertical axis is larger than the distance between A and B—which is equal to 1 billion. ▶

With the help of the graph, it becomes easier to tell how and why the economy moves from A to A'. The initial increase in consumption leads to an increase in demand of \$1 billion. At the initial level of income, Y, the level of demand is now given by point B: Demand is \$1 billion higher. To satisfy this higher level of demand, firms increase production by \$1 billion. The economy moves to point C, with both demand and production higher by \$1 billion. But this is not the end of the story. The higher level of production implies an increase in income of \$1 billion (recall that income = production), and to a further increase in demand, so demand is now given by point D. Point D leads to a higher level of production, and so on, until the economy is at A', where production and demand are again equal, and is therefore the new equilibrium.

Figure 3-3

The Effects of an Increase in Autonomous Spending on Output

An increase in autonomous spending has a more than one-for-one effect on equilibrium output.

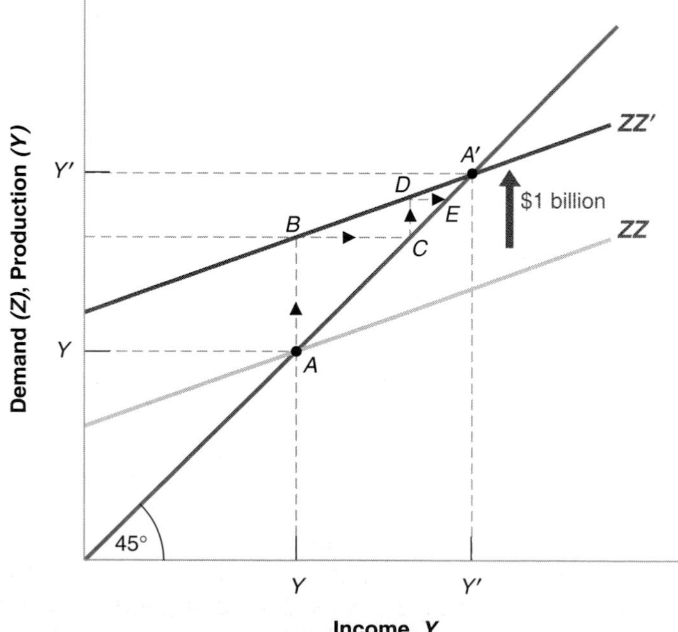

We can pursue this line of explanation a bit further, and this will give us another way of thinking about the multiplier.

- The first-round increase in demand, given by the distance *AB* in Figure 3-3, equals \$1 billion.
- This first-round increase in demand leads to an equal increase in production, also given by the distance *AB*, thus \$1 billion.
- This first-round increase in production leads to an equal increase in income, given by the distance *BC*, also equal to \$1 billion.
- The second-round increase in demand, given by the distance *CD*, equals \$1 billion (the increase in income in the first round) times the propensity to consume out of income, c_1—hence, \$$c_1$ billion.
- This second-round increase in demand leads to an equal increase in production, also given by the distance *CD*, and thus an equal increase in income, given by the distance *DE*.
- The third-round increase in demand equals \$$c_1$ billion (the increase in income in the second round), times c_1, the marginal propensity to consume out of income; it is equal to \$$c_1 * c_1 =$ \$$c_1^2$ billion, and so on.

Following this logic, the total increase in production after, say, *n* rounds equals \$1 billion times the sum:

$$1 + c_1 + c_1^2 + \cdots + c_1^n$$

Such a sum is called a **geometric series**. Geometric series will come up often in this book. (A refresher is given in Appendix 2.) One main property is that, when c_1 is less than one (as it is here) and as *n* gets larger and larger, the sum keeps increasing but approaches a limit. That limit is $1/(1 - c_1)$, making the eventual increase in output equal to \$$1/(1 - c_1)$ billion.

The expression $1/(1 - c_1)$ should be familiar: It is the multiplier, derived another way. This gives us an equivalent, but more intuitive way of thinking about the multiplier. We can think of the original increase in demand as triggering successive increases in production, with each increase in production implying an increase in income, which leads to an increase in demand, which leads to a further increase in production, which leads . . . and so on. The multiplier is the sum of all these successive increases in production.

Trick question: Think about the multiplier as the result of these successive rounds. What would happen in each successive round if c_1, the propensity to consume, were larger than one?

Using Words

How can we summarize our findings in words?

Production depends on demand, which depends on income, which is itself equal to production. An increase in demand, such as an increase in government spending, leads to an increase in production and a corresponding increase in income. This increase in income leads to a further increase in demand, which leads to a further increase in production, and so on. The end result is an increase in output that is larger than the initial shift in demand, by a factor equal to the multiplier.

The size of the multiplier is directly related to the value of the propensity to consume: The higher the propensity to consume, the higher the multiplier. What is the value of the propensity to consume in the United States today? To answer this question, and more generally to estimate behavioral equations and their parameters, economists use **econometrics**, the set of statistical methods used in economics. To give you a sense of what econometrics is and how it is used, read Appendix 3. This appendix gives you a quick introduction, using as an application the estimation of the propensity to consume. The conclusion from the appendix is that, in the United States today, the propensity to consume is around 0.6. An additional dollar of income leads on average to an increase in consumption of 60 cents. This implies a multiplier equal to $1/(1 - c_1) = 1/(1 - 0.6) = 2.5$.

How Long Does It Take for Output to Adjust?

Let's return to our example one last time. Suppose that c_0 increases by \$1 billion. We know that output will increase by an amount equal to the multiplier $1/(1 - c_1)$ times \$1 billion. But how long will it take for output to reach this higher value?

Under the assumptions we have made so far, the answer is: Right away! In writing the equilibrium condition (3.6), I have assumed that production is always equal to demand—in other words, production responds to demand instantaneously. In writing the consumption function (3.2), I have assumed that consumption responds to disposable income instantaneously. Under these two assumptions, the economy goes instantaneously from point A to point A' in Figure 3-3: The increase in demand leads to an immediate increase in production, the increase in income associated with the increase in production leads to an immediate increase in demand, and so on. We can think of the adjustment in terms of successive rounds as we did earlier, but all these rounds happen at once.

In the model we saw earlier, we ruled out this possibility by assuming firms did not hold inventories and so could not rely on inventories to respond to demand.

This instantaneous adjustment does not seem plausible. And it is not: A firm that faces an increase in demand may decide to wait before adjusting its production, meanwhile drawing down its inventories to satisfy demand. A worker who gets a pay raise may not adjust her consumption right away. And these delays imply that the adjustment of output will take time.

Describing formally this adjustment of output over time—describing what economists call the **dynamics** of adjustment—would be too hard. But it is easy to do it in words:

- Suppose, for example, that firms make decisions about their production level at the beginning of each quarter; once the decision is made, production cannot be adjusted for the rest of the quarter. If purchases are higher than production, firms draw down inventories to satisfy purchases. If purchases are lower than production, firms accumulate inventories.
- Now, return to our example, and suppose consumers decide to spend more, that they increase c_0. During the quarter in which this happens, demand increases, but—because of our assumption that production was set at the beginning of the quarter—production does not yet change. Therefore, income does not change either.
- In the following quarter, firms having observed an increase in demand in the previous quarter are likely to set a higher level of production. This increase in production leads to a corresponding increase in income and a further increase in demand. If purchases still exceed production, firms further increase production in the following quarter, and so on.
- In short, in response to an increase in consumer spending, output does not jump to the new equilibrium, but rather increases over time from Y to Y'.

  How long this adjustment takes depends on how and how often firms revise their production schedule. The more often firms adjust their production schedule, and the larger the response of production to past increases in purchases, the faster the adjustment.

I shall often do in this book what I just did here. Having looked at changes in equilibrium output, I shall then describe informally how the economy moves from one equilibrium to the other. This will not only make the description of what happens in the economy feel more realistic, but it will often reinforce your intuition about why the equilibrium changed.

I have focused in this section on *increases* in demand. But the mechanism is symmetric: *Decreases* in demand lead to decreases in output. The 1990–1991 recession in the United States was largely the result of a sudden drop in consumer confidence, leading to a sharp decrease in consumption demand, which led, in turn, to a sharp decline in output. The origins of the 1990–1991 recession are examined in the Focus box, "Consumer Confidence and the 1990–1991 Recession."

Consumer Confidence and the 1990–1991 Recession

FOCUS

In the third quarter of 1990, after the invasion of Kuwait by Iraq but before the beginning of the Persian Gulf War, U.S. GDP growth turned negative, and remained negative for the following two quarters. This episode is known as the 1990–1991 recession.

Column 1 of the table shows the size and the timing of the recession. It gives the change in GDP—in billions of 1992 dollars—for each quarter from the second quarter of 1990 to the second quarter of 1991. In 1990:3, 1990:4, and 1991:1, the change in GDP is negative. This is the 1990–1991 recession.

- Had the recession been forecast by economists? The answer is no. Column 2 gives the **forecast error,** the difference between the actual value of GDP and the value of GDP that had been forecast by economists one quarter earlier. A positive forecast error indicates that actual GDP turned out to be higher than was forecast; a negative forecast error indicates that actual GDP turned out lower than was forecast. As you can see, the forecast errors are negative during all three quarters of the recession. They are larger than the actual declines in GDP in each of the first two quarters of the recession. What this means is that at the beginning of each of these two quarters, the forecasts were of positive GDP growth, while growth actually turned out to be negative.
- Where did these forecast errors come from? In terms of equation (3.8), which of the determinants of spending was the main culprit? Was it c_0, or $\bar{I}$, or G, or T? Research looking at the evolution of each of the components of spending suggests that the main culprit, for the last two quarters of the recession, was an adverse shift in consumption, an unexpected decrease in c_0. Forecast errors of c_0 are given in column 3. There are two large negative errors for the last two quarters of the recession.
- A large decrease in c_0 is a drop in consumption given disposable income. Why did consumption drop so much, given disposable income, in late 1990 and early 1991? The direct cause is shown in the last column of the table, which gives the value of the **consumer confidence index.** This index is computed from a monthly survey of about 5,000

Table 1 GDP, Consumption, and Forecast Errors, 1990–1991

Quarter	(1) Change in Real GDP	(2) Forecast Error for GDP	(3) Forecast Error for c_0	(4) Index of Consumer Confidence
1990:2	19	−17	−23	105
1990:3	−29	−57	−1	90
1990:4	−63	−88	−37	61
1991:1	−31	−27	−30	65
1991:2	27	47	8	77

Source: Olivier Blanchard, "Consumption and the Recession of 1990–1991," *American Economic Review*, May 1993.

Continued

households; the survey asks consumers how confident they are about both current and future economic conditions, from job opportunities to their expected family income six months in the future. As you can see, there was a very large decrease in the index in the fourth quarter of 1990. Consumers lost confidence, leading them to cut consumption given disposable income, thus triggering the recession.

- This brings us to the last question: Why did consumers lose confidence in late 1990? Why did they become more pessimistic about the future? Even today, economists are not sure. It is more than likely that this change in mood was related to the increasing probability of a war in the Middle East—a war that started in early 1991, after the beginning of the recession. People worried that the United States might get involved in a prolonged and costly war. They also worried that a war in the Middle East could lead to a large increase in oil prices and to a recession: The two previous large increases in oil prices in the 1970s had both been associated with recessions. Whatever the reason, the decrease in consumer confidence was a major factor behind the 1990–1991 recession.

What about the 2001–2002 slowdown? So far, things look quite different from the 1990–1991 recession. The slowdown has come primarily from a decline in investment rather than a decline in consumption. Indeed, until September 11, consumer confidence and consumer spending had remained surprisingly high. One of the main worries, following September 11, was that consumer confidence would drop, leading to a decline in consumption, and a further decline in output. Consumer confidence dropped, but by less than had been feared: The index, which was at 110 in August, dropped to 85 in October—a much smaller decline than in 1990. And, at the time of this writing, there are reasons to be optimistic: In December 2001, the index has rebounded and stands at 94.

3-4 Investment Equals Saving: An Alternative Way of Thinking About Goods-Market Equilibrium

Thus far, we have been thinking of equilibrium in the goods market in terms of the equality of the production and the demand for goods. An alternative—but equivalent—way of thinking about equilibrium focuses instead on investment and saving. This is how John Maynard Keynes first articulated this model in 1936, in *The General Theory of Employment, Interest and Money.*

- Let's start by looking at saving. By definition, **private saving (*S*)**, saving by consumers, is equal to their disposable income minus their consumption:

$$S \equiv Y_D - C$$

Using the definition of disposable income, we can rewrite private saving as income minus taxes minus consumption

$$S \equiv Y - T - C$$

- Now return to the equation for equilibrium in the goods market. Production must be equal to demand, which, in turn, is the sum of consumption, investment, and government spending:

$$Y = C + I + G$$

Subtract taxes (T) from both sides and move consumption to the left side:

$$Y - T - C = I + G - T$$

The left side of this equation is simply private saving (S), so,

$$S = I + G - T$$

Or equivalently,

$$I = S + (T - G) \tag{3.10}$$

The term on the left is investment. The first term on the right is *private saving*. The second term is **public saving**—taxes minus government spending. If taxes exceed government spending, the government is running a **budget surplus**—public saving is positive. If taxes are less than government spending, the government is running a **budget deficit**—public saving is negative.

Equation (3.10) gives us another way of thinking about equilibrium in the goods market: It says that equilibrium in the goods market requires that investment equals **saving**—the sum of private and public saving. This way of looking at the equilibrium explains why the equilibrium condition for the goods market is called the ***IS* relation**, for "**I**nvestment equals **S**aving." What firms want to invest must be equal to what people and the government want to save.

To strengthen your intuition for equation (3.10), think of an economy where there is only one person who has to decide how much to consume, invest, and save—a "Robinson Crusoe" economy. For Robinson Crusoe, the saving and the investment decisions are one and the same: What he invests (say, by keeping rabbits for reproduction, rather than having them for dinner), he automatically saves. In a modern economy, however, investment decisions are made by firms, whereas saving decisions are made by consumers and the government. In equilibrium, equation (3.10) tells us, all those decisions have to be consistent: Investment must be equal to saving.

To summarize: There are two equivalent ways of stating the condition for equilibrium in the goods market:

Production = Demand
Investment = Saving

Earlier, we characterized the equilibrium using the first condition, equation (3.6). We now do the same using the second condition, equation (3.10). The results will be the same, but the derivation will give you another way of thinking about the equilibrium.

- Note first that *consumption and saving decisions are one and the same*: Given their disposable income, once consumers have chosen consumption, their saving is determined, and vice versa. The way we specified consumption behavior implies that private saving is given by:

$$\begin{aligned} S &= Y - T - C \\ &= Y - T - c_0 - c_1(Y - T) \end{aligned}$$

Rearranging, we get

$$S = -c_0 + (1 - c_1)(Y - T) \tag{3.11}$$

- In the same way that we called c_1 the propensity to consume, we can call $(1 - c_1)$ the **propensity to save**. The propensity to save tells us how much people save out of an additional unit of income. The assumption we made earlier that the propensity to consume (c_1) is between zero and one implies that the propensity to save $(1 - c_1)$ is also between zero and one. Private saving increases with disposable income, but by less than one dollar for each additional dollar of disposable income.

In equilibrium, investment must be equal to saving, the sum of private and public saving. Replacing private saving in equation (3.10) by its expression from above

$$\bar{I} = -c_0 + (1 - c_1)(Y - T) + (T - G)$$

The Paradox of Saving

FOCUS

As we grow up, we are told of the virtues of thrift. Those who spend all their income are condemned to end up poor. Those who save are promised a happy life. Similarly, governments tell us that an economy that saves is an economy that will grow strong and prosper. The model we have seen in this chapter, however, tells a different and surprising story.

Suppose that, at a given level of disposable income, consumers decide to save more. In other words, suppose consumers decrease c_0, therefore decreasing consumption and increasing saving at a given level of disposable income. What happens to output and to saving?

Equation (3.12) makes clear that equilibrium output decreases: As people save more at their initial level of income, they decrease their consumption. But this decrease in consumption decreases demand, which decreases production.

Can we tell what happens to saving? Return to the equation for private saving, equation (3.11) (by assumption, there is no change in public saving, so saving and private saving move together)

$$S = -c_0 + (1 - c_1)(Y - T)$$

On one hand, $-c_0$ is higher (less negative): Consumers are saving more at any level of income; this tends to increase saving. But, on the other hand, their income, Y, is lower: This decreases saving. The net effect would seem to be ambiguous. In fact, we can tell which way it goes.

To see how, go back to equation (3.10), the equilibrium condition that investment and saving must be equal:

$$I = S + (T - G)$$

By assumption, investment does not change: $I = \bar{I}$. Nor does T or G. So, the equilibrium condition tells us, in equilibrium, private saving, S, cannot change, either. While people want to save more at a given level of income, income decreases by an amount such that saving is unchanged.

This means that attempts by people to save more lead both to a decline in output and to unchanged saving. This surprising pair of results is known as the **paradox of saving** (or the paradox of thrift).

So, should you forget the old wisdom? Should the government tell people to be less thrifty? No. The results of this simple model are of much relevance in the short run. The desire of consumers to save more led to the 1990–1991 recession (as we saw in the Focus box earlier in this chapter). But—as we shall see later in this book when we look at the medium run and the long run—other mechanisms come into play over time, and an increase in the saving rate is likely to lead eventually to higher saving and higher income. A warning remains, however: Policies that encourage saving may be good in the medium run and in the long run, but may lead to a recession in the short run.

Solving for output

$$Y = \frac{1}{1 - c_1}[c_0 + \bar{I} + G - c_1 T] \qquad (3.12)$$

Equation (3.12) is exactly the same as equation (3.8). This should come as no surprise. We are looking at the same equilibrium condition, just in a different way. This alternative way will prove useful in various applications later in the book. The Focus box above looks at such an application, which was first emphasized by Keynes, and is often called the "paradox of saving."

3-5 Is the Government Omnipotent? A Warning

Equation (3.8) implies that the government, by choosing the level of spending, G, or the level of taxes, T, can choose the level of output it wants. If it wants output to be higher by, say, \$1 billion, all it needs to do is to increase G by \$$(1 - c_1)$ billion; this increase in government spending, in theory, will lead to an output increase of \$$(1 - c_1)$ billion times the multiplier $1/(1 - c_1)$, thus \$1 billion.

Can governments really choose the level of output they want? Obviously not. There are many aspects of reality that we have not yet incorporated in our model, and all complicate the governments' task. We shall incorporate them in due time. But it is useful to list them briefly here:

For a glimpse at the longer list, go to the Focus box "Fiscal Policy: What You Have Learned and Where" in Chapter 26.

- Changing government spending or taxes may be far from easy. Getting the U.S. Congress to pass bills always takes time, and can often turn into a president's nightmare (Chapters 24 and 26).
- We have focused on the behavior of consumption. But investment is also likely to respond—and so are imports, as some of the increased demand by consumers and firms falls not on domestic goods but on foreign goods. All these responses are hard to assess with much certainty, and likely to come with complex dynamic effects (Chapters 5, 18, and 19).
- Anticipations are likely to matter. For example, the reaction of consumers to a tax cut is likely to depend very much on whether they think of the tax cut as transitory or permanent. The more they perceive the tax cut as permanent, the larger will be their consumption response (Chapters 16 and 17).
- Achieving a given level of output may come with unpleasant side effects. Trying to achieve too high a level of output may, for example, lead to increasing inflation and, for that reason, may become unsustainable in the medium run (Chapters 7 and 8).
- Cutting taxes or increasing government spending may lead to large budget deficits and an accumulation of public debt. Such debt may have adverse implications in the long run (Chapters 11 and 26).

As of January 2002, the fiscal "stimulus package" aimed at helping the U.S. economy after September 11 was still in limbo in Congress, because Democrats and Republicans could not agree on its content.

In short, the proposition that, by using fiscal policy, the government can affect demand and output in the short run, is an important and correct one. But, as we refine our analysis, we shall see that the role of the government in general, and the successful use of fiscal policy in particular, becomes increasingly difficult: Governments will never again have it so good as they had it in this chapter!

Summary

What you should remember about the components of GDP:

- GDP is the sum of consumption, plus investment, plus government spending, plus exports, minus imports, plus inventory investment.
- Consumption (C) is the purchase of goods and services by consumers. Consumption is the largest component of demand.
- Investment (I) is the sum of nonresidential investment—the purchase of new plants and new machines by firms—and of residential investment—the purchase of new houses or apartments by people.
- Government spending (G) is the purchase of goods and services by federal, state, and local governments.
- Exports (X) are purchases of U.S. goods by foreigners. Imports (IM) are purchases of foreign goods by U.S. consumers, U.S. firms, and the U.S. government.
- Inventory investment is the difference between production and purchases. It can be positive or negative.

What you should remember about our first model of output determination:

- In the short run, demand determines production. Production is equal to income. And income determines demand.
- The consumption function shows how consumption depends on disposable income. The propensity to consume describes how much consumption increases for a given increase in disposable income.
- Equilibrium output is the level of output at which production equals demand. In equilibrium, output equals autonomous spending times the multiplier. Autonomous spending is that part of demand that does not depend on income. The multiplier is equal to $1/(1 - c_1)$, where c_1 is the propensity to consume.
- Increases in consumer confidence, in investment demand, in government spending, or decreases in taxes, all increase equilibrium output in the short run.
- An alternative way of stating the goods-market equilibrium condition is that investment must be equal to saving, the sum of private and public saving. For this reason, the equilibrium condition is called the IS relation (I for investment, S for saving).

Key Terms

- consumption (C), 46
- investment (I), 47
- fixed investment, 47
- nonresidential investment, 47
- residential investment, 47
- government spending (G), 47
- government transfers, 47
- imports (IM), 47
- exports (X), 47
- net exports ($X - IM$), 47
- trade balance, 47
- trade surplus, 47
- trade deficit, 47
- inventory investment, 47
- identity, 48
- disposable income (Y_D), 48
- consumption function, 48
- behavioral equation, 48
- linear relation, 49
- parameter, 49
- propensity to consume (c_1), 49
- endogenous variables, 50
- exogenous variables, 50
- fiscal policy, 50
- equilibrium, 51
- equilibrium in the goods market, 51
- equilibrium condition, 51
- autonomous spending, 52
- balanced budget, 52
- multiplier, 52
- geometric series, 55
- econometrics, 55
- dynamics, 56
- forecast error, 57
- consumer confidence index, 57
- private saving (S), 58
- public saving ($T - G$), 59
- budget surplus, 59
- budget deficit, 59
- saving, 59
- *IS* relation, 59
- propensity to save, 59
- paradox of saving, 60

Questions and Problems

Quick Check

1. *Using the information in this chapter, label each of the following statements* true, false, *or* uncertain. *Explain briefly.*
   a. The largest component of GDP is consumption.
   b. Government spending, including transfers, was equal to 17% of GDP in 2001.
   c. The propensity to consume has to be positive, but otherwise it can take on any positive value.
   d. Fiscal policy describes the choice of government spending and taxes, and is treated as exogenous in our goods market model.
   e. The equilibrium condition for the goods market states that consumption equals output.
   f. An increase of one unit in government spending leads to an increase of one unit in equilibrium output.
   g. An increase in the propensity to consume leads to a decrease in output.

2. *Suppose that the economy is characterized by the following behavioral equations:*

$$C = 160 + 0.6\,Y_D$$
$$I = 150$$
$$G = 150$$
$$T = 100$$

   Solve for
   a. Equilibrium GDP (Y)
   b. Disposable income (Y_D)
   c. Consumption spending (C)

3. *For the economy in problem 2,*
   a. Solve for equilibrium output. Compute total demand. Is it equal to production? Explain.
   b. Assume that G is now equal to 110. Solve for equilibrium output. Compute total demand. Is it equal to production? Explain.
   c. Assume that G is equal to 110, so output is given by your answer to (b). Compute private plus public saving. Is it equal to investment? Explain.

Dig Deeper

4. *The balanced budget multiplier*

   For both political and macroeconomic reasons governments are often reluctant to run budget deficits. Here, we examine whether policy changes in G and T that maintain a balanced budget are macroeconomically neutral. Put another way, we examine whether it is possible to affect output through changes in G and T so that the government budget remains balanced.

   Start from equation (3.7).
   a. By how much does Y increase when G increases by one unit?
   b. By how much does Y decrease when T increases by one unit?
   c. Why are your answers to (a) and (b) different?

   Suppose that the economy starts with a balanced budget: T = G. If the increase in G is equal to the increase in T, then the budget remains in balance. Let us now compute the balanced budget multiplier.

d. Suppose that both G and T increase by one unit. Using your answers to (a) and (b), what is the change in equilibrium GDP? Are balanced budget changes in G and T macroeconomically neutral?

e. How does the specific value of the propensity to consume affect your answer to (d)? Why?

5. *Automatic stabilizers*

So far in this chapter we have been assuming that the fiscal policy variables G and T are independent of the level of income. In the real world, however, this is not the case. Taxes typically depend on the level of income, and so tend to be higher when income is higher. In this problem we examine how this automatic response of taxes can help reduce the impact of changes in autonomous spending on output.

Consider the following behavioral equations:

$$C = c_0 + c_1 Y_D$$
$$T = t_0 + t_1 Y$$
$$Y_D = Y - T$$

G and I are both constant.

Assume that t_1 is between zero and one.

a. Solve for equilibrium output.

b. What is the multiplier? Does the economy respond more to changes in autonomous spending when t_1 is zero or when t_1 is positive? Explain.

c. Why is fiscal policy in this case called an automatic stabilizer?

6. *Balanced budget versus automatic stabilizers*

It is often argued that a balanced budget amendment would actually be destabilizing. To understand this argument, consider the economy of problem 5.

a. Solve for equilibrium output.

b. Solve for taxes in equilibrium.

Suppose that the government starts with a balanced budget and that there is a drop in c_0.

c. What happens to Y? What happens to taxes?

d. Suppose that the government cuts spending in order to keep the budget balanced. What will be the effect on Y? Does the cut in spending required to balance the budget counteract or reinforce the effect of the drop in c_0 on output? (Don't do the algebra. Use your intuition and give the answer in words.)

We invite you to visit the Blanchard page on the Prenctice Hall Web site at:
www.prenhall.com/blanchard
for this chapter's World Wide Web exercises

Financial Markets

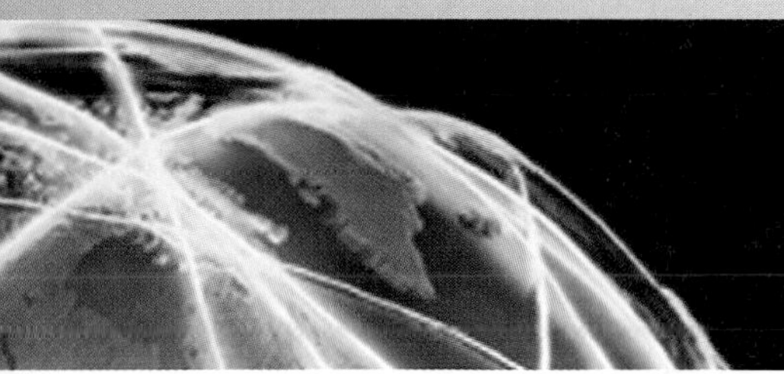

CHAPTER 4

Barely a day goes by without the media speculating whether the **Fed** (short for the **Federal Reserve Bank**—the central bank of the United States) is going to change the interest rate, and what the change is likely to do to the economy. Alan Greenspan, the chairman of the Fed, is widely perceived as the most powerful policy maker in the United States, if not in the world (see the accompanying cartoon).

The model of economic activity we developed in Chapter 3 did not include the interest rate, so there was no role for Alan Greenspan. This was a strong simplification; it is time to relax it. This requires that we take two steps:

First, we must look at what determines the interest rate, and at the role the Fed plays in this determination—the topic of this chapter. Second, we must look at how the interest rate affects demand and output—the topic of the next chapter.

The chapter has four sections:

- Section 4-1 looks at the demand for money.
- Section 4-2 assumes that the central bank directly controls the supply of money, and shows how the interest rate is determined by the condition that the demand for money be equal to the supply of money.
- Section 4-3—an optional section—introduces banks as suppliers of money, and revisits the determination of the interest rate, and the role of the central bank.
- Section 4-4—also an optional section—presents two alternative ways to think about the equilibrium. One focuses on the federal funds market. The other focuses on the money multiplier. ■

4-1 The Demand for Money

This section looks at the determinants of *the demand for money*. (A warning before we start: Words such as *money* or *wealth* have very specific meanings in economics, often not the same meanings as in everyday conversations. The purpose of the Focus box "Semantic Traps: Money, Income, and Wealth" is to help you avoid some of these traps. Read it carefully, and come back to it once in a while.)

Suppose, as a result of having steadily saved part of your income in the past, your financial wealth today is $50,000. You may intend to keep saving in the future and to increase your wealth further, but its value today is given. The only choice you can make today is how to allocate this $50,000 between money and bonds:

Make sure you see the difference between the decision about how much to save (a decision that determines how wealth changes over time), and the decision about how to allocate a given stock of wealth between money and bonds.

- **Money**, which you can use for transactions, pays no interest.

  In reality, there are two types of money: **Currency**, coins and bills, and **checkable deposits**, the bank deposits on which you can write checks. The distinction between the two will be important when we look at the supply of money. For the moment, it does not matter.
- **Bonds** pay a positive interest rate, i, but they cannot be used for transactions.

  In reality, there are many types of bonds, each associated with a specific interest rate. For the time being, we shall ignore this aspect of reality, and assume there is just one type of bond, so i is the interest rate.

We shall abandon this assumption and look at a large menu of interest rates when we focus on the role of expectations, starting in Chapter 14.

Think of buying or selling bonds as implying some cost, for example, a phone call to a broker and the payment of a transaction fee. How much of your $50,000 should you hold in money, and how much in bonds?

Holding all your wealth in the form of money is clearly very convenient. It avoids the need to call a broker or pay transaction fees. But it also means receiving no interest income.

Holding all your wealth in the form of bonds implies receiving interest on all your wealth, but having to call your broker whenever you need money to take the subway or pay for a cup of coffee is an inconvenient way of going through life!

Semantic Traps: Money, Income, and Wealth

Every day we use *money* to denote many things. We use it as a synonym for income: "making money." We use it as a synonym for wealth: "She has a lot of money." In economics, you must be more careful. Here is a basic guide to some terms and their precise meanings in economics.

Income is what you earn from working plus what you receive in interest and dividends. It is a **flow**—that is, it is expressed per unit of time: weekly income, monthly income, or yearly income. J. Paul Getty was once asked what his income was. Getty answered, "$1,000." What he meant but did not say was, "$1,000 per minute."

Saving is that part of after-tax income that is not spent. It is also a flow. If you save 10% of your income and your income is $3,000 per month, then you save $300 per month. **Savings** (plural) is sometimes used as a synonym for wealth—the value of what you have accumulated over time. To avoid confusion, I shall not use "savings" (plural) in this book.

Your **financial wealth,** or simply **wealth,** is the value of all your financial assets minus all your financial liabilities. In contrast to income or saving, which are flow variables, financial wealth is a **stock** variable. It is the value of wealth at a given moment in time.

At a given moment in time, you cannot change the total amount of your financial wealth. You can change it only over time, as you save or dissave, or as the value of your assets change. But you can change the composition of your wealth; you can, for example, decide to pay back part of your mortgage by writing a check on your checking account. This leads to a decrease in your liabilities (a smaller mortgage) and a corresponding decrease in your assets (a smaller checking account balance); but it does not change your wealth.

Financial assets that can be used directly to buy goods are called money. Money includes currency and checkable deposits, deposits against which you can write checks. Money is also a stock. Somebody can have a large wealth but small money holdings, for example $1,000,000 worth of stocks, but only $500 in her checking account. Or somebody can have a large income but small money holdings, for example, be paid $10,000 a month, but have a very small positive balance on her checking account.

Investment is a term economists reserve for the purchase of new capital goods, from machines to plants to office buildings. When you want to talk about the purchase of shares or other financial assets, you should call it **financial investment.**

Learn how to be economically correct:

Do not say "Mary is making a lot of money"; say "Mary receives a high income."

Do not say "Joe has a lot of money"; say "Joe is very wealthy."

Therefore, it is clear that you should hold both money *and* bonds. In what proportions should you do so? This will depend mainly on two variables:

- Your level of transactions. You want to have enough money, on average, to avoid having to sell bonds to get money too often. Say that you typically spend $3,000 a month. You may want to have on average, say, two months worth of spending on hand, or $6,000 in money, and the rest, $50,000 – $6,000 = $44,000, in bonds. If, instead, you typically spend $4,000 a month, you may want to have $8,000 in money and only $42,000 in bonds.
- The interest rate on bonds. The only reason to hold any of your wealth in bonds is that they pay interest. If bonds paid no interest, you would hold all of your wealth in money: Bonds and money would pay the same interest rate (namely, zero), and money, which can be used for transactions, would therefore be more convenient.

  The higher the interest rate, the more you will be willing to incur the hassle and the costs associated with buying and selling bonds. If the interest rate is very high, you may decide to squeeze your money holdings to an average of only two weeks' worth of spending, or $1,500 (assuming your monthly spending is $3,000). This way, you will be able to keep, on average, $48,500 in bonds, getting more interest as a result.

Let's make this last point more concrete. Most of you probably do not hold bonds; few of you have a broker. But many of you hold bonds indirectly, through a money market account. **Money market funds** (the full name is *money market mutual funds*) receive funds from people, and use these funds to buy bonds, typically government bonds. The funds pay an interest rate close to the interest rate on the bonds that they hold—the difference coming from the administrative costs of running the funds and from their profit margin.

In the early 1980s, with the interest rate on these funds reaching 14% per year, many people who had previously kept all their financial wealth in their checking account (which paid little or no interest) realized how much interest they could earn by holding part of their financial wealth in a money market account instead. Money market funds became very popular. Since then, however, the interest rate has decreased. In 2001, the interest rate paid by money market funds was under 5.0%. This is better than zero—the rate paid on many checking accounts—but is much less attractive than the rate in the early 1980s. As a result, people are now less careful about putting as much as they can in their money market fund. Put another way, for a given level of transactions, people now keep more in their checking account than they did in the early 1980s.

Deriving the Demand for Money

Let's move from this discussion to an equation describing the demand for money.

Revisit Chapter 2's example of an economy composed of a steel company and a car company. Calculate the volume of transactions in that economy, and its relation to GDP. If the steel and the car companies double in size, what happens to transactions and to GDP? (Harder: What happens if the two firms merge?) ▶

Denote the amount of money people want to hold—their *demand for money*—by M^d (the superscript *d* stands for *demand*). The demand for money for the economy as a whole is just the sum of all the individual demands for money. Thus, money demand for the economy as a whole depends on the overall level of transactions in the economy and on the interest rate. The overall level of transactions in the economy is hard to measure, but it is likely to be roughly proportional to nominal income: If nominal income increases by 10%, it is reasonable to think that the amount of transactions in the economy also increases by roughly 10%. So we can write the relation between the demand for money, nominal income, and the interest rate as

$$M^d = \$Y\,\underset{(-)}{L(i)} \qquad (4.1)$$

where $\$Y$ denotes nominal income. Read this equation in the following way: *The demand for money, M^d, is equal to nominal income, $\$Y$, times a function of the interest rate, i, with the function denoted by $L(i)$.* The minus sign under i in $L(i)$ captures the fact that the interest rate has a negative effect on money demand: An increase in the interest rate decreases the demand for money.

Equation (4.1) summarizes what we have discussed so far:

What matters here is nominal income—income in dollars, not real income. If real income does not change but prices double, leading to a doubling of nominal income, people will need to hold twice as much money to buy the same consumption basket. ▶

- First, the demand for money increases in proportion to nominal income. If nominal income doubles, increasing from $\$Y$ to $\$2Y$, then the demand for money also doubles, increasing from $\$YL(i)$ to $\$2YL(i)$.
- Second, the demand for money depends negatively on the interest rate. This is captured by the function $L(i)$ and the negative sign underneath: An increase in the interest rate decreases the demand for money.

The relation between the demand for money, nominal income, and the interest rate implied by equation (4.1) is represented in Figure 4-1. The interest rate, i, is measured on the vertical axis. Money, M, is measured on the horizontal axis.

The relation between the demand for money and the interest rate *for a given level of nominal income* is represented by the M^d curve. The curve is downward sloping: The lower the interest rate (the lower i), the higher the amount of money people want to hold (the higher M).

For a given interest rate, an increase in nominal income increases the demand for money. In other words, an increase in nominal income shifts the demand for money to

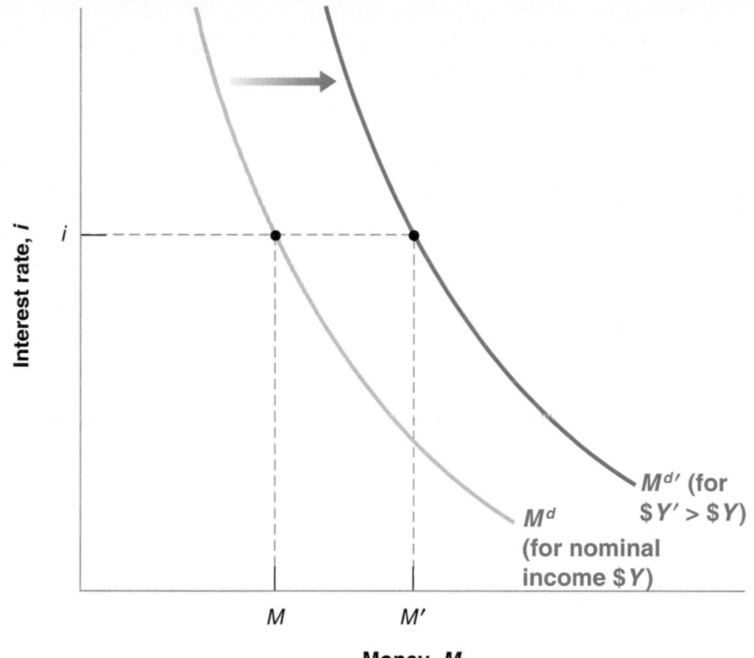

Figure 4-1

The Demand for Money

For a given level of nominal income, a lower interest rate increases the demand for money. At a given interest rate, an increase in nominal income shifts the demand for money to the right.

the right, from M^d to $M^{d\prime}$. For example, at interest rate i, an increase in nominal income from $\$Y$ to $\$Y'$ increases the demand for money from M to M'.

4-2 The Determination of the Interest Rate. I

Having looked at the demand for money, we now look at the supply of money, and then at the equilibrium.

In reality, there are two suppliers of money: Checkable deposits are supplied by banks. Currency is supplied by the central bank. In this section, we shall assume that people hold only currency as money, so all money is currency, supplied by the central bank. In the next section, we shall reintroduce checkable deposits, and look at the role of banks. Introducing banks makes the discussion more realistic. But it also makes the mechanics of money supply more complicated, and it is better to build the intuition in two steps.

Money Demand, Money Supply, and the Equilibrium Interest Rate

Suppose the central bank decides to supply an amount of money equal to M, so $M^s = M$. The superscript s stands for *supply*. (Let's leave aside for the moment the issue of how the central bank determines the amount of money in the economy. We shall return to it in a few paragraphs.)

Throughout this section, "money" stands for "central bank money," or "currency."

Equilibrium in financial markets requires that money supply be equal to money demand, that $M^s = M^d$. Then, using $M^s = M$, and equation (4.1) for money demand, the equilibrium condition is

$$\begin{aligned} \text{Money supply} &= \text{Money demand} \\ M &= \$Y\,L(i) \end{aligned} \qquad (4.2)$$

The Demand for Money and the Interest Rate: The Evidence

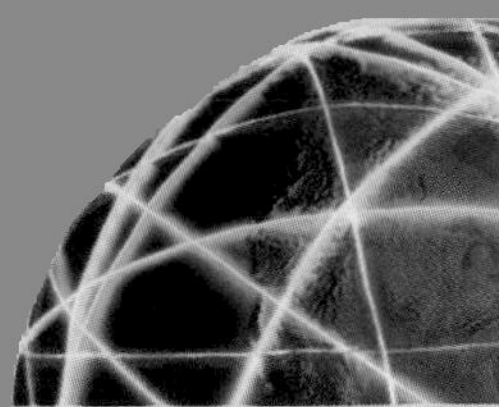

How well does equation (4.1) fit the facts? In particular, how much does the demand for money respond to changes in the interest rate? To get at the answer, first divide both sides of equation (4.1) by $\$Y$:

$$\frac{M^d}{\$Y} = L(i)$$

The term on the left side of the equation is the ratio of money demand to nominal income—in other words, how much money people want to hold in relation to their income. Because $L(i)$ is a decreasing function of the interest rate, i, this equation says

- When the interest rate is high, then $L(i)$ is low and the ratio of money to nominal income should be low.
- When the interest rate is low, then $L(i)$ is high and the ratio of money to nominal income should be high.

So if equation (4.1)—and, by implication, this equation—is a good description of reality, we should observe an inverse relation between the ratio of money to nominal income and the interest rate. This provides the motivation for Figure 1, which plots both the ratio of money to nominal income and the interest rate against time, for the period 1960 to 2000.

The ratio of money to nominal income is constructed as follows. Money, M, is the sum of currency, travelers' checks, and checkable deposits. This measure of money, is called **M1**. Nominal income is measured by nominal GDP $\$Y$. The interest rate, i, is the average interest rate paid by government bonds during each year.

Figure 1 suggests two main conclusions:

- The first is that there has been a large decline in the ratio of money to nominal income since 1960. The interest rate was roughly the same in 2000 as it was in the 1960s. Yet, in 2000, the ratio of money to nominal income was less than half what it was in 1960 (11% in 2000, compared to 27% in 1960).

  Economists sometimes refer to the inverse of the ratio of money to nominal income—that is, to the ratio of nominal income to money—as the **velocity** of money. The use of the word *velocity* comes from the intuitive idea that when the ratio of nominal income to money is higher, the number of transactions for a given quantity of money is higher, and it must be the case that money is changing hands faster; in other words, the velocity of money is higher. Therefore, another, equivalent, way of stating the first characteristic of Figure 1 is that the velocity of money has increased from about 3.7 (1/0.27) in 1960 to about 9.1 (1/0.11) in 2000.

  Why has velocity more than doubled over the last 40 years? The reason is not hard to find. Many innovations in financial markets have made it possible to hold lower money balances for a given

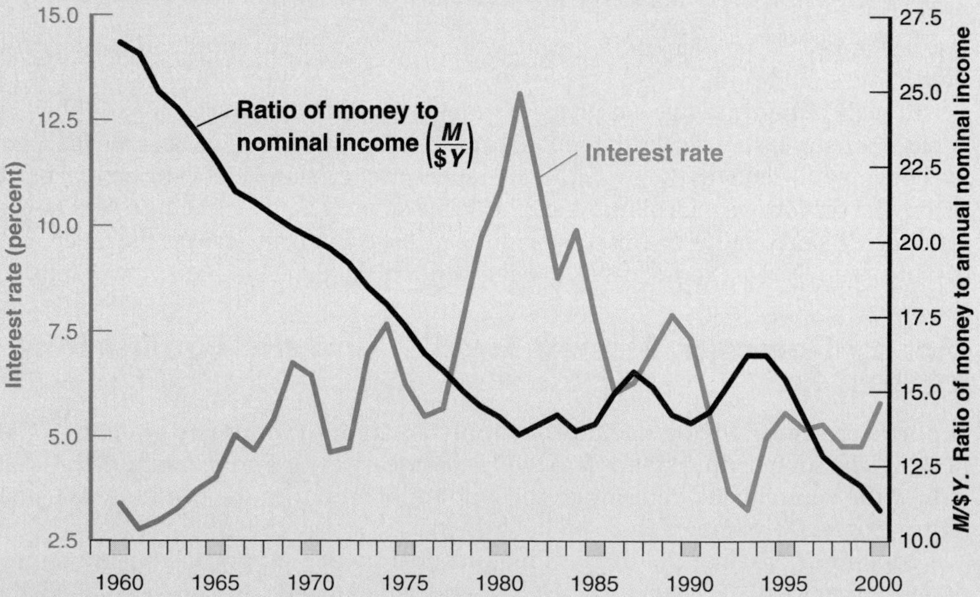

Figure 1 *The Ratio of Money to Nominal Income and the Interest Rate, 1960–2000*
The ratio of money to nominal income has decreased over time. Leaving aside this trend, the interest rate and the ratio of money to nominal income typically move in opposite directions.

FOCUS

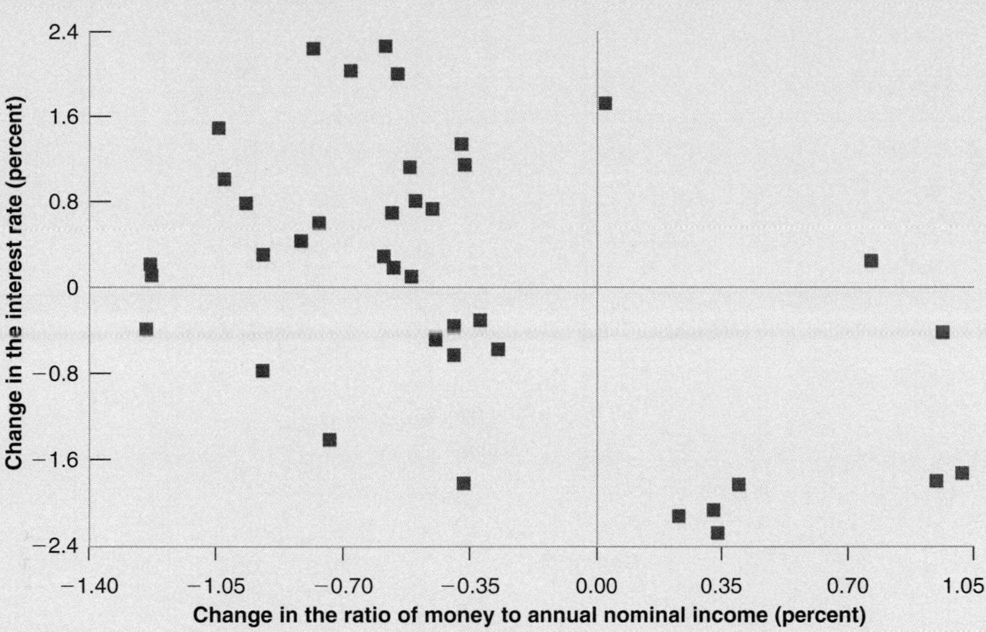

Figure 2 *Changes in the Interest Rate versus Changes in the Ratio of Money to Nominal Income, 1960–2000*
Increases in the interest rate have typically been associated with a decrease in the ratio of money to nominal income, decreases in the interest rate with an increase in that ratio.

amount of transactions. Perhaps the most important development here is the increased use of credit cards. At first glance, credit cards would appear to be money: When we go to a store, aren't we asked whether we want to pay with cash, check, or credit card? But, despite what they may seem, credit cards are not money. You actually do not pay when you use your credit card at the store; you pay when you receive your bill and send your monthly payment. What credit cards allow you to do is to concentrate many of your payments in one day, and thus to decrease the average amount of money you need to have during the rest of the month. (Some credit cards also allow you to defer payment, and thus to borrow, often at a high interest rate. This is a separate service, and not what is relevant here.) You would expect the introduction of credit cards to reduce money demand in relation to nominal income over time. Figure 1 shows that this has been the case.

- The second conclusion is that there is a negative relation between year-to-year movements in the ratio of money to nominal income and year-to-year movements in the interest rate. The trend of decline in the ratio of money to nominal income in the figure makes it difficult, however, to see this relation clearly. A better way to look at year-to-year movements is with a scatter diagram.

Figure 2 plots the change in the ratio of money to nominal income versus the change in the interest rate from year to year. Changes in the interest rate are measured on the vertical axis. Changes in the ratio of money to nominal income are measured on the horizontal axis. Each point (shown as a square) in the figure corresponds to a given year (the years are not identified in the figure). The vertical and horizontal lines give the mean values of the change in the ratio and in the interest rate for the period 1960–2000. The figure shows a negative relation between year-to-year changes in the interest rate and changes in the ratio. Note that most of the points lie either in the northwest quadrant (increases in the interest rate, decreases in the ratio) or the southeast quadrant (decreases in the interest rate, increases in the ratio). The relation is not tight, but if we were to draw a line that best fits the cloud of points, it would clearly be downward sloping, as predicted by our money demand equation.

Figure 4-2

The Determination of the Interest Rate

The interest rate must be such that the supply of money (which is independent of the interest rate) is equal to the demand for money (which does depend on the interest rate).

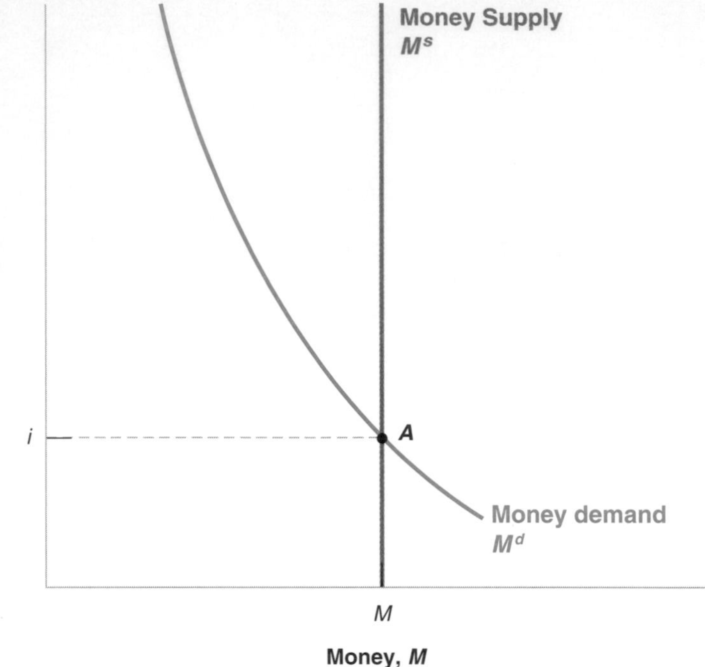

As for the *IS* relation, the name of the *LM* relation is more than 50 years old. The letter L stands for "liquidity": Economists use liquidity as a measure of how easily an asset can be exchanged for money. Money is *fully liquid,* other assets less so; we can think of the demand for money as a demand for liquidity. The letter M stands for money. The demand for liquidity must equal the supply of money. ▶

Equation (4.2) tells us that the interest rate i must be such that, given their income $\$Y$, people are willing to hold an amount of money equal to the existing money supply M. This equilibrium relation is called the ***LM* relation.**

This equilibrium condition is represented graphically in Figure 4-2. As in Figure 4-1, money is measured on the horizontal axis, and the interest rate is measured on the vertical axis. The demand for money, M^d, drawn for a given level of nominal income $\$Y$, is downward sloping: A higher interest rate implies a lower demand for money. The supply of money is drawn as the vertical line denoted M^s: The money supply equals M, and is independent of the interest rate. Equilibrium is at point A, with interest rate i.

With this characterization of the equilibrium, we can look at the effects of changes in nominal income or in the money stock on the equilibrium interest rate.

- Figure 4-3 shows the effects of an increase in nominal income on the interest rate.

  The figure replicates Figure 4-2, so the initial equilibrium is at point A. An increase in nominal income from $\$Y$ to $\$Y'$ increases the level of transactions, which increases the demand for money at any interest rate. The money demand curve *shifts* to the right, from M^d to $M^{d'}$. The equilibrium moves from A up to A'; the equilibrium interest rate increases from i to i'.

  In words: *An increase in nominal income leads to an increase in the interest rate.* The reason is that at the initial interest rate, the demand for money exceeds the unchanged supply of money. An increase in the interest rate is needed to decrease the amount of money people want to hold and reestablish equilibrium.

- Figure 4-4 shows the effects of an increase in the money supply on the interest rate.

  The initial equilibrium is at point A, with interest rate i. An increase in the money supply, from $M^s = M$ to $M^{s'} = M'$, leads to a shift of the money supply curve to the right, from M^s to $M^{s'}$. The equilibrium moves from A down to A'; the interest rate decreases from i to i'.

  In words: *An increase in the supply of money leads to a decrease in the interest rate.* The decrease in the interest rate increases the demand for money so it equals the larger money supply.

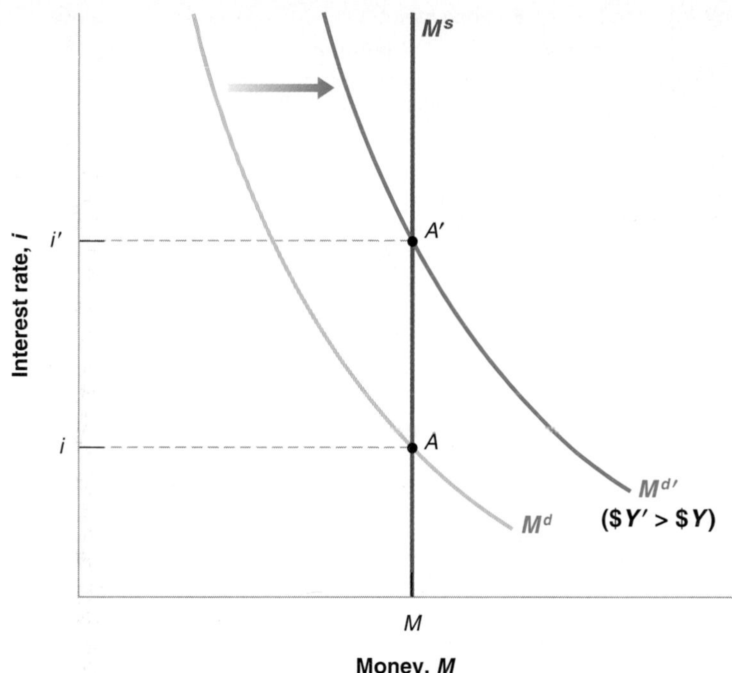

Figure 4-3

The Effects of an Increase in Nominal Income on the Interest Rate

An increase in nominal income leads to an increase in the interest rate.

Monetary Policy and Open-Market Operations

We can get a better feel for the results in Figures 4-3 and 4-4 by looking more closely at how the central bank actually changes the money supply, and what happens when it does so.

Assume the central bank changes the supply of money by buying or selling bonds in the bonds market. If it wants to increase the amount of money in the economy, it

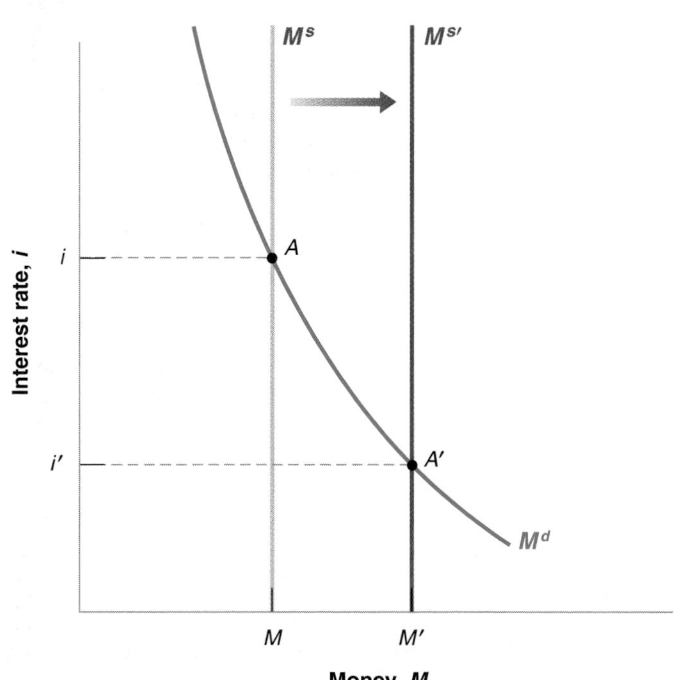

Figure 4-4

The Effects of an Increase in the Money Supply on the Interest Rate

An increase in the supply of money leads to a decrease in the interest rate.

Figure 4-5

The Balance Sheet of the Central Bank, and the Effects of an Expansionary Open-Market Operation

The assets of the central bank are the bonds it holds. The liabilities are the stock of money in the economy. An open-market operation in which the central bank buys bonds and issues money increases both assets and liabilities by the same amount.

(a) Balance sheet

Assets	Liabilities
Bonds	Money (currency)

(b) The Effects of an Expansionary Open-Market Operation

Assets	Liabilities
Change in bond holdings: +$1 million	Change in money stock: +$1 million

buys bonds and pays for them by creating money. If it wants to decrease the amount of money in the economy, it sells bonds, and removes from circulation the money it receives in exchange for the bonds. Such operations are called **open-market operations**, so-called because they take place in the "open-market" for bonds. They are the standard method central banks use to change the money stock in modern economies.

The balance sheet of a bank (or firm, or individual) is a list of its assets and liabilities at a point in time. The assets are the sum of what the bank owns and what is owed to the bank at that time. The liabilities are what the bank owes to others, also at that time. ▶

The balance sheet of the central bank is given in Figure 4-5. The assets of the central bank are the bonds it holds in its portfolio. Its liabilities are the stock of money in the economy. Open-market operations lead to equal changes in assets and liabilities.

If the central bank buys, say, $1 million worth of bonds, the amount of bonds it holds is higher by $1 million, and so is the amount of money in the economy. Such an operation is called an **expansionary open-market operation**, because the central bank increases (*expands*) the supply of money.

If the central bank sells $1 million worth of bonds, both the amount of bonds held by the central bank, and the amount of money in the economy are lower by $1 million. Such an operation is called a **contractionary open-market operation**, because the central bank decreases (*contracts*) the supply of money.

One more step is needed before we can describe the effects of open-market operations. We have focused so far on the interest rate on bonds. In fact, what is determined in bonds markets is not interest rates, but bond *prices*; the interest rate on a bond can then be inferred from the price of the bond. Understanding the relation between the interest rate and the price of a bond will prove useful both here and later in this book.

- Suppose the bonds in our economy are one-year bonds—bonds that promise a payment of a given number of dollars, say, $100, a year hence. In the United States, such bonds, when issued by the government and promising payment in a year or less, are called **Treasury bills** or **T-bills**. Let the price of a bond today be $\$P_B$, where the subscript B stands for "bond." If you buy the bond today and hold it for a year, the rate of return on holding the bond for a year is $(\$100 - \$P_B)/\$P_B$ Therefore, the interest rate on the bond is given by:

The interest rate is what you get for the bond a year from now ($100) minus what you pay for the bond today ($\$P_B$), divided by the price of the bond today, ($\$P_B$). ▶

$$i = \frac{\$100 - \$P_B}{\$P_B}$$

  If $\$P_B$ is $95, the interest rate equals $5/$95 = 0.053, or 5.3% per year. If $\$P_B$ is $90, the interest rate is 11.1% per year. *The higher the price of the bond, the lower the interest rate.*

- Equivalently, if we are given the interest rate, we can infer the price of the bond. Reorganizing the formula above, the price today of a one-year bond paying $100 a year from today is given by

$$\$P_B = \frac{\$100}{1+i}$$

The price of the bond today is equal to the final payment divided by 1 plus the interest rate. If the interest rate is positive, the price of the bond is less than the final payment. The higher the interest rate, the lower the price today. When newspapers write that "bonds markets went up today," they mean that *the prices of bonds went up*, and therefore that *interest rates went down*.

In Japan today, the one-year interest rate is (nearly) equal to zero. If a one-year Japanese government bond promises 100 yen in one year, for what price will it sell today?

We are now ready to return to the effects of an open-market operation. Consider first an expansionary open-market operation, in which the central bank buys bonds in the bonds market and pays for them by creating money. As the central bank buys bonds, the demand for bonds goes up, increasing the price of bonds. Equivalently, the interest rate on bonds goes down. If, instead, the central bank decreases the supply of money—a contractionary open-market operation—it sells bonds in the bonds market. This leads to a decrease in their price, and an increase in the interest rate.

To summarize:

- The interest rate is determined by the equality of the supply of money and the demand for money.
- By changing the supply of money, the central bank can affect the interest rate.
- The central bank changes the supply of money through open-market operations, which are purchases or sales of bonds for money.
- Open-market operations in which the central bank increases the money supply by buying bonds lead to an increase in the price of bonds—equivalently, a decrease in the interest rate.
- Open-market operations in which the central bank decreases the money supply by selling bonds lead to a decrease in the price of bonds—equivalently, an increase in the interest rate.

We have been looking at an economy with only two assets, money and bonds. This is obviously a much simplified version of actual economies with their many financial assets and many financial markets. But, as you shall see in later chapters, the basic lessons we have just seen apply very generally. The only change we shall have to make is to replace "interest rate" in our conclusions by "short-term interest rate." You shall see that the short-term interest rate is determined by the condition that money supply equals money demand; the central bank can, through open-market operations, change the short-term interest rate; and open-market operations are indeed the basic tool used by most modern central banks, including the Fed, to affect interest rates.

The complication: The short-term interest rate—the rate directly affected by monetary policy—is not the only interest rate in the economy, and not the only interest rate that affects spending. The determination of other interest rates and asset prices (such as stock prices) is the topic of Chapter 15.

There is one dimension, however, in which our model must be extended. We have assumed that all money was currency, supplied by the central bank. In the real world, money includes not only currency but also checkable deposits. Checkable deposits are supplied not by the central bank, but by (private) banks. How the presence of banks changes our conclusions is the topic of the next two sections.

You can skip the next two sections and still go through most of the arguments in the rest of the book. If you do so, let me give you the bottom line: Even in this more complicated case, the central bank can, by changing the amount of central bank money, affect the interest rate.

4-3 The Determination of Interest Rates. II*

To understand what determines the interest rate in an economy with both currency and checkable deposits, we must first look at what banks do.

What Banks Do

Modern economies are characterized by the existence of many types of **financial intermediaries**, institutions that receive funds from people and firms, and use these

**This section is optional.*

Figure 4-6

The Balance Sheet of Banks, and the Balance Sheet of the Central Bank Revisited

(a) **Central Bank**

Assets	**Liabilities**
Bonds	Central Bank Money = Reserves + Currency

(b) **Banks**

Assets	**Liabilities**
Reserves Loans Bonds	Checkable deposits

funds to buy bonds or stocks, or to make loans to other people and firms. Their liabilities are what they owe to the people and firms from whom they have received funds. Their assets are the stocks and bonds they own, and the loans they have made.

Banks are one type of financial intermediary. What makes banks special—and the reason we focus on banks here rather than financial intermediaries in general—is that their liabilities are money: People can pay for transactions by writing checks up to the amount of their account balance. Let's look at what they do more closely.

As always, this description is a simplification. Banks have liabilities other than checkable deposits, and are engaged in more activities than holding bonds or making loans. But these complications are not relevant here.

Banks receive funds from depositors. They keep some of these funds as reserves, and use the rest to make loans and purchase bonds. Their balance sheet is shown in Figure 4-6, panel (b). Their liabilities consist of checkable deposits, the funds deposited by people and firms. Their assets consist of reserves, loans, and bonds.

- Banks receive funds from people and firms who either deposit funds or have funds sent directly to their checking account (their paycheck, for example.) At any point in time, people and firms can write checks or withdraw up to the full amount of their account balance. Thus, the liabilities of the banks are equal to the value of *checkable deposits*.
- Banks keep as **reserves** some of the funds they have received. These reserves are reserves of central bank money; they are held partly in cash, partly on an account the banks have at the central bank, on which they can draw when they need to. Banks hold reserves for three reasons:

  1. On any given day, some depositors withdraw cash from their checking account, while others deposit cash into their account. There is no reason for the inflows and outflows of cash to be equal, so the bank must keep some cash on hand.
  2. In the same way, on any given day, people with accounts at the bank write checks to people with accounts at other banks, and people with accounts at other banks write checks to people with accounts at the bank. What the bank, as a result of these transactions, owes to other banks may be greater or smaller than what other banks owe to the bank. For this reason also, the bank needs to keep reserves.
  3. The first two reasons imply that banks would want to keep some reserves even if they were not required to. But, in addition, banks are subject to legal reserve requirements, which require them to hold reserves in some proportion to checkable deposits. In the United States, reserve requirements are set by the Fed, which can set them anywhere between 7 and 22% of deposits. The actual **reserve ratio**, the ratio of bank reserves to checkable deposits, is about 10% in the United States today.

- Leaving aside reserves, banks use the remainder of their funds to make loans to firms and consumers or to buy bonds. Loans represent roughly 70% of banks' nonreserve assets. Bonds account for the rest, 30%. The distinction between bonds and loans is unimportant for our purpose—which is understanding the determination of the money supply. So, in what follows, I shall assume for simplicity that banks do not make loans, that they hold only reserves and bonds as assets. But the distinction between loans and bonds is important for other purposes, from the possibility of "bank runs"' to the role of federal deposit insurance. These topics are explored in the Focus box "Bank Runs."

Figure 4-6, panel (a) returns to the balance sheet of the central bank, in an economy in which there are banks. It is very similar to the balance sheet of the central bank we saw in Figure 4-5. The asset side is the same as before: The assets of the central bank are the bonds it holds. The liabilities of the central bank are the money it has issued, **central bank money**. The new feature is that not all of central bank money is held as currency by the public. Some is held as reserves by banks.

Bank Runs

Is bank money (checkable deposits) just as good as central bank money (currency)? To answer, we must look at what banks do with the funds they receive from depositors, and at the distinction between making loans and holding bonds.

Making a loan to a firm and buying a government bond are actions more similar than they may seem. In one case, the bank lends to a firm. In the other, the bank lends to the government. This is why, for simplicity, I have assumed in the text that banks hold only bonds.

But, in one respect, making a loan is very different from buying a bond. Bonds, especially government bonds, are very liquid: In case of need, they can be sold easily in the bonds market. Loans are often not liquid at all. Calling them back may be impossible: The firm, which has used the loan to buy inventories or a new machine, no longer has the cash. The bank could in principle sell the loan itself to a third party and get cash; but selling the loan may be very difficult, as potential buyers know little about how reliable the firm is as a borrower.

This fact has one important implication: Take a healthy bank, a bank with a good portfolio of loans. Suppose rumors start that the bank is not doing well and some loans will not be repaid. Believing that the bank may fail, people with deposits at the bank will want to close their accounts and withdraw cash. If enough people do so, the bank will run out of reserves. Given that the loans cannot be called back, the bank will not be able to satisfy the demand for cash, and it will have to close.

Conclusion: The belief that a bank may close may lead it to close, even if all its loans are good. The financial history of the United States up to the 1930s is full of such **bank runs.** One bank fails for the right reason (that is, it has made bad loans), leading depositors at other banks to get scared and run on their own banks, thus forcing them to close, whether or not their loans are good. You may have seen *It's a Wonderful Life,* an old movie with James Stewart; it runs on TV every year around Christmas. Because of the failure of another bank in town, depositors at the savings and loans of which James Stewart is the manager get scared and come to get their money back. It takes all of James Stewart's persuasion to avoid closure. The movie has a happy ending. In real life, most bank runs didn't.

What can be done to avoid such runs? The United States has dealt with this problem since 1934 with **federal deposit insurance.** The U.S. government insures each account up to a ceiling of $100,000. As a result, there is no reason for depositors to run and get their money out, and healthy banks do not fail.

However, federal deposit insurance leads to problems of its own. Depositors who do not have to worry about their deposits no longer look at the activities of the banks in which they have their deposits, and banks may misbehave, for example making loans they would not have made absent the insurance (more on this when we discuss Japan's current economic problems in Chapter 22).

An alternative solution, which has been often proposed but never implemented, is **narrow banking.** Narrow banking would restrict banks to holding liquid, safe, government bonds, such as T-bills. It would eliminate bank runs, as well as the need for federal insurance. Loans to firms would have to be made by other financial intermediaries.

FOCUS

The Supply and the Demand for Central Bank Money

The easiest way to think about the determination of the interest rate in this economy is by thinking in terms of the supply and the demand for *central bank money*:

- The demand for central bank money is equal to the demand for currency plus the demand for reserves by banks.
- The supply of central bank money is under the direct control of the central bank.
- The equilibrium interest rate is such that the demand and the supply for central bank money are equal.

Figure 4-7 shows the structure of demand and supply in more detail. (Look only at the top part of the figure for the moment. The bottom part shows how the equations we shall derive later relate to the various boxes in the figure.)

Start from the left side. The demand for money is a demand for both checkable deposits and currency. Banks have to hold reserves against checkable deposits: The demand for checkable deposits leads to a demand for reserves by banks. The demand for central bank money is equal to the demand for reserves by banks plus the demand for currency. Go to the right side: The supply of central bank money is determined by the central bank. The interest rate must be such that the demand and the supply are equal.

We now go through each of the boxes in Figure 4-7 and ask:

What determines the demand for checkable deposits and the demand for currency?

What determines the demand for reserves by banks?

How does the condition that the demand and the supply of central bank money be equal determines the interest rate?

Be careful to distinguish among:

- **demand for money (demand for currency and checkable deposits)**
- **demand for bank money (demand for checkable deposits)**
- **demand for central bank money (demand for currency by people, and demand for reserves by banks)**

The Demand for Money

When people can hold both currency and checkable deposits, the demand for money involves *two* decisions. First, people must decide how much money to hold. Second, they must decide how much of this money to hold in currency and how much to hold in checkable deposits.

It is reasonable to assume that the overall demand for money (currency plus checkable deposits) is given by the same factors as before. People will hold more money, the higher the level of transactions, and the lower the interest rate on bonds. So we can assume that overall money demand is given by the same equation as before (equation [4.1]):

$$M^d = \$Y \underset{(-)}{L(i)} \qquad (4.3)$$

Figure 4-7

Determinants of the Demand and the Supply of Central Bank Money

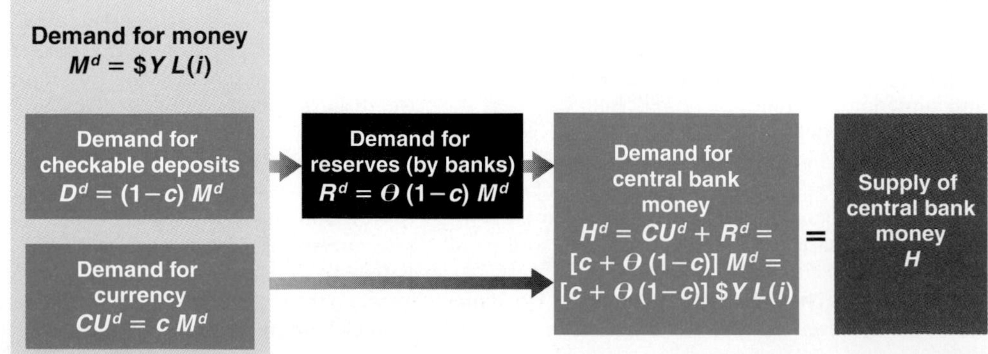

That brings us to the second decision. How do people decide how much to hold in currency, and how much in checkable deposits? Currency is more convenient for small transactions (it is also more convenient for illegal transactions!) Checks are more convenient for large transactions. Holding money in your checking account is safer than holding it in cash.

◀ A Fed study suggests that more than half of U.S. currency is held abroad! It is a reasonable guess that part of these foreign holdings of U.S. currency is associated with illegal transactions, and that U.S. currency is the currency of choice for illegal transactions around the world.

Let us simply assume that people hold a fixed proportion of their money in currency—call this proportion c—and, by implication, a fixed proportion $(1 - c)$ in checkable deposits. In the United States, people hold 40% of their money in the form of currency, thus $c = 0.4$. Call the demand for currency CU^d (CU for currency, and d for demand). Call the demand for checkable deposits D^d (D for deposits, and d for demand). The two demands are given by

$$CU^d = cM^d \qquad (4.4)$$

$$D^d = (1-c)M^d \qquad (4.5)$$

Equation (4.4) gives the first component of the demand for central bank money, the demand for currency by the public. Equation (4.5) gives the demand for checkable deposits.

We now have a description of the behavior in the first box, "Demand for Money," on the left side of Figure 4-7. Equation (4.3) gives the overall demand for money; equations (4.4) and (4.5) give the demand for checkable deposits and the demand for currency, respectively. The three demand equations are written in the bottom part of the box in the figure.

The demand for checkable deposits leads to a demand by banks for reserves, the second component of the demand for central bank money. To see how, let us turn to the behavior of banks.

The Demand for Reserves

The larger the amount of checkable deposits, the larger the amount of reserves the banks must hold, both for precautionary and for legal reasons. Let θ (the Greek lowercase theta) be the reserve ratio, the amount of reserves banks hold per dollar of checkable deposits. Let R denote the reserves of banks. Let D denote the dollar amount of checkable deposits. Then, by the definition of θ, the following relation holds between R and D:

$$R = \theta D \qquad (4.6)$$

We saw earlier that, in the United States today, the reserve ratio is roughly equal to 10%. Thus, θ is roughly equal to 0.1.

If people want to hold D^d in deposits, then from equation (4.6) banks must hold θD^d in reserves. Combining equations (4.5) and (4.6), the second component of the demand for central bank money—the demand for reserves by banks—is given by

$$R^d = \theta(1-c)M^d \qquad (4.7)$$

We now have the equation corresponding to the second box, "Demand for reserves by corresponding to banks," on the left side of Figure 4-7.

The Demand for Central Bank Money

Call H^d the demand for central bank money. This demand is equal to the sum of the demand for currency and the demand for reserves:

$$H^d = CU^d + R^d \qquad (4.8)$$

Replace CU^d and R^d by their expressions from equations (4.4) and (4.7) to get

$$H^d = cM^d + \theta(1-c)M^d = [c+\theta(1-c)]M^d$$

Finally, replace the overall demand for money, M^d, by its expression from equation (4.3) to get:

$$H^d = [c+\theta(1-c)]\,\$Y\,L(i) \tag{4.9}$$

This gives us the equation corresponding to the third box, "Demand for central bank money," on the left side of Figure 4-7.

The Determination of the Interest Rate

We are now ready to characterize the equilibrium. Let H be the supply of central bank money; H is directly controlled by the central bank; just as in the previous section, the central bank can change the amount of H through open market operations. The equilibrium condition is that the supply of central bank money be equal to the demand for central bank money:

$$H = H^d \tag{4.10}$$

Or, using equation (4.9):

$$H = [c+\theta(1-c)]\,\$Y\,L(i) \tag{4.11}$$

The supply of central bank money (the left side of equation [4.11]) is equal to the demand for central bank money (the right side of equation [4.11]), which is itself equal to the term in brackets times the overall demand for money.

Look at the term in brackets more closely. Assume that people held only currency, so $c = 1$. Then, the term in brackets would be equal to 1, and the equation would be exactly the same as equation (4.2) in Section 4-2 (with the letter H replacing the letter M on the left side, but H and M both stand for the supply of central bank money). In this case, people would hold only currency, and banks would play no role in the supply of money. We would be back to the case we looked at in Section 4-2.

Assume instead that people do not hold currency at all, but hold only checkable deposits. In this case, $c = 0$, and the term in brackets is equal to θ. Suppose, for example, that $\theta = 0.1$, so that the term in brackets is equal to 0.1. Then, the demand for central bank money is equal to one-tenth of the overall demand for money. This is easy to understand: People hold only checkable deposits. For every dollar they want to hold, banks need to have 10 cents in reserves. The demand for reserves is one-tenth of the overall demand for money.

Leaving aside these two extreme cases, note that, as long as people hold some checkable deposits (so that $c < 1$), the term in brackets is less than 1: The demand for central bank money is less than the overall demand for money. This comes from the fact that the demand for reserves by banks is only a fraction of the demand for checkable deposits.

We can represent the equilibrium condition, equation (4.11), graphically, and we do this in Figure 4-8. The figure looks the same as Figure 4-2, but with central bank money rather than money on the horizontal axis. The interest rate is measured on the vertical axis. The demand for central bank money, $CU^d + R^d$, is drawn for a given level of nominal income. A higher interest rate implies a lower demand for central bank money for two reasons: The demand for currency goes down; the demand for checkable deposits also goes down, leading to a decrease in the demand for reserves by banks. The supply of money is fixed, and is represented by a vertical line at H. Equilibrium is at point A, with interest rate i.

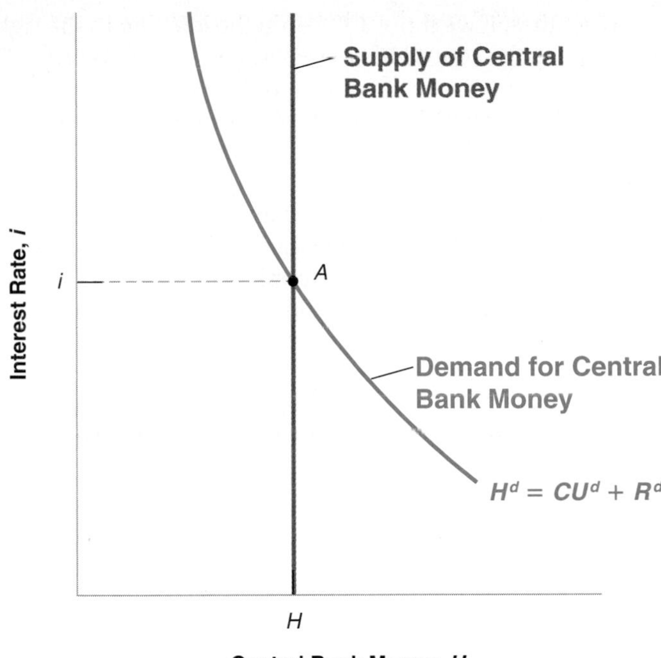

Figure 4-8

Equilibrium in the Market for Central Bank Money, and the Determination of the Interest Rate

The equilibrium interest rate is such that the supply of central bank money is equal to the demand for central bank money.

The effects of either changes in nominal income or changes in the supply of central bank money are qualitatively the same as in the previous section. In particular, an increase in the supply of central bank money leads to a shift in the vertical supply line to the right. This leads to a lower interest rate. As before, an increase in central bank money leads to a decrease in the interest rate; symmetrically, a decrease in central bank money leads to an increase in the interest rate.

4-4 Two Alternative Ways to Think About the Equilibrium*

In Section 4-3, we looked at the equilibrium through the condition that the supply and the demand of central bank money be equal. There are two other ways of looking at the equilibrium. While they are all equivalent, each provides a different way of thinking about the equilibrium, and going through each will strengthen your understanding.

The Federal Funds Market and the Federal Funds Rate

Instead of thinking in terms of the supply and the demand for central bank money, we can think in terms of the supply and the demand for bank reserves.

The supply of reserves is equal to the supply of central bank money, H, minus the demand for currency by the public, CU^d. The demand for reserves by banks is R^d. So the equilibrium condition that the supply and the demand for bank reserves be equal is given by:

$$H - CU^d = R^d$$

*This section is optional.

Note that, if we move CU^d from the left side to the right side, and use the fact that the demand for central bank money, H^d, is given by $H^d = CU^d + R^d$, then this equation is equivalent to $H = H^d$. In other words, looking at the equilibrium in terms of the supply and the demand for reserves is equivalent to looking at the equilibrium in terms of the supply and the demand for central bank money—the approach we followed in Section 4-3.

Nevertheless, this alternative way of looking at the equilibrium is attractive because, in the United States, there is indeed a market for bank reserves, in which the interest rate moves so the supply and demand for reserves are equal. This market is called the **federal funds market**. Banks that have excess reserves at the end of the day lend them to banks that have insufficient reserves. In equilibrium, the total demand for reserves by all banks, R^d, must be equal to the supply of reserves to the market, $H - CU^d$—the equilibrium condition stated above. The interest rate determined in the market is called the **federal funds rate**. Because the Fed can choose the federal funds rate it wants by appropriately changing the supply of central bank money, H, the federal funds rate is typically thought of as an indicator of U.S. monetary policy, reflecting what the Fed wants the interest rate to be. This is why, when we looked in Chapter 1 at the sharp decline in the federal funds rate during 2001, we interpreted the decline as reflecting the decision by the Fed to decrease the interest rate in order to stimulate economic activity.

The Supply of Money, the Demand for Money, and the Money Multiplier

Instead of thinking in terms of the supply and the demand for central bank money, we can look at the equilibrium in terms of the overall supply and the overall demand for money (currency and checkable deposits).

To derive an equilibrium condition in terms of the overall supply and the overall demand for money, take the equilibrium condition (4.11) and divide both sides by $[c + \theta(1 - c)]$:

$$\begin{array}{ccc} \dfrac{1}{[c+\theta(1-c)]}H & = & \$Y\,L(i) \\ \text{Supply of money} & = & \text{Demand for money} \end{array} \qquad (4.12)$$

The right side of the equation gives the overall demand for money (currency plus checkable deposits.) The left side gives the overall supply of money (currency plus checkable deposits). Condition (4.12) therefore says that, in equilibrium, the overall supply and the overall demand of money must be equal.

- If you compare equation (4.12) with equation (4.2), the equation characterizing the equilibrium in an economy without banks, you will see that the only difference is that the overall supply of money is not equal just to central bank money, but to central bank money times a constant term $1/[c + \theta(1 - c)]$.

  Note also that, because $[c + \theta(1 - c)]$ is less than one, its inverse—the constant term on the left of (4.12)—is greater than one. For this reason, this constant term is called the **money multiplier**. The overall supply of money is therefore equal to central bank money times the money multiplier. If the money multiplier is 4, for example, then the overall supply of money is equal to 4 times the supply of central bank money.
- To reflect the fact that the overall supply of money depends in the end on the amount of central bank money, central bank money is often called **high-powered money** (this is where the letter H we used to denote central bank money comes

from), or the **monetary base**. The term *high-powered* reflects the fact that increases in H lead to more than one-for-one increases in the overall money supply, and are therefore "high powered." In the same way, the term *monetary base* reflects the fact that the overall money supply depends ultimately on a "base"—the amount of central bank money in the economy.

The presence of a multiplier in equation (4.12) implies that a given change in central bank money has a larger effect on the money supply—and in turn a larger effect on the interest rate—in an economy with banks than in an economy without banks. To understand why, it is useful to return to the description of open-market operations, this time in an economy with banks.

Understanding the Money Multiplier

To make things easier, let us consider the special case where people hold only checkable deposits, which means $c = 0$. In this case, the multiplier is $1/\theta$: an increase of a dollar of high-powered money leads to an increase of $1/\theta$ dollars in the money supply. Assume further that $\theta = 0.1$, so that the multiplier equals $1/0.1 = 10$. The purpose of what follows is to get more intuition for where this multiplier comes from, and, more generally, for how the initial increase in central bank money leads to a 10-fold increase in the overall money supply.

Suppose the Fed buys \$100 worth of bonds in an open-market operation. It pays the seller—call him seller 1—\$100. To pay the seller, the Fed creates \$100 in central bank money. The increase in central bank money is \$100. When we looked earlier at the effects of an open-market operation in an economy in which there were no banks, this was the end of the story. Here it is just the beginning:

- Seller 1 (who, we have assumed, does not want to hold any currency) deposits the \$100 in a checking account at his bank—call it bank A. This leads to an increase in checkable deposits of \$100.
- Bank A keeps \$100 times 0.1 = \$10 in reserves, and buys bonds with the rest, \$100 times 0.9 = \$90. It pays \$90 to the seller of those bonds—call her seller 2.
- Seller 2 deposits \$90 in a checking account in her bank—call it bank B. This leads to an increase in checkable deposits of \$90.
- Bank B keeps \$90 times 0.1 = \$9 in reserves, and buys bonds with the rest, \$90 times 0.9 = \$81. It pays \$81 to the seller of those bonds, call him seller 3.
- Seller 3 deposits \$81 in a checking account in his bank, call it bank C.
- And so on.

By now, the chain of events should be clear. What is the eventual increase in the money supply? The increase in checkable deposits is \$100 when seller 1 deposits the proceeds of his sale of bonds in bank A, plus \$90 when seller 2 deposits the proceeds of her sale of bonds in bank B, plus \$81 when seller 3 does the same, and so on. Let's write the sum as

$$\$100\,(1 + 0.9 + 0.9^2 + \cdots)$$

The series in parentheses is a geometric series, so its sum is equal to $1/(1 - 0.9) = 10$. The money supply increases by \$1,000, ten times the initial increase in central bank money.

This derivation gives us another way of thinking about the money multiplier: We can think of the ultimate increase in the money supply as the result of *successive rounds of purchases of bonds*—the first started by the Fed in its open-market operation, the following rounds by banks. Each successive round leads to an increase in the money supply; eventually the increase in the money supply is equal to 10 times the initial increase in the central bank money.

See Appendix 2 at the end of this book for a refresher on geometric series.

Note the parallel between our interpretation of the money multiplier as the result of successive purchases of bonds and the interpretation of the goods market multiplier (Chapter 3) as the result of successive rounds of spending. Multipliers can often be derived as the sum of a geometric series, and be interpreted as the result of successive rounds of decisions. This interpretation often gives a better intuition for the process at work.

Summary

- The demand for money depends positively on the level of income and negatively on the interest rate.
- The interest rate is determined by the equilibrium condition that the supply of money be equal to the demand for money.
- Given the supply of money, an increase in income leads to an increase in the demand for money and an increase in the interest rate. An increase in the supply of money leads to a decrease in the interest rate.
- The way the central bank changes the supply of money is through open-market operations.
- Expansionary open-market operations, in which the central bank increases the money supply by buying bonds, lead to an increase in the price of bonds—equivalently, a decrease in the interest rate.
- Contractionary open-market operations, in which the central bank decreases the money supply by selling bonds, lead to a decrease in the price of bonds—equivalently, an increase in the interest rate.
- When money includes both currency and checkable deposits, we can think of the interest rate as determined by the condition that the supply of central bank money be equal to the demand for central bank money.
- The supply of central bank money is under the control of the central bank. The demand for central bank money depends on the overall demand for money, the proportion of money people keep in currency, and the ratio of reserves to checkable deposits chosen by banks.
- Another, but equivalent, way to think about the determination of the interest rate is in terms of the equality of the supply and demand for bank reserves. The market for bank reserves is called the federal funds market. The interest rate determined in that market is called the federal funds rate.
- Yet another way to think about the determination of the interest rate is in terms of the equality of the overall supply and overall demand for money. The overall supply of money is equal to central bank money times the money multiplier.

Key Terms

- Federal Reserve Bank (Fed), 65
- money, 66
- currency, 66
- checkable deposits, 66
- bonds, 66
- income, 67
- flow, 67
- saving, 67
- savings, 67
- financial wealth, wealth, 67
- stock, 67
- investment, 67
- financial investment, 67
- money market funds, 68
- *M*1, 70
- velocity, 70
- *LM* relation, 72
- open-market operation, 74
- expansionary, and contractionary, open-market operation, 74
- Treasury bill, T-bill, 74
- financial intermediaries, 75
- (bank) reserves, 76
- reserve ratio, 76
- central bank money, 77
- bank run, 77
- federal deposit insurance, 77
- narrow banking, 77
- federal funds market, federal funds rate, 82
- money multiplier, 82
- high-powered money, 82
- monetary base, 83

Questions and Problems

Quick Check

1. *Using the information in this chapter, label each of the following statements* true, false, *or* uncertain. *Explain briefly.*
   a. Income and financial wealth are both examples of stock variables.
   b. The demand for money does not depend on the interest rate because only bonds earn interest.
   c. Given their financial wealth, if people are satisfied with the amount of money they hold, then they must also be satisfied with the amount of bonds they hold.
   d. Financial innovations are the reason why velocity has increased dramatically in the last 40 years.
   e. In the last 40 years, the ratio of money to nominal income has moved in the same direction as the interest rate.
   f. The central bank can increase the supply of money by selling bonds in the market for bonds.
   g. By construction, bond prices and interest rates always move in opposite directions.

2. Suppose that a person's wealth is $50,000 and that her yearly income is $60,000. Also, suppose that her money demand function is given by

$$M^d = \$Y(.35 - i)$$

a. What is her demand for money and her demand for bonds when the interest rate is 5%? 10%?
b. Describe the effect of the interest rate on money demand and bond demand. Explain.
c. Suppose that the interest rate is 10%. In percentage terms, what happens to her demand for money if her yearly income is reduced by 50%?
d. Suppose that the interest rate is 5%. In percentage terms, what happens to her demand for money if her yearly income is reduced by 50%?
e. Summarize the effect of income on money demand. How does it depend on the interest rate?

3. A bond promises to pay $100 in one year.

a. What is the interest rate on the bond if its price today is $75? $85? $95?
b. What is the relation between the price of the bond and the interest rate?
c. If the interest rate is 8%, what is the price of the bond today?

4. Suppose that money demand is given by

$$M^d = \$Y(.25 - i)$$

where $Y is $100. Also, suppose that the supply of money is $20. Assume equilibrium in financial markets.

a. What is the interest rate?
b. If the Federal Reserve Bank wants to increase i by 10% (that is, from, say, 2 to 12%), at what level should it set the supply of money?

5. Suppose that a person's wealth is $50,000 and that her yearly income is $60,000. Also suppose that her money demand function is given by

$$M^d = \$Y(.35 - i)$$

a. Derive the demand for bonds. What is the effect of an increase in the interest rate by 10% on the demand for bonds?
b. What are the effects of an increase in wealth on money and on bond demand? Explain in words.
c. What are the effects of an increase in income on money and on bond demand? Explain in words.
d. "When people earn more money, they obviously will hold more bonds." What is wrong with this sentence?

Dig Deeper

6. The money multiplier

Suppose the following assumptions hold:

1. The public holds no currency.
2. The ratio of reserves to deposits is 0.1
3. The demand for money is given by

$$M^d = \$Y(.8 - 4i)$$

Initially, the monetary base is $100 billion and nominal income is $5 trillion.

a. What is the demand for central bank money?
b. Find the equilibrium interest rate by setting the demand for central bank money equal to the supply of central bank money.
c. What is the overall supply of money? Is it equal to the overall demand for money at the interest rate you found in (b)?
d. What is the impact on the interest rate if central bank money is increased to $300 billion?
e. If the overall money supply increases to $3,000 billion what will be the impact on i? (*Hint*: Use what you learned in (c).)

7. Bank runs and the money multiplier.

During the Great Depression, the U.S. economy experienced many bank runs, to the point where people became unwilling to keep their money in banks, preferring to keep it in cash.

How would you expect such a shift away from checkable deposits toward currency to affect the size of the money multiplier? (To find what happened to the money multiplier during the Great Depression, go to Chapter 22.)

8. ATMs and credit cards

This problem examines the effect of the introduction of ATMs and credit cards on money demand. For simplicity, let's examine a person's demand for money over a period of four days.

Suppose that before ATMs and credit cards this person goes to the bank once at the beginning of each four-day period and withdraws from his savings account all the money he needs for four days. He spends $4 per day.

a. How much does he withdraw each time he goes to the bank?

Compute this person's money holdings for days 1 through 4 (in the morning, before he spends any of the money he withdraws).

b. What is the amount of money he holds on average?

Suppose now that with the advent of ATMs he withdraws money once every 2 days.

c. Same as (a).
d. Same as (b).

Finally, with the advent of credit cards, this person pays for all his purchases using his card. He withdraws no money until the fourth day, when he withdraws the whole amount necessary to pay for his credit card purchases over the previous four days.

e. Compute this person's money holdings for days 1 through 4.
f. Same as (b).
g. Based on your answers to (b), (d), and (f), what has been the effect of ATMs and credit cards on money demand?

9. The velocity of money

Let money demand be given by

$$M^d = \$Y L(i)$$

a. Derive an expression for velocity as a function of *i*. How does it depend on *i*?

b. Look at Figure 1 in the Focus box "The Demand for Money and the Interest Rate: The Evidence." What has happened to the velocity of money from 1960 to 2000?

c. According to Figure 1, the interest rate was roughly the same in 2000 as it was in 1960. In light of this fact, what do you think explains the decline in the velocity of money from 1960 to 2000? (*Hint*: Look at problem 8.)

We invite you to visit the Blanchard page on the Prentice Hall Web site at:
www.prenhall.com/blanchard
for this chapter's World Wide Web exercises

Further Readings

For more on financial markets and institutions, read a textbook on money and banking. An excellent one is *Money, the Financial System and the Economy,* by R. Glenn Hubbard (Reading, MA: Addison-Wesley, 3rd ed., 2000).

The Fed maintains a useful Web site, which contains not only data on financial markets, but also information on what the Fed does, on recent testimonies by the Fed chairman, and so on (**www.federalreserve.gov**).

There are many cartoons about Alan Greenspan. If you have nothing better to do, look at (**cagle.slate.msn.com/news/greenspan2/main.asp**).

Goods and Financial Markets: The *IS-LM* Model

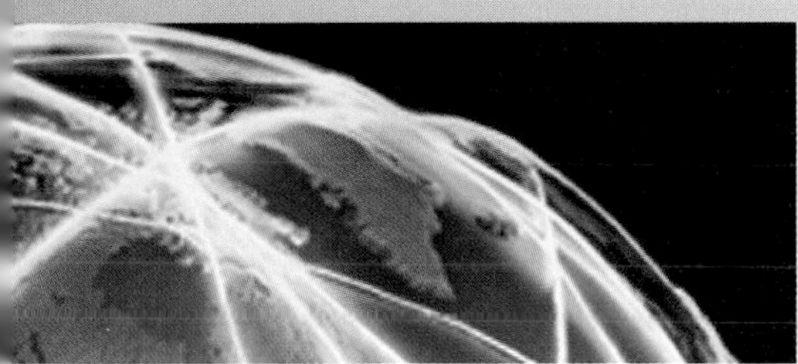

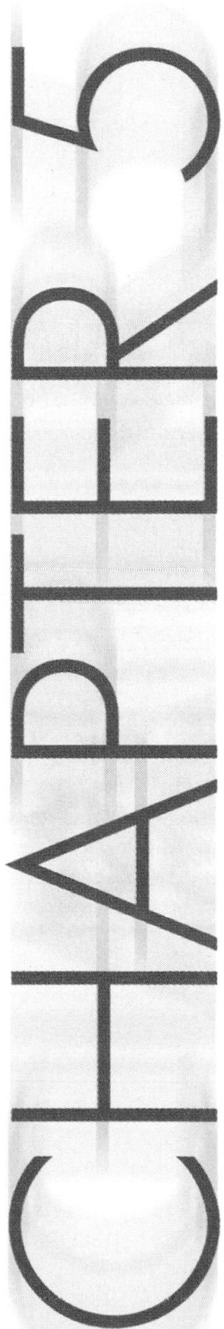

In Chapter 3, we looked at the goods market. In Chapter 4, we looked at financial markets. We now look at goods and financial markets together. By the end of this chapter you will have a framework to think about how output and the interest rate are determined in the short run.

In developing this framework, we follow a path first traced by two economists, John Hicks and Alvin Hansen, in the late 1930s and the early 1940s. When the economist John Maynard Keynes published his *General Theory* in 1936, there was much agreement that his book was both fundamental and nearly impenetrable (look at it, and you will agree). There were many debates about what Keynes "really meant." In 1937, John Hicks summarized what he saw as one of Keynes's main contributions: the joint description of goods and financial markets. His analysis was later extended by Alvin Hansen. Hicks and Hansen called their formalization the *IS-LM* model.

Macroeconomics has made substantial progress since the early 1940s. This is why the *IS-LM* model is treated in Chapter 5 rather than in Chapter 27 of this book. (If you had taken this course 40 years ago, you would be nearly done!) But to most economists, the *IS-LM* model still represents an essential building block—one that, despite its simplicity, captures much of what happens in the economy in *the short run*. This is why the *IS-LM* model is still taught and used today.

The chapter has five sections:

- Section 5-1 looks at equilibrium in the goods market, and derives the *IS* relation.
- Section 5-2 looks at equilibrium in financial markets, and derives the *LM* relation.
- Sections 5-3 and 5-4 put the *IS* and the *LM* relations together and use the resulting *IS-LM* model to study the effects of fiscal and monetary policy, first separately, then together.
- Section 5-5 introduces dynamics, and explores how the *IS-LM* model captures what happens in the economy in the short run. ■

5-1 The Goods Market and the *IS* Relation

Let's first summarize what we learned in Chapter 3:

- We characterized equilibrium in the goods market as the condition that production, Y, be equal to the demand for goods, Z. We called this condition the *IS* relation.
- We defined demand as the sum of consumption, investment, and government spending. We assumed that consumption was a function of disposable income (income minus taxes), and took investment spending, government spending, and taxes as given. The equilibrium condition was given by

$$Y = C(Y - T) + \bar{I} + G$$

(In Chapter 3, we assumed, to simplify the algebra, that the relation between consumption, C, and disposable income, $Y - T$, was linear. Here, we shall not make this assumption, and use the more general form, $C = C(Y - T)$ instead.)

- Using this equilibrium condition, we then looked at the factors that changed equilibrium output. We looked in particular at the effects of changes in government spending and of shifts in consumption demand.

The main simplification of this first model was that the interest rate did not affect the demand for goods. Our first task in this chapter is to remove this simplification, to introduce the interest rate in our model of equilibrium in the goods market. For the time being, we focus only on the effect of the interest rate on investment and leave a discussion of its effects on the other components of demand to later.

See Chapter 16 for more on the effects of the interest rate on both consumption and investment.

Investment, Sales, and the Interest Rate

In Chapter 3, investment was left unexplained—we assumed investment was constant, even when output changed. Investment—spending on new machines and plants by firms—is in fact far from constant, and it depends primarily on two factors:

- The level of sales. A firm facing an increase in sales needs to increase production. To do so, it may need to buy additional machines, or to build an additional plant. A firm facing low sales will feel no such need and will spend little, if anything on investment.
- The interest rate. Consider a firm deciding whether to buy a new machine. Suppose that to buy the new machine, the firm must borrow. The higher the interest rate, the less attractive it is to borrow and buy the machine. At a high enough interest rate, the additional profits from using the new machine will not cover interest payments, and the new machine will not be worth buying.

The argument still holds if the firm uses its own funds: The higher the interest rate, the more attractive it is to lend the funds rather than to use them to buy the new machine.

To capture these two effects, we write the investment relation as follows:

$$I = I(\underset{(+,\ -)}{Y,\ i}) \tag{5.1}$$

Equation (5.1) states that investment, I, depends on production, Y, and the interest rate, i. (We continue to assume that inventory investment is equal to zero, so sales and production are always equal. As a result, Y denotes sales and it also denotes production.) The positive sign under Y indicates that an increase in production (equivalently, sales) leads to an increase in investment. The negative sign under the interest rate, i, indicates that an increase in the interest rate leads to a decrease in investment.

$Y\uparrow \Rightarrow I\uparrow$
$i\uparrow \Rightarrow I\downarrow$

The Determination of Output

Taking into account the investment relation (5.1), the condition for equilibrium in the goods market becomes

$$Y = C(Y - T) + I(Y, i) + G \qquad (5.2)$$

Production (the left side of the equation) must be equal to the demand for goods (the right side). Equation (5.2) is our expanded *IS relation.* We can now look at what happens to output when the interest rate changes.

Start with Figure 5-1. Measure the demand for goods on the vertical axis. Measure output on the horizontal axis. For a given value of the interest rate, i, demand is an increasing function of output, for two reasons:

- An increase in output leads to an increase in income, and so to an increase in disposable income, and so to an increase in consumption; we studied this relation in Chapter 3.
- An increase in output also leads to an increase in investment; this is the relation between investment and production that we have introduced in this chapter.

In short, an increase in output leads, through its effects on both consumption and investment, to an increase in the demand for goods. This relation between demand and output, for a given interest rate, is represented by the upward-sloping curve ZZ.

Note two characteristics of ZZ in Figure 5-1:

- Since we have not assumed that the consumption and investment relations in equation (5.2) are linear, ZZ is in general a curve rather than a line. Thus, I have drawn it as a curve in Figure 5-1. All the arguments that follow would apply if we assumed that the consumption and investment relations were linear, and that ZZ was a straight line instead.

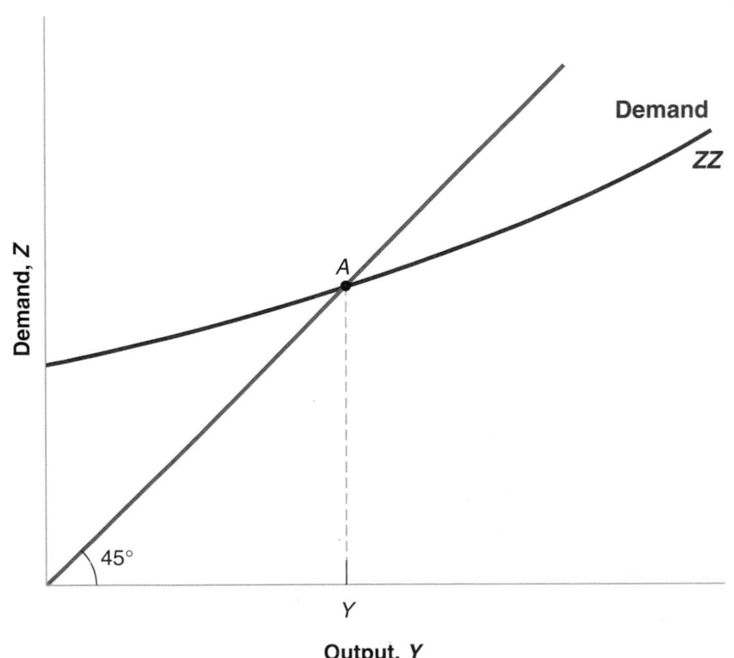

Figure 5-1

Equilibrium in the Goods Market

The demand for goods is an increasing function of output. Equilibrium requires that the demand for goods be equal to output.

- I have drawn ZZ so that it is flatter than the 45-degree line. Put another way, I have assumed that an increase in output leads to a less than one-for-one increase in demand.

  In Chapter 3, where investment was constant, this restriction naturally followed from the assumption that consumers spend only part of their additional income on consumption. But now that we allow investment to respond to production, this restriction may no longer hold. When output increases, the sum of the increase in consumption and the increase in investment could exceed the initial increase in output. Although this is a theoretical possibility, the empirical evidence suggests that it is not the case in practice. That's why I shall assume the response of demand to output is less than one for one and draw ZZ flatter than the 45-degree line.

Equilibrium in the goods market is reached at the point where the demand for goods equals output, so at point A, the intersection of ZZ and the 45-degree line. The equilibrium level of output is given by Y.

So far, what we have done is extend, in straightforward fashion, the analysis of Chapter 3. But we are now ready to derive the *IS* curve.

Deriving the *IS* Curve

We have drawn the demand relation, ZZ, in Figure 5-1 for a given value of the interest rate. Let's now ask what happens if the interest rate changes.

Suppose that, in Figure 5-2, the demand curve is given by ZZ, and the initial equilibrium is at point A. Suppose now that the interest rate increases from its initial value, i, to a new higher value, i'. At any level of output, the higher interest rate implies a decrease in investment, so a decrease in demand. The demand curve ZZ shifts down to ZZ': At a given level of output, demand is lower. The new equilibrium is at the intersection of the lower demand curve ZZ' and the 45-degree line, so at point A'. The equilibrium level of output is now equal to Y'.

Equilibrium in the goods market $\Rightarrow i\uparrow \Rightarrow Y\downarrow$

Figure 5-2

The Effects of an Increase in the Interest Rate on Output

An increase in the interest rate decreases the demand for goods at any level of output.

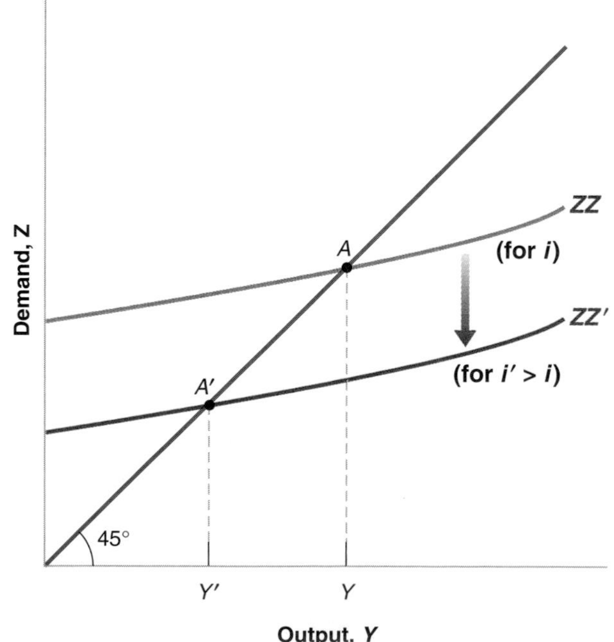

In words: The increase in the interest rate decreases investment. The decrease in investment leads to a decrease in output, which further decreases consumption and investment. In other words, the initial decrease in investment leads to a larger decrease in output through the multiplier effect.

Can you show graphically what the size of the multiplier is? (Hint: Look on the vertical axis at the ratio of the decrease in equilibrium output to the initial decrease in investment.)

Using Figure 5-2, we can find the equilibrium value of output associated with *any* value of the interest rate. The relation between equilibrium output and the interest rate is derived in Figure 5-3.

- Figure 5-3, panel (a) reproduces Figure 5-2. The interest rate, i, implies a level of output equal to Y. The higher interest rate, i', implies a lower level of output, Y'.

Figure 5-3

The Derivation of the* IS *Curve

Equilibrium in the goods market implies that an increase in the interest rate leads to a decrease in output. The *IS* curve is downward sloping.

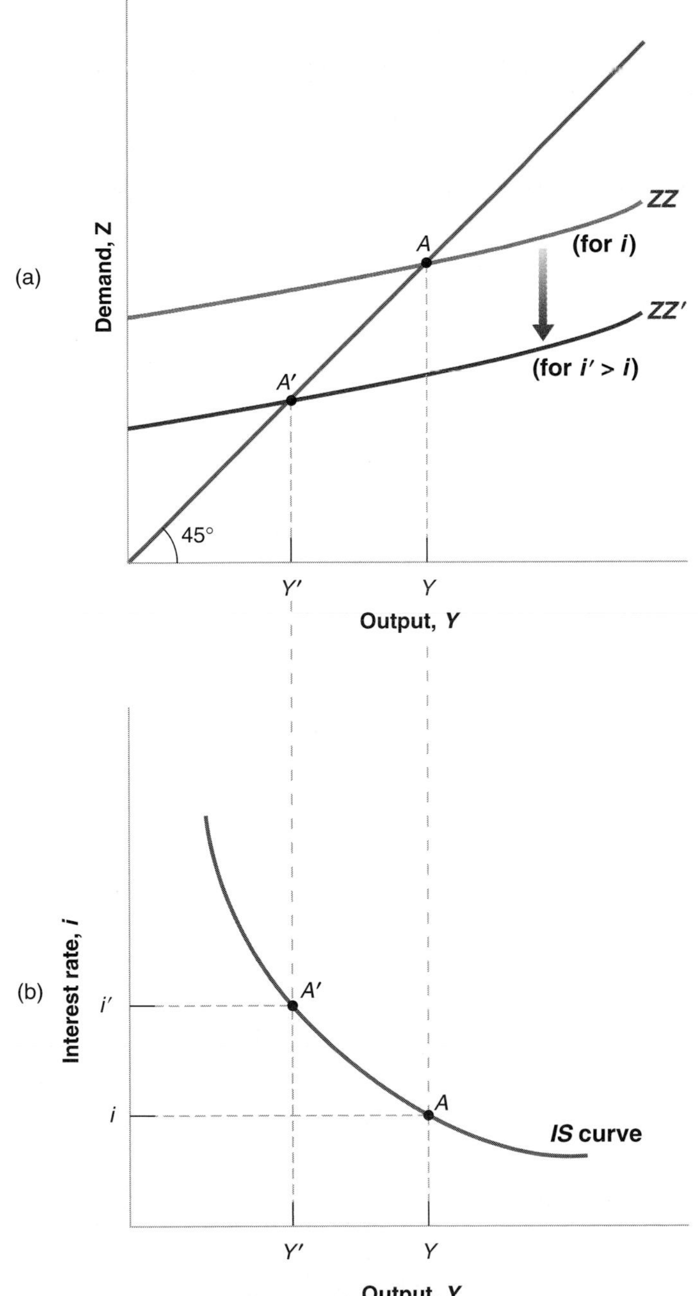

Equilibrium in the goods market implies that an increase in the interest rate leads to a decrease in output. This relation is represented by the downward-sloping *IS* curve. ▶

- Figure 5.3, panel (b) plots equilibrium output Y on the horizontal axis against the interest rate on the vertical axis. Point A in Figure 5-3, panel (b) corresponds to point A in Figure 5-3, panel (a), and point A' in Figure 5-3, panel (b) corresponds to A' in Figure 5-3, panel (a). More generally, equilibrium in the goods market implies that the higher the interest rate, the lower the equilibrium level of output.
- This relation between the interest rate and output is represented by the downward-sloping curve in Figure 5-3, panel (b). This curve is called the ***IS* curve**.

Shifts of the *IS* Curve

Note the *IS* curve in Figure 5-3 is drawn for given values of taxes, T, and government spending, G. Changes in either T or G will shift the *IS* curve.

To see how, consider Figure 5-4. The *IS* curve gives the equilibrium level of output as a function of the interest rate. It is drawn for given values of taxes and spending. Now consider an increase in taxes, from T to T'. At a given interest rate, say, i, disposable income decreases, leading to a decrease in consumption, leading in turn to a decrease in the demand for goods and a decrease in equilibrium output. The equilibrium level of output decreases from Y to Y'. Put another way, the *IS* curve shifts to the left: At any interest rate, the equilibrium level of output is lower than it was before the increase in taxes.

For given i, $T\uparrow \Rightarrow Y\downarrow$: An increase in taxes shifts the *IS* curve to the left. ▶

More generally, any factor that, for a given interest rate, decreases the equilibrium level of output, leads the *IS* curve to shift to the left. We have looked at an increase in taxes. But the same would hold for a decrease in government spending, or a decrease in consumer confidence (which decreases consumption given disposable income). In contrast, any factor that, for a given interest rate, increases the equilibrium level of output—a decrease in taxes, an increase in government spending, an increase in consumer confidence—leads the *IS* curve to shift to the right.

Let's summarize:

- Equilibrium in the goods market implies that an increase in the interest rate leads to a decrease in output. This relation is represented by the downward-sloping *IS* curve.

Figure 5-4

Shifts of the IS *Curve*

An increase in taxes shifts the *IS* curve to the left.

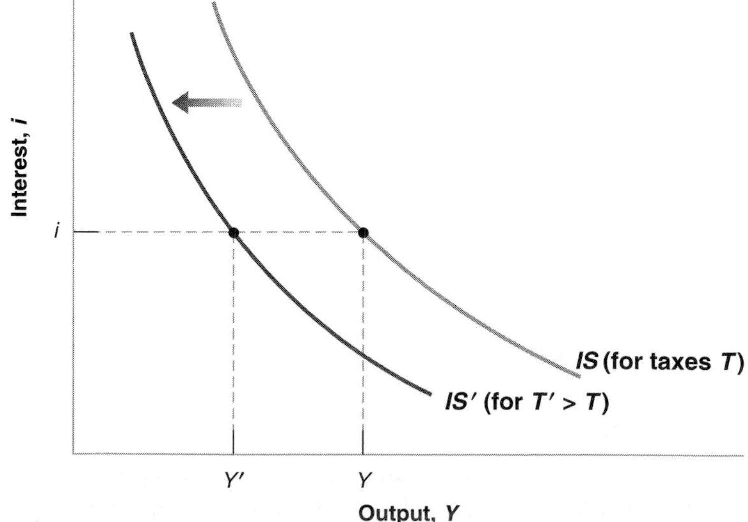

- Changes in factors that decrease the demand for goods given the interest rate shift the *IS* curve to the left. Changes in factors that increase the demand for goods given the interest rate shift the *IS* curve to the right.

5-2 Financial Markets and the *LM* Relation

Let's now turn to financial markets. We saw in Chapter 4 that the interest rate is determined by the equality of the supply of and the demand for money:

$$M = \$Y\,L(i)$$

The variable M on the left side is the nominal money stock. I shall ignore here the details of the money-supply process that we saw in Section 4-3, and simply think of the central bank as controlling M directly.

The right side gives the demand for money, which is a function of nominal income, $\$Y$, and of the nominal interest rate, i. As we saw in Section 4-1, an increase in nominal income increases the demand for money; an increase in the interest rate decreases the demand for money. Equilibrium requires that money supply (the left side of the equation) be equal to money demand (the right side of the equation).

Real Money, Real Income, and the Interest Rate

The equation $M = \$Y\,L(i)$ gives a relation between money, nominal income, and the interest rate. It will be more convenient here to rewrite it as a relation between real money (that is, money in terms of goods), real income (that is, income in terms of goods), and the interest rate.

Recall that nominal income divided by the price level equals real income, Y. Dividing both sides of the equation by the price level, P, gives

From Chapter 2: ◄ **Nominal GDP = Real GDP multiplied by the GDP deflator: $\$Y = YP$. Equivalently, Real GDP = Nominal GDP divided by the GDP deflator: $\$Y/P = Y$.**

$$\frac{M}{P} = Y\,L(i) \qquad (5.3)$$

Hence, we can restate our equilibrium condition as the condition that the *real money supply*—that is, the money stock in terms of goods, not dollars—be equal to the *real money demand*, which depends on real income, Y, and the interest rate, i.

The notion of a "real" demand for money may feel a bit abstract, so an example may help. Think not of your demand for money in general but just of your demand for coins. Suppose you like to have coins in your pocket to buy four cups of coffee during the day. If a cup costs 60 cents, you will want to keep about \$2.40 in coins: This is your nominal demand for coins. Equivalently, you want to keep enough coins in your pocket to buy four cups of coffee. This is your demand for coins in terms of goods—here in terms of cups of coffee.

From now on, I shall refer to equation (5.3) as the *LM relation*. The advantage of writing things this way is that *real income*, Y, appears on the right side of the equation instead of *nominal income* $\$Y$. And real income (equivalently, real output) is the variable we focus on when looking at equilibrium in the goods market. To make the reading lighter, I shall refer to the left and right sides of equation (5.3) simply as "money supply" and "money demand" rather than the more accurate but heavier "real money supply" and "real money demand." Similarly, I shall refer to Y as income rather than "real income."

Deriving the *LM* Curve

To see the relation between output and the interest rate implied by equation (5.3), let's begin by looking at Figure 5-5. Let the interest rate be measured on the vertical

Figure 5-5

The Effects of an Increase in Income on the Interest Rate

An increase in income leads, at a given interest rate, to an increase in the demand for money. Given the money supply, this leads to an increase in the equilibrium interest rate.

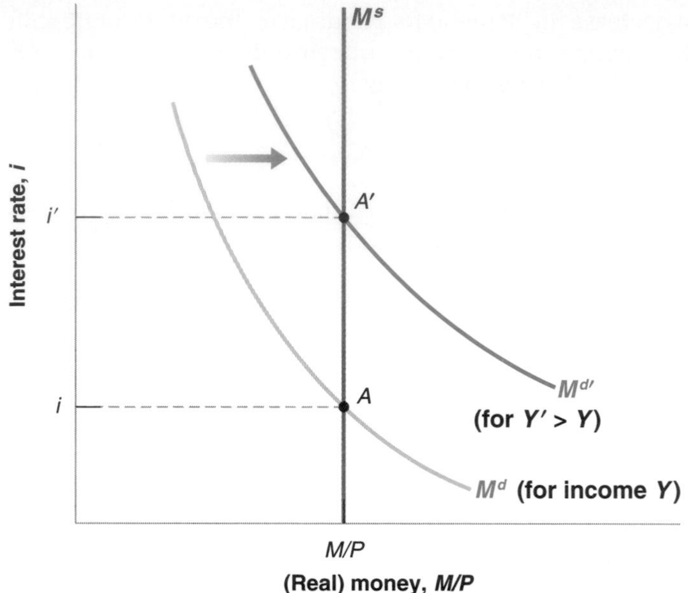

axis, and (real) money be measured on the horizontal axis. (Real) money supply is given by the vertical line at M/P, and is denoted M^s. For a given level of (real) income, Y, (real) money demand is a decreasing function of the interest rate. It is drawn as the downward-sloping curve denoted M^d. Except for the fact that we measure real rather than nominal money on the horizontal axis, the figure is similar to Figure 4-3 in Chapter 4. The equilibrium is at point A, where money supply is equal to money demand, and the interest rate is equal to i.

Now consider an increase in income from Y to Y', which leads people to increase their demand for money at any given interest rate. Money demand shifts to the right, to $M^{d'}$. The new equilibrium is at A', with a higher interest rate, i'. Why does an increase in income lead to an increase in the interest rate? When income increases, money demand increases. But the money supply is given. Thus, the interest rate must go up until the two opposite effects on the demand for money—the increase in income that leads people to want to hold more money, and the increase in the interest rate that leads people to want to hold less money—cancel each other. At that point, the demand for money is equal to the unchanged money supply, and financial markets are again in equilibrium.

Equilibrium in financial markets: For given M, $Y\uparrow \Rightarrow i\uparrow$

Using Figure 5-5, we can find the value of the interest rate associated with *any* value of income for a given money stock. The relation is derived in Figure 5-6.

- Figure 5-6, panel (a) reproduces Figure 5-5. When income is equal to Y, money demand is given by M^d and the equilibrium interest rate is equal to i. When income is equal to the higher value Y', money demand is given by $M^{d'}$ and the equilibrium interest rate is equal to i'.
- Figure 5-6, panel (b) plots the equilibrium interest rate i on the vertical axis against income on the horizontal axis. Point A in Figure 5-6, panel (b) corresponds to point A in Figure 5-6, panel (a), and point A' in Figure 5-6, panel (b) corresponds to point A' in Figure 5-6, panel (a). More generally, equilibrium in financial markets implies that the higher the level of output, the higher the demand for money, and therefore the higher the equilibrium interest rate.

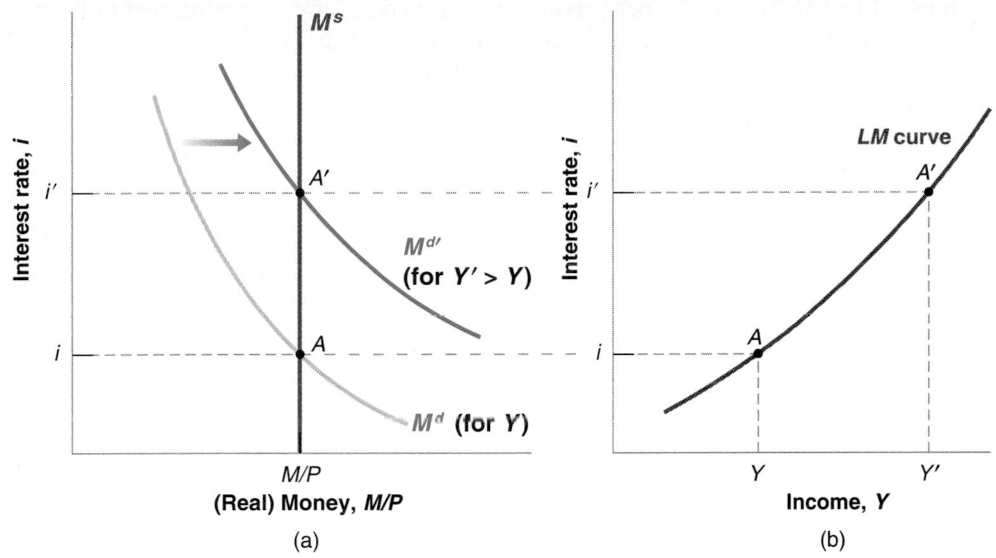

Figure 5-6

The Derivation of the LM *Curve*

Equilibrium in financial markets implies that an increase in income leads to an increase in the interest rate. The *LM* curve is upward sloping.

- This relation between output and the interest rate is represented by the upward-sloping curve in Figure 5-6, panel (b). This curve is called the ***LM* curve.** Economists sometimes characterize this relation by saying "higher economic activity puts pressure on interest rates." Make sure you understand the steps behind this statement.

Equilibrium in financial markets implies that for a given money stock, the interest rate is an increasing function of the level of income. This relation is represented by the upward-sloping *LM* curve.

Shifts of the *LM* Curve

We have derived the *LM* curve in Figure 5-6 taking both the nominal money stock, *M*, and the price level, *P*—and, by implication, their ratio, the real money stock, *M/P*—as given. Changes in *M/P*, whether they come from changes in the nominal money stock, *M*, or from changes in the price level, *P*, will shift the *LM* curve.

To see how, let us look at Figure 5-7, and consider an increase in the nominal money supply, from *M* to *M′*, so that, at the same price level, the real money supply

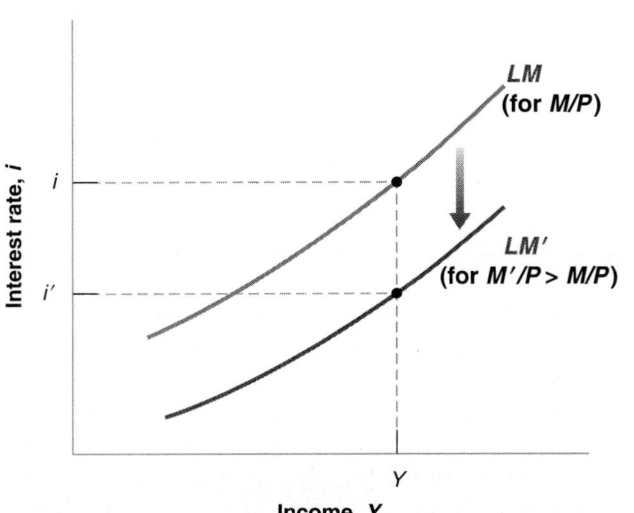

Figure 5-7

Shifts of the LM *Curve*

An increase in money leads the *LM* curve to shift down.

For given Y, $M/P\uparrow \Rightarrow i\downarrow$: An increase in money shifts the *LM* curve down.

Why do we think about shifts of the *IS* curve to the left and to the right, but about shifts of the *LM* curve up or down?

We think of the goods market as determining Y given i; so we want to know what happens to Y when an exogenous variable changes. Y is on the horizontal axis, and moves right or left.

We think of financial markets as determining i given Y; so we want to know what happens to i when an exogenous variable changes. i is on the vertical axis, and moves up or down.

increases from M/P to M'/P. Then, at any level of income, say, Y, the interest rate consistent with equilibrium in financial markets is lower, going down from i to, say, i'. The *LM* curve shifts down, from *LM* to *LM'*. By the same reasoning, at any level of income, a decrease in the money supply leads to an increase in the interest rate. It leads the *LM* curve to shift up.

Let's summarize:

- Equilibrium in financial markets implies that for a given real money supply, an increase in the level of income, which increases the demand for money, leads to an increase in the interest rate. This relation is represented by the upward-sloping *LM* curve.
- Increases in the money supply shift the *LM* curve down; decreases in the money supply shift the *LM* curve up.

5-3 Putting the *IS* and the *LM* Relations Together

We now put the *IS* and *LM* relations together. At any point in time, the supply of goods must be equal to the demand for goods. And the supply of money must be equal to the demand for money. Both the *IS* and the *LM* relations must hold.

$$IS \text{ relation:} \quad Y = C(Y - T) + I(Y, i) + G$$

$$LM \text{ relation:} \quad \frac{M}{P} = Y L(i)$$

Figure 5-8 plots both the *IS* curve and the *LM* curve on one graph. Output—equivalently, production or income—is measured on the horizontal axis. The interest rate is measured on the vertical axis.

Any point on the downward-sloping *IS* curve corresponds to equilibrium in the goods market. *Any point* on the upward-sloping *LM* curve corresponds to equilibrium in financial markets. *Only at point A* are both equilibrium conditions satisfied. That means point *A*, with associated level of output *Y* and interest rate *i*, is the overall equilibrium, the point at which there is equilibrium in both the goods market and the financial markets.

Figure 5-8

The IS–LM *Model*

Equilibrium in the goods market implies that an increase in the interest rate leads to a decrease in output. This is represented by the *IS* curve. Equilibrium in financial markets implies that an increase in output leads to an increase in the interest rate. This is represented by the *LM* curve. Only at point *A*, which is on both curves, are both goods and financial markets in equilibrium.

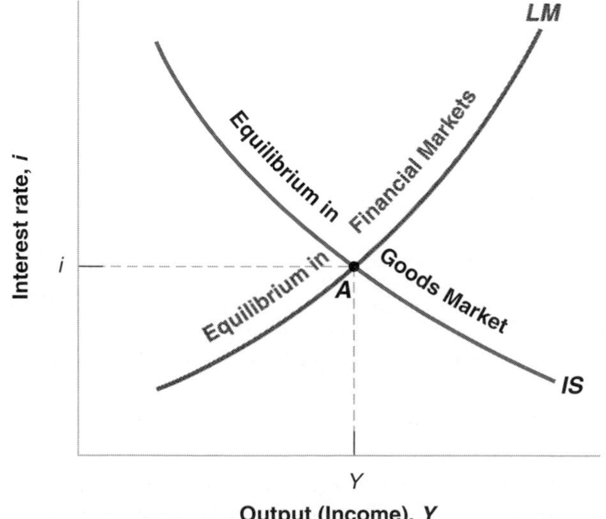

The *IS* and *LM* relations that underlie Figure 5-8 contain a lot of information about consumption, investment, money demand, and equilibrium conditions. But you may ask: So what if the equilibrium is at point *A*? How does this fact translate into anything directly useful about the world? Don't despair: Figure 5-8 holds the answer to many questions in macroeconomics. Used properly, it allows us to study what happens to output and the interest rate when the central bank decides to increase the money stock, or when the government decides to increase taxes, or when consumers become more pessimistic about the future, and so on.

Let's now see what the *IS-LM* model can do.

Fiscal Policy, Output, and the Interest Rate

Suppose the government decides to reduce the budget deficit, and does so by increasing taxes while keeping government spending unchanged. Such a change in fiscal policy is often called a **fiscal contraction** or a **fiscal consolidation**. (An *increase* in the deficit, either due to an increase in government spending or to a decrease in taxes, is called a **fiscal expansion**.) What are the effects of this fiscal contraction on output, on its composition, and on the interest rate?

Decrease in $G - T \Leftrightarrow$ fiscal contraction $\Leftrightarrow$ fiscal consolidation

Increase in $G - T \Leftrightarrow$ fiscal expansion

In answering this or any question about the effects of changes in policy, always go through the following three steps:

1. Ask how this change affects goods and financial markets equilibrium relations, how it shifts the *IS* or the *LM* curve.
2. Characterize the effects of these shifts on the intersection of the *IS* and the *LM* curve, and thus, on the equilibrium.
3. Describe the effects in words.

With time and experience, you will often be able to go directly to step 3; by then you will be ready to give an instant commentary on the economic events of the day. But until you get to that level of expertise, go step by step.

- Going through step 1, the first question is how the increase in taxes affects equilibrium in the goods market—that is, how it affects the *IS* curve.

  Let's draw, in Figure 5-9, panel (a), the *IS* curve corresponding to equilibrium in the goods market before the increase in taxes. Now take an arbitrary point, *B*, on this *IS* curve. By construction of the *IS* curve, output, Y_B, and the corresponding interest rate, i_B, are such that the supply of goods is equal to the demand for goods.

  At the interest rate, i_B, ask what happens to output if taxes increase from T to T'. We saw the answer in Section 5-1. Because people have less disposable income, the increase in taxes decreases consumption, and through the multiplier, decreases output. At interest rate, i_B, output decreases from Y_B to Y_C. More generally, at *any* interest rate, higher taxes lead to lower output: The *IS* curve shifts to the left, from *IS* to *IS'*.

  Taxes appear in the *IS* relation $\Leftrightarrow$ Taxes shift the *IS* curve.

  Next, let's see if anything happens to the *LM* curve. Figure 5-9, panel (b) draws the *LM* curve corresponding to financial-markets equilibrium before the increase in taxes. Take an arbitrary point, *F*, on this *LM* curve. By construction of the *LM* curve, the interest rate, i_F, and income, Y_F, are such that the supply of money is equal to the demand for money.

  What happens to the *LM* curve when taxes are increased? The answer: Nothing. At the given level of income, Y_F, the interest rate at which the supply of

Figure 5-9

The Effects of an Increase in Taxes

An increase in taxes shifts the *IS* curve to the left, and leads to a decrease in the equilibrium level of output and the equilibrium interest rate.

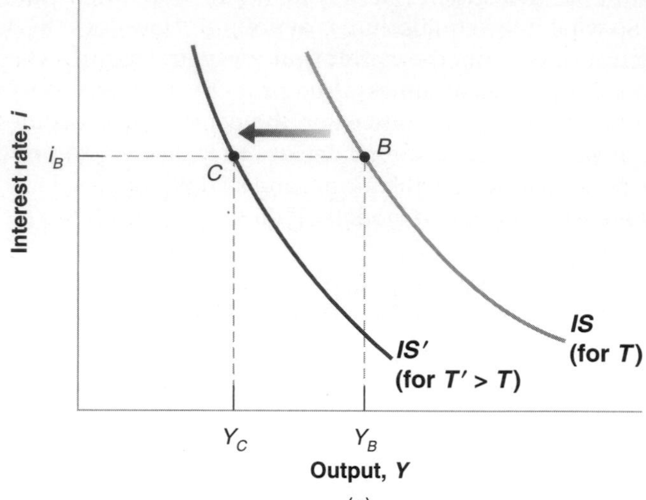

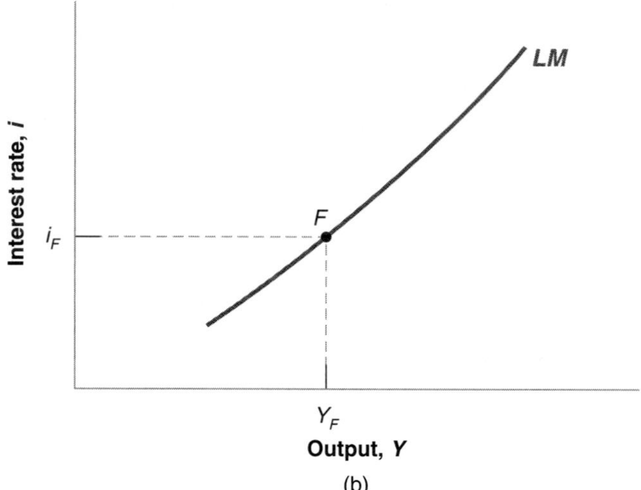

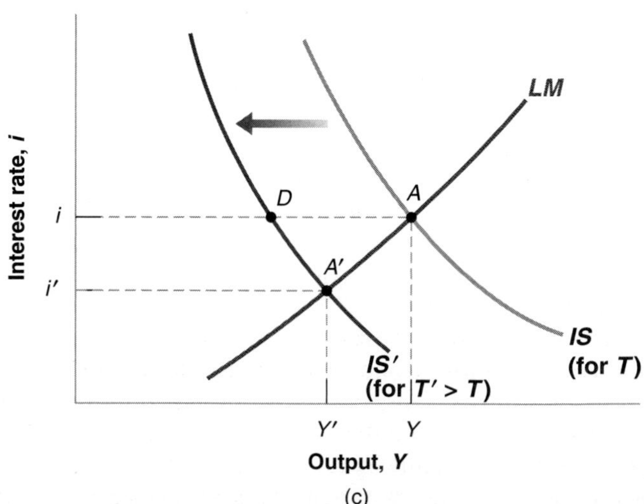

money is equal to the demand for money is the same as before, namely, i_F. In other words, because taxes do not appear in the *LM* relation, they do not affect the equilibrium condition. They do not affect the *LM* curve. Taxes enter equation (5.2), so, when taxes change, the *IS* curve shifts. But taxes do not enter equation (5.3), so the *LM* curve does not shift.

- Now let's consider the second step, the determination of the equilibrium. Let the initial equilibrium in Figure 5-9, panel (c) be at point *A*, at the intersection of the initial *IS* curve and the *LM* curve. The *IS* curve is the same as the *IS* curve in Figure 5-9, panel (a), the *LM* curve is the same as the *LM* curve in Figure 5-9, panel (b).

  After the increase in taxes, the *IS* curve shifts to the left—from *IS* to *IS'*. The new equilibrium is at the intersection of the new *IS* curve and the unchanged *LM* curve, so at point *A'*. Output decreases from *Y* to *Y'*. The interest rate decreases from *i* to *i'*. Thus, as the *IS* curve *shifts*, the economy *moves along* the *LM* curve, from *A* to *A'*. The reason these words are italicized is that it is important to always distinguish *shifts of* curves (here the shift of the *IS* curve) and *movements along* a curve (here the movement along *LM* curve). Many mistakes result from not distinguishing between shifts of and movements along a curve.
- The third and final step is to tell the story in words: The increase in taxes leads to lower disposable income, which causes people to decrease their consumption. The result through the multiplier effect is a decrease in output and income. The decrease in income reduces the demand for money, leading to a decrease in the interest rate. The decline in the interest rate reduces but does not completely offset the effect of higher taxes on the demand for goods.

Taxes do not appear in the *LM* relation ⇔ Taxes do not shift the *LM* curve.

Note the general principle here: A curve shifts in response to a change in an exogenous variable only if this variable appears directly in the equation represented by that curve.

A reminder: An exogenous variable is a variable we take as given, unexplained within the model. Here, it is taxes.

$T\uparrow \Rightarrow$ The *IS* curve shifts. The *LM* curve does not shift. The economy moves along the *LM* curve.

If the interest rate did not decline, the economy would go from point *A* to point *D* in Figure 5-9, panel (c), and output would be directly below point *D*. Because of the decline in the interest rate—which stimulates investment—the decline in activity is only to point *A'*.

What happens to the components of demand? By assumption, government spending remains unchanged: We have assumed that the reduction in the budget deficit takes place through an increase in taxes. Consumption surely goes down: Taxes go up and income goes down, so disposable income goes down on both counts. The question is: What happens to investment? On one hand, lower output means lower sales and lower investment. On the other, a lower interest rate leads to higher investment. Without knowing more about the exact form of the investment relation, equation (5.1), we cannot tell which effect dominates.

If investment depends only on the interest rate, then investment surely increases; if investment depends only on sales, then investment surely decreases. In general, investment depends on both the interest rate and on sales, so we cannot tell. Contrary to what is often stated by politicians, a reduction in the budget deficit does not necessarily lead to an increase in investment. (The Focus box "Deficit Reduction: Good or Bad for Investment?" discusses this at more length.)

We shall return to the relation between fiscal policy and investment many times in this book, and we shall qualify this first answer in many ways. But the result that, *in the short run, deficit reduction may decrease investment,* will remain.

Monetary Policy, Output, and the Interest Rate

An increase in the money supply is called a **monetary expansion**. A decrease in the money supply is called a **monetary contraction** or **monetary tightening**.

Increase in *M* ⇔ monetary expansion.

Decrease in *M* ⇔ monetary contraction ⇔ monetary tightening.

Let's take the case of a monetary expansion. Suppose that the central bank increases nominal money, *M*, through an open-market operation. Given our assumption that the price level is fixed, this increase in nominal money leads to a one-for-one increase in real money, *M/P*. Let us denote the initial real money supply by *M/P*, the new higher one by *M'/P*, and trace the effects of the increase in the money supply on output and the interest rate.

For a given price level *P*: *M* increases by 10% ⇒ *M/P* increases by 10%.

FOCUS

Deficit Reduction: Good or Bad for Investment?

You may have heard this argument before: "Private saving goes either toward financing the budget deficit or financing investment. It does not take a genius to conclude that reducing the budget deficit leaves more saving available for investment, so investment increases."

This argument sounds simple and convincing. How do we reconcile it with what we just saw, namely, that deficit reduction may decrease rather than increase investment?

To make progress, first go back to Chapter 3, equation (3.10). There we saw that we can also think of the goods-market equilibrium condition as:

Investment		Private saving	+	Public saving
I	$=$	S	$+$	$(T - G)$

In equilibrium, investment is equal to private saving plus public saving. If public saving is positive, the government is said to run a budget surplus; if public saving is negative, the government runs a budget deficit. So it is true that given private saving, if the government reduces its deficit—either by increasing taxes or reducing government spending, so $T - G$ goes up—investment must go up: Given S, $T - G$ going up implies that I goes up.

The crucial part of this statement, however, is "given private saving." The point is a fiscal contraction affects private saving as well: The contraction leads to lower output, and so to lower income. As consumption goes down by less than income, private saving also goes down. And it may go down by more than the reduction in the budget deficit, leading to a decrease rather than an increase in investment. In terms of the preceding equation: If S decreases by more than $T - G$ increases, then T will decrease, not increase.

To sum up, a fiscal contraction may decrease investment. Or, looking at the reverse policy, a fiscal expansion—a decrease in taxes or an increase in spending—may actually increase investment.

- Again, the first step is to see whether and how the *IS* and the *LM* curves shift.

  Money does not appear in the *IS* relation ⇔ Money does not shift the *IS* curve.

  Let's look at the *IS* curve first. The money supply does not *directly* affect either the supply of or the demand for goods. In other words, M does not appear in the *IS* relation. Thus, a change in M does not shift the *IS* curve.

  Money appears in the *LM* relation ⇔ Money shifts the *LM* curve.

  Money enters the *LM* relation, however, so that the *LM* curve shifts when the money supply changes. As we saw in Section 5-2, an increase in money shifts the *LM* curve down, from *LM* to *LM′*: At a given level of income, an increase in money leads to a decrease in the interest rate.

  $M\uparrow \Rightarrow$ The *IS* curve does not shift. The *LM* curve shifts down. The economy moves along the *IS* curve.

- The second step is to see how these shifts affect the equilibrium. The monetary expansion shifts the *LM* curve. It does not shift the *IS* curve. Thus, in Figure 5-10, the economy moves along the *IS* curve, and the equilibrium moves from point A to point A'. Output increases from Y to Y', and the interest rate decreases from i to i'.
- The third step is to say it in words: The increase in money leads to a lower interest rate. The lower interest rate leads to an increase in investment and, through the multiplier, to an increase in demand and output.

In contrast to the case of a fiscal contraction, we can tell exactly what happens to the different components of demand after a monetary expansion: Because income is higher and taxes are unchanged, disposable income goes up, and so does consumption. Because sales are higher, and the interest rate is lower, investment also unambiguously goes up. So a monetary expansion is more investment friendly than a fiscal expansion.

To summarize:

- You should remember the three-step approach (characterize the shifts, show the effect on the equilibrium, tell the story in words) we have developed in this section

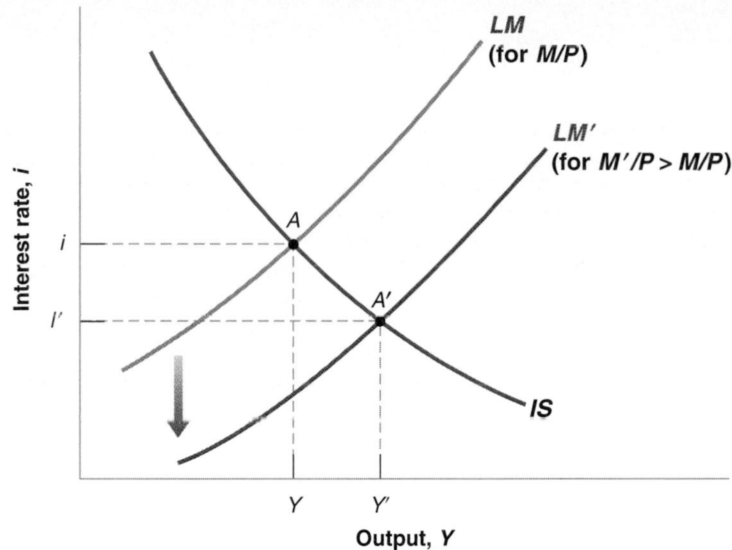

Figure 5-10

The Effects of a Monetary Expansion

A monetary expansion leads to higher output and a lower interest rate.

to look at the effects of changes in policy on activity and the interest rate. We shall use it throughout the book.

- Table 5-1 summarizes what we have learned about the effects of fiscal and monetary policy. Use the same method to look at other changes. For example, trace the effects of a decrease in consumer confidence through its effect on consumption demand, or of the introduction of new, more convenient credit cards through their effect on the demand for money.

5-4 Using a Policy Mix

We have looked so far at fiscal policy and monetary policy in isolation. Our purpose was to show how each policy worked. In practice, the two are often used together. The combination of monetary and fiscal policies is known as the **monetary-fiscal policy mix**, or, simply, the **policy mix**.

Sometimes monetary and fiscal policies are used for a common goal. For example, expansionary monetary policy is used to offset the adverse effect on the demand for goods of a fiscal contraction. This was the case in the 1990s in the United States, where fiscal policy and monetary policy, used in combination, delivered both sustained deficit reduction and output growth. How it was done, and how much of the credit should go to President Clinton, to Alan Greenspan (the chairman of the Fed), and to sheer luck is described in the Focus box "The Clinton-Greenspan Policy Mix."

Fiscal contraction ⇔ Reduction in budget deficit.

See the related Focus box "Did Rules Help Reduce the U.S. Budget Deficit?" in Chapter 24.

Table 5-1 The Effects of Fiscal and Monetary Policy

	Shift of *IS*	Shift of *LM*	Movement in Output	Movement in Interest Rate
Increase in taxes	left	none	down	down
Decrease in taxes	right	none	up	up
Increase in spending	right	none	up	up
Decrease in spending	left	none	down	down
Increase in money	none	down	up	down
Decrease in money	none	up	down	up

The Clinton-Greenspan Policy Mix

When Bill Clinton was elected president at the end of 1992, he faced a tough macroeconomic problem. The federal budget deficit was 4.5% of GDP—the second largest percentage since World War II—and there was a wide consensus that something should be done about it (for why deficits are so bad, have a peek at Chapter 26). At the same time, the U.S. economy was just coming out of the 1990–1991 recession; while we now know that output growth was positive in 1992, many economists at the time worried that the recession might not yet have ended.

The problem facing Clinton was clear: As desirable as a deficit reduction might be, implementing it might lead to a decrease in demand, and perhaps put the United States back into recession. In terms of the *IS-LM* model, a shift of the *IS* to the left might lead to a decrease in output, to a recession.

Yet, five years later, in 1998, the federal deficit was gone, replaced by a surplus of 0.8% of GDP, and the U.S. economy was in the seventh year of a sustained expansion. (Table 1 gives the basic numbers for the budget, output growth and interest rates, from 1991 to 1998.) How did Clinton do it? He did it with the help of Alan Greenspan, and with some luck.

Even before the election, Alan Greenspan had stated that he was worried about the size of the fiscal deficit. When Clinton was elected, Greenspan made it clear he would be happy to help. While not stating this explicitly, he indicated that if Clinton were to embark on a path of deficit reduction, the Fed would be willing to counteract the adverse effects of a fiscal contraction on output with a more expansionary monetary policy. In terms of the *IS-LM* diagram in Figure 1, the Fed agreed (that is, implicitly: nothing was signed, or even written down) that, if deficit reduction took place (leading to a shift to the left of the *IS* curve, from *IS* to *IS′*), the Fed would shift the *LM* curve down (from *LM* to *LM′*). In effect, it agreed to offset the adverse effects of fiscal contraction on activity, to get the economy to go from *A* to *A′* rather than to *B* (which is where the economy would have gone, absent monetary expansion).

On the basis of this implicit understanding, in February 1993 Clinton sent a deficit reduction plan to

Table 1 Selected Macro Variables for the United States, 1991–1998

	1991	1992	1993	1994	1995	1996	1997	1998
Budget surplus (% of GDP) (minus sign = deficit)	−3.3	−4.5	−3.8	−2.7	−2.4	−1.4	−0.3	0.8
GDP growth (%)	−0.9	2.7	2.3	3.4	2.0	2.7	3.9	3.7
Interest rate (%)	7.3	5.5	3.7	3.3	5.0	5.6	5.2	4.8

Source: Bureau of Economic Analysis. Interest rate: average interest rate over the year on one-year government bonds.

Sometimes the monetary-fiscal mix emerges from tensions or even disagreements between the government (which is in charge of fiscal policy) and the central bank (which is in charge of monetary policy). A typical scenario is one in which the central bank, disagreeing with what it considers a dangerous fiscal expansion, embarks on a course of monetary contraction to offset some of the effects of fiscal expansion on activity. An example of such a tension is Germany after unification in the early 1990s, described in the Focus box "German Unification and the German Monetary-Fiscal Tug of War."

See also two related Focus boxes: "German Unification, Interest Rates, and the EMS" in Chapter 20, and "Anatomy of a Crisis: The September 1992 EMS Crisis" in Chapter 21.

5-5 How Does the *IS-LM* Model Fit the Facts?

We have so far ignored dynamics. For example, when looking at the effects of an increase in taxes in Figure 5-9—or the effects of a monetary expansion in Figure 5-10—we made it look as if the economy moved instantaneously from A to A', as if output went instantaneously from Y to Y'. This is clearly not realistic: The adjustment of output clearly takes some time. To capture this time dimension, we need to reintroduce dynamics.

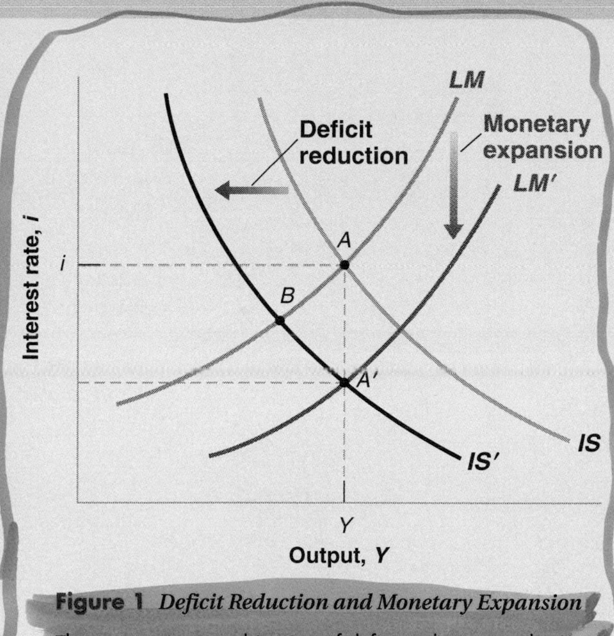

Figure 1 *Deficit Reduction and Monetary Expansion*

The appropriate combination of deficit reduction and monetary expansion can achieve a reduction in the deficit without adverse effects on output.

Congress. This plan was intended to get the deficit slowly down to 2.5% of GDP by 1998, with the reduction coming in roughly equal parts from tax increases and spending decreases. The limited size of the deficit reduction was due to the worry that, even with help from the Fed, too fast a deficit reduction would lead to a recession. As this deficit reduction package was implemented, the Fed delivered on its implicit promise: Interest rates, which had already been reduced in 1991 and 1992, were further decreased in 1993 and 1994. The interest rate in 1994 was 3.3%, down from 7.3% in 1991. The result of this policy mix (fiscal contraction and monetary expansion) was a steady output expansion in the face of deficit reduction.

Was the expansion of output from 1992 to 1998 only due to a smart policy mix? No, it was also due to luck. Especially from 1995 on, various factors, from unusually strong consumer and firm confidence, to a strong stock market, led to favorable shifts of the *IS* curve, and in turn to strong output growth (which, as we have seen in Chapter 1, lasted until year 2000). This had two implications:

- First, the Fed did not have to decrease interest rates further; shifts to the right in the *IS* curve were enough to sustain activity. Indeed, from 1994 on, the Fed had to slightly increase interest rates, so as to prevent the economy from "overheating" (more on this in the next four chapters).
- Second, the mechanical effect of this strong expansion was to further reduce the deficit: When an economy grows, tax revenues (which depend directly on output) tend to increase while spending is largely unaffected: The deficit is automatically reduced. (A useful rule of thumb for the United States is that every additional increase in the growth rate of 1% per year leads to a decrease in the ratio of the deficit to GDP of 0.5%.) Thus, the mechanical effect of sustained growth was a much larger reduction of the deficit than had been anticipated, even by the Clinton administration.

Introducing dynamics formally would be difficult. But, as we did in Chapter 3, we can describe the basic mechanisms in words. Some of the mechanisms are familiar from Chapter 3, some are new:

- Consumers are likely to take some time to adjust their consumption to a change in disposable income.
- Firms are likely to take some time to adjust investment spending following a change in their sales.
- Firms are likely to take some time to adjust investment spending following a change in the interest rate.
- Firms are likely to take some time to adjust production following a change in their sales.

So, in response to, say, an increase in taxes, it is likely to take some time for consumption spending to decrease in response to the change in disposable income, to take some time for production to decrease in response to the decrease in consumption spending, to take some time for investment to decrease in response to lower sales, to take some time for consumption to decrease in response to the decrease in income, and so on.

German Unification and the German Monetary-Fiscal Tug of War

FOCUS

In 1990 East Germany and West Germany again became one country. Whereas the two parts had been at a roughly comparable level of economic development before World War II, this was no longer the case by 1990. West Germany was far richer and far more productive than East Germany. There were many economic consequences of unification. We focus here only on its implications for fiscal and monetary policy in Germany.

Upon unification, it became clear that most firms in the Eastern Lander (as the ex–German Democratic Republic is now known) were just not competitive. Many simply had to be closed in part or in total, and the others needed new and more modern equipment. It soon became obvious that transition would require large increases in government spending on new infrastructure, on cleaning up environmental damage, on unemployment benefits to workers losing their jobs, and on government subsidies to firms to keep them operating until they turned around.

Faced with this large increase in spending, the German government decided to rely partly on increased taxes and partly on a larger deficit. Table 1 gives basic numbers for some of the major macroeconomic variables from 1988 to 1991 (for West Germany only).

The numbers show that, even before unification, Germany was experiencing a strong expansion. GDP growth in 1988 and 1989 was close to 4%. Investment was booming. And, because tax revenues depend on economic activity, the strong growth in GDP was the source of high government revenues in 1989, leading to a fiscal surplus of 0.2% of GDP in 1989.

The effects of unification were to increase demand further. In 1990, investment increased even faster than it had in 1989. And, because of the increase in spending and transfers due to unification, West Germany's fiscal position went from a budget surplus in 1989 to a budget deficit of 1.8% of GDP in 1990. In terms of the *IS-LM* model, 1990 was thus characterized by a sharp increase in investment and government spending, a large shift of the *IS* curve to the right, from *IS* to *IS′* in Figure 1.

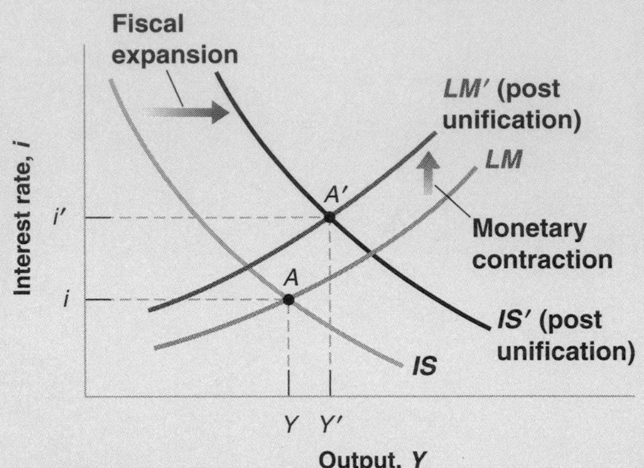

Figure 1 *The Monetary-Fiscal Policy Mix in Post-Unification Germany*

Seeing these developments, the Bundesbank (as the German central bank is called) worried that growth was too strong, that the economy was operating at too high a level of activity, and that the result would be inflation (a mechanism we explore in the next four chapters). It concluded that output growth should be slowed. Even though the interest rate had already increased from 4.3% in 1988 to 7.1% in 1989, the Bundesbank decided on a policy of even tighter money; it let the interest rate go even higher, to 9.2% in 1991. In terms of the *IS-LM* diagram in Figure 1, the central bank decided to shift the *LM* curve up, to slow down economic activity.

The result was fast growth (from the fiscal expansion) and high interest rates (from tight money). These high interest rates had important implications not only for Germany, but for all of Europe. Indeed, some economists argue that the high interest rates were one of the main causes of the recession in the rest of Europe in the early 1990s. We shall discuss this argument in more detail in Chapter 20.

Table 1 Selected Macroeconomic Variables for West Germany, 1988–1991

	1988	1989	1990	1991
GDP growth (%)	3.7	3.8	4.5	3.1
Investment growth (%)	5.9	8.5	10.5	6.7
Budget surplus (% of GDP) (minus sign = deficit)	−2.1	0.2	−1.8	−2.9
Interest rate (short term)	4.3	7.1	8.5	9.2

Source: OECD Economic Outlook, June 1992. "Investment" refers to nonresidential investment.

In response to, say, a monetary expansion, it is likely to take some time for investment spending to increase in response to the decrease in the interest rate, to take some time for production to increase in response to the increase in investment spending, to take some time for consumption and investment to increase in response to the induced change in output, and so on.

Describing the adjustment process implied by all these sources of dynamics is obviously complicated. But the basic implication is straightforward: It will take some time for output to adjust to changes in fiscal policy, or to changes in monetary policy. How much time? This question can only be answered by looking at the data and using econometrics. Figure 5-11 shows the results of such an econometric study, which uses data from the United States from 1960 to 1990.

The study focuses on the effects of changes in the *federal funds rate,* the interest rate that is most directly affected by changes in monetary policy. It traces the typical effects of such a change on several macroeconomic variables.

We discussed the federal funds market and the federal funds rate in Section 4-4.

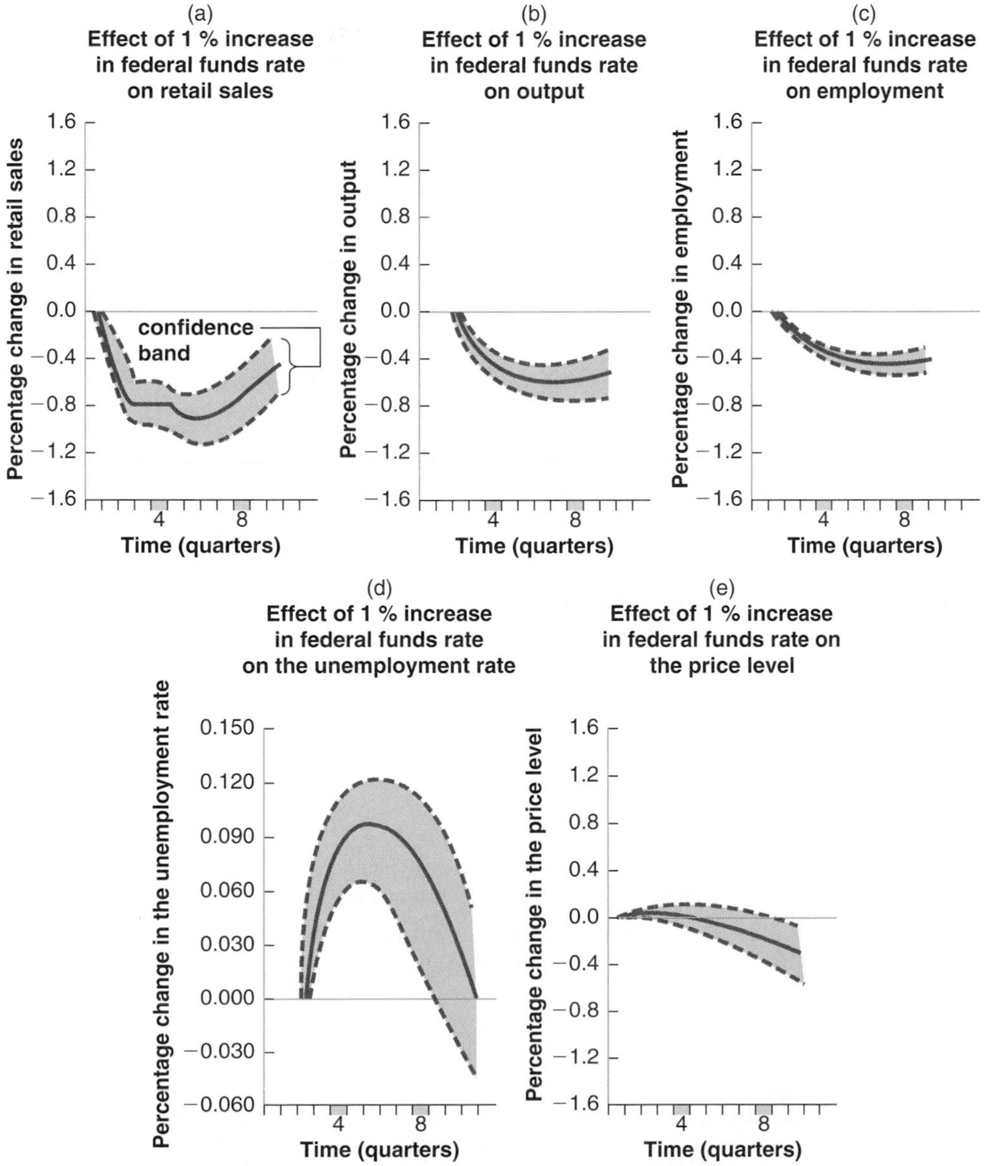

Figure 5-11

The Empirical Effects of an Increase in the Federal Funds Rate

In the short run, an increase in the federal funds rate leads to a decrease in output and to an increase in unemployment, but has little effect on the price level.

Source: Lawrence Christiano, Martin Eichenbaum, and Charles Evans, "The Effects of Monetary Policy Shocks: Evidence From the Flow of Funds," Review of Economics and Statistics, *February 1996, volume 78–1.*

ACTIVE GRAPH

Each panel in Figure 5-11 represents the effects of the change in the interest rate on a given variable. Each panel plots three lines. The solid line in the center of a band gives the best estimate of the effect of the change in the interest rate on the variable we look at in the panel. The two dashed lines and the tinted space between the dashed lines represents a **confidence band**, a band within which the true value of the effect lies with 60% probability.

There is no such thing in econometrics as learning the exact value of a coefficient or the exact effect of one variable on another. Rather, the best econometrics can do is to provide us a best estimate—here, the thick line—and a measure of confidence we can have in the estimate—here, the confidence band.

- Figure 5-11, panel (a) shows the effects of an increase in the federal funds rate of 1% on retail sales over time. The percentage change in retail sales is plotted on the vertical axis; time, measured in quarters, on the horizontal axis.

  Focusing on the best estimate—the solid line—we see that the increase in the federal funds rate leads to a decline in retail sales. The largest decrease in retail sales, −0.9%, is achieved after five quarters.
- Figure 5-11, panel (b) shows how lower sales lead to lower output. In response to the decrease in sales, firms cut production, but by less initially than the decrease in sales. Put another way, firms accumulate inventories for some time. The adjustment of production is smoother and slower than the adjustment of sales. The largest decrease, −0.7%, is reached after eight quarters. In other words, monetary policy works, but it works with long lags. It takes nearly two years for monetary policy to have its full effect on production.

This is why monetary policy could not prevent the 2001 slowdown. When, at the start of 2001, the Fed realized that the U.S. economy was slowing down and started cutting the federal funds rate, it was already too late for these cuts to have much effect on output in 2001.

- Figure 5-11, panel (c) shows how lower output leads to lower employment: As firms cut production, they also cut employment. As with output, the decline in employment is slow and steady, reaching −0.5% after eight quarters. The decline in employment is reflected in an increase in the unemployment rate, shown in Figure 5-11, panel (d).
- Figure 5-11, panel (e) looks at the behavior of the price level. Remember that one of the *assumptions* of the *IS-LM* model is that the price level is given and so does not change in response to changes in demand. Figure 5-11, panel (e) shows that this assumption is not a bad approximation of reality in the short run. The price level is nearly unchanged for the first six quarters or so. Only after the first six quarters does the price level appear to decline. This gives a strong hint as to why the *IS-LM* model becomes less reliable as we look at the medium run: In the medium run, we can no longer assume that the price level is given, and movements in the price level become important.

Figure 5-11 contains two lessons.

First, it gives us a sense of the dynamic adjustment of output and other variables to monetary policy.

Second, and more fundamentally, it shows that what we observe in the economy is consistent with the implications of the *IS-LM* model. This does not *prove* that the *IS–LM* model is the right model. It may be that what we observe in the economy is the result of a completely different mechanism, and the fact that the *IS-LM* model fits well is a coincidence. But this seems unlikely. The *IS-LM* model looks like a solid basis on which to build when looking at movements in activity in the short run. Later, we shall extend the model to look at the role of expectations (Chapters 14 to 17) and the implications of openness both in the goods and in the financial markets (Chapters 18 to 21). But we must first understand what determines output in the medium run. This is the topic of the next four chapters.

Summary

- The *IS-LM* model characterizes the implications of equilibrium in both the goods and the financial markets.
- The *IS* relation and the *IS* curve show the combinations of the interest rate and the level of output that are consistent with equilibrium in the goods market. An

increase in the interest rate leads to a decline in output. The *IS* curve is downward sloping.

- The *LM* relation and the *LM* curve show the combinations of the interest rate and the level of output consistent with equilibrium in financial markets. Given the real money supply, an increase in output leads to an increase in the interest rate. The *LM* curve is upward sloping.
- A fiscal expansion shifts the *IS* curve to the right, leading to an increase in output and an increase in the interest rate. A fiscal contraction shifts the *IS* curve to the left, leading to a decrease in output and a decrease in the interest rate.
- A monetary expansion shifts the *LM* curve down, leading to an increase in output and a decrease in the interest rate. A monetary contraction shifts the *LM* curve up, leading to a decrease in output and an increase in the interest rate.
- The combination of monetary and fiscal policies is known as the monetary-fiscal policy mix, or simply the policy mix. Sometimes monetary and fiscal policy are used for a common goal. Sometimes they are not, and the monetary-fiscal mix reflects tensions or even disagreements between the government (which is in charge of fiscal policy) and the central bank (which is in charge of monetary policy).
- The *IS-LM* model appears to describe well the behavior of the economy in the short run. In particular, the effects of monetary policy appear to be similar to those implied by the *IS-LM* model once dynamics are introduced in the model. An increase in the interest rate due to a monetary contraction leads to a steady decrease in output, with the maximum effect taking place after about eight quarters.

Key Terms

- *IS* curve, 92
- *LM* curve, 95
- fiscal contraction, fiscal consolidation, 97
- fiscal expansion, 97
- monetary expansion, 99
- monetary contraction, tightening, 99
- monetary-fiscal policy mix, or policy mix, 101
- confidence band, 106

Questions and Problems

Quick Check

1. *Using the information in this chapter, label each of the following statements* true, false, *or* uncertain. *Explain briefly.*
   a. The main determinants of investment are the level of sales and the interest rate.
   b. If all the exogenous variables in the *IS* relation are constant, then a higher level of output can be achieved only by lowering the interest rate.
   c. The *IS* curve is downward sloping because goods-market equilibrium implies that an increase in taxes leads to a lower level of output.
   d. If both government spending and taxes increase by the same amount, the *IS* curve does not shift.
   e. The *LM* curve is upward sloping because a higher level of the money supply is needed to increase output.
   f. An increase in government spending decreases investment.
   g. An increase in output at a constant interest rate can only be achieved using a monetary-fiscal policy mix.

2. *Consider first the goods market model with constant investment that we saw in Chapter 3:*

$$C = c_0 + c_1\,(Y - T),\ \text{and}\ \bar{I},\ G,\ \text{and}\ T\ \text{are given}$$

   a. Solve for equilibrium output. What is the value of the multiplier?

   Now, let investment depend on both sales and the interest rate:

$$I = b_0 + b_1 Y - b_2 i$$

   b. Solve for equilibrium output. At a given interest rate, is the effect of a change in autonomous spending bigger than what it was in (a)? Why? (Assume $c_1 + b_1 < 1$.)

   Next, write the LM relation as:

$$M/P = d_1 Y - d_2 i$$

   c. Solve for equilibrium output. (*Hint*: Eliminate the interest rate from the *IS* and *LM* relations.) Derive the multiplier (the effect of a change of 1 in autonomous spending on output).
   d. Is the multiplier you obtained smaller or larger than the multiplier you derived in your answer to (a)? Please explain how your answer depends on the parameters in the behavioral equations for consumption, investment, and money demand.

3. *The response of investment to fiscal policy*

   Using the IS-LM graph, show the effects on output and the interest rate of a decrease in government spending. Can you tell what happens to investment? Why?

Now, consider the following IS-LM model:

$$C = c_0 + c_1(Y - T)$$
$$I = b_0 + b_1 Y - b_2 i$$
$$M/P = d_1 Y - d_2 i$$

a. Solve for equilibrium output. (*Hint*: You may want to work through problem 2 if you're having trouble with this step.)
b. Solve for the equilibrium interest rate. (*Hint*: Use the *LM* relation.)
c. Solve for investment.
d. Under what conditions on the parameters of the model (e.g., c_0, c_1, and so on) will investment increase when G decreases? (*Hint*: If G decreases by 1 unit, by how much does I increase? Be careful, you want the change in I to be positive when the change in G is negative.)
e. Explain the condition you derived in (d).

4. *Consider the following IS-LM model:*

$$C = 200 + .25Y_D$$
$$I = 150 + .25Y - 1000i$$
$$G = 250$$
$$T = 200$$
$$(M/P)^d = 2Y - 8{,}000i$$
$$M/P = 1{,}600$$

a. Derive the *IS* relation. (*Hint*: You want an equation with Y on the left side, all else on the right.)
b. Derive the *LM* relation. (*Hint*: It will be convenient for later use to rewrite this equation with i on the left side, all else on the right.)
c. Solve for equilibrium real output. (*Hint*: Substitute the expression for the interest rate given by the *LM* equation into the *IS* equation and solve for output.)
d. Solve for the equilibrium interest rate. (*Hint*: Substitute the value you obtained for Y in [c] into either the *IS* or *LM* equations and solve for i. If your algebra is correct you should get the same answer from both equations.)
e. Solve for the equilibrium values of C and I and verify the value you obtained for Y by adding up C, I, and G.
f. Now suppose that the money supply increases to $M/P = 1{,}840$. Solve for Y, i, C, and I, and describe in words the effects of an expansionary monetary policy.
g. Set M/P equal to its initial value of 1,600. Now suppose that government spending increases to $G = 400$. Summarize the effects of an expansionary fiscal policy on Y, i, and C.

Dig Deeper

5. *Investment and the interest rate*

The chapter argues that the reason investment depends negatively on the interest rate is that, when the interest rate increases, the cost of borrowing also increases and this discourages investment. However, firms often finance their investment projects using their own funds. Since no borrowing actually occurs, will higher interest rates discourage investment in this case? Explain. (Hint: *Think of yourself as the owner of a firm who is considering either financing new investment projects in that firm using the profits your firm just earned, or buying bonds. Will your decision to invest in new projects in your firm be affected by the interest rate?)*

6. *The liquidity trap*

a. Suppose the interest rate on bonds was negative. Would people want to hold bonds or to hold money? Explain.
b. Draw the demand for money as a function of the interest rate, for a given level of real income. How does your answer to (a) affect your answer? (*Hint*: Show that the demand for money becomes very flat as the interest rate gets very close to zero.)
c. Derive the *LM* curve. What happens to the *LM* curve as the interest rate gets very close to zero? (*Hint*: It becomes very flat.)
d. Take your *LM* curve. Suppose that the interest rate is very close to zero, and the central bank increases the supply of money. What happens to the interest rate at a given level of income?
e. Can an expansionary monetary policy increase output when the interest rate is already very close to zero?

This inability of the central bank to decrease the interest rate when it is already very close to zero is known as the "liquidity trap," and was first mentioned by Keynes in 1936 in his General Theory*—which laid the foundations of the* IS-LM *model. As we shall see in Chapter 22, Japan is now in such a liquidity trap. This liquidity trap sharply limits the ability of monetary policy to get Japan out of its economic slump.*

7. *The Bush-Greenspan policy mix*

In 2001, the Fed pursued a very expansionary monetary policy. At the same time, President George W. Bush pushed through legislation lowering income taxes.

a. Illustrate the effect of such a policy mix on output.
b. How does this policy mix differ from the Clinton-Greenspan mix?
c. What happened to output in 2001? How do you reconcile this fact with the fact that growth was so low in 2001? (*Hint*: What else happened?)

8. *Policy mixes*

Suggest a policy mix to achieve the following objectives:

a. Increase Y while keeping i constant.
b. Decrease the fiscal deficit while keeping Y constant. What happens to i? to investment?

We invite you to visit the Blanchard page on the Prentice Hall Web site at:
www.prenhall.com/blanchard
for this chapter's World Wide Web exercises

Further Readings

"Vulgar Keynesians," by Paul Krugman, discusses the role of monetary policy in the U.S. economy. Read it and try to see if you can restate his arguments in terms of the *IS-LM* model. (Internet address: **web.mit.edu/krugman/www/vulgar.html**)

Another interesting Web page is by Brad DeLong, an economist at the University of California at Berkeley (Internet address: **econ161.berkeley.edu/**). For more information on deficit reduction and the Clinton-Greenspan policy mix, read his article, "The Budget Deficit."

The Medium Run

In the medium run, the economy returns to a level of output associated with the natural rate of unemployment.

Chapter 6

Chapter 6 looks at equilibrium in the labor market. It characterizes the natural rate of unemployment, the unemployment rate to which the economy tends to return in the medium run. Associated with the natural rate of unemployment is a natural level of output.

Chapter 7

Chapter 7 looks at equilibrium in all three markets—goods, financial, labor—together. It shows that, while output typically deviates from the natural level of output in the short run, it returns to the natural level of output in the medium run. The model developed in Chapter 7 is called the *AS-AD* model, and, with the *IS-LM* model, is one of the workhorses of macroeconomics.

Chapter 8

Chapter 8 looks more closely at the relation between inflation and unemployment, a relation known as the Phillips curve. It shows that, in the United States today, unemployment below the natural rate of unemployment leads to an increase in inflation; unemployment above the natural rate of unemployment leads to a decrease in inflation.

Chapter 9

Chapter 9 looks at the determination of output, unemployment, and inflation, and the effects of money growth. It shows how, in the short run, a decrease in money growth can trigger a recession. It shows how, in the medium run, such a decrease in money growth is neutral; it is reflected one for one in a decrease in the rate of inflation, with no change in unemployment and no change in output.

The Labor Market

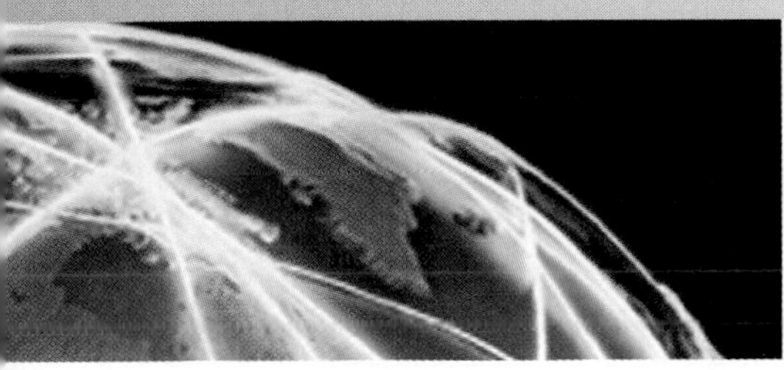

Think about what happens when firms respond to an increase in demand by increasing production:

- Higher production leads to higher employment.
- Higher employment leads to lower unemployment.
- Lower unemployment leads to higher wages.
- Higher wages increase production costs, leading firms to increase prices.
- Higher prices lead workers to ask for higher wages.
- And so on.

So far, we have simply ignored this sequence of events: By assuming a constant price level, we in effect assumed that firms were willing to supply any amount of output at a given price level. As long as our focus was on the *short run,* this assumption was acceptable. But, as our attention turns to the *medium run,* we must now abandon this assumption, explore how prices and wages adjust over time, and how this, in turn, affects the response of output. This will be our task in this and the next three chapters.

At the center of the sequence of events sketched above is *the labor market,* the market in which wages are determined. This chapter focuses on the labor market.

- Section 6-1 provides an overview of the labor market.
- Section 6-2 focuses on unemployment, how it moves over time, and how its movements affect individual workers.

- Sections 6-3 and 6-4 look at wage and price determination.
- Section 6-5 then looks at equilibrium in the labor market. It characterizes the *natural rate of unemployment,* the rate of unemployment to which the economy tends to return in the medium run.
- Section 6-6 gives the map of where we go next. ■

6-1 A Tour of the Labor Market

The total U.S. population in 2000 was 275.1 million (Fig. 6-1). Excluding those who were either under working age (under 16), in the armed forces, or behind bars, the number of people potentially available for civilian employment, the **noninstitutional civilian population**, was 209.6 million.

The civilian **labor force**—the sum of those either working or looking for work—was only 140.8 million, however. The other 68.8 million people were **out of the labor force**, neither working in the market place nor looking for work. So, the **participation rate**, defined as the ratio of the labor force to the noninstitutional civilian population, was 140.8/209.6, or 67%. The participation rate has steadily increased over time, reflecting mostly the increasing participation rate of women: In 1950, one woman out of three was in the labor force; now the number is close to two out of three.

Work in the home, such as keeping house and raising children, is not classified as work in official statistics. The reason is the difficulty of measuring these activities, not a value judgment as to what is work or not work.

Of those in the labor force, 135.2 million were employed, and 5.6 million were unemployed—looking for work. So, the **unemployment rate**, defined as the ratio of the unemployed to the labor force, was 5.6/140.8 = 4.0%. As we discussed in Chapter 1, this unemployment rate was unusually low, the lowest in the United States in three decades.

Figure 6-1

Population, Labor Force, Employment, and Unemployment in the United States, 2000

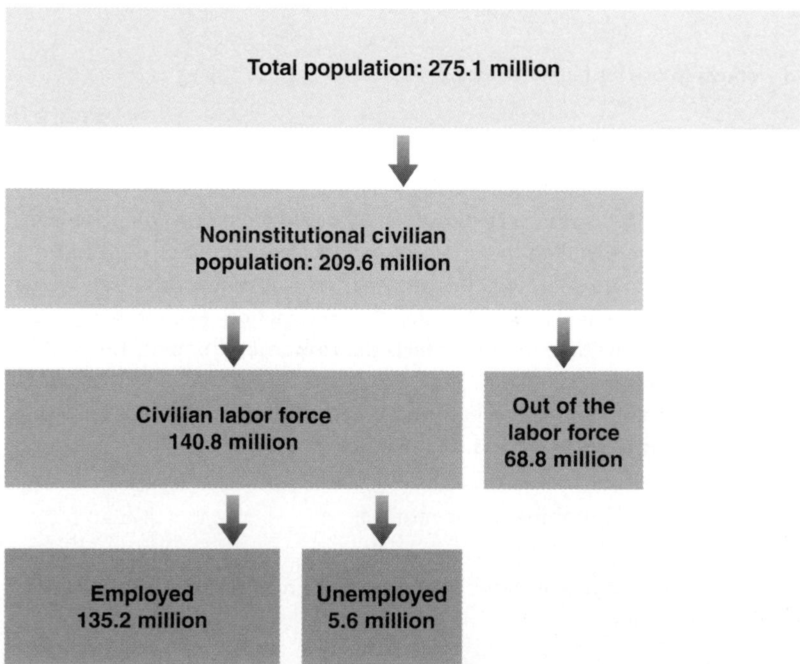

The Large Flows of Workers

To think further about unemployment, and what it implies for individual workers, consider the following analogy:

Take an airport full of passengers. It may be full because many planes are coming and going, and many passengers are quickly moving in and out of the airport. Or it may be full because bad weather is delaying flights and passengers are stuck, waiting for the weather to improve. The number of passengers in the airport will be high in both cases, but their plight will be quite different.

In the same way, an unemployment rate may reflect two very different realities. It may reflect an active labor market, with many **separations** and many **hires**, and so with many workers entering and exiting unemployment; or it may reflect a sclerotic labor market, with few separations, few hires, and a stagnant unemployment pool.

Sclerosis, a medical term, means hardening of the arteries. By analogy, it is used in economics to describe markets (such as the labor market) that function poorly and have few transactions.

Finding out which reality hides behind the aggregate unemployment rate requires data on movements of workers. Such data are available in the United States from a monthly survey called the **Current Population Survey (CPS)**. Average monthly flows, computed from the CPS for the United States from 1994 to 1999, are reported in Figure 6-2. (For more on the ins and outs of the CPS, see the Focus box "The Current Population Survey.")

Figure 6-2 has three striking features:

The numbers for employment, unemployment, and those out of the labor force in Figure 6-1 refer to 2000. The numbers for the same variables in Figure 6-2 refer to averages from 1994 to 1999. For this reason, they are slightly different.

- The flows of workers in and out of employment are very large.

  On average, there are 6.7 million separations each month in the United States (out of an employment pool of 127 million): 3.5 million workers move directly from one job to another (the circle arrow at the top). Another 1.5 million move from employment to unemployment (the arrow from employment to unemployment). And 1.7 million move from employment to out of the labor force (the arrow from employment to out of the labor force).

  Why are there so many separations each month? About three-fourths of all separations are **quits**, workers leaving their jobs for a better alternative. The remaining one fourth are **layoffs**. Layoffs come mostly from changes in employment levels across firms: The slowly changing aggregate employment numbers hide a reality of continual job destruction and job creation across firms. At any time, some firms are suffering decreases in demand and decreasing their employment; other firms are enjoying increases in demand and increasing employment.

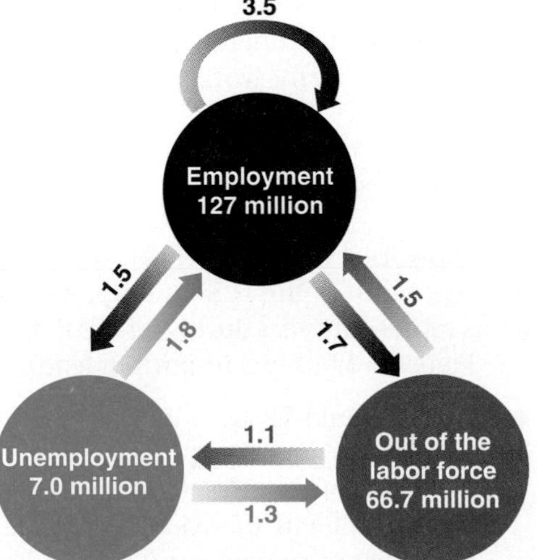

Figure 6-2

Average Monthly Flows Between Employment, Unemployment, and Nonparticipation in the United States, 1994–1999

(1) The flows of workers in and out of employment are large. (2) The flows in and out of unemployment are large in relation to the number of unemployed. (3) There are also large flows in and out of the labor force, much of them directly to and from employment.

- The flows in and out of unemployment are large in relation to the number of unemployed:

    The average flow out of unemployment each month is 3.1 million: 1.8 million get a job, and 1.3 million stop searching and drop out of the labor force. Put another way, the proportion of unemployed leaving unemployment equals 3.1/7.0 or about 44% each month. Put yet another way, the average **duration of unemployment**—the average length of time people spend unemployed—is about three months.

    This fact has an important implication. You should not think of the unemployed in the United States as a stagnant pool of workers waiting indefinitely for jobs. For most (obviously not all) of the unemployed, being unemployed is more a quick transition than a long wait between jobs: In this respect, the United States is unusual among rich countries. Evidence from Western Europe shows a much smaller proportion of the unemployed leaving unemployment each month, a much longer average duration of unemployment.

- The flows in and out of the labor force are also surprisingly large: Each month 3 million workers drop out of the labor force (1.7 + 1.3), and a roughly equal number join the labor force (1.5 + 1.1).

    You might have expected these two flows to be small, composed on one side of those finishing school and entering the labor force for the first time, and on the other side of workers entering retirement. But both of these groups actually represent a small fraction of the total flows. Each month only about 400,000 new people enter the labor force, and about 250,000 retire. The actual flows in and out of the labor force are 5.6 million (1.7 + 1.3 + 1.5 + 1.1) or about 8 times larger.

    What this fact implies is that many of those classified as "out of the labor force" are in fact willing to work, and move back and forth between participation and nonparticipation. Indeed, among those classified as out of the labor force, nearly 5 million report that although they are not looking, they "want a job." What they mean exactly is unclear, but the evidence is that many do take jobs when offered one.

    This fact also has an important implication. The sharp focus on the unemployment rate by economists, policy makers, and news media is partly misdirected. Some of the people classified as "out of the labor force" are very much like the unemployed; they are in effect **discouraged workers**, and while they are not actively looking for a job, they will take it if they find it. This is why economists sometimes focus on the **nonemployment rate**, the ratio of population minus employment to population, rather than the unemployment rate. I shall follow tradition in this book and focus on the unemployment rate, but you should keep in mind that the unemployment rate is not the best estimate of the number of people available for work.

The average duration of unemployment equals the inverse of the proportion of unemployed leaving unemployment each month. To see why, consider this example. Suppose the number of unemployed is constant and equal to 100, and each unemployed person remains unemployed for 2 months. So, at any time, there are 50 people who have been unemployed for one month, 50 for two months. Each month, the 50 unemployed who have been unemployed for two months leave unemployment. In this example, the proportion of unemployed leaving unemployment each month is 50/100 = 50%. The duration of unemployment is 2 months—the inverse of 1/50%.

Working in the opposite direction, some of the unemployed may be unwilling to accept any job offered to them, and should probably not be counted as unemployed since they are not really looking for a job.

6-2 Movements in Unemployment

Let's now look more closely at movements in unemployment. Figure 6-3 shows the average value of the U.S. unemployment rate for each year since 1948. The shaded areas represent years during which there was a recession.

Figure 6-3 has two important features:

- Until the mid-1980s, it looked as if the U.S. unemployment rate was on an upward trend, from an average of 4.5% in the 1950s to 4.7% in the 1960s, 6.2% in the 1970s, 7.3% in the 1980s. Since then, however, the unemployment rate has steadily declined, and in the 1990s, the average unemployment rate stood at 5.2%. This decrease has led a number of economists to conclude that the trend has been reversed, and that the

The evolution of the unemployment rate has been very different in Western Europe. As we saw in Chapter 1, the unemployment rate in the European Union, which was around 3% in the 1960s, is now around 9%. More on this in Chapters 8 and 13.

The Current Population Survey

The Current Population Survey (CPS) is the main source of statistics on the labor force, employment, participation, and earnings in the United States.

When the CPS began in 1940, it was based on interviews of 8,000 households. The sample has grown considerably, and now more than 60,000 households are interviewed every month. The households are chosen so that the sample is representative of the U.S. population. Each household stays in the sample for four months, leaves the sample for the following eight months, then returns for another four months before leaving the sample permanently.

The survey is now based on computer-assisted interviews. Interviews are either done in person, in which case interviewers use laptop computers to enter data, or by phone. Some questions are the same every month. Other questions are specific to a particular survey and are used to find out about particular aspects of the labor market.

The Labor Department uses the data to compute and publish numbers on employment, unemployment, and participation by age, sex, education, and industry. Economists use these data, which are available in large computer files, in two ways.

The first is to get snapshots of how things are at various points in time, to answer questions such as: What is the distribution of wages for Hispanic-American workers with only primary education, and how does it compare with the same distribution 10 or 20 years ago?

The second, of which Figure 6-2 is an example, is by exploiting the fact that the survey follows people through time. By looking at those who are in the sample in two adjacent months, economists can find out, for example, how many of those who were unemployed last month are employed this month. This number gives them an estimate of the probability of finding a job for those who were unemployed last month.

For more on the CPS, read "How the Government Measures Unemployment" at **www.bls.gov/**.

FOCUS

U.S. economy is likely to operate at a lower average unemployment rate in the future than in the last 20 years. We shall return to this issue in Chapter 8.

- Leaving aside these trend changes, year-to-year movements in the unemployment rate are closely associated with recessions and expansions. Note, for example, the last two peaks in unemployment. The most recent, in which

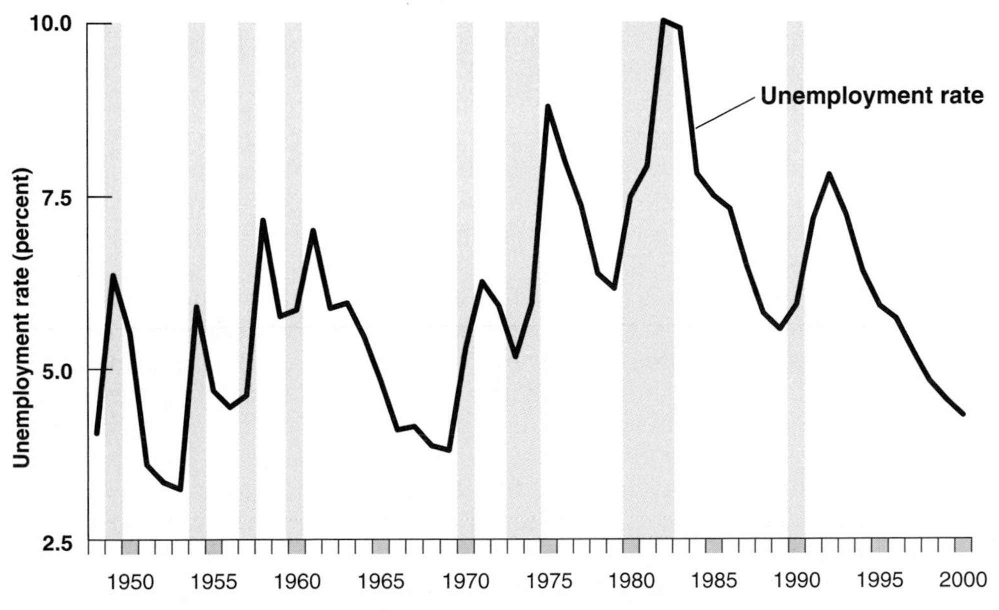

Figure 6-3

Movements in the U.S. Unemployment Rate, 1948–2000

Since 1948, the average yearly U.S. unemployment rate has fluctuated between 3 and 10%.

9.7% is the average unemployment rate for the year. The unemployment rate reached 10.8% in November 1982.

unemployment peaked at 7.7%, was associated with the recession of 1990–1991 (the peak in unemployment actually came one year after the end of the recession, in 1992). The peak before that, in which unemployment peaked at 9.7% (a postwar high) was during the recession of 1982.

How do these fluctuations in the *aggregate unemployment rate* affect *individual workers*? This is an important question, because the answer determines:

- the effect of movements in the aggregate unemployment rate on the welfare of individual workers, and
- the effect of the aggregate unemployment rate on wages.

Think about how firms can decrease their employment in response to a decrease in demand. They can hire fewer new workers, or they can lay off the workers they currently employ. Typically, firms prefer first to slow or stop the hiring of new workers, relying on quits and retirements to achieve a decrease in employment. But doing only this may not be enough if the decrease in demand is large, so firms may then have to lay off workers.

Now think about the implications for both employed and unemployed workers.

- If the adjustment takes place through a decrease in hires, the effect is to decrease the chance that an unemployed worker will find a job. Fewer hires means fewer job openings; higher unemployment means more job applicants. Fewer openings and more applicants combine to make it harder for the unemployed to find jobs.
- If, instead, the adjustment takes place through higher layoffs, then the employed workers are at a higher risk of losing their jobs.

In general, as firms use both margins of adjustment, higher unemployment is associated with both a lower chance of finding a job if unemployed and a higher chance of losing it if employed. Figures 6-4 and 6-5 show these two effects at work in the United States over the period 1968–1999.

Figure 6-4 plots two variables against time: the unemployment rate (measured on the left vertical axis); and the proportion of unemployed workers finding a job each month (measured on the right vertical axis). This proportion is constructed by dividing the flow from unemployment to employment during each month by the number of unemployed at the beginning of the month. To show the relation between the two variables more clearly, the proportion of unemployed finding jobs is plotted on an inverted scale: Be sure you see that on the right vertical scale, the proportion is lowest at the top, highest at the bottom.

The relation between movements in the proportion of unemployed workers finding jobs and the unemployment rate is striking: Periods of higher unemployment are associated with much lower proportions of unemployed workers finding jobs. At the peak of the 1980–1982 recession for example, the proportion of unemployed workers finding jobs was down to about 17% per month, compared to an average value of 25% over the whole period.

Similarly, Figure 6-5 plots two variables against time: the unemployment rate (measured on the left vertical axis), and the monthly separation rate from employment, constructed by dividing the flow from employment (to unemployment and to "out of the labor force") during each month by the number of employed at the beginning of the month (measured on the right vertical axis). The relation between the separation rate and the unemployment rate plotted in Figure 6-5 is less tight than the relation plotted in Figure 6-4, but it is nevertheless quite visible. Higher unemployment implies a higher separation rate, a higher chance for employed workers to lose their jobs.

To be precise, we learn from Figure 6-5 only that, when unemployment is higher, separations are higher. Separations equal quits plus layoffs. We know from other sources that quits are lower when unemployment is high: It is more attractive to quit when there are plenty of jobs. So, if separations go up and quits go down, this implies that layoffs (which equal separations minus quits) go up even more than separations.

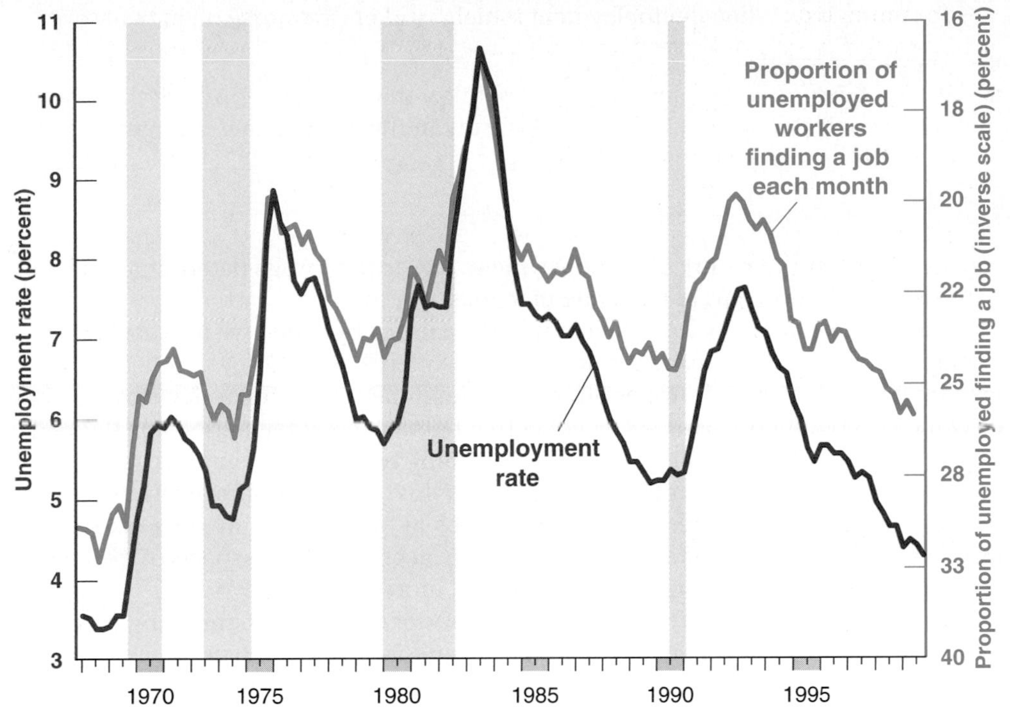

Figure 6-4

The Unemployment Rate and the Proportion of Unemployed Finding Jobs, 1968–1999

When unemployment is high, the proportion of unemployed finding jobs is low. Note that the scale on the right is an inverse scale.

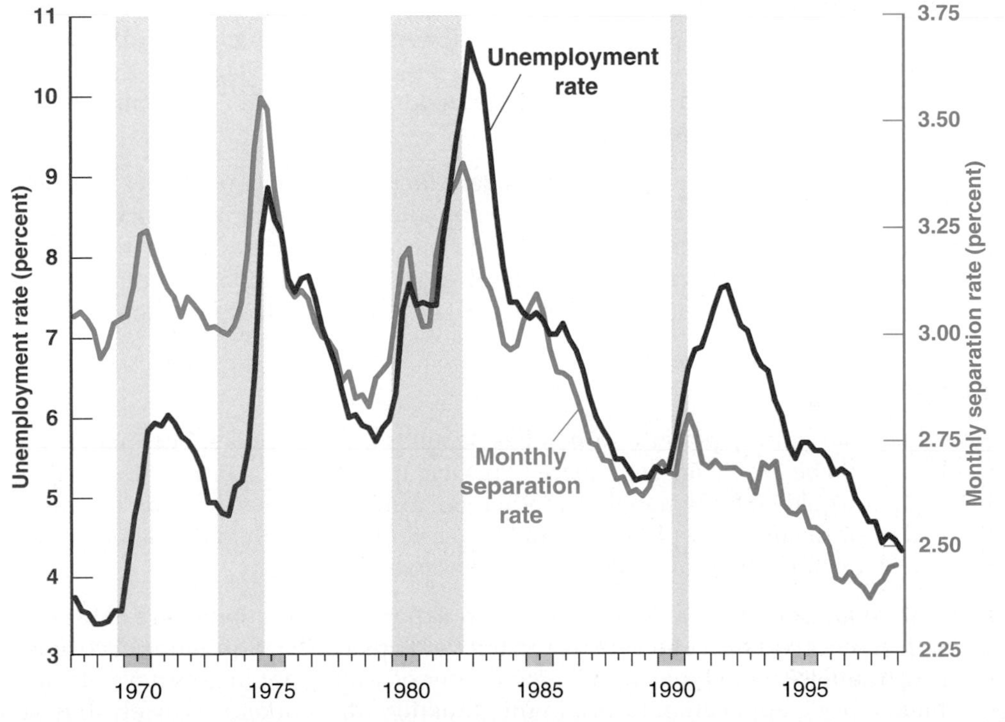

Figure 6-5

The Unemployment Rate and the Monthly Separation Rate from Employment, 1968–1999

When unemployment is high, a higher proportion of workers lose their jobs.

To summarize: When unemployment is high, workers are worse off in two ways:

- They are more likely to lose their job.
- If they become unemployed, the probability that they will find another job is lower; equivalently, they can expect to be unemployed for a longer length of time.

6-3 Wage Determination

Having looked at the nature of unemployment, let's turn to wage determination, and to the relation between wages and unemployment.

Wages are set in many ways. Sometimes they are set by **collective bargaining**, that is, bargaining between firms and unions. In the United States, however, collective bargaining plays a limited role, especially outside manufacturing. Today, fewer than 25% of workers have their wages set in collective bargaining agreements. For the rest, wages are either set by employers, or by bargaining between the employer and individual employees. The higher the skills needed to do the job, the more likely there is to be bargaining. Wages offered for entry-level jobs at McDonald's are on a take-it-or-leave-it basis. New college graduates can typically negotiate a few aspects of their contract. CEOs and baseball stars can negotiate a lot more.

Collective bargaining: bargaining between a union (or a group of unions) and a firm (or a group of firms).

There are also large differences across countries. Collective bargaining plays an important role in Japan and in most European countries. Negotiations may take place at the level of the firm, at the level of industry, or at the national level. Sometimes contract agreements apply only to firms that have signed the agreement; sometimes they are automatically extended to all firms and all workers in the sector or the economy.

Given these differences across workers and across countries, can we hope for anything like a general theory of wage determination? Yes. Although institutional differences influence wage determination, there are common forces at work in all countries. Two sets of facts stand out:

- Workers are typically paid a wage that exceeds their **reservation wage**, the wage that would make them indifferent to working or becoming unemployed. In other words, most workers are paid a high enough wage that they prefer to be employed than rather unemployed.
- Wages typically depend on labor-market conditions. The lower the unemployment rate, the higher are wages.

To think about these facts, economists have focused on two broad lines of explanation. The first is that even in the absence of collective bargaining, workers have some bargaining power, which they can and do use to obtain wages above their reservation wage. The second is that firms themselves may, for a number of reasons, want to pay wages higher than the reservation wage. Let's look at each explanation in turn.

Bargaining

How much **bargaining power** a worker has depends on two factors. The first is how costly it would be for the firm to replace him, were he to leave the firm. The second is how hard it would be for him to find another job, were he to leave the firm. The more costly it is for the firm to replace him, and the easier it is for him to find another job, the more bargaining power he will have. This has two implications:

- How much bargaining power a worker has depends first on the nature of his job. Replacing a worker at McDonald's is not very costly; the required skills can be taught quickly, and typically a large number of willing applicants have already filled out job application forms. In this situation, the worker is unlikely to have much bargaining power. If he asks for a higher wage, the firm can lay him off and find a replacement at minimum cost. In contrast, a highly skilled worker who knows in detail how the firm operates may be very difficult and costly to replace. This gives him more bargaining power. If he asks for a higher wage, the firm may decide that it is best to give it to him.

- How much bargaining power a worker has depends on labor-market conditions. When the unemployment rate is low, it is more difficult for firms to find acceptable replacements; at the same time, it is easier for workers to find other jobs. Workers are in a stronger bargaining position, and may be able to obtain a higher wage. When the unemployment rate is high, finding good replacements is easier for firms, while finding another job is harder for workers. Being in a weak bargaining position, workers may have no choice but to accept a lower wage.

Efficiency Wages

Leaving aside workers' bargaining power, firms themselves may want to pay more than the reservation wage. Firms want their workers to be productive, and a higher wage can help them achieve that goal.

If, for example, it takes a while for workers to learn how to do a job correctly, firms will want their workers to stay for some time. But if workers are paid only their reservation wage, they will be indifferent to staying or leaving. Many of them will quit, and turnover will be high. Paying a wage above the reservation wage makes it financially attractive for workers to stay. It decreases turnover, and increases productivity.

◀ Before September 11, 2001, the approach to airport security was to hire workers at low wages, and accept the resulting high turnover. Now that airport security has become a much higher priority, the approach is to make the jobs more attractive and better paying, so as to get more motivated and more competent workers, and reduce turnover.

Behind this example lies a more general proposition: Most firms want their workers to feel good about their jobs. Feeling good promotes good work, which leads to higher productivity. Paying a high wage is one instrument the firm can use to achieve these goals. (See the Focus box "Henry Ford and Efficiency Wages.") Economists call the theories that link the *productivity* or the *efficiency* of workers to the wage they are paid **efficiency wage theories**.

Like theories based on bargaining, efficiency wage theories suggest that wages depend on both the nature of the job and on labor-market conditions:

- Firms—such as high-tech firms—that see employees' morale and commitment as essential to the quality of their work will pay more than firms in sectors where workers' activity is more routine.
- Labor-market conditions will affect the wage. A low unemployment rate makes it more attractive for employed workers to quit: When unemployment is low, it is easy to find another job. That means when unemployment decreases, a firm that wants to avoid an increase in quits will have to increase wages to induce workers to stay with the firm. Thus, lower unemployment will again lead to higher wages.

Wages, Prices, and Unemployment

We capture our discussion of wage determination by the following equation:

$$W = P^e F(\underset{(-,+)}{u, z}) \qquad (6.1)$$

The aggregate nominal wage W depends on three factors:

- The expected price level, P^e
- The unemployment rate, u
- A catchall variable, z, that stands for all other variables that may affect the outcome of wage setting.

FOCUS

Henry Ford and Efficiency Wages

In 1914, Henry Ford—the builder of the most popular car in the world at the time, the model-T —made a stunning announcement. His company would pay all qualified employees a minimum of $5 a day for an 8-hour day. This was a very large salary increase for most employees, who previously, had earned, on average, $2.30, for 9-hour days. Although company profits were substantial, this increase in pay was far from negligible—it represented about half of the company's profits at the time.

What Ford's motivations were are not entirely clear. Ford himself gave too many reasons for us to know which ones he actually believed. The reason was not that the company had a hard time finding workers at the previous wage. But the company clearly had a hard time retaining workers. There was a very high turnover rate, as well as high dissatisfaction among workers.

Whatever the reasons behind Ford's decision, the results of the wage increase were astounding, as Table 1 shows.

The annual turnover rate (the ratio of separations to employment) plunged from a high of 370% in 1913 to a low of 16% in 1915. (An annual turnover rate of 370% means that, on average, 31% of the company's workers left each month, so that over the year the ratio of separations to employment was 31% × 12 = 370%.) The layoff rate collapsed from 62% to nearly 0%. Other measures point in the same direction. The average rate of absenteeism (not shown in the table), which ran at 10% in 1913, was down to 2.5% one year later. There is little question that higher wages were the main source of these changes.

Did productivity at the Ford plant increase enough to offset the cost of increased wages? The answer to this question is less clear. Productivity was much higher in 1914 than in 1913; estimates of productivity increases range from 30 to 50%. Despite higher wages, profits were also higher in 1914 than in 1913. But how much of this increase in profits was due to changes in workers' behavior and how much was due to the increasing success of model-T cars is harder to establish.

While the effects support efficiency-wage theories, it may be that the increase in wages to $5 a day was excessive, at least from the point of view of profit maximization. But Henry Ford probably had other objectives as well, from keeping the unions out—which he did—to generating publicity for himself and the company—which he surely did.

Source: Dan Raff and Lawrence Summers, "Did Henry Ford Pay Efficiency Wages?" NBER Working Paper, 2101, *December 1986.*

Table 1 Annual Turnover and Layoff Rates (%) at Ford, 1913–1915

	1913	1914	1915
Turnover rate	370	54	16
Layoff rate	62	7	0.1

Let's look at each factor:

The Expected Price Level

First leave aside the difference between the expected and the actual price level, and ask: Why does the price level affect wages?

The answer: Both workers and firms care about *real wages,* not nominal wages.

- Workers care not about how many dollars they receive, but about how many goods they can buy with their wages. In other words, they care about their wage in terms of goods, about *W/P*.
- In the same way, firms do not care about the nominal wages they pay workers, but about the nominal wages they pay in relation to the price of the output they sell. So firms also care about *W/P*.

If workers expected the price level—the price of the goods they buy— to double, they would ask for a doubling of their nominal wage. If firms expected the price level—the price of the goods they sold—to double, they would be willing to double the nominal wage. So if both workers and firms expected the price level were going to double, they would agree to doubling the nominal wage, keeping the real wage constant. This is captured in equation (6.1): A doubling in the expected price level leads to a doubling of the nominal wage chosen in wage setting.

◀ **In short:** $P^e\uparrow \Rightarrow W\uparrow$

Returning to the distinction we put aside at the start of the paragraph: Why do wages depend on the *expected price level, P^e*, rather than the *actual price level, P*? The answer is that wages are set in nominal (dollar) terms, and when they are set, what the relevant price level will be is not yet known.

For example, in union contracts in the United States, nominal wages are typically set in advance for three years. Unions and firms have to decide what nominal wages will be over the following three years based on what they expect the price level to be over those three years. Even when wages are set by firms, or by bargaining between the firm and each worker, nominal wages are typically set for a year. If the price level goes up unexpectedly during the year, nominal wages are typically not readjusted. (How workers and firms form expectations of the price level will occupy us for much of the next three chapters; we leave this issue aside for the moment.)

The Unemployment Rate

Also affecting the aggregate wage in equation (6.1) is the unemployment rate, u. The minus sign under u indicates that an increase in the unemployment rate decreases wages.

That wages depend on unemployment was one of the main conclusions of our earlier discussion of wage determination. If we think of wages as being determined by bargaining, then higher unemployment weakens workers' bargaining power, forcing workers to accept lower wages. If we think of wages as being determined by efficiency wage considerations, then higher unemployment allows firms to pay lower wages and still keep workers willing to work.

◀ **In short:** $u\uparrow \Rightarrow W\downarrow$

The Other Factors

The third variable in equation (6.1), z, is a catchall variable that stands for all the factors that affect wages given the expected price level and the unemployment rate. By convention, let's define z so that an increase in z implies an increase in the wage (thus, the positive sign under z in the equation.) Our earlier discussion suggests a long list of potential factors here.

◀ **In short:** $z\uparrow \Rightarrow W\uparrow$

Take, for example, **unemployment insurance**—the payment of unemployment benefits to workers who lose their jobs. There are good reasons why society should provide some insurance to workers who lose a job and find it difficult to find another. But there is little question that by making the prospects of unemployment less distressing, more generous unemployment benefits do increase wages at a given unemployment rate. To take an extreme example, suppose unemployment insurance did not exist. Workers would then be willing to accept very low wages to avoid remaining unemployed. But unemployment insurance does exist, and it allows unemployed workers to hold out for higher wages. In this case, we can think of z as representing the level of unemployment benefits: At a given unemployment rate, higher unemployment benefits increase the wage.

It is easy to think of other factors. An increase in the minimum wage may increase not only the minimum wage itself, but also wages just above the minimum wage, leading to an increase in the average wage, W, at a given unemployment rate. Or take an increase in employment protection, which makes it more expensive for firms to lay off workers. Such a change is likely to increase the bargaining power of workers covered by this protection (laying them off and hiring other workers is more costly for firms), increasing the wage for a given unemployment rate.

We shall explore some of these factors as we go along.

6-4 Price Determination

Having looked at wage determination, let's now turn to price determination.

Prices depend on costs. Costs depend on the nature of the **production function**—the relation between the inputs used in production and the quantity of output produced, and on the price of these inputs.

We shall assume here that firms produce goods using labor as the only factor of production and according to the production function:

$$Y = AN$$

where Y is output, N is employment, and A is labor productivity. This way of writing the production function implies that **labor productivity**—output per worker—is constant and equal to A.

Using a term from microeconomics, this assumption implies *constant returns to labor in production.* If firms double the number of workers they employ, they double the amount of output they produce.

It should be clear that this is a strong simplification. In reality, firms use factors of production other than labor. They use capital—machines and factories. They use raw materials—oil, for example. There is technological progress, so that labor productivity, A, is not constant but instead steadily increases over time. We shall introduce these complications later. We shall introduce raw materials in Chapter 7 when we discuss the oil crises of the 1970s. We shall focus on the role of capital and technological progress when we turn to the determination of output in the *long run* in Chapters 10 to 13. For the moment however, this simple relation between output and employment will make our life easier, and still serve our purposes.

Given the assumption that labor productivity, A, is constant, we can make one further simplification. We can choose the units for output so that one worker produces one unit of output—so that $A = 1$. (This way, we do not have to carry the letter A around, and this will simplify notation.) With that assumption, the production function becomes

$$Y = N \tag{6.2}$$

The production function $Y = N$ implies that the cost of producing one more unit of output is the cost of employing one more worker, at wage W. Using the terminology introduced in your microeconomics course, the marginal cost of production is equal to W.

If there were perfect competition in the goods market, the price of a unit of output would be equal to marginal cost: P would be equal to W. But many goods markets are not competitive, and firms charge a price higher than their marginal cost. A simple way of capturing this fact is to assume that firms set their price according to

$$P = (1 + \mu)W \tag{6.3}$$

where μ is the **markup** of the price over the cost. If goods markets were perfectly competitive, μ would be equal to zero, and the price, P, would simply equal the wage W.

To the extent that they are not competitive and that firms have market power, μ is positive, and the price, P, will exceed the cost, W, by a factor equal to $(1 + \mu)$.

6-5 The Natural Rate of Unemployment

Let's now look at the implications of wage and price determination for unemployment.

To do so, let's make one additional assumption, namely that nominal wages depend on the actual price level, P, rather than on the expected price level, P^e (why we make this assumption will become clear soon.)

◀ **The rest of the chapter is based on the assumption that $P^e = P$.**

Under this additional assumption, wage setting and price setting determine the equilibrium rate of unemployment. Let's see how.

The Wage-Setting Relation

Given the assumption that nominal wages depend on the actual price level, P, rather than on the expected price level, P^e, equation (6.1), which characterizes wage determination, becomes

$$W = P\,F(u, z)$$

Dividing both sides by the price level,

$$\frac{W}{P} = \underset{(-,+)}{F(u, z)} \qquad (6.4)$$

Wage determination implies a negative relation between the real wage, W/P, and the unemployment rate, u: *The higher the unemployment rate, the lower the real wage chosen by wage setters.* The intuition is straightforward: The higher the unemployment rate, the weaker workers are in bargaining, and so the lower the real wage.

◀ **"Wage setters" means unions and firms if wages are set by collective bargaining; individual workers and firms if wages are set on a case-by-case basis; firms if wages are set on a take-it-or-leave-it basis.**

This relation between the real wage and the rate of unemployment—let's call it the **wage-setting relation**—is drawn in Figure 6-6. The real wage is measured on the vertical axis. The unemployment rate is measured on the horizontal axis. The wage-setting

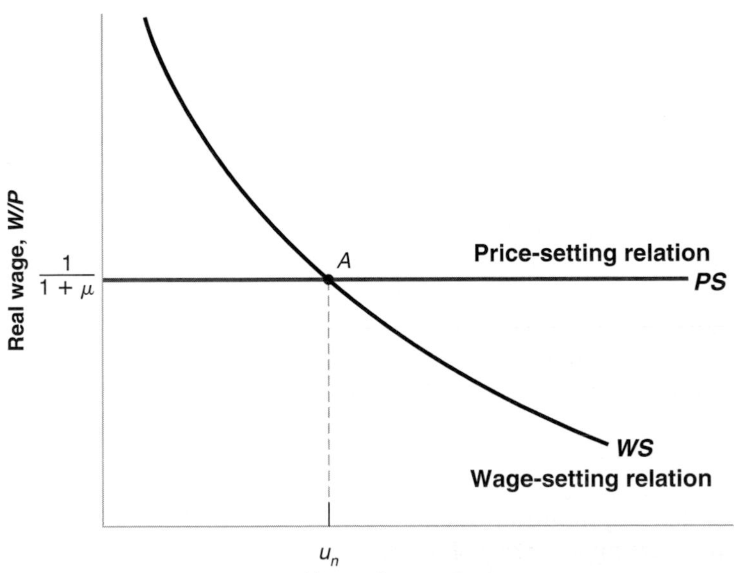

Figure 6-6

The Wage-Setting Relation, the Price-Setting Relation, and the Natural Rate of Unemployment

The real wage chosen in wage setting is a decreasing function of the unemployment rate. The real wage implied by price setting is constant, independent of the unemployment rate. The natural rate of unemployment is the unemployment rate such that the real wage chosen in wage setting is equal to the real wage implied by price setting.

ACTIVE GRAPH

relation is drawn as the downward-sloping curve, *WS* (for wage setting): The higher the unemployment rate, the lower the real wage.

The Price-Setting Relation

Turn now to the implications of price determination. If we divide both sides of the price-determination equation, (6.3), by the nominal wage, we get

$$\frac{P}{W} = 1 + \mu \qquad (6.5)$$

The ratio of the price level to the wage implied by the price-setting behavior of firms equals 1 plus the markup. Now invert both sides of this equation to get the implied real wage

$$\frac{W}{P} = \frac{1}{1+\mu} \qquad (6.6)$$

Note what this equation says: *Price-setting decisions determine the real wage paid by firms.* An increase in the markup leads firms to increase their price given the wage; equivalently, it leads to a decrease in the real wage.

The step from equation (6.5) to equation (6.6) is algebraically straightforward. But how price setting actually determines the real wage paid by firms may not be intuitively obvious.

Think of it this way: Suppose the firm in which you work increases its markup, and so increases the price of its product. Your real wage does not change very much. You are still paid the same nominal wage, and the product produced by the firm is likely to be a small part of your consumption basket. Suppose now that not only the firm you work for but all the firms in the economy increase their markup. Now, all prices go up. Even if you are paid the same nominal wage, your real wage goes down. So, the higher the markup set by firms, the lower your real wage.

The **price-setting relation** in equation (6.6) is drawn as the horizontal line *PS* (for price setting) in Figure 6-6. The real wage implied by price setting is $1/(1+\mu)$; it does not depend on the unemployment rate.

Equilibrium Real Wages and Unemployment

Equilibrium in the labor market requires that the real wage implied by wage setting be equal to the real wage implied by price setting. (This way of stating equilibrium may sound strange if you learned to think in terms of labor supply and labor demand in your microeconomics course. The relation between the wage-setting and price-setting relations on one hand, and labor supply and labor demand on the other, is closer than it looks at first and is explored further in the appendix at the end of this chapter.)

In Figure 6-6, equilibrium is therefore given by point *A*. The equilibrium unemployment rate is given by u_n.

We can characterize the equilibrium unemployment rate algebraically; eliminating W/P between equations (6.4) and (6.6) gives

$$F(u_n, z) = \frac{1}{1+\mu} \qquad (6.7)$$

The equilibrium unemployment rate, u_n, is such that the real wage chosen in wage setting—the left side of equation (6.7)—is equal to the real wage implied by price setting—the right side of equation (6.7).

The equilibrium unemployment rate u_n is called the **natural rate of unemployment** (which is why I have used the subscript n to denote it). The terminology has become standard, and I shall adopt it, but this is a bad choice of words. The word *natural* suggests a constant of nature, one that is unaffected by institutions and policy. As its derivation makes clear, however, the "natural" rate of unemployment is anything but natural. The positions of the wage-setting and price-setting curves, and thus the equilibrium unemployment rate, depend on both z and μ. Consider two examples:

◄ *Natural*, as defined by Webster's Dictionary, means "in a state provided by nature, without man-made changes."

- *An increase in unemployment benefits.* An increase in unemployment benefits can be represented by an increase in z: Since an increase in benefits makes the prospect of unemployment less painful, it increases the wage set by wage setters at a given unemployment rate. So it shifts the wage-setting relation up, from *WS* to *WS'* in Figure 6-7. The economy moves along the *PS* line, from *A* to *A'*. The natural rate of unemployment increases from u_n to u'_n.

  In words: At a given unemployment rate, higher unemployment benefits lead to a higher real wage. A higher unemployment rate is needed to bring the real wage back to what firms are willing to pay.
- *A less stringent enforcement of existing antitrust legislation.* To the extent that this allows firms to collude more easily, and so increases their market power, it leads to an increase in their markup—an increase in μ. The increase in μ implies a decrease in the real wage paid by firms, and so it shifts the price-setting relation down, from *PS* to *PS'* in Figure 6-8. The economy moves along *WS*. The equilibrium moves from *A* to *A'*, and the natural rate of unemployment increases from u_n to u'_n.

  In words: By letting firms increase their price given the wage, less stringent enforcement of antitrust legislation leads to a decrease in the real wage. Higher unemployment is required to make workers accept this lower real wage, leading to an increase in the natural rate of unemployment.

Factors such as the generosity of unemployment benefits or antitrust legislation can hardly be thought of as the result of nature. Rather, they reflect various characteristics of

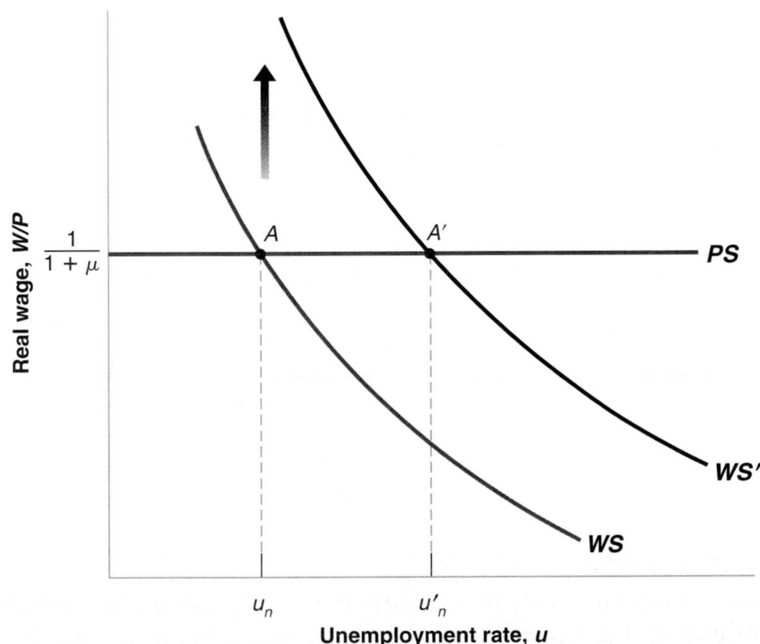

Figure 6-7

Unemployment Benefits and the Natural Rate of Unemployment

An increase in unemployment benefits leads to an increase in the natural rate of unemployment.

Figure 6-8

Markups and the Natural Rate of Unemployment

An increase in the markup decreases the real wage, and leads to an increase in the natural rate of unemployment.

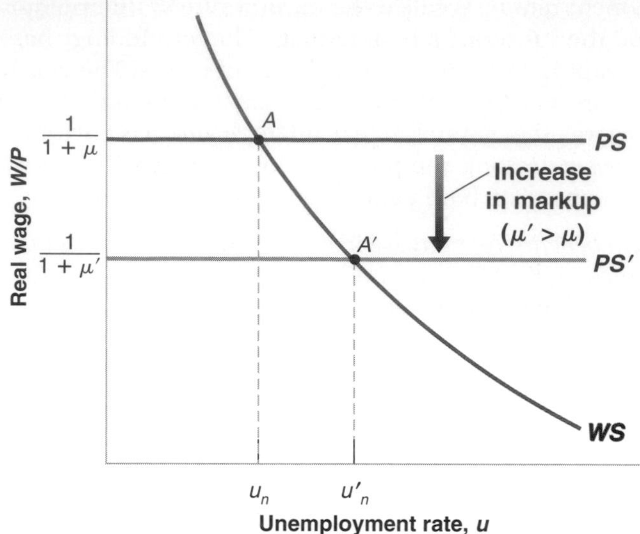

This name has been suggested by Edmund Phelps, of Columbia University. For more on Phelps's contributions, see Chapters 8 and 27.

the structure of the economy. For that reason, a better name for the equilibrium rate of unemployment would be the **structural rate of unemployment**, but so far, the name has not caught on.

From Unemployment to Employment

Associated with the natural rate of unemployment is a **natural level of employment**, the level of employment that prevails when unemployment is equal to its natural rate.

Let's review the relation between unemployment, employment, and the labor force. Let U denote unemployment, N denote employment, and L the labor force. Then,

$$u \equiv \frac{U}{L} = \frac{L-N}{L} = 1 - \frac{N}{L}$$

The first step follows from the definition of the unemployment rate u. The second follows from the fact that, from the definition of the labor force, the level of unemployment, U, equals the labor force, L, minus employment, N. The third step follows from simplifying the fraction. Putting all three steps together, the unemployment rate, u, equals 1 minus the ratio of employment, N, to the labor force, L.

Rearranging to get employment in terms of the labor force and the unemployment rate gives

$$N = L(1-u)$$

Employment, N, is equal to the labor force, L, times 1 minus the unemployment rate, u.

So, if the natural rate of unemployment is u_n, and the labor force is equal to L, the natural level of employment, N_n, is given by:

$$N_n = L(1-u_n)$$

For example, if the labor force is 100 million and the natural rate of unemployment is 5%, then the natural level of employment is 95 million.

From Employment to Output

Finally, associated with the natural level of employment is a **natural level of output**, the level of production when employment is equal to the natural level of employment.

Given the production function we have been using in this chapter ($Y = N$), the relation takes the simple form. The natural level of output Y_n is given by

$$Y_n = N_n = L(1 - u_n)$$

For use in the next chapter, note that, using equation (6.7) and the relations between the unemployment rate, employment, and output we just derived, the natural level of output satisfies

$$F\left(1 - \frac{Y_n}{L}, z\right) = \frac{1}{1+\mu} \qquad (6.8)$$

The natural level of output (Y_n) is such that, at the associated rate of unemployment ($u_n = 1 - Y_n/L$), the real wage chosen in wage setting—the left side of equation (6.8)—is equal to the real wage implied by price setting—the right side of equation (6.8).

We have gone through many steps in this section. It is time to summarize: Suppose that the expected price level is equal to the actual price level. Then:

- The real wage chosen in wage setting is a decreasing function of the unemployment rate.
- The real wage implied by price setting is constant.
- Equilibrium in the labor market requires that the real wage chosen in wage setting be equal to the real wage implied by price setting. This determines the unemployment rate.
- This equilibrium unemployment rate is known as the natural rate of unemployment.
- Associated with the natural rate of unemployment is a natural level of employment, and a natural level of output.

6-6 Where We Go from Here

We have just seen how equilibrium in the labor market determines the rate of unemployment (we have called this equilibrium rate of unemployment the *natural rate of unemployment*), which in turn determines the level of output (we have called this level of output the *natural level of output*).

So, you may ask, what did we do in the previous three chapters? If equilibrium in the labor market determines the unemployment rate and, by implication, the level of output, why did we spend so much time looking at the goods and financial markets? What about our earlier conclusions that the level of output was determined by factors such as monetary policy, fiscal policy, consumer confidence, and so on—all factors which do not enter equation (6.8) and therefore do not affect the natural level of output?

The key to the answers is simple, yet important.

- We have derived the natural rate of unemployment, and the associated levels of employment and output, under two assumptions. First, we have assumed equilibrium in the labor market. Second, we have assumed that the price level was equal to the expected price level.
- There is no reason for the second assumption to be true in the *short run*. The price level may well turn out to be different from what was expected by wage setters when nominal wages were set. Hence, in the short run, there is no reason for unemployment to be equal to the natural rate, or for output to be equal to its natural level.

  As we shall see in the next chapter, the factors that determine movements in output *in the short run* are indeed the factors we focused on in the preceding

In the short run, the factors that determine movements in output are the factors we focused on in the preceding three chapters: monetary policy, fiscal policy, and so on.

In the medium run, output tends to return to the natural level, and the factors that determine output are the factors we have focused on in this chapter.

three chapters: monetary policy, fiscal policy, and so on. Your time (and mine) was not wasted.

- But expectations are unlikely to be systematically wrong (say, always too high, or always too low) forever. That is why, *in the medium run*, unemployment tends to return to the natural rate, and output tends to return to the natural level.

In the medium run, the factors that determine unemployment and output are the factors which appear in equations (6.7) and (6.8).

These, in short, are the answers to the questions asked in the first two paragraphs of this section. Developing these answers in detail will be our task in the next three chapters.

Summary

- The labor force is composed of those who are working (employed) or looking for work (unemployed). The unemployment rate is equal to the ratio of the number of unemployed to the number in the labor force. The participation rate is equal to the ratio of the labor force to the population of working age.
- The U.S. labor market is characterized by large flows between employment, unemployment, and "out of the labor force." Each month, on average, about 40% of the unemployed move out of unemployment, either to take a job or to drop out of the labor force.
- Unemployment is high in recessions, low in expansions. During periods of high unemployment, the probability of losing a job increases, and the probability of finding a job if unemployed decreases.
- Wages are set unilaterally by firms, or by bargaining between workers and firms. They depend negatively on the unemployment rate, and positively on the expected price level. The reason why wages depend on the expected price level is that they are typically set in nominal terms for some period of time. During that time, even if the price level turns out to be different from what was expected, wages are typically not readjusted.
- The price set by firms depends on the wage and on the markup of prices over wages. The higher the markup chosen by firms, the lower the real wage implied by price-setting decisions.
- Equilibrium in the labor market requires that the real wage chosen in wage setting be equal to the real wage implied by price setting. Under the additional assumption that the expected price level is equal to the actual price level, equilibrium in the labor market determines the unemployment rate. This unemployment rate is known as the *natural rate of unemployment.*
- In general, the actual price level may turn out to be different from the price level expected by wage setters. Therefore the unemployment rate need not be equal to the natural rate.
- The coming chapters will show that in the short run, unemployment and output are determined by the factors we focused on in the preceding three chapters, but that in the medium run, unemployment tends to return to the natural rate, and output tends to return to its natural level.

Key Terms

- noninstitutional civilian population, 114
- labor force; out of the labor force, 114
- participation rate, 114
- unemployment rate, 114
- separations, hires, 115
- Current Population Survey (CPS), 115
- quits, layoffs, 115
- duration of unemployment, 116
- discouraged workers, 116
- nonemployment rate, 116
- collective bargaining, 120
- reservation wage, 120
- bargaining power, 120
- efficiency wage theories, 121
- unemployment insurance, 123
- production function, 124
- labor productivity, 124
- markup, 124
- wage-setting relation, 125
- price-setting relation, 126
- natural rate of unemployment, 127
- structural rate of unemployment, 128
- natural level of employment, 128
- natural level of output, 128

Questions and Problems

Quick Check

1. *Using the information in this chapter, label each of the following statements* true, false, *or* uncertain. *Explain briefly.*
   a. Since 1950, the participation rate in the United States has remained roughly constant at 60%.
   b. Each month, the flows in and out of employment are very small compared to the size of the labor force.
   c. One third of all unemployed workers exit the unemployment pool each year.
   d. The unemployment rate tends to be high in recessions, low in expansions.
   e. Most workers are typically paid their reservation wage.
   f. Workers who do not belong to unions have no bargaining power.
   g. It may be in the best interest of employers to pay wages higher than their workers' reservation wage.
   h. The natural rate of unemployment is unaffected by policy changes.

2. *Answer the following questions using the information provided in this chapter.*
   a. As a percentage of the employed workers, what is the size of the flows in and out of employment (i.e., hires and separations) each month?
   b. As a percentage of the unemployed workers, what is the size of the flows from unemployment into employment each month?
   c. As a percentage of the unemployed, what is the size of the total flows out of unemployment each month? What is the average duration of unemployment?
   d. As a percentage of the labor force, what is the size of the total flows in and out of the labor force each month?
   e. What percentage of the flows in the labor force is due to new workers entering the labor force?

3. *The natural rate of unemployment*

   Suppose that the firms' markup over costs is 5%, and the wage-setting equation is $W = P(1 - u)$, where u is the unemployment rate.
   a. What is the real wage as determined by the price-setting equation?
   b. What is the natural rate of unemployment?
   c. Suppose that the markup of prices over costs increases to 10%. What happens to the natural rate of unemployment? Explain the logic behind your answer.

Dig Deeper

4. *Reservation wages*

   In the mid-1980s, a famous supermodel once said that she would not get out of bed for less than $10,000 (presumably per day).
   a. What is your own reservation wage?
   b. Did your first job pay more than your reservation wage at the time?
   c. Relative to your reservation wage at the time you accept each job, which job pays more: your first one or the one you expect to have in 10 years?
   d. Explain your answers in terms of the efficiency wage theory.

5. *Bargaining power and wage determination*

   Even in the absence of collective bargaining, workers do have some bargaining power that allows them to receive wages higher than their reservation wage. Each worker's bargaining power depends both on the nature of his job and on the economy-wide labor market conditions. Let's consider each factor in turn.
   a. Compare the job of a delivery person and a computer network administrator. In which of these jobs does a worker have more bargaining power? Why?
   b. For any given job, how do labor market conditions affect the worker's bargaining power? Which labor market variable would you look at to assess labor market conditions?

Explore Further

6. *Unemployment spells and long-term unemployment*

   According to the data presented in this chapter, about one out of every three unemployed workers leaves unemployment each month.
   a. What is the probability a worker will still be unemployed after one month? Two months? Six months?
   b. If we look at the unemployment pool at one point in time, what proportion of the unemployed will have been unemployed for six months or more?
   c. Using Table B44 of the Economic Report of the President (**www.access.gpo.gov/eop/**), look for the proportion of unemployed who have been unemployed 6 months or more (27 weeks or more). Compute the average proportion for the 1990s. Does the number correspond to the answer obtained in (b)? Can you guess what may cause the difference between the two? (*Hint*: Suppose that the probability of exiting unemployment goes down with how long you have been unemployed.)

7. *Go to the Web site maintained by the U.S. Bureau of Labor Statistics at the address (***stats.bls.gov***). Look under the link "Economy at a glance."*
   a. What are the latest monthly data on the size of the U.S. civilian labor force, on the number of unemployed, and on the unemployment rate?
   b. How many people are employed?
   c. Compute the change in the number of unemployed from the first number in the table to the most recent month in the table. Do the same for the number of employed workers. Is the decline in unemployment equal to the increase in employment? Explain in words.

Further Reading

A further discussion of unemployment along the lines of this chapter is given by Richard Layard, Stephen Nickell, and Richard Jackman in *The Unemployment Crisis* (Oxford: Oxford University Press, 1994).

We invite you to visit the Balanchard page on the Prentice Hall Web site at:
www.prenhall.com/blanchard
for this chapter's World Wide Web exercises

Appendix: Wage- and Price-Setting Relations Versus Labor Supply and Labor Demand

In your microeconomics course, you probably saw a representation of labor-market equilibrium in terms of labor supply and labor demand. You may therefore be asking yourself: How does the representation in terms of wage setting and price setting relate to the representation of the labor market I saw in my microeconomics course?

In an important sense, the two representations are similar:

To see why, let's redraw Figure 6-6, but in terms of the real wage and the level of *employment* (rather than the unemployment rate). We do this in Figure A6-1.

Employment, N, is measured on the horizontal axis. The level of employment must be somewhere between zero and L, the labor force: Employment cannot exceed the number of people available for work, the labor force. For any employment level, N, unemployment is given by $U = L - N$. Knowing that, we can measure unemployment by starting from L and moving to the left on the horizontal axis: Unemployment is given by the distance between L and N. The lower is employment, N, the higher is unemployment, and by implication the higher is the unemployment rate, u.

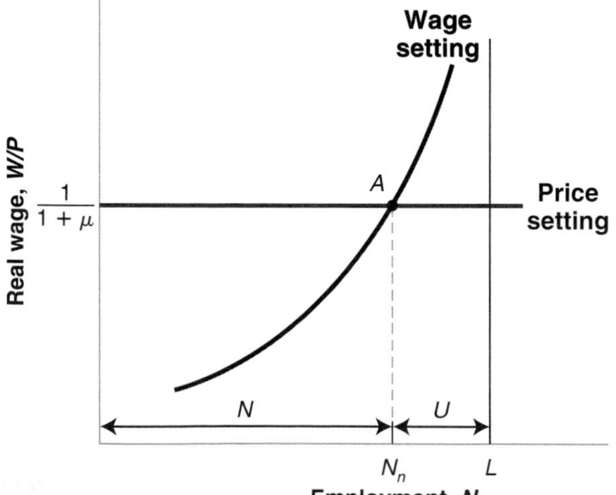

Figure A6-1 *Wage Setting and Price Setting and the Natural Level of Employment*

Let's now draw the wage-setting and price-setting relations, and characterize the equilibrium:

- An increase in employment (a movement to the right along the horizontal axis) implies a decrease in unemployment, and so an increase in the real wage chosen in wage setting. Thus, the wage-setting relation is now *upward sloping*: Higher employment implies a higher real wage.
- The price-setting relation is still a horizontal line at $W/P = 1/(1 + \mu)$.
- The equilibrium is given by point A, with "natural" employment level N_n (and an implied natural unemployment rate equal to $u_n = (L - N_n)/L$).

In this figure the wage-setting relation looks like a labor-supply relation. As the level of employment increases, the real wage paid to workers increases as well. For that reason, the wage-setting relation is sometimes called the "labor supply" relation (in quotes).

What we have called the price-setting relation looks like a flat labor-demand relation. The reason it is flat rather than downward sloping has to do with our simplifying assumption of constant returns to labor in production. Had we assumed, more conventionally, that there were decreasing returns to labor in production, our price-setting curve would, like the standard labor-demand curve, be downward sloping: As employment increased, the marginal cost of production would increase, forcing firms to increase their price given the wage. In other words, the real wage implied by price setting would decrease as employment increased.

But, in a number of ways, the two approaches are different:

- The standard labor-supply relation gives the wage at which a given number of workers are willing to work: The higher the wage, the larger the number of workers who are willing to work.

  In contrast, the wage corresponding to a given level of employment in the wage-setting relation is the result of a process of bargaining between workers and firms, or unilateral wage setting by firms. Factors such as the structure of collective bargaining or the use of wages to deter quits affect the wage-setting relation. They seem to play an important role in reality. Yet they play no role in the standard labor-supply relation.

- The standard labor-demand relation gives the level of employment chosen by firms at a given real wage. It is derived under the assumption that firms operate in competitive goods and labor markets and therefore take wages and prices—and, by implication, the real wage—as given.

  In contrast, the price-setting relation takes into account the fact that in most markets firms actually set prices. Factors such as the degree of competition in the goods market affect the price setting relation by affecting the markup; these factors have no place in the standard labor-demand relation.
- While the labor-supply/labor-demand framework generates unemployment in equilibrium, those who are unemployed are *willingly unemployed*: At the equilibrium real wage, they prefer to be unemployed rather than work.

  In contrast, in the wage-setting/price-setting framework, unemployment is likely to be involuntary. In the efficiency wage interpretation we saw in the text, for example, firms pay a wage above the reservation wage, and thus workers would rather be employed than unemployed. Yet, in equilibrium, there is unemployment. Those who are unemployed are not indifferent. They would rather be working than be unemployed. This also seems to capture reality better than does the labor-supply/labor-demand framework.

These are the three reasons why I have relied on the wage-setting and the price-setting relations rather than on the labor-supply/labor-demand approach to characterize labor market equilibrium in this chapter.

Putting All Markets Together: The *AS-AD* Model

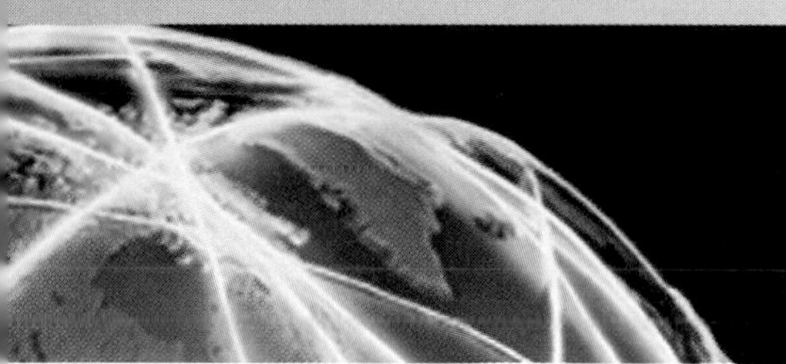

We looked in Chapter 5 at the determination of output in the short run. We looked in Chapter 6 at the determination of output in the medium run. We are now ready to put the two together, and look at the determination of output in the short and the medium run.

To do so, we use the equilibrium conditions for *all* the markets we have looked at so far—the goods and financial markets in Chapter 5, the labor market in Chapter 6. Then, using these equilibrium conditions, we derive two relations:

- One, which we call the *aggregate supply relation,* captures the implications of equilibrium in the labor market; it builds on what you saw in Chapter 6.

- The other, which we call the *aggregate demand relation,* captures the implications of equilibrium in both the goods market and financial markets; it builds on what you saw in Chapter 5.

Combining these two relations gives us the *AS-AD* model (for aggregate supply–aggregate demand). This chapter presents the basic version of the model. When confronted with a macroeconomic question, it is the version I typically use to organize my thoughts. For some questions, however (in particular for the study of inflation), the basic *AS-AD* model must be extended—this is what we shall do in the next two chapters.

This chapter is organized as follows:

- Section 7-1 derives the aggregate supply relation and Section 7-2 derives the aggregate demand relation.

- Section 7-3 combines the two to characterize equilibrium output in the short run and in the medium run.

- Sections 7-4 to 7-6 show how we can use the model to look at the dynamic effects of monetary policy, of fiscal policy, and of changes in the price of oil.

- Section 7-7 summarizes. ■

7-1 Aggregate Supply

The **aggregate supply relation** captures the effects of output on the price level. It is derived from the behavior of wages and prices we described in Chapter 6.

Recall the equations for wage determination (equation [6.1]), and for price determination (equation [6.3]) we derived in Chapter 6:

$$W = P^e F(u,z)$$
$$P = (1+\mu)W$$

- The nominal wage, W, set by wage setters, depends on the expected price level, P^e, on the unemployment rate, u, and on the catchall variable, z, which stands for all the other factors that affect wage determination, from unemployment benefits to the form of collective bargaining.
- The price, P, set by firms (equivalently, the price level) is equal to the nominal wage, W, times 1 plus the markup, μ.

In Section 6-5 we used these two relations together with the additional assumption that the price level was equal to the expected price level. Under this additional assumption, we derived the natural rate of unemployment and, by implication, the natural level of output.

The difference in this chapter is that we do not impose this additional assumption (it will turn out that the price level is equal to the expected price level in the medium run, but will typically not be equal to the expected price level in the short run). Without this additional assumption, the price-setting relation and the wage-setting relation give us a relation, which we now derive, between the *price level*, the *output level*, and the *expected price level*.

- The first step is to eliminate the nominal wage, W, between the two equations. Replacing the nominal wage in the second equation above by its expression from the first gives:

$$P = P^e(1+\mu)F(u,z) \qquad (7.1)$$

  This tells us that the price level, P, depends on the expected price level, P^e, on the unemployment rate, u (as well as on the markup, μ, and on the catchall variable, z; but we shall take both μ and z as constant here).
- The second step is to replace the unemployment rate, u, by its expression in terms of output. To replace u, recall the relation between the unemployment rate, employment, and output we derived in Chapter 6:

$$u = \frac{U}{L} = \frac{L-N}{L} = 1 - \frac{N}{L} = 1 - \frac{Y}{L}$$

The first equality, $u = U/L$, follows from the definition of the unemployment rate. The second equality, $U/L = (L-N)/L$, follows from the definition of unemployment ($U \equiv L-N$). The third equality, $(L-N)/L = 1-(N/L)$, just simplifies the fraction. The fourth equality, $1-(N/L) = 1-(Y/L)$, follows from the specification of the production function, which says that to produce one unit of output requires one worker, so that $Y = N$.

What we get then is

$$u = 1 - \frac{Y}{L}$$

In words: For a given labor force, the higher is output, the lower is the unemployment rate.

Replacing u by $1-(Y/L)$ in equation (7.1) gives us the *aggregate supply relation*, or *AS relation for short*:

A better name would be "the labor market relation." But, because the relation looks graphically like a supply curve (there is a positive relation between output and the price), it is called "the aggregate supply relation." I shall follow tradition. But be aware: The aggregate supply curve is very different from a regular supply curve.

$$P = P^e(1+\mu)F\left(1-\frac{Y}{L}, z\right) \tag{7.2}$$

The price level, P, depends on the expected price level, P^e, and on the level of output, Y (and also on the markup, μ, on the catchall variable, z, and on the labor force, L; but we take them as constant here).

The *AS* relation has two important properties:

- *An increase in output leads to an increase in the price level.* This is the result of four underlying steps: ◀ $Y\uparrow \Rightarrow P\uparrow$

  1. An increase in output leads to an increase in employment. ◀ $Y\uparrow \Rightarrow N\uparrow$
  2. The increase in employment leads to a decrease in unemployment, so to a decrease in the unemployment rate. ◀ $N\uparrow \Rightarrow u\downarrow$
  3. The lower unemployment rate leads to an increase in the nominal wage. ◀ $u\downarrow \Rightarrow W\uparrow$
  4. The increase in the nominal wage leads to an increase in the price set by firms—equivalently, an increase in the price level. ◀ $W\uparrow \Rightarrow P\uparrow$

- *An increase in the expected price level leads, one for one, to an increase in the actual price level.* For example, if the expected price level doubles, then the price level will also double. This effect works through wages: ◀ $P^e\uparrow \Rightarrow P\uparrow$

  1. If wage setters expect the price level to be higher, they set a higher nominal wage. ◀ $P^e\uparrow \Rightarrow W\uparrow$
  2. The increase in the nominal wage leads to an increase in costs, which leads to an increase in the price set by firms—equivalently, a higher price level. ◀ $W\uparrow \Rightarrow P\uparrow$

The relation between the price level, P, and output, Y, for a given value of the expected price level, P^e, is represented by the curve *AS* in Figure 7-1. The *AS* curve has three properties which will prove useful in what follows:

- *The aggregate supply curve is upward sloping.* Put another way, an increase in output, Y, leads to an increase in the price level, P. You saw why earlier.

An informal way of saying the same thing: High economic activity puts pressure on prices.

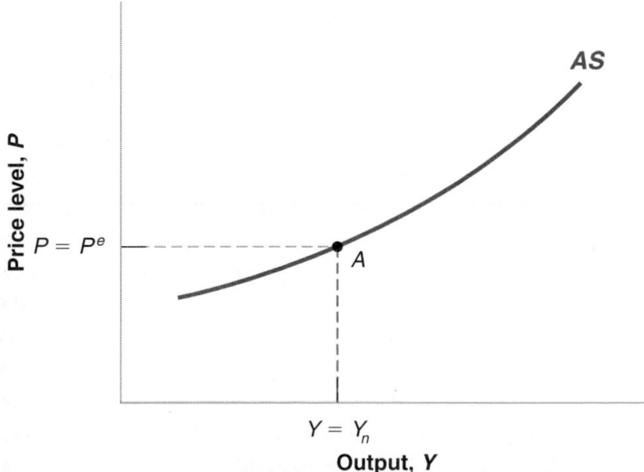

Figure 7-1

The Aggregate Supply Curve

Given the expected price level, an increase in output leads to an increase in the price level. If output is equal to the natural level of output, the price level is equal to the expected price level.

- *The aggregate supply curve goes through point A, where $Y = Y_n$ and $P = P^e$. Put another way, when output, Y, is equal to the natural level of output, Y_n, the price level, P, turns out to exactly equal the expected price level, P^e.*

  How do we know this? From the definition of the natural level of output in Chapter 6. Recall, we defined the natural rate of unemployment (and, by implication, the natural level of output) as the rate of unemployment (and, by implication, the level of output) that prevails if the price level and the expected price level are equal.

  This property—that the price level equals the expected price level when output is equal to the natural level of output—has two straightforward implications:

  When output is above the natural level of output, the price level is higher than expected. In Figure 7-1, if Y is to the right of Y_n, P is higher than P^e.

  Conversely, when output is below the natural level of output, the price level is lower than expected. In Figure 7-1, if Y is to the left of Y_n, P is lower than P^e.
- *An increase in the expected price level P^e shifts the aggregate supply curve up. Conversely, a decrease in the expected price level shifts the aggregate supply curve down.*

This third property is shown in Figure 7-2. Suppose the expected price level increases from P^e to P'^e. At a given level of output, and so at a given unemployment rate, the increase in the expected price level leads to an increase in wages, leading in turn to an increase in prices. So at any level of output, the price level is higher: The aggregate supply curve shifts up. In particular, instead of going through point A (where $Y = Y_n$ and $P = P^e$), the aggregate supply curve now goes through point A' (where $Y = Y_n$, $P = P'^e$).

Recall that when output equals the natural level of output, the price level turns out to be equal to the expected price level.

To summarize:

- Starting from wage determination and price determination in the labor market, we have derived the *aggregate supply relation.*
- This relation implies that for a given expected price level, the price level is an increasing function of the level of output, and of the expected price level. It is represented by an upward-sloping curve, called the *aggregate supply curve.*
- Increases in the expected price level shift the aggregate supply curve up; decreases in the expected price level shift the aggregate supply curve down.

Figure 7-2

The Effect of an Increase in the Expected Price Level on the Aggregate Supply Curve

An increase in the expected price level shifts the aggregate supply curve up.

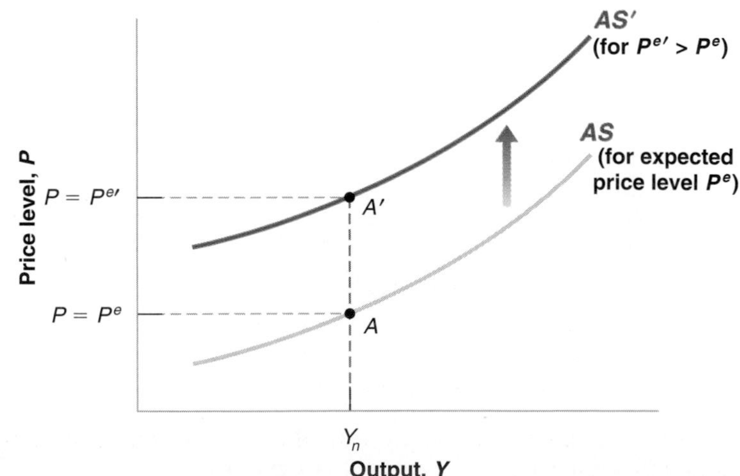

7-2 Aggregate Demand

The **aggregate demand relation** captures the effect of the price level on output. It is derived from the equilibrium conditions in the goods and financial markets.

Start with the description of equilibrium in the goods and financial markets (the *IS-LM* model) you saw in equations (5.2) and (5.3) of Chapter 5:

$$\text{Goods market} \qquad IS: \; Y = C(Y-T) + I(Y, i) + G$$

$$\text{Financial markets} \qquad LM: \; \frac{M}{P} = Y\,L(i)$$

- Equilibrium in the goods market requires that output equal the demand for goods—the sum of consumption, investment, and government spending. This is the *IS* relation.
- Equilibrium in financial markets requires that the supply of money equal the demand for money. This is the *LM* relation.

  Note that what appears on the left side of the *LM* equation is the real money stock, M/P. We focused in Chapter 5 on changes in the real money stock that came from changes in nominal money, M. But changes in the real money stock, M/P, can also come from changes in the price level, P. An increase of 10% in the price level, P, has the same effect on the real money stock as a 10% decrease in the stock of nominal money, M: Either leads to a 10% decrease in the real money stock.

Using the *IS* and the *LM* relations, we can derive the relation between the price level and the level of output implied by equilibrium in the goods and financial markets. We do this in Figure 7-3.

- Figure 7-3, panel (a) draws the *IS* curve and the *LM* curve. The *IS* curve is drawn for given values of G and T. It is downward sloping: An increase in the interest rate leads to a decrease in output. The *LM* curve is drawn for a given value of M/P. It is upward sloping: An increase in output increases the demand for money, and the interest rate increases so as to maintain equality of money demand and the (unchanged) money supply. The point at which the goods market and the financial markets are both in equilibrium is at the intersection of the *IS* curve and the *LM* curve, at point A.

  Now consider the effects of an increase in the price level from P to P'. Given the stock of nominal money, M, the increase in the price level, P, decreases the real money stock, M/P. This implies that the *LM* curve shifts up: At a given level of output, the lower real money stock leads to an increase in the interest rate. The economy moves along the *IS* curve. The equilibrium moves from A to A'; the interest rate increases from i to i', and output decreases from Y to Y'. In short, the increase in the price level leads to a decrease in output.

  In words: The increase in the price level leads to a decrease in the real money stock, which leads to an increase in the interest rate. The increase in the interest rate leads to a decrease in the demand for goods and to a decrease in output.
- The implied negative relation between output and the price level is drawn as the downward-sloping curve *AD* in Figure 7-3, panel (b). Points A and A' in Figure 7-3, panel (b) correspond to points A and A' in Figure 7-3, panel (a). An increase in the price level from P to P' leads to a decrease in output from Y to Y'. This curve is called the *aggregate demand curve*. The underlying negative relation between output and the price level is called the *aggregate demand relation*.

A better name would be "the goods market and financial markets relation." But, because it is a long name, and because the relation looks graphically like a demand curve (i.e., a negative relation between output and the price), it is called the "aggregate demand relation." I shall follow tradition. But again be aware: The aggregate demand curve is very different from a regular demand curve.

Any variable other than the price level that shifts either the IS curve or the LM curve also shifts the aggregate demand relation.

The Derivation of the Aggregate Demand Curve

(a)

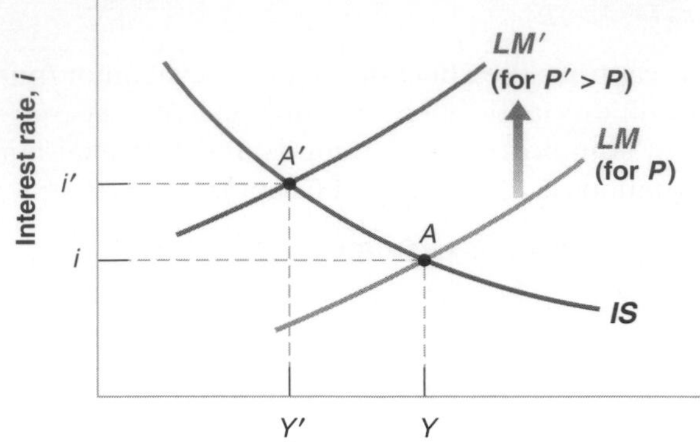

An increase in the price level leads to a decrease in output.

(b)

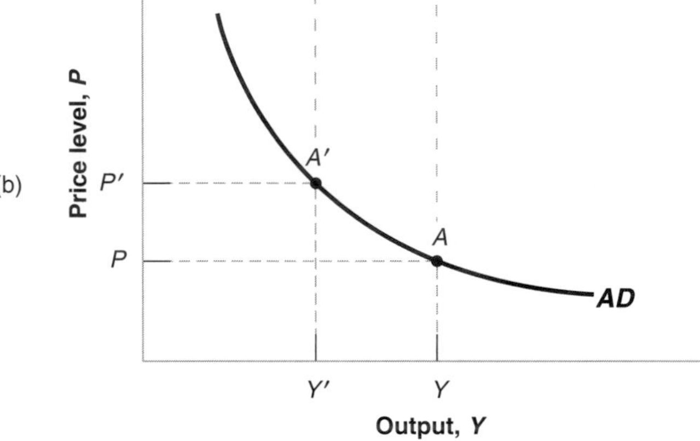

Take, for example, an increase in government spending G. At a given price level, the level of output implied by equilibrium in the goods and the financial markets is higher: In Figure 7-4, the aggregate demand curve shifts to the right, from AD to AD'.

Recall that a contractionary open-market operation is a decrease in nominal money, M, through the sales of bonds by the central bank.

Or take a contractionary open-market operation—a decrease in M. At a given price level, the level of output implied by equilibrium in the goods and the financial markets is lower. In Figure 7-4, the aggregate demand curve shifts to the left, from AD to AD''.

Let's represent what you have learned by the following aggregate demand relation:

$$Y = Y\left(\frac{M}{P},\ G,\ T\right) \qquad (7.3)$$
$$(+,\quad +,\quad -)$$

Output, Y, is an increasing function of the real money stock, M/P, an increasing function of government spending, G, and a decreasing function of taxes, T.

Given monetary and fiscal policy—that is, given M, G, and T—an increase in the price level, P, leads to a decrease in the real money stock, M/P, which leads to a decrease in output. This is the relation captured by the AD curve back in Figure 7-3, panel (b).

$P\uparrow \Rightarrow Y\downarrow$

To summarize:

- Starting from the equilibrium conditions for the goods and financial markets, we have derived the *aggregate demand relation.*

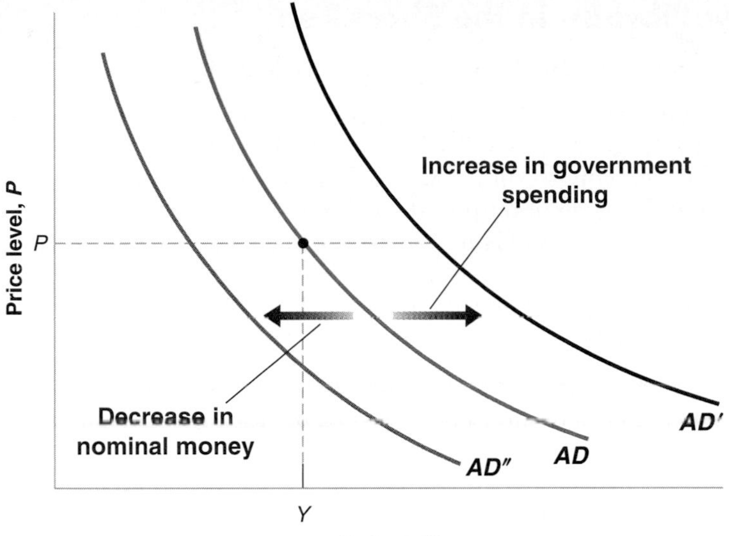

Figure 7-4

Shifts of the Aggregate Demand Curve

An increase in government spending increases output at a given price level, shifting the aggregate demand curve to the right. A decrease in nominal money decreases output at a given price level, shifting the aggregate demand curve to the left.

- This relation implies that the level of output is a decreasing function of the price level. It is represented by a downward-sloping curve, called the *aggregate demand curve.*
- Changes in monetary or fiscal policy—or more generally in any variable, other than the price level, that shifts the *IS* or the *LM* curves—shift the aggregate demand curve.

7-3 Equilibrium in the Short Run and in the Medium Run

We now put together the *AS* and the *AD* relations. From Sections 7-1 and 7-2, the two relations are given by

$$AS \textbf{ relation} \qquad P = P^e(1+\mu)F\left(1-\frac{Y}{L}, z\right)$$

$$AD \textbf{ relation} \qquad Y = Y\left(\frac{M}{P}, G, T\right)$$

For a given value of the expected price level, P^e, (which enters the aggregate supply relation), and for given values of the monetary and fiscal policy variables *M*, *G*, and *T* (which enter the aggregate demand relation), these two relations determine the equilibrium values of output, *Y*, and the price level, *P*.

Note the equilibrium clearly depends on the value of P^e. The value of P^e determines the position of the aggregate supply curve (go back to Figure 7-2), and the position of the aggregate supply curve affects the equilibrium. In the short run, we can take P^e, the price level expected by wage setters when they last set wages, as given. But, over time, P^e is likely to change, shifting the aggregate supply curve, and changing the equilibrium. With this in mind, we first characterize equilibrium in the short run—that is, taking P^e as given. We then look at how P^e changes over time, and how that change affects the equilibrium.

Equilibrium in the Short Run

The short-run equilibrium is characterized in Figure 7-5:

- The aggregate supply curve, *AS*, drawn for a given value of P^e, is upward sloping: The higher the level of output, the higher the price level. The position of the curve depends on P^e. Recall from Section 7-1 that when output is equal to the natural level of output, the price level is equal to the expected price level. This implies that, in Figure 7-5, the aggregate supply curve goes through point *B*: If $Y = Y_n$, then $P = P^e$.
- The aggregate demand curve, *AD*, drawn for given values of *M*, *G*, and *T*, is downward sloping: The higher the price level, the lower the level of output.

The equilibrium is given by the intersection of the *AS* and *AD* curves at point *A*. By construction, at point *A*, the goods market, the financial markets, and the labor market are *all* in equilibrium. That the labor market is in equilibrium comes from the fact that point *A* is on the aggregate supply curve. That goods and financial markets are in equilibrium comes from the fact that point *A* is on the aggregate demand curve. The equilibrium level of output and price level are given by *Y* and *P*.

There is no reason why, in general, equilibrium output *Y* should be equal to the natural level of output, Y_n. Equilibrium output depends both on the position of the aggregate supply curve—thus on the value of P^e—and on the position of the aggregate demand curve—thus on the values of *M*, *G*, and *T*. As I have drawn the two curves, *Y* is greater than Y_n: The equilibrium level of output exceeds the natural level of output. But I could clearly have drawn the *AS* and the *AD* curves so equilibrium output, *Y* was smaller than the natural level of output, Y_n.

Figure 7-5 gives our first result: In the *short run*, there is no reason why output should equal the natural level of output. It all depends on the specific values of the expected price level, and the values of the variables affecting the position of aggregate demand.

So, we must now ask: What happens over time? More specifically, suppose, in the short run, output is above the natural level of output—as is the case in Figure 7-5. Will output eventually return to the natural level of output? If so, how? These are the questions we take up in the rest of the section.

Figure 7-5

The Short-Run Equilibrium

The equilibrium is given by the intersection of the aggregate supply curve and the aggregate demand curve. At point *A*, the labor market, the goods market, and financial markets are all in equilibrium.

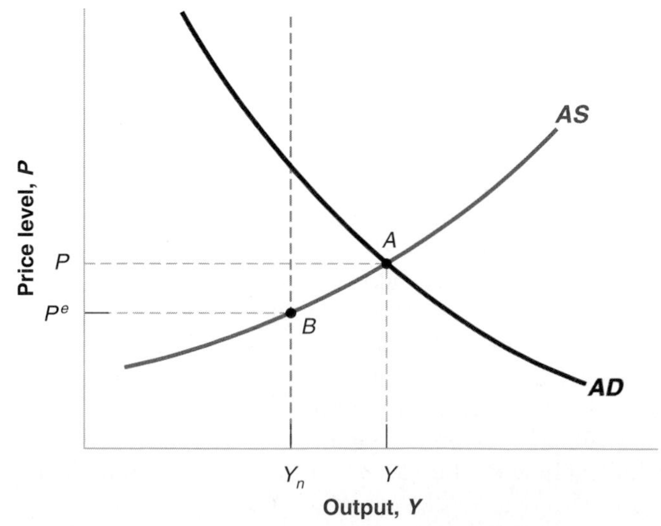

From the Short Run to the Medium Run

To think about what happens over time, consider Figure 7-6. The curves denoted *AS* and *AD* are the same as in Figure 7-5, and so the short-run equilibrium is at point *A*—which corresponds to point *A* in Figure 7-5. Output is equal to *Y*, and is higher than the natural level of output Y_n.

- At point *A*, output exceeds the natural level of output. So we know from Section 7-1 that the price level is higher than the expected price level—higher than the price level wage setters expected when they set nominal wages.

  The fact that the price level is higher than wage setters expected is likely to lead wage setters to revise upwards their expectations of what the price level will be in the future. So, next time they set nominal wages, they are likely to make that decision based on a higher expected price level, say, based on $P^{e\prime}$, where $P^{e\prime} > P^e$.

  This increase in the expected price level implies that, next period, the aggregate supply curve shifts up, from *AS* to *AS′*: At a given level of output, wage setters expect a higher price level. So they set a higher nominal wage, which in turn leads firms to set a higher price. The price level increases.

  This upward shift in the *AS* curve implies that the economy moves up along the *AD* curve. The equilibrium moves from *A* to *A′*. Equilibrium output decreases from *Y* to *Y′*.

  In words: The fact that output initially exceeds the natural level of output leads to an increase in the expected price level. This expectation leads to an increase in nominal wages, which leads to an increase in the price level. This higher price level leads to a decrease in the real money stock. The interest rate increases, leading to a decrease in output.
- The adjustment does not end at point *A′*. At point *A′*, output *Y′* still exceeds the natural level of output Y_n, so the price level is still higher than the expected price level. Wage setters are likely to continue to revise upwards their expectation of the price level.

  This implies that so long as equilibrium output exceeds the natural level of output Y_n, the expected price level increases, shifting the *AS* curve upward. As the

If you live in an economy where the inflation rate is typically positive, then, even if the price level this year turns out equal to what you expected, you may still take into account the presence of inflation and expect the price level to be higher next year. In this chapter, we look at an economy in which there is no steady inflation. We shall focus on the dynamics of output and inflation in the next two chapters.

There are many steps here:
- **A higher expected price level leads to a higher price level.**
- **A higher price level leads to a lower real money stock.**
- **A lower real money stock leads to a higher interest rate.**
- **A higher interest rate leads to a lower demand for goods, and so to a decrease in output.**

Fear not: You will have more opportunities to think about these steps in the next three sections.

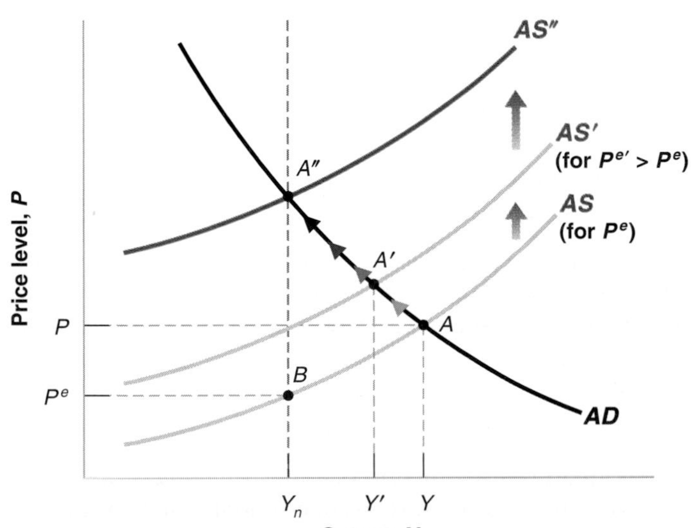

Figure 7-6

The Adjustment of Output over Time

If output is above the natural level of output, the *AS* curve shifts up over time, until output has decreased back to the natural level of output.

ACTIVE GRAPH

AS curve shifts upward and the economy moves up along the *AD* curve, equilibrium output continues to decrease.

Does this adjustment eventually come to an end? Yes. It ends when the *AS* curve has shifted all the way to *AS″*, when the equilibrium has moved all the way to *A″*, and the equilibrium level of output is equal to Y_n. At *A″*, equilibrium output is equal to the natural level of output, so the price level is equal to the expected price level. Wage setters have no reason to change their expectations; the *AS* curve no longer shifts, and the economy stays at *A″*.

In words: So long as output exceeds the natural level of output, the price level exceeds the expected price level. This leads wage setters to revise their expectations of the price level upward, leading to an increase in the price level. The increase in the price level leads to a decrease in the real money stock, which leads to an increase in the interest rate, which leads to a decrease in output. The adjustment stops when output is equal to the natural level of output. At that point, the price level is equal to the expected price level, expectations no longer change, and so, output remains at the natural level of output. Put another way, in the *medium run*, output returns to the natural level of output.

- We have looked at the dynamics of adjustment starting from a case in which initial output was higher than the natural level of output. Clearly, a symmetric argument holds when initial output is below the natural level of output. In this case, the price level is lower than the expected price level, leading wage setters to lower their expectations of the price level. Lower expectations of the price level lead the *AS* curve to shift down, and the economy to move down the *AD* curve until output has increased back to the natural level of output.

To summarize:

Short run $Y \neq Y_n$ ▶

- In the *short run*, output can be above or below the natural level of output. Changes in any of the variables that enter either the aggregate supply relation or the aggregate demand relation lead to changes in output and to changes in the price level.

Medium run $Y \rightarrow Y_n$ ▶

- In the *medium run*, output eventually returns to the natural level of output. The adjustment works through changes in the price level. When output is above the natural level of output, the price level increases. The higher price level leads to a decrease in demand and output. When output is below the natural level of output, the price level decreases, increasing demand and output.

In the rest of the chapter, we use the *AS-AD* model to look at the dynamic effects of changes in policy or in the economic environment. We focus on three such changes. The first two are old favorites by now: an open-market operation, which changes the stock of nominal money, and a decrease in the budget deficit. The third, which we could not examine until we had developed a theory of wage and price determination, is an increase in the price of oil. Each of these changes is interesting in its own right:

- Monetary policy was responsible for the recession of 1980–1982.
- Budget deficit reduction made headlines throughout the 1990s.
- Increases in the price of oil were the main cause of the 1973–1975 recession.

7-4 The Effects of a Monetary Expansion

We take up the more difficult question of the effects of a change in the rate of growth of money—rather than a change in the level of money—in the next two chapters. ▶

What are the short-run and medium-run effects of an expansionary monetary policy, say, of an increase in the level of nominal money from *M* to *M′*?

The Dynamics of Adjustment

Look at Figure 7-7. Assume that before the change in nominal money, output is at the natural level of output, so aggregate demand and aggregate supply cross at point A, the level of output equals Y_n, and the price level equals P.

Now consider an increase in nominal money. Recall the specification of aggregate demand from equation (7.3):

$$Y = Y\left(\frac{M}{P}, G, T\right)$$

For a given price level, P, the increase in nominal money, M, leads to an increase in the real money stock, M/P, leading to an increase in output. The aggregate demand curve shifts to the right, from AD to AD'. In the short run, the economy goes from A to A'. Output increases from Y_n to Y'; the price level increases from P to P'.

We think of shifts in the *AD* curve as shifts to the right or to the left because we think of the *AD* relation as telling us what output is for a given price level. We then ask: At a given price level, does output increase (a shift to the right), or decrease (a shift to the left)?

We think of shifts in the *AS* curve as shifts up or down because we think of the *AS* relation as telling us what the price level is for a given level of output. We then ask: At a given output level, does the price level increase (a shift up), or decrease (a shift down)?

Over time, the adjustment of price expectations comes into play. As output is higher than the natural level of output, the price level is higher than wage setters expected. They revise their expectations, leading the aggregate supply curve to shift up over time. The economy moves up along the aggregate demand curve AD'. The adjustment process stops when output has returned to the natural level of output. At that point, the price level is equal to the expected price level. In the medium run, the aggregate supply curve is given by AS'', and the economy is at point A'': Output is back to Y_n, and the price level is equal to P''.

We can actually pin down the exact size of the eventual increase in the price level. If output is back to the natural level of output, the real money stock must also be back to its initial value. In other words, the proportional increase in prices must be equal to the proportional increase in the nominal money stock: If the initial increase in nominal money is equal to 10%, then the price level ends up 10% higher than it was initially.

Look at the equation above. If *Y* is unchanged (and *G* and *T* are also unchanged), then *M/P* must also be unchanged.

If *M/P* is unchanged, it must be that *M* and *P* increase in the same proportion.

Going Behind the Scenes

To get a better sense of what is going on, it is useful to go behind the scenes and look at what happens not only to output and to the price level, but also what happens to the interest rate. We can do this by looking at what happens in terms of the *IS-LM* model.

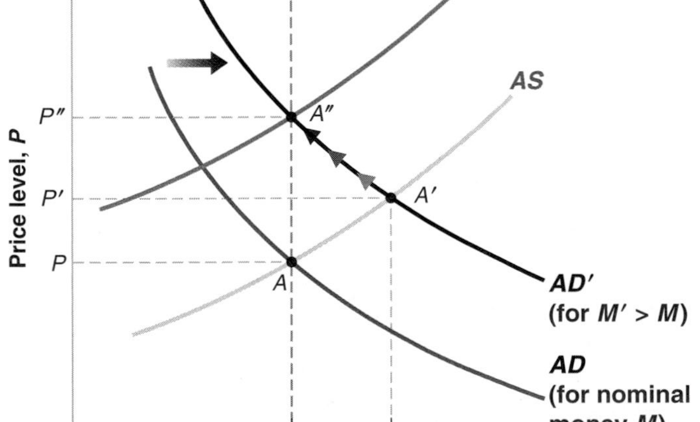

Figure 7-7

The Dynamic Effects of a Monetary Expansion

A monetary expansion leads to an increase in output in the short run, but has no effect on output in the medium run.

Figure 7-8, panel (a) reproduces Figure 7-7 (although leaving out the *AS″* curve to keep things visually simple), and shows the adjustment of output and the price level in response to the increase in nominal money. Figure 7-8, panel (b) shows the adjustment of output and the interest rate, by looking at the same adjustment process, but in terms of the *IS-LM* model.

Look at Figure 7-8, panel (b). Before the change in nominal money, the equilibrium is given by the intersection of the *IS* and *LM* curves, at point *A*—which corresponds to point *A* in Figure 7-8, panel (a). Output is equal to the natural level of output, Y_n, and the interest rate is given by *i*.

The short-run effect of the monetary expansion is to shift the *LM* curve down from *LM* to *LM′*, moving the equilibrium from point *A* to point *A′*—which corresponds to point *A′* in Figure 7-8, panel (a). The interest rate is lower, output is higher.

There are two effects at work behind the shift from *LM* to *LM′*: One is due to the increase in nominal money. The other, which partly offsets the first, is due to the increase in the price level. Let's look at these two effects more closely:

Figure 7-8

The Dynamic Effects of a Monetary Expansion on Output and the Interest Rate

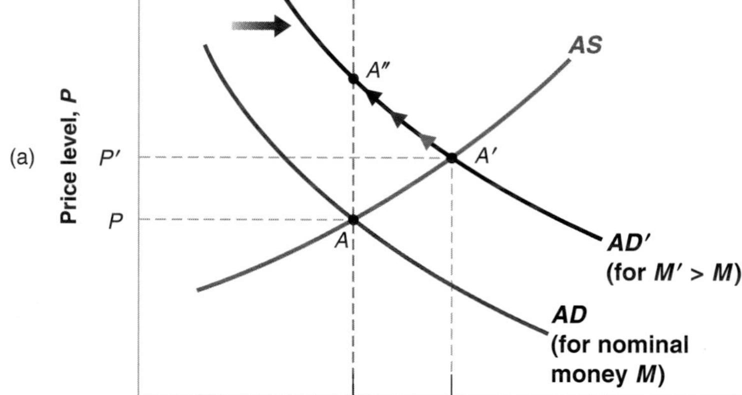

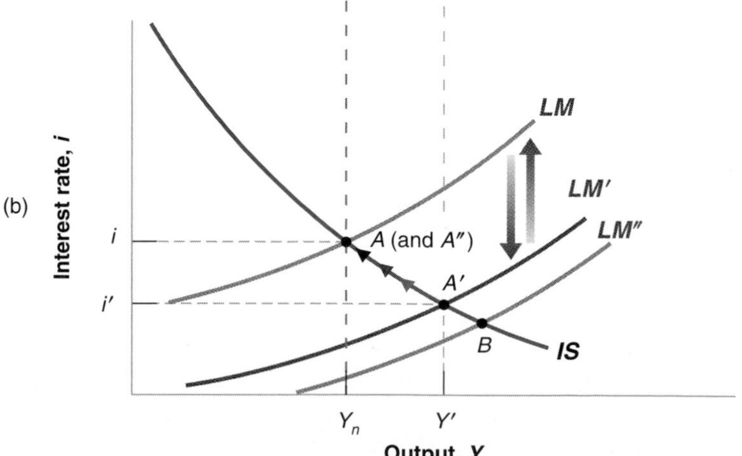

The increase in nominal money initially shifts the *LM* curve down, decreasing the interest rate and increasing output. Over time, the price level increases, shifting the *LM* curve back up until output is back at the natural level of output.

- If the price level did not change, the increase in nominal money would shift the *LM* curve down to *LM*″. So, if the price level did not change—as was our assumption in Chapter 5—the equilibrium would be at the intersection of *IS* and *LM*″, so at point *B*.
- But even in the short run, the price level increases—from *P* to *P*′ in Figure 7-8, panel (a). This increase in the price level shifts the *LM* curve upward from *LM*″ to *LM*′, partially offsetting the effect of the increase in nominal money.
- The net effect of these two shifts—down from *LM* to *LM*″ in response to the increase in nominal money, and up from *LM*′ to *LM*″ in response to the increase in the price level—is a shift of the *LM* curve from *LM* to *LM*′, and the short run equilibrium is given by *A*′.

Why only partially? Suppose the price level increased in the same proportion as nominal money, leaving the real money stock unchanged. If the real money stock were unchanged, output would remain unchanged as well. But if output were unchanged, the price level would not increase, in contradiction with our premise.

Over time, the fact that output is above the natural level of output implies that the price level continues to increase. As the price level increases, it further reduces the real money stock and shifts the *LM* back up. The economy moves along the *IS* curve: The interest rate increases and output declines. Eventually, the *LM* curve returns to where it was before the increase in nominal money.

The economy ends up at point *A*, which corresponds to point *A*″ in Figure 7-8, panel (a): The increase in nominal money is exactly offset by a proportional increase in the price level. The real money stock is therefore unchanged. With the real money stock unchanged, output is back to its initial value, Y_n, which is the natural level of output, and the interest rate is also back to its initial value, *i*.

The Neutrality of Money

Let's summarize what you have just learned about the effects of monetary policy:

- In the *short run*, a monetary expansion leads to an increase in output, a decrease in the interest rate, and an increase in the price level.

  How much of the effect of a monetary expansion falls initially on output and how much on the price level depends on the slope of the aggregate supply curve. In Chapter 5, we assumed the price level did not respond at all to an increase in output—we assumed in effect that the aggregate supply curve was flat. Although we intended this as a simplification, empirical evidence does show that the initial effect of changes in output on the price level is quite small. We saw this when we looked at estimated responses to changes in the federal funds rate in Figure 5-11: Despite the increase in output, the price level remained practically unchanged for nearly a year.
- Over time, the price level increases, and the effects of the monetary expansion on output and on the interest rate disappear. *In the medium run, the increase in nominal money is reflected entirely in a proportional increase in the price level; the increase in nominal money has no effect on output or on the interest rate.* (How long it takes in reality for the effects of money on output to disappear is the topic of the Focus box "How Long Lasting Are the Real Effects of Money?".) Economists refer to the absence of medium-run effects of money on output and on the interest rate by saying that money is neutral in the medium run.

  The **neutrality of money** in the medium run does not mean that monetary policy cannot or should not be used to affect output: An expansionary monetary policy can, for example, help the economy move out of a recession and return faster to the natural level of output. But it is a warning that monetary policy cannot sustain higher output forever.

Actually, the way the proposition is typically stated is that money is neutral in the *long run*. This is because many economists use "long run" to refer to what I call in this book the "medium run."

How Long Lasting Are the Real Effects of Money?

How long lasting are the effects of an increase in money on output?

One way to answer is to turn to macroeconometric models. These models, which are used both to forecast activity, and to look at the effects of alternative macroeconomic policies, are large-scale versions of the aggregate supply and aggregate demand model presented in this chapter. Figure 1 shows the effects in such a model (built by John Taylor of Stanford University) of a 3% permanent increase in nominal money. The increase in nominal money takes place over the four quarters of year 1: 0.1% in the first quarter, another 0.6% in the second, another 1.2% in the third, and another 1.1% in the fourth. After these four step increases, nominal money remains at its new higher level forever.

The effects of money on output reach a maximum after three quarters. By then, output is 1.8% higher than it would have been without the increase in nominal money. Over time, however, the price level increases and output returns to its initial level. In year 4, the price level is up by 2.5%, while output is up by only 0.3%. Therefore, the Taylor model suggests, it takes roughly four years for output to return to its initial level, four years for changes in nominal money to become neutral.

Some economists are skeptical of the results of simulations from such large models. Building such a model requires making decisions about which equations to include, which variables to include in each equation and which ones to leave out. Some decisions are bound to be wrong. Because the models are so large, it is often difficult to know how each of these decisions affects the outcome of a particular simulation. So, these economists argue, whenever possible simpler methods should be used.

One such method is simply to trace out, using econometrics, the effects of a change in money on output. This method is not without its own problems: A strong relation between money and output may not come from an effect of money on output, but rather from an effect of output on the conduct of monetary policy and thus on nominal money (the econometric problems raised by such two-way causation are discussed further in Appendix 3 at the end of the book). But the method can provide a useful first pass. The results of such a study by Frederic Mishkin, building on earlier work by Robert Barro, are summarized in Table 1.

Following Barro, Mishkin first separates movements in nominal money into those movements that could have been predicted based on the information available up to that time (a component he calls **anticipated money**) and those movements that could not have been predicted (a component he calls **unanticipated**

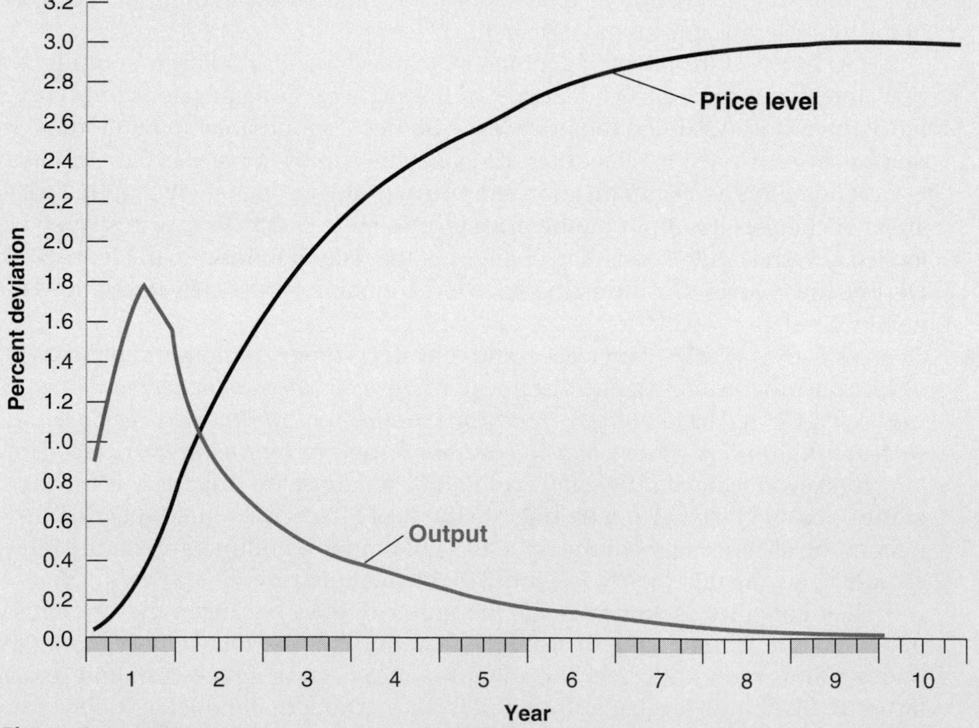

Figure 1 *The Effects of an Expansion in Nominal Money in the Taylor Model*

FOCUS

Table 1 The Effects of a 1% Increase in Nominal Money (Anticipated or Unanticipated) on Output

Quarters	0	2	4	6	12	16
Effects on output						
Anticipated	1.3	1.9	1.8	1.3	0.7	−0.6
Unanticipated	2.0	2.3	2.2	2.0	0.5	−0.4

money). The motivation for this distinction should be clear from this chapter: If wage setters anticipate increases in money, they may anticipate that the price level will be higher and therefore they will ask for higher wages. Thus, to the extent that changes in money are anticipated, they may have a larger effect on the price level and a smaller effect on output.

The results in Table 1 confirm that changes in money have stronger effects when they are unanticipated. Whether anticipated or unanticipated, the effects of changes in money on output peak after about two quarters. The effects are substantially larger than in the Taylor model (which looked at a 3% increase in nominal money; Table 1 looks at the effects of 1% increase). As in the Taylor model, the effects disappear after three to four years (12 to 16 quarters).

Although results using the two approaches are not identical, they share a number of features. Money has a strong effect on output in the short run. But the effect is largely gone after four years. By then, the effect of higher nominal money is largely reflected in a higher price level, not in a higher level of output.

Sources: Figure 1 is reproduced from John Taylor, Macroeconomic Policy in a World Economy *(New York: W. W. Norton, 1993) Figure 5.1A, p. 138.*

Table 1 is taken from Frederic Mishkin, A Rational Expectations Approach to Macroeconometrics *(Chicago: NBER and University of Chicago, 1983), Table 6.5, p. 122. The study by Mishkin builds on Robert Barro, "Unanticipated Money Growth in the United States,"* American Economic Review, *March 1977, p. 101–115.*

7-5 A Decrease in the Budget Deficit

The policy we just looked at—a monetary expansion—led to a shift in aggregate demand coming from a shift in the *LM* curve. Let's now look at the effects of a shift in aggregate demand coming from a shift in the *IS* curve.

Suppose the government decides to reduce its budget deficit by decreasing its spending from G to G' while leaving taxes, T, unchanged. How will this affect the economy in the short run and in the medium run?

Assume that output is initially at the natural level of output, so that the economy is at point A in Figure 7-9: Output equals Y_n. The decrease in government spending from G to G' shifts the aggregate demand curve to the left, from AD to AD': For a given price level, output is lower. In the short run, the equilibrium moves from A to A', output decreases from Y_n to Y' and the price level decreases from P to P'.

The initial effect of deficit reduction is thus to trigger a decrease in output. We first derived this result in Chapter 3, and it holds here as well.

What happens over time? As long as output is below the natural level of output, we know that the aggregate supply curve keeps shifting down. The economy moves down along the aggregate demand curve AD' until the aggregate supply curve is given by AS'' and the economy reaches point A''. By then, the initial recession is over, and output is back at Y_n.

Like an increase in nominal money, a reduction in the budget deficit does not affect output forever. Eventually, output returns to the natural level of output.

Figure 7-9

The Dynamic Effects of a Decrease in the Budget Deficit

A decrease in the budget deficit leads initially to a decrease in output. Over time, output returns to the natural level of output.

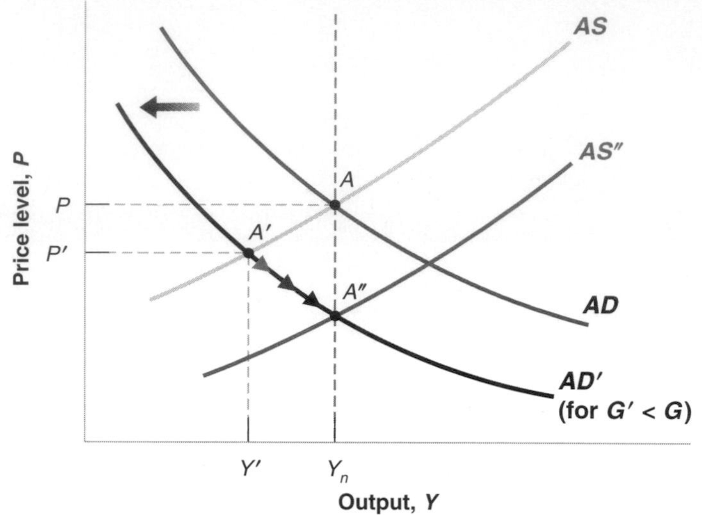

That the price level decreases for some time feels strange: We rarely observe deflation (although recall Japan, in Chapter 1). This result comes from the fact that we are looking at an economy in which money growth is zero (we are assuming that M is constant, not growing), and so there is no inflation in the medium run. When we introduce money growth in the next chapter, we shall see that a recession typically leads to a decrease in inflation, not to a decrease in the price level.

But there is an important difference between the effects of a change in money and the effects of a change in the deficit: At point A'', not everything is the same as before: In particular, the interest rate is lower than before the shift. The best way to see this is to look at the adjustment in terms of the underlying *IS-LM* model.

Deficit Reduction, Output, and the Interest Rate

Figure 7-10, panel (a) reproduces Figure 7-9, showing the adjustment of output and the price level in response to the decrease in the budget deficit (but leaving out AS'' to keep things visually simple). Figure 7-10, panel (b) shows the adjustment of output and the interest rate, by looking at the same adjustment process, but in terms of the *IS-LM* model.

Look at Figure 7-10, panel (b). Before the change in fiscal policy, the equilibrium is given by the intersection of the *IS* curve and the *LM* curve, at point A—which corresponds to point A in Figure 7-10, panel (a). Output is equal to the natural level of output, Y_n, and the interest rate is given by i.

As the government reduces the budget deficit, the *IS* curve shifts to the left, to IS'. If the price level did not change (the assumption we made in Chapter 5), the economy would move from point A to point B. But, because the price level declines in response to the decrease in output, the real money stock increases, leading to a partly offsetting shift of the *LM* curve, down to LM'. So, the initial effect of deficit reduction is to move the economy from point A to point A'; point A' in Figure 7-10, panel (b) corresponds to point A' in Figure 7-10, panel (a). Both output and the interest rate are lower than before the fiscal contraction. Note that whether investment increases or decreases in the short run is ambiguous: Lower output decreases investment, but the lower interest rates increase investment.

As long as output remains below the natural level of output, the price level continues to decline, leading to a further increase in the real money stock. The *LM* curve continues to shift down. In Figure 7-10, panel (b), the economy moves down from point A' along IS', and eventually reaches A'' (which corresponds to A'' in Figure 7-10, panel [a]). At A'', the *LM* curve is given by LM'':

At A'', output is back at the natural level of output. But the interest rate is lower than it was before deficit reduction, down from i to i''. The composition of output, in terms of

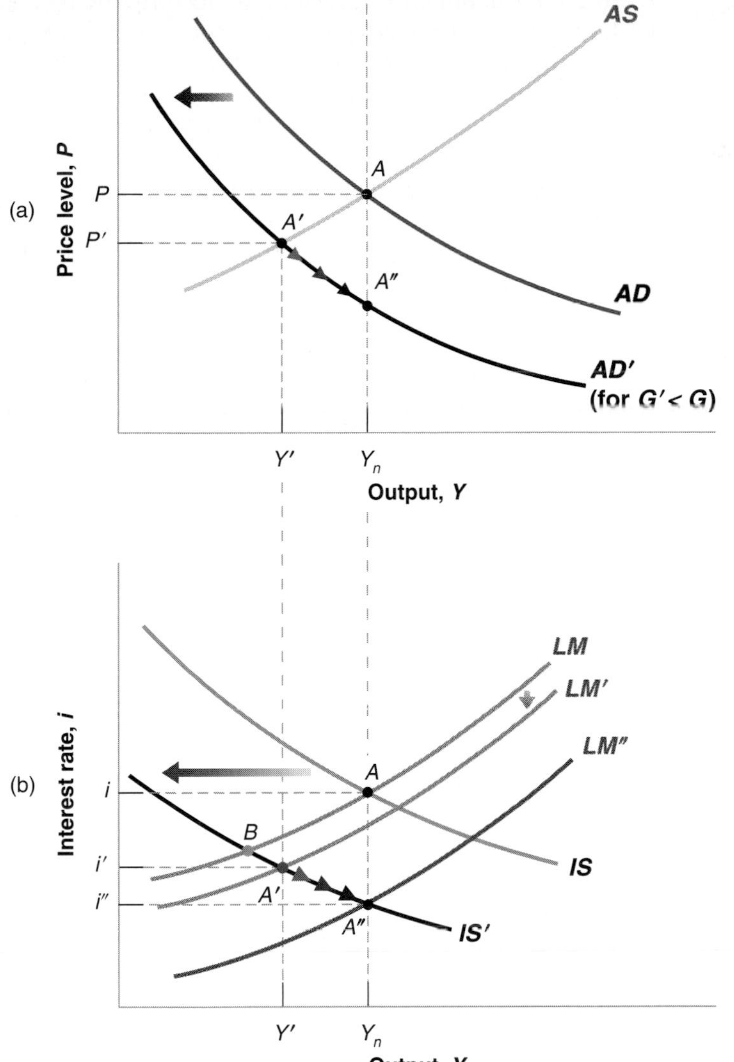

Figure 7-10

The Dynamic Effects of a Decrease in the Budget Deficit on Output and the Interest Rate

Deficit reduction leads in the short run to a decrease in output and to a decrease in the interest rate. In the medium run, output returns to its natural level, while the interest rate declines further.

spending, is also different. To see how and why, let us rewrite the *IS* relation, taking into account that at *A″*, output is back at the natural level of output, so that $Y = Y_n$

$$Y_n = C(Y_n - T) + I(Y_n, i) + G$$

Because income, Y_n, and taxes, T, are unchanged, consumption, C, is the same as before deficit reduction. By assumption, government spending, G, is lower than before; therefore, investment, I, must be higher than before deficit reduction—higher by an amount exactly equal to the decrease in G. Put another way, *in the medium run,* a reduction in the budget deficit unambiguously leads to a decrease in the interest rate and an increase in investment.

Budget Deficits, Output, and Investment

Let's summarize what you have just learned about the effects of fiscal policy:

- In the *short run,* a budget deficit reduction, if implemented alone—i.e., without an accompanying change in monetary policy—leads to a decrease in output, and may lead to a *decrease* in investment.

Note the qualification "without an accompanying change in monetary policy." In principle, these adverse short-run effects on output can be avoided by using the right monetary-fiscal mix. What is needed is for the central bank to decrease the interest rate enough to offset the adverse effects of the decrease in government spending on aggregate demand. As you saw in Chapter 5, this is what happened in the United States in the 1990s: The Fed made sure that, even in the short run, deficit reduction did not lead to a recession and to a decrease in output.

- In the *medium run*, output returns to the natural level of output, and the interest rate is lower. In the medium run, deficit reduction leads unambiguously to an *increase* in investment.

  We have not taken into account so far the effects of investment on capital accumulation, and the effects of capital on production (we shall do so when we look at the long run, starting in Chapter 10). But it is easy to see how our conclusions would be modified if we did take into account the effects on capital accumulation. In the long run, the level of output depends on the capital stock in the economy. So if a lower government budget deficit leads to more investment, it will lead to a higher capital stock, and the higher capital stock will lead to higher output.

Effects of a deficit reduction: ▶
⇒ Short run
$Y\downarrow$ $I \uparrow\downarrow$?
Medium run
$Y \rightarrow I\uparrow$
Long run
$Y\uparrow I\uparrow$

Everything we have just said about the effects of deficit reduction would apply equally to measures aimed at increasing private (rather than public) saving. An increase in the saving rate increases output and investment in the medium run and in the long run. But it may also create a recession and a decrease in investment in the short run.

Disagreements among economists about the effects of measures aimed at increasing either public saving or private saving often come from differences in time frames. Those who are concerned with short-run effects worry that measures to increase saving, public or private, may create a recession and decrease saving and investment for some time. Those who look beyond the short run see the eventual increase in saving and investment, and emphasize the favorable medium-run and long-run effects on output.

7-6 Changes in the Price of Oil

In the 1970s, the price of oil increased dramatically. This large increase was the result of the formation of the Organization of Petroleum Exporting Countries (OPEC), a cartel of oil producers. Behaving as a monopolist, OPEC reduced the supply of oil and in doing so, increased its price. Figure 7-11, which plots the ratio of the price of crude petroleum to the producer price index since 1960, shows the effects of the formation of OPEC (the ratio is set to 100 in 1960.) The relative price of petroleum, which had remained roughly constant throughout the 1960s, almost tripled between 1970 and 1982. There were two particularly sharp increases in the price, the first in 1973–1975 and the second in 1979–1981.

These high prices did not last very long. From 1982 to 1998, the OPEC cartel became steadily weaker, unable to enforce the production quotas it had set for its members. Some member countries started to produce more than their assigned quota, and the supply of oil increased, leading to a large decline in the price. From a high of 264 in 1982, the relative price bottomed out at 65 in 1998.

In the late 1990s, however, the OPEC cartel became stronger, and the price of oil increased again. In 2000, the relative price stood at 130, twice its 1998 value. While the relative price was still far from its peak in the 1970s, the increase was similar in size to the increase of the mid-1970s, triggering fears that the U.S. economy may be in for a repeat of the 1974–1975 recession. But, in 2001, the price of oil fell again, and, for the time being, earlier fears have been alleviated. Nevertheless, these movements in the

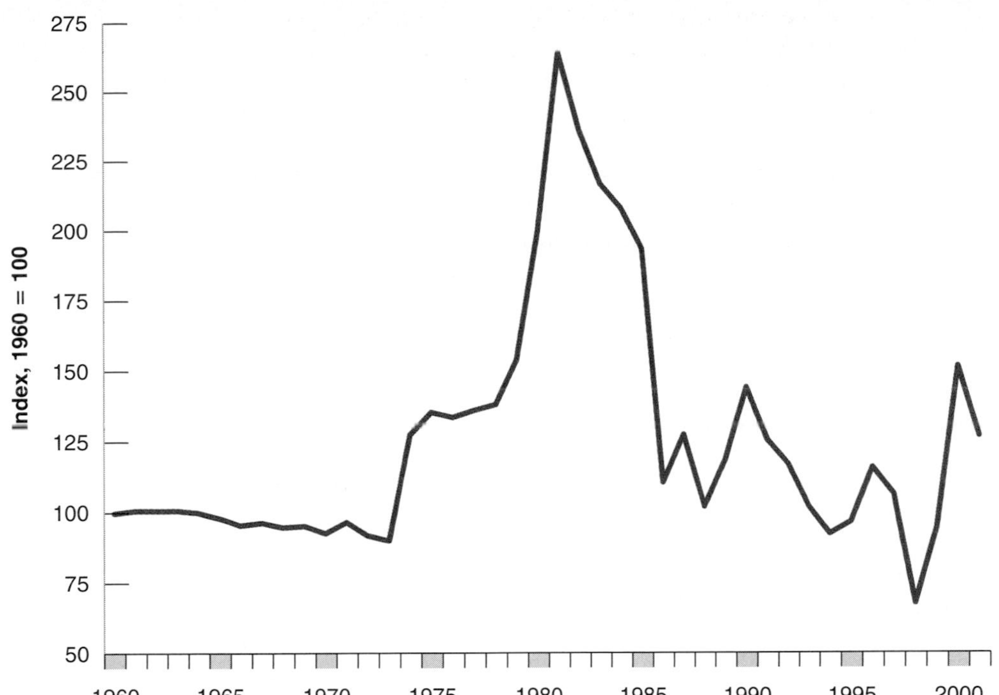

Figure 7-11

The Price of Crude Petroleum, 1960–2001

There were two sharp increases in the relative price of oil in the 1970s, followed by a decrease in the 1980s and the 1990s.

price of oil are still more than enough motivation for us to ask: What are the effects of an increase in the price of oil in our model?

We face a problem in thinking about the macroeconomic effects of an increase in the price of oil: The price of oil appears neither in our aggregate supply relation nor in our aggregate demand relation! The reason is that we have assumed so far that output was produced using only labor. One way of proceeding would be to relax this assumption, recognize explicitly that output is produced using labor and other inputs (including energy), and derive the implications for the relation of prices both to wages and to the price of oil. I shall instead use a shortcut and capture the increase in the price of oil by an increase in μ, the markup of the price over the nominal wage. The justification is straightforward: Given wages, an increase in the price of oil increases the cost of production, forcing firms to increase prices.

We can then track the dynamic effects of an *increase in the markup* on output and the price level. It is easiest here to work backward in time, first asking what happens in the medium run, and then working out the dynamics of adjustment from the short run to the medium run.

Effects on the Natural Rate of Unemployment

Let's start by asking what happens to the natural rate of unemployment as a result of the increase in the price of oil. Figure 7-12 reproduces the characterization of labor-market equilibrium from Chapter 6:

The wage-setting curve is downward sloping. The price-setting relation is represented by the horizontal line at $W/P = 1/(1 + \mu)$. The initial equilibrium is at point A, and the initial natural unemployment rate is u_n.

Do not be confused: u and μ are not the same; u is the unemployment rate, μ is the markup.

An increase in the markup leads to a downward shift of the price-setting line, from *PS* to *PS′*: The higher the markup, the lower the real wage implied by price setting. The equilibrium moves from A to A'. The real wage is lower. The natural unemployment

Figure 7-12

The Effects of an Increase in the Price of Oil on the Natural Rate of Unemployment

An increase in the price of oil leads to a lower real wage and a higher natural rate of unemployment.

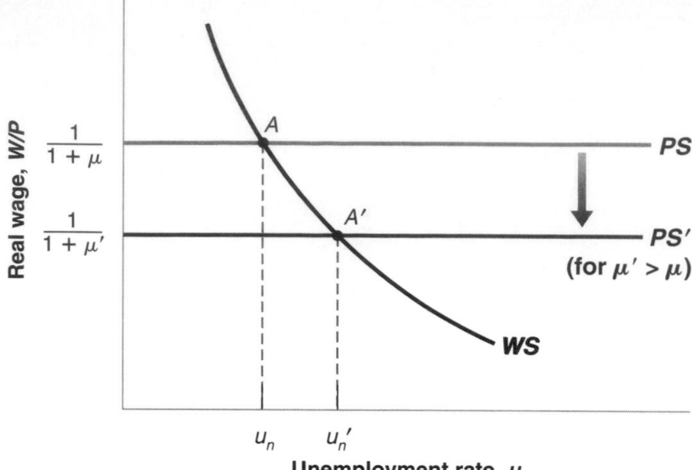

rate is higher: Getting workers to accept the lower real wage requires an increase in unemployment.

The increase in the natural rate of unemployment implies a decrease in the natural level of employment. If we assume that the relation between employment and output is unchanged—that is, that each unit of output still requires one worker, in addition to the energy input—then the decrease in the natural level of employment leads to an identical decrease in the natural level of output. In short, an increase in the price of oil leads to a decrease in the natural level of output.

The Dynamics of Adjustment

Let's now turn to dynamics. Suppose that before the increase in the price of oil, the aggregate demand curve and the aggregate supply curve are given by *AD* and *AS*, respectively, so the economy is at point *A* in Figure 7-13, with output at the natural level of output, Y_n, and, by implication, $P = P^e$.

We have just established that the increase in the price of oil decreases the natural level of output from Y_n to Y'_n. We now want to know what happens in the short run and how the economy moves from Y_n to Y'_n.

To think about the short run, recall from equation (7.2) that the aggregate supply relation is given by

$$P = P^e(1+\mu)\, F\left(1-\frac{Y}{L}, z\right)$$

Recall that we capture the effect of an increase in the price of oil by an increase in the markup, μ. So, in the short run (given P^e), the increase in the price of oil shows up as an increase in the markup, μ. This increase in the markup leads firms to increase their prices, leading to an increase in the price level, *P*, at any level of output, *Y*. The aggregate supply curve shifts up.

We can be more specific about the size of the shift, and knowing the size of this shift will be useful in what follows. We know from Section 7-1 that the aggregate supply curve always goes through the point where output equals the natural level of output and the price level equals the expected price level. Before the increase in the price of oil, the aggregate supply curve in Figure 7-13 goes through point *A*, where output equals Y_n and the price level is equal to P^e. After the increase in the price of oil, the new aggregate supply curve goes through point *B*, where output equals the new lower

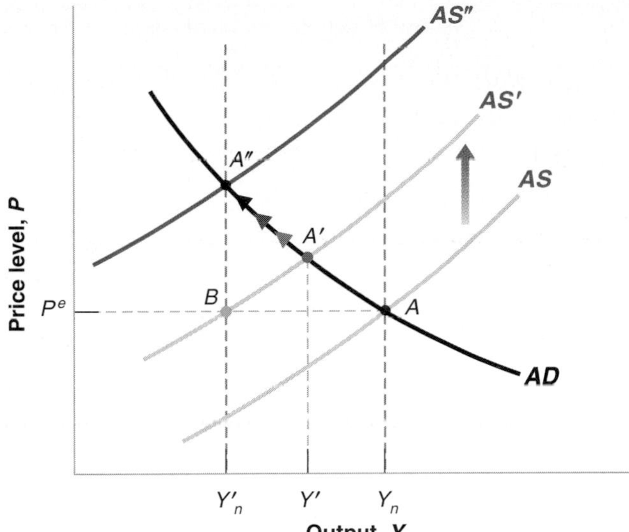

Figure 7-13

The Dynamic Effects of an Increase in the Price of Oil

An increase in the price of oil leads, in the short run, to a decrease in output and an increase in the price level. Over time, output decreases further and the price level increases further.

natural level of output Y'_n and the price level equals the expected price level, P^e. So, the aggregate supply curve shifts from *AS* to *AS′*.

Does the *aggregate demand curve* shift as a result of the increase in the price of oil? The answer is: Maybe. There are many channels through which demand might be affected at a given price level. The higher price of oil may lead firms to change their investment plans, canceling some investment projects or shifting to less energy-intensive equipment. The increase in the price of oil also redistributes income from oil buyers to oil producers. Oil producers may have a higher propensity to save than oil buyers. Let's take the easy way here: Because some of the effects shift the aggregate demand curve to the right and others shift the aggregate demand curve to the left, let's simply assume that the effects cancel each other out and that aggregate demand does not shift.

This was the case in the 1970s. The OPEC countries realized that high oil revenues might not last forever. Many of them saved a large proportion of the income from oil revenues.

Under this assumption, only the *AS* shifts in the short run. The economy therefore moves along the *AD* curve, from *A* to *A′*. Output decreases from Y_n to Y'. The increase in the price of oil leads firms to increase their price; the increase in the price level decreases demand and output.

What happens over time? While output has decreased, the natural level of output has decreased even more: At point *A′*, output Y' is still above the new natural level of output Y'_n, so the aggregate supply curve continues to shift up. The economy therefore moves over time along the aggregate demand curve, from *A′* to *A″*. At point *A″*, output Y' is equal to the new lower natural level of output Y'_n, and the price level is higher than before the oil shock: Shifts in aggregate supply affect output not only in the short run but in the medium run as well.

How does our story compare to what actually happened after the first oil shock? Table 7-1 gives the basic macroeconomic facts.

From 1973 to 1975, the cumulative increase in petroleum prices (that is, the sum of the rates of change of petroleum prices in 1973, 1974, and 1975, in dollars) was 77.3%. The effects on output and the price level were very much what our model predicts: a combination of a recession and large increases in the price level. In 1974 and 1975, GDP growth was negative. In both 1974 and 1975, inflation (as measured by the rate of change of the GDP deflator) was higher than the year before. At the time, this combination of negative growth and high inflation—which was baptized **stagflation,** to capture the combination of *stagnation* and *inflation*—came as a surprise to economists. It was the trigger for a large amount of research on the effects of supply shocks (shocks that shift

Table 7-1 The Effects of the Increase in the Price of Oil, 1973–1975

	1973	1974	1975
Rate of change of petroleum price (%)	10.4	51.8	15.1
Rate of change of GDP deflator (%)	5.6	9.0	9.4
Rate of GDP growth (%)	5.8	−0.6	−0.4
Unemployment rate (%)	4.9	5.6	8.5

the aggregate supply curve) for the rest of the decade. By the time of the second oil shock in the late 1970s, macroeconomists were better equipped to understand it.

7-7 Conclusions

This chapter has covered a lot of ground. Let me repeat some key concepts and develop some of the conclusions.

The Short Run Versus the Medium Run

One message in this chapter is that changes in policy, and changes in the economic environment—from changes in consumer confidence to changes in the price of oil—typically have different effects in the short run and in the medium run. We looked at the effects of a monetary expansion, of a deficit reduction, and of an increase in the price of oil. The main results are summarized in Table 7-2. A monetary expansion, for example, affects output in the short run but not in the medium run. In the short run, a reduction in the budget deficit decreases output and the interest rate, and may decrease investment. But in the medium run, the interest rate decreases and output returns to the natural level of output, so investment increases. An increase in the price of oil decreases output not only in the short run but also in the medium run. And so on.

This difference between the short-run effects and the medium-run effects of policies is one of the reasons economists disagree in their policy recommendations. Some economists believe the economy returns quickly to its medium-run equilibrium, and so they emphasize medium-run implications of policy. Others believe the adjustment mechanism through which output returns to the natural level of output can be very slow, so they put more emphasis on the short-run effects of policy. They are more

Table 7-2 Short-Run Effects and Medium-Run Effects of a Monetary Expansion, a Budget Deficit Reduction, and an Increase in the Price of Oil on Output, the Interest Rate, and the Price Level

	Short Run			Medium Run		
	Output	Interest Rate	Price Level	Output	Interest Rate	Price Level
Monetary expansion	increase	decrease	increase (small)	no change	no change	increase
Deficit reduction	decrease	decrease	decrease (small)	no change	decrease	decrease
Increase in oil price	decrease	increase	increase	decrease	increase	increase

willing to use monetary policy or budget deficits to get out of a recession, even if money is neutral in the medium run, and budget deficits have adverse implications in the long run.

We shall return to these issues many times in this book. See the discussion of the Great Depression and of the current situation in Japan in Chapter 22, and Chapter 24 to 26 on policy.

Shocks and Propagation Mechanisms

This chapter also gives you a general way of thinking about **output fluctuations** (sometimes called **business cycles**)—movements in output around its trend (a trend that we have ignored so far, but on which we shall focus in Chapters 10 to 13).

The economy is constantly hit by **shocks** to aggregate supply, or to aggregate demand, or to both. These shocks may be shifts in consumption coming from changes in consumer confidence, shifts in investment, shifts in the demand for money, shifts in labor productivity, changes in oil prices, and so on. Or they may come from changes in policy—from the introduction of a tax law, to a program of infrastructure investment, to the decision by the central bank to fight inflation through tight money, and so on.

How to define *shocks* is harder than it looks. Suppose a failed economic program in an eastern European country leads to political chaos in that country, which leads to increased risk of nuclear war in the region, which leads to a fall in consumer confidence in the United States, which leads to a recession in the United States. What is the "shock"? The failed program? The fall of democracy? The increased risk of nuclear war? Or the decrease in consumer confidence? In practice, we have to cut the chain of causation somewhere. Thus, we may refer to the drop in consumer confidence as "the shock," ignoring its underlying causes.

Each shock has dynamic effects on output and its components. These dynamic effects are called the **propagation mechanism** of the shock. Propagation mechanisms are different for different shocks. The effects on output may be largest at the beginning and then decrease over time. Or the effects may build up for a while, and then decrease and disappear. We saw, for example, that the effects of an increase in money on output, reach a peak after six to nine months and then slowly decline afterward. Some shocks have effects even in the medium run. This is the case for any shock that has a permanent effect on aggregate supply, such as a permanent change in the price of oil.

Fluctuations in output come from the continual appearance of new shocks, each with its propagation mechanism. At times, some shocks are sufficiently bad, or come in sufficiently bad combinations, that they create a recession. The two recessions of the 1970s were due largely to increases in the price of oil; the recession of the early 1980s was due to a sharp change in monetary policy; the recession of the early 1990s was due primarily to a sudden decline in consumer confidence; the slowdown of 2001 appears to be due to a sharp drop in investment spending and to the events of September 11 of that year. What we call economic fluctuations are the result of these shocks and their dynamic effects on output.

Where We Go from Here: Output, Unemployment, and Inflation

In developing the model of this chapter, we assumed the nominal money stock was constant. That is, although we considered the effects of a one-time change in the level of nominal money (in Section 7-4), we did not allow for sustained nominal money growth. We are now ready to relax this assumption and allow for nominal money growth. Only by considering positive nominal money growth can we explain why inflation is typically positive, and think about the relation between economic activity and inflation. Movements in unemployment, output, and inflation are the topics of the next two chapters.

Summary

- The model of aggregate supply and aggregate demand describes movements in output and the price level when account is taken of equilibrium in the goods market, the financial markets, and the labor market.
- The aggregate supply relation captures the effects of output on the price level. It is derived from equilibrium in the labor market. The aggregate supply relation is a relation between the price level, the expected price level, and the level of output. An increase in output decreases unemployment, increasing wages and, in turn, increasing the price level. An increase in the expected price level leads, one for one, to an increase in the actual price level.

The Natural Rate of Unemployment and the Phillips Curve

In 1958, A. W. Phillips drew a diagram plotting the rate of inflation against the rate of unemployment in the United Kingdom for each year from 1861 to 1957. He found clear evidence of a negative relation between inflation and unemployment: When unemployment was low, inflation was high, and when unemployment was high, inflation was low, often even negative.

Two years later, Paul Samuelson and Robert Solow replicated Phillips' exercise for the United States, using data from 1900 to 1960. Figure 8-1 shows their findings, using CPI inflation as a measure of the inflation rate. Apart from the period of very high unemployment during the 1930s (the years from 1931 to 1939 are denoted by black triangles and are clearly to the right of the other points in the figure), there also appeared to be a negative relation between inflation and unemployment in the United States.

This relation, which Samuelson and Solow baptized the **Phillips curve**, rapidly became central to macroeconomic thinking and policy. It appeared to imply that countries could choose between different combinations of unemployment and inflation. A country could achieve low unemployment if it were willing to tolerate higher inflation, or it could achieve price-level stability—zero inflation—if it were willing to tolerate higher unemployment. Much of the discussion about macroeconomic policy became a discussion about which point to choose on the Phillips curve.

In the 1970s, however, the relation broke down. In the United States and most OECD countries, there was both high inflation *and* high unemployment, clearly contradicting the original Phillips curve. A relation reappeared, but it reappeared as a relation between the unemployment rate and the *change* in the inflation rate. Today in the United States, high unemployment leads not to low inflation, but to a decrease in inflation.

The purpose of this chapter is to explore the mutations of the Phillips curve and, more generally, to help you understand the relation between inflation and unemployment. You will see that what Phillips discovered was the aggregate supply relation, and that the mutations of the Phillips curve came from changes in the way people and firms formed expectations.

The chapter has three sections:

- Section 8-1 shows how we can think of the aggregate supply relation as a relation between inflation, expected inflation, and unemployment.
- Section 8-2 uses this relation to interpret the mutations in the Phillips curve over time.

Figure 8-1

Inflation Versus Unemployment in the United States, 1900–1960

During the period 1900–1960 in the United States, a low unemployment rate was typically associated with a high inflation rate, and a high unemployment rate was typically associated with a low or negative inflation rate.

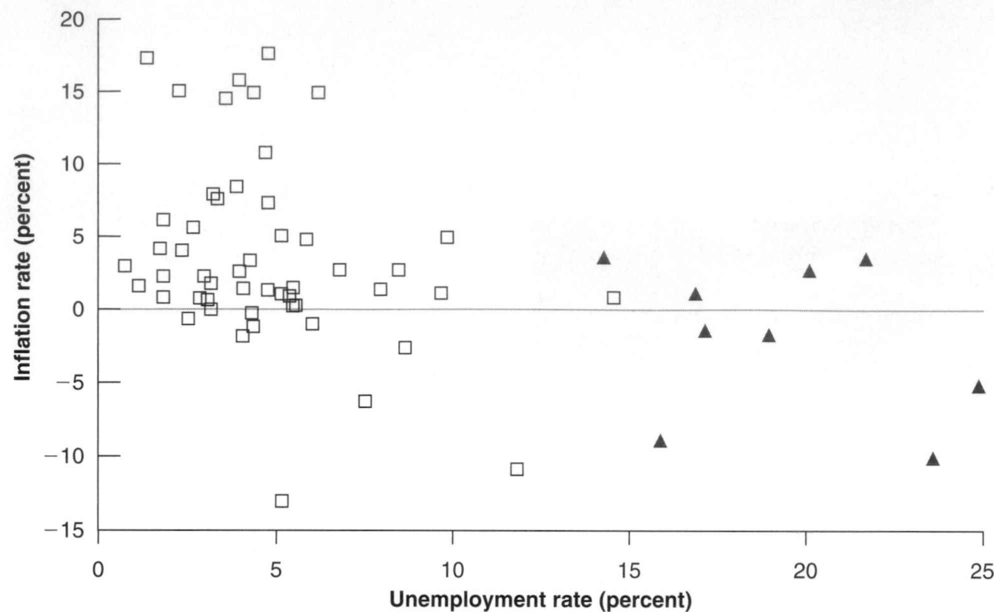

■ Section 8-3 further discusses the relation between unemployment and inflation, across countries and over time. ■

8-1 Inflation, Expected Inflation, and Unemployment

We then replaced the unemployment rate by its expression in terms of output to obtain a relation between the price level, the expected price level, and output. This step is not needed here.

Our first step will be to show that the aggregate supply relation we derived in Chapter 7 can be rewritten as a relation between *inflation, expected inflation,* and the *unemployment rate.*

Go back to the aggregate supply relation between the price level, the expected price level, and the unemployment rate we derived in Chapter 7 (equation [7.1]):

$$P = P^e(1 + \mu)F(u,z)$$

Recall the wage setting relation, equation (6.1):

$$W = P^e F(u, z)$$

Recall that the function, F, captures the effects on the wage of the unemployment rate, u, and of the other factors that affect wage setting, represented by the catchall variable, z. It will be convenient here to assume a specific form for this function:

$$F(u, z) = 1 - \alpha u + z$$

This captures the notion that the higher the unemployment rate, the lower is the wage; and the higher z (for example, the more generous unemployment benefits are), the higher is the wage. The parameter α (the Greek lowercase alpha) captures the strength of the effect of unemployment on the wage.

Replace the function, F, by this specific form in the aggregate supply relation we began with

$$P = P^e(1 + \mu)(1 - \alpha u + z) \qquad (8.1)$$

Finally, let π denote the *inflation rate,* and π^e denote the expected inflation rate. Then, equation (8.1) can be rewritten as

$$\pi = \pi^e + (\mu + z) - \alpha u \qquad (8.2)$$

Deriving equation (8.2) from equation (8.1) is not difficult, but it is tedious, so it is left to an appendix at the end of this chapter. What is important is that you understand each of the effects at work in equation (8.2):

From now on, to lighten your reading, I shall often refer to "the inflation rate" simply as "inflation," and to "the unemployment rate" simply as "unemployment."

- *An increase in expected inflation π^e leads to an increase in inflation, π.*

  To see why, return to equation (8.1). An increase in the expected price level, P^e, leads, one for one, to an increase in the actual price level, P. If wage setters expect a higher price level, they set a higher nominal wage, which leads to an increase in the price level.

  Now note that, given last period's price level, a higher price level this period implies a higher rate of increase in the price level from last period to this period, i.e., higher inflation.

  Similarly, given last period's price level, a higher expected price level this period implies a higher expected rate of increase in the price level from last period to this period, i.e., higher expected inflation.

  So the fact that an increase in the expected price level leads to an increase in the actual price level can be restated as: An increase in expected inflation leads to an increase in inflation.
- *Given expected inflation, π^e, an increase in the markup, μ, or an increase in the factors that affect wage determination—an increase in z—lead to an increase in inflation, π.*

  From equation (8.1): Given the expected price level P^e, an increase in either μ or z increases the price level, P. Using the same argument as in the previous bullet to restate this proposition in terms of inflation and expected inflation: Given expected inflation, π^e, an increase in either μ or z lead to an increase in inflation, π.
- *Given expected inflation, π^e, an increase in the unemployment rate u leads to a decrease in inflation, π.*

  From equation (8.1): Given the expected price level, P^e, an increase in the unemployment rate u leads to a lower nominal wage, which leads to a lower price level, P. Restating this in terms of inflation and expected inflation: Given expected inflation, π^e, an increase in the unemployment rate, u, leads to a decrease in inflation, π.

We need just one more step before we can return to a discussion of the Phillips curve: When we look at movements in inflation and unemployment below, it will be convenient to use time indexes, so that we can refer to variables such as inflation, or expected inflation, or unemployment, in a specific year. So we rewrite equation (8.2) as

$$\pi_t = \pi_t^e + (\mu + z) - \alpha u_t \qquad (8.3)$$

The variables π_t, π_t^e, and u_t refer to inflation, expected inflation, and unemployment in year t. Note that there are no time indexes on μ and z. This is because we shall typically think of both μ and z as constant while we look at movements in inflation, expected inflation, and unemployment over time.

8-2 The Phillips Curve

We can now return the relation between unemployment and inflation as it was first discovered by Phillips, Samuelson, and Solow, circa 1960.

The Early Incarnation

Think of an economy where inflation is equal to zero on average, positive in some years, negative in others. This is not the way things are in the United States today: The last year during which inflation was negative—the last year during which there was deflation—was 1955, when inflation was −0.3%. But as we shall see later in this chapter, average inflation *was* close to zero during much of the period at which Phillips, Samuelson, and Solow were looking.

Think of wage setters choosing nominal wages for the coming year and thus having to forecast what inflation will be over the year. With the average inflation rate equal to zero in the past, it is reasonable for wage setters to expect that inflation will be equal to zero over the next year as well. So, let's assume they set $\pi_t^e = 0$. Equation (8.3) then becomes

$$\pi_t = (\mu + z) - \alpha u_t \tag{8.4}$$

This is precisely the negative relation between unemployment and inflation that Phillips found for the United Kingdom, and Solow and Samuelson found for the United States. The story behind it is simple: Given the expected price level, which workers simply take to be last year's price level, lower unemployment leads to a higher nominal wage. A higher nominal wage leads to a higher price level. Putting the steps together, lower unemployment leads to a higher price level this year relative to last year's price level, i.e., to higher inflation.

This mechanism has sometimes been called the **wage-price spiral**, an expression that captures well the basic mechanism at work:

- Low unemployment leads to a higher nominal wage.
- In response to the higher nominal wage, firms increase their prices. The price level increases.
- In response to the higher price level, workers, next time the wage is set, ask for a higher nominal wage.
- The higher nominal wage leads firms to further increase their prices. The price level increases further.
- In response to this further increase in the price level, workers, when they set the wage again, ask for a further increase in the nominal wage.
- And so on, resulting in steady wage and price inflation.

Mutations

The combination of an apparently reliable empirical relation, together with a plausible story to explain it, led to the adoption of the Phillips curve by macroeconomists and policy makers. U.S. macroeconomic policy in the 1960s was aimed at maintaining unemployment in the range that appeared consistent with moderate inflation. And, throughout the 1960s, the negative relation between unemployment and inflation provided a reliable guide to the joint movements in unemployment and inflation.

Figure 8-2 plots the combinations of the inflation rate and the unemployment rate in the United States for each year from 1948 to 1969. Note how well the Phillips relation held during the long economic expansion that lasted during most of the 1960s. During the years 1961 to 1969, denoted by black diamonds in the figure, the unemployment rate declined steadily from 6.8 to 3.4%; the inflation rate steadily increased, from 1.0 to 5.5%. Put informally, from 1961 to 1969, the U.S. economy moved up along the Phillips curve.

Around 1970, however, the relation between the inflation rate and the unemployment rate, so visible in Figure 8-2, broke down. Figure 8-3 gives the combination of the

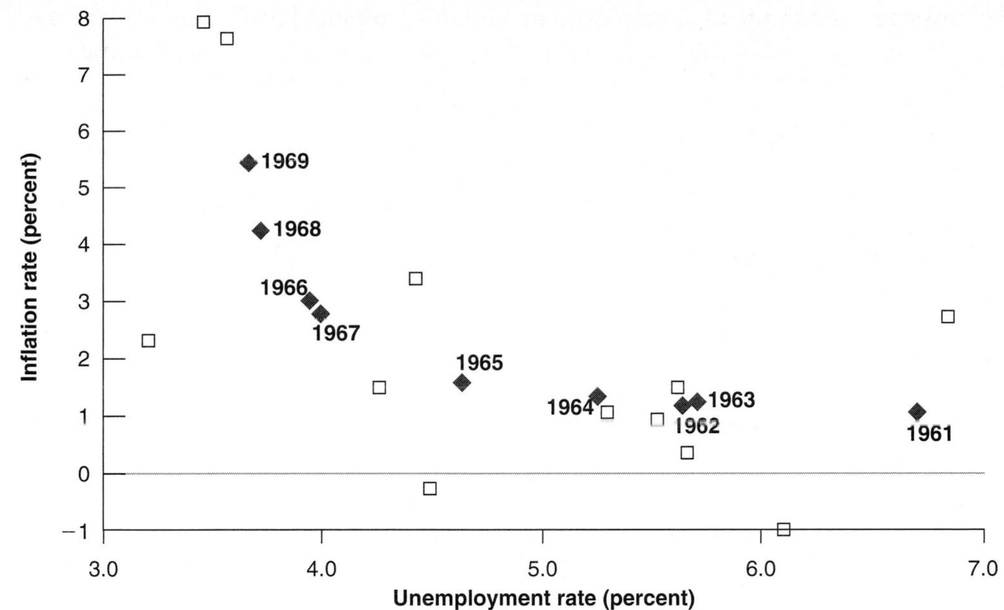

Figure 8-2

Inflation Versus Unemployment in the United States, 1948–1969

The steady decline in the U.S. unemployment rate throughout the 1960s was associated with a steady increase in the inflation rate.

inflation rate and the unemployment rate in the United States for each year since 1970. The points are scattered in a roughly symmetric cloud: There is no visible relation between the unemployment rate and the inflation rate.

Why did the original Phillips curve vanish? There are two main reasons:

- The United States was hit twice in the 1970s by a large increase in the price of oil (see Chapter 7). The effect of this increase in nonlabor costs was to force firms to increase their price relative to the wage they were paying, to increase the markup, μ. As shown in equation (8.3), an increase in μ leads to an increase in inflation,

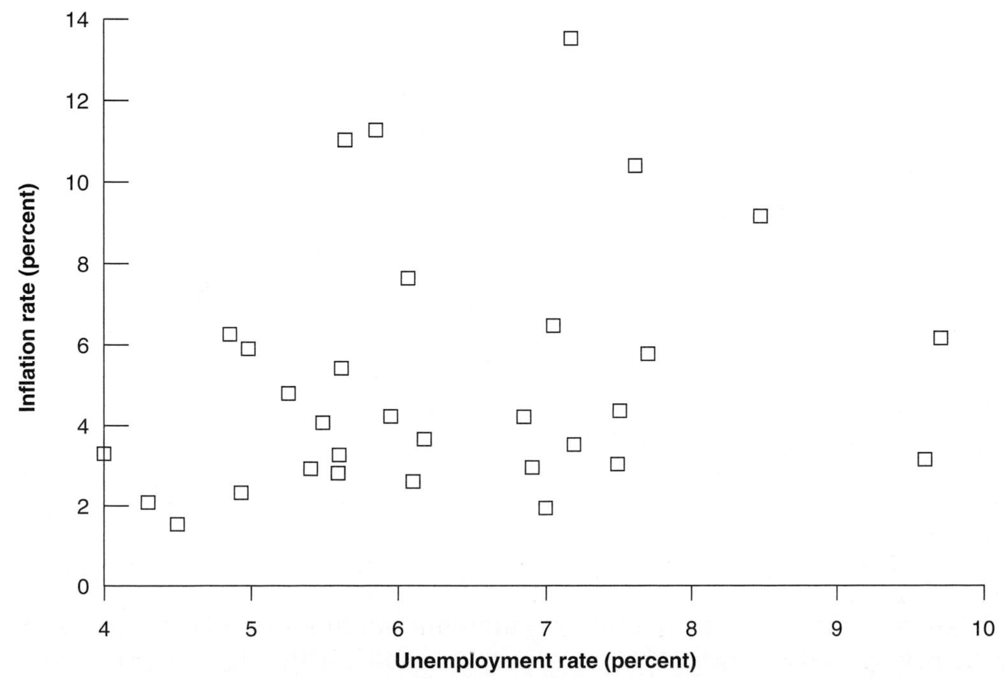

Figure 8-3

Inflation Versus Unemployment in the United States, 1970–2000

Beginning in 1970, the relation between the unemployment rate and the inflation rate disappeared in the United States.

even at a given rate of unemployment, and this happened twice in the 1970s. But the main reason for the breakdown of the Phillips curve relation was elsewhere:

- Wage setters changed the way they formed their expectations. This change came in turn from a change in the behavior of inflation. Look at Figure 8-4 which shows the U.S. inflation rate since 1900. Starting in the 1960s (the decade shaded in the figure), you can see a clear change in the behavior of the rate of inflation. First, rather than being sometimes positive, sometimes negative, as it had for the first part of the century, the rate of inflation became consistently positive. Second, inflation became more persistent: High inflation in one year became more likely to be followed by high inflation the next year.

  The persistence of inflation led workers and firms to revise the way they formed their expectations. When inflation is consistently positive year after year, expecting that the price level this year will be the same as the price level last year—which is the same as expecting zero inflation—becomes systematically incorrect; worse, it becomes foolish. People do not like to make the same mistake repeatedly. So, as inflation became consistently positive and more persistent, people, when forming expectations, started to take into account the presence and the persistence of inflation. This change in expectation formation changed the nature of the relation between unemployment and inflation.

Let's look at the argument in the previous sentence more closely. First, suppose expectations of inflation are formed according to

$$\pi_t^e = \theta \pi_{t-1} \qquad (8.5)$$

The value of the parameter θ (the Greek lowercase theta) captures the effect of last year's inflation rate, π_{t-1}, on this year's expected inflation rate, π_t^e. The higher the value of θ, the more last year's inflation leads workers and firms to revise their expectations of what inflation will be this year, and so the higher the expected inflation rate. We can think of what happened from 1970 on as an increase in the value of θ over time:

Figure 8-4

U.S. Inflation, 1900–2000

Since the 1960s, the U.S. inflation rate has been consistently positive. Inflation has also become more persistent: A high inflation rate this year is more likely to be followed by a high inflation rate next year.

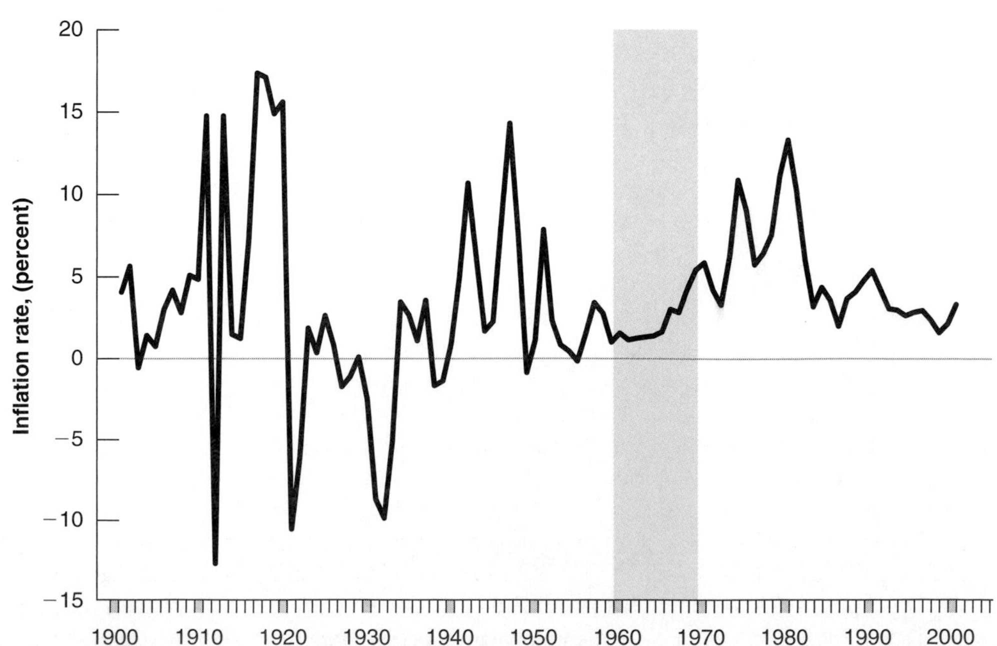

- As long as inflation was low and not very persistent, it was reasonable for workers and firms to ignore past inflation and to assume that this year's price level would be roughly the same as last year's price level. For the period that Samuelson and Solow had looked at, θ was close to zero, and expectations were roughly given by $\pi_t^e = 0$.
- But, as inflation became more persistent, workers and firms started changing the way they formed expectations. They started assuming that if inflation had been high last year, inflation was likely to be high this year as well. The parameter θ, the effect of last year's inflation rate on this year's expected inflation rate, steadily increased. The evidence suggests that, by the mid-1970s, people formed expectations by expecting this year's inflation rate to be the same as last year's inflation rate—in other words, that θ was now equal to 1.

Think about how *you* form expectations. What do you expect inflation to be next year? How did you come to this conclusion?

Now turn to the implications of different values of θ for the relation between inflation and unemployment. To do so, replace equation (8.5) in equation (8.3):

$$\pi_t = \overbrace{\theta \pi_{t-1}}^{\pi_t^e} + (\mu + z) - \alpha u_t$$

- When θ equals zero, we get the original Phillips curve, a relation between the inflation rate and the unemployment rate:

$$\pi_t = (\mu + z) - \alpha u_t$$

- When θ is positive, the inflation rate depends not only on the unemployment rate but also on last year's inflation rate:

$$\pi_t = \theta\, \pi_{t-1} + (\mu + z) - \alpha u_t$$

- When θ equals 1, the relation becomes (moving last year's inflation rate to the left side of the equation):

$$\pi_t - \pi_{t-1} = (\mu + z) - \alpha u_t \tag{8.6}$$

So, when $\theta = 1$, the unemployment rate affects not *the inflation rate*, but rather the *change in the inflation rate*: High unemployment leads to decreasing inflation; low unemployment leads to increasing inflation.

This discussion gives the key to what happened from 1970 on. As θ increased from 0 to 1, the simple relation between the unemployment rate and the inflation rate disappeared. This disappearance is what we saw in Figure 8-3. But a new relation emerged, this time between the unemployment rate and the change in the inflation rate—as predicted by equation (8.6). This relation is shown in Figure 8-5, which plots the change in the inflation rate versus the unemployment rate observed for each year since 1970. The figure shows a clear negative relation between the unemployment rate and the change in the inflation rate. The line that best fits the scatter of points for the period 1970–2000 is

This line, called a regression line, is obtained using econometrics. (See Appendix 3 at the end of the book.) Note the line does not fit the cloud of points very tightly. There are years when the change in inflation is much larger than implied by the line, and years when the change in inflation is much smaller than implied by the line. We return to this point later.

$$\pi_t - \pi_{t-1} = 6\% - 1.0\, u_t \tag{8.7}$$

The line is drawn in Figure 8-5. For low unemployment, the change in inflation is positive. For high unemployment, the change in inflation is negative. This is the form the Phillips curve relation takes in the United States today.

To distinguish it from the original Phillips curve (equation [8.4]), equation (8.6) (or its empirical counterpart, equation [8.7]) is often called the **modified Phillips curve**, or the **expectations-augmented Phillips curve** (to indicate that π_{t-1} stands for expected inflation), or the **accelerationist Phillips curve** (to indicate that a low

Figure 8-5

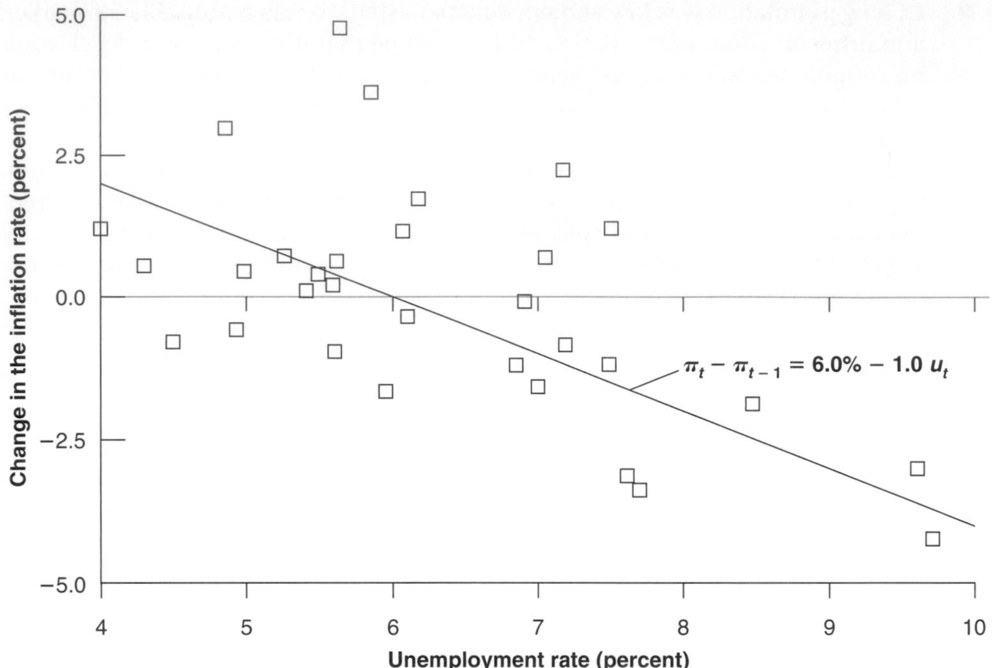

Change in Inflation Versus Unemployment in the United States, 1970–2000

Since 1970, there has been a negative relation between the unemployment rate and the change in the inflation rate in the United States.

Original Phillips curve: $u_t \uparrow \Rightarrow \pi_t \downarrow$

(Modified) Phillips curve: $u_t \uparrow \Rightarrow (\pi_t - \pi_{t-1}) \downarrow$ ►

unemployment rate leads to an increase in the inflation rate and thus an *acceleration* of the price level). I shall simply call equation (8.6) the Phillips curve, and refer to the earlier incarnation, equation (8.4), as the *original* Phillips curve.

Back to the Natural Rate of Unemployment

The history of the Phillips curve is closely related to the discovery of the concept of the natural unemployment rate that we introduced in Chapter 6.

The original Phillips curve implied that there was no such thing as a natural unemployment rate: If policy makers were willing to tolerate a higher inflation rate, they could maintain a lower unemployment rate forever.

In the late 1960s, while the original Phillips curve still gave a good description of the data, two economists, Milton Friedman and Edmund Phelps, questioned the existence of such a trade-off between unemployment and inflation. They questioned it on logical grounds, arguing that such a trade-off could exist only if wage setters systematically underpredicted inflation, and that they were unlikely to make the same mistake forever. Friedman and Phelps also argued that if the government attempted to sustain lower unemployment by accepting higher inflation, the trade-off would ultimately disappear; the unemployment rate could not be sustained below a certain level, a level they called the "natural rate of unemployment." Events proved them right, and the trade-off between the unemployment rate and the inflation rate indeed disappeared. (See the Focus box "Theory Ahead of the Facts: Milton Friedman and Edmund Phelps.") Today, most economists accept the notion of a *natural rate of unemployment*—subject to the many caveats we shall see in the next section.

Let's make explicit the connection between the Phillips curve and the natural rate of unemployment. By definition (see Chapter 6), the natural rate of unemployment is the unemployment rate such that the actual price level is equal to the expected price level. Equivalently, and more conveniently here, the natural rate of unemployment is the unemployment rate such that the actual inflation rate is equal to the expected inflation rate. Denote the natural unemployment rate by u_n. Then, imposing the condition that actual inflation and expected inflation be the same ($\pi_t = \pi_t^e$) in equation (8.3) gives

$$0 = (\mu + z) - \alpha u_t$$

Solving for the natural rate u_n:

$$u_n = \frac{\mu + z}{\alpha} \qquad (8.8)$$

The higher the markup, μ, or the higher the factors that affect wage setting, z, the higher the natural rate of unemployment.

From equation (8.8), $\alpha u_n = \mu + z$. Replacing $(\mu + z)$ by αu_n in equation (8.3) and rearranging gives

$$\pi_t - \pi_t^e = -\alpha(u_t - u_n) \qquad (8.9)$$

If—as is the case in the United States today—the expected rate of inflation, π_t^e, is well approximated by last year's inflation rate, π_{t-1}, the equation finally becomes

$$\pi_t - \pi_{t-1} = -\alpha(u_t - u_n) \qquad (8.10)$$

Start from equation (8.3):

$\pi_t = \pi_t^e + (\mu + z) - \alpha u_t \Rightarrow$

$\pi_t - \pi_t^e = (\mu + z) - \alpha u_t$

If $\pi_t = \pi_t^e$, then

$0 = (\mu - z) - \alpha u_t$

Start from equation (8.3):

$\pi_t = \pi_t^e + (\mu + z) - \alpha u_t$

If $\alpha u_n = (\mu + z)$, then:

$\pi_t = \pi_t^e + \alpha u_n - \alpha u_t$

Rearranging:

$\pi_t = \pi_t^e + \alpha (u_t - u_n)$

Equation (8.10) is an important relation because

- It gives us another way of thinking about the *Phillips curve*, as a relation between the actual unemployment rate, u_t, the natural unemployment rate, u_n, and the change in the inflation rate, $\pi_t - \pi_{t-1}$:
  The change in the inflation rate depends on the difference between the actual and the natural unemployment rates. When the actual unemployment rate is higher than the natural unemployment rate, the inflation rate decreases; when the actual unemployment rate is lower than the natural unemployment rate, the inflation rate increases.
- It gives us another way of thinking about the *natural rate of unemployment*: The natural rate of unemployment is the rate of unemployment required to keep the inflation rate constant. This is why the natural rate is also called the **nonaccelerating inflation rate of unemployment (NAIRU)**.

Calling the natural rate "the nonaccelerating inflation rate of unemployment" is actually wrong: It should be called "the nonincreasing inflation rate of unemployment," or NIIRU. But NAIRU has now become standard and it is too late to change it.

What has been the natural rate of unemployment in the United States since 1970? Put another way, what has been the unemployment rate that, on average, has led to constant inflation?

To answer this question, all we need to do is to return to equation (8.7), the estimated relation between the change in inflation and the unemployment rate since 1970. Putting the change in inflation equal to zero in that equation implies a value for the natural unemployment rate of 6%/1.0 = 6%. In words: The evidence suggests that, since 1970 in the United States, the average rate of unemployment required to keep inflation constant has been equal to 6%.

From 1995 to 2000, the average unemployment rate was 4.7%. Yet the inflation rate did not increase. This suggests the U.S. natural rate of unemployment may now be lower than 6%. More on this in the next section.

8-3 A Summary and Many Warnings

To summarize what we have learned so far:

- The aggregate supply relation is well captured in the United States today by a relation between the change in the inflation rate and the deviation of the unemployment rate from the natural rate of unemployment (equation [8.8]).
- When the unemployment rate exceeds the natural rate of unemployment, the inflation rate decreases. When the unemployment rate is below the natural rate of unemployment, the inflation rate increases.

Theory Ahead of the Facts: Milton Friedman and Edmund Phelps

FOCUS

Economists are usually not very good at predicting major changes before they happen, and most of their insights are derived after the fact. Here is an exception.

In the late 1960s—precisely as the original Phillips curve relation was working like a charm—two economists, Milton Friedman and Edmund Phelps, argued that the appearance of a trade-off between inflation and unemployment was an illusion.

Here are a few quotes from Milton Friedman. About the Phillips curve, he said:

> Implicitly, Phillips wrote his article for a world in which everyone anticipated that nominal prices would be stable and in which this anticipation remained unshaken and immutable whatever happened to actual prices and wages. Suppose, by contrast, that everyone anticipates that prices will rise at a rate of more than 75% a year—as, for example, Brazilians did a few years ago. Then, wages must rise at that rate simply to keep real wages unchanged. An excess supply of labor [by this, Friedman means high unemployment] will be reflected in a less rapid rise in nominal wages than in anticipated prices, not in an absolute decline in wages.

He went on:

> To state [my] conclusion differently, there is always a temporary trade-off between inflation and unemployment; there is no permanent trade-off. The temporary trade-off comes not from inflation per se, but from a rising rate of inflation.

He then tried to guess how much longer the apparent trade-off between inflation and unemployment would last in the United States:

> But how long, you will say, is "temporary"? . . . I can at most venture a personal judgment, based on some examination of the historical evidence, that the initial effect of a higher and unanticipated rate of inflation lasts for something like two to five years; that this initial effect then begins to be reversed; and that a full adjustment to the new rate of inflation takes as long for employment as for interest rates, say, a couple of decades.

Friedman could not have been more right. A few years later, the original Phillips curve started to disappear, in exactly the way Friedman had predicted.

Source: Milton Friedman, "The Role of Monetary Policy," March 1968, American Economic Review, *58–1, p. 1–17. (The article by Phelps, "Money-Wage Dynamics and Labor-Market Equilibrium,"* Journal of Political Economy, *August 1968, part 2, pp. 678–711, made many of the same points more formally.)*

This relation has held quite well since 1970. But evidence from its earlier history, as well as the evidence from other countries, point to the need for a number of warnings. All of them are on the same theme: The relation between inflation and unemployment can and does vary across countries and time.

Variations in the Natural Rate of Unemployment Across Countries

Recall from equation (8.8) that the natural rate of unemployment depends on all the factors that affect wage setting, represented by the catchall variable z; the markup, μ, set by firms; and the response of inflation to unemployment, represented by α. If these factors differ across countries, there is no reason to expect all countries to have the same natural rate of unemployment. And natural rates indeed differ across countries, sometimes considerably.

For example, compare Japan and the United States. The natural rate of unemployment is not directly observable, but under the assumption that the economy fluctuates around it—sometimes above, sometimes below—a simple strategy is to look at the average unemployment rate over a long period. Since 1960 the unemployment rate in Japan has averaged 2.0%, compared to 6.1% in the United States. There is little question that, over this period, the Japanese natural rate has been much lower than the U.S. natural rate.

In 2000, the *actual* unemployment rate was *higher* in Japan than it was in the United States: 4.7% in Japan versus 4.0% in the United States. But this reflected the facts that (1) Japan was in a slump, with an actual unemployment rate far above its natural rate, and (2) the United States was in an expansion, with an actual unemployment rate probably below the natural rate.

The Japanese Unemployment Rate

FOCUS

The average unemployment rate in Japan since 1960 has been 2.0%, compared to 6.1% in the United States. If we take the average unemployment rate to be a rough estimate of the underlying natural rate of unemployment, it would appear that, over the period, the natural rate in Japan has been equal to roughly one-third of the U.S. natural rate. Why the difference?

One of the main reasons appears to be the widespread reliance on lifetime employment in the Japanese labor market. The typical pattern of working life is one in which new workers quickly settle on a job and keep it until retirement. Table 1 shows the sharp contrast with the United States. By age 24, U.S. workers have had on average more than four jobs, Japanese workers only about two. By age 64, U.S. workers have had on average nearly 11 jobs; Japanese workers have had fewer than five.

To give workers incentives to stay in their jobs, Japanese firms offer wages that increase steeply with seniority, rely mostly on seniority-based promotions, and offer large lump-sum retirement payments. In exchange for job security, Japanese workers allow firms to reassign them to other divisions or even to affiliated companies. When car sales at Nissan declined in the 1980s, for example, Nissan sent some of its workers from idle production lines to the dealerships, to help promote sales.

One implication of these labor arrangements is that flows of workers through the labor market are much smaller in Japan than they are in the United States. In Japan, there are no temporary layoffs and many fewer permanent layoffs. A much larger proportion of the needed reallocation of workers takes place within firms rather than through the labor market.

To see why lower flows lead to a lower natural rate of unemployment, think of two countries that are identical in all respects except for the size of the labor-market flows.

In country 1 (think Japan), 2% of the workers become unemployed every quarter. In country 2 (think the United States), 6% of the workers become unemployed every quarter. In both countries, the average duration of unemployment—the average time it takes an unemployed worker to find employment—is the same, one quarter.

Under these assumptions, the unemployment rate in country 1 (Japan) will be equal to 2% (the flow into unemployment—2% per quarter times a duration of unemployment of one quarter). The unemployment rate in country 2 (the United States) will be equal to 6% (6% per quarter times a duration of unemployment of one quarter). The country with the lower flows will have a lower natural rate of unemployment.

Should we expect the natural rate of unemployment to remain very low in Japan? Some economists believe the answer is no. They point out that Japanese firms, facing increasing international competition, may find it too costly to continue to offer lifetime employment in the future. If this is the case, flows of workers and, by implication, the natural rate of unemployment, are likely to be higher in Japan in the future than in the past.

Table 1 Cumulative Number of Jobs Held by Males of Different Ages, in Japan and the United States

Age Group	*16–19*	*20–24*	*25–29*	...	*55–64*
Japan	0.72	2.06	2.71	...	4.91
United States	2.00	4.40	6.15	...	10.95

(The numbers for Japan are for 1977, those for the United States for 1978.)

The question of where the differences between the U.S. and the Japanese natural rates of unemployment come from is taken up in the Focus box "The Japanese Unemployment Rate." The answer, in short, is that the internal organization of firms is very different in the two countries. Flows of separations and hires are much smaller in Japan than in the United States, resulting in a much lower natural rate of unemployment in Japan.

Variations in the Natural Rate of Unemployment over Time

When writing equation (8.6) and when estimating equation (8.7), we treated $(\mu + z)$ as a constant. But there are good reasons to believe that μ and z vary over time. The degree of monopoly power of firms, the structure of wage bargaining, the system of unemployment benefits, and so on are likely to change over time, leading to changes in either μ or z, and by implication, leading to changes in the natural rate of unemployment.

Changes in the natural unemployment rate over time are hard to measure. The reason is again that we do not observe the natural rate, only the actual rate. But broad evolutions can be established by comparing average unemployment rates across decades. We saw in Chapter 6 that, from the 1950s to the 1980s, the U.S. unemployment rate fluctuated around a slowly increasing trend: Average unemployment was 4.5% in the 1950s, 7.3% in the 1980s. In the 1990s, the trend appears to have been reversed, with average unemployment down to 5.2%. In 2000, the unemployment rate was equal to 4.0%, with little or no increase in the inflation rate. This has led a number of economists to conclude that the U.S. natural rate of unemployment has decreased. Whether this is the case is discussed in the Focus box "Did the U.S. Natural Rate of Unemployment Decrease in the 1990s and, If So, Why?". The conclusion is that the natural rate has decreased; the natural rate is probably between 4% and 5% in the United States today. What is less clear is whether it will remain that low in the future.

In 2001, the U.S. unemployment rate increased a lot, and the forecast for 2002 is that it will exceed 6%. This increase reflects however an increase of the actual unemployment rate due to the slowdown, not an increase in the natural unemployment rate.

Thus far, we have focused on the United States. But if our purpose is to show that the natural unemployment rate can change over time, the evidence from Europe is actually much stronger. Recall our discussion of the evolution of European unemployment in Chapter 1. The European unemployment rate, which until the early 1970s had been much lower than the U.S. rate, has steadily increased. After exceeding 10% in the 1980s and 1990s, it has started decreasing. But in 2000, it still stood at 8.1%, compared to 4.0% for the United States.

A high unemployment rate does not necessarily reflect a high natural rate of unemployment; it can reflect instead a large deviation of the actual unemployment rate from the natural rate of unemployment. How can we tell? Equation (8.10) gives us a clue: By looking at the change in inflation, $\pi_t - \pi_{t-1}$. If inflation is decreasing fast, this is an indication that the actual unemployment rate, u_t, is far above the natural rate of unemployment, u_n. If inflation is stable, this is an indication that the actual unemployment rate and the natural rate of unemployment are roughly equal, and that the natural rate itself is high, around 8%.

Looking at the change in inflation to infer whether high unemployment reflects a high natural rate of unemployment, or unemployment above the natural rate of unemployment. From equation (8.10):

$$\pi_t - \pi_{t-1} = -\alpha(u_t - u_n)$$

If $\pi_t - \pi_{t-1} < 0$, it must be that $u_t > u_n$.

If $\pi_t - \pi_{t-1} = 0$, it must be that $u_t = u_n$.

As you saw in Table 1-2, EU countries have roughly stable inflation today. This suggests that the actual and the natural rates of unemployment are roughly equal. Equivalently, the high rate of unemployment in Europe today reflects a high natural rate of unemployment. The average rate of unemployment for the countries now members of the European Union was about 3% in the 1960s. If we take this average as an estimate of what the natural unemployment rate was then, this argument suggests that the natural rate in the European Union has therefore increased by about 5% since the 1960s.

This point is reinforced in Figure 8-6 (on page 175), which plots the change in the EU inflation rate against the unemployment rate for each year since 1961. Each decade is represented by different symbols—the 1960s by squares, the 1970s by diamonds, the 1980s by inverted triangles, and the 1990s by stars. The points for each successive decade make clear that the relation between the change in the inflation rate and the unemployment rate has shifted to the right over time. This suggests a

Did the U.S. Natural Rate of Unemployment Decrease in the 1990s and, If So, Why?

In 2000, the U.S. unemployment rate was 4%, the lowest rate since 1969. Despite the low rate, there was little pressure on inflation. The inflation rate, measured using the GDP deflator, was flat, 2.1% in 2000, compared to 2.2% in 1999. The inflation rate measured using the CPI was up a bit, from 2.1% in 1999 to 3.3% in 2000; but this largely reflected an increase in the price of oil rather than pressure from wages. (For a discussion of the difference between the two inflation rates, and the effect of changes in oil prices, see Chapter 2.)

This combination of low unemployment and stable inflation has led some economists to proclaim the emergence of a "new labor market" where unemployment can be kept much lower than before without risk of increasing inflation—an economy with a much lower natural rate of unemployment. What should we make of this claim? Has the natural rate of unemployment decreased? And, if so, why?

Let us first look at the relation between the change in the inflation rate and the unemployment rate in the 1990s. Figure 1 replicates Figure 8-5, with the points corresponding to the years since 1990 indicated by black diamonds. The line drawn in the figure gives the historical relation between the change in the inflation rate and the unemployment rate, based on observations from 1970 to 2000 (equation [8.7]). Note that since 1994, all the points have remained below the line: In other words, given the unemployment rate, the change in the inflation rate in each of these years has been less than would have been predicted by the average relation between the change in the inflation rate and the unemployment rate for the period 1970 to 2000.

Does this mean the relation between the change in the inflation rate and the unemployment rate has shifted, that the line corresponding to the 1990s is lower than the line drawn in the figure? Figure 1 makes clear that the relation between the change in the inflation rate and the unemployment rate has never been tight. There have been many years since 1970 when the change in inflation was much larger or much smaller than predicted by the line: It would have been wrong to conclude, in each of those years, that the natural rate of

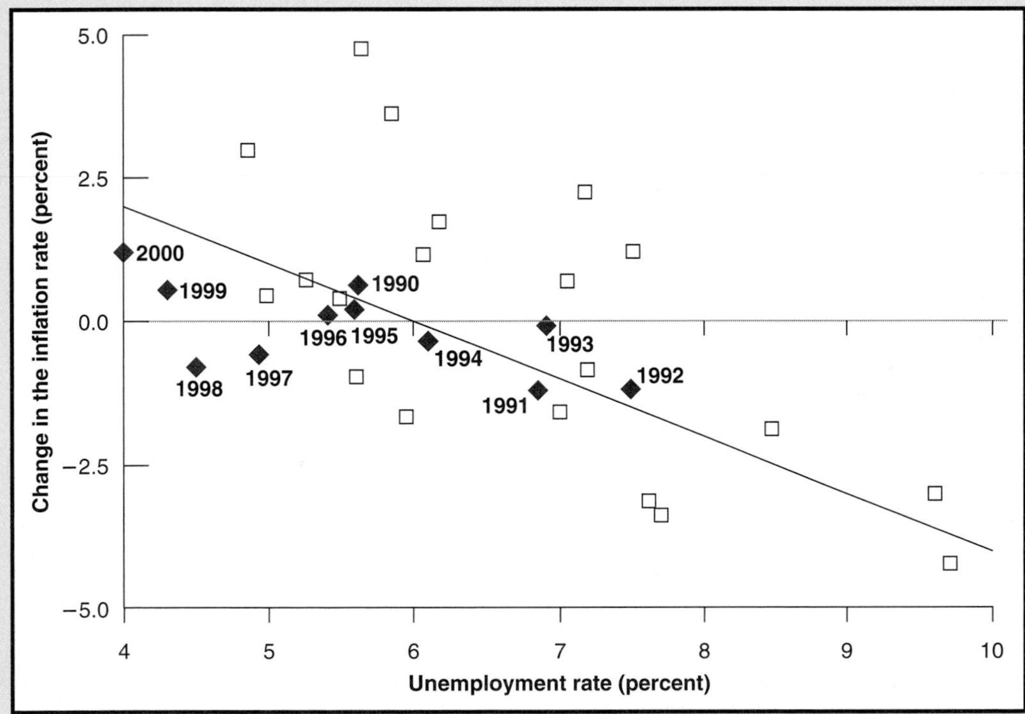

FIGURE 1 *Change in Inflation Versus Unemployment in the United States in the 1990s*
Since 1994, the change in inflation has been less than would have been predicted by the average relation between inflation and unemployment for the period 1970 to 2000.

FOCUS

Continued

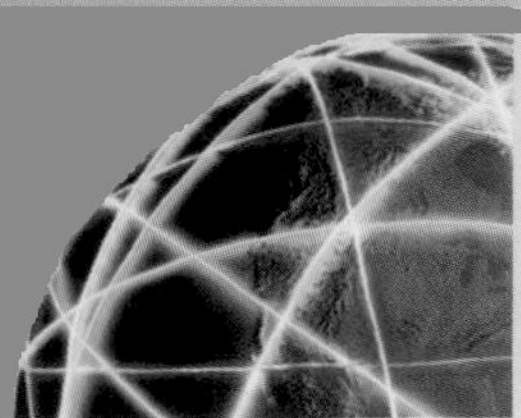

unemployment had drastically decreased or increased. The favorable outcomes from 1994 to 2000 could represent a series of such lucky breaks, with the underlying relation between the change in inflation and unemployment remaining the same as before. But having lucky breaks seven years in a row is not a very likely outcome, and the evidence points to a downward shift in the relation, implying a decrease in the rate of unemployment consistent with zero change in inflation—a decrease in the natural rate of unemployment.

Does the decrease in the natural rate of unemployment reflect the emergence of a "new labor market"? The most extreme claims that, in a new global economy, we should no longer expect any relation between unemployment and inflation, have no basis either in facts or in theory: In a tight labor market, firms still need to increase wages to attract and keep workers, and wage increases still lead to price increases. But the argument that globalization may decrease the natural rate of unemployment is not without merits: Stronger competition between U.S. and foreign firms may lead to a decrease in monopoly power, leading to a decrease in the markup. The option firms have to move some of their operations abroad surely makes them stronger in bargaining. The evidence points to a decreasing role of unions in the United States economy: The unionization rate in the United States, which stood at 25% in the mid-1970s, is below 10% today. So, part of the decrease in the natural rate may come from globalization.

Part of the decrease, however, seems attributable to other factors. Among them:

- The aging of the U.S. population. The proportion of young workers (workers between the ages of 16 and 24) has decreased from 24% in 1980 to 16% in 1998. Young workers tend to start their working life by going from job to job, and typically have a higher unemployment rate. So, a decrease in the proportion of young workers leads to a decrease in the overall unemployment rate. Estimates are that this effect can account for a decrease in the natural unemployment rate of up to 0.6% since 1980.
- The increase in the prison population. The proportion of the population in prison or in jail has tripled in the last 20 years in the United States. In 1980, 0.3% of the U.S. population was in prison; in 1998, the proportion had increased to 0.9%. As many of those in prison would likely have been unemployed, were they not in prison today, this is likely to have had an effect on the unemployment rate. Estimates are that this effect can account for a decrease in the natural unemployment rate of about 0.2% since 1980.
- The increase in temporary help employment. In 1980, employment in temporary help agencies accounted for less than 0.5% of total U.S. employment. Today, it accounts for more than 2%. This is likely to have reduced the natural rate of unemployment. In effect, it allows many workers to look for jobs while being employed rather than unemployed. Estimates are that this can account for a 0.3% decrease in the natural unemployment rate in the 1990s.
- The unexpectedly high rate of productivity growth at the end of the 1990s. As you saw in Chapter 1, productivity growth was very high in the United States at the end of the 1990s. This had been expected neither by firms nor by workers. Given nominal wage inflation, this higher productivity growth led to a smaller increase in costs, which led to lower price inflation. There is little question that this is part of the reason why, despite low unemployment, there was so little increase in inflation at the end of the 1990s.

Will the natural rate of unemployment remain low in the future? The answer is that it depends on the exact contribution of the factors we just listed. Globalization, demographics, prisons, and temporary help agencies are here to stay. The effects of high productivity growth on the natural unemployment rate may not stay: Productivity growth may slow down. Even if it does not, higher productivity growth is likely to be reflected in higher wage increases (we return to these issues in Chapters 12 and 13). In short, some of the decrease in the natural unemployment rate is likely to be permanent; some is not. We should not expect the U.S. economy to be able to remain forever at 4% unemployment with stable inflation.

For more on this issue, read "The High-Pressure U.S. Labor Market of the 1990s," by Lawrence Katz and Alan Krueger, Brookings Papers on Economic Activity, *1999–1, 1–87.*

steady increase in the natural unemployment rate (the rate at which inflation remains stable) over the period.

Why has the natural unemployment rate increased so much in Europe? To answer, we need to look more closely at the nature and the effects of technological change on the economy, and so we defer a discussion to Chapter 13. What you should take from what we have seen so far is a strong warning: The natural unemployment rate can change and does change over time.

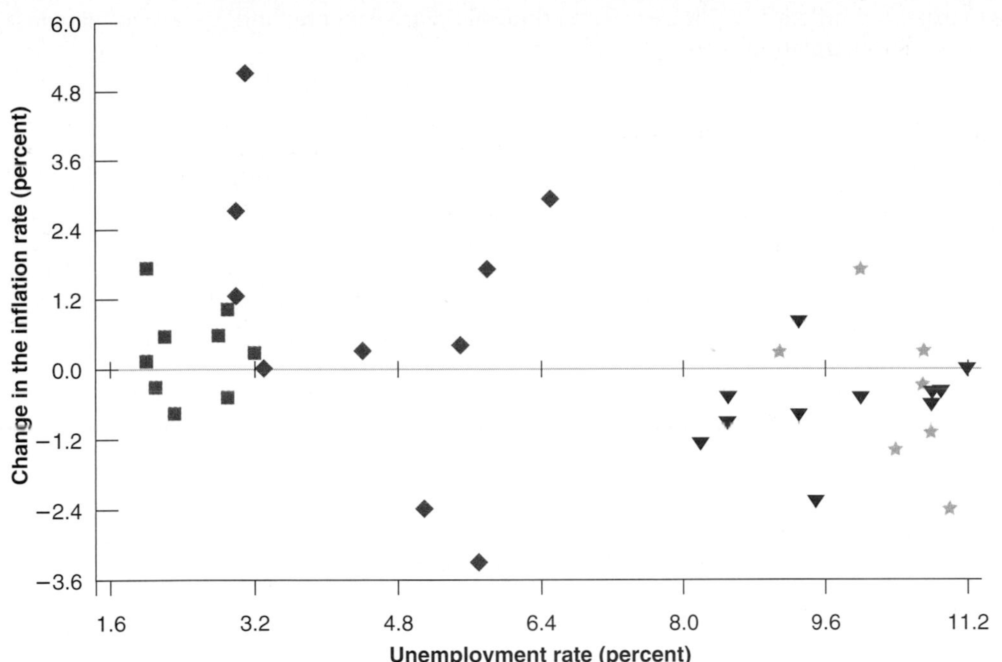

Figure 8-6

Change in Inflation Versus Unemployment—European Union, 1961–2000

The Phillips curve relation between the change in the inflation rate and the unemployment rate has shifted to the right over time, suggesting a steady increase in the natural unemployment rate in the European Union since 1960.

High Inflation and the Phillips Curve Relation

Recall how, in the 1970s, the U.S. Phillips curve changed as inflation became more persistent and wage setters changed the way they formed expectations. The lesson is a general one: The relation between unemployment and inflation is likely to change with the level and the persistence of inflation. Evidence from countries with high inflation confirms this lesson. Not only does the way workers and firms form their expectations change, but so do institutional arrangements.

When the inflation rate becomes high, inflation also tends to become more variable. As a result, workers and firms become more reluctant to enter into labor contracts that predetermine nominal wages for a long period of time: If inflation turns out higher than expected, real wages may plunge and workers may suffer a large cut in their standard of living. If inflation turns out lower than expected, real wages may go up sharply. Firms may not able to pay their workers; some firms may go bankrupt.

More concretely, when inflation runs on average at 5% a year, wage setters can be confident inflation will be between 3 and 7%. When inflation runs on average at 30% a year, wage setters can be confident inflation will be between 20 and 40%. In the first case, if they set a nominal wage, their real wage may end up 2% higher or lower than they expected; in the second case, it may end up 10% higher or lower than they expected. There is much more uncertainty in the second case.

For this reason, the form of wage agreements changes with the level of inflation. Nominal wages are set for shorter periods of time, down from a year to a month or even less. **Wage indexation**, a rule that automatically increases wages in line with inflation, becomes more prevalent.

These changes lead in turn to a stronger response of inflation to unemployment. To see this, an example based on wage indexation will help. Think of an economy that has two types of labor contracts. A proportion, λ (the Greek lowercase lambda), of labor contracts is indexed: Nominal wages in those contracts move one for one with variations in the actual price level. A proportion $1 - \lambda$ of labor contracts is not indexed: Nominal wages are set on the basis of expected inflation. Expected inflation is equal to last year's inflation.

This assumption is too strong. Indexation clauses typically adjust wages not for current inflation (which is only known with a lag), but for inflation in the recent past, so there remains a short delay between inflation and wage adjustments. I ignore this delay here.

Under this assumption, equation (8.9) becomes

$$\pi_t = [\lambda \pi_t + (1 - \lambda)\pi_t^e] - \alpha(u_t - u_n)$$

The term in brackets on the right reflects the fact that a proportion λ of contracts is indexed and thus responds to actual inflation (π_t) and a proportion $(1 - \lambda)$ responds to expected inflation, π_t^e. If we assume that this year's expected inflation is equal to last year's actual inflation ($\pi_t^e = \pi_{t-1}$), we get

$$\pi_t = [\lambda\pi_t + (1-\lambda)\pi_{t-1}] - \alpha(u_t - u_n) \tag{8.11}$$

When $\lambda = 0$, all wages are set on the basis of expected inflation—which is equal to last year's inflation, π_{t-1}—and the equation reduces to equation (8.10):

$$\pi_t - \pi_{t-1} = -\alpha(u_t - u_n)$$

When λ is positive, however, a proportion λ of wages is set on the basis of actual inflation rather than expected inflation. To see what this implies, reorganize equation (8.11): Move the term in brackets to the left, factor $(1 - \lambda)$ on the left of the equation, and divide both sides by $(1 - \lambda)$ to get

$$\pi_t - \pi_{t-1} = -\frac{\alpha}{(1-\lambda)}(u_t - u_n)$$

Wage indexation increases the effect of unemployment on inflation. The higher the proportion of wage contracts which are indexed—the higher λ—the larger the effect of the unemployment rate on the change in inflation—the higher the coefficient $\alpha/(1 - \lambda)$.

The intuition is as follows: Without wage indexation, lower unemployment increases wages, which in turn increases prices. But because wages do not respond to prices right away, there is no further effect within the year. With wage indexation, however, an increase in prices leads to a further increase in wages within the year, which leads to a further increase in prices, and so on, so that the effect of unemployment on inflation within the year is higher.

If and when λ gets close to 1—which is when most labor contracts allow for wage indexation—small changes in unemployment can lead to very large changes in inflation. Put another way, there can be large changes in inflation with nearly no change in unemployment. This is what happens in countries where inflation is very high: The relation between inflation and unemployment becomes more and more tenuous and eventually disappears altogether.

High inflation is the topic of Chapter 23.

Deflation and the Phillips Curve Relation

We have just looked at what happens to the Phillips curve when inflation is very high. Another issue is what happens when inflation is low, and possibly negative—when there is deflation.

The motivation for asking the question is given by an aspect of Figure 8-1 we mentioned at the start of the chapter but then left aside. In that figure, note how the points corresponding to the 1930s (they are denoted by triangles) lie to the right of the others. Not only is unemployment unusually high—this is no surprise as we are looking at the years corresponding to the Great Depression—but, *given the high unemployment rate* the inflation rate is surprisingly high. In other words, given the very high unemployment rate, we would have expected not merely deflation, but a large rate of deflation. In fact, deflation was limited, and from 1934 to 1937 inflation was actually positive.

How do we interpret that fact? There are two potential explanations.

One is that the Great Depression was associated with an increase not only in the actual unemployment rate, but also in the natural unemployment rate. This seems unlikely. Most economic historians see the depression primarily as the result of a large adverse shift in aggregate demand, thus as an increase in the actual unemployment rate over the natural rate of unemployment, rather than an increase in the natural rate of unemployment.

For more on the Great Depression, see Chapter 22.

The other is that, when the economy starts experiencing deflation, the Phillips curve relation breaks down. One possible reason: The reluctance of workers to accept nominal wage decreases. Workers may be willing to accept a cut in real wages, which comes from nominal wages increasing more slowly than inflation; they may, however, fight the same cut in real wages, if it comes with an absolute decrease in nominal wages. If this argument is correct, this implies that the Phillips curve relation between the change in inflation and unemployment may disappear or at least become weaker when the economy is close to zero inflation.

This issue is a crucial one at this stage because, in many countries, inflation is now very low. As you saw in Chapter 1, Japan is actually having negative inflation. What happens to the Phillips curve relation in this environment of low inflation or even deflation is one of the developments closely watched by macroeconomists today.

Consider two scenarios: In one, inflation is 4%, and your nominal wage goes up by 2%. In the other, inflation is 0%, and your nominal wage is cut by 2%. Which do you dislike most? You should be indifferent between the two: In both cases, your real wage goes down by 2%. There is some evidence, however, that most people find the first scenario less painful. More on this in Chapter 25.

For more on the Japanese economic slump, see Chapter 22.

Summary

- The aggregate supply relation can be expressed as a relation between inflation, expected inflation, and unemployment. The higher expected inflation, the higher is actual inflation. The higher unemployment, the lower is inflation.
- When inflation is not very persistent, expected inflation does not depend very much on past inflation. Thus, the aggregate supply relation becomes a relation between inflation and unemployment. This is what Phillips, in the United Kingdom, and Solow and Samuelson, in the United States, discovered when they looked, in the late 1950s, at the joint behavior of unemployment and inflation.
- As inflation became more persistent in the 1970s and 1980s, expectations of inflation became based more and more on past inflation. In the United States today, the aggregate supply relation takes the form of a relation between unemployment and the change in inflation. High unemployment leads to decreasing inflation; low unemployment leads to increasing inflation.
- The natural unemployment rate is the unemployment rate at which the inflation rate remains constant. When the actual unemployment rate is above the natural rate of unemployment, the inflation rate decreases; when the actual unemployment rate is below the natural unemployment rate, the inflation rate increases.
- The natural rate of unemployment depends on many factors that differ across countries and can change over time. This is why the natural rate of unemployment varies across countries: It is much lower in Japan than in the United States. Also, the natural unemployment rate varies over time: In the United States, the natural unemployment rate increased by 1 to 2% from the 1960s to the 1980s, and appears to have decreased in the 1990s. In Europe, the natural unemployment rate has increased by about 5% since the 1960s.
- Changes in the way the inflation rate varies over time affect the way wage setters form expectations and also affects how much they use wage indexation. When wage indexation is widespread, small changes in unemployment can lead to very large changes in inflation. At high rates of inflation, the relation between inflation and unemployment disappears altogether.
- At very low or negative rates of inflation, the Phillips curve relation appears to become weaker. During the Great Depression, even very high unemployment led only to limited deflation. The issue is important because many countries have low inflation today.

Key Terms

- Phillips curve, 161
- wage-price spiral, 164
- modified, or expectations-augmented, or accelerationist Phillips curve, 167
- nonaccelerating inflation rate of unemployment (NAIRU), 169
- wage indexation, 175

Questions and Problems

Quick Check

1. *Using the information in this chapter, label each of the following statements* true, false, *or* uncertain. *Explain briefly.*
   a. The original Phillips curve is the negative relation between unemployment and inflation first observed in the U.K.
   b. The original Phillips curve relation has proven to be very stable across countries and over time.
   c. The aggregate supply relation is consistent with the Phillips curve as observed before the 1970s, but not since.
   d. Policy makers can only exploit the inflation-unemployment trade-off temporarily.
   e. Before the 1970s, there was no natural rate of unemployment, and policy makers could achieve as low a rate of unemployment as they wanted.
   f. The expectations-augmented Phillips curve is consistent with workers and firms adapting their expectations following the macroeconomic experience of the 1960s.
2. *Discuss the following statements:*
   a. The Phillips curve implies that when unemployment is high, inflation is low and vice versa. Therefore, we may experience either high inflation or high unemployment, but we will never experience both together.
   b. As long as we do not mind having high inflation, we can achieve as low a level of unemployment as we want. All we have to do is increase the demand for goods and services by using, for example, expansionary fiscal policy.
3. *Mutations of the Phillips curve*

   Suppose that the Phillips curve is given by

$$\pi_t = \pi_t^e + 0.1 - 2u_t$$

where

$$\pi_t^e = \theta\,\pi_{t-1}$$

Also, suppose that θ is initially equal to zero.

   a. What is the natural rate of unemployment?

   Suppose that the rate of unemployment is initially equal to the natural rate. In year t the authorities decide to bring the unemployment rate down to 3% and hold it there forever.

   b. Determine the rate of inflation in years t, $t + 1$, $t + 2$, $t + 5$.
   c. Do you believe the answer given in (b)? Why or why not? (*Hint*: Think about how people are likely to form expectations of inflation.)

   Now suppose that in year t + 5θ increases from 0 to 1. Suppose that the government is still determined to keep u at 3% forever.

   d. Why might θ increase in this way?
   e. What will the inflation rate be in years $t + 5$, $t + 6$, $t + 7$?
   f. Do you believe the answer given in (e)? Why or why not?
4. *Oil shocks, inflation, and unemployment*

   Suppose that the Phillips curve is given by

$$\pi_t - \pi_t^e = 0.08 + 0.1\mu - 2u_t$$

where μ is the markup of prices over wages.

Suppose that μ is initially equal to 20%, but that as a result of a sharp increase in oil prices, μ increases to 40% in year t and after.

   a. Why would an increase in oil prices result in an increase in μ?
   b. What is the effect of the increase in μ on the natural rate of unemployment? Explain in words.

Dig Deeper

5. *The macroeconomic effects of the indexation of wages*

   Suppose that the Phillips curve is given by

$$\pi_t - \pi_t^e = 0.1 - 2u_t$$

where

$$\pi_t^e = \pi_{t-1}$$

Suppose inflation in year t − 1 is zero. In year t, the authorities decide to keep the unemployment rate at 4% forever.

   a. Compute the rate of inflation for years t, $t + 1$, $t + 2$, and $t + 3$.

   Now suppose that half the workers have indexed labor contracts.

   b. What is the new equation for the Phillips curve?
   c. Answer (a) again.
   d. What is the effect of wage indexation on the relation between π and u?
6. *The price of oil has substantially declined in the 1990s.*
   a. Can this help explain the evidence on inflation and unemployment in the 1990s, presented in this chapter?
   b. What has been the likely effect on the natural rate of unemployment?

Explore Further

7. *Estimating the natural rate of unemployment*

   To answer this question, you will need data on the annual U.S. unemployment and inflation rates since, 1970, which can be obtained from the Web site of the Bureau of Labor Statistics: **stats.bls.gov/data/**

   Select the "most requested series." Under "Employment and Unemployment," pick "Labor force statistics from the Current Population Survey" and make an extract of the "Unemployment Rate—Civilian Labor Force." This is a monthly series, so use the year's average for that year's unemployment rate.

   Similarly, under the "most requested series," look under "Prices and Living Conditions" and make an extract of the "Consumer Price Index—All Urban Consumers." Define the inflation rate in year t as the percentage change in the CPI between year t and year t − 1. Once you have computed the rate of inflation for each year, compute also the change in the inflation rate from one year to the next.

a. Construct a scatter diagram for all the years since 1970, with the change in inflation on the vertical axis and the rate of unemployment on the horizontal axis. Print out the graph. Is your graph similar to Figure 8-5?
b. Using a ruler, draw the line that appears to fit best the cloud of points in the figure. Approximately what is the slope of your line? What is the intercept? Write down the corresponding equation.
c. According to your analysis in (b), what has been the natural rate of unemployment since 1970?

8. *Changes in the natural rate of unemployment*

Repeat Problem 7(a), now drawing separate graphs for the period 1970–1990 and 1990 on. Do you find that the relation between inflation and unemployment is different in the two subperiods? If so, what does this imply for natural rate of unemployment?

We invite you to visit the Blanchard page on the Prentice Hall Web site at:
www.prenhall.com/blanchard
for this chapter's World Wide Web exercises

Appendix: From the Aggregate Supply Relation to a Relation Between Inflation, Expected Inflation, and Unemployment

This appendix shows how to go from the relation between the price level, the expected price level, and the unemployment rate given by equation (8.1):

$$P = P^e(1+\mu)(1-\alpha u+z)$$

to the relation between inflation, expected inflation, and the unemployment rate given by equation (8.2):

$$\pi = \pi^e + (\mu+z) - \alpha u$$

First, introduce time subscripts for the price level, the expected price level, and the unemployment rate, so P_t, P_t^e and u_t refer to the price level, the expected price level, and the unemployment rate in year *t*. Equation (8.1) becomes

$$P_t = P_t^e(1+\mu)(1-\alpha u_t+z)$$

Next, go from an expression in terms of price levels to an expression in terms of inflation rates. Divide both sides by last year's price level, P_{t-1},

$$\frac{P_t}{P_{t-1}} = \frac{P_t^e}{P_{t-1}}(1+\mu)(1-\alpha u_t+z) \qquad (8A.1)$$

Rewrite the fraction P_t/P_{t-1} on the left side as

$$\frac{P_t}{P_{t-1}} = \frac{P_t - P_{t-1} + P_{t-1}}{P_{t-1}} = 1 + \frac{P_t - P_{t-1}}{P_{t-1}} = 1 + \pi_t$$

where the first equality follows from adding and subtracting P_{t-1} in the numerator of the fraction, the second equality follows from the fact that $P_{t-1}/P_{t-1} = 1$, and the third follows from the definition of the inflation rate ($\pi_t \equiv (P_t - P_{t-1})/P_{t-1}$).

Do the same for the fraction P_t^e/P_{t-1} on the right side, using the definition of the expected inflation rate: ($\pi_t^e \equiv (P_t^e - P_{t-1})/P_{t-1}$):

$$\frac{P_t^e}{P_{t-1}} = \frac{P_t^e - P_{t-1} + P_{t-1}}{P_{t-1}} = 1 + \frac{P_t^e - P_{t-1}}{P_{t-1}} = 1 + \pi_t^e$$

Replacing P_t/P_{t-1} and P_t^e/P_{t-1} in equation (8A.1) by the expressions we have just derived,

$$(1+\pi_t) = (1+\pi_t^e)(1+\mu)(1-\alpha u_t+z)$$

This gives us a relation between inflation π_t, expected inflation π_t^e, and the unemployment rate, u_t. The remaining steps make the relation look more friendly.

Divide both sides by $(1+\pi_t^e)(1+\mu)$:

$$\frac{(1+\pi_t)}{(1+\pi_t^e)(1+\mu)} = 1 - \alpha u_t + z$$

As long as inflation, expected inflation, and the markup are not too large, a good approximation to this equation is given by

$$1 + \pi_t - \pi_t^e - \mu = 1 - \alpha u_t + z$$

(See Propositions 3 and 6 in Appendix 2 at the end of the book.) Rearranging gives

$$\pi_t = \pi_t^e + (\mu+z) - \alpha u_t$$

Dropping the time indexes, this is equation (8.2) in the text. (With the time indexes kept, this is equation [8.3] in the text.) The inflation rate, π_t, depends on the expected inflation rate, π_t^e, and the unemployment rate, u_t. The relation also depends on the markup, μ, on the factors that affect wage setting, z, and on the effect of the unemployment rate on wages, α.

Inflation, Activity, and Nominal Money Growth

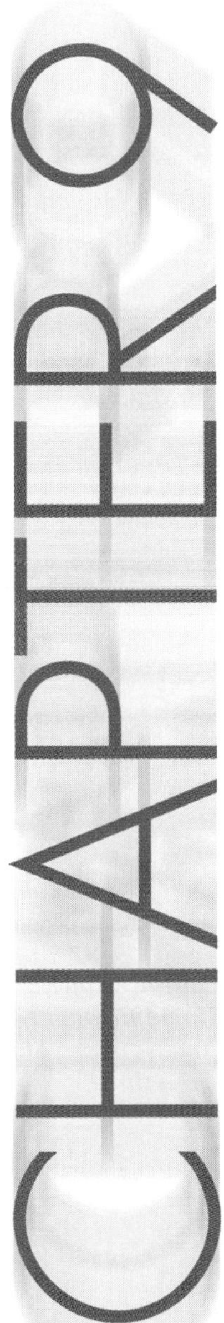

In October 1979, the Fed decided to reduce nominal money growth and decrease inflation, then close to 14% per year. Five years later, after a deep recession, inflation was down to 4% per year.

Why did the Fed decide to reduce inflation? How did it do it? Why was there a recession? More generally, what are the effects of nominal money growth on inflation and on output? Our treatment of expectations in Chapter 7 was too simple to allow us to take up these questions. But, with our discussion of expectations and the introduction of the Phillips curve relation in Chapter 8, we now have what we need to answer them. This is what we do in this chapter.

- Section 9-1 looks at the three relations between output, unemployment, and inflation: Okun's law, the Phillips curve, and the aggregate demand relation.

- Section 9-2 shows that, in the medium run, changes in nominal money growth are reflected one for one in changes in inflation, with no effect on either output or unemployment.

- Section 9-3 shows that in the short run, changes in nominal money growth affect both output and unemployment. A decrease in nominal money growth leads to a period of lower output growth and higher unemployment.

- Section 9-4 discusses the role of credibility and of expectations in the adjustment of the economy to a decrease in nominal money growth.

- Section 9-5 returns to the U.S. disinflation of 1979–1985. ■

9-1 Output, Unemployment, and Inflation

The discussion in this chapter builds on three relations between output, unemployment, and inflation:

- Okun's law, which shows how output growth affects unemployment.
- The Phillips curve, which shows how unemployment affects inflation.
- The aggregate demand relation, which shows how inflation and money growth affect output growth.

The three relations are shown in Figure 9-1. Okun's law is represented by the arrow from output growth to unemployment. The Phillips curve is represented by the arrow from unemployment to inflation. The aggregate demand relation is represented by the two arrows—the arrow from inflation to output growth, and the arrow from nominal money growth to output growth. Together, the three relations determine the effects of nominal money growth on output growth, unemployment, and inflation. In this section, we look at each relation on its own. In the rest of the chapter, we put them together and look at their joint implications.

Okun's Law: From Output Growth to Unemployment

When we wrote the relation between output and unemployment in Chapter 6, we did so under two convenient but restrictive assumptions. We assumed that output moved one for one with employment, so changes in output led to equal changes in employment. And we assumed the labor force was constant, so changes in employment were reflected one for one in opposite changes in unemployment.

We assumed that $Y = N$ and L (the labor force) is constant.

We must now move beyond these assumptions. To understand why, let's see what they imply for the relation between the rate of output growth and the unemployment rate. If output and employment move together, a 1% increase in output leads to a 1% increase in employment. And if movements in employment are reflected in opposite movements in unemployment, a 1% increase in employment leads to a decrease of 1% in the unemployment rate. Let u_t denote the unemployment rate in year t, u_{t-1} the unemployment rate in year $t - 1$, and g_{yt} denote the growth rate of output from year $t - 1$ to year t. Then, under these two assumptions, the following relation should hold:

$$u_t - u_{t-1} = -g_{yt} \qquad (9.1)$$

The change in the unemployment rate should be equal to the negative of the growth rate of output. If output growth is, say, 4%, then the unemployment rate should decline by 4%.

Figure 9-1

Output Growth, Unemployment, Inflation, and Nominal Money Growth

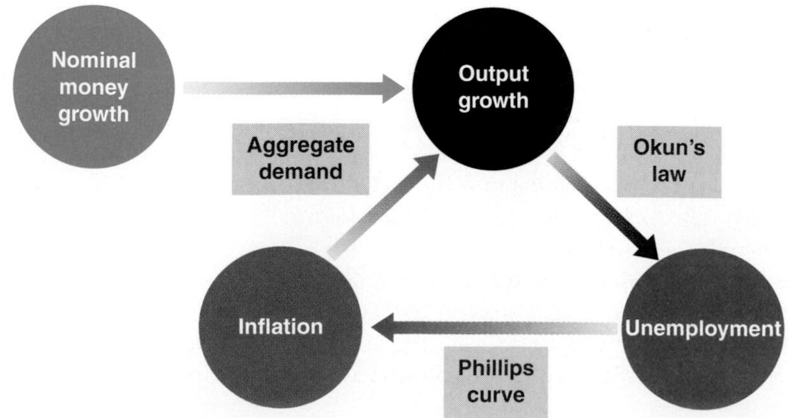

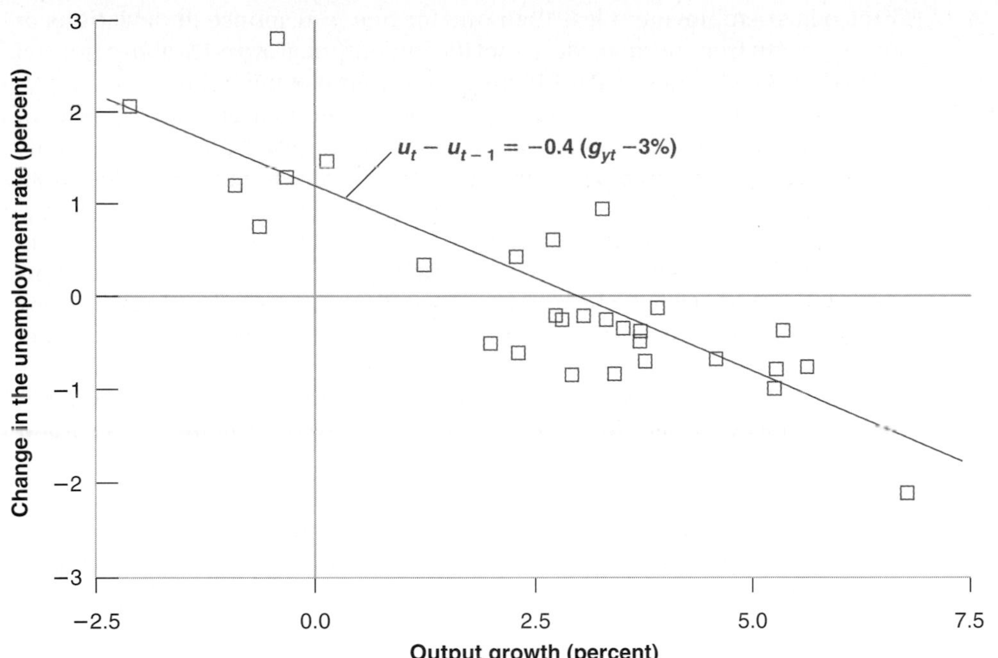

Figure 9-2

Changes in the Unemployment Rate Versus Output Growth in the United States, 1970–2000

High output growth is associated with a reduction in the unemployment rate; low output growth is associated with an increase in the unemployment rate.

Contrast this with the actual relation between output growth and the change in the unemployment rate, the relation known as **Okun's law**. Figure 9-2 plots the change in the unemployment rate against the rate of output growth for each year since 1970. It also plots the regression line that best fits the scatter of points. The relation corresponding to the line is given by

$$u_t - u_{t-1} = -0.4(g_{yt} - 3\%) \quad (9.2)$$

Like equation (9.1), equation (9.2) gives a negative relation between the change in unemployment and output growth. But it differs from equation (9.1) in two ways:

- Annual output growth has to be at least 3% to prevent the unemployment rate from rising. This is because of two factors we have neglected so far: Both the size of the labor force and the productivity of labor are growing over time.

  To maintain a constant unemployment rate, employment must grow at the same rate as the labor force. Suppose the labor force grows at 1.7% per year; then employment must grow at 1.7% per year. If, in addition, labor productivity—output per worker—grows at 1.3% per year, this implies that output must grow at 1.7% + 1.3% = 3% per year. In other words, to maintain a constant unemployment rate, output growth must be equal to 3% per year.

  In the United States, the sum of the rate of labor-force growth and of labor–productivity growth has been equal to 3% per year on average since 1960, and this is why the number 3% appears on the right side of equation (9.2). I shall call the rate of output growth needed to maintain a constant unemployment rate the **normal growth rate** in what follows.
- The coefficient on the right side of equation (9.2) is −0.4, compared to −1.0 in equation (9.1). Put another way, output growth 1% above normal leads only to a 0.4% reduction in the unemployment rate in equation (9.2) rather than to a 1% reduction in the unemployment rate in equation (9.1). There are two reasons why:

1. Firms adjust employment less than one for one in response to deviations of output growth from normal. More specifically, output growth 1% above normal for one year leads to only a 0.6% increase in the employment rate.

   One reason is that some workers are needed no matter what the level of output is. The accounting department of a firm, for example, needs roughly the same number of employees whether the firm is selling more or less than normal.

   Another reason is that training new employees is costly; for this reason, firms prefer to keep current workers around rather than lay them off when output is lower than normal, and ask them to work overtime rather than hire new employees when output is higher than normal. In bad times, firms in effect hoard labor; this behavior is called **labor hoarding**.

Putting the two steps together:

- 1% increase in output above normal ⇒
- 0.6% increase in employment ⇒
- 0.4% decrease in the unemployment rate.

2. An increase in the employment rate does not lead to a one-for-one decrease in the unemployment rate. More specifically, a 0.6% increase in the employment rate leads to only a 0.4% decrease in the unemployment rate. The reason is that labor force participation increases. When employment increases, not all the new jobs are filled by the unemployed. Some of the jobs go to people who were classified as *out of the labor force*, meaning they were not actively looking for a job. And, as labor-market prospects improve for the unemployed, some discouraged workers—who were previously classified as out of the labor force—decide to start actively looking for a job, and become classified as unemployed.

Let's write equation (9.2) using letters rather than numbers. Let $\bar{g}_y$ denote the normal growth rate of the economy (about 3% per year for the United States). Let the coefficient β (the Greek lowercase beta) measure the effect of output growth above normal on the change in the unemployment rate (As you saw in equation [9.2], in the United States, β equals 0.4. The evidence for other countries is given in the Focus box "Okun's Law Across Countries."). We can then write

$$u_t - u_{t-1} = -\beta(g_{yt} - \bar{g}_y) \tag{9.3}$$

Okun's law:

$g_{yt} > \bar{g}_y \Rightarrow u_t < u_{t-1}$

$g_{yt} < \bar{g}_y \Rightarrow u_t > u_{t-1}$

Output growth above normal leads to a decrease in the unemployment rate; output growth below normal leads to an increase in the unemployment rate.

The Phillips Curve: From Unemployment to Inflation

We derived in Chapter 8 the following relation between inflation, expected inflation, and unemployment (equation [8.7])

$$\pi_t = \pi_t^e - \alpha(u_t - u_n) \tag{9.4}$$

Inflation depends on expected inflation and on the deviation of unemployment from the natural rate of unemployment.

We then argued that in the United States today, expected inflation is well approximated by last year's inflation, so that we can replace π_t^e by π_{t-1}. With this assumption, the relation between inflation and unemployment takes the form

$$\pi_t - \pi_{t-1} = -\alpha(u_t - u_n) \tag{9.5}$$

Phillips curve:

$u_t < u_n \Rightarrow \pi_t > \pi_{t-1}$

$u_t > u_n \Rightarrow \pi_t < \pi_{t-1}$

Unemployment below the natural rate leads to an increase in inflation; unemployment above the natural rate leads to a decrease in inflation. The parameter α gives the effect of unemployment on the change in inflation. You saw in Chapter 8 that, since 1970 in the United States, the natural unemployment rate has been on average equal to 6%, and α roughly equal to 1.0. This value of α means that an unemployment

Okun's Law Across Countries

FOCUS

The coefficient β in Okun's law gives the effect on the unemployment rate of deviations of output growth from normal. A value for β of 0.4 tells us that output growth 1% above the normal growth rate for one year decreases the unemployment rate by 0.4%.

The coefficient β depends in part on how firms adjust employment in response to fluctuations in their production. This adjustment of employment depends in turn on such factors as the internal organization of firms and the legal and social constraints on hiring and firing. We would expect the coefficient to be different across countries, and it is. Table 1 gives the estimated coefficient β for a number of countries.

The first column gives estimates of β based on data from 1960 to 1980. The United States has the highest coefficient, 0.39, followed by Germany, 0.20, the United Kingdom, 0.15, and by Japan, 0.02.

The ranking in the first column fits well what we know about the behavior of firms and the structure of firing and hiring regulations across countries. β is smallest in Japan. As you saw in Chapter 8, Japanese firms offer a high degree of job security to their workers, so variations in output have little effect on employment and so also little effect on unemployment. β is largest in the United States, where there are few social and legal constraints on firms' adjustment of employment. And legal restrictions on firing—from severance pay to the need for legal permission from the state to terminate employment—explain why the coefficients estimated for the two European countries are in between those of Japan and the United States.

The second column gives estimates based on data from 1981 to 2000. The coefficient is unchanged for the United States, but higher for the other three countries. This again fits with what we know about firms and regulations. Increased competition in goods markets since the early 1980s has led firms in most countries to reconsider and reduce their commitment to job security. And, at the urging of firms, legal restrictions on hiring and firing have been considerably weakened in many countries. Both factors have led to a larger response of employment to fluctuations in output, thus to a larger value of β.

Table 1 Okun's Law Coefficients Across Countries and Time

Country	β, 1960–1980	β, 1981–2000
United States	0.39	0.39
United Kingdom	0.15	0.51
Germany	0.20	0.37
Japan	0.02	0.12

Source: Author's computations.

rate of 1% above the natural rate for one year leads to a decrease in the inflation rate of about 1%.

The Aggregate Demand Relation: From Nominal Money Growth and Inflation to Output Growth

We derived in Chapter 7 an aggregate demand relation between output and the real money stock, government spending, and taxes (equation [7.3]), based on equilibrium in goods and financial markets:

$$Y_t = Y\left(\frac{M_t}{P_t}, G_t, T_t\right)$$

We are simplifying aggregate demand $Y(M/P, G, T)$ in two ways:

We focus on the relation between the real money stock, M/P, and output, Y, ignoring the two fiscal policy variables, G and T. We can then write the aggregate demand relation as $Y = Y(M/P)$.

We assume the relation between the real money stock and output is linear. This implies we can write the aggregate demand relation as $Y = \gamma M/P$.

where I have added time indices—which we did not need in Chapter 7 but we shall need in this chapter.

To focus on the relation between the real money stock and output, I shall ignore changes in factors other than real money here, and write the aggregate demand relation simply as

$$Y_t = \gamma \frac{M_t}{P_t} \tag{9.6}$$

where γ (the Greek lowercase gamma) is a positive parameter. This equation states that the demand for goods, and thus output, is simply proportional to the real money stock. This simplification will make our life easier. You should keep in mind, however, that behind this relation hides the mechanisms you saw in the *IS–LM* model:

- An increase in the real money stock leads to a decrease in the interest rate.
- The decrease in the interest rate leads to an increase in the demand for goods, and so to an increase in output.

If a variable is the ratio of two variables, its growth rate is equal to the difference between the growth rates of these two variables (see proposition 8 in Appendix 2 at the end of the book). So if $Y = \gamma M/P$ and γ is constant, $g_y = g_m - \pi$.

Equation (9.6) gives a relation between levels—the output level, the level of money, and the price level. We need to go from this relation to a relation between growth rates—of output, money, and the price level. Fortunately, this is easy.

Let g_{yt} be the growth rate of output. Let π_t be the growth rate of the price level—the rate of inflation—and g_{mt} be the growth rate of nominal money. Then, from equation (9.6), it follows that

$$g_{yt} = g_{mt} - \pi_t \tag{9.7}$$

Aggregate demand relation:

$g_{mt} > \pi_t \Rightarrow g_{yt} > 0$

$g_{mt} < \pi_t \Rightarrow g_{yt} < 0$

If nominal money growth exceeds inflation, real money growth is positive, and so is output growth. If nominal money growth is less than inflation, real money growth is negative, and so is output growth. In other words, given inflation, expansionary monetary policy (high nominal money growth) leads to high output growth; contractionary monetary policy (low nominal money growth) leads to low, possibly negative, output growth.

9-2 The Medium Run

Let's collect the three relations between inflation, unemployment, and output growth we derived in Section 9-1:

- Okun's law shows how the deviation of output growth from normal leads to a change in the unemployment rate (equation [9.3])

$$u_t - u_{t-1} = -\beta(g_{yt} - \bar{g}_y)$$

- The Phillips curve shows how the deviation of the unemployment rate from the natural rate leads to a change in the inflation rate (equation [9.5])

$$\pi_t - \pi_{t-1} = -\alpha(u_t - u_n)$$

- The aggregate demand relation shows how the difference between nominal money growth and inflation affects output growth (equation [9.7])

$$g_{yt} = g_{mt} - \pi_t$$

Our task is now to see what these three relations imply for the effects of nominal money growth on output, unemployment, and inflation. The easiest way to proceed is to work backward in time, i.e., to start by looking at the medium run—that is, where the economy ends up when all the dynamics have worked themselves out—and then to look at dynamics—i.e., to see how the economy gets there. This section looks at the *medium run.* The following sections look at dynamics.

Assume that the central bank maintains a constant growth rate of nominal money, call it $\bar{g}_m$. What will be the values of output growth, unemployment, and inflation in the medium run?

- In the medium run, the unemployment rate must be constant; the unemployment rate cannot be increasing or decreasing forever. Putting $u_t = u_{t-1}$ in Okun's law implies that $g_{yt} = \bar{g}_y$. *In the medium run, output must grow at its normal rate of growth,* $\bar{g}_y$.

◀ Medium run: $g_y = \bar{g}_y$

- With nominal money growth equal to $\bar{g}_m$ and output growth equal to $\bar{g}_y$, the aggregate demand relation implies that inflation is constant and satisfies

$$\bar{g}_y = \bar{g}_m - \pi$$

Moving π to the left, and $\bar{g}_y$ to the right gives an expression for inflation:

$$\pi = \bar{g}_m - \bar{g}_y \tag{9.8}$$

In the medium run, inflation must be equal to nominal money growth minus normal output growth. If we define **adjusted nominal money growth** as equal to nominal money growth minus normal output growth, equation (9.8) can be stated as: *In the medium run, inflation equals adjusted nominal money growth.*

◀ Medium run: $\pi = \bar{g}_m - \bar{g}_y$

The way to think about this result is as follows: A growing level of output implies a growing level of transactions and thus a growing demand for real money. So, if output is growing at 3%, the real money stock must also grow at 3% per year. If the nominal money stock grows at a rate different from 3% per year, the difference must show up in inflation (or deflation). For example, if nominal money growth is 10% per year, then inflation must be equal to 7% per year.

- If inflation is constant, then inflation this year is equal to inflation last year: $\pi_t = \pi_{t-1}$. Putting $\pi_t = \pi_{t-1}$ in the Phillips curve implies that $u_t = u_n$. *In the medium run, the unemployment rate must be equal to the natural rate of unemployment.*

◀ Medium run: $u = u_n$

These results are the natural extension of the results we derived in Chapter 7. There, you saw that *changes in the level of nominal money* were neutral in the medium run: They had no effect on either output or unemployment, but were reflected one for one in changes in the price level. We see here that a similar neutrality result applies to *changes in the rate of growth of nominal money*: Changes in nominal money growth have no effect on output or unemployment in the medium run, but are reflected one for one in changes in the rate of inflation.

◀ **In the medium run, changes in nominal money growth have no effect on output or on unemployment. They are reflected one for one in changes in the rate of inflation.**

Another way to state this last result is that the only determinant of inflation in the medium run is adjusted nominal money growth. Milton Friedman put it this way: *Inflation is always and everywhere a monetary phenomenon.* Unless they lead to higher nominal money growth, factors such as the monopoly power of firms, strong unions, strikes, fiscal deficits, the price of oil, and so on have no effect on inflation *in the medium run.*

◀ "Unless" is important. During episodes of very high inflation (Chapter 23), you will see that fiscal deficits often lead to nominal money creation, and to higher nominal money growth.

We summarize the results of this section in Figure 9-3, which plots the unemployment rate on the horizontal axis, and the inflation rate on the vertical axis.

- In the medium run, the unemployment rate is equal to the natural rate of unemployment. The economy must be somewhere on the vertical line at $u = u_n$.
- In the medium run, inflation must be equal to adjusted nominal money growth—the rate of nominal money growth minus the normal rate of growth of output. This is represented by the (upper) horizontal line at $\pi = \bar{g}_m - \bar{g}_y$.

Figure 9-3

Inflation and Unemployment in the Medium Run

In the medium run, unemployment is equal to the natural rate, and inflation is equal to adjusted nominal money growth.

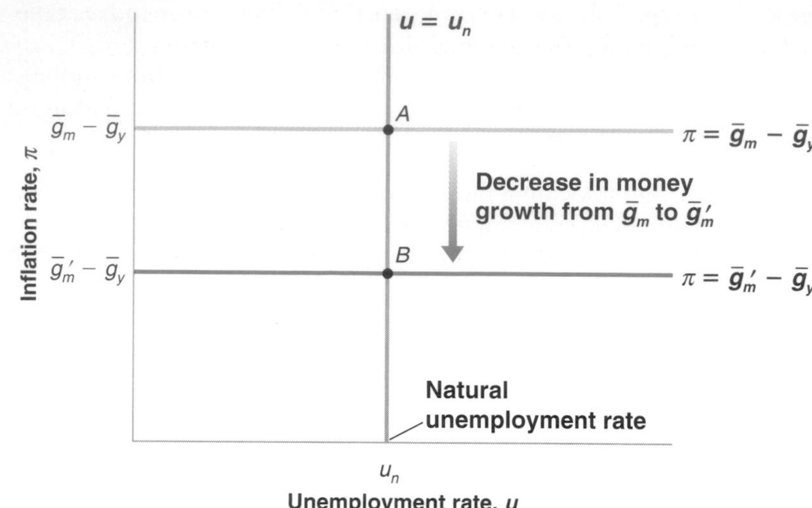

A decrease in nominal money growth from $\bar{g}_m$ to $\bar{g}'_m$ shifts the horizontal line downward, moving the equilibrium from point *A* to point *B*. The inflation rate decreases by the same amount as the decrease in the rate of nominal money growth. There is no change in the unemployment rate, which is still equal to u_n.

Having looked at where the economy ends up in the medium run, we now look at how it gets there. In other words, we look at the dynamics of adjustment. This is the focus of the next three sections.

9-3 Disinflation

Assume the economy is in medium-run equilibrium: Unemployment is at the natural rate of unemployment; The rate of growth of output is equal to the normal growth rate. The inflation rate is equal to adjusted nominal money growth.

You may ask: What is so bad about high inflation if growth is proceeding at a normal rate, and unemployment is at the natural rate of unemployment? To answer, we need to discuss the costs of inflation. We shall do so in Chapter 23.

Suppose, however, that the rate of nominal money growth and, by implication, the inflation rate are high, and there is a consensus that inflation must be reduced. From the previous section, we know the only way to achieve lower inflation is to reduce the rate of nominal money growth: Only lower nominal money growth will lead to lower inflation in the medium run. The question we now take up is what will happen along the way.

A First Pass

Suppose that the central bank decreases the rate of nominal money growth. Just by looking at our three relations, we can tell the beginning of the story.

$g_m \downarrow \Rightarrow g_m - \pi \downarrow \Rightarrow g_y \downarrow$

- Look at the aggregate demand relation: Given the initial rate of inflation, lower nominal money growth leads to lower real nominal money growth, and thus to a decrease in output growth.

$g_y \downarrow \Rightarrow u \uparrow$

- Look at Okun's law: Output growth below normal leads to an increase in unemployment.

$u \uparrow \Rightarrow \pi \downarrow$

- Look at the Phillips curve relation: Unemployment above the natural rate leads to a decrease in inflation.

So we have our first set of results: Initially, lower nominal money growth decreases output growth and increases unemployment. The increase in unemployment leads to a decrease in inflation.

We can actually go a bit further in thinking about what happens to the economy over time (rely on your intuition here; we shall go through the arithmetic step by step later):

- Look at the Phillips curve relation: So long as unemployment remains above the natural rate, inflation keeps decreasing. So, eventually, inflation becomes less than nominal money growth.
- Look at the aggregate demand equation: Eventually, inflation is sufficiently low that real money growth, and, in turn, output, start increasing faster than the normal growth rate.
- Look at Okun's law: If output growth is above normal, then unemployment starts decreasing.

$u > u_n \Rightarrow \pi\downarrow$

$\pi << g_m \Rightarrow g_y > \bar{g}_y$

$g_y > \bar{g}_y \Rightarrow u\downarrow$

This gives us a second set of results. So long as unemployment remains above the natural rate, inflation decreases. Eventually, inflation is sufficiently low, and, by implication, real money growth is sufficiently high that unemployment must start decreasing. Unemployment does not stay high forever.

This is an important pair of results: After a decrease in nominal money growth, unemployment initially increases (the first result), but eventually turns around (the second result). We want to know more, however: For how long does unemployment increase? By how much? How does it return to the natural rate of unemployment in the medium run? If the central bank cares about unemployment in addition to inflation, should it decrease nominal money growth at once, or should it decrease it slowly over time? To answer these questions, we need to look more closely at our three relations.

How Much Unemployment? And for How Long?

Start with the Phillips curve relation (equation [9.5])

$$\pi_t - \pi_{t-1} = -\alpha(u_t - u_n)$$

This relation makes it clear that **disinflation**—a decrease in inflation—can be obtained only at the cost of higher unemployment: For the left side of the equation to be negative—that is, for inflation to decrease—the term $(u_t - u_n)$ must be positive: The unemployment rate must exceed the natural rate.

Make sure to distinguish between

Deflation: Decrease in the price level.

Disinflation: Decrease in the inflation rate.

The equation actually has a stronger implication: The total amount of unemployment required for a given decrease in inflation does not depend on the speed at which disinflation is achieved. In other words, disinflation can be achieved quickly, at the cost of very high unemployment for a few years; or it can be achieved more slowly, with a smaller increase in unemployment spread over more years. In both cases, the total amount of unemployment, summing over the years, will be the same.

Let's see why. Define first a **point-year of excess unemployment** as a difference between the actual and the natural unemployment rate of one percentage point for one year. For example, if the natural rate of unemployment is 6%, an unemployment rate of 8% four years in a row corresponds to 4 times (8 − 6) = 8 point-years of excess unemployment.

When should you use "percentage point" rather than "percent"? Suppose you are told the unemployment rate, which was equal to 10%, has increased by 5%. Is it 5% of itself, in which case the unemployment rate is (1.05) times 10% = 10.5%? Or is it 5 percentage points, in which case it is 10% + 5% = 15%? The use of "percentage point" rather than "percent" helps avoid the ambiguity. If you are told the unemployment rate has increased by 5 percentage points, this means that the unemployment rate is 10% + 5% = 15%.

Now look at a central bank that wants to reduce inflation by x percentage points. To make things simpler, let's use specific numbers: Assume that the central bank wants to reduce inflation from 14 to 4%, so that x is equal to 10. Let's also assume that α equals 1.

- Suppose the central bank wants to achieve the reduction in inflation in one year. Equation (9.5) tells us that what is required is one year of unemployment at 10% above the natural rate. In this case, the right side of the equation is equal to −10%, and the inflation rate decreases by 10% within a year.

- Suppose the central bank wants to achieve the reduction in inflation over two years. Equation (9.5) tells us that what is then required is two years of unemployment at 5% above the natural rate. During each of the two years, the right side of the equation is equal to −5%, so the inflation rate decreases by 5% each year, thus by 2 times 5% = 10% over two years.
- By the same reasoning, reducing inflation over 5 years requires 5 years of unemployment at 2% above the natural rate (5 times 2% = 10%); reducing inflation over 10 years requires 10 years of unemployment at 1% above the natural rate (10 times 1% = 10%) and so on.

Note that in each case the number of point-years of excess unemployment required to decrease inflation is the same, namely, 10: 1 year times 10% excess unemployment in the first scenario, 2 years times 5% in the second, 10 years times 1% in the last. The implication is straightforward: The central bank can choose the distribution of excess unemployment over time, but it cannot change the total number of point-years of excess unemployment.

Sacrifice ratio = Point-years of excess unemployment / Decrease in inflation ▶

We can state this conclusion another way. Define the **sacrifice ratio** as the number of point-years of excess unemployment needed to achieve a decrease in inflation of 1%. Then equation (9.5) implies that this ratio is independent of policy and simply equal to $(1/\alpha)$. If α roughly equals one, as the estimated Phillips curve suggests, then the sacrifice ratio is roughly equal to one.

From equation (9.5), excess unemployment of 1% for one year decreases the inflation rate by α times 1%. Put the other way, to reduce the inflation rate by 1%, excess unemployment must be equal to $1/\alpha$ for one year. ▶

If the sacrifice ratio is constant, does this imply that the speed of disinflation is irrelevant? No. Suppose that the central bank tried to achieve the decrease in inflation in one year. As you have just seen, this would require an unemployment rate of 10% above the natural rate for one year. With a natural unemployment rate of 6%, this would require increasing the actual unemployment rate to 16% for one year. From Okun's law, using a value of 0.4 for β and a normal output growth rate of 3%, output growth would have to satisfy

$$u_t - u_{t-1} = -\beta(g_{yt} - \bar{g}_y)$$
$$16\% - 6\% = -0.4\,(g_{yt} - 3\%)$$

This implies a value for $g_{yt} = -(10\%)/0.4 + 3\% = -22\%$. In words, output growth would have to equal −22% for a year! For comparison, the largest negative growth rate in the United States in the twentieth century was −15% in 1931, during the Great Depression. It is fair to say that macroeconomists do not know with great confidence what would happen if monetary policy were aimed at inducing such a large negative growth rate. But most would surely be unwilling to try. The increase in the overall unemployment rate would lead to extremely high unemployment rates for some groups—specifically the young and the unskilled, whose unemployment typically increases more than the average unemployment rate. Not only would the welfare costs for these groups be large, but such high unemployment might leave permanent scars. The sharp drop in output would most likely also lead to a large number of bankruptcies, with long-lasting effects on economic activity. In short, the disruptions from a fast disinflation are likely to be very large. For this reason, the central bank will want to go more slowly, and achieve disinflation over a number of years rather than all in one year.

Working Out the Path of Nominal Money Growth

Let's assume that, based on the computations we just went through, the central bank decides to decrease the inflation rate from 14 to 4% over five years. Clearly, it does not control either inflation or unemployment directly. Look at Figure 9-1 again: What the central bank does control is nominal money growth, which in turn affects output growth, which in turn affects unemployment, which in turn affects inflation.

You saw in Chapter 4 that the central bank actually controls central bank money, not the money stock itself. We shall ignore this complication here. ▶

TABLE 9-1 Engineering Disinflation

	Year								
	Before	Disinflation					After		
	0	1	2	3	4	5	6	7	8
Inflation (%)	14	12	10	8	6	4	4	4	4
Unemployment rate (%)	6	8	8	8	8	8	6	6	6
Output growth (%)	3	−2	3	3	3	3	8	3	3
Nominal money growth (%)	17	10	13	11	9	7	12	7	7

Using our equations, however, we can solve for the path of nominal money growth that will achieve the disinflation. This is what we do in the rest of this section. Let's make the same numerical assumptions as before. Normal output growth is 3%. The natural rate of unemployment is 6%; α in the Phillips curve is equal to 1; β in Okun's law is equal to 0.4. Table 9.1 shows how to derive the path of nominal money growth needed to achieve 10% disinflation over five years.

For the rest of this section: First follow the logic of the step-by-step computations; this will give you a better sense of the relations between output growth, unemployment, inflation, and nominal money growth. Do not worry yet about understanding the broader picture. When you have gone through the whole argument, step back and look at the way the economy adjusts over time. Make sure you can tell the story in words.

In year 0, before the disinflation, output growth is 3%: unemployment is equal to the natural rate, 6%; inflation is running at 14%; nominal money growth is 17%. Real money growth equals 17%−14% = 3%, the same as output growth.

The central bank then makes the decision to reduce inflation from 14% to 4% over five years, starting in year 1. The easiest way to solve for the required path of nominal money growth is to work backwards: To start from the desired path of inflation, derive the required path of unemployment and the required path of output growth, and, finally, derive the required path of nominal money growth.

- *The path of inflation.* The first line of Table 9-1 gives the path of inflation required to achieve the decrease in inflation over five years:

  Inflation starts at 14% before the change in monetary policy, decreases by 2 percentage points in each year from year 1 to year 5, and then remains at its lower level of 4% thereafter.
- *The path of unemployment.* The second line gives the path of unemployment required to achieve the decrease in inflation.

  This step is derived by using the Phillips curve relation. If inflation is to decrease by 2 percentage points per year for five years and $\alpha = 1$, the economy must accept five years of unemployment at 2 percentage points above the natural rate ($5 \times 2\% = 10\%$, the required decrease in inflation). Thus, from year 1 to year 5, the unemployment rate in each of those years must equal 6% + 2% = 8%.
- *The path of output.* The third line gives the *path of output growth* required to achieve the required path of unemployment.

  This step is derived by using Okun's law. From Okun's law, we know that the initial increase in unemployment requires lower output growth. With β equal to 0.4, the initial increase in unemployment of 2% requires the rate of output growth to be lower than normal by 2%/0.4 = 5 percentage points. Given a normal growth rate of 3%, the economy must therefore have a growth rate of 3% − 5% = −2% in year 1. There must be a recession in year 1.

  From years 2 to 5, growth must proceed at a rate sufficient to maintain the unemployment rate constant at 8%. Thus, output must grow at its normal rate, 3%. In other words, from years 2 to 5, the economy grows at a normal rate, but has an unemployment rate that exceeds the natural rate of unemployment by 2 percentage points.

Once disinflation is achieved, higher output growth in year 6 is needed to return unemployment to the natural rate: To decrease the unemployment rate by 2 percentage points in one year, Okun's law tells us that the rate of output growth must exceed normal growth by 2%/0.4, thus, by 5%. The economy must therefore grow at 3% + 5% = 8% for one year.

- *The path of nominal money growth.* The last line gives the path of nominal money growth required to achieve the required path of output.

  From the aggregate demand relation, (equation [9.7]), we know that output growth equals nominal money growth minus inflation, or equivalently that nominal money growth equals output growth plus inflation. Adding the numbers for inflation in the first line and for output growth in the third gives us the required path for the rate of nominal money growth.

  The path looks surprising at first: Nominal money growth goes down sharply in year 1, then up again, then slowly down for three years, then up again in the year following disinflation, to finally reach its permanent lower level of 7%. But this is easy to explain:

  To start the disinflation, the central bank must increase unemployment. To increase unemployment requires a sharp contraction in nominal money growth in year 1. The decrease in nominal money growth—from 17 to 10%—is much sharper than the decrease in inflation—from 14 to 12%. The result is thus a sharp decrease in real money growth, a recession, and an increase in the unemployment rate.

  For the next four years, monetary policy is aimed at maintaining unemployment at 8%, not at increasing unemployment further. Nominal money growth is aimed at allowing demand and therefore output to grow at the normal growth rate. Put another way, nominal money growth is set equal to inflation plus the normal growth rate of 3%. And as inflation decreases—because of high unemployment—so does nominal money growth.

  At the end of the disinflation the central bank must allow unemployment to go back to the natural rate of unemployment (otherwise inflation would continue to decrease.) So, in year 6, there must be a one-time increase in nominal money growth before the central bank returns, from year 7 on, to the new lower rate of nominal money growth.

Figure 9-4 shows the path of unemployment and inflation implied by this disinflation path. In year 0, the economy is at point *A*: The unemployment rate is 6% and the inflation rate is 14%. Years 1 to 5 are years of disinflation, during which the economy moves from *A* to *B*. Unemployment is higher than the natural rate of unemployment, leading to a steady decline in inflation. Inflation decreases until it reaches 4%. From year 6 on, the economy remains at point *C*, with unemployment back down to the natural rate of unemployment and an inflation rate of 4%. *In the medium run, nominal money growth and inflation are lower, and the unemployment rate and output growth are back to normal;* this is the neutrality result we obtained in Section 9-2. *But the transition to lower nominal money growth and lower inflation is associated with a period of higher unemployment.*

The disinflation path drawn in Figure 9-4 is one of many possible paths. We could have looked instead at a path that front-loaded the increase in the unemployment rate and allowed it to return slowly to the natural rate of unemployment, avoiding the sharp increase in nominal money growth that takes place at the end of our scenario (year 6 in Table 9-1). Or we could have looked at a path where the central bank decreased the rate of nominal money growth from 14 to 4% at once, letting inflation and unemployment adjust over time. But all the paths we would draw would share one characteristic: The total unemployment cost—that is, the number of point-years of

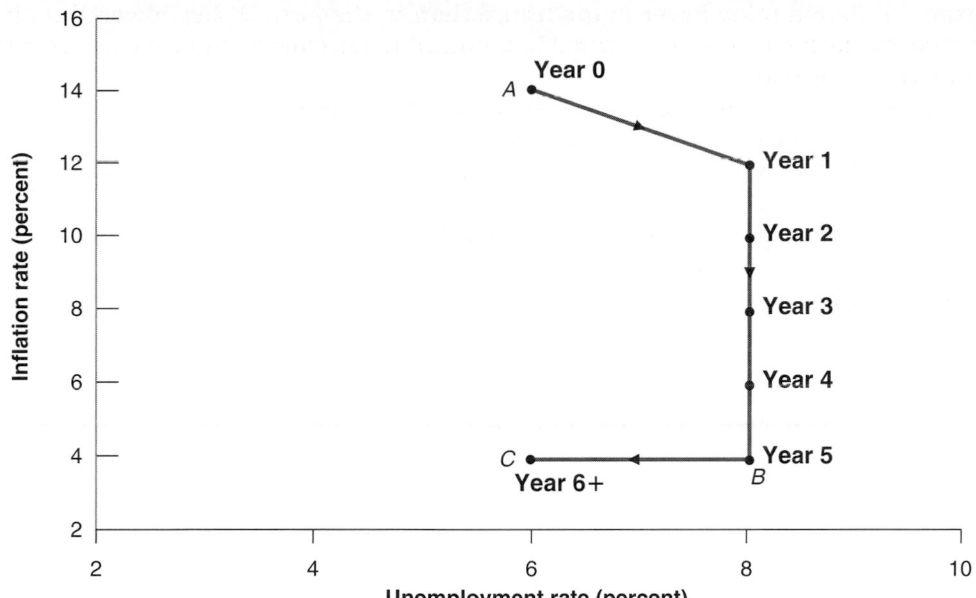

Figure 9-4

A Disinflation Path

Five years of unemployment above the natural rate of unemployment lead to a permanent decrease in inflation.

excess unemployment—would be the same. Put another way, *unemployment has to remain above the natural rate by a large enough amount, or long enough, to achieve disinflation.*

The analysis we have just developed is very much the type of analysis economists at the Fed were conducting in the late 1970s. The econometric model they used, as well as most econometric models in use at the time, shared our simple model's property that policy could change the timing, but not the number of point-years of excess unemployment. I shall call this the *traditional approach* in what follows. This traditional approach was challenged by two separate groups of macroeconomists. The next section presents their arguments, and the discussion that followed.

9-4 Expectations, Credibility, and Nominal Contracts

The focus of both groups was the role of expectations, and how changes in expectation formation might affect the unemployment cost of disinflation. But despite this common focus, they reached quite different conclusions.

Expectations and Credibility: The Lucas Critique

The conclusions of the first group were based on the work of Robert Lucas and Thomas Sargent, of the University of Chicago. In what has become known as the **Lucas critique**, Lucas pointed out that when trying to predict the effects of a major change in policy—such as the change considered by the Fed at the time—it could be very misleading to take as given the relations estimated from past data.

In the case of the Phillips curve, taking equation (9.5) as given was equivalent to assuming that wage setters would keep expecting inflation in the future to be the same as in the past, that the way wage setters formed expectations would not change in response to the change in policy. This was an unwarranted assumption, Lucas argued: Why shouldn't wage setters take policy changes into account? If wage setters believed that the Fed was committed to lower inflation, they might well expect inflation to be lower in the future than in the past. If they lowered their expectations of inflation, then actual inflation would decline without the need for a protracted recession.

The logic of Lucas's argument can be seen by returning to equation (9.4), the Phillips curve with expected inflation on the right:

$$\pi_t = \pi_t^e - \alpha(u_t - u_n)$$

If $\pi_t^e = \pi_{t-1}$, the Phillips curve is given by

$$\pi_t - \pi_{t-1} = -\alpha(u_t - u_n)$$

To achieve $\pi_t < \pi_{t-1}$, it must be that $u_t > u_n$.

If wage setters kept forming expectations of inflation by looking at last year's inflation (if $\pi_t^e = \pi_{t-1}$), then the only way to decrease inflation would be to accept higher unemployment for some time; we explored the implications of this assumption in the preceding section.

But if wage setters could be convinced that inflation was indeed going to be lower than in the past, they would decrease their expectations of inflation. This would in turn reduce actual inflation, without necessarily any change in the unemployment rate. For example, if wage setters were convinced that inflation, which had been running at 14% in the past, would be only 4% in the future, and if they formed expectations accordingly, then inflation would decrease to 4% *even if unemployment remained at the natural rate of unemployment*

$$\begin{aligned} \pi_t &= \pi_t^e - \alpha(u_t - u_n) \\ 4\% &= 4\% - \quad 0\% \end{aligned}$$

Nominal money growth, inflation, and expected inflation could all be reduced without the need for a recession. Put another way, decreases in nominal money growth could be neutral not only in the medium run, but also in the short run.

Lucas and Sargent did not believe that disinflation could really take place without some increase in unemployment. But Sargent, looking at the historical evidence on the end of several very high inflations, concluded that the increase in unemployment could be small. The sacrifice ratio—the amount of excess unemployment needed to achieve disinflation—might be much lower than suggested by the traditional approach. The essential ingredient of successful disinflation, he argued, was **credibility** of monetary policy—the belief by wage setters that the central bank was truly committed to reducing inflation. Only credibility would lead wage setters to change the way they formed expectations. Furthermore, he argued, a clear and quick disinflation program was much more likely to be credible than a protracted one that offered plenty of opportunities for reversal and political infighting along the way.

The "credibility view":

Fast disinflation is likely to be more credible than slow disinflation. Credibility decreases the unemployment cost of disinflation. Thus, the central bank should go for fast disinflation.

Nominal Rigidities and Contracts

A contrary view was taken by Stanley Fischer, from MIT, and John Taylor, then at Columbia University. Both emphasized the presence of **nominal rigidities**, meaning that, in modern economies, many wages and prices are set in nominal terms for some time and are typically not readjusted when there is a change in policy.

Fischer argued that even with credibility, too rapid a decrease in nominal money growth would lead to higher unemployment. Even if the Fed fully convinced workers and firms that nominal money growth was going to be lower, the wages set before the change in policy would reflect expectations of inflation prior to the change in policy. In effect, inflation would already be built into existing wage agreements, and could not be reduced instantaneously and without cost. At the very least, Fischer said, a policy of disinflation should be announced sufficiently in advance of its actual implementation to allow wage setters to take it into account when setting wages.

Taylor's argument went one step further. An important characteristic of wage contracts, he argued, is that they are not all signed at the same time. Instead, they are staggered over time. He showed that this **staggering of wage decisions** imposed strong limits on how fast disinflation could proceed without triggering higher unemployment, even if the Fed's commitment to inflation was fully credible. Why the limits? If workers cared about relative wages—that is, cared about their wages relative to the wages of other workers—each wage contract would choose a wage not very different from wages in the other contracts in force at the time. Too rapid a decrease in nominal money growth would not lead to a proportional decrease in inflation. Rather, the real money stock would decrease, triggering a recession and an increase in the unemployment rate.

Taking into account the time pattern of wage contracts in the United States, Taylor then showed that, under full credibility of monetary policy, there *was* a path of disinflation consistent with no increase in unemployment. This path is shown in Figure 9-5.

Disinflation starts in quarter 1 and lasts for 16 quarters. Once it is achieved, the inflation rate, which started at 10%, is 3%. The striking feature is how slowly disinflation proceeds at the beginning. One year (four quarters) after the announcement of the change in policy, inflation is still 9.9%. But then disinflation proceeds more quickly. By the end of the third year inflation is down to 4%, and by the end of the fourth year the desired disinflation is achieved.

The reason for the slow decrease in inflation at the beginning—and, behind the scene, for the slow decrease in nominal money growth—is straightforward: Wages in force at the time of the policy change are the result of decisions made before the policy change, so that the path of inflation in the near future is largely predetermined. If nominal money growth were to decrease sharply, inflation could not decrease very much right away, and the result would be a decrease in real money and a recession. So the best policy is for the Fed to proceed slowly at the beginning while announcing it will proceed faster in the future. This announcement leads new wage agreements to take the new policy into account. When most wage decisions in the economy come from decisions made after the change in policy, disinflation can proceed much more quickly. This is what happens in the third year following the policy change.

Like Lucas and Sargent, Taylor did not believe that disinflation could really be implemented without an increase in unemployment. For one thing, he realized that

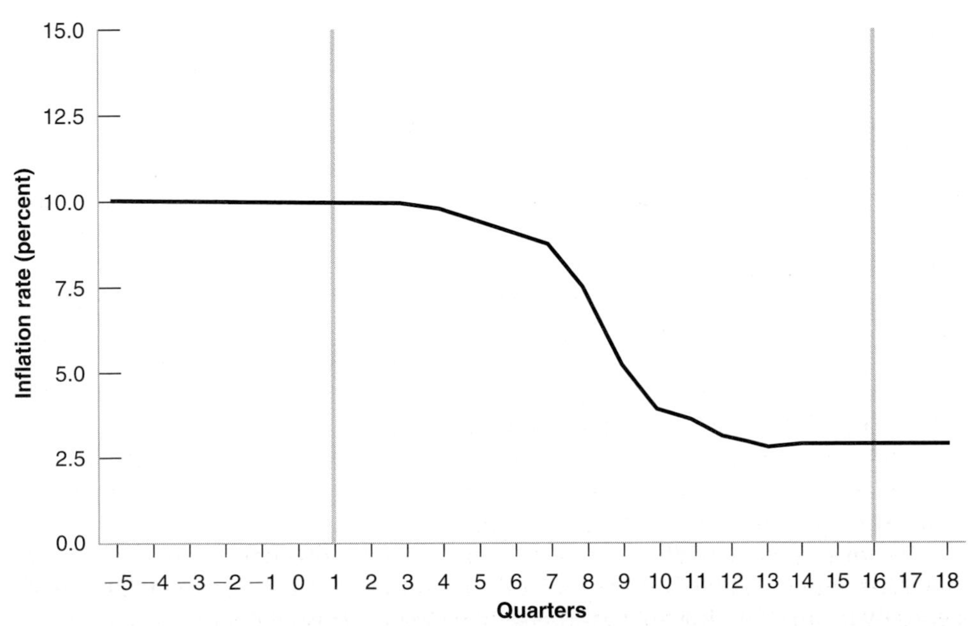

Figure 9-5

Disinflation Without Unemployment in the Taylor Model

With staggering of wage decisions, disinflation must be phased in slowly to avoid an increase in unemployment.

The "nominal rigidities view": Many wages are set in nominal terms, sometimes for many years. The way to decrease the unemployment cost of disinflation is to give wage setters time to take the change in policy into account. Thus, the central bank should go for slow disinflation.

the path of disinflation drawn in Figure 9-5 might not be credible. The announcement, say, this year, that nominal money growth will be decreased two years from now is likely to run into a serious credibility problem. Wage setters are likely to ask themselves: If the decision has been made to disinflate, why should the central bank wait two years? Without credibility, inflation expectations might not change, defeating the hope that disinflation can be achieved without an increase in the unemployment rate. But Taylor's analysis had two clear messages: First, like Lucas and Sargent, Taylor's analysis emphasized the role of expectations. Second, it suggested that a slow but credible disinflation might have a cost lower than that implied by the traditional approach.

With this discussion in mind, let us end the chapter with a look at what actually happened in the United States from 1979 to 1985.

9-5 The U.S. Disinflation, 1979–1985

In 1979, the U.S. unemployment rate was 5.8%; GDP growth was 2.5%; the inflation rate (using the CPI deflator) was a high 13.3%. The question the Federal Reserve faced was no longer whether it should reduce inflation, but how fast it should reduce it. In August 1979, President Carter appointed Paul Volcker chairman of the Federal Reserve Board. Volcker, who had served in the Nixon administration, was considered an extremely qualified chairman who could and would lead the fight against inflation.

In October 1979, the Fed announced a number of changes in its operating procedures. In particular, it indicated that it would shift from targeting a given level of the short-term interest rate to targeting the growth rate of nominal money.

This change would hardly seem to be the stuff of history books. The Fed made no announcement of a battle against inflation, nor of a targeted path of disinflation, nor various other ambitious-sounding plans. Nevertheless, financial markets widely interpreted this technical change as a sign of a major change in monetary policy. In particular, the change was interpreted as indicating that the Fed had become committed to reducing inflation and, if needed, ready to let interest rates increase, perhaps to very high levels.

The federal funds rate (the rate at which banks lend and borrow reserves overnight) is the rate most directly under the control of the Fed (Chapter 4).

Over the following seven months, the Fed let the federal funds rate increase by more than 6 percentage points, from 11.4% in September 1979 to 17.6% in April 1980. But then there was a halt, followed by a rapid reversal. By July 1980, the rate was back down to 9%, dropping 8.6 percentage points in four months. This roller-coaster movement of the federal funds rate is shown in Figure 9-6, which plots the federal funds rate and the inflation rate, measured as the rate of change of the CPI over the previous 12 months, for the period January 1979 to December 1984.

The reason for the decrease in the federal funds rate in the middle of 1980 was the accumulation of signs that the economy was entering a sharp recession. In March 1980, believing that high consumer spending was one of the causes of inflation, the Carter administration had imposed controls on consumer credit—limits on how much consumers could borrow to buy some durable goods. The effect of these controls turned out to be much larger than the Carter administration had anticipated. The combination of the fear of a sharp recession and the political pressure coming from the proximity of Presidential elections was enough to lead the Fed to decrease interest rates sharply.

Cumulative increases in the federal funds rate of 3 percentage points just before the 1980 election surely did not improve Carter's reelection prospects.

By the end of 1980, with the economy apparently in recovery, the Fed again sharply increased the federal funds rate. By January 1981, the rate was back up to 19%.

By the end of 1981, signs accumulated that the very high interest rates had triggered a second recession. The Fed decided not to repeat its mistake of 1980—the abandonment of its disinflation target in the face of a recession. In contrast to its actions in 1980, it kept interest rates high. The federal funds rate decreased to 12.3% in December 1981, but then increased back to 14.9% in April 1982.

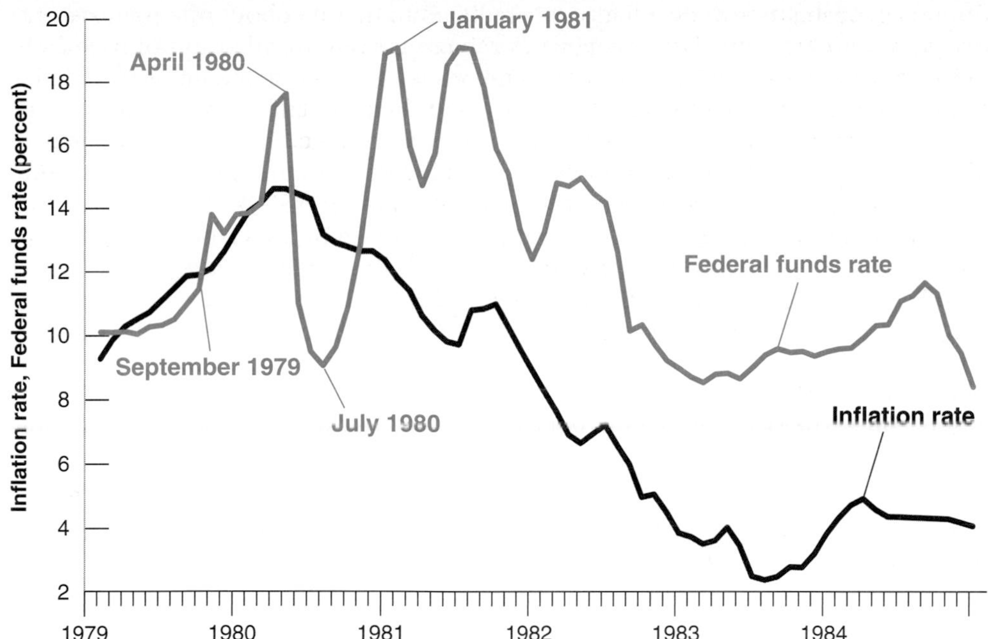

Figure 9-6

The Federal Funds Rate and Inflation, 1979–1984

A sharp increase in the interest rate from September 1979 to April 1980 was followed by a sharp decline in mid-1980, and then a second and sustained increase from July 1980 on, lasting for most of 1981 and 1982.

I have gone through the events of 1979–1982 in some detail to show the practical difficulties of establishing "credibility." Paul Volcker had credibility when he came to office. However, the credibility of the Fed's disinflation stance was surely eroded by the Fed's behavior in 1980. Credibility was progressively reestablished in 1981 and 1982, especially when, despite clear indications that the economy was in recession, the Fed increased the federal funds rate in the spring of 1982.

Did this credibility—to the extent that it was present—lead to a more favorable trade-off between unemployment and disinflation than implied by the traditional approach? Table 9-2 gives the relevant numbers.

The first two lines of the table makes clear that there was no expectation miracle: Line 2 shows disinflation was associated with substantial unemployment. The average unemployment rate was above 9% in both 1982 and 1983, peaking at 10.8% in the month of December 1982.

The answer to whether the unemployment cost was lower than implied by the traditional approach is given in the rest of the table. Under the traditional

TABLE 9-2 Inflation and Unemployment, 1979–1985

	1979	1980	1981	1982	1983	1984	1985
1. GDP growth (%)	2.5	−0.5	1.8	−2.2	3.9	6.2	3.2
2. Unemployment rate (%)	5.8	7.1	7.6	9.7	9.6	7.5	7.2
3. CPI inflation (%)	13.3	12.5	8.9	3.8	3.8	3.9	3.8
4. Cumulative unemployment (%)		1.0	2.6	6.3	9.9	11.4	12.6
5. Cumulative disinflation (%)		0.8	4.4	9.5	9.5	9.4	9.5
6. Sacrifice ratio		1.2	0.6	0.7	1.0	1.2	1.3

Cumulative unemployment is the sum of point-years of excess unemployment from 1980 on, assuming a natural rate of unemployment of 6.0%. Cumulative disinflation is the difference between inflation in a given year and inflation in 1979. The sacrifice ratio is the ratio of cumulative unemployment to cumulative disinflation.

approach, each point of disinflation is predicted to require about one point-year of excess unemployment. Line 4 computes the cumulative number of point-years of excess unemployment from 1980 on, assuming a natural rate of unemployment of 6%. Line 5 computes cumulative disinflation—the decrease in inflation starting from its 1979 level. Line 6 gives the sacrifice ratio, the ratio of the cumulative point-years of unemployment above the natural rate of unemployment to cumulative disinflation.

The table shows there were no obvious "credibility gains". By 1982, the sacrifice ratio looked quite attractive: The cumulative decrease in inflation since 1979 was nearly 9.5%, at a cost of 6.3 point-years of unemployment—a sacrifice ratio of about 0.7, relative to the sacrifice ratio of 1 predicted by the traditional approach. But by 1985, the sacrifice ratio had reached 1.3. A 9.5% disinflation had been achieved with 12.6 point-years of excess unemployment, an outcome actually worse than the outcome predicted by the traditional approach.

In short: The U.S. disinflation of the early 1980s was associated with a substantial increase in unemployment. The Phillips curve relation between the change in inflation and the deviation of the unemployment rate from the natural rate proved more robust than many economists anticipated. Was this outcome due to a lack of credibility of the change in monetary policy, or to the fact that credibility is not enough to substantially reduce the cost of disinflation? One way of learning more is to look at other disinflation episodes. This is the approach followed in a recent paper by Laurence Ball, from Johns Hopkins University. Ball estimates sacrifice ratios for 65 disinflation episodes in 19 OECD countries over the last 30 years. He reaches three main conclusions.

- Disinflations typically lead to a period of higher unemployment. Put another way, even if a decrease in nominal money growth is neutral in the medium run, unemployment increases for some time before returning to the natural rate of unemployment.
- Faster disinflations are associated with smaller sacrifice ratios. This conclusion provides some evidence to support the expectation and credibility effects emphasized by Lucas and Sargent.
- Sacrifice ratios are smaller in countries that have shorter wage contracts. This provides some evidence to support Fischer and Taylor's emphasis on the structure of wage agreements.

Summary

- There are three relations linking output, unemployment, and inflation:

  Okun's law shows how the deviation of output growth from normal leads to a change in the unemployment rate. In the United States today, output growth of 1% above normal for a year leads to a decrease in the unemployment rate of about 0.4%.

  The Phillips curve shows how the deviation of the unemployment rate from the natural rate leads to a change in the inflation rate. In the United States today, an unemployment rate 1% below the natural rate for a year leads to an increase in the inflation rate of about 1%.

  The aggregate demand relation shows how the difference between nominal money growth and inflation affects output growth. Given nominal money growth, higher inflation leads to a decrease in output growth.

- In the medium run, the unemployment rate is equal to the natural rate of unemployment, and output grows at its normal growth rate. Nominal money growth determines the inflation rate: A 1% increase in nominal money growth leads to a 1% increase in the inflation rate. As Milton Friedman put it: Inflation is always and everywhere a monetary phenomenon.
- In the short run, a decrease in nominal money growth leads to a slowdown in growth and an increase in unemployment for some time. Thus, disinflation (a decrease in the inflation rate) can be achieved only at the cost of more unemployment. How much unemployment is a controversial issue.

- The traditional approach assumes that people do not change the way they form expectations when monetary policy changes, so that the relation between inflation and unemployment is unaffected by the change in policy. This approach implies that disinflation can be achieved by a short but large increase in unemployment, or by a longer and smaller increase in unemployment. But policy cannot affect the total number of point-years of excess unemployment.
- An alternative view is that, if the change in monetary policy is credible, expectation formation may change, leading to a smaller increase in unemployment than predicted by the traditional approach. In its extreme form, this alternative view implies that if policy is fully credible, it can achieve disinflation with no increase in unemployment. A less extreme form recognizes that while expectation formation may change, the presence of nominal rigidities is likely to imply some increase in unemployment, although less than implied by the traditional approach.
- The U.S. disinflation of the early 1980s, during which inflation decreased by approximately 10%, was associated with a large recession. The unemployment cost was close to the predictions of the traditional approach.

Key Terms

- Okun's law, 183
- normal growth rate, 183
- labor hoarding, 184
- adjusted nominal money growth, 187
- disinflation, 189
- point-year of excess unemployment, 189
- sacrifice ratio, 190
- Lucas critique, 193
- credibility, 194
- nominal rigidities, 194
- staggering of wage decisions, 194

Questions and Problems

Quick Check

1. Using the information in this chapter, label each of the following statements true, false, *or* uncertain. *Explain briefly.*

a. The U.S. unemployment rate will remain constant as long as there is positive output growth.

b. Many firms prefer to keep workers around when demand is low (rather than lay them off) even if the workers are underutilized.

c. The behavior of Okun's law across countries and across decades is consistent with our knowledge of firm behavior and labor market regulations.

d. There is a reliable negative relation between the rate of inflation and the growth rate of output.

e. In the medium run, the rate of inflation is equal to the rate of nominal money growth.

f. According to the Phillips curve relation, the sacrifice ratio is independent of the speed of disinflation.

g. If Lucas and Sargent were right, and monetary policy was fully credible, there would be no relation between inflation and unemployment—no Phillips curve relation.

h. Contrary to the traditional Phillips curve analysis, Taylor's analysis of staggered wage contracts makes the case for a slow approach to disinflation.

i. Ball's analysis of disinflation episodes provides some support for both the credibility effects of Lucas and Sargent and for the wage-contract effects of Fischer and Taylor.

2. As shown by equation (9.2), the estimated Okun's law for the United States is given by

$$u_t - u_{t-1} = -0.4\,(g_{yt} - 3\%)$$

a. What growth rate of output leads to an increase in the unemployment rate of 1% per year? How can the unemployment rate increase even though the growth rate of output is positive?

b. What rate of growth of output do we need if we want to decrease unemployment by two percentage points over the next four years?

c. Suppose that we experience a second baby boom. How do you expect Okun's law to change if the rate of growth of the labor force increases by two percentage points?

3. Suppose that the economy can be described by the following three equations:

$$u_t - u_{t-1} = -0.4\,(g_{yt} - 3\%) \qquad \text{Okun's law}$$
$$\pi_t - \pi_{t-1} = -(u_t - 5\%) \qquad \text{Phillips curve}$$
$$g_{yt} = g_{mt} - \pi_t \qquad \text{Aggregate demand}$$

a. What is the natural rate of unemployment for this economy?

b. Suppose that the unemployment rate is equal to the natural rate, and that the inflation rate is 8%. What is the growth rate of output? What is the growth rate of the money supply?

c. Suppose that conditions are as in (b), when, in year t, the authorities use monetary policy to reduce the inflation rate to 4% in year t and keep it there. What must happen to the unemployment rate in years $t, t+1, t+2, \ldots$? What must happen to the rate of growth of output in years $t, t+1, t+2, \ldots$? What must be the rate of nominal money growth in years $t, t+1, t+2, \ldots$?

4. Suppose that you are advising a government that wants to reduce the inflation rate. It is considering two options: a gradual reduction over several years or an immediate reduction.

a. Lay out the arguments for and against each option.
b. If the only criterion you were to consider was the sacrifice ratio, which option would you take? Why might you want to consider other criteria?
c. What particular features of the economy would you want to look at before giving your advice?

5. *Markups, unemployment, and inflation*

Suppose that the Phillips curve is given by

$$\pi_t - \pi_{t-1} = -(u_t - 5\%) + 0.1\,\mu$$

where μ is the markup.

Suppose that unemployment is initially at its natural rate. Suppose now that an oil shock increases μ, but that the monetary authority continues to keep the unemployment rate at its previous value.

a. What will happen to inflation?
b. What should the monetary authority do instead?

Dig Deeper

6. *Credibility and disinflation*

Suppose that the Phillips curve is given by

$$\pi_t = \pi_t^e - (u_t - 5\%)$$

and expected inflation is given by

$$\pi_t^e = \pi_{t-1}$$

a. What is the sacrifice ratio in this economy?

Suppose that unemployment is initially equal to the natural rate and $\pi = 12\%$. The central bank decides that 12% inflation is too high and that, starting in year t, it will maintain the unemployment rate one percentage point above the natural rate of unemployment until the inflation rate has decreased to 2%.

b. Compute the rate of inflation for years $t, t+1, t+2, \ldots$
c. For how many years must the central bank keep the unemployment rate above the natural rate of unemployment? Is the implied sacrifice ratio consistent with your answer to (a)?

Now suppose that people know that the central bank wants to lower inflation to 2%, but they are not sure of the central bank's willingness to accept an unemployment rate above the natural rate of unemployment. So, their expectation of inflation is a weighted average of the target of 2% and last year's inflation, i.e.,

$$\pi_t^e = \beta\, 2\% + (1 - \beta)\,\pi_{t-1}$$

where β is the weight they put on the central bank's target of 2%.

d. Let $\beta = .25$. How long will it take before the inflation rate is equal to 2%? What is the sacrifice ratio? Why is it different from the answer in (c)?
e. *Suppose that after the policy has been in effect for one year, people believe that the central bank is indeed committed to reducing inflation to 2%. So, they now set their expectations according to*

$$\pi_t^e = 2\%$$

From what year onward can the central bank let the unemployment rate return to the natural rate? What is the sacrifice ratio now?

f. What advice would you give to a central bank that wants to lower the rate of inflation by increasing the rate of unemployment as little and for as short a time period as possible?

7. *The effects of a permanent decrease in the rate of nominal money growth*

Suppose that the economy can be described by the following three equations:

$u_t - u_{t-1} = -0.4\,(g_{yt} - 3\%)$	Okun's law
$\pi_t - \pi_{t-1} = -(u_t - 5\%)$	Phillips curve
$g_{yt} = g_{mt} - \pi_t$	Aggregate demand

a. Reduce the three equations to two by substituting g_{yt} from the aggregate demand equation into Okun's law.

Assume initially that $u_t = u_{t-1} = 5\%$, $g_{mt} = 13\%$, and $\pi_t = 10\%$. Now suppose that money growth is permanently reduced from 13 to 3%, starting in year t.

b. Compute (using a calculator, or a spreadsheet program) unemployment and inflation in year $t, t+1, \ldots, t+10$.
c. Does inflation smoothly decline from 10 to 3%? Why or why not?
d. Compute the values of the unemployment rate and the inflation rate in the medium run.

We invite you to visit the Blanchard page on the Prentice Hall Web site at:
www.prenhall.com/blanchard
for this chapter's World Wide Web exercises

Further Reading

A description of U.S. monetary policy in the 1980s is given by Michael Mussa in Chapter 2 of Martin Feldstein, ed., *American Economic Policy in the 1980s* (University of Chicago Press and NBER, 1994) pp. 81–164. Read also the comments on the chapter by Paul Volcker, who was chairman of the Fed from 1979 to 1987.

The Long Run

The next four chapters focus on the long run. In the long run, what dominates is not fluctuations, but growth. So now we need to ask: What determines growth?

Chapter 10

Chapter 10 looks at the facts of growth. It first documents the large increase in output in rich countries over the past fifty years. Then, taking a wider look, it shows that, on the scale of human history, such growth is a recent phenomenon. And it shows that it is not a universal phenomenon: Many poor countries are suffering from no or low growth.

Chapter 11

Chapter 11 focuses on the role of capital accumulation in growth. It shows that capital accumulation cannot by itself sustain output growth, but that it does affect the level of output. A higher saving rate leads to lower consumption initially, but is likely to lead to higher consumption in the long run.

Chapter 12

Chapter 12 turns to the role of technological progress. It shows how, in the long run, the growth rate of an economy is determined by the rate of technological progress. It then looks at the role of R&D in generating such progress. It returns to the facts of growth presented in Chapter 10, and shows how to interpret them using the theory developed in Chapters 11 and 12.

Chapter 13

Chapter 13 (an optional chapter), shows how we can integrate the study of the long run with our earlier study of the short run and the medium run. It discusses whether and when technological progress can cause unemployment, and whether technological progress should be blamed for the increase in wage inequality in the United States over the last 20 years.

The Facts of Growth

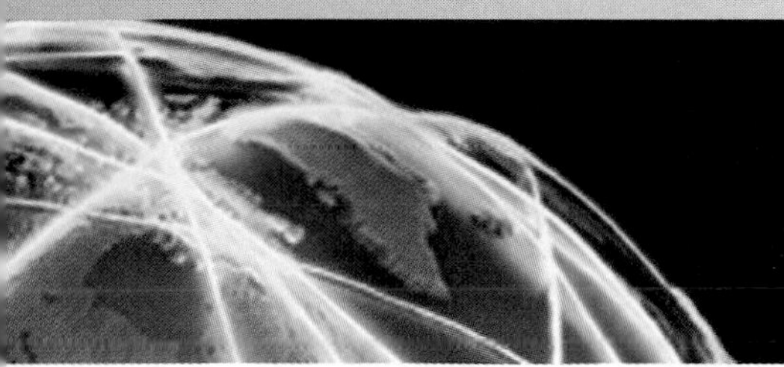

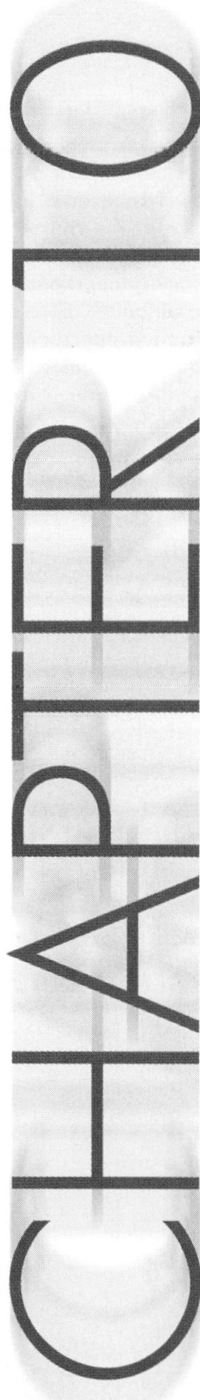

Our perceptions of how the economy is doing are often dominated by year-to-year fluctuations in economic activity. A recession leads to gloom, an expansion to optimism. But if we step back to get a look at activity over longer periods—say, over many decades—the picture changes. Fluctuations fade. **Growth**—the steady increase in aggregate output over time—dominates the picture.

Figure 10-1 shows the evolution of U.S. GDP (in 1996 dollars) since 1890. The years from 1929 to 1933 correspond to the large decrease in output during the Great Depression, and the years 1980 to 1982 correspond to the largest postwar recession. Note how small these two episodes appear compared to the steady increase in output over the last 100 years.

With this in mind, we now shift our focus from fluctuations to growth. Put another way, we turn from the study of the determination of output in the *short and medium run*—where fluctuations dominate—to the determination of output in the *long run*—where growth dominates.

- Section 10-1 looks at growth in the United States and other rich countries over the last fifty years.
- Section 10-2 takes a broader look, across both time and space.
- Section 10-3 then gives a primer on growth and introduces the framework to be developed in the next three chapters. ■

Figure 10-1

U.S. GDP Since 1890

Aggregate U.S. output has increased by a factor of 43 since 1890.

Source: 1890–1929: Historical Statistics of the United States; 1929–2000: National Income and Product Accounts.

The scale used to measure GDP on the vertical axis in Figure 10-1 is called a logarithmic scale. The characteristic of a logarithmic scale is that the same proportional increase in a variable is represented by the same distance on the vertical axis. For more discussion, see Appendix 2 at the end of the book.

10-1 Growth in Rich Countries Since 1950

Table 10-1 gives the evolution of **output per capita** (GDP divided by population) for France, Germany, Japan, the United Kingdom, and the United States, since 1950. I have chosen these five countries not only because they are the world's major economic powers, but because what has happened to them is broadly representative of what has happened in other advanced countries over the last half century or so.

There are two reasons for looking at the numbers for output *per capita* rather than the numbers for total output. The evolution of the **standard of living** is given by the evolution of output per capita, not a country's total output. And, when comparing countries with different populations, output numbers must be adjusted to take into

Table 10-1 The Evolution of Output per Capita in Five Rich Countries Since 1950

	Annual Growth Rate Output per Capita (%)		*Real Output per Capita (1996 dollars)*		
	1950–1973	1974–2000	1950	2000	2000/1950
France	4.1	1.6	5,489	21,282	3.9
Germany	4.8	1.7	4,642	21,910	4.7
Japan	7.8	2.4	1,940	22,039	11.4
United Kingdom	2.5	1.9	7,321	21,647	3.0
United States	2.2	1.7	11,903	30,637	2.6
Average	4.3	1.8	6,259	23,503	3.7

Source: 1950–1992: Penn World Tables, constructed by Robert Summers and Alan Heston (**pwt.econ.upenn.edu**). Extended from 1992 to 2000 by using rates of real GDP growth from the OECD Economic Outlook, and population growth rates from the IMF International Financial Statistics (IFS). The average in the last line is a simple (unweighted) average.

account these differences in population size. This is exactly what output per capita does.

Output: GDP
Output per capita: GDP divided by population

Before discussing the table, we must look into how the output numbers are constructed. So far, in constructing output numbers for countries other than the United States, we have used the straightforward method of taking that country's GDP expressed in that country's currency, then multiplying it by the current exchange rate to express it in terms of dollars (see Chapter 1). But this simple computation will not do here, for two reasons.

- First, exchange rates can vary a lot (more on this in Chapters 18 to 21). The dollar increased and then decreased in the 1980s by roughly 50% vis-à-vis the currencies of its trading partners. But, surely, the standard of living in the United States did not increase by 50% and then decrease by 50% compared to the standard of living of its trading partners in the 1980s. Yet this is the conclusion we would reach if we compared GDP per capita using current exchange rates.
- The second reason goes beyond fluctuations in exchange rates. In 2000, GDP per capita in India, using the current exchange rate, was $450, compared to $35,900 in the United States. Surely nobody could live on $450 a year in the United States. But people live on it—admittedly, not very well—in India, where the prices of basic goods, those goods needed for subsistence, are much lower than in the United States. The level of consumption of the average person in India, who consumes mostly basic goods, is not 80 (35,900 divided by 450) times smaller than that of the average person in the United States. This pattern applies to other countries besides the United States and India: In general, the lower a country's output per capita, the lower the prices of food and basic services in that country.

Constructing PPP numbers is a lot of work. At this point, the "Penn World Tables" project (described in the Focus box) has constructed PPP numbers only up to the early 1990s. In Table 10-1, I extended those numbers to 2000 for the five major OECD countries. To do the same for the larger sets of countries we look at in the rest of this chapter would be too much work. So I show evolutions of output per capita only up to the latest year available in the Penn World Tables data set (1992 for most countries, 1990 or 1991 for the others).

So when our focus is on comparing standards of living, either across time or across countries, we get more meaningful comparisons by correcting for the effects we just discussed—variations in exchange rates, and systematic differences in prices across countries. The numbers in Table 10-1 are obtained by making these corrections. The details of construction are complicated, but the principle is simple: The numbers for GDP in Table 10-1 are constructed using a common set of prices for all countries. Such adjusted real GDP numbers, which you can think of as measures of **purchasing power** across time or across countries, are called **purchasing power parity (PPP)** numbers. Further discussion is given in the Focus box "The Construction of PPP Numbers."

The differences between PPP numbers and the numbers based on current exchange rates can be substantial. Return to our comparison between India and the United States. We saw that, at current exchange rates, the ratio of GDP per capita in the United States to GDP per capita in India was 80. Using PPP numbers, the ratio is only 17; while this is still a large difference, it is much smaller than the ratio we obtained using current exchange rates. Or take comparisons among rich countries. Based on the numbers we saw in Chapter 1—numbers constructed using current exchange rates—GDP per capita in the United States in 2000 was equal to 94% of the GDP per capita in Japan. But, based on the PPP numbers in Table 10-1 , GDP per capita in the United States is in fact equal to 139% of GDP per capita in Japan. More generally, PPP numbers suggest that the United States still has the highest GDP per capita among the world's major countries.

The bottom line: When comparing standard of living across countries, use PPP numbers.

We can now return to Table 10-1. You should draw three main conclusions from the table:

1. *The standard of living has increased significantly since 1950.* Growth from 1950 to 2000 has increased real output per capita by a factor of 2.6 in the United States, by a factor of 4.7 in Germany, and by a factor of 11.4 in Japan.

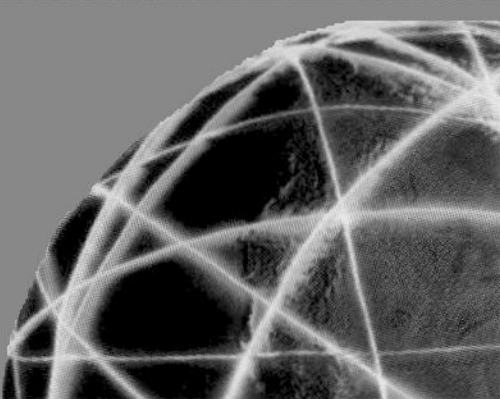

The Construction of PPP Numbers

FOCUS

Consider two countries—say, the United States and Russia—but without attempting to fit the characteristics of these two countries very closely.

In the United States, annual consumption per capita equals $20,000. Individuals buy two goods: Every year, they buy a new car for $10,000, and spend the rest on food. The price of a yearly bundle of food is $10,000.

In Russia, annual consumption per capita equals 60,000 rubles. People keep their cars for 15 years. The price of a car is 300,000 rubles, so that individuals spend on average 20,000 rubles—300,000/15—a year on cars. They buy the same yearly bundle of food as their U.S. counterparts, at a price of 40,000 rubles.

Russian and U.S. cars are of identical quality, and so are Russian and U.S. food. (You may dispute the realism of these assumptions. Whether a car in country X is the same as a car in country Y is very much the type of problem confronting economists constructing PPP measures.) The exchange rate is such that one dollar is equal to 30 rubles. What is consumption per capita in Russia relative to consumption per capita in the United States?

One way to answer is by taking consumption per capita in Russia and converting it into dollars using the exchange rate. Using that method, Russian consumption per capita in dollars is $2,000 (60,000 rubles divided by the exchange rate, 30 rubles to the dollar). According to these numbers, consumption per capita in Russia is only 10% of U.S. consumption per capita.

Does this answer make sense? True, Russians are poorer, but food is much cheaper in Russia. A U.S. consumer spending all of his 20,000 dollars on food would buy 2 bundles of food ($20,000/$10,000). A Russian consumer spending all of his 60,000 rubles on food would buy 1.5 bundles of food (60,000 rubles/40,000 rubles). In terms of food bundles, the difference looks much smaller between U.S. and Russian consumption per capita. And given that one-half of consumption in the United States and two-thirds of consumption in Russia go to spending on food, this seems like a relevant computation.

Can we improve on our initial answer? Yes. One way is to use the same set of prices for both countries and then measure the quantities of each good consumed in each country using this common set of prices. Suppose we use U.S. prices. In terms of U.S. prices, annual consumption per capita in the United States is obviously still $20,000. What is it in Russia? Every year, the average Russian buys approximately 0.07 car (one car every 15 years) and one bundle of food. Using U.S. prices—specifically, $10,000 for a car and $10,000 for a bundle of food—gives Russian consumption per capita as [(0.07 × $10,000) + (1 × $10,000)] = [$700 + $10,000] = $10,700. So, using U.S. prices to compute consumption in both countries puts annual Russian consumption per capita at $10,700/$20,000 = 53.5% of annual U.S. consumption per capita, a better estimate of relative standards of living than we obtained using our first method (which gave only 10%).

This type of computation, namely, the construction of variables across countries using a common set of prices, underlies PPP estimates. Rather than using U.S. dollar prices as in our example (why use U.S. rather than Russian or, for that matter, French prices?), these estimates use average prices across countries; these prices are called international dollar prices. The estimates we use in Table 10-1 and elsewhere in this chapter are the result of an ambitious project known as the "Penn World Tables." (Penn is for the University of Pennsylvania, where the project is located). Led by three economists—Irving Kravis, Robert Summers, and Alan Heston—over more than 15 years, this project has constructed PPP series not only for consumption (as we just did in our example), but more generally for GDP and its components, going back to 1950, for most countries in the world.

For more on the construction of PPP numbers, go to the Web site listed under Table 10-1.

These numbers show what is sometimes called the *force of compounding*. In a different context, you probably have heard how saving even a little while you are young will build to a large amount by the time you retire. For example, if the interest rate is 4.9% a year, an investment of one dollar, with the proceeds reinvested every year, will grow to about 11 dollars 50 years later ($[1 + 0.049]^{50} = 10.93$ dollars). The same logic applies to growth rates. The average annual growth rate in Japan over the period 1950 to 2000 was equal to 4.9% [(7.8% a year times 23 years + 2.4% a year times 27 years), divided by 50 years]. This high growth rate has led to an 11-fold increase in real output per capita over the period.

Clearly, a better understanding of growth, if it leads to the design of policies that stimulate growth, can have a very large effect on the standard of living. Suppose we could find a policy measure that increased the growth rate permanently by 1%. This would lead, after 40 years, to a standard of living 50% higher than it would have been without the policy, a substantial difference.

Policy measures with such magic results have proven difficult to discover!

2. *Growth rates of output per capita have decreased since the mid-1970s.* The first two columns of Table 10-1 show growth rates of output per capita for both pre- and post-1973. Pinpointing the exact date of the decrease in growth is difficult; 1973, the date used to split the sample in the table, is as good as any date in the mid-1970s.

   Growth has decreased in all five countries. The decrease has been stronger in the countries that were growing fast pre-1973, such as France, Germany, and especially Japan, with the result that the differences in growth rates across countries are smaller post-1973 than they were pre-1973.

   If it continues, this decline in growth will have profound implications for the evolution of the standard of living in the future. At a growth rate of 4.3% per year—the average growth rate across our five countries from 1950 to 1973—it takes only 16 years for the standard of living to double. At a growth rate of 1.8% per year—the average from 1973 to 1998—it takes 39 years, so more than twice as long. Expectations of fast growth in individual income that had developed in the 1950s and 1960s have had to confront the reality of lower growth since 1973. In this context, it is easy to see why the increase in U.S. productivity growth in the second half of the 1990s we saw in Chapter 1 is potentially big news. It may be the sign that the United States is poised for a return to the high pre-1973 growth rates. We shall return to the issue in Chapter 12.

The "rule of 70": If a variable grows at x% a year, then it will take approximately $70/x$ years for the variable to double. If $x = 4.3$, it will take about 16 (70 divided by 4.3) years for the variable to double. If $x = 1.8$, it will take about 39 (70 divided by 1.8) years.

3. *Levels of output per capita across the five countries have converged (become closer) over time.* Put another way, those countries that were behind have grown faster, reducing the gap between them and the United States.

   In 1950, output per capita in the United States was around twice the level of output per capita in the United Kingdom, Germany, and France, and more than six times the level of output per capita in Japan. From the perspectives of Japan and Europe, the United States looked like the land of plenty, where everything was bigger and better. Today these perceptions have faded, and the numbers explain why. Using PPP numbers, U.S. output per capita is still the highest, but, in 2000, it was only 37% above average output per capita in the other four countries, a much smaller difference than in the 1950s.

From the Focus box in Chapter 1: the OECD (which stands for "Organization for Economic Cooperation and Development) is an international organization that includes most of the world's rich economies. The complete list is given in Chapter 1.

This **convergence** of levels of output per capita across countries is not specific to the five countries we are looking at, but extends to the set of OECD countries. This is shown in Figure 10-2, which plots the average annual growth rate of output per capita from 1950 to 1992 against the initial level of output per capita in 1950 for the countries that are members of the OECD today. There is a clear negative relation between the initial level of output per capita and the growth rate since 1950: Countries that were behind in 1950 have typically grown faster. The relation is not perfect: Turkey, which had roughly the same low level of output per capita as Japan in 1950, has had a growth rate equal to only about half that of Japan. But the relation is clearly there.

At this time, 1992 is the latest year for which Summers and Heston have constructed PPP numbers.

Some economists have pointed to a problem in graphs like Figure 10-2. By looking at the set of countries that are members of the OECD today, what we have done in effect is to look at a club of economic winners: OECD membership is not officially based on economic success, but economic success is surely an important determinant of membership. But when you look at a club whose membership is based on economic success, you will find that those who came from behind had the fastest growth: This is precisely why they made it to the club. Thus, the finding of convergence could come in part from the way we selected the countries in the first place.

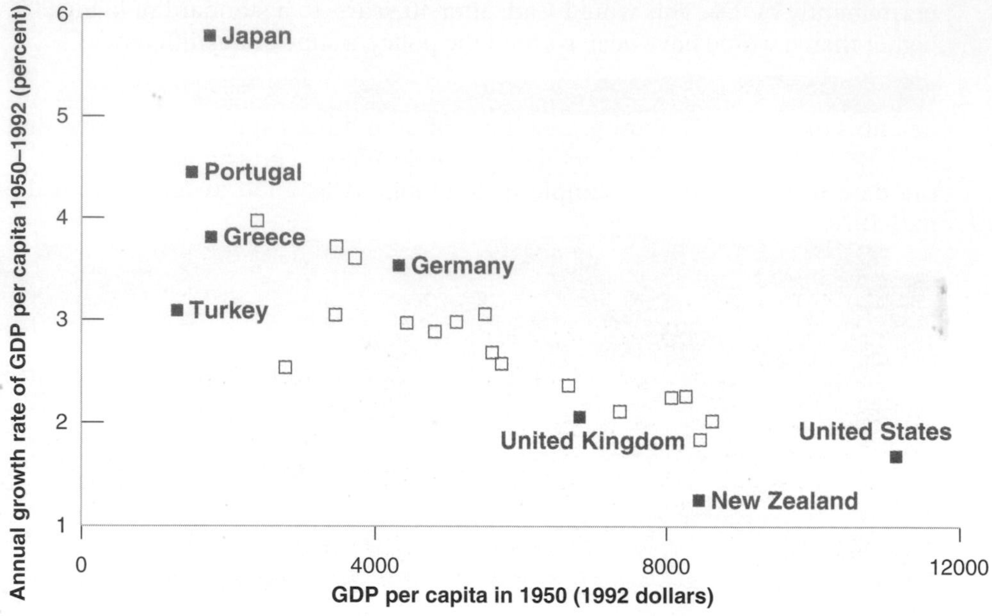

Figure 10-2

Growth Rate of GDP per Capita Since 1950 Versus GDP per Capita in 1950; OECD Countries

Countries that had a lower level of output per capita in 1950 have typically grown faster.

Source: See Table 10-1. South Korea, the Czech Republic, Hungary, and Poland are not included because of missing data.

So a better way of looking at convergence is to define the set of countries we look at not on the basis of where they are today—as we did in Figure 10-2 by taking today's OECD members—but on the basis of where they were in, say, 1950. For example, we can look at all countries that had an output per capita of at least one-fourth of U.S. output per capita in 1950, then look for convergence within that group. It turns out that most of the countries in that group have indeed converged, and therefore convergence is not solely an OECD phenomenon. However, a few countries—Uruguay, Argentina, and Venezuela among them—have not converged. Perhaps the most striking case is Argentina. In 1950, output per capita in Argentina was $5,574 (in 1996 dollars), roughly similar to output per capita in France. In 1990, it stood at $6,506 (in 1996 dollars), a meager 17% increase in 40 years—far below the 1990 French level of $19,227.

1990 is the latest year for which PPP numbers are available for Argentina.

10-2 A Broader Look Across Time and Space

You should remember three basic facts about growth in rich countries since 1950:

- The large increase in the standard of living.
- The decrease in growth since the mid-1970s.
- Convergence of output per capita among rich countries.

These are the three facts we shall keep in mind and try to explain as we think about growth in the next three chapters. Before we do so, however, it is useful to put them in broader perspective. This is what we do in this section, by looking at the evidence both over a much longer time span and a wider set of countries.

Looking Across Two Millennia

Has output per capita in the currently rich economies always grown at growth rates similar to the growth rates in Table 10-1? The answer is no. Estimates of growth are clearly harder to construct as we look further back in time. But there is agreement among economic historians about the main evolutions over the last 2,000 years.

- From the end of the Roman Empire to roughly 1500, there was essentially no growth of output per capita in Europe: Most workers were employed in agriculture, in which there was little technological progress. Because agriculture's share of output was so large, inventions with applications outside agriculture could contribute little to overall production and output. While there was some output growth, a roughly proportional increase in population led to roughly constant output per capita.
- From about 1500 to 1700, growth of output per capita turned positive but small, around 0.1% per year, increasing to 0.2% per year from 1700 to 1820.
- Even during the Industrial Revolution, growth rates were not high by current standards. The growth rate of output per capita from 1820 to 1950 in the United States was only 1.5% per year.
- On the scale of human history, therefore, growth of output per capita is a recent phenomenon. In light of the growth record of the last 200 years or so, what appears unusual is the high growth rate achieved in the 1950s and the 1960s, rather than the lower growth rate since 1973.

This period of stagnation of output per capita is often called the **Malthusian era.** That is because Thomas Robert Malthus, an English economist writing at the end of the eighteenth century, argued that this proportional increase in output and population was not a coincidence. Any increase in output, he argued, would lead to a decrease in mortality, which would in turn lead to an increase in population until output per capita was back at its initial level. Europe was in a trap, unable to increase its output per capita. Eventually, Europe was able to escape that trap. But the issue remains very relevant in many poor countries.

History also puts into context the convergence of OECD countries to the level of U.S. output per capita since 1950. The United States was not always the world's economic leader. History looks more like a long-distance race in which one country assumes leadership for some time, only to lose it to another and return to the pack or disappear from sight. For much of the first millennium, and until the fifteenth century, China probably had the world's highest level of output per capita. For a couple of centuries, leadership moved to the cities of northern Italy. It was then assumed by the Netherlands until around 1820, and then by the United Kingdom from 1820 to around 1870. Since then, the United States has been in the lead. Seen in this light, history looks more like **leapfrogging** (in which countries get close to the leader and then overtake it) than like convergence (in which the race becomes closer and closer). If history is any guide, the United States may not remain in the lead forever.

Looking Across Countries

We have seen how output per capita has converged among OECD countries. But what about the other countries? Are the poorest countries also growing faster? Are they converging toward the United States, even if they are still far behind?

A first answer is given in Figure 10-3, which plots the annual growth rate of output per capita from 1960 to 1992 against output per capita for the year 1960, for 101 countries.

The numbers for 1950 are missing for too many countries to use 1950 as the initial year, as we did in Figure 10-2. Figure 10-3 includes all the countries for which PPP estimates of GDP per capita exist for both 1960 and 1992 (or, in some cases, 1990 or 1991). There are some notable absences, such as China and a number of eastern European countries, for which the numbers for 1960 are not available.

The striking feature of Figure 10-3 is that there is no clear pattern: It is not the case that, in general, countries that were behind in 1960 have grown faster. Some have, but many have not.

The cloud of points in Figure 10-3 hides, however, several interesting subpatterns, which appear when we put countries into different groups. In Figure 10-4, we identify three groups. The diamonds represent the OECD countries we looked at earlier. The squares represent African countries. The triangles represent Asian countries. Together, these three groups account for 63 countries. To avoid cluttering, Figure 10-4 leaves out all other countries; these do not show obvious patterns.

The figure yields three main conclusions:

1. The picture for the OECD countries (for the rich countries) is much the same as in Figure 10-2, which looked at a slightly longer period of time (from 1950 on, rather than from 1960 on here). Nearly all start at high levels of output per capita (say, at least one-third of the U.S. level in 1960), and there is clear evidence of convergence.

The Reality of Growth: A Workingman's Budget in 1851

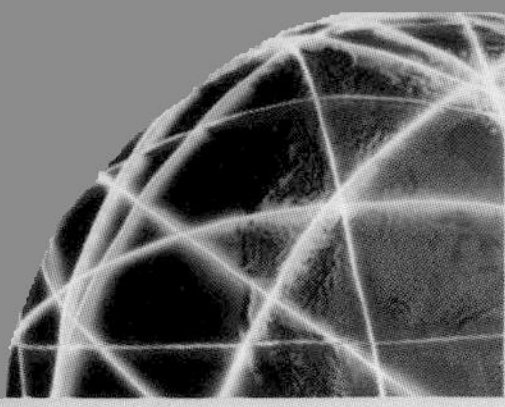

FOCUS

Data on GDP per capita do not fully convey the reality of growth and the accompanying increase in the standard of living. An examination of an annual "workingman's budget" in 1851 Philadelphia gives a much better sense of the improvement (Table 1).

Note how much a family spent on food in 1851: 41% of expenditures. Today's corresponding share—as reflected in the composition of the consumption basket used to compute the Consumer Price Index—is only 14%. And food at home—as opposed to food in restaurants—accounts for only 8.6% of total consumption today. But perhaps more revealing is the composition of food consumption. Compare the food in the table to the richness and diversity of the food we eat today.

Table 1 Annual Workingman's Budget, Philadelphia, 1851

Item of expenditure	Amount (dollars)	Percent of total
Butcher's meat (2 lb a day)	72.80	13.5
Flour (6-1/2 lb a year)	32.50	6.0
Butter (2 lb a week)	32.50	6.0
Potatoes (2 pk a week)	26.00	4.8
Sugar (4 lb a week)	16.64	3.0
Coffee and tea	13.00	2.4
Milk	7.28	1.4
Salt, pepper, vinegar, starch, soap, yeast, cheese, eggs	20.80	3.9
Total expenditures for food	221.52	41.0
Rent	156.00	29.0
Coal (3 tons a year)	15.00	2.8
Charcoal, chips, matches	5.00	0.9
Candles and oil	7.28	1.4
Household articles (wear, tear, and breakage)	13.00	2.4
Bedclothes and bedding	10.40	1.9
Wearing apparel	104.00	19.3
Newspapers	6.24	1.2
Total expenditures other than food	316.92	58.9

Source: Productivity and American Leadership; (Chapter 3, Table 3.2), by William Baumol et al., Cambridge, MA: MIT Press, 1989. The composition of expenditures today comes from Table 712 (average annual income and expenditures of all consumer units, 1995) in the *Statistical Abstract of the United States, 1997.*

2. Convergence is also visible for most Asian countries. While Japan (represented as a diamond, as it is a member of the OECD) was the first of the Asian countries to grow rapidly and now has the highest level of output per capita in Asia, a number of other Asian countries are trailing it closely. The four triangles in the top left corner of the figure correspond to Singapore, Taiwan, Hong Kong, and South Korea—four countries sometimes called the **four tigers**. All four have had average annual growth rates of GDP per capita in excess of 6% over the last 30 years. In 1960, their average output per capita was about 16% of the U.S.; by 1992, it had increased to 62% of U.S. output.

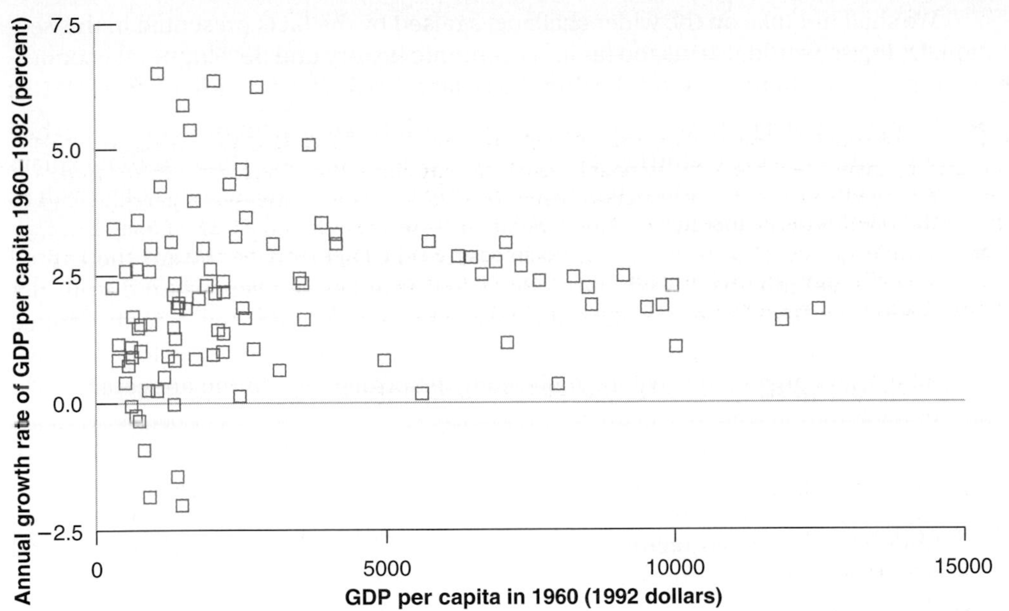

Figure 10-3

Growth Rate of GDP per Capita, 1960–1992, Versus GDP per Capita in 1960 (1992 dollars); 101 Countries

There is no clear relation between the growth rate of output since 1960 and the level of output per capita in 1960.

Source: See Table 10-1.

3. The picture is very different, however, for African countries. Convergence is certainly not the rule in Africa. Most African countries were very poor in 1960, and many have had negative growth of output per capita—an absolute decline in their standard of living—since then. Even in the absence of major wars, output per capita has declined at about 2% a year in Chad and Madagascar since 1960 (the two lowest squares in the figure); as a result, output per capita in these two countries stands at 55% of its 1960 level. Why so many African countries are not growing is one of the main questions facing development economists today.

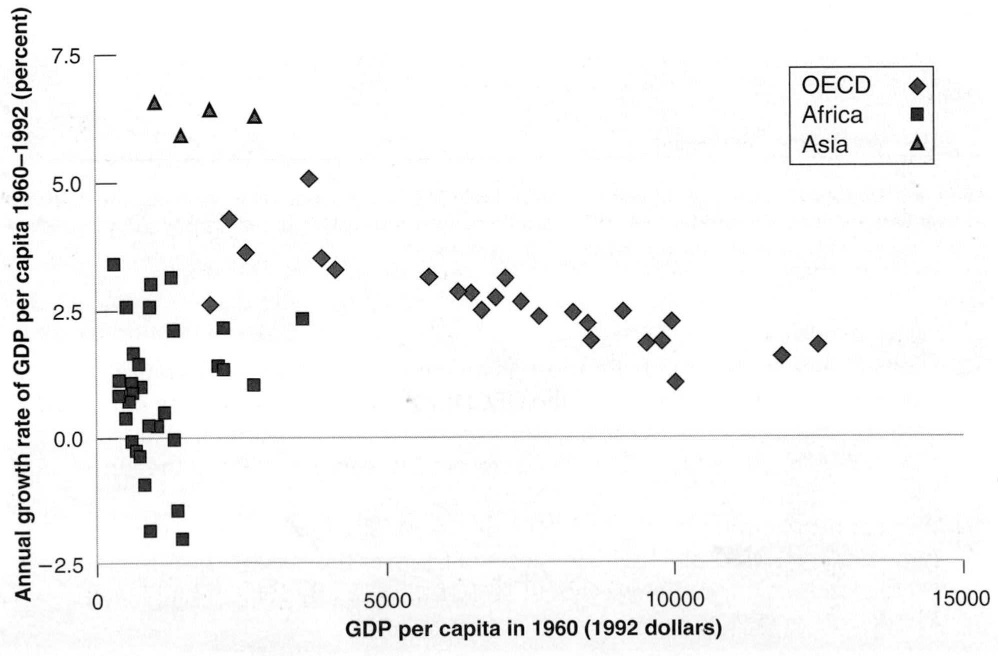

Figure 10-4

Growth Rate of GDP per Capita, 1960–1992, Versus GDP per Capita in 1960; OECD, Africa, and Asia.

Asian countries are converging to OECD levels. There is no evidence of convergence for African countries.

Source: See Figure 10-2.

We shall not take on the wider challenges raised by the facts presented in this section. Doing so would take us too far into economic history and development economics. But they put in perspective the three basic facts we discussed earlier for the OECD:

The distinction between *growth theory* and *development economics* is fuzzy. A rough distinction is that growth theory takes many institutions (for example, the legal system, the form of government) as given. Development economics asks what institutions are needed to sustain growth.

- Growth is not a historical necessity. There was little growth for most of human history, and in many countries today growth remains elusive. Theories that explain growth in the OECD today must also be able to explain the absence of growth in the past, and its absence in much of Africa today.
- Convergence of output per capita in many OECD countries toward the United States level may well be the prelude to leapfrogging, a stage when output per capita in one or more countries increases above output per capita in the United States. Theories that explain convergence must therefore also allow for the possibility that convergence will be followed by leapfrogging and the appearance of a new economic leader.
- Finally, in a longer historical perspective, it is not so much the lower growth since 1973 in the OECD that is unusual. More unusual is the earlier period of exceptionally fast growth. Finding the explanation for lower growth today may come from understanding what factors contributed to fast growth post-World War II, and whether these factors have disappeared.

10-3 Thinking About Growth: A Primer

How do we go about explaining the facts we have seen in Sections 10-1 and 10-2? What determines growth? What is the role of capital accumulation? What is the role of technological progress? To think about and answer these questions, economists use a framework originally developed by Robert Solow, from MIT, in the late 1950s. The framework has proven sturdy and useful, and we shall use it here. This section provides an introduction. Chapters 11 and 12 provide a more detailed analysis, first of the role of capital accumulation and then of the role of technological progress in the process of growth.

Solow's article, "A Contribution to the Theory of Economic Growth," appeared in the *Quarterly Journal of Economics*, February 1956, pp. 65–94. Solow received the Nobel Prize for economics in 1987 for his work on growth.

The Aggregate Production Function

The starting point of any theory of growth must be an **aggregate production function**, a specification of the relation between aggregate output and the inputs in production.

The aggregate production function we introduced in Chapter 6 to study the determination of output in the short run and the medium run took a particularly simple form. Output was simply proportional to the amount of labor used by firms—more specifically, proportional to the number of workers employed by firms (equation [6.2]). So long as our focus was on fluctuations in output and employment, the assumption was acceptable. But, now that our focus shifts to growth, that assumption will no longer do: It implies that output per worker is constant, ruling out growth (or at least growth of output per worker) altogether. It is time to relax it. From now on, we shall assume that there are two inputs, capital and labor, and that the relation between aggregate output and the two inputs is given by

$$Y = F(K, N) \tag{10.1}$$

The aggregate production function is

$Y = F(K, N)$

Aggregate output (Y) depends on the aggregate capital stock (K), and aggregate employment (N).

As before, Y is aggregate output. K is capital—the sum of all the machines, plants, and office buildings in the economy. N is labor—the number of workers in the economy. The function F, which tells us how much output is produced for given quantities of capital and labor, is the *aggregate production function.*

This way of thinking about aggregate production is an improvement on our treatment in Chapter 6. But it should be clear that it is still a drastic simplification of reality. Surely, machines and office buildings play very different roles in production, and should be treated as separate inputs. Surely, workers with Ph.D.'s are different from high-school dropouts; yet, by constructing the labor input as simply equal to the *number* of workers in the economy, we treat all workers as identical. We shall relax some of these simplifications later. For the time being, equation (10.1), which emphasizes the role of both labor and capital in production, will do.

The next step must be to think about where the aggregate production function, F, which relates output to the two inputs, comes from. In other words, what determines how much output can be produced for given quantities of capital and labor? The answer: The **state of technology**. A country with a more advanced technology will produce more output from the same quantities of capital and labor than will an economy with only a primitive technology.

The function F depends on the state of technology. The higher the state of technology, the higher $F(K, N)$ for a given K and a given N.

How should we define the *state of technology*? As the list of blueprints defining both the range of products that can be produced in the economy as well as the techniques available to produce them? Or as not only the list of blueprints, but also the organization of firms, the organization and sophistication of markets, the system of laws and the quality of their enforcement, the political system, and so on? For most of the next two chapters, I shall think of the state of technology according to the narrow definition—the set of blueprints. At the end of Chapter 12, however, I shall consider the broader definition, and return to what we know about the role of the other factors, from legal institutions to the quality of government.

Following up on growth theory versus development economics: Think of growth theory as focusing on the role of technology in the narrow sense, and development economics as focusing on the role of technology in the broader sense.

Returns to Scale and Returns to Factors

Now that we have introduced the aggregate production function, what restrictions can we reasonably impose on this function?

Consider first a thought experiment in which we double both the number of workers and the amount of capital in the economy. What do you expect will happen to output? A reasonable answer is that output will double as well: In effect, we have cloned the original economy, and the clone economy can produce output in the same way as the original economy. This property is called **constant returns to scale**: If the scale of operation is doubled—that is, if the quantities of capital and labor are doubled—then output will also double.

$$2Y = F(2K, 2N)$$

Or, more generally, for any number x (this will be useful below),

$$xY = F(xK, xN) \tag{10.2}$$

We have looked at what happens to production when *both* capital and labor are increased. Let's now ask a different question. What should we expect to happen if *only one* of the two inputs in the economy—say, capital—is increased?

Constant returns to scale:

$$F(xK, xN) = xY$$

Surely output will increase. That part is clear. But it is reasonable to assume that the same increase in capital will lead to smaller and smaller increases in output as the level of capital increases. In other words, if there is little capital to start with, a little more capital will help a lot. If there is a lot of capital to start with, a little more capital may make little difference. Why? Think, for example, of a secretarial pool, composed of a given number of secretaries. Think of capital as computers. The introduction of the first computer will substantially increase the pool's production, because some of the more time-consuming tasks can now be done automatically by the computer. As the number of computers increases and more secretaries in the pool get their own computer, production will further increase, although perhaps by less per additional computer than was the case when the first one was introduced. Once each and every secretary has a PC, increasing the number of computers further is unlikely to increase production very much, if at all. Additional computers may simply remain unused and left in their shipping boxes, and lead to no increase in output whatsoever.

Output here is secretarial services. The two inputs are secretaries and computers. The production function relates secretarial services to the number of secretaries and the number of computers.

Even under constant returns to scale, there are decreasing returns to each factor, keeping the other factor constant:

- Given labor, there are decreasing returns to capital: Increases in capital lead to smaller and smaller increases in output as the level of capital increases.
- Given capital, there are decreasing returns to labor: Increases in labor lead to smaller and smaller increases in output as the level of labor increases.

We shall refer to the property that increases in capital lead to smaller and smaller increases in output as the level of capital increases as **decreasing returns to capital** (a property that will be familiar to those who have taken a course in microeconomics). A similar property holds for the other input, labor: Increases in labor, given capital, lead to smaller and smaller increases in output as the level of labor increases. (Return to our example, and think of what happens as you increase the number of secretaries for a given number of computers.) There are **decreasing returns to labor** as well.

Output and Capital per Worker

The production function we have written down, together with the two properties we have just introduced, implies a simple relation between output per worker and capital per worker.

Constant returns to scale implies that we can rewrite equation (10.1) as a relation between *output per worker* and *capital per worker*. To get this result algebraically, let $x = 1/N$ in equation (10.2), so that

$$\frac{Y}{N} = F\left(\frac{K}{N}, \frac{N}{N}\right) = F\left(\frac{K}{N}, 1\right) \qquad (10.3)$$

Make sure you understand what is behind the algebra. Suppose capital and the number of workers both double. What happens to output per worker?

Note that Y/N is output per worker, K/N is capital per worker. So equation (10.3) says that the amount of output per worker depends on the amount of capital per worker. This relation between output per worker and capital per worker is drawn in Figure 10-5.

Output per worker (Y/N) is measured on the vertical axis, capital per worker (K/N) on the horizontal axis. The relation between the two is given by the upward sloping curve. As capital per worker increases, so does output per worker. Note that the curve is drawn so that increases in capital lead to smaller and smaller increases in output. This follows from the property that there are *decreasing returns to capital*: At point A, where capital per worker is low, an increase in capital per worker, represented by the horizontal distance AB, leads to an increase in output per worker equal to the vertical distance $A'B'$. At point C, where capital per worker is larger, the same increase in capital per worker, represented by the horizontal distance CD (where the distance CD is equal to the distance AB) leads to a much smaller increase in output per worker, only $C'D'$. This is just as in our example of the secretarial pool, where additional computers led to less and less effect on total output.

Increases in capital per worker lead to smaller and smaller increases in output per worker as the level of capital per worker increases.

Figure 10-5

Output and Capital per Worker

Increases in capital per worker lead to smaller and smaller increases in output per worker.

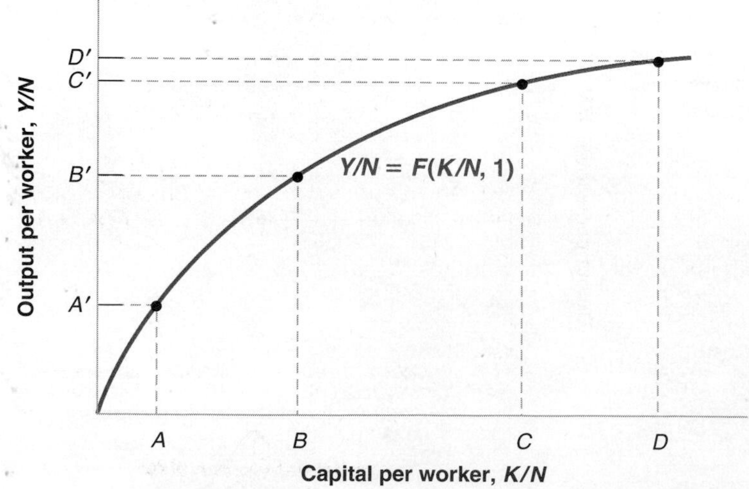

The Sources of Growth

We are now ready to return to our basic question: Where does growth come from? Why does output per worker—or output per capita, if we assume the ratio of workers to the population as a whole remains roughly constant over time—go up over time? Equation (10.3) gives a first answer:

- Increases in output per worker (Y/N) can come from increases in capital per worker (K/N). This is the relation we just looked at in Figure 10-5. As (K/N) increases—as we move to the right on the horizontal axis—(Y/N) increases.

◄ **Increases in capital per worker: Movements along the production function.**

- Or they can come from improvements in the state of technology, which shift the production function, F, and so lead to more output per worker *given* capital per worker. This is shown in Figure 10-6. An improvement in the state of technology shifts the production function up, from $F(K/N, 1)$ to $F(K/N, 1)'$. For a given level of capital per worker, the improvement in technology leads to an increase in output per worker. For example, for the level of capital per worker corresponding to point A, output per worker increases from A' to B'. (To return to our secretarial pool example, a reallocation of tasks within the pool may lead to better division of labor, and an increase in the output per secretary.)

◄ **Improvements in the state of technology: Shifts of the production function.**

Hence, we can think of growth as coming from **capital accumulation** and from **technological progress**—the improvement in the state of technology. We shall see, however, that these two factors play very different roles in the growth process:

- Capital accumulation *by itself* cannot sustain growth. A formal argument will have to wait until Chapter 11. But you can already get the intuition for this answer from Figure 10-5. Because of decreasing returns to capital, sustaining a steady increase in output per worker would require larger and larger increases in the level of capital per worker. At some stage, the economy will not be willing or able to save and invest enough to further increase capital. At that stage, output per worker will stop growing.

  Does this mean that an economy's **saving rate**—the proportion of income that is saved—is irrelevant? No. It is true that a higher saving rate cannot permanently increase the *growth rate of output*. But a higher saving rate can sustain a higher *level of output*. Let me state this in a slightly different way. Take two economies that differ only in their saving rate. The two economies will grow at the

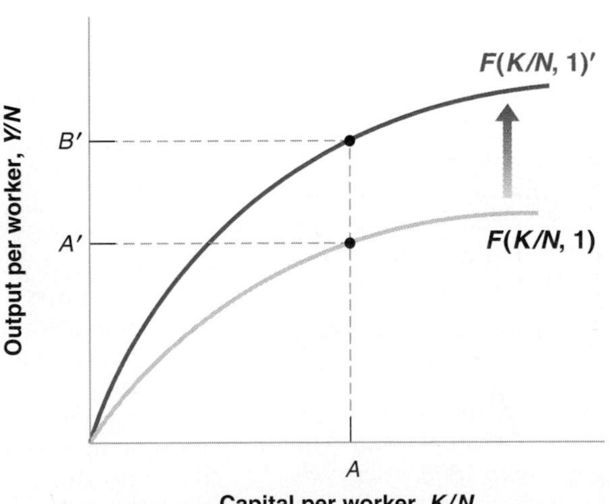

Figure 10-6

The Effects of an Improvement in the State of Technology

An improvement in technology shifts the production function up, leading to an increase in output per worker for a given level of capital per worker.

same rate; but, at any point in time, the economy with the higher saving rate will have a higher level of output per capita than the other. How and how much the saving rate affects the level of output, and whether a country such as the United States (which has a very low saving rate) should try to increase its saving rate, will be one of the topics we take up in Chapter 11.

- Sustained growth requires sustained technological progress. This really follows from the first proposition: Given that the two factors that can lead to an increase in output are capital accumulation and technological progress, if capital accumulation cannot sustain growth forever, then technological progress must be key. And it is. We shall see in Chapter 12 that the economy's rate of growth of output per capita is eventually determined by the economy's rate of technological progress.

  This has a strong implication. In the long run, an economy that sustains a higher rate of technological progress will eventually overtake all other economies. This raises the question of what determines the rate of technological progress. What we know about the determinants of technological progress—from the role of spending on fundamental and applied research, to the role of patent laws, to the role of education and training—will be one of the topics we take up in Chapter 12.

Summary

- Over long periods, fluctuations in output are dwarfed by growth, the steady increase of aggregate output over time.
- Looking at growth in five rich countries (France, Germany, Japan, the United Kingdom, and the United States) since 1950, three main facts emerge:

  1. All five countries have experienced strong growth and a large increase in the standard of living. Growth from 1950 to 2000 has increased real output per capita by a factor of 2.6 in the United States, by a factor of 4.7 in Germany, and by a factor of 11.4 in Japan.
  2. Growth has decreased since the mid-1970s. The average growth rate of output per capita has gone from 4.3% per year from 1950 to 1973 to 1.8% from 1974 to 2000.
  3. The levels of output per capita across the five countries have converged over time. Put another way, those countries that were behind have grown faster, reducing the gap between them and the current world economic leader, the United States.

- Looking at the evidence across a broader set of countries and a longer period, the following facts emerge:

  1. On the scale of human history, sustained output growth is a recent phenomenon. From the end of the Roman Empire to roughly year 1500, there was essentially no growth of output per capita in Europe. Even during the Industrial Revolution, growth rates were not high by current standards. The growth rate of output per capita from 1820 to 1950 in the United States was 1.5%.
  2. Convergence of levels of output per capita is not a worldwide phenomenon. Many Asian countries are rapidly catching up, but most African countries have both very low levels of output per capita and low growth rates.

- To think about growth, economists start from an aggregate production function relating aggregate output to two factors of production, capital and labor. How much output is produced given these inputs depends on the state of technology.
- Under the assumption of constant returns, the aggregate production function implies that increases in output per worker can come either from increases in capital per worker, or from improvements in the state of technology.
- Capital accumulation by itself cannot permanently sustain growth of output per capita. Nevertheless, how much a country saves is very important because the saving rate determines the *level* of output per capita, if not its growth rate.
- Sustained growth of output per capita is ultimately due to technological progress. Perhaps the most important question in growth theory is what determines technological progress.

Key Terms

- growth, 203
- logarithmic scale, 204
- output per capita, 204
- standard of living, 204
- purchasing power, purchasing power parity (PPP), 205
- convergence, 207
- Malthusian era, 209
- leapfrogging, 209
- four tigers, 210
- aggregate production function, 212
- state of technology, 213
- constant returns to scale, 213
- decreasing returns to capital, 214
- decreasing returns to labor, 214
- capital accumulation, 215
- technological progress, 215
- saving rate, 215

Questions and Problems

Quick Check

1. *Using the information in this chapter, label each of the following statements* true, false, *or* uncertain. *Explain briefly.*

a. Despite the Great Depression, U.S. output was higher in 1940 than in 1929.

b. On a log scale, a variable that increases at 5% a year will move along an upward-sloping line, with a slope of 0.05.

c. The price of food is higher in poor countries than in rich countries.

d. Output per capita in most countries in the world is converging to the level of output per capita in the United States.

e. For much of human history, any increase in output led to a proportional increase in population, so to stagnation of output per capita.

f. Capital accumulation does not affect the level of output in the long run. Only technological progress does.

g. The aggregate production function is a relation between output on one hand, labor and capital on the other.

h. Because eventually we shall know everything, growth will have to come to an end.

2. *Use Table 10-1 to answer the following questions:*

a. Compute what output per capita would have been in 2000 for each of the five countries if the growth rate during 1974–2000 for each country had remained the same as during 1950–1973.

b. What would have been the ratio of output per capita in Japan relative to output per capita in the United States?

c. Did convergence continue during the growth slowdown from 1974–2000?

3. *Assume that the average consumer in Mexico and the United States buys the quantities and pays the prices indicated in the following table:*

	Food		Transportation Services	
	Price	Quantity	Price	Quantity
Mexico	5 pesos	400	20 pesos	200
United States	$1	1,000	$2	2,000

a. Compute U.S. consumption per capita in dollars.

b. Compute Mexican consumption per capita in pesos.

c. Suppose that the exchange rate is 0.1 ($0.10 per peso). Compute Mexico's consumption per capita in dollars.

d. Using the purchasing power parity method and U.S. prices, compute Mexican consumption per capita in dollars.

e. Under each method, how much smaller is the standard of living in Mexico than in the United States? Does the choice of method make a difference?

4. *Consider the production function* $Y = \sqrt{K}\sqrt{N}$

a. Compute output when $K = 49$ and $N = 81$.

b. If both capital and labor double, what happens to output?

c. Is this production function characterized by constant returns to scale? Explain.

d. Write this production function as a relation between output per worker and capital per worker.

e. Let $K/N = 4$. What is Y/N? Now double K/N to 8. Does Y/N more or less than double?

f. Does the relation between output per worker and capital per worker exhibit constant returns to scale?

g. Is your answer in (f) the same as your answer in (c)? Why or why not?

h. Plot the relation between output per worker and capital per worker. Does it have the same general shape as the relation in Figure 10-5? Explain.

Dig Deeper

5. *Consider the production function given in problem 4. Assume that N is constant and equal to 1.*

a. Derive the relation between the growth rate of output and the growth rate of capital.

b. Suppose we want to achieve output growth equal to 2% a year. What is the required rate of growth of capital?

c. In (b), what happens to the ratio of capital to output over time?

d. Is it possible to sustain output growth of 2% forever in this economy? Why or why not?

6. *Between 1950 and 1973, France, Germany, and Japan all experienced growth rates that were at least two percentage*

points higher than those in the United States. Yet the most important technological advances of that period were made in the United States. How can this be?

Explore Further

7. In Table 10-1 we saw that the levels of output per capita in the United Kingdom, Germany, France, Japan, and the United States were much closer to each other in 2000 than they were in 1950. Here we will examine convergence for another set of countries.

Go to the Web address containing the Penn World Tables (see Table 10-1 and the Focus box on the construction of PPP numbers) (**pwt.econ.upenn.edu/**).

a. Find GDP per capita for France, Belgium, Italy, and the United States, for 1950 to 1992.

b. Once the numbers appear on your Web browser, save them as a text file and import them to your favorite spreadsheet program. Define for each country for each year the ratio of its real GDP to that of the United States for that year (so that this ratio will be equal to one for the United States for all years).

c. Graph the ratios for France, Belgium, and Italy over the period for which you have data, 1950–1992 (all in the same graph). Does your graph support the notion of convergence among the four countries listed in (a)?

d. Repeat the same exercise for Argentina, Venezuela, Chad, Madagascar, and the United States. Does your new graph support the notion of convergence among this group of countries?

We invite you to visit the Blanchard page on the Prentice Hall Web site at:
www.prenhall.com/blanchard
for this chapter's World Wide Web exercises

Further Readings

Brad deLong, an economist at the University of California at Berkeley, has several fascinating articles on growth on his Web page (**www.j-bradford-delong.net/**). Read in particular "Berkeley Faculty Lunch Talk: Main Themes of Twentieth Century Economic History," which covers many of the themes of this chapter.

A broad presentation of facts about growth is given by Angus Maddison in *The World Economy. A Millenium Perspective* (Paris: OECD, 2001). The associated site **www.theworldeconomy.org** has a large number of facts and data on growth over the last two millenia.

Chapter 3 in *Productivity and American Leadership*, by William Baumol, Sue Anne Batey Blackman, and Edward Wolff (Cambridge, MA: MIT Press, 1989) gives a vivid description of how life has been transformed by growth in the United States since the mid-1880s.

Saving, Capital Accumulation, and Output

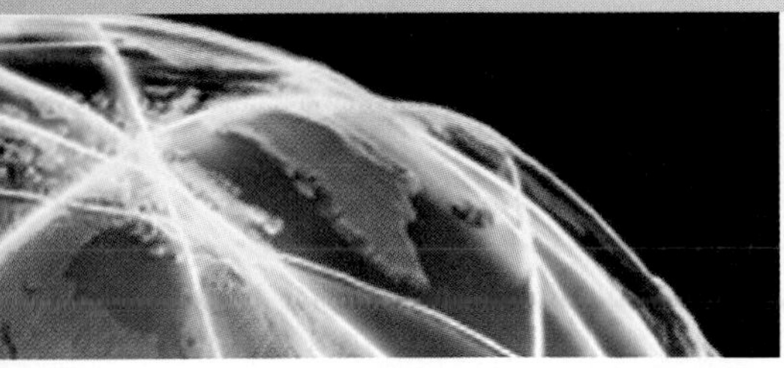

CHAPTER 11

Since 1950 the U.S. saving rate—the ratio of saving to GDP—has averaged only 18%, compared to 24% in Germany and 34% in Japan. Can this explain why the U.S. growth rate has been lower than in most OECD countries in the last 50 years? Would increasing the U.S. saving rate lead to sustained higher U.S. growth in the future?

I have already given the basic answer to these questions at the end of Chapter 10, and the answer is no. Over long periods—an important qualification to which we shall return—an economy's growth rate does not depend on its saving rate. It does not appear that lower U.S. growth in the last 50 years comes primarily from a low saving rate. Nor should we expect that an increase in the saving rate would lead to sustained higher U.S. growth.

This conclusion does not imply, however, that we should not be concerned about the low U.S. saving rate. Even if the saving rate does not permanently affect the growth rate, it does affect the level of output and the standard of living. An increase in the saving rate would lead to higher growth for some time and eventually to a higher standard of living in the United States.

The effects of the saving rate on capital and output per capita are the topics of this chapter.

- Sections 11-1 and 11-2 look at the interactions between output and capital accumulation, and the effects of the saving rate.

- Section 11-3 plugs in numbers to give a better sense of the magnitudes involved.

- Section 11-4 extends our discussion to take into account not only physical capital but also human capital. ■

11-1 Interactions Between Output and Capital

At the center of the determination of output in the long run are two relations between output and capital:

- The amount of capital determines the amount of output being produced.
- The amount of output determines the amount of saving and investment, and so the amount of capital being accumulated.

Together, these two relations, which are represented in Figure 11-1, determine the evolution of output and capital over time. Let's look at each relation in turn.

The Effects of Capital on Output

We started discussing the first of these two relations, the effect of capital on output, in Section 10-3. There we introduced the aggregate production function and you saw that, under the assumption of constant returns to scale, we can write the following relation between output per worker and capital per worker:

$$\frac{Y}{N} = F\left(\frac{K}{N}, 1\right)$$

Output per worker (Y/N) is an increasing function of capital per worker (K/N). Under the assumption of decreasing returns to capital, the larger the initial ratio of capital per worker, the smaller the effects of an increase in capital per worker. When capital per worker is already very high, further increases in capital per worker have only a small effect on output.

To simplify notation, we shall rewrite this relation between output and capital per worker simply as

$$\frac{Y}{N} = f\left(\frac{K}{N}\right)$$

where the function f represents the same relation between output and capital per worker as the function F.

Suppose, for example, the function F has the "double square root" form, so

$$Y = F(K, N) = \sqrt{K}\sqrt{N}$$

Divide both sides by N:

$$Y/N = \sqrt{K}\sqrt{N}/N = \sqrt{K/N}$$

So, in this case, the function f giving the relation between output per worker and capital per worker is simply the square root function:

$$f(K/N) = \sqrt{K/N}$$

$$f\left(\frac{K}{N}\right) = F\left(\frac{K}{N}, 1\right)$$

In this chapter, we shall make two further assumptions:

- The first is that the size of the population, the participation rate, and the unemployment rate are all constant. This implies that employment, N, is also constant. To see why, go back to the relations we saw in Chapter 2, and again in Chapter 6, between population, the labor force, unemployment, and employment.
  —The labor force is equal to population times the participation rate. So, if the size of the population is constant, and the participation rate is constant, the labor force is also constant.

Figure 11-1

Capital, Output, and Saving/Investment

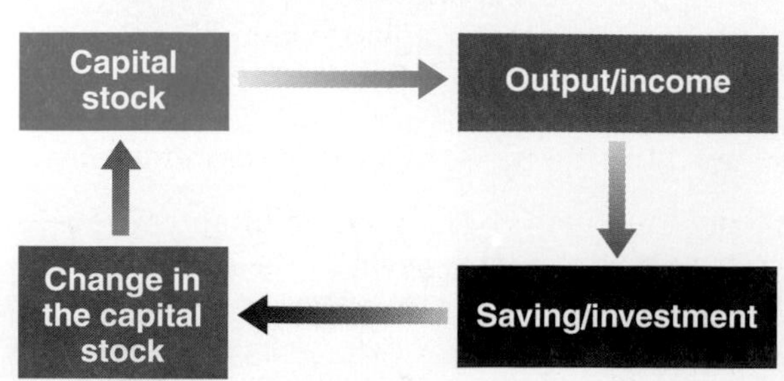

—Employment, in turn, is equal to the labor force times 1 minus the unemployment rate. If, for example, the size of the labor force is 100 million, and the unemployment rate is 5%, then employment is equal to 95 million (100 million times (1 – .05)). So, if the labor force is constant, and the unemployment rate is constant, employment is also constant.

Under these assumptions, output per worker (output divided by employment), output per capita (output divided by population), and output itself all move proportionately. Although I shall usually refer to movements in output or capital *per worker*, to lighten the text I shall sometimes just talk about movements in output or capital, leaving out the "per worker" or "per capita" qualification.

The reason for assuming that N is constant is to make it easier to focus on the role of capital accumulation in growth: If N is constant, the only factor of production that changes over time is capital. The assumption is not very realistic, however, and we shall relax it in the next two chapters. In Chapter 12, we shall allow for steady population and employment growth. And in Chapter 13, we shall see how we can integrate our analysis of the long run—which ignores fluctuations in employment—with our earlier analysis of the short and medium run—which focused precisely on these fluctuations in employment (and the fluctuations in output and unemployment). But both steps are better left to later.

- The second assumption is that there is no technological progress, so the production function f (or, equivalently, F) does not change over time.

  Again, the reason for making this assumption—which is obviously contrary to fact—is to focus just on the role of capital accumulation. In Chapter 12, we shall introduce technological progress and see that the basic conclusions we derive here about the role of capital in growth also hold when there is technological progress. Again, this step is better left to later.

To summarize: With these two assumptions, our first relation between output and capital per worker, from the production side, can be written as

$$\frac{Y_t}{N} = f\left(\frac{K_t}{N}\right) \tag{11.1}$$

where I have introduced time indexes for output and capital—but not for labor, N, which we assume to be constant and so does not need a time index (in other words, we could write labor in equation [11.1] with a time index, i.e., as N_t. But our assumption that it is constant implies that $N_t = N$.)

In words: Higher capital per worker leads to higher output per worker.

From the production side: The level of capital per worker determines the level of output per worker.

The Effects of Output on Capital Accumulation

To derive the second relation, between output and capital accumulation, we proceed in two steps.

First, we derive the relation between output and investment.

Then we derive the relation between investment and capital accumulation.

Output and Investment

To derive the relation between output and investment, we make three assumptions:

- We continue to assume that the economy is closed. As we saw in Chapter 3 (equation [3.10]), this implies that investment, I, is equal to saving—the sum of private saving, S, and public saving, $T - G$.

$$I = S + (T - G)$$

As you shall see in Chapter 19, saving and investment need not be equal in an open economy. A country may save more than it invests, and lend the difference to the rest of the world. Japan, for example, has been running a large trade surplus for a long time, lending part of its saving to the rest of the world.

- To focus on the behavior of private saving, we ignore both taxes and government spending, so $T = G$, and by implication public saving, the difference between taxes and government spending, $T - G = 0$. (We shall relax this assumption later on when we discuss the implications of fiscal policy on growth). With this assumption, the previous equation becomes:

$$I = S$$

Investment is equal to private saving.

- We assume that private saving is proportional to income, so,

$$S = sY$$

The parameter s is the saving rate, and has a value between zero and 1. This assumption captures two basic facts about saving: (1) The saving rate does not appear to systematically increase or decrease as a country becomes richer. (2) Richer countries do not appear to have systematically higher or lower saving rates than poorer ones.

You have now seen two specifications of saving behavior (equivalently, consumption behavior): one for the short run in Chapter 3, and one for the long run in this chapter. You may wonder how the two specifications relate to each other, and whether they are consistent. The answer is yes. A full discussion is given in Chapter 16.

Combining these two relations, and introducing time indexes gives

$$I_t = sY_t$$

Investment is proportional to output: The higher output, the higher saving, and so the higher investment.

Investment and Capital Accumulation

The second step relates investment, which is a flow (the new machines produced and new plants built during a given period), to capital, which is a stock (the existing machines and plants in the economy at a point in time).

Recall that flows are variables that have a time dimension (i.e., they are defined per unit of time); stocks are variables that do not have a time dimension (they are defined at a point in time). Output, saving, and investment are flows. Employment and the capital stock are stocks.

Think of time as measured in years, so t denotes year t, $t + 1$ denotes year $t + 1$, and so on. Think of the capital stock as being measured at the beginning of each year, so K_t refers to the capital stock at the beginning of year t, K_{t+1} to the capital stock at the beginning of year $t + 1$ and so on.

Assume that capital depreciates at rate δ (the lowercase Greek delta) per year: That is, from one year to the next, a proportion δ of the capital stock breaks down and becomes useless; equivalently a proportion $(1 - \delta)$ of the capital stock remains intact from one year to the next.

The evolution of the capital stock is then given by

$$K_{t+1} = (1 - \delta)K_t + I_t$$

The capital stock at the beginning of year $t + 1$, K_{t+1} is equal to the capital stock at the beginning of year t which is still intact in year $t + 1$, $(1 - \delta)K_t$, plus the new capital stock put in place during year t, i.e., investment during year t, I_t.

We can now combine the relation from output and investment, and the relation from investment to capital accumulation to obtain the second relation we need to think about growth, the relation from output to capital accumulation.

Replacing investment by saving in the previous equation, and dividing both sides by N (the number of workers in the economy) gives

$$\frac{K_{t+1}}{N} = (1 - \delta)\frac{K_t}{N} + s\frac{Y_t}{N}$$

In words: Capital per worker at the beginning of year $t + 1$ is equal to capital per worker at the beginning of year t, adjusted for depreciation, plus investment per worker during year t, itself equal to the saving rate times output per worker during year t.

Expanding the term $(1 - \delta)K_t/N$ to $K_t/N - \delta K_t/N$, moving K_t/N to the left, and reorganizing the right side:

$$\frac{K_{t+1}}{N} - \frac{K_t}{N} = s\frac{Y_t}{N} - \delta\frac{K_t}{N} \tag{11.2}$$

In words: The change in the capital stock per worker—represented by the difference between the two terms on the left—is equal to saving per worker—represented by the first term on the right—minus depreciation—represented by the second term on the right. This equation gives us the second relation between output and capital per worker.

From the saving side: The level of output per worker determines the change in the level of capital per worker over time.

11-2 Implications of Alternative Saving Rates

We have derived two relations:

From the production side, equation (11.1) shows how capital determines output.

From the saving side, equation (11.2) shows how output in turn determines capital accumulation.

Let's now put them together to see what they imply for the behavior of output and capital over time.

Dynamics of Capital and Output

Replacing output per worker (Y_t/N) in equation (11.2) by its expression in terms of capital per worker from equation (11.1) gives

$$\underbrace{\frac{K_{t+1}}{N} - \frac{K_t}{N}}_{\substack{\text{change in capital}\\ \text{from year } t \text{ to year } t+1}} = \underbrace{sf\left(\frac{K_t}{N}\right)}_{\substack{\text{investment}\\ \text{during year } t}} - \underbrace{\delta\frac{K_t}{N}}_{\substack{\text{depreciation}\\ \text{during year } t}} \tag{11.3}$$

This relation describes what happens to capital per worker. The change in capital per worker from this year to the next depends on the difference between two terms:

- Investment per worker, the first term on the right. The level of capital per worker this year determines output per worker this year. Given the saving rate, output per worker determines the amount of saving per worker and thus of investment per worker this year.

$K_t/N \rightarrow f(K_t/N) \rightarrow sf(K_t/N)$

- Depreciation per worker, the second term on the right. The capital stock per worker determines the amount of depreciation per worker this year.

$K_t/N \rightarrow \delta K_t/N$

If investment per worker exceeds depreciation per worker, the change in capital per worker is positive: Capital per worker increases.

If investment per worker is less than depreciation per worker, the change in capital per worker is negative: Capital per worker decreases.

Given capital per worker, output per worker is then given by equation (11.1):

$$\frac{Y_t}{N} = f\left(\frac{K_t}{N}\right)$$

Equations (11.3) and (11.1) contain all the information we need to understand the dynamics of capital and output over time. The easiest way to interpret them is to use a graph. We do this in Figure 11-2, where output per worker is measured on the vertical axis, capital per worker is measured on the horizontal axis.

In Figure 11-2, look first at the curve representing output per worker, $f(K_t/N)$, as a function of capital per worker. The relation is the same as in Figure 10-5: Output per

Figure 11-2

Capital and Output Dynamics

When capital and output are low, investment exceeds depreciation, and capital increases. When capital and output are high, investment is less than depreciation and capital decreases.

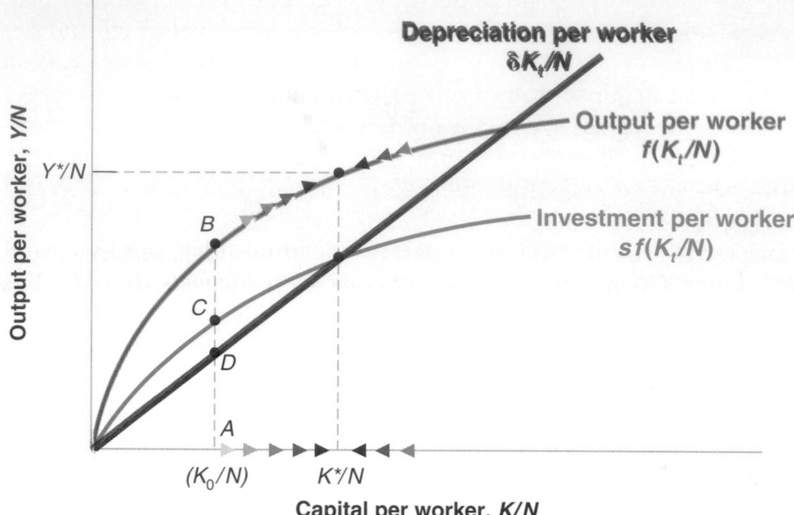

worker increases with capital per worker, but—because of decreasing returns to capital—the effect is smaller the higher the level of capital per worker.

Now look at the two curves representing the two components on the right of equation (11.3).

To make the graph easier to read, I have assumed an unrealistically high saving rate. (Can you tell roughly what value I have assumed for s? What would be a plausible value for s?)

- The relation representing investment per worker, $sf(K_t/N)$, has the same shape as the production function, except that it is lower by a factor s (the saving rate). Suppose the level of capital per worker is equal to K_0/N in Figure 11-2. Output per worker is then given by the distance AB, and investment per worker is given by the vertical distance AC, which is equal to s times the vertical distance AB. Thus, just as for output per worker, investment per worker increases with capital per worker, but by less and less as capital per worker increases. When capital per worker is already very high, the effect of a further increase in capital per worker on output per worker, and thus in turn on investment per worker, is very small.
- The relation representing depreciation per worker, $\delta K_t/N$, is represented by a straight line. Depreciation per worker increases in proportion to capital per worker, so the relation is represented by a straight line with slope equal to δ. At the level of capital per worker K_0/N, depreciation per worker is given by the vertical distance AD.

The change in capital per worker is given by the difference between investment per worker and depreciation per worker. At K_0/N, the difference is positive; investment per worker exceeds depreciation per worker by an amount represented by the vertical distance $CD = AC - AD$; capital per worker increases. As we move to the right along the horizontal axis and look at higher and higher levels of capital per worker, investment increases by less and less, while depreciation keeps increasing in proportion to capital. For some level of capital per worker, K^*/N in Figure 11-2, investment is just enough to cover depreciation, and so, capital per worker remains constant. To the left of K^*/N, investment exceeds depreciation and capital per worker increases. This is indicated by the arrows pointing to the right along the curve representing the production function. To the right of K^*/N, depreciation exceeds investment, and capital per worker decreases. This is indicated by the arrows pointing to the left along the curve representing the production function.

When capital per worker is low, capital per worker and output per worker increase over time. When capital per worker is high, capital per worker and output per worker decrease over time.

Characterizing the evolution of capital per worker and output per worker over time is now easy. Consider an economy that starts with a low level of capital per worker—say, K_0/N in Figure 11-2. Because investment exceeds depreciation, capital per worker increases. And because output moves with capital, output per worker increases as well. Capital per worker eventually reaches K^*/N, the level at which investment is equal to depreciation. Once the economy has reached the level of capital per worker K^*/N, output per worker and capital per worker remain constant at Y^*/N and K^*/N, their long-run equilibrium levels.

Think, for example, of a country that loses part of its capital stock, say, as a result of bombing during a war. The mechanism we have just seen suggests that, if it has suffered much larger capital losses than population losses, it will come out of the war with a low level of capital per worker, so at a point to the left of K^*/N. The country will then experience a large increase in both capital per worker and output per worker for some time. This appears to describe well what happened after World War II to countries that had proportionately larger destructions of capital than of human lives (see the Focus box, "Capital Accumulation and Growth in France in the Aftermath of World War II").

What does the model predict for postwar growth if a country suffers proportional losses in population and in capital? Do you find this answer convincing? What elements may be missing from the model?

If a country starts instead from a high level of capital per worker, from a point to the right of K^*/N, then depreciation will exceed investment, and capital per worker and output per worker will decrease: The initial level of capital per worker cannot be sustained given the saving rate. This decrease in capital per worker will continue until the economy again reaches the point where investment is equal to depreciation, where capital per worker is equal to K^*/N. From then on, capital per worker and output per worker will remain constant.

Steady-State Capital and Output

Let's look more closely at the levels of output per worker and capital per worker to which the economy converges in the long run. The state in which output per worker and capital per worker are no longer changing is called the **steady state** of the economy. Putting the left side of equation (11.3) equal to zero (in steady state, by definition, the change in capital per worker is zero), the steady-state value of capital per worker, K^*/N, is given by

$$sf\left(\frac{K^*}{N}\right) = \delta\frac{K^*}{N} \tag{11.4}$$

The steady-state value of capital per worker is such that the amount of saving per worker (the left side) is just sufficient to cover depreciation of the capital stock per worker (the right side).

Given steady state capital per worker (K^*/N), the steady-state value of output per worker (Y^*/N), is given by the production function

$$\frac{Y^*}{N} = f\left(\frac{K^*}{N}\right) \tag{11.5}$$

We now have all the elements we need to discuss the effects of the saving rate on output per worker, both over time and in steady state.

The Saving Rate and Output

We can now return to the question asked at the beginning of the chapter: What are the effects of the saving rate on the growth rate of output per worker? Our analysis leads to a three-part answer:

1. *The saving rate has no effect on the long-run growth rate of output per worker, which is equal to zero.*

Capital Accumulation and Growth in France in the Aftermath of World War II

When World War II ended in 1945, France had suffered some of the heaviest losses of all European countries. The losses in lives were large; more than 550,000 people had died, out of a population of 42 million. The losses in capital were much larger. Estimates are that the French capital stock in 1945 was about 30% below its prewar value. A more vivid picture of the destruction of capital is provided by the numbers in Table 1.

The model of growth we have just seen makes a clear prediction about what will happen to a country that loses a large part of its capital stock: The country will experience fast capital accumulation and output growth for some time. In terms of Figure 11-2, a country with capital per worker initially far below K^*/N will grow rapidly as it converges to K^*/N and output per worker converges to Y^*/N.

This prediction fares well in the case of postwar France. There is plenty of anecdotal evidence that small increases in capital led to large increases in output. Minor repairs to a major bridge would lead to the reopening of that bridge. Reopening the bridge would lead in turn to large reductions in the travel time between two cities, leading to a large reduction in transport costs. A large reduction in transport costs would then allow a plant to get much needed inputs and increase production and so on.

The more convincing evidence, however, comes directly from the numbers on growth of aggregate output itself. From 1946 to 1950, the annual growth rate of French real GDP was a very high 9.6% per year, leading to an increase in real GDP of about 60% over five years.

Was all the increase in French GDP due to capital accumulation? The answer is no. There were other forces in addition to the mechanism in our model. Much of the remaining capital stock in 1945 was old. Investment had been low in the 1930s (a decade dominated by the Great Depression), and nearly nonexistent during the war. Much of the postwar capital accumulation was associated with the introduction of more modern capital and the use of more modern production techniques. This was another reason for the high growth rates of the postwar period.

Source: Gilles Saint-Paul, "Economic Reconstruction in France, 1945–1958," in Rudiger Dornbusch, Willem Nolling, and Richard Layard, eds. Postwar Economic Reconstruction and Lessons for the East Today *(Cambridge, MA: MIT Press, 1993), 83–114.*

TABLE 1 Proportion of the French Capital Stock Destroyed by the End of World War II

Railways (%)	Tracks	6	*Rivers* (%)	Waterways	86
	Stations	38		Canal locks	11
	Engines	21		Barges	80
	Hardware	60	*Buildings* (numbers)		
Roads (%)	Cars	31		Dwellings	1,229,000
	Trucks	40		Industrial	246,000

Source: See source note for this box.

FOCUS

This conclusion is rather obvious: We have seen that, eventually, the economy converges to a constant level of output per worker. In other words, in the long run, the growth rate of output is equal to zero, whatever the value of the saving rate.

There is, however, a way of thinking about it that will be useful when we introduce technological progress in Chapter 12. Think of what would be needed to sustain a constant positive growth rate of output per worker in the long run. Capital per worker would have to increase. Not only that, but, because of decreasing returns to capital, it would have to increase faster than output per worker. This implies that each year the economy would have to save a larger and larger fraction of output and put it toward capital accumulation. At some point, the fraction of output it would need to save would be greater than one—something clearly impossible. This is why it is impossible to sustain a constant positive growth rate forever. In the long run, capital per worker must be constant and so must be output per worker.

2. Nonetheless, *the saving rate determines the level of output per worker in the long run.* Other things equal, countries with a higher saving rate will achieve higher output per worker in the long run.

   Figure 11-3 illustrates this point. Consider two countries with the same production function, the same level of employment, and the same depreciation rate, but different saving rates, say, s_0 and $s_1 > s_0$. Figure 11-3 draws their common production function, $f(K_t/N)$, and the functions giving saving/investment per worker as a function of capital per worker for each of the two countries, $s_0 f(K_t/N)$ and $s_1 f(K_t/N)$. In the long run, the country with saving rate s_0 will reach the level of capital per worker, K_0/N, and output per worker, Y_0/N. The country with saving rate s_1 will reach the higher levels K_1/N and Y_1/N.

3. *An increase in the saving rate will lead to higher growth of output per worker for some time, but not forever*

   This conclusion follows from the two propositions we just discussed. From the first, we know that an increase in the saving rate does not affect the long-run *growth rate of output per worker,* which remains equal to zero. From the second, we know that an increase in the saving rate leads to an increase in the long-run *level of output per worker.* It follows that, as output per worker increases to its new higher level in response to the increase in the saving rate, the economy will undergo a period of positive growth. This period of growth will end when the economy reaches its new steady state.

   We can use Figure 11-3 again to illustrate this point. Consider a country that has an initial saving rate of s_0. Assume that capital per worker is initially equal to K_0/N, with associated output per worker Y_0/N. Now consider the effects of an increase in the saving rate from s_0 to s_1. (You can think of this increase as coming from tax changes that make it more attractive to save or from reductions in the budget deficit; the origin of the increase in the saving rate does not matter here.) The function giving saving/investment per worker as a function of capital per worker shifts upward from $s_0 f(K_t/N)$ to $s_1 f(K_t/N)$.

   At the initial level of capital per worker, K_0/N, investment now exceeds depreciation, so capital per worker increases. As capital per worker increases, so does

Some economists argue that the high output growth achieved by the Soviet Union from 1950 to 1990 was the result of such a steady increase in the saving rate over time, and so could not be sustained forever. Paul Krugman has used the term "Stalinist growth" to denote this type of growth—growth resulting from a higher and higher saving rate over time.

Note that the first proposition is a statement about the growth rate of output per worker. The second proposition is a statement about the level of output per worker.

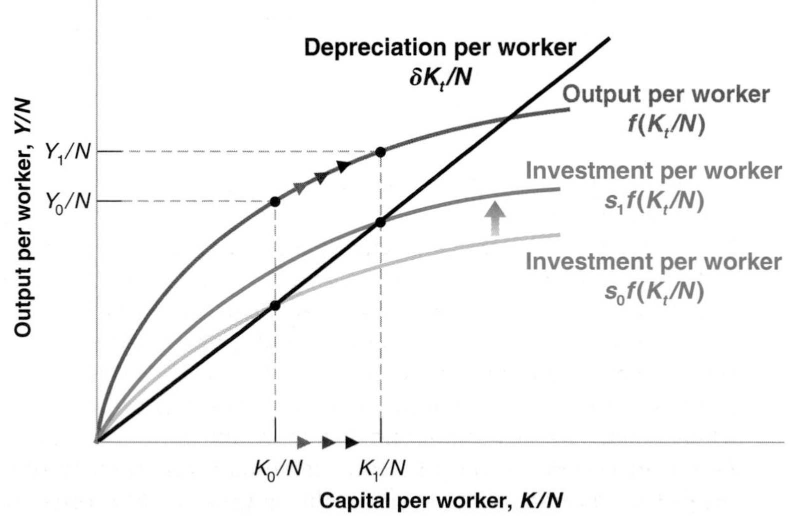

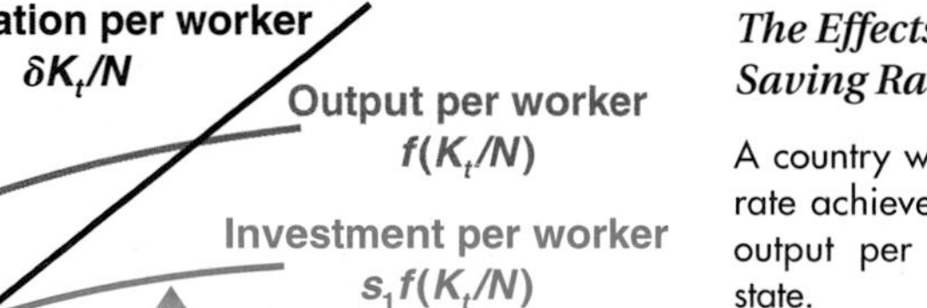

Figure 11-3

The Effects of Different Saving Rates

A country with a higher saving rate achieves a higher level of output per worker in steady state.

Figure 11-4

The Effects of an Increase in the Saving Rate on Output per Worker

An increase in the saving rate leads to a period of growth until output reaches its new higher steady-state level.

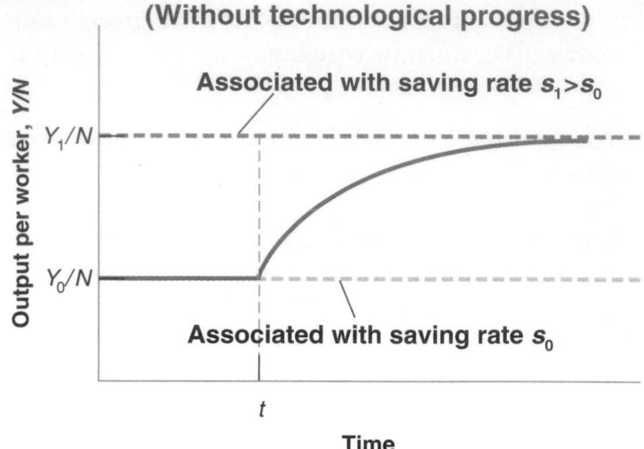

output per worker, and the economy undergoes a period of positive growth. When capital per worker eventually reaches K_1/N, investment is again equal to depreciation and growth ends. The economy remains from then on at K_1/N, with associated output per worker at Y_1/N. The movement of output per worker is plotted against time in Figure 11-4. Output per worker is initially constant at level Y_0/N. After the increase in the saving rate, say, at time t, output per worker increases for some time until it reaches the higher level of output per worker, Y_1/N, and the growth rate returns to zero.

We have derived these three results under the assumption of no technological progress and thus no growth of output per worker in the long run. But, as we shall see in Chapter 12, the three results extend directly to an economy in which there is technological progress. Let me briefly indicate how.

An economy where there is technological progress has a positive growth rate of output per worker even in the long run. This long-run growth rate is independent of the saving rate—the extension of the first result just discussed. The saving rate affects however the level of output per worker—the extension of the second result. So, an increase in the saving rate leads to growth greater than steady-state growth rate for some time until the economy reaches its new higher path—the extension of our third result.

These three results are illustrated in Figure 11-5, which extends Figure 11-4 by plotting the effect of an increase in the saving rate in an economy with positive technological progress. The figure uses a logarithmic scale to measure output per worker, so that an economy where output per worker grows at a constant rate is represented by a line with slope equal to that growth rate. At the initial saving rate, s_0, the economy moves along *AA*. If, at time t, the saving rate increases to s_1, the economy experiences higher growth for some time until it reaches its new higher path, *BB*. On path *BB*, the growth rate is again the same as before the increase in the saving rate (that is, the slope of *BB* is the same as the slope of *AA*).

See the discussion of logarithmic scales in Appendix 2 at the end of the book.

The Saving Rate and Consumption

Governments can use various instruments to affect the saving rate. They can run budget deficits or surpluses. They can give tax breaks to savers, making it more attractive to save. What saving rate should governments aim for? To think about the answer, we must shift our focus from the behavior of *output* to the behavior of *consumption*: What matters to people is not how much is produced, but how much they consume.

It is clear that an increase in saving must come initially at the expense of lower consumption. (Except when I think it helpful, I shall drop the "per worker" in this

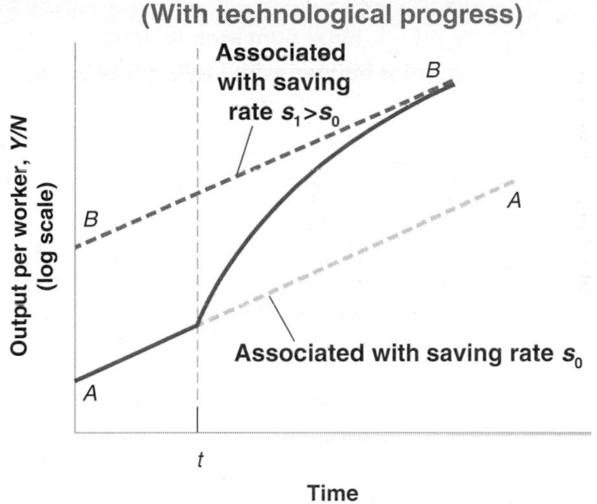

Figure 11-5

The Effects of an Increase in the Saving Rate on Output per Worker in an Economy with Technological Progress

An increase in the saving rate leads to a period of higher growth until output reaches a new, higher path.

subsection and just refer to consumption rather than consumption per worker, capital rather than capital per worker, and so on). A change in the saving rate this year has no effect on capital this year, and so no effect on output and income *this year*. So an increase in saving comes initially with an equal decrease in consumption.

Investment this year does not affect the capital stock this year: I_t affects K_{t+1}, not K_t.

Because we assume that employment is constant, we are ignoring the short-run effect of an increase in the saving rate on output we focused on in Chapter 3. In the short run, not only does an increase in the saving rate reduce consumption given income, but it may also create a recession, and decrease income further. We shall return to a discussion of short-run and long-run effects of changes in saving at various points in the book. See, for example, Chapter 26.

Does an increase in saving lead to an increase in consumption in the long run? Not necessarily. Consumption may decrease, not only initially, but also in the long run. You may find this surprising. After all, we know from Figure 11-3 that an increase in the saving rate always leads to an increase in the level of *output* per worker. But output is not the same as consumption. To see why not, consider what happens for two extreme values of the saving rate:

An economy in which the saving rate is (and has always been) zero is an economy in which capital is equal to zero. In this case, output is also equal to zero, and so is consumption. A saving rate equal to zero implies zero consumption in the long run.

Now go to the opposite extreme and consider an economy in which the saving rate is equal to one: People save all their income. The level of capital, and thus output, will be very high. But because people save all of their income, consumption is equal to zero. What happens is that the economy is carrying an excessive amount of capital: Simply maintaining that level of output requires that all output be devoted to replacing depreciation! A saving rate equal to 1 also implies zero consumption in the long run.

These two extreme cases imply that there must be some value of the saving rate between 0 and 1 that maximizes the steady-state level of consumption. Increases in the saving rate below this value lead to a decrease in consumption initially, but to an increase in consumption in the long run. Increases in the saving rate beyond this value decrease consumption not only initially, but also in the long run. This happens because the increase in capital associated with the increase in the saving rate leads to only a small increase in output, an increase that is too small to cover the increased depreciation: The economy carries too much capital. The level of capital associated with the value of the saving rate that yields the highest level of consumption in steady state is known as the **golden-rule level of capital**. Increases in capital beyond the golden-rule level reduce steady-state consumption.

This argument is illustrated in Figure 11-6, which plots consumption per worker in steady state (on the vertical axis) against the saving rate (on the horizontal axis).

Figure 11-6

The Effects of the Saving Rate on Consumption per Worker in Steady State

An increase in the saving rate leads to an increase, then to a decrease in consumption per worker in steady state.

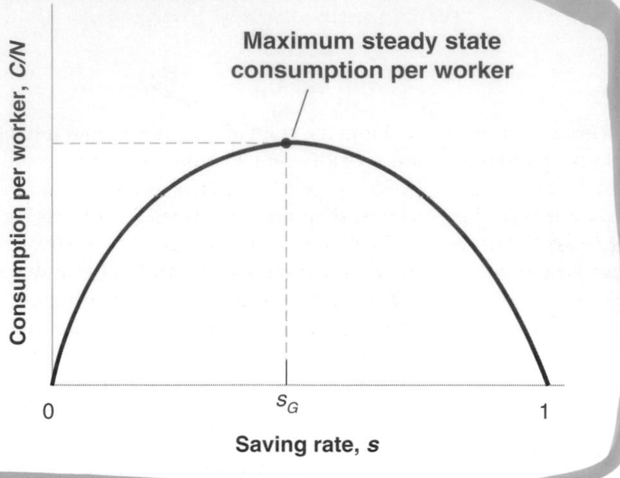

A saving rate equal to zero implies a capital stock per worker equal to zero, a level of output per worker equal to zero, and, by implication, a level of consumption per worker equal to zero. For s between 0 and s_G, (G for golden rule) higher values of the saving rate imply higher values for capital per worker, output per worker, and consumption per worker. For s larger than s_G, increases in the saving rate still lead to higher values of capital per worker and output per worker; but they lead to lower values of consumption per worker: This is because the increase in output is more than offset by the increase in depreciation due to the larger capital stock. For $s = 1$, consumption per worker is equal to zero. Capital per worker and output per worker are high, but all of output is used just to replace depreciation, leaving nothing for consumption.

If an economy already has so much capital that it is operating beyond the golden rule, then increasing saving further will decrease consumption not only in the short run, but also in the long run. Is this a relevant worry? Do some countries actually have too much capital? The empirical evidence indicates that most OECD countries are actually far below their golden-rule level of capital. If they were to increase the saving rate, it would lead to higher consumption in the future.

This conclusion implies that, in practice, governments face a trade-off: An increase in the saving rate implies lower consumption for some time, higher consumption later. What should they do? How close to the golden rule should governments try to get? That depends on how much weight they put on the welfare of current generations—who are more likely to lose from policies aimed at increasing the saving rate—versus the welfare of future generations, who are more likely to gain. Enter politics: Future generations do not vote. This implies that governments are unlikely to ask current generations for large sacrifices, which in turn means that capital is likely to stay far below its golden-rule level. These intergenerational issues are very much in evidence in the current debate on social security reform; this is explored in the Focus box, "Social Security, Social Security Reform, and Capital Accumulation in the United States."

11-3 Getting a Sense of Magnitudes

How large is the effect of a change in the saving rate on output in the long run? For how long and by how much does an increase in the saving rate affect growth? How far is the United States from the golden-rule level of capital? To get a better sense of the answers

Social Security, Social Security Reform, and Capital Accumulation in the United States

Social Security was introduced in the United States in 1935. Its goal was to make sure the elderly would have enough income to live on. It has become the largest transfer program in the United States. Benefits paid to retirees now exceed 4% of GDP. For two-thirds of retirees, Social Security benefits account for more than 50% of their income.

One can think of two ways to set up and run a social security system:

- One is to tax workers and distribute the tax contributions as benefits to retirees. Such a system is called a **pay-as-you-go system**: The system pays benefits out "as it goes," i.e., as it collects them in contributions.
- The other is to tax workers, invest the contributions in financial assets, and pay back the principal plus the interest to workers when they retire. Such a system is called a **fully funded system**: At any time, the system has funds equal to the accumulated contributions of workers, and from which it will be able to pay out benefits when these workers retire.

From the point of view of retirees, the two systems feel quite similar, although not identical:

What the retirees receive in a pay-as-you-go system depends on demographics—the ratio of retirees to workers—and on the evolution of the tax rate set by the system.

What the retirees receive in a fully funded system depends on the rate of return on the financial assets held by the fund.

But, in both cases, workers pay contributions when they work, and receive benefits when they have retired.

From the point of view of the economy, the two systems are very different: In a pay-as-you-go system, the contributions are redistributed, not invested; in a fully funded system, they are invested, leading to a higher capital stock.

Most actual social security systems are somewhere between pay-as-you-go and fully funded systems. The U.S. system is close to a pay-as-you-go system. When it was set up in 1935, the intention was to partially fund it. But this did not happen. Contributions from workers were used to pay benefits to the retirees; for the first few decades of the system, retirees received benefits without having contributed, or without having contributed for very long. This gift to the initial retirees was widely perceived as fair: These were the generations that had suffered during the Great Depression, and then through World War II. Also, it was not very costly: The number of eligible retirees was small at the beginning—only 7% of the population over 65 received benefits in 1940 (compared to 91% today)—so the Social Security tax rate required to finance benefits was low.

The system is now in trouble.

The reason: Demographic changes. Life expectancy, and with it the average length of retirement, has steadily increased. The large baby-boom generations are approaching retirement. As a result, the ratio of workers to retirees has steadily decreased, and will continue to decrease over the next 50 years. As Figure 1 shows, there are 3.3 workers for every retiree in the United States; projections are that this number will decrease to less than 2 by 2075. At given benefit and tax rates, this means a growing imbalance between benefits and contributions.

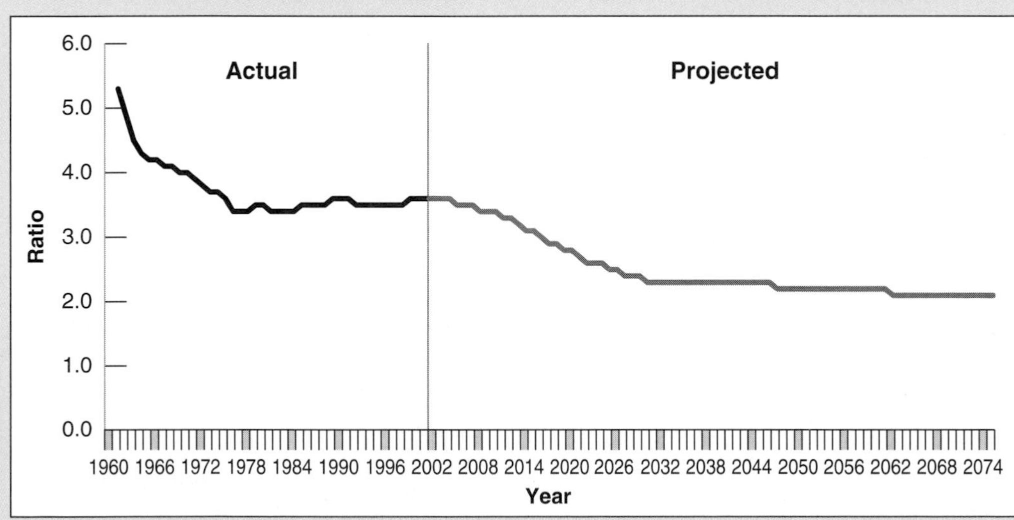

FIGURE 1 *Ratio of Workers to Retirees, 1960 to 2075*

The ratio of workers to retirees will steadily decline in the future.
***Source:** 2001 Social Security Trustees Report.*

Continued

FOCUS

In anticipation of these demographic evolutions, the Social Security tax rate has already been increased, and contributions have been higher than benefits for some time, leading to the accumulation of a **Social Security trust fund**. This does not mean the Social Security system is now fully funded, the fund is small relative to the benefits to be paid in the future. Under current rules, benefits are expected to start exceeding contributions by 2020, and the trust fund is expected to be depleted by 2040.

It is clear that something will have to be done to balance the system over the next century. This means either an increase in the tax rate, or a decrease in the benefit rate, or an increase in the retirement age. These measures can be implemented now, and used to accumulate a larger trust fund, or they can be implemented later. The longer the wait, the larger the needed adjustment: Suppose the adjustment takes place only through an increase in the tax rate. Computations suggest that the rate would have to increase today from 12.5% to about 15%. If we waited until 2030, the rate would have to increase to about 17%.

In this context, some economists and politicians have suggested that Social Security reform should do more than just balance the existing system. They argue that the goal should be a shift to a fully funded system. Their argument is that the U.S. saving rate is too low and that funding the Social Security system would increase it. Martin Feldstein, an advocate of such a shift, has concluded that it could lead to a 34% increase of the capital stock in the long run.

How should we think about such a proposal? It might have been a good idea to fully fund the system at the start: The United States would have a higher saving rate. The U.S. capital stock would be higher, output and consumption would also be higher. But we cannot rewrite history. The existing system has promised benefits to retirees and these promises have to be honored. This means that, if we wanted to shift to a fully funded system, current workers would have, in effect, to contribute twice. Once to finance the benefits owed to retirees, and then again, to fund the system and finance their own retirement. This would be good for the United States in the long run, but would impose a disproportionate cost on current workers. The practical implication is that, if it is to happen, the move to a fully funded system will have to be very slow, so that the burden of adjustment does not fall too much on one generation relative to the others.

A recent review of the history, the problems, and the choices facing the U.S. Social Security system is Social Security Reform: Links to Saving, Investment, and Growth, *Federal Reserve Bank of Boston, Conference Series No 41, June 1997.*

to these questions, let us now make more specific assumptions, plug in some numbers, and see what we get.

Assume the production function is given by

$$Y = \sqrt{K}\sqrt{N} \tag{11.6}$$

Output equals the product of the square root of capital and the square root of labor. Note that this production function exhibits both constant returns to scale, and decreasing returns to either capital or labor.

Dividing both sides by N (because we are interested in output per worker):

$$\frac{Y}{N} = \frac{\sqrt{K}\sqrt{N}}{N} = \frac{\sqrt{K}}{\sqrt{N}} = \sqrt{\frac{K}{N}}$$

The second equality follows from $\sqrt{N}/N = \sqrt{N}/(\sqrt{N}\sqrt{N}) = 1/\sqrt{N}$

▶ Output per worker equals the square root of capital per worker. Put another way, the production function, f, relating output per worker to capital per worker is given by

$$f\left(\frac{K_t}{N}\right) = \sqrt{\frac{K_t}{N}}$$

Now return to equation (11.3), repeated here for convenience:

$$\frac{K_{t+1}}{N} - \frac{K_t}{N} = s\, f\left(\frac{K_t}{N}\right) - \delta \frac{K_t}{N}$$

Replace $f(K_t/N)$ by $\sqrt{K_t/N}$:

$$\frac{K_{t+1}}{N} - \frac{K_t}{N} = s\sqrt{\frac{K_t}{N}} - \delta \frac{K_t}{N} \qquad (11.7)$$

This equation describes the evolution of capital per worker over time. Let's look at what it implies.

The Effects of the Saving Rate on Steady-State Output

How large is the effect of an increase in the saving rate on the steady-state level of output per worker?

Start with equation (11.7). In steady state, the amount of capital per worker is constant, so the left side of the equation equals zero. This implies

$$s\sqrt{\frac{K}{N}} = \delta \frac{K}{N}$$

(I have dropped time indexes, which are no longer needed because in steady state K/N is constant.) Square both sides:

$$s^2 \frac{K}{N} = \delta^2 \left(\frac{K}{N}\right)^2$$

Divide both sides by (K/N) and reorganize:

$$\frac{K}{N} = \left(\frac{s}{\delta}\right)^2 \qquad (11.8)$$

Steady-state capital per worker is equal to the square of the ratio of the saving rate to the depreciation rate.

From equations (11.6) and (11.8), steady-state output per worker is then given by

$$\frac{Y}{N} = \sqrt{\frac{K}{N}} = \sqrt{\left(\frac{s}{\delta}\right)^2} = \frac{s}{\delta} \qquad (11.9)$$

Steady-state output per worker is equal to the ratio of the saving rate to the depreciation rate.

A higher saving rate and a lower depreciation rate both lead to higher steady-state capital per worker (equation [11.8]) and higher steady-state output per worker (equation [11.9]). To see what this implies, let's take a numerical example. Suppose the depreciation rate is 10% per year, and suppose the saving rate is also 10%. Then, from equations (11.8) and (11.9), steady-state capital per worker and output per worker are both equal to 1. Now suppose that the saving rate doubles, from 10 to 20%. It follows from equation (11.8) that in the new steady state, capital per worker increases from 1 to 4. And from equation (11.9), output per worker doubles, from 1 to 2. Thus doubling the saving rate leads, in the long run, to doubling output per worker: This is a large effect.

The Dynamic Effects of an Increase in the Saving Rate

After an increase in the saving rate, how long does it take for output to reach its new steady-state level? Put another way, by how much and for how long does an increase in the saving rate affect the growth rate?

To answer these questions, we must use equation (11.7) and solve it for capital per worker in year 0, in year 1, and so on.

Suppose that the saving rate, which had always been equal to 0.1, increases in year 0 from 0.1 to 0.2 and remains at this higher value forever after. In year 0, nothing happens to the capital stock (recall that it takes one year for higher saving and higher investment to show up in higher capital). So, capital per worker remains equal to the steady state value associated with a saving rate of 0.1. From equation (11.8):

$$K_0/N = (0.1/0.1)^2 = 1^2 = 1$$

In year 1, equation (11.7) gives

$$\frac{K_1}{N} - \frac{K_0}{N} = s\sqrt{\frac{K_0}{N}} - \delta\frac{K_0}{N}$$

With a depreciation rate equal to 0.1 and a saving rate now equal to 0.2, this equation implies that:

$$\frac{K_1}{N} - 1 = [(0.2)(\sqrt{1})] - [(0.1)1]$$

so,

$$\frac{K_1}{N} = 1.1$$

In the same way, we can solve for K_2/N and so on. Once we have the values of capital per worker in year 0, in year 1, and so on, we can then use equation (11.6) to solve for output per worker in year 0, in year 1, and so on. The results of this computation are presented in Figure 11-7. Panel (a) plots the *level* of output per worker against time. (Y/N) increases over time from its initial value of 1 in year 0 to its steady-state value of 2 in the long run. Panel (b) gives the same information in a different way, plotting instead the *growth rate* of output per worker against time. As panel (b) shows, growth of output per worker is highest at the beginning and then decreases over time. As the economy reaches its new steady state, growth of output per worker returns to zero.

What Figure 11-7 clearly shows is that the adjustment to the new, higher, long-run equilibrium takes a long time. It is only 40% complete after 10 years, 63% complete after 20 years. Put another way, the increase in the saving rate increases the growth rate of output per worker for a long time. The average annual growth rate is 3.1% for the first 10 years, 1.5% for the next 10. While changes in the saving rate have no effect on growth in the long run, they do lead to higher growth for quite some time.

To go back to the question raised at the beginning of the chapter, can the low saving rate in the United States explain why the U.S. growth rate has been so low—relative to other OECD countries—since 1950? The answer would be yes if the United States had had a higher saving rate in the past, and *if this saving rate had decreased substantially in the last 50 years.* If this were the case, this could explain the period of lower growth in the United States in the last 50 years along the lines of the mechanism in Figure 11-7 (with the sign reversed, as we would be looking at a decrease—not an increase—in the saving rate.) But this is not the case: The U.S. saving rate has been low for a long time. Low saving cannot explain the poor U.S. growth performance over the last 50 years.

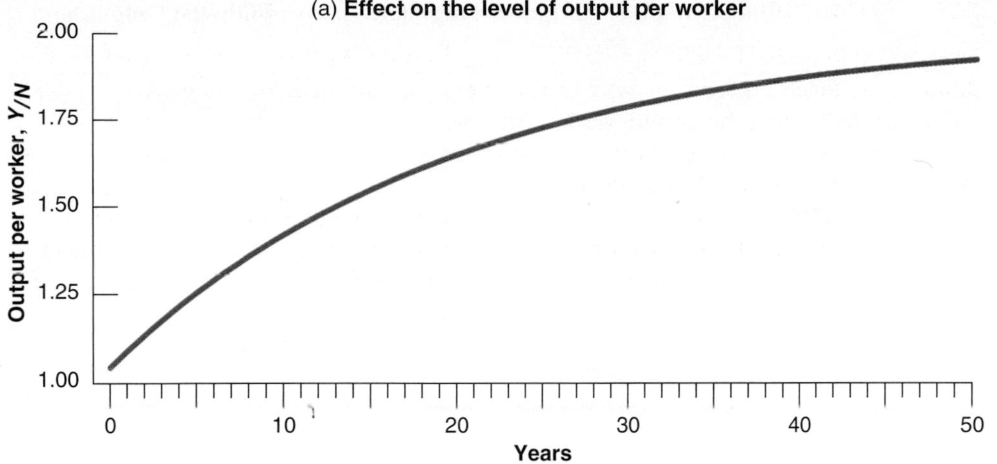

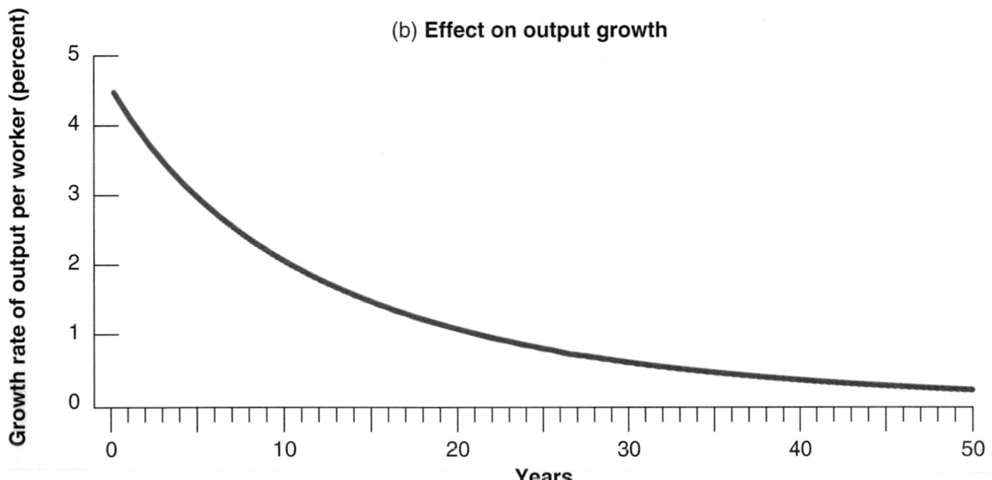

Figure 11-7

Dynamic Effects of an Increase in the Saving Rate from 10 to 20% on the Level and the Growth Rate of Output per Worker

It takes a long time for output to adjust to its new higher level after an increase in the saving rate. Put another way, an increase in the saving rate leads to a long period of higher growth.

The U.S. Saving Rate and the Golden Rule

What is the saving rate that would maximize steady-state consumption per worker? Recall that in steady state, consumption is equal to what is left after enough is put aside to maintain a constant level of capital. More formally, in steady state, consumption per worker is equal to output per worker minus depreciation per worker.

$$\frac{C}{N} = \frac{Y}{N} - \delta \frac{K}{N}$$

Using equations (11.8) and (11.9) for the steady-state values of output per worker and capital per worker, consumption per worker is thus given by

$$\frac{C}{N} = \left(\frac{s}{\delta}\right) - \delta\left(\frac{s}{\delta}\right)^2$$
$$= \frac{s(1-s)}{\delta}$$

Using this equation, together with equations (11.8) and (11.9), Table 11-1 gives the steady-state values of capital per worker, output per worker, and consumption per worker for different values of the saving rate (and for a depreciation rate equal to 10%).

Table 11-1 The Saving Rate and the Steady-State Levels of Capital, Output, and Consumption per Worker

Saving Rate s	Capital per worker K/N	Output per worker Y/N	Consumption per worker C/N
0.0	0.0	0.0	0.0
0.1	1.0	1.0	0.9
0.2	4.0	2.0	1.6
0.3	9.0	3.0	2.1
0.4	16.0	4.0	2.4
0.5	25.0	5.0	2.5
0.6	36.0	6.0	2.4
—	—	—	—
1.0	100.0	10.0	0.0

Steady-state consumption per worker is largest when s equals one-half: The golden-rule level of capital is associated with a saving rate of 50%. Below that level, increases in the saving rate lead to an increase in long-run consumption per worker. Above that level, they lead to a decrease. Few economies in the world today have saving rates above 40%, and (as we saw at the beginning of the chapter) the U.S. saving rate is actually less than 20%. As rough as it is, our computation suggests that, in most economies, an increase in the saving rate would increase both output per worker and consumption per worker in the long run.

Check your understanding of the issues: Using the equations in this section, argue the pros and cons of policy measures aimed at increasing the U.S. saving rate from its current value of about 18% to, say, 20%.

11-4 Physical Versus Human Capital

We have concentrated so far on physical capital—on machines, plants, office buildings, and so on. But economies have another type of capital: the set of skills of the workers in the economy, what economists call **human capital**. An economy with many highly skilled workers is likely to be much more productive than an economy in which most workers cannot read or write.

The increase in human capital has been as large as the increase in physical capital over the last two centuries. At the beginning of the Industrial Revolution, only 30% of the population knew how to read. Today, the literacy rate in OECD countries is above 95%. Schooling was not compulsory prior to the Industrial Revolution. Today it is compulsory, usually until the age of 16. Still, there are large differences across countries. Today in OECD countries, nearly 100% of children get a primary education, 90% get a secondary education, and 38% get a higher education. The corresponding numbers in poor countries, countries with GDP per capita below $400 in 1985, are 95%, 32%, and 4%, respectively.

Even this comparison may be misleading. The quality of education may be quite different across countries.

How should we think about the effect of human capital on output? How does the introduction of human capital change our earlier conclusions? These are the questions we take up in this last section.

Extending the Production Function

The most natural way of extending our analysis to allow for human capital is to modify the production function relation (11.1) to read

$$\frac{Y}{N} = f\left(\frac{K}{N}, \frac{H}{N}\right) \qquad (11.10)$$
$$\left(+\ ,\ +\right)$$

The level of output per worker depends on both the level of physical capital per worker, K/N, and the level of human capital per worker, H/N. As before, an increase in capital per worker (K/N) leads to an increase in output per worker. And an increase in the average level of skill (H/N) also leads to more output per worker. More skilled workers can use more complex machines; they can deal more easily with unexpected complications; they can adapt faster to new tasks. All of these lead to higher output per worker.

◀ **Note that we are using the same symbol, *H*, to denote the monetary base in Chapter 4, and human capital in this chapter. Both uses are traditional. Do not be confused.**

We assumed earlier that increases in physical capital per worker increased output per worker, but that the effect became smaller as the level of capital per worker increased. The same assumption is likely to apply to human capital per worker. Think of increases in H/N as coming from increases in the number of years of education. The evidence is that the returns to increasing the proportion of children acquiring a primary education are very large. At the very least, the ability to read and write allows people to use equipment that is more complicated but more productive. For rich countries, however, primary education—and, for that matter, secondary education—are no longer the relevant margins: Most children now get both. The relevant margin is higher education. The evidence here—and I am sure this will come as good news to most of you—is that higher education increases skills, at least as measured by the increase in wages for those who acquire it. But, to take an extreme example, it is not clear that forcing everybody to acquire an advanced college degree would increase aggregate output very much. Many people would end up overqualified and probably more frustrated rather than more productive.

◀ **We look at this evidence in Chapter 13.**

How should we construct the measure for human capital, H? The answer is: Very much in the same way we construct the measure for physical capital, K. In constructing K, we just add the values of the different pieces of capital, so that a machine that costs \$2,000 gets twice the weight of a machine that costs \$1,000. Similarly, we construct the measure of H such that workers who are paid twice as much get twice the weight. Take, for example, an economy with 100 workers, half of them unskilled and half of them skilled. Suppose the relative wage of skilled workers is twice that of unskilled workers. We can then construct H as $[(50 \times 1) + (50 \times 2)] = 150$. Human capital per worker, H/N, is equal to $150/100 = 1.5$.

◀ **The rationale for using relative wages as weights is that they reflect relative marginal products. A worker who is paid three times more than another is assumed to have a marginal product equal to three times that of the other worker.**

An issue is whether relative wages accurately reflect marginal products. To take a controversial example: in the same job, with the same seniority, women still often earn less than men. Is it because their marginal product is lower? Should they be given a lower weight than men in the construction of human capital?

Human Capital, Physical Capital, and Output

How does the introduction of human capital change the analysis of the previous sections?

Our conclusions about *physical capital accumulation* remain valid: An increase in the saving rate increases steady-state physical capital per worker, and therefore increases output per worker. But our conclusions now extend to *human capital accumulation* as well. An increase in how much society "saves" in the form of human capital—through education and on-the-job training—increases steady-state human capital per worker, which leads to an increase in output per worker.

Our extended model therefore gives us a richer picture of the determination of output per worker. In the long run, it tells us, output per worker depends on both how much society saves and how much it spends on education.

What is the relative importance of human capital and physical capital in the determination of output per worker? A place to start is to compare how much is spent on formal education to how much is invested in physical capital. In the United States, spending on formal education is about 6.5% of GDP. This number includes both government expenditures on education and private expenditures by people on education.

This number is between one third and one half of the gross investment rate for physical capital (which is around 16%). But this comparison is only a first pass. Consider the following complications:

- Education, especially higher education, is partly consumption—done for its own sake—and partly investment. We should include only the investment part for our purposes. However, the 6.5% number in the preceding paragraph includes both.
- At least for postsecondary education, the opportunity cost of a person's education is also foregone wages while acquiring the education. Spending on education should include not only the actual cost of education but also the opportunity cost. The 6.5% number does not include this opportunity cost.
- Formal education is only part of education. Much of what we learn comes from on-the-job training, formal or informal. Both the actual costs and the opportunity costs of on-the-job training should also be included. The 6.5% number does not include the costs associated with on-the-job training.
- We should compare investment rates net of depreciation. Depreciation of physical capital, especially of machines, is likely to be higher than depreciation of human capital. Skills deteriorate, but do so slowly. Unlike physical capital, skills deteriorate more slowly the more they are used.

How large is your opportunity cost relative to your tuition? ▶

For all these reasons, it is difficult to come up with reliable numbers for investment in human capital. A recent study concludes that investment in physical capital and in education play roughly similar roles in the determination of output. This conclusion implies that output per worker depends roughly equally on the amount of physical capital and the amount of human capital in the economy. Countries that save more, or spend more on education, can achieve substantially higher steady-state levels of output per worker.

See N. Gregory Mankiw, David Romer, and David Weil, "A Contribution to the Empirics of Economic Growth," *Quarterly Journal of Economics*, 1992, 407–437. ▶

Endogenous Growth

Note what the conclusion we just reached did say and did not say. It did say that a country that saves more or spends more on education will achieve a *higher level* of output per worker in steady state. It did not say that by saving or spending more on education, a country can sustain permanently *higher growth* of output per worker.

This conclusion, however, has been challenged in the past decade. Following the lead of Robert Lucas and Paul Romer, researchers have explored the possibility that the combination of physical capital and human capital accumulation may actually be enough to sustain growth. Given human capital, increases in physical capital will run into decreasing returns. And given physical capital, increases in human capital will also run into decreasing returns. But, these researchers have asked, what if both physical and human capital increase in tandem? Can't an economy grow forever just by having steadily more capital and more skilled workers?

We have mentioned Lucas once already, in connection with the Lucas critique in Chapter 9. ▶

Models that generate steady growth even without technological progress are called **models of endogenous growth**, to reflect the fact that in those models—in contrast to the model we saw in earlier sections of this chapter—growth depends, even in the long run, on variables such as the saving rate and the rate of spending on education. The jury on this class of models is still out, but the indications so far are that the conclusions we drew earlier need to be qualified, not abandoned. The current consensus is as follows:

- Output per worker depends on the level of both physical capital per worker and human capital per worker. Both forms of capital can be accumulated, one through physical investment, the other through education and training. Increasing either the saving rate and/or the fraction of output spent on education and training can lead to much higher levels of output per worker in the long run. However, given the rate of technological progress, such measures do not lead to a permanently higher growth rate.

- Note the qualifier in the last proposition: *given the rate of technological progress.* But is technological progress unrelated to the level of human capital in the economy? Can't a better educated labor force lead to a higher rate of technological progress? These questions take us to the topic of the next chapter, the sources and the implications of technological progress.

Summary

- In the long run, the evolution of output is determined by two relations. (To make the reading of this summary easier, I shall omit "per worker" in what follows.) First, the level of output depends on the amount of capital. Second, capital accumulation depends on the level of output, which determines saving and investment.
- These interactions between capital and output imply that, starting from any level of capital (and ignoring technological progress, the topic of Chapter 12), an economy converges in the long run to a *steady-state* (constant) level of capital. Associated with this level of capital is a steady-state level of output.
- The steady-state level of capital and thus the steady-state level of output depend positively on the saving rate. A higher saving rate leads to a higher steady-state level of output; during the transition to the new steady state, a higher saving rate leads to positive output growth. But in the long run (again ignoring technological progress), the growth rate of output is equal to zero, and is thus independent of the saving rate.
- An increase in the saving rate requires an initial decrease in consumption. In the long run, the increase in the saving rate may lead to an increase or to a decrease in consumption, depending on whether the economy is below or above the *golden-rule level of capital,* the level of capital at which steady-state consumption is highest.
- Most countries have a level of capital below the golden-rule level. Thus, an increase in the saving rate will lead to an initial decrease in consumption, followed by an increase in the long run. In thinking about whether to take policy measures aimed at changing the saving rate, policy makers must decide how much weight to put on the welfare of current generations versus the welfare of future generations.
- While most of the analysis of this chapter focuses on the effects of physical capital accumulation, output depends on the levels of both physical *and* human capital. Both forms of capital can be accumulated, one through investment, the other through education and training. Increasing the saving rate or the fraction of output spent on education and training can lead to large increases in output in the long run.

Key Terms

- saving rate, 219
- steady state, 225
- golden-rule level of capital, 229
- pay-as-you-go social security system, 231
- fully funded social security system, 231
- Social Security trust fund, 232
- human capital, 236
- models of endogenous growth, 238

Questions and Problems

Quick Check

1. *Using the information in this chapter, label each of the following statements* true, false, *or* uncertain. *Explain briefly.*
   a. The saving rate is always equal to the investment rate.
   b. A higher investment rate can sustain higher growth of output forever.
   c. If capital never depreciated, growth could go on forever.
   d. The higher the saving rate, the higher consumption in steady state.
   e. Output per capita in the United States is roughly equal to 60% of output per worker.
   f. We should fund Social Security. This would increase consumption, now and in the future.
   g. The U.S. capital stock is far below the golden rule level. The government should give tax breaks for saving.
   h. For many countries, an increase in the education level is the key to sustained growth.
   i. Education increases human capital, and so output. It follows that governments should subsidize education.

2. *"The Japanese growth rate of output per worker will remain higher than that of the United States for as long as the Japanese saving rate exceeds that of the United States." Do you agree or disagree?*

3. In Chapter 3 we saw that an increase in the saving rate can lead to a recession in the short run (the paradox of saving). We can now examine the effects beyond the short run. What is the effect of an increase in the saving rate on output per worker likely to be after one decade? After five decades?

Dig Deeper

4. Discuss the likely impact of the following changes on the level of output per worker in the long run:

a. The right to exclude saving from income when paying the income tax.

b. A higher rate of female participation (but constant population).

5. Suppose that the production function is given by

$Y = 0.5\sqrt{K}\sqrt{N}$

a. Derive the steady state levels of output per worker and output per worker in terms of the saving rate (s) and the depreciation rate (δ).

b. Derive the equation for steady-state output per worker and steady-state consumption per worker in terms of s and δ.

c. Suppose that $\delta = 5\%$. With your favorite spreadsheet software, compute steady-state output per worker and steady-state consumption per worker for $s = 0, 0.1, 0.2, \ldots, 1$. Explain.

d. Use your software to graph the steady-state level of output per worker and the steady-state level of consumption per worker as a function of the saving rate (i.e., measure the saving rate on the horizontal axis of your graph and the corresponding values of output per worker and consumption per worker on the vertical axis).

e. Does the graph show that there is a value of s that maximizes output per worker? Does the graph show that there is a value of s that maximizes consumption per worker? If so, what is this value?

6. (This problem is based on the material in the appendix.) Suppose that the economy's production is given by $Y = K^{\alpha} N^{1-\alpha}$. Assume that $\alpha = 1/3$.

a. Is this production function characterized by constant returns to scale? Explain.

b. Are there decreasing returns to capital?

c. Are there decreasing returns to labor?

d. Transform the production function into a relationship between output per worker and capital per worker.

e. For a given saving rate (s) and a depreciation rate (δ), give an expression for capital per worker in the steady state.

f. Give an expression for output per worker in the steady state.

g. Solve for the steady-state level of output per worker when $\delta = 0.08$ and $s = 0.32$.

h. Suppose that the depreciation rate remains constant at $\delta = 0.08$ while the saving rate is reduced by half to $s = 0.16$. What is the new steady-state output per worker?

8. Suppose that the economy's production function is given by $Y = K^{1/3}N^{2/3}$, and that both the saving rate (s) and the depreciation rate (δ) are equal to 0.10.

a. What is the steady-state level of capital per worker?

b. What is the steady-state level of output per worker?

Suppose that the economy is in steady state, and that, in period t, the depreciation rate increases permanently from 0.10 to 0.20.

c. What will be the new steady-state levels of capital per worker and output per worker?

d. Compute the path of capital per worker and output per worker over the first three periods after the change in the depreciation rate.

We invite you to visit the Blanchard page on the Prentice Hall Web site at:
www.prenhall.com/blanchard
for this chapter's World Wide Web exercises

Further Readings

The classic treatment of the relation between the saving rate and output is by Robert Solow, *Growth Theory: An Exposition* (New York: Oxford University Press, 1970).

An easy-to-read discussion of whether and how to increase saving and improve education in the United States is given in Memoranda 23 to 27 in *Memos to the President: A Guide Through Macroeconomics for the Busy Policymaker*, by Charles Schultze (the chairman of the Council of Economic Advisers during the Carter administration), (Washington, D.C.: Brookings Institution, 1992).

Appendix: The Cobb-Douglas Production Function and the Steady State

In 1928, Charles Cobb (a mathematician) and Paul Douglas (an economist, who went on to become a U.S. senator) concluded that the following production function gave a very good description of the relation between output, physical capital, and labor in the United States from 1899 to 1922:

$$Y = K^{\alpha}N^{1-\alpha} \qquad (11\text{-A1})$$

with α being a number between zero and 1. Their findings proved surprisingly robust. Even today, the production function (11-A1), now known as the **Cobb-Douglas production function**, still gives a good description of the relation between output, capital, and labor in the United States. And the Cobb-Douglas production function has become a standard tool in the economists' toolbox. (Verify for yourself that it satisfies the two properties we discussed in the text: constant returns to scale, and decreasing returns to capital and to labor.)

The purpose of this appendix is to characterize the steady state of an economy when the production function is given by (11-A1). (All you need to follow the steps is a knowledge of the properties of exponents.)

Recall that, in steady state, saving per worker must be equal to depreciation per worker. Let us see what this implies.

- To derive saving per worker, we must derive first the relation between output per worker and capital per worker implied by equation (11-A1). Divide both sides of equation (11-A1) by N:

$$Y/N = K^{\alpha}N^{1-\alpha}/N$$

Using the properties of exponents

$$N^{1-\alpha}/N = N^{1-\alpha}N^{-1} = N^{-\alpha}$$

so, replacing in the preceding equation, we get

$$Y/N = K^{\alpha}N^{-\alpha} = (K/N)^{\alpha}$$

Output per worker Y/N is equal to the ratio of capital per worker K/N raised to the power α.

Saving per worker is equal to the saving rate times output per worker, so using the previous equation, is equal to

$$s(K/N)^{\alpha}$$

- Depreciation per worker is equal to the depreciation rate times capital per worker:

$$\delta(K/N)$$

- The steady state level of capital, K^*, is determined by the condition that saving per worker be equal to depreciation per worker, so,

$$s(K^*/N)^{\alpha} = \delta(K^*/N)$$

To solve this expression for the steady state level of capital per worker K^*/N, divide both sides by $(K^*/N)^{\alpha}$:

$$s = \delta(K^*/N)^{1-\alpha}$$

Divide both sides by δ, and change the order of the equality:

$$(K^*/N)^{1-\alpha} = s/\delta$$

Finally, raise both sides to the power $1/(1-\alpha)$:

$$(K^*/N) = (s/\delta)^{1/(1-\alpha)}$$

This gives the steady state level of capital per worker.

- From the production function, the steady state level of output per worker is then equal to

$$(Y^*/N) = (K/N)^{\alpha} = (s/\delta)^{\alpha/(1-\alpha)}$$

Let's see what this last equation implies.

- First, note that, in the text, we worked with a special case of equation (11-A1), the case where $\alpha = 0.5$. (Taking a variable to the power 0.5 is the same as taking the square root of the variable.) If $\alpha = 0.5$, the preceding equation implies that

$$\frac{Y^*}{N} = \frac{s}{\delta}$$

Output per worker is equal to the ratio of the saving rate to the depreciation rate. This is the equation we discussed in the text. A doubling of the saving rate leads to a doubling in steady state output per worker.

- The empirical evidence suggests, however, that, if we think of K as physical capital, α is closer to one third than to one half. Assuming $\alpha = 1/3$, then $(1/3)/[1-(1/3)] = (1/3)/(2/3) = 1/2$, and the equation for output per worker yields:

$$\frac{Y^*}{N} = \left(\frac{s}{\delta}\right)^{1/2} = \sqrt{\frac{s}{\delta}}$$

This implies smaller effects of the saving rate on output per worker than was suggested by the computations in the text. A doubling of the saving rate for example implies an increase in output per worker by a factor of $\sqrt{2}$, or only about 1.4 (put another way, a 40% increase in output per worker).

- There is, however, an interpretation of our model in which the appropriate value of α is close to 1/2, so the computations in the text are applicable. If, along the lines of Section 11-4, we allow for both physical and human capital, then a value of α around 1/2 for the contribution of this broader definition of capital to output is indeed roughly appropriate. Thus, one interpretation of the numerical results in Section 11-3 is that they give the effects of a given saving rate, but with saving interpreted to include saving in both physical capital and in human capital (more machines, and more education).

Key Terms

- Cobb-Douglas production function, 240

Technological Progress and Growth

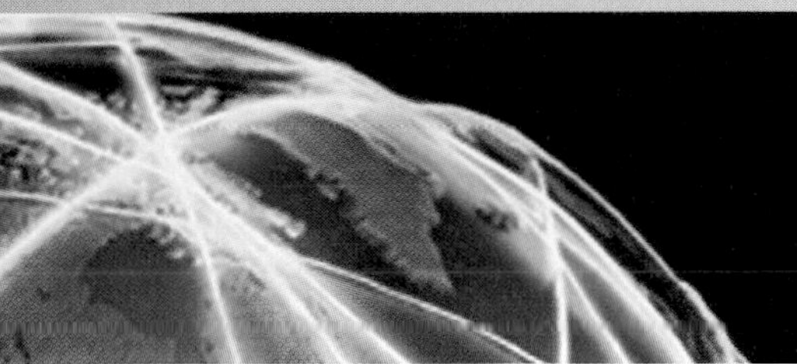

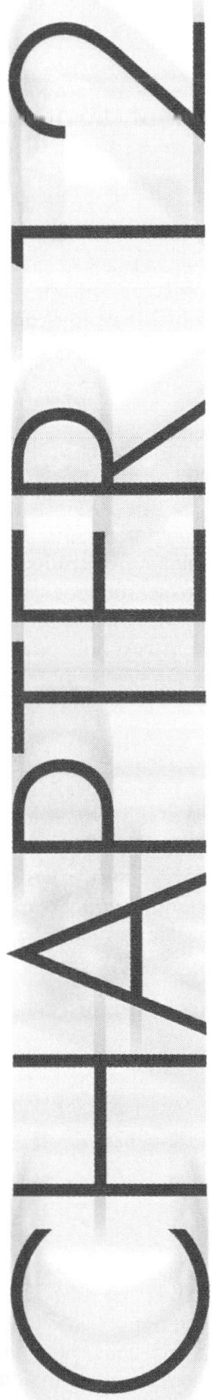

Our conclusion in Chapter 11 that capital accumulation cannot by itself sustain growth has a straightforward implication: Sustained growth *requires* technological progress. This chapter looks at the role of technological progress in growth.

- Section 12-1 looks at the respective role of technological progress and capital accumulation in growth. It shows how, in steady state, the rate of growth of output per capita is simply equal to the rate of technological progress. This does not mean, however, that the saving rate is irrelevant: The saving rate affects the level of output per capita—but not its rate of growth.
- Section 12-2 turns to the determinants of technological progress, focusing in particular on the role of research and development (R&D).
- Section 12-3 returns to the facts of growth presented in Chapter 10, and interprets them in the light of what we have learned in this chapter and in Chapter 11.
- Section 12-4 takes a broader look at the role of institutions in growth. ■

12-1 Technological Progress and the Rate of Growth

In an economy in which there is both capital accumulation and technological progress, at what rate will output grow? To answer this question, we need to extend the model developed in Chapter 11 to allow for technological progress. To introduce technological progress into the picture, we must revisit the aggregate production function.

Technological Progress and the Production Function

Technological progress has many dimensions:

- It may mean larger quantities of output for given quantities of capital and labor: Think of a new type of lubricant that allows a machine to run at a higher speed, and so to produce more.
- It may mean better products: Think of the steady improvement in car safety and comfort over time.
- It may mean new products: Think of the introduction of the CD player, the fax machine, cell phones, flat screen monitors.
- It may mean a larger variety of products: Think of the steady increase in the number of breakfast cereals available at your local supermarket.

The average number of items carried by a supermarket increased from 2,200 in 1950 to 17,500 in 1985. To get a sense of what this means, see Robin Williams in the supermarket scene in the movie *Moscow on the Hudson*, in which he plays an immigrant from the Soviet Union.

These dimensions are more similar than they appear. If we think of consumers as caring not about the goods themselves, but about the services these goods provide, then they all have something in common: In each case, consumers receive more services. A better car provides more safety, a new product, such as the fax machine, or the Internet, provides more information services, and so on.

As you saw in the Focus box "Real GDP, Technological Progress, and the Price of Computers" in Chapter 2, thinking of products as providing a number of underlying services is the method used to construct the price index for computers.

If we think of output as the set of underlying services provided by the goods produced in the economy, we can think of technological progress as leading to increases in output for given amounts of capital and labor. We can then think of the *state of technology* as a variable that tells us how much output can be produced from given amounts of capital and labor at any time. Let's denote the state of technology by A and rewrite the production function as

$$Y = F(K, N, A)$$
$$(+, +, +)$$

This is our extended production function. Output depends on both capital and labor, K and N, and on the state of technology, A: Given capital and labor, an improvement in the state of technology, A, leads to an increase in output.

For simplicity, we shall ignore human capital here. We return to it later in the chapter.

It will be convenient to use a more restrictive form of the preceding equation, namely,

$$Y = F(K, AN) \qquad (12.1)$$

This equation states that production depends on capital and on labor multiplied by the state of technology. This way of introducing the state of technology makes it easier to think about the effect of technological progress on the relation between output, capital, and labor. Equation (12.1) implies that we can think of technological progress in two equivalent ways:

- Technological progress reduces the number of workers needed to achieve a given amount of output. Doubling A produces the same quantity of output with only half the original number of workers, N.
- Technological progress increases AN, which we can think of as the amount of **effective labor** in the economy. If the state of technology, A, doubles, it is as if the economy had twice as many workers. In other words, we can think of output being produced by two factors: capital, K, and effective labor, AN.

AN is also sometimes called labor in efficiency units. The use of "efficiency" for "efficiency units" here and for "efficiency wages" in Chapter 6 is a coincidence: The two notions are unrelated.

What restrictions should we impose on the extended production function (12.1)? We can build directly here on our discussion in Chapter 10.

It is again reasonable to assume constant returns to scale: *For a given state of technology (A)*, doubling both the amount of capital (K) and the amount of labor (N) is likely to lead to a doubling of output:

$$2Y = F(2K, 2AN)$$

More generally, for any number x,

$$xY = F(xK, xAN)$$

It is also reasonable to assume decreasing returns to each of the two factors, capital and effective labor. Given effective labor, an increase in capital is likely to increase output, but at a decreasing rate. Symmetrically, given capital, an increase in effective labor is likely to increase output, but at a decreasing rate.

It was convenient in Chapter 11 to think in terms of output *per worker* and capital *per worker*. That was because the steady state of the economy was a state where output *per worker* and capital *per worker* were constant. It is convenient here to look at output *per effective worker* and capital *per effective worker*. The reason is the same: As we shall soon see, in steady state, output *per effective worker* and capital *per effective worker* are constant.

Per worker: divided by the number of workers (N)

Per effective worker: divided by the number of effective workers (AN)—the number of workers, N, times the state of technology, A.

To get a relation between output per effective worker and capital per effective worker, take $x = 1/AN$ in the preceding equation. This gives

$$\frac{Y}{AN} = F\left(\frac{K}{AN}, 1\right)$$

Or, if we define the function f so that $f(K/AN) \equiv F(K/AN, 1)$:

$$\frac{Y}{AN} = f\left(\frac{K}{AN}\right) \qquad (12.2)$$

Suppose that F has the "double square root" form:

$$Y = F(K, AN) = \sqrt{K}\sqrt{AN}$$

Then,

$$\frac{Y}{AN} = \frac{\sqrt{K}\sqrt{AN}}{AN} = \frac{\sqrt{K}}{\sqrt{AN}} = \sqrt{\frac{K}{AN}}$$

So the function f is simply the square root function:

$$f\left(\frac{K}{AN}\right) = \sqrt{\frac{K}{AN}}$$

In words: *Output per effective worker* (the left side) is a function of *capital per effective worker* (the expression in the function on the right side).

The relation between output per effective worker and capital per effective worker is drawn in Figure 12-1. It looks very much the same as the relation we drew in Figure 11-2 between output per worker and capital per worker in the absence of technological progress. There, increases in K/N led to increases in Y/N, but at a decreasing rate. Here, increases in K/AN lead to increases in Y/AN, but at a decreasing rate.

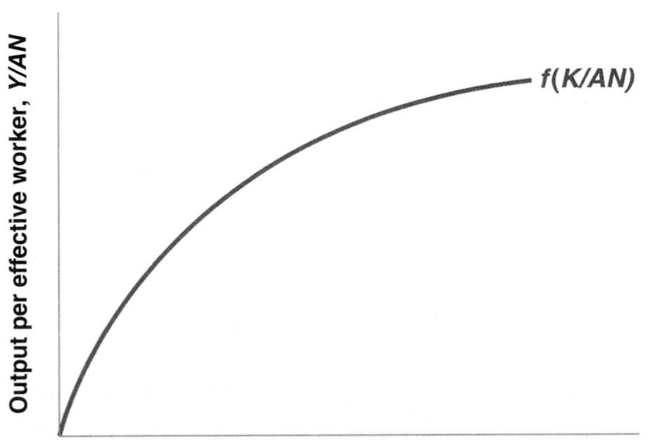

Figure 12-1

Output per Effective Worker Versus Capital per Effective Worker

Because of decreasing returns to capital, increases in capital per effective worker lead to smaller and smaller increases in output per effective worker.

Interactions Between Output and Capital

The key to understanding the results in this chapter: The results we derived for *output per worker* in Chapter 11 still hold in this chapter, but now for *output per effective worker*. For example, in Chapter 11, we saw that output per worker was constant in steady state. In this chapter, we shall see that output per effective worker is constant in steady state. And so on.

We now have the elements we need to think about the determinants of growth. Our analysis will parallel the analysis of Chapter 11. There we looked at the dynamics of *output per worker* and *capital per worker*. Here we look at the dynamics of *output per effective worker* and *capital per effective worker*.

In Chapter 11, we characterized the dynamics of output and capital per worker using Figure 11-2. In that figure, we drew three relations:

- The relation between output per worker and capital per worker.
- The relation between investment per worker and capital per worker.
- The relation between depreciation per worker—equivalently, the investment per worker needed to maintain a constant level of capital per worker—and capital per worker.

The dynamics of capital per worker, and by implication of output per worker, were determined by the relation between investment per worker and depreciation per worker. Depending on whether investment per worker was greater or smaller than depreciation per worker, capital per worker increased or decreased over time, as did output per worker.

We follow exactly the same approach in building Figure 12-2. The difference is that we focus on output, capital, and investment *per effective worker*, rather than per worker.

- The relation between output per effective worker and capital per effective worker was derived in Figure 12-1. The relation is repeated in Figure 12-2. Output per effective worker increases with capital per effective worker, but at a decreasing rate.
- Under the same assumptions as in Chapter 11—investment is equal to private saving, and the private saving rate is constant—investment is given by

$$I = S = sY$$

Divide both sides by the number of effective workers, AN, to get

$$\frac{I}{AN} = s\frac{Y}{AN}$$

Figure 12-2

Dynamics of Capital per Effective Worker and Output per Effective Worker

Capital per effective worker and output per effective worker converge to constant values in the long run.

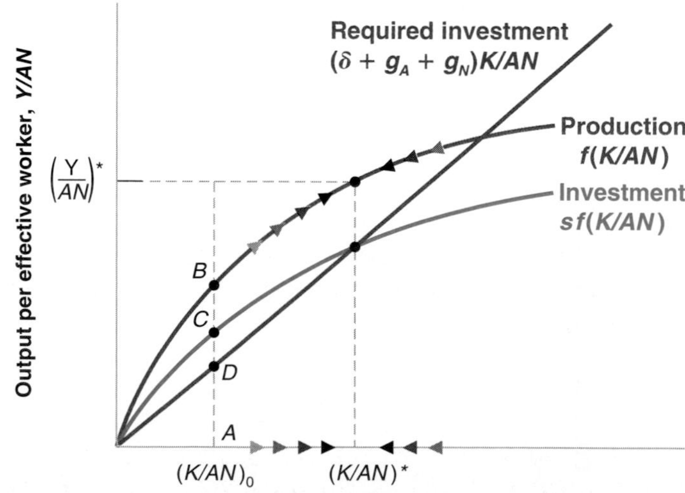

Replacing output per effective worker, Y/AN, by its expression from equation (12.2) gives

$$\frac{I}{AN} = sf\left(\frac{K}{AN}\right)$$

The relation between investment per effective worker and capital per effective worker is drawn in Figure 12-2. It is the same as the upper curve—the relation between output per effective worker and capital per effective worker—times the saving rate, s.

- Finally, we need to ask what level of investment per effective worker is needed to maintain a given level of capital per effective worker.

In Chapter 11, the answer was simple; for capital to be constant, investment had to be equal to the depreciation of the existing capital stock. Here, the answer is slightly more complicated. The reason is as follows: Now that we allow for technological progress (so A is increasing over time), the number of effective workers (AN) is increasing over time. Thus, maintaining the same ratio of capital to effective workers (K/AN) requires an increase in the capital stock (K) proportional to the increase in the number of effective workers (AN). Let's look at this condition more closely.

In Chapter 11, we assumed $g_A = 0$ and $g_N = 0$. Our focus in this chapter is on the implications of technological progress, $g_A > 0$. But, once we allow for technological progress, introducing population growth, $g_N > 0$, is straightforward. Thus, I allow for both $g_A > 0$ and $g_N > 0$.

Let δ be the depreciation rate of capital. Let the rate of population growth be equal to g_N. If we assume that the ratio of employment to the total population remains constant, the number of workers (N) also grows at annual rate g_N. And let the rate of technological progress be equal to g_A. Together, these last two assumptions imply that the growth rate of effective labor (AN) equals $g_A + g_N$. For example: If the number of workers is growing at 1% per year and the rate of technological progress is 2% per year, then the growth rate of effective labor is equal to 3% per year.

The growth rate of the product of two variables is the sum of the growth rates of the two variables. See Proposition 7 in Appendix 2 at the end of the book.

These assumptions imply that the level of investment needed to maintain a given level of capital per effective worker is given by:

$$\delta K + (g_A + g_N)K$$

or equivalently,

$$(\delta + g_A + g_N)K$$

An amount δK is needed just to keep the capital stock constant. If the depreciation rate is 10%, then investment must be equal to 10% of the capital stock just to maintain the same level of capital. And an additional amount $(g_A + g_N)K$ is needed to ensure that the capital stock increases at the same rate as effective labor. If effective labor increases at 3% per year, then capital must increase by 3% per year to maintain the same level of capital per effective worker. Putting δK and $(g_A + g_N)K$ together in this example: If the depreciation rate is 10% and the growth rate of effective labor is 3%, then investment must equal 13% of the capital stock to maintain a constant level of capital per effective worker.

Dividing the preceding expression by the number of effective workers to get the amount of investment per effective worker required to maintain a constant level of capital per effective worker gives

$$(\delta + g_A + g_N)\frac{K}{AN}$$

The level of investment per effective worker needed to maintain a given level of capital per effective worker is represented by the upward sloping line, "Required investment" in Figure 12-2. The slope of the line equals $\delta + g_A + g_N$.

Dynamics of Capital and Output

We can now give a graphical description of the dynamics of capital per effective worker and output per effective worker. Consider in Figure 12-2 a given level of capital per effective worker, say, $(K/AN)_0$. At that level, output per effective worker equals the vertical distance *AB*. Investment per effective worker is equal to *AC*. The amount of investment required to maintain that level of capital per effective worker is equal to *AD*. Because actual investment exceeds the investment level required to maintain the existing level of capital per effective worker, *K/AN* increases.

- Hence, starting from $(K/AN)_0$, the economy moves to the right, with the level of capital per effective worker increasing over time. This goes on until investment per effective worker is just sufficient to maintain the existing level of capital per effective worker, until capital per effective worker reaches $(K/AN)^*$.
- In the long run, capital per effective worker reaches a constant level, and so does output per effective worker. Put another way, the steady state of this economy is such that *capital per effective worker and output per effective worker are constant, and equal to* $(K/AN)^*$ *and* $(Y/AN)^*$*, respectively.*

  Note what this conclusion implies: *In steady state, in this economy, what is constant is not output but rather output per effective worker.* This implies that, in steady state, output, *Y*, is growing at the same rate as effective labor, *AN* (so that the ratio of the two is constant). Because effective labor grows at rate $(g_A + g_N)$, output growth in steady state must also equal $(g_A + g_N)$. The same reasoning applies to capital. Because capital per effective worker is constant in steady state, capital is also growing at rate $(g_A + g_N)$.

If the number of effective workers is constant, then constant output per effective worker implies constant output. This was the case in Chapter 11 where we assumed there was neither population growth nor technological progress. But this is not the case here.

If Y/AN is constant, Y must grow at the same rate as AN. So, it must grow at rate $g_A + g_N$.

These conclusions give us our first important result. *In steady state, the growth rate of output equals the rate of population growth* (g_N) *plus the rate of technological progress,* (g_A)*. By implication, the growth rate of output is independent of the saving rate.*

To strengthen your intuition, go back to the argument we used in Chapter 11 to show that without technological progress and population growth, the economy could not sustain positive growth forever.

- The argument went as follows: Suppose the economy tried to achieve positive output growth. Because of decreasing returns to capital, capital would have to grow faster than output. The economy would have to devote a larger and larger proportion of output to capital accumulation. At some point there would be no more output to devote to capital accumulation. Growth would come to an end.
- Exactly the same logic is at work here. Effective labor grows at rate $(g_A + g_N)$. Suppose the economy tried to sustain output growth in excess of $(g_A + g_N)$. Because of decreasing returns to capital, capital would have to increase faster than output. The economy would have to devote a larger and larger proportion of output to capital accumulation. At some point this would prove impossible. Thus, the economy cannot permanently grow faster than $(g_A + g_N)$.

The standard of living is given by output per worker (or, more accurately, output per capita), not output per effective worker.

We have focused on the behavior of aggregate output. To get a sense of what happens not to aggregate output, but rather to the standard of living over time, we must look instead at the behavior of output per worker (not output per *effective* worker). Because output grows at rate $(g_A + g_N)$ and the number of workers grows at rate g_N, output per worker grows at rate g_A. In other words, *in steady state, output per worker grows at the rate of technological progress.*

The growth rate of Y/N is equal to the growth rate of Y minus the growth rate of N (see Proposition 8 in Appendix 2 at the end of the book). So the growth rate of Y/N is given by $(g_Y - g_N) = (g_A + g_N) - g_N = g_A$.

Because output, capital, and effective labor all grow at the same rate, $(g_A + g_N)$, in steady state, the steady state of this economy is also called a state of **balanced growth**: In steady state, output and the two inputs, capital and effective labor, grow in balance

Table 12-1 The Characteristics of Balanced Growth

		Rate of growth of:
1	Capital per effective worker	0
2	Output per effective worker	0
3	Capital per worker	g_A
4	Output per worker	g_A
5	Labor	g_N
6	Capital	$g_A + g_N$
7	Output	$g_A + g_N$

(at the same rate). The characteristics of balanced growth will be helpful later in the chapter, and are summarized in Table 12-1.

On the balanced growth path (equivalently, in steady state; equivalently, in the long run):

- *Capital per effective worker* and *output per effective worker* are constant; this is the result we derived in Figure 12-2.
- Equivalently, *capital per worker* and *output per worker* are growing at the rate of technological progress, g_A.
- Or, in terms of labor, capital, and output: *Labor* is growing at the rate of population growth, g_N; *capital* and *output* are growing at a rate equal to the sum of population growth and the rate of technological progress, $(g_A + g_N)$.

The Effects of the Saving Rate

In steady state, the growth rate of output depends *only* on the rate of population growth and the rate of technological progress. Changes in the saving rate do not affect the steady-state growth rate. But changes in the saving rate do increase the steady-state level of output per effective worker.

This result is best seen in Figure 12-3, which shows the effect of an increase in the saving rate from s_0 to s_1. The increase in the saving rate shifts the investment relation from $s_0 f(K/AN)$ to $s_1 f(K/AN)$. It follows that the steady-state level of capital per effective

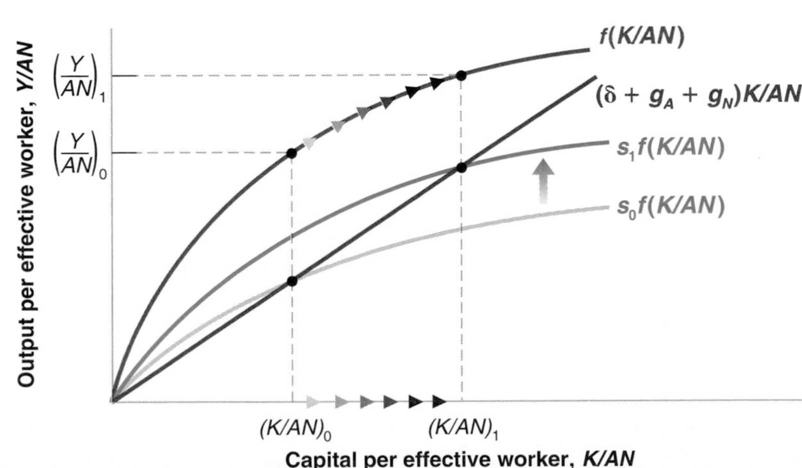

Figure 12-3

The Effects of an Increase in the Saving Rate: I

An increase in the saving rate leads to an increase in the steady-state levels of output per effective worker and capital per effective worker.

worker increases from $(K/AN)_0$ to $(K/AN)_1$, with a corresponding increase in the level of output per effective worker from $(Y/AN)_0$ to $(Y/AN)_1$.

Figure 12-4 is the same as Figure 11-5, which anticipated the derivation presented here.

For a description of logarithmic scales, see Appendix 2 at the end of the book.

Following the increase in the saving rate, capital per effective worker and output per effective worker increase for some time as they converge to their new higher level. Figure 12-4 plots capital against time (upper graph) and output against time (lower graph). Both capital and output are measured on logarithmic scales. The economy is initially on the balanced growth path *AA*: Capital and output are growing at rate $(g_A + g_N)$—the slope of *AA* is equal to $(g_A + g_N)$. After the increase in the saving rate at time *t*, output and capital grow faster for some period of time. Eventually, capital and output end up at higher levels than they would have been without the increase in saving. But their growth rate returns to $g_A + g_N$. In the new steady state, the economy grows at the same rate, but on a higher growth path *BB*—the line *BB*, which is parallel to *AA*, also has a slope equal to $(g_A + g_N)$.

When a logarithmic scale is used, a variable growing at a constant rate moves along a straight line. The slope of the line is equal to the rate of growth of the variable.

To summarize: In an economy with technological progress and population growth, output grows over time. In steady state, output *per effective worker* and capital *per effective worker* are constant. Put another way, output *per worker* and capital *per worker* grow at the rate of technological progress. Put yet another way, output and capital grow at the same rate as effective labor, thus at a rate equal to the growth rate of the number of workers plus the rate of technological progress. When the economy is in steady state, it is said to be on a balanced growth path.

Figure 12-4

The Effects of an Increase in the Saving Rate: II

The increase in the saving rate leads to higher growth until the economy reaches its new, higher, balanced growth path.

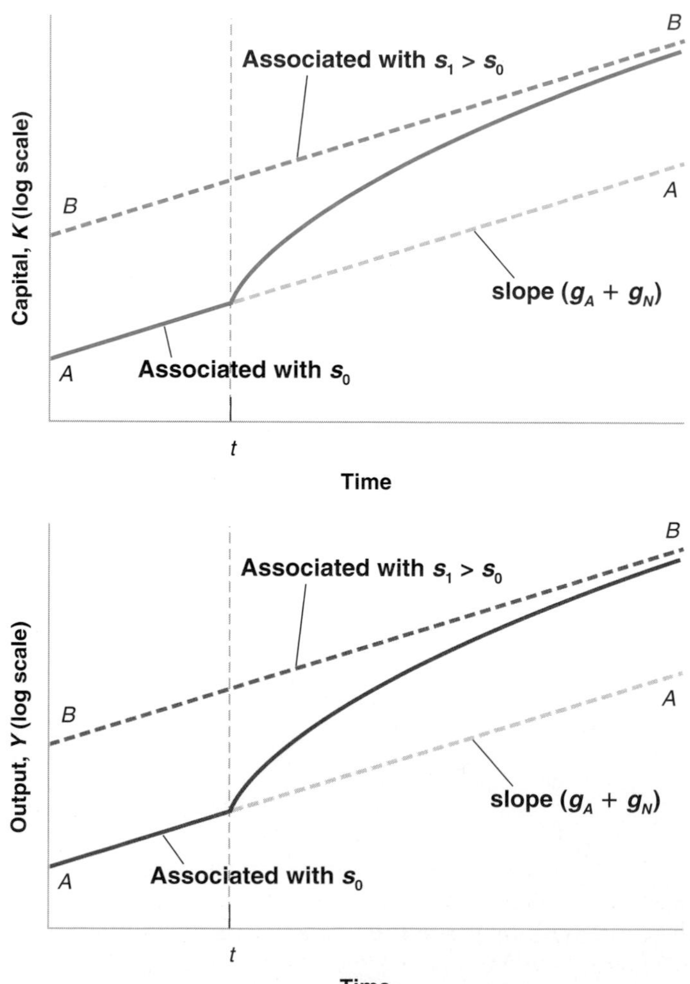

The rate of output growth in steady state is independent of the saving rate. The saving rate affects the steady-state level of output per effective worker however. And increases in the saving rate lead, for some time, to an increase in the growth rate above the steady-state growth rate.

12-2 The Determinants of Technological Progress

You have just seen that the growth rate of output per worker is ultimately determined by the rate of technological progress. But what determines the rate of technological progress? This is the question we take up in this section.

The term *technological progress* brings to mind images of major discoveries: the invention of the microchip, the discovery of the structure of DNA, and so on. These discoveries suggest a process driven largely by scientific research and chance rather than by economic forces. But the truth is that most technological progress in modern economies is the result of a humdrum process: the outcome of firms' **research and development (R&D)** activities. Industrial R&D expenditures account for between 2 and 3% of GDP in each of the five major rich countries we looked at in Chapter 10 (the United States, France, Germany, Japan, and the United Kingdom). About 75% of the roughly 1 million U.S. scientists and researchers working in R&D are employed by firms. U.S. firms' R&D spending equals more than 20% of their spending on gross investment, and more than 60% of their spending on net investment—investment net of depreciation.

Firms spend on R&D for the same reason they buy new machines or build new plants: to increase profits. By increasing spending on R&D, a firm increases the probability that it will discover and develop a new product. (I shall use the word *product* as a generic term to denote new goods or new techniques of production.) If the new product is successful, the firm's profits will increase. There is, however, an important difference between purchasing a machine and spending more on R&D. The difference is that the outcome of R&D is fundamentally *ideas*. And, unlike a machine, an idea can potentially be used by many firms at the same time. A firm that has just acquired a new machine does not have to worry that another firm will use that particular machine. A firm that has discovered and developed a new product can make no such assumption.

This last point implies that the level of R&D spending depends not only on the **fertility of the research** process—how spending on R&D translates into new ideas and new products, but also on the **appropriability** of research results—the extent to which firms benefit from the results of their own R&D. Let's look at each aspect.

The Fertility of the Research Process

If research is very fertile—if R&D spending leads to many new products—then, other things equal, firms will have more incentives to spend on R&D; R&D and technological progress will be higher. The determinants of the fertility of research lie largely outside the realm of economics. Many factors interact here:

- The fertility of research depends on the successful interaction between basic research (the search for general principles and results) and applied research and development (the application of these results to specific uses, and the development of new products). Basic research does not lead, by itself, to technological progress. But the success of applied research and development depends ultimately on basic research. Much of the computer industry's development can be traced to a few breakthroughs, from the invention of the transistor to the invention of the microchip.

- Some countries appear more successful at basic research; others are more successful at applied research and development. Studies point to the relevance of the education system. For example, it is often argued that the French higher education system, with its strong emphasis on abstract thinking, produces researchers who are better at basic research than at applied research and development. Studies also point to the importance of a "culture of entrepreneurship," in which a big part of technological progress comes from the entrepreneurs' ability to organize the successful development and marketing of new products.
- It takes many years, and often many decades, for the full potential of major discoveries to be realized. The usual sequence is one in which a major discovery leads to the exploration of potential applications, then to the development of new products, then to the adoption of these new products. The Focus box "The Diffusion of New Technology: Hybrid Corn" shows the results of one of the first studies of this process of diffusion of ideas. Closer to us is the example of personal computers. Twenty years after the commercial introduction of personal computers, it often feels as if we have just started discovering their uses.

In Chapter 11, we looked at the role of human capital as an input in production: More educated people can use more complex machines, or handle more complex tasks. Here, we see a second role of human capital: Better researchers and scientists, and, by implication, a higher rate of technological progress.

An age-old worry is that research will become less and less fertile, that most major discoveries have already taken place, and that technological progress will now slow down. This fear may come from what happened to the mining industry, where higher-grade mines were exploited first, and where we have had to exploit increasingly lower-grade mines. But this is only an analogy, and so far there is no evidence that it is correct.

The Appropriability of Research Results

The second determinant of the level of R&D and of technological progress is the degree of *appropriability* of research results. If firms cannot appropriate the profits from the development of new products, they will not engage in R&D and technological progress will be slow. Many factors are also at work here:

- The nature of the research process itself is important. For example, if it is widely believed that the discovery of a new product will quickly lead to the discovery of an even better product, there may be little payoff to being first. A highly fertile field of research may not generate high levels of R&D. This example is extreme, but revealing.
- Even more important is the degree of protection given to new products by the law. Without legal protection, profits from developing a new product are likely to be small. Except in rare cases where the product is based on a trade secret (such as Coca Cola), it will generally not take long for other firms to produce the same product, eliminating any advantage the innovating firm may initially have had. This is why countries have patent laws. **Patents** give a firm that has discovered a new product—usually a new technique or device—the right to exclude anyone else from the production or use of the new product for a period of time.

How should governments design patent laws? On one hand, protection is needed to provide firms with the incentives to spend on R&D. On the other, once firms have discovered new products, it would be best for society if the knowledge embodied in those new products was made available without restrictions to other firms and to people. Take, for example, biogenetic research. Only the prospect of large profits is leading bioengineering firms to embark on expensive research projects. Once a firm has found a new product, and this product can save many lives, it would clearly be best to make it available at cost to all potential users. But if such a policy was systematically followed, it would eliminate incentives for firms to do research in the first place. Patent law must strike a difficult balance. Too little protection will lead to little

This type of dilemma is known as "time inconsistency." We shall see other examples and discuss it at length in Chapter 24.

The Diffusion of New Technology: Hybrid Corn

New technologies are not developed or adopted overnight. One of the first studies of the diffusion of new technologies was carried out in 1957 by Zvi Griliches, who looked at the diffusion of hybrid corn in different states in the United States.

Hybrid corn is, in the words of Griliches, "the invention of a method of inventing." Producing hybrid corn entails crossing different strains of corn to develop a type adapted to local conditions. Introduction of hybrid corn can increase yield by up to 20%.

While the idea of hybridization was first developed at the beginning of the twentieth century, the first commercial application did not take place until the 1930s in the United States. Figure 1 shows the rate at which hybrid corn was adopted in a number of U.S. states from 1932 to 1956.

The figure shows two dynamic processes at work. One is the process through which hybrid corns appropriate to each state were discovered. Hybrid corn became available in southern states (Texas, Alabama) more than 10 years after it had become available in northern states (Iowa, Wisconsin, Kentucky). The other is the speed at which hybrid corn was adopted within each state. Within eight years of hybrid corn's introduction, practically all corn in Iowa was hybrid corn. The process was much slower in the south. More than 10 years after its introduction, hybrid corn accounted for only 60% of total acreage in Alabama.

Why was the speed of adoption higher in Iowa than in the South? Griliches's article showed that the reason was economic: The speed of adoption in each state was a function of the profitability of introducing hybrid corn. And profitability was higher in Iowa than in the southern states.

Source: Zvi Griliches, "Hybrid Corn: An Exploration in the Economics of Technological Change," Econometrica, *October 1957, 25–24.*

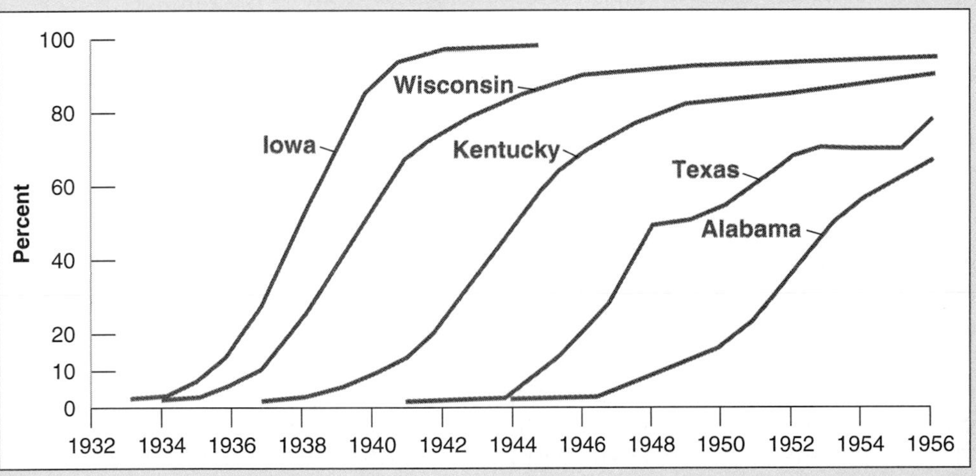

Figure 1 *Percentage of Total Corn Acreage Planted with Hybrid Seed—Selected U.S. States, 1932–1956*

Source: See source note for this box.

R&D. Too much protection will make it difficult for new R&D to build on the results of past R&D, and may also lead to little R&D.

Countries that are less technologically advanced often have poorer patent protection. China, for example, is a country with poor enforcement of patent rights. Our discussion helps explain why. Those countries are typically users rather than producers of new technologies. Much of their improvement in productivity comes not from inventions within the country, but from the adaptation of foreign technologies. In this case, the costs of weak patent protection are small, because there would be few domestic inventions anyway. But the benefits of low patent protection are clear: They allow domestic firms to use and adapt foreign technology without having to pay royalties to the foreign firms that developed the technology.

◀ **The issues go beyond patent laws. To ask two controversial questions: Should Microsoft be kept in one piece, or broken up to stimulate R&D? Should the government impose caps on the prices of AIDS drugs?**

12-3 The Facts of Growth Revisited

In Chapter 10, we looked at growth in rich countries since 1950 and we identified three main facts:

- Sustained growth, especially from 1950 to the mid-1970s.
- A slowdown in growth since the mid-1970s.
- Convergence: Countries that were further behind have been growing faster.

Let us now use the theory we have developed to see what light it sheds on these facts.

Capital Accumulation Versus Technological Progress

Suppose we see an economy growing unusually fast—either in relation to its own growth in the past, or in relation to growth in other countries. Our theory implies this fast growth may come from two sources:

- It may be due to a higher rate of technological progress, so that faster output growth reflects faster balanced growth. In other words, if g_A is higher, balanced output growth ($g_Y = g_A + g_N$) will also be higher.
- Or it may reflect the adjustment of capital per effective worker, K/AN, to a higher level. As we saw in Figure 12-4, such an adjustment leads to a period of higher growth, even if the rate of technological progress has not increased.

Can we tell how much of the growth comes from one source, how much comes from the other? Yes. If high growth reflects high balanced growth, output per worker should be growing at a rate *equal* to the rate of technological progress (see Table 12-1, line 4). If high growth reflects instead the adjustment to a higher level of capital per effective worker, this adjustment should be reflected in a growth rate of output per worker that *exceeds* the rate of technological progress.

This discussion suggests a simple strategy, that of computing the growth rate of output per worker and the rate of technological progress for our five countries since 1950, then comparing the two numbers. Angus Maddison recently implemented this strategy; his results are summarized in Table 12-2. (What Maddison has computed, and thus what is reported in Table 12-2, is the growth rate of output *per capita* rather than the growth rate of output *per worker*. If the ratio of employment to population had remained constant, the growth rates of output per capita and of output per worker would be identical. They are not, but they are close, so we can ignore the difference here.)

In the United States, for example, the ratio of employment to population increased from 55% in 1950 to 65% in 2000. This represents an increase of 0.17% per year. Thus, in the United States, output per capita has increased 0.17% more per year than output per worker—a small difference, relative to the numbers in the table.

The first two columns correspond roughly to the first two columns of Table 10-1. They give the average annual growth rates of output per capita during 1950–1973 and 1973–1987, respectively. (Unfortunately, the data put together by Maddison stop in 1987. But, based on what we know, the basic conclusions would be very similar if we were to extend the second period to include the 1990s.) The third column gives the change in the growth rate from the first to the second period.

There are minor differences between the two tables, due to differences in sources and in time periods.

Columns 4 and 5 give the average annual rates of technological progress during 1950–1973 and 1973–1987, respectively. The sixth column gives the change in the rate of technological progress from the first period to the second. The method of construction of the rate of technological progress—which is not directly observable—is presented in the appendix at the end of this chapter.

With the help of the table, let's return to and interpret our three main facts:

1. *The period of high growth of output per capita, from 1950 to 1973, was due to rapid technological progress, not to unusually high capital accumulation.*

   Look at columns 1 and 4 of the table. In all five countries, the growth rate of output per capita from 1950 to 1973 was roughly equal to the rate of technological

Table 12-2 Average Annual Rates of Growth of Output per Capita and of Technological Progress in Five Rich Countries, 1950–1987

	Rate of Growth of Output per Capita (%)			Rate of Technological Progress (%)		
	1950–1973 (1)	1973–1987 (2)	Change (3)	1950–1973 (4)	1973–1987 (5)	Change (6)
France	4.0	1.8	−2.2	4.9	2.3	−2.6
Germany	4.9	2.1	−2.8	5.6	1.9	−3.7
Japan	8.0	3.1	−4.9	6.4	1.7	−4.7
United Kingdom	2.5	1.8	−0.7	2.3	1.7	−0.6
United States	2.2	1.6	−0.6	2.6	0.6	−2.0
Average	4.3	2.1	−2.2	4.4	1.6	−2.8

Average is a simple average of the growth rates in each column. Germany refers to West Germany only.

Source: Constructed from Tables 3-3, 5-3, 5-4, and 5-19 in Angus Maddison, *Dynamic Forces in Capitalist Development* (New York: Oxford University Press, 1991).

progress. This is what we would expect when countries are growing along their balanced growth path; so the main source of high growth from 1950 to 1973 was a high rate of technological progress.

This is an important conclusion, because it rejects one hypothesis for why growth was so high from 1950 to 1973. The hypothesis is that fast growth was the result of the destruction of capital during World War II, leading to rapid rates of capital growth after the war. As we saw in the Focus box in Chapter 11, this explanation does explain some of the high growth in the immediate postwar period in France, and probably in some of the other countries as well. But it is not the reason for the sustained growth of the 1950s and 1960s in the five countries we are looking at.

2. *The slowdown in growth of output per capita since 1973 has come from a decrease in the rate of technological progress, not from unusually low capital accumulation.*

   This conclusion comes from looking at columns 3 and 6 of Table 12-2. If lower capital accumulation were to blame for the growth slowdown, we would see a larger decline in the growth rate of output per capita than in the rate of technological progress. But this is not what the table shows. In all five countries, the decrease in technological progress has been roughly equal to the decrease in the growth rate of output per capita.

   So, contrary to some popular beliefs, the slowdown in growth since the mid-1970s is not due to a sharp drop in the saving rate, not due to the "disappearance of thrift." It is due to the decrease in the rate of technological progress, which declined from an average of 4.4% per year during 1950–1973 to only 1.6% per year from 1973–1987.

3. *Convergence of output per capita across countries has come from higher technological progress, rather than from faster capital accumulation, in the countries that started behind.*

   Look at column 4 of Table 12-2. During 1950–1973, the average annual rate of technological progress was 3.8% higher in Japan than in the United States, 3.0% higher in Germany than in the United States, 2.3% higher in France than in the United States. Only the U.K. rate was slightly below that of the United States.

During 1973–1987, the differences narrowed to 1.1% for Japan, 1.3% for Germany, and 1.7% for France.

These facts yield an important conclusion:

One can think, in general, of two sources of convergence between countries. First, poorer countries are poorer because they have less capital to start with. Over time, they accumulate capital faster than the others, generating convergence. Second, Poorer countries are poorer because they are less technologically advanced than the others. Thus, over time, they become more sophisticated, either by importing technology from advanced countries or developing their own. As technological levels converge, so does output per capita.

The conclusion we can draw from Table 12-2 is that the more important source of convergence in this case has clearly been the second one. For example, Japan's output per worker has increased relative to that of the United States; not so much because Japan has accumulated capital extremely quickly, but rather because the state of technology has improved very quickly in Japan over the last 40 years.

Why Did Technological Progress Slow Down in the mid-1970s?

The conclusions we reached in the preceding section represent (intellectual, if not technological) progress. But, by putting the focus on the role of technological progress in growth, these conclusions raise a number of questions, chief among them: *Why* has technological progress slowed down since the mid-1970s? Much research has been devoted to answering this question. A number of hypotheses have been suggested, from measurement error, to the rise of the service sector, to decreased spending on R&D. Let's look at each hypothesis in turn.

Measurement Error

The first hypothesis is that there has been in fact no slowdown in technological progress, and that the measured slowdown is solely the result of measurement error.

That measurement error could be important is obvious to anybody who looks at how measures of output (such as GDP) are actually constructed. In a number of sectors, productivity is not easily measured: How do you measure the evolution of the productivity of doctors (not to mention lawyers) over time? Due to the difficulties in measuring productivity in these sectors, the National Income and Product Accounts make simple assumptions about technological progress in those sectors. And these assumptions may well be wrong. To take an example, technological progress in financial services is assumed equal to zero. But there is plenty of evidence that there has been substantial technological progress in financial services. In check processing, for example, the average number of checks processed per worker per hour increased from 265 in 1971 to 825 in 1986, an increase of 7.6% per year.

There is an interesting connection here between the measurement of inflation and the measurement of productivity growth—growth of output per worker. If an increase in the price of a good reflects in fact an increase in its quality, and if this quality increase is ignored by statisticians, what should be counted as productivity growth (an increase in quality-adjusted output) will be counted instead as inflation (an increase in the price.) A recent study of the U.S. CPI has concluded that the failure to fully adjust for quality improvements in the basket of goods underlying the index has led the Bureau of Labor Statistics (which is in charge of constructing the CPI) to overstate CPI inflation by about 0.6% a year. If the conclusion of this study is right, and if the findings extend to the GDP deflator, this implies that productivity growth has been understated by 0.6% a year.

The conclusion of the report is that CPI inflation actually exceeds true inflation by more than 1% a year. But some of the problems discussed in the report are not related to the issues discussed in this chapter. (For more, read "Measuring the CPI," *Journal of Economic Perspectives*, 1998-1, volume 12.

There is no question that there is measurement error and that we may be systematically understating technological progress and output growth. This is an important point: Our standard of living may be increasing faster than the official statistics suggest. To explain the slowdown, however, it would have to be the case that the error has become larger since the mid-1970s, so technological progress is *more* understated now than it was earlier. There is little evidence so far that this is the case.

The Rise of the Service Sector

The second hypothesis is that the slowdown in technological progress reflects the fact that the United States, and the other rich countries, have become **postindustrial economies** in which manufacturing's share of GDP is steadily declining, and the share of services is steadily increasing. And, the argument goes, the scope for technological progress is more limited in services than in manufacturing. How much technological progress can take place in haircuts?

This argument is plausible. However, the facts show that the shift toward services has played a limited role in the slowdown. We can see why in Figure 12-5, which plots the change in average annual labor productivity growth from 1948–1973 to 1973–1987, by industry. What is striking about Figure 12-5 is how the slowdown in productivity growth has affected nearly all sectors. Only farming and nonelectrical machinery (mainly computers) have seen increases in labor productivity growth from the first period to the second. The decline has been largest in mining (reflecting the depletion of the most easily available reserves) and in utilities (where it is in large part the result of more stringent environmental regulations). More directly relevant for our purposes here, the decline has been roughly the same in manufacturing sectors as in service sectors. Thus, the shift in composition from manufacturing toward services cannot account for the slowdown in overall productivity growth.

For reasons of data availability, the numbers in the figure refer to labor productivity growth—that is, the growth rate of output per worker ($g_Y - g_N$)—rather than to the rate of technological progress, g_A. Based on what we know for specific industries, the results would be very similar if we used estimates of the rate of technological progress instead.

Decreased R&D Spending

The third hypothesis focuses on R&D. Because of the roughly equal decline in the productivity of the manufacturing and service sectors, the search for explanations must center on factors that can explain why there has been a slowdown in most sectors. A natural hypothesis is that there was a general decline in R&D, which has led to a

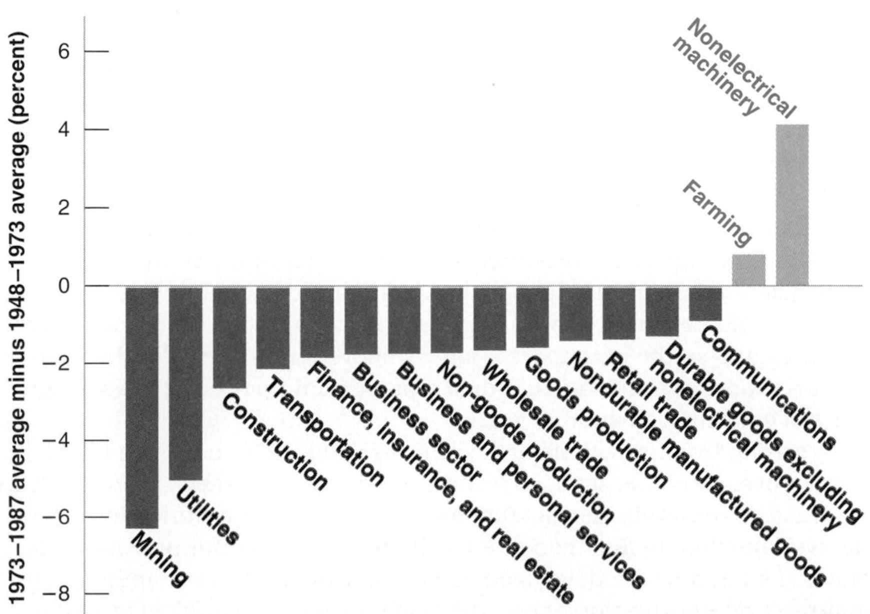

Figure 12-5

Changes in Average Annual Labor Productivity Growth, 1948–1973 to 1973–1987, by Industry

Most sectors of the U.S. economy have experienced a slowdown in productivity growth.

Source: Martin N. Baily and Robert Gordon, "The Productivity Slowdown, Measurement Issues, and the Explosion of Computer Power," Brookings Papers on Economic Activity, *1988:2, 347–431.*

Table 12-3 Spending on R&D as a Percentage of GDP

	1963	1975	1989
France	1.6	1.8	2.3
Germany	1.4	2.2	2.9
Japan	1.5	2.0	3.0
United Kingdom	2.3	2.0	2.3
United States	2.7	2.3	2.8

Source: Kumiharu Shigehara, "Causes of Declining Growth in Industrialized Countries," in *Policies for Long-Run Economic Growth* (Kansas City, MO: Kansas City Fed, 1993), Table 4, p. 22.

decline in the rate of technological progress. It turns out that the facts do not support this hypothesis. Table 12-3 shows the evolution of spending on R&D in each of our five countries. In all five countries, spending on R&D remained constant or increased as a percentage of GDP between 1963 and 1989.

The facts therefore suggest that the proximate reason for the decline in the rate of technological progress is a decline not in the amount but in the fertility of R&D. While rich countries are spending as much or more than they used to spend on R&D, measured technological progress has slowed down. This is unfortunately the extent of our knowledge at this point. Some economists argue that this reflects that there were no major discoveries during the period. Others argue that different sectors have developed sector-specific technologies, with the result that discoveries affect a smaller number of sectors than in the past, leading to smaller spillovers of research across sectors. In the light of this debate, the recent increase in productivity growth in the United States is particularly interesting. Could it be that we have just entered, as some claim, a New Economy, an economy with higher productivity growth than in the past? The evidence to date is reviewed in the Focus box "The New Economy and Productivity Growth." The basic conclusion: The claims made by new economy proponents are too strong; but there is indeed some basis for optimism.

12-4 Epilogue: The Secrets of Growth

Why the rate of technological progress has declined since the mid-1970s is not the only unanswered question in the economics of growth. Many questions remain.

We understand the basic mechanisms of growth in rich countries. But we are not very good at answering more specific questions. For example: Are governments spending the right amount on basic research? Should patent laws be modified? Is there a case for an **industrial policy**, a policy aimed at helping specific sectors of the economy (for example, those sectors with the potential for high technological progress, and so the potential for large spillovers for the rest of the economy)? What can we expect in terms of additional growth from increasing the average number of years of education by another year?

Turning from growth in rich countries since 1950 to growth over a longer time span or over a broader set of countries, our knowledge is even more limited.

Take, for example, the fact that most countries in the world have a level of output per worker equal to less than one-tenth the level of output per worker of the United States. The framework developed in this and the previous chapter gives us a way of approaching the question of why this might be so. If we think of output per worker as

FOCUS

The New Economy and Productivity Growth

Average annual productivity growth in the United States from 1996 to 2000 was 2.7%—a high number relative to the anemic 1% average achieved over the previous 20 years.

Is it a sign, as proponents of the New Economy argue, that the U.S. economy has entered an era of high productivity growth? Research to date gives reasons both for optimism and for caution.

It suggests that a sharp distinction must be drawn between what is happening in the information technology (IT) sector—the sector that produces computers, computer software and software services, and communications equipment—and the rest of the economy—which uses this information technology.

- In the IT sector, technological progress has been proceeding at an extraordinary pace.

  In 1965, Gordon Moore, then research director at Fairchild Semiconductor, and, later, founder of Intel Corporation, predicted that the number of transistors in a chip would double every 18 to 24 months, allowing for steadily more powerful computers. As shown in Figure 1, this relation—now known as **Moore's law**—has held extremely well over time. The first logic chip produced in 1971 had 2300 transistors; the Pentium 4, released in 2000 had 42 million.

  While proceeding at a less extreme pace, technological progress in the rest of the IT sector has also been very high. And the share of the IT sector in GDP is steadily increasing, from 3% of GDP in 1980, to 4.5% in 1990, and to close to 7% today. The combination of high technological progress in the IT sector and of an increasing IT share implies a steady increase in the economy-wide rate of technological progress. This is one of the factors behind the high productivity growth in the second half of the 1990s.

  In the non-IT sector (the "old economy," which still accounts for more than 90% of the U.S. economy), however, there is little evidence of a parallel technological revolution.

- On one hand, the steady decrease in the price of IT equipment (reflecting technological progress in

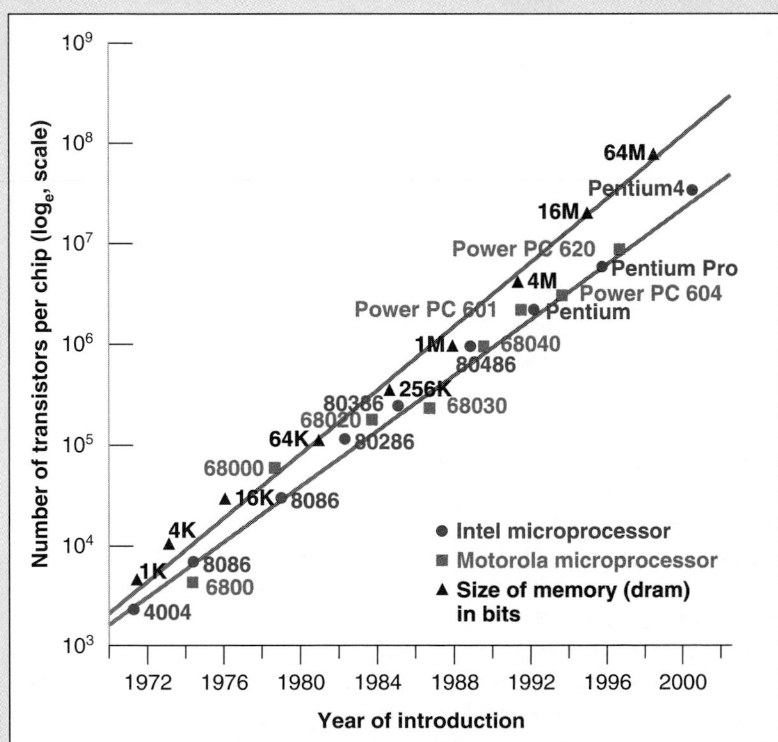

Figure 1 *Moore's Law: Number of Transistors per Chip, 1970–2000*

(*Source: Dale Jorgenson*, post.economics.harvard.edu/faculty/ jorgenson/papers/aea5.ppt)

Continued

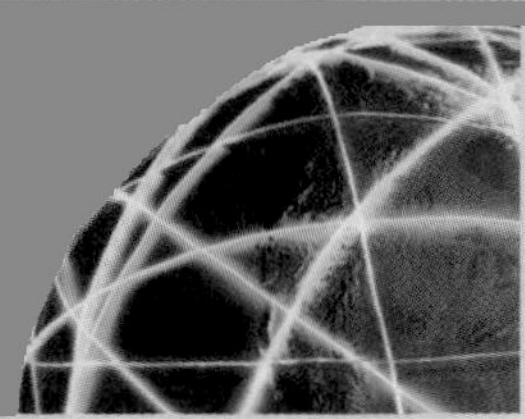

the IT sector) has led firms in the non-IT sector to increase their stock of IT capital. This has led to an increase in the ratio of capital per worker and an increase in productivity growth in the non-IT sector.

Let's go through this argument a bit more formally. Go back to equation (12.2), which gives the relation of output per effective worker to the ratio of capital per effective worker:

$$\frac{Y}{AN} = f\left(\frac{K}{AN}\right)$$

Think of this equation as giving us the relation between output per effective worker and capital per effective worker in the non-IT sector. The evidence is that the decrease in the price of IT capital has led firms to increase their stock of IT capital, and, by implication, their overall capital stock. In other words, K/AN has increased in the non-IT sector, leading to an increase in Y/AN.

- On the other hand, the IT revolution does not appear to have had a direct effect on the pace of technological progress in the non-IT sector. You have surely heard claims that the information technology revolution was forcing firms to drastically reorganize, leading to large gains in productivity. Firms may be reorganizing, but so far there is no evidence that this is leading to large gains in productivity: Measures of technological progress show no rise in the rate of technological progress in the non-IT sector relative to the post-1973 average.

In terms of the production function relation we just discussed, there is no evidence that the technological revolution has led to a higher rate of growth of A in the non-IT sector.

Are there reasons to expect productivity growth to be higher in the future than in the last 25 years? The answer is yes: The factors we have just discussed are here to stay. Technological progress in the IT sector is likely to remain high. The share of IT will continue to increase. Firms in the non-IT sector are likely to further increase their stock of IT capital, leading to further increases in productivity.

How high can we expect productivity growth to be in the future? Surely not as high as it was in the second half of the 1990s: Much of it was luck and the result of a strong expansion. But, according to some estimates, perhaps 0.5 percentage points higher than its post-1973 average: This may not be the miracle some have claimed, but it is an increase, which, if sustained, will make a substantial difference to the U.S. standard of living in the future.

For more on these issues, read "Information Technology and the U.S. Economy," by Dale Jorgenson, American Economic Review, *March 2001, 91-1, 1–32.*

depending on physical capital per worker, human capital per worker (the two factors emphasized in Chapter 11), and on the state of technology (the factor emphasized in this chapter), we can ask: Are these countries poorer because they have less physical and human capital, or because the state of their technology is lower?

The answer turns out to be that most of the difference comes from differences in the measured level of technology across countries. Take, for example, the United States and China. Using PPP measures, GDP per worker, Y/N, is 16 times higher in the United States than in China. If this ratio reflected only differences in the level of physical capital and human capital per worker between the two countries, then we would find that, adjusting for differences in physical and human capital, the two economies had the same value of A: The level of technology would be the same in both countries. Existing estimates imply that A is, in fact, 10 times higher in the United States than in China. In short, even if China suddenly acquired the same levels of physical capital and education per worker as the United States, output per worker would still be only a fraction of what it is in the United States.

See Robert Hall and Charles Jones, "Why Do Some Countries Produce So Much More Output per Worker Than Others?" *Quarterly Journal of Economics*, February 1999, 114-1, 83–116.

This answer is a useful first step, but it only raises another question. Poor countries have access to most of the technological knowledge in the world. What prevents these poor countries from simply adapting much of the advanced countries' technology, quickly closing a good part of their **technology gap**? It is clear that the answer to that question requires us to take a broader interpretation of technology than we have so far in this chapter, and to look at many of the factors we left aside in thinking about the determinants of the production function in Chapter 10. These include poorly

These factors take us from the realm of growth theory to the realm of development economics.

established property rights, political instability, the lack of entrepreneurs, and poorly developed financial markets. The list is easy to draw up. But the specific role of each of these factors is hard to pinpoint. And solving these problems is not easy: Many are as much the result of low income as they are the cause of low income.

The importance of these factors has been painfully obvious during the transition of eastern European countries from central planning to a market economy in the 1990s. In many of these countries, poorly defined property rights, poorly enforced laws, and corrupt public officials, have severely constrained the growth of new firms.

Looking at the poor countries that have grown rapidly in the last 20 years (such as the "four tigers": Hong Kong, Taiwan, Singapore, and South Korea) or looking at the even more recent fast growers (such as China, Indonesia, Malaysia, and Thailand) would seem to be the best way of uncovering the secrets of growth. But here again the lessons are not proving simple. In all these countries, growth has come with the rapid accumulation of both physical capital and human capital. And in all these countries growth has also come with an increase in the importance of foreign trade, an increase in exports and imports. But beyond these two factors, clear differences emerge. Some economies, such as Hong Kong, have relied mostly on free markets and limited government intervention. Others, such as Korea and Singapore, have relied instead on government intervention and an industrial policy aimed at fostering the growth of specific industries. (The cases of Hong Kong and Singapore are discussed in detail in the Focus box, "Hong Kong and Singapore: A Tale of Two Cities.") The bottom line is that we have not yet unraveled the secrets of growth.

For example, political instability and ethnic conflicts are at the source of output stagnation in a number of African countries. And, in turn, output stagnation contributes to political instability and exacerbates ethnic conflicts.

Hong Kong and Singapore: A Tale of Two Cities

Between 1960 and 1985, the average growth rate of output in both Hong Kong and Singapore was 6.1% per year.* How did both Hong Kong and Singapore grow so fast? Looking closely, one is struck both by the similarities and by the differences in their economic evolutions.

The Similarities

Hong Kong and Singapore have several things in common. Both are ex-British colonies. Both are essentially cities, which served initially as trading ports with little manufacturing activity. The postwar population of both countries was composed primarily of immigrant Chinese from southern China. During the course of their rapid growth, they have gone through a similar sequence of industries, with Singapore starting later than Hong Kong by 10 to 15 years. The respective sequences are summarized in Table 1.

The Differences

A closer look shows, however, major differences in the way the two countries have grown.

Hong Kong has grown under a policy of minimal government intervention. For the most part, the government has limited its intervention to providing infrastructure and selling land as it became required for further growth. In contrast, growth in Singapore has been dominated by government intervention. Through budget surpluses, as well as forced saving through pension contributions, the government has achieved a very high national saving rate. Singapore's share of gross investment in GDP increased from 9% in 1960 to 43% in 1984, one of the highest investment rates in the world. The development of specific industries has been the result of systematic government targeting, implemented through large tax incentives for mostly foreign investors.

These differences in strategies are reflected in the relative roles of capital accumulation and technological progress. In Hong Kong, the annual growth rate of output per worker from 1970 to 1990 was 2.4%; the growth rate of technological progress over the same period was 2.3%. Using the interpretation provided by the model we developed in this chapter, growth in Hong Kong has been roughly balanced. In Singapore, the growth rate of output per worker from 1971 to 1990 was 1.5%. In the article on which this box is based, Alwyn Young, an economist at the University of Chicago, concludes that the rate of technological progress during that period was a surprisingly low 0.1%. If his computation is right (and, after an intense controversy triggered by his article, it appears to be largely right), this implies that Singapore has grown nearly entirely through unusually high capital accumulation, not technological progress. Singapore's growth has been very much unbalanced.

Continued

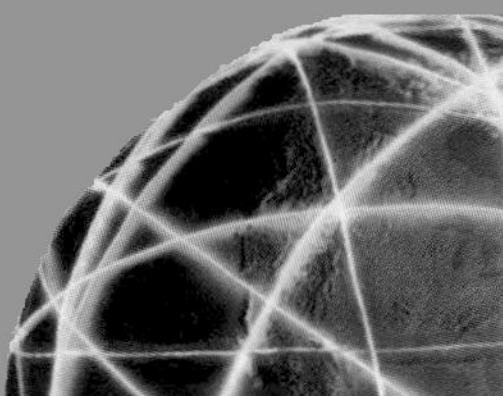

Why has Singapore achieved so little technological progress? Alwyn Young argues that, in effect, Singapore has moved too fast from one industry to the next. By moving so fast, it has not had time to learn how to produce any of them very efficiently. And, by relying largely on foreign investment, it has not allowed a class of domestic entrepreneurs to learn from and replace foreign investment in the future.

If Alwyn Young is right, what lies in store for Singapore? The model we have developed in this chapter suggests that a slowdown in growth is inevitable. High investment rates can lead to high growth only for a while. The numbers would appear brighter for Hong Kong, which seems to be growing on a balanced growth path. But major changes are in store for Hong Kong as well: In 1997, Hong Kong became again part of China; whether this will help or hinder its growth remains to be seen.

Source: Alwyn Young, "A Tale of Two Cities: Factor Accumulation and Technical Change in Hong Kong and Singapore," NBER Macroeconomics Annual, *1992, 13–63.*

**These numbers are computed using PPP measures of GDP, from Heston and Summers (see the Focus box on PPP measures in Chapter 10).*

Table 1 The Sequence of Activities in Hong Kong and Singapore Since the Early 1950s

Hong Kong		Singapore	
Early 1950s	Textiles	Early 1960s	Textiles
Early 1960s	Clothing, Plastics	Late 1960s	Electronics, Petroleum refining
Early 1970s	Electronics	Early 1970s	Electronics, Petroleum refining, Textiles, Clothing
1980s	Trade, Banking		
		1980s	Banking, Electronics

Source: See Source note for this box.

Summary

- In thinking about the implications of technological progress for growth, it is useful to think of technological progress as increasing the amount of effective labor available in the economy (that is, labor multiplied by the state of technology). We can then think of output as being produced with capital and effective labor.
- In steady state, output *per effective worker* and capital *per effective worker* are constant. Put another way, output *per worker* and capital *per worker* grow at the rate of technological progress. Put yet another way, output and capital grow at the same rate as effective labor, thus at a rate equal to the growth rate of the number of workers plus the rate of technological progress.
- When the economy is in steady state, it is said to be on a balanced growth path. Output, capital, and effective labor are all growing "in balance," i.e., at the same rate.
- The rate of output growth in steady state is independent of the saving rate. However, the saving rate affects the steady-state level of output per effective worker. And increases in the saving rate lead, for some time, to an increase in the growth rate above the steady-state growth rate.
- Technological progress depends on both (1) the fertility of research and development—how spending on R&D translates into new ideas and new products, and (2) the appropriability of the results of R&D—the extent to which firms benefit from the results of their R&D.
- In designing patent laws, governments must trade off protection for future discoveries with a desire to make existing discoveries available to potential users without restrictions.
- Germany, France, Japan, the United Kingdom, and the United States have had roughly balanced growth since 1950. The slowdown in growth since the mid-1970s comes from a decrease in the rate of technological progress. Convergence of output appears to have come primarily from a convergence in technology levels.

- There is no good explanation for the decline in the average rate of technological progress since the mid-1970s. More generally, our understanding of the determinants of technological progress, and its relation to factors such as the legal system or the political system, remains limited.

Key Terms

- effective labor, or labor in efficiency units, 244
- balanced growth, 248
- research and development (R&D), 251
- fertility of research, 251
- appropriability of research, 251
- patents, 252
- postindustrial economies, 257
- industrial policy, 258
- Moore's law, 259
- technology gap, 260

Questions and Problems

Quick Check

1. *Using the information in this chapter, label each of the following statements* true, false, *or* uncertain. *Explain briefly.*
   a. Writing the production function in terms of capital and effective labor implies that as the level of technology increases by a certain percentage, the number of workers required to achieve the same level of output decreases by the same percentage.
   b. If the rate of technological progress increases, the investment rate (the ratio of investment to output) must increase in order to keep capital per effective worker constant.
   c. In steady state, output per effective worker grows at the rate of population growth.
   d. In steady state, output per worker grows at the rate of technological progress.
   e. A higher saving rate implies a higher level of capital per effective worker in the steady state, and thus a higher rate of growth of output per effective worker.
   f. Even if the potential returns from R&D spending are identical to the potential returns from investing in a new machine, R&D spending is much riskier for firms than investing in new machines.
   g. The fact that one cannot patent a theorem implies that private firms will not engage in basic research.
   h. The slowdown in technological progress since the 1970s seems to be driven by the widespread decline in R&D spending in most industrialized countries.
   i. In the future, Singapore and Hong Kong are likely to grow at roughly the same rate.

2. *R&D and growth*
   a. Why is the amount of R&D spending important for growth? How do the appropriability and fertility of research affect the amount of R&D spending?

   For each of the following policy proposals, determine how the appropriability and fertility of research are affected and what you expect the long-run effect to be on R&D and on output:
   b. An international treaty that ensures that each country's patents are legally protected all over the world.
   c. Tax credits for each dollar of R&D spending.
   d. A decrease in funding of government-sponsored conferences between universities and corporations.
   e. The elimination of patents on breakthrough drugs, so the drugs can be sold at low cost as soon as they are available.

3. *The current Social Security system is best described as a pay-as-you-go system where current benefits are largely paid by current taxes. An alternative system is a fully funded system where workers' contributions are saved and repaid with interest upon retirement. How would a shift to a fully funded system affect output per worker and the growth of output per worker in the long run?*

4. *Where does technological progress come from for the economic leaders of the world? Do developing countries have other alternatives? Do you see any reasons why developing countries may choose to have poor patent protection? Are there any dangers in such a policy (for developing countries)?*

Dig Deeper

5. *Consider the following two scenarios:*

   i. The rate of technological progress declines forever.
   ii. The saving rate declines forever.

   a. What is the impact of each of these scenarios on economic growth over the next five years?
   b. Over the next seven decades?

   In both cases, make sure to consider the effects on both the growth rate and the level of output.

6. *Measurement error, inflation, and productivity growth*

   Suppose that there are only two goods produced in the economy, haircuts and banking services. Prices, quantities, and the number of workers occupied in the production of each good for Year 1 and for Year 2 are given by

	Year 1			Year 2		
	P1	Q1	W1	P2	Q2	W2
Haircut	10	100	50	12	100	50
Banking	10	200	50	12	230	60

a. What is nominal GDP in each year?
b. Using Year 1 prices, what is real GDP in Year 2? What is the growth rate of real GDP?
c. What is the rate of inflation using the GDP deflator?
d. Using Year 1 prices, what is real GDP per worker in Year 1 and Year 2? What is labor productivity growth between Year 1 and Year 2 for the whole economy?

Now suppose that banking services in Year 2 are not the same as banking services in Year 1 because they include telebanking that Year 1 banking services did not include. The technology for telebanking was available in Year 1 but the price of banking services with telebanking in Year 1 was $13 and no one chose that package. However, in Year 2 the price of banking services with telebanking was $12 and everyone chose to have that package in Year 2 (i.e., in Year 2 no one chose to have the Year 1 banking services package without telebanking).

e. Using Year 1 prices, what is real GDP for Year 2? What is the growth rate of real GDP?
f. What is the rate of inflation using the GDP deflator?
g. What is the labor productivity growth between Year 1 and Year 2 for the whole economy?
h. "If banking services are mismeasured—for example, by not taking into account the introduction of telebanking—we shall overestimate inflation and underestimate productivity growth." Discuss in the light of the answers to (a) to (g).

7. *Suppose that the economy's production function is*

$$Y = \sqrt{K}\,\sqrt{NA}$$

and that the saving rate (s) is equal to 16% and that the rate of depreciation (δ) is equal to 10%. Further, suppose that the number of workers grows at 2% per year and that the rate of technological progress is 4% per year.

a. Find the steady-state values of
   The capital stock per effective worker.
   Output per effective worker.
   The growth rate of output per effective worker.
   The growth rate of output per worker.
   The growth rate of output.
b. Suppose that the rate of technological progress doubles to 8% per year. Recompute the answers to part (a). Explain.
c. Now suppose that the rate of technological progress is still equal to 4% per year, but the number of workers now grows at 6% per year. Recompute the answers to (a). Are people better off in (a) or in (c)? Explain.

8. *Discuss the potential role of the following factors on the steady-state level of output per worker. In each case, indicate whether the effect is through A, or/and through K or through H.*

a. Geographic location
b. Education
c. Protection of property rights
d. Openness to trade
e. Low tax rates
f. Good public infrastructure
g. Low population growth

Explore Further

9. *Growth accounting*

In the appendix to this chapter, it is shown how data on output, capital, and labor can be used to construct estimates of the rate of growth of technological progress. Consider the following production function, which gives a good description of production in rich countries:

$$Y = K^{1/3}(NA)^{2/3}$$

Following the same steps as in the appendix, you can show that:

$$Residual = \left[g_Y - \frac{1}{3} g_K - \frac{2}{3} g_N \right]$$

or reorganizing:

$$Residual = \left[\left(g_Y - g_N\right) - \frac{1}{3}\left(g_K - g_N\right) \right]$$

The rate of technological progress is then obtained by dividing the residual by the share of labor, which, given the production function we have assumed, is equal to 2/3:

$$g_A = \text{Residual}/(2/3) = (3/2)\ \text{Residual}$$

Now go to the Web site for the National Bureau of Economic Research at **www.nber.org/data/** *and open the Penn World Tables. Search for the series "Real GDP per worker" and "Nonresidential capital stock per worker" for both Japan and the United States for the period 1965–1992. (Unfortunately, the series on K/N is not available for years prior to 1965.)*

Input the series into your favorite spreadsheet program.

a. Compute the growth rate of $Y/N (g_Y - g_N)$ and K/N $(g_K - g_N)$ for each year and for each country.
b. For each country, calculate the average growth rate of Y/N and K/N for the subperiods 1965–1973 and 1974–1992.
c. Using the equations above, compute the rate of technological progress for both subperiods for both countries.
d. Do you find evidence of a slowdown? For which subperiod?
e. The United States was the technological leader in both periods. So why is it that Japan's growth rate of technological progress is so much higher than that of the United States in both periods? Why does the difference become smaller in the later subperiod?
f. Does the difference in g_A explain all the difference in $(g_Y - g_N)$? If not, where does the rest come from?

WWW *We invite you to visit the Blanchard page on the Prentice Hall Web site at:*
www.prenhall.com/blanchard
for this chapter's World Wide Web exercises

Further Readings

For an issue we have not explored in the text, growth and the environment, read *Development and the Environment, World Development Report* (World Bank: Oxford University Press, 1992).

For more on the theory of growth, read Charles Jones, *Introduction to Economic Growth* (New York, NY: Norton, 1998).

For more on what the future may hold, read "The Next Society. A Survey of the Near Future," *The Economist*, November 2001.

Appendix: Constructing a Measure of Technological Progress

In 1957, Robert Solow suggested a way of constructing an estimate of technological progress. The method, still used today, relies on one important assumption: that each factor of production is paid its marginal product.

Under this assumption, it is easy to compute the contribution of an increase in any factor of production to the increase in output. For example, if a worker is paid $30,000 a year, the assumption implies that her contribution to output is equal to $30,000. Now suppose that this worker increases the amount of hours she works by 10%. The increase in output coming from the increase in her hours will therefore be equal to $30,000 × 10%, or $3,000.

Let us write this more formally. Denote output by Y, labor by N, and the real wage by W/P. Then, we just established, the change in output is equal to the real wage multiplied by the change in labor.

$$\Delta Y = \frac{W}{P}\Delta N$$

Divide both sides of the equation by Y, divide and multiply the right side by N, and reorganize

$$\frac{\Delta Y}{Y} = \frac{WN}{PY}\frac{\Delta N}{N}$$

Note that the first term on the right (WN/PY) is equal to the share of labor in output—the total wage bill in dollars divided by the value of output in dollars. Denote this share by α. Note that $\Delta Y/Y$ is the rate of growth of output, and denote it by g_Y. Note similarly that $\Delta N/N$ is the rate of change of the labor input, and denote it by g_N. Then the previous relation can be written as

$$g_Y = \alpha g_N$$

More generally, this reasoning implies that the part of output growth attributable to growth of the labor input is equal to α times g_N. If, for example, employment grows by 2%, and the share of labor is 0.7, then the output growth due to the growth in employment is equal to 1.4% (0.7 times 2%).

Similarly, we can compute the part of output growth attributable to growth of the capital stock. As there are only two factors of production, labor and capital, and as the share of labor is equal to α, the share of capital in income must be equal to $(1-\alpha)$. If the growth rate of capital is equal to g_K, then the part of output growth attributable to growth of capital is equal to $(1-\alpha)$ times g_K. If for example, capital grows by 5%, and the share of capital is 0.3, then the output growth due to the growth of the capital stock is equal to 1.5% (0.3 times 5%).

Putting the contributions of labor and capital together, the growth in output attributable to growth in both labor and capital is equal to $[\alpha g_N + (1-\alpha)g_K]$.

We can then measure the effects of technological progress by computing what Solow called the residual, the excess of actual growth of output g_Y over the growth attributable to growth of labor and the growth of capital $[\alpha g_N + (1-\alpha)g_K]$.

$$\text{residual} \equiv g_Y - [\alpha g_N + (1-\alpha)g_K]$$

This measure is called the **Solow residual**. It is easy to compute: All we need to know to compute it are the growth rate of output, g_Y, the growth rate of labor, g_N, and the growth rate of capital, g_K, together with the shares of labor, α and capital, $(1-\alpha)$.

To continue with our previous numerical examples. Suppose employment grows by 4%, the capital stock grows by 5%, the share of labor is 0.7 (and so the share of capital is 0.3). Then the part of output growth attributable to growth of labor and growth of capital is equal to 2.9% (0.7 times 2% plus 0.3 times 5%). If output growth is equal, for example, to 4%, then the Solow residual is equal to 1.1% (4% minus 2.9%).

The Solow residual is sometimes called the **rate of growth of total factor productivity** (or the **rate of TFP growth,** for short). The use of "total factor productivity" is to distinguish it from the *rate of growth of labor productivity*, which is defined as $(g_Y - g_N)$, the rate of output growth minus the rate of labor growth.

The Solow residual is related to the rate of technological progress in a simple way. The residual is equal to the share of labor times the rate of technological progress

$$\text{residual} = \alpha g_A$$

I shall not derive this result here. But the intuition for this relation comes from the fact that what matters in the production function $Y = F(K, AN)$ (equation [12.1]) is the product of the state of technology times labor, AN. We saw that to get the contribution of labor growth to output growth, we must multiply the growth rate of labor by its share. Because N and A enter in the same way in the production function, it is clear that to get the contribution of technological progress to output growth, we must also multiply it by the share of labor.

If the Solow residual is equal to zero, so is technological progress. To construct an estimate of g_A, we must construct the Solow residual and then divide it by the share of labor. This is how the estimates of g_A presented in the text are constructed.

In the numerical example we saw earlier, the Solow residual is equal to 1.1% and the share of labor is equal to 0.7. So, the rate of technological progress, g_A, is equal to 1.6% (1.1% divided by 0.7).

Keep straight the two definitions of productivity growth you have seen in this chapter:

- Labor productivity growth (equivalently, the rate of growth of output per worker): $g_Y - g_N$
- The rate of technological progress: g_A

In steady state, labor productivity growth $(g_Y - g_N)$ equals the rate of technological progress, g_A. Outside of the steady state however, they need not be equal: An increase in the ratio of capital per effective worker, due, for example, to an increase in the saving rate, increases $g_Y - g_N$ over g_A for some time.

Key Terms

- Solow residual, or rate of growth of total factor productivity, or rate of TFP growth, 265

Source: Robert Solow, "Technical Change and the Aggregate Production Function," *Review of Economics and Statistics*, 1957, 312–320.

Technological Progress, Wages, and Unemployment

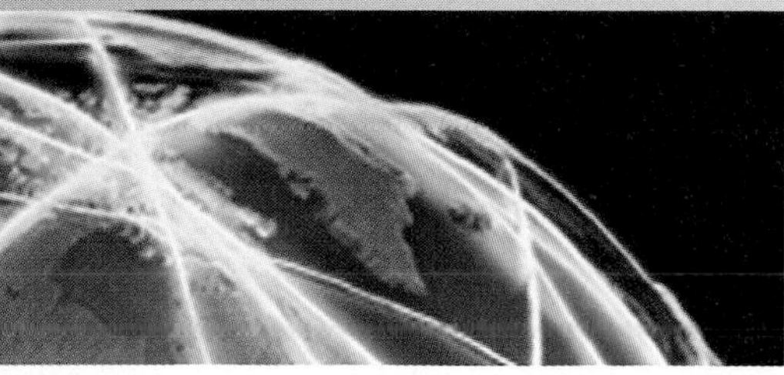

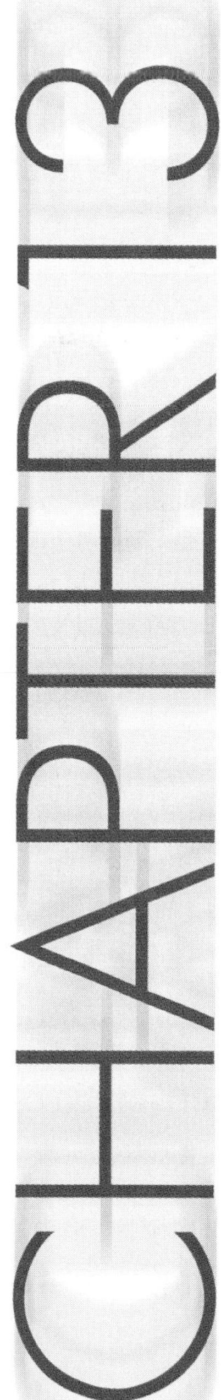

We spent much of Chapter 12 celebrating the merits of technological progress. In the long run, technological progress, we argued, is the key to steady increases in output per capita, to increases in the standard of living.

Popular discussions of technological progress are often more ambivalent. Since the beginning of the Industrial Revolution, workers have worried that technological progress will eliminate their jobs and throw them into unemployment. In early nineteenth-century England, groups of textile industry workers, known as the Luddites, destroyed the new machines that they saw as a direct threat to their jobs. Similar movements took place in other countries. *"Saboteur"* comes from one of the ways French workers destroyed machines: by putting their sabots (their heavy wooden shoes) in the machines.

The theme of **technological unemployment** typically resurfaces whenever unemployment is high. During the Great Depression, adherents to a movement called the *technocracy movement* argued that high unemployment came from the introduction of machinery, and that things would only get worse if technological progress were allowed to continue. Today in Europe—where unemployment is high—there is widespread support in many countries for a shorter workweek, down to 35 or even 30 hours. Because of technological progress, the argument goes, there is no longer enough work for all workers to have full-time jobs. The proposed solution is to have each worker work fewer hours (at the same hourly wage) so that more workers can be employed.

In its crudest form, the argument that technological progress must lead to unemployment is obviously false. The very large improvements in the standard of living that advanced countries have enjoyed during the twentieth century have come with large *increases* in employment and no systematic increase in the unemployment rate. In the United States, output per capita has increased by a factor of 6 since 1900 and, far from declining, employment has increased by a factor of 5 (reflecting a parallel increase in the size of the U.S. population.) Nor, looking across countries, is there any evidence of a systematic positive relation between the unemployment rate and the level of productivity. Japan and the United States, two of the countries with the highest levels of productivity, have two of the lowest unemployment rates among OECD countries.

Do these facts mean that the fears reflected in popular perceptions are groundless? The answer is no, or at least not necessarily. To organize the discussion here, let's distinguish between two related but separate dimensions of technological progress:

1. Technological progress makes it feasible to produce a larger quantity of goods using the same number of workers.

   This can be stated in two ways. Optimistic: Technological progress allows the economy to produce *more and more* output with the same number of workers. Pessimistic: Technological

progress implies that the economy can produce the same amount of output with *fewer and fewer* workers. Those who see technological progress as increasing output and the standard of living think in terms of the first. Those who worry about technological unemployment think in terms of the second.

The evidence we saw in previous chapters clearly shows that, in the long run, the adjustment to technological progress is through increases in output, not a decrease in employment. But how much time does this adjustment take? Does output increase quickly enough in response to an increase in productivity to avoid a prolonged period of unemployment? By assuming in Chapter 12 that employment remained constant—or grew at a constant rate—we assumed away the issue. We take it up in the first two sections of this chapter.

- Section 13-1 looks at the short-run response of output and unemployment to increases in productivity.

- Section 13-2 looks at the medium-run response of output and unemployment to increases in productivity.

  As you shall see, neither theory nor evidence supports the fear that faster technological progress leads to more unemployment. If anything, the effect seems to go the other way: Productivity slowdowns, not productivity increases, appear to be associated with more unemployment for some time.

2. **Technological progress leads to the production of new goods and the disappearance of old ones.**

   With technological progress comes a complex process of job creation and job destruction. This theme was central to the work of Joseph Schumpeter, a Harvard economist who in the 1930s emphasized that the process of growth was fundamentally a process of creative destruction. For those who lose their jobs and have to find new ones, or for those who have skills that are no longer in demand, technological progress can be a curse, not a blessing. As consumers, they benefit from the availability of new goods. As workers, they may suffer from prolonged unemployment and settle for lower wages when taking a new job. Concerns that technological change may have adverse effects on specific groups of workers is particularly relevant in the United States today. The last 20 years have been characterized by a decline in the relative wages of low-skill workers. Most signs point to technological progress as the main cause.

- Section 13-3 considers the distribution effects of technological progress. ■

13-1 Productivity, Output, and Unemployment in the Short Run

In Chapter 12, we represented technological progress as an increase in A, the *state of technology*, in the production function:

$$Y = F(K, AN)$$

Technological progress, not capital accumulation, is central to the issues we shall be discussing in this chapter. So, for simplicity, we shall leave aside capital here, and assume that output is produced according to the following production function:

$$Y = AN \qquad (13.1)$$

Under this assumption, output is produced using only labor, N, and each worker produces A units of output. Increases in A represent technological progress.

The variable A has two interpretations here. One is indeed as the state of technology. The other, which follows from the fact that $Y/N = A$, is as labor productivity (output per worker). So, when referring to increases in A, I shall use *technological progress* or (labor) *productivity growth* interchangeably.

"Output per worker" (Y/N) and "the state of technology" (A) are in general not the same. Recall from Chapter 12 that an increase in output per worker may come from an increase in capital per worker, even if the state of technology has not changed. They are the same here because, in writing the production function as equation (13.1), we ignore the role of capital in production.

Rewrite equation (13.1) as

$$N = Y/A \tag{13.2}$$

Employment is equal to output divided by productivity. Given output, the higher the level of productivity, the lower the level of employment. This naturally leads to the question: When productivity increases, does output increase enough to avoid a decrease in employment—equivalently, an increase in unemployment? In this section, we look at the short-run responses of output, employment, and unemployment. In the next, we look at their medium-run responses and, in particular, at the relation between the natural rate of unemployment and the rate of technological progress.

Technological Progress, Aggregate Supply, and Aggregate Demand

The right model to use when thinking about the short-run and medium-run response of output to a change in productivity in the short run is the aggregate supply and aggregate demand model that we developed in Chapter 7. Recall its basic structure:

- Output is determined by the intersection of the aggregate supply curve and the aggregate demand curve.
- The *aggregate supply* relation captures the effects of output on the price level. The aggregate supply curve is upward sloping: An increase in the level of output leads to an increase in the price level. Behind the scenes, the mechanism is that an increase in output leads to a decrease in unemployment. The decrease in unemployment leads to an increase in nominal wages, which leads to an increase in prices—an increase in the price level.
- The *aggregate demand* relation captures the effects of the price level on output. The aggregate demand curve is downward sloping: An increase in the price level leads to a decrease in the demand for output. The mechanism behind the scenes: An increase in the price level leads to a decrease in the real money stock. The decrease in real money leads in turn to an increase in the interest rate. The increase in the interest rate leads to a decrease in the demand for goods, decreasing output.

Aggregate supply curve: Given P^e, $Y\uparrow \Rightarrow u\downarrow \Rightarrow W\uparrow \Rightarrow P\uparrow$

Aggregate demand curve: $P\uparrow \Rightarrow (M/P)\downarrow \Rightarrow i\uparrow \Rightarrow Y\downarrow$

The aggregate supply curve is drawn as *AS* in Figure 13-1. The aggregate demand curve is drawn as *AD*. The intersection of the aggregate supply curve and the aggregate demand curve gives the level of output, Y, consistent with equilibrium in labor, goods, and financial markets. Given the equilibrium level of output Y, the level of employment is determined by $N = Y/A$. For a given level of output, the higher the level of productivity, the smaller the number of workers needed to produce it.

Suppose productivity increases from level A to level A'. What happens to output, and to employment and unemployment in the short run? The answer depends on how the increase in productivity shifts the aggregate supply curve and the aggregate demand curve.

A and A' refer to levels of productivity here, not points on the graph. (To avoid confusion, points in the graph are denoted by B and B'.)

Take the aggregate supply curve first. The effect of an increase in productivity is to decrease the amount of labor needed to produce a unit of output, reducing cost for firms. This leads firms to reduce the price they charge at any level of output. The aggregate supply curve shifts down, from *AS* to *AS'* in Figure 13-2.

Now take the aggregate demand curve. Does an increase in productivity increase or decrease the demand for goods at a given price level? There is no general answer

Figure 13-1

Aggregate Supply and Aggregate Demand for a Given Level of Productivity

The aggregate supply curve is upward sloping: An increase in output leads to an increase in the price level. The aggregate demand curve is downward sloping: An increase in the price level leads to a decrease in output.

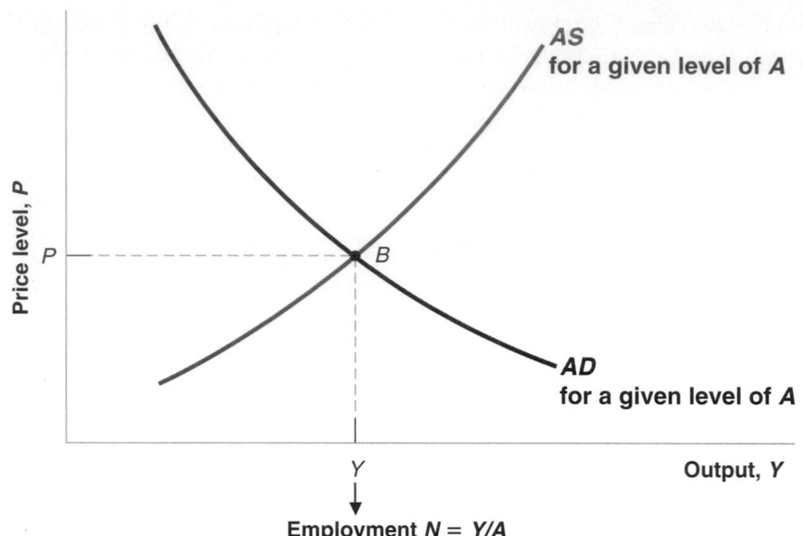

because productivity increases do not appear in a vacuum; what happens to aggregate demand depends on what triggered the increase in productivity in the first place:

- Take the case where productivity increases come from the widespread implementation of a major technological breakthrough. It is easy to see how this change may be associated with an increase in demand at a given price level. The prospect of higher growth in the future leads consumers to feel more optimistic about the future, and so to increase their consumption given their current income. The prospect of higher profits in the future, as well as the need to put the new technology in place, may also lead to a boom in investment. In this case, the demand for goods increases at a given price level; the aggregate demand curve shifts to the right.
- Now take the case where productivity growth comes not from the introduction of new technologies but from the more efficient use of existing technologies. One of the implications of increased international trade has been an increase in foreign competition. This competition has forced many firms to cut costs by reorganizing

Figure 13-2

The Effects of an Increase in Productivity on Output in the Short Run

An increase in productivity shifts the aggregate supply curve down. It has an ambiguous effect on the aggregate demand curve, which may shift to the left or to the right. In this figure, we assume a shift to the right.

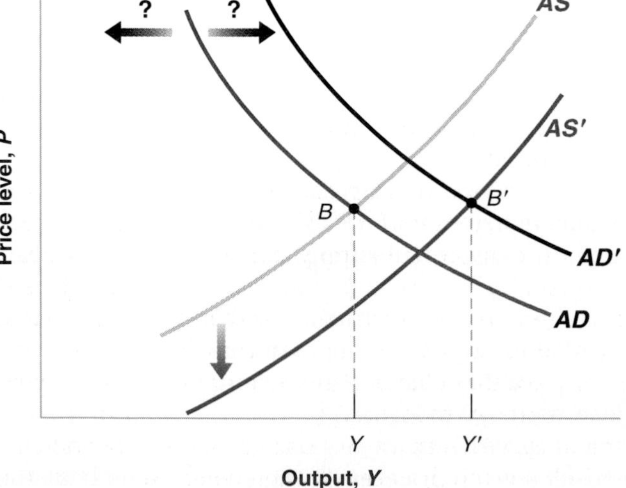

production and eliminating jobs (this is often called *downsizing*). When such reorganizations are the source of productivity growth, there is no presumption that aggregate demand will increase: Reorganization of production may require little or no new investment. Increased uncertainty and worries about job security may well lead workers to want to save more, and so to reduce consumption spending given their current income. In this case, aggregate demand may shift to the left rather than to the right.

Let's assume the most favorable case (most favorable from the point of view of output and employment), namely, the case where the aggregate demand curve shifts to the right. In this case, the increase in productivity shifts the aggregate supply curve down, from *AS* to *AS'*, and shifts the aggregate demand curve to the right, from *AD* to *AD'*. These shifts are drawn in Figure 13-2. Both shifts contribute to an increase in equilibrium output, from *Y* to *Y'*. In this case, the increase in productivity unambiguously leads to an increase in output. In words, lower costs and high demand combine to create an economic boom. (If this reminds you of what happened in the United States in the 1990s, you are right. See the Focus Box, "Technological Progress, Unemployment, and the U.S. Expansion in the 1990s," at the end of the next section.)

Without more information however, we cannot tell what happens to employment. To see why, note that equation (13.2) implies the following relation:

% change in employment = % change in output − % change in productivity

Start from the production function $Y = AN$. From proposition 7 in Appendix 2 at the end of the book, this relation implies that $g_Y = g_A + g_N$. Or equivalently: $g_N = g_Y - g_A$.

Thus, what happens to employment depends on whether output increases proportionately more or less than productivity. If productivity increases by 2%, it takes an increase in output of at least 2% to avoid a decrease in employment—that is, an increase in unemployment. And without a lot more information about the slopes and the size of the shifts of the *AS* and *AD* curves, we cannot tell whether this condition is satisfied in Figure 13-2. In the short run, increases in productivity may or may not lead to an increase in unemployment. Theory alone cannot settle the issue.

The discussion has assumed that macroeconomic policy was given. But, by shifting the aggregate demand curve, fiscal policy and monetary policy can clearly affect the outcome. Suppose you were in charge of monetary policy in this economy: What level of output would you try to achieve?

The Empirical Evidence

Can empirical evidence help us reach a conclusion? At first glance, it would seem to. Look at Figure 13-3, which plots the behavior of labor productivity and the behavior of output for the U.S. business sector from 1960 to 2000.

The figure shows a strong positive relation between year-to-year movements in output growth and productivity growth. Furthermore, the movements in output are typically larger than the movements in productivity. This would seem to imply that, when productivity growth is high, output increases by more than enough to avoid any adverse effect on employment. But this conclusion would be wrong. The reason is that, *in the short run*, the causal relation runs mostly the other way, from output growth to productivity growth. That is, in the short run, output growth leads to productivity growth, not the other way around.

Correlation versus causality: If we see a positive correlation between output growth and productivity growth, should we conclude that high productivity growth leads to high output growth, or that high output growth leads to high productivity growth?

We saw why when we discussed Okun's law in Chapter 9: In bad times, firms hoard labor—they keep more workers than is necessary for current production. When the demand for goods increases for any reason, firms respond partly by increasing employment and partly by having currently employed workers work harder. This is why increases in output lead to increases in productivity. And this is what we see in Figure 13-3: High output growth leads to higher productivity growth. This is not the relation we are after. Rather, we want to know what happens to output and unemployment when there is an *exogenous* change in productivity—a change in productivity that comes from a change in technology, not from the response of firms to movements in output. Figure 13-3 does not help us much here. And the conclusion from the

Figure 13-3

U.S. Labor Productivity and Output Growth, 1960–2000

There is a strong positive relation between output growth and productivity growth. But the causality runs from output growth to productivity growth, not the other way around.

Source: U.S. Department of Labor; Bureau of Labor Statistics.

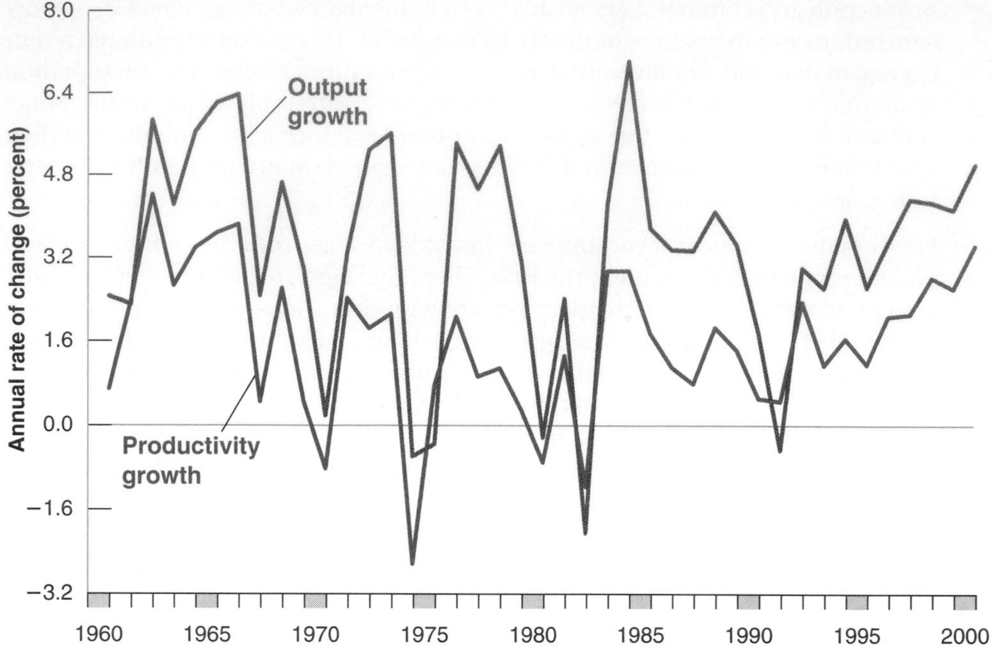

research that has looked at the effects of exogenous movements in productivity growth on output is that the data give an answer just as ambiguous as the answer given by the theory:

- Sometimes increases in productivity lead to increases in output sufficient to maintain or even increase employment in the short run.
- Sometimes they do not, and unemployment increases in the short run.

13-2 Productivity and the Natural Rate of Unemployment

We have looked so far at the *short-run* effects of a change in productivity on output, employment, and unemployment. In the medium run, we know the economy returns to the natural level of output—the level of output consistent with the natural rate of unemployment. Now we must ask: Is the natural rate of unemployment itself affected by changes in productivity?

Recall from Chapter 6, the natural rate of unemployment is determined by two relations, the price-setting relation and the wage-setting relation. Our first step must be to think about how changes in productivity affect each of these two relations.

Price Setting and Wage Setting Revisited

Consider price setting first.

- From equation (13.1), each worker produces A units of output; equivalently, producing 1 unit of output requires $1/A$ workers.
- If the nominal wage is equal to W, the nominal cost of producing 1 unit of output is therefore equal to $(1/A)W = W/A$.
- If firms set their price equal to $1 + \mu$ times cost (where μ is the markup), the price level is given by:

$$\text{Price setting} \qquad P = (1+\mu)\frac{W}{A} \qquad (13.3)$$

The only difference between this equation and equation (6.3) is the presence of the productivity term, A (which we had implicitly set to 1 in Chapter 6). An increase in productivity decreases cost, which decreases the price level given the nominal wage.

Turn to wage setting. The evidence suggests that other things being equal, wages are typically set to reflect the increase in productivity over time. If productivity has been growing at 3% a year on average for some time, then wage contracts will build in a wage increase of 3% a year. This suggests the following extension of our earlier wage-setting equation

$$\text{Wage setting} \qquad W = A^e P^e F(u,z) \qquad (13.4)$$

Look at the three terms on the right side of equation (13.4).

- Two of them, P^e and $F(u, z)$, are familiar from equation (6.1). Wages depend (negatively) on the unemployment rate, u, and on institutional factors captured by the variable z. And workers care about real wages, not nominal wages, so wages depend on the (expected) price level, P^e.
- The new term is A^e: Wages now also depend on the expected level of productivity, A^e. If workers and firms both expect productivity to increase, they will incorporate those expectations into the wages set in bargaining.

Think of workers and firms setting the wage to divide (expected) output between workers and firms according to their relative bargaining power. If both sides expect higher productivity and so higher output, this will be reflected in the bargained wage. How productivity affects wage setting is one of the questions examined in the book by Edmund Phelps, *Structural Slumps* (Cambridge, MA: Harvard University Press, 1994), already mentioned in Chapter 6.

The Natural Rate of Unemployment

We can now characterize the natural rate of unemployment. Recall that the natural rate of unemployment is determined by the price-setting and wage-setting relations, and the additional condition that expectations be correct. In this case, this condition requires that expectations of *both* prices *and* productivity be correct, so $P^e = P$ and $A^e = A$.

The price-setting equation determines the real wage paid by firms. Reorganizing equation (13.3), we can write

$$\frac{W}{P} = \frac{A}{1+\mu} \qquad (13.5)$$

The real wage paid by firms, W/P, increases one for one with productivity A: The higher the level of productivity, the lower the price set by firms given the nominal wage, and therefore the higher the real wage paid by firms.

This equation is represented in Figure 13-4. The real wage is measured on the vertical axis. The unemployment rate is measured on the horizontal axis. Equation (13.5)

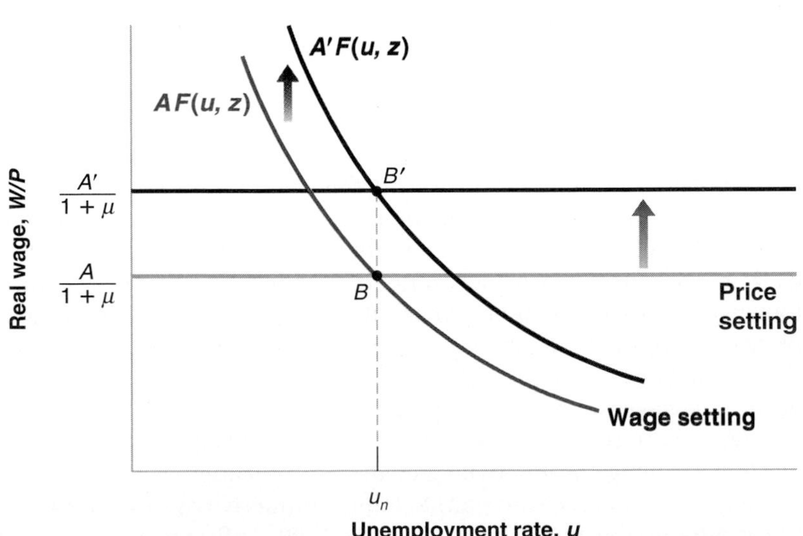

Figure 13-4

The Effects of an Increase in Productivity on the Natural Rate of Unemployment

An increase in productivity shifts both the wage- and the price-setting curves in the same proportion and thus has no effect on the natural rate of unemployment.

is represented by the solid horizontal line at $W/P = A/(1 + \mu)$: The real wage implied by price setting is independent of the unemployment rate.

Turn to the wage-setting equation. Under the condition that expectations are correct—so both $P^e = P$ and $A^e = A$—the wage-setting equation (13.4) becomes

$$\frac{W}{P} = A\,F(u, z) \qquad (13.6)$$

The real wage, W/P, implied by wage bargaining depends on both the level of productivity and the unemployment rate. The higher the level of productivity, the higher the real wage. The higher the unemployment rate, the lower the real wage. For a given level of productivity, equation (13.6) is represented by the solid downward-sloping curve in Figure 13-4: The real wage implied by wage setting is a decreasing function of the unemployment rate.

The reason for using *B* rather than *A* to denote the equilibrium is that we are already using the letter *A* to denote the level of productivity. ▶

Equilibrium in the labor market is given by point *B*, and the natural rate of unemployment is u_n. Let's now ask what happens to the natural rate of unemployment in response to an increase in productivity. Suppose that *A* increases by 5%, so the new level of productivity A' equals 1.05 times *A*.

- From equation (13.5) we see that the real wage implied by price setting is now higher by 5%: The price-setting curve shifts up.
- From equation (13.6), we see that at a given unemployment rate, the real wage implied by wage setting is also higher by 5%: The wage-setting curve shifts up.
- Note that at the initial unemployment rate, u_n, both curves shift up by the same amount, namely, 5% of the initial real wage. That is why the new equilibrium is at B', directly above *B*: The real wage is higher by 5%, and the natural rate of unemployment remains the same.

The intuition for this result is straightforward. A 5% increase in productivity leads firms to reduce prices by 5% given wages, leading to a 5% increase in real wages. This increase exactly matches the increase in real wages from wage bargaining at the initial unemployment rate. Real wages increase by 5%, and the natural unemployment rate remains the same.

We have looked at a one-time increase in productivity, but the argument we have developed also applies to productivity growth. Suppose that productivity steadily increases, so that each year *A* increases by 5%. Then, each year, real wages will increase by 5%, and the natural rate of unemployment will remain unchanged.

The Empirical Evidence

We have derived two strong results: *The natural rate of unemployment should depend neither on the level of productivity nor on the rate of productivity growth.* How do these two results fit the facts?

An obvious problem in answering this question is that we do not observe the natural rate of unemployment. But we can work around this problem by looking at the relation between average productivity growth and the average unemployment rate over decades. Because the actual unemployment rate moves around the natural rate, looking at the average unemployment rate over a decade should give us a good estimate of the natural rate of unemployment for that decade. Looking at average productivity growth over a decade also takes care of another problem we discussed earlier: While changes in labor hoarding can have a large effect on yearly changes in labor productivity, these changes in labor hoarding are unlikely to make much difference when we look at average productivity growth over a decade.

Figure 13-5 plots average U.S. labor productivity growth and the average unemployment rate during each decade since 1890. At first glance, there seems to be little

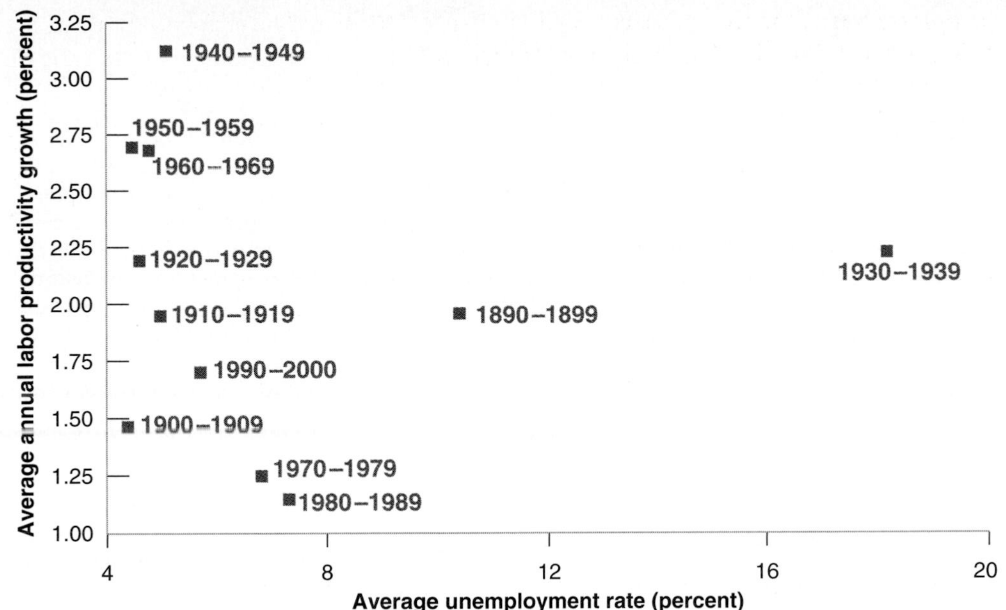

Figure 13-5

Productivity Growth and Unemployment—Averages by Decade, 1890–2000

There is little relation between the 10-year averages of productivity growth and the 10-year averages of the unemployment rate. If anything, higher productivity growth is associated with lower unemployment.

Source: U.S. Bureau of the Census, *Historical Statistics of the United States.*

relation between the two. But it is possible to argue that the decade of the Great Depression is so different that it should be left aside. If we ignore the 1930s (the decade of the Great Depression), then a relation—although not a very strong one—emerges between productivity growth and the unemployment rate. But it is the opposite of the relation predicted by those who believe in technological unemployment:

Periods of *high productivity growth,* such as the 1940s to the 1960s, have been associated with *a lower unemployment rate.* Periods of *low productivity growth,* such as the United States saw in the 1970s and 1980s, have been associated with *a higher unemployment rate.*

There is also substantial evidence that the slowdown in productivity growth has played an important role in the rise of European unemployment since the 1970s. We return to this issue in the Focus box "European Unemployment, Productivity Growth, and Technological Change" at the end of this chapter.

Can the theory we have developed be extended to explain this inverse relation in the medium run between productivity growth and unemployment? The answer is yes. To see why, we must look more closely at the formation of expectations of productivity in wage setting.

Up to this point, we have looked at the rate of unemployment that prevails when *both* price expectations *and* expectations of productivity are correct. However, one of the lessons of the 1970s and 1980s is that it takes a very long time for expectations of productivity to adjust to the reality of lower productivity growth. When productivity growth slows down for any reason, it takes a long time for society in general, and workers in particular, to adjust their expectations. In the meantime, workers keep asking for wage increases that are no longer consistent with the new lower rate of productivity growth.

To see what this description implies, let's look at what happens to the unemployment rate when price expectations are correct (that is, $P^e = P$), but expectations of productivity, A^e, may not be (A^e may not be equal to A). In this case, the relations implied by price setting and wage setting are

$$\textit{Price setting} \qquad \frac{W}{P} = \frac{A}{1+\mu}$$

$$\textit{Wage setting} \qquad \frac{W}{P} = A^e F(u, z)$$

Technological Progress, Unemployment, and the U.S. Expansion in the 1990s

FOCUS

Why did the U.S. economy do so well in the second half of the 1990s? (Table 1 repeats the basic numbers for growth, unemployment, inflation, and labor productivity.) We first asked the question in Chapter 1. In later chapters, we looked at various pieces of the answer. Here, we put these pieces together.

- The buzz in the second half of the 1990s was of the New Economy and the rise of the high-tech sector. As you saw in Chapter 12, there is indeed some evidence of a pickup in the underlying rate of productivity growth, coming mainly from a high rate of technological progress in the IT sector, combined with an increasing share of the sector in the U.S. economy. In terms of Figure 13-2, there was a downward shift of the aggregate supply curve.
- This evolution was associated with a strong increase in aggregate demand. Hopes of high profits led to a boom in investment, mainly, but not only, in the IT sector. Anticipations of higher incomes in the future led to a boom in consumption. In terms of Figure 13-2, there was a large shift of the aggregate demand to the right, resulting in a large increase in output, a large increase in employment, and a steady decrease in unemployment during the period.
- The decrease in the unemployment rate to historically low levels was not associated with an increase in inflation, suggesting a decrease in the natural unemployment rate. As you saw in Chapter 8, there were many factors behind this decrease. But the major factor was probably the increase in productivity growth. The increase in productivity growth was largely unexpected, leading, along the lines developed in this section, to a decrease in the natural rate of unemployment.
- Can the U.S. economy hope to continue to operate at high output growth, low unemployment, and low inflation? It is useful here to distinguish between the actual rate of unemployment and the natural rate of unemployment. In the short run, the actual

Table 1 Selected U.S. Macroeconomic Variables, 1995–2000 (percent)

	1995	1996	1997	1998	1999	2000
GDP growth	2.7	3.6	4.4	4.4	4.2	5.0
Unemployment rate	5.6	5.4	4.9	4.5	4.2	4.0
Inflation rate	2.2	1.9	1.9	1.3	1.5	2.0
Labor productivity	1.2	2.1	2.1	2.9	2.7	3.7

Source: OECD Economic Outlook, June 2001. The inflation rate is measured using the GDP deflator.

Suppose productivity growth declines: A increases more slowly than before. If expectations of productivity growth adjust slowly, then A^e will increase for some time by more than A does. What will then happen to unemployment is shown in Figure 13-6. If A^e increases by more than A, the wage-setting relation will shift up by more than the price-setting relation. The equilibrium will move from B to B', and the natural rate of unemployment will increase from u_n to u'_n. The natural rate of unemployment will remain higher until expectations of productivity have adjusted to the new reality, until A^e and A are again equal.

The price-setting relation shifts up by a factor A. The wage-setting relation shifts up by a factor, A^e. If $A^e > A$, the wage-setting relation shifts up by more than the price-setting relation.

To summarize what we have seen in this and the preceding section: There is not much support, either in theory or in the data, for the idea that faster productivity growth leads to higher unemployment:

- In the short run, there is no reason to expect, nor does there appear to be, a systematic relation between movements in productivity growth and movements in unemployment.
- In the medium run, if there is a relation between productivity growth and unemployment, it appears to be an inverse relation. Lower productivity growth leads to higher

rate of unemployment depends largely on what happens to aggregate demand. Here, it is clear that some of the optimism that led firms to invest and consumers to spend in the second half of the 1990s has been tempered. Investment spending is sharply down, the U.S. economy is now in a slowdown, and the actual rate of unemployment is sharply up. Most forecasts for 2002 are that it will reach or exceed 6%—two percentage points above its average value in 2000. What about the natural rate of unemployment? As we argued in this section, the effect of higher productivity growth, even if it continues, will not last forever. Sooner or later, the natural rate of unemployment will increase from its low level at the end of 1990s. When and by how much is difficult to predict.

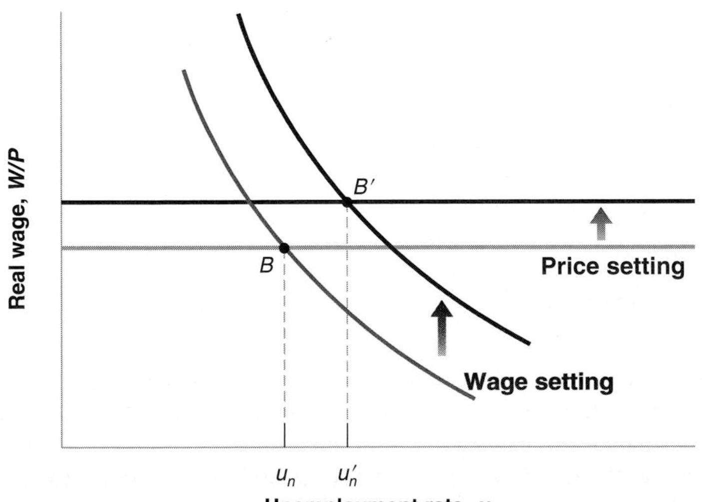

Figure 13-6

The Effects of a Decrease in Productivity Growth on the Unemployment Rate When Expectations of Productivity Growth Adjust Slowly

If it takes time for workers to adjust their expectations of productivity growth, a slowdown in productivity growth will lead to an increase in the natural rate of unemployment for some time.

unemployment. Higher productivity growth leads to lower unemployment. Indeed, many economists see a connection between the decrease in the natural unemployment rate and the increase in the rate of technological progress in the United States in the second half of the 1990s. We take up the issue in the Focus box "Technological Progress, Unemployment, and the U.S. Expansion in the 1990s."

Given this evidence, where do fears of technological unemployment come from? They probably come from the dimension of technological progress we have neglected so far, **structural change**—the change in the structure of the economy induced by technological progress. For some workers, those with skills no longer in demand, structural change may indeed mean unemployment, or lower wages, or both.

13-3 Technological Progress and Distribution Effects

Technological progress is a process of structural change. New goods are developed, making old ones obsolete. New techniques of production are introduced, requiring new skills and making some old skills less useful. The essence of this **churning** process is nicely reflected in the following quote from the president of the Federal Reserve Bank of Dallas in his introduction to a report, *The Churn*:

The Churn: The Paradox of Progress (Dallas, TX: Federal Reserve Bank of Dallas, 1993). ▶

> My grandfather was a blacksmith, as was his father. My dad, however, was part of the evolutionary process of the churn. After quitting school in the seventh grade to work for the sawmill, he got the entrepreneurial itch. He rented a shed and opened a filling station to service the cars that had put his dad out of business. My dad was successful, so he bought some land on the top of a hill, and built a truck stop. Our truck stop was extremely successful until a new interstate went through 20 miles to the west. The churn replaced US 411 with Interstate 75, and my visions of the good life faded.

Many professions, from those of blacksmiths to harness makers, have vanished forever. There were more than 11 million farm workers in the United States at the beginning of the twentieth century; because of very high productivity growth in agriculture, there are less than 1 million today. There are now more than 3 million truck, bus, and taxi drivers in the United States; there were none in 1900. There are more than 1 million computer programmers; there were practically none in 1960. The Focus box "U.S. Occupations with the Largest Job Growth, and Occupations with the Largest Job Decline, 1998–2008" gives you a sense of current and projected evolutions in the United States.

The Increase in Wage Inequality

For those in growing sectors, or those with the right skills, technological progress leads to new opportunities and higher wages. But for those in declining sectors, or those with skills that are no longer in demand, technological progress can mean the loss of their job, a period of unemployment, and possibly much lower wages. The last 20 years in the United States have seen a large increase in wage inequality. Most economists believe that one of the main culprits behind this increase is technological change.

Figure 13-7 shows the evolution of relative wages for various groups of workers, by education level, from 1973 to 1999. The figure is based on information on individual workers from the CPS. Each of the lines in the figure shows the evolution of the wage of workers with a given level of education—"some high school," "high school diploma," "some college," "college degree," "advanced degree"—*relative to* the wage of workers who have just a high school diploma. All relative wages are further divided by their

We described the CPS survey and some of its uses in Chapter 6. ▶

Occupations with the Largest Job Growth, and Occupations with the Largest Job Decline, 1998–2008

The U.S. Department of Labor regularly makes projections of the future number of workers in different occupations. Table 1 gives the 10 occupations that are forecast to have the largest job growth from 1998 to 2008. Table 2 gives the 10 occupations that are forecast to have the largest job decline over the same period.

Technological progress is surely the main force behind the rise of systems analysts and computer support specialists, the decline in the number of farmers and farm workers, and the demise of typists and switchboard operators. But both tables show that there are other forces at work:

- Trade is important. The decline in the number of textile machine operators reflects the fact that these activities are moving to low-wage countries.
- Increases in income and the aging of the U.S. population, which both change the structure of demand, are also important. Note the increase in the number of registered nurses, and in the number of home health aides.

Table 1 Occupations with the Largest Job Growth

	1998 (thousands)	2008 (thousands)	change (thousands)	change (%)
Systems analysts	617	1194	577	+ 94
Retail salespersons	4056	4620	563	+ 14
Cashiers	3198	3754	556	+ 17
General managers	3362	3913	551	+ 16
Truck drivers	2970	3463	493	+ 17
Office clerks	3021	3484	463	+ 15
Registered nurses	2079	2530	451	+ 22
Computer support specialists	429	869	439	+102
Home health aides	746	1179	433	+ 58
Teacher assistants	1192	1567	375	+ 61

Source: Bureau of Labor Statistics, Monthly Labor Review, November 1999.

Table 2 Occupations with the Largest Job Decline

	1998 (thousands)	2008 (thousands)	change (thousands)	change (%)
Farmers	1306	1135	−173	−13
Sewing machine operators	369	257	−112	−30
Child care workers, private household	305	209	−97	−40
Word processors, typists	459	365	−93	−20
Bookkeeping clerks	2078	1997	−81	−4
Cleaners and servants, private household	600	530	−71	−12
Farm workers	851	794	−57	−7
Computer operators, mainframes	224	170	−54	−24
Textile machine operators	192	141	−50	−26
Switchboard operators	214	185	−30	−14

Source: Bureau of Labor Statistics, Monthly Labor Review, November 1999.

FOCUS

Figure 13-7

Evolution of Relative Wages, by Education Level, 1973–1999

Since the early 1980s, the relative wage of workers with a low education level has decreased; the relative wage of workers with a high education level has increased.

Source: Economic Policy Institute Datazone, **www.epinet.org**.

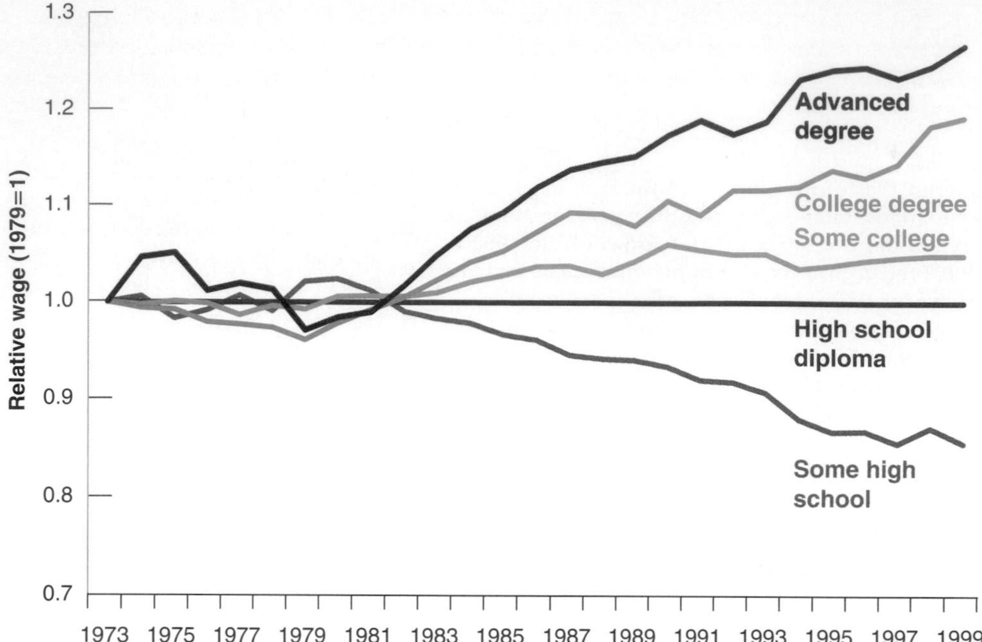

value in 1973, so the resulting wage series are all equal to one in 1973. The figure yields a very striking conclusion.

Starting in the early 1980s, workers with a low level of education have seen their relative wage steadily decrease over time, while workers with a high level of education have seen their relative wage steadily increase. At the low end of the education ladder, the relative wage of workers who have not completed high school has declined by nearly 15%. This implies that, in many cases, these workers have seen a decrease not only in their relative wage, but in their absolute real wage as well. At the high end of the education ladder, the relative wage of those with an advanced degree has increased by 20% since the early 1980s. In short, wage inequality has increased a lot in the United States over the last 20 years.

The Causes of Increased Wage Inequality

What are the causes of this increase in wage inequality? There is general agreement that the main factor behind the increase in the wage of high-skill relative to the wage of low-skill workers is a steady increase in the demand for high-skill workers relative to the demand for low-skill workers.

This trend in relative demand is not new; it was already present to some extent in the 1960s and 1970s. But it was offset then by a steady increase in the relative supply of high-skill workers: A steadily larger proportion of children finished high school, went to college, finished college, and so on. Since the early 1980s, relative supply has continued to increase, but not fast enough to match the continuing increase in relative demand. The result has been a steady increase in the relative wage of high-skill workers versus low-skill workers.

What explains this steady shift in relative demand?

- One line of argument focuses on the role of international trade. Those U.S. firms that employ higher proportions of low-skill workers, the argument goes, are increasingly driven out of markets by imports from similar firms in low-wage countries. Alternatively, to remain competitive, firms must relocate some of their production to low-wage countries. In both cases, the result is a steady decrease in the relative demand for low-skill workers in the United States. There are clear similarities between the effects of trade and the effects of technological progress: While both trade and technological progress are good for the economy as a whole, they both lead to structural change, and leave some workers worse off.

There is no question that trade is partly responsible for increased wage inequality. The presence of textile machine operators in the list of the 10 occupations with the largest job decline in the United States (see this chapter's earlier Focus box) is testimony to this fact: The U.S. textile industry has largely moved to low-wage countries. But a closer examination shows that trade accounts for only part of the shift in relative demand. The most telling fact against explanations based solely on trade is that the shift in relative demand toward high-skill workers appears to be present even in those sectors that are not exposed to foreign competition.

Pursuing the effects of international trade would take us too far afield. For a more thorough discussion of who gains and who loses from trade, look at the textbook by Paul Krugman and Maurice Obstfeld, *International Economics*, 5th ed. (New York: HarperCollins, 2000).

- The other line of argument focuses on **skill-biased technological progress**. New machines and new methods of production, the argument goes, require high-skill workers, more so today than in the past. The development of computers requires workers to be increasingly computer literate. The new methods of production require workers to be more flexible, better able to adapt to new tasks. Greater flexibility in turn requires more skills and more education.

  Unlike explanations based on trade, skill-biased technological progress can explain why the shift in relative demand appears to be present in nearly all sectors of the economy. At this point, most economists believe that it is the dominant factor in explaining the increase in wage dispersion.

Does all this imply that the United States is condemned to steadily increasing wage inequality? Not necessarily. There are at least three reasons to think that the future may be different from the recent past:

- The trend in relative demand may simply slow down. For example, it is likely that computers will become easier and easier to use in the future, even by low-skill workers. Computers may even replace high-skill workers, those workers whose skills involve primarily the ability to compute or to memorize. Paul Krugman has argued—only partly tongue in cheek—that accountants, lawyers, and doctors may be next on the list of professions to be replaced by computers.
- Technological progress is not exogenous: This is a theme we explored in Chapter 12. How much firms spend on R&D and in what directions they direct their research depend on expected profits. The low relative wage of low-skill workers may lead firms to explore new technologies that take advantage of low-skill workers. In other words, market forces may lead technological progress to become less skill biased in the future.
- The relative supply of high-skill versus low-skill workers is also not exogenous. The large increase in the relative wage of more educated workers implies that the returns to acquiring more education and training are higher than they were one or two decades ago. Higher returns to training and education can increase the relative supply of high-skill workers, and, as a result, work to stabilize relative wages. Many economists believe that policy has an important role to play here, to make sure that the quality of primary and secondary education for the children of low-wage workers does not further deteriorate, and that those who want to acquire more education can borrow in order to pay for it.

This ends our discussion of the interactions between technological progress, wages, and unemployment. Throughout the chapter, I have used examples from the United States. But, in fact, the discussion may be even more relevant for Europe today. This is explored at more length in the Focus Box "European Unemployment, Productivity Growth, and Technological Change."

European Unemployment, Productivity Growth, and Technological Change

FOCUS

You saw in Chapter 1 how European unemployment started increasing in the 1970s, continued to increase in the 1980s, and has remained high since then. What triggered the initial increase? Why has unemployment remained so high for so long? Despite a large amount of research, economists still have few answers. What is clear, however, is that various dimensions of technological progress play a central role in the story. This is the focus of this box.

1. How much of the increase in the unemployment rate in Europe reflect an increase in the natural rate? Or instead an increase of the actual rate above the natural rate?

To answer, recall the main conclusion from Chapter 8: The change in inflation depends (negatively) on the difference between the actual rate of unemployment and the natural rate of unemployment. So, if we observe that inflation is roughly constant, then we can infer that the actual rate of unemployment and the natural rate of unemployment are roughly equal. If instead, inflation is decreasing, then the actual rate is above the natural rate. If inflation is increasing, then the actual rate is below the natural rate.

With this motivation in mind, Figure 1 looks at the evolution of both unemployment inflation in the European Union since 1970. The figure suggests four conclusions:

- Inflation increased in the 1970s. This suggests that during this period, the actual unemployment rate was below the natural rate of unemployment. In other words, the evidence suggests that the 1970s were associated not only with a large increase in the actual rate of unemployment, but also with an even larger increase in the natural rate of unemployment.
- Inflation then decreased sharply in the early 1980s. This suggests that, during that period, the actual rate of unemployment exceeded the natural unemployment rate.
- Since the late 1980s, inflation has declined, but slowly. This suggests that during that period, the natural rate of unemployment has been higher than—but close to—the actual rate of unemployment.
- Since the late 1990s, inflation has been roughly stable. This suggests that the natural rate of unemployment today in Europe is close to the actual rate of

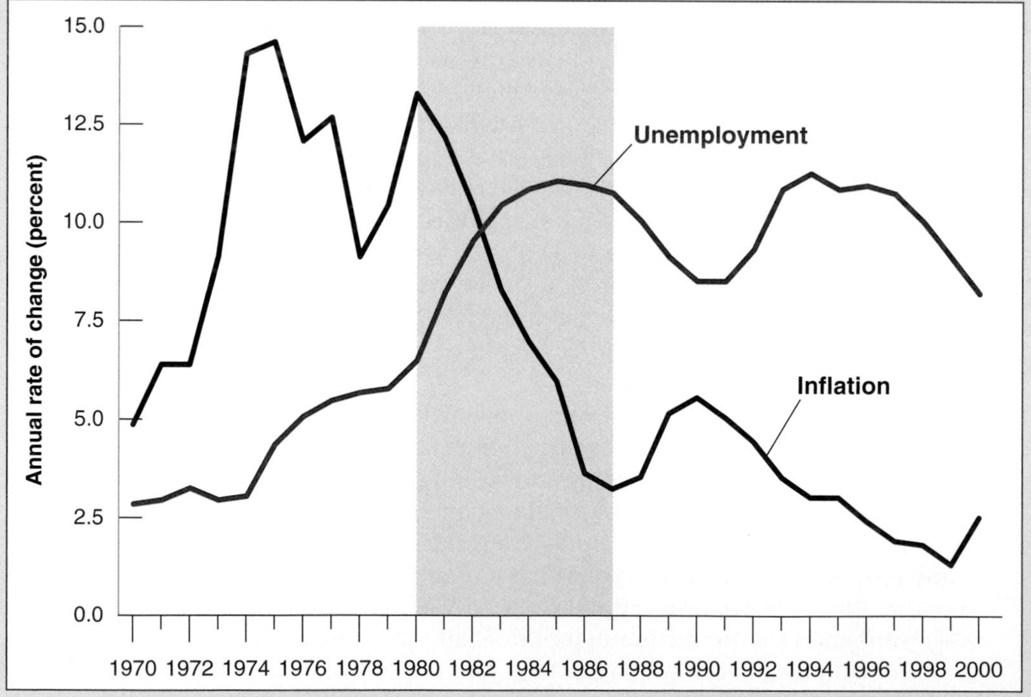

Figure 1 *EU Unemployment and Inflation, 1970–2000*

Today, inflation is roughly stable in Europe. This suggests that the high rate of unemployment reflects a high natural rate of unemployment.

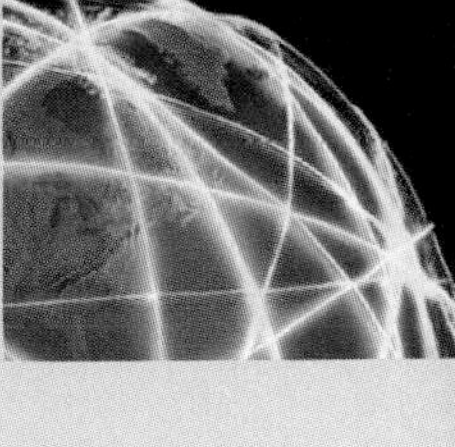

unemployment, at about 8%. This represents an increase in the natural rate of unemployment of 5 to 6 percentage points since the 1960s.

In short, the natural rate clearly increased a lot in the 1970s. It has remained high since, and stands today around 8%.

2. Why did the natural rate increase so much in the 1970s and the 1980s? Economists point to two major adverse shocks:

- One is the 3-fold increase in the price of oil in the 1970s. We discussed its effects on the U.S. economy in Chapter 7. Its effects on European countries were very similar: Higher inflation, and an increase in both the natural and the actual unemployment rate.

  This shock surely contributed to the initial increase in unemployment. It does not easily explain, however, why unemployment continued to increase during most of the 1980s. By the mid-1980s, the price of oil (in real terms) had sharply decreased, roughly returning to its level of the early 1970s (look back at Figure 7-11). Yet, unemployment continued to increase.
- The other, and probably the more important, shock is the decrease in the rate of technological progress, starting in the mid-1970s. We discussed it in Chapter 10 and again in Chapter 12. From 1950 to 1973, countries such as Germany and France had experienced very fast technological progress: 4% a year for France, 4.9% a year for Germany. (See Table 12-2.) Starting in the mid-1970s, this rate of technological progress suddenly dropped, averaging only 1.8% for France over the period 1973–1987, and 2.1% for Germany.

  The effect of this large decrease in the rate of technological progress was exactly what we described in Section 12-2. It took a long time for workers, who had seen their real wages increase at 4 to 5% a year in the past, to adjust. During that time, they—and the unions that represented them—continued to ask for large wage increases, wage increases that were now too large given the new, lower rate of technological progress. The result was a steady increase in the natural rate of unemployment.

That it takes many years for workers to adjust to a decrease in the rate of technological progress is plausible. That it would take 25 years is less plausible. Yet, in most European countries, the natural rate of unemployment is still very high. (It is not high in all countries: In the Netherlands, for example, the unemployment rate is now around 3%. But the unemployment rate remains high in the four largest EU countries: France, Germany, Italy, and Spain).

So, what accounts for the high natural rate today? Economists have explored a two lines of arguments; each line known by greek name, hysteresis for the first, and Eurosclerosis for the second:

3. Hysteresis.

The hysteresis line of argument holds that the natural rate of unemployment is not independent of actual unemployment—contrary to what we have assumed until now. In fact, the argument goes, the "natural rate" depends on the history of actual unemployment. (The word *hysteresis* comes from physics. Outside of physics, it is typically used to describe any system whose equilibrium position depends on the history of the system. Here, the fact that the rate of unemployment to which the economy eventually returns depends on the history of unemployment.)

According to this line of argument, the long period of high unemployment in Europe has led to an increase in the natural rate. High unemployment has led governments to offer more generous unemployment benefits; this made it easier for the unemployed to survive, but it has also led to an increase in the natural rate of unemployment. (You saw in Chapter 6 how an increase in unemployment benefits leads to an increase in the natural rate.) High persistent unemployment has led some workers to remain unemployed for such a long time that they have become unemployable. They have lost skills, morale, or connections. While they might be counted as unemployed, they become in effect irrelevant to the labor market. This again has increased the natural rate.

Each of these explanations clearly contains some truth. The question is whether these effects are strong enough to account for why the natural rate of unemployment is still so high today.

4. Eurosclerosis

The Eurosclerosis line of argument reasons that the high natural rate today reflects a structural problem: European labor market institutions (unemployment benefits, minimum wages, and so on) are not well adapted to the high level of technological change that characterizes modern economies. One of the implications of this lack of adaptation, the argument goes, is a high natural rate of unemployment. (*Sclerosis* means hardening of the tissues. The argument is that the labor market institutions are hardening the economic structure.)

One particular argument is closely related to the discussion of biased technological progress we had in Section 13-3. It goes as follows: In both the United States and in Europe, the demand for low-skill workers has declined; the demand for high-skill workers has increased. In the United States, the decrease in demand

Continued

Expectations

The next four chapters represent the first major extension of the core. They look at the role of expectations in output fluctuations.

Chapter 14

Chapter 14 introduces two important concepts. The first is the distinction between the real interest rate and the nominal interest rate. The second is the concept of expected present discounted value. The chapter ends by discussing the Fisher hypothesis, the proposition that, in the medium run, nominal interest rates fully reflect inflation and money growth.

Chapter 15

Chapter 15 focuses on the role of expectations in financial markets. It first looks at the determination of bond prices and bond yields. It shows how we can learn about the course of expected future interest rates by looking at the yield curve. It then turns to stock prices, and shows how they depend on expected future dividends and interest rates. Finally, it discusses whether stock prices always reflect fundamentals, or may instead reflect bubbles or fads.

Chapter 16

Chapter 16 focuses on the role of expectations in consumption and investment decisions. The chapter shows how consumption depends partly on current income, partly on human wealth, and partly on financial wealth. It shows how investment depends partly on current cash flow, and partly on the expected present value of future profits.

Chapter 17

Chapter 17 looks at the role of expectations in output fluctuations. Starting from the *IS-LM* model, it modifies the description of goods market equilibrium (the *IS* relation) to reflect the effect of expectations on spending. It revisits the effects of monetary and fiscal policy on output. It shows, for example, that in contrast to the results derived in the core, a fiscal contraction may sometimes increase output, even in the short run.

Expectations: The Basic Tools

CHAPTER 14

The consumer who considers buying a new car must ask: Can I safely take a new car loan? How much of a wage raise can I expect over the next few years? Is a recession coming? How safe is my job?

The manager who observes an increase in current sales must ask: Is this a temporary boom that I should meet with the existing production capacity? Or is it likely to last, in which case I should order new machines?

The pension fund manager who observes a boom in the stock market must ask: Are stock prices going to increase further, or is the boom likely to fizzle? Does the increase in stock prices reflect expectations of firms' higher profits in the future? Do I share those expectations? Should I move some of my funds in or out of the stock market?

These examples make clear that many economic decisions depend not only on what is happening today, but also on expectations of what will happen in the future. Indeed, some decisions should depend very little on what is happening today. For example, why should an increase in sales today, if it is not accompanied by expectations of continued higher sales in the future, lead a firm to alter its investment plans? The new machines may not be in operation before sales have returned to normal. By then, they might sit idle, gathering dust.

We have not paid systematic attention until now to the role of expectations in goods and financial markets. We ignored expectations in our construction of both the *IS-LM* model, and the aggregate demand component of the *AS-AD* model that builds on the *IS-LM*. When looking at the goods market, we assumed that consumption depended on current income and that investment depended on current sales. When looking at financial markets, we lumped assets together and called them "bonds"; we then focused on the choice between bonds and money, and ignored the choice between bonds and stocks, the choice between short-term bonds and long-term bonds, and so on. We introduced these simplifications to build the intuition for the basic mechanisms at work. It is now time to think about the role and the determination of expectations in economic fluctuations. We do so in this and the next three chapters.

This chapter lays the groundwork. The first two sections introduce two key concepts:

- Section 14-1 introduces the distinction between the *real* interest rate and the *nominal* interest rate.
- Section 14-2 introduces the concept of *expected present discounted value.*

- Sections 14-3 and 14-4 then build on the distinction between real and nominal interest rates to revisit the effects of money growth on interest rates. They derive a surprising but important result: Higher money growth leads to *lower* nominal interest rates in the short run, but to *higher* nominal interest rates in the medium run. ■

14-1 Nominal Versus Real Interest Rates

In January 1981, the *one-year T-bill rate*—the interest rate on one-year government bonds—was 12.6%. In January 2001, the one-year T-bill rate was only 4.6%. Although most of us cannot borrow at the same interest rate as the government, the interest rates we face as consumers were also substantially lower in 2001 than in 1981. It was much cheaper to borrow in 2001 than it was in 1981.

Or was it? In 1981, inflation was around 12%. In 2001, inflation was around 2%. This would seem relevant: The interest rate tells us how many dollars we shall have to pay in the future in exchange for having one more dollar today. But we do not consume dollars. We consume goods.

When we borrow, what we really want to know is how many goods we have to give up in the future in exchange for the goods we get today. Likewise, when we lend, we want to know how many goods—not how many dollars—we shall get in the future for the goods we give up today. The presence of inflation makes the distinction important. What is the point of receiving high interest payments in the future if inflation between now and then is so high that we are able to buy few goods with the proceeds?

This is where the distinction between nominal interest rates and real interest rates comes into play:

Nominal interest rate: Interest rate in terms of dollars. ▶

- Interest rates expressed in terms of dollars (or, more generally, in units of the national currency) are called **nominal interest rates**. The interest rates printed in the financial pages of newspapers are nominal interest rates. For example, when we say that the one-year T-bill rate is 4.6%, we mean that for every dollar the government borrows by issuing one-year T-bills, it promises to pay 1.046 dollars a year from now. More generally, if the nominal interest rate for year t is i_t, borrowing one dollar this year requires you to pay $1 - i_t$ dollars next year. (I shall use interchangeably "this year" for "today," and "next year" for "one year from today.")

Real interest rate: Interest rate in terms of a basket of goods. ▶

- Interest rates expressed *in terms of a basket of goods* are called **real interest rates**. If we denote the real interest rate for year t by r_t, then, by definition, borrowing the equivalent of one basket of goods this year requires you to pay the equivalent of $1 + r_t$ baskets of goods next year.

What is the relation between nominal and real interest rates? How do we go from nominal interest rates—that we observe—to real interest rates—that we typically do not observe? The answer: We must adjust the nominal interest rate to take into account expected inflation.

Let's go through the step-by-step derivation:

Assume there is only one good in the economy, bread (we shall add jam and other goods later). Denote the one-year nominal interest rate, in terms of dollars, by i_t: If you borrow one dollar this year, you will have to repay $1 + i_t$ dollars next year. But you are not interested in dollars. You want to know: If you borrow enough to eat one more pound of bread this year, how much will you have to repay, in terms of pounds of bread, next year?

Figure 14-1 helps us derive the answer. The top part repeats the definition of the one-year real interest rate. The bottom part shows how we can derive the one-year real

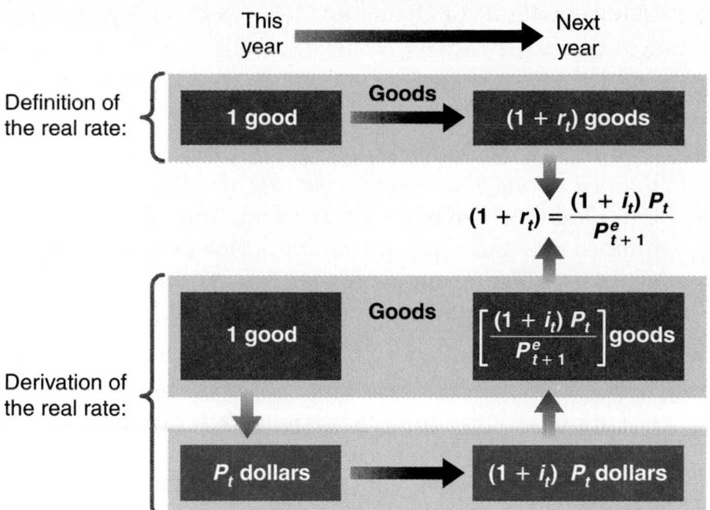

Figure 14-1

Definition and Derivation of the Real Interest Rate

interest rate from information about the one-year nominal interest rate and the price of bread.

- Start with the arrow pointing down in the lower left of Figure 14-1. You want to eat one more pound of bread this year. If the price of a pound of bread this year is P_t dollars, to eat one more pound of bread, you must borrow P_t dollars.
- If i_t is the one-year nominal interest rate—the interest rate in terms of dollars—and if you borrow P_t dollars, you will have to repay $(1 + i_t)P_t$ dollars next year. This is represented by the arrow from left to right at the bottom of Figure 14-1.
- What you care about is not dollars, but pounds of bread. Thus, the last step involves converting dollars to pounds of bread next year. Let P^e_{t+1} be the price of bread you expect for next year. (The superscript *e* indicates this is an expectation: You do not know yet what the price of bread will be next year.) How much you expect to repay next year, in terms of pounds of bread, is therefore equal to $(1 + i_t)P_t$ (the amount of dollars you have to repay next year) divided by P^e_{t+1} (the price of bread in terms of dollars you expect for next year), so $(1 + i_t)P_t/P^e_{t+1}$. This is represented by the arrow pointing up in the lower right of Figure 14-1.

If you have to pay \$10 next year, and you expect the price of bread next year to be \$2 a loaf, you expect to have to repay the equivalent of 10/2 = 5 loaves of bread next year. This is why we divide the dollar amount $(1 + i_t)P_t$ by the expected price of bread next year, P^e_{t+1}.

Putting together what you see in the top part and what you see in the bottom part of Figure 14-1, it follows that the one-year real interest rate, r_t, is given by

$$1+r_t = (1 + i_t)\frac{P_t}{P^e_{t+1}} \tag{14.1}$$

This relation looks intimidating. Two simple manipulations make it look friendlier:

- Denote expected inflation by π^e_t. Given there is only one good—bread—the expected rate of inflation equals the expected change in the dollar price of bread between this year and next year, divided by the dollar price of bread this year:

$$\pi^e_t \equiv \frac{(P^e_{t+1} - P_t)}{P_t} \tag{14.2}$$

Add 1 to both sides in (14.2):

$$1+\pi_t^e = 1+\frac{(P_{t+1}^e - P_t)}{P_t}$$

Reorganize:

$$1+\pi_t^e = \frac{P_{t+1}^e}{P_t}$$

Take the inverse on both sides:

$$\frac{1}{1+\pi_t^e} = \frac{P_t}{P_{t+1}^e}$$

Using equation (14.2), rewrite P_t/P_{t+1}^e as $1/(1+\pi_t^e)$. Replace in (14.1) to get

$$(1+r_t) = \frac{1+i_t}{1+\pi_t^e} \tag{14.3}$$

One plus the real interest rate equals the ratio of one plus the nominal interest rate, divided by one plus the expected rate of inflation.

- Equation (14.3) gives us the *exact* relation of the real interest rate to the nominal interest rate and expected inflation. However, when the nominal interest rate and expected inflation are not too large—say, less than 20% per year—a close approximation to this equation is given by the simpler relation

$$r_t \approx i_t - \pi_t^e \tag{14.4}$$

Equation (14.4) is simple. Remember it. It says that *the real interest rate is (approximately) equal to the nominal interest rate minus expected inflation.* (In the rest of the book, I shall often treat the relation (14.4) as if it were an equality. Remember, however, it is only an approximation.)

See Proposition 6, Appendix 2 at the end of the book.

Suppose i = 10% and π^e = 5%. The exact relation (14.3) gives r_t = 4.8%.

The approximation given by equation (14.4) gives 5%—close enough.

The approximation can be quite bad when i and π^e are high. If i = 100% and π^e = 80%, the exact relation gives r = 11%; the approximation gives r = 20%—a big difference.

Note some of the implications of equation (14.4):

- When expected inflation equals zero, the nominal and the real interest rates are equal.
- Because expected inflation is typically positive, the real interest rate is typically lower than the nominal interest rate.
- For a given nominal interest rate, the higher the expected rate of inflation, the lower the real interest rate.

The case where expected inflation happens to be equal to the nominal interest rate is worth looking at more closely. Suppose the nominal interest rate and expected inflation both equal 10%, and you are a borrower. For every dollar you borrow this year, you will have to repay 1.10 dollars next year. But dollars will be worth 10% less in terms of bread next year. So, if you borrow the equivalent of one pound of bread, you will have to repay the equivalent of one pound of bread next year: The real cost of borrowing—the real interest rate—is equal to zero. Now suppose you are a lender: For every dollar you lend this year, you will receive 1.10 dollars next year. This looks attractive, but dollars next year will be worth 10% less in terms of bread. If you lend the equivalent of one pound of bread this year, you will get the equivalent of one pound of bread next year: Despite the 10% nominal interest rate, the real interest rate is equal to zero.

We have assumed so far that there was only one good—bread. But what we have done generalizes easily. All we need to do is to substitute the *price level*—the price of a basket of goods—for the price of bread in equation (14.1) or equation (14.3). If we use the consumer price index (the CPI) to measure the price level, the real interest rate tells us how much consumption we must give up next year to consume more today.

Nominal and Real Interest Rates in the United States Since 1978

Let us return to the question at the start of this section. We can now restate it as follows: Was the *real interest rate* lower in 2001 than it was in 1981? More generally, what has happened to the real interest rate in the United States since the early 1980s?

The answer is given in Figure 14-2, which plots both nominal and real interest rates since 1978. For each year, the nominal interest rate is the one-year T-bill rate at the beginning of the year. To construct the real interest rate, we need a measure for

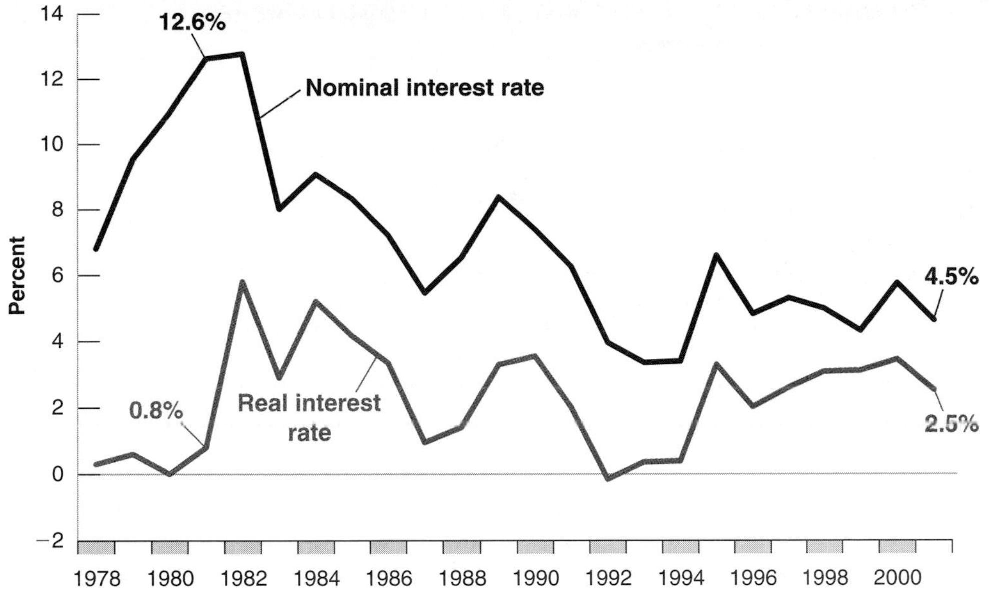

Figure 14-2

Nominal and Real One-Year T-bill Rates in the United States, 1978–2001

While the nominal interest rate has declined considerably since the early 1980s, the real interest rate is actually higher in 2001 than it was then.

expected inflation—more precisely, the rate of inflation expected as of the beginning of each year. We use, for each year, the forecast of inflation for that year published at the end of the previous year by the OECD. For example, the forecast of inflation used in constructing the real interest rate for 2001 is the forecast of inflation published by the OECD in December 2000—2.1%.

Figure 14-2 shows the importance of adjusting for inflation. While the nominal interest was much lower in 2001 than it was in 1981, the real interest rate was actually *higher* in 2001 than it was in 1981: 2.5% in 1999 versus 0.8% in 1981. Put another way, despite the large decline in interest rates, borrowing is actually more expensive in 2001 than it was 1981. This comes from the fact that inflation (and, with it, expected inflation) has steadily declined since the early 1980s.

The real interest rate ($i - \pi^e$) is based on expected inflation. If actual inflation turns out to be different from expected inflation, the realized real interest rate ($i - \pi$) will be different from the real interest rate.

For this reason, the real interest rate is sometimes called the *ex-ante* real interest rate (*ex-ante* means "before the fact": here, before inflation is known).

The realized real interest rate is called the *ex-post* real interest rate (*ex-post* means "after the fact": here, after inflation is known).

14-2 Expected Present Discounted Values

Let's now turn to the second key concept we introduce in this chapter, that of expected present discounted value.

To motivate this concept, let's return to the example of the manager considering whether to buy a new machine. On one hand, buying and installing the machine involves a cost today. On the other, the machine allows for higher production, higher sales, and thus higher profits in the future. The question facing the manager is whether the value of these expected profits is higher than the cost of buying and installing the machine. This is where the concept of expected present discounted value comes in handy: The **expected present discounted value** of a sequence of future payments is the value today of this expected sequence of payments. Once the manager has computed the expected present discounted value of the sequence of profits, her problem becomes simple. If this value exceeds the initial cost, she should go ahead and buy the machine. If it does not, she should not.

As in the case of the real interest rate in Section 14-1, the practical problem is that expected present discounted values are not directly observable. They must be constructed from information on the sequence of expected payments and expected interest rates. Let's first look at the mechanics of construction.

Figure 14-3

Computing Present Discounted Values

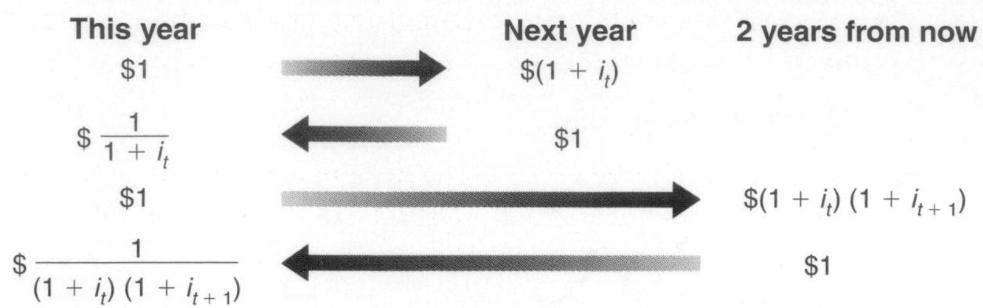

Computing Expected Present Discounted Values

If the one-year nominal interest rate is i_t, lending one dollar this year yields $1 + i_t$ dollars next year. Equivalently, borrowing one dollar this year implies paying back $1 + i_t$ dollars next year. In that sense, one dollar this year is worth $1 + i_t$ dollars next year. This relation is represented graphically in the first line of Figure 14-3.

Turn the argument around and ask: One dollar *next year* is worth how many dollars this year? The answer, shown in the second line of Figure 14-3, is $1/(1 + i_t)$ dollars. Think of it this way: If you lend $1/(1 + i_t)$ dollars this year, you will receive $1/(1 + i_t)$ times $(1 + i_t) = 1$ dollar next year. Equivalently, if you borrow $1/(1 + i_t)$ dollars this year, you will have to repay exactly one dollar next year. So, one dollar next year is worth $1/(1 + i_t)$ dollars this year.

More formally, we say that $1/(1 + i_t)$ is the *present discounted value* of one dollar next year.

The word *present* comes from the fact that we are looking at the value of a payment next year in terms of dollars *today*.

The word *discounted* comes from the fact that the value next year is discounted, with $1/(1 + i_t)$ being the **discount factor** (the one-year nominal interest rate, i_t, is sometimes called the **discount rate**).

i_t: discount rate

$1/(1 + i_t)$: discount factor

If the discount rate goes up, the discount factor goes down.

Because the nominal interest rate is always positive, the discount factor is always less than 1: A dollar next year is worth less than a dollar today. The higher the nominal interest rate, the lower the value today of a dollar next year. If $i = 5\%$, the value this year of a dollar next year is $1/1.05 \approx 95$ cents. If $i = 10\%$, the value today of a dollar next year is $1/1.10 \approx 91$ cents.

Now apply the same logic to the value today of a dollar *two years from now*. For the moment, assume that current and future one-year nominal interest rates are known with certainty. Let i_t be the nominal interest rate for this year, and i_{t+1} be the one-year nominal interest rate next year.

If, today, you lend one dollar for two years, you will get $(1 + i_t)(1 + i_{t+1})$ dollars two years from now. Put another way, one dollar today is worth $(1 + i_t)(1 + i_{t+1})$ dollars two years from now. This relation is represented in the third line of Figure 14-3.

What is one dollar two years from now worth today? By the same logic as before, the answer is $1/(1 + i_t)(1 + i_{t+1})$ dollars: If you lend $1/[(1 + i_t)(1 + i_{t+1})]$ dollars this year, you will get exactly one dollar in two years. So, the *present discounted value of a dollar two years from today* is equal to $1/(1 + i_t)(1 + i_{t+1})$ dollars. This relation is shown in the fourth line of Figure 14-3. If, for example, the one-year nominal interest rate is the same this year and next, and equal to 5%, so $i_t = i_{t+1} = 5\%$, then the present discounted value of a dollar in two years is equal to $1/(1.05)^2$ or about 91 cents today.

A General Formula

Having gone through these steps, it is easy to derive the present discounted value for the general case.

Consider a sequence of payments in dollars, starting today and continuing into the future. Assume for the moment that these future payments are known with certainty. Denote today's payment by $\$z_t$, the payment next year by $\$z_{t+1}$, the payment two years from today by $\$z_{t+2}$, and so on.

The present discounted value of this sequence of payments—that is the value in today's dollars of the sequence of payments—which we shall call $\$V_t$, is given by

$$\$V_t = \$z_t + \frac{1}{1+i_t}\$z_{t+1} + \frac{1}{(1+i_t)(1+i^e_{t+1})}\$z_{t+2} + \cdots$$

Each payment in the future is multiplied by its respective discount factor. The more distant the payment, the smaller the discount factor, and thus the smaller today's value of that distant payment. In other words, future payments are discounted more heavily, so their present discounted value is lower.

We have assumed so far that future payments and future interest rates were known with certainty. Actual decisions, however, have to be based on expectations of future payments rather than on actual values for these payments. In our earlier example, the manager cannot be sure of how much profit the new machine will actually bring; nor can she be sure what interest rates will be in the future. The best she can do is get the most accurate forecasts she can, and then compute the *expected present discounted value* of profits, based on these forecasts.

How do we compute the expected present discounted value when future payments or interest rates are uncertain? Basically in the same way as before, but replacing the *known* future payments and *known* interest rates by *expected* future payments and *expected* interest rates. Formally, denote expected payments next year by $\$z^e_{t+1}$, expected payments two years from now by $\$z^e_{t+2}$, and so on. Similarly, denote the expected one-year nominal interest rate next year by i^e_{t+1}, and so on (the one-year nominal interest rate this year, i_t, is known today, so it does not need a superscript e). The expected present discounted value of this expected sequence of payments is given by

◀ This statement glosses over an important issue—risk. If people dislike risk, the value of an uncertain (and therefore risky) payment, now or in the future, will be lower than the value of a riskless payment, even if both have the same expected value. We ignore this effect here, but return to it in Chapter 15.

$$\$V_t = \$z_t + \frac{1}{(1+i_t)}\$z^e_{t+1} + \frac{1}{(1+i_t)(1+i^e_{t+1})}\$z^e_{t+2} + \cdots \qquad (14.5)$$

"Expected present discounted value" is a heavy expression to carry; I shall often use, for short, just **present discounted value**, or even just **present value**. Also, it will be convenient to have a shorthand way of writing expressions like equation (14.5). To denote the present value of a expected sequence for $\$z$, I shall write $V(\$z_t)$, or just $V(\$z)$.

Using Present Values: Examples

Equation (14.5) has two important implications:

- The present value depends positively on current and expected future payments. An increase in either today's $\$z$ or any future $\$z^e$ leads to an increase in the present value.

◀ $\$z$ or future $\$z^e\uparrow \Rightarrow V\uparrow$

- The present value depends negatively on current and expected future interest rates. An increase in either current i or in any future i^e leads to a decrease in the present value.

◀ i or future $i^e\uparrow \Rightarrow V\downarrow$

Equation (14.5) is not simple, however, and intuition for these effects is best built by going through some examples.

Constant Interest Rates

To focus on the effects of the sequence of payments on the present value, assume that interest rates are expected to be constant over time, so that $i_t = i^e_{t+1} = \ldots$, and denote their common value by i. The present value formula—equation (14.5)—becomes

$$\$V_t = \$z_t + \frac{1}{(1+i)}\,\$z^e_{t+1} + \frac{1}{(1+i)^2}\,\$z^e_{t+2} + \cdots \qquad (14.6)$$

The weights correspond to the terms of a geometric series. See geometric series in Appendix 2 at the end of the book.

In this case, the present value is a *weighted sum* of current and expected future payments: The weights decline *geometrically* through time. The weight on a payment this year is one, the weight on the payment n years from now is $(1/(1+i))^n$. With a positive interest rate, the weights get closer and closer to zero as we look further and further into the future. For example, with an interest rate equal to 10%, the weight on a payment 10 years from today is equal to $1/(1+0.10)^{10} = 0.386$, so that a payment of $1,000 in 10 years is worth $386 today. The weight on a payment in 30 years is $1/(1+0.10)^{30} = .057$, so that a payment of $1,000 in 30 years is worth only $57 today!

Constant Interest Rates and Payments

In some cases, the sequence of payments for which we want to compute the present value is simple. For example, a typical fixed-rate 30-year mortgage requires constant dollar payments over 30 years. Consider a sequence of equal payments—call them $\$z$ without a time index—over n years including this year. In this case, the present value formula in equation (14.6) simplifies to

$$\$V_t = \$z\left[1 + \frac{1}{(1+i)} + \cdots + \frac{1}{(1+i)^{n-1}}\right]$$

By now, geometric series should not hold any secret, and you should have no problem deriving this relation. But if you do, see Appendix 2 at the end of the book.

Because the terms in the expression in brackets represent a geometric series, we can compute the sum of the series, and get

$$\$V_t = \$z\,\frac{1-[1/(1+i)^n]}{1-[1/(1+i)]}$$

What is the present value if i equals 4%? 8%? (Answers: $706,000, $530,000)

Suppose you have just won 1 million dollars from your state lottery and have been presented with a 6-foot $1,000,000 check on TV. Afterward, you are told that, to protect you from your worst spending instincts as well as from your many new "friends," the state will pay you the million dollars in equal yearly installments of $50,000 over the next 20 years. What is the present value of your prize? Taking, for example, an interest rate of 6% per year, the preceding equation gives $V = \$50{,}000\,(.688)/(.057) =$ or about $608,000. Not bad, but winning the prize did not make you a millionaire.

Constant Interest Rates and Payments, Going on Forever

Let's go one step further and assume that payments are not only constant, but go on forever. Real-world examples are harder to come by for this case, but one example comes from nineteenth-century England, when the government issued *consols,* bonds paying a fixed yearly amount forever. Let $\$z$ be the constant payment. Assume that payments start next year, rather than right away, as in the previous example (this makes for simpler algebra). From equation (14.6), we have

Most consols were bought back by the British government during the end of the nineteenth century and the early part of twentieth century. A few are still around.

$$\begin{aligned}\$V_t &= \frac{1}{(1+i)}\$z + \frac{1}{(1+i)^2}\$z + \cdots \\ &= \frac{1}{(1+i)}\left[1 + \frac{1}{(1+i)} + \cdots\right]\$z\end{aligned}$$

where the second line follows by factoring out $1/(1 + i)$. The reason for factoring out $1/(1 + i)$ should be clear from looking at the term in brackets: It is an infinite geometric sum, so we can use the property of geometric sums to rewrite the present value as

$$\$V_t = \frac{1}{1+i}\frac{1}{[1-(1/(1+i))]}\$z$$

Or, simplifying

$$\$V_t = \frac{\$z}{i}$$

The present value of a constant sequence of payments $\$z$ is equal to the ratio of $\$z$ to the interest rate i. If, for example, the interest rate is expected to be 5% per year forever, the present value of a consol that promises \$10 per year forever equals \$10/.05 = \$200. If the interest rate increases and is now expected to be 10% per year forever, the present value of the consol decreases to \$10/.10 = \$100.

Zero Interest Rates

Because of discounting, computing present discounted values typically requires the use of a calculator. There is, however, a case where computations simplify. This is the case where the interest rate is equal to zero: If $i = 0$, then $1/(1 + i)$ equals one, and so does $[1/(1 + i)^n]$ for any power n. For that reason, the present discounted value of a sequence of expected payments is just the *sum* of those expected payments.

Because the interest rate is in fact typically positive, assuming the interest rate is zero is only an approximation. But it is a very useful one for back-of-the-envelope computations.

Nominal Versus Real Interest Rates, and Present Values

So far, we have computed the present value of a sequence of dollar payments by using interest rates in terms of dollars—nominal interest rates. Specifically, we have written equation (14.5) as

$$\$V_t = \$z_t + \frac{1}{(1+i_t)}\$z^e_{t+1} + \frac{1}{(1+i_t)(1+i^e_{t+1})}\$z^e_{t+2} + \cdots$$

where i_t, i^e_{t+1},..., is the sequence of current and expected future nominal interest rates, and $\$z_t$, $\$z^e_{t+1}$, $\$z^e_{t+2}$,..., is the sequence of current and expected future dollar payments.

Suppose we want instead to compute the present value of a sequence of *real* payments—that is, payments in terms of a basket of goods rather than in terms of dollars. Following the same logic as before, what we need to do is to use the right interest rates for this case: namely, interest rates in terms of the basket of goods—*real interest rates*. Specifically, we can write the present value of a sequence of real payments as

$$V_t = z_t + \frac{1}{1+r_t}z^e_{t+1} + \frac{1}{(1+r_t)(1+r^e_{t+1})}z^e_{t+2} + \cdots \qquad (14.7)$$

where r_t, r^e_{t+1},..., is the sequence of current and expected future real interest rates, z_t, z^e_{t+1}, z^e_{t+2}..., is the sequence of current and expected future real payments, and V_t is the real present value of future payments.

These two ways of writing the present value turn out to be equivalent. That is, the real value obtained by constructing $\$V_t$ using equation (14.5) and dividing by P_t, the

The proof is given in the appendix to this chapter. Go through it to test your understanding of the two tools introduced in this chapter: real interest rate versus nominal interest rate, and expected present values.

price level, is equal to the real value V_t obtained from equation (14.7), so

$$\$V_t/P_t = V_t$$

In words: We can compute the present value of a sequence of payments in two ways. One way is to compute it as the present value of the sequence of payments expressed in dollars, discounted using nominal interest rates, and then dividing by the price level today. The other way is to compute it as the present value of the sequence of payments expressed in real terms, discounted using real interest rates. The two ways give the same answer.

Do we need both formulas? Yes. Deciding which one is more helpful depends on the context:

Take bonds, for example. Bonds typically are claims to a sequence of nominal payments over a period of years. For example, a 10-year bond may promise $50 each year for 10 years, plus a final payment of $1,000 in the last year. So, when we look at the pricing of bonds in Chapter 15, we shall rely on equation (14.5) (which is expressed in terms of dollar payments) rather than on equation (14.7) (which is expressed in real terms).

But, sometimes, we have a better sense of future expected real values than of future expected dollar values. You may have little idea of what your dollar income will be in 20 years: Its value depends very much on what happens to inflation between now and then. But you may be confident that your nominal income will increase at least as much as inflation—equivalently, that your real income will not decrease. In this case, using equation (14.5), which requires you to form expectations of future dollar income, may be difficult; using equation (14.7), which requires you to form expectations of future real income, will be easier. For that reason, when we discuss consumption and investment decisions in Chapter 16, we shall rely on equation (14.7) rather than equation (14.5).

14-3 Nominal and Real Interest Rates, and the *IS-LM* Model

We shall spend the next three chapters using the tools we have just developed. In the rest of this chapter we take a first step, introducing the distinction between real and nominal interest rates in the *IS-LM* model, and then exploring the relation between money growth, inflation, and real and nominal interest rates.

In the *IS-LM* model we developed in the core (Chapter 5), the interest rate entered in two places: It affected investment in the *IS* relation, and affected the choice between money and bonds in the *LM* relation. Which interest rate—nominal or real—were we talking about in each case?

I shall ignore time subscripts here; they are not needed for the rest of the chapter.

- Take the *IS* relation first. Our discussion earlier in this chapter should make it clear that, in deciding how much investment to undertake, firms care about the *real interest rate*: Firms produce goods. They want to know how much they will have to repay, not in terms of dollars but in terms of goods. So what belongs in the *IS* relation is the real interest rate. Let r denote the real interest rate. The *IS* relation must therefore be modified to read

$$Y = C(Y - T) + I(Y, r) + G \qquad (14.8)$$

For the time being, we shall focus only on the effect of the interest rate on investment. In Chapters 16 and 17, you will see how the real interest rate affects both investment and consumption decisions.

Investment spending, and thus the demand for goods, depends on the *real* interest rate (not the nominal interest rate, as we assumed until now).

- Now turn to the *LM* relation. In deriving the *LM* relation, we argued that the demand for money depends on the interest rate. Were we referring to the nominal interest rate or the real interest rate?

The answer is the *nominal interest rate.* Remember why the interest rate affects the demand for money. When thinking about whether to hold money or bonds, people take into account the opportunity cost of holding money rather than bonds—the opportunity cost is what they give up by holding money rather than bonds. Money pays a zero nominal interest rate. Bonds pay a nominal interest rate of i. Hence, the opportunity cost of holding money is equal to the difference between the interest rate from holding bonds minus the interest from holding money, so $i - 0 = i$, which is just the nominal interest rate. Therefore, the *LM* relation is still given by

$$\frac{M}{P} = YL(i)$$

Collecting this equation, equation (14.8), and the relation between the real interest rate and the nominal interest rate, the extended *IS-LM* model is given by

$$\begin{array}{rll} IS & Y & = C(Y - T) + I(Y, r) + G \\ LM & M/P & = YL(i) \\ \text{Real interest rate} & r & \approx i - \pi^e \end{array}$$

Note an immediate implication of these three equations:

- The interest rate directly affected by monetary policy (the interest rate that enters the *LM* equation) is the nominal interest rate.
- The interest rate that affects spending and output (the rate that enters the *IS* relation) is the real interest rate.
- So, the effects of monetary policy on output depend, therefore, on how movements in the nominal interest rate translate into movements in the real interest rate. To further explore this question, the next section looks at the effects of an increase in money growth on the nominal interest rate and the real interest rate, both in the short run and in the medium run.

◀ **Interest rate in the *LM* relation: nominal interest rate, *i***

◀ **Interest rate in the *IS* relation: real interest rate, *r***

14-4 Money Growth, Inflation, and Nominal and Real Interest Rates

"The Fed's decision to allow for higher money growth is the main factor behind the decline in interest rates in the last six months." (imaginary quote, circa 1991)

"The nomination to the Board of the Federal Reserve of two left-leaning economists, both perceived to be soft on inflation, has led financial markets to worry about higher money growth, higher inflation, and higher interest rates in the future." (imaginary quote, circa May 1994)

These two quotes are made up, but they are composites of what was written at the time. Which one is right? Does higher money growth lead to lower interest rates, or does higher money growth lead to higher interest rates? The answer: Both! There are two keys to the answer. One, the distinction we just introduced between the real and the nominal interest rate. The other, the distinction we developed in the core between the short run and the medium run. As you shall see, the full answer is:

- Higher money growth leads to lower nominal interest rates in the short run, but to higher nominal interest rates in the medium run.
- Higher money growth leads to lower real interest rates in the short run, but has no effect on real interest rates in the medium run.

The purpose of this section is to develop this answer, and draw its implications.

Revisiting the *IS-LM* Model

We have derived three equations—the *IS* relation, the *LM* relation, and the relation between the real and the nominal interest rate. It will be more convenient to reduce them to two equations. To do so, replace the real interest rate in the *IS* relation by the nominal interest rate minus expected inflation. This gives

$$\begin{aligned} IS\text{:} \quad Y &= C(Y - T) + I(Y, i - \pi^e) + G \\ LM\text{:} \quad M/P &= Y L(i) \end{aligned}$$

These two equations are the same as in Chapter 5, but with just one difference: Investment spending in the *IS* relation depends on the real interest rate, which is equal to the nominal interest rate minus expected inflation.

The associated *IS* and *LM* curves are drawn in Figure 14-4, for given values of *P*, *M*, *G*, and *T*, and for a given expected rate of inflation, π^e.

If $r = i - \pi^e$, then $\Delta r = \Delta i - \Delta\pi^e$. If π^e is constant, $\Delta\pi^e = 0$, so $\Delta r = \Delta i$.

- For a given expected rate of inflation (π^e), the nominal interest rate and the real interest rate move together. Hence, a decrease in the nominal interest rate implies an equal decrease in the real interest rate, leading to an increase in spending and in output: The *IS* curve is downward sloping.
- The *LM* curve is upward sloping: Given the money stock, an increase in output, which leads to an increase in the demand for money, requires an increase in the nominal interest rate.
- The equilibrium is at the intersection of the *IS* curve and the *LM* curve, at point *A*, with output level, Y_A, nominal interest rate, i_A. Given the nominal interest rate, i_A, the real interest rate, r_A, is given by $r_A = i_A - \pi^e$.

Nominal and Real Interest Rates in the Short Run

Assume the economy is initially at the natural rate of output, so $Y_A = Y_n$. Now suppose the central bank increases the rate of growth of money. What happens to output, to the nominal interest rate, and to the real interest rate in the short run?

Figure 14-4

Equilibrium Output and Interest Rates

The equilibrium level of output and the equilibrium nominal interest rate are given by the intersection of the *IS* curve and the *LM* curve. The real interest rate equals the nominal interest rate minus expected inflation.

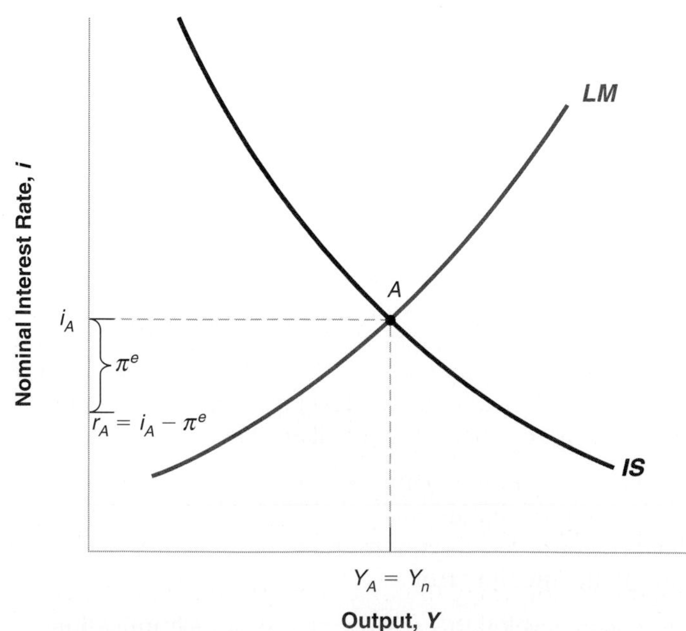

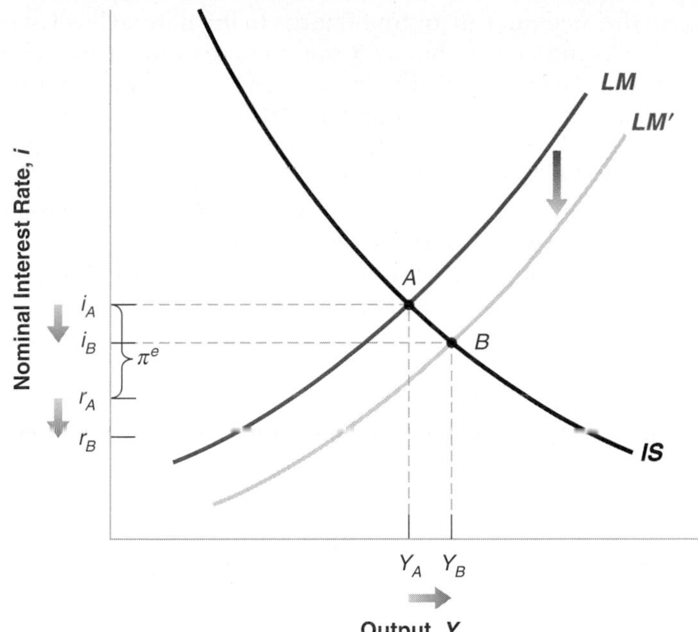

Figure 14-5

The Short-Run Effects of an Increase in Money Growth

An increase in money growth increases the real money stock in the short run. This increase in real money leads to an increase in output and a decrease in both the nominal and the real interest rate.

One of the lessons from our analysis of monetary policy in the core is that, in the short run, the faster increase in nominal money will not be matched by an equal increase in the price level. In other words, the higher rate of growth of nominal money will lead, in the short run, to an increase in the real money stock (M/P). This is all we need to know for our purposes. What happens to output and to interest rates in the short run is shown in Figure 14-5.

The increase in the real money stock leads to a shift in the *LM* curve down, from *LM* to *LM'*: For a given level of output, the increase in the real money stock leads to a decrease in the nominal interest rate. If we assume—as seems reasonable—that people and firms do not revise their expectations of inflation immediately, the *IS* curve does not shift: Given expected inflation, a given nominal interest rate corresponds to the same real interest rate and to the same level of spending and output. The economy moves down the *IS* curve; the equilibrium moves from *A* to *B*. Output is higher. The nominal interest rate is lower, and given expected inflation, so is the real interest rate.

In the short run, when the rate of money growth increases, M/P increases. Both i and r decrease, and Y increases.

To summarize: In the short run, the increase in nominal money growth leads to an increase in the real money stock.

This increase in real money leads to a decrease in both the nominal and the real interest rate, and to an increase in output.

Go back to our first quote: The goal of the Fed, circa 1991, was precisely to achieve this outcome. Worried that the recession might get worse, the Fed increased money growth to decrease the real interest rate and increase output.

Nominal and Real Interest Rates in the Medium Run

Turn now to the medium run. Suppose that the central bank increases the rate of money growth permanently. What will happen to output and nominal and real interest rates in the medium run?

To answer that question, we rely on two of the central propositions we derived in the core:

- In the medium run, output returns to the natural level of output.

  As you saw in Chapter 6, output returns to the natural level of output because, in the medium run, the unemployment rate must return to the natural rate of unemployment. The natural level of output is simply the level of output associated with the natural rate of unemployment.

  While we spent Chapters 10 to 13 looking at growth of output over time, we shall, for simplicity, ignore output growth here. So we shall assume that Y_n, the natural level of output, is constant over time.

In the medium run: $Y = Y_n$. ▶

- In the medium run, the rate of inflation is equal to the rate of money growth minus the rate of growth of output.

  We derived this conclusion in Chapter 9. The intuition for it is simple: A growing level of output implies a growing level of transactions and thus a growing demand for real money. If output is growing at 3% per year, the real money stock must also grow at 3% per year. If the nominal money stock grows at a rate different from 3% per year, the difference must show up in inflation (or deflation). For example, if nominal money growth is 10% per year, then inflation must be equal to 7% per year.

  If, as we assume here, output growth is equal to zero, this proposition takes an even simpler form: In the medium run, the rate of inflation is equal to the rate of nominal money growth.

In the medium run (if $g_y = 0$): $\pi = g_m$. ▶

The implications of these two propositions for the behavior of the real interest rate and the nominal interest rate in the medium run are then straightforward:

- Take the real interest rate first. For convenience, let me rewrite the *IS* equation:

$$Y = C(Y - T) + I(Y, r) + G$$

ACTIVE GRAPH

  One way of thinking about the *IS* relation is that it tells us, for given values of G and T, what real interest rate, r, is needed to sustain a given level of spending, and so a given level of output, Y. If, for example, output is equal to the natural level of output, Y_n, then, for given values of G and T, the real interest rate must be such that

$$Y_n = C(Y_n - T) + I(Y_n, r) + G$$

  By analogy with our use of the word *natural* to denote the level of output in the medium run, let us call this value of the real interest rate the *natural real interest rate*, and denote it by r_n. Then, our earlier proposition that, in the medium run, output returns to its natural level, Y_n, has a direct implication: For given G and T, in the medium run, the real interest rate returns to the natural interest rate, r_n. In other words, in the medium run, both output and the real interest rate are unaffected by the rate of money growth.

- Turn to the nominal interest rate. Recall the relation between the nominal interest rate and the real interest rate:

$$i = r + \pi^e$$

  You have just seen that in the medium run, the real interest rate equals the natural interest rate, r_n. So,

$$i = r_n + \pi^e$$

  In the medium run, expected inflation is equal to actual inflation (people cannot have incorrect expectations of inflation forever). So,

$$i = r_n + \pi$$

  In the medium run, inflation is equal to money growth (recall we are assuming that the rate of growth of output equals zero), so,

$$i = r_n + g_m$$

In words: In the medium run, the nominal interest rate is equal to the natural real interest rate plus the rate of money growth. So an increase in money growth leads to an equal increase in the nominal interest rate.

To summarize: In the medium run, money growth does not affect the real interest rate, but affects inflation and the nominal interest rate one-for-one.

A permanent increase in nominal money growth of, say, 10% is eventually reflected in a 10% increase in the inflation rate, and a 10% increase in the nominal interest rate—leaving the real interest rate unchanged. The result that, in the medium run, the nominal interest rate increases one for one with inflation is known as the **Fisher effect**, or the **Fisher hypothesis**, after Irving Fisher, an economist at Yale University who first stated it and its logic at the beginning of the twentieth century.

Irving Fisher, *The Rate of Interest* (New York: Macmillan, 1906).

This result underlies the second quote we saw at the beginning of the section: If financial investors were worried that the appointment of new board members at the Fed might lead to higher money growth, they were right to expect higher nominal interest rates in the future.

In this case, their fears turned out to be unfounded. The Fed remained committed to low inflation throughout the 1990s.

From the Short to the Medium Run

We have now seen how to reconcile the two quotes at the beginning of the section: An increase in money growth (a monetary expansion) is likely to lead to *a decrease* in nominal interest rates in the short run, but to *an increase* in nominal interest rates in the medium run.

What happens between the short run and the medium run? A full characterization of the movements of the real interest rate and the nominal interest rate over time would take us beyond what we can do here. But the basic features of the adjustment process are easy to describe.

In the short run, the real interest rate and the nominal interest rate both go down. Why don't they stay down forever? Because there are many steps, let me first state the answer in short: Because low interest rates lead to high output, which eventually leads to high inflation; high inflation leads in turn to a decrease in the real money stock, and to an increase in interest rates. Now, the answer step by step:

- As long as the real interest rate is below the natural real interest rate—that is, the value corresponding to the natural level of output—output is higher than the natural level. Equivalently, unemployment is below the natural rate. From the Phillips curve relation, we know that as long as unemployment is below the natural rate, inflation increases.
- As inflation increases, it eventually becomes higher than nominal money growth, leading to negative real money growth. When real money growth turns negative, the nominal interest rate starts increasing. And, given expected inflation, so does the real interest rate.
- In the medium run, the real interest rate increases back to its initial value. Output is then back to the natural level of output, unemployment is back to the natural rate of unemployment, and inflation is no longer changing. As the real interest rate converges back to its initial value, the nominal interest rate converges to a new higher value, equal to the real interest rate plus the new, higher, rate of nominal money growth.

In the short run: $i\downarrow\ r\downarrow$

$r < r_n \Rightarrow Y > Y_n$

$Y > Y_n \Rightarrow u < u_n$

$u < u_n \Rightarrow \pi\uparrow$

Over time:

Eventually: $\pi > g'_m$

$\pi > g'_m \Rightarrow g'_m - \pi < 0$

$g'_m - \pi < 0 \Rightarrow i\uparrow$

In the medium run:

$r = r_n$

$Y = Y_n$

$u = u_n$

$\pi = g_m$

$i = r_n + g_m$

Figure 14-6 summarizes these results by showing the adjustment over time of the real interest rate and the nominal interest rate to an increase in nominal money growth from, say, 0 to 10%, starting at time t. Before time t, both interest rates are constant and equal to each other. The real interest rate is equal to r_n. The nominal interest rate is also equal to r_n (as inflation and expected inflation are equal to zero.)

Figure 14-6

The Adjustment of the Real and the Nominal Interest Rates to an Increase in Money Growth

An increase in money growth leads initially to a decrease in both the real and the nominal interest rate. Over time, the real interest rate returns to its initial value. The nominal interest rate converges to a new higher value, equal to the initial value plus the increase in money growth.

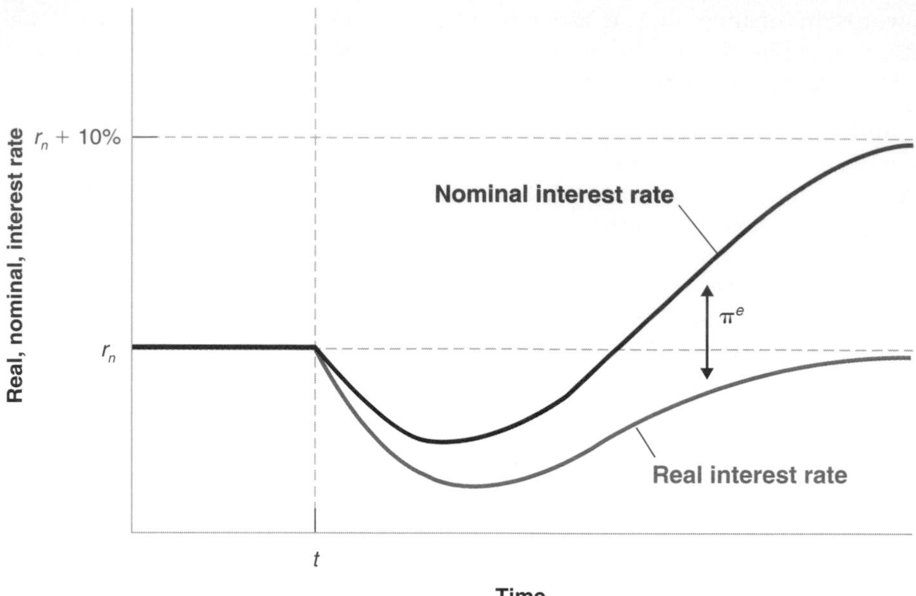

At time t, the rate of money growth increases from 0 to 10%. The increase in the rate of nominal money growth leads, for some time, to an increase in real money, and to a decrease in the nominal interest rate. As expected inflation increases, the decrease in the real interest rate is larger than the decrease of the nominal interest rate.

Eventually, the nominal interest rate and the real interest rate start increasing. In the medium run, the real interest rate returns to its initial value. Inflation and expected inflation converge to the new rate of money growth, thus 10%. The nominal interest rate converges to a value equal to the real interest rate plus 10%.

Evidence on the Fisher Hypothesis

There is plenty of evidence that a monetary expansion decreases nominal interest rates in the short run (see, for example, Section 5-5.) But how much evidence is there for the Fisher hypothesis, the proposition that in the medium run, increases in inflation lead to one-for-one increases in nominal interest rates?

Economists have tried to answer this question by looking at two types of evidence. One is the relation between nominal interest rates and inflation *across countries*. Because the relation holds only in the medium run, we should not expect inflation and nominal interest rates to be close to each other in any one country at any one time, but the relation should hold on average. This approach is explored further in the Focus box "Nominal Interest Rates and Inflation Across Latin America in the Early 1990s," which finds substantial support for the Fisher hypothesis.

The other type of evidence is the relation between the nominal interest rate and inflation over time for one country. Again, the Fisher hypothesis does not imply that the two should move together from year to year. But it does suggest that the long swings in inflation should eventually be reflected in similar swings in the nominal interest rate. To see evidence of these long swings, we need to look at as long a period of time as we can. Figure 14-7 looks at the nominal interest rate and inflation in the United States since 1927. The nominal interest rate is the three-month Treasury bill rate, and inflation is the rate of change of the CPI.

Nominal Interest Rates and Inflation Across Latin America in the Early 1990s

Figure 1 plots nominal interest rate–inflation pairs for eight Latin American countries (Argentina, Bolivia, Chile, Ecuador, Mexico, Peru, Uruguay, and Venezuela) for 1992 and 1993. Because the Brazilian numbers would dwarf those from other countries, they are not included in the figure. (In 1992, Brazil's inflation rate was 1,008% and its nominal interest rate was 1,560%. In 1993, inflation was 2,140% and the nominal interest rate was 3,240%.) The numbers for inflation refer to the rate of change of the consumer price index (CPI). The numbers for nominal interest rates refer to the "lending rate." The exact definition of this term varies with each country, but you can think of it as corresponding to the prime interest rate in the United States—the rate charged to borrowers with the best credit rating.

Note the wide range of inflation rates, from 10 to about 100%. This is precisely why I have chosen to present numbers from Latin America in the early 1990s. With this much variation in inflation, we can learn a lot about the relation between nominal interest rates and inflation. And the figure indeed shows a clear relation between inflation and nominal interest rates. The line drawn in the figure plots what the nominal interest rate should be under the Fisher hypothesis, assuming an underlying real interest rate of 5%, so that $i = 5\% + \pi$. The slope of the line is one: Under the Fisher hypothesis, a 1% increase in inflation should be reflected in a 1% increase in the nominal interest rate.

As you can see, the line fits well; roughly half of the points are above the line, the other half below. The Fisher hypothesis appears roughly consistent with the cross-country evidence from Latin America in the early 1990s.

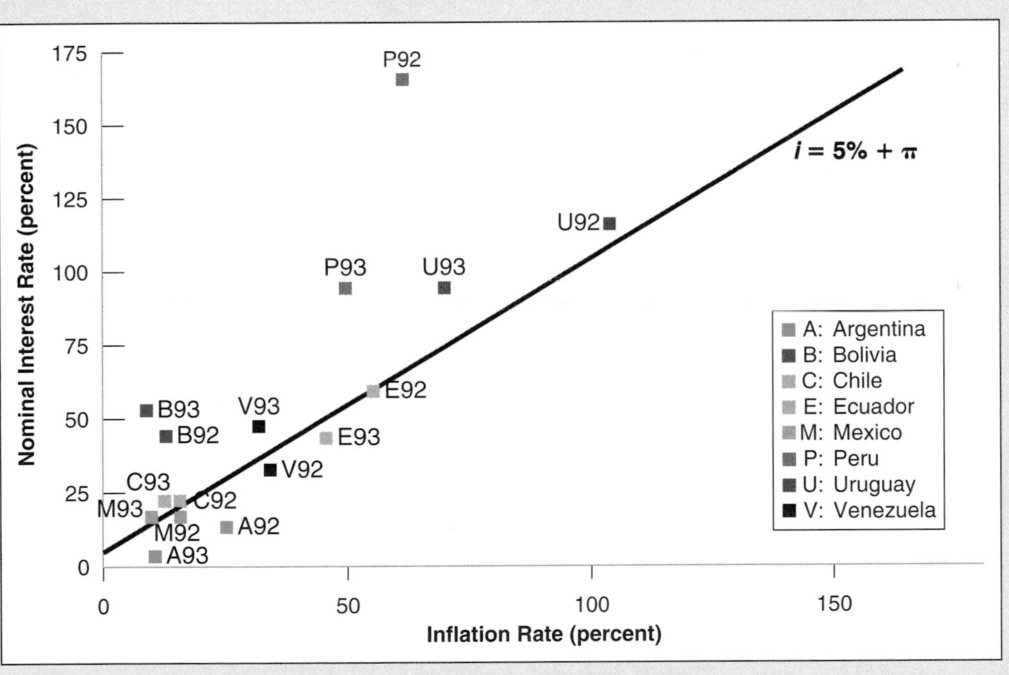

Figure 1 *Nominal Interest Rates and Inflation: Latin America, 1992–1993.*

Brazil is not shown; its four-digit nominal interest rate and inflation rate would be way off the scale.

FOCUS

Figure 14-7 has at least three interesting features:

- The steady increase in inflation from the early 1960s to the early 1980s was associated with a roughly parallel increase in the nominal interest rate. The decrease in inflation since the mid-1980s has been associated with a decrease in the nominal interest rate. These evolutions support the Fisher hypothesis.

Figure 14-7

The Three-Month Treasury Bill Rate and Inflation, 1927–2000

The increase in inflation from the early 1960s to the early 1980s was associated with an increase in the nominal interest rate. The decrease in inflation since the mid-1980s has been associated with a decrease in the nominal interest rate.

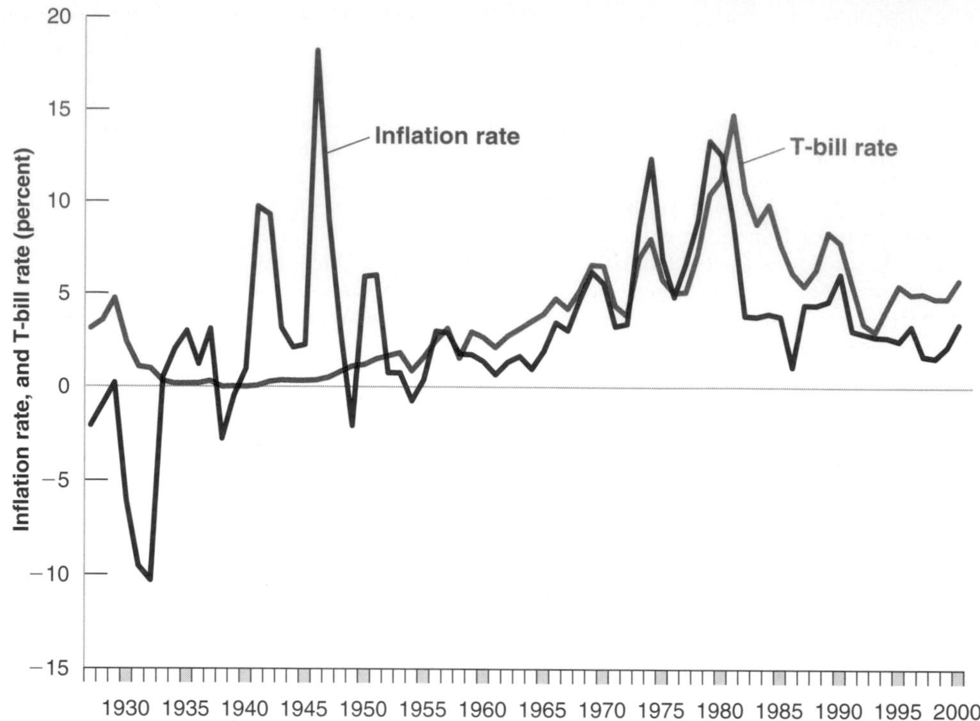

- Evidence of the short-run effects that we discussed earlier is also easy to see. The nominal interest rate lagged behind the increase in inflation in the 1970s, while the disinflation of the early 1980s was associated with an initial *increase* in the nominal interest rate, followed by a much slower decline in the nominal interest rate than in inflation.
- The other episode of inflation, during and after World War II, underlines the importance of the "medium run" qualifier in the Fisher hypothesis. During that period, inflation was high but short-lived. And it was gone before it had time to be reflected in a higher nominal interest rate. The nominal interest rate remained very low throughout the 1940s.

This was the result of a deliberate policy by the Fed to maintain a very low nominal interest rate to reduce interest payments on the large government debt created during World War II. ▶

More careful studies confirm our basic conclusion. The Fisher hypothesis that, in the medium run, increases in inflation are reflected in a higher nominal interest rate appears to fit the data quite well. But the adjustment takes a long time. The data confirm the conclusion reached by Milton Friedman, which we quoted in a Focus box in Chapter 8, that it typically takes a "couple of decades" for nominal interest rates to reflect the higher inflation rate.

Summary

- The nominal interest rate tells you how many dollars you need to repay in the future in exchange for one dollar today.
- The real interest rate tells you how many goods you need to repay in the future in exchange for one good today.
- The real interest rate is approximately equal to the nominal interest rate minus expected inflation.
- The expected present discounted value of a sequence of payments equals the value today of the expected sequence of payments. It depends positively on current

and future expected payments. It depends negatively on current and future expected interest rates.

- In discounting a sequence of current and expected future nominal payments, one should use current and expected future nominal interest rates. In discounting a sequence of current and expected future real payments, one should use current and expected future real interest rates.
- Investment decisions depend on the real interest rate. The choice between money and bonds depends on the nominal interest rate. Thus, the real interest rate enters the *IS* relation, while the nominal interest rate enters the *LM* relation.
- In the short run, an increase in money growth typically leads to a decrease of both the nominal interest rate and the real interest rate.

  In the medium run, an increase in money growth has no effect on the real interest rate, and increases the nominal interest rate one for one.
- The proposition that in the medium run, changes in inflation are reflected one for one in changes in the nominal interest rate is known as the Fisher effect or the Fisher hypothesis. The empirical evidence suggests that while it takes a long time, changes in inflation are eventually reflected in changes in the nominal interest rate.

Key Terms

- nominal interest rate, 290
- real interest rate, 290
- expected present discounted value, 293
- discount factor, 294
- discount rate, 294
- present discounted value, 295
- present value, 295
- Fisher effect, Fisher hypothesis, 303

Questions and Problems

Quick Check

1. *Using the information in this chapter, label each of the following statements* true, false, *or* uncertain. *Explain briefly.*
   a. As long as inflation remains roughly constant, the movements in the real interest rate are roughly equal to the movements in the nominal interest rate.
   b. If inflation turns out to be higher than expected then the realized real cost of borrowing turns out to be lower than the real interest rate.
   c. Looking across countries, the real interest rate is likely to vary much less than the nominal interest rate.
   d. The real interest rate is equal to the nominal interest rate divided by the price level.
   e. In the medium run, the real interest rate is not affected by money growth.
   f. The Fisher effect states that in the medium run, the nominal interest rate is not affected by money growth.
   g. The experience of Latin American countries in the early 1990s supports the Fisher hypothesis.
   h. The value today of a nominal payment in the future cannot be greater than the nominal payment itself.
   i. The real value today of a real payment in the future cannot be greater than the real payment itself.
2. *For which of the following problems would you want to use real payments and real interest rates, or nominal payments and nominal interest rates, to compute the expected present discounted value? In each case, explain why.*
   a. Estimating the present discounted value of the profits from an investment in a new machine.
   b. Estimating the present value of a 20-year U.S. government bond.
   c. Deciding whether to lease or buy a car.
3. *For each of the following, compute the real interest rate using the exact formula and the approximation formula:*
   a. $i = 4\%$; $\pi^e = 2\%$
   b. $i = 15\%$; $\pi^e = 11\%$
   c. $i = 54\%$; $\pi^e = 46\%$
4. *Nominal and real interest rates around the world*
   a. Can the nominal interest rate ever be negative? Explain.
   b. Can the real interest rate ever be negative? Under what circumstances? If so, why not just hold cash instead?
   c. What are the effects of a negative real interest rate on borrowing and lending?
   d. Find a recent issue of *The Economist* and look at the tables in the back (Economic Indicators and Financial Indicators). Use the three-month money market rate as the nominal interest rate and the most recent three-month rate of change in consumer prices as the expected rate of inflation (both are in annual terms). Which countries have the lowest nominal interest rates? Which countries have the lowest real interest rates? Are these real interest rates close to being negative?
5. *You want to save $2,000 today for retirement in 40 years. You have to choose between two plans:*

   i. *Pay no taxes today, put the money in an interest-yielding account, and pay taxes equal to 25% of the total amount withdrawn at retirement. (In the United States, such an account is known as a regular individual retirement account, or IRA.)*

ii. *Pay taxes equivalent to 20% of the investment amount today, put the remainder in an interest-yielding account, and pay no taxes when you withdraw your funds at retirement. (In the United States, this is known as a Roth IRA.)*

a. What is the expected present discounted value of each of these plans if the interest rate is 1%? 10%?
b. Which plan would you pick in each case?

6. *The present value of an infinite stream of dollar payments of \$z (that starts next year) is \$z/i when the nominal interest rate, i, is constant. This formula gives the price of a consol—a bond paying a fixed nominal payment each year, forever. It is also a good approximation for the present discounted value of a stream of constant payments over long but not infinite periods, as long as i is constant. Let's examine how close the approximation is. Suppose that i = 10%.*

a. Let $\$z = 100$. What is the present value of the consol?
b. What is the expected present discounted value for a bond that pays \$*z* over the next 10 years? 20 years? 30 years? 60 years? (*Hint*: Use the formula from Chapter 14 but remember to adjust for the first payment.)
c. Repeat the exercise for $i = 2\%$ and $i = 5\%$.

7. *The Fisher hypothesis*

a. What is the Fisher hypothesis?
b. Does the experience of Latin American countries in the 1990s support or refute the Fisher hypothesis? Explain.
c. Look at the figure in the Focus box on Latin America. Note that the line drawn through the scatter of points does not go through the origin. Does the "Fisher effect" suggest that it should go through the origin? Explain.
d. "If the Fisher hypothesis is true, then changes in the growth rate of the money stock translate one-for-one into changes in *i*, and the real interest rate is left unchanged. Thus, there is no room for monetary policy to affect real economic activity." Discuss.

Dig Deeper

8. *When looking at the short run in Section 14-4, we showed how an increase in nominal money growth led to higher output, a lower nominal interest rate, and a lower real interest rate.*

The analysis in the text (as summarized in Figure 14-5) assumed that expected inflation, π^e, did not change. Let's now relax this assumption, and assume that expected inflation increases by $\Delta\pi^e$.

a. Show the effect on the *IS* curve. Explain in words.
b. Show the effect on the *LM* curve. Explain in words.
c. Show the effect on output and on the nominal interest rate. Could the nominal interest rate end up higher—not lower—than before the change in money growth? Why?
d. Even if what happens to the nominal interest rate is ambiguous, can you tell what happens to the real interest rate? (*Hint*: What happens to output relative to Figure 14-5? What does this imply for what happens to the real interest rate?)

We invite you to visit the Blanchard page on the Prentice Hall Web site at:
www.prenhall.com/blanchard
for this chapter's World Wide Web exercises

Appendix: Deriving the Expected Present Discounted Value Using Real or Nominal Interest Rates

This appendix shows that the two ways of expressing present discounted values, equations (14.5) and (14.7), are equivalent.

Equation (14.5) gives the present value as the sum of current and future expected *nominal payments*, discounted using current and future expected *nominal interest rates*

$$\$V_t = \$z_t + \frac{1}{1+i_t}\$z_{t+1} + \frac{1}{(1+i_t)(1+i^e_{t+1})}\$z_{t+2} + \cdots \quad (14.5)$$

Equation (14.7) gives the present value as the sum of current and future expected *real payments*, discounted using current and future expected *real interest rates*

$$V_t = z_t + \frac{1}{1+r_t}z^e_{t+1} + \frac{1}{(1+r_t)(1+r^e_{t+1})}z^e_{t+2} + \cdots \quad (14.7)$$

Divide both sides of equation (14.5) by the current price level, P_t. So:

$$\frac{\$V_t}{P_t} = \frac{\$z_t}{P_t} + \frac{1}{1+i_t}\frac{\$z^e_{t+1}}{P_t} + \frac{1}{(1+i_t)(1+i^e_{t+1})}\frac{\$z^e_{t+2}}{P_t} + \cdots \quad (14.A1)$$

Let's look at each term on the right side of equation (14.A1), and show that it is equal to the corresponding term in equation (14.7):

- Take the first term, $\$z_t/P_t$. Note $\$z_t/P_t = \$z_t$, the real value of the current payment. So, this term is the same as the first term on the right of equation (14.7).
- Take the second term:

$$\frac{1}{(1+i_t)} \frac{\$z^e_{t+1}}{P_t}$$

Multiply the numerator and the denominator by P^e_{t+1}, the price level expected for next year, to get

$$\frac{1}{(1+i_t)} \frac{P^e_{t+1}}{P_t} \frac{\$z^e_{t+1}}{P^e_{t+1}}$$

Note that the fraction on the right, $\$z^e_{t+1}/P^e_{t+1}$, is equal to z^e_{t+1}, the expected real payment at time $t+1$. Note that the fraction in the middle, P^e_{t+1}/P_t, can be rewritten as $1 + [(P^e_{t+1} - P_t)/P_t]$, thus using the definition of expected inflation, as $(1 + \pi^e_t)$.

Using these two results, rewrite the second term as

$$\frac{(1+\pi^e_t)}{(1+i_t)} z^e_{t+1}$$

Recall the relation between the real interest rate, the nominal interest rate, and expected inflation, in equation (14.3) $[(1 + r_t) = (1 + i_t)/(1 + \pi^e_t)]$. Using this relation in the previous equation gives

$$\frac{1}{(1+r_t)} z^e_{t+1}$$

This term is the same as the second term on the right side of equation (14.7).
- The same method can be used to rewrite the other terms; make sure that you can derive the next one.

We have shown that the right side of equations (14.7) and (14.A1) are equal to each other. It follows that the terms on the left side are equal, so,

$$V_t = \frac{\$V_t}{P_t}$$

This says:

The present value of current and future expected *real payments,* discounted using current and future expected *real interest rates* (the term on the left side) is equal to:

The present value of current and future expected *nominal payments,* discounted using current and future expected *nominal interest rates,* divided by the current price level (the term on the right side).

Financial Markets and Expectations

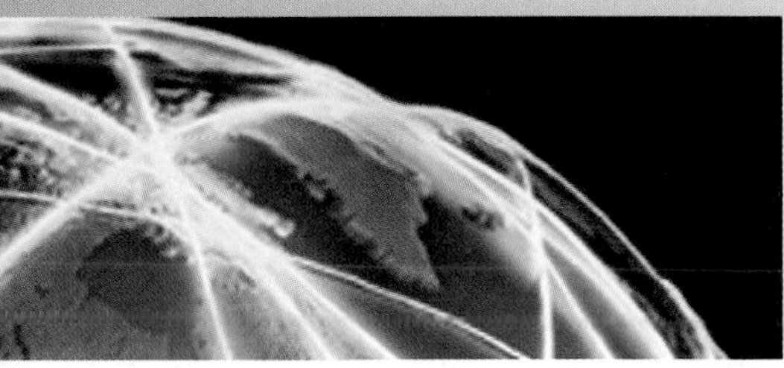

CHAPTER 15

In our first pass at financial markets in the core (Chapter 4), we assumed there were only two assets: money and one type of bond—a one-year bond. We now look at an economy with a richer and more realistic menu of nonmoney assets: short-term bonds, long-term bonds, and stocks.

Our focus throughout this chapter is on the role of expectations in the determination of bond and stock prices.

- Section 15-1 looks at the determination of bond prices and bond yields. It shows how bond prices and yields depend on current and expected future short-term interest rates. It then shows how we can use the yield curve to learn about the expected course of future short-term interest rates.
- Section 15-2 looks at the determination of stock prices. It shows how stock prices depend on current and expected future profits, as well as on current and expected future interest rates. It then discusses the effects of movements in economic activity on stock prices.
- Section 15-3 discusses fads and bubbles in the stock market—episodes when stock prices appear to move for reasons unrelated to either profits or interest rates. ■

15-1 Bond Prices and Bond Yields

Bonds differ in two basic dimensions:

1. **Default risk**, the risk that the issuer of the bond (it could be a government, or a company) will not pay back the full amount promised by the bond.

2. **Maturity**, the length of time over which the bond promises to make payments to the holder of the bond. A bond that promises to make one payment of $1,000 in six months has a maturity of six months; a bond that promises $100 per year for the next 20 years and a final payment of $1,000 at the end of those 20 years has a maturity of 20 years. Maturity is the more important dimension for our purposes and we shall focus on it here.

Do not worry: I am just introducing the terms here. They will be defined and explained in this section. ▶

Bonds of different maturities each have a price and an associated interest rate called the *yield to maturity*, or simply the *yield*. Yields on bonds with a short maturity, typically a year or less, are called *short-term interest rates*. Yields on bonds with a longer maturity are called *long-term interest rates*.

Term structure ⇔ Yield curve ▶

On any given day, we observe the yields on bonds of different maturities, and so we can trace graphically how the yield depends on the maturity of a bond. This relation between maturity and yield is called the **yield curve**, or the **term structure of interest rates** (the word *term* is synonymous with maturity). Figure 15-1 gives, for example, the term structure on U.S. government bonds on November 1, 2000, and the term structure on U.S. government bonds on June 1, 2001. The choice of the two dates is not accidental; why I chose them will become clear shortly.

To find out what the term structure of interest rates is at the time you read this chapter, look for "Treasury Bonds, Notes and Bills" in the "Money & Investing" section of the *Wall Street Journal*. ▶

Note how, on November 1, 2000, the yield curve is slightly downward sloping, declining from a three-month interest rate of 6.2% to a 30-year interest rate of 5.8%. In other words, long-term interest rates are slightly lower than short-term interest rates. Note how, seven months later, on June 1, 2001, the yield curve is sharply upward sloping, increasing from a three-month interest rate of 3.5% to a 30-year interest rate of 5.7%. In other words, long-term interest rates are now much higher than short-term interest rates.

Why is the yield curve downward sloping in November 2000, but upward sloping in June 2001? Put another way, why are long-term interest rates slightly lower than short-term interest rates in November 2000, but higher than short-term interest rates in June 2001? What were financial market participants thinking at each date? To answer these questions, and more generally to think about the determination of the

Figure 15-1

U.S. Yield Curves: November 1, 2000 and June 1, 2001

The yield curve, which was slightly downward sloping in November 2000, was sharply upward sloping seven months later.

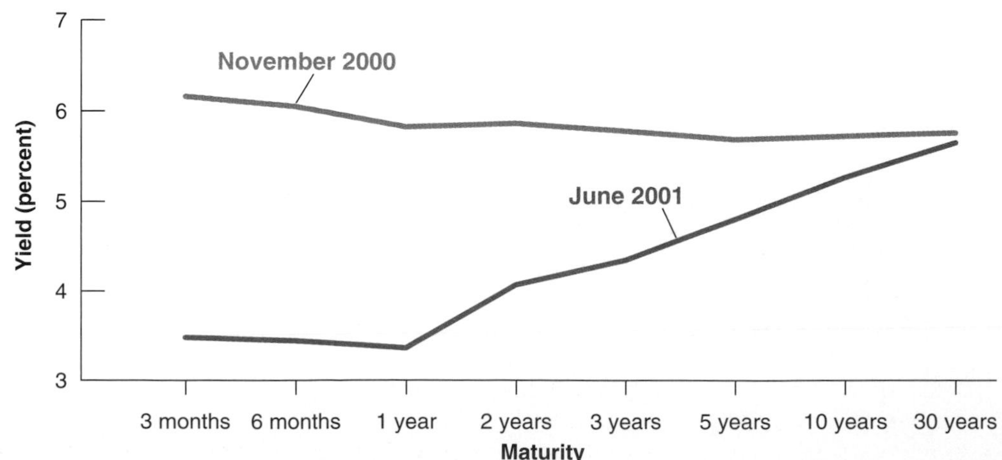

The Vocabulary of Bond Markets

Understanding the basic vocabulary of financial markets will help make them less mysterious. Here is a basic vocabulary review.

- Bonds are issued by governments or by firms. If issued by the government or government agencies, the bonds are called **government bonds**. If issued by firms, they are called **corporate bonds**.
- In the United States, bonds are rated for their default risk (the risk that they will not be repaid) by two private firms, the Standard & Poor's Corporation (S&P) and Moody's Investors Service. Moody's **bond ratings** range from Aaa for bonds with nearly no risk of default, such as U.S. government bonds, to C for bonds where the default risk is high. A lower rating typically implies that the bond has to pay a higher interest rate, or else investors will not buy it. The difference between the interest rate paid on a given bond and the interest rate paid on the bond with the highest (best) rating is called the **risk premium** associated with the bond. Bonds with high default risk are sometimes called **junk bonds**.
- Bonds that promise a single payment at maturity are called **discount bonds**. The single payment is called the **face value** of the bond.
- Bonds that promise multiple payments before maturity and one payment at maturity are called **coupon bonds**. The payments before maturity are called **coupon payments**. The final payment is called the face value of the bond. The ratio of coupon payments to the face value is called the **coupon rate**. The **current yield** is the ratio of the coupon payment to the price of the bond.

  For example, a bond with coupon payments of \$5 each year, a face value of \$100, and a price of \$80 has a coupon rate of 5% and a current yield of $5/80 = 0.0625 = 6.25\%$. From an economic viewpoint, neither the coupon rate nor the current yield are interesting measures. The correct measure of the interest rate on a bond is its yield to maturity, or simply yield; you can think of it as roughly the average interest rate paid by the bond over its **life** (the life of a bond is the amount of time left until the bond matures). We shall define the yield to maturity more precisely later in the chapter.
- U.S. government bonds range in maturity from a few days to 30 years. Bonds with a maturity of up to a year when they are issued are called **Treasury bills**, or **T-bills**. They are discount bonds, making only one payment at maturity. Bonds with a maturity of one to 10 years when they are issued are called **Treasury notes**. Bonds with a maturity of 10 or more years when they are issued are called **Treasury bonds**. Treasury notes and bonds are coupon bonds.
- Bonds are typically nominal bonds: They promise a sequence of fixed nominal payments—payments in terms of domestic currency. However, there are other types of bonds. Among them are **indexed bonds**, bonds that promise payments adjusted for inflation rather than fixed nominal payments. Instead of promising to pay, say, 100 dollars in a year, a one-year indexed bond promises to pay $100(1 + \pi)$ dollars, where π is the rate of inflation that will take place over the coming year. Because they protect bondholders against the risk of inflation, indexed bonds are popular in many countries. They play a particularly important role in the United Kingdom, where, over the last 20 years, people have increasingly used them to save for retirement. By holding long-term indexed bonds, people can make sure that the payments they receive when they retire will be protected from inflation. Indexed bonds (called inflation-indexed bonds) were introduced in the United States in 1997. They account only for a small proportion of U.S. government bonds at this point, but their role will surely increase in the future.

FOCUS

yield curve, and the relation between short-term interest rates and long-term interest rates, we proceed in two steps:

First, we derive *bond prices* for bonds of different maturities.

Second, we go from bond prices to *bond yields*, and examine the determinants of the yield curve, the determinants of the relation between long-term interest rates and short-term interest rates.

Bond Prices as Present Values

In much of the section, we shall look at just two types of bonds, a bond that promises one payment of \$100 in one year—a one-year bond, and a bond that promises one payment of \$100 in two years—a two-year bond. Once you understand how their

◄ Note that both bonds are *discount bonds* (see the Focus box).

prices and their yields are determined, it will be easy to generalize our results to bonds of any maturity. We shall do so later on.

Let's start by deriving the prices of the two bonds.

- Given that the one-year bond is a promise to pay \$100 next year, it follows from Section 14-2 that its price, call it $\$P_{1t}$, must be equal to the present value of a payment of \$100 next year. Let the current one-year nominal interest rate be i_{1t}. Note that I now denote the one-year interest rate in year t by i_{1t} rather than simply by i_t as I did in earlier chapters. This is to make it easier for you to remember that it is the *one-year* interest rate. So,

$$\$P_{1t} = \frac{\$100}{1 + i_{1t}} \tag{15.1}$$

  The price of the one-year bond varies inversely with the current one-year nominal interest rate.

- Given that the two-year bond is a promise to pay \$100 in two years, its price, call it P_{2t}, must be equal to the present value of \$100 two years from now:

$$\$P_{2t} = \frac{\$100}{(1 + i_{1t})(1 + i^e_{1t+1})} \tag{15.2}$$

  where i_{1t} denotes the one-year interest rate this year and i^e_{1t+1} denotes the one-year rate expected by financial markets for next year. The price of the two-year bond depends inversely on both the current one-year rate and the one-year rate expected for next year.

Arbitrage and Bond Prices

Before exploring further the implications of equations (15.1) and (15.2), let us look at an alternative derivation of equation (15.2). This alternative derivation will introduce you to the important concept of *arbitrage*.

Suppose you have the choice between holding one-year bonds or two-year bonds. What you care about is how much you will have one year from now. Which bonds should you hold?

- Suppose you hold one-year bonds. For every dollar you put in one-year bonds, you will get $(1 + i_{1t})$ dollars next year. This relation is represented in the first line of Figure 15-2.
- Suppose you hold two-year bonds. Because the price of a two-year bond is $\$P_{2t}$, every dollar you put in two-year bonds buys you $\$1/\$P_{2t}$ bonds today.

  When next year comes, the bond will have only one more year before maturity, and thus one year from today, the two-year bond will now be a one-year bond. Therefore the price at which you can expect to sell it next year is $\$P^e_{1t+1}$, which is the expected price of a one-year bond next year.

  So for every dollar you put in two-year bonds, you can expect to receive $\$1/\$P_{2t}$ times $\$P^e_{1t+1}$, or equivalently $\$P^e_{1t+1}/\$P_{2t}$ dollars next year. This is represented in the second line of Figure 15-2.

Figure 15-2

Returns from Holding One-Year and Two-Year Bonds for One Year

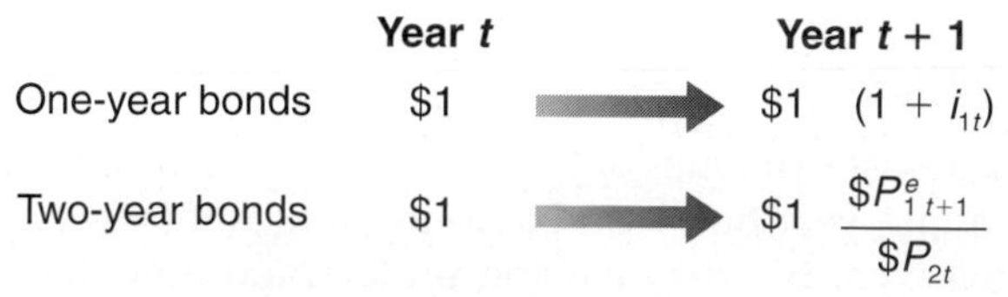

	Year t		Year $t + 1$
One-year bonds	\$1	→	\$1 $(1 + i_{1t})$
Two-year bonds	\$1	→	\$1 $\dfrac{\$P^e_{1t+1}}{\$P_{2t}}$

Which bonds should you hold? Suppose you, and other financial investors, care *only* about *expected return*. (This assumption is known as the **expectations hypothesis**. It is a strong simplification: You, and other financial investors, are likely to care not only about the expected return, but also about the risk associated with holding each bond. If you hold a one-year bond, you know with certainty what you will get next year. If you hold a two-year bond, the price at which you will sell it next year is uncertain; holding the two-year bond is risky. We leave this consideration aside here, but we briefly discuss it in the appendix to this chapter.)

Under the assumption that investors only care about expected return, it follows that the two bonds must offer the same expected one-year return. Suppose this condition was not satisfied. Suppose that, for example, the one-year return on one-year bonds was lower than the expected one-year return on two-year bonds. Nobody would want to hold the existing supply of one-year bonds, and the market for one-year bonds could not be in equilibrium. Only if the expected one-year return is the same on both bonds will financial investors be willing to hold both one-year bonds and two-year bonds.

If the two bonds offer the same expected one-year return, it follows from Figure 15-2 that

$$1 + i_{1t} = \frac{\$P^e_{1t+1}}{\$P_{2t}} \tag{15.3}$$

The left side gives the return per dollar from holding a one-year bond for one-year; the right side gives the expected return per dollar from holding a two-year bond for one year. I shall call equations such as (15.3)—equations that state that the expected returns on two assets have to be equal—**arbitrage** relations. Rewrite equation (15.3) as

I use *arbitrage* to denote the proposition that expected returns on two assets must be equal. Some economists reserve *arbitrage* for the narrower proposition that *riskless* profit opportunities do not go unexploited.

$$\$P_{2t} = \frac{\$P^e_{1t+1}}{1 + i_{1t}} \tag{15.4}$$

Arbitrage implies that the price of a two-year bond today is the present value of the expected price of the bond next year. This raises the next question: What does the expected price of one-year bonds next year, $\$P^e_{1t+1}$, depend on?

The answer is straightforward. Just as the price of a one-year bond this year depends on this year's one-year interest rate, the price of a one-year bond next year will depend on the one-year rate next year. Writing equation (15.1) for next year (year $t + 1$) and denoting expectations in the usual way:

$$\$P^e_{1t+1} = \frac{\$100}{(1 + i^e_{1t+1})}$$

The price of the bond next year is expected to equal the final payment, \$100, discounted by the one-year interest rate expected for next year.

Replacing $\$P^e_{1t+1}$ by $\$100/(1 + i^e_{1t+1})$ in equation (15.4) gives

$$\$P_{2t} = \frac{\$100}{(1 + i_{1t})(1 + i^e_{1t+1})} \tag{15.5}$$

This expression is the same as equation (15.2). What we have shown is that *arbitrage* between one- and two-year bonds implies that the price of a two-year bond is the *present value* of the payment in two years, namely, \$100, discounted using current and next year's expected one-year interest rates.

The relation between arbitrage and present values: Arbitrage between bonds of different maturities implies that bond prices are equal to the expected present values of payments on these bonds.

From Bond Prices to Bond Yields

Having looked at bond prices, we now go on to bond yields. To begin, we need a definition of the yield to maturity: The **yield to maturity** on an n-year bond, or, equivalently, the ***n*-year interest rate**, is defined as that constant annual interest rate that makes the bond price today equal to the present value of future payments on the bond.

This definition is simpler than it sounds. Take, for example, the two-year bond we introduced earlier. Denote its yield by i_{2t}, where the subscript 2 is there to remind us that this is the yield to maturity on a two-year bond, or, equivalently, the two-year interest rate. Following the definition of the yield to maturity, this yield is the constant annual interest rate that would make the present value of $100 in two years equal to the price of the bond today. So, it satisfies the following relation:

$$\$P_{2t} = \frac{\$100}{(1 + i_{2t})^2} \tag{15.6}$$

$$\$90 = \frac{\$100}{(1 + i_{2t})^2}$$
$$\Rightarrow (1 + i_{2t})^2 = \$100 / \$90$$
$$\Rightarrow (1 + i_{2t}) = \sqrt{\$100 / \$90}$$
$$\Rightarrow i_{2t} = 5.4\%$$

Suppose the bond sells for $90 today. Then, the two-year interest rate i_{2t} is given by $\sqrt{100/90} - 1\$$, or 5.4%. In other words, holding the bond for two years—until maturity—yields an interest rate of 5.4% per year.

What is the relation of the two-year interest rate to the current one-year interest rate and to the expected one-year interest rate? To answer, look at equation (15.6) and equation (15.5). Eliminating $\$P_{2t}$ between the two gives

$$\frac{\$100}{(1+i_{2t})^2} = \frac{\$100}{(1+i_{1t})(1+i^e_{1t+1})}$$

Rearranging:

$$(1 + i_{2t})^2 = (1 + i_{1t})(1 + i^e_{1t+1})$$

This gives us the exact relation between the two-year interest rate i_{2t}, the current one-year interest rate i_{1t}, and next year's expected one-year interest rate i^e_{t+1}. A useful approximation to this relation is given by

We used a similar approximation when we looked at the relation between the nominal interest rate and the real interest rate in Chapter 14. See Proposition 3 in Appendix 2.

$$i_{2t} \approx \frac{1}{2}(i_{1t} + i^e_{1t+1}) \tag{15.7}$$

Equation (15.7) simply says that the two-year interest rate is (approximately) the average of the current one-year interest rate and next year's expected one-year interest rate.

We have focused so far on the relation between the prices and yields of one-year and two-year bonds. But our results generalize to bonds of any maturity.

- We could have looked at bonds with maturities shorter than a year. For example, the yield on a bond with a maturity of six months is (approximately) equal to the average of the current three-month interest rate and next quarter's expected three-month interest rate.
- Or, we could have looked instead at bonds with maturities longer than two years. For example, the yield on a 10-year bond is (approximately) equal to the average of the current one-year interest rate and the one-year interest rates expected for the next nine years.

Put simply, long-term interest rates reflect current and future expected short-term interest rates.

Interpreting the Yield Curve

The relations we just derived give us the keys we need to interpret the slope of the yield curve. By looking at yields for bonds of different maturities, we can infer what financial markets expect short-term interest rates will be in the future.

Suppose we want to find out what financial markets expect the one-year interest rate to be one year from now. All we need to do is to look at the yield on a two-year bond, i_{2t}, and the yield on a one-year bond, i_{1t}. From equation (15.7), multiplying both sides by 2 and reorganizing, we get

$$i^e_{1t+1} = 2i_{2t} - i_{1t} \qquad (15.8)$$

The one-year interest rate expected for next year is equal to twice the yield on a two-year bond minus the current one-year interest rate. Take, for example, the yield curve for June 1, 2001 shown in Figure 15-1.

- On June 1, 2001, the one-year interest rate, i_{1t}, was 3.4%.
- On June 1, 2001, the two-year interest rate, i_{2t}, was 4.1%.
- From equation (15.8), it follows that, on June 1, 2001, financial markets expected the one-year interest rate one year later—that is, the one-year interest rate on June 1, 2002—to equal $2 \times 4.1\% - 3.4\% + 4.8\%$—that is, 1.4% higher than the one-year interest rate on June 1, 2001. In words: On June 1, 2001, financial markets expected the one-year interest rate to be substantially higher one year later.

More generally, when the yield curve is upward sloping, i.e., when long-term interest rates are higher than short-term interest rates, this tells us that financial markets expect short-term rates to be higher in the future. When the yield curve is downward sloping, i.e., when long-term interest rates are lower than short-term interest rates, this tells us that financial markets expect short-term interest rates to be lower in the future.

The Yield Curve and Economic Activity

We can now return to the question: Why did the yield curve go from being downward sloping in November 2000 to being upward sloping in June 2001? Equivalently, why did long-term interest rates go from being lower than short-term interest rates in November 2000, to being much higher than short-term interest rates in June 2001?

The answer in short: Because an unexpected slowdown in economic activity in the first half of 2001 led to a sharp decline in short-term interest rates. And because, even as the slowdown was taking place, financial markets expected output to recover, and short-term interest rates to return to higher levels in the future, leading long-term interest rates to decrease much less than short-term interest rates.

To go through the answer step by step, let's use the *IS-LM* model we developed in the core (Chapter 5). Think of the interest rate measured on the vertical axis as a short-term nominal interest rate. And to keep things simple, let's assume that expected inflation is equal to zero, so we do not have to worry about the distinction between the nominal and real interest rate we introduced in Chapter 14. This distinction is not central here.

We shall extend the *IS-LM* model in Chapter 17 to take explicitly into account what we have learned about the role of expectations on decisions. For the moment, the basic *IS-LM* model will do.

It would be easy (and more realistic) to allow for constant, but positive (rather than zero), expected inflation. The conclusions would be the same.

Go back to November 2000. At the time, economic indicators suggested that, after many years of high growth, the U.S. economy had started to slow down. This slowdown was perceived as largely for the better: Most economists believed output was above the natural level of output (equivalently, that the unemployment rate was below the natural rate), so a mild slowdown was desirable. And the forecasts were indeed for

Figure 15-3

The U.S. Economy as of November 2000

In November 2000, the U.S. economy was operating above the natural level of output. Forecasts were for a "soft landing," a return of output to the natural level of output, and a small decrease in interest rates.

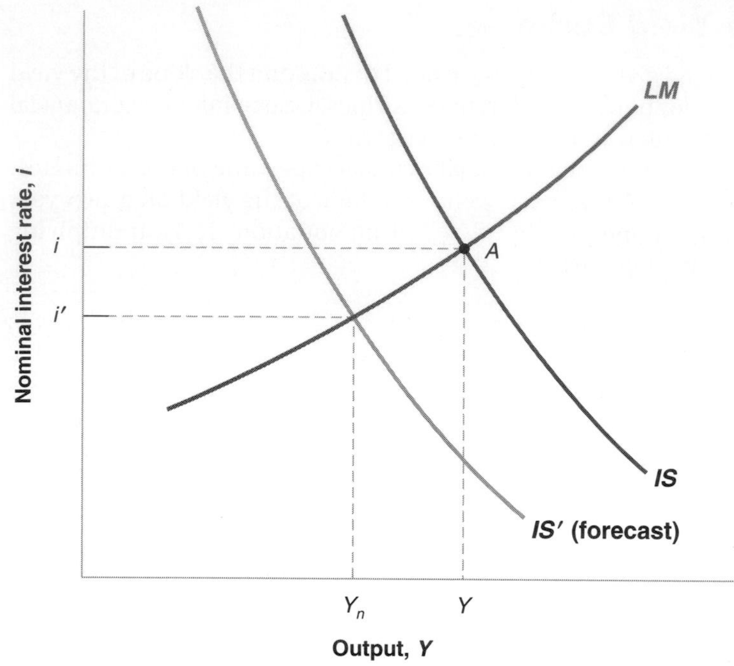

a mild slowdown, for what was called a **soft landing** of output back to the natural level of output.

The economic situation at the time is represented in Figure 15-3. The U.S. economy was at a point such as *A*, with interest rate *i*, and output *Y*. The level of output, *Y*, was perceived to be above the natural level of output Y_n. The forecasts were that the *IS* curve would gradually shift to the left, from *IS* to *IS'*, leading to a return of output to the natural level of output Y_n, and a small decrease in the interest rate from *i* to *i'*. This small expected decrease in the interest rate was the reason why the yield curve was slightly downward sloping in November 2000.

Forecasts for a mild slowdown turned out however to be too optimistic. Starting in late 2000, the economic situation deteriorated more than had been forecast. What happened is represented in Figure 15-4. There were two major developments:

- The adverse shift in spending was stronger than had been expected. Instead of shifting from *IS* to *IS'* as forecast (see Figure 15-3), the *IS* curve shifted by much more, from *IS* to *IS''* in Figure 15-4. Had monetary policy remained unchanged, the economy would have moved along the *LM* curve; the equilibrium would have moved from *A* to *B*, leading to a decrease in output and a decrease in the short-term interest rate.
- There was however, more at work. Realizing that the slowdown was stronger than it had anticipated, the Fed shifted in early 2001 to a policy of monetary expansion, leading to a downward shift in the *LM* curve. As a result of this shift in the *LM* curve, the economy was, in June 2001, at a point such as *A'*—rather than at point *B*. Output was higher and the interest rate lower than they would have been in the absence of the monetary expansion.

Look back at Figure 1-2, which gives the evolution of the federal funds rate in 2001. ▶

In words: The decrease in short-term interest rates—and thus, the decline at the short-term end of the yield curve from November 1, 2000, to June 1, 2001, shown in Figure 15-1—was the result of an unexpectedly large adverse shift in spending, combined with the strong response of the Fed aimed at limiting the size of the decrease in output. This

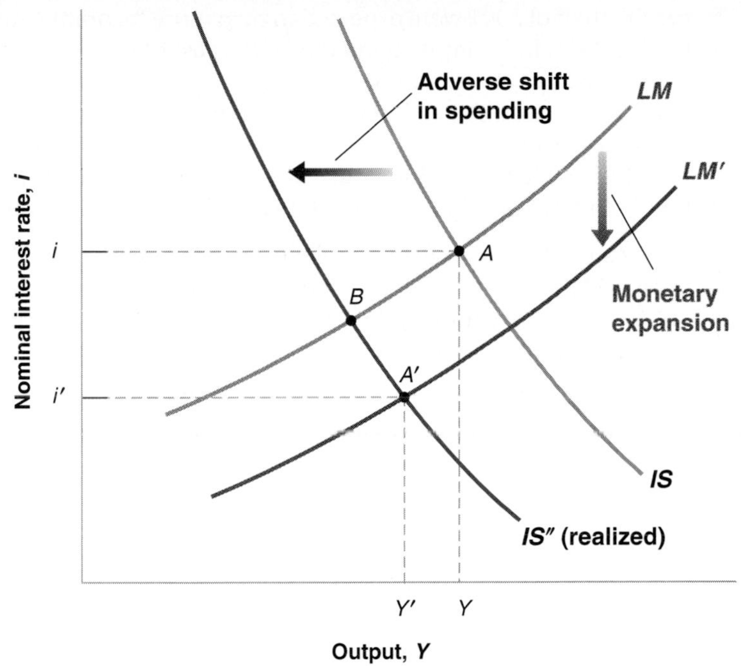

Figure 15-4

The U.S. Economy from November 2000 to June 2001

From November 2000 to June 2001, an adverse shift in spending, together with a monetary expansion, combined to lead to a decrease in the short-term interest rate.

still leaves one question: Why was the yield curve upward sloping in June 2001? Equivalently, why were long-term interest rates higher than short-term interest rates?

To answer that question, we must look at what markets expected to happen to the U.S. economy in the future, as of June 2001. This is represented in Figure 15-5. Financial markets expected two main developments:

- They expected a pickup in spending, a shift of the *IS* curve to the right, from *IS* to *IS′*. The reasons: Some of the factors that had contributed to the adverse shift in

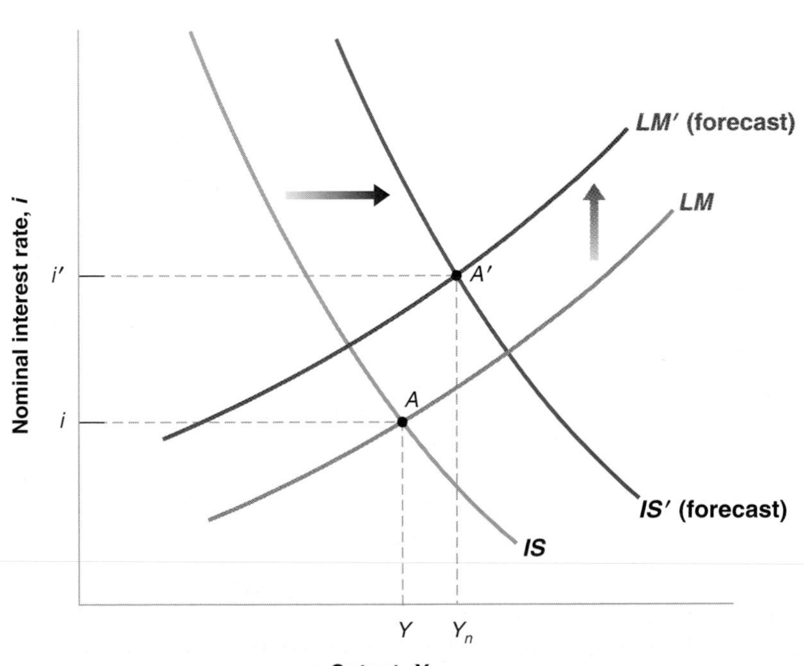

Figure 15-5

The Expected Path of the U.S. Economy as of June 2001

In June 2001, financial markets expected stronger spending and tighter monetary policy to lead to higher short-term interest rates in the future.

See the discussion of the 2001 ▶ tax cut in Chapter 3.

the first half of 2001 were expected to turn more favorable. Also, the tax cut passed in May 2001, to be implemented over the rest of the year, was expected to lead to an increase in consumption spending.

- They also expected that, once the *IS* curve started shifting to the right and output started to recover, the Fed would start shifting from the policy of monetary accomodation which it had followed during the first half of 2001, to a tighter monetary policy. In terms of Figure 15-5, they expected the *LM* curve to shift up.

Note that the yield curve in June 2001 was nearly flat for maturities up to one year. What does this tell you about when financial markets expected the economy to turn around, and short-term interest rates to start rising? (The answer: Not right away. Make sure you can explain why.) ▶

As a result of both shifts, financial markets expected the U.S. economy to move from point *A* to point *A'*; they expected both output to recover and short-term interest rates to increase. The anticipation of higher short-term interest rates was the reason why long-term interest rates remained high, why the yield curve was upward sloping in June 2001.

15-2 The Stock Market and Movements in Stock Prices

We have so far focused on bonds. But while governments finance themselves by issuing bonds, the same is not true of firms. Firms raise funds in two ways: through **debt finance**—bonds and loans; and through **equity finance**, through issues of **stocks**—or **shares**, as stocks are also called. Instead of paying predetermined amounts as bonds do, stocks pay **dividends** in an amount decided by the firm. Dividends are paid from the firm's profits. They are typically less than profits, as firms retain some of their profits to finance their investment. But dividends move with profits: When profits increase, so do dividends.

Our focus in this section is on the determination of stock prices. As a way of introducing the issues,Figure 15-6 shows the behavior of an index of U.S. stock prices, the *Standard & Poor's 500 Composite Index* (or the S&P index, for short) from 1960 to 2000. Movements in the S&P index measure movements in the average stock price of 500 large companies. (Another and better-known index is the *Dow Jones*

Figure 15-6

Standard & Poor's Stock Price Index, in Nominal and Real Terms, 1960–2000

Nominal stock prices have been multiplied by 25 since 1960. Real stock prices have only multiplied by 4. Real stock prices went through a slump until the late 1980s. Only since then have they grown rapidly.

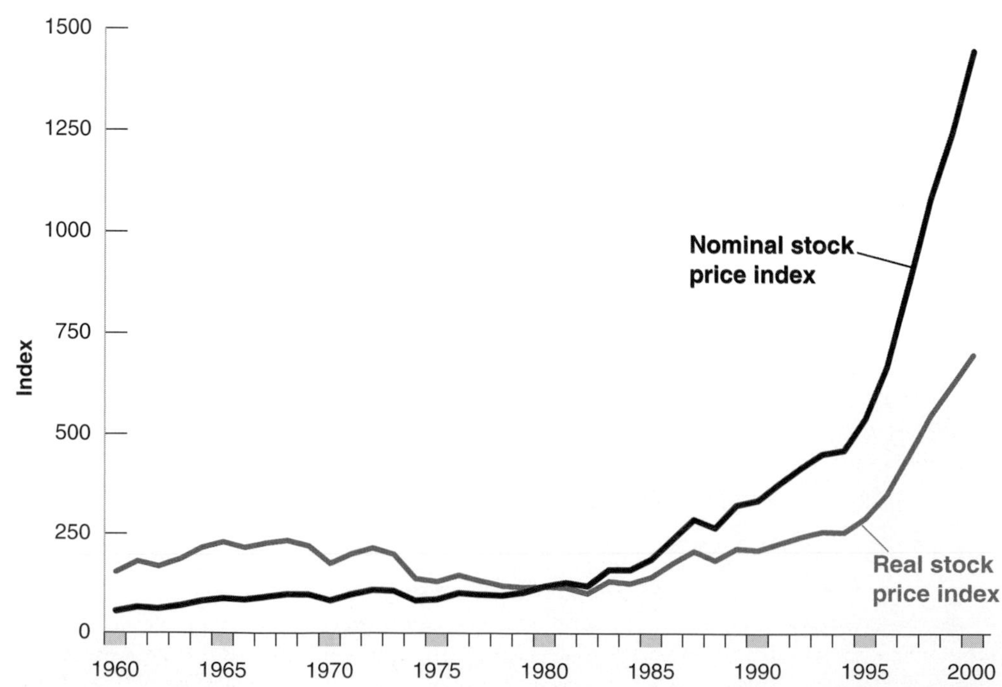

Industrial Index, an index of stocks of industrial firms only, and therefore less representative of the average price of stocks than the S&P index. Similar indexes exist for other countries. The *Nikkei Index* reflects movements in stock prices in Tokyo, and the *FT* and *CAC* indexes reflect stock price movements in London and Paris, respectively.)

Figure 15-6 plots two lines. One gives the evolution of the stock price index as it was published in newspapers or flashed on the evening news. The index shows near constancy until 1980, and a rapid increase since. It rose from 120 in 1980 to more than 330 in 1990, and to 1300 in December 2000. (The value given in Figure 15-6 for 2000 [1450] is the average value for the year. Because the index decreased substantially in the last quarter of 2000, the December value is lower than the average value for the year.)

◀ The S&P index is defined so that its average value for the period 1941–1943 is equal to 10. (No one seems to know why this strange normalization was chosen.)

This index, however, is *nominal*—that is, it gives the evolution of stock prices in terms of dollars. Of more interest to us is the evolution of the price index in real terms (that is, adjusted for inflation). The evolution of the real price index, constructed by dividing the nominal price index by the CPI for each year, is also shown in Figure 15-6. The CPI is chosen equal to 1.0 in January 1980, so the nominal price index and the real price index are equal by construction in January 1980.

The plot of the real price index shows a somewhat different picture. It shows how dismal the stock market's performance was in the late 1960s and 1970s: Roughly constant nominal stock prices and a steadily increasing price level implied steadily decreasing real stock prices. And while real stock prices have increased since about 1980, it took until 1992 for them to reach their level of the mid-1960s. Since then, however, real stock prices have increased a lot more. In December 2000, the real price index stood at 630, about 2.5 times its value of 240 in 1992 (the value given in Figure 15-6 for 1998 is the average value for the year, which is higher than the December value).

Why did the stock market do so badly for so long? Why did it rebound in the early 1980s? Why did it increase so much in the 1990s? More generally, how do stock prices respond to changes in the economic environment and in macroeconomic policy? This is the question we take up in the rest of this section.

Stock Prices as Present Values

What determines the price of a stock that promises a sequence of dividends in the future? By now, I am sure the material in Chapter 14 has become second nature, and you already know the answer: The stock price must equal the present value of future expected dividends.

Let $\$Q_t$ be the price of the stock. Let $\$D_t$ denote the dividend this year, $\$D^e_{t+1}$ the expected dividend next year, $\$D^e_{t+2}$ the expected dividend two years from now, and so on.

Suppose we look at the price of the stock after the dividend has been paid this year—this price is known as the *ex-dividend price*—so that the first dividend to be paid after the purchase of the stock is next year's dividend. (This is just a matter of convention; we could alternatively look at the price before this year's dividend has been paid. What term would we have to add?) The price of the stock is then given by

$$\$Q_t = \frac{\$D^e_{t+1}}{1 + i_{1t}} + \frac{\$D^e_{t+2}}{(1 + i_{1t})(1 + i^e_{1t+1})} + \cdots \qquad (15.9)$$

The price of the stock is equal to the present value of the dividend next year, discounted using the current one-year interest rate, plus the present value of the

Two equivalent ways of writing the stock price:

The nominal stock price equals the expected present discounted value of future nominal dividends, discounted by current and future nominal interest rates.

The real stock price equals the expected present discounted value of future real dividends, discounted by current and future real interest rates.

dividend two years from now, discounted using both this year's one-year interest rate and the next year's expected one-year interest rate, and so on.

As in the case of long-term bonds, the present value relation in equation (15.9) can be derived from arbitrage, from the assumption that the expected return per dollar from holding a stock for one year must be equal to the return from holding a one-year bond. The derivation is given in the appendix to this chapter. Going through the appendix will improve your understanding of the relation between arbitrage and present values, but it can be skipped without harm.

Equation (15.9) gives the stock price as the present value of *nominal* dividends, discounted by *nominal* interest rates. From Chapter 14, we know we can rewrite this equation to express the *real* stock price as the present value of *real* dividends, discounted by *real* interest rates. So we can rewrite the real stock price as

$$Q_t = \frac{D^e_{t+1}}{(1 + r_{1t})} + \frac{D^e_{t+2}}{(1 + r_{1t})(1 + r^e_{1t+1})} + \cdots \tag{15.10}$$

Q_t and D_t, without a dollar sign, denote the real price and the real dividend at time *t. The real stock price is the present value of future real dividends, discounted by the sequence of one-year real interest rates.*

This relation has two important implications:

Higher expected future real dividends lead to a higher real stock price.

Higher current and expected future one-year real interest rates lead to a lower real stock price.

Let's now see what light this relation sheds on movements in the stock market.

The Stock Market and Economic Activity

Figure 15-6 showed the large movements in stock prices over the last 40 years. It is not unusual for the price index to go up or down by 15% within a year. In 1974, the stock market went down by 30% (in real terms); in 1983, it went up by 30%. Daily movements of 2% or more are not unusual. What causes these movements?

The first point to be made is that these movements should be, and they are for the most part, unpredictable. The reason why is best understood by thinking in terms of the choice people have between stocks and bonds. If it were widely believed that, a year from now, the price of a stock was going to be 20% higher than today's price, holding the stock for a year would be unusually attractive, much more attractive than holding short-term bonds. There would be a very large demand for the stock. Its price would increase *today* to the point where the expected return from holding the stock was back in line with the expected return on other assets. In other words, the expectation of a high stock price next year would lead to a high stock price today.

There is indeed a saying in economics that it is a sign of a *well-functioning stock market* that movements in stock prices are unpredictable. The saying is too strong: At any moment, a few financial investors may have better information or simply be better at reading the future. If they are only a few, they may not buy enough of the stock to bid its price all the way up today. Thus, they may get large expected returns. But the basic idea is nevertheless right. The financial market gurus who regularly predict large imminent movements in the stock market over the next few months are quacks. Major movements in stock prices cannot be predicted.

You may have heard the proposition that stock prices follow a **random walk.** This is a technical term, but with a simple interpretation: Something—it can be a molecule, or the price of an asset—follows a random walk if each step it takes is as likely to be up as it is to be down. Its movements are therefore unpredictable.

If movements in the stock market cannot be predicted, if they are the result of news, where does this leave us? We can still do two things:

- We can do Monday-morning quarterbacking, looking back and identifying the news to which the market reacted.

- We can ask "what if" questions. For example: What would happen to the stock market if the Fed were going to embark on a more expansionary policy, or if consumers were to become more optimistic and increase spending?

Let us look at two "what if" questions, using the *IS-LM* model. To simplify, let's assume, as we did earlier, that expected inflation equals zero, so that the real interest rate and the nominal interest rate are equal.

A Monetary Expansion and the Stock Market

Suppose the economy is in a recession and the Fed decides to adopt a more expansionary monetary policy. The increase in money shifts the *LM* curve down in Figure 15-7. Equilibrium output moves from point *A* to point *A′*. How will the stock market react?

The answer depends on what the stock market expected monetary policy to be before the Fed's move:

If the stock market fully anticipated the expansionary policy, then the stock market will not react: Neither its expectations of future dividends nor its expectations of future interest rates are affected by a move it had already anticipated. Thus, in equation (15.9), nothing will change, and stock prices will remain the same.

Suppose instead that the Fed's move is at least partly unexpected. In that case, stock prices will increase. They will increase for two reasons: First, a more expansionary monetary policy implies lower interest rates for some time. Second, it also implies higher output for some time (until the economy returns to the natural level of output), and so higher dividends. As equation (15.9) tells us, both lower interest rates and higher dividends, current and expected, will lead to an increase in stock prices.

On September 30, 1998, the Fed lowered the target federal funds rate by 0.5%. This decrease was expected by financial markets. The Dow Jones index remained roughly unchanged (actually, going *down* 28 points for the day).

Less than a month later, on October 15, 1998, the Fed lowered the target federal funds rate again, that time by 0.25%. In contrast to the September cut, that move by the Fed came as a complete surprise to financial markets. The Dow Jones index increased by 330 points on that day, an increase of more than 3%.

An Increase in Consumer Spending and the Stock Market

Now consider an unexpected shift of the *IS* curve to the right, resulting for example from stronger-than-expected consumer spending. As a result of the shift, output in Figure 15-8, panel (a) increases from *A* to *A′*.

Will stock prices go up? You might be tempted to say yes: A stronger economy means higher profits and higher dividends for some time. But this answer is incomplete, for at least two reasons.

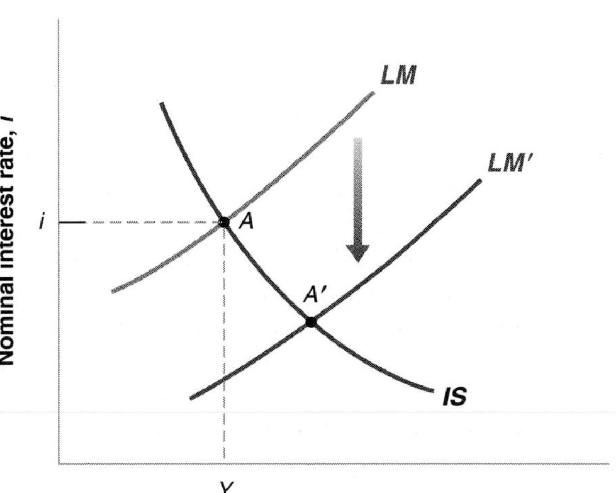

Figure 15-7

An Expansionary Monetary Policy and the Stock Market

A monetary expansion decreases the interest rate and increases output. What it does to the stock market depends on whether financial markets anticipated the monetary expansion.

Figure 15-8

An Increase in Consumption Spending and the Stock Market

Panel (a): The increase in consumption spending leads to a higher interest rate and a higher level of output. What happens to the stock market depends on the slope of the *LM* curve and on the Fed's behavior:

Panel (b): If the *LM* curve is steep, the interest rate increases a lot, and output increases little. Stock prices go down. If the *LM* curve is flat, the interest rate increases little, and output increases a lot. Stock prices go up.

Panel (c): If the Fed accommodates, the interest rate does not increase, but output does. Stock prices go up. If the Fed decides instead to keep output constant, the interest rate increases, but output does not. Stock prices go down.

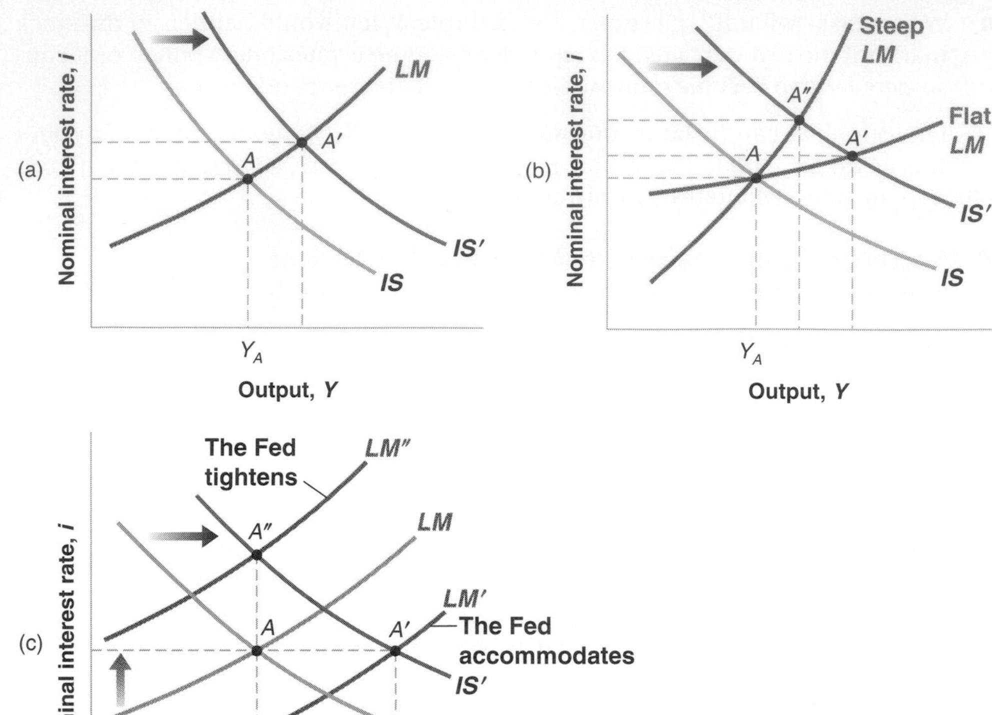

First, the answer ignores the effect of higher activity on interest rates: The movement along the *LM* curve implies an increase in both output and interest rates. Higher output implies higher profits, and so higher stock prices. Higher interest rates imply lower stock prices. Which of the two effects, higher profits or higher interest rates, dominates? The answer depends on the slope of the *LM* curve. This is shown in Figure 15-8, panel (b). A very flat *LM* curve leads to a movement from *A* to *A*′, with small increases in interest rates, large increases in output, and so an increase in stock prices. A very steep *LM* curve leads to a movement from *A* to *A*″, with large increases in interest rates, small increases in output, and so a decrease in stock prices.

Second, the answer ignores the effect of the shift in the *IS* curve on the Fed's behavior. In practice, this is the effect that financial investors often care the most about. When receiving the news of unexpectedly strong economic activity, the main question on Wall Street is: How will the Fed react?

- Will the **Fed accommodate** the shift in the *IS* curve—*accommodate* meaning: Will the Fed increase the money supply in line with money demand so as to avoid an increase in the interest rate?

  Accommodation corresponds to a downward shift of the *LM* curve, from *LM* to *LM*′ in Figure 15-8, panel (c). In this case, the economy will go from point *A* to point *A*′. Stock prices will increase, as output is expected to be higher, and interest rates are not expected to increase.
- Will the Fed instead keep the same monetary policy, leaving the *LM* curve unchanged? In that case the economy will move along the *LM* curve. As we saw earlier, what happens to stock prices is ambiguous. The economy will have higher profits, but the interest rate will be higher as well.

Making (Some) Sense of (Apparent) Nonsense: Why the Stock Market Moved Yesterday, and Other Stories

Here are some quotes from the *Wall Street Journal* from April 1997 to August 2001. Try to make sense of them, using what you've just learned.

- April 1997. Good news on the economy leading to an increase in stock prices:

  Bullish investors celebrated the release of market-friendly economic data by stampeding back into the stock market, pushing the Dow Jones Industrial Average to its second-largest point gain ever and putting the blue-chip index within shooting distance of a record just weeks after it was reeling.

- December 1999. Good news on the economy leading to a decline in stock prices:

  Good economic news was bad news for stocks and worse news for bonds. . . . The announcement of stronger-than-expected November retail-sales numbers wasn't welcome. Economic strength creates inflation fears and sharpens the risk that the Federal Reserve will raise interest rates again.

- September 1998. Bad news on the economy leading to a decrease in stock prices:

  Nasdaq stocks plummeted as worries about the strength of the U.S. economy and the profitability of U.S. corporations prompted widespread selling.

- August 2001. Bad news on the economy leading to an increase in stock prices:

  Investors shrugged off more gloomy economic news, and focused instead on their hope that the worst is now over for both the economy and the stock market. The optimism translated into another 2% gain for the Nasdaq Composite Index.

- Or will the Fed worry that an increase in output above Y_A may lead to an increase in inflation? This will be the case if the economy is already close to the natural level of output, if, in Figure 15-8, panel (c), Y_A is close to Y_n. In this case, a further increase in output would lead to an increase in inflation, something that the Fed wants to avoid. A decision by the Fed to counteract the rightward shift of the *IS* curve with a monetary contraction implies an upward shift of the *LM* curve from *LM* to *LM''*, so the economy goes from *A* to *A''* and output does not change. In that case, stock prices will surely go down: There is no change in expected profits, but the interest rate is now likely to be higher for some time.

To summarize:

Changes in output may or may not be associated with changes in stock prices in the same direction. Whether they are depends on:

What the market expected in the first place,

The source of the shocks, and

How the market expects the central bank to react to the output change.

15-3 Bubbles, Fads, and Stock Prices

Do all movements in stock prices come from news about future dividends or interest rates? Many economists doubt it. They point to times such as Black October in 1929, when the U.S. stock market fell by 23% in two days, or to October 19, 1987, when the Dow Jones index fell by 22.6% in a single day. They point to the amazing rise of Japanese stock prices in the 1980s, followed by a sharp fall in the 1990s: As we saw in Chapter 1 (Figure 1-6), the Nikkei index increased from around 13,000 in 1985 to around 35,000 in 1989, only to decline back to around 16,000 in 1992. In each case, they point to the lack of obvious news, or at least of news important enough to justify such enormous movements.

What they argue is that stock prices are not always equal to their **fundamental value**, defined as the present value of expected dividends given in equation (15.10), and that stocks are sometimes underpriced or overpriced. Overpricing eventually comes to an end, sometimes with a crash as in October 1929, or with a long slide as in the case of the Nikkei index.

Recall that arbitrage is the condition that the expected rates of return on two financial assets be equal.

Under what conditions can such mispricing occur? The surprising answer is that it can occur even when investors are rational, and when arbitrage holds. To see why, consider the case of a truly worthless stock (i.e., the stock of a company that all financial investors know will never make profits and will never pay dividends). Putting D^e_{t+1}, D^e_{t+2}, and so on equal to zero in equation (15.10) yields a simple and unsurprising answer: The fundamental value of such a stock is equal to zero.

Might you nevertheless be willing to pay a positive price for such a stock? Yes. You might if you expect the price at which you can sell the stock next year to be higher than this year's price. And the same applies to a buyer next year: He may well be willing to buy at a high price if he expects to sell at an even higher price in the following year. This process suggests that stock prices may increase just because investors expect them to. Such movements in stock prices are called **rational speculative bubbles**: Financial investors may well be behaving rationally as the bubble inflates. Even those investors who hold the stock at the time of the crash, and therefore sustain a large loss, may also have been rational. They may have realized there was a chance of a crash, but also a chance that the bubble would continue, and they could sell at an even higher price.

In a speculative bubble, the price of a stock is higher than its fundamental value. Investors are willing to pay a high price for the stock, in anticipation of being able to resell the stock at an even higher price.

To make things simple, our example assumed the stock to be fundamentally worthless. But the argument is general and applies to stocks with a positive fundamental value as well. People might be willing to pay more than the fundamental value of a stock if they expect its price to further increase in the future. And the same argument applies to other assets, such as housing, gold, and paintings. Two such bubbles are described in the Focus box "Famous Bubbles: From Tulipmania in Seventeenth-Century Holland to Russia in 1994."

In the context of the U.S. stock market, Alan Greenspan has called it "irrational exuberance."

Are all deviations from fundamental values in financial markets rational bubbles? Probably not. Many financial investors are not rational. An increase in stock prices in the past, say, due to a succession of good news, often creates excessive optimism. If investors simply extrapolate from past returns to predict future returns, a stock may become "hot" (high priced) for no reason other than its price has increased in the past. Such deviations of stock prices from their fundamental value are often called **fads**. We

Famous Bubbles: From Tulipmania in Seventeenth-Century Holland to Russia in 1994

Tulipmania in Holland

In the seventeenth century, tulips became increasingly popular in western European gardens. A market developed in Holland for both rare and common forms of tulip bulbs.

The episode called the "tulip bubble" took place from 1634 to 1637. In 1634, the price of rare bulbs started increasing. The market went into a frenzy, speculators buying tulip bulbs in anticipation of even higher prices later. The price of one such bulb, "Admiral Van de Eyck," increased from 1,500 guineas in 1634 to 7,500 guineas in 1637, the equivalent of a price of a house at the time. There are stories about a sailor mistakenly eating bulbs, only to realize the cost of his "meal" later. In early 1637, prices increased faster. Even the price of some common bulbs exploded, rising by a factor of up to 20 in January. But, in February 1637, prices collapsed. A few years later, bulbs were trading for roughly 10% of their value at the peak of the bubble.

The MMM Pyramid in Russia

In 1994 a Russian "financier," Sergei Mavrody, created a company called MMM and proceeded to sell shares, promising shareholders a rate of return of at least 3,000% per year!

The company was an instant success. The share price increased from 1,600 rubles (then equivalent to $1) in February to 105,000 rubles ($51) in July. And by July, according to the company claims, the number of shareholders had increased to 10 million.

The trouble was that the company was not involved in any type of production and held no assets, except for its 140 offices in Russia. The shares were intrinsically worthless. The company's initial success was based on a standard pyramid scheme, with MMM using the funds from the sale of new shares to pay the promised returns on the old shares. Despite repeated warnings by government officials, including Boris Yeltsin, that MMM was a scam and that the increase in the price of shares was a bubble, the promised returns were just too attractive to many Russian people, especially in the midst of a deep economic recession.

The scheme could work only as long as the number of new shareholders—and thus new funds to be distributed to existing shareholders—increased fast enough. By the end of July 1994, the company could no longer make good on its promises and the scheme collapsed. The company closed. Mavrody tried to blackmail the government into paying the shareholders, claiming that not doing so would trigger a revolution or a civil war. The government refused, leading many shareholders to be angry at the government rather than at Mavrody. Later on in the year, Mavrody actually ran for Parliament, as a self-appointed defender of the shareholders who had lost their savings. He won!

The account of tulipmania is taken from Peter Garber, "Tulipmania," Journal of Political Economy, *June 1989, 535–560.*

are all aware of fads outside of the stock market; there are good reasons to believe they exist in the stock market as well.

How much of the movement in stock prices is due to movements in the fundamental value of stocks, and how much to fads and bubbles? At the time of this writing, the question is very much on the minds of many economists and financial investors. They are wondering whether the large increase in the U.S. stock market in the 1990s was not, in part, a bubble. Some worry that the decline in stock prices that has taken place since the middle of 2000 (the S&P index declined by 20% from July 2000 to July 2001) may not be the beginning of a larger decline. The Focus box "Is the U.S. Stock Market Overvalued?" looks at the evidence, and concludes that the current level of the stock market seems high relative to fundamentals.

The general question of what determines stock prices—fundamentals only, or also fads and bubbles—is an important question, not only for participants in financial markets but also for macroeconomics. The stock market is more than just a sideshow: As we shall explore in the next two chapters, not only are stock prices affected by economic activity, but economic activity is affected by stock prices, through their influence on both consumption and investment spending. Many economists believe the stock market crash of 1929 was one of the sources of the Great Depression. And, as we discussed briefly in Chapter 1 and shall discuss at more length in Chapter 22, the long and large decline of the Nikkei after what was probably in large part a speculative bubble in the 1980s appears to be one of the causes of the slump in Japan since the early 1990s.

◄ See Chapter 22.

Is the U.S. Stock Market Overvalued?

At the end of 2000, U.S. stock prices stood in real terms at more than three times their 1990 level. This large increase has led a number of economists, financial investors, and policy makers to worry that the stock market might be overvalued, and that a large market correction (as large declines in stock prices are euphemistically called) may be in store.

The fact that stock prices increased during the 1990s is not by itself a puzzle. After the 1990–1991 recession, the U.S. economy went through a long expansion—an expansion lasting much longer than most economists and financial investors had anticipated. With the long expansion came high profits, and high dividends—much higher than had been expected as of 1990. In other words, there was plenty of good news in the 1990s. This good news should have led to higher-than-expected stock prices—and indeed it did!

The question is whether the strong performance of stock prices can be fully explained by the strong performance of dividends. The evidence here suggests that it cannot. If higher dividends fully accounted for higher prices, stock prices should have increased roughly in line with dividends. Put another way, the dividend-price ratio (also called the dividend yield) should have remained roughly constant. Figure 1 plots the evolution of the dividend-price ratio for the stocks in the S&P index from 1990 to 2000. The conclusion is clear: The dividend-price ratio declined steadily throughout the decade, from 3.6% in 1990 to 1.2% in 2000—a historical low. In other words, stock prices increased much more than dividends during the decade.

That stock prices are high in relation to current dividends does not, however, prove the stock market is overvalued, for at least three reasons:

- High stock prices may reflect anticipations of much higher dividends in the future. Return to equation (15.10): The higher future expected dividends, the higher the stock price, even given the current dividend.
- High stock prices may reflect a decrease in real interest rates since 1990. Again, return to equation (15.10): Given current and expected dividends, the lower current and future expected real interest rates, the higher the stock price.
- High stock prices may reflect a factor we have ignored in this chapter, a decrease in the risk premium associated with stocks relative to bonds. To the extent that investors perceive stocks as less risky than earlier, they may be willing to pay a higher price for stocks than earlier. (The appendix shows how a decrease in the risk premium leads to an increase in the stock price.)

Whether these factors together can explain the full increase in stock prices is the subject of much current research and is far from settled. In a recent article, John Campbell, from Harvard, and Robert Shiller, from Yale, have shown that, based on historical evidence, there are some reasons to worry. When the dividend-price ratio has been low in the past, stock prices have typically done poorly over the following 20 years, leading to a much lower return on holding stocks than holding bonds.

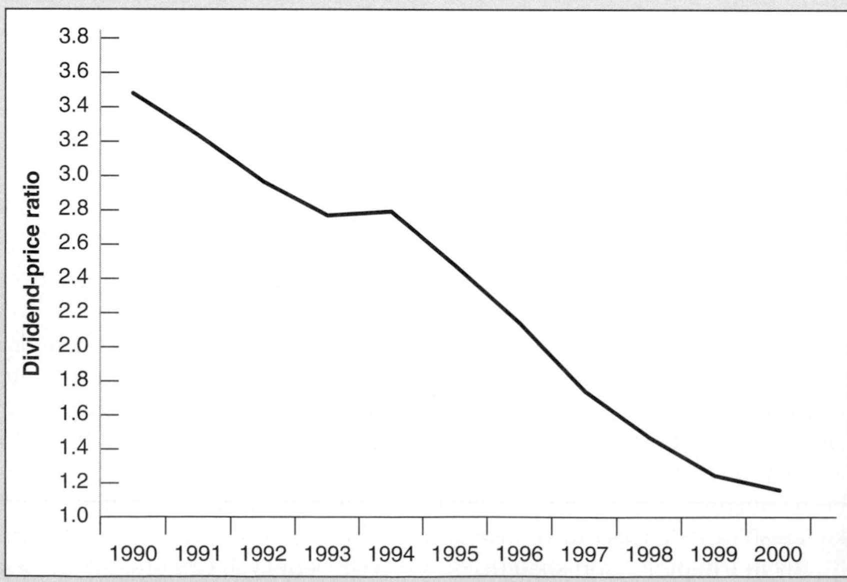

Figure 1 *The Evolution of the Dividend-Price Ratio from 1990 to 2000*

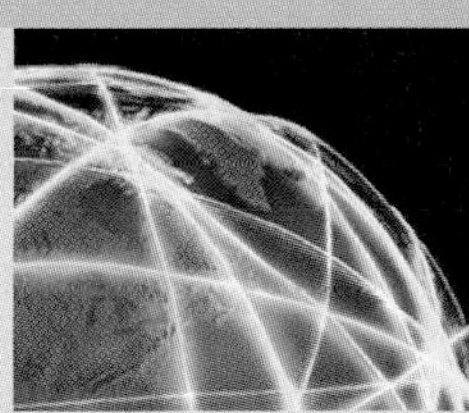

This is shown in Figure 2, which plots two variables for each year since 1870. The variable on the horizontal axis is the dividend-price ratio. The variable on the vertical axis is the rate of change of real stock prices over the following 20 years. Each point corresponds to a different year. For example, the point for 1980 gives the dividend-price ratio for 1980, and the rate of change of real stock prices between 1980 and 2000.

The plot clearly shows that, historically, a low dividend-price ratio has been followed by a poor performance of the stock market over the following years. (For example, on the eve of the stock market crash of 1929, the dividend-price ratio was the lowest it had been in decades; over the following 20 years, stock prices declined by 86%!) The figure also plots the regression line, the line that fits the scatter of points best. The equation for the line is

$$\text{20-year rate of change} = -76\% + 0.22 \text{ Dividend-price ratio}$$

This equation implies that a dividend-price ratio of 1.2% (the value of the ratio in 2000) should be followed on average by a decrease in real stock prices of 49.6% ($-76\% + 0.22$ times 1.2%) over the following 20 years! The fit of the line to the scatter of points is not very tight and things may be different this time—but it is a serious warning nevertheless.

Source: John Campbell and Robert Shiller, "Valuation Ratios and the Long-Run Stock Market Outlook: An Update," Cowles Foundation Discussion Paper number 1295, March 2001, (cowles.econ.yale.edu /P/au/d_shiller/ online.html).

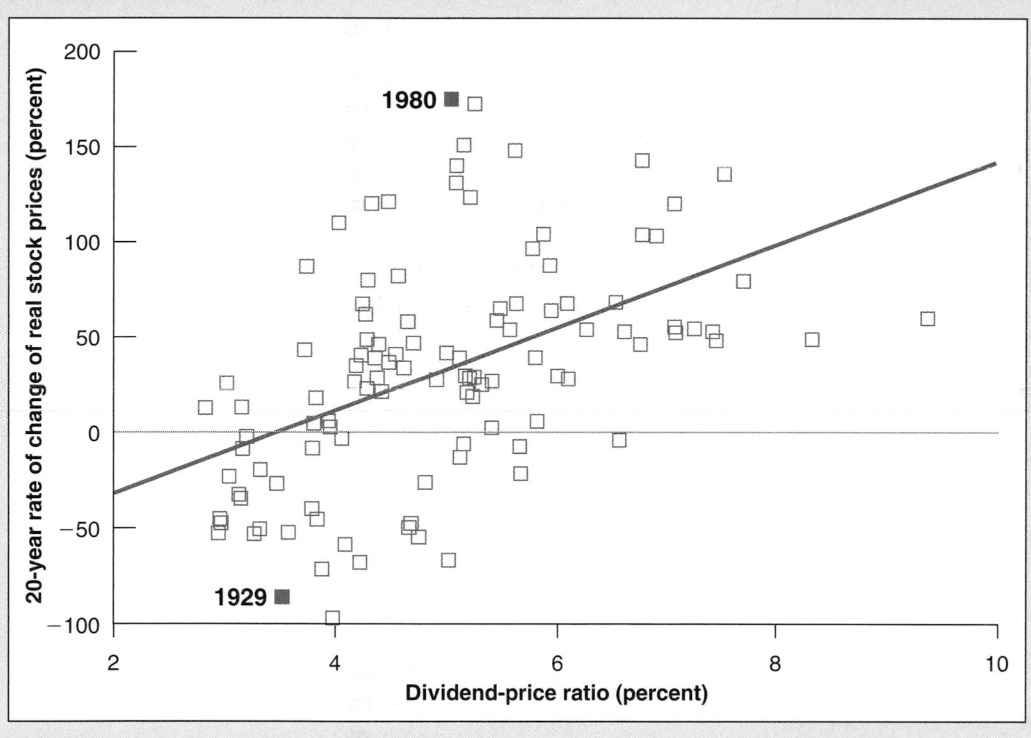

Figure 2 *Twenty-Year Rate of Change in the Real Stock Price Versus Dividend-Price Ratio, 1870–1890 to 1980–2000*

Summary

- Arbitrage between bonds of different maturities implies that the price of a bond is the present value of the payments on the bond, discounted using current and expected short-term interest rates over the life of the bond. Hence, higher current or expected short-term interest rates lead to lower bond prices.
- The yield to maturity on a bond is (approximately) equal to the average of current and expected short-term interest rates over the life of a bond.
- The slope of the yield curve (equivalently, the term structure) tells us what financial markets expect to happen to short-term interest rates in the future.

Further Readings

There are many bad books written about the stock market. A good one, and fun to read, is Burton Malkiel, *A Random Walk Down Wall Street*, 7th ed. (New York, NY: Norton, 2000).

Peter Garber gives an account of historical bubbles in "Famous First Bubbles," *Journal of Economic Perspectives*, Spring 1990, 35–54.

Appendix: Arbitrage and Stock Prices

This appendix has two parts.

The first shows that, in the absence of rational speculative bubbles, arbitrage between stocks and bonds implies that the price of a stock is equal to the expected present value of dividends.

The second shows how to modify the arbitrage relation to take into account the fact that financial investors care about risk. It then shows how this modifies the present value relation between stock prices and dividends.

Arbitrage and Stock Prices

You face the choice of investing either in one-year bonds or in stocks for a year. What should you choose?

- Suppose you decide to hold one-year bonds. Then, for every dollar you put in one-year bonds, you will get $(1+i_{1t})$ dollars next year. This payoff is represented in the upper line of Figure 15A-1.
- Suppose you decide instead to hold stocks for a year. This implies buying a stock today, receiving a dividend next year and then selling the stock. As the price of a stock is $\$Q_t$, every dollar you put in stocks buys you $\$1/\$Q_t$ stocks. And for each stock you buy, you expect to receive $(\$D^e_{t+1} + \$Q^e_{t+1})$, the sum of the expected dividend and the stock price next year. Therefore, for every dollar you put in stocks, you expect to receive $(\$D^e_{t+1} + \$Q^e_{t+1})/\$Q_t$. This payoff is represented in the lower line of Figure 15A-1.

Let's use the same arbitrage argument we used for bonds earlier. If financial investors care only about expected rates of return, then equilibrium requires that the expected rate of return from holding stocks for one year be the same as the rate of return on one-year bonds:

$$\frac{(\$D^e_{t+1} + \$Q^e_{t+1})}{\$Q_t} = 1 + i_{1t}$$

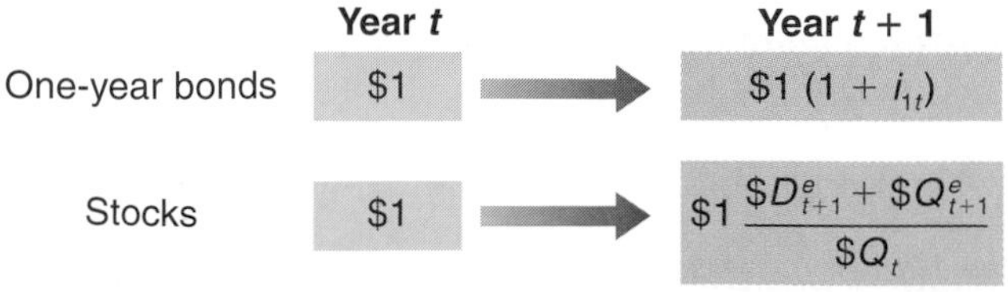

	Year t		Year $t+1$
One-year bonds	\$1	→	$\$1\,(1+i_{1t})$
Stocks	\$1	→	$\$1\,\dfrac{\$D^e_{t+1} + \$Q^e_{t+1}}{\$Q_t}$

Figure 15A-1 *Returns from Holding One-year Bonds or Stocks for One Year*

Rewrite this equation as

$$\$Q_t = \frac{\$D^e_{t+1}}{(1 + i_{1t})} + \frac{\$Q^e_{t+1}}{(1 + i_{1t})} \qquad (15\text{-}A1)$$

Arbitrage implies that the price of the stock today is equal to the present value of the expected dividend plus the present value of the expected stock price next year.

The next step is to think about what determines $\$Q^e_{t+1}$, the expected stock price next year. Next year, financial investors will again face the choice between stocks and one-year bonds. Thus, the same arbitrage relation will hold. Writing the previous equation, but now for time $t+1$, and taking expectations into account gives

$$\$Q^e_{t+1} = \frac{\$D^e_{t+2}}{(1 + i^e_{1t+1})} + \frac{\$Q^e_{t+2}}{(1 + i^e_{1t+1})}$$

The expected price next year is simply the present value next year of the sum of the expected dividend and price two years from now. Replacing the expected price $\$Q^e_{t+1}$ in equation (15-A1) gives

$$\$Q_t = \frac{\$D^e_{t+1}}{(1 + i_{1t})} + \frac{\$D^e_{t+2}}{(1 + i_{1t})(1 + i^e_{1t+1})} + \frac{\$Q^e_{t+2}}{(1 + i_{1t})(1 + i^e_{1t+1})}$$

The stock price is the present value of the expected dividend next year, plus the present value of the expected dividend two years from now, plus the expected price two years from now.

If we replace the expected price in two years as the present value of the expected price and dividends in three years, and so on for n years, we get

$$\$Q_t = \frac{\$D^e_{t+1}}{(1 + i_{1t})} + \cdots + \frac{\$D^e_{t+n}}{(1 + i_{1t})\ldots(1 + i^e_{1t+n-1})} + \frac{\$Q^e_{t+n}}{(1 + i_{1t})\ldots(1 + i^e_{1t+n-1})} \qquad (15\text{-}A2)$$

Look at the last term in equation (15-A2)—the present value of the expected price in n years. As long as people do not expect the stock price to explode in the future, then, as we keep replacing $\$Q^e_{t+n}$ and n increases, this term will go to zero. To see why, suppose the interest rate is constant and equal to i. The last term becomes

$$\frac{\$Q^e_{t+n}}{(1+i_{1t})\ldots(1+i^e_{1t+n-1})} = \frac{\$Q^e_{t+n}}{(1+i)^n}$$

Suppose further that people expect the price of the stock to converge to some value, call it $\$\bar{Q}$ in the far future. Then, the last term becomes

$$\frac{\$Q^e_{t+n}}{(1+i)^n} = \frac{\$\bar{Q}}{(1+i)^n}$$

If the interest rate is positive, this expression goes to zero as n becomes large. Equation (15-A2) reduces to equation (15.9) in the text: The price today is the present value of expected future dividends.

(A subtle point: The condition that people expect the price of the stock to converge to some value over time seems reasonable. And, indeed, most of the time it is likely to be satisfied. When, however, prices are subject to rational bubbles [Section 15-3], that is, when people are expecting large increases in the stock price in the future and this is when the condition that the expected stock price does not explode is not satisfied. This is why, when there are bubbles, the argument I just gave fails, and the stock price is no longer equal to the present value of expected dividends.)

An Extension to the Present Value Formula to Take Risk into Account

In this and the previous chapter, we have assumed that people cared only about expected return, and did not care about risk. Put another way, we have assumed that people were **risk neutral**. In fact, most people are **risk averse**. They care both about expected return—which they like—and risk—which they dislike.

Most of **finance theory** is indeed concerned with how people make decisions when they are risk averse, and what risk aversion implies for asset prices. Exploring these issues would take us too far. But we can nevertheless explore a simple extension of our framework, which captures the fact that people are risk averse, and shows how to modify the arbitrage and the present value relations.

If people perceive stocks as more risky than bonds, and people dislike risk, they are likely to require a *risk premium* to hold stocks rather than bonds. In the case of stocks, this risk premium is called the **equity premium**. Denote it by θ (the Greek lowercase theta). If θ is, for example, 5%, then people will hold stocks only if the expected rate of return on stocks exceeds the expected rate of return on short-term bonds by 5% a year.

In that case, the arbitrage equation between stocks and bonds becomes

$$\frac{\$D^e_{t+1} + \$Q^e_{t+1}}{\$Q_t} = 1 + i_{1t} + \theta$$

The only change is the presence of θ on the right side of the equation. Going through the same steps as above (replacing Q^e_{t+1} by its expression at time $t+1$, and so on), the stock price equals:

$$\$Q_t = \frac{\$D^e_{t+1}}{(1+i_{1t}+\theta)} + \cdots + \frac{\$D^e_{t+n}}{(1+i_{1t}+\theta)\ldots(1+i_{1t+n-1}+\theta)} + \cdots$$

The stock price is still equal to the present value of expected future dividends. But the discount rate here equals the interest rate plus the equity premium. Note that the higher the premium, the lower the stock price. Over the last 100 years in the United States, the average equity premium has been equal to roughly 5%. But (in contrast to the assumption we made earlier, where we took θ to be constant) it is not constant. The equity premium appears, for example, to have decreased since the early 1950s, from around 7% to less than 3% today. Variations in the equity premium are another source of fluctuations in stock prices.

Key Terms

- risk neutral, 333
- risk averse, 333
- finance theory, 333
- equity premium, 333

Expectations, Consumption, and Investment

Having looked at the role of expectations in financial markets, we now turn to the role expectations play in determining the two main components of spending—consumption and investment. This description of consumption and investment will be the main building block of the expanded *IS-LM* model we shall develop in Chapter 17.

- Section 16-1 looks at consumption, and shows how consumption decisions depend not only on current income, but also on expected future income, as well as on financial wealth.
- Section 16-2 turns to investment, and shows how investment decisions depend on current and expected profits, and on current and expected real interest rates.
- Section 16-3 looks at the movements in consumption and investment over time, and shows how to interpret those movements in light of what you learned in this chapter. ■

16-1 Consumption

How do people decide how much to consume and how much to save? Until now, we have assumed that consumption and saving depended only on current income. By now, you realize they depend on much more, particularly on expectations of the future. We now explore how those expectations affect the consumption decision.

The theory of consumption on which this section is based was developed independently in the 1950s by Milton Friedman, of the University of Chicago, who called it the **permanent income theory of consumption**, and by Franco Modigliani, of MIT, who called it the **life cycle theory of consumption**. Each chose his label carefully. Friedman's "permanent income" emphasized that consumers look beyond current income. Modigliani's "life cycle" emphasized that consumers' natural planning horizon is their entire lifetime.

Friedman received the Nobel Prize in economics in 1976; Modigliani received the Nobel Prize in economics in 1985.

The behavior of aggregate consumption has remained a hot area of research ever since, for two reasons. One is simply the sheer size of consumption as a component of GDP, and therefore the need to understand movements in consumption. The other is the increasing availability of large surveys of individual consumers, such as the PSID described in the Focus box "Up Close and Personal: Learning from Panel Data Sets." These surveys, which were not available when Friedman and Modigliani developed their theories, have allowed economists to steadily improve their understanding of how consumers actually behave. This section summarizes what we know today.

From Chapter 3: Consumption spending accounts for 69% of total spending in the United States.

The Very Foresighted Consumer

Let's start with an assumption that will surely—and rightly—strike you as extreme, but will serve as a convenient benchmark. We'll call it the theory of the *very foresighted consumer*. How would a very foresighted consumer decide how much to consume? He would proceed in two steps:

- First, he would add up the value of the stocks and bonds he owns, the value of his checking and savings accounts, the value of the house he owns minus the mortgage still due, and so on. This would give him a notion of his **financial wealth** and his **housing wealth**.

  He would also estimate what his after-tax labor income was likely to be over his working life, and compute the present value of expected after-tax labor income. This would give him an estimate of what economists call his **human wealth**—to contrast it with his **nonhuman wealth**, defined as the sum of financial wealth and housing wealth.
- Adding his human wealth and nonhuman wealth, he would have an estimate of his **total wealth**. He would then decide how much to spend out of this total wealth. A reasonable assumption is that he would decide to spend a proportion of total wealth to maintain roughly the same level of consumption each year throughout his life. If that level of consumption was higher than his current income, he would then borrow the difference. If it were lower than his current income, he would instead save the difference.

With a slight abuse of language, I shall use "housing wealth" to refer not only to housing, but also to the other goods that the consumer may own, from cars to paintings and so on.

Human wealth + Nonhuman wealth = Total wealth

Let's write this formally. What we have described is a consumption decision of the form

$$C_t = C\,(\text{total wealth}_t) \qquad (16.1)$$

where C_t is consumption at time t, and (total wealth$_t$) is the sum of nonhuman wealth (financial plus housing wealth) and human wealth at time t (the expected present value, as of time t, of current and future after-tax labor income).

This description contains much truth: Like the foresighted consumer, we surely do think about our wealth and our expected future labor income in deciding how

Up Close and Personal: Learning from Panel Data Sets

Panel data sets are data sets that give the value of one or more variables for many individuals or many firms over time. I described one such survey, the Current Population Survey (or CPS), in Chapter 6. Another is the Panel Study of Income Dynamics, or PSID.

The PSID was started in 1968, with approximately 4,800 families. Interviews of these families have been conducted every year since, and are still continuing. The survey has grown as new individuals have joined the original families, either by marriage or by birth. Each year, the survey asks people about their income, wage rate, number of hours worked, health, and food consumption. (The focus on food consumption is because one of the survey's initial aims was to better understand the living conditions of poor families. The survey would be more useful if it asked about all of consumption rather than food consumption. Unfortunately, it does not.)

By giving 30 years of information about individuals and about extended families, the survey has allowed economists to ask and answer questions for which there was previously only anecdotal evidence. Among the many questions for which the PSID has been used are

- How much does (food) consumption respond to transitory movements in income—For example, to the loss of income from becoming unemployed?
- How much risk sharing is there within families—for example, when a family member becomes sick or unemployed, how much help does he or she get from other family members?
- How much do people care about staying geographically close to their families? When somebody becomes unemployed, for example, how does the probability that he will migrate to another city depend on how many family members live in the city in which he currently lives?

much to consume today. But one cannot help thinking that it assumes too much computation and foresight on the part of the typical consumer.

To get a better sense of what that description implies and what is wrong with it, let's apply this decision process to the problem facing a typical U.S. college student.

◀ Because each of us is a consumer, we can use introspection as a way of checking the plausibility of a particular theory.

An Example

Let's assume you are 21 years old, with three more years of college before you start your first job. You may be in debt today, having borrowed to go to college. You may own a car and a few other worldly possessions. For simplicity, let's assume your debt and your possessions roughly offset each other, so that your nonhuman wealth is equal to zero. Your only wealth, therefore, is your human wealth, the present value of your expected after-tax labor income.

You expect your starting annual salary in three years to be around $40,000 (in year 2000 dollars) and to increase by an average of 3% a year in real terms, until your retirement at age 60. About 25% of your income will go to taxes.

◀ You are welcome to use your own numbers, and see where the computation takes you.

Building on what you saw in Chapter 14, let's compute the present value of your labor income as the value of *real* expected after-tax labor income, discounted using *real* interest rates (equation [14.7]).

Let Y_{Lt} denote real labor income in year *t*.

Let T_t denote real taxes in year *t*.

Let $V(Y^e_{Lt} - T^e_t)$ denote your human wealth, i.e., the expected present value of your after-tax labor income—expected as of year *t*.

To make the computation simple, assume the real interest rate equals zero—so the expected present value is simply the sum of expected labor income over your working life and is therefore given by

$$V(Y^e_{Lt} - T^e_t) = (\$40{,}000)(0.75)[1 + (1.03) + (1.03)^2 + \cdots + (1.03)^{36}]$$

The first term ($40,000) is your initial level of labor income, in year 2000 dollars.

The computation of the consumption level you can sustain is made easier by our assumption that the real interest rate equals zero. In this case, if you consume one fewer good today, you can consume exactly one more good next year, and the condition you must satisfy is simply that the sum of consumption over your lifetime is equal to your wealth. So, if you want to consume a constant amount each year, you just need to divide your wealth by the remaining number of years in your life.

The second term (0.75) comes from the fact that, because of taxes, you keep only 75% of what you earn.

The third term $[1 + (1.03) + (1.03)^2 + \cdots + (1.03)^{36}]$ reflects the fact that you expect your real income to increase at 3% a year for 37 years (you will start earning income at age 24, and work until age 60).

Using the properties of geometric series to solve for the sum in brackets gives:

$$V(Y^e_{Lt} - T^e_t) = .75\ (66.2)(\$40{,}000) = \$1{,}986{,}000$$

Your wealth today, the expected value of your lifetime after-tax labor income, is around $2 million.

How much should you consume? You can expect to live about 16 years after retirement, so that your expected remaining life today is 56 years. If you want to consume the same amount every year, the constant level of consumption that you can afford equals your total wealth divided by your expected remaining life, or $1,986,000/56 = ► $35,464 a year. Given that your income until you get your first job is equal to zero, this implies borrowing $35,464 a year for the next three years, and starting to save when you get your first job.

Toward a More Realistic Description

Your first reaction to this computation may be that this is a stark and slightly sinister way of summarizing your life prospects. Your second reaction may be that while you agree with most of the ingredients that went into the computation, you surely do not intend to borrow $35,464 × 3 = $106,392 over the next three years.

1. You may not want to plan for constant consumption over your lifetime and may be quite happy with deferring higher consumption until later. Student life usually does not leave much time for expensive activities. You may want to defer memberships in golf clubs and trips to the Galapágos islands to later in life. You also have to think about the additional expenses that will come with having children, sending them to nursery school, summer camp, college, and so on.

2. You may find that the amount of computation and foresight involved in the computation we just went through far exceeds the amount you use in your own decisions. You may never have thought until now about exactly how much income you are going to make, and for how many years. You may feel that most consumption decisions are made in a simpler, less forward-looking fashion.

3. The computation of total wealth is based on forecasts of what can reasonably be expected to happen. But things can turn out better or worse. What happens if you are unlucky, and you become unemployed or sick? How will you pay back what you borrowed? You may well want to be prudent, make sure that you can adequately survive even the worst outcomes, and thus borrow much less than $106,392.

4. Even if you decided to borrow $106,392, you are likely to find the bank from which you try to borrow that amount to be unreceptive. Why? The bank may worry that you are taking on a commitment you will not be able to afford if times turn bad, and that you may not be able or willing to repay the loan.

These reasons, all good ones, imply that to characterize consumers' actual behavior, we must modify the description we gave earlier. The last three reasons in particular suggest consumption depends not only on total wealth but also on current income.

Take the second reason: You may, because it is a simple rule, decide to let your consumption follow your income and not think about what your wealth might be. In that case, consumption will depend on current income, not on your wealth.

Now take the third reason: It implies that a safe rule may be to consume no more than your current income. This way, you do not run the risk of accumulating debt that you could not repay if times were to turn bad.

Or take the fourth reason: It implies that you may have little choice anyway. Even if you wanted to consume more than your current income, you may be unable to do so, since no bank will give you a loan.

If we want to allow for a direct effect of current income on consumption, what measure of current income should we use? A convenient variable is after-tax labor income, introduced earlier in defining human wealth. This leads to a consumption function of the form

$$C_t = C(\text{Total wealth}_t,\ Y_{Lt} - T_t) \qquad (16.2)$$
$$(\quad + \qquad , \quad + \quad)$$

In words: *Consumption is an increasing function of total wealth, and also an increasing function of current after-tax labor income. Total wealth is the sum of nonhuman wealth—financial wealth plus housing wealth—and of human wealth—the present value of expected after-tax labor income.*

How much does consumption depend on total wealth (and thus on expectations of future income) and how much on current income? Some consumers, especially those who have a temporarily low income and poor access to credit, are likely to consume their current income, regardless of what they expect will happen to them in the future. A worker who becomes unemployed and has no financial wealth may have a hard time borrowing to maintain her level of consumption, even if she is fairly confident that she will soon find another job. Consumers who are richer and have easier access to credit are more likely to give more weight to the expected future and to try to maintain roughly constant consumption over time. The relative importance of wealth and income in consumption decisions can be settled only by looking at the empirical evidence. This is not easy to do, and the Focus box "How Much Do Expectations Matter? Looking for Natural Experiments" explains why. But even if some details still need to be filled in, the basic evidence is clear and unsurprising: Both total wealth and current income affect consumption.

Putting Things Together: Current Income, Expectations, and Consumption

Let's go back to what motivates this chapter—the importance of expectations in the determination of spending. Note first that, with consumption behavior described by equation (16.2), expectations affect consumption in two ways:

- Expectations affect consumption directly through human wealth: To compute their human wealth, consumers have to form their own expectations of future labor income, real interest rates, and taxes.
- Expectations affect consumption indirectly, through nonhuman wealth—stocks, bonds, housing. Consumers do not need to do any computation here, and can take the value of these assets as given. But as you saw in Chapter 15, the computation is in effect done for them by financial markets: The price of their stocks, for example, depends itself on expectations of future dividends and interest rates.

How expectations of higher output in the future affect consumption today:

Expected future output ↑ leads to Expected future labor income ↑ leads to Human wealth ↑ leads to Consumption today ↑

Expected future income ↑ leads to Expected future dividends ↑ leads to Stock prices ↑ leads to Nonhuman wealth ↑ leads to Consumption today ↑

How Much Do Expectations Matter? Looking for Natural Experiments

FOCUS

How much does consumption depend on current income versus expected future income? This is not easy to answer because, most of the time, expectations of future income move very much with current income. If we get promoted and receive a raise, not only does our current income go up, but so typically does the income we can expect to receive in future years. Whether or not we are very foresighted, our consumption will typically move closely with our current income.

What can economists do to disentangle the effects of current versus expected future income? They must look for times and events where current income and expected future income move in different ways, and then look at what happens to consumption. Such events are called **natural experiments.** "Experiments" in the sense that, like laboratory experiments, these events allow us to test a theory or to get a better estimate of an important parameter. "Natural" meaning that, unlike researchers in the physical sciences, economists typically cannot run experiments themselves. They must rely on experiments given by nature—or, as you shall see in the second example, created by policy makers.

Here are two examples from recent research on consumption:

Retirement

Retirement implies a large, predictable change in labor income: Labor income drops to zero! . . . . By looking at how people save for retirement, we can, in principle, find out whether, when, and by how much people take into account the predictable decline in their future labor income.

A study based on a panel data set called the *Survey of Income and Program Participation* sheds some light on retirement behavior. Table 1, taken from the study, shows the mean level and the composition of (total) wealth for people between 65 and 69 years in 1991:

Table 1 Mean Wealth of People, Ages 65–69, in 1991 (in current dollars)

Social Security pension	$99,682
Employer-provided pension	62,305
Personal retirement assets	10,992
Other financial assets	42,018
Home equity	64,955
Other equity	33,855
Total	$313,807

Source: Venti and Wise, Table A1.

(The first two items are expected present values of future payments).

A mean wealth of $313,807 is substantial (U.S. per capita personal disposable income was $16,205 in 1991), suggesting an image of forward-looking individuals making careful saving decisions and retiring with enough wealth to enjoy a comfortable retirement.

A closer look at the table, and at differences across individuals, suggests two caveats:

- The largest component of wealth is the present value of Social Security benefits, an amount over which workers have no control. Indeed, one of the main motivations behind the introduction of the Social Security program in the United States was to make sure people contributed to their retirement, whether or not they would have done so on

This dependence of consumption on expectations has in turn two main implications for the relation between consumption and income:

- *Consumption is likely to respond less than one for one to fluctuations in current income.* In deciding how much to consume, consumers look at more than current income. If they conclude that a decrease in income is permanent, they may decrease consumption one for one with the decrease in income. But if they conclude that the decrease in current income is transitory, they will adjust their consumption by less. In a recession, consumption adjusts less than one for one to decreases in income. This is because consumers know that recessions typically do not last for more than a few quarters, and that the economy will eventually return to the natural level of output. The same is true in expansions. Faced with an unusually rapid increase in income, consumers are unlikely to increase consumption by as much as income. They are likely to assume that the boom is transitory, and that things will return to normal.

Go back to the two consumption functions we used in the core:

- Looking at the short run (Chapter 3), we assumed $C = c_0 + c_1 Y$ (ignoring taxes here). This implied that, when income increased, consumption increased less than proportionately with income (C/Y went down). This was appropriate, as our focus was on fluctuations, on transitory movements in income.
- Looking at the long run (Chapter 10), we assumed

(*Continued*)

their own. The third largest component is an employer-provided pension, another a component over which workers have limited control. The only components that clearly reflect an individual saving decision (personal retirement assets + other financial assets) account only for $53,010, or about 17% of total wealth. So, one can also read the evidence as suggesting that people save enough for retirement, partly because they are forced to, through Social Security and other contributions.

- The numbers in the table are averages and hide substantial differences across individuals. The same study shows that many people retire with little more than their Social Security pensions. More generally, studies of retirement saving give the following picture: Most people appear to give little thought to retirement saving until some time during their 40s. At that point, many start saving for retirement. But many also save little and rely mostly on Social Security benefits when they retire.

Announced Tax Cuts

In 1981 the Reagan administration designed a fiscal package with phased-in tax cuts over 1981–1983. Income tax rates were to be reduced in three steps: 5% in 1981, 10% in 1982, and 8% in 1983, implying a cumulative reduction of 23%, a very large tax reduction. Congress passed the package in July 1981 and it became law in August 1981.

This tax change provides us with a natural experiment. The experiment is a change in expected future after-tax labor income coming from an anticipated decrease in taxes. And the question we want to answer is simple: Did consumers react in 1981 to the expected decrease in taxes to come in 1982 and 1983, and, if so, by how much?

This is exactly the question asked by James Poterba, from MIT, in a 1988 article. Using econometrics, Poterba looked for evidence of an unusual increase in consumption, given disposable income, in the summer of 1981 (the time when Congress passed the package). He found no evidence of such an increase.

Is this conclusive evidence that consumers do not take into account changes in expected future income in their consumption decision? Not necessarily. There are at least two alternative interpretations of the facts. People may have believed that Congress would change its mind, leading them to take a wait-and-see attitude and wait for the actual decreases in taxes to adjust their consumption. Or maybe people do not take into account expected changes in taxes, but take into account other expected changes in their income (say, an expected promotion or the coming of retirement). These arguments cannot be dismissed. But what can be safely said is that the evidence from that particular natural experiment does not provide evidence for a strong effect of expected future tax changes on consumption.

Sources: On retirement: Steven Venti and David Wise, "The Wealth of Cohorts: Retirement and Saving and the Changing Assets of Older Americans," mimeo, Kennedy School, Harvard University, October 1993.

On the Reagan tax cuts: James Poterba, "Are Consumers Forward Looking? Evidence from Fiscal Experiments," American Economic Review, *May 1988, 413–418.*

- *Consumption may move even if current income does not change.* The election of a charismatic president who articulates the vision of an exciting future may lead people to become more optimistic about the future in general, and about their own future income in particular, leading them to increase consumption even if their current income does not change. You saw in Chapter 3 that the U.S. recession of 1990–1991 was caused in large part by a large decrease in consumption, caused in turn by a large decrease in consumer confidence. Even today, economists are not sure why people became suddenly so pessimistic. But they did, and their expectations of the future turned somber. Consumer pessimism was one of the main causes of the 1990–1991 recession.

$S = sY$, or, equivalently, $C = (1 - s)Y$. This implied that, when income increased, consumption proportionately with income (C/Y remained the same). This was appropriate, as our focus was on permanent—long run—movements in income.

◀ What does this suggest will happen to the saving rate in a recession?

One of the main worries macroeconomists had after the events of September 11, 2001 was that we would see a repeat of 1990–1991: Consumers would become pessimistic, consumption would drop, leading to a deeper recession. As you saw in Chapter 3, this has not been the case. While consumer confidence fell in the months following September 11, 2001 the fall was much smaller than in 1990–1991, and, at the time of this writing—the start of 2002—confidence appears to be recovering.

16-2 Investment

How do firms make investment decisions? In our first pass at the answer in the core (Chapter 5), we took investment to depend on the current interest rate and the current level of sales. We improved on that answer in Chapter 14 by pointing out that what mattered was the real interest rate, not the nominal interest rate. It should now be clear that investment decisions, just as consumption decisions, depend on more than the current real interest rate and current sales. They also depend very much on expectations of the future. We now explore how those expectations affect investment decisions.

Just like the basic theory of consumption, the basic theory of investment is straightforward. A firm deciding whether to invest—say, whether to buy a new machine—must make a simple comparison. The firm must first compute the present value of profits it can expect from having this machine. It must then compare the present value of profits to the cost of buying the machine. If the present value exceeds the cost, the firm should buy the machine—invest; if the present value is less than the cost, then the firm should not buy the machine—not invest. This, in a nutshell, is the theory of investment. Let's look at it in more detail.

Investment and Expectations of Profit

Let's go through the steps a firm must take to determine whether to buy a new machine. (While I refer to a machine, the same reasoning applies to the other components of investment—the building of a new factory, the renovation of an office complex, and so on.)

Depreciation

To compute the present value of expected profits, the firm must first estimate how long the machine will last. Most machines are like cars. They can last nearly forever; but as time passes, they become more and more expensive to maintain, less and less reliable.

Assume a machine loses its usefulness at rate δ (the Greek lowercase delta) per year. A machine that is new this year is worth only $(1-\delta)$ machines next year, $(1-\delta)^2$ machines in two years, and so on. The *depreciation rate*, δ, measures how much usefulness the machine loses from one year to the next. What are reasonable values for δ? This is a question that the statisticians in charge of computing how the U.S. capital stock changes over time have had to answer. Based on their studies of depreciation of specific machines and buildings, they use numbers between 4 and 15% for machines, and between 2 and 4% for buildings and factories.

If the firm has a large number of machines, we can think of δ as the proportion of machines that die every year. (Think of lightbulbs—which work perfectly until they die.) If the firm starts the year with K working machines and does not buy new ones, it has only $K(1-\delta)$ machines left one year later, and so on.

The Present Value of Expected Profits

The firm must then compute the present value of expected profits.

To capture the fact that it takes some time to put machines in place (and even more time to build a factory or an office building), let's assume that a machine bought in year t becomes operational—and starts depreciating—only one year later, in year $t+1$. Denote profit per machine in real terms by Π (this is an uppercase Greek pi as opposed to the lowercase Greek pi, which we use to denote inflation).

If the firm buys a machine in year t, the machine generates its first expected profit in year $t + 1$; denote this expected profit by Π^e_{t+1}. The present value, in year t, of this expected profit in year $t + 1$, is given by

$$\frac{1}{1+r_t}\Pi^e_{t+1}$$

This term is represented by the arrow pointing left in the upper line of Figure 16-1. Because we are measuring profit in real terms, we are using real interest rates to discount future profits. This is one of the lessons we learned in Chapter 14.

Denote expected profit per machine in year $t + 2$ by Π^e_{t+2}. Because of depreciation, only $(1-\delta)$ of the machine bought in year t is left in year $t + 2$, so the expected profit from the machine is equal to $(1-\delta)\Pi^e_{t+2}$. The present value of this expected profit as of year t is equal to

$$\frac{1}{(1+r_t)(1+r^e_{t+1})}(1-\delta)\,\Pi^e_{t+2}$$

This computation is represented by the arrow pointing left in the lower line of Figure 16-1.

The same reasoning applies to expected profit in following years. Putting the pieces together gives us *the present value of expected profits* from buying the machine in year t, call it $V(\Pi^e_t)$:

$$V(\Pi^e_t) = \frac{1}{1+r_t}\Pi^e_{t+1} + \frac{1}{(1+r_t)(1+r^e_{t+1})}(1-\delta)\,\Pi^e_{t+2} + \cdots \qquad (16.3)$$

The expected present value is equal to the discounted value of expected profit next year, plus the discounted value of expected profit two years from now (taking into account the depreciation of the machine), and so on.

The Investment Decision

The firm must then decide whether to buy the machine. This decision depends on the relation between the present value of expected profits and the price of the machine. To simplify notation, let's assume the real price of a machine—that is, the machine's price in terms of the basket of goods produced in the economy—equals 1. What the firm must then do is compare the present value of profits to 1.

If the present value is less than 1, the firm should not buy the machine: If it did, it would be paying more for the machine than it expects to get back in profits later. If the present value exceeds 1, the firm has an incentive to buy the new machine.

Let's now go from this one-firm, one-machine example to investment in the economy as a whole.

Let I_t denote aggregate investment.

Denote profit per machine, or, more generally, profit per unit of capital (where capital includes machines, factories, office buildings, and so on) for the economy as a whole by Π_t.

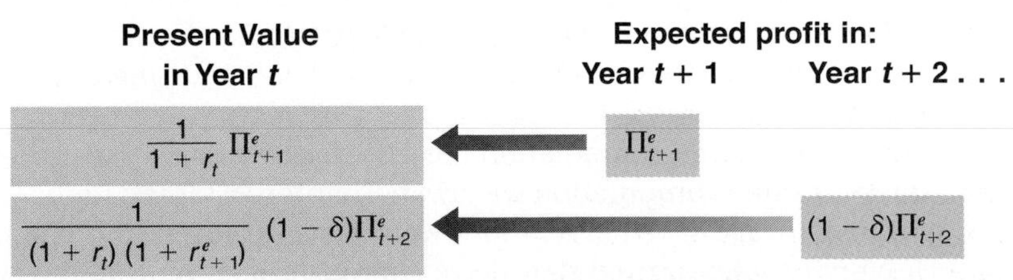

Figure 16-1 *Computing the Present Value of Expected Profits*

Investment and the Stock Market

FOCUS

Suppose a firm has 100 machines and 100 shares outstanding—one share per machine. Suppose the price per share is $2, and the purchase price of a machine is only $1. Obviously, the firm should invest—buy a new machine and finance it by issuing a share: Each machine costs the firm $1 to purchase, but stock market participants are willing to pay $2 for a share corresponding to this machine when it is installed in the firm.

This is an example of a more general argument made by James Tobin that there should be a tight relation between the stock market and investment. In deciding whether to invest, he argued, firms may not need to go through the type of complicated computation you saw in the text. In effect, the stock price tells firms how much the stock market values each unit of capital already in place. The firm then has a simple problem: Compare the purchase price of an additional unit of capital to the price the stock market is willing to pay for it. If the stock market value exceeds the purchase price, the firm should buy the machine; otherwise, it should not.

Tobin then constructed a variable corresponding to the value of a unit of capital in place relative to its purchase price, and looked at how closely it moved with investment. He used the symbol "q" to denote the variable, and the variable has become known as **Tobin's q**. Its construction is as follows.

1. Take the total value of U.S. corporations, as assessed by financial markets. That is, compute the sum of their stock market value (the price of a share times the number of shares). Compute also the total value of their bonds outstanding (firms finance themselves not only through stocks but also through bonds). Add together the value of stocks and bonds.
2. Divide this total value by the value of the capital stock of U.S. corporations at replacement cost (the price firms would have to pay to replace their machines, their plants, and so on).

The ratio gives us, in effect, the value of a unit of capital in place relative to its current purchase price. This ratio is Tobin's q. Intuitively, the higher q, the higher the value of capital relative to its current purchase price, and the higher should be investment. (In the example at the beginning of this Focus box, Tobin's q is equal to 2; the firm should definitely invest.)

How tight is the relation between Tobin's q and investment? The answer is given in the adjacent figure, which plots the two variables for each year from 1960 to 1999 for the United States.

Measured on the left vertical axis is the rate of change of the ratio of investment to capital.

Measured on the right vertical axis is the rate of change of Tobin's q. This variable is lagged once. For 1987; for example, the figure shows the rate of change of investment to capital for 1987, and the rate of change of Tobin's q for 1986—that is, a year earlier. The reason for presenting the two variables this way is that the strongest relation in the data appears to be between investment *this year* and Tobin's q *last year*. Put another way, movements in investment are more closely associated with movements in the stock market last year rather than with movements this year; this may be because it takes time for firms to make investment decisions, build new factories, and so on.

Denote the expected present value of profit per unit of capital by $V(\Pi_t^e)$, defined as in equation (16.3).

Our discussion suggests an investment function of the form:

$$I_t = I(V(\Pi_t^e)) \quad (16.4)$$
$$(+)$$

In words: *Investment depends positively on the expected present value of future profits (per unit of capital). The higher current or expected profits, the higher the expected present value and the higher the level of investment. The higher current or expected real interest rates, the lower the expected present value, and thus the lower the level of investment.*

If the present value computation the firm has to make strikes you as quite similar to the present value computation we saw in Chapter 15 for the fundamental value of a stock, you are right. This relation was first explored by James Tobin, from Yale University, who argued that there should indeed be a tight relation between

The message from the figure is clear: There is a strong relation between Tobin's q and investment. This is probably not because firms follow blindly the signals from the stock market, but because investment decisions and stock market prices depend very much on the same factors—expected future profits and expected future interest rates.

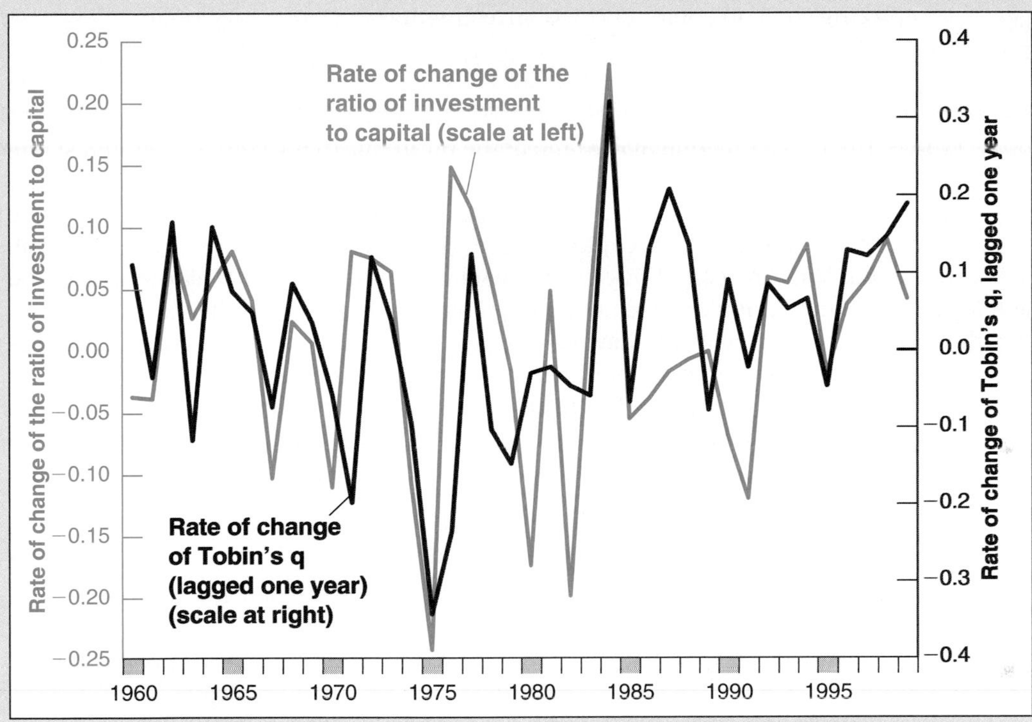

Figure 1 *Tobin's q Versus the Ratio of Investment to Capital—Annual Rates of Change, 1960–1999*

investment and the value of the stock market. His argument and the evidence are presented in the Focus box "Investment and the Stock Market."

◀ **Tobin received the Nobel Prize in economics in 1981.**

A Convenient Special Case

Before exploring further implications and extensions of equation (16.4), it is useful to go through a special case where the relation between investment, profit, and interest rates becomes very simple.

Suppose firms expect both future profits (per unit of capital) and future interest rates to remain at the same level as today, so that

$$\Pi^e_{t+1} = \Pi^e_{t+2} = \cdots = \Pi_t$$

and

$$r^e_{t+1} = r^e_{t+2} = \cdots = r_t$$

Economists call such expectations (in which people expect the future to be like the present) **static expectations**. Under these two assumptions, equation (16.3) becomes

$$V(\Pi_t^e) = \left(\frac{\Pi_t}{r_t + \delta}\right) \quad (16.5)$$

(the derivation is given in the appendix to this chapter).

The present value of expected profits is simply the ratio of the profit rated—that is, profit per unit of capital—to the sum of the real interest rate and the depreciation rate.

Replacing (16.5) in equation (16.4), investment is

$$I_t = I\left(\frac{\Pi_t}{r_t + \delta}\right) \quad (16.6)$$

Investment is a function of the ratio of the profit rate to the sum of the interest rate and the depreciation rate. Look more closely at the expression in parentheses. The denominator—the sum of the real interest rate and the depreciation rate—is called the **user cost** or the **rental cost of capital**. To see why it is called the rental cost of capital, suppose the firm, instead of buying the machine, rented it by the year from a rental agency. How much would the rental agency have to charge? Even if the machine did not depreciate, the agency would have to charge an interest charge equal to r_t times the price of the machine (we have assumed the price of a machine to be 1 in real terms, so r_t times 1 is just r_t): The agency has to get at least as much from buying and then renting the machine as it would from, say, buying bonds. In addition, the rental agency would have to charge for depreciation, δ times the price of the machine, 1. Therefore,

Such arrangements exist: Many firms lease cars and trucks from leasing companies.

$$\text{Rental cost} = (r_t + \delta)$$

Even though firms typically do not rent their machines, $(r_t + \delta)$ still captures the implicit cost—sometimes called the *shadow cost*—to the firm of using the machine for one year.

The investment function given by equation (16.6) then has a simple interpretation: *Investment depends on the ratio of profit to the user cost. The higher the profit rate, the higher the level of investment. The higher the real interest rate, the higher the user cost, the lower the level of investment.*

This relation between profit, the real interest rate, and investment relies on a strong assumption: that the future is expected to be the same as the present. It is nevertheless a useful relation to remember, and a relation macroeconomists keep handy in their toolbox.

If the future is expected to be the same as the present, investment depends on the ratio of profit to the user cost—the sum of the real interest rate and the depreciation rate.

Profit $\uparrow \Rightarrow$ investment $\uparrow$

Interest rate $\uparrow \Rightarrow$ investment $\downarrow$

Current Versus Expected Profit

The theory we have developed so far implies that investment should be forward looking, and depends primarily on *expected future profits*. (Under our assumption that new capital starts being operational only one year after purchase, current profit does not even appear in equation [16.3].) One striking empirical fact about investment, however, is how strongly it moves with fluctuations in *current profit*.

This relation is shown in Figure 16-2, which plots yearly changes in investment and in profit since 1960 for the U.S. economy. Investment is measured as the ratio of *fixed nonresidential investment* to the *fixed nonresidential capital stock*. Profit is constructed as the ratio of the sum of *after-tax profits plus interest payments paid by U.S. corporations*, divided by their capital stock. The average value of this ratio is equal to approximately 6% a year; put another way, one dollar of capital generates on average 6 cents of profit a year. The shaded areas in the figure represent years in which there was a recession—a decline in output for at least two consecutive quarters of the year.

For definitions of all these terms, see Appendix 1 on National Income Accounts at the end of the book.

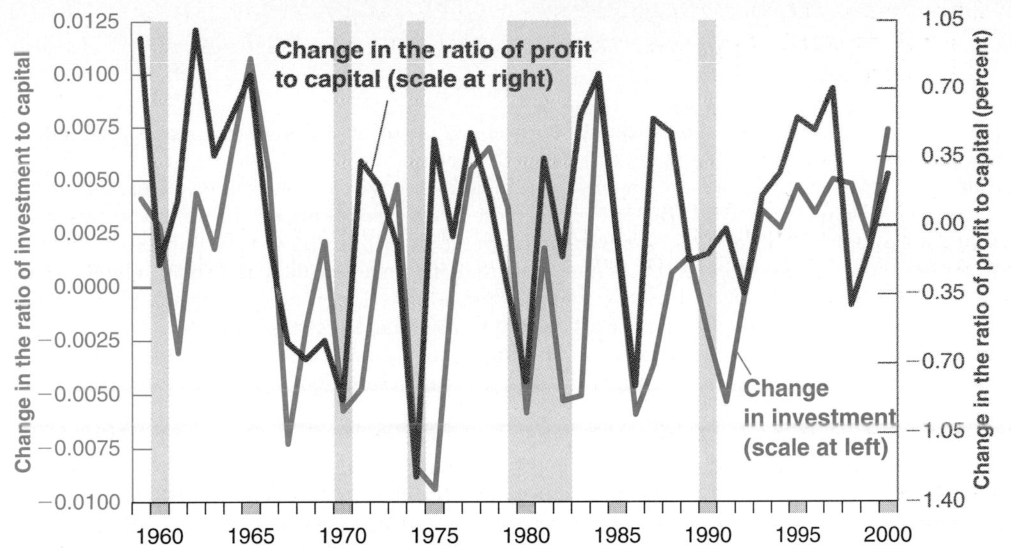

Figure 16-2

Changes in Investment and Changes in Profit in the United States, 1960–2000

Investment and profit move very much together.

There is a clear positive relation between changes in investment and changes in current profit in Figure 16-2. Is this relation inconsistent with the theory we have just developed, which holds that investment should be related to the present value of expected future profits rather than to current profit? Not necessarily: If firms expect future profits to move very much like current profit, then the present value of profits will move very much like current profit, and so will investment.

Economists who have looked at the question more closely have concluded, however, that the effect of current profit on investment is stronger than would be predicted by the theory we have developed so far. How they have gathered some of the evidence is described in the Focus box "Profitability Versus Cash Flow." On one hand, some firms with highly profitable investment projects but low current profits appear to be investing too little. On the other hand, some firms that have high current profit appear sometimes to invest in projects of doubtful profitability. In short, current profit appears to affect investment, even after controlling for the expected present value of profits.

Why does current profit play a role in the investment decision? The answer lurks in Section 16-1, where we discussed why consumption depends directly on current income: Some of the reasons we used to explain the behavior of consumers also apply to firms:

- If its current profit is low, a firm that wants to buy new machines can get the funds it needs only by borrowing. It may be reluctant to borrow: While expected profits may look good, things may turn bad, leaving the firm unable to repay the debt. But if current profit is high, the firm may be able to finance its investment just by retaining some of its earnings and without having to borrow. The bottom line is that higher current profit may lead the firm to invest more.
- Even if the firm wants to invest, it may have difficulty borrowing. Potential lenders may not be convinced the project is as good as the firm says, and may worry the firm will be unable to repay. If the firm has large current profits, it does not have to borrow and so does not need to convince potential lenders. It can proceed and invest as it pleases, and is more likely to do so.

In summary: To fit the investment behavior we observe, the investment equation is better written as

$$I_t = I(V(\Pi_t^e), \Pi_t) \qquad (16.7)$$
$$(\; + \quad , + \;)$$

Profitability Versus Cash Flow

FOCUS

How much does investment depend on the expected present value of profits, and how much does it depend on current profit? In other words, what is more important for investment decisions: **profitability** (the expected present discounted value of profits), or **cash flow** (current profit, the net flow of cash the firm is receiving)?

The difficulty in answering this question is similar to the problem of identifying the relative importance of current income and expected future income on consumption—a problem we discussed in the first Focus box in this chapter: Most of the time, cash flow and profitability are likely to move together. Firms that do well typically have both large cash flows and good future prospects. Firms that suffer losses often also have poor future prospects.

As in the case for consumption, the best way to isolate the effects of cash flow and profitability is to identify times or events when cash flow and profitability move in different directions, and then look at what happens to investment. This is the approach taken by Owen Lamont, an economist at the University of Chicago. An example will help you understand Lamont's strategy.

Think of two firms, A and B. Firm A is involved only in steel production. Firm B is composed of two parts, one part steel production, the other part oil exploration.

Suppose there is a sharp drop in the price of oil, leading to losses in oil exploration. This shock decreases firm B's cash flow. If the losses in oil exploration are large enough to offset the profits from steel production, firm B may show an overall loss.

The question we can now ask is: As a result of the decrease in the price of oil, will firm B invest less in its steel operation than firm A does? If only profitability in steel production matters, there is no reason for firm B to invest less in its steel operation than firm A. But if current cash flow also matters, the fact that firm B has a lower cash flow may prevent it from investing as much as firm A in its steel operation. Looking at investment in the steel operations of the two firms can tell us how much investment depends on cash flow versus profitability.

This is the empirical strategy followed by Lamont. He focuses on what happened in 1986 when the price of oil in the United States dropped by 50%, leading to large losses in oil-related activities. He then looks at whether firms that had substantial oil activities cut investment in their non-oil activities relatively more than other firms in the same non-oil activities. He concludes that they did. He finds that for every $1 decrease in cash flow due to the decrease in the price of oil, investment spending in non-oil activities was reduced by 10 to 20 cents. In short: Current cash flow matters.

Source: Owen Lamont, "Cash Flow and Investment: Evidence from Internal Capital Markets," Journal of Finance, *March 1997.*

A general review of studies along these lines is given by R. Glenn Hubbard in "Capital-market Imperfections and Investment," Journal of Economic Literature, *1995.*

In words: *Investment depends both on the expected present value of profits and on the current level of profit.*

Profit and Sales

We have argued that investment depends on both current and expected profit. We must now ask: What determines profit? Answer: Primarily two factors: (1) the level of sales, and (2) the existing capital stock. If sales are low relative to the capital stock, profits per unit of capital are likely to be depressed as well.

Let's write this more formally. Ignore the distinction between sales and output, and let Y_t denote output—equivalently, sales. Let K_t denote the capital stock at time t. Our discussion suggests the following relation:

$$\Pi_t = \Pi\left(\underset{(+)}{\frac{Y_t}{K_t}}\right) \qquad (16.8)$$

Profit per unit of capital is an increasing function of the ratio of sales to the capital stock. For a given capital stock, the higher the sales, the higher is profit. For given sales, the higher the capital stock, the lower is profit.

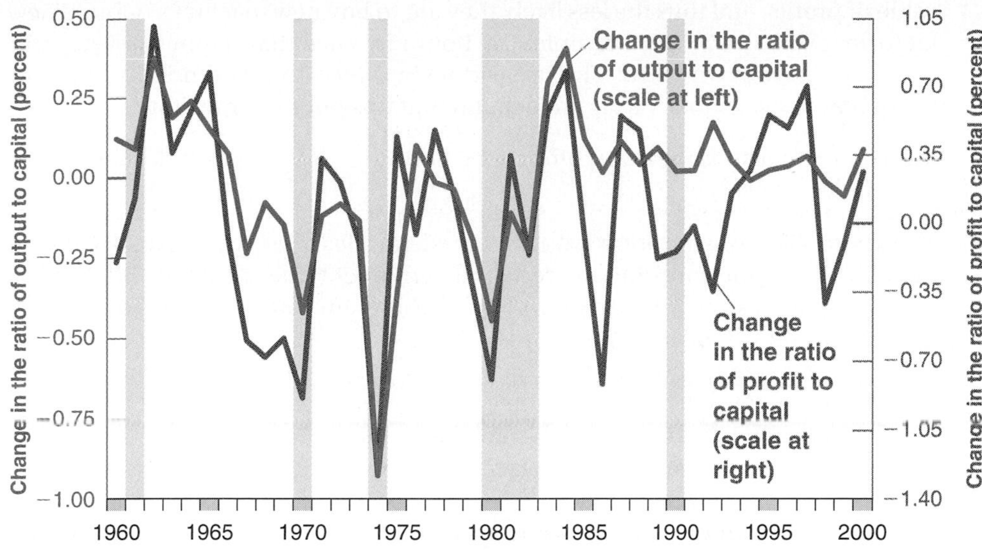

Figure 16-3

Changes in Profit and Changes in the Ratio of Output to Capital in the United States, 1960–2000

Profit and output move largely together.

How does this relation hold in practice? Figure 16-3 plots yearly changes in profit per unit of capital (measured on the right vertical axis) and changes in the ratio of output to capital (measured on the left vertical axis), for the United States since 1960. As in Figure 16-2, profit per unit of capital is defined as the sum of after-tax profits plus interest payments for U.S. corporations, divided by their capital stock, measured at replacement cost. The ratio of output to capital is constructed as the ratio of GDP to the aggregate capital stock. The shaded areas are years during which the U.S. economy was in recession.

The figure shows a tight relation between changes in profit and changes in the ratio of output to capital. Given that most of the year-to-year changes in the ratio of output to capital come from movements in output (capital moves slowly over time; even large swings in investment lead to slow changes in the capital stock), we can state the relation as follows: Profit decreases in recessions, and increases in expansions.

Why is this relation between output and profit relevant here? Because it implies a link between *current output and expected future output* on one hand, and *investment* on the other: Current output affects current profit, expected future output affects expected future profit, and current and expected future profits in turn affect investment. For example, the anticipation of a long, sustained economic expansion leads firms to expect high profits, now and for some time in the future. These expectations in turn lead to higher investment. The effect of current and expected output on investment, together with the effect of investment back on demand and output, will play a crucial role when we return to the determination of output in Chapter 17.

◀ High expected output leads to High expected profit leads to High investment today

16-3 The Volatility of Consumption and Investment

You will surely have noticed the similarities between our treatment of consumption and of investment behavior in Sections 16-1 and 16-2:

- Whether consumers perceive current movements in income to be transitory or permanent affects their consumption decisions.
- In the same way, whether firms perceive current movements in sales to be transitory or permanent affects their investment decisions. The less they expect a current increase in sales to last, the less they revise their assessment of the present

value of profits, and thus the less likely they are to buy new machines or build new factories. This is why, for example, the boom in sales that happens every year between Thanksgiving and Christmas does not lead to a boom in investment every year in December. Firms understand that this boom is transitory.

In the United States, retail sales are 24% higher on average in December than in other months. In France and Italy, sales are 60% higher in December.

But there are also important differences between consumption decisions and investment decisions:

- The theory of consumption we developed implies that when faced with an increase in income consumers perceive as permanent, they respond with *at most* an equal increase in consumption. The permanent nature of the increase in income implies that they can afford to increase consumption now and in the future by the same amount as the increase in income. Increasing consumption more than one for one would require cuts in consumption later, and there is no reason for consumers to want to plan consumption this way.
- Now consider the behavior of firms faced with an increase in sales they believe to be permanent. The present value of expected profits increases, leading to an increase in investment. In contrast to consumption, there is no implication that the increase in investment should be no greater than the increase in sales. Rather, once a firm has decided that an increase in sales justifies the purchase of a new machine or the building of a new factory, it may want to proceed quickly, leading to a large but short-lived increase in investment spending. This increase may exceed the increase in sales.

  More concretely, take a firm that has a ratio of capital to its annual sales of, say, 3:1. An increase in sales of $10 million this year, if expected to be permanent, requires the firm to spend $30 million on additional capital if it wants to maintain the same ratio of capital to output. If the firm buys the additional capital right away, the increase in investment spending this year will equal *three times* the increase in sales. Once the capital stock has adjusted, the firm will return to its normal pattern of investment. This example is extreme, because firms are unlikely to adjust their capital stock right away. But even if they do adjust their capital stock more slowly, say over a few years, the increase in investment may still exceed the increase in sales for a while.

  We can tell the same story in terms of equation (16.8). As we make no distinction here between output and sales, the initial increase in sales leads to an equal increase in output, Y, so that Y/K—the ratio of the firm's output to its existing capital stock—also increases. The result is higher profit, which leads the firm to undertake more investment. Over time, the higher level of investment leads to a higher capital stock, K, so that Y/K decreases back to normal. Profit per unit of capital returns to normal, and so does investment. Thus, in response to a permanent increase in sales, investment may increase a lot initially, and then return to normal over time.

These differences suggest that investment should be more volatile than consumption. How much more volatile? The answer from the data is given in Figure 16-4, which plots yearly rates of change in U.S. consumption and investment since 1960. To make the figure easier to interpret, both rates of change are plotted as deviations from the average rate of change, so that they are on average equal to zero.

The figure yields three conclusions:

- Consumption and investment usually move together: Recessions, for example, are typically associated with decreases in *both* investment and consumption. Given our discussion, which has emphasized that consumption and investment depend largely on the same determinants, this should not come as a surprise.

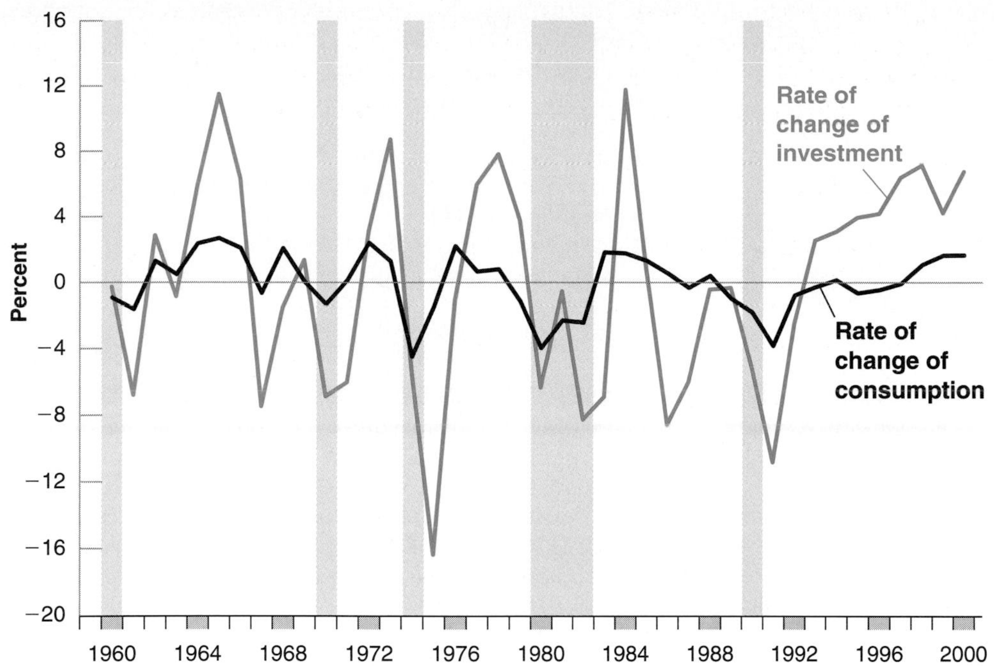

Figure 16-4

Rates of Change of Consumption and Investment, 1960–2000

Relative movements in investment are much larger than relative movements in consumption.

- Investment is much more volatile than consumption. Relative movements in investment range from −17 to 12%, while relative movements in consumption range only from −4 to 3%.
- Another way of stating the same fact is that, whereas the level of investment is much smaller than the level of consumption (recall that investment accounts for 17% of GDP, versus 69% for consumption), changes in investment from one year to the next are typically of the same magnitude as changes in consumption. Both components contribute roughly equally to fluctuations in output over time.

Summary

- Consumption depends both on wealth and current income. Wealth is the sum of nonhuman wealth (financial wealth and housing wealth) and human wealth (the present value of expected after-tax labor income).
- The response of consumption to changes in income depends on whether consumers perceive these changes as transitory or as permanent.
- Consumption is likely to respond less than one for one to movements in income, and consumption may move even if current income does not change.
- Investment depends on both current profit and the present value of expected future profits.
- Under the simplifying assumption that firms expect profits and interest rates to be the same in the future as they are today, we can think of investment as depending on the ratio of profit to the user cost of capital, where the user cost is the sum of the real interest rate and the depreciation rate.
- Movements in profit are closely related to movements in output. Hence, we can think of investment as depending indirectly on current and expected future output movements. Firms that anticipate a long output expansion, and thus a long sequence of high profits, will invest. Movements in output that are not expected to last will have a small effect on investment.
- Investment is much more volatile than consumption. While investment accounts only for 17% of GDP and consumption accounts for 69%, movements in investment and consumption are of roughly equal magnitude.

Key Terms

- permanent income theory of consumption, 336
- life cycle theory of consumption, 336
- financial wealth, 336
- housing wealth, 336
- human wealth, 336
- nonhuman wealth, 336
- total wealth, 336
- panel data sets, 337
- natural experiment, 340
- Tobin's q, 344
- static expectations, 346
- user cost of capital, or rental cost of capital, 346
- profitability, 348
- cash flow, 348

Questions and Problems

Quick Check

1. *Using the information in this chapter, label each of the following statements* true, false, *or* uncertain. *Explain briefly.*
   a. For the typical college student, human wealth and nonhuman wealth are approximately equal.
   b. Natural experiments, such as retirement and announced tax cuts, do not suggest that expectations of future income are a major factor affecting consumption.
   c. Buildings and factories depreciate much faster than machines do.
   d. A high value for Tobin's q indicates that the stock market believes that capital is overvalued and thus investment should be lower.
   e. Economists have found that the effect of current profit on investment can be fully explained by the effect of current profit on expectations of future profits.
   f. Data from the last three decades in the United States suggest that corporate profits are closely tied to the business cycle.
   g. Changes in consumption and investment are typi–cally in the same direction and roughly of the same magnitude.

2. *A consumer has nonhuman wealth equal to $100,000. She earns $40,000 this year, and expects her salary to rise by 5% in real terms each year for the following two years. She will then retire. The real interest rate is equal to 0% and is expected to remain at 0% in the future. Labor income is taxed at a rate of 25%.*
   a. What is this consumer's human wealth?
   b. What is her total wealth?
   c. If she expects to live for seven years after retirement and wants her consumption to remain the same (in real terms) every year from now on, how much can she consume this year?
   d. If she received a bonus of $20,000 in the current year only, with all future salary payments remaining as stated earlier, by how much could she increase consumption now and in the future?
   e. Suppose now that at retirement, Social Security will start paying benefits each year equal to 60% of her earnings during her last working year. (Assume benefits are not taxed.) How much can she consume this year (and still maintain constant consumption)?

3. *A pretzel manufacturer is considering buying another pretzel-making machine that costs $100,000. The machine will depreciate by 8% per year. It will generate real profits equal to $18,000 next year, $18,000(1 − 8%) two years from now (that is, the same real profits, but adjusted for depreciation), $18,000(1 − 8%)^2 three years from now, and so on. Determine whether the manufacturer should buy the machine if the real interest rate is assumed to remain constant at*
   a. 5%
   b. 10%
   c. 15%

4. *Suppose that at age 22, you have just finished college and have been offered a job with a starting salary of $40,000. Your salary will remain constant in real terms. However, you have also been admitted to a professional school. The school takes two years to complete and upon graduation you expect your starting salary to be 10% higher in real terms, and remain constant in real terms thereafter. The tax rate on labor income is 40%.*
   a. If the real interest rate is zero and you expect to retire at age 60 (i.e., if you do not go to professional school, you expect to work for 38 years total), what is the maximum you should be willing to pay in tuition to attend this professional school?
   b. What is your answer to (a) if you expect to pay 30% in taxes?

Dig Deeper

5. *Individual saving and aggregate capital accumulation*

   Suppose that every consumer is born without any financial wealth and lives for three periods: young, middle age, and retirement age. Consumers work in the first two periods and retire in the last one. Their income is $5 in the first period, $25 in the second, and $0 in the last one. Inflation and expected inflation is zero, and the real interest rate is also zero.
   a. What is the present discounted value of future labor income at the beginning of life? What is the highest sustainable level of consumption such that consumption is equal in all three periods?
   b. For each age group, what is the amount of saving that allows consumers to maintain the constant level of consumption you found in (a)? (*Hint*: Saving can be a negative number if the consumer needs to borrow in order to maintain a certain level of consumption.)

c. Suppose there are n people born each period. What is total saving? (*Hint*: Compute the total amount saved by the generations that save and subtract the total amount dissaved by the generations that dissave.) Explain.

d. What is total financial wealth in the economy? (*Hint*: Compute the financial wealth of people at the beginning of the first period of life, the second period of life, the third period of life. [Remember that people can be in debt, so financial wealth can be negative.] Add them up.)

Suppose now that restrictions on borrowing do not allow young consumers to borrow. At each age group, consumers once again compute their total wealth and then determine their desired level of consumption as the highest level that allows their consumption to be equal in all three periods. However, if that is greater than their income plus total financial wealth, then they are constrained to consuming exactly their income plus total financial wealth.

e. Derive consumption in each period of life. Explain the difference between your answer here and your answer to (a).

f. Derive total saving. Explain the difference, if any, with your answer to (c).

g. Derive total financial wealth. Explain the difference with your answer to (d).

h. Financial liberalization may be good for people, but it is bad for overall capital accumulation. Discuss.

Explore Further

6. *For this exercise, you will need annual data on consumption and investment. Go to the NIPA Web page:* **www.bea.doc.gov/bea/dn/nipaweb/**. *Go to Table 1-2. Find annual data for the years 1959 to 2000 for*

- Personal Consumption Expenditures
- Gross Private Domestic Investment
- Gross Domestic Product

a. On average, how much larger is consumption than investment?

b. Compute the change in the levels of consumption and investment from one year to the next, and graph them for the period 1959–2000. Are the year-to-year changes in consumption and investment of the same magnitude?

c. What do your answers in (a) and (b) imply about the volatility of consumption and investment? Is this implication consistent with Figure 16-4?

d. Use Figure 16-4 to identify the years corresponding to the last two recessions. Using your graph from (b), which component played the largest role in each of these recessions, consumption or investment? Is this consistent with what we have learned so far about these recessions?

We invite you to visit the Blanchard page on the Prentice Hall Web site at:
www.prenhall.com/blanchard
for this chapter's World Wide Web exercises

Appendix: Derivation of the Expected Present Value of Profits Under Static Expectations

You saw in the text that the expected present value of profits is given by

$$V(\Pi_t^e) = \frac{1}{1+r_t}\Pi_{t+1}^e + \frac{1}{(1+r_t)(1+r_{t+1}^e)}(1-\delta)\,\Pi_{t+2}^e + \cdots \quad (16.3)$$

If firms expect both future profits (per unit of capital) and future interest rates to remain at the same level as today, so that $\Pi_{t+1}^e = \Pi_{t+2}^e = \cdots = \Pi_t$, and $r_{t+1}^e = r_{t+2}^e = \cdots = r_t$, equation (16.3) becomes

$$V(\Pi_t^e) = \frac{1}{1+r_t}\Pi_t + \frac{1}{(1+r_t)^2}(1-\delta)\,\Pi_t + \cdots$$

Factoring out $[1/(1+r_t)]\,\Pi_t$,

$$V(\Pi_t^e) = \frac{1}{1+r_t}\Pi_t\left(1 + \frac{1-\delta}{1+r_t} + \cdots\right) \quad (16.A1)$$

The term in parentheses in this equation is a geometric series, a series of the form $1 + x + x^2 + \cdots$, and so it is equal to $1/(1-x)$ (Proposition 2 in Appendix 2 at the end of the book):

$$(1 + x + x^2 + \ldots) = \frac{1}{1-x}$$

Here x equals $(1-\delta)/(1+r_t)$, so,

$$\left(1 + \frac{1-\delta}{1+r_t} + \left(\frac{1-\delta}{1+r_t}\right)^2 + \ldots\right) = \frac{1}{1-(1-\delta)/(1+r_t)} = \frac{1+r_t}{r_t+\delta}$$

Replacing in equation (16-A1) gives

$$V(\Pi_t^e) = \frac{1}{1+r_t}\,\frac{1+r_t}{r_t+\delta}\,\Pi_t$$

Simplifying gives equation (16.5) in the text:

$$V(\Pi_t^e) = \left(\frac{\Pi_t}{r_t+\delta}\right) \quad (16.5)$$

Expectations, Output, and Policy

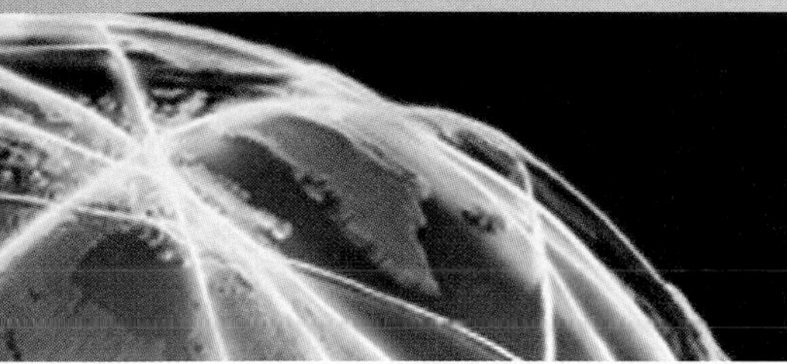

CHAPTER 17

In Chapter 15, you saw how expectations affected bond and stock prices. In Chapter 16, you saw how expectations affected consumption decisions and investment decisions. In this chapter we put the pieces together and take another look at the effects of monetary and fiscal policy.

- Section 17-1 draws the major implication of what we have learned, namely, that expectations of both future output and future interest rates affect current spending and therefore current output.

- Section 17-2 looks at monetary policy. It shows how the effects of monetary policy depend crucially on how expectations respond to policy: Monetary policy directly affects only the short-term interest rate. What happens to spending and output then depends on how changes in the short-term interest rate lead people and firms to change their expectations of future interest rates and of future income, and, by implication, lead them to change their spending.

- Section 17-3 turns to fiscal policy. It shows how, in sharp contrast to the simple model you saw back in the core, a fiscal contraction may, under some circumstances, lead to an increase in output, even in the short run. Again, how expectations respond to policy are at the center of the story. ■

17-1 Expectations and Decisions: Taking Stock

Let's start by reviewing what you have learned, and then discuss how we should modify the characterization of goods and financial markets—the *IS-LM* model—we developed in the core.

Expectations, Consumption, and Investment Decisions

The theme of Chapter 16 was that both consumption and investment decisions depend very much on expectations of future income and interest rates. The channels through which expectations affect consumption and investment spending are summarized in Figure 17-1.

Note the many channels through which expected future variables affect current decisions, both directly and through asset prices:

- An increase in current and expected future after-tax real labor income, or a decrease in current and expected future real interest rates increase human wealth (the expected present discounted value of after-tax real labor income), which in turn leads to an increase in consumption.
- An increase in current and expected future real dividends, or a decrease in current expected future real interest rates increase stock prices, which lead to an increase in nonhuman wealth, and in turn, to an increase in consumption.
- A decrease in current and expected future nominal interest rates leads to an increase in bond prices, which leads to an increase in nonhuman wealth, and, in turn, to an increase in consumption. (Note that in the case of bonds, it is nominal rather than real interest rates which matter, because bonds are claims to dollars rather than goods in the future.)
- An increase in current and expected future real after-tax profits, or a decrease in current and expected future real interest rates, increase the present value of real after-tax profits, which lead, in turn, to an increase in investment.

Expectations and the *IS* Relation

A model that gave a detailed treatment of consumption and investment along the lines suggested in Figure 17-1 would be very complicated. It can be done—and it is done in the large empirical models that macroeconomists build to understand the economy

Figure 17-1

Expectations and Spending. The Channels

Expectations affect consumption and investment decisions, both directly and through asset prices.

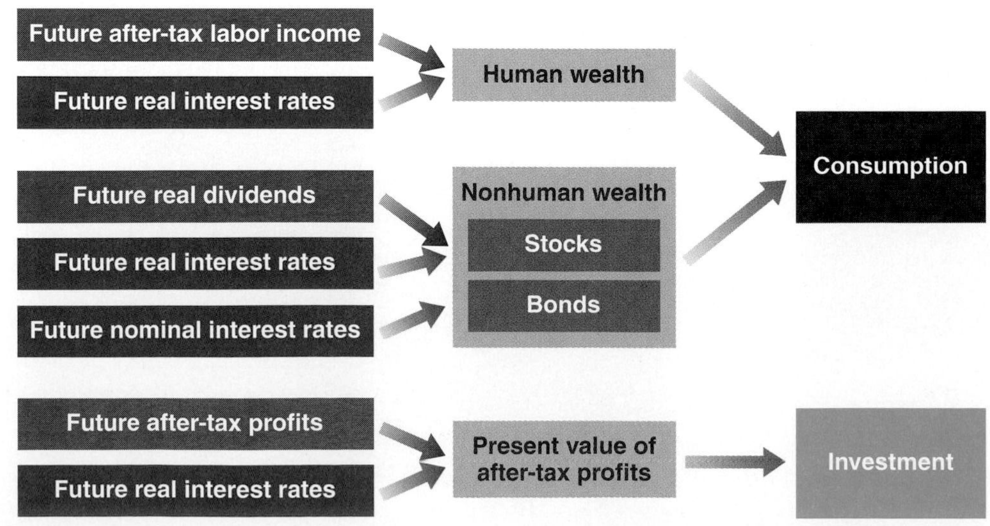

and analyze policy; but this is not the place for such complexity. We want to capture the essence of what you have learned so far, how consumption and investment depend on expectations of the future—without getting lost in the details.

To do so, we make a major simplification. We reduce the present and the future to only two periods: (1) a *current* period, which you can think of as the current year, and (2) a *future* period, which you can think of as all future years lumped together. This way, we do not have to keep track of expectations about each future year.

This way of dividing time between "today" and "later" is the way many of us organize our own life: Think of "things to do today" versus "things that can wait."

Having made this assumption, the question becomes: How we should write the *IS* relation for the current period. Earlier, we derived the following equation for the *IS* relation:

See equation (14.8) in Chapter 14, which itself extended the relation derived in Chapter 5 (equation 5.2) to allow for a distinction between the real interest rate and the nominal interest rate.

$$Y = C(Y - T) + I(Y, r) + G$$

We assumed that consumption depended only on current income, and investment depended only on current output and the current real interest rate. We now want to modify this to take into account the effect of expectations both on consumption and on investment. We proceed in two steps:

- First, we simply rewrite the equation in more compact form, but without changing its content. For that purpose, let's define aggregate private spending as the sum of consumption and investment spending:

$$A(Y, T, r) \equiv C(Y - T) + I(Y, r)$$

where A stands for **aggregate private spending**, or, simply, **private spending**. With this notation we can rewrite the *IS* relation as

The reason for doing so is to group together the two components of demand, C and I, which both depend on expectations. We continue to treat G, government spending, as exogenous—unexplained within our model.

$$\underset{(+,\ -,\ -)}{Y = A(Y, T, r)} + G \qquad (17.1)$$

The properties of aggregate private spending, A, follow from the properties of consumption and investment that we derived in earlier chapters.

Aggregate private spending is an increasing function of income, Y: Higher income (equivalently, output) increases consumption and investment.

Aggregate private spending is a decreasing function of taxes, T: Higher taxes decrease consumption.

Aggregate private spending is a decreasing function of the real interest rate, r: A higher real interest rate decreases investment.

- The first step only simplified notation. Now comes the task of extending equation (17.1) to reflect the role of expectations. The natural extension is to allow spending to depend not only on current variables but also on their expected values in the future period

$$Y = \underset{(+,\ -,\ -,\ +,\ -,\ -)}{A(Y, T, r, Y'^e, T'^e, r'^e)} + G \qquad (17.2)$$

Primes denote future values and the superscript e denotes an expectation, so Y'^e, T'^e, and r'^e denote future expected income, future expected taxes, and the future expected real interest rate, respectively. The notation is a bit heavy, but what it captures is straightforward:

Notation:
Primes stand for values of the variables in the future period.
The superscript e stands for "expected."

Increases in either current or expected future income increase private spending.

Increases in either current or expected future taxes decrease private spending.

Increases in either the current or expected future real interest rate decrease private spending.

Y or $Y'^e \uparrow \rightarrow A \uparrow$
T or $T'^e \uparrow \rightarrow A \downarrow$
r or $r'^e \uparrow \rightarrow A \downarrow$

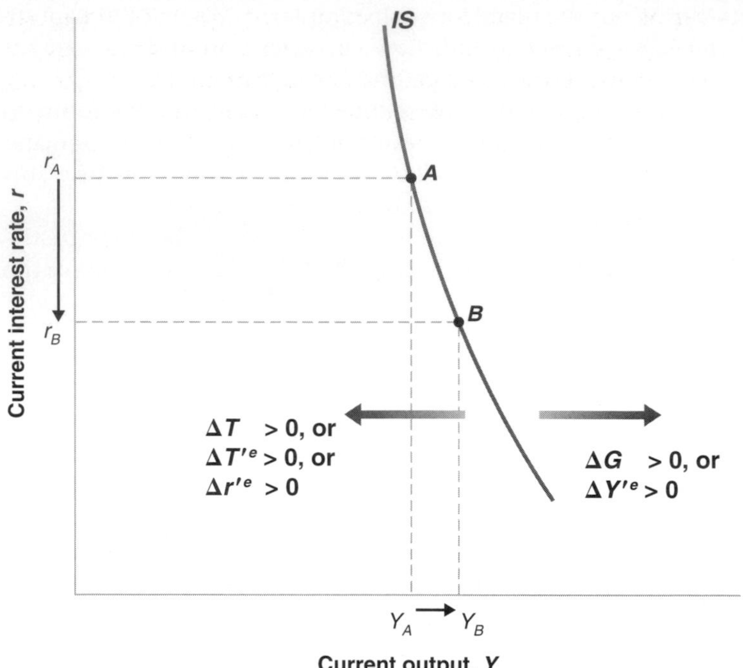

Figure 17-2

The New IS Curve

Given expectations, a decrease in the real interest rate leads to a small increase in output: The *IS* curve is steeply downward sloping. Increases in government spending, or in expected future output shift the *IS* curve to the right. Increases in taxes, in expected future taxes, or in the expected future real interest rate shift the *IS* curve to the left.

With goods market equilibrium now given by equation (17.2), Figure 17-2 shows the new *IS* curve. As usual, to draw the curve, we take all variables other than current output, Y, and the current real interest rate, r, as given. Thus, the *IS* curve is drawn for given values of current and future expected taxes, T and T'^e, for given values of expected future output, Y'^e, and for given values of the expected future real interest rate, r'^e.

The new *IS* curve, based on equation (17-2), is still downward sloping, for the same reason as in Chapter 5: A decrease in the current real interest rate leads to an increase in spending. This increase in spending leads, through a multiplier effect, to an increase in output. We can say more, however: The new *IS* curve is much steeper than the *IS* curve we drew in earlier chapters. Put another way, *everything being the same*, a large decrease in the current interest rate is likely to have only a small effect on equilibrium output.

To see why the effect is small, take point A on the *IS* curve in Figure 17-2, and consider the effects of a decrease in the real interest rate. The effect of the decrease in the real interest rate on output depends on the strength of two effects: the effect of the real interest rate on spending given income, and the size of the multiplier. Let's examine each one in turn.

Suppose you want a 30-year loan, and the one-year interest rate goes down from 5 to 2%. All future expected one-year rates remain the same. By how much does the 30-year interest rate come down? (If you need to, look at the relation between short-term interest rates and long-term interest rates in Chapter 15.)

- A decrease in the current real interest rate, *given unchanged expectations of the future real interest rate,* does not have much effect on spending. We saw why in the previous chapters: A change in only the current real interest rate does not lead to large changes in present values, and so does not lead to large changes in spending. For example, firms are not likely to change their investment plans very much in response to a decrease in the current real interest rate if they do not expect future real interest rates to be lower as well.
- The multiplier is likely to be small. Recall that the size of the multiplier depends on the size of the effect of a change in current income (output) on spending. But a change in current income, *given unchanged expectations of future income,* is

unlikely to have a large effect on spending. The reason: Changes in income that are not expected to last have only a limited effect on both consumption and investment. Consumers who expect their income to be higher only for a year will increase consumption, but by much less than the increase in income. Firms which expect sales to be higher only for a year are unlikely to change their investment plans much if at all.

Suppose your firm decides to give all employees a one-time bonus of $10,000. This is not expected to happen again. By how much will you increase your consumption this year? (If you need to, look at the discussion of consumption behavior in Chapter 16.)

Putting things together, a large decrease in the current real interest rate—from r_A to r_B in Figure 17-2—leads to only a small increase in output, from Y_A to Y_B. The *IS* curve, which goes through points *A* and *B*, is steeply downward sloping.

Changes in all variables in equation (17.2) other than *Y* and *r* *shift* the *IS* curve:

- Changes in current taxes (T) or in current government spending (G) shift the *IS* curve. An increase in current government spending increases spending at a given interest rate, shifting the *IS* curve to the right, an increase in taxes shifts the *IS* curve to the left. These shifts are represented in Figure 17-2.
- Changes in expected future variables also shift the *IS* curve. An increase in expected future output, Y'^e, shifts the *IS* curve to the right: Higher expected future income leads consumers to feel wealthier and spend more. Higher expected future output implies higher expected profits, leading firms to invest more. Higher spending leads, through the multiplier effect, to higher output. By a similar argument, an increase in expected future taxes leads consumers to decrease current spending and shifts the *IS* curve to the left. And an increase in the expected future real interest rate decreases current spending, also leading to a decrease in output, shifting the *IS* curve to the left. These shifts are also represented in Figure 17-2.

The *LM* Relation Revisited

The *LM* relation we derived in Chapter 4 and have used until now was given by

$$\frac{M}{P} = Y\,L(i) \tag{17.3}$$

where *M*/*P* is the supply of money and *YL*(i) is the demand for money. Equilibrium in financial markets requires that the supply of money be equal to the demand for money. The demand for money depends on real income and on the short-term nominal interest rate—the opportunity cost of holding money. We derived this demand for money before thinking about expectations. Now that we have, the question is whether we should modify equation (17.3). The answer—I am sure this will be good news—is: No.

Think of your own demand for money. How much money you want to hold today depends on your *current* level of transactions, not on the level of transactions you expect next year or the year after; there will be time to adjust your money balances to your transaction level if it changes in the future. And the opportunity cost of holding money today depends on the *current* nominal interest rate, not on the expected nominal interest rate next year or the year after. If short-term interest rates were to increase in the future, increasing the opportunity cost of holding money then, the time to reduce your money balances would be then, not now.

So, in contrast to the consumption decision, the decision as to how much money to hold is myopic, depending primarily on current income and the current short-term nominal interest rate. We can still think of the demand for money as depending on the current level of output and the current nominal interest rate, and use equation (17.3) to describe the determination of the nominal interest rate in the current period.

To summarize: We have seen that expectations about the future play a major role in spending decisions. This implies that expectations enter the *IS* relation: Private spending depends not only on current output and the current real interest rate, but also on expected future output, and the expected future real interest rate.

In contrast, the decision about how much money to hold is largely myopic: The two variables entering the *LM* relation are still current income, and the current nominal interest rate.

17-2 Monetary Policy, Expectations, and Output

In the basic *IS-LM* model we developed in Chapter 5, there was only one interest rate, i, which entered both the *IS* relation and the *LM* relation. When the Fed expanded the money supply, "the" interest rate went down, and spending increased. From the previous three chapters, you have learned there are in fact many interest rates, and that we must keep two distinctions in mind:

1. The distinction between the nominal interest rate and the real interest rate.
2. The distinction between current and expected future interest rates.

The interest rate that enters the *LM* relation, which is the interest rate that the Fed affects directly, is the *current nominal interest rate.* In contrast, spending in the *IS* relation depends on both *current and expected future real interest rates.* Economists sometimes state this distinction even more starkly by saying that while the Fed controls the *short-term nominal interest rate,* what matters for spending and output is the *long-term real interest rate.*

Let's look at this distinction more closely. Recall from Chapter 14 that the real interest rate is equal to the nominal interest rate minus expected current inflation:

Expected current inflation: inflation expected, as of today, for the current period (the current year).

$$r = i - \pi^e$$

Similarly, the expected future real interest rate is equal to the expected future nominal interest rate minus expected future inflation.

Expected future inflation: inflation expected, as of today, for the future period (all future years).

$$r'^e = i'^e - \pi'^e$$

When the Fed increases the money supply—therefore decreasing the current nominal interest rate, i—the effect on the current and the expected future real interest rates depends on two factors:

- Whether the increase in the money supply leads financial markets to revise their expectations of the future nominal interest rate, i'^e.
- Whether the increase in the money supply leads financial markets to revise their expectations of both current inflation and future inflation, π^e and π'^e. If, for example, the change in money leads financial markets to expect more inflation in the future—so π'^e increases—the expected future real interest rate, r'^e, will decrease for a given expected future nominal interest rate, i'^e.

To make things simpler, I shall leave aside here the second factor—the role of changing expectations of inflation—and focus on the first, the role of changing expectations of the future nominal interest rate. Thus, I shall assume that expected current inflation and expected future inflation are both equal to zero. In this case, we need not distinguish between the nominal interest rate and the real interest rate, as they are equal, and we can use the same letter to denote both. Let r denote the current real (and nominal) interest rate, and r'^e denote the expected future real (and nominal) interest rate.

We explored the role of changing expectations of inflation on the relation between the nominal interest rate and the real interest rate in Chapter 14. Leaving changes in expected inflation aside will keep the analysis simpler here. You have, however, all the elements you need to think through what would happen if we also allowed expectations of current inflation and future inflation to adjust. How would these expectations adjust? Would this lead to a larger or a smaller effect on output in the current period?

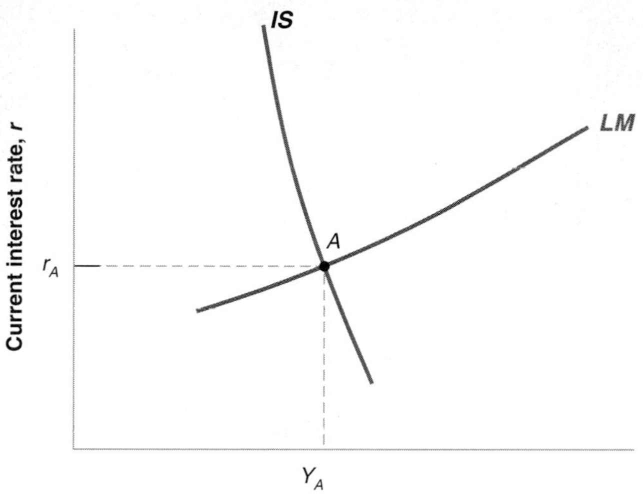

Figure 17-3

The New IS-LM

The *IS* curve is steeply downward sloping: Other things being equal, a change in the current interest rate has a small effect on output. The *LM* curve is upward sloping. The equilibrium is at the intersection of the *IS* and *LM* curves.

With this simplification we can rewrite the *IS* and *LM* relations in equations (17.2) and (17.3) as

The *IS* relation is the same as equation (17.2). The *LM* relation is now in terms of the real interest rate—which, here, is equal to the nominal interest rate.

$$IS: \quad Y = A(Y, T, r, Y'^e, T'^e, r'^e) + G \tag{17.4}$$

$$LM: \quad \frac{M}{P} = Y\, L(r) \tag{17.5}$$

The corresponding *IS* and *LM* curves are drawn in Figure 17-3. The vertical axis measures the current interest rate, r; the horizontal axis measures current output Y. The *IS* curve is steeply downward sloping. We saw earlier the reason why: For given expectations, a change in the current interest rate has a limited effect on spending, and the multiplier is small. The *LM* is upward sloping. An increase in income leads to an increase in the demand for money. Given the supply of money, the result is an increase in the interest rate. Equilibrium in goods and financial markets implies that the economy is at point *A*, on both the *IS* and the *LM* curves.

There is no need to distinguish here between the real interest rate and the nominal interest rate: Given zero expected inflation, they are the same.

Now suppose the economy is in a recession, and the Fed decides to increase the money supply.

Assume first that this expansionary monetary policy does not change expectations of either the future interest rate or future output. In Figure 17-4, the *LM* shifts down, from *LM* to *LM″*. (Because I already use primes to denote future values of the variables, I shall use double primes [such as in *LM″*] to denote shifts in curves in this chapter.) The equilibrium moves from point *A* to point *B*, with higher output and a lower interest rate. The steep *IS* curve, however, implies that the increase in the money supply has only a small effect on output: Changes in the current interest rate, unaccompanied by changes in expectations, have only a small effect on spending, and in turn a small effect on output.

Given expectations, an increase in the money supply leads to a shift in the *LM* and, so, a movement down the steep *IS*. The result is a large decrease in r, a small increase in Y.

Is it reasonable, however, to assume that expectations are unaffected by an expansionary monetary policy? Isn't it likely that as the Fed decreases the current interest rate, financial markets anticipate lower interest rates in the future as well, along with higher future output stimulated by this lower future interest rate? What happens if they do? At a given current interest rate, prospects of a lower future interest rate and of higher future output both increase spending and output; they shift the *IS* curve to the right, from *IS* to *IS″*. The new equilibrium is given by point *C*. Thus, while the direct effect of the expansion in the money supply on output is limited, the full effect, once changes in expectations are taken into account, is much larger.

If the increase in money leads to an increase in Y'^e and a decrease in r'^e, the *IS* curve shifts to the right, leading to a larger increase in Y.

Figure 17-4

The Effects of an Expansionary Monetary Policy

The effects of monetary policy on output depend very much on whether and how monetary policy affects expectations.

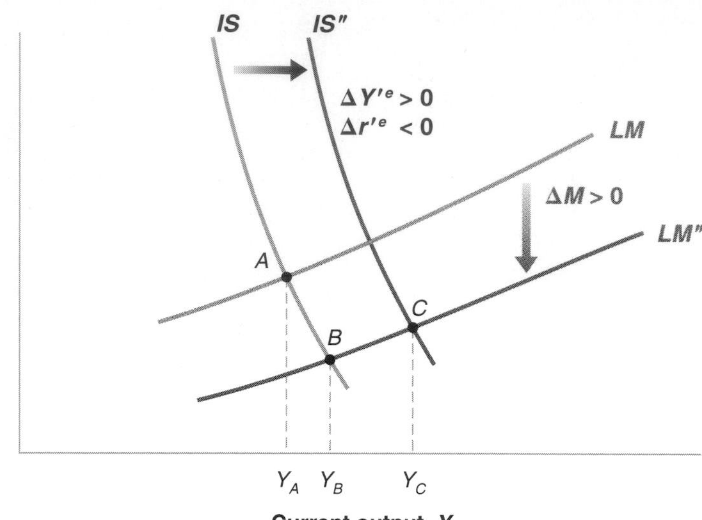

To summarize: You have just learned an important lesson. The effects of monetary policy—of any type of macroeconomic policy, for that matter—depend crucially on their effect on expectations.

If a monetary expansion leads financial investors, firms, and consumers to revise their expectations of future interest rates and output, then the effects of the monetary expansion on output may be very large.

But if expectations remain unchanged, the effects of the monetary expansion on output will be small.

We can link this discussion to our discussion in Chapter 15, of the effects of changes in monetary policy in the stock market. Many of the same issues were present there. If, when the change in monetary policy takes place, it comes as no surprise to investors, firms, and consumers, then expectations will not change. The stock market will react only a little, if at all. And output will change only a little, if at all. But, if the change comes as a surprise and is expected to last, expectations of future output go up, expectations of future interest rates come down, the stock market booms, and output increases.

At this stage, you may have become very skeptical that macroeconomists can say much about the effects of policy, or the effects of other shocks: If the effects depend so much on what happens to expectations, can macroeconomists have any hope of predicting what will happen? The answer is yes:

Saying that the effect of a particular policy depends on its effect on expectations is not the same as saying that anything can happen. Expectations are not arbitrary. The manager of a fund who has to decide whether to invest in stocks or bonds, or the firm thinking about whether to build a new plant, or a consumer thinking about how much he should save for retirement—all give a lot of thought to what may happen in the future. We can think of each of them as forming expectations about the future by assessing the likely course of future expected policy and then working out the implications for future activity. If they do not do it themselves—surely most of us do not spend our time solving macroeconomic models before taking decisions—they do so indirectly, by watching TV and reading newsletters and newspapers, which themselves rely on the predictions of public and private forecasters. Economists refer to expectations formed in this forward-looking manner as **rational expectations**. The

Rational Expectations

Most macroeconomists today routinely solve their models under the assumption of rational expectations. This was not always the case. The last 25 years in macroeconomic research are often called the "rational expectations" revolution.

The importance of expectations is an old theme in macroeconomics. But until the early 1970s, macroeconomists thought of expectations in one of two ways.

- One was as **animal spirits** (from an expression Keynes introduced in the *General Theory* to refer to movements in investment that could not be explained by movements in current variables): Shifts in expectations were considered important but unexplained.
- The other was as the result of simple, backward-looking rules. For example, people were often assumed to have static expectations, to expect the future to be like the present (we used this assumption in discussing the Phillips curve in Chapter 8, and in exploring investment decisions in Chapter 16). Or people were assumed to have **adaptive expectations**: If, for example, their forecast of a given variable in a given period turned out to be too low, people were assumed to "adapt" by raising their expectation for the value of the variable for the following period. For example, seeing an inflation rate higher than they had expected led people to predict more inflation in the future than they had previously anticipated.

In the early 1970s, a group of macroeconomists led by Robert Lucas (at Chicago) and Thomas Sargent (then at Chicago, now at Stanford) argued that these assumptions did not reflect the way people form expectations. (Robert Lucas received the Nobel Prize in 1995 for his work on expectations.) They argued that, in thinking about the effects of alternative policies, economists should assume that people have rational expectations, that people look to the future and do the best job they can in predicting it. This is not the same as assuming that people know the future, but rather that they use the information they have in the best possible way.

Using the popular macroeconomic models of the time, Lucas and Sargent showed how replacing traditional assumptions about expectations formation by the assumption of rational expectations could fundamentally alter the results. We saw, for example, in Chapter 9 how Lucas challenged the notion that disinflation necessarily required an increase in unemployment for some time. Under rational expectations, he argued, a credible disinflation policy might be able to decrease inflation without any increase in unemployment. More generally, Lucas and Sargent's research showed the need for a complete rethinking of macroeconomic models under the assumption of rational expectations, and this is what has happened since.

Most macroeconomists today use rational expectations as a working assumption in their models and in their analyses of policy. This is not because they believe that people always have rational expectations. Surely there are times when people, firms, or financial market participants lose sight of reality and become too optimistic or too pessimistic. But these are more the exception than the rule, and it is not clear that economists can say much about those times, anyway. In thinking about the likely effects of a particular economic policy, the best assumption to make seems to be that financial markets, people, and firms will do the best they can to work out its implications. Designing a policy on the assumption that people will make systematic mistakes in responding to it is unwise.

So why did it take until the 1970s for rational expectations to become a standard assumption in macroeconomics? Largely because of technical problems. Under rational expectations, what happens today depends on expectations of what will happen in the future. But what happens in the future depends on what happens today. The success of Lucas and Sargent in convincing most macroeconomists to use rational expectations comes not only from the strength of their case, but also from showing how it could actually be done. Much progress has been made since in developing solution methods for larger and larger models. Today, a number of large macroeconometric models are solved under the assumption of rational expectations. (I presented a simulation from such a model in Chapter 7. You shall see another example in Chapter 24.)

FOCUS

introduction of the assumption of rational expectations is one of the most important developments in macroeconomics in the last 25 years. It has largely shaped the way macroeconomists think about policy. It is discussed further in the Focus box "Rational Expectations."

We could go back and think about the implications of rational expectations in the case of a monetary expansion we have just studied. It will be more fun to do this in the context of a change in fiscal policy, and this is what we now turn to.

17-3 Deficit Reduction, Expectations, and Output

Recall the conclusions we reached in the core about the effects of a budget deficit reduction:

We discussed the short-run and medium-run effects of changes in fiscal policy in Section 7-5. ▶

We discussed the long-run ▶ effects of changes in fiscal policy in Section 11-2.

- In the medium run and in the long run, a budget deficit reduction is likely to be beneficial for the economy. In the medium run, a lower budget deficit implies higher saving and higher investment. In the long run, higher investment translates into higher capital and thus higher output.
- In the short run, however, a reduction in the budget deficit, unless it is offset by a monetary expansion, leads to a reduction in spending, and so to a contraction in output.

It is this adverse short-run effect that—in addition to the unpopularity of increases in taxes or reductions in government programs—often deters governments from tackling their budget deficit: Why take the risk of a recession now, for benefits that will accrue not now, but later in the future?

In the recent past, however, several economists have argued that a deficit reduction may actually increase output even in the *short run*. Their argument: If people take into account the future beneficial effects of deficit reduction, their expectations about the future may improve enough to lead to an increase—rather than a decrease—in current spending, and so to an increase in current output. This section presents their argument more formally. The Focus box "Can a Budget Deficit Reduction Lead to an Output Expansion? Ireland in the 1980s" reviews some of the supporting evidence.

Assume the economy is described by equation (17.4) for the *IS* relation and equation (17.5) for the *LM* relation. Now suppose the government announces a program to reduce the deficit, through decreases both in current spending, G, and in future spending, G'^e. What will happen to output *this period*?

The Role of Expectations About the Future

Suppose first that expectations of future output (Y'^e) and of the future interest rate (r'^e) do not change. Then, we get the standard answer: The decrease in government spending in the current period leads to a shift in the *IS* curve to the left, and so to a decrease in equilibrium output.

The crucial question, therefore, is what happens to expectations. To answer, let us go back to what you learned in the core about the effects of a deficit reduction in the medium run and the long run:

- In the medium run, a deficit reduction has no effect on output. It leads, however, to a lower interest rate, and to higher investment. These were two of the main lessons of Chapter 7. Let's review the logic behind each:

  Recall that, when we look at the medium run, we ignore the effects of capital accumulation on output. So, in the medium run, the natural level of output depends on the level of productivity (taken as given) and on the natural level of employment. The natural level of employment depends in turn on the natural rate of unemployment. If spending by the government on goods and services does not affect the natural rate of unemployment—and there is no obvious reason why it should—then changes in spending will not affect the natural level of output. Therefore, deficit reduction has no effect on the level of output in the medium run.

  Now recall that output must be equal to spending, and that spending is the sum of public spending and private spending. Given that output is unchanged and that public spending is lower, private spending must be higher. Higher private spending requires a lower equilibrium interest rate: The lower interest rate leads to higher investment, and thus to higher private spending, which offsets the decrease in public spending and leaves output unchanged.

In the medium run: Output does not change ◀ Investment increases.

- In the long run—that is, taking into account the effects of capital accumulation on output—higher investment leads to a higher capital stock, and thus a higher level of output.

  This was the main lesson of Chapter 11. The higher the proportion of output saved (or invested, investment and saving must be equal for the goods market to be in equilibrium), the higher the capital stock, and thus the higher the level of output in the long run.

◀ In the long run: Investment increases Capital increases Output increases

We can think of our *future period* as including both the medium and the long run. If people, firms, and financial market participants have rational expectations, then, in response to the announcement of a deficit reduction, they will expect these developments to take place in the future. Thus, they will revise their expectation of future output (Y'^e) up, and their expectation of the future interest rate (r'^e) down.

Back to the Current Period

We can now return to the question of what happens *this period* in response to the announcement and start of the deficit reduction program. Figure 17-5 draws the *IS* and *LM* curves for the current period. In response to the announcement of the deficit reduction, there are now three factors shifting the *IS* curve:

- Current government spending (G) goes down, leading to a shift of the *IS* curve to the left. At a given interest rate, the decrease in government spending leads to a decrease in total spending and, so, a decrease in output. This is the standard effect of a reduction in government spending, and the only one taken into account in the basic *IS-LM* model.
- Expected future output (Y'^e) goes up, leading to a shift of the *IS* curve to the right. At a given interest rate, the increase in expected future output leads to an increase in private spending, increasing output.
- The expected future interest rate goes down, leading to a shift of the *IS* curve to the right. At a given current interest rate, a decrease in the future interest rate stimulates spending and increases output.

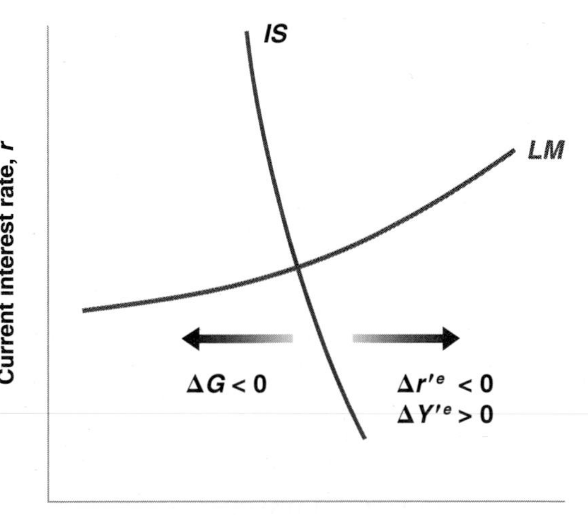

Figure 17-5

The Effects of a Deficit Reduction on Current Output

When account is taken of its effect on expectations, the decrease in government spending need not lead to a decrease in output.

What is the net effect of these three shifts in the *IS* curve? Can the effect of expectations on consumption and investment spending offset the decrease in government spending? Without much more information about the exact form of the *IS* and *LM* relations and about the details of the deficit reduction program, we cannot tell which shifts will dominate, and whether output will go up or down. But our analysis tells us that both cases are possible, that output may go up in response to the deficit reduction. And it gives us a few hints about when this might happen: Note that the smaller the decrease in current government spending (G), the smaller the adverse effect on spending today. Note also that the larger the decrease in expected future government spending (G'^e), the larger the effect on expected future output and interest rates, thus the larger the favorable effect on spending today. This suggests that **backloading** the deficit reduction program toward the future, with small cuts today and larger cuts in the future, is more likely to lead to an increase in output:

On the other hand, backloading raises other issues. Announcing the need for painful cuts in spending, and then leaving them to the future, is likely to seriously decrease the program's **credibility**—the perceived probability that the government will do what it has promised when the time comes to do it. The government must play a delicate balancing act: enough cuts in the current period to show a commitment to deficit reduction; enough cuts left to the future to reduce the adverse effects on the economy in the short run.

More generally, our analysis suggests that anything in a deficit reduction program that improves expectations of how the future will look is likely to make the short-run effects of deficit reduction less painful. Let me give two examples:

- Measures that are perceived by firms and financial markets as reducing some of the distortions in the economy may improve expectations, and make it more likely that output increases in the short run. Take, for example, unemployment benefits. You saw in Chapter 6 that lower unemployment benefits lead to a decline in the natural rate of unemployment, resulting in a higher natural level of output. So, a reform of the social insurance system, which includes a reduction in the generosity of unemployment benefits, is likely to have two effects on spending and thus on output in the short run.

  One is to decrease the consumption of the unemployed: Lower unemployment benefits will reduce their income and their consumption.

  The other is to increase spending through expectations: The anticipation of higher output in the future may lead to both higher consumption and higher investment.

  If the second effect dominates, the outcome may be an increase in overall spending, increasing output not only in the medium run but also in the short run. (Even if a reduction in unemployment benefits increases output, this surely does not imply that unemployment benefits should be eliminated. Even if aggregate income goes up, we must worry about the effects on the distribution of income: The consumption of the unemployed goes down, and the pain associated with being unemployed goes up.)
- Or take an economy where the government has, in effect, lost control of its budget: Government spending is high, tax revenues are low, and the deficit is very large. In such an environment, a credible deficit reduction program is also more likely to increase output in the short run. Before the annoucement of the program, people may have expected major political and economic trouble in the future. The announcement of a program of deficit reduction may well reassure people that the government has regained control, and that the future is less bleak than they anticipated. This decrease in pessimism about the future may lead to an increase in spending and output, even if taxes are increased as part of the deficit reduction program.

As you will see in Chapter 23, a very large deficit often leads to very high money creation and, soon after, to very high inflation. Very high inflation leads not only to economic trouble, but also to political instability.

To summarize: A program of deficit reduction may increase output even in the short run. Whether it does or not depends on many factors, in particular:

- The credibility of the program: Will spending be cut or taxes increased in the future as announced?
- The timing of the program: How large are spending cuts in the future relative to current spending cuts?
- The composition of the program: Does the program remove some of the distortions in the economy?
- The state of government finances in the first place: How large is the initial deficit? Is this a "last chance" program? What will happen if it fails?

This gives you a sense of both the importance of expectations in determining the outcome, and of the complexities involved in the use of fiscal policy in such a context.

Note how far we are from the results of Chapter 3 where, by choosing spending and taxes wisely, the government could achieve any level of output it wanted. Here, even the direction of the effect of a deficit reduction on output is ambiguous.

Can a Budget Deficit Reduction Lead to an Output Expansion? Ireland in the 1980s

FOCUS

Ireland went through two major deficit reduction programs in the 1980s:

1. The first program was started in 1982. In 1981, the budget deficit had reached a very high 13.0% of GDP. Government debt, the result of the accumulation of current and past deficits, was 77% of GDP, also a very high level. The government clearly had to regain control of its finances. Over the next three years, it embarked on a program of deficit reduction, based mostly on tax increases. This was an ambitious program: Had output continued to grow at its normal rate, the program would have reduced the deficit by 5% of GDP.

   The results were dismal. As shown in line 2 of Table 1, output growth was low in 1982, negative in 1983. Low growth was associated with a major increase in unemployment, from 9.5% in 1981 to 15% in 1984 (line 3). Because of low output growth, tax revenues—which depend on the level of activity—were lower than anticipated. The actual deficit reduction, shown in line 1, was only 3.5% of GDP. And the result of continuing high deficits and low GDP growth was a further increase in the ratio of debt to GDP, to 97% in 1984.
2. A second attempt was made starting in February 1987. At the time, things were still very bad. The 1986 deficit was 10.7% of GDP; debt stood at 116% of GDP, a record high in Europe at the time. This new program of deficit reduction was different from the first. The focus was more on a reduction of the role of government, and a decrease in government spending rather than on an increase in taxes. The tax increases in the program were achieved through a tax reform widening the tax base, and without an increase in the marginal tax rate (the highest tax rate on income). The program was again very ambitious: Had output grown at its normal rate, the reduction in the deficit would have been 6.4% of GDP.

   The results of the second program could not have been more different from the results of the first. The years 1987 to 1989 showed strong growth, with average GDP growth exceeding 5%. The unemployment

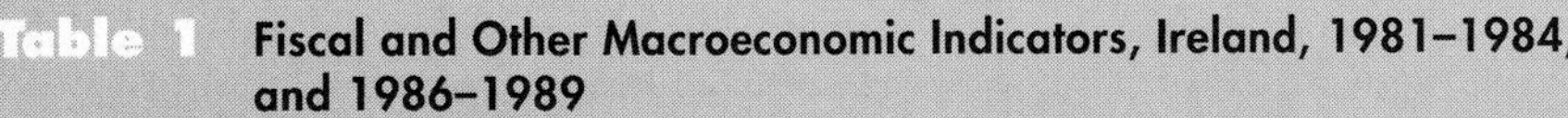

Table 1 Fiscal and Other Macroeconomic Indicators, Ireland, 1981–1984, and 1986–1989

	1981	1982	1983	1984	1986	1987	1988	1989
1. Budget deficit (% of GDP)	−13.0	−13.4	−11.4	−9.5	−10.7	−8.6	−4.5	−1.8
2. Output growth rate (%)	3.3	2.3	−0.2	4.4	−0.4	4.7	5.2	5.8
3. Unemployment rate (%)	9.5	11.0	13.5	15.0	17.1	16.9	16.3	15.1
4. Household saving rate (% of disposable income)	17.9	19.6	18.1	18.4	15.7	12.9	11.0	12.6

Source: OECD Economic Outlook, June 1998

(*Continued*)

rate was reduced by 2%. Because of strong output growth, tax revenues were stronger than anticipated, and the deficit was reduced by nearly 9% of GDP.

Several economists have argued that the striking difference between the results of the two programs can be traced to the different reaction of expectations in each case. The first package, they argue, focused on tax increases and did not change what many people saw as too large a role of government in the economy. The second, with its focus on cuts in spending and on tax reform, had a much more positive impact on expectations, and so a positive impact on spending and output.

Are these economists right? One variable, the household saving rate— defined as disposable income minus consumption, divided by disposable income—strongly suggests that expectations are an important part of the story. To interpret the behavior of the saving rate, recall the lessons from Chapter 16 about consumption behavior. When disposable income grows unusually slowly or goes down—as it does in a recession—consumption typically slows down or declines by less than disposable income, as people expect things to improve in the future. Put another way, when the growth of disposable income is unusually low or negative, the saving rate typically comes down. Now look (in line 4) at what happened from 1981 to 1984: Despite low growth throughout and a recession in 1983, the household saving rate actually increased a little during that period. Put another way, people reduced their consumption by more than the reduction in disposable income: The reason must be that they were very pessimistic about the future.

Now turn to 1986 to 1989. During that period, economic growth was unusually strong. By the same argument as in the previous paragraph, we would have expected consumption to increase less strongly, and thus the saving rate to increase. Instead, the saving rate decreased very strongly, from 15.7% in 1986 to 12.6% in 1989. Consumers must have become much more optimistic about the future to increase their consumption by more than the increase in disposable income.

The next question is whether this difference in the adjustment of expectations over the two episodes can be attributed fully to the differences in the two fiscal programs. The answer: No. Ireland was changing in many ways at the time of the second fiscal program. Productivity was increasing much faster than real wages, reducing the cost of labor for firms. Attracted by tax breaks, low labor costs, and an educated labor force, many foreign firms were coming to Ireland to create new plants: These factors played a major role in the expansion of the late 1980s. Irish growth has been very strong ever since, with average output growth exceeding 6% since 1990. Surely this long expansion is due to other factors than fiscal policy. Nevertheless, the change in fiscal policy in 1987 probably played a role in convincing people, firms (including foreign firms), and financial markets that the government was regaining control of its finances. And the fact remains that the substantial deficit reduction of 1987–1989 was accompanied by a strong output expansion, not by the recession predicted by the basic *IS-LM* model.

For a more detailed discussion, look at Francesco Giavazzi and Marco Pagano, "Can Severe Fiscal Contractions Be Expansionary? Tales of Two Small European Countries," NBER Macroeconomics Annual, *1990, 75–110.*

A survey of what we have learned by looking at programs of deficit reduction around the world is given in "An Empirical Analysis of Fiscal Adjustments," by John McDermott and Robert Wescott, IMF working paper, June 1996.

Summary

- Spending in the goods market depends on current and expected future output and on the current and the expected future real interest rate.
- Expectations affect demand and, in turn, affect output: Changes in expected future output or in the expected future real interest rate lead to changes in spending and in output today.
- By implication, the effects of any policy on spending and output depends on whether and how policy affects expectations of future output and expectations of the future real interest rate.
- Rational expectations is the assumption that people, firms, and participants in financial markets form expectations of the future by assessing the course of future expected policy and then working out the implications for future output, future interest rates, and so on. While it is clear that most people do not go through this exercise themselves, we can think of them as doing so indirectly by relying on the predictions of public and private forecasters.
- Although there are surely cases where people, firms, or financial investors do not have rational expectations, the assumption of rational expectations seems to be the best benchmark to evaluate the potential effects of alternative policies. Designing a policy on the assumption that people will make systematic mistakes in responding to it would be unwise.
- Changes in the money supply affect the short-term nominal interest rate. Spending, however, depends instead on the current and the expected future real

interest rate. Thus, the effect of monetary policy on activity depends crucially on whether and how changes in the short-term nominal interest rate lead to changes in the current and the expected future real interest rate.

- A budget deficit reduction may lead to an increase rather than a decrease in output. This is because expectations of higher output and lower interest rates in the future may lead to an increase in spending that more than offsets the reduction in spending coming from the direct effect of the deficit reduction on total spending.

Key Terms

- aggregate private spending, or private spending, 357
- rational expectations, 362
- animal spirits, 363
- adaptive expectations, 363
- backloading, 366
- credibility, 366

Questions and Problems

Quick Check

1. *Using the information in this chapter, label each of the following statements* true, false, *or* uncertain. *Explain briefly.*
   a. Changes in expected future one-year real interest rates have a much larger effect on spending than changes in the current one-year real interest rate.
   b. The introduction of expectations in the goods market model means that the *IS* curve is still downward sloping but is now much flatter.
   c. Current money demand depends on current and expected future nominal interest rates.
   d. The rational expectations assumption implies that consumers must take into account the effects of future fiscal policy on output.
   e. Expected future fiscal policy affects expected future economic activity but not current economic activity.
   f. Depending on its effect on expectations, a fiscal contraction may actually lead to an economic expansion.
   g. The very different effects of Ireland's deficit reduction programs in 1982 and in 1987 provide little support for a single theory of expectations.

2. *During the late 1990s, many observers claimed that the United States had transformed into a New Economy, and this justified the very high values for stock prices observed at the time.*
   a. Discuss how this affected consumption spending.
   b. The stock market subsequently decreased. Discuss how this might have affected consumption.

3. *For each of the following, determine whether the IS curve, the LM curve, both curves, or neither shift. In each case, assume that expected current and future inflation are equal to zero, and that no other exogenous variable is changing.*
   a. A decrease in the expected future real interest rate.
   b. The yield curve becomes steeper.
   c. An increase in the current money supply.
   d. An increase in the expected future money supply.
   e. An increase in expected future taxes.
   f. A decrease in expected future income.

4. *"The rational expectations assumption is unrealistic because, essentially, it amounts to the assumption that every consumer has perfect knowledge of the economy." Discuss.*

5. *A new president, who promised during the campaign that she would cut taxes, has just been elected. People trust that she will keep her promise, but that the tax cuts will be implemented only in the future. Determine the impact of the election on current output, the current interest rate, and current private spending, under each of the following assumptions. (In each case, indicate what you think will happen to Y'^e, r'^e, and T'^e, and then how these changes in expectations affect output today.)*
   a. The Fed will not change its policy.
   b. The Fed will act to prevent any change in future output.
   c. The Fed will act to prevent any increase in the future interest rate.

Dig Deeper

6. *The Clinton deficit package*

   In 1992, the U.S. deficit was \$290 billion. During the presidential campaign, the large deficit emerged as a major issue. So, when President Clinton won the election, deficit reduction was the first item on the new administration's agenda.
   a. What does deficit reduction imply for the medium run and the long run? What are the advantages of reducing the deficit?

   In the final version passed by Congress in August 1993, the deficit reduction package included a reduction of \$20 billion in its first year, increasing gradually to \$131 billion four years later.
   b. Why was the deficit reduction package back-loaded? Are there any advantages or disadvantages to this approach?

   In February 1993, President Clinton presented the budget in his State of the Union address. He asked Alan Greenspan, the Fed chairman, to sit next to First Lady Hillary Clinton during the delivery of the address.
   c. What was the purpose of this symbolic gesture? How can the Fed's decision to use expansionary monetary policy in the future affect the short run response of the economy?

Explore Further

7. *Go to the Web page for the Federal Reserve Bank of St. Louis,* **www.stls.frb.org/fred/**, *and download the following three series:*
   i. *Three-Month Treasury Constant Maturity Rate*
   ii. *Three-Year Treasury Constant Maturity Rate*
   iii. *Twenty-Year Treasury Constant Maturity Rate*

   a. Plot the yield curve for November 1992 (the election month) and for August 1993 (the month during which the deficit reduction plan was passed). What can you tell from the change in the yield curve about the financial markets' expectation of what the Fed would do?

   Download "Federal Government surplus or deficit, National Income and Products Account" series for the 1990s. Download nominal and real GDP for the 1990s.

   b. Did the economy go into a recession following the passing of the deficit reduction package in 1993? Is this consistent with your answer to (a)?
   c. Was the budget deficit reduced (as a percentage of GDP)?
   d. Are there any reasons to think that factors other than the budget deficit reduction package may have helped reduce the deficit in the 1990s? (*Hint*: Look at the growth rate of real GDP in the 1990s.)

We invite you to visit the Blanchard page on the Prentice Hall Web site at:
www.prenhall.com/blanchard
for this chapter's World Wide Web exercises

The Open Economy

The next four chapters represent the second major extension of the core. They look at the implications of openness—the fact that most economies trade both goods and assets with the rest of the world.

Chapter 18

Chapter 18 discusses the implications of openness in goods and financial markets. Openness in goods markets allows people to choose between domestic goods and foreign goods. An important determinant of their decisions is the real exchange rate—the relative price of foreign goods in terms of domestic goods. Openness in financial markets allows people to choose between domestic assets and foreign assets. This imposes a tight relation between the exchange rate, both current and expected, and domestic and foreign interest rates—a relation known as the interest parity condition.

Chapter 19

Chapter 19 focuses on equilibrium in the domestic goods market in an open economy. It shows how the demand for domestic goods now depends also on the real exchange rate. It shows how fiscal policy affects both output and the trade balance. It discusses the conditions under which a real depreciation improves the trade balance, and increases output.

Chapter 20

Chapter 20 characterizes goods and financial markets' equilibrium in an open economy. In other words, it gives an open economy version of the *IS-LM* model we saw in the core. It shows how, under flexible exchange rates, monetary policy affects output not only through its effect on the interest rate, but also through its effect on the exchange rate. It shows how fixing the exchange rate also implies giving up the ability to change the interest rate.

Chapter 21

Chapter 21 looks at the properties of different exchange rate regimes. It shows how, in the medium run, the real exchange rate can adjust even under a fixed exchange rate regime. It then looks at exchange rate crises under fixed exchange rates, and at movements in exchange rates under flexible exchange rates. It ends by discussing the pros and cons of various exchange rate regimes, from the adoption of a common currency such as the Euro, to the use of a currency board, to dollarization.

Openness in Goods and Financial Markets

CHAPTER 18

We have assumed so far that the economy was closed—that it did not interact with the rest of the world. We had to start this way, to keep things simple and build up your intuition for the basic macroeconomic mechanisms. We are now ready to relax this assumption. Understanding the macroeconomic implications of openness will occupy us for this and the next three chapters.

Openness has three distinct dimensions:

1. **Openness in goods markets**—the ability of consumers and firms to choose between domestic goods and foreign goods.

   In no country is this choice completely free of restrictions: Even the countries most committed to free trade have **tariffs**—taxes on imported goods—and **quotas**—restrictions on the quantity of goods that can be imported—on at least some foreign goods. At the same time, in most countries, average tariffs are low and getting lower.

2. **Openness in financial markets**—the ability of financial investors to choose between domestic financial assets and foreign financial assets.

   Until recently even some of the richest countries, such as France and Italy, had **capital controls**, restrictions on the foreign assets their domestic residents could hold as well as on the domestic assets foreigners could hold. These restrictions are rapidly disappearing. As a result, world financial markets are becoming more and more closely integrated.

3. **Openness in factor markets**—the ability of firms to choose where to locate production, and of workers to choose where to work.

   Here also trends are clear. Multinational companies operate plants in many countries and move their operations around the world to take advantage of low costs. Much of the debate about the **North American Free Trade Agreement (NAFTA)** signed in 1993 by the United States, Canada, and Mexico centered on its implications for the relocation of U.S. firms to Mexico. And immigration from low-wage countries is a hot political issue in countries ranging from Germany to the United States.

In the short run and in the medium run—the focus of this and the next three chapters—openness in factor markets plays much less of a role than openness in either goods markets or

financial markets. Thus, I shall ignore openness in factor markets, and focus on the implications of the first two dimensions of openness here.

- Section 18-1 looks at openness in the goods market, the determinants of the choice between domestic goods and foreign goods, and the role of the real exchange rate.
- Section 18–2 looks at openness in financial markets, the determinants of the choice between domestic financial assets and foreign financial assets, and the role of interest rates and exchange rates.
- Section 18–3 gives the map to the next three chapters. ■

18-1 Openness in Goods Markets

Let's start by looking at how much the United States sells to and buys from the rest of the world. Then, we shall be better able to think about the choice between domestic goods and foreign goods, and the role of the relative price of foreign goods in terms of domestic goods—the real exchange rate.

Exports and Imports

Figure 18-1 plots the evolution of U.S. exports and U.S. imports, as ratios to GDP, since 1929 ("U.S. exports" means exports *from* the United States; "U.S. imports" means imports *to* the United States.) Note how these ratios have increased over time. Exports and imports, which were equal to 5% of GDP during the 1960s, now stand around 13% of GDP (11.1% for exports, 14.7% for imports). The United States trades nearly three times as much (relative to its GDP) with the rest of the world as it did just 40 years ago.

A closer look at Figure 18-1 reveals two other interesting features.

- Both exports and imports sharply declined between 1929 and 1936. This decline was due in large part to the now-infamous *Smoot-Hawley Act of 1930*. In a misguided attempt to help the U.S. economy recover from the Great Depression,

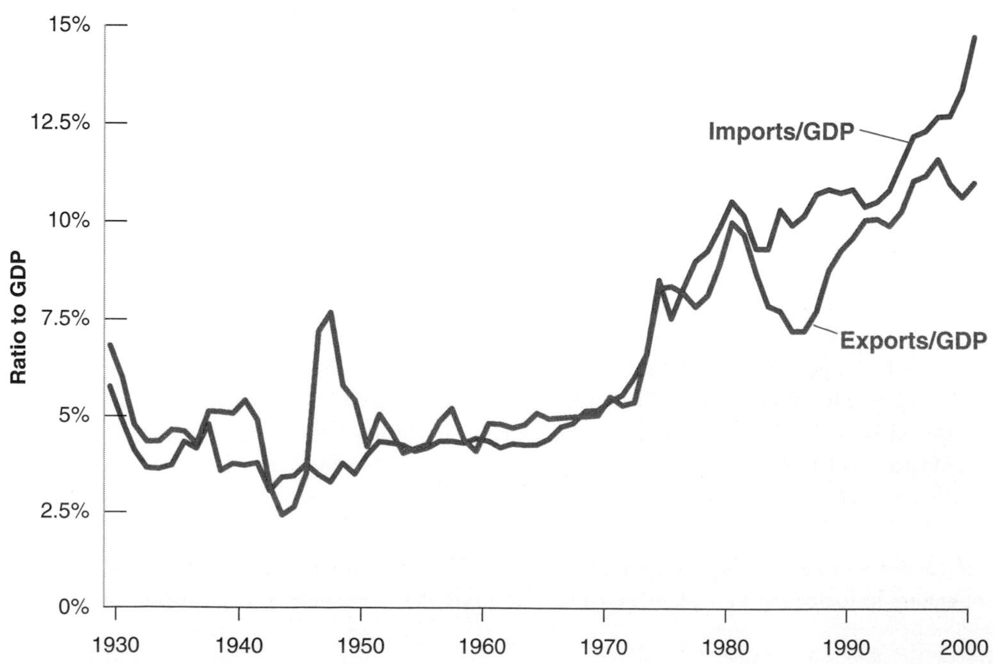

Figure 18-1

U.S. Exports and Imports as Ratios of GDP, 1929–2000

Exports and imports, which were equal to 5% of GDP as recently as the 1960s, now stand around 13% of GDP.

Smoot-Hawley sharply increased tariffs on foreign goods in the hope of increasing the demand for domestic goods. The results were retaliation by other countries (in the form of higher tariffs on U.S. goods) and a sharp decrease in world trade.

- Although imports and exports have followed broadly the same trend, they have also diverged for long periods, generating sustained trade surpluses or trade deficits. Three episodes stand out:

    1. The trade surpluses of the late 1940s, which were due to the post–World War II reconstruction effort in Europe, leading to large exports from the United States to Europe.
    2. The trade deficits of the mid-1980s; we shall return to them in Chapter 20.
    3. The current trade deficit—the ratio of the trade deficit to GDP reached 3.6% in 2000, a historical record; we shall return to it in Chapter 19.

Mr. Smoot and Mr. Hawley had a brief moment of renewed fame during a TV debate on NAFTA in 1993, when U.S. Vice President Albert Gore presented their picture to H. Ross Perot as a way of reminding Americans of the dangers of opposing free trade.

From Chapter 3: The trade balance is the difference between exports and imports:
Exports > imports:
Trade surplus (equivalently, positive trade balance)
Exports < imports:
Trade deficit (equivalently, negative trade balance)

Given all the talk in the media about *globalization*, a volume of trade (measured by the ratio of exports or imports to GDP) around 13% of GDP may strike you as small. However, the volume of trade is not necessarily a good measure of openness. Many sectors can be exposed to foreign competition without the effects of this competition showing up in high imports: By being competitive and keeping their prices low enough, these sectors can retain their domestic market share and keep imports out. This suggests that a better index of openness than export or import ratios is the proportion of aggregate output composed of **tradable goods**—goods that compete with foreign goods in either domestic markets or foreign markets. Estimates are that tradable goods represent around 60% of aggregate output in the United States today.

Tradable goods: Cars, computers . . . Nontradable goods: Housing, medical services, haircuts . . .

It remains true that, with exports around 11% of GDP, the United States has one of the smallest ratios of exports to GDP among the rich countries of the world. Table 18-1 gives ratios for a number of OECD countries:

For more on the OECD and for the list of member countries, see Chapter 1.

The United States and Japan are at the low end of the range of export ratios. The large European countries, such as Germany and the United Kingdom, have ratios that are two to three times larger. And the smaller European countries have even larger ratios, from 45% in Switzerland to 84% in Belgium. (Belgium's 84% ratio of exports to GDP raises an odd possibility: Could a country have exports larger than its GDP, an export ratio greater than one? The answer is: Yes. The reason why is given in the Focus box "Can Exports Exceed GDP?")

Do these numbers indicate that the United States has more trade barriers than, say, the United Kingdom or Belgium? No. The main factors behind these differences are geography and size. Distance from other markets explains a good part of the low Japanese ratio. Size also matters: The smaller the country, the more it must specialize in only a few products, producing and exporting them, and relying on imports for the others. Belgium can hardly afford to produce the same range of goods as the United States, a country roughly 40 times its economic size.

Iceland is both isolated and small. What would you expect its export ratio to be? (Answer: 34%)

Table 18-1 Ratios of Exports to GDP for Selected OECD Countries, 2000

Country	Export Ratio (%)	Country	Export Ratio (%)
United States	11	Switzerland	45
Japan	10	Austria	48
Germany	33	Netherlands	74
United Kingdom	27	Belgium	84

Source: International Financial Statistics, IMF.

FOCUS

Can Exports Exceed GDP?

Can a country have exports larger than its GDP—have an export ratio greater than one?

It would seem that the answer must be no. Countries cannot export more than they produce, so the export ratio must be less than one. Not so. The key to the answer is to realize that exports and imports may include exports and imports of intermediate goods.

Take, for example, a country that imports intermediate goods for $1 billion. Suppose it transforms them into final goods using only labor. Say, total wages equal $200 million and there are no profits. The value of these final goods is thus equal to $1,200 million. Assume that $1 billion worth of final goods is exported and the rest is consumed domestically.

Exports and imports therefore both equal $1 billion. What is GDP in this economy? Remember that GDP is value added in the economy (see Chapter 2). So, in this example, GDP equals $200 million, and the ratio of exports to GDP equals $1000/$200 = 5.

Hence, exports can exceed GDP. This is actually the case for a number of small countries where most economic activity is organized around a harbor and import-export activities. This is even the case for small countries where manufacturing plays an important role, such as Singapore (for more on Singapore, look at the Focus box in Chapter 12). In 1999, the ratio of exports to GDP in Singapore was 135%.

The Choice Between Domestic Goods and Foreign Goods

How does openness in goods markets force us to rethink the way we look at equilibrium in the *goods market*?

Until now, when we were thinking about consumers' decisions in the goods market, we focused on their decision to save or to consume. When goods markets are open, domestic consumers face a second decision: whether to buy domestic goods or to buy foreign goods. Indeed, all buyers—other domestic buyers such as firms or the government, and foreign buyers—face a similar decision. This decision has a direct effect on domestic output: If buyers decide to buy more domestic goods, the demand for domestic goods increases, and so does domestic output. If they decide to buy more foreign goods, then foreign output increases instead of domestic output.

In a closed economy, people face one decision: Save, or buy (consume). In an open economy, they face two decisions: Save, or buy (buy domestic, or buy foreign).

Central to this second decision (to buy domestic goods or foreign goods) is the price of foreign goods relative to domestic goods. We call this relative price the **real exchange rate**. The real exchange rate is not directly observable, and you will not find it in the newspapers. What you will find in newspapers are *nominal exchange rates*, the relative prices of currencies. So, in the rest of this section, we start by looking at nominal exchange rates, and then see how we can use them to construct real exchange rates.

Nominal Exchange Rates

Nominal exchange rates between two currencies can be quoted in one of two ways:

- As the price of the domestic currency in terms of the foreign currency. If, for example, we look at the United States and the United Kingdom, and think of the dollar as the domestic currency and the pound as the foreign currency, we can express the nominal exchange rate as the price of a dollar in terms of pounds. In August 2001, the exchange rate defined this way was 0.66 (1 $ = 0.66 £).

- As the price of the foreign currency in terms of the domestic currency. Continuing with the same example, we can express the nominal exchange rate as the price of a pound in terms of dollars. In August 2001, the exchange rate defined this way was 1.5 (1 £ = 1.5 $).

Either definition is fine; the important thing is to remain consistent. In this book, I shall always define the **nominal exchange rate** as *the price of the foreign currency in terms of domestic currency*, and denote it by *E*. When looking, for example, at the exchange rate between the United States and the United Kingdom (from the viewpoint of the United States, so the dollar is the domestic currency), *E* will denote the price of a pound in terms of dollars—so, as of August 2001, *E* was 1.5.

E: Nominal exchange rate—Price of foreign currency in terms of domestic currency. (From the point of view of the U.S., the price of a pound in terms of dollars.)

Warning: Defining exchange rates as the price of foreign currency in terms of domestic currency is the convention in economic articles and books on the U.S. side of the Atlantic. On the other side of the Atlantic, however, economists more often use the alternative definition, defining exchange rates as the price of domestic currency in terms of foreign currency.

Exchange rates between the dollar and most foreign currencies change every day, every minute of the day. These changes are called *nominal appreciations* or *nominal depreciations*—appreciations or depreciations, for short. An **appreciation** of the domestic currency is an increase in the price of the domestic currency in terms of a foreign currency.

Given our definition of the exchange rate as the price of the foreign currency in terms of domestic currency, an appreciation of the domestic currency corresponds to a *decrease* in the exchange rate, *E*. A **depreciation** of the domestic currency is a decrease in the price of the domestic currency in terms of a foreign currency. So, given our definition of the exchange rate as the price of the foreign currency in terms of domestic currency, a depreciation of the domestic currency corresponds to an *increase* in the exchange rate, *E*.

This is more intuitive than it seems: Consider again the dollar and the pound (from the viewpoint of the United States):

- An *appreciation* of the dollar (also called a *dollar appreciation*) means the price of a dollar in terms of pounds goes up. Equivalently, the price of a pound in terms of dollars goes down, the same as saying the exchange rate has decreased.
- A *depreciation* of the dollar (a *dollar depreciation*) means the price of a dollar in terms of pounds goes down. Equivalently, the price of a pound in terms of dollars goes up, the same as saying the exchange rate has increased.

From the point of view of United States looking at U.K.

Nominal exchange rate E
Price of pounds in terms of dollars

Appreciation of the dollar
Price of dollars in pounds increases equivalently Price of pounds in dollars decreases equivalently Nominal exchange rate decreases: E↓

Depreciation of the dollar
Price of dollars in pounds decreases equivalently Price of pounds in dollars increases equivalently Nominal exchange rate increases: E↑

Figure 18-2

The Nominal Exchange Rate Between the Dollar and the Pound (from the Point of View of the United States): Appreciation and Depreciation

That an *appreciation* corresponds to a *decrease* in the exchange rate, and a *depreciation* to an *increase* in the exchange rate, will almost surely be confusing to you at first—it confuses many professional economists—but it will eventually become second nature as your understanding of open-economy macroeconomics deepens. Until then, consult Figure 18-2, which summarizes the terminology. (You may have encountered two other words to denote movements in exchange rates: *revaluations* and *devaluations*. These two terms are used when countries operate under **fixed exchange rates**—a system in which two or more countries maintain a constant exchange rate between their currencies. Under such a system, decreases in the exchange rate—which are infrequent by definition—are called **revaluations** (rather than appreciations). Increases in the exchange rate are called **devaluations** (rather than depreciations). We discuss fixed exchange rates in Chapter 20.)

Keep these definitions in mind as we move on to Figure 18-3, which plots the nominal exchange rate between the dollar and the pound since 1975. Note two things in this figure:

- *The trend decrease in the exchange rate.* In 1975, one pound was worth 2.4 dollars. In 2000, the value of the pound had declined to only 1.5 dollars.

  Put another way, there was a strong appreciation of the dollar vis-à-vis the pound over the period.

- *The large fluctuations in the exchange rate.* In the space of less than 10 years in the 1980s, the value of the pound dropped from 2.4 dollars in 1981 to 1.1 dollars in 1985, and then back up to 1.8 dollars by early 1988.

  Put another way, there was a large appreciation of the dollar in the first half of the 1980s, followed by a large depreciation later in the decade. What caused these swings? What effects did they have on the U.S. economy? This is one of the issues we shall return to later on in this and the next two chapters.

Remember:
Increase in the exchange rate ⇔ Depreciation.
Decrease in the exchange rate ⇔ Appreciation.

If we are interested, however, in the choice between buying domestic goods or foreign goods, the nominal exchange rate gives us only part of the information we need. Figure 18-3, for example, tells us only about movements in the relative price of the two currencies, the dollar and the pound. To British tourists thinking of visiting the United States, the question

Figure 18-3

The Nominal Exchange Rate Between the Dollar and the Pound, 1975–2000

While the dollar has strongly appreciated vis-à-vis the pound over the past 25 years, this appreciation has come with large swings in the nominal exchange rate between the two currencies, especially in the 1980s.

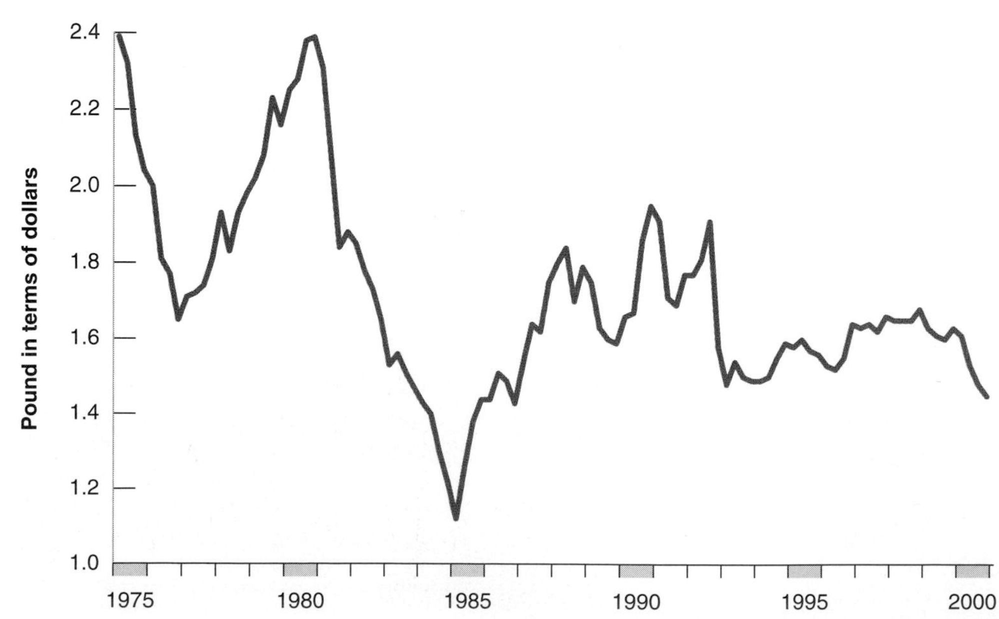

is not only how many dollars they will get in exchange for their pounds, but how much goods will cost in the United States, relative to how much they cost in the United Kingdom. This takes us to our next step—the construction of real exchange rates.

From Nominal to Real Exchange Rates

How can we construct the real exchange rate between the United States and the United Kingdom—the price of British goods in terms of U.S. goods?

Suppose the United Kingdom produced only one good, a Jaguar S-type Luxury Sedan, and the United States also produced only one good, a Cadillac Seville Luxury Sedan (this is one of those "Suppose" statements that run completely against the facts, but we shall become more realistic shortly). Constructing the real exchange rate, the price of the British good in terms of the U.S. good, would be straightforward.

- The first step would be to take the price of a Jaguar in pounds and convert it to a price in dollars. The price of a Jaguar in the United Kingdom is £30,000. A pound is worth 1.5 dollars, so the price of a Jaguar in dollars is 30,000 pounds $\times$ \$1.5 per pound = \$45,000.
- The second step would be to compute the ratio of the price of the Jaguar in dollars to the price of the Cadillac in dollars. The price of a Cadillac in the United States is \$40,000. So the price of a Jaguar in terms of Cadillacs—that is, the real exchange rate between the United States and the United Kingdom—would be \$45,000/\$40,000 = 1.12.

Computing the relative price of a Jaguar in terms of Cadillacs:
Jaguar: £ 30,000 × \$1.5 per pound = \$45,000
Cadillac: \$40,000

Relative price of a Jaguar in terms of Cadillacs:

$$\frac{\$45{,}000}{\$40{,}000} = 1.12$$

The example is straightforward, but how do we generalize it? The United Kingdom and the United States produce more than Jaguars and Cadillacs, and we want to construct a real exchange rate that reflects the relative price of *all* the goods produced in the United Kingdom in terms of *all* the goods produced in the United States.

The computation we just went through tells us how to proceed. Rather than use the pound price of a Jaguar and the dollar price of a Cadillac, we must use a pound price index for all goods produced in the United Kingdom and a dollar price index for all goods produced in the United States. This is exactly what the GDP deflators we introduced in Chapter 2 do: They are by definition price indexes for the set of final goods and services produced in the economy.

So let P be the GDP deflator for the United States, P^* be the GDP deflator for the United Kingdom (as a rule, I shall denote foreign variables by an asterisk), and E be the pound-dollar nominal exchange rate. Figure 18-4 goes through the steps needed to construct the real exchange rate.

- The price of British goods in pounds is P^*. Multiplying it by the exchange rate, E—the price of pounds in terms of dollars—gives us the price of British goods in dollars, EP^*.
- The price of U.S. goods in dollars is P. The *real exchange rate*, the price of British goods in terms of U.S. goods, which we shall call ϵ (the Greek lowercase epsilon), is thus given by

ϵ: Real exchange rate—Price of foreign goods in terms of domestic goods (for example, from the point of view of the U.S., the price of U.K. goods in terms of U.S. goods).

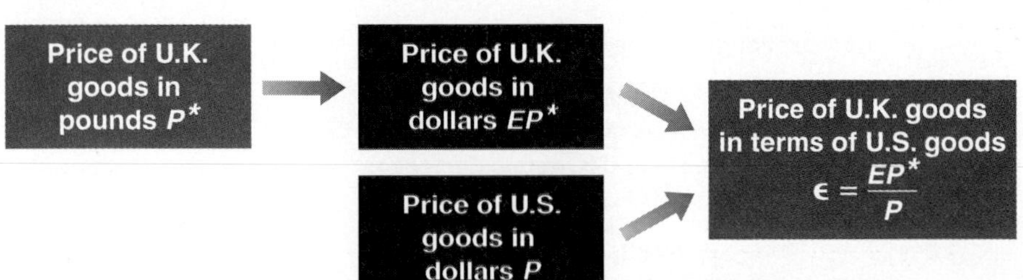

Figure 18-4

The Construction of the Real Exchange Rate

$$\epsilon = \frac{EP^*}{P} \qquad (18.1)$$

The real exchange rate is constructed by multiplying the nominal exchange rate by the foreign price level, and then dividing by the domestic price level—a straightforward extension of the computation we made in our Jaguar/Cadillac example. Note, however, an important difference between our example and this more general computation:

An index number is a number that is set equal to an arbitrary value (often 1 or 100) in an arbitrary year, called the base year. Because the choice of both the value in the base year and of the base year itself is arbitrary, the level of an index number is arbitrary, and so contains no information. But the rate of change of an index number does not depend on the choice of the value in the base year, and is, therefore, informative. For example, the fact that the GDP deflator is, say, 200, is uninformative. The fact that the GDP deflator changes during the year from 200 to 210, a 5% increase, is informative: It tells us that inflation was 5% during the year.

Unlike the price of Jaguars in terms of Cadillacs, the real exchange rate is an index number: That is, its level is arbitrary, and so, uninformative. It is uninformative because the GDP deflators used in the construction of the real exchange rate are themselves index numbers; as we saw in Chapter 2, they are equal to 1 (or 100) in whatever year is chosen as the base year. But all is not lost. Although the level of the real exchange rate is uninformative, relative changes in the real exchange rate are informative: If for example, the real exchange rate between the United States and the United Kingdom increases by 10%, this 10% increase tells us U.S. goods are now 10% cheaper relative to British goods than they were before.

Like nominal exchange rates, real exchange rates move over time. An increase in the relative price of domestic goods in terms of foreign goods is called a **real appreciation**. A decrease in the relative price of domestic goods in terms of foreign goods is called a **real depreciation**.

Real (as opposed to *nominal*) indicates we are referring to changes in the relative price of *goods*, not the relative price of currencies.

- Given our definition of the real exchange rate as the price of foreign goods in terms of domestic goods, a real appreciation corresponds to a *decrease* in the real exchange rate, ϵ.
- Similarly, a real depreciation corresponds to an *increase* in the real exchange rate, ϵ. These definitions are summarized in Figure 18-5, which does for the real exchange rate what Figure 18-2 did for the nominal exchange rate.

Figure 18-6 plots the evolution of the real exchange rate between the United States and the United Kingdom from 1975 to 2000, constructed using equation (18.1). For

Figure 18-5

The Real Exchange Rate Between U.S. Goods and U.K. Goods (from the Point of View of the United States): Real Appreciation and Real Depreciation

From the point of view of United States looking at U.K.

Real exchange rate, ϵ
Price of U.K. goods in terms of U.S. goods

Real appreciation
Price of U.S. goods in terms of U.K. goods increases equivalently: Price of U.K. goods in terms of U.S. goods decreases equivalently: Real exchange rate decreases: $\epsilon\downarrow$

Real depreciation
Price of U.S. goods in terms of U.K. goods decreases equivalently: Price of U.K. goods in terms of U.S. goods increases equivalently: Real exchange rate increases: $\epsilon\uparrow$

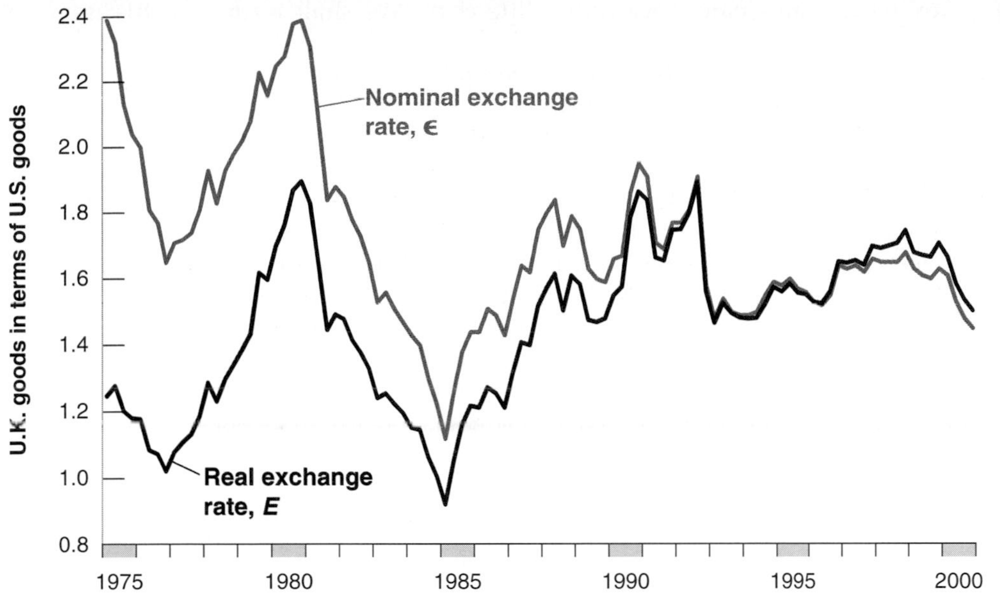

Figure 18-6

Real and Nominal Exchange Rates Between the United States and the United Kingdom, 1975–2000

Except for the difference in trend reflecting higher average inflation in the United Kingdom than in the United States, the nominal and the real exchange rates have moved largely together since 1970.

convenience, it also reproduces the evolution of the nominal exchange rate from Figure 18-3. The GDP deflators have both been set equal to 1 in 1996, so that in that year the nominal exchange rate and the real exchange rate are equal by construction.

Note two things about Figure 18-6:

- *In 2000, the real exchange rate was equal to 1.5, slightly higher than its 1975 value of 1.3.* In other words, there was a (small) real depreciation of U.S. goods vis-à-vis British goods over the period.

  How do we reconcile the fact that there was both a nominal appreciation (of the dollar vis-à-vis the pound) and a real depreciation (of U.S. goods vis-à-vis British goods) during the period? To see how, return to the definition of the real exchange rate:

$$\epsilon = E\frac{P^*}{P}$$

  Two things have happened since 1975:

  First, E has gone down: The pound has gone down in terms of dollars—this is the nominal appreciation we saw earlier.

  Second, inflation has been higher in the United Kingdom than in the United States, leading to a larger increase in the U.K. price level, P^*, than in the U.S. price level, P. This increase in P^*/P has been slighly larger than the decrease in E, leading to an increase in ϵ, a real depreciation.

  Let's go back to our British tourists thinking of visiting the United States. They can buy fewer dollars per pound than in 1975. Does this imply their trip will be more expensive (in terms of British goods)? No: When they arrive in the United States, they will discover that the prices of goods in the United States have increased much less than the prices of goods in the United Kingdom, and this more than cancels the decrease in the value of the pound in terms of dollars. They will find that their trip will actually be cheaper (in terms of British goods) than it was in 1975.

  There is a general lesson here. Over long periods of time, depending on differences in inflation rates across countries, nominal exchange rates and real

Can there be a real appreciation with no nominal appreciation?

Can there be a nominal appreciation with no real appreciation?

(The answer to both questions: Yes.)

exchange rates can move quite differently. We shall return to this issue in Chapter 20.

- *The large fluctuations in the nominal exchange rate we saw in Figure 18-3 also show up in the real exchange rate.*

  The reason is not hard to find: As inflation rates have not been very different in the United Kingdom and the United States, year-to-year movements in the price ratio, P^*/P, have been small compared to the often sharp movements in the nominal exchange rate, E. Thus, from year to year, or even over a few years, movements in the real exchange rate, ϵ, have been driven mostly by movements in the nominal exchange rate, E. Note that since the early 1990s, the nominal exchange rate and the real exchange rates have moved nearly together. This reflects the fact that, since the mid-1980s, inflation rates have been very similar in both countries.

If inflation rates were equal, P^*/P would be constant, and ϵ and E would move together.

From Bilateral to Multilateral Exchange Rates

We need one last step. We have concentrated so far on the exchange rate between the United States and the United Kingdom. But the United States trades with many countries besides the United Kingdom. Table 18-2 gives the geographic composition of U.S. trade for both exports and imports. The numbers refer only to **merchandise trade**—exports and imports of goods. They do not include exports and imports of services, such as travel services and tourism, for which the decomposition by country is not available.

Canada and Western Europe account for 39 to 46% (depending on whether one looks at imports or exports) of U.S. merchandise trade. But trade with Japan and the rest of Asia accounts for a steadily increasing proportion of U.S. merchandise trade. Interestingly, trade is much more unbalanced with Japan and the rest of Asia than with Canada and Western Europe: In 2000, the dollar volume of U.S. exports of goods to Japan was less than half the dollar volume of U.S. imports of goods from Japan. This merchandise trade deficit with Japan has indeed been a major source of tension between the two countries for some time.

How do we go from **bilateral exchange rates**, such as the real exchange rate between the United States and the United Kingdom, to **multilateral exchange rates**? The answer is straightforward. If we want to measure the average price of U.S. goods

***Bi* means two. *Multi* means many.**

Table 18-2 The Country Composition of U.S. Merchandise Trade, 2000

	Exports to		Imports from	
Countries	$ Billions	Percent	$ Billions	Percent
Canada	179	23	232	19
Western Europe	178	23	243	20
Japan	64	8	146	12
Mexico	86	11	136	11
Asia*	130	17	340	28
OPEC	20	3	42	3
Others	116	15	83	7
Total	773	100	1222	100

Source: *Survey of Current Business*, April 2001.
*Not including Japan.
OPEC: Organization of Petroleum Exporting Countries.

Figure 18-7

The U.S. Multilateral Real Exchange Rate, 1975–2000

The large real appreciation of U.S. goods in the first half of the 1980s was followed by an even larger real depreciation in the second half of the 1980s. This large swing in the 1980s is sometimes called the "dance of the dollar."

relative to the average price of goods of U.S. trading partners, we should use the U.S. share of trade with each country as the weight for that country. Using export shares we can construct an "export" real exchange rate, and using import shares we can construct an "import" real exchange rate. Because economists usually do not want to keep track of two different exchange rates, they typically use an exchange rate that takes an average of export and import shares. This is the variable we shall think of when talking about the **U.S. multilateral real exchange rate**, or the U.S. real exchange rate, for short.

Here is an example using Table 18-2. The share of exports to Canada in U.S. exports is 23%. The share of imports from Canada in U.S. imports is 19%. The share used to compute the multilateral U.S. exchange rate is (23% + 19%)/2 = 21%.

You may encounter the following names for the relative price of foreign goods vis-à-vis U.S. goods:

- **The U.S. multilateral real exchange rate**
- **The U.S. trade-weighted real exchange rate**
- **The U.S. effective real exchange rate**

Figure 18-7 shows the evolution of this multilateral real exchange rate, the average price of foreign goods relative to U.S. goods from 1975 to 2000. Like the bilateral real exchange rates we saw a few pages earlier, it is an index number. So, its level is also arbitrary; here it is set equal to 1 in 1996.

The most striking aspect of the figure is something we already saw when looking at the bilateral exchange rate between the United States and the United Kingdom in Figure 18-6, the large swing in the real exchange rate in the 1980s. Foreign goods were substantially less expensive compared to U.S. goods in the mid-1980s than they were either at the beginning or the end of the decade. In other words, there was a large real appreciation of U.S. goods in the first half of the 1980s, followed by an even larger real depreciation in the second half. This large swing, which as we have seen has its origins in the movement of the nominal exchange rate, is so striking that it has been given various names, from the "dollar cycle" to the more graphic "dance of the dollar." In the coming chapters, we shall look at where this swing came from and what effects these movements in the real exchange rate had on the trade deficit and on economic activity.

Once more, just to make sure: Increase in the real exchange rate ⇔ Real depreciation

Decrease in the real exchange rate ⇔ Real appreciation

18-2 Openness in Financial Markets

Openness in financial markets allows financial investors to hold both domestic assets and foreign assets, to diversify their portfolios, to speculate on movements in foreign interest rates versus domestic interest rates, on movements in exchange rates, and so on.

Diversify and speculate they do. Given that buying or selling foreign assets implies buying or selling foreign currency—sometimes called **foreign exchange**—the volume of transactions in foreign-exchange markets gives a sense of the importance of international financial transactions. In 2000 the recorded *daily* volume of foreign-exchange transactions in the world was about $3.0 trillion, of which 80%—about $2.4 trillion—involved dollars on one side of the transaction.

To get a sense of the magnitude of these numbers, the sum of U.S. exports and imports in 2000 totaled $2.5 trillion *for the year,* or about $7 billion a day. Suppose the only dollar transactions in foreign-exchange markets had been on one side by U.S. exporters selling their foreign currency earnings, and on the other side by U.S. importers buying the foreign currency they needed to buy foreign goods. Then, the volume of transactions would have been $7 billion a day, or about 0.3% of the actual daily volume of dollar transactions ($2.4 trillion) involving dollars in foreign-exchange markets. This computation tells us that most of the transactions are associated not with trade, but with purchases and sales of financial assets. The volume of transactions in foreign-exchange markets is not only high but also rapidly increasing. The volume of foreign-exchange transactions in New York is now about 25 times what it was in 1980. Again, this activity reflects mostly an increase in financial transactions rather than an increase in trade over the last 15 years.

Daily volume of foreign exchange transactions with dollars in one side of the transaction: $2.4 trillion.

Daily volume of trade of the United States with the rest of the world: $7 billion (0.3% of the volume of foreign exchange transactions).

For a country as a whole, openness in financial markets has another important implication. It allows the country to run trade surpluses and trade deficits. Recall that a country running a trade deficit is buying more from the rest of the world than it is selling to the rest of the world. In order to pay for the difference between what it buys and what it sells, the country must borrow from the rest of the world. It borrows by making it attractive for foreign financial investors to increase their holdings of domestic assets—in effect, to lend to the country.

Let's start by looking more closely at the relation between trade flows and financial flows. When this is done, we shall then be able to look at the determinants of these financial flows.

The Balance of Payments

A country's transactions with the rest of the world, including both trade flows and financial flows, are summarized by a set of accounts called the **balance of payments**. Table 18-3 presents the U.S. balance of payments for 2001. The table has two parts, separated by a line. Transactions are referred to either as **above the line** or **below the line**.

The Current Account

The transactions above the line record payments to and from the rest of the world. They are called **current account** transactions.

- The first two lines record the exports and imports of goods and services. Exports lead to payments from the rest of the world, imports to payments to the rest of the world. In 2001, imports exceeded exports, leading to a U.S. trade deficit of $348 billion. (Note that the numbers for exports and imports are different from those in Table 18-2; this is because the numbers in Table 18-2 refer only to goods and the numbers here include both goods *and* services.)
- Exports and imports are not the only sources of payments to and from the rest of the world. U.S. residents receive **investment income** on their holdings of foreign assets, and foreign residents receive investment income on their holdings of U.S. assets. In 2001, investment income received from the rest of the world was $293 billion and investment income paid to foreigners was $312 billion, for a net balance of −$19 billion.
- Finally, countries give and receive foreign aid; the net value of these payments is recorded as **net transfers received**. These net transfers amounted in 2001 to −$50 billion. This negative amount reflects the fact that, in 2001, the United States was—as it has traditionally been—a net donor of foreign aid.

Table 18-3 The U.S. Balance of Payments, 2001 ($ billions)

Current Account		
Exports	1004	
Imports	1352	
Trade balance (deficit = −) (1)		−348
Investment income received	293	
Investment income paid	312	
Net investment income (2)		−19
Net transfers received (3)		−50
Current account balance (deficit = −) (1) + (2) + (3)		−417
Capital Account		
Increase in foreign holdings of U.S. assets (4)	895	
Increase in U.S. holdings of foreign assets (5)	439	
Capital account balance (deficit = −) (4) − (5)		456
Statistical discrepancy		−39

Source: Survey of Current Business, March 2002. All numbers in billions.

The sum of net payments to and from the rest of the world is called the **current account balance**. If net payments from the rest of the world are positive, the country is running a **current account surplus**; if they are negative, the country is running a **current account deficit**. Adding all payments to and from the rest of the world, net payments from the United States to the rest of the world were equal in 2001 to −$348 − $19 − $50 = −$417 billion. Put another way, in 2001, the United States ran a current account deficit of $417 billion, a deficit equal to roughly 4.1% of its GDP.

◀ **Can a country have: A trade deficit and no current account deficit? A current account deficit and no trade deficit? (The answer to both questions: Yes.)**

The Capital Account

The fact that the United States had a current account deficit of $417 billion in 2001 implies that it had to borrow $417 billion from the rest of the world—or, equivalently, that net foreign holdings of U.S. assets had to increase by $417 billion. The numbers below the line describe how this was achieved. Transactions below the line are called **capital account** transactions.

The increase in foreign holdings of U.S. assets was $895 billion. But there was also an increase in U.S. holdings of foreign assets in 2001 of $439 billion, so the net increase in U.S foreign indebtedness (the increase in foreign holdings of U.S. assets, minus the increase in U.S. holdings of foreign assets), also called **net capital flows** to the United States, was $895 − $439 = $456 billion. Another name for net capital flows is the **capital account balance**: Positive net capital flows are called a **capital account surplus**; negative net capital flows are called a **capital account deficit.** So, put another way, in 2001, the United States ran a capital account surplus of $456 billion, or close to 4.5% of U.S. GDP.

◀ **A country that runs a current account deficit must finance it through positive net capital flows. Equivalently, it must run a capital account surplus.**

Shouldn't net capital flows (equivalently, the capital account surplus) be exactly equal to the current account deficit (which we saw from above was equal to $417 billion in 2001)?

In principle, yes. In practice, no.

The numbers for current and capital account transactions are constructed using different sources; although they should give the same answers, they typically do not. In 2001, the difference between the two—the **statistical discrepancy**—was

GDP Versus GNP: The Example of Kuwait

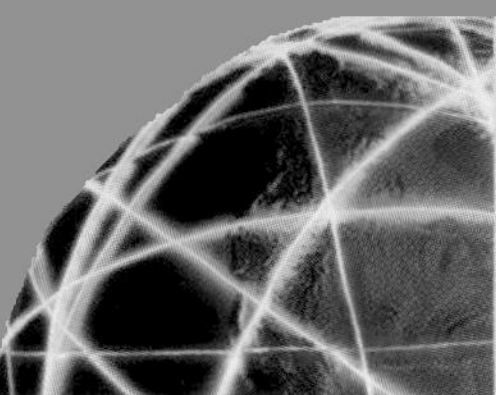

FOCUS

Should value added in an open economy be defined as

- The value added domestically (that is, within the country), or
- The value added by domestically owned factors of production?

The two definitions are not the same: Some domestic output may be produced by capital owned by foreigners, while some foreign output may be produced by capital owned by domestic residents.

The answer is that either definition is fine, and economists use both. **Gross domestic product (GDP)**, the measure we have used so far, corresponds to value added domestically. **Gross national product (GNP)** corresponds to the value added by domestically owned factors of production. GNP is equal to GDP plus net factor payments from the rest of the world (factor payments from the rest of the world minus factor payments to the rest of the world). While GDP is now the measure most commonly mentioned, GNP was widely used until the early 1990s, and you will still often encounter it in newspapers and academic publications.

For most countries, the difference between GNP and GDP is typically small, because factor payments to and from the rest of the world roughly cancel. For the United States in 2001, the difference between GDP and GNP was less than 0.2% of GDP (this is an unusually small number, by historical standards. But, for the United States, the difference between the two has never exceeded more than 1% of GDP).

There are a few exceptions. One is Kuwait. When oil was discovered in Kuwait, Kuwait's government decided that a portion of oil revenues would be saved and invested abroad rather than spent, to provide future Kuwaiti generations with investment income when oil revenues came to an end. Kuwait ran a large current account surplus, steadily accumulating foreign assets. As a result, it now has large holdings of foreign assets, and receives substantial investment income from the rest of the world. Table 1 gives GDP, GNP, and net factor payments for Kuwait, from 1989 to 1994.

Note how much larger GNP is compared to GDP throughout the period. But note also how net factor payments decreased after 1989. This is because Kuwait had to pay its allies for part of the cost of the 1990–1991 Gulf War *and* to pay for reconstruction after the war. It did so by running a current account deficit—equivalently, by decreasing its net holdings of foreign assets. This in turn led to a decrease in the income from foreign assets, and, by implication, a decrease in net factor payments.

Table 1 GDP, GNP, and Net Factor Payments in Kuwait, 1989–1994

Year	GDP	GNP	Net Factor Payments
1989	7143	9616	2473
1990	5328	7560	2232
1991	3131	4669	1538
1992	5826	7364	1538
1993	7231	8386	1151
1994	7380	8321	941

Source: International Financial Statistics, IMF. All numbers are in millions of Kuwaiti dinars. 1 dinar = \$3.3 (2001).

−\$39 billion, nearly 10% of the current account balance. This is yet another reminder that, even for the United States, economic data are far from perfect. (This problem of measurement manifests itself in another way as well. The sum of the current account deficits of all the countries in the world should be equal to zero: One country's deficit should show up as a surplus for the other countries taken as a whole. This is not, however, the case in the data: If we just add the published current account deficits of all the countries in the world, it would appear that the world is running a [measured] large current account deficit. Some economists speculate that the explanation is unrecorded trade with the Martians. Most others believe that mismeasurement is the explanation.)

Now that we have looked at the current account, we can return to an issue we touched on in Chapter 2, the difference between GDP, the measure of output we have used so far, and GNP, another measure of aggregate output. This is done in the Focus box "GDP Versus GNP: The Example of Kuwait."

The Choice Between Domestic and Foreign Assets

Openness in financial markets implies that financial investors face a new financial decision, holding domestic versus holding foreign assets.

It would seem that we actually have to think about at least *two* new decisions, the choice of holding domestic *money* versus foreign *money*, and the choice of holding domestic *interest-paying assets* versus foreign *interest-paying assets*. But remember why people hold money: to engage in transactions. For somebody who lives in the United States, and whose transactions are mostly or fully in dollars, there is little point in holding foreign currency: Foreign currency cannot be used for transactions in the United States, and if the goal is to hold foreign assets, holding foreign currency is clearly less desirable than holding foreign bonds, which pay interest. This leaves us with only one new choice to think about, the choice between domestic interest-paying assets and foreign interest-paying assets.

Two qualifications:

- **Foreigners involved in illegal activities often hold dollars, because dollars can be exchanged easily and cannot be traced.**
- **In times of very high inflation, people sometimes switch to a foreign currency, often the dollar, even for some domestic transactions.**

Let's think of these assets for now as domestic one-year bonds and foreign one-year bonds. To continue with our focus on the United States and the United Kingdom, consider for example, the choice between U.S. one-year bonds and U.K. one-year bonds, from the point of view of a U.S. investor.

- Suppose you decide to hold U.S. bonds.

  Let i_t be the one-year U.S. nominal interest rate. Then, as Figure 18-8 shows, for every dollar you put in U.S. bonds, you will get $(1 + i_t)$ dollars next year. (This is represented by the arrow pointing to the right at the top of the figure.)
- Suppose you decide instead to hold U.K. bonds.

  To buy U.K. bonds, you must first buy pounds. Let E_t be the nominal exchange rate between the dollar and the pound. For every dollar, you get $(1/E_t)$ pounds. (This is represented by the arrow pointing downward in the figure.)

  Let i_t^* denote the one-year nominal interest rate on U.K. bonds (in pounds). When next year comes, you will have $(1/E_t)(1 + i_t^*)$ pounds. (This is represented by the arrow pointing right at the bottom of the figure.)

  You will then have to convert your pounds back into dollars. If you expect the nominal exchange rate next year to be E^e_{t+1}, you can expect to have $(1/E_t)(1 + i_t^*)$ E^e_{t+1} dollars next year for every dollar you invested. (This is represented by the arrow pointing upward in the figure.)

  We shall look at the expression we just derived in more detail soon. But note its basic implication already: In assessing the attractiveness of U.K. versus U.S. bonds, you cannot look just at the U.K. interest rate and the U.S. interest rate; you must also assess what you think will happen to the dollar/pound exchange rate between this year and next.

The decision whether to invest abroad or at home depends on more than interest rates. It also depends on what you think will be the course of the exchange rate in the future.

Let's now make the same assumption we made in Chapter 14 when discussing the choice between short-term bonds and long-term bonds, or between bonds and stocks. Let's assume that you and other financial investors care only about the expected rate of

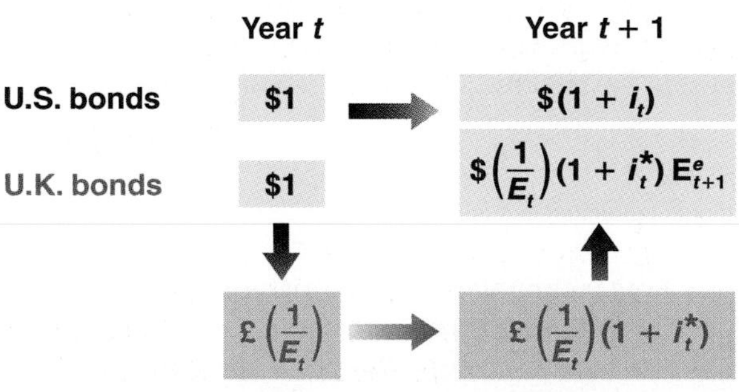

Figure 18-8

Expected Returns from Holding One-Year U.S. Bonds or U.K. Bonds

return and therefore want to hold only the asset with the highest expected rate of return. In that case, if both U.K. bonds and U.S. bonds are to be held, they must have the same expected rate of return, so that the following *arbitrage relation* must hold:

$$1+i_t = \left(\frac{1}{E_t}\right)(1+i_t^*)\,(E_{t+1}^e)$$

Reorganizing that equation:

$$1+i_t = (1+i_t^*)\left(\frac{E_{t+1}^e}{E_t}\right) \quad (18.2)$$

The word *uncovered* is to distinguish this relation from another relation called the *covered interest parity* condition. The covered interest parity condition is derived by looking at the following choice:

Buy and hold U.S. bonds for one year. Or buy pounds today, buy one-year U.K. bonds with the proceeds, and agree to sell the pounds for dollars a year ahead at a predetermined price, called the *forward exchange rate.*

The rate of return of these two alternatives, which can both be realized at *no risk today*, must be the same. The covered interest parity condition is a *riskless arbitrage* condition.

Equation (18.2) is called the **uncovered interest parity** relation, or simply the **interest parity condition**.

The assumption that financial investors will hold only the bonds with the highest expected rate of return is obviously too strong, for two reasons:

- It ignores transaction costs. Going in and out of U.K. bonds requires three separate transactions, each with a transaction cost.
- It ignores risk. The exchange rate a year from now is uncertain; that means that holding U.K. bonds is more risky, in terms of dollars, than holding U.S. bonds.

Whether holding U.K. bonds or U.S. bonds is more risky actually depends on which investors we are looking at. Holding U.K. bonds is more risky from the point of view of U.S. investors. Holding U.S. bonds is more risky from the point of view of British investors. (Why?)

But as a characterization of capital movements among the major world financial markets (New York, Frankfurt, London, and Tokyo), the assumption is not far off. Small changes in interest rates and rumors of impending appreciation or depreciation can lead to movements of tens of billions of dollars within minutes. For the rich countries of the world, the arbitrage assumption in equation (18.2) is a good approximation of reality. Other countries whose capital markets are smaller and less developed, or countries that have various forms of capital controls, have more leeway in choosing their domestic interest rate than is implied by equation (18.2). We shall return to this issue at the end of Chapter 20.

Interest Rates and Exchange Rates

Let's get a better sense of what the interest parity condition implies. Rewrite equation (18.2) as

$$1+i_t = (1+i_t^*)\left(1+\frac{E_{t+1}^e-E_t}{E_t}\right) \quad (18.3)$$

This follows from Proposition 3 in Appendix 2 at the end of the book.

This gives a relation between the domestic nominal interest rate, i_t, the foreign nominal interest rate, i_t^*, and the expected rate of depreciation, $(E_{t+1}^e - E_t)/E_t$. (Remember, an increase in E is a depreciation, so that $[E_{t+1}^e - E_t]/E_t$ is the expected rate of depreciation of the domestic currency. If the domestic currency is expected to appreciate, then this term is negative.) As long as interest rates or the expected rate of depreciation are not too large—say, below 20% a year—a good approximation to this equation is given by

$$i_t \approx i_t^* + \frac{E_{t+1}^e - E_t}{E_t} \quad (18.4)$$

An important relation to remember:

Under the uncovered interest parity condition, the domestic interest rate must approximately equal the foreign interest rate plus the expected depreciation of the domestic currency.

This is the relation you must remember: Arbitrage implies that *the domestic interest rate must be (approximately) equal to the foreign interest rate plus the expected depreciation rate of the domestic currency.*

Let's apply this equation to U.S. bonds versus U.K. bonds. Suppose the one-year nominal interest rate is 4.0% in the United States, 2.5% in the United Kingdom. Should you hold U.K. bonds or U.S. bonds? The answer:

- It depends whether you expect the dollar to depreciate vis-à-vis the pound over the coming year by more or less than the difference between the U.S. interest rate and the U.K. interest rate, 4.0% − 2.5% = 1.5%.
- If you expect the dollar to depreciate by more than 1.5%, then, despite the fact that the interest rate is lower in the United Kingdom than in the United States, investing in U.K. bonds is more attractive than investing in U.S. bonds. By holding U.K. bonds, you will get smaller interest payments next year, but the pound will also be worth more in terms of dollars next year, making investing in U.K. bonds more attractive than investing in U.S. bonds.
- But if you expect the dollar to depreciate by less than 1.5% or even to appreciate, then the reverse holds, and U.S bonds are more attractive than U.K. bonds.

In other words, the uncovered interest parity condition tells us that financial investors must be expecting on average a depreciation of the dollar with respect to the pound of about 1.5% over the coming year, and this is why they are willing to hold U.K. bonds despite their lower interest rate. (Another example is provided in the Focus box "Buying Brazilian Bonds.")

Buying Brazilian Bonds

Go back to September 1993 (the very high interest rate in Brazil at the time helps make the point I want to get across here). Brazilian bonds are paying a *monthly* interest rate of 36.9%. This seems very attractive compared to the *annual* rate of 3% on U.S. bonds—corresponding to a monthly interest rate of about 0.2%. Shouldn't you buy Brazilian bonds?

The discussion in this chapter tells you that to decide, you need one more crucial element, the expected rate of change of the dollar vis-à-vis the cruzeiro (the name of the Brazilian currency at the time; the currency is now called the *real*). You need this information because (as Figure 18-8 makes clear) the return in dollars from investing in Brazilian bonds for a month is

$$(1+i_t^*)\frac{E_{t+1}^e}{E_t} = (1.369)\frac{E_{t+1}^e}{E_t}$$

What rate of cruzeiro depreciation should you expect over the coming month? Assume the rate of depreciation next month will be equal to the rate of depreciation last month. You know that 100,000 cruzeiros, worth \$1.01 at the end of July 1993, were worth only \$.75 at the end of August 1993. If depreciation continues at the same rate, the return from investing in Brazilian bonds for a month is

$$(1+i_t^*)\frac{E_{t+1}^e}{E_t} = (1.369)\left(\frac{.75}{1.01}\right) = 1.016$$

The expected rate of return in dollars from holding Brazilian bonds is only (1.016 − 1) = 1.6% per month, not the 36.9% per month that looked so attractive. Note that 1.6% per month is still much higher than the monthly interest rate on U.S. bonds (about 0.2%.) But think of the risk and the transaction costs—all the elements we ignored when we wrote the arbitrage condition. When these are taken into account, you may well decide to keep your funds out of Brazil.

FOCUS

Figure 18-9

One-Year Nominal Interest Rates in the United States and in the United Kingdom, 1975–2000

U.S. and U.K. nominal interest rates have largely moved together over the last 25 years.

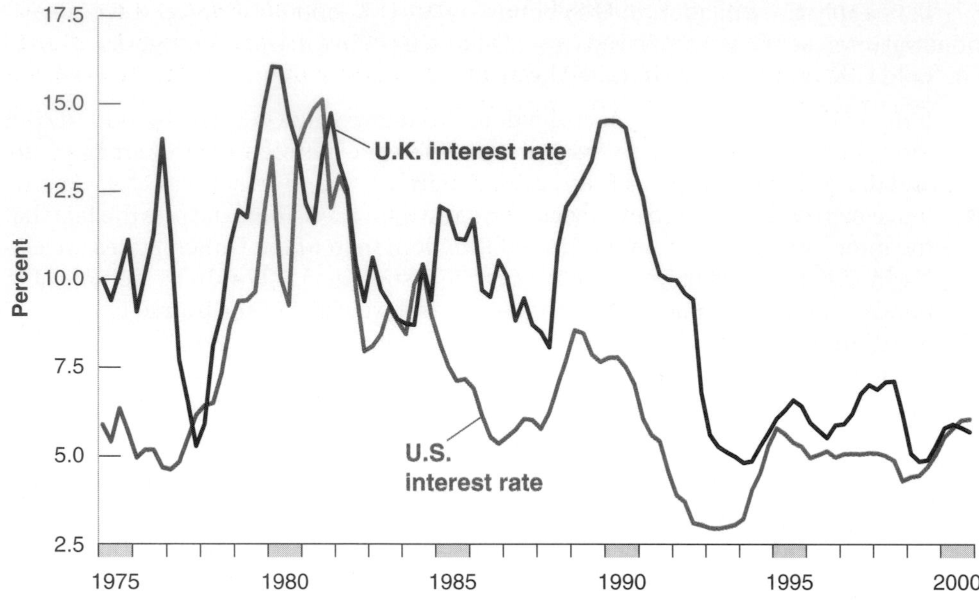

The arbitrage relation between interest rates and the exchange rate in equation (18.4) will play a central role in the following chapters. It suggests that unless countries are willing to tolerate large movements in their exchange rate, domestic and foreign interest rates are likely to move very much together. Take the extreme case of two countries that commit to maintaining their bilateral exchange rate at a fixed value. If markets have faith in this commitment, they will expect the exchange rate to remain constant, and the expected depreciation will be zero. In that case, the arbitrage condition implies that interest rates in the two countries will have to move exactly together. Most of the time, as we shall see, governments do not make such absolute commitments to maintain the exchange rate, but they often do try to avoid large movements in the exchange rate. This puts sharp limits on how much they can allow their interest rate to deviate from interest rates elsewhere in the world.

If $E^e_{t+1} = E_t$, then the interest parity condition implies $i_t = i^*_t$.

How much do nominal interest rates actually move together between major countries? Figure 18-9 plots the one-year nominal interest rate in the United States and the one-year nominal interest rate in the United Kingdom since 1975. The impression from the figure is of related but not identical movements. Interest rates were very high in both countries in the early 1980s, and high again—although much more so in the United Kingdom than in the United States—in the late 1980s. Both have been low since the early to mid-1990s. At the same time, differences between the two have sometimes been quite large: In 1990, for example, the U.K. interest rate was nearly 7% above the U.S. interest rate. In the coming chapters, we shall return to why such differences emerge, and what their implications may be.

Meanwhile, do the following: Look at the back pages of a recent issue of *The Economist* for short-term interest rates in different countries relative to the United States. Which are the currencies against which the dollar is expected to depreciate?

18-3 Conclusions and a Look Ahead

We have now set the stage for the study of the open economy:

- Openness in goods markets allows a choice between domestic goods and foreign goods. This choice depends primarily on the *real exchange rate*—the relative price of foreign goods in terms of domestic goods.

- Openness in financial markets allows a choice between domestic assets and foreign assets. This choice depends on their relative rates of return, which, in turn, depend on domestic interest rates and foreign interest rates, and on the expected rate of depreciation of the domestic currency.

In the next chapter, Chapter 19, we look at the implications of openness in goods markets. Chapter 20 brings in openness in financial markets. In Chapter 21, we discuss the pros and cons of different exchange rate regimes.

Summary

- Openness in goods markets allows people and firms to choose between domestic goods and foreign goods. Openness in financial markets allows financial investors to hold domestic financial assets or foreign financial assets.
- The nominal exchange rate is the price of foreign currency in terms of domestic currency. From the viewpoint of the United States, the nominal exchange rate between the United States and the United Kingdom is the price of a pound in terms of dollars.
- A nominal appreciation (an appreciation, for short) is an increase in the price of the domestic currency in terms of foreign currency; given the definition of the exchange rate, a nominal appreciation corresponds to a decrease in the exchange rate.

  A nominal depreciation (a depreciation, for short) is a decrease in the price of the domestic currency in terms of foreign currency; a nominal depreciation corresponds to an increase in the exchange rate.
- The real exchange rate is the relative price of foreign goods in terms of domestic goods. It is equal to the nominal exchange rate times the foreign price level divided by the domestic price level.
- A real appreciation is an increase in the relative price of domestic goods in terms of foreign goods; a real appreciation corresponds to a decrease in the real exchange rate.

  A real depreciation is a decrease in the relative price of domestic goods; a real depreciation corresponds to an increase in the real exchange rate.
- The multilateral real exchange rate, or real exchange rate, for short, is a weighted average of bilateral real exchange rates, with the weight for each foreign country equal to its share in trade.
- The balance of payments records a country's transactions with the rest of the world. The current account balance is equal to the sum of the trade balance, net investment income, and net transfers received from the rest of the world. The capital account balance is equal to capital flows from the rest of the world minus capital flows to the rest of the world.
- The current account and the capital account are mirror images of each other. Leaving aside statistical problems, the current account balance plus the capital account balance must sum to zero. A current account deficit is financed by net capital flows from the rest of the world, thus by a capital account surplus. Similarly, a current account surplus corresponds to a capital account deficit.
- Uncovered interest parity, or interest parity, for short, is an arbitrage condition stating that the expected rates of return in terms of domestic currency on domestic bonds and foreign bonds must be equal. Interest parity implies that the domestic interest rate approximately equals the foreign interest rate plus the expected rate of depreciation of the domestic currency.

Key Terms

- openness in goods markets, 373
- tariffs, 373
- quotas, 373
- openness in financial markets, 373
- capital controls, 373
- openness in factor markets, 373
- North American Free Trade Agreement (NAFTA), 373
- tradable goods, 375
- real exchange rate, 376
- nominal exchange rate, 377
- appreciation (nominal), 377
- depreciation (nominal), 377
- fixed exchange rates, 378
- revaluation, 378
- devaluation, 378
- real appreciation, 380
- real depreciation, 380
- merchandise trade, 382
- bilateral exchange rate, 382
- multilateral exchange rate, 382
- multilateral real exchange rate, 383
- trade-weighted real exchange rate, 383

- effective real exchange rate, 383
- foreign exchange, 383
- balance of payments, 384
- above the line, below the line, 384
- current account, 384
- investment income, 384
- net transfers received, 384
- current account balance, 385
- current account surplus, deficit, 385
- capital account, 385
- net capital flows, 385
- capital account balance, 385
- capital account surplus, deficit, 385
- statistical discrepancy, 385
- gross domestic product (GDP) versus gross national product (GNP), 386
- uncovered interest parity relation, or interest parity condition, 388

Questions and Problems

Quick Check

1. *Using the information in this chapter, label each of the following statements* true, false, *or* uncertain. *Explain briefly.*
   a. Countries with net capital inflows must run current account deficits.
   b. While the export ratio can be larger than one—as it is in Singapore—the same cannot be true of the ratio of imports to GDP.
   c. That a rich country like Japan has such a small ratio of imports to GDP is clear evidence of an unfair playing field for American exporters to Japan.
   d. Uncovered interest parity implies that real interest rates must be the same across countries.
   e. If the nominal exchange rate between the Euro and the dollar is 0.90, it means that one Euro is worth 90 cents.
   f. If the real exchange rate between the United Kingdom and the United States is 2, this means that goods are twice as expensive in the United Kingdom than in the United States.

2. *Consider two fictional economies, one called the domestic country and the other the foreign country. Construct the balance of payments for each country given the following list of transactions:*

   The domestic country purchased $100 in oil from the foreign country.
   Foreign tourists spent $25 on domestic ski slopes.
   Domestic residents purchased $45 in life insurance in the foreign country.
   Domestic residents purchased $5 in illegal substances from foreigners.
   Foreign investors were paid $15 in dividends from their holdings of domestic equities.
   Domestic residents gave $25 to foreign charities.
   Foreign businessmen gave $35 in bribes to domestic government officials.
   Domestic businesses borrowed $65 from foreign banks.
   Foreign investors purchased $15 in domestic junk bonds.
   Domestic investors sold off $50 in holdings of foreign government bonds.

3. *Consider two bonds, one issued in euros in Germany, one issued in dollars in the United States. Assume that both government securities are one-year bonds—paying the face value of the bond one year from now. The exchange rate, E, stands at 1 euro = 0.95 dollars.*

   The face values and prices on the two bonds are given by

	Face Value	Price
United States 1-year bond	$10,000	$9,615.38
Germany 1-year bond	€13,333	€12,698.10

The symbol € represents the euro.

   a. Compute the nominal interest rate on each of the bonds.
   b. Compute the expected exchange rate next year consistent with uncovered interest parity.
   c. If you expect the dollar to depreciate relative to the Euro, which bond should you buy?
   d. Assume you are a U.S. investor. You exchange dollars for euros and purchase the German bond. One year from now it turns out *E* is actually 0.90 (1 euro = 0.90 dollars). What is your realized rate of return in dollars compared to the realized rate of return you would have made had you held the U.S. bond?
   e. Are the differences in rates of return in (d) consistent with the uncovered interest parity condition? Why or why not?

Dig Deeper

4. *When Ronald Reagan was president, the U.S. trade deficit increased substantially. Democrats pointed to the trade deficit as a sign that the U.S. economy was no longer competitive. Ronald Reagan pointed to the large net capital inflows instead as a sign that the U.S. economy had become a very attractive place for foreign investors. Who was right? Can you tell?*

5. *Assume that there exists a market for buying and selling foreign exchange one year in the future, at a price determined today—this price is called the forward exchange rate. Denote the forward price of 1 Euro in terms of dollars by* F. *In other words, you can enter into a contract today to sell 1 Euro for* F *dollars one year in the future.*
   a. Derive the following approximation to covered interest parity, where i denotes the one-year interest rate and an asterisk denotes a foreign variable:

$$i = i^* + \left(\frac{F-E}{E}\right)$$

b. Given the two government bonds and exchange rate from problem 3, find the forward exchange rate of 1 euro consistent with covered interest parity.

c. What should you do if the forward exchange rate is actually different from the value you just derived?

d. Suppose the forward exchange rate is as you computed it in (b). You buy euros today, buy the German bond today, and enter a contract today to sell the euros you will receive in a year at the forward exchange rate.

Does a surprise in the exchange rate between now and next year affect the returns on your investment? Why or why not?

Explore Further

6. Retrieve the nominal exchange rates between Japan and the United States from the Internet. A useful and free Canadian site, which allows you to construct graphs online, is located at **pacific.commerce.ubc.ca/xr**.

a. Plot the yen versus the dollar since 1979. During which period did the yen appreciate? During which period did the yen depreciate?

b. Given the current Japanese slump, one way of increasing demand would be to make Japanese goods more attractive. Does this require an appreciation or a depreciation of the yen?

c. What has happened to the yen in the past few years? Has it appreciated or depreciated? Is this good or bad for Japan?

7. Go to the Federal Reserve Bank of St. Louis' Web site for trade data at **www.stls.frb.org/fred/data/exchange.html**. *Find data for "Balance on the Current Account" and for "U.S. Assets Abroad, Net: Outflow (−)." (Note that a negative number is a net outflow.) Look at the data for 1990–2000. Why was there such a large flow of U.S. assets moving out of the United States?*

We invite you to visit the Blanchard page on the Prentice Hall Web site at:
www.prenhall.com/blanchard
for this chapter's World Wide Web exercises

Further Readings

If you want to learn more about international trade and international economics, a very good textbook is one by Paul Krugman and Maurice Obstfeld, *International Economics, Theory and Policy*, 5th ed. (New York, NY: HarperCollins, 2000).

If you want to know current exchange rates between nearly any pair of currencies in the world, look at the "currency converter" at **www.oanda.com**.

The Goods Market in an Open Economy

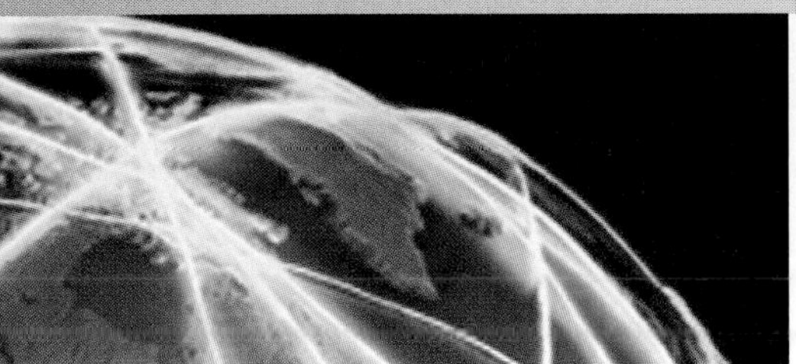

At the time of this writing, countries around the world are worried about a U.S. slowdown. Their concerns are not for the United States, but for themselves. To them, a U.S. slowdown means lower exports to the United States, a deterioration of their trade position, and a higher risk of a slowdown for their own economy.

Are their worries justified? Can a slowdown in the United States really lead to a world slowdown? If there are such strong interactions between countries, shouldn't macroeconomic policies be coordinated between countries? If so, why does it seem so difficult to achieve such coordination? To answer these questions, we must expand our treatment of the goods market in the core (Chapter 3), to take into account openness in goods markets. This is what we do in this chapter.

- Section 19-1 characterizes equilibrium in the goods market for an open economy.
- Sections 19-2 and 19-3 show the effects of domestic shocks and foreign shocks on the domestic economy's output and trade balance.
- Sections 19-4 and 19-5 look at the effects of a real depreciation on output and on the trade balance.
- Section 19-6 gives an alternative description of the equilibrium, which shows the close connection between saving, investment, and the trade balance. ■

"Domestic demand for goods" and "demand for domestic goods" sound close. But, in an open economy, they are not the same. Part of domestic demand falls on foreign goods. Part of foreign demand falls on domestic goods.

19-1 The *IS* Relation in the Open Economy

When we were assuming the economy was closed to trade, there was no need to distinguish between the *domestic demand for goods* and the *demand for domestic goods*: They were clearly the same. Now, we must distinguish between the two: Some domestic demand falls on foreign goods, and some of the demand for domestic goods comes from foreigners. Let's look at this distinction more closely.

The Demand for Domestic Goods

In an open economy, the **demand for domestic goods** is given by

$$Z \equiv C + I + G - \epsilon IM + X \qquad (19.1)$$

The first three terms—consumption, C, investment, I, and government spending, G—constitute the **domestic demand for goods**. If the economy were closed, $C + I + G$ would also be the demand for domestic goods. This is why, until now, we looked only at $C + I + G$. But now we have to make two adjustments:

In Chapter 3, I ignored the real exchange rate and subtracted *IM*, not ϵ *IM*. This was a cheat; I did not want to have to talk about the real exchange rate—and complicate matters—so early in the book.

- First, we must subtract *imports*, that part of domestic demand that falls on foreign goods—rather than on domestic goods.

  We must be careful here: Foreign goods are different from domestic goods, so we cannot just subtract the quantity of imports, IM. If we were to do so, we would be subtracting apples (foreign goods) from oranges (domestic goods). We must first express the value of imports in terms of domestic goods. This is what ϵIM in equation (19.1) stands for: As we saw in Chapter 18, ϵ is the real exchange rate—the price of foreign goods in terms of domestic goods. So ϵIM (the price times the quantity of imports) is the value of imports in terms of domestic goods.
- Second, we must add *exports*, the demand for domestic goods that comes from abroad. This is captured by the term X in equation (19.1).

Domestic demand for goods $(C + I + G)$
Minus
Domestic demand for foreign goods (imports, ϵIM)
Plus
Foreign demand for domestic goods (exports, X) equals
Demand for domestic goods $(C + I + G - \epsilon IM + X)$

The Determinants of the Demand for Domestic Goods

Having listed the five components of demand, our next task is to specify their determinants. Let's start with the first three: C, I, and G.

The Determinants of *C*, *I*, and *G*

Now that we are assuming the economy is open, how should we modify our earlier descriptions of consumption, investment, and government spending? The answer: Not very much, if at all. How much consumers decide to spend still depends on their income and their wealth. While the real exchange rate surely affects the *composition* of consumption spending between domestic goods and foreign goods, there is no obvious reason why it should affect the overall *level* of consumption. The same is true of investment: The real exchange rate may affect whether firms buy domestic machines or foreign machines, but it should not affect total investment.

This is good news because it implies that we can use the descriptions of consumption, investment, and government spending that we developed earlier. Therefore,

$$\textit{Domestic demand}: C + I + G = \underset{(+)}{C(Y - T)} + \underset{(+,-)}{I(Y, r)} + G$$

Domestic demand, $C + I + G$, depends on income, Y, the interest rate, r, taxes, T, and the level of government spending, G.

We assume that consumption depends positively on disposable income, $Y - T$, and that investment depends positively on production, Y, and negatively on the real interest rate, r. We continue to take government spending, G, as given. Note that we leave aside the refinements introduced in Chapters 14 to 17, where we looked at the role of expectations in affecting spending. We want to take things one step at a time and understand the effects of opening the economy; we shall reintroduce some of those refinements later.

The Determinants of Imports

What does the quantity of imports, IM, depend on? Primarily on the overall *level of domestic demand*: The higher the level of domestic demand, the higher the demand for all goods, both domestic and foreign. This is what started this chapter: The rest of the world is worried about a U.S. recession because a U.S. recession leads to lower U.S. imports. But IM also clearly depends on *the real exchange rate*: The higher the price of foreign goods relative to the price of domestic goods, the lower the domestic demand for foreign goods relative to the domestic demand for domestic goods, and so, the lower the quantity of imports.

Thus, we write imports as

$$IM = IM(Y, \epsilon) \quad (19.2)$$
$$(+,-)$$

- The quantity of imports depends on income (or, equivalently, on output—income and output are still equal in an open economy), Y: Higher income leads to higher imports.
- The quantity of imports also depend on the real exchange rate. Recall that the real exchange rate, ϵ, is defined as the price of foreign goods in terms of domestic goods. A higher real exchange rate makes foreign goods relatively more expensive, leading to a decrease in the quantity of imports, IM. This negative effect of the real exchange rate on the quantity of imports is captured by the negative sign under ϵ in equation (19.2). (As ϵ goes up while IM goes down, note that what happens to $\epsilon\, IM$, the *value* of imports in terms of domestic goods, is ambiguous. We return to this point shortly.)

Again, we cheat a bit here. Our discussion suggests that we should be using domestic demand, $C + I + G$, instead of income, Y. You might also dispute the assumption that imports depend on total domestic demand and not on its composition. For example, many poor countries import most of their capital equipment but consume mostly domestic goods. In that case, the composition of demand would matter for imports. I leave these complications aside here.

The quantity of imports, IM, depends on the level of output, Y, and the real exchange rate, ϵ.

The Determinants of Exports

The export of one country is, by definition, the import of another. In thinking about what determines U.S. exports, we can ask, equivalently, what determines foreign imports. From our discussion of the determinants of imports in the preceding paragraph, we know that foreign imports are likely to depend on foreign activity, and on the relative price of foreign goods. Let Y^* denote output in the rest of the world, call it *foreign output.*

Recall that asterisks refer to foreign variables.

Thus, we can write exports as

$$X = X(Y^*, \epsilon) \quad (19.3)$$
$$(+\ ,+)$$

- An increase in foreign output leads to an increase in the foreign demand for all goods, some of which falls on U.S. goods, leading to higher U.S. exports.
- An increase in epsilon—an increase in the relative price of foreign goods in terms of U.S. goods—makes U.S. goods more attractive relative to foreign goods, leading to an increase in exports.

Exports depend on the level of foreign output, Y^*, and the real exchange rate, ϵ.

We can show graphically what we have learned so far in Figure 19-1, which plots the various components of demand against output, keeping constant all other variables (the interest rate, taxes, government spending, foreign output, and the real exchange rate) that affect demand.

In Figure 19-1, panel (a), the line DD plots domestic demand, $C + I + G$, as a function of output, Y. This relation between demand and output is familiar from Chapter 3. Under our standard assumptions, the slope of the relation between demand and

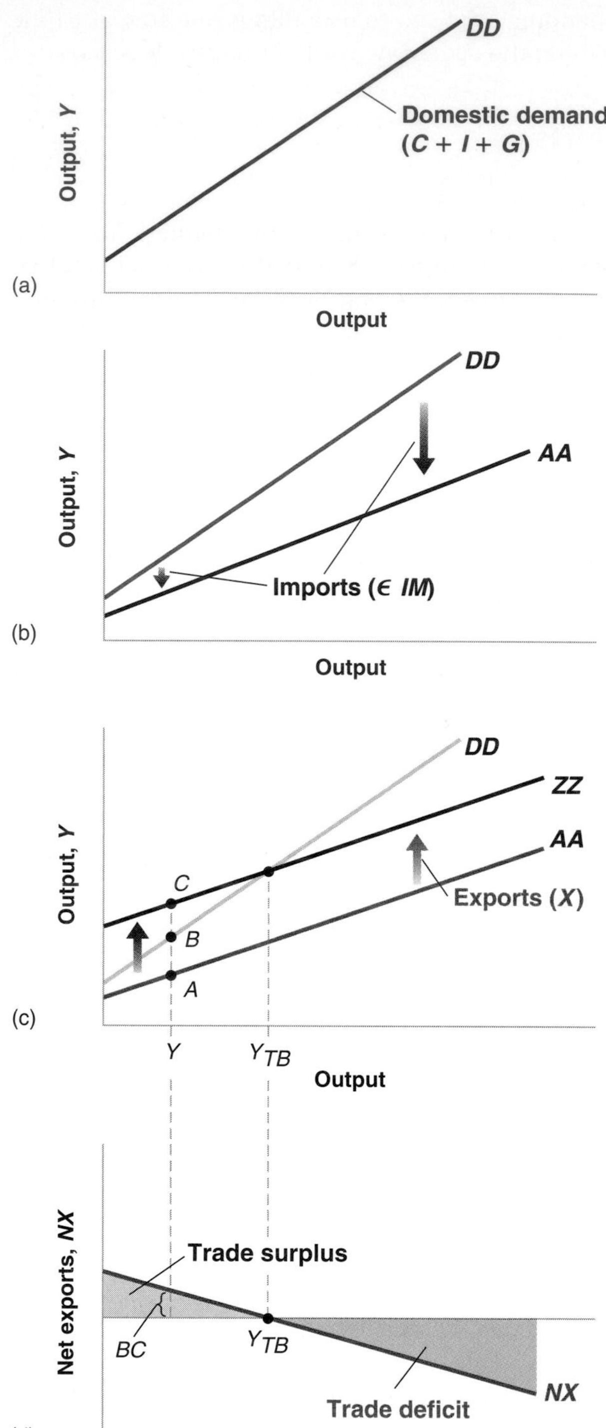

Figure 19-1

The Demand for Domestic Goods and Net Exports

The domestic demand for goods is an increasing function of income. The demand for domestic goods is obtained by subtracting the value of imports from domestic demand, and then adding exports. The trade balance is a decreasing function of output.

output is positive but less than 1: An increase in output—equivalently, an increase in income, as output and income are still the same in an open economy—increases demand but less than one for one. (In the absence of good reasons to the contrary, I draw the relation between demand and output, and the other relations in this chapter, as lines rather than curves. This is purely for convenience, and none of the discussions that follow depend on this assumption.)

To arrive at the demand for domestic goods, we must first *subtract imports*. This is done in Figure 19-1, panel (b) and gives us the line *AA*. The line *AA* represents the domestic demand for domestic goods. The distance between *DD* and *AA* equals the value of imports, $\epsilon\, IM$. Because the quantity of imports increases with income, the distance between the two lines increases with income. We can establish two facts about line *AA*, which will be useful later in the chapter:

For a given real exchange rate, ϵ, $\epsilon\, IM$—the value of imports in terms of domestic goods—moves exactly with *IM*—the quantity of imports.

1. *AA* is flatter than *DD*: As income increases, some of the additional domestic demand falls on foreign goods rather than on domestic goods. As income increases, the domestic demand for domestic goods increases less than total domestic demand.

2. As long as some of the additional demand falls on domestic goods, *AA* has a positive slope: An increase in income leads to some increase in the demand for domestic goods.

Next we must *add exports*. This is done in Figure 19-1, panel (c) and gives us the line *ZZ*, which is above *AA*. The line *ZZ* represents the demand for domestic goods. The distance between *ZZ* and *AA* equals exports. Because exports do not depend on domestic output, the distance between *ZZ* and *AA* is constant, which is why the two lines are parallel. Because *AA* is flatter than *DD*, *ZZ* is flatter than *DD* as well.

From the information in panel (c) we can characterize the behavior of net exports—the difference between exports and imports ($X - \epsilon\, IM$)—as a function of output. At output level *Y*, for example, exports are given by the distance *AC* and imports by the distance *AB*, so net exports are given by the distance *BC*.

This relation between net exports and output is represented as the line *NX* (for Net eXports) in Figure 19-1, panel (d). Net exports are a decreasing function of output: As output increases, imports increase and exports are unaffected, leading to lower net exports. Call Y_{TB} (*TB* for trade balance) the level of output at which the value of imports is just equal to exports, so that net exports are equal to zero. Levels of output above Y_{TB} lead to higher imports, leading to a trade deficit. Levels of output below Y_{TB} lead to lower imports, and a trade surplus.

Recall that *net exports* is synonymous with trade balance. Positive net exports correspond to a trade surplus, negative net exports to a trade deficit.

19-2 Equilibrium Output and the Trade Balance

The goods market is in equilibrium when domestic output equals the demand for domestic goods:

$$Y = Z$$

Equilibrium in the goods market requires that domestic output be equal to the demand for domestic goods.

Collecting the relations we derived for the components of the demand for domestic goods, *Z*:

$$Y = C(Y - T) + I(Y, r) + G - \epsilon\, IM(Y, \epsilon) + X(Y^*, \epsilon) \qquad (19.4)$$

This equilibrium condition determines output as a function of all the variables we take as given, from taxes to the real exchange rate to foreign output. This is not a simple relation; Figure 19-2 represents it graphically, in a more user-friendly way.

In Figure 19-2, panel (a), demand is measured on the vertical axis, output (equivalently, production or income) on the horizontal axis. The line *ZZ* plots demand as a function of output. This line just replicates the line *ZZ* in Figure 19-1: *ZZ* is upward sloping, but with slope less than 1.

Equilibrium output is at the point where demand equals output, at the intersection of the line *ZZ* and the 45-degree line: point *A* in the figure, with associated output level *Y*.

Figure 19-2

Equilibrium Output and Net Exports

The goods market is in equilibrium when production is equal to the demand for domestic goods. At the equilibrium level of output, the trade balance may show a deficit or a surplus.

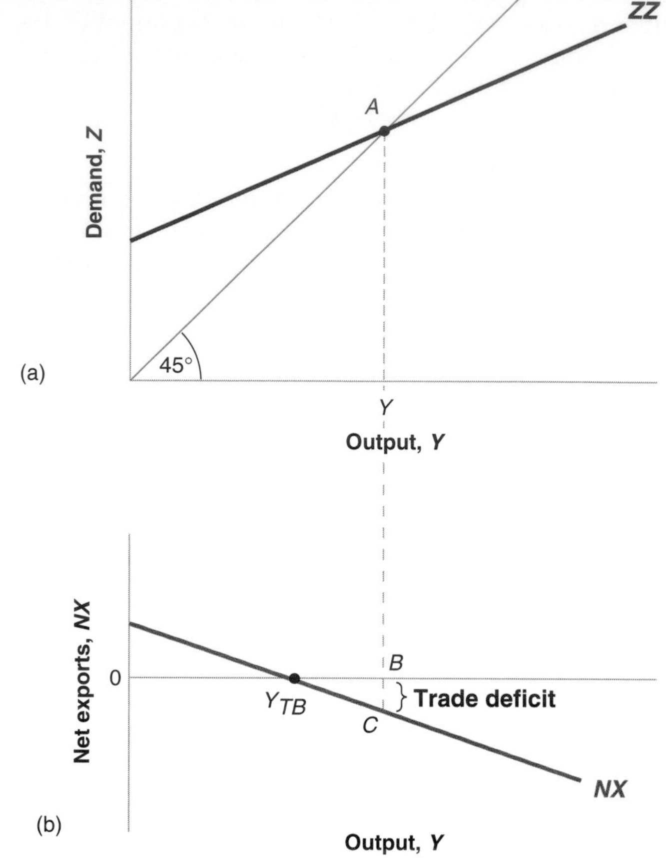

The equilibrium level of output is given by the condition $Y = Z$. The level of output at which there is trade balance is given by the condition $X = \epsilon IM$. These are two different conditions.

Figure 19-2, panel (b) replicates Figure 19-1, panel (d), drawing net exports as a decreasing function of output. There is in general no reason why the equilibrium level of output, Y, should be the same as the level of output at which trade is balanced, Y_{TB}. As I have drawn the figure, equilibrium output is associated with a trade deficit, equal to the distance BC.

We now have the tools needed to answer the questions we asked at the beginning of this chapter.

19-3 Increases in Demand, Domestic or Foreign

How do changes in demand affect output in an open economy? Let's start with an old favorite—an increase in government spending—then turn to a new exercise, the effects of an increase in foreign activity.

Increases in Domestic Demand

As in the core, we start with the goods market; the conclusions we derive here will still largely be correct when we introduce financial markets and labor markets later on.

Suppose the economy is in recession and the government decides to increase government spending—so as to increase domestic demand and output. What will be the effects on output and on the trade balance?

The answer is given in Figure 19-3. Before the increase in government spending, demand is given by ZZ in panel (a), and the equilibrium is at point A, where output

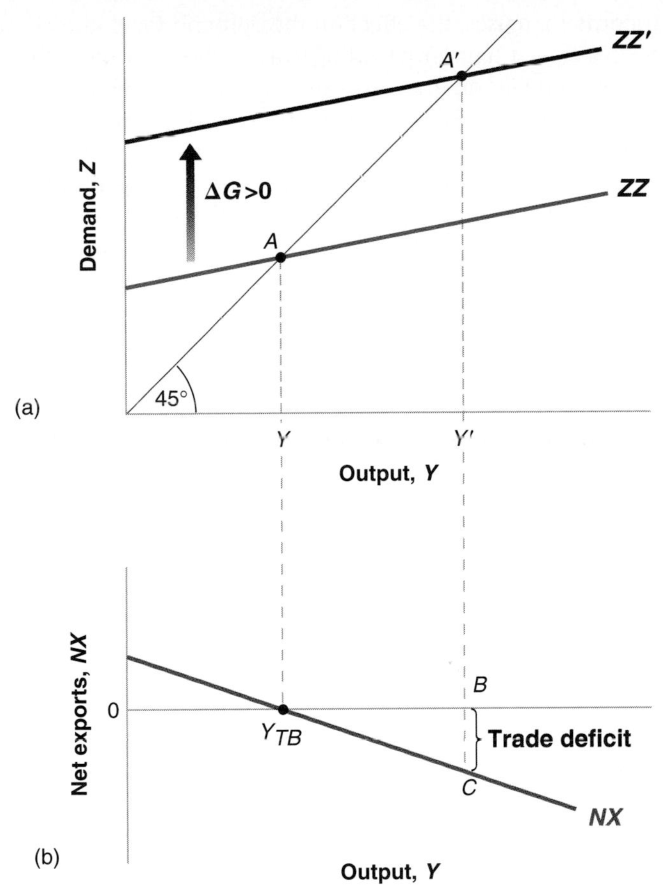

Figure 19-3

The Effects of an Increase in Government Spending

An increase in government spending leads to an increase in output and to a trade deficit.

equals Y. Let's assume—though, as we have seen, there is no reason why this should be true in general—that trade is initially balanced, so, in panel (b), $Y = Y_{TB}$.

What happens if the government increases spending by ΔG? At any level of output, demand is higher by ΔG, shifting the demand relation up by ΔG from ZZ to ZZ'. The equilibrium point moves from A to A', and output increases from Y to Y'. The increase in output is larger than the increase in government spending: There is a multiplier effect.

So far, the story sounds the same as the story for a closed economy in Chapter 3. There are two important differences, however:

- There is now an effect on the trade balance. Because government spending enters neither the exports relation nor the imports relation directly, the relation between net exports and output in Figure 19-3, panel (b) does not shift. So the increase in output from Y to Y' leads to a *trade deficit* equal to BC.
- Not only does government spending now generate a trade deficit, but the effect of government spending on output is smaller than it would be in a closed economy. Recall from Chapter 3 that the smaller the slope of the demand relation, the smaller the multiplier (for example, if ZZ were horizontal, the multiplier would be 1). And recall from Figure 19-1 that the demand relation, ZZ, is flatter than the demand relation in the closed economy, DD. That means the *multiplier is smaller in the open economy.*

◀ **Starting from trade balance, an increase in government spending leads to a trade deficit.**

◀ **An increase in government spending increases output. The multiplier is smaller than in the closed economy.**

The trade deficit and the smaller multiplier have the same origin: An increase in demand now falls not only on domestic goods, but also on foreign goods. So, when

The smaller multiplier and the trade deficit have the same underlying cause: Some domestic demand falls on foreign goods, not on domestic goods.

income increases, the effect on the demand for domestic goods is smaller than it would be in a closed economy, leading to a smaller multiplier. And, because some of the increase in demand falls on imports—and exports are unchanged—the result is a trade deficit.

These two implications are important. In an open economy, an increase in domestic demand has a smaller effect on output than in a closed economy, as well as an adverse effect on the trade balance. Indeed, the more open the economy, the smaller the effect on output and the larger the adverse effect on the trade balance. Take Belgium, and its ratio of imports to GDP close to 90%. When domestic demand increases in Belgium, most of the increase in demand is likely to take the form of an increase in the demand for foreign goods rather than an increase in the demand for domestic goods. The effect of an increase in government spending is thus likely to be a large increase in Belgium's trade deficit and only a small increase in its output, making domestic demand expansion a rather unattractive policy for Belgium. Even for the United States, which has an import ratio of only 14%, an increase in demand will be associated with a worsening of the trade balance. (This conclusion is developed further in the first appendix to this chapter, "Multipliers: Belgium Versus the United States.")

Increases in Foreign Demand

Consider now an increase in foreign output, an increase in Y^*. This could be due to an increase in foreign government spending, G^*—the policy change we just analyzed, but now taking place abroad. But we do not need to know where the increase comes from to analyze the effects on the U.S. economy.

Figure 19-4 shows the effects of an increase in foreign activity on domestic output and the trade balance. The initial demand for domestic goods is given by ZZ in panel (a). The equilibrium is at point A, with output level Y. Let's assume trade is balanced, so that in panel (b) the net exports associated with Y are equal to zero ($Y = Y_{TB}$).

Recall that *DD* is the domestic demand for goods. *ZZ* is the demand for domestic goods. The difference between the two is equal to the trade deficit.

It will be useful for use below to draw the line which gives the *domestic demand for goods* $C + I + G$ as a function of income. This line is denoted by DD in Figure 19–4, panel (a). Recall from Figure 19-1 that DD is steeper than ZZ. The difference between ZZ and DD equals net exports, so that if trade is balanced at point A, then ZZ and DD intersect at point A.

Now consider the effects of an increase in foreign output, ΔY^*. Higher foreign output means higher foreign demand, including higher foreign demand for U.S. goods. So the direct effect of the increase in foreign output is to increase U.S. exports by some amount, call it ΔX.

- For a given level of output, this increase in exports leads to an increase in the demand for U.S. goods by ΔX, so the line giving the demand for domestic goods as a function of output shifts up by ΔX, from ZZ to ZZ'.
- For a given level of output, net exports go up by ΔX. So the line giving net exports as a function of output in Figure 19-4, panel (b) also shifts up by ΔX, from NX to NX'.

*Y** directly affects exports and so enters the relation between the demand for domestic goods and output. An increase in *Y** shifts *ZZ* up.

*Y** does not affect either consumption, investment, or government spending directly, and so does not enter the relation between the domestic demand for goods and output. An increase in *Y** does not shift *DD*.

The new equilibrium is at point A' in Figure 19-4, panel (a), with output level Y'. The increase in foreign output leads to an increase in domestic output. The channel is clear: Higher foreign output leads to higher exports of domestic goods, which increases domestic output and the domestic demand for goods through the multiplier.

What happens to the trade balance? We know that exports go up. But could it be that the increase in domestic output leads to such a large increase in imports that the trade balance actually deteriorates? No: The trade balance must improve. To see why, note that when foreign demand increases, the demand for domestic goods shifts up from ZZ to ZZ'; but the line DD, which gives domestic demand for goods as a function of output, does not shift. At the new equilibrium level of output Y', domestic demand

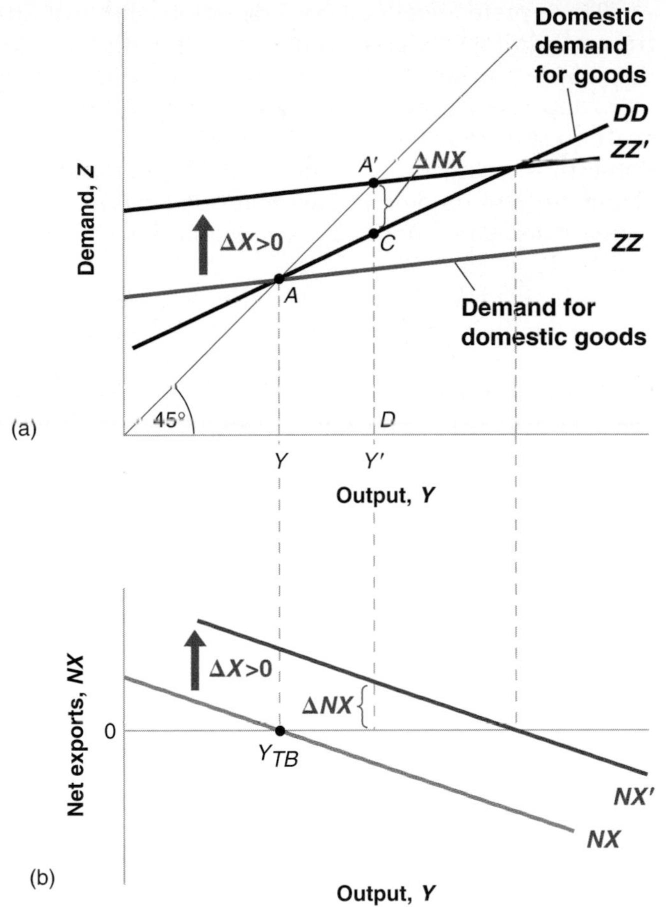

Figure 19-4

The Effects of an Increase in Foreign Demand

An increase in foreign demand leads to an increase in output and to a trade surplus.

is given by the distance *DC*, and the demand for domestic goods is given by *DA′*. Net exports are thus given by the distance *CA′*—which, because *DD* is necessarily below *ZZ′*, is necessarily positive. Thus, while imports increase, the increase does not offset the increase in exports, and the trade balance improves.

An increase in foreign output increases domestic output and improves the trade balance.

Games That Countries Play

We have derived two basic results so far:

1. An increase in domestic demand leads to an increase in domestic output, but leads also to a trade deficit. (We looked at an increase in government spending, but the results would have been the same for a decrease in taxes, an increase in consumer spending, and so on.)
2. An increase in foreign demand (which could come from the same types of changes taking place abroad) leads to an increase in domestic output and a trade surplus.

Governments do not like trade deficits, and for good reasons. The main reason: A country that consistently runs a trade deficit accumulates debt vis-à-vis the rest of the world, and therefore has to pay steadily higher interest payments to the rest of the world. Thus, it is no wonder that countries prefer increases in foreign demand (which lead to an improvement in the trade balance) to increases in domestic demand (which lead to a deterioration in the trade balance).

These preferences may have disastrous implications. Consider a group of countries, all doing a large amount of trade with each other, so that an increase in demand in any one country falls largely on the goods produced in the other countries. Suppose all these countries are in recession and each has roughly balanced trade to start. Each country may be very reluctant to take measures to increase domestic demand. Were it to do so, this might result in a small increase in output but also a large trade deficit. Each country may just wait for the other countries to increase demand. But if they all wait, nothing happens and the recession may last a long time.

Is there a way out of this situation? There is—at least in theory. If all countries coordinate their macroeconomic policies to increase domestic demand simultaneously, each can expand without increasing its trade deficit (vis-à-vis the others; their combined trade deficit with respect to the rest of the world will still increase). The reason is clear: The coordinated increase in demand leads to increases in both exports and imports in each country. It is still true that domestic demand expansion leads to larger imports; but this increase in imports is offset by the increase in exports, which comes from the foreign demand expansions.

Coordination is a word governments often invoke. The seven major countries of the world—the so-called **G-7** (the United States, Japan, France, Germany, the United Kingdom, Italy, and Canada; the *G* stands for "group of")—meet regularly to discuss their economic situation; the communiqué at the end of the meeting rarely fails to mention coordination. But the evidence is that there is in fact very limited macrocoordination among countries. Here are some reasons why:

- Coordination may imply that some countries have to do more than others. They may not want to do so.

  Suppose that only some countries are in recession. Countries that are not in a recession will be reluctant to increase their own demand; but if they do not, the countries that expand will run a trade deficit vis-à-vis countries that do not.

  Or suppose some countries are already running a large budget deficit. These countries will not want to cut taxes or increase spending further, and will ask other countries to take on more of the adjustment. Those other countries may be reluctant to do so.
- Countries have a strong incentive to promise to coordinate, and then not deliver on that promise.

  Once all countries have agreed, say, to an increase in spending, each country has an incentive not to deliver, so as to benefit from the increase in demand elsewhere and thereby improve its trade position. But if each country cheats, or does not do everything it promised, there will be insufficient demand expansion to get out of the recession.

These reasons are far from abstract concerns. Countries in the European Union, which are highly integrated with one another, have in the past 30 years often suffered from such coordination problems. In the late 1970s, a bungled attempt at coordination left most countries weary of trying again. In the early 1980s, an attempt by the French socialists to go at it alone led to a large French trade deficit, and eventually to a change in policy (this is described in the Focus box "The French Socialist Expansion, 1981–1983"). Thereafter, most countries decided that it was better to wait for an increase in foreign demand than to increase their own demand. There has been very little coordination of fiscal policy since then in Europe.

European countries embarked on fiscal expansion too late. By the time they increased spending, their economies were already recovering, and there was no longer a need for higher government spending. ▶

The French Socialist Expansion, 1981–1983

In May 1981, the Socialist Party won the elections in France. Faced with an economy suffering from more than 7% unemployment, the Socialists offered a program aimed at increasing demand through more generous social policies and subsidies to job creation. Welfare benefits and pensions were increased. Public jobs were created, as were new training programs for the young and the unemployed. Table 1 summarizes the macroeconomic results of the policy.

The fiscal expansion is quite visible in the data: The budget, which was balanced in 1980, was in deficit by 2.8% of GDP in 1982. The effects on growth are equally visible. Average growth in 1981–1982 was 1.85%—not an impressive growth rate, but still much above the EU's dismal 0.45% average growth rate over the same two years.

Nevertheless, the Socialists abandoned their policy in March 1983. The last line of Table 1 tells us why. As France was expanding faster than its trading partners, it experienced a sharp increase in its trade deficit. While the government may have tolerated those trade deficits, financial markets—which were very nervous about the Socialists in the first place—forced three devaluations of the franc in 18 months. (Recall from Chapter 18 that when countries try to maintain a fixed exchange rate—as was the case for France at the time—depreciations are called *devaluations.* We shall see the mechanisms that lead to such devaluations in the next two chapters.) The first was in October 1981, by 8.5% against the DM; the second in June 1982, by 10% against the DM; and the third in March 1983, by 8% against the DM. In March 1983, unwilling to face further attacks on the franc and worried about the trade deficits, the French government gave up its attempt to use demand policies to decrease unemployment and shifted to a new policy of "austerity"—a policy aimed at achieving low inflation, budget and trade balance, and no further devaluations. This policy has been maintained by the various French governments, from both the left and the right, to this day.

Table 1 Macroeconomic Aggregates, France: 1980–1983

	1980	1981	1982	1983
GDP growth (%)	1.6	1.2	2.5	0.7
EU growth (%)	1.4	0.2	0.7	1.6
Budget surplus	0.0	−1.9	−2.8	−3.2
Current account surplus	−0.6	−0.8	−2.2	−0.9

The budget and current account surpluses are measured as ratios to GDP, in percent. A minus sign indicates a deficit. EU growth refers to the average growth rate for the countries of the European Union.

Source: OECD Economic Outlook, December 1993.

FOCUS

19-4 Depreciation, the Trade Balance, and Output

Suppose the U.S. government takes policy measures that lead to a depreciation of the dollar. (We shall see in Chapter 20 how this can be achieved using monetary policy; for the moment we assume the government can simply choose the exchange rate.)

Recall that the real exchange rate is given by

$$\epsilon \equiv \frac{EP^*}{P}$$

The real exchange rate, ϵ (the price of foreign goods in terms of domestic goods), equals the nominal exchange rate, E (the price of foreign currency in terms of domestic currency), times the foreign price level, P^*, divided by the domestic price level, P. Under the assumption we have made in this chapter that the price levels are given, it follows that a nominal depreciation is reflected one for one in a real depreciation. More concretely, if the dollar depreciates vis-à-vis the yen by 10% (a 10% nominal

Given P and P^*, $E \uparrow \Rightarrow \epsilon \equiv EP^*/P \uparrow$

In words: Given the domestic price level and the foreign price level, a nominal depreciation leads to a real depreciation.

A look ahead: In Chapter 21, we shall look at the effects of a nominal depreciation when we allow the price level to adjust over time. You will see that a nominal depreciation leads to a real depreciation in the short run, but not in the medium run.

depreciation), and if the price levels in Japan and the United States do not change, U.S. goods will be 10% cheaper compared to Japanese goods (a 10% real depreciation).

Let's now ask what the effects of this real depreciation will be on the U.S. trade balance and on U.S. output.

Depreciation and the Trade Balance: The Marshall-Lerner Condition

Return to the definition of net exports:

$$NX \equiv X - \epsilon\, IM$$

Replace X and IM by their expressions from equations (19.2) and (19.3):

$$NX = X(Y^*, \epsilon) - \epsilon\, IM(Y, \epsilon)$$

If the dollar depreciates vis-à-vis the yen by 10%:

- U.S. goods will be cheaper in Japan, leading to a larger quantity of U.S. exports to Japan.
- Japanese goods will be more expensive in the United States, leading to a smaller quantity of imports of Japanese goods to the United States.
- Japanese goods will be more expensive, leading to a higher import bill for a given quantity of imports of Japanese goods to the United States.

Note that as the real exchange rate, ϵ, enters the right side of the equation in three places: The real depreciation—an increase in ϵ—affects the trade balance through three separate channels.

1. *Exports, X, increase.* The real depreciation makes U.S. goods relatively less expensive abroad. This leads to an increase in foreign demand for U.S. goods—an increase in U.S. exports.
2. *Imports, IM, decrease.* The real depreciation makes foreign goods relatively more expensive in the United States. This leads to a shift in domestic demand toward domestic goods, to a decrease in the quantity of imports.
3. *The relative price of foreign goods, ϵ, increases.* This *increases* the import bill, $\epsilon\, IM$. The same quantity of imports now costs more to buy (in terms of domestic goods).

The condition is named after the two economists, Alfred Marshall and Abba Lerner, who were the first to derive it.

For the trade balance to improve following a depreciation, exports must increase enough (the first channel) and imports must decrease enough (the second channel) to compensate for the increase in the price of imports (the third channel). The condition under which a real depreciation leads to an increase in net exports is known as the **Marshall-Lerner condition**. (It is derived formally in the second appendix, "Derivation of the Marshall-Lerner Condition," at the end of the chapter.) It turns out—with a caveat we shall state when we introduce dynamics later in this chapter—that this condition is satisfied in reality. So, for the rest of the book, we shall assume that a real depreciation—an increase in ϵ—leads to an increase in net exports—an increase in NX.

The Effects of a Depreciation

We have just looked at the *direct* effects of a depreciation on the trade balance—that is, the effects *given U.S. and foreign output.* But the effects do not end there. The change in net exports changes domestic output, which affects net exports further.

Because the effects of a real depreciation are very much like those of an increase in foreign output, we can use Figure 19-4, the same figure that we used to show the effects of an increase in foreign output earlier.

Marshall-Lerner condition: Given output, a real depreciation leads to an increase in net exports.

Just like an increase in foreign output, a depreciation leads to an increase in net exports (assuming, as we do, that the Marshall-Lerner condition holds), at any level of output. Both the demand relation (ZZ in Figure 19-4, panel [a]) and the net exports relation (NX in Figure 19-4, panel [b]) shift up. The equilibrium moves from A to A'; output increases from Y to Y'. By the same argument we used earlier, the trade balance improves: The increase in imports induced by the increase in output is less than the direct improvement in the trade balance induced by the depreciation.

To summarize: *The depreciation leads to a shift in demand, both foreign and domestic, toward domestic goods. This shift in demand leads in turn both to an increase in domestic output and to an improvement in the trade balance.*

While a depreciation and an increase in foreign output each have the same effect on domestic output and the trade balance, there is, however, a subtle but important difference between the two. A depreciation works by making foreign goods relatively more expensive. But this means that given their income, people—who now have to pay more to buy foreign goods because of the depreciation—are worse off. This mechanism is strongly felt in countries that undergo a large depreciation. Governments trying to achieve a large depreciation often find themselves with strikes and riots in the streets, as people react to the much higher prices of imported goods. This was for example the case in Mexico in 1994–1995, where a large depreciation of the peso—from 3.44 pesos per dollar in November 1994 to 5.88 pesos per dollar in May 1995—led to a large decline in workers' living standards. The depreciation helped the Mexican economy recover, but not without substantial social unrest.

There is an alternative to riots—asking for and obtaining an increase in wages. But, if wages increase, the prices of domestic goods will follow and increase as well, leading to a smaller real depreciation. To discuss this mechanism, we need to look at the supply side in more detail than we have done so far. We return to the dynamics of depreciation, and wage and price movements in ◀ Chapter 21.

Combining Exchange-Rate and Fiscal Policies

Suppose a government wants to reduce the trade deficit without changing the level of output. A depreciation alone will not do: It will reduce the trade deficit, but it will also increase output. Nor will a fiscal contraction do: It will reduce the trade deficit, but it will decrease output.

What should the government do? Answer: Use the right combination of depreciation and fiscal contraction. Figure 19-5 shows what this combination should be.

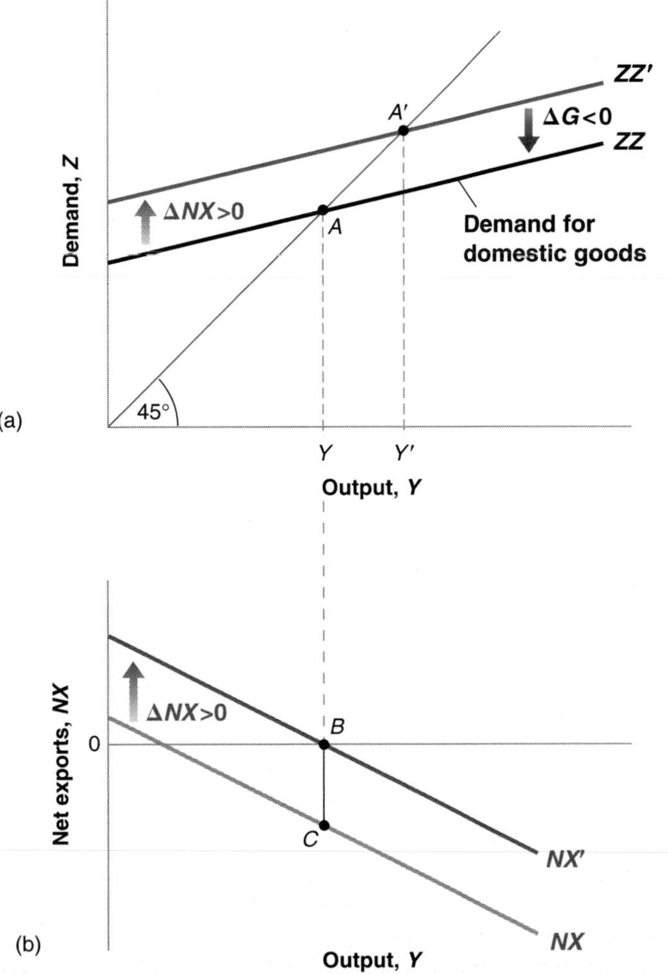

Figure 19-5

Reducing the Trade Deficit Without Changing Output

To reduce the trade deficit without changing output, the government must both achieve a depreciation and decrease government spending.

Table 19-1 Exchange-Rate and Fiscal Policy Combinations

Initial Conditions	Trade Surplus	Trade Deficit
Low output	ϵ ? G↑	ϵ ↑ G?
High output	ϵ ↓ G?	ϵ ? G↓

The initial equilibrium in Figure 19-5, panel (a), is at *A*, associated with output *Y*. The trade deficit is given by the distance *BC* in panel (b). If the government wants to eliminate the trade deficit without changing output, it must do two things:

1. It must achieve a depreciation sufficient to eliminate the trade deficit at the initial level of output. So, the depreciation must be such as to shift the net exports relation from *NX* to *NX′* in Figure 19-5, panel (b).

 The problem is that this depreciation, and the associated increase in net exports, also shifts the demand relation in Figure 19-5, panel (a) from *ZZ* to *ZZ′*. In the absence of other measures, the equilibrium would move from *A* to *A′*, and output would increase from *Y* to *Y′*.

2. In order to avoid the increase in output, the government must reduce government spending so as to shift *ZZ′* back to *ZZ*. This combination of a depreciation and a fiscal contraction leads to the same level of output and an improved trade balance.

A general lesson: If you want to achieve two targets (here, output and trade balance), you better have two instruments (here, fiscal policy and the exchange rate).

There is a general point behind this example. To the extent that governments care about *both* the level of output and the trade balance, they have to use *both* fiscal policy and the exchange-rate. We just saw one such combination. Table 19-1 shows others, depending on the initial output and trade situation. Take, for example, the formula in the top right corner of the table. Initial output is too low (put another way, unemployment is too high), and the economy has a trade deficit. A depreciation will help on both the trade and the output fronts: It reduces the trade deficit and increases output. But there is no reason for the depreciation to achieve both the correct increase in output and the elimination of the trade deficit. Depending on the initial situation and the relative effects of the depreciation on output and the trade balance, the government may need to complement the depreciation with either an increase or a decrease in government spending. This ambiguity is captured by the question mark in the formula. Make sure that you understand the logic behind each of the other three formulas. An application of the arguments developed in this section is given in the Focus box "The U.S. Trade Deficit: Origins and Implications."

19-5 Looking at Dynamics: The J-Curve

We have ignored dynamics so far in this chapter. It is time to reintroduce them. The dynamics of consumption, investment, sales, and production we discussed in Chapter 3 are as relevant to the open economy as they are to the closed economy. But there are additional dynamic effects as well, which come from the dynamics of exports and imports. I focus on these effects here.

Return to the effects of the exchange rate on the trade balance. I argued earlier that a depreciation leads to an increase in exports and to a decrease in imports. But these effects do not happen overnight. Think of the dynamic effects of, say, a 10% dollar depreciation.

The U.S. Trade Deficit: Origins and Implications

The U.S. trade deficit steadily increased in the late 1990s, reaching 3.6% of GDP in 2000. The U.S. current account deficit—which adds net interest payments to the rest of the world to the trade deficit—grew even larger, reaching 4.5% of GDP in 2000. (Numbers for the 1990s for both the trade and current account deficit are given in the first two lines of Table 1. Can you tell why the current account deficit increased more than the trade deficit?)

These are the largest trade and current account deficits (both absolutely, and in proportion to GDP) in recorded U.S. history. And, given the size of the U.S. economy, they represent a very large amount—more than $400 billion for the current account deficit—that the United States has to borrow from the rest of the world.

Where does the trade deficit, and by implication the current account deficit, come from? There are two main causes:

- *The very high U.S. growth rate during the second half of the 1990s, relative to the growth rate of its main trading partners.* From 1996 to 2000, the average annual growth rate in the United States was 4.3% (leading to an increase in real GDP of 21% over those five years), compared to 2.6% in the European Union (for an increase in GDP of 12.5%), and 1.3% in Japan (for an increase in GDP of only 6.7%). The result was a much faster growth of imports—which depend on U.S. GDP—than of exports—which depend on what happens in the rest of the world—and thus a steadily increasing trade deficit.

  Higher growth does not necessarily lead to a higher trade deficit: If the main source of the increase in demand and growth in a country is an increase in foreign demand, the country can grow fast and maintain trade balance, or even sustain a trade surplus. In the case of the United States in the late 1990s, however, the main source of increased demand was domestic demand, with high consumption and investment demand as the main factors behind the sustained expansion. Thus, high growth came with an increasing trade deficit.

- *The steady real appreciation of U.S. goods—a decrease in the real U.S. effective exchange rate.*

  Even if, at a given real exchange rate, growth leads to an increase in the trade deficit, a real depreciation can help maintain trade balance by making domestic goods more competitive. But just the opposite happened to the U.S. real exchange rate in the late 1990s: The United States experienced a real appreciation, not a real depreciation. As shown in Table 1, the real effective exchange rate, normalized to equal 1.0 in 1996:1, decreased to 0.80 in 2000—implying a 20% real appreciation. The result was a further deterioration of the trade balance.

Should we expect the large trade deficit and current account deficit to naturally disappear in the future? At an unchanged real exchange rate, the answer is: Probably not. If there were good reasons to expect U.S. trading partners to experience much higher growth than the United States over the coming decade, then we could expect to see the same process we saw in the 1990s, but this time in reverse: Lower growth in the United States would lead to a steady reduction in the trade deficit. But there are few reasons to expect such a scenario. While the United States cannot expect to replicate the growth rates of the late 1990s, there is also no reason either to expect much lower growth than average over the coming decade. And nobody is predicting sustained high growth in the European Union, much less so for Japan.

Can the United States afford to sustain a large trade deficit and a large current account deficit for many

Table 1 U.S. Trade and Current Account Deficits, the U.S. Real Exchange Rate, and U.S., E.U., and Japanese Growth Rates

	1990–1995 (average)	1996	1997	1998	1999	2000
Trade deficit (% of GDP)	−0.9	−1.1	−1.1	−1.7	−2.7	−3.6
Current account deficit (% of GDP)	−1.0	−1.6	−1.7	−2.5	−3.6	−4.5
Real exchange rate (1996:1=1)	0.97	1.00	0.92	0.86	0.85	0.80
Growth rate, U.S. (%)	2.3	3.6	4.4	4.4	4.2	4.1
Growth rate, E.U. (%)	1.8	1.6	2.6	2.8	2.6	3.3
Growth rate, Japan (%)	2.0	3.5	1.8	−1.1	0.8	1.5

(*Continued*)

FOCUS

more years? The answer, again: Probably not. While financial investors have been willing to lend to the United States until now, it may be difficult for the United States to continue to borrow $400 billion per year or so in the future. And, even if financial investors were willing to continue to lend, it is not clear that it would be a wise policy for the United States to accumulate such a large debt vis-à-vis the rest of the world.

These arguments have two implications:

1. The U.S. trade and current account deficits will need to be reduced.
2. This is unlikely to happen without a real depreciation of the dollar. How large a depreciation? Estimates range from 20 to 40%—in short, a substantial real depreciation.

Return to the issues discussed in Table 19-1 in the text: Will this depreciation need to be accompanied by other macroeconomic policy measures, such as a fiscal contraction, to make sure that output remains close to its natural level? This depends on what happens to domestic demand. If, for example, the real depreciation takes place as domestic demand is low and the U.S. economy is still in a slowdown, then there may be no need to offset the real depreciation with a fiscal contraction. Indeed, by increasing foreign demand, the real depreciation may counteract the weakness in domestic demand, and help the economy grow. In other words, a real depreciation may help the United States both to reduce its trade deficit, and get out of the slowdown—a nice combination.

In the first few months following the depreciation, the effect of the depreciation is likely to be reflected much more in prices than in quantities. The price of imports in the United States goes up, the price of U.S. exports abroad goes down. But the quantity of imports and exports is likely to adjust slowly: It takes a while for consumers to realize that relative prices have changed, it takes a while for firms to shift to cheaper suppliers, and so on. So a depreciation may well lead to an initial deterioration of the trade balance; ϵ increases, but neither X nor IM adjusts very much initially, leading to a decline in net exports ($X - \epsilon IM$).

As time passes, the effects of the change in the relative prices of both exports and imports become stronger. Cheaper U.S. goods lead U.S. consumers and firms to decrease their demand for foreign goods: U.S. imports decrease. Cheaper U.S. goods abroad lead foreign consumers and firms to increase their demand for U.S. goods: U.S. exports increase. If the Marshall-Lerner condition eventually holds—and we have argued that it does—the response of exports and imports eventually becomes stronger than the adverse price effect, and the eventual effect of the depreciation is to improve the trade balance.

The response of the trade balance to the real exchange rate:

Initially:
(X, IM) unchanged, $\epsilon\uparrow$
$\Rightarrow (X - \epsilon IM)\downarrow$

Eventually:
($X\uparrow$, $IM\downarrow$, $\epsilon\uparrow$)
$\Rightarrow (X - \epsilon IM)\uparrow$

Figure 19-6 captures this adjustment by plotting the evolution of the trade balance against time in response to a real depreciation. The predepreciation trade deficit is OA. The depreciation initially *increases* the trade deficit to OB: ϵ goes up, but neither IM nor

Figure 19-6

The J-Curve

A real depreciation leads initially to a deterioration, then to an improvement of the trade balance.

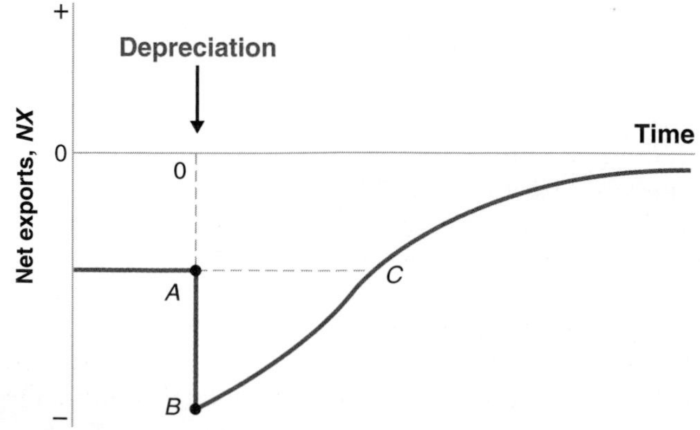

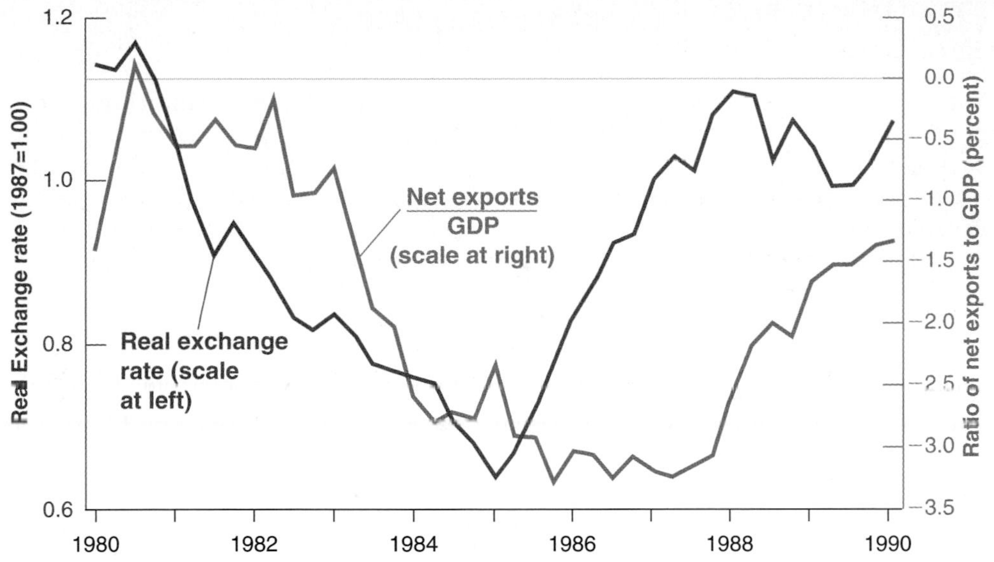

Figure 19-7

The Real Exchange Rate and the Ratio of Net Exports to GDP: United States, 1980–1990

The real appreciation and the depreciation of the dollar in the 1980s were reflected in increasing, then decreasing trade deficits. There were, however, substantial lags in the effects of the real exchange rate on the trade balance.

X changes right away. Over time, exports increase and imports decrease, reducing the trade deficit. Eventually (if the Marshall-Lerner condition is satisfied), the trade balance improves beyond its initial level; this is what happens from point *C* on in the figure. Economists refer to this adjustment process as the **J-curve**, because—admittedly, with a bit of imagination—the curve in the figure resembles a *J*: first down, then up.

The importance of the dynamic effects of the real exchange rate on the trade balance can be seen from the evidence from the United States in the mid-1980s: Figure 19-7 plots the U.S. trade balance against the U.S. real exchange rate in the 1980s. As we saw in the last chapter, the period from 1980 to 1985 was one of sharp real appreciation and the period from 1985 to 1988 one of sharp real depreciation. Turning to the trade balance, which is expressed as a proportion of GDP, two facts are clear:

1. Movements in the real exchange rate were reflected in parallel movements in net exports. The appreciation was associated with a large deterioration of the trade balance, and the later depreciation was associated with a large improvement in the trade balance.

2. There were, however, substantial lags in the response of the trade balance to changes in the real exchange rate. Note how from 1981 to 1983, the trade deficit remained small while the dollar was appreciating. And note how the steady depreciation of the dollar from 1985 on was not reflected in an improvement in the trade balance before 1987: The dynamics of the J-curve were very much at work in both episodes.

The delays in 1985–1988 were unusually long, prompting some economists at the time to question whether there was still a relation between the real exchange rate and the trade balance. In retrospect, the relation was still there—the delays were just longer than usual.

In general, the econometric evidence on the dynamic relation between exports, imports, and the real exchange rate suggests that in all OECD countries a real depreciation eventually leads to a trade balance improvement. But it also suggests that this process takes some time, typically between six months and a year. These lags have implications not only for the effects of a depreciation on the trade balance but also for the effects of a depreciation on output. If a depreciation initially decreases net exports, it also initially exerts a contractionary effect on output. Thus, if a government relies on a depreciation both to improve the trade balance and to expand domestic output, the effects will go the "wrong" way for a while.

19-6 Saving, Investment, and the Trade Balance

You saw in Chapter 3 how we could rewrite the condition for equilibrium in the goods market as the condition that investment equals saving—the sum of private saving and public saving. Let us now derive the corresponding condition for the open economy, and show how useful this alternative way of looking at the equilibrium can be.

Start from our equilibrium condition:

$$Y = C + I + G - \epsilon IM + X$$

Subtract $C + T$ from both sides, and use the fact that private saving is given by $S = Y - C - T$, to get

$$S = I + G - T - \epsilon IM + X$$

Using the definition of net exports $NX \equiv X - \epsilon IM$, and reorganizing gives

$$NX = S + (T - G) - I \qquad (19.5)$$

This condition says that in equilibrium, the trade balance, NX, must equal saving—private saving, S, and public saving, $T - G$—minus investment, I. It follows that a trade surplus must correspond to an excess of saving over investment; a trade deficit must correspond to an excess of investment over saving.

One way of getting more intuition for this relation is to return to the discussion of the current account and the capital account in Chapter 18. There, we saw that a trade surplus implies net lending from the country to the rest of the world, and a trade deficit implies net borrowing by the country from the rest of the world. So, consider a country that invests more than it saves, so that $S + (T - G) - I$ is negative. That country must be borrowing the difference from the rest of the world; it must therefore be running a trade deficit.

Note some of the things that equation (19.5) says:

- An increase in investment must be reflected in either an increase in private saving or public saving, or in a deterioration of the trade balance (a smaller trade surplus, or a larger trade deficit).
- An increase in the budget deficit must be reflected in an increase in either private saving, or a decrease in investment, or a deterioration of the trade balance.
- A country with a high saving rate, private and public, must have either a high investment rate or a large trade surplus.

Note also, however, what equation (19.5) *does not say*. It does not say, for example, whether a budget deficit will lead to a trade deficit, or, instead, to an increase in private saving, or to a decrease in investment. To find out what happens in response to a budget deficit, we must explicitly solve for what happens to output and its components using the assumptions that we have made about consumption, investment, exports, and imports. We can do so using either equation (19.1)—as we have done throughout this chapter—or equation (19.5), as the two are equivalent. However, let me strongly recommend that you use equation (19.1). Using equation (19.5) can, if you are not careful, be very misleading. To see how misleading, consider, for example, the following argument (which is so common that you may have read it in some form in newspapers):

"It is clear the United States cannot reduce its large trade deficit (currently close to 4% of GDP) through a depreciation." Look at equation (19.5). It shows that the trade deficit is equal to investment minus saving. Why should a depreciation affect either saving or investment? So, how can a depreciation affect the trade deficit?

The argument may sound convincing, but we know it is wrong. We showed earlier that a depreciation leads to an increase in output and an improvement in the trade position. So what is wrong with the argument? A depreciation actually affects saving and investment: It does so by affecting the demand for domestic goods, thereby increasing output. Higher output leads to an increase in saving over investment, or equivalently to a decrease in the trade deficit.

A good way of making sure that you understand the material in this chapter is to go back and look at the various cases we have considered, from changes in government spending, to changes in foreign output, to combinations of depreciation and fiscal contraction, and so on. Trace what happens in each case to each of the four components of equation (19.5): private saving, public saving (equivalently, the budget surplus), investment, and the trade balance. Make sure, as always, that you can tell the story in words. If you can, you are ready to go on to Chapter 20.

Show, for example, that an increase in foreign demand leads to:

- **An increase in private saving,**
- **An increase in investment (but by less than private saving),**
- **No change in the budget deficit,**
- **An improvement in the trade balance.**

Summary

- In an open economy, the demand for domestic goods is equal to the domestic demand for goods (consumption, plus investment, plus government spending) minus the value of imports (in terms of domestic goods), plus exports.
- In an open economy, an increase in domestic demand leads to a smaller increase in output than it would in a closed economy because some of the additional demand falls on imports. For the same reason, an increase in domestic demand also leads to a deterioration of the trade balance.
- An increase in foreign demand leads, as a result of increased exports, to both an increase in domestic output and an improvement in the trade balance.
- Because increases in foreign demand improve the trade balance and increases in domestic demand worsen the trade balance, countries may be tempted to wait for increases in foreign demand to move them out of a recession. When a group of countries is in recession, coordination can help them get out of it.
- If the Marshall-Lerner condition is satisfied—and the empirical evidence suggests that it is—a real depreciation leads to an improvement in net exports.
- A real depreciation leads first to a deterioration of the trade balance, and then to an improvement. This adjustment process is known as the J-curve.
- The condition for equilibrium in the goods market can be rewritten as the condition that saving (public and private) minus investment must be equal to the trade balance. A trade surplus corresponds to an excess of saving over investment. A trade deficit corresponds to an excess of investment over saving.

Key Terms

- demand for domestic goods, 396
- domestic demand for goods, 396
- coordination, 404
- G-7, 404
- Marshall-Lerner condition, 406
- J-curve, 411
- marginal propensity to import, 415

Questions and Problems

Quick Check

1. *Using the information in this chapter, label each of the following statements* true, false, *or* uncertain. *Explain briefly.*
   a. Trade deficits generally reflect high investment.
   b. Budget deficits cause trade deficits.
   c. It is much easier for the government of a small open economy to maintain output at a given level than for the government of a large closed economy.
   d. The only way a country can eliminate a trade surplus is through a real appreciation.
   e. A small open economy can reduce its trade deficit through fiscal contraction at a smaller cost in output than a large economy can.

f. If the trade deficit is equal to zero, the domestic demand for goods and the demand for domestic goods are equal.

g. The current high U.S. trade deficit is the result of higher growth in the United States than in the rest of the world since the mid-1990s.

2. *The nominal exchange rate, the real exchange rate, and foreign and domestic inflation*

a. Using the definition of the real exchange rate, verify that the following is true (you may want to use propositions 7 and 8 in Appendix 2 at the end of the book):

$$\frac{\Delta\epsilon}{\epsilon} = \frac{\Delta E}{E} + \frac{\Delta P^*}{P^*} - \frac{\Delta P}{P}$$

b. If domestic inflation is higher than foreign inflation, but the domestic country has a fixed exchange rate, what happens to the real exchange rate over time? Assume the Marshall-Lerner condition holds. What happens to the trade balance over time? Explain in words.

3. *The potential effects of a recession in Japan on the U.S. economy*

a. The share of Japanese spending on U.S. goods is about 10% of U.S. exports, which are themselves equal to about 10% of U.S. GDP. What is the share of Japanese spending on U.S. goods relative to U.S. GDP?

b. Assume the multiplier in the United States is 2, and that a recession in Japan has reduced output by 5% (relative to its natural level). What is the impact on U.S. GDP of the Japanese slowdown?

c. If the Japanese recession also leads to a slowdown of the other economies that import goods from the U.S., the effect could be larger. Assume U.S. exports fall by 5% (of themselves). What is the impact on U.S. GDP?

d. Comment on the following statement from an economist on television: "Unless Japan recovers from recession quickly, growth will grind to a halt in the rest of the world."

4. *Consider an economy with a fixed exchange rate. Assume that the price level is fixed.*

a. What is the effect on output and the trade balance of a depreciation in the first six months after the depreciation?

b. What is the effect on output and the trade balance of the depreciation after six months?

Dig Deeper

5. *Interactions and coordination between countries.*

Consider the following open economy. The real exchange rate is fixed and equal to one. Consumption, investment, government spending, and taxes are given by

$$C = 10 + 0.8(Y - T);\ I = 10;\ G = 10;\ T = 10$$

Imports and exports are given by

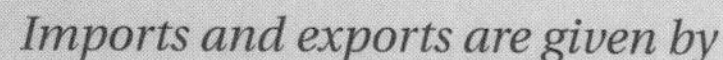

$$IM = 0.3Y;\ X = 0.3Y^*$$

where an asterisk denotes a foreign variable.

a. Solve for equilibrium output in the domestic economy, given Y^*. What is the multiplier in this economy? If we were to close the economy—so exports and imports were identically equal to zero—what would the multiplier be? Why are they different?

b. Assume the foreign economy has the same equations as the domestic economy (with asterisks reversed). Use the two sets of equations to solve for the equilibrium output of each country. What is the multiplier for each country now? Why is it different from the open economy multiplier above?

c. Assume both countries have a target level of output of 125. What is the increase in G necessary in either of these countries, assuming the other country does not change its level of government spending, to achieve target output? Solve for net exports and the budget deficit in each country.

d. What is the common increase in G necessary to achieve target output in both countries?

e. Why is fiscal coordination (such as the common increase in G in [d]) difficult to achieve in practice?

6. *Macroeconomic effects of tariff wars*

Consider two open IS-LM economies.

a. Consider a tax, at rate τ on imports of foreign goods (such a tax on foreign goods is called a tariff). How does this affect the import relation? The export relation?

b. What are the consequences of the introduction of a tax on foreign goods in the domestic country on equilibrium output and net exports?

c. What are the consequences of the same tax on foreign equilibrium output and net exports?

d. Suppose that, in response to the domestic tariff, the foreign country responds by introducing a similar tax on its imports. What are the additional effects of this foreign retaliation on equilibrium output and the volume of trade? (Assume identical economies and a foreign tax equal to the domestic one.)

7. *Get from your library a recent issue of the "International Financial Statistics," published monthly by the IMF. Look at the list of countries in the table of contents. Make a list of five countries you would expect to have high ratios of exports to GDP. Then, go to the page corresponding to each country, and look up the numbers for exports and for GDP, for the most recent available year. (Make sure that you are comparing exports and GDP measured in the same units—either domestic currency or dollars. If one variable is in domestic currency and the other variable is in dollars, use the exchange rate to convert the two to the same currency.) Compute the export ratios. How good were your guesses?*

We invite you to visit the Blanchard page on the Prentice Hall Web site at:
www.prenhall.com/blanchard
for this chapter's World Wide Web exercises

Further Reading

A good discussion of the relation among trade deficits, budget deficits, private saving, and investment is given in Barry Bosworth's *Saving and Investment in a Global Economy* (Washington, DC: Brookings Institution, 1993).

Appendix 1: Multipliers—Belgium Versus the United States

"If we assume that the various relations in equation (19.4) are linear, we can compute the effects of government spending, foreign output, and so forth, both on output and on the trade balance. In this appendix we look at the differences between the effects of government spending in a large country such as the United States and in a small country such as Belgium.

Assume consumption and investment for a given country are given by

$$C = c_0 + c_1(Y - T)$$
$$I = d_0 + d_1 Y - d_2 r$$

Consumption, C, increases with disposable income, $Y - T$. Investment, I, increases with output, Y, and decreases with the real interest rate, r. Parameters are c_0, c_1, d_0, d_1, d_2.

For simplicity, ignore movements in the real exchange rate, ϵ, and assume $\epsilon = 1$. Assume imports and exports are given by

$$IM = im_1 Y$$
$$X = x_1 Y^*$$

Imports, IM, are proportional to domestic output, Y. Exports, X, are proportional to foreign output Y^*. Parameters are im_1 and x_1. In the same way we referred to c_1 as the marginal propensity to consume in Chapter 3, im_1 is the **marginal propensity to import**.

The equilibrium condition is that output equals the demand for domestic goods

$$Y = C + I + G - IM + X$$

(Recall that we are assuming that ϵ equals 1, so $\epsilon\, IM$ is simply equal to IM.) Replace C, I, G, IM, and X by their expressions from above:

$$Y = [c_0 + c_1(Y - T)] + (d_0 + d_1 Y - d_2 r) + G - im_1 Y + x_1 Y^*$$

Regroup terms:

$$Y = (c_1 + d_1 - im_1)Y + (c_0 + d_0 - c_1 T - d_2 r + G + x_1 Y^*)$$

Bring the terms in output together, and solve for output:

$$Y = \left[\frac{1}{1-(c_1+d_1-im_1)}\right](c_0+d_0-c_1T-d_2r+G+x_1Y^*)$$

Output equals the multiplier (the term in brackets) times autonomous spending (the term in parentheses, which captures the effect of all the variables we take as given in explaining output.

Consider the multiplier. Specifically, consider $(c_1 + d_1 - im_1)$ in the denominator. As in the closed economy, $(c_1 + d_1)$ gives the effects of an increase in output on consumption and investment demand; $(-im_1)$ captures the fact that some of the increased demand falls not on domestic goods but on foreign goods.

- In the extreme case where all the additional demand falls on foreign goods—when $im_1 = c_1 + d_1$—an increase in output has no effect back on the demand for domestic goods; in that case, the multiplier equals 1.
- In general, im_1 is less than $(c_1 + d_1)$, so that the multiplier is greater than 1. But the multiplier is smaller than it would be in a closed economy.

Using this equation, we can easily characterize the effects of an increase in government spending of ΔG:

The increase in output is equal to the multiplier times the change in government spending:

$$\Delta Y = \frac{1}{1-(c_1+d_1-im_1)}\Delta G$$

And the increase in imports that follows from the increase in output implies the following change in net exports:

$$\Delta NX = -im_1 \Delta Y$$
$$= -\frac{im_1}{1-(c_1+d_1-im_1)}\Delta G$$

Let's see what these formulas imply by choosing numerical values for the parameters.

Let $c_1 + d_1$ be equal to 0.6. What value should we choose for im_1? We saw in Chapter 18 that, in general, the larger the country, the more self-sufficient it is, and the less it imports. So let's choose two values of im_1—a small value, say, 0.1, for a large country such as the United States, and a larger one, say, 0.5, for a small country such as Belgium. Note that the proportion of an increase in demand that falls on imports is given by $im_1/(c_1 + d_1)$. (An increase in output of one dollar leads to an increase in spending of $(c_1 + d_1)$ dollars, of which im_1 dollars is spent on foreign goods.) So, an equivalent way of stating our choice of im_1 is that, in the large country, 1/6 (0.1 divided by 0.6) of demand falls on imports, versus 5/6 (0.5 divided by 0.6) in the small country.

Now return to the expressions for output and the trade balance.

For the large country:

- The effects of the change in government spending on output are given by

$$\Delta Y = \frac{1}{1-(0.6-0.1)}\Delta G = 2.0\ \Delta G$$

- The effects of the change in government spending on the trade balance are given by

$$\Delta NX = -0.1\ \Delta Y = \frac{-0.1}{1-(0.6-0.1)}\Delta G = -0.2\ \Delta G$$

For the small country:

- The effects of the change in government spending on output are given by

$$\Delta Y = \frac{1}{1-(0.6-0.5)}\Delta G = 1.11\ \Delta G$$

- The effects of the change in government spending on the trade balance are given by

$$\Delta NX = -0.5\ \Delta Y = \frac{-0.5}{1-(0.6-0.5)}\Delta G = -0.65\ \Delta G$$

These computations show the very different trade-offs faced by each country:

- In the large country, the effect of an increase in *G* on output is large and the effect on the trade balance is small.
- In the small country, the effect of an increase in *G* on output is small, and the deterioration of the trade balance is large—equal to half of the increase in government spending.

This example shows how openness makes it more difficult to use fiscal policy to affect output, especially in small countries. The more open the economy, the smaller the effect of fiscal policy on output and the larger the effect on the trade balance. We shall see more examples of this proposition as we go along.

Appendix 2: Derivation of the Marshall-Lerner Condition

Start from the definition of net exports, $NX \equiv X - \epsilon IM$, and assume trade to be initially balanced, so that $X = \epsilon IM$. The Marshall-Lerner condition is the condition under which a real depreciation, an increase in ϵ, leads to an increase in net exports.

To derive this condition, consider an increase in the real exchange rate of $\Delta\epsilon$. The change in the trade balance is given by

$$\Delta NX = \Delta X - \epsilon(\Delta IM) - IM(\Delta\epsilon)$$

The first term on the right, ΔX, gives the change in exports. The second, $\epsilon(\Delta IM)$, is equal to the real exchange rate times the change in the quantity of imports. The third, $IM(\Delta\epsilon)$, is equal to the quantity of imports times the change in the real exchange rate.

Divide both sides of the equation by *X* to get

$$\frac{\Delta NX}{X} = \frac{\Delta X}{X} - \epsilon\frac{\Delta IM}{X} - \frac{IM\,\Delta\epsilon}{X}$$

Use the fact that $\epsilon IM = X$ to replace ϵ/X by $1/IM$ in the second term on the right, and to replace IM/X by $1/\epsilon$ in the third term on the right. This substitution gives

$$\frac{\Delta NX}{X} = \frac{\Delta X}{X} - \frac{\Delta IM}{IM} - \frac{\Delta\epsilon}{\epsilon}$$

The change in the trade balance (as a ratio to exports) in response to a real depreciation is equal to the sum of three terms:

- The first is the proportional change in exports, $\Delta X/X$, induced by the real depreciation.
- The second term is equal to minus the proportional change in imports, $-\Delta IM/IM$, induced by the real depreciation.
- The third term is equal to minus the proportional change in the real exchange rate, $-\Delta\epsilon/\epsilon$, or equivalently, minus the rate of real depreciation.

The Marshall-Lerner condition is the condition that the sum of these three terms be positive. If it is satisfied, a real depreciation leads to an improvement in the trade balance.

A numerical example will help here. Suppose that a 1% depreciation leads to a relative increase in exports of 0.9% and to a relative decrease in imports of 0.8%. (Econometric evidence on the response of exports and imports to the real exchange rates suggests that these are indeed reasonable numbers.) In that case, the right-hand side of the equation is equal to 0.9% − (−0.8%) − 1% = 0.7%. Thus, the trade balance improves: The Marshall-Lerner condition is satisfied.

Output, the Interest Rate, and the Exchange Rate

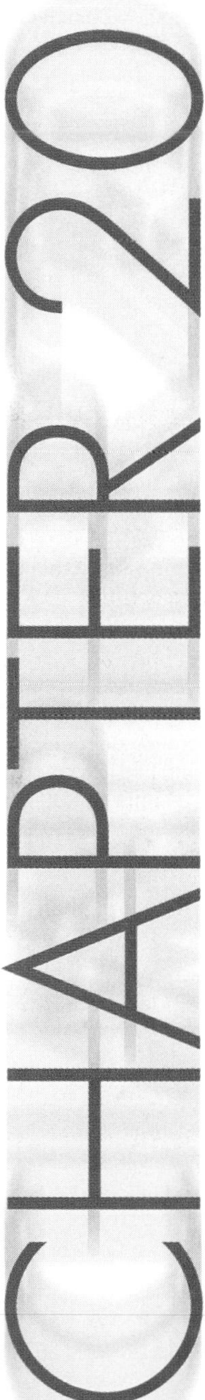

In Chapter 19, we treated the exchange rate as one of the policy instruments available to the government. But the exchange rate is not a policy instrument. Rather, it is determined in the foreign-exchange market—a market where, as you saw in Chapter 18, there is an enormous amount of trading. This fact raises two obvious questions: What determines the exchange rate? How can policy makers affect it?

These are the questions that motivate this chapter. More generally, we examine the implications of equilibrium in both the goods market and financial markets, including the foreign exchange market. This allows us to characterize the joint movements of output, the interest rate, and the exchange rate in an open economy. The model we develop is an extension to the open economy of the *IS-LM* model you saw in Chapter 5, and is known as the **Mundell-Fleming model**—after the two economists, Robert Mundell and Marcus Fleming, who first put it together in the 1960s. (The model presented here keeps the spirit but differs in its details from the original Mundell-Fleming model.)

- Section 20-1 looks at equilibrium in the goods market.
- Section 20-2 looks at equilibrium in financial markets, including the foreign exchange market.
- Section 20-3 puts the two equilibrium conditions together and looks at the determination of output, the interest rate, and the exchange rate.
- Section 20-4 looks at the role of policy under flexible exchange rates.
- Section 20-5 looks at the role of policy under fixed exchange rates. ■

20-1 Equilibrium in the Goods Market

Equilibrium in the goods market was the focus of Chapter 19, where we derived the equilibrium condition (equation [19.4]):

$$Y = \underset{(+)}{C(Y-T)} + \underset{(+,-)}{I(Y,r)} + G - \epsilon \underset{(+,-)}{IM(Y,\epsilon)} + \underset{(+,+)}{X(Y^*,\epsilon)}$$

Goods market equilibrium (*IS*): Output = Demand for domestic goods.

For the goods market to be in equilibrium, output (the left side of the equation) must be equal to the demand for domestic goods (the right side of the equation).

This demand is equal to consumption, *C*, plus investment, *I*, plus government spending, *G*, minus imports, $\epsilon\, IM$, plus exports, *X*.

Consumption, *C*, depends positively on disposable income, $Y - T$.

Investment, *I*, depends positively on output, *Y*, and negatively on the real interest rate, *r*.

Government spending, *G*, is taken as given.

The volume of imports, *IM*, depends positively on output, *Y*, negatively on the real exchange rate, ϵ.

Exports, *X*, depend positively on foreign output, Y^*, and positively on the real exchange rate, ϵ.

It will be convenient in what follows to regroup the last two terms under "net exports," defined as exports minus imports, $X - \epsilon\, IM$:

$$NX(Y,Y^*,\epsilon) \equiv X(Y^*,\epsilon) - \epsilon\, IM(Y,\epsilon)$$

Reminder: A real depreciation is represented by an increase in the real exchange rate—an increase in the price of foreign goods in terms of domestic goods.

It follows from our assumptions about imports and exports that net exports, *NX*, depend on domestic output, *Y*, foreign output, Y^*, and the exchange rate, ϵ. An increase in domestic output increases imports, thus decreasing net exports. An increase in foreign output increases exports, thus increasing net exports. An increase in ϵ—a real depreciation—leads to an increase in net exports.

I shall assume, throughout the chapter, that the Marshall-Lerner condition—that is, the condition that a real depreciation improves the trade balance—holds (see Chapter 19).

Using this definition of net exports, we can rewrite the equilibrium condition as

$$Y = \underset{(+)}{C(Y-T)} + \underset{(+,-)}{I(Y,r)} + G + \underset{(-,+,+)}{NX(Y,Y^*,\epsilon)} \tag{20.1}$$

For our purposes, the main implication of equation (20.1) is the dependence of demand, and so of equilibrium output, both on the real interest rate and on the real exchange rate:

- An increase in the real interest rate leads to a decrease in investment spending, and so to a decrease in the demand for domestic goods. This leads, through the multiplier, to a decrease in output.
- An increase in the real exchange rate—a real depreciation—leads to a shift in demand towards domestic goods, and so an increase in net exports. The increase in net exports increases the demand for domestic goods and so increases output.

For the remainder of the chapter, I shall make two simplifications to equation (20.1):

First simplification: $P = P^* = 1$, so, $\epsilon = E$

- Given our focus on the short run, we assumed in our previous treatment of the *IS-LM* model that the (domestic) price level was given. I shall extend this assumption to the foreign price level, so the real exchange rate ($\epsilon \equiv EP^*/P$) and the nominal exchange rate (E) move together. A nominal depreciation leads, one for one, to a real depreciation. If, for notational convenience, we choose P and P^* so that $P^*/P = 1$ (and we can do so because they are index numbers), then $\epsilon = E$ and we can replace ϵ by E in equation (20.1).

- As we take the domestic price level as given and fixed, there is no inflation, neither actual nor expected. The nominal interest rate and the real interest rate are the same, and we can replace the real interest rate, r, in equation (20.1) by the nominal interest rate, i.

Second simplification: ◀ $\pi^e = 0$, so, $r = i$

With these two simplifications, equation (20.1) becomes

$$Y = \underset{(+)}{C(Y-T)} + \underset{(+,-)}{I(Y,i)} + G + \underset{(-,+,+)}{NX(Y,Y^*,E)} \tag{20.2}$$

Output depends on both the nominal interest rate and the nominal exchange rate.

20-2 Equilibrium in Financial Markets

When we looked at financial markets in the *IS-LM* model, we assumed that people chose between only two financial assets, money and bonds. Now that we look at a financially open economy, we must take into account the fact that people have a choice between domestic bonds and foreign bonds. Let's consider each choice in turn.

◀ We leave aside the other choices—between short-term and long-term bonds, and between short-term bonds and stocks—studied in Chapter 15.

Money Versus Bonds

When looking at the determination of the interest rate in the *IS-LM* model, we wrote the condition that the supply of money be equal to the demand for money as

$$\frac{M}{P} = Y\,L(i) \tag{20.3}$$

We took the real supply of money (the left side of equation [20.3]) as given. We assumed that the real demand for money (the right side of equation [20.3]) depended on the level of transactions in the economy, measured by real output, Y, and on the opportunity cost of holding money rather than bonds, the nominal interest rate on bonds, i.

How should we change this characterization now that the economy is open? You will like the answer: Not very much, if at all.

In an open economy, the demand for domestic money is still mostly a demand by domestic residents. There is not much reason for, say, the British to hold U.S. currency or dollar denominated demand deposits. Transactions in the United Kingdom require payment in pounds, not in dollars. If residents of the U.K. want to hold dollar-denominated assets, they are better off holding U.S. bonds, which at least pay a positive interest rate. And the demand for money by domestic residents in any country still depends on the same factors as before: their level of transactions that we measure by domestic real output, and the opportunity cost of holding money, the nominal interest rate on bonds.

◀ Two qualifications from Chapter 18: (1) the dollars used for illegal transactions abroad, and (2) the dollars used for domestic transactions in countries with very high inflation. I shall ignore both qualifications here.

Therefore, we can still use equation (20.3) to think about the determination of the nominal interest rate in an open economy. The interest rate must be such that the supply of money and the demand for money are equal. An increase in the money supply leads to a decrease in the interest rate. An increase in money demand, say as a result of an increase in output, leads to an increase in the interest rate.

◀ Financial markets equilibrium. Condition 1 (*LM*): Supply of money = Demand for money

Domestic Bonds Versus Foreign Bonds

In looking at the choice between domestic bonds and foreign bonds, we shall rely on the assumption we introduced in Chapter 18: Financial investors, domestic or foreign, go for the highest expected rate of return. This implies that, in equilibrium, both domestic bonds and foreign bonds must have the same expected rate of return; otherwise, investors would be willing to hold only one or the other, but not both, and this could not be an equilibrium.

As you saw in Chapter 18, this assumption implies that the following arbitrage relation—the *interest parity condition*—must hold:

$$i_t = i_t^* + \frac{E_{t+1}^e - E_t}{E_t}$$

The domestic interest rate, i_t, must be equal to the foreign interest rate, i_t^*, plus the expected rate of depreciation of the domestic currency, $(E_{t+1}^e - E_t)/E_t$.

Financial markets equilibrium. Condition 2 (Arbitrage): The expected rates of return on domestic and foreign bonds must be equal. Equivalently, the domestic interest rate must equal the foreign interest rate plus the expected rate of depreciation of the domestic currency.

For now, we shall take the expected future exchange rate as given and denote it as $\bar{E}^e$ (we shall relax this assumption in Chapter 21). Under this assumption, and dropping time indexes, the interest parity condition becomes

$$i = i^* + \frac{\bar{E}^e - E}{E} \tag{20.4}$$

Multiplying both sides by E, bringing the terms in E to the left side, and dividing both sides by $(1 + i - i^*)$ gives the current exchange rate as a function of the expected future exchange rate, the domestic interest rate, and the foreign interest rate:

$$E = \frac{\bar{E}^e}{1 + i - i^*} \tag{20.5}$$

Equation (20.5) implies a negative relation between the domestic interest rate and the exchange rate. Given the expected future exchange rate and the foreign interest rate, *an increase in the domestic interest rate leads to a decrease in the exchange rate—equivalently, to an appreciation of the domestic currency. A decrease in the domestic interest rate leads to an increase in the exchange rate—to a depreciation of the domestic currency.*

$i\uparrow \Rightarrow E\downarrow$
$i\downarrow \Rightarrow E\uparrow$

This relation between the exchange rate and the domestic interest rate plays a central role in the real world, and will play a central role in the rest of this chapter. To understand it further, think about the sequence of events that takes place in financial markets and foreign exchange markets after an increase in the U.S. interest rate above the U.K. interest rate:

- Start from a situation where the U.S. and U.K. interest rates are equal, so that $i = i^*$. This implies, from equation (20.5), that the current exchange rate equals the expected future exchange rate: $E = E^e$.
- Suppose, as a result of a U.S. monetary contraction, the U.S. interest rate increases. At an unchanged exchange rate, it becomes more attractive to hold U.S. bonds, so financial investors want to shift out of U.K. bonds and into U.S. bonds. To do so, they must sell U.K. bonds for pounds, then sell pounds for dollars, then use the dollars to buy U.S. bonds. As investors sell pounds and buy dollars, the dollar appreciates.
- That an increase in the U.S. interest rate leads to an appreciation of the dollar is intuitively straightforward: An increase in the demand for dollars leads to an increase in the price of dollars. What is less intuitive is *by how much* the dollar must appreciate. The important point here: If financial investors do not change their expectation of the future exchange rate, then *the more the dollar appreciates today*, the more investors expect it to *depreciate in the future* (as they expect it to return to the same value in the future). Other things being equal, this expectation makes U.K. bonds more attractive: When the dollar is expected to depreciate, a given rate of return in pounds means a higher rate of return in dollars.

- This gives us the answer: The initial dollar appreciation must be such that the expected future depreciation compensates for the increase in the U.S. interest rate. When this is the case, investors are again indifferent and equilibrium prevails.

A numerical example will help. Assume that, until now, the one-year U.S. interest rate and the one-year U.K. interest rate were both equal to 4%. Suppose the U.S. interest rate now increases to 10%. If the expected exchange rate for next year does not change, the dollar will appreciate by 6% today. Why? Because, if the dollar appreciates by 6% today and investors do not change their expectation of the exchange rate one year ahead, the dollar is now expected to depreciate by 6% over the coming year. Put the other way, the pound is expected to appreciate by 6% over the dollar over the coming year, so that holding U.K. bonds yields an expected rate of return of 10%: the 4% rate of return in pounds, plus the expected 6% appreciation of the pound vis-à-vis the dollar. Holding U.S. bonds or holding U.K. bonds both yield an expected rate of return of 10% in dollars. Financial investors are willing to hold either one, so there is equilibrium in the foreign exchange market.

In terms of equation (20.4),

$$i \quad = i^* \quad + \frac{\bar{E}^e - E}{E}$$
$$10\% = 4\% + 6\%$$

The rate of return from holding U.S. bonds (the left side) is equal to 10%. The expected rate of return from holding U.K. bonds, expressed in dollars, (the right side) is equal to the U.K. interest rate, 4%, plus the expected depreciation of the dollar, 6%.

◀ Make sure you understand the steps in the argument:
- The one-year interest rate on U.S. bonds increases by 6%.
- Investors then buy U.S. bonds. To pay for them, they must first buy dollars.
- The dollar appreciates until it is expected to depreciate by 6% during the coming year.
- This happens when the dollar has appreciated today by 6%.

Figure 20-1 plots the relation between the (domestic) interest rate and the exchange rate implied by equation (20.5)—the interest parity relation. The relation is drawn for a given expected future exchange rate, $\bar{E}^e$, and a given foreign interest rate, i^*. The lower the interest rate, the higher the exchange rate: The relation is represented by a downward-sloping curve. Equation (20.5) also implies that when the domestic interest rate is equal to the foreign interest rate, the exchange rate is equal to the expected future exchange rate: When $i = i^*$, then $E = \bar{E}^e$. This point is denoted A in the figure.

◀ What happens to the curve if i^* increases? if $\bar{E}^e$ increases?

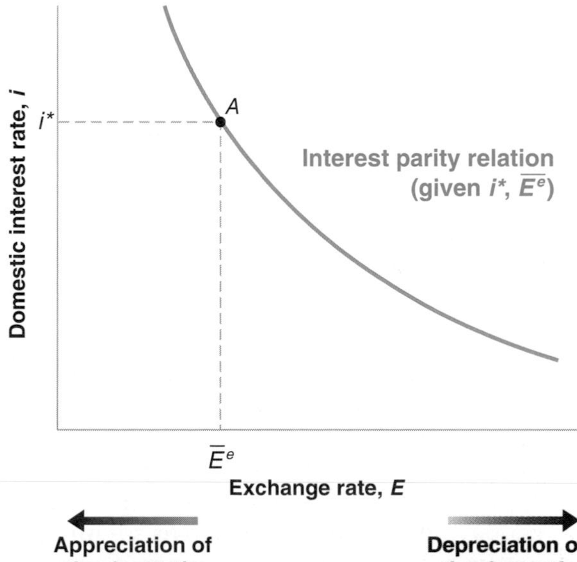

The Relation Between the Interest Rate and the Exchange Rate Implied by Interest Parity

A lower domestic interest rate leads to a higher exchange rate—to a depreciation of the domestic currency. A higher domestic interest rate leads to a lower exchange rate—to an appreciation of the domestic currency.

Note that our argument relies heavily on the assumption that when the interest rate changes, the expected exchange rate remains unchanged. This implies that an appreciation today leads to an expected depreciation in the future—as the exchange rate is expected to return to the same, unchanged, value in the future. We shall relax the assumption that the future exchange rate is fixed in Chapter 21. But the basic conclusion will remain: *An increase in the domestic interest rate relative to the foreign interest rate leads to an appreciation.*

20-3 Putting Goods and Financial Markets Together

We now have the elements we need to understand the movements of output, the interest rate, and the exchange rate.

Goods-market equilibrium implies that output depends, among other factors, on the interest rate and the exchange rate:

$$Y = C(Y - T) + I(Y, i) + G + NX(Y, Y^*, E)$$

The interest rate in turn is determined by the equality of money supply and money demand:

$$\frac{M}{P} = Y\,L(i)$$

And the interest-parity condition implies a negative relation between the domestic interest rate and the exchange rate:

$$E = \frac{\bar{E}^e}{1 + i - i^*}$$

Together, these three relations determine output, the interest rate, and the exchange rate. Working with three relations is not very easy. But we can easily reduce them to two by using the interest parity condition to eliminate the exchange rate in the goods-market equilibrium relation. Doing this gives us the following two equations, the *open-economy versions of our familiar IS and LM relations*:

$$IS: \quad Y = C(Y - T) + I(Y, i) + G + NX\left(Y, Y^*, \frac{\bar{E}^e}{1 + i - i^*}\right)$$

$$LM: \quad \frac{M}{P} = Y\,L(i)$$

Take the *IS relation* first and consider the effects of an increase in the interest rate on output. An increase in the interest rate now has two effects:

- The first effect, which was already present in a closed economy, is the direct effect on investment. A higher interest rate leads to a decrease in investment, so to a decrease in the demand for domestic goods and a decrease in output.
- The second effect, which is only present in the open economy, is the effect through the exchange rate. An increase in the domestic interest rate leads to an appreciation of the domestic currency. The appreciation, which makes domestic goods more expensive relative to foreign goods, leads to a decrease in net exports, so to a decrease in the demand for domestic goods and a decrease in output.

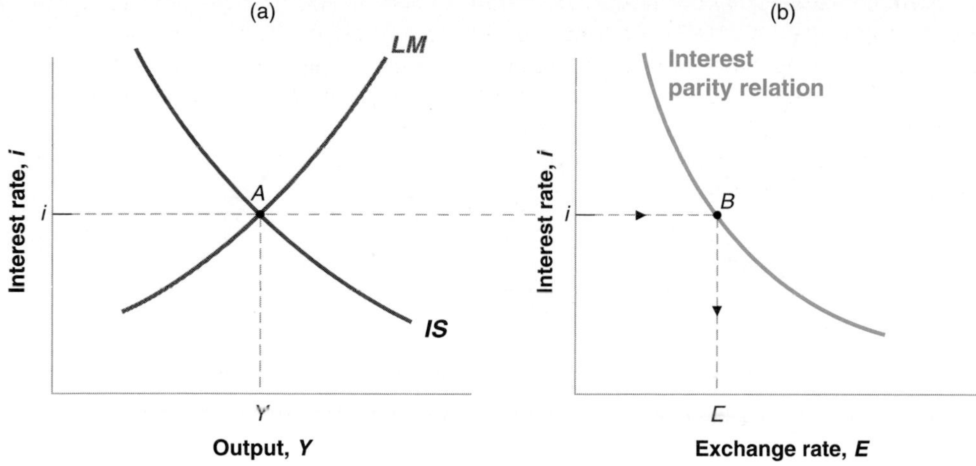

Figure 20-2

The* IS-LM *Model in the Open Economy

An increase in the interest rate reduces output both directly and indirectly (through the exchange rate): The *IS* curve is downward sloping. Given the real money stock, an increase in income increases the interest rate: The *LM* curve is upward sloping.

Both effects work in the same direction: An increase in the interest rate decreases demand directly, and indirectly—through the adverse effect of the appreciation on demand.

The *IS* relation between the interest rate and output is drawn in Figure 20-2, panel (a) for given values of all the other variables in the relation, namely, T, G, Y^*, i^*, and $\bar{E}^e$. The *IS* curve is downward sloping: An increase in the interest rate leads to a decrease in output. It looks very much the same as in the closed economy, but it hides a more complex relation than before: The interest rate affects output not only directly, but also indirectly through the exchange rate.

An increase in the interest rate leads, both directly and indirectly (through the exchange rate), to a decrease in output.

The *LM relation* is exactly the same as in the closed economy. The *LM* curve is upward sloping. For a given value of the real money stock, M/P, an increase in output leads to an increase in the demand for money, and to an increase in the equilibrium interest rate.

Equilibrium in the goods and financial markets is attained at point A in panel (a), with output level Y and interest rate i. The equilibrium value of the exchange rate cannot be read directly from the graph. But it is easily obtained from panel (b), which replicates Figure 20-1, and gives the exchange rate associated with a given interest rate. The exchange rate associated with the equilibrium interest rate i is equal to E.

To summarize: We have derived the *IS* and the *LM* relations for an open economy.

The IS curve is downward sloping: An increase in the interest rate leads directly, and indirectly through the exchange rate, to a decrease in demand and a decrease in output.

The LM curve is upward sloping: An increase in income increases the demand for money, requiring an increase in the equilibrium interest rate.

Equilibrium output and the equilibrium interest rate are given by the intersection of the *IS* and the *LM* curves. *Given the foreign interest rate and the expected future exchange rate, the equilibrium interest rate determines the equilibrium exchange rate.*

20-4 The Effects of Policy in an Open Economy

Having derived the *IS-LM* model for the open economy, we now put it to use and look at the effects of policy.

The Effects of Fiscal Policy in an Open Economy

Let's look again at a change in government spending. Suppose that, starting from a balanced budget, the government decides to increase defense spending without

FLEXIBLE EXCHANGE RATES

Figure 20-3

The Effects of an Increase in Government Spending

An increase in government spending leads to an increase in output, an increase in the interest rate, and an appreciation.

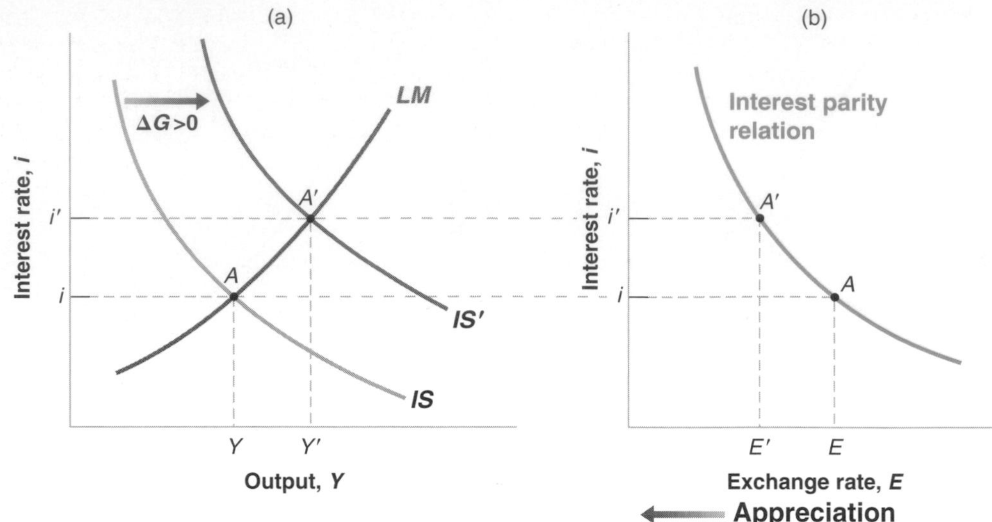

raising taxes, and so runs a budget deficit. What happens to the level of output? To the composition of output? To the interest rate? To the exchange rate?

The answers are given in Figure 20-3. The economy is initially at point A. The increase in government spending by $\Delta G > 0$ increases output at a given interest rate, shifting the *IS* curve to the right, from *IS* to *IS'* in panel (a). Because government spending does not enter the *LM* relation, the *LM* curve does not shift. The new equilibrium is at point A', with a higher level of output and a higher interest rate. In panel (b), the higher interest rate leads to a decrease in the exchange rate—an appreciation of the domestic currency. So *an increase in government spending leads to an increase in output, an increase in the interest rate, and an appreciation of the domestic currency.*

An increase in government spending shifts the *IS* curve to the right. It shifts neither the *LM* curve nor the interest-parity curve.

In words: An increase in government spending leads to an increase in demand, leading to an increase in output. As output increases, so does the demand for money, leading to upward pressure on the interest rate. The increase in the interest rate, which makes domestic bonds more attractive, leads to an appreciation of the domestic currency. The higher interest rate and the appreciation of the domestic currency both decrease the domestic demand for goods, offsetting some of the effect of government spending on demand and output.

Can we tell what happens to the various components of demand?

- Consumption and government spending clearly both go up—consumption goes up because of the increase in income, government spending goes up by assumption.
- What happens to investment is ambiguous. Recall that investment depends on both output and the interest rate: $I = I(Y, i)$. On one hand, output goes up, leading to an increase in investment. But on the other, the interest rate also goes up, leading to a decrease in investment. Depending on which of these two effects dominates, investment can go up or down. In short: The effect of government spending on investment was ambiguous in the closed economy; it remains ambiguous in the open economy.
- Recall that net exports depend on domestic output, foreign output, and the exchange rate: $NX = NX(Y, Y^*, E)$. Thus, both the appreciation and the increase in output combine to decrease net exports: The appreciation decreases exports and

increases imports, and the increase in output further increases imports. So, the budget deficit leads to a deterioration of the trade balance. If trade is balanced to start, then the budget deficit leads to a trade deficit. Note that, while an increase in the budget deficit increases the trade deficit, the effect is far from mechanical. It works through the effect of the budget deficit on output and on the exchange rate, and, in turn, on the trade deficit.

The Effects of Monetary Policy in an Open Economy

The effects of our other favorite policy experiment, a monetary contraction, are shown in Figure 20-4. Look at panel (a). At a given level of output, a decrease in the money stock by $\Delta M < 0$ leads to an increase in the interest rate: The *LM* curve shifts up, from *LM* to *LM'*. Because money does not directly enter the *IS* relation, the *IS* curve does not shift. The equilibrium moves from point *A* to point *A'*. In panel (b), the increase in the interest rate leads to an appreciation of the domestic currency.

A monetary contraction shifts the *LM* curve up. It shifts neither the *IS* curve nor the interest-parity curve.

So *a monetary contraction leads to a decrease in output, to an increase in the interest rate, and to an appreciation of the domestic currency.* The story is easy to tell. A monetary contraction leads to an increase in the interest rate, making domestic bonds more attractive and triggering an appreciation. The higher interest rate and the appreciation both decrease demand and output. As output decreases, money demand decreases, leading to a decrease in the interest rate, offsetting some of the initial increase in the interest rate and some of the initial appreciation.

Can you tell what happens to consumption, to investment, and to net exports?

This version of the *IS-LM* model for the open economy was first put together in the 1960s by two economists, Robert Mundell, at Columbia University, and Marcus Fleming, at the IMF. For this reason, it is called the *Mundell-Fleming model.* How well does it fit the facts? To answer, one could hardly design a better experiment than the sharp monetary and fiscal policy changes the U.S. economy underwent in the early 1980s. The evidence is shown in the Focus box "Monetary Contraction and Fiscal Expansion: The United States in the Early 1980s." Conclusion: The Mundell-Fleming model and its predictions pass with flying colors.

Robert Mundell received the Nobel Prize in economics in 1999.

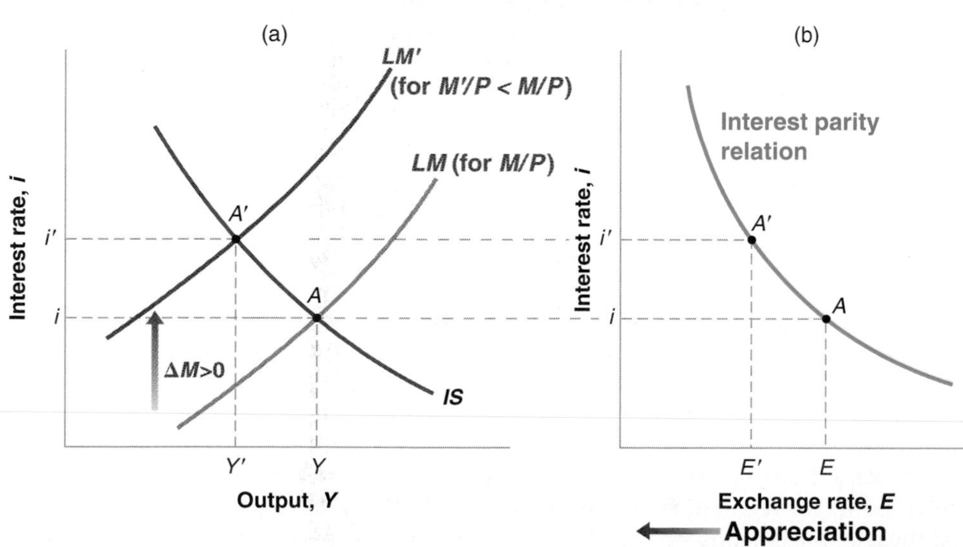

Figure 20-4

The Effects of a Monetary Contraction

A monetary contraction leads to a decrease in output, an increase in the interest rate, and an appreciation.

FLEXIBLE EXCHANGE RATES

Monetary Contraction and Fiscal Expansion: The United States in the Early 1980s

FOCUS

The early 1980s in the United States were dominated by sharp changes both in monetary policy and in fiscal policy.

We have already discussed the origins of the change in monetary policy in Chapter 9. By the late 1970s, the Chairman of the Fed, Paul Volcker, concluded U.S. inflation was too high and had to be reduced. Starting in late 1979, Volcker embarked on a path of sharp monetary contraction, realizing this might lead to a recession in the shortrun, but would lead to lower inflation in the medium run.

The change in fiscal policy was triggered by the election of Ronald Reagan in 1980. Reagan was elected on the promise of more conservative policies, namely, a scaling down of taxation and the government's role in economic activity. This commitment was the inspiration for the Economic Recovery Act of August 1981. Personal income taxes were cut by a total of 23%, in three installments from 1981 to 1983. Corporate taxes were also reduced. These tax cuts were not, however, accompanied by corresponding decreases in government spending, and the result was a steady increase in budget deficits, which reached a peak in 1983 at 5.6% of GDP. Table 1 gives spending and revenue numbers for 1980–1984.

What were the Reagan administration's motivations for cutting taxes without implementing corresponding cuts in spending? These are still being debated today, but there is agreement that there were two main motivations.

One motivation came from the beliefs of a fringe, but influential, group of economists called the **supply siders**, who argued that a cut in tax rates would lead people and firms to work much harder and more productively, and that the resulting increase in activity would lead to an increase, not a decrease, in tax revenues. Whatever the merits of the argument appeared to be then, it proved wrong: Even if some people did work harder and more productively after the tax cuts, tax revenues decreased and the fiscal deficit increased.

The other motivation was the hope that the cut in taxes, and the resulting increase in deficits, would scare

Table 1 The Emergence of Large U.S. Budget Deficits, 1980–1984

	1980	1981	1982	1983	1984
Spending	22.0	22.8	24.0	25.0	23.7
Revenues	20.2	20.8	20.5	19.4	19.2
Personal taxes	9.4	9.6	9.9	8.8	8.2
Corporate taxes	2.6	2.3	1.6	1.6	2.0
Budget surplus (−: deficit)	−1.8	−2.0	−3.5	−5.6	−4.5

Numbers are for fiscal years, which start in October of the previous calendar year. All numbers are expressed as a percentage of GDP.

Source: Historical Tables, Office of Management and Budget.

20-5 Fixed Exchange Rates

We have assumed so far that the central bank chose the money supply and let the exchange rate adjust in whatever manner was implied by equilibrium in the foreign-exchange market. In most countries, this assumption does not reflect reality: Central banks act under implicit or explicit exchange-rate targets and use monetary policy to achieve those targets. The targets are sometimes implicit, sometimes explicit; they are sometimes specific values, sometimes bands or ranges. These exchange-rate arrangements (or *regimes*, as they are called) come under many names. Let's first see what these names mean.

Congress into cutting spending, or, at the very least, into not increasing spending further. This motivation turned out to be partly right; Congress found itself under enormous pressure not to increase spending, and the growth of spending in the 1980s was surely lower than it would have been otherwise. Nonetheless, this decrease in spending was not enough to offset the shortfall in taxes and avoid the rapid increase in deficits.

Whatever the reason for the deficits, the combined effects of the monetary contraction and the fiscal expansion were in line with what the Mundell-Fleming model predicts. Table 2 gives the evolution of the main macroeconomic variables from 1980 to 1984.

From 1980 to 1982, the evolution of the economy was dominated by the effects of the monetary contraction. Interest rates, both nominal and real, increased sharply, leading both to a large dollar appreciation (a decrease in the exchange rate) and to a recession. The goal of lowering inflation was achieved, although not right away; by 1982, inflation was down to about 4%. Lower output and dollar appreciation had opposing effects on the trade balance (lower output leading to lower imports and an improvement in the trade balance; the appreciation of the dollar leading to a deterioration in the trade balance), resulting in little change in the trade deficit before 1982.

From 1982 on, the evolution of the economy was dominated by the effects of the fiscal expansion. As our model predicts, these effects were strong output growth, high interest rates, and further dollar appreciation. The effects of high output growth and dollar appreciation were an increase in the trade deficit to 2.7% of GDP by 1984. By the mid-1980s, the main macroeconomic policy issue had become that of the **twin deficits**, the budget deficit and the trade deficit. It was to remain one of the central macroeconomic issues throughout the 1980s and the first part of the 1990s.

Table 2 Major U.S. Macroeconomic Variables, 1980–1984

	1980	1981	1982	1983	1984
GDP growth (%)	−0.5	1.8	−2.2	3.9	6.2
Unemployment rate (%)	7.1	7.6	9.7	9.6	7.5
Inflation (CPI) (%)	12.5	8.9	3.8	3.8	3.9
Interest rate (nominal) (%)	11.5	14.0	10.6	8.6	9.6
(real) (%)	2.5	4.9	6.0	5.1	5.9
Real exchange rate	117	99	89	85	77
Trade surplus (−: deficit) (% of GDP)	−0.5	−0.4	−0.6	−1.5	−2.7

Inflation: Rate of change of the CPI. The nominal interest rate is the three-month T-bill rate. The real interest rate is equal to the nominal rate minus the forecast of inflation by DRI, a private forecasting firm. The real exchange rate is the U.S. multilateral real exchange rate, normalized so that 1973 = 100.

Pegs, Crawling Pegs, Bands, the EMS, and the Euro

At one end of the spectrum are countries with *flexible exchange rates* such as the United States and Japan. These countries have no explicit exchange-rate targets. While their central banks surely do not ignore movements in the exchange rate, they have shown themselves quite willing to let their exchange rates fluctuate considerably.

Like the "dance of the dollar" in the 1980s (Chapter 18), there was a "dance of the yen" in 1990s, with a sharp appreciation of the yen in the first half of the 1990s, followed by a sharp depreciation later in the decade.

At the other end are countries that operate under *fixed exchange rates*. These countries maintain a fixed exchange rate in terms of some foreign currency. Some **peg** their currency to the dollar. For example, from 1991 to 2001, Argentina pegged its currency, the peso, at the highly symbolic exchange rate of one dollar for one peso (more on this in Chapter 21). Others used to peg their currency to the French franc (most of these are former French colonies in Africa); as the French franc has been replaced by the Euro, they are now pegged to the Euro. Yet, others peg to a basket of currencies, with the weights reflecting the composition of their trade.

The label "fixed" is a bit misleading: It is not the case that the exchange rate in countries with fixed exchange rates actually never changes. But changes are rare. An extreme case is that of the African countries pegged to the French franc. When their exchange rates were readjusted in January 1994, this was the first adjustment in 45 years. Because these changes are rare, economists use specific words to distinguish them from the daily changes that occur under flexible exchange rates. They refer to an increase in the exchange rate under a regime of fixed exchange rates as a *devaluation* rather than a depreciation, and to a decrease in the exchange rate under a regime of fixed exchange rates as a *revaluation* rather than an appreciation.

Recall the definition of the real exchange rate, $\epsilon = EP^*/P$.

If domestic inflation is higher than foreign inflation, then:

- **P increases faster than P^*.**
- **Equivalently, P^*/P decreases.**
- **If E is fixed, EP^*/P decreases.**

Equivalently, there is a steady real appreciation: Domestic goods become steadily more expensive relative to foreign goods.

Between these extremes are countries with various degrees of commitment to an exchange rate target. For example, some countries operate under a **crawling peg**. The name describes it well: These countries often have inflation rates that exceed the U.S. inflation rate. If they were to peg their nominal exchange rate against the dollar, the increase in their domestic price level relative to the U.S. price level would lead to a steady real appreciation and rapidly make their goods noncompetitive. To avoid this effect, these countries choose a predetermined rate of depreciation against the dollar. They choose to "crawl" (move slowly) vis-à-vis the dollar.

Yet another arrangement is for a group of countries to maintain their bilateral exchange rates (the exchange rate between each pair of countries) within some bands. Perhaps the most prominent example was the **European Monetary System (EMS)**, which determined the movements of exchange rates within the European Union from 1978 to 1998. Under EMS rules, member countries agreed to maintain their exchange rate vis-à-vis the other currencies in the system within narrow **bands** around a **central parity**—a given value for the exchange rate. Changes in the central parity and devaluations or revaluations of specific currencies could occur, but only by common agreement among member countries. After a major crisis in 1992, which led several countries to drop out of the EMS altogether, exchange rate adjustments became more and more infrequent, leading several countries to move one step further and adopt a common currency, the **Euro**. Conversion from domestic currencies to the Euro started on January 1, 1999, and was completed in early 2002. We shall return to the implications of the move to the Euro in Chapter 21.

We look at the 1992 crisis in Chapter 21.

You can think of countries adopting a common currency as adopting an extreme form of fixed exchange rates: Their "exchange rate" is fixed at one to one between any pair of countries.

We shall discuss the pros and cons of these different exchange regimes in the next chapter. But first, you must understand how pegging the exchange rate affects monetary policy and fiscal policy. This is what we do in the rest of this section.

Pegging the Exchange Rate, and Monetary Control

Suppose a country decides to peg its exchange rate at some chosen value, call it $\bar{E}$. How does it actually achieve this? The government cannot just announce the value of the exchange rate and stand there. Rather, it must take measures so that its chosen exchange rate will prevail in the foreign-exchange market. Let's look at this more closely.

Pegging or no pegging, the exchange rate and the nominal interest rate must satisfy the interest parity condition:

$$i_t = i_t^* + \frac{E_{t+1}^e - E_t}{E_t}$$

Now suppose the country pegs the exchange rate at $\bar{E}$, so the current exchange rate $E_t = \bar{E}$. If financial and foreign exchange markets believe that the exchange rate will remain pegged at this value, then their expectation of the future exchange rate, E^e_{t+1}, is also equal to $\bar{E}$, and the interest parity relation becomes

$$i_t = i^*_t + \frac{\bar{E} - \bar{E}}{\bar{E}} = i^*_t$$

In words: If financial investors expect the exchange rate to remain unchanged, they will require the same nominal interest rate in both countries. *Under a fixed exchange rate and perfect capital mobility, the domestic interest rate must be equal to the foreign interest rate.*

This condition has one further important implication. Return to the equilibrium condition that the supply of money and demand for money be equal. Now that $i = i^*$, this condition becomes

Under perfect capital mobility, fixing the exchange rate means giving up the freedom to choose the domestic interest rate, which must remain equal to the foreign interest rate.

$$\frac{M}{P} = Y\,L(i) \qquad (20.6)$$

Suppose an increase in domestic output increases the demand for money. In a closed economy, the central bank could leave the money stock unchanged, leading to an increase in the equilibrium interest rate. In an open economy, and under flexible exchange rates, the central bank can still do the same: The result will be both an increase in the interest rate and an appreciation of the domestic currency. But under fixed exchange rates, the central bank cannot keep the money stock unchanged. If it did, the domestic interest rate would increase above the foreign interest rate, leading to an appreciation of the domestic currency. To maintain the exchange rate, the central bank must increase the supply of money in line with the increase in the demand for money so the equilibrium interest rate does not change. Given the price level, P, nominal money, M, must adjust so that equation (20.6) holds.

To summarize, *under fixed exchange rates, the central bank gives up monetary policy as a policy instrument.* A fixed exchange rate implies a domestic interest rate equal to the foreign rate. And the money supply must adjust to maintain the interest rate.

These results depend very much on the interest rate parity condition, which in turn depends on the assumption of perfect capital mobility (financial investors go for the highest expected rate of return). The case of fixed exchange rates with imperfect capital mobility—which is more relevant for middle-income countries, such as in Latin America or Asia—is treated in the appendix to this chapter.

Fiscal Policy Under Fixed Exchange Rates

If monetary policy can no longer be used under fixed exchange rates, what about fiscal policy? To answer this, we use Figure 20-5.

Figure 20-5 starts by replicating Figure 20-3, panel (a), which we used earlier to analyze the effects of fiscal policy under flexible exchange rates. In that case, we saw that a fiscal expansion ($\Delta G > 0$) shifted the *IS* curve to the right. Under flexible exchange rates, the money stock remained unchanged, leading to a movement in the equilibrium from point *A* to point *B*, with an increase in output from Y_A to Y_B, an increase in the interest rate, and a decrease in the exchange rate—an appreciation of the domestic currency.

However, under fixed exchange rates the central bank cannot let the currency appreciate. As the increase in output leads to an increase in the demand for money, the central bank must accommodate this increased demand for money by increasing the money supply. In terms of Figure 20-5, the central bank must shift the LM curve down as the *IS* curve shifts to the right, so that the interest rate, and thus the exchange rate, do not change. The equilibrium therefore moves from *A* to *C*, with higher output Y_C and unchanged interest and exchange rates. So, *under fixed exchange rates, fiscal policy is more powerful than it is under flexible exchange rates. This is because fiscal policy triggers monetary accommodation.*

Is the effect of fiscal policy stronger in a closed economy or in an open economy with fixed exchange rates? (*Hint:* The answer is ambiguous.)

Figure 20-5

The Effects of a Fiscal Expansion Under Fixed Exchange Rates

Under flexible exchange rates, a fiscal expansion increases output from Y_A to Y_B. Under fixed exchange rates, output increases from Y_A to Y_C.

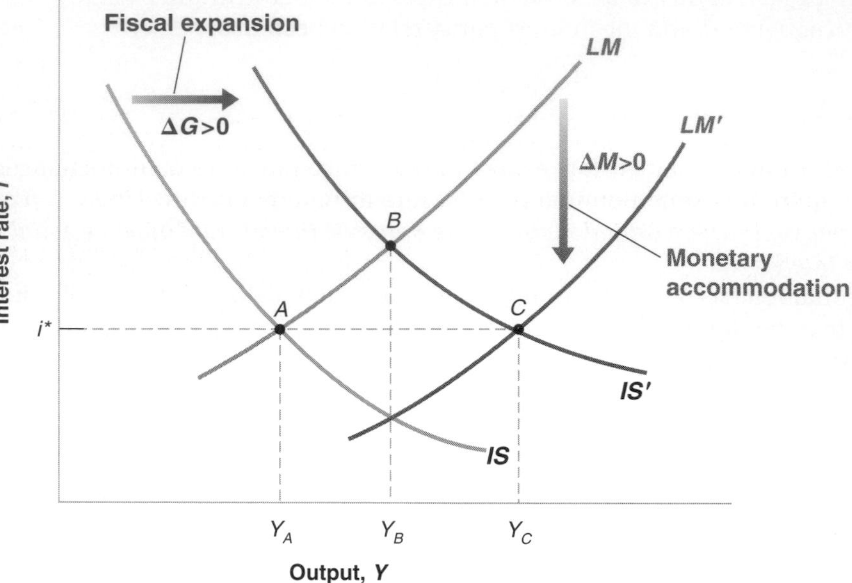

As this chapter comes to an end, a question should have started to form in your mind. Why would a country choose to fix its exchange rate? You have seen several reasons why this appears to be a bad idea:

- By fixing the exchange rate, a country gives up a powerful tool for correcting trade imbalances or changing the level of economic activity.
- By committing to a particular exchange rate, a country also gives up control of its interest rate. Not only that, but the country must match movements in the foreign interest rate, at the risk of unwanted effects on its own activity. This is what happened in the early 1990s in Europe. Because of the increase in demand due to reunification, Germany felt it had to increase its interest rate. To maintain their parity with the DM (the Deutsche Mark, the German currency at the time), other countries in the European Monetary System were also forced to increase their interest rate, something that they would rather have avoided. (This is the topic of the Focus box "German Unification, Interest Rates, and the EMS.")
- While the country retains control of fiscal policy, one policy instrument is not enough. As you saw in Chapter 19, for example, a fiscal expansion can help the economy get out of a recession, but only at the cost of a larger trade deficit. And, under fixed exchange rates, a country that wants, for example, to decrease its budget deficit cannot use monetary policy to offset the contractionary effect of its fiscal policy on output.

So why do some countries fix their exchange rate? Why have 11 European countries just adopted a common currency? To answer these questions, we must do some more work. We must look at what happens not only in the short run—which is what we did in this chapter—but also in the medium run, when the price level can adjust. We must look at the nature of exchange rate crises. Once we have done all this, we shall then be able to give an assessment of the pros and cons of exchange rate regimes. These are the topics we take up in Chapter 21.

German Unification, Interest Rates, and the EMS

Under a fixed exchange rate regime such as the European Monetary System (EMS) (let's ignore here the degree of flexibility that was afforded by the bands), no individual country can change its interest rate if the other countries do not change theirs as well. So, how do interest rates actually change? Two arrangements are possible: One is for all the member countries to coordinate changes in their interest rates. Another is for one of the countries to take the lead and for the other countries to follow—this is what happened in the EMS, with Germany as the leader.

During the 1980s, most European central banks shared similar goals and were happy to let the Bundesbank (the German central bank) take the lead. But in 1990, German unification led to a sharp divergence in goals between the Bundesbank and the other EMS nations' central banks. Recall the macroeconomic implications of unification from Chapter 5: The need for large transfers to eastern Germany and an investment boom both led to a large increase in demand in Germany. The Bundesbank's fear that this shift would generate too strong an increase in activity led it to adopt a restrictive monetary policy. The result was, as we saw, strong growth in Germany together with a large increase in interest rates.

This may have been the right policy mix for Germany. But for other countries, this policy mix was much less appealing. The other countries had not experienced the same increase in demand, but to stay in the EMS, they had to match the high German interest rates. The net result was a sharp decrease in demand and in output in the other countries. These results are presented in Table 1, which gives nominal interest rates, real interest rates, inflation rates, and GDP growth from 1990 to 1992 for Germany and for two of its EMS partners, France and Belgium.

Note first how the high German nominal interest rates were matched by both France and Belgium. Nominal interest rates were actually higher in France than in Germany in all three years! This is because France needed higher interest rates than Germany to maintain the DM/franc parity; the reason is that financial markets were not sure that France would actually keep the parity of the franc vis-à-vis the DM. Worried about a possible devaluation of the franc, financial investors asked for a higher interest rate on French bonds than on German bonds.

While France and Belgium had to match—or, as we have just seen, more than match—German nominal rates, both countries had less inflation than Germany. The result was very high real interest rates, higher than in Germany. In both France and Belgium, average real interest rates from 1990 to 1992 were close to 7%. And in both countries, the period 1990–1992 was characterized by slow growth and rising unemployment. Unemployment in France in 1992 was 10.4%, up from

Table 1 German Unification, Interest Rates, and Output Growth: Germany, France, and Belgium, 1990–1992

	Nominal Interest Rates (%)			Inflation (%)		
	1990	1991	1992	1990	1991	1992
Germany	8.5	9.2	9.5	2.7	3.7	4.7
France	10.3	9.6	10.3	2.9	3.0	2.4
Belgium	9.6	9.4	9.4	2.9	2.7	2.4
	Real Interest Rates (%)			**GDP Growth (%)**		
	1990	1991	1992	1990	1991	1992
Germany	5.7	5.5	4.8	5.7	4.5	2.1
France	7.4	6.6	7.9	2.5	0.7	1.4
Belgium	6.7	6.7	7.0	3.3	2.1	0.8

The nominal interest rate is the short-term nominal interest rate. The real interest rate is the realized real interest rate over the year—that is, the nominal interest rate minus actual inflation over the year. All rates are annual.

Source: OECD Economic Outlook.

(**Continued**)

FOCUS

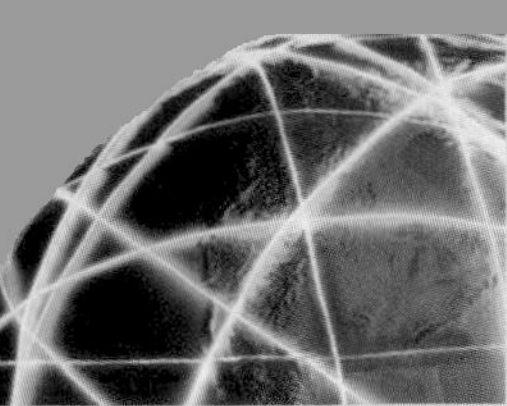

8.9% in 1990. The corresponding numbers for Belgium were 12.1 and 8.7%.

While we have looked at only two of Germany's EMS partners, a similar story was unfolding in the other EMS countries. By 1992, average unemployment in the European Union, which had been 8.7% in 1990, had increased to 10.3%. The effects of high real interest rates on spending were not the only source of this slowdown, but they were the main one.

By 1992, an increasing number of countries were wondering whether to keep defending their EMS parity or to give it up and lower their interest rates. Worried about the risk of devaluations, financial markets started to ask for higher interest rates in those countries where they thought devaluation was more likely. The result was two major exchange rate crises, one in the fall of 1992 and the other in the summer of 1993. By the end of these two crises, two countries, Italy and the United Kingdom, had left the EMS. We shall look at these crises, their origins and their implications, in Chapter 21.

Summary

- In an open economy, the demand for goods depends both on the interest rate and on the exchange rate. A decrease in the interest rate increases the demand for goods. An increase in the exchange rate—a depreciation—increases the demand for goods.
- The interest rate is determined by the equality of money demand and money supply. The exchange rate is determined by the interest parity condition, which states that the domestic interest rate must equal the foreign interest rate plus the expected rate of depreciation.
- Given the expected future exchange rate and the foreign interest rate, increases in the domestic interest rate lead to a decrease in the exchange rate (an appreciation). Decreases in the domestic interest rate lead to an increase in the exchange rate (a depreciation).
- Under flexible exchange rates, an expansionary fiscal policy leads to an increase in output, to an increase in the interest rate, and to an appreciation. A contractionary monetary policy leads to a decrease in output, to an increase in the interest rate, and to an appreciation.
- There are many types of exchange-rate arrangements. They range from fully flexible exchange rates to crawling pegs, to pegs, to fixed exchange rates, to the adoption of a common currency. Under fixed exchange rates, a country maintains a fixed exchange rate in terms of a foreign currency or a basket of currencies.
- Under fixed exchange rates and the interest parity condition, a country must maintain an interest rate equal to the foreign interest rate. The central bank loses the use of monetary policy as a policy instrument. Fiscal policy becomes more powerful than under flexible exchange rates, however, because fiscal policy triggers monetary accommodation and so does not lead to offsetting changes in the domestic interest rate and exchange rate.

Key Terms

- Mundell-Fleming model, 417
- supply siders, 426
- twin deficits, 427
- peg, 427
- crawling peg, 428
- European Monetary System (EMS), 428
- bands, 428
- central parity, 428
- Euro, 428

Questions and Problems

Quick Check

1. *Using the information in this chapter, label each of the following statements* true, false, *or* uncertain. *Explain briefly.*
   a. Because the multiplier is smaller in an open economy than in a closed economy, fiscal policy is less effective in an open economy than in a closed economy.
   b. Monetary policy is more effective in a closed economy than in an open economy with flexible exchange rates.
   c. If financial investors expect the exchange rate to be higher next year, interest parity implies that it will be higher today.

d. If financial investors expect the dollar to depreciate vis-à-vis the yen over the coming year, one-year interest rates will be higher in the United States than in Japan.
e. If the Japanese interest rate is equal to zero, foreigners will not want to hold Japanese bonds.
f. Under fixed exchange rates, the money stock must be constant.

2. *Devaluation and credibility*
   a. Suppose a country devalues. Also suppose that markets believe that the new parity will hold, and therefore do not expect a further depreciation in the future. What are the consequences of the devaluation on output and the interest rate?
   b. Now suppose that, having witnessed the devaluation, markets now expect further depreciation in the future. What are the effects of the devaluation and of the change in expectations on output and the interest rate? How does your answer differ from your answer to (a) and why?

3. *Follow the leader*

   Consider a group of open economies; assume perfect capital mobility.
   a. Assume there is a Leader country. All other countries (referred to as Follower countries) fix their exchange rates vis-à-vis the Leader country. Discuss the effectiveness of monetary policy in the Follower countries.
   b. If all countries fix their exchange rate vis-à-vis the Leader country, isn't the Leader country's exchange rate also fixed? What does this imply for the effectiveness of the Leader country's monetary policy?
   c. If the Leader country reduces its money supply to fight inflation, what must the Follower countries do to maintain their fixed exchange rates? What is the effect on their economy? What would happen in Follower countries if they did not change their money supply?

4. *Consider the IS and LM equations in Section 20-3.*
   a. Show the effect of a decrease in foreign output, Y^*, on domestic output, Y. Explain in words.
   b. Show the effect of an increase in the foreign interest rate, i^*, on domestic output, Y. Explain in words.
   c. "A monetary contraction abroad is likely to lead to a recession at home." Discuss.

5. *Consider a small open IS-LM economy with flexible exchange rates, where output is at the natural level of output, but there is a trade deficit. What is the appropriate fiscal-monetary policy mix?*

6. *Consider a monetary expansion in an economy operating under flexible exchange rates. Discuss the effects on consumption, investment, and net exports.*

Dig Deeper

7. *In the early 1980s, the U.S. economy was dominated by contractionary monetary policy followed by expansionary fiscal policy.*
   a. What does the Mundell-Fleming model predict should be the effect of a contractionary monetary policy?
   b. What does the Mundell-Fleming model predict should be the effect of an expansionary fiscal policy?
   c. Look at Table 2 in the Focus box. "Monetary Contraction and Fiscal Expansion: The United States in the Early 1980s." Does the data for the U.S. economy support the Mundell-Fleming model?

We invite you to visit the Blanchard page on the Prentice Hall Web site at:
www.prenhall.com/blanchard
for this chapter's World Wide Web exercises

Further Readings

A fascinating account of the politics behind fiscal policy under the Reagan administration is given by David Stockman—who was then the director of the Office of Management and Budget (OMB)—in *The Triumph of Politics: Why the Reagan Revolution Failed* (New York, NY: Harper & Row, 1986).

A good book on the evolution of exchange rate arrangements in Europe is *European Monetary Integration: From the European Monetary System to Economic and Monetary Union*, 2nd ed., by Daniel Gros and Niels Thygesen (New York, NY: Addison-Wesley-Longman, 1998).

Appendix: Fixed Exchange Rates, Interest Rates, and Capital Mobility

The assumption of perfect capital mobility is a good approximation to what happens in countries with highly developed financial markets and few capital controls, such as the United States, the United Kingdom, and Japan. But the assumption is more questionable in countries that have less-developed financial markets or have capital controls in place. There, domestic financial investors may have neither the savvy nor the legal right to buy foreign bonds when domestic interest rates are low. The central bank may be able both to decrease interest rates and to maintain a given exchange rate.

To look at these issues, we need to have another look at the balance sheet of the central bank. In Chapter 4, we assumed the only asset held by the central bank was domestic bonds. In an open economy, the central bank actually holds two types of assets: (1) domestic bonds and (2) **foreign-exchange reserves**, which we shall think of as foreign currency—although they also take the form of foreign bonds or foreign interest-paying assets. Think of the balance sheet of the central bank as represented in Figure 20A-1.

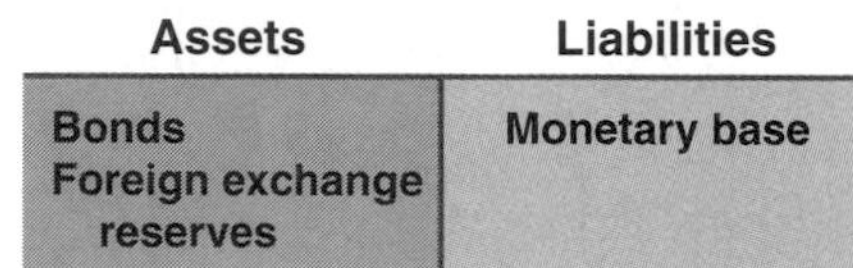

Assets	Liabilities
Bonds Foreign exchange reserves	Monetary base

Figure 20A-1 *Balance Sheet of the Central Bank*

On the asset side are bonds and foreign-exchange reserves, and on the liability side is the monetary base. There are now two ways in which the central bank can change the monetary base: either by purchases or sales of bonds in the bond market, or by purchases or sales of foreign currency in the foreign-exchange market. (If you did not read Section 4-3 in the core, replace "monetary base" by "money supply," and you will get the flavor of the argument. If you have read it, recall that the money supply is equal to the monetary base times the money multiplier. Take the money multiplier as given, and our conclusions about the monetary base extend straightforwardly to the money supply.)

Perfect Capital Mobility and Fixed Exchange Rates

Consider first the effects of an open market operation under the joint assumptions of perfect capital mobility and fixed exchange rates (the assumptions we made in the last section of this chapter).

- Assume the domestic interest rate and the foreign interest rate are initially equal, so $i = i^*$. Suppose the central bank embarks on an expansionary open-market operation, buying bonds in the bond market in amount ΔB, and creating money—increasing the monetary base—in exchange. This purchase of bonds leads to a decrease in the domestic interest rate, i. This is, however, only the beginning of the story:
- Now that the domestic interest rate is lower than the foreign interest rate, financial investors prefer to hold foreign bonds. To buy foreign bonds, they must first buy foreign currency. They go to the foreign exchange market and sell domestic currency for foreign currency.
- If the central bank did nothing, the price of domestic currency would fall, and the result would be a depreciation. Under its commitment to a fixed exchange rate, the central bank cannot allow the currency to depreciate. So, it must intervene in the foreign-exchange market and sell foreign currency for domestic currency. As it sells foreign currency and buys domestic money, the monetary base decreases.
- How much foreign currency must the central bank sell? It must keep selling until the monetary base is back to where it was before its open-market operation level, so the domestic interest rate is again equal to the foreign interest rate. Only then are financial investors willing to hold domestic bonds.

How long do all these steps take? Under perfect capital mobility, all this may happen within minutes or so of the original open-market operation. After these steps, the balance sheet of the central bank looks as represented in Figure 20A-2. Bond holdings are up by ΔB, reserves of foreign currency are down by ΔB, and the monetary base is unchanged, having gone up by ΔB in the open-market operation and down by ΔB as a result of the sale of foreign currency in the foreign exchange market.

Assets	Liabilities
Bonds: ΔB	Monetary base $\Delta B - \Delta B$
Reserves: $-\Delta B$	$= 0$

Figure 20A-2 *Balance Sheet of the Central Bank after an Open-Market Operation, and the Induced Intervention in the Foreign-Exchange Market*

To summarize, under fixed exchange rates and perfect capital mobility, the only effect of the open-market operation is to change the *composition* of the central bank's balance sheet but not the monetary base.

Imperfect Capital Mobility and Fixed Exchange Rates

Let's now move away from the assumption of perfect capital mobility. Suppose it takes some time for financial investors to shift between domestic bonds and foreign bonds.

Now an expansionary open-market operation can initially bring the domestic interest rate below the foreign interest rate. But over time, investors shift to foreign bonds, leading to an increase in the demand for foreign currency in the foreign-exchange market. To avoid a depreciation of the domestic currency, the central bank must again stand ready to sell foreign currency and buy domestic currency. Eventually, the central bank buys enough domestic currency to offset the effects of the initial open-market operation. The monetary base is back to where it was before the open-market operation, and so is the interest rate. The central bank holds more domestic bonds and smaller reserves of foreign currency.

The difference between this case and the preceding one is that, by accepting a loss in foreign-exchange reserves, the central bank is now able to decrease interest rates *for some time*. If it takes just a few days for financial investors to adjust, the trade-off can be very unattractive—as many countries, who have suffered large losses in reserves without much effect on the interest rate, have discovered at their expense. But, if the central bank can affect the domestic interest rate for a few weeks or months, it may, in some circumstances, be willing to do so.

Now let's deviate further from perfect capital mobility. Suppose, in response to a decrease in the domestic interest rate, financial investors are either unwilling or unable to move much of their portfolio into foreign bonds. For example, there are administrative and legal controls on financial transactions, making it either illegal or very expensive for domestic residents to invest outside the country. This is the relevant case for most middle-income countries, from Latin America, to eastern Europe, to Asia.

After an expansionary open-market operation, the domestic interest rate decreases, making domestic bonds less attractive. Some domestic investors move into foreign bonds, selling domestic currency for foreign currency. To maintain the exchange rate, the central bank must buy domestic currency and supply foreign currency. However, the foreign-exchange intervention by the central bank may now be small compared to the initial open-market operation. And if capital controls truly prevent investors from moving into foreign bonds at all, there may be no need at all for such a foreign-exchange intervention.

Even leaving this extreme case aside, the net effects of the initial open-market operation and the following foreign-exchange interventions are likely to be *an increase in the monetary base; a decrease in the domestic interest rate; an increase in the central bank's bond holdings; and some—but limited—loss in reserves of foreign currency.* With imperfect capital mobility, a country has some freedom to move the domestic interest rate while maintaining its exchange rate. This freedom depends primarily on three factors:

- The degree of development of its financial markets, and how willing domestic and foreign investors are to shift between domestic assets and foreign assets.
- The degree of capital controls it is able to impose on both domestic investors and foreign investors.
- The amount of foreign-exchange reserves it holds: The higher the reserves, the more it can afford the loss in reserves it is likely to sustain if it decreases the interest rate at a given exchange rate.

Key Term

- foreign-exchange reserves, 434

Exchange Rate Regimes

CHAPTER 21

In July 1944, representatives of 44 countries met in Bretton Woods, New Hampshire, to design a new international monetary and exchange rate system. The system they adopted was based on fixed exchange rates, with all member countries other than the United States pegging the price of their currency in terms of the dollar. In 1973, a series of exchange rate crises brought an abrupt end to the system—and an end to what is now called "the Bretton Woods period." Since then, the world has been characterized by many exchange rate arrangements. Some countries operate under flexible exchange rates; some operate under fixed exchange rates; some go back and forth between regimes. Which exchange rate regime is best for a country is one of the most debated issues in macroeconomics. This chapter discusses this issue.

- Section 21-1 looks at the medium run. It shows that, in contrast to the results we derived for the short run in Chapter 20, an economy ends up with the same real exchange rate and output level in the medium run, regardless of whether it operates under fixed exchange rates or flexible exchange rates. This obviously does not make the exchange rate regime irrelevant—the short run matters very much—but it is an important extension and qualification to our previous analysis.

- Section 21-2 looks at another aspect of fixed exchange rates, exchange rate crises. During a typical exchange rate crisis, a country operating under a fixed exchange rate is forced, often under dramatic conditions, to abandon its parity and to devalue. Such crises were behind the breakdown of the Bretton Woods system. They rocked the European Monetary System in the early 1990s, and were a major element of the Asian Crisis of the late 1990s. It is important to understand why they happen, and what they imply.

- Section 21-3 turns to the behavior of exchange rates under a flexible exchange rate regime. It shows that the behavior of exchange rates, and the relation of the exchange rate to monetary policy, are in fact more complex than we assumed in Chapter 20. Large fluctuations in the exchange rate, and the difficulty of using monetary policy to affect the exchange rate, make a flexible exchange rate regime less attractive than it appeared to be in Chapter 20.

- Section 21-4 puts these results together, reviewing the case for flexible or fixed rates. It discusses two recent and important developments, the move to a common currency in Europe, and the move towards strong forms of fixed exchange rate regimes, from currency boards to dollarization. ■

21-1 Fixed Exchange Rates and the Adjustment of the Real Exchange Rate in the Medium Run

The results we derived in Chapter 20, where we focused on the short run, drew a sharp contrast between the behavior of the economy under flexible exchange rates and under fixed exchange rates.

- Under flexible exchange rates, a country that needed to achieve a real depreciation—for example, to reduce its trade deficit or to get out of a recession—could do so by using monetary policy to decrease the interest rate and increase the exchange rate (achieve a depreciation).
- Under fixed exchange rates, a country lost both of these instruments: By definition, its nominal exchange rate was fixed, and thus could not be adjusted. And the fixed exchange rate and the interest parity condition implied that the country could not adjust its interest rate; the domestic interest rate had to remain equal to the foreign interest rate.

This appeared to make a flexible exchange rate regime much more attractive than a fixed exchange rate regime: Why give up two macroeconomic instruments? As we now shift focus from the short run to the medium run, you will see that this earlier conclusion needs to be qualified. While the conclusions about the short run were valid, you will see that, in the medium run, the difference between the two regimes fades away. More specifically, in the medium run, *the economy reaches the same real exchange rate and the same level of output, whether it operates under fixed exchange rates or under flexible exchange rates.*

The intuition for this result is straightforward. Recall the definition of the real exchange rate:

$$\epsilon = \frac{EP^*}{P}$$

The real exchange rate, ϵ, is equal to the nominal exchange rate, E (the price of foreign currency in terms of domestic currency); times the foreign price level, P^*, divided by the domestic price level, P. There are, therefore, two ways in which the real exchange rate can adjust:

- Through a change in the nominal exchange rate, E: This can be done only under flexible exchange rates. And if we assume the foreign price level, P^*, and the domestic price level, P, do not change in the short run, it is the only way to adjust the real exchange rate in the short run.
- Through a change in the domestic price level, P, relative to the foreign price level, P^*: In the medium run, this option is open even to a country operating under a fixed (nominal) exchange rate. And this is indeed what happens under fixed exchange rates. The adjustment takes place through the price level rather than through the nominal exchange rate.

Let us go through this argument step by step. To begin, let us derive the aggregate demand and aggregate supply relations for an open economy under fixed exchange rates.

Aggregate Demand Under Fixed Exchange Rates

Start from the condition for goods-market equilibrium we derived in Chapter 20, equation (20.1):

$$Y = C(Y - T) + I(Y, r) + G + NX(Y, Y^*, \epsilon) \qquad (21.1)$$

Warning: **The next paragraphs rely on what you learned in earlier chapters. Make sure you remember the definitions of: the real interest rate (Chapter 14), the real exchange rate (Chapter 18), and the interest rate parity condition (Chapter 18).**

This condition states that for the goods market to be in equilibrium, output must be equal to the demand for domestic goods—that is, the sum of consumption, investment, government spending, and net exports.

Next, recall the following relations:

- The real interest rate, r, equals the nominal interest rate, i^*, minus expected inflation, π^e:

$$r = i - \pi^e$$

- The real exchange rate, ϵ, is defined as

$$\epsilon = \frac{EP^*}{P}$$

- Under fixed exchange rates, the nominal exchange rate, E, is, by definition, fixed. Denote by $\bar{E}$ the value at which the nominal exchange rate is fixed, so,

$$E = \bar{E}$$

- Under fixed exchange rates and perfect capital mobility, the domestic interest rate, i, must be equal to the foreign interest rate, i^*:

$$i = i^*$$

Using these four relations, rewrite equation (21.1) as

$$Y = C(Y - T) + I(Y, i^* - \pi^e) + G + NX\left(Y, Y^*, \frac{\bar{E}P^*}{P}\right) \qquad (21.2)$$

This is a rich—and complicated—equilibrium condition. It tells us that in an open economy with fixed exchange rates, equilibrium output (or, more precisely, the level of output implied by equilibrium in the goods, financial, and foreign exchange markets) depends on:

- Government spending, G, and taxes, T. An increase in government spending increases output. So does a decrease in taxes.
- The foreign nominal interest rate, i^*, minus expected inflation, π^e. An increase in the foreign nominal interest rate requires a parallel increase in the domestic nominal interest rate. Given expected inflation, this increase in the domestic nominal interest rate leads to an increase in the domestic real interest rate, and, so, decreases demand and output.
- Foreign output, Y^*. An increase in foreign output increases exports, so increases net exports. The increase in net exports increases domestic output.
- The real exchange rate, ϵ, equal to the fixed nominal exchange rate, $\bar{E}$, times the foreign price level, P^*, divided by the domestic price level, P. An increase in the real exchange rate, equivalently, a real depreciation, leads to an increase in net exports, and so, to an increase in output.

We shall focus here on the effects of only three of these variables: the real exchange rate, government spending, and taxes. Let me write the relation between these three variables and output as

In the closed economy, we had to use both the *IS* and the *LM* relations to derive the aggregate demand relation. Under fixed exchange rates, we do not need the *LM* relation. The reason is that the nominal interest rate, rather than being determined jointly by the *IS* and *LM* relations, is determined by (must be equal to) the foreign interest rate. (The *LM* relation still holds, but, as we saw in Chapter 20, it simply determines the money stock.)

$$Y = Y\left(\frac{EP^*}{P}, G, T\right) \tag{21.3}$$
$$= \quad (\;+\;, +, -)$$

An increase in the real exchange rate—a real depreciation—increases output. So does an increase in government spending, or a decrease in taxes. All the other variables that affect output in equation (21.2) are taken as given and, to simplify notation, I simply omit them from equation (21.3).

Equation (21.3) gives us our *aggregate demand relation,* the relation between output and the price level implied by equilibrium in the goods market and in financial markets. As in the closed economy, this aggregate demand relation implies a negative relation between the price level and output. But, while the sign of the effect of the price level on output in the aggregate demand relation is the same as in the closed economy, the channel is very different:

In a closed economy:

$P\uparrow \Rightarrow (M/P)\downarrow \Rightarrow i\uparrow \Rightarrow Y\downarrow$

In an open economy with fixed exchange rates:

$P\uparrow \Rightarrow (EP^*/P)\downarrow \Rightarrow NX\downarrow \Rightarrow Y\downarrow$

- In the closed economy, the price level affects output through its effect on the real money stock and in turn on the interest rate.
- In the open economy under fixed exchange rates, the interest rate is fixed—pinned down by the foreign interest rate. The way the price level affects output here is, instead, through its effect on the real exchange rate. Given the fixed nominal exchange rate, $\bar{E}$, and the foreign price level, P^*, an increase in the domestic price level, P, leads to a decrease in the real exchange rate, $\bar{E}P^*/P$—a real appreciation. This real appreciation leads to a decrease in net exports, and a decrease in demand and, in turn, a decrease in output. Put simply, an increase in the price level makes domestic goods more expensive, thus decreasing the demand for domestic goods, and in turn decreasing output.

Equilibrium in the Short Run and in the Medium Run

The aggregate demand curve implied by equation (21.3) is drawn as the *AD* curve in Figure 21-1. It is downward sloping: An increase in the price level decreases output. As always, the relation is drawn for given values of all other variables, in this case, for given values of $\bar{E}$, P^*, G, and T.

For the aggregate supply curve, we rely on the relation we derived in the core. Going back to the *aggregate supply relation* we derived in Chapter 7, equation (7.2):

$$P = P^e(1+\mu)F\left(1-\frac{Y}{L}, z\right) \tag{21.4}$$

The price level, P, depends on the expected price level, P^e, and on the level of output, Y. Recall the two mechanisms at work:

- The expected price level matters because it affects nominal wages, which in turn affect the price level.

$P^e\uparrow \Rightarrow W\uparrow \Rightarrow P\uparrow$

- Higher output matters because it leads to higher employment, which leads to lower unemployment, which leads to higher wages, which lead to a higher price level.

$Y\uparrow \Rightarrow u\downarrow \Rightarrow W\uparrow \Rightarrow P\uparrow$

The aggregate supply curve is drawn as the *AS* curve in Figure 21-1 for a given value of the expected price level. It is upward sloping: Higher output leads to a higher price level.

The short-run equilibrium is given by the intersection of the aggregate demand curve and the aggregate supply curve, point *A* in Figure 21-1. As was the case in the closed economy, there is no reason why the short-run equilibrium level of output, Y,

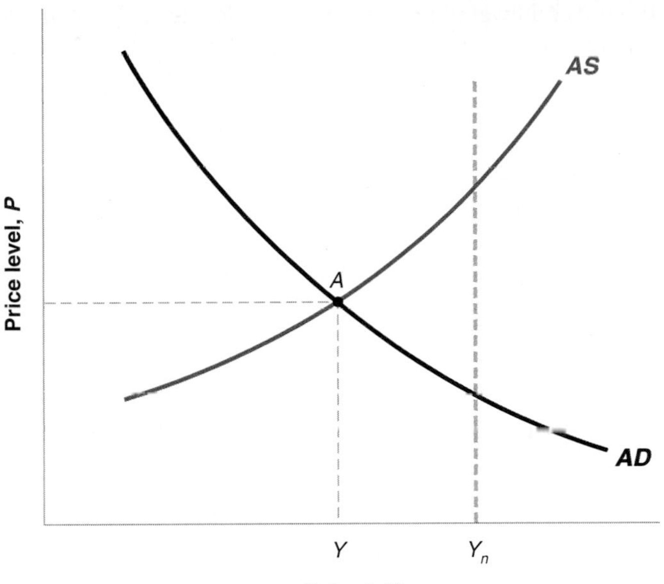

Figure 21-1

Aggregate Demand and Aggregate Supply in an Open Economy Under Fixed Exchange Rates

An increase in the price level leads to a real appreciation and a decrease in output: The aggregate demand curve is downward sloping. An increase in output leads to an increase in the price level: The aggregate supply curve is upward sloping.

should be equal to the natural level of output, Y_n. As the figure is drawn, Y is lower than Y_n, so output is below the natural level of output.

What happens over time? The basic answer is familiar from our earlier study of adjustment in a closed economy, and is shown in Figure 21-2. So long as output remains below the natural level of output, the aggregate supply shifts down. The reason: When output is below the natural level of output, the price level turns out to be lower than was expected. This leads wage setters to revise their expectation of the price level downward, leading to a lower price level at a given level of output, and thus a shift down of the aggregate supply curve. So, starting from *A*, the economy moves over time along the aggregate demand curve, until it reaches *B*. At *B*, output is equal to

Make sure you understand this step. If you need a refresher, return to Section 7-1.

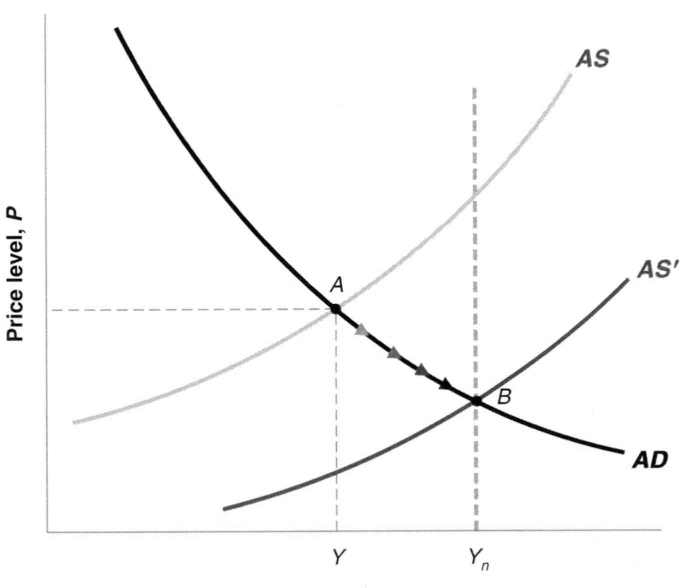

Figure 21-2

Adjustment Under Fixed Exchange Rates

The aggregate supply shifts down over time, leading to a decrease in the price level, to a real depreciation, and to an increase in output. The process ends when output has returned to the natural level of output.

The result that the price level decreases along the path of adjustment comes from our assumption that the foreign price level is constant. If we had assumed instead that the foreign price level was increasing over time, what would be needed is that the domestic price level increases less than the foreign price level, or, put another way, that domestic inflation is lower than foreign inflation for some time.

the natural level of output. The price level is lower than it was at A; by implication, the real exchange rate is higher than it was at A. In words: So long as output is below the natural level of output, the price level decreases. The decrease in the price level over time leads to a steady real depreciation. This real depreciation leads to an increase in output until output has returned to the natural level of output.

To summarize: In the medium run, despite the fact that the nominal exchange rate is fixed, the economy achieves the real depreciation needed to return output to its natural level. This is an important qualification to the conclusions we reached in the previous chapter—where we were focusing only on the short run:

- In the short run, a fixed nominal exchange rate implies a fixed real exchange rate.
- In the medium run, a fixed nominal exchange rate is consistent with an adjustment of the real exchange rate. The adjustment is achieved through movements in the price level.

The Case for and Against a Devaluation

The result that, even under fixed exchange rates, the economy returns to the natural level of output in the medium run, is important. But it does not eliminate the fact that the process of adjustment may be long and painful, during which output remains too low and unemployment remains too high for a long time. This raises the issue of whether there are faster and better ways to return output to normal. The answer, within the model we have just developed, is a clear yes.

Suppose that the government decides, while keeping the fixed exchange rate regime, to allow for a *one-time devaluation*. For a given price level, a devaluation (an increase in the nominal exchange rate) leads to a real depreciation (an increase in the real exchange rate), and thus to an increase in output. In other words, a devaluation shifts the aggregate demand curve to the right: Output is higher at a given price level.

This has a straightforward implication: A devaluation of the right size can take the economy directly from Y to Y_n. This is shown in Figure 21-3. Suppose the economy is

Figure 21-3

Adjustment with a Devaluation

The right size devaluation can shift aggregate demand to the right, leading the economy to point C. At point C, output is back to the natural level of output.

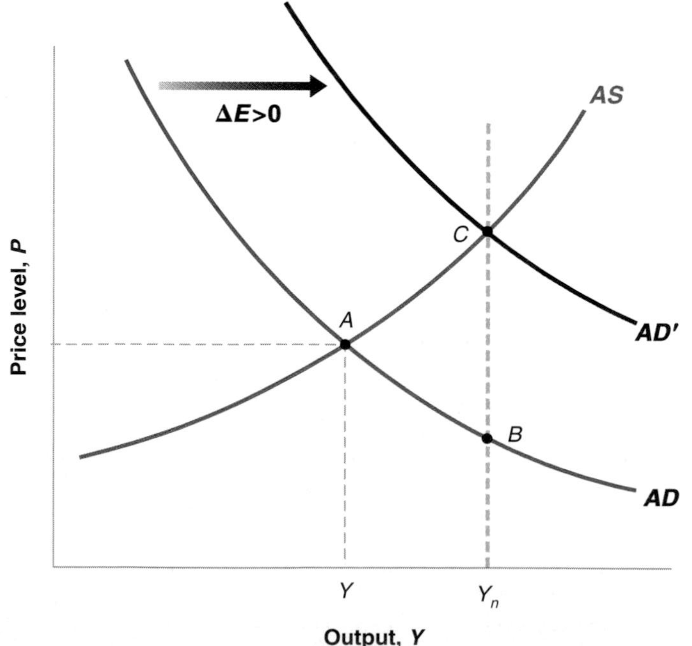

initially at A, the same point A as in Figure 21-2. The right size depreciation shifts the aggregate demand curve from AD to AD', taking the equilibrium from A to C. At C, output is equal to the natural level of output Y_n. The real exchange rate is the same as at B. (We know this because output is the same at points B and C. From equation [21.3], and without changes in G or T, this implies that the real exchange rate must also be the same.)

That the "right size" devaluation can return output to the natural level of output right away—rather than over time, as was the case absent the devaluation—sounds too good to be true—and, in practice, it is. Achieving the "right size" devaluation—the devaluation that takes output to Y_n right away—is easier to achieve in a graph than in reality:

- In contrast to our simple aggregate demand relation (21.3), the effects of the depreciation on output do not happen right away. As you saw in Chapter 19, the initial effects of a depreciation on output may be contractionary, as people pay more for imports, and the quantities of imports and exports have not yet adjusted.

See Section 19-5 on the J curve.

The Return of Britain to the Gold Standard: Keynes Versus Churchill

In 1925, Britain decided to return to the **gold standard.** The gold standard was a system in which each country fixed the price of its currency in terms of gold and stood ready to exchange gold for currency at the stated parity. This system implied fixed nominal exchange rates between countries.

The gold standard had been in place from 1870 until World War I. Because of the need to finance the war, and to do so in part by money creation, Britain suspended the gold standard in 1914. In 1925, Winston Churchill, then Britain's Chancellor of the Exchequer (the English equivalent of Secretary of the Treasury in the United States), decided to return to the gold standard, and to return at the prewar parity—that is, at the prewar value of the pound in terms of gold. But, because prices had increased faster in Britain than in many of its trading partners, returning to the prewar parity implied a large real appreciation: At the same nominal exchange rate as before the war, British goods were now more expensive relative to foreign goods. (Go back to the definition of the real exchange rate, $\epsilon = EP^*/P$: The price level in Britain, P, had increased more than the foreign price level, P^*. At a given nominal exchange rate, E, this implied that ϵ was lower, that Britain suffered from a real appreciation.)

Keynes severely criticized the decision to return to the prewar parity. In *The Economic Consequences of Mr. Churchill*, a book he published in 1925, Keynes argued as follows: If Britain was going to return to the gold standard, it should have done so at a higher price of gold in terms of currency, at a nominal exchange rate higher than the prewar nominal exchange rate. In a newspaper article, he articulated his views as follows:

> There remains, however, the objection to which I have never ceased to attach importance, against the return to gold in actual present conditions, in view of the possible consequences on the state of trade and employment. I believe that our price level is too high, if it is converted to gold at the par of exchange, in relation to gold prices elsewhere; and if we consider the prices of those articles only which are not the subject of international trade, and of services, i.e., wages, we shall find that these are materially too high—not less than 5 per cent, and probably 10 per cent. Thus, unless the situation is saved by a rise of prices elsewhere, the Chancellor is committing us to a policy of forcing down money wages by perhaps 2 shillings in the pound.
>
> I do not believe that this can be achieved without the gravest danger to industrial profits and industrial peace. I would much rather leave the gold value of our currency where it was some months ago than embark on a struggle with every trade union in the country to reduce money wages. It seems wiser and simpler and saner to leave the currency to find its own level for some time longer rather than force a situation where employers are faced with the alternative of closing down or of lowering wages, cost what the struggle may.
>
> For this reason, I remain of the opinion that the Chancellor of the Exchequer has done an ill-judged thing—ill judged because we are running the risk for no adequate reward if all goes well.

Keynes's prediction turned out to be right. While other countries were growing, Britain was in recession for the rest of the decade. Most economic historians attribute a good part of the blame to the initial overvaluation.

Source: "The Nation and Athenaeum," May 2, 1925.

- Also, in contrast to our simple aggregate supply relation (21.4), there is likely to be a direct effect of the devaluation on the price level. As the price of imported goods increases, the price of a consumption basket increases. This increase is likely to lead workers to ask for higher nominal wages, forcing firms to increase their prices as well.

But these complications do not affect the basic conclusion: Allowing the nominal exchange rate to adjust can help output return to its natural level, if not right away, at least faster than without a devaluation. And so, whenever a country under fixed exchange rates faces either a large trade deficit or a large recession, there is a lot of political pressure either to give up the fixed exchange rate regime altogether, or, at least, to have a one-time devaluation. Perhaps the most forceful presentation of this view was made nearly 80 years ago by Keynes, who argued against Winston Churchill's decision to return the British pound in 1925 to its pre–World War I parity. His arguments are presented in the Focus Box "The Return of Britain to the Gold Standard: Keynes Versus Churchill." Most economic historians believe that history proved Keynes right, and that overvaluation of the pound was one of the main reasons for Britain's poor economic performance after World War I.

Those who oppose a shift to flexible exchange rates or oppose a devaluation argue that there are good reasons to choose fixed exchange rates, and that too much willingness to devalue defeats the purpose of adopting a fixed exchange rate regime in the first place. They argue that too much willingness on the part of governments to consider devaluations actually leads to an increased likelihood of exchange rate crises. To understand their arguments, we now turn to these crises, what triggers them, and what their implications might be.

21-2 Exchange Rate Crises Under Fixed Exchange Rates

Suppose a country is operating under a fixed exchange rate. Suppose financial investors start believing there may soon be an exchange rate adjustment—either a devaluation or a shift to a flexible exchange rate regime accompanied by a depreciation.

We just saw why this might be the case:

- The domestic currency may be overvalued. A real depreciation is called for. While this could be achieved in the medium run without a devaluation, financial investors may conclude that the government will take the quickest way out—and devalue.

  Such an overvaluation often happens in countries that fix the nominal exchange rate while having an inflation rate higher than the inflation rate in the country they are pegging to. Higher relative inflation implies a steadily increasing price of domestic goods relative to foreign goods, a steady real appreciation, and so a steady worsening of the trade position. As time passes, the need for an adjustment of the real exchange rate increases, and financial investors become more and more nervous.
- Internal conditions may call for a decrease in the domestic interest rate. A decrease in the domestic interest rate cannot be achieved under fixed exchange rates. But it can be achieved if the country is willing to shift to a flexible exchange rate regime. If a country lets the exchange rate float and then decreases its domestic interest rate, we know from Chapter 20 that this will trigger an increase in the nominal exchange rate—a nominal depreciation.

As soon as financial markets believe a devaluation may be coming, then maintaining the exchange rate requires an increase, often a large one, in the domestic interest rate. To see this, return to the interest parity condition we derived in Chapter 18:

$$i_t = i_t^* + \frac{(E_{t+1}^e - E_t)}{E_t} \qquad (21.5)$$

Because it is more convenient, we use the approximation, equation (18.4), rather than the original interest parity condition, equation (18.2).

In Chapter 18, we interpreted this equation as a relation between the *one-year* domestic and foreign nominal interest rates, the current exchange rate, and the expected exchange rate a year hence. But the choice of one year as the period was arbitrary. The relation holds over a day, a week, a month. If financial markets expect the exchange rate to be 2% higher a month from now, they will hold domestic bonds only if the one-month domestic interest rate exceeds the one-month foreign interest rate by 2% (or, if we express interest rates at an annual rate, if the domestic interest rate exceeds the foreign interest rate by 2% × 12 = 24%).

Under fixed exchange rates, the current exchange rate, E_t, is set at some level, say, $E_t = \bar{E}$. If markets expect the parity will be maintained over the period, then $E_{t+1}^e = \bar{E}$, and the interest parity condition simply states that the domestic and the foreign interest rates must be equal.

Suppose, however, participants in financial markets start anticipating a devaluation—an increase in the exchange rate. Suppose they believe that, over the coming month, there is a 75% chance the parity will be maintained and a 25% chance there will be a 20% devaluation. The term $(E_{t+1}^e - E_t)/E_t$ in the interest parity equation (21.5), which we assumed equal to zero earlier, now becomes 0.75 × 0% + 0.25 × 20% (a 75% chance of no change plus a 25% chance of a devaluation of 20%), so equals 5%.

This implies that, if the central bank wants to maintain the existing parity, it must now offer a monthly interest rate 5% higher—60% higher at annual rate (12 months × 5% per month)! 60% is the interest differential needed to convince investors to hold domestic bonds rather than foreign bonds.

What, then, are the choices confronting the government and the central bank?

In most countries, the government is formally in charge of choosing the parity, the central bank formally in charge of maintaining it. In practice, choosing and maintaining the parity are joint responsibilities of the government and the central bank.

- First, they can try to convince markets they have no intention of devaluing. This is always the first line of defense: Communiqués are issued, and prime ministers or presidents appear on TV to reiterate their absolute commitment to the existing parity. But words are cheap, and they rarely convince financial investors.
- Second, the central bank can increase the interest rate, but by less than would be needed to satisfy equation (21.5)—in our example, by less than 60%. Although domestic interest rates are high, they are not high enough to fully compensate for the perceived risk of devaluation. This action typically leads to a large capital outflow, as financial investors still prefer to get out of domestic bonds and into foreign bonds. This implies selling domestic bonds, getting the proceeds in domestic currency, going to the foreign exchange market to sell domestic currency for foreign currency, and then buying foreign bonds. If the central bank did not intervene in the foreign exchange market, the large sales of domestic currency for foreign currency would lead to a depreciation. If it wants to maintain the exchange rate, the central bank must therefore stand ready to buy domestic currency and sell foreign currency at the current exchange rate. In doing so, it often loses most of its reserves of foreign currency. (The mechanics of central bank intervention were described in the appendix to Chapter 20.)
- Eventually—after a few hours or a few months—the choice for the central bank becomes either to increase the interest rate enough to satisfy equation (21.5) or to validate the market's expectations and devalue. Setting a very high short-term domestic interest rate can have a devastating effect on demand and on output.

In the summer of 1998, Boris Yeltsin announced that the Russian government had no intention of devaluing the ruble. Two weeks later, the ruble collapsed.

This course of action makes sense only if (1) the perceived probability of a devaluation is small, so the interest rate does not have to be too high, and (2) the government believes markets will soon become convinced that no devaluation is coming, allowing domestic interest rates to decrease. Otherwise, the only option is to devalue.

To summarize; expectations that a devaluation may be coming can trigger an exchange rate crisis. Faced with such expectations, the government has two options:

1. Give in and devalue, or

2. Fight and maintain the parity, at the cost of very high interest rates and a potential recession. Fighting may not work anyway: The recession may force the government to change policy later on, or force the government out of office.

An interesting twist here is that a devaluation may happen even if the belief that a devaluation was coming was initially groundless. Even if the government initially had no intention of devaluing, it may be forced to devalue if financial markets believe that it will devalue: The cost of maintaining the parity would be a long period of high interest rates and a recession; the government prefers to devalue instead.

The 1992 EMS Crisis

An example of the problems we discussed in this section is the exchange rate crisis that shook the European Monetary System (EMS) in the early 1990s.

At the start of the 1990s, the EMS appeared to work well. Started in 1979, it was an exchange rate system based on fixed parities with bands: Each member country (among them France, Germany, Italy, and, starting in 1990, the United Kingdom) had to maintain its exchange rate vis-à-vis all other member countries within narrow bands. The first few years had been rocky, with many **realignments**—adjustments of parities—among member countries, but, from 1987 to 1992, there were only two realignments. There was increasing talk about narrowing the bands further and even moving to the next stage—to a common currency.

See the Focus box in Chapter 5, "German Reunification and the German Monetary Fiscal Tug of War" and the Focus box in Chapter 20, "German Unification, Interest Rates, and the EMS." ▶

In 1992, however, financial markets became increasingly convinced that more realignments were soon to come. The reason was one we have seen already, namely, the macroeconomic implications of German reunification. Because of the pressure on demand coming from reunification, the Bundesbank (the German central bank) was maintaining high interest rates to avoid too large an increase in output and an increase in inflation in Germany. While Germany's EMS partners needed lower interest rates to reduce growing unemployment, they had to match the German interest rates to maintain their EMS parities. To financial markets, the position of Germany's EMS partners looked increasingly untenable. Lower interest rates outside Germany, and thus devaluations of many currencies vis-à-vis the DM, appeared increasingly likely.

Throughout 1992, the perceived probability of a devaluation forced several of Germany's trading partners to maintain higher nominal interest rates than Germany. But the first major crisis did not come until September 1992. The day-by-day story is told in the Focus box "Anatomy of a Crisis: The September 1992 EMS Crisis." The belief that several countries were soon going to devalue led in early September to speculative attacks on several currencies, with financial investors selling in anticipation of an oncoming devaluation. All the lines of defense described earlier were used by the monetary authorities and the governments of the countries under attack. First, solemn communiqués were issued, but with no discernible effect. Then, interest rates were increased, up to 500% for the **overnight interest rate** (the rate for lending and borrowing overnight) in Sweden (expressed at an annual rate). But they were not increased enough to prevent capital outflows and large losses of foreign exchange reserves by the central banks under pressure. Next came different courses of action in different countries: Spain devalued its exchange rate, Italy and the United Kingdom suspended their participation in the EMS, and France decided to tough it out through higher interest rates until the storm was over.

By the end of September, financial markets believed no further devaluations were imminent. Some countries were no longer in the EMS, others had devalued but remained in the EMS, and those that had maintained their parity had shown their determination to stay in the EMS, even if this meant very high interest rates. But the underlying problem—the high German interest rates—was still present, and it was only a matter of time until the next crisis. In November 1992, further speculation forced a devaluation of the Spanish peseta, the Portuguese escudo, and the Swedish krona. The peseta and the escudo were further devalued in May 1993. In July 1993, after yet another large speculative attack, EMS countries decided to adopt large fluctuation bands (plus or minus 15%) around central parities, in effect moving to a system that allowed for very large exchange rate fluctuations. This system with wider bands was kept until the adoption of a common currency in January 1999.

Anatomy of a Crisis: The September 1992 EMS Crisis

- September 5–6. The Ministers of Finance of the European Union meet in Bath, England. The official communiqué at the end of the meeting reaffirms their commitment to maintaining existing parities within the exchange rate mechanism (ERM) of the European Monetary System (EMS).
- September 8: The first attack. The attack comes not against one of the currencies in the EMS, but against the currencies of Scandinavian countries, which are also pegged to the DM. The Finnish authorities give in and decide to let their currency, the markka, **float**—that is, be determined in the foreign exchange market without central bank intervention. The markka depreciates by 13% vis-à-vis the DM. Sweden decides to maintain its parity and increases its overnight interest rate to 24% (at an annual rate). Two days later, it increases it further, to 75%.
- September 10–11: The second attack. The Bank of Italy intervenes heavily to maintain the parity of the lira, leading the bank to sustain large losses of foreign exchange reserves. But on September 13, the lira is devalued by 7% vis-à-vis the DM.
- September 16–17: The third attack. Speculation starts against the British pound, leading to large losses in foreign exchange reserves by the Bank of England. The Bank of England increases its overnight rate from 10 to 15%. However, speculation continues against both the pound and (despite the previous devaluation) against the lira. Both England and Italy announce they are temporarily suspending their participation in the ERM. Over the following weeks, both currencies depreciate by roughly 15% vis-à-vis the DM.
- September 16–17. With the pound and the lira out of the ERM, the attack turns against the other currencies. To maintain its parity, Sweden increases its overnight rate to 500%! Ireland increases its overnight rate to 300%. Spain decides to stay in the ERM, but to devalue by 5%.
- September 20. French voters narrowly approve the Maastricht Treaty (the treaty that sets the time table for the transition to a common currency) in a referendum. A negative vote would surely have amplified the crisis. The narrow, but positive, vote is seen as the sign that the worst may be over, and that the treaty will eventually be accepted by all EU members.
- September 23–28. Speculation against the franc forces the Banque de France to increase its short-term interest rate by 2.5%. To defend their parity without having to resort to very high short-term interest rates, both Ireland and Spain reintroduce capital controls.
- End of September. The crisis ends. Two countries, the United Kingdom and Italy, have left the ERM and let their currency depreciate. Spain remains within the ERM, but only after a devaluation. The other countries have maintained their parity, but, for some of them, at the cost of large reserve losses.

Source: World Economic Outlook, *October 1993.*

To summarize: The 1992 EMS crisis came from the perception by financial markets that the high interest rates forced by Germany upon its partners under the rules of the EMS were becoming very costly.

The belief that some countries might want to devalue or get out of the EMS led investors to ask for even higher interest rates, making it even more costly for those countries to maintain their parity.

In the end, some countries could not bear the cost; some devalued, some dropped out. Others remained in the system, but at a substantial cost in terms of output.

21-3 Exchange Rate Movements under Flexible Exchange Rates

In the model we developed in Chapter 20, there was a simple relation between the interest rate and the exchange rate: The lower the interest rate, the higher the exchange rate. This implied that a country that wanted to maintain a stable exchange rate just had to maintain its interest rate close to the foreign interest rate. A country that wanted to achieve a given depreciation just had to decrease its interest rate by the right amount.

See the relation between the two in Figure 20-1.

In reality, the relation between the interest rate and the exchange rate is not so simple. Exchange rates often move even absent movements in interest rates. The size of the effect of a given decrease in the interest rate on the exchange rate is hard to predict, making it much harder for monetary policy to achieve its desired outcome.

To see why things are more complicated, we must return once again to the interest parity condition we derived in Chapter 18 (equation 18.2):

$$1 + i_t = \left(\frac{1}{E_t}\right)(1 + i_t^*)(E_{t+1}^e)$$

Rewrite it as

$$E_t = \frac{1+i_t^*}{1+i_t}E_{t+1}^e \tag{21.6}$$

Think of the time period (from t to $t+1$) as one year. The exchange rate this year depends on the one-year domestic interest rate, the one-year foreign interest rate, and the exchange rate expected for next year. We assumed in Chapter 20 that the expected exchange rate next year (E_{t+1}^e) was constant. But this was a simplification. The exchange rate expected one year hence is not constant. Using equation (21.6), but now for next year, it is clear that the exchange rate next year will depend on next year's one-year domestic interest rate, the one-year foreign interest rate, and the exchange rate expected for the year after, and so on. So, any change in expectations of *current and future* domestic and foreign interest rates, as well as changes in the expected exchange rate in the far future, will affect the exchange rate today.

Let's explore this more closely. Write equation (21.6) for year $t+1$ rather than year, t:

$$E_{t+1} = \frac{1+i_{t+1}^*}{1+i_{t+1}}E_{t+2}^e$$

The exchange rate in year $t+1$ depends on the domestic interest rate and the foreign interest rate for year $t+1$, as well as on the expected future exchange rate in year $t+2$. So, the expectation of the exchange rate in year $t+1$, held as of year t, is given by

$$E_{t+1}^e = \frac{1+i_{t+1}^{*e}}{1+i_{t+1}^e}E_{t+2}^e$$

The expected exchange rate in year $t+1$ depends on the domestic interest rate expected for year $t+1$, the foreign interest rate expected for year $t+1$, and the expected future exchange rate in year $t+2$. Replacing E^e_{t+1} in equation (21.6) gives

$$E_t = \frac{(1+i^*_t)(1+i^{*e}_{t+1})}{(1+i_t)(1+i^e_{t+1})} E^e_{t+2}$$

The current exchange rate depends on both this year's and next year's expected domestic and foreign interest rates, and on the expected exchange rate two years from now. Continuing to solve forward in time in the same way (by replacing E^e_{t+2}, E^e_{t+3}, and so on until, say, year $t+n$) we get

$$E_t = \frac{(1+i^*_t)(1+i^{*e}_{t+1})\ldots(1+i^{*e}_{t+n})}{(1+i_t)(1+i^e_{t+1})\ldots(1+i^e_{t+n})} E^e_{t+n} \qquad (21.7)$$

Suppose we take n to be large, say, 10 years (equation [21.7] holds for any value of n). This relation tells us that the current exchange rate depends on two sets of factors:

- Current and expected domestic and foreign interest rates for each year over the next 10 years.
- The expected exchange rate 10 years from now.

For some purposes, it is useful to go further and derive a relation between current and expected future domestic and foreign *real* interest rates, the current *real* exchange rate, and the expected future *real* exchange rate. This is done in the appendix to this chapter. (The derivation is not much fun, but it is a useful way of brushing up on the relation between real interest rates and nominal interest rates, and real exchange rates and nominal exchange rates.) Equation (21.7) is sufficient, however, to make the three points I want to emphasize here:

1. Any factor that moves the expected future exchange rate, E_{t+n}, moves the current exchange rate, E_t. Indeed, if the domestic interest rate and the foreign interest rate are expected to be the same in both countries from t to $t+n$, the fraction on the right in equation (21.7) is equal to one, so the relation reduces to $E_t = E^e_{t+n}$: The effect of any change in the expected future exchange rate on the current exchange rate is one for one.

   If we think of n as large (say, 10 years or more), we can think of E_{t+n} as the exchange rate required to achieve current account balance in the medium or long run: Countries cannot borrow—run a current account deficit—forever, and will not want to lend—run a current account surplus—forever, either. Thus, any news that affects forecasts of the current account balance in the future is likely to have an effect on the expected future exchange rate, and, in turn, on the exchange rate today. For example, the announcement of a larger-than-expected trade deficit may lead investors to conclude that a depreciation will be needed at some point to reestablish trade balance. Thus, E^e_{t+n} will increase, leading in turn to an increase in E_t today.

2. Any factor that moves current or expected future domestic or foreign interest rates between year t and $t+n$ moves the current exchange rate. For example, given foreign interest rates, an increase in current or expected future domestic interest rates leads to a decrease in E_t, so to an appreciation.

   This implies that any variable that leads investors to change their expectations of future interest rates will lead to a change in the exchange rate today. For example, the "dance of the dollar" in the 1980s we discussed in earlier chapters— the sharp appreciation of the dollar in the first half of the decade, followed by an equally sharp depreciation later—can be largely explained by the movement in

◄ See Chapter 18 and Chapter 20.

For more on the relation between long-term interest rates and current and expected future short-term interest rates, go back to Chapter 15.

current and expected future U.S. interest rates relative to interest rates in the rest of the world during that period. During the first half of the 1980s, tight monetary policy and expansionary fiscal policy combined to increase both U.S. short-term interest rates and long-term interest rates, with the increase in long-term rates reflecting anticipations of high short-term interest rates in the future. This increase in both current and expected future interest rates was in turn the main cause of the dollar appreciation. Both fiscal and monetary policy were reversed in the second half of the decade, leading to lower U.S. interest rates, and a dollar depreciation.

3. The third implication follows from the first two. In reality, and in contrast to our analysis in Chapter 20, the relation between the interest rate i_t, and the exchange rate, E_t, is all but mechanical. When the central bank cuts the interest rate, financial markets have to assess whether this action signals a major shift in monetary policy and the cut in the interest rate is just the first of many such cuts, or whether this cut is just a temporary movement in interest rates. Announcements by the central bank may not be very useful: The central bank itself may not even know what it will do in the future. Typically, it will be reacting to early signals, which may be reversed later. Financial markets also have to assess how foreign central banks will react, whether they will stay put, or follow suit and cut their interest rates. All this makes it much harder to predict what the effect of the change in the interest rate will be on the exchange rate.

   Let's be more concrete. Go back to equation (21.7). Assume that $E^e_{t+n} = 1$. Assume that current and expected future domestic interest rates and current and expected future foreign interest rates are all equal to 5%. The current exchange rate is then given by

$$E_t = \frac{(1.05)^n}{(1.05)^n} 1 = 1$$

If this reminds you of our discussion of the effect of monetary policy on stock prices in Chapter 15, you are right. This is more than a coincidence: Like stock prices, the exchange rate depends very much on expectations of variables far into the future. How expectations change in response to a change in a current variable (here, the interest rate) very much determines the outcome.

Now consider a monetary expansion, which decreases the current domestic interest rate, i_t, from 5 to 3%. Will this lead to an increase in E_t—to a depreciation—and if so by how much? The answer: It all depends.

Suppose the interest rate is expected to be lower just for one year, so the $n - 1$ expected future interest rates are unchanged. The current exchange rate then increases to

$$E_t = \frac{(1.05)^n}{(1.03)(1.05)^{n-1}} = \frac{1.05}{1.03} = 1.02$$

The expansionary monetary policy leads to an increase in the exchange rate—a depreciation—of only 2%.

Suppose instead that when the current interest rate declines from 5 to 3%, investors expect the decline to last for five years (so $i_{t+4} = \ldots = i_{t+1} = i_t = 3\%$.) The exchange rate then increases to

$$E_t = \frac{(1.05)^n}{(1.03)^5(1.05)^{n-5}} = \frac{1.05^5}{1.03^5} = 1.10$$

The expansionary monetary policy now leads to an increase in the exchange rate—a depreciation—of 10%, a much larger effect.

You can surely think of yet other outcomes. Suppose investors had anticipated that the central bank was going to decrease interest rates, and the actual decrease turns out to be smaller than they anticipated. They will revise their expectations of future nominal interest rates *upward*, leading to an appreciation rather than a depreciation of the currency!

When, at the end of the Bretton Woods period, countries moved from fixed exchange rates to flexible exchange rates, most economists had expected that exchange rates would be stable. The large fluctuations in exchange rates that followed (and have continued to this day) came as a surprise. For some time, these fluctuations were thought to be the result of irrational speculation in foreign exchange markets. It was not until the mid-1970s that economists realized that these large movements could be explained, as we have here, by the rational reaction of financial markets to news about future interest rates and the future exchange rate. This has an important implication: A country that decides to operate under flexible exchange rates must accept the fact that it will be exposed to substantial exchange rate fluctuations over time.

The explanation was first given by Rudiger Dornbusch, from MIT, in 1976. More on his contribution in Chapter 27.

21-4 Choosing Between Exchange Rate Regimes

Let us now return to the question that motivates this chapter: Should countries choose flexible exchange rates or fixed exchange rates? Are there circumstances when flexible rates dominate, others when fixed rates dominate?

Much of what we have seen in this and the previous chapter would seem to favor flexible exchange rates:

- Section 21-1 argued that the exchange rate regime may not matter in the medium run. But it is still the case that it does in the short run. In the short run, countries that operate under fixed exchange rates and perfect capital mobility give up two macroeconomic instruments, the interest rate and the exchange rate. This not only reduces their ability to respond to shocks, but may also lead to exchange rate crises.
- Section 21-2 argued that the anticipation that a country that operates under a fixed exchange rate may have to devalue leads investors to ask for very high interest rates, making the economic situation worse, and putting more pressure on the country to devalue—so, another argument against fixed exchange rates.
- Section 21-3 introduced one argument against flexible exchange rates, namely, that under flexible exchange rates, the exchange rate may move a lot and may be difficult to control through monetary policy.

On net, it would appear that from a macroeconomic viewpoint, flexible exchange rates dominate fixed exchange rates. This indeed appears to be the consensus that has emerged among economists and policy makers.

The consensus goes like this: In general, flexible exchange rates are preferable, with two exceptions:

1. When a group of countries is already tightly integrated, in which case a common currency may be the right solution.

2. When the central bank cannot be trusted to follow a responsible monetary policy under flexible exchange rates. In this case, a strong form of fixed exchange rates, such as a currency board or dollarization, may provide a solution.

Let me discuss each of these two exceptions.

Common Currency Areas

Countries that operate under a fixed exchange rate regime are constrained to have the same interest rate. But how costly is that constraint? If the countries face roughly the same macroeconomic problems and the same shocks, they would have chosen similar

The Euro: A Short History

FOCUS

- As the European Union celebrated its thirtieth birthday in 1988, several governments decided that the time had come to plan a move to a common currency. They asked Jacques Delors, the president of the European Union, to prepare a report, which he presented in June 1989.

  The Delors report suggested moving to a European Monetary Union (EMU) in three stages:

  Stage I was the abolition of capital controls.

  Stage II was the choice of fixed parities, to be maintained except for "exceptional circumstances."

  Stage III was the adoption of a single currency.
- Stage I was implemented in July 1990.
- Stage II began in 1994, after the exchange rate crises of 1992–1993 had subsided. A new institution, the European Monetary Institute (EMI), was created to work out both the details of the transition and the rules of the new regime. A minor but symbolic decision involved choosing the name of the new common currency. The French liked "Ecu" (European currency unit), which is also an old French currency name. But its partners preferred **Euro,** and the name was adopted in 1995.
- In parallel, EU countries held referendums on whether they should adopt the **Maastricht Treaty.** The treaty, negotiated in 1991, set three main conditions for joining the EMU: low inflation, a budget deficit below 3%, and a public debt below 60%. The treaty was not very popular and, in many countries, the outcome of the popular vote was close. In France, the treaty passed with only 51% of the votes. In Denmark, the treaty was rejected.
- In 1996–1997, it looked as if few European countries would satisfy the Maastricht conditions. But several countries took drastic measures to reduce their budget deficit. When the time came to decide, in May 1998, which countries would be members of the Euro, 11 countries made the cut: Austria, Belgium, Finland, France, Germany, Italy, Ireland, Luxembourg, the Netherlands, Portugal, and Spain. The United Kingdom, Denmark, and Sweden decided to stay out, at least at the beginning. Greece did not qualify.
- Stage III started in January 1999. Parities between the 11 currencies and the Euro were "irrevocably" fixed. The new **European Central Bank (ECB)**, based in Frankfurt, became responsible for monetary policy for the Euro area. In 2001, Greece finally qualified and joined.

  From 1999 to 2002, the Euro existed as a unit of account but Euro coins and bank notes did not exist. In effect, the Euro area was still functioning as an area with fixed exchange rates. The next and final step was the introduction of Euro coins and bank notes in January 2002. For the first few months of 2002, national currencies and the Euro then circulated side by side, after which national currencies were taken out of circulation.

  Today, the Euro is the only currency used in the Euro area. The Euro area, as the group of member countries is called, has become a common currency area.

For more on the Euro, go to **www.euro.ecb.int/**

policies in the first place. Forcing them to have the same monetary policy may not be much of a constraint.

This is the same Mundell who put together the Mundell-Fleming model you saw in Chapter 20.

This argument was first explored by Robert Mundell, who looked at the conditions under which a set of countries might want to operate under fixed exchange rates, or even adopt a common currency. For countries to constitute an **optimal currency area**, Mundell argued, they need to satisfy one of two conditions:

- The countries have to experience similar shocks. We just saw the rationale for this: If they have similar shocks, then they would have chosen roughly the same monetary policy anyway.
- Or, if the countries experience different shocks, they must have high factor mobility. If workers, for example, are willing to move from countries that are doing poorly to countries that are doing well, factor mobility rather than macroeconomic policy can allow countries to adjust to shocks. When the unemployment rate is high in a country, workers leave that country to take jobs elsewhere, and the unemployment rate in that country decreases back to normal. If the unemployment rate is low, workers come to the country, and the unemployment rate in the country increases back to normal. The exchange rate is not needed.

Source: ECB

Following Mundell's analysis, most economists believe, for example, that the common currency area composed of the 50 states of the United States is close to an optimal currency area. True, the first condition is not satisfied: Individual states suffer from different shocks. California is more affected by shifts in demand from Asia than the rest of the United States. Texas is more affected by what happens to the price of oil, and so on. But the second condition is largely satisfied. There is considerable labor mobility across states in the United States. When a state does poorly, workers leave that state. When it does well, workers come to that state. State unemployment rates quickly return to normal, not because of state-level macroeconomic policy, but because of labor mobility.

Each U.S. state could have its own currency that freely floated against other state currencies. But this is not the way things are: The United States is a common currency area, with one currency, the U.S. dollar.

And there are clearly many advantages to the use of a common currency. For firms and consumers within the United States, the benefits of having a common currency are obvious; think of how complicated life would be if you had to change money every time you crossed a state line. The benefits go beyond these lower transaction costs. When prices are quoted in the same currency, it becomes much easier for buyers to compare prices, and competition between firms increases, benefiting consumers. Given these benefits and the limited macroeconomic costs, it makes good sense for the United States to have a single currency.

In adopting the Euro, Europe has made the same choice as the United States. When the process of conversion from national currencies to the Euro ended in early 2002, the Euro became the common currency for at least 12 European countries (look at the Focus box "The Euro: A Short History"). Is the economic argument for this new common currency area as compelling as it is for the United States?

There is little question that a common currency will yield for Europe many of the same benefits as it does for the United States. A report by the European Commission estimates that the elimination of foreign exchange transactions within the Euro area will lead to a reduction in costs of 0.5% of the combined GDP of these countries. There are also clear signs that the use of a common currency is already increasing competition. When shopping for cars, for example, European consumers are now looking for the lowest Euro price anywhere in the Euro area. This has already led to a decline in the price of cars in several countries.

There is, however, less agreement on whether Europe constitutes an optimal common currency area. This is because neither of the two Mundell conditions appears to be satisfied. While the future may be different, European countries have experienced very different shocks in the past; recall German reunification, and how differently it has affected Germany and the other European countries. And labor mobility is very low in Europe, and likely to remain so. Workers move much less *within* European countries than workers move within the United States. Given the language and cultural differences between European countries, mobility *between* countries is likely to

Argentina's Currency Board

FOCUS

When Carlos Menem became president of Argentina in 1989, he inherited an economic mess. Inflation was running at more than 30% a month. Output growth was negative.

Menem and his economy minister, Domingo Cavallo, quickly came to the conclusion that, under the circumstances, the only way to bring money growth—and, by implication, inflation—under control, was to peg the peso (Argentina's currency) to the dollar, and to do this through a very hard peg. So, in 1991, Cavallo announced that Argentina would adopt a currency board. The central bank would stand ready to exchange pesos for dollars, on demand. Furthermore, it would do so at the highly symbolic rate of one dollar for one peso.

The creation of a currency board and the choice of a symbolic exchange rate, both had the same purposes: To convince financial markets that the government was serious about the peg. And to make it more difficult for future governments to give up the parity and devalue. And so, by making the fixed exchange rate more credible in this way, decrease the risk of a foreign exchange crisis.

For a while, the currency board appeared to work extremely well. Inflation, which had exceeded 2,300% in 1990, was down to 4% by 1994! This was clearly the result of the tight constraints the currency board put on money growth. Even more impressive, this large decrease in inflation was accompanied by strong output growth. Output growth averaged 5% a year from 1991 to 1999.

Starting in 1999 however, growth turned negative, and Argentina went into a long and deep recession. Was the recession due to the currency board? Yes and no:

- **Throughout the second half of the 1990s, the dollar steadily appreciated vis-à-vis other major world currencies. Because the peso was pegged to the dollar, the peso also appreciated. By the late 1990s, it was clear that the peso was overvalued, leading to a decrease in demand for goods from Argentina, a decline in output, and an increase in trade deficit.**
- **The currency board was not fully responsible for the recession. There were other causes as well. But the currency board made it much harder to fight it: Lower interest rates and a depreciation of the peso would have helped the economy recover, but under the currency board this was not an option.**

In 2001, the economic crisis turned into a financial and an exchange rate crisis, along the lines we described in Section 21-2:

be even lower. The risk, therefore, is that, at some time in the future, one or more Euro members suffers from a large decline in demand and output, and can neither use the interest rate or use the exchange rate to increase activity. As we saw in Section 21-1, the adjustment will still take place in the medium run. But, as you also saw there, this adjustment may be long and painful. So far, such a pessimistic scenario has not yet taken place; some economists worry that it will in the future.

Hard Pegs, Currency Boards, and Dollarization

The second case for fixed exchange rates is very different from the first. It is based on the argument that there may be times when a country wants to limit its ability to use monetary policy. We shall look at this argument in more detail in Chapter 23, where we look at the dynamics of hyperinflation, and in Chapter 25, where we look at monetary policy in general—but the essence of the argument is simple.

Look at a country that has had very high inflation in the recent past. This may be, for example, because it was unable to finance its budget deficit by any other means than through money creation, resulting in high money growth and high inflation. Suppose the country decides to reduce money growth and inflation. One way of convincing financial markets that it is serious about reducing money growth is to fix its exchange rate: The need to use the money supply to maintain the parity then ties the hands of the monetary authority. To the extent that financial markets expect the parity

- Because of the recession, the fiscal deficit increased, leading to an increase in government debt. Worried that the government might default on its debt, financial investors started asking for very high interest rates on government debt, making the fiscal deficit even larger, and, by doing so, further increasing the risk of default.
- Worried that the government would give up the currency board and devalue in order to fight the recession, financial investors started asking for very high interest rates in pesos, making it more costly for the government to sustain the parity with the dollar, and so making it more likely that the currency board would be abandoned.

In December 2001, the government defaulted on part of its debt. In early 2002, it gave up the currency board, and let the peso float.

At the time of this writing, the macroeconomic situation in Argentina is glum. The peso has depreciated to 1.8 pesos for 1 dollar. Whether the government will repay its debt is unclear. What will happen to borrowers who had borrowed in dollars and must now pay back a much larger amount in pesos is equally unclear. Argentina has gone through three presidents in a month. The task facing the current president is a tough one.

Does this mean that the currency board was a bad idea? Economists still disagree.

- Some argue that it was a good idea, but it did not go far enough. Argentina should simply have dollarized, i.e., adopted the dollar as the currency, and eliminated the peso altogether. By eliminating the domestic currency, this solution would have eliminated the risk of a devaluation. The lesson, they argue, is that a currency board does not provide a sufficiently hard peg for the exchange rate. Only dollarization will do.
- Others argue that the currency board may have been a good idea at the start, but that it should not have been kept for so long. Once inflation was under control, Argentina should have moved from a currency board, and returned to a floating exchange rate regime. The problem is that Argentina kept the fixed parity with the dollar too long, to the point where the peso was overvalued, and an exchange rate crisis was inevitable.

The debate is likely to continue. Meanwhile, Argentina has to reconstruct its economy.

to be maintained, they will stop worrying about money growth being used to finance the budget deficit.

Note the qualifier "To the extent that financial markets expect the parity to be maintained." Fixing the exchange rate is not a magic solution. The country needs to convince financial investors that not only is the exchange rate fixed today, the exchange rate will remain fixed in the future. This has two implications:

1. Fixing the exchange rate must be part of a more general macroeconomic package. Fixing the exchange rate while continuing to run a large budget deficit will only convince financial markets that money growth will start again, and that a devaluation is soon to come.

2. Making it symbolically or technically harder to change the parity may also be useful, an approach known as a **hard peg**.

An extreme form of a hard peg is simply to replace the domestic currency with a foreign currency. Because the foreign currency typically chosen is the dollar, this is known as **dollarization**.

Few countries are willing, however, to give up their currency and adopt the currency of another country. A less extreme way is the use of a **currency board**. Under a currency board, a central bank stands ready to exchange foreign currency for domestic currency at the official exchange rate; furthermore, it cannot engage in open-market operations, that is, buy or sell government bonds.

When Israel was suffering from high inflation in the 1980s, an Israeli finance minister proposed dollarization as part of a stabilization program. His proposal was perceived as an attack on the sovereignty of Israel, and he was quickly fired.

Perhaps the best-known example of a currency board is that adopted by Argentina in 1991, but abandoned in a crisis at the end of 2001. The story is told in the Focus box "Argentina's Currency Board." Economists differ on what conclusions one should draw from what happened in Argentina. Some conclude that currency boards are not *hard* enough: They do not prevent exchange rate crises. So, if a country decides to adopt a fixed exchange rate, it should go all the way and dollarize. Others conclude that fixed exchange rates are a bad idea. If currency boards are used at all, they should be used for a short period of time, before the country returns to a floating exchange rate regime.

Summary

- Even under a fixed exchange rate regime, countries can adjust their *real* exchange rate in the medium run. They can do so by relying on adjustments in the price level. Nevertheless, the adjustment may be long and painful. Exchange rate adjustments allow the economy to adjust faster, and thus reduce the pain that comes from a long adjustment.
- Exchange rate crises typically start when participants in financial markets believe a currency may soon be devalued. Defending the parity then requires very high interest rates, with potentially large adverse macroeconomic effects. These adverse effects may force the country to devalue, even if there were no initial plans for such a devaluation.
- The exchange rate today depends both on (1) the difference between current and expected future domestic interest rates, and current and expected future foreign interest rates, and (2) the exchange rate expected in the future.

  Any factor that increases current or expected future domestic interest rates leads to a decrease in the exchange rate today.

  Any factor that increases current or expected future foreign interest rates leads to an increase in the exchange rate today.

  Any factor that changes expectations of the exchange rate in the future leads to a change in the exchange rate today.
- There is wide agreement among economists that flexible exchange regimes generally dominate fixed exchange rate regimes, except in two cases:

1. When a group of countries is highly integrated and forms an optimal currency area. (You can think of a common currency for a group of countries as an extreme form of fixed exchange rates among this group of countries.) For countries to form an optimal currency area, they must either face largely similar shocks, or there must be high labor mobility between these countries.

2. When a central bank cannot be trusted to follow a responsible monetary policy under flexible exchange rates. In this case, a strong form of fixed exchange rates such as dollarization or a currency board, provides a way of tying the hands of the central bank.

Key Terms

- gold standard, 443
- realignments, 446
- overnight interest rate, 446
- float, 447
- optimal currency area, 452
- Euro, 452
- Maastricht Treaty, 452
- European central bank (ECB), 452
- hard peg, 456
- dollarization, 456
- currency board, 456

Questions and Problems

Quick Check

1. Using the information in this chapter, label each of the following statements true, false, *or* uncertain. *Explain briefly.*

a. Britain's return to the gold standard caused years of high unemployment.

b. Investors who suddenly expect a large devaluation in a country operating under a fixed exchange rate may force a crisis.

c. Because speculative behavior by foreign investors can cause currency crises, small countries would be better off not allowing foreigners to hold domestic assets.

d. The countries of southeast Asia should form a common currency area as they produce similar goods, and are subject to largely similar shocks.

e. The large number of immigrants from Mexico to the United States every year indicates there is substantial labor mobility between the two countries, and thus they constitute an optimal currency area.

2. Consider the specification of the aggregate demand relation in an open economy with fixed exchange rates given in equation (21.2):

$$Y = C(Y-T) + I(Y, i^* - \pi^e) + G + NX\left(Y, Y^*, \frac{\overline{E}P^*}{P}\right)$$

Discuss the effects on output, given the domestic price level, of

a. An increase in the foreign price level. Explain in words.

b. An increase in expected inflation. Explain in words.

c. Discuss the following: "Why do economists say inflation is bad? High inflation abroad, and high expected inflation at home, both increase output."

3. Consider a country operating under fixed exchange rates, with aggregate demand and aggregate supply given by

$$Y_t = Y\left(\frac{\overline{E}P^*}{P_t}, G, T\right)$$

$$P_t = P_{t-1}(1+\mu)F\left(1 - \frac{Y_t}{L}, z\right)$$

Assume the economy is initially in medium run equilibrium, with constant prices and output equal to the natural level of output. Describe the short-run and the medium-run effects of an increase in government spending on

a. Output, the real exchange rate, the interest rate.

b. The components of spending: consumption, investment, and net exports.

c. Comment on the proposition: "Budget deficits lead to trade deficits."

4. Expected nominal and real depreciations. (This problem is based on the appendix to this chapter.)

Assume that the one-year nominal interest rate is 10% at home and 6% abroad. Further, assume inflation over the coming year is expected to be 6% at home and 3% abroad. Suppose interest parity holds.

a. What must be the expected annual nominal depreciation of the domestic currency over the coming year?

b. What must be the expected annual real depreciation?

c. If you expected a nominal appreciation of the currency over the coming year, which bond would you purchase?

Dig Deeper

5. When East and West Germany were reunited in 1990, the exchange rate between the two countries was fixed forever. In a symbolic gesture of equality between the two countries, it was decreed that one East German mark would be worth the same as one West German mark, while the currency of the East was probably worth much less.

a. Think of East Germany as the domestic economy. Suppose East Germany was initially in medium-run equilibrium before reunification (obviously a counterfactual assumption here, but one has to start somewhere!) and suppose that the exchange rate (vis-à-vis West Germany) was then set much too low. Discuss the impact of that decision on equilibrium output and unemployment in East Germany using the *AS-AD* model. Explain in words.

b. What is the adjustment process back to the medium-run equilibrium?

c. Suppose that prices in Western Germany are constant—that there is no inflation. What has to happen to prices and wages in Eastern Germany?

6. In January 1999, Brazil was forced to devalue its currency, the "real," by 8% against the dollar despite receiving a multibillion-dollar package from the IMF in November to defend the currency. During the week before the devaluation, Brazilian stock prices decreased by nearly half. But after the devaluation was announced, the stock market indices returned to their precrisis levels.

Can you explain these movements in equity prices, both before and after the devaluation?

(To read more about the crisis itself, check out the January 16–22, 1999, issue of The Economist, *either in your library or in an online archive at* **www.economist.com***)*

We Invite you to visit the Blanchard page on the Prentice Hall Web site at:
www.prenhall.com/blanchard
for this chapter's World Wide Web exercises

Appendix: The Real Exchange Rate, and Domestic and Foreign Real Interest Rates

We derived in Section 21-3 a relation between the current nominal exchange rate, current and expected future domestic and foreign nominal interest rates, and the expected future nominal exchange rate (equation [21.7]). This appendix derives a similar relation, but in terms of real interest rates and the real exchange rate. It then briefly discusses how this alternative relation can be used to think about movements in the real exchange rate.

Deriving the Real Interest Parity Condition

Start from the nominal interest parity condition, equation (18.2):

$$(1+i_t) = (1+i_t^*)\frac{E^e_{t+1}}{E_t}$$

Recall the definition of the real interest rate from Chapter 14, equation (14.3):

$$(1+r_t) \equiv \frac{(1+i_t)}{(1+\pi^e_t)}$$

where $\pi^e_t \equiv (P^e_{t+1} - P_t)/P_t$ is the expected rate of inflation. Similarly, the foreign real interest rate is given by

$$(1+r_t^*) = \frac{(1+i_t^*)}{(1+\pi_t^{*e})}$$

where $\pi_t^{*e} \equiv (P^{*e}_{t+1} - P^*_t)/P^*_t$ is the expected foreign rate of inflation.

Use these two relations to eliminate nominal interest rates in the interest-parity condition, so,

$$(1+r_t) = (1+r_t^*)\left[\frac{E^*_{t+1}(1+\pi_t^{*e})}{E_t(1+\pi^e_t)}\right] \qquad (21.A1)$$

Note from the definition of inflation that $(1+\pi^e_t) = P^e_{t+1}/P_t$ and, similarly, $(1+\pi_t^{*e}) = P^{*e}_{t+1}/P^*_t$.

Using these two relations in the term in brackets gives

$$\frac{E^e_{t+1}(1+\pi_t^{*e})}{E_t(1+\pi^e_t)} = \frac{E^e_{t+1}P^{*e}_{t+1}/P^*_t}{E_t P^e_{t+1}/P_t}$$

Reorganizing terms:

$$\frac{E^e_{t+1}P^{*e}_{t+1}/P^*_t}{E_t P^e_{t+1}/P_t} = \frac{E^e_{t+1}P^{*e}_{t+1}/P^e_{t+1}}{E_t P^*_t/P_t}$$

Using the definition of the real exchange rate at time t and time $t+1$:

$$\frac{E^e_{t+1}P^{*e}_{t+1}/P^e_{t+1}}{E_t P^*_t/P_t} = \frac{\epsilon^e_{t+1}}{\epsilon_t}$$

Replacing in equation (21.A1) gives

$$(1+r_t) = (1+r_t^*)\frac{\epsilon^e_{t+1}}{\epsilon_t}$$

Or, equivalently,

$$\epsilon_t = \frac{1+r_t^*}{1+r_t}\epsilon^e_{t+1} \qquad (21.A2)$$

The real exchange rate today depends on the domestic and foreign real interest rates this year, and the expected future real exchange rate next year. This equation corresponds to equation (21.6) in the text, but now in terms of the real rather than nominal exchange rate and interest rates.

Solving the Real Interest Parity Condition Forward

The next step is to solve equation (21.A2) forward, exactly in the same way as we did it for equation (21.6) in the text. The equation above implies that the real exchange rate in year $t+1$ is given by

$$\epsilon_{t+1} = \frac{1+r^*_{t+1}}{1+r_{t+1}}\epsilon^e_{t+2}$$

Taking expectations, as of year t:

$$\epsilon^e_{t+1} = \frac{1+r^{*e}_{t+1}}{1+r^e_{t+1}}\epsilon^e_{t+2}$$

Replacing in the previous relation:

$$\epsilon_t = \frac{(1 + r_t^*)(1 + r_{t+1}^{*e})}{(1 + r_t)(1 + r_{t+1}^e)} \epsilon_{t+2}^e$$

Solving for ϵ_{t+2}^e and so on gives

$$\epsilon_t = \frac{(1 + r_t^*)(1 + r_{t+1}^{*e})\ldots(1 + r_{t+n}^{*e})}{(1 + r_t)(1 + r_{t+1}^e)\ldots(1 + r_{t+n}^e)} \epsilon_{t+n}^e$$

This relation gives the current real exchange rate as a function of the difference between current and expected future domestic real interest rates and current and expected future foreign real interest rates, and of the expected real exchange rate in year $t + n$.

The advantage of this relation over the relation we derived in the text between the nominal exchange rate and nominal interest rates, equation (21.7), is that it is typically easier to predict the future real exchange rate than to predict the future nominal exchange rate. If, for example, the economy suffers from a large trade deficit, we may be fairly confident that there will have to be a real depreciation—that ϵ_{t+n}^e will have to be higher. Whether there will be a nominal depreciation—what happens to E_{t+n}^e—is harder to tell: It depends on what happens to inflation, both at home and abroad over the next n years.

Pathologies

Sometimes, (macroeconomic) things go very wrong: There is a sharp drop in output. Or unemployment remains high for very long. Or inflation increases to very high levels. These pathologies are the focus of the next two chapters.

Chapter 22

Chapter 22 looks at depressions and slumps, periods during which output drops far below and stays far below the natural level of output. The chapter discusses the adverse effects of deflation, and what happens when an economy is caught in a liquidity trap. It then looks at the Great Depression, what triggered it, what made it so bad, and what eventually led to recovery. It then turns to the current Japanese economic slump, a slump that started in the early 1990s, and is still ongoing today. It shows that many of the factors that contributed to the Great Depression are also operating in Japan today.

Chapter 23

Chapter 23 looks at episodes of high inflation, from Germany in the early 1920s to Latin America in the 1980s and early 1990s. It shows the role of both fiscal and monetary policy in generating high inflation. Budget deficits lead to high nominal money growth. High nominal money growth leads to high inflation. It then looks at how high inflations end, and at the role and the nature of stabilization programs.

Depressions and Slumps

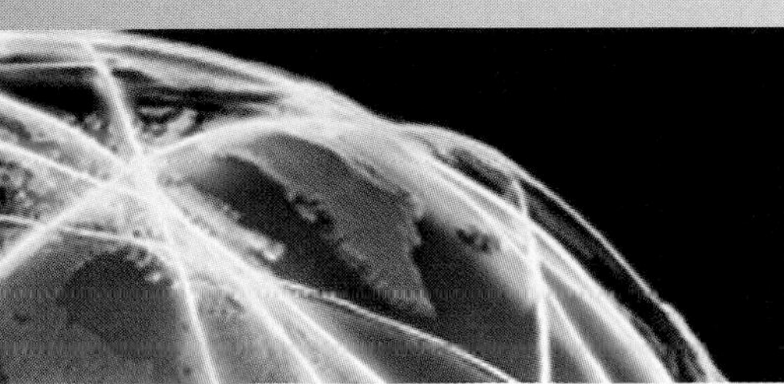

A major theme of this book so far has been that, while economies go through fluctuations in the short run, they tend to return to normal in the medium run. An adverse shock may lead to a recession, but fairly quickly the economy turns around, and output returns to its natural level.

Most of the time, this is what happens. But once in a while, things go wrong. Output remains far below its natural level for many years. Unemployment remains stubbornly high. Simply put, the economy appears to be stuck, unable to return to normal. The most infamous case is surely that of the Great Depression, which affected most of the world from the late 1920s to the start of World War II. (While there is no agreed-upon definition, economists use **depression** to describe a deep and long-lasting recession.) For a long time after the Great Depression, economists were confident that they had learned their lessons: Macroeconomic policy could ensure such a depression would never happen again. Now, they are not so confident. Since the early 1990s, Japan has been in a prolonged economic slump. (Again, while there is no agreed-upon definition, most economists use **slump** to denote a long period of low or no growth, longer than a typical recession, but less deep than a depression.) While not as bad as the Great Depression, the Japanese slump shares many features with the Great Depression. And, at the time of this writing, it is far from clear how the Japanese economy will emerge from its slump and return to growth.

What goes wrong in such episodes?

Are the shocks particularly bad?

Do the usual adjustment mechanisms break down?

Or, are macroeconomic policies particularly misguided?

These are the questions we take up in this chapter.

- Section 22-1 looks at two of the mechanisms which have played a central role in both the Great Depression and in Japan: The adverse effects of deflation, and the liquidity trap.
- Section 22-2 then gives an account of the Great Depression.
- Section 22-3 does the same for the Japanese slump. ■

22-1 Disinflation, Deflation, and the Liquidity Trap

Let's go back to the argument we developed earlier about why output tends to return to the natural level of output in the medium run. The easiest way to present the argument is in terms of the *IS-LM* graph in Figure 22-1, with the nominal interest rate on the vertical axis, output on the horizontal axis.

The argument we developed in Chapter 7 went like this:

Recall that the natural level of output is the level of output that prevails when the unemployment rate is equal to the natural unemployment rate. See Chapter 6.

- Suppose an adverse shock has led to a decrease in output, so the economy is at point *A*, with a level of output, *Y*, below the natural level of output, Y_n. The nature of the shock is not important here: It could be a decrease in spending by consumers, or a decrease in investment spending by firms. What is important here is that output is now below the natural level of output.
- The fact that output is below the natural level of output will lead, in turn, to a decrease in the price level over time. Given the nominal money stock, the decrease in the price level will increase the real money stock. This increase in the real money stock will shift the *LM* curve down, leading to a lower interest rate and higher output. After some time, the economy will be, for example, at point *B*, with output equal to Y'.
- So long as output remains below its natural level, the price level will continue to decrease, the *LM* curve will continue to shift down. The economy will move down the *IS* curve until it reaches point *C*, and output has returned to Y_n. In short, output below the natural level of output will lead to a decrease in the price level, which will continue until the economy has returned to normal.

For given *M*: $P\downarrow \Rightarrow M/P\uparrow \Rightarrow$ *LM* shifts down, $Y\uparrow$.

The argument in Chapter 7 was based on the strong simplifying assumption that the nominal money stock was constant. This implied that in the medium run, the price level was also constant. And it also implied that if output was below the natural level of output, the adjustment of output back to its natural level was achieved through a *decrease* in the price level—something we rarely observe in practice. Chapters 8 and 9 explored a more realistic version of the model, where we

Figure 22-1

The Return of Output to Its Natural Level

Low output leads to a decrease in the price level. The decrease in the price level leads to an increase in the real money stock. The *LM* curve shifts down. The *LM* curve continues to shift down until output has returned to the natural level of output.

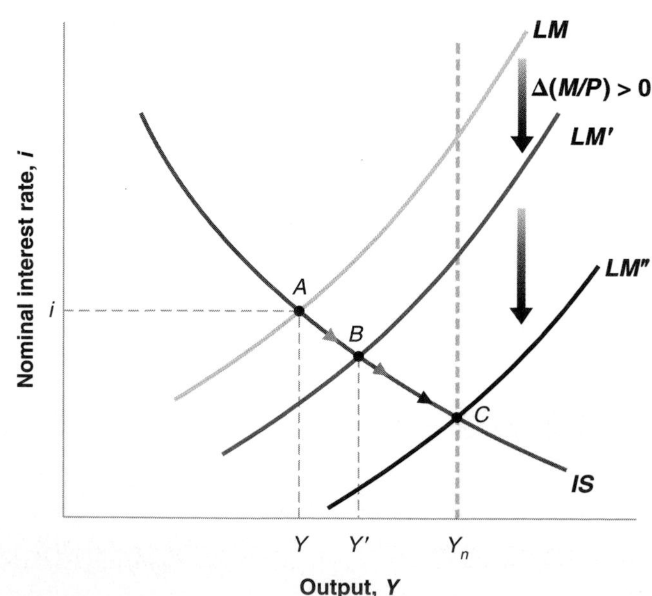

allowed for positive nominal money growth—and so allowed for positive inflation in the medium run. This model gave a richer description of the adjustment of output and inflation to shocks. But, for our present purposes, it delivered the same basic implication as the simpler version of the model presented in Chapter 7: The economy will tend to return to the natural level of output over time.

The argument goes now as follows:

- Suppose that, as in Figure 22-1, output is below the natural level of output—equivalently, the unemployment rate is higher than the natural rate of unemployment.

  Then, from the Phillips curve relation, inflation will decrease over time.
- Suppose nominal money growth and inflation were initially equal to each other, so real money growth (the difference between nominal money growth and inflation) was initially equal to zero.

  If inflation decreases, and so, becomes lower than the rate of nominal money growth, then real money growth will now turn positive. Equivalently, the real money stock will increase.
- This increase in the real money stock will shift the *LM* curve down, leading to an increase in output. The *LM* curve will continue to shift down until, eventually, output is back to the natural level of output.

  So, the adjustment looks the same as in Figure 22-1: Lower output will lead to an increase in the real money stock, until output is back to the natural level of output.

From equation (8.10): If the unemployment rate exceeds the natural rate of unemployment, inflation decreases.

Assume the rate of nominal money growth, g_m, and the rate of inflation, π, are initially equal: $g_m = \pi$.
Then, for given g_m
$\pi\downarrow \Rightarrow g_m - \pi > 0 \Rightarrow$
$M/P\uparrow \Rightarrow$ *LM* shifts down, $Y\uparrow$.

It would therefore appear that economies have a strong built-in stabilizing mechanism to lift them out of recessions:

- Output below the natural level of output leads to lower inflation.
- Lower inflation leads in turn to higher real money growth.
- Higher real money growth leads to an increase in output over time.

The study of depressions and slumps tells us, however, that this built-in mechanism is not foolproof, and that things may go wrong in several ways. We now look at some of them.

The Nominal Interest Rate, the Real Interest Rate, and Expected Inflation

Looking at the adjustment of output in Figure 22-1, we ignored the distinction between the nominal interest rate and the real interest rate. We need now to reintroduce this distinction. Recall from Chapter 14 that

- What matters for spending decisions, and thus what enters the *IS* relation, is the *real interest rate*—the interest rate in terms of goods.
- What matters for the demand for money, and thus what enters the *LM* relation, is the *nominal interest rate*—the interest rate in terms of dollars.

Recall also the relation between the two interest rates: The real interest rate is equal to the nominal interest rate minus expected inflation.

Let r be the real interest rate, i be the nominal interest rate, and π^e be expected inflation. Then, from equation (14.4): $r = i - \pi^e$.

What this distinction between the two interest rates implies is shown in Figure 22-2. Suppose the economy is initially at *A*: Output is initially below the natural level of output.

Because output is below the natural level of output, inflation decreases.

- The decrease in inflation leads to an increase in the real money stock and a shift in the *LM* curve down, from *LM* to *LM'*. The shift of the *LM* curve—due to the

Figure 22-2

The Effects of Lower Inflation on Output

When inflation decreases in response to low output, there are two effects. (1) The real money stock increases, leading the *LM* curve to shift down. (2) Expected inflation decreases, leading to a shift of the *IS* curve to the left. The result may be a further decrease in output.

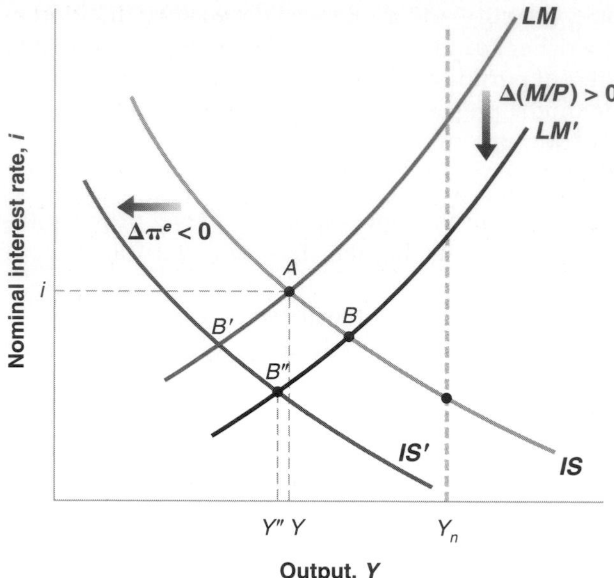

increase in M/P—is the shift we saw in Figure 22-1. This shift of the *LM* curve tends to increase output. If this were the only shift, the economy would go from *A* to *B*.

- But there is now a second effect at work: Suppose the decrease in inflation leads to a decrease in expected inflation. Then, for a given nominal interest rate, the decrease in expected inflation increases the real interest rate. The higher real interest rate leads in turn to lower spending and lower output. So, at a given nominal interest rate, the level of output implied by equilibrium in the goods market is lower. The *IS* curve shifts to the left, from *IS* to *IS'*. The shift in the *IS* curve—due to the decrease in π^e—tends to decrease output. If this were the only shift, the economy would go from *A* to *B'*.

$r = i - \pi^e$. So, for a given i, $\pi^e \downarrow \Rightarrow r \uparrow \Rightarrow Y \downarrow$. The *IS* curve shifts to the left.

Does output go up or down as a result of these two shifts? The answer: We cannot tell. The combined effect of the two shifts is to move the economy from *A* to *B''*, with output *Y''*. Whether *Y''* is greater or smaller than *Y* depends on which shift dominates, and is in general ambiguous.

As I have drawn the figure, *Y''* is smaller than *Y*. In this case, rather than returning to its natural level, output declines further away from it: Things get worse rather than better.

A numerical example will help you keep straight the two effects of inflation on output:

In Chapter 9, you saw that in the medium run, inflation is equal to nominal money growth minus normal output growth. The example assumes for simplicity that normal output growth is zero, so inflation and nominal money growth are equal.

- Suppose nominal money growth, inflation, and expected inflation are all equal initially to 5%.

  Suppose the nominal interest rate is equal to 7%, so the real interest rate is equal to 7% – 5% = 2%.
- Suppose that because output is lower than the natural level of output, inflation decreases from 5 to 3% after a year.
- Real money growth—nominal money growth minus inflation—is now equal to 5% – 3% = 2%. Equivalently, the real money stock increases by 2%.

  Suppose this increase in the real money stock leads to a decrease in the nominal interest rate from, say, 7 to 6%. This is the first effect you saw above: Lower inflation leads to an increase in the real money stock, and a lower nominal interest rate.

- Suppose the decrease in inflation leads people to expect that inflation this year will be 2% lower than it was last year, so expected inflation decreases from 5 to 3%.

  This implies that, at any given nominal interest rate, the real interest rate increases by 2%. This is the second effect you saw earlier: At a given nominal interest rate, lower expected inflation leads to an increase in the real interest rate.
- Combining the two effects, the nominal interest rate decreases from 7 to 6%. Expected inflation decreases from 5 to 3%. So, the real interest rate moves from 7% − 5% = 2% to 6% − 3% = 3%.

  In words: The net effect of lower inflation is to increase the real interest rate, not to decrease it.

We have just looked at what happens at the start of the adjustment process. But it is easy to describe a scenario in which things go from bad to worse over time. The decrease in output from Y to Y'' leads to a further decrease in inflation, a further decrease in expected inflation. This leads to a further increase in the real interest rate, which leads to a further decrease in output, and so on. In other words, the initial recession can turn into a full-fledged depression, with output continuing to decline rather than returning to the natural level of output. The stabilizing mechanism we described in earlier chapters simply breaks down.

The Liquidity Trap

One reaction to the scenario just described is to conclude that, while we should worry about it, it can easily be avoided by the appropriate use of macroeconomic policy, in particular, monetary policy: The scenario was derived under the assumption that monetary policy (in our case, the rate of growth of nominal money) remained unchanged. But if the central bank is worried about a decrease in output, it would seem that all it needs to do is to embark on an expansionary monetary policy. In terms of Figure 22-2, all the central bank needs to do is to increase the stock of nominal money to shift the *LM* curve down further, and make sure that the shift in the *LM* curve will be enough to increase output.

That monetary policy can and should be used in this context is clearly the right prescription. But there is a limit to what the central bank can do: It cannot decrease the nominal interest rate below zero. If expected inflation is low or even negative (if people expect a deflation), the implied real interest rate may still not be low enough to get the economy out of a recession. This issue is at the center of discussions about Japan today. Let's now look at it more closely.

Go back first to our characterization of the demand and the supply of money in Chapter 4. There, we drew the demand for money, for a given level of income, as a decreasing function of the nominal interest rate. The lower the nominal interest rate, the larger the demand for money—equivalently, the smaller the demand for bonds. What we did not ask in Chapter 4 is what happens when the interest rate goes down to zero. The answer: Once people hold enough money for transaction purposes, they are then indifferent to holding the rest of their financial wealth in the form of money or in the form of bonds. The reason they are indifferent is that both money and bonds pay the same nominal interest rate, namely, zero. Thus, the demand for money is as shown in Figure 22-3:

◀ Look at Figure 4-1. We avoided the issue, by not drawing the demand for money for interest rates close to zero. . . .

- As the nominal interest rate decreases, people want to hold more money (and thus fewer bonds): The demand for money increases.

Figure 22-3

Money Demand, Money Supply, and the Liquidity Trap

As the nominal interest rate decreases to zero, once people have enough money for transaction purposes, they are indifferent between holding money and holding bonds. The demand for money becomes horizontal. This implies that, when the nominal interest rate is equal to zero, further increases in the money supply have no effect on the nominal interest rate.

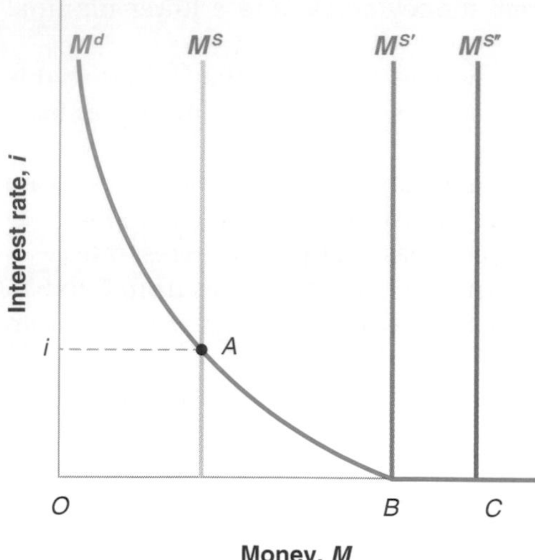

- As the nominal interest rate becomes equal to zero, people want to hold an amount of money at least equal to the distance *OB*: This is what they need for transaction purposes. But they are willing to hold even more money (and therefore hold fewer bonds) because they are indifferent between money and bonds. Therefore, the demand for money becomes horizontal beyond point *B*.

Now consider the effects of an increase in the money supply.

- Consider the case where the money supply is M^s, so the nominal interest rate consistent with financial market equilibrium is positive and equal to i (this is the case we considered in Chapter 4). Starting from that equilibrium in Figure 22-3, an increase in the money supply—a shift of the M^s line to the right—leads to a decrease in the nominal interest rate.
- Now consider the case where the money supply is $M^{s\prime}$, so the equilibrium is at point *B*; or consider the case where the money supply is $M^{s\prime\prime}$, so the equilibrium is given at point *C*. In either case, the initial nominal interest rate is zero. And, in either case, an increase in the money supply has no effect on the nominal interest rate. Think of it this way: Suppose the central bank increases the money supply. It does so through an open-market operation in which it buys bonds and pays for them by creating money. As the nominal interest rate is zero, people are indifferent to how much money or bonds they hold, so they are willing to hold fewer bonds and more money at the same nominal interest rate, namely, zero. The money supply increases, but with no effect on the nominal interest rate.

From Chapter 4: The central bank changes the money stock through open market operations, in which it buys or sells bonds in exchange for money. ▶

In short, once the nominal interest rate is equal to zero, expansionary monetary policy becomes powerless. Or to use the words of Keynes, who was the first to point to the problem, the increase in money falls into a **liquidity trap**: People are willing to hold more money (*more liquidity*) at the same nominal interest rate.

Having looked at equilibrium in the financial markets, let's now turn to the *IS-LM*, and see how it must be modified to take into account the liquidity trap.

The derivation of the *LM* curve is shown in Figure 22-4, panels (a) and (b). Recall that the *LM* curve gives, for a given real money stock, the relation between the nominal interest rate and the level of income implied by equilibrium in financial markets. To derive the *LM* curve, panel (a) looks at equilibrium in the financial markets for a given value of the real money stock, and three money demand curves, each corresponding to a different level of income:

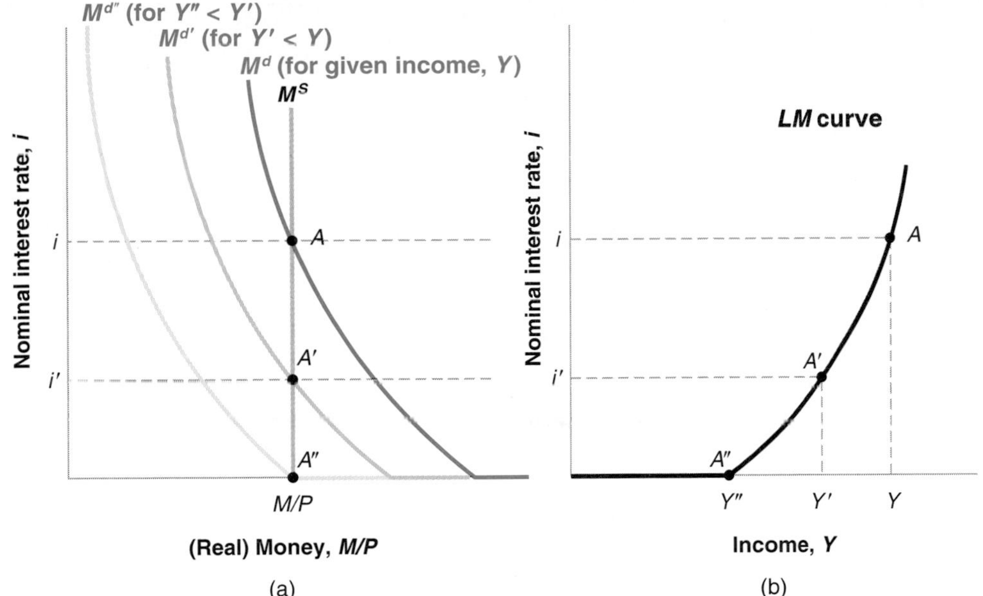

Figure 22-4

The Derivation of the* LM *Curve in the Presence of a Liquidity Trap

For low levels of output, the *LM* curve is a flat segment, with a nominal interest rate equal to zero. For higher levels of output, it is upward sloping: An increase in income leads to an increase in the nominal interest rate.

- M^d gives the demand for money for a given level of income Y. The equilibrium is given by point A, with nominal interest rate equal to i. This combination of income Y and nominal interest rate i gives us a first point on the LM curve, point A in panel (b).
- $M^{d'}$ gives the demand for money for a lower level of income, $Y' < Y$. Lower income means fewer transactions, and so a lower demand for money at any interest rate. In this case, the equilibrium is given by point A', with nominal interest rate equal to i'. This combination of income, Y' and nominal interest rate, i' gives us a second point on the LM curve, point A' in panel (b).
- $M^{d''}$ gives the demand for money for a still lower level of income $Y'' < Y'$. In this case, the equilibrium is given by point A'' in panel (a), with nominal interest rate exactly equal to zero. Point A'' in panel (b) corresponds to A'' in panel (a).
- What happens if income decreases below Y'', shifting the demand for money further to the left in panel (a)? The intersection between the money supply curve and the money demand curve takes place on the horizontal portion of the money demand curve. The equilibrium remains at A'', and the nominal interest rate remains equal to zero.

So far, the derivation of the *LM* curve is exactly the same as in Chapter 5. It is only when income is below Y'' that things become different.

To summarize, in the presence of a liquidity trap, the *LM* curve looks as drawn in Figure 22-4, panel (b).

For values of income greater than Y'', it is upward sloping—just as it was in Chapter 5 when we first characterized the *LM* curve.

For values of income less than Y'', it is flat at $i = 0$: The nominal interest rate cannot go below zero.

Having derived the *LM* curve in the presence of a liquidity trap, we can look at the properties of the *IS-LM* model modified in this way. Suppose the economy is initially at point A in Figure 22-5. Equilibrium is at the intersection of the *IS* curve and the *LM* curve, with output, Y, and nominal interest rate, i. And suppose that this level of output is far below the natural level of output, Y_n. The question is: Can monetary policy help the economy return to Y_n?

Suppose the central bank increases the money supply, shifting the *LM* curve from *LM* to *LM'*. The equilibrium moves from point A down to point B. The nominal

Figure 22-5

The IS-LM *Model and the Liquidity Trap*

In the presence of a liquidity trap, there is a limit to how much monetary policy can increase output. Monetary policy may not be able to increase output back to its natural level.

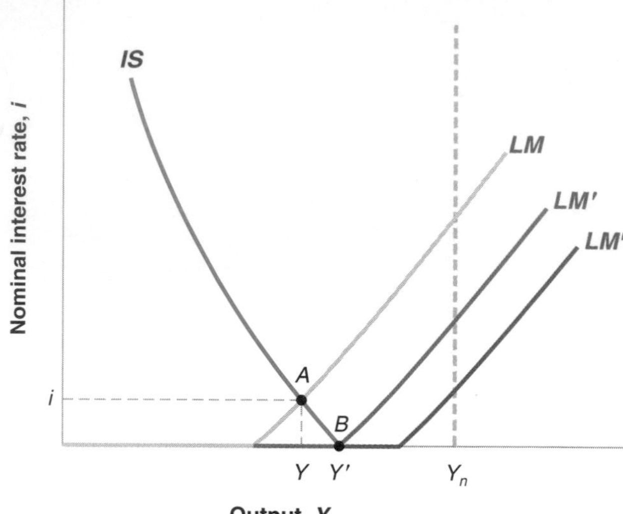

interest rate decreases from i to zero, and output increases from Y to Y'. Thus, to this extent, expansionary policy can indeed increase output.

What happens, however, if, starting from point B, the central bank increases the money supply further, shifting the LM curve from LM' to, say, LM''? The intersection of IS and LM'' remains at point B, and output remains equal to Y'. Expansionary monetary policy no longer has an effect on output; it cannot therefore help output return to Y_n.

In words: When the nominal interest rate is equal to zero, the economy falls in a "liquidity trap": The central bank can increase "liquidity"—that is, increase the money supply. But this "liquidity" falls into a "trap": The additional money is willingly held by financial investors at an unchanged interest rate, namely, zero. If at this zero nominal interest rate, the demand for goods is still too low, then there is nothing further monetary policy can do to return output to its natural level.

Putting Things Together: The Liquidity Trap and Deflation

Just as you may have been skeptical when we were discussing the adverse effects of lower inflation earlier, you may well remain skeptical that the liquidy trap is a serious issue: After all, a zero nominal interest rate is a very low interest rate. Shouldn't a zero nominal interest rate be enough to strongly stimulate spending, and avoid a recession?

The answer is no. And to explain it, we must again draw the distinction between the real interest rate and the nominal interest rate. What matters for spending is the real interest rate. What the real interest rate corresponding to a zero nominal interest rate is depends on the rate of expected inflation:

$r = i - \pi^e = 0\% - 10\% = -10\%$

Revisit our discussion of investment decisions in Chapter 16. Why is investment likely to be very high if firms can borrow at a real interest rate of −10%? (*Hint*: To what do firms compare the real interest rate?)

- Suppose the rate of inflation, actual or expected, is high, say, equal to 10%. Then, a zero nominal interest rate corresponds to a real interest rate of −10%. At such a negative real interest rate, consumption and investment spending are likely to be very high, high enough to make sure that demand is sufficient to return output to the natural level of output. So, at high inflation, the liquidity trap is unlikely to be a serious problem.
- Suppose the rate of inflation is negative—the economy is experiencing deflation. Say, the rate of inflation is −5% (equivalently, the rate of deflation is 5%). Then,

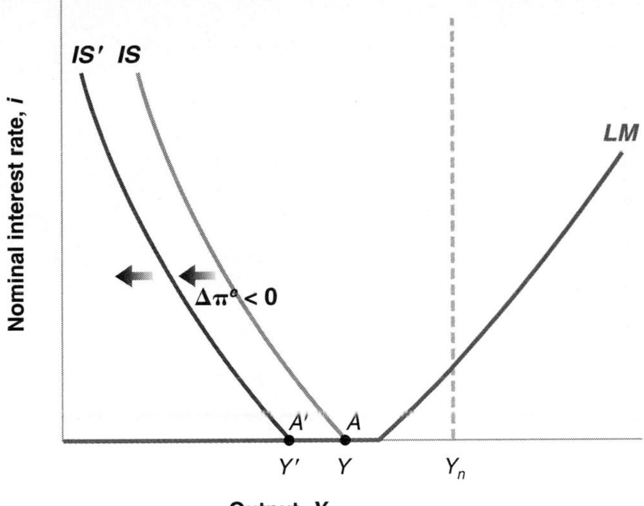

Figure 22-6

The Liquidity Trap and Deflation

Suppose the economy is in a liquidity trap, and there is deflation. Output below the natural level of output leads to more deflation over time, which leads to a further increase in the real interest rate, and leads a further shift of the *IS* curve to the left. This shifts leads to a further decrease in output, which leads to more deflation ... and so on.

even if the nominal interest rate is equal to zero, the real interest rate is equal to 5%. This real interest rate may still be too high to stimulate spending enough, and, in this case, there is nothing monetary policy can do to increase output.

◀ $r = i - \pi^e = 0\% - (-5\%) = 5\%$

You can now see how the two mechanisms—the effects of expected inflation on the real interest rate, and the liquidity trap—we described in this section can come together to turn recessions into slumps or depressions.

Suppose the economy has been in a recession for some time, so inflation has steadily decreased and turned into deflation. Suppose monetary policy has decreased the nominal interest rate down to zero. Even at this zero nominal interest rate, expected deflation implies the real interest rate is still positive.

Suppose that, as a result, the economy is at a point such as *A* in Figure 22-6, at the intersection of the *IS* and the *LM* curves. The nominal interest rate is equal to zero, and output, *Y*, is below the natural level of output, Y_n.

There is clearly nothing monetary policy can do in this case to increase output. And things are likely to get worse over time.

As output is below the natural level of output, the rate of deflation, actual and expected, is likely to increase (inflation is likely to become more negative). At a given nominal interest rate, higher expected deflation leads to an increase in the real interest rate; the *IS* curve shifts to the left in Figure 22-6, from *IS* to, say, *IS'*, leading to a further decrease in output, from *Y* down to *Y'*.

This leads to further deflation, which leads to a further increase in the real interest rate, a further decrease in output, which leads. . . and so on.

The economy gets in a vicious cycle: Low output leads to more deflation. More deflation leads to a higher real interest rate and even lower output, and there is nothing monetary policy can do about it. The scenario may sound exotic. Exotic it may be, but, as we shall now see when looking first at the Great Depression, and then at the Japanese slump, it is far from irrelevant.

22-2 The Great Depression

In 1929, the U.S. unemployment rate was 3.2%. By 1933, it had increased to 24.9%! Not until 10 years later in 1942, was it back down to 4.7%. (Figure 22-7 shows the evolution of the unemployment rate from 1920 to 1950.) This **Great Depression** was

Figure 22-7

The U.S. Unemployment Rate, 1920–1950

The Great Depression was characterized by a sharp increase in unemployment, followed by a slow decline.

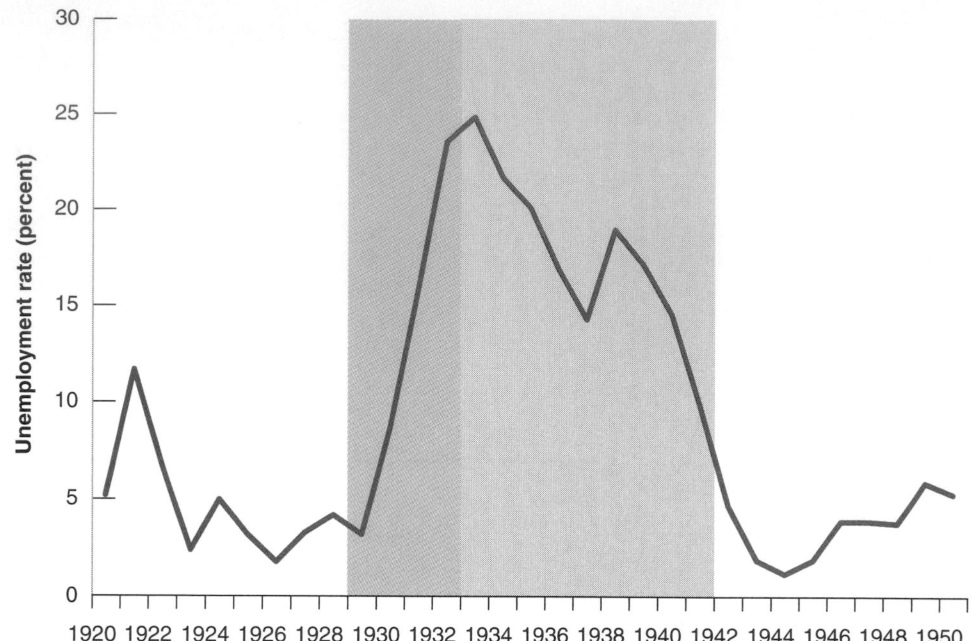

Warning: *Warning:* **The quality of unemployment data is much lower before World War II than after World War II. Cross-country comparisons are particularly dangerous.**

For a look at other countries, read Peter Temin's *Lessons from the Great Depression* (Cambridge, MA: MIT Press, 1989).

From Section 9-1: Okun's law relates the change in the unemployment rate to the deviation of output growth from normal output growth. In the United States today, output growth of 1% above normal for a year leads to a decrease in the unemployment rate of about 0.4%. If normal output growth is 2%, show, using Table 22-1, how this quantitative relation fits the relation between output growth and unemployment from 1933 to 1941.

worldwide: The average unemployment rate from 1930 to 1938 was 15.4% in the United Kingdom, 10.2% in France, and 21.2% in Germany. But I shall focus here only on what happened in the United States, and take up three questions:

What triggered the initial increase in unemployment?
What made the depression last so long?
How did the economy eventually return to low unemployment?

Table 22-1 gives the evolution of the U.S. unemployment rate, the growth rate of output, the consumer price index, and the money stock from 1929 to 1942. Focusing only on unemployment and output for the moment, two facts emerge from the data:

- The size and the speed of the initial output decline. The average annual growth rate from 1929 to 1932 was an astounding −8.6%, leading to an increase in the unemployment rate of more than 20 percentage points (3.2 to 24.9%) in four years.
- The length of the recovery. The average annual growth rate from 1933 to 1941 was a high 7.7%. But, in 1941, at the eve of U.S. entry into World War II, the unemployment rate was still a high 9.9%. (There is no contradiction here, just an application of Okun's law: A long period of high growth was needed to decrease the unemployment rate.)

Let's look at both aspects in turn.

The Initial Fall in Spending

Popular accounts often say that the Great Depression was caused by the stock market crash of 1929. Not so. A recession had actually started before the crash, and other factors played a central role later in the Depression.

Nevertheless, the crash was important. The stock market had boomed from 1921 to 1929. Stock prices had increased much faster than the dividends paid by firms—and

Table 22-1 U.S. Unemployment, Output Growth, Prices, and Money, 1929–1942

Year	Unemployment Rate (%)	Output Growth Rate (%)	Price Level	Nominal Money Stock
1929	3.2	−9.8	100.0	26.4
1930	8.7	−7.6	97.4	25.4
1931	15.9	−14.7	88.8	23.6
1932	23.6	−1.8	79.7	19.4
1933	24.9	9.1	75.6	21.5
1934	21.7	9.9	78.1	25.5
1935	20.1	13.9	80.1	29.2
1936	16.9	5.3	80.9	30.3
1937	14.3	−5.0	83.8	30.0
1938	19.0	8.6	82.2	30.0
1939	17.2	8.5	81.0	33.6
1940	14.6	16.1	81.8	39.6
1941	9.9	12.9	85.9	46.5
1942	4.7	13.2	95.1	55.3

Sources: Unemployment rate: Series D85–86; output growth: GNP growth (in 1958 prices), Series F31; price level: CPI (1929 = 100), Series E135; Money stock: M1 (in billions of dollars), Series X414. *Historical Statistics of the United States*, U.S. Department of Commerce.

as a result the dividend-price ratio had decreased from 6.5% in 1921 to 3.5% in 1929. On October 28, 1929, the stock market price index dropped from 298 to 260. The next day, it dropped further to 230. This was a fall of 23% in two days, and a drop of 40% from the peak of early September. By November the index was down to 198. A brief stock market recovery in early 1930 was followed by further declines in stock prices as the depth of the depression became increasingly clear to the market participants. By June 1932, the index bottomed out, at 47. (The evolution of the index from January 1920 to December 1950 is shown in Figure 22-8.)

◀ Note the parallel between the evolution of stock prices during the 1920s and during the 1990s. The U.S. dividend-price ratio was 3.2% in 1991, 1.2% at the end of 2000. (See the Focus box "Is the U.S. Stock Market Overvalued?" in Chapter 15.)

Was the October 1929 crash caused by the sudden realization that a depression was coming? The answer is no. There is no evidence of major news in October. The source of the crash was almost surely the end of a speculative bubble. Stockholders who had purchased stocks at high prices in the anticipation of further increases in prices got scared and attempted to sell their stocks. The result was a large drop in prices.

◀ Revisit dividends and prices, and bubbles and crashes, in Section 15-3.

The crash not only decreased consumers' wealth, it also increased their uncertainty about the future. Unsettled by the crash and feeling uncertain about the future, consumers and firms decided to see how things evolved and to postpone purchases of durable goods and investment goods. There was, for example, a large decrease in car sales—the type of purchase that can easily be deferred—in the months just following the crash. Industrial production, which had declined by 1.8% from August to October 1929, declined by 9.8% from October to December, and by another 24% from December 1929 to December 1930.

The Contraction in Nominal Money

The impact of the crash was compounded by a major policy mistake, namely, a large decrease in the nominal money stock. The first column of Table 22-2 gives the evolution

Figure 22-8

The S&P Composite Index, 1920:1–1950:12

From September 1929 to June 1932, the stock market index decreased from 313 to 47, to slowly recover thereafter.

of the nominal money stock, measured by $M1$ ($M1$ is the sum of currency, travelers' checks, and checkable deposits). From 1929 to 1933, $M1$ *decreased* from \$26.4 billion to \$19.4 billion, a decrease of 27%.

To understand why the nominal money stock went down so much, you must go back to what you learned in Chapter 4 about the relation between the nominal money stock and the monetary base: In an economy in which some of the money held by people and firms takes the form of checkable deposits, the money stock (the sum of currency and checkable deposits) is larger than the monetary base, H (currency plus banks' reserves). The relation between the two is given by

What follows relies on the presentation of equilibrium in financial markets in terms of (overall) money supply and (overall) money demand presented in Chapter 4.

$$M1 = H \times \text{money multiplier}$$

The money multiplier depends in turn both on how much reserves banks keep in proportion to their deposits, and on what proportion of money people keep in the form of currency as opposed to checkable deposits. Now note that from 1929 to

Table 22-2 Money, Nominal and Real, 1929–1933

Year	Nominal Money Stock ($M1$)	Monetary Base (H)	Money Multiplier ($M1/H$)	Real Money Stock ($M1/P$)
1929	26.4	7.1	3.7	26.4
1930	25.4	6.9	3.7	26.0
1931	23.6	7.3	3.2	26.5
1932	20.6	7.8	2.6	25.8
1933	19.4	8.2	2.4	25.6

Source: $M1$: Series X414; H: Series X422 plus Series X423: P: Series E135. *Historical Statistics of the United States*, U.S. Department of Commerce.

1933, the monetary base, H (shown in the second column of Table 22-2), *increased* from $7.1 to $8.2 billion. This means the decrease in $M1$ did not come from a decrease in the monetary base, but came instead from a decrease in the money multiplier, $M1/H$ (shown in the third column of Table 22–2), which fell from 3.7 in 1929 to 2.4 in 1933. Why did the money multiplier decline so much? The answer: Because of bank failures:

The classic description of what happened then is by Milton Friedman and Anna Schwartz, *A Monetary History of the United States, 1867–1960* (Princeton, NJ: Princeton University Press, 1963).

With the large decline in output, more and more borrowers found themselves unable to repay their loans to banks, causing more and more banks to become insolvent and close down. Bank failures increased steadily from 1929 until 1933, when the number of failures reached a peak of 4,000, out of about 20,000 banks in operation at the time.

Bank failures had a direct effect on the money supply: Checkable deposits at the failed banks became worthless. But the major effect on the money supply was indirect: Worried that their bank might also fail, many people took their money out of banks, and shifted from checkable deposits to currency. The increase in the ratio of currency to deposits led to a decrease in the money multiplier, and so to a decrease in the money supply. Think of the mechanism this way: If people had liquidated *all* their deposits and asked banks for currency in exchange, the multiplier would have decreased all the way down to 1: People would have held only central bank money; $M1$ would have been just equal to the monetary base H. The actual shift was less dramatic; nevertheless, the multiplier dropped from 3.7 in 1929 to 2.4 in 1933, leading to a decrease in the money supply despite an increase in the monetary base.

From Chapter 4: The multiplier is $1/(c + \theta\,(1 - c))$ where c is the proportion of money people want to hold as currency, and θ is the ratio of reserves to checkable deposits. The higher c, the lower the multiplier. And if $c = 1$—if people want to hold only currency—then the multiplier equals 1.

The implication for our purposes is simple: With a decrease in the nominal money stock from 1929 to 1933 roughly proportional to the decrease in the price level, the real money stock (shown in the fourth column of Table 22-2) remained roughly constant, eliminating one of the mechanisms that could have led to a recovery. In other words, the *LM* curve remained roughly unchanged—it did not shift down as it would have done if the nominal money stock had remained constant, implying an increase in the real money stock.

This is why Milton Friedman and Anna Schwartz have argued that the Fed was responsible for the depth of the Depression: It was not directly responsible for the decrease in the nominal money supply. But it should have taken steps to offset the decrease in the money multiplier by expanding the monetary base much more than it did.

The Adverse Effects of Deflation

With the fall in spending, and the decrease in the nominal money supply, the stage was set for the mechanisms we studied in Section 22-1 to turn the decline in output into a full-fledged depression.

As shown in the first column of Table 22-3, the result of the contraction in nominal money was to lead to only a limited decline in the nominal interest rate. The nominal interest rate, measured by the interest rate on one-year corporate bonds, reached 5.3% in 1929 (up from 4.1% in 1928), only to slowly decline over time, reaching 2.6% in 1933.

At the same time, as shown in the second column of Table 22-3, the result of low output was a strong *deflation,* with the rate of deflation reaching 9.2% in 1931, and 10.8% in 1932! If we make the assumption that expected deflation was equal to actual deflation in each year, we can construct a series for the real interest rate. This is done in the last column of Table 22-3, and gives a convincing explanation for why output continued to decline until 1933. The *real interest rate* reached 12.3% in 1931, 14.8% in 1932, and still a very high 7.8% in 1933. It is no great surprise that, at those interest rates, both consumption and investment demand remained very low, and the depression got worse.

Table 22-3 The Nominal Interest Rate, Inflation, and the Real Interest Rate, 1929–1933

Year	One-Year Nominal Interest Rate (%), i	Inflation Rate (%), π	One-Year Real Interest Rate (%), r
1929	5.3	−0.0	5.3
1930	4.4	−2.5	6.9
1931	3.1	−9.2	12.3
1932	4.0	−10.8	14.8
1933	2.6	−5.2	7.8

Source: Interest rate, series X487-491, Inflation rate constructed from CPI, E135-166. The real rate is constructed as the nominal rate minus inflation. *Historical Statistics of the United States,* U.S. Department of Commerce.

The Recovery

The recovery started in 1933. Except for another sharp decrease in the growth rate of output in 1937 (see Table 22-1), growth was consistently high, running at an average annual rate of 7.7% from 1933 to 1941. Macroeconomists and economic historians have studied the recovery much less than they studied the initial decline. And many questions remain.

One of the factors that contributed to the recovery is clear. Following the election of Franklin Roosevelt in 1932, there was a change in monetary policy and a dramatic increase in nominal money growth. From 1933 to 1941, the nominal money stock increased by 140%, the real money stock by 100%. These increases were due to increases in the monetary base, not in the money multiplier. Christina Romer, an economic historian from the University of California at Berkeley, has argued that if monetary policy had been unchanged from 1933 on, output would have been 25% lower than it actually was in 1937, and 50% lower than it was in 1942. These are very large numbers. Even if we believe these numbers overestimate the effect of monetary policy, the conclusion that monetary policy played an important role in the recovery is still surely warranted.

Christina Romer, "What Ended the Great Depression?" ***Journal of Economic History,*** **December 1992, 757–784.**

The role of other factors, from budget deficits to the **New Deal**—the set of programs put in place by the Roosevelt administration to get the U.S. economy out of the Great Depression—is less clear.

One New Deal program was aimed at improving the functioning of banks by creating the *Federal Deposit Insurance Corporation (FDIC)* to insure checkable deposits and to avoid bank runs and bank failures. And, indeed, there were few bank failures after 1933.

Other programs included relief and public works programs for the unemployed, and a program administered by the **National Recovery Administration (NRA)** to establish "orderly competition" in industry. Economists generally agree that these programs had few direct effects on the recovery. But some economists argue that the indirect effects of these programs—particularly the perception of the government's commitment to getting the economy out of the depression—were important in changing expectations in 1933 and after. We saw in earlier chapters how such expectational effects of policy can be important. However, showing their importance in 1933 and after is difficult and remains largely to be done.

The recovery also presents us with a puzzle. In 1933, deflation stopped. The rest of the decade was characterized by small but positive inflation. The CPI was 81.8 in 1940, compared to 75.6 in 1933. The end of deflation probably helped the recovery. The shift from deflation to rough price stability implied much lower real interest rates than had been the case from 1929 until 1933.

The puzzle is *why* deflation ended in 1933: With a large deflation in 1932 and unemployment at an all-time high, the theory of wage determination we developed in previous chapters implies that there should have been further large wage cuts and further deflation. This is not what happened. As we saw in the Phillips curve diagram constructed for the United States by Samuelson and Solow (Figure 8-1), the years 1933 to 1939 are clear outliers. So why did deflation stop?

- One proximate cause may be the set of measures taken by the Roosevelt administration. The **National Industrial Recovery Act (NIRA)**, signed in June 1933, asked industries to establish minimum wages, and not to take advantage of the high unemployment rate to impose further wage cuts on workers. Economists are usually doubtful that such admonitions to firms have much effect. But the NIRA offered firms a carrot in exchange, in effect a decrease in competition in goods markets under the guise of "orderly competition," and thus the potential for higher profits if they complied. The evidence suggests that the NIRA did have an effect on wage setting.
- Another factor may be that while unemployment was still high, output growth was high as well. As a result, there were bottlenecks in production, leading firms to increase their prices given wages. Because of the sharp increase in demand, the price of raw materials was also bid up, increasing costs, and again forcing firms to increase their prices given wages. In short, and in contrast to our simple specification of price setting where we assumed prices depended only on wages, the effect of fast growth was to increase prices given wages, thereby reducing the deflationary pressure of unemployment.
- A relevant fact in this discussion is that deflation ended in the mid-1930s in most countries, even in countries that did not have programs similar to the New Deal and did not have the same fast growth rates after 1933 as the United States. This suggests that, perhaps, other more general factors were at work. One possibility, which has been explored in the case of European unemployment in the 1980s and 1990s is that, after a while, high unemployment exerts less pressure on inflation. The idea is that once people have been unemployed for a long time, they give up on finding a job, becoming in effect irrelevant to the wage determination process. As a result, unemployment has less effect on wages, and in turn less effect on inflation.

Why should we care about how deflation turned to inflation in the United States in 1933? Because, as you shall see next, the answer is very relevant to Japan today. How to get rid of deflation, and, in so doing, decrease the real interest rate and stimulate growth, is one of the main issues confronting Japan today.

22-3 The Japanese Slump

From the end of World War II to the beginning of the 1990s, Japan's economic performance was spectacular: From 1950 to 1973, the average growth rate was 8% per year. As in other OECD countries, the average growth rate decreased after 1973. But, from 1973 to 1991, it was still a very respectable 4% per year, a higher rate than in most other OECD countries. As a result of this growth, Japanese output per capita (measured in PPP terms), which was equal to only 17% of the U.S. level in 1950, had climbed to 80% of the U.S. level in 1990.

See the discussion of the post-1973 growth slowdown in major OECD countries in Chapter 12.

Forgotten the definition of GDP in PPP terms? See Chapter 10.

Table 22-4 Output Growth, Unemployment, Inflation, Japan, 1990–2001

Year	Output Growth Rate (%)	Unemployment Rate (%)	Inflation Rate (%)
1990	5.3	2.1	2.4
1991	3.1	2.1	3.0
1992	0.9	2.2	1.7
1993	0.4	2.5	0.6
1994	1.0	2.9	0.1
1995	1.6	3.1	−0.4
1996	3.5	3.4	−0.8
1997	1.8	3.4	0.4
1998	−1.1	3.4	−0.1
1999	0.8	4.1	−1.4
2000	1.5	4.7	−1.6
2001	−0.7	5.0	−1.6

Source: OECD Economic Outlook, December 2001.

This growth came to an abrupt end in the early 1990s. Table 22-4 gives the evolution of the growth rate of GDP, the unemployment rate, and the inflation rate from 1990 to 2001.

- Since 1992, the annual growth rate has been either positive and small, or negative. Overall, the average growth rate from 1992 to 2001 has been under 1%, far below the performance of earlier decades. This long period of low growth is what is called the *Japanese slump*. This slump is obviously not as sharp and as deep as the Great Depression. (Recall from Table 22-1 that the average annual growth rate in the United States from 1929 to 1932 was −8.6%.) But it is substantial. Think of it this way: If output growth had continued at the same rate as output had grown from 1973 to 1991, output in Japan would be 30% higher than it is today.
- Low output growth has led to a steady increase in unemployment. Looking at the evolution of the unemployment rate since 1990 in the second column of Table 22-4, you might conclude that Japan was not doing so badly. True, the unemployment rate has increased, from 2.1% in 1990 to 5.0% in 2001. But 5.0% is still lower than the average unemployment rate in the United States over the last 40 years, and is a rate that many European countries can only dream of achieving. Yet, it is the highest unemployment rate Japan has had since World War II.

  The reason why it is so low has to do with the organization of firms, and of the labor market in Japan. As we saw in Chapter 8, Japanese firms offer substantial employment protection to their workers. So, when Japanese firms experience a decrease in production, they tend to keep their workers, leading to a small effect of the decrease in output on employment, and in turn, a small effect on unemployment.

  See the Focus box "The Japanese Unemployment Rate" in Chapter 8. ►

  Another way to think about the evolution of unemployment in Japan is in terms of Okun's law, the relation between output growth and unemployment we saw in Chapter 9: In the United States, the *Okun coefficient* is equal to 0.4. A decrease in the growth rate of 1% for one year leads to an increase in the unemployment rate of 0.4%. In Japan, the Okun coefficient is equal to 0.1. A decrease in the growth rate of 1% for one year leads to an increase in the unemployment rate of only 0.1%. As cumulative output growth in Japan since 1992 has been about 30% below normal, this has resulted in an increase in the unemployment rate of $0.1 \times 30\% = 3\%$. In the United States, the same shortfall in growth would have led to an increase in unemployment of $0.4 \times 30\% = 12\%$, a much larger increase.

◀ See the Focus box "Okun's Law Across Countries" in Chapter 9.

- Low growth and high unemployment (by Japanese standards) have led to a steady decrease in the inflation rate over time. As shown in Table 22-4, the inflation rate was already low at the start of the 1990s. Since 1995, inflation has turned into deflation, something which had not been observed in OECD countries since the Great Depression.

The numbers in Table 22-4 raise an obvious set of questions:
What triggered this slump?
Why has it lasted so long?
Were monetary and fiscal policies misused, or did they fail?
What happens next?

The Rise and Fall of the Nikkei

The 1980s were associated with a stock market boom in Japan: The Nikkei index, a broad index of Japanese stock prices, increased from 7,000 in 1980 to 35,000 at the end of 1989—a 5-fold increase. Then, within two years, the index fell sharply—down to 16,000 at the end of 1992. For the rest of the decade, the index has remained low. At the end of 2001, it stood slightly above 10,000, less than one-third of its value at the peak.

◀ The evolution of the Nikkei index is shown in Figure 1-7 in Chapter 1.

Why did the Nikkei rise so much in the 1980s, and then fall so quickly in the early 1990s? Recall from Chapter 15 that there can be two reasons for a stock price to increase:

- A change in the fundamental value of the stock price, coming, for example, from an increase in current or future expected dividends. Knowing that the stock will pay higher dividends either now or in the future, investors are willing to pay more for the stock today. Its price goes up.
- A speculative bubble: Investors buy at a higher price simply because they expect the price to go even higher in the future.

◀ Recall from Chapter 15 that in the absence of a speculative bubble, the price of a stock is equal to the expected present value of future dividends.

Figure 22-9 gives the evolution of dividends and stock prices in Japan from 1980 to 2001. The upper line shows the evolution of the stock price index (the Nikkei); the lower line shows the evolution of the corresponding index for dividends. For convenience, both variables are normalized to be equal to one in 1980. A look at the figure yields a simple conclusion: While the stock price index increased in the 1980s, the dividend remained flat. This is not proof that the increase in the Nikkei was a bubble: Investors may have expected large increases in future dividends, even if current dividends were not increasing. But it strongly suggests that the increase in the Nikkei had a large bubble component, and that the later fall was largely a bursting of that bubble.

Whatever its origin, the rapid fall in stock prices had a major impact on spending, and, in turn, a big impact on output. Table 22-5 shows the evolution of GDP growth, consumption growth, and investment growth from 1988 to 1993. Investment, which had been very strong during the rise of the Nikkei, collapsed. In contrast to the Great Depression—where consumption had fallen sharply after the stock market crash—consumption was less affected. But the strength in consumption was not enough to avoid a sharp decline in total spending and in GDP growth, from 6.5% in 1999 to 0.4% in 1993.

◀ See the discussion of the effects of stock prices on consumption and investment in Chapters 16 and 17.

Figure 22-9

Stock Prices and Dividends, Japan, 1980–2001

The increase in stock prices in the 1980s and the subsequent decrease have not been associated with a parallel movement in dividends.

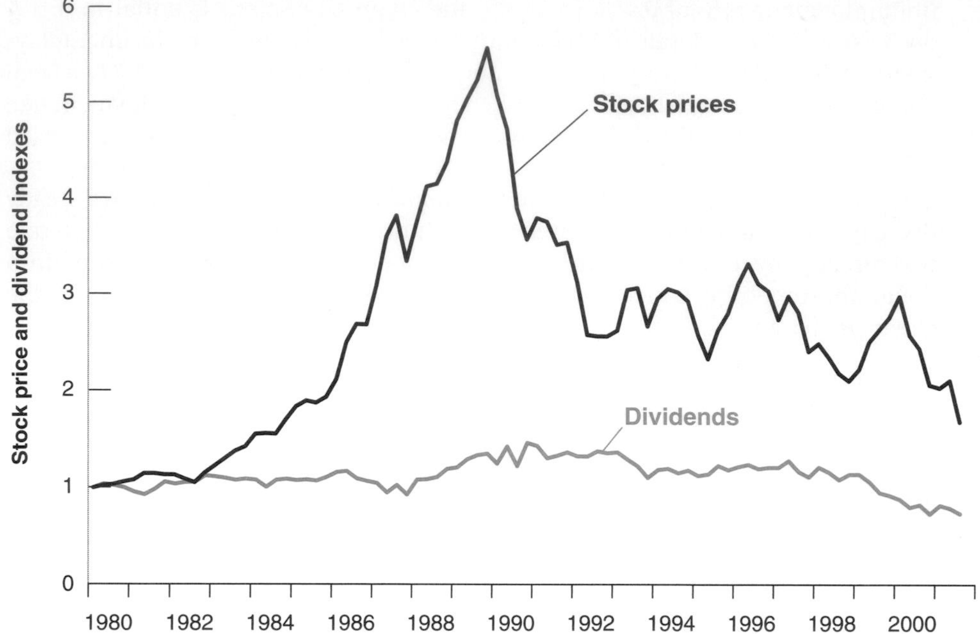

In short, there is no mystery about how the Japanese slump started. The more difficult question is why it continued for so long. After all, perhaps the main lesson from the Great Depression was that macroeconomic policies could and should be used to help the economy recover. Were they used in Japan? If so, why did they fail? These are the next two questions we take up.

The Failure of Monetary and Fiscal Policy

Monetary policy was used. But it was used too late, and when it was used, it was faced with the twin problems of the liquidity trap and deflation we discussed in Section 22-1.

Table 22-5 GDP, Consumption, and Investment Growth, Japan, 1988–1993

Year	GDP (%)	Consumption (%)	Investment (%)
1988	6.5	5.1	15.5
1989	5.3	4.7	15.0
1990	5.3	4.4	11.5
1991	3.1	2.1	4.4
1992	0.9	2.2	−7.3
1993	0.4	2.5	−11.6

Source: OECD Economic Outlook. December 2001. Investment is private, fixed, nonresidential.

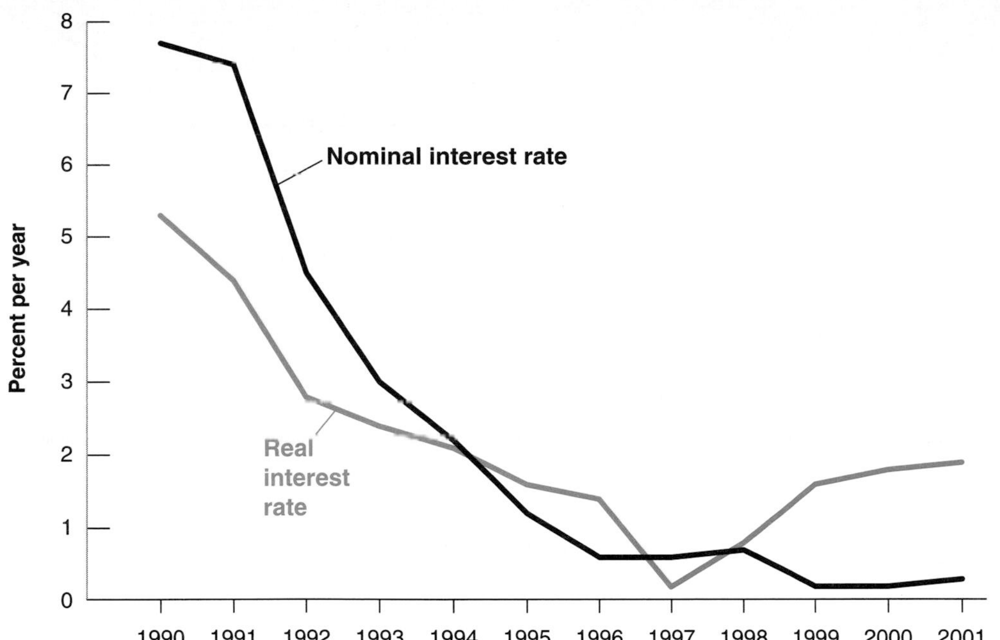

Figure 22-10

The Nominal Interest Rate and the Real Interest Rate in Japan, 1990–2001

Japan is now in a liquidity trap: The nominal interest rate is close to zero. Deflation implies that even at a zero nominal interest rate, the real interest rate is positive.

The point is made in Figure 22-10, which shows the evolution of the nominal interest rate and the real interest rate in Japan, from 1990 to 2001. (Because we do not observe expected inflation, I construct the real interest rate as the nominal interest rate minus actual—rather than expected—inflation.)

The nominal interest rate was high in 1990, close to 8%. This was in part because the Bank of Japan (often refered to as the *BoJ*), worried about the rise of the Nikkei, had tried to decrease stock prices by increasing the interest rate. With inflation around 2%, this nominal interest rate implied a real interest rate of about 6%.

Recall that the stock price depends positively on current and expected future dividends, and negatively on current and future interest rates.

As growth slowed down, the BoJ cut the nominal interest rate. But it did so slowly, and by 1996, when the nominal interest rate was down to less than 1%, the cumulative effect of low growth was such that inflation had turned to deflation. As a result, the real interest rate was higher than the nominal interest rate.

Since the mid-1990s, Japan has, in effect, been in a liquidity trap. At times, the nominal short-term interest rate has been equal to zero. At the time of this writing, it equals 0.02%, two-hundredths of 1%! It cannot decrease further. At the same time, unemployment remains high, leading to a larger and larger rate of deflation, so the real interest rate is increasing. At the time of this writing, it stands around 2%, not low enough to stimulate demand and increase output. Japan is clearly in the vicious cycle we described in Section 22-1: high unemployment leading to larger deflation, leading to a higher real interest rate, leading to lower demand, leading to higher unemployment.

Fiscal policy was used as well. Figure 22-11 shows what happened to tax revenues and to government spending as a proportion of GDP from 1990 to 2001. It shows both the decrease in taxes at the start of the slump, and the steady increase in spending throughout the decade—an increase of close to 8% of GDP. Much of this increased spending has taken the form of public work projects, many of them of doubtful usefulness. But, from the point of view of increasing demand, one project is as good as another, and so this increase in government spending should have contributed to an overall increase in demand.

A joke circulating in Japan is that, as a result of public works projects, by the end of the slump, the entire shoreline of the Japanese archipelago will be covered in concrete.

Figure 22-11

Government Spending and Revenues, Japan, 1990 to 2001

The budget deficit steadily increased in the 1990s, mostly as a result of increased government spending.

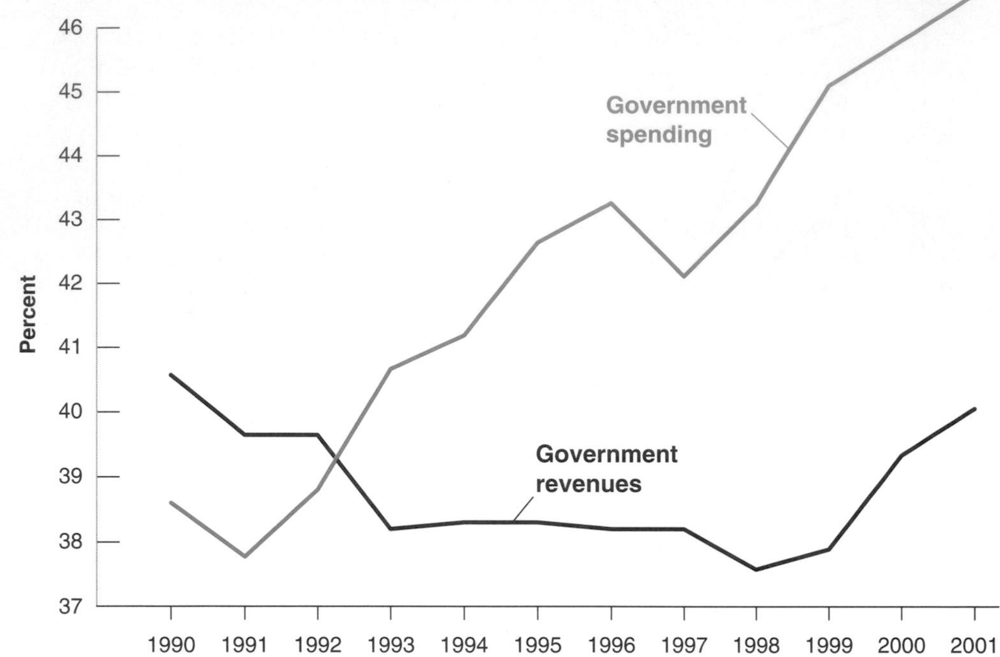

Has it? The economists who have looked at this question have concluded that it has, but that it was just not enough to increase spending and output. Put another way, in the absence of increased government spending, output would have declined even more. Fiscal policy limited the decline, but did not lead to a recovery. And here is the problem faced by the Japanese government today: High government spending and low taxes have led to a long string of budget deficits, and a steady accumulation of government debt. The ratio of government debt to GDP has increased from 61% of GDP in 1991 to 130% in 2001. At a current interest rate on government bonds very close to zero, interest payments on the debt are small. But if the interest rate were to increase in the future, interest payments might represent a very heavy burden on the government budget. For this reason, the Japanese government is understandably reluctant to continue to use fiscal policy. This is reflected in the increase in the ratio of taxes to GDP since 1999.

At an interest rate of 1% per year, a 130% debt-to-GDP ratio implies interest payments equal to 1.3% of GDP. At an interest rate of, say, 6% per year, the same debt-to-GDP ratio implies interest payments equal to 7.8% of GDP.

What Comes Next?

It is not hard to see why most macroeconomists are gloomy about Japan's immediate prospects: Monetary policy cannot decrease the interest rate further. The scope for fiscal policy, after a decade of large budget deficits, is limited at best. So, what tools remain for policy makers to use? At this stage, policy recommendations fall in two main categories:

- *Create inflation.*

  In the strange world of the liquidity trap, more inflation is good. If the Japanese suddenly became convinced that there was going to be inflation in the future, the real interest rate would decrease. This would stimulate spending and output. And actual inflation would also increase; remember that the Phillips curve relation implies that an increase in expected inflation leads, one for one, to an increase in actual inflation.

$\pi = \pi^e - \alpha(u - u_n)$. Given unemployment, u, an increase in π^e leads to an equal increase in π.

The issue then is whether and how the BoJ can convince the Japanese that there will be inflation in the future. Various proposals have been made. One is that the BoJ should announce an *inflation target,* a rate of inflation it will try to achieve over the next few years. If people believe the announcement, then expected inflation—and in turn actual inflation—will indeed increase, helping the Japanese economy to get out of the slump. But this is not a sure thing: If people do not believe the announcement and continue to expect deflation, then deflation will continue, and there is little the BoJ will be able to do to avoid it.

Note the symmetry with our discussion in Chapter 9 of whether a central bank can achieve disinflation at little or no output cost. The answer there was: If the central bank can credibly convince people that inflation will be lower, then it may be able to achieve lower inflation at little output cost.

In short, there is a clear, self-fulfilling element to the success of such an announcement: If the announcement is believed, it is likely to succeed. If the annoucement is not believed, it will not succeed. What happened in 1933 in the Great Depression may be relevant here. One may interpret what Roosevelt did in 1933 as coordinating a shift from deflation to inflation, helping the U.S. economy to recover. We may hope—but we can hardly be sure—that Japan is able to do the same.

- *Clean up the banking system.*

  Another line of policy recommendations starts from the proposition that the Japanese economy suffers today from a large number of structural problems.

  One of the main structural problems, the argument goes, is the poor health of the banking system: Largely as a result of the slump, many firms are doing poorly. And banks carry on their books many *bad loans,* loans that the borrowers will not be able to repay. (Why this is, and how it happened, is discussed in the Focus Box "The Japanese Banking Problem.") One result is that a number of bad firms—firms that are making losses and should close—continue to be financed by the banks, and so continue to operate. Another result is, as a large proportion of bank financing continues to go to the firms with bad loans, "good firms"—firms with good prospects and good investment projects—cannot find financing and thus cannot invest.

  The right policy, the argument continues, is therefore to eliminate the problem of bad bank loans, by closing or reorganizing the firms that cannot repay their loans, and by closing or reorganizing the banks that have made too many bad loans. These measures will have two effects:

  They will eliminate the bad firms, leading eventually—as these firms are replaced by more productive ones—to higher productivity and to a higher natural level of output.

  They will allow firms with good investment projects to invest, leading to an increase in investment spending, and so an increase in demand and output.

  Not all economists agree. There is no disagreement about the fact that many bank loans are bad in Japan, and that a cleanup of the banking system is needed. Where there is disagreement is whether such a cleanup will help Japan get out of the slump in the short run. In the short run, a cleanup of the banking system implies closing a number of firms and a number of banks. Many economists worry this may actually lead to a further decrease in output in the short run, and thus to a worsening of the output slump, before the positive effects of the cleanup start appearing. The concern that the economy will get worse before it gets better is one of the main reasons why the successive Japanese governments have been reluctant, so far, to embark on a general bank cleanup.

In short, it may be that either Japanese consumers or Japanese firms soon become more optimistic, increase spending, and this leads to an increase in output. But, unless this happens, with the two main macroeconomic policy tools being unavailable, there does not appear to be any simple solution to getting Japan out of its current slump. The solutions being considered are neither sure to succeed, nor likely to be painless.

The Japanese Banking Problem

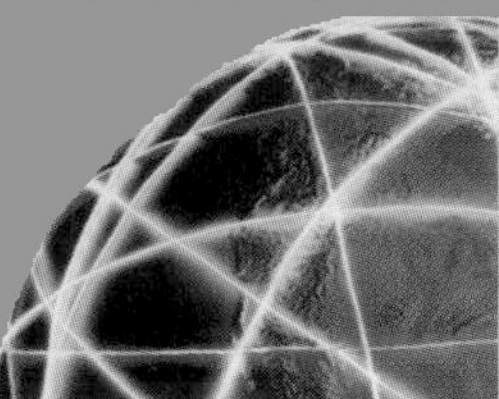

Just as was the case in the Great Depression, one of the implications of the sharp decrease in output growth in Japan in the early 1990s was that many firms found themselves unable to repay their bank loans.

The situation was made worse by two facts:

In the 1980s, the banks had started losing their best borrowers—the large Japanese firms, which increasingly financed themselves by issuing bonds rather than by borrowing from banks. As a result, banks had made loans to more risky borrowers, some of whom would have a hard time repaying their loans even in the absence of a slump.

Also, for many of the loans, firms had used land as collateral ("collateral" stands for any asset that the borrower promises to give to the bank if the loan is not repaid). And, together with stock prices, land prices collapsed in the early 1990s, decreasing the value of that collateral.

In the Great Depression, the result of bad bank loans had been a series of bank failures and bank runs (see the Focus box "Bank Runs" in Chapter 4). Indeed, one of the lessons of the Great Depression was that to avoid such bank runs, governments should provide insurance to the depositors. Federal deposit insurance was introduced in 1934 in the United States. And a similar insurance system was later put in place in most countries, including Japan.

Deposit insurance solves one problem: It eliminates the risk of bank runs. But it creates other problems, which have been in evidence in Japan in the 1990s. To understand what these problems are, think of a bank that has the balance sheet described in Figure 1.

- On the asset side, it has one loan at $100.
- On the liability side, it has $50 in deposits.
- The net worth of the bank, the difference between assets and liabilities is therefore $100 − $50 = $50.

(Note two differences with the balance sheets we studied in Chapter 4. First, I ignore reserves. They were important for the arguments developed in Chapter 4; they are not important here. Second, I assumed in Chapter 4 that assets were equal to liabilities, that net worth was zero. Net worth is typically positive, and this plays an important role here.)

Now suppose the loan turns bad: The firm to which the loan was made cannot pay any of it back. What should happen?

- The value of the loan is now zero: The bank should write the loan off. The bank still owes $50 in deposits, but cannot pay them back. Thus, deposit insurance should pay $50 to the depositors, and the bank should close.
- But that is unlikely to happen. To keep his job, the manager of the bank may pretend that nothing has happened, and the loan is still good. Indeed, the manager may decide to lend further to the firm, so the firm can pay off the old loan, and it looks like business as usual. This is clearly throwing good money after bad, but by doing so, the manager buys time and keeps his job, at least for some time.
- Even the owners of the bank may go along: If the bank closes now, they lose everything (net worth is clearly equal to zero). If there is the slightest chance that the firm will recover and be able to pay back, they may end up with positive net worth (this is known as "gambling for resurrection"). So, even if the odds are very bad, the bank may continue to lend to the firm.
- Depositors do not care what the bank does: Their deposits are insured, whatever the bank does. Even the regulator, if there is one, may prefer to close his eyes: Acknowledging the existence of bad loans, and the fact that the bank must be closed, may reflect badly on him—again, better to wait.

The result is that banks are likely to renew the bad loans, or even to make new loans to the bad firms, and to do so at the expense of good firms. And so, the more time passes, the worse the problem of bad loans becomes.

This is exactly what has happened in Japan in the 1990s. Until 1993, the banks did not disclose any information about bad loans. Since then, they have reluctantly acknowledged the presence of bad loans on their books. And the total amount of bad loans (self-reported by banks) has steadily increased, from 12 trillion yen in 1993, to 30 trillion yen in 1998, to 44 trillion yen in 2001. But even that amount may be far below the true number. An estimate by the OECD puts the total value of bad loans at 237 trillion yen, or close to 45% of GDP. And there lies one on the main problems confronting Japan today.

Assets	Liabilities
Loan: $100	Deposits: $50 Net worth: $50

Figure 1 *The Bank's Balance Sheet*

FOCUS

Summary

- In general, a recession leads to a decrease in inflation. Given nominal money growth, the decrease in inflation leads to an increase in real money growth, decreasing the nominal interest rate, and increasing output back to its natural level.
- One reason why this adjustment back to the natural level of output may fail is that the decrease in inflation may lead to an increase in the real interest rate. If expected inflation decreases more than the nominal interest rate, the real interest rate will increase. As spending depends on the real interest rate, the increase in the real interest rate will lead to a further decrease in output.
- Monetary policy can be used to decrease the nominal interest rate further, which helps increase output. Monetary policy, however, cannot decrease the nominal interest rate below zero. When this happens, the economy is said to be in a liquidity trap.
- The combination of the liquidity trap and deflation can transform a recession into a slump or a depression. If the nominal interest rate is zero, and the economy is experiencing a deflation, the real interest rate is positive, and may be too high to lead to an increase in spending and output. Output may continue to decline, leading to higher deflation, a higher real interest rate, and so on.

On the Great Depression in the United States:

- The unemployment rate increased from 3.2% in 1929 to 24.9% in 1933.
- The initial cause of this increase in unemployment was a large adverse shift in demand, brought about by the stock market crash of 1929 and the resulting increase in uncertainty about the future.
- The result of high unemployment was a large deflation from 1929 to 1933.
- The favorable effect of the decrease in the price level on the real money stock was offset, however, by a roughly equal decrease in nominal money. This decrease in nominal money was due to bank failures and a decrease in the money multiplier. The main effect of deflation was a large increase in the real interest rate, leading to a further decrease in demand and output.
- Recovery started in 1933. Average growth was high, 7.7% per year from 1933 to 1941. Unemployment decreased, but it was still equal to 9.9% in 1941. In contrast to the predictions of the Phillips curve, deflation turned to inflation from 1934 on, despite a very high unemployment rate.
- Many questions remain about the recovery. What is clear is that high nominal money growth, leading to high real money growth, was an important factor in the recovery.

On the Japanese slump:

- After a long period of very high growth, Japan has had very low growth since 1992. This long period of low growth is called the Japanese slump.
- The slump was triggered by the fall of Japanese stock prices at the end of the 1980s, which led to a sharp decrease in investment spending, and in turn a decrease in output.
- Monetary policy was used to try to increase output in the 1990s. But Japan is now in a liquidity trap, with a nominal interest rate very close to zero. Because Japan is experiencing deflation, the real interest rate is positive.
- Fiscal policy was also used to try to increase output in the 1990s. But after a decade of deficits, government debt has increased to 130% of GDP, and the Japanese government is reluctant to increase its debt further.
- Turning deflation into inflation would decrease the real interest rate and help the Japanese economy recover. The question is how the Bank of Japan can engineer such a change.
- Cleaning up the banking system of its bad loans is clearly desirable. What is not clear is whether such a cleanup would lead to an increase in output in the short run.

Key Terms

- depression, 463
- slump, 463
- liquidity trap, 468
- Great Depression, 471
- New Deal, 476
- National Recovery Administration (NRA), National Industrial Recovery Act (NIRA), 476, 477

Questions and Problems

Quick Check

1. Using the information in this chapter, label each of the following statements true, false, *or* uncertain. *Explain briefly.*

a. The stock market crash of 1929 reflected the realization by financial investors that the Great Depression was coming.

b. The Fed could have done more either to prevent, or at least to limit, the scope of the Great Depression.

c. We have learned how to use fiscal and monetary policy to avoid another Great Depression.

d. The Japanese slump in the 1990s was triggered by the sharp fall of Japanese stock prices at the end of the 1980s.

e. The Japanese central bank can help the Japanese economy recover by keeping inflation very low.

2. The effects of long-term unemployment on the natural rate. Suppose that price setting is given by

$$\frac{W}{P} = \frac{1}{1+0.1}$$

And wage setting is given by

$$\frac{W}{P} = 1 - (u_S + 0.5u_L)$$

where

u_S is the ratio of the number of short-term unemployed to the labor force.

u_L is the ratio of the number of long-term unemployed to the labor force.

Suppose further that the proportion of unemployed who are long-term unemployed is equal to β *so* $u_L = \beta u$, *and* $u_S = (1 - \beta)\, u$.

a. According to the wage-setting equation, which type of unemployment has a greater impact on wages—long term or short term? Explain.

b. Derive the natural rate. (*Hint*: Substitute $u_L = \beta u$ and $u_S = (1 - \beta)\, u$ in the wage-setting equation. The natural rate will depend on β.)

c. Compute the natural rate if $\beta = 0.0$; 0.4; 0.8. Explain.

3. The effect of long-term unemployment on inflation. Recall equation (8.6) in Chapter 8:

$$\pi_t - \pi_{t-1} = (\mu + z) - \alpha u_t$$

a. Interpret the equation. Why does higher unemployment lead to lower inflation given past inflation? Draw the change in inflation against the unemployment rate.

Write the overall unemployment rate, u, as $u = u_S + u_L$ *with* u_S *the short-term unemployment rate (the ratio of the short-term unemployed to the labor force), and* u_L *the long-term unemployment rate (the ratio of the long-term unemployed to the labor force).*

b. Now assume that the long-term unemployed have no effect on wage bargaining. Show how the equation above should be modified.

c. Suppose the proportion of long-term unemployed in unemployment increases (for a given u, u_L increases, and u_S decreases). Show what happens to the curve relating the change in inflation to the overall unemployment rate.

d. *"Disinflation requires high unemployment for some time. High unemployment leads to a higher proportion of long-term unemployed. If the long-term unemployed play no role in bargaining, the unemployment cost of disinflation will be higher than the cost derived in Chapter 8."* Discuss.

4. "The Japanese central bank should simply increase the growth rate of nominal money to get the economy out of its slump." Discuss.

Dig Deeper

5. Consider an economy in a recession and with a nominal interest rate very close to zero. (Think of Japan in 2001). Assume that there are only two relevant periods for economic decision making, corresponding to the current and the future period.

a. Draw the *IS-LM* for the current period. (Draw it so the equilibrium interest rate is very close to zero.)

b. Can current monetary policy increase current output? (*Hint*: Can the *LM* curve cross the horizontal axis?)

c. Can expected future monetary policy increase current output? How? Under what conditions?

d. If you were the head of the central bank, how would you convince people, firms, and financial investors that you will implement this monetary policy in the future?

e. Can we infer how successful the central bank is in convincing people it will implement this monetary policy in the future by looking at what happens to the term structure of interest rates today?

(For more discussion in the context of Japan, look at Krugman's "Japan: Still Trapped," at web.mit.edu/krugman/www/japtrap2.html.)

We invite you to visit the Blanchard page on the Prentice Hall Web site at:
www.prenhall.com/blanchard
for this chapter's World Wide Web exercises

Further Readings

For more on the Great Depression, Lester Chandler, *America's Greatest Depression* (New York, NY: Harper & Row, 1970) gives the basic facts. So does the book by John A. Garraty, *The Great Depression* (New York, NY: Harcourt Brace Jovanovich, 1986).

Peter Temin's *Did Monetary Forces Cause the Great Depression?* (New York, NY: W.W. Norton, 1976) looks more specifically at the macroeconomic issues. So do the articles in a symposium on the Great Depression in the *Journal of Economic Perspectives*, Spring 1993.

A description of the Great Depression through the eyes of those who suffered through it is given in Studs Terkel's *Hard Times: An Oral History of the Great Depression in America* (New York, NY: Pantheon Books, 1970).

A good book on the Japanese economy, although a bit out of date, is Takatoshi Ito's *The Japanese Economy* (Cambridge, MA: MIT Press, 1992).

For a discussion of the current Japanese economic problems, see Paul Krugman's Japan Web page at **www.wws.princeton.edu/pkrugman**. See also Adam Posen's *Restoring Japan's Economic Growth* (Washington, D.C.: Institute for International Studies, 1998).

CHAPTER 23

High Inflation

In 1913, the value of all currency circulating in Germany was 6 billion marks. Ten years later, in October 1923, 6 billion marks was barely enough to buy a one-kilo loaf of rye bread in Berlin. A month later, the price had increased to 428 billion marks.

The German hyperinflation of the early 1920s is probably the most famous hyperinflation. (**Hyperinflation** simply means very high inflation.) But it is not the only one. Table 23-1 (see below) summarizes the seven major hyperinflations that followed World War I and World War II. They share several features. They were all short (lasting a year or so) but intense, with inflation running at 50% per month or more. In all, the increase in the price level was staggering. As you can see, the largest price increase was actually not reached during the German hyperinflation, but in Hungary after World War II. What cost one Hungarian pengö in August 1945 cost 3,800 trillions of trillions of pengös less than a year later.

Such rates of inflation had not been seen before nor have they been seen since. The closest such rate in the recent past occurred in Bolivia. From January 1984 to September 1985,

Table 23-1 Seven Hyperinflations of the 1920s and 1940s

Country	Beginning	End	P_T/P_0	Average Monthly Inflation (%)	Average Monthly Money Growth (%)
Austria	Oct. 1921	Aug. 1922	70	47	31
Germany	Aug. 1922	Nov. 1923	1.0×10^{10}	322	314
Greece	Nov. 1943	Nov. 1944	4.7×10^{6}	365	220
Hungary 1	Mar. 1923	Feb. 1924	44	46	33
Hungary 2	Aug. 1945	Jul. 1946	3.8×10^{27}	19,800	12,200
Poland	Jan. 1923	Jan. 1924	699	82	72
Russia	Dec. 1921	Jan. 1924	1.2×10^{5}	57	49

P_T/P_0: Price level in the last month of hyperinflation divided by the price level in the first month.

Source: Philip Cagan, "The Monetary Dynamics of Hyperinflation," in Milton Friedman, ed., *Studies in the Quantity Theory of Money* (Chicago: University of Chicago Press, 1956), Table 1.

Table 23-2 High Inflation in Latin America, 1976–2000

	Average Monthly Inflation Rate (%)				
	1976–1980	1981–1985	1986–1990	1991–1995	1996–2000
Argentina	9.3	12.7	20.0	2.3	0.0
Brazil	3.4	7.9	20.7	19.0	0.6
Nicaragua*	1.4	3.6	35.6	8.5	0.8
Peru	3.4	6.0	23.7	4.8	0.8

Source: International Financial Statistics, IMF, various issues.
*Nicaragua: last column is for 1996 to 1999.

Bolivian inflation averaged 40% per month, implying a roughly 1,000-fold increase in the price level over 21 months. [With an inflation rate of 40% per month, the price level at the end of 21 months is $(1 + 0.4)^{21} = 1{,}171$ times the price level at the beginning.] But many countries, especially in Latin America, have struggled with prolonged bouts of high inflation. Table 23-2 gives average monthly inflation rates for four Latin American countries since 1976. All four had at least five years with average monthly inflation running above 20% a month. Both Argentina and Brazil had monthly inflation rates in excess of 10% a month for more than a decade. All four countries have now returned to low inflation—inflation has even turned to deflation in the case of Argentina.

What causes hyperinflations? You saw in Chapter 9 that inflation ultimately results from nominal money growth. The relation between nominal money growth and inflation is confirmed by the last two columns of Table 23-1: Note how, in each country, high inflation was associated with correspondingly high nominal money growth. Why was nominal money growth so high? The answer turns out to be common to all hyperinflations: Nominal money growth is high because the budget deficit is high. The budget deficit is high because the economy is affected by major shocks that make it difficult or impossible for the government to finance its expenditures in any way other than money creation.

In this chapter, we look at this answer in more detail, relying on examples from various hyperinflations.

- Section 23-1 looks at the relation between the budget deficit and money creation.
- Section 23-2 looks at the relation between inflation and real money balances.
- Section 23-3 puts the two together, and shows how a large budget deficit can lead to high and increasing inflation.
- Section 23-4 looks at how hyperinflations end.
- Section 23-5 draws conclusions from our two chapters on pathologies—depressions and slumps in Chapter 22, and high inflation in this chapter. ■

23-1 Budget Deficits and Money Creation

A government can finance its budget deficit in one of two ways:

- It can borrow, the way you or I would. We borrow by taking a loan. Governments borrow by issuing bonds.

- It can do something that neither you nor I can do. It can, in effect, finance the deficit by creating money. I say "in effect" because, as you will remember from Chapter 4, governments do not create money; the central bank creates money. But with the central bank's cooperation, the government can in effect finance itself by money creation: It can issue bonds and ask the central bank to buy them. The central bank then pays the government with money it creates, and the government uses that money to finance its deficit. This process is called **debt monetization**.

Most of the time, and in most countries, deficits are financed primarily through borrowing rather than through money creation. But, at the start of hyperinflations, two changes usually take place:

- *There is a budget crisis.* The source is typically a major social or economic upheaval.

  It may be a civil war or a revolution that destroys the state's ability to collect taxes. This was the case, for example, in Nicaragua in the 1980s.

  It may come, as in the case of the post–World War I and World War II hyperinflations, from the aftermath of a war that leaves the government with both smaller tax revenues and the large expenditures needed for reconstruction. This is what happened in Germany in 1922 and 1923. Burdened with payments for the war (called "war reparations") it had to pay to Allied forces, Germany had a budget deficit equal to more than two-thirds of its expenditures.

  It may come from a large adverse economic shock—for example, a large decline in the price of a raw material that is both the country's major export and its main source of revenues. As you shall see in this chapter's Focus box on Bolivian hyperinflation, this is what happened in Bolivia in the 1980s. The decline in the price of tin, Bolivia's principal export, was one of the main causes of Bolivian hyperinflation.
- *The government becomes increasingly unable to borrow from the public or from abroad to finance its deficit.* The reason is the size of the deficit itself. Worried that the government may not be able to repay the debt in the future, potential lenders start asking the government for higher and higher interest rates. Sometimes, foreign lenders decide to stop lending to the government altogether. As a result, the government turns increasingly to the other source of finance—money creation. Eventually, most of the deficit is financed by money creation.

How large is the rate of nominal money growth needed to finance a given amount of revenues?

- Let M be the nominal money stock, measured, say, at the end of each month. (In the case of hyperinflation, things change so quickly that it is useful to look at what happens from month to month, rather than from quarter to quarter, or from year to year.) Let ΔM be the change in the nominal money stock from the end of last month to the end of this month—nominal money creation during the month.
- The revenue, in real terms (that is, in terms of goods), that the government generates by creating an amount of money equal to ΔM is therefore equal to $\Delta M/P$—nominal money creation during the month, divided by the price level. This real revenue from money creation is called **seignorage**. The word is revealing: The right to issue money was a precious source of revenue for the "seigneurs" of the past: They could buy the goods they wanted by issuing their own money and using it to pay for the goods.

We can summarize what we have just learned by writing

$$\text{seignorage} = \frac{\Delta M}{P} \qquad (23.1)$$

◀ **We are taking a shortcut here. What should be on the right-hand side of the equation is the change in the monetary base—the money created by the central bank—not the change in the money stock (which includes both currency and checkable deposits). I ignore the distinction here; it does not play an important role in the argument that follows.**

Seignorage is equal to money creation, divided by the price level. To see what rate of nominal money growth is required to generate a given amount of seignorage, note that we can rewrite $\Delta M/P$ as

$$\frac{\Delta M}{P} = \frac{\Delta M}{M}\frac{M}{P}$$

"Real money balances" is just another name for the real money stock.

In words: We can think of seignorage, $\Delta M/P$, as the product of the rate of nominal money growth, $\Delta M/M$, times real money balances, M/P. The larger the real money balances held in the economy, the larger the amount of seignorage corresponding to a given rate of nominal money growth. Replacing this expression in equation (23.1) gives

$$\text{seignorage} = \frac{\Delta M}{M}\frac{M}{P} \qquad (23.2)$$

Remember: Income is a flow. *Y* here is real income per month.

This gives us the relation we wanted between seignorage, the rate of nominal money growth, and real money balances. To think about relevant magnitudes, it is convenient to divide both sides of equation (23.2) by real income, Y, (measured at a monthly rate):

$$\frac{\text{seignorage}}{Y} = \frac{\Delta M}{M}\left(\frac{M/P}{Y}\right) \qquad (23.3)$$

Suppose the government is running a budget deficit equal to 10% of real income, and decides to finance it through seignorage, so deficit$/Y$ = seignorage$/Y = 0.1$. Suppose people hold real balances equal to two months of income, so $(M/P)/Y = 2$. Then this implies that nominal money growth must satisfy

$$0.1 = \frac{\Delta M}{M} \times 2 \Rightarrow \frac{\Delta M}{M} = 0.05$$

To finance a deficit of 10% of real income through seignorage, the monthly growth rate of nominal money must be equal to 5%.

Does this imply that the government can finance a deficit equal to 20% of real income through a rate of nominal money growth of 10%, a deficit of 40% of real income through a rate of nominal money growth of 20%, and so on? No. As nominal money growth increases, so does inflation. And, as inflation increases, the opportunity cost of holding money increases, leading people to reduce their real money balances. In terms of equation (23.2), an increase in nominal money growth, $\Delta M/M$, leads to a decrease in real money balances, M/P, so that an increase in nominal money growth will generate a less proportional increase in seignorage. What is crucial here is how much people adjust their real money balances in response to inflation, and it is the issue to which we turn next.

23-2 Inflation and Real Money Balances

What determines the amount of real money balances that people are willing to hold? And how does this amount depend on nominal money growth?

Let's go back to the *LM* relation we derived in Chapter 5:

$$\frac{M}{P} = Y\,L(\underset{(-)}{i})$$

Higher real income leads people to hold larger real money balances. A higher nominal interest rate increases the opportunity cost of holding money rather than bonds and leads people to reduce their real money balances.

This characterization holds in both stable economic times and times of hyperinflations. But in times of hyperinflation, we can simplify it further. Here's how:

- First, rewrite the *LM* relation using the relation between the nominal interest rate and the real interest rate, $i = r + \pi^e$:

$$\frac{M}{P} = Y\,L\,(r + \pi^e)$$

Real money balances depend on real income, *Y*, on the real interest rate, *r*, and on expected inflation, π^e.

- Second, note that while all three variables (Y, r, and π^e) are likely to vary over time during a hyperinflation, expected inflation is likely to move much more than the other two variables: During a typical hyperinflation, actual inflation—and presumably expected inflation—may move from 0 to 50% a month or more.

So, it is not a bad approximation to assume that both income and the real interest rate are constant, and focus just on the movements in expected inflation. So, we write

$$\frac{M}{P} = \bar{Y}L\,\underset{(\;-\;)}{(\bar{r} + \pi^e)} \qquad (23.4)$$

where the bars over *Y* and *r* mean that we now take both income and the real interest rate as constant. In times of hyperinflation, equation (23.4) tells us we can think of real money balances as depending primarily on expected inflation. As expected inflation increases and it becomes more and more costly to hold money, people will reduce their real money balances.

Recall, from Chapter 14, that $r = i - \pi^e$. Equivalently, $i = r + \pi^e$.

During a hyperinflation people indeed find many ways of reducing their real money balances. When the monthly rate of inflation is 100%, for example, keeping currency for a month implies losing half of its real value (because things cost twice as much a month later). **Barter**, the exchange of goods for other goods rather than for money, increases. Payments for wages become much more frequent—often twice weekly. Once people are paid, they rush to stores to buy goods. While the government often makes it illegal to use other currencies than the one it is printing, people shift to foreign currencies as stores of value. And even if it is illegal, an increasing proportion of transactions takes place in foreign currency. During the Latin American hyperinflations of the 1980s, people shifted to U.S. dollars. The shift to dollars has become so widespread in the world that it has a name: **dollarization** (the use of dollars in another country's domestic transactions).

In describing the Austrian hyperinflation of the 1920s, Keynes noted: "In Vienna, during the period of collapse, mushroom exchange banks sprang up at every street corner, where you could change your krone into Zurich francs within a few minutes of receiving them, and so avoid the risk of loss during the time it would take you to reach your usual bank."

One of the hopes of the European Union is that the Euro may replace the dollar as the foreign currency of choice. (Why would the European Union want this to happen?) If it happens, we may have to speak of "euroization" rather than of "dollarization."

By how much do real money balances actually decrease as inflation increases? Figure 23-1 examines the evidence from the Hungarian hyperinflation of the early 1920s and provides some insights.

- Panel (a) plots real money balances and the monthly inflation rate from November 1922 to February 1924. Note how movements in inflation are reflected in opposite movements in real money balances. The short-lived decline in Hungarian inflation from July to October 1923 is reflected in an equally short-lived increase in real money balances. At the end of the hyperinflation in February 1924, real money balances are roughly half what they were at the beginning.
- Panel (b) presents the same information as panel (a), but in the form of a scatter diagram. It plots monthly real money balances on the horizontal axis against inflation on the vertical axis. (We do not observe expected inflation, which is the variable we would like to plot, so I use actual inflation instead.) Note how the points nicely describe a downward-sloping demand for money: As actual

Figure 23-1

Inflation and Real Money Balances in Hungary, November 1922 to February 1924

At the end of the Hungarian hyperinflation, real money balances stood at roughly half their pre-hyperinflation level.

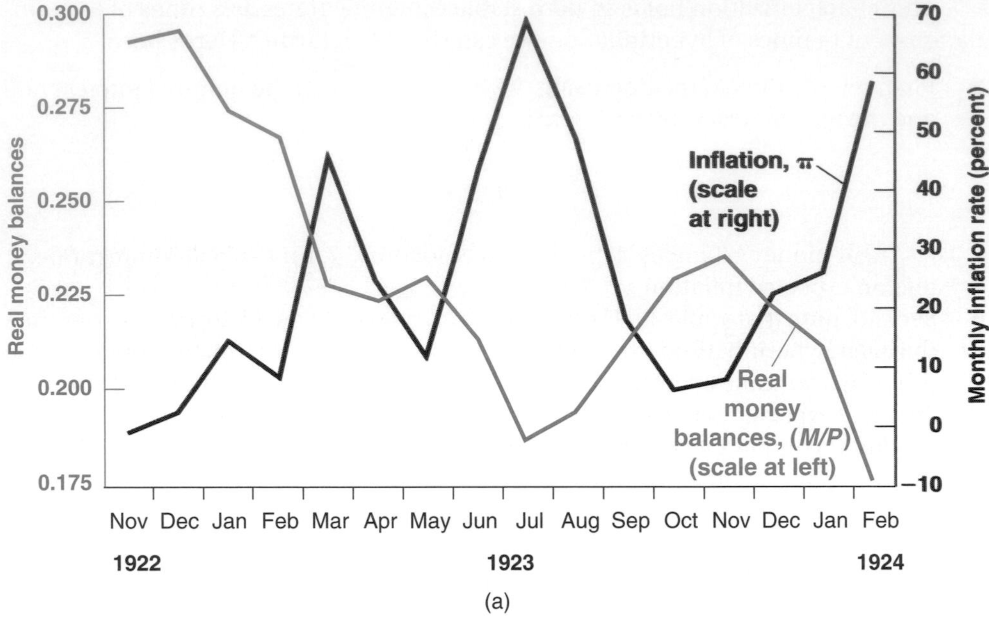

(a)

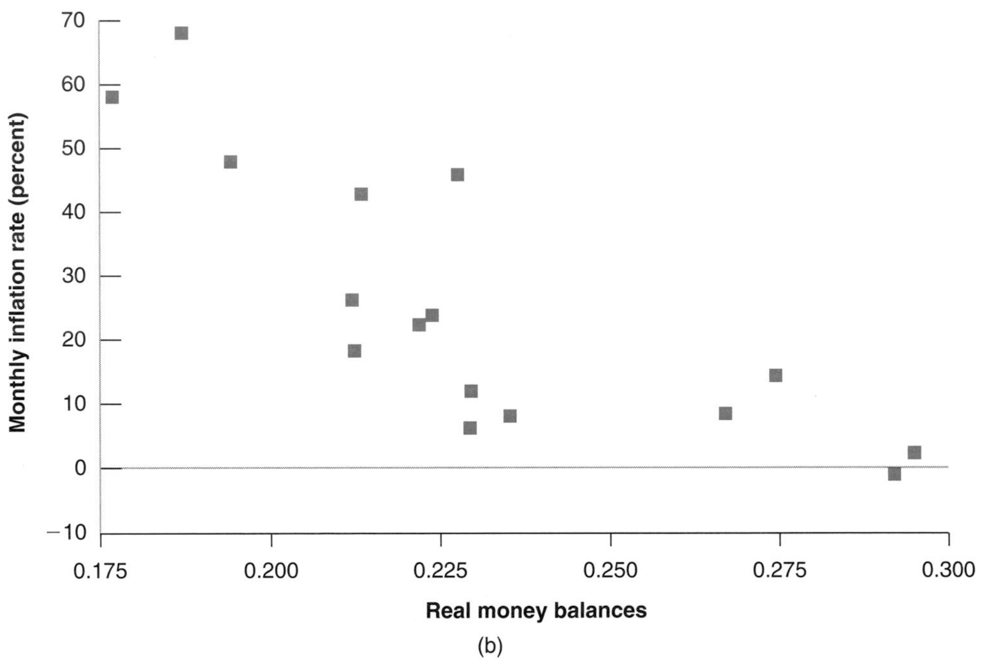

(b)

This decrease in real money balances explains why, in Table 23-1, average inflation is higher than average nominal money growth in each of the seven postwar hyperinflations: That real money balances, M/P, decrease during a hyperinflation implies that prices, P, must increase more than M—average inflation must be higher than average nominal money growth.

inflation—and, presumably, expected inflation as well—increases, the demand for money strongly decreases.

To summarize, increases in inflation lead people to decrease their use of money, and lead to a decrease in real money balances.

23-3 Deficits, Seignorage, and Inflation

We have derived two relations:

- A relation between seignorage, nominal money growth, and real money balances (equation [23.2]).

- A relation between real money balances and inflation (equation [23.4]).

Combining the two gives

$$\text{seignorage} = \left(\frac{\Delta M}{M}\right)\left(\frac{M}{P}\right) = \left(\frac{\Delta M}{M}\right)\left[\bar{Y}L(\bar{r}+\pi^e)\right] \qquad (23.5)$$

The first line repeats equation (23.2): Seignorage equals the rate of nominal money growth times real money balances. And the second line replaces real money balances by their expression in terms of expected inflation, from equation (23.4).

Using the relation between seignorage, the rate of nominal money growth, and the expected rate of inflation implied by the second line of (23.5), we can now show how the need to finance a large budget deficit through seignorage can lead not only to *high inflation*, but also, as is the case during hyperinflations, to *high and increasing inflation.*

The Case of Constant Nominal Money Growth

Suppose the government chooses a *constant* rate of nominal money growth and maintains that rate forever. (Clearly, this is not what happens during hyperinflations, where the rate of nominal money growth typically increases over the course of the hyperinflation; we shall get more realistic later.) How much seignorage will this constant rate of nominal money growth generate?

If nominal money growth is constant forever, then inflation and expected inflation must eventually be constant as well. Assume output growth equals zero. Then, actual inflation and expected inflation must both equal nominal money growth:

Recall that in the medium run (equation [9.8]):

$$\pi = g_m - \bar{g}_y$$

$$\bar{g}_y = 0 \Rightarrow \pi = g_m$$

$$\pi^e = \pi = \frac{\Delta M}{M}$$

Replacing π^e by $\Delta M/M$, in equation (23.5) gives

$$\text{seignorage} = \frac{\Delta M}{M}\left[\bar{Y}L\left(\bar{r}+\frac{\Delta M}{M}\right)\right] \qquad (23.6)$$

Note that nominal money growth, $\Delta M/M$, enters the equation in two places, and has two opposite effects on seignorage:

- Given real money balances, nominal money growth increases seignorage. This effect is captured by the first term in $\Delta M/M$ in equation (23.6).
- An increase in nominal money growth increases inflation and thus decreases real money balances. This effect is captured by $\Delta M/M$ in the second term on the right of equation (23.6).

$\Delta M/M\uparrow \Rightarrow$ Seignorage $\uparrow$

$\Delta M/M\uparrow \Rightarrow \pi\uparrow \Rightarrow \pi^e\uparrow \Rightarrow L(\bar{r}+\pi^e)\downarrow \Rightarrow M/P\downarrow \Rightarrow$ Seignorage $\downarrow$

So, the net effect of nominal money growth on seignorage is ambiguous. The empirical evidence is that the relation between seignorage and nominal money growth looks as shown in Figure 23-2. The relation is hump shaped:

At low rates of nominal money growth, such as we observe in Europe or the United States today, an increase in nominal money growth leads to a small reduction in real money balances. Thus, higher money growth leads to an increase in seignorage.

When nominal money growth (and therefore inflation) is very high, however, the reduction in real money balances induced by higher nominal money growth becomes larger and larger. Eventually, there is a rate of nominal money growth—point *A* in Figure 23-2—beyond which further increases in nominal money growth *decrease* seignorage.

Figure 23-2

Seignorage and Nominal Money Growth

Seignorage is first an increasing function, then a decreasing function of nominal money growth.

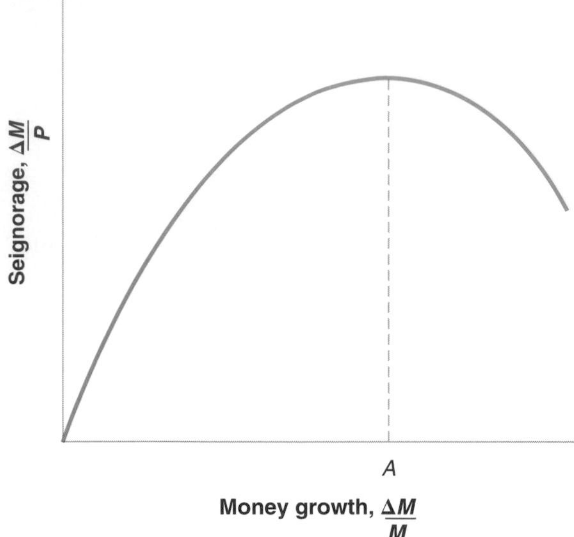

The shape of the relation in Figure 23-2 may look familiar to those of you who have studied the economics of taxation. Income tax revenues equal the *tax rate on income* times income—the *tax base*. At low tax rates, the tax rate has little influence on how much people work, and tax revenues increase with the tax rate. But as tax rates increase further, some people start working less—or stop declaring part of their income—and the tax base decreases. As the income tax reaches very high levels, increases in the tax rate lead to a decline in tax revenues. Obviously, tax rates of 100% lead to no tax revenue at all: Why work if the government takes all your income?

See the Focus box "Monetary Contraction and Fiscal Expansion: The United States in the Early 1980s," in Chapter 20.

This relation between tax revenues and the tax rate is often called the **Laffer curve**, after the economist Arthur Laffer, who argued in the early 1980s that a cut in U.S. tax rates would lead to more tax revenues. He was clearly wrong about where the United States was on the curve: The effect of the decrease in tax rates was to lower tax revenues, not increase them. But the general point still stands: When tax rates are high enough, a further increase in the tax rate can lead to a decrease in tax revenues.

If the inflation rate is 5%, you lose 5% of the value of your real money balances. It is as if you were paying a tax of 5% on these balances.

There is more than a simple analogy here. Inflation can be thought of as a tax on money balances. The tax rate is the rate of inflation, π, which reduces the real value of money holdings. The tax base is real money balances, M/P. The product of these two variables, $\pi(M/P)$, is called the **inflation tax**. There is a subtle difference from other forms of taxation: What the government receives from money creation at any point in time is not the inflation tax, but rather seignorage, $(\Delta M/M)\ (M/P)$. However, the two are closely related. When nominal money growth is constant, inflation must eventually be equal to nominal money growth, so that

$$\text{Inflation tax} = \pi \left(\frac{M}{P}\right)$$
$$= \left(\frac{\Delta M}{M}\right)\left(\frac{M}{P}\right)$$
$$= \text{Seignorage}$$

What rate of nominal money growth leads to the *most seignorage*, and how much seignorage does it generate? These are the questions that Philip Cagan asked in a classic paper on hyperinflations written in 1956. In one of the earliest uses of econometrics,

Table 23-3 Nominal Money Growth and Seignorage

	Rate of Money Growth Maximizing Seignorage (% per month)	Implied Seignorage (% of output)	Actual Rate of Money Growth (% per month)
Austria	12	13	31
Germany	20	14	314
Greece	28	11	220
Hungary 1	12	19	33
Hungary 2	32	6	12,200
Poland	54	5	72
Russia	39	1	49

Monthly rate of nominal money growth, in percent.

Source: Philip Cagan, "The Monetary Dynamics of Hyperinflation," in Milton Friedman, ed., *Studies in the Quantity Theory of Money* (Chicago: University of Chicago Press, 1956).

Cagan estimated the relation between the demand for money and expected inflation (equation [23.4]) during each of the hyperinflations in Table 23-1. Then, using equation (23.6), he computed the rate of nominal money growth that maximized seignorage, and the associated amount of seignorage. The answers he obtained are given in the first two columns of Table 23-3. The third column repeats the actual nominal money growth numbers from Table 23-1.

This table shows something very interesting: In all seven hyperinflations, actual average nominal money growth (column 3) far exceeded the rate of nominal money growth that would have maximized seignorage (column 1). Compare the actual rate of nominal money growth in Hungary after World War II, 12,200%, to the rate of nominal money growth that would have maximized seignorage, 32%. This would seem to be a serious problem for the story we have developed so far. If the reason for money creation was to finance the budget deficit, why was the actual rate of nominal money growth so much higher than the number that maximized seignorage? The answer lies in the dynamics of the economy's adjustment to high nominal money growth. We now turn to that.

Dynamics and Increasing Inflation

Return to the argument we just developed: *If maintained forever*, a higher rate of nominal money growth will *eventually* lead to a proportional increase in both actual inflation and expected inflation, and so lead to a decrease in real money balances. If nominal money growth is higher than the amount that maximizes seignorage, the increase in nominal money growth will lead to a decrease in seignorage.

The crucial words in the argument are "if maintained forever" and "eventually." Consider a government that needs to finance a suddenly much larger deficit, and decides to do so by creating money. As the rate of money growth increases, it may take a while for inflation and expected inflation to adjust. Even as expected inflation increases, it will take a while longer for people to fully adjust their real money balances: Creating barter arrangements takes time, the use of foreign currencies in transactions develops slowly, and so on.

Let's state this conclusion more formally. Recall our equation for seignorage:

$$\text{seignorage} = \left(\frac{\Delta M}{M}\right)\left(\frac{M}{P}\right)$$

- In the short run, an increase in the rate of nominal money growth, $\Delta M/M$, may lead to little change in real money balances, M/P. Put another way, if it is willing to increase nominal money growth sufficiently, a government will be able to generate nearly any amount of seignorage that it wants *in the short run*, far in excess of the numbers in the second column of Table 23-3.
- But over time, as prices adjust and real money balances decrease, this government will find that the same rate of nominal money growth yields less and less seignorage (M/P will decrease, leading to lower seignorage for a given rate of nominal money growth $\Delta M/M$).
- So, if the government keeps trying to finance a deficit larger than the deficit shown in the second column of Table 23-3(for example, if Austria tries to finance a deficit that is more than 13% of GDP), it will find that it cannot do so with a constant rate of nominal money growth. The only way it will succeed is by continually *increasing* the rate of nominal money growth. This is why actual nominal money growth exceeds the numbers in the first column, and why hyperinflations are nearly always characterized by increasing nominal money growth and inflation.

There is also another effect at work, which we have ignored until now. We have taken the deficit as given. But as inflation becomes very high, the budget deficit typically becomes larger. Part of the reason has to do with lags in tax collection. This effect is known as the **Tanzi-Olivera effect**, for Vito Tanzi and Julio Olivera, two economists who have emphasized its importance. As taxes are collected on past nominal income, their real value goes down with inflation. For example, if income taxes are paid this year on income received last year, and if the price level this year is 10 times higher than last year's price level, the actual tax rate is only one-tenth of the official tax rate. Thus, high inflation typically decreases real government revenues, making the deficit problem worse. The problem is often compounded by other effects on the expenditure side: Governments often try to slow inflation by prohibiting firms under state control from increasing their prices, although their costs are increasing with inflation. The direct effect on inflation is small at best, but the firms then run a deficit that must in turn be financed by the government, further increasing the budget deficit. As the budget deficit increases, so does the need for more seignorage, and so does the need for even higher nominal money growth.

Hyperinflations and Economic Activity

We have focused so far on movements in nominal money growth and inflation—which clearly dominate the economic scene during a hyperinflation. But hyperinflations affect the economy in many other ways:

Initially, higher nominal money growth leads to an *increase* in output. It takes some time for increases in nominal money growth to be reflected in inflation, and during that time, the effects of higher nominal money growth are expansionary: As you saw in Chapter 14, the initial effects of an increase in nominal money growth are actually to *decrease* nominal interest rates and real interest rates, leading to an increase in demand and an increase in output.

In the short run:
$g_m\uparrow \Rightarrow i\downarrow$
and
$g_m\uparrow \Rightarrow \pi^e\uparrow$
So, for both reasons
$r = i - \pi^e\downarrow$

But as inflation becomes very high, the adverse effects of hyperinflation dominate:

- The transaction system works less and less well. One famous example of inefficient exchange is the story of people using wheelbarrows to carry all the currency needed for transactions at the end of the German hyperinflation.

- Price signals become less and less useful: Because prices change so often, it is difficult for consumers and producers to assess the relative prices of goods and to make informed decisions. The evidence shows that the higher the rate of inflation, the higher the variation in the relative prices of different goods. Thus, the price system, which is crucial to the functioning of a market economy, also becomes less and less efficient.
- Swings in the inflation rate become larger. It becomes harder to predict what inflation will be in the near future, whether it will be, say, 500 or 1,000% over the next year. Borrowing at a given nominal interest rate becomes more and more a gamble. If you borrow at, say, 1,000% for a year, you may end up paying a real interest rate of 500% or 0%: A large difference! The result is that borrowing and lending typically come to a near stop in the last months of hyperinflation, leading to a large decline in investment.

The following joke was told in Israel during the high inflation of the 1980s: "Why is it cheaper to take the taxi rather than the bus? Because in the bus, you have to pay the fare at the beginning of the ride. In the taxi, you pay only at the end."

We have discussed here the costs of very high inflation. The discussion today in OECD countries is about the costs of, say, 5% inflation versus 0%. The issues are quite different in that case, and we return to them in Chapter 25.

So, as inflation increases and its costs become larger, there is typically an increasing consensus that it should be stopped. This takes us to the next section, how hyperinflations actually end.

23-4 How Do Hyperinflations End?

Hyperinflations do not die a natural death. Rather, they have to be stopped through a **stabilization program**.

The Elements of a Stabilization Program

What needs to be done to end a hyperinflation follows from our analysis of the causes of hyperinflation:

- There must be a fiscal reform and a credible reduction of the budget deficit. This reform must take place on both the expenditure side and the revenue side of the budget.

  On the expenditure side, reform typically implies reducing the government subsidies that have often mushroomed during the hyperinflation. Obtaining a temporary suspension of interest payments on foreign debt also helps decrease expenditures. An important component of stabilization in Germany in 1923 was the reduction in "reparation payments"—precisely those payments that had triggered the hyperinflation in the first place.

  On the revenue side, what is required is not so much an increase in overall taxation but rather a change in the composition of taxation. This is important: As you saw, during a hyperinflation, people are in effect paying a tax, namely, the inflation tax. Stabilization implies replacing the inflation tax with other taxes. The challenge is to put in place and collect these other taxes. This cannot be done overnight, but it is essential that people become convinced that it will be done and that the budget deficit will be reduced.
- The central bank must make a credible commitment that it will no longer automatically monetize the government debt. This credibility may be achieved in several ways. The central bank can be prohibited, by decree, from buying any government debt, so that no monetization of the debt is possible. Or the central bank can peg the exchange rate to the currency of a country with low inflation. An even more drastic step is to dollarize, to make a foreign currency such as the U.S. dollar the country's official currency. This step is drastic because it implies giving up seignorage altogether, and is often perceived as a decrease in the country's independence.

This is what Argentina did in 1991, adopting a currency board and fixing the exchange rate at one dollar for one peso. See the discussion of currency boards and of the evolution of the Argentine economy since 1991 in Chapter 21.

- Are other measures needed as well? Some economists argue that **incomes policies**—that is, wage and price guidelines or controls—should be used, in addition to fiscal and monetary measures, to help the economy reach a new lower rate of inflation. Incomes policies, they argue, help coordinate expectations around a new lower rate of inflation. If firms know wages will not increase, they will not increase prices. If workers know prices will not increase, they will not ask for wage increases, and inflation is eliminated more easily.

This argument was particularly relevant in the stabilizations in eastern Europe in the early 1990s where, because of central planning, the initial structure of relative prices was very different from the structure of relative prices in a market economy. Imposing wage or price controls would have prevented relative prices from adjusting to their appropriate market value. ▶

Others argue that credible deficit reduction and central bank independence are all that is required. They argue that the appropriate policy changes, if credible, can lead to drastic changes in expectations and therefore lead to the elimination of expected and actual inflation nearly overnight. They point to the potential dangers of wage and price controls. Governments may end up relying on the controls, and may not take the painful but needed fiscal and policy measures, leading ultimately to failure. Also, if the structure of relative prices is distorted to start with, price controls run the risk of maintaining these distortions.

Stabilization programs that do not include incomes policies are called **orthodox**; those that do are called **heterodox** (because they rely on both monetary-fiscal changes and incomes policies). The hyperinflations of Table 23-1 were all ended through orthodox programs. Many of the Latin American stabilizations of the 1980s and 1990s have relied on heterodox programs.

Can Stabilization Programs Fail?

Can stabilization programs fail? Yes. They can fail, and they often do. Argentina went through five stabilization plans from 1984 to 1989 before succeeding in stabilizing inflation in the early 1990s. Brazil only succeeded in 1995, in its sixth attempt in 12 years.

Sometimes failure comes from a botched or half-hearted effort at stabilization. A government puts wage controls in place, but does not take the measures needed to reduce the deficit and nominal money growth. Wage controls cannot work if nominal money growth continues, and the stabilization program eventually fails.

See, for example, the failed stabilization attempt in April 1984 in Bolivia described in the Focus box in this chapter. ▶

Sometimes failure comes from political opposition. If social conflict was one of the causes of the initial budget deficit and thus was at the root of the hyperinflation, it may still be present and just as hard to resolve at the time of stabilization. Those who lose from the fiscal reform required to decrease the deficit will oppose the stabilization program and may force the government to retreat. Often, workers who perceive an increase in the price of public services or an increase in taxation, but who do not fully perceive the decrease in the inflation tax, go on strike or even riot, leading to failure of the stabilization plan.

This is a variation on the theme of self-fulfilling exchange rate crises developed in Chapter 21. ▶

Failure can also come from the anticipation of failure. Suppose the exchange rate is fixed to the dollar as part of the stabilization program. Also suppose participants in financial markets anticipate that the government will soon be forced to devalue. To compensate for the risk of devaluation, they require very high interest rates to hold domestic bonds rather than U.S. bonds. These very high interest rates cause a large recession. The recession forces the government to devalue, validating the markets' initial fears. If instead, markets had believed that the government would maintain the exchange rate, the risk of devaluation would have been lower, interest rates would have been lower, and the government would have been able to proceed with stabilization. To many economists, the successes and failures of stabilization plans appear to have an element of self-fulfilling prophecy. Even well-conceived plans work only if they are expected to work. In other words, luck and good public relations both play a role.

The Costs of Stabilization

You saw in Chapter 9 how the U.S. disinflation of the early 1980s was associated with a recession and a large increase in unemployment. Similarly, disinflation in Europe in the

1980s was also associated with a large increase in unemployment. We might therefore expect the much larger disinflations associated with the end of a hyperinflation to be associated with very large recessions or even with depressions. This is typically not the case.

To understand why, recall our discussion of disinflation in Section 9-3. We argued that there were three reasons why inflation might not decrease as fast as nominal money growth, leading to a recession:

Remember that the rate of real money growth equals the rate of nominal money growth minus the rate of inflation. If inflation decreases by less than nominal money growth, this implies negative real money growth—a decrease in the real money stock. This decrease in the real money stock then leads to high interest rates, which can trigger a recession.

- Wages are typically set in nominal terms for some period of time (up to three years in the United States) and, as a result, many of them are already determined when the decision to disinflate is made.
- Wage contracts are typically staggered, making it difficult to implement a slowdown in all wages at the same time.
- The change in monetary policy may not be fully and instantaneously credible.

Hyperinflation eliminates the first two problems. During hyperinflation, wages and prices are adjusted so often that both nominal rigidities and the staggering of wage decisions become nearly irrelevant.

But the issue of credibility remains. The fact that even coherent programs may not succeed implies that *no program is fully credible from the start.* If, for example, the government decides to fix the exchange rate, a high interest rate may be needed initially to maintain the parity. Those programs that turn out to be successful are those programs where increased credibility leads to lower interest rates over time. But, even when credibility eventually arrives, the initial high interest rate often leads to a recession. Overall, the evidence is that most, but not all, hyperinflations involve some cost in output.

How should a stabilization package be designed so as to reduce this output cost? Should the stabilization program be orthodox or heterodox? Should there be restrictions on nominal money growth, or should the exchange rate be fixed? At this point, few countries are experiencing high inflation, so that the questions are not at the top of the policy makers' agendas. But, if history is any guide, some countries will again lose control of their budget, finance the budget deficit through money creation, and experience high, if not hyperinflation. These questions are then sure to come back.

All rich and most middle-income countries in the world have low inflation at this point. A few, such as Japan, have deflation. The middle-income country with the highest inflation rate at the time of this writing is Turkey, where the annual inflation rate is now above 60%.

After 10 years of low inflation under a currency board arrangement, Argentina is again at risk. The currency board has collapsed, the peso has depreciated, and the budget deficit is getting larger. It is too early to say whether this will lead to high inflation.

23-5 Conclusions

An underlying theme of the core of this book was that, while in the short run, output fluctuated around its natural level, it would tend to return to the natural level of output in the medium run. And, if the adjustment was too slow, fiscal and monetary policy could be used to help and shape the adjustment. Most of the time, this is indeed what happens. But the last two chapters tell us, it does not always happen:

- Sometimes, the adjustment mechanism that is supposed to return the economy to its natural level of output breaks down. An economy in a slump or in a depression experiences deflation, and deflation makes things worse rather than better.
- Monetary and fiscal policy may prove unable to help. In a slump, monetary policy may be constrained by the liquidity trap: Nominal interest rates cannot be negative. The government cannot run budget deficits to sustain higher demand and higher output forever; if it tries, the increase in government debt eventually becomes a problem in itself.
- And governments may lose control of both fiscal policy and monetary policy. Faced with major adverse shocks—war, civil war, a collapse of their exports, a social explosion—they may lose control of their budget, run a larger and larger budget deficit, and have no other choice than to finance the deficit through money creation. The result of this loss of control may be high inflation or even hyperinflation.

The Bolivian Hyperinflation of the 1980s

In the 1970s, Bolivia achieved strong output growth, in large part because of high world prices for its exports: tin, silver, coca, oil, and natural gas. But by the end of the decade, the economic situation started deteriorating. The price of tin declined. Foreign borrowing, which had financed a large part of Bolivian spending in the 1970s, was sharply curtailed as foreign lenders started worrying about repayment. Partly as a result, and partly because of long-running social conflicts, political chaos ensued. From 1979 to 1982, the country had 12 presidents, nine military and three civilian.

When the first freely elected president in 18 years came to power in 1982, he faced a nearly impossible task. U.S. commercial banks and other foreign lenders were running scared. They surely did not want to make new loans to Bolivia, and they wanted previous loans to be repaid. Net private (medium-term and long-term) foreign lending to the Bolivian government had decreased from 3.5% of GDP in 1980 to −0.3% in 1982, and to −1.0% in 1983. Because the government had no other choice, it turned to money creation to finance the budget deficit.

Inflation and Budget Deficits

The next three years were characterized by the interaction of steadily higher inflation and budget deficits.

Table 1 gives the budget numbers for the period 1981–1986. Because of the lags in tax collection, the effect of rising inflation was to sharply reduce real tax revenues. And the government's attempt to maintain low prices for public services was the source of large deficits for state-run firms. As these deficits were financed by subsidies from the state, the result was a further increase in the budget deficit. In 1984, the budget deficit reached a staggering 31.6% of GDP.

The result of higher budget deficits and the need for higher seignorage was to increase nominal money growth and inflation. Inflation, which had run at an average 2.5% a month in 1981, increased to 7% in 1982 and to 11% in 1983. As shown in Figure 1, which gives Bolivia's monthly inflation rate from January 1984 to April 1986 (the vertical line indicates the beginning of stabilization), inflation kept increasing in 1984 and 1985, reaching 182% in February 1985.

Stabilization

There were many attempts at stabilization along the way. Stabilization programs were launched in November 1982, November 1983, April 1984, August 1984, and February 1985. The April 1984 package was an orthodox program involving a large devaluation, the announcement of a tax reform, and an increase in public-sector prices. But the opposition of trade unions was too strong, and the program was abandoned.

After the election of a new president, yet another attempt at stabilization was made in September 1985. This one proved successful. The stabilization plan was organized around the elimination of the budget deficit. Its main features were

- Fiscal policy: Public-sector prices were increased; food and energy prices were increased; public-sector wages were frozen; and a tax reform, aimed at reestablishing and broadening the tax base, was announced.
- Monetary policy: The official exchange rate of the peso was adjusted to what the black market rate (the actual exchange rate at which one could exchange pesos for dollars before the stabilization program) had been pre-stabilization. The exchange rate was set at 1.1 million pesos to the dollar, up from 67,000 pesos to the dollar the month before (a 1,600% devaluation). The exchange rate was then left to float, within limits.
- Reestablish international creditworthiness: Negotiations were started with international organizations and commercial banks to restructure the debt. An agreement with foreign creditors and the IMF was reached nine months later, in June 1986.

Table 1 Revenues, Expenditures, and the Deficit, as a Percentage of Bolivian GDP

Percent of GDP	1981	1982	1983	1984	1985	1986
Revenues	9.4	4.6	2.6	2.6	1.3	10.3
Expenditures	15.1	26.9	20.1	33.2	6.1	7.7
Budget Balance (deficit)	−5.7	−22.3	−17.5	−31.6	−4.8	2.6

Revenues and expenditures of the central government.

Source: Jeffrey Sachs, "The Bolivian Hyperinflation and Stabilization," National Bureau of Economic Research, working paper No. 2073, November 1986, Table 3.

FOCUS

Continued

As in the previous attempt at stabilization, the unions called a general strike. In response, the government declared a state of siege, and the strike was quickly disbanded. After so many failed attempts to end hyperinflation, public opinion was clearly in favor of stabilization.

The effects on inflation were dramatic. By the second week of September, the inflation rate was actually negative! Inflation did not remain negative for very long, but the average monthly rate of inflation was below 2% during 1986–1989. As Table 1 shows, the budget deficit was drastically reduced in 1986, and the average deficit was below 5% of GNP for the rest of the decade.

Did stabilization have a negative effect on output? It probably did. Real interest rates remained very high for more than a year after stabilization. The full effect of these high real interest rates on output is hard to establish because, at the same time stabilization was implemented, Bolivia was hit with further large declines in the price of tin and natural gas. In addition, a major campaign against narcotics had the effect of disrupting coca production. How much of the Bolivian recession of 1986 was due to stabilization, and how much was due to these other factors, is difficult to assess.

References:

The material in this box draws largely from Jeffrey Sachs, "The Bolivian Hyperinflation and Stabilization," NBER working paper, 1986. Sachs was one of the architects of the stabilization program.

See also Juan Antonio Morales, "The Transition from Stabilization to Sustained Growth in Bolivia," in Michael Bruno et al., eds., Lessons of Economic Stabilization and Its Aftermath *(Cambridge, MA: MIT Press, 1991).*

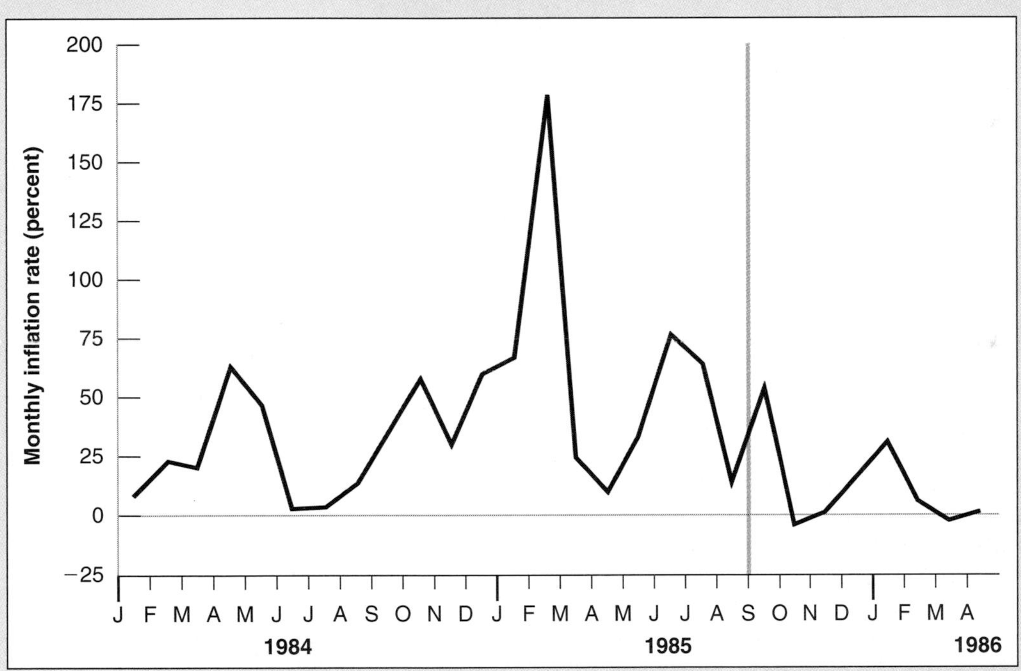

Figure 1 *Bolivian Monthly Inflation Rate, January 1984 to April 1986*

Summary

- Hyperinflations are periods of high inflation. The most extreme episodes took place after World Wars I and II in Europe. But Latin America has had episodes of high inflation as recently as the early 1990s.
- High inflation comes from high nominal money growth. High nominal money growth comes from the combination of large budget deficits and the inability to finance these large budget deficits through borrowing, either from the public or from abroad.
- The revenues from money creation are called seignorage. Seignorage is equal to the product of nominal money growth and real money balances. The smaller

are real money balances, the higher the required rate of nominal money growth, and therefore the higher the rate of inflation required to generate a given amount of seignorage.

- Hyperinflations are typically characterized by increasing inflation. There are two reasons why. One is that higher nominal money growth leads to higher inflation, inducing people to reduce real money balances, requiring even higher nominal money growth (and thus leading to even higher inflation) to finance the same real deficit. The other reason is that higher inflation often increases the deficit, which requires higher nominal money growth, and even higher inflation.
- Hyperinflations are ended through stabilization programs. To be successful, stabilization programs must include fiscal measures aimed at reducing the deficit and monetary measures aimed at reducing or eliminating money creation as a source of financing for the deficit. Some stabilization plans also include wage and price guidelines or controls.
- A stabilization program that imposes wage and price controls without changes in fiscal policy and monetary policy will fail. But even coherent and well-conceived programs do not always succeed. Anticipations of failure may lead to failure of even a coherent plan.

Key Terms

- hyperinflation, 489
- debt monetization, 491
- seignorage, 491
- barter, 493
- dollarization, 493
- Laffer curve, 496
- inflation tax, 496
- Tanzi-Olivera effect, 498
- stabilization program, 499
- incomes policies, 499
- orthodox stabilization program; heterodox stabilization program, 500

Questions and Problems

Quick Check

1. *Using the information in this chapter, label each of the following statements* true, false, *or* uncertain. *Explain briefly.*
   a. In the short run, governments can finance a deficit of any size through money growth.
   b. The inflation tax is always equal to seignorage.
   c. Hyperinflations may distort prices, but have no effect on real output.
   d. The solution to ending hyperinflations is simple: Institute a wage and price freeze, and inflation will stop.
   e. As inflation is generally good for those who borrow money, hyperinflations are the best times in which to take out large loans.
   f. Budget deficits usually shrink during hyperinflations.

2. *Assume that money demand takes the following form:*

$$\frac{M}{P} = Y[1-(r+\pi^e)]$$

where $Y = 1{,}000$ and $r = 0.1$.
   a. Assume that, in the short run, π^e is constant and equal to 25%. Calculate the amount of seignorage if the rate of money growth, $\Delta M/M$, equals:
      1. 25%.
      2. 50%.
      3. 75%.
   b. In the medium run, $\pi^e = \pi = \Delta M/M$. Compute the amount of seignorage associated with the three rates of money growth in question (a). Explain why the answers differ from those in (a).

3. *How would each of the following change the Tanzi-Olivera effect?*
   a. Requiring monthly instead of yearly tax payments by households.
   b. Assessing greater penalties for under-withholding of taxes from monthly paychecks.
   c. Decreasing the income tax, and increasing the sales tax.

4. *You are the economic adviser to a country suffering from a hyperinflation. Discuss the following statements made by politicians debating the proper course for stabilization:*

   "This crisis will not end until workers begin to pay their fair share of taxes."
   "The central bank has demonstrated that it cannot responsibly wield its power to create money, so we have no choice but to adopt a currency board."
   "Price controls are necessary to end this madness."
   "Stabilization will only be successful if there is a large recession and a substantial increase in unemployment."
   "Let's not blame the central bank. The problem is fiscal policy, not monetary policy."

Dig Deeper

5. *Referring to question 2, in the medium run, what is the rate of money growth that maximizes seignorage?*

WWW *We invite you to visit the Blanchard page on the Prentice Hall Web site at:*
www.prenhall.com/blanchard
for this chapter's World Wide Web exercises

Further Readings

For more on the German hyperinflation, read Steven Webb, *Hyperinflation and Stabilization in the Weimar Republic* (New York, NY: Oxford University Press, 1989).

Two good reviews of what economists know and don't know about hyperinflation are

Rudiger Dornbusch, Federico Sturzenegger, and Holger Wolf, "Extreme Inflation: Dynamics and Stabilization," *Brookings Papers on Economic Activity*, 1990–2, pp. 1–84.

Pierre Richard Agenor and Peter Montiel, *Development Macroeconomics* (Princeton, NJ: Princeton University Press, 1995), Chapters 8 to 11. Chapter 8 makes for easy reading; the other chapters are more difficult.

The experience of Israel, which went through high inflation and stabilization in the 1980s, is described in Michael Bruno's *Crisis, Stabilization and Economic Reform* (New York, NY: Oxford University Press, 1993), especially Chapters 2 to 5. Michael Bruno was the head of Israel's central bank for most of that period.

On how to end hyperinflations:

One of the classic articles is "The Ends of Four Big Inflations," by Thomas Sargent, in Robert Hall, ed., *Inflation: Causes and Effects* (Chicago: NBER and the University of Chicago, 1982), 41–97. In that article, Sargent argues that a credible program can lead to stabilization at little or no cost in terms of activity.

Rudiger Dornbusch and Stanley Fischer, "Stopping Hyperinflations, Past and Present," *Weltwirtschaftlichers Archiv*, 1986–1, 1–47, gives a very readable description of the end of hyperinflations in Germany, Austria, and Poland in the 1920s, and of Italy in 1947, Israel in 1985, and Argentina in 1985.

Back to Policy

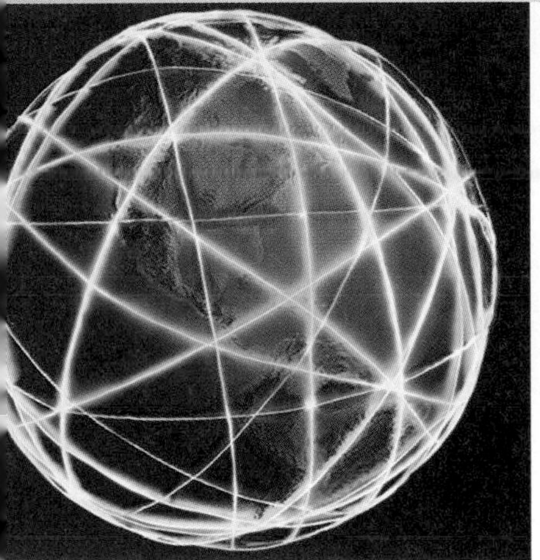

Nearly every chapter of this book has looked at the role of policy. The next three chapters put it all together.

BACK TO POLICY

Chapter 24

Chapter 24 asks two questions: Given the uncertainty about the effects of macroeconomic policies, wouldn't it be better not to use policy at all? And, even if policy can in principle be useful, can we trust policy makers to carry out the right policy? The bottom line: Uncertainty limits the role of policy; policy makers do not always do the right thing. But, with the right institutions, policy can help and should be used.

Chapter 25

Chapter 25 looks at monetary policy. It reviews what we have learned, chapter by chapter, and then focuses on two issues. The first is the optimal rate of inflation: High inflation is bad, but how low a rate of inflation should the central bank aim for? The second is the design of policy: Should the central bank target money growth, or should it target inflation? What rule should the central bank use to adjust the interest rate? The chapter ends with a description of the way monetary policy is conducted in the United States today.

Chapter 26

Chapter 26 looks at fiscal policy. It reviews what we have learned, and then looks more closely at the mechanics of debt, taxes, and spending implied by the government budget constraint. It then considers several issues, from how wars should be financed to the dangers of accumulating too high a level of debt. It ends with a description of the current budget situation in the United States, and a discussion of the problems on the horizon.

Back to Policy

Back to Policy

Should Policy Makers Be Restrained?

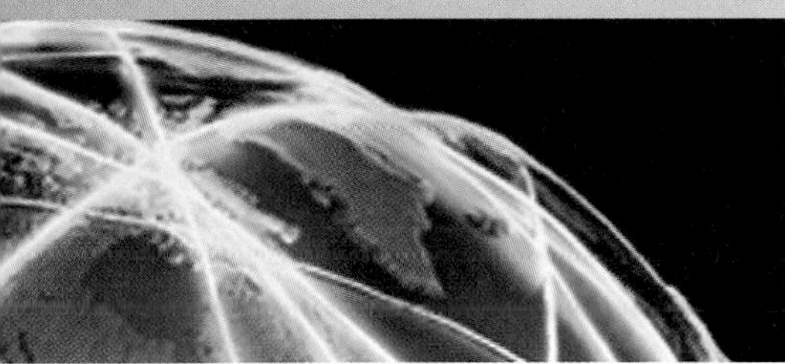

CHAPTER 24

At many points in this book, you saw how the right mix of fiscal and monetary policy could help a country out of a recession, improve its trade position without increasing activity and igniting inflation, slow down an overheating economy, stimulate investment and capital accumulation, and so on.

This conclusion, however, appears at odds with growing demands that policy makers be tightly restrained: In the European Union, countries that have adopted the Euro are required to keep their budget deficit under 3% of GDP. In the United States, the first item in the "Contract with America," the program drawn up by Republicans for the midterm U.S. elections in 1994, was the introduction of a balanced-budget amendment to the Constitution (Figure 24-1.) With the elimination of the U.S. budget deficit in the second half of the 1990s, the push for a balanced-budget amendment has weakened; but, if deficits were to come back, the issue would surely return to center stage. Monetary policy is also under fire. For example, the charter of the central bank of New Zealand, written in 1989, defines monetary policy's role as the maintenance of price stability, to the exclusion of any other macroeconomic goal.

This chapter looks at the case for restraints on macroeconomic policy.

- Sections 24-1 and 24-2 look at one line of argument, namely, that policy makers may have good intentions, but they end up doing more harm than good.

- Section 24-3 looks at another, more cynical, line—that policy makers do what is best for them, which is not necessarily what is best for the country. ■

HOUSE REPUBLICAN

CONTRACT WITH AMERICA

A PROGRAM FOR ACCOUNTABILITY

We've listened to your concerns and we hear you loud and clear. If you give us the majority, on the first day of Congress, a Republican House will:

Force Congress to live under the same laws as every other American
Cut one out of three Congressional committee staffers
Cut the Congressional budget

Then, in the first 100 days there will be votes on the following 10 bills:

1. Balanced budget amendment and the line item veto: It's time to force the government to live within its means and restore accountability to the budget in Washington.

2. Stop violent criminals: Let's get tough with an effective, able, and timely death penalty for violent offenders. Let's also reduce crime by building more prisons, making sentences longer and putting more police on the streets.

3. Welfare reform: The government should encourage people to work, not have children out of wedlock.

4. Protect our kids: We must strengthen families by giving parents greater control over education, enforcing child support payments, and getting tough on child pornography.

5. Tax cuts for families: Let's make it easier to achieve the American Dream: save money, buy a home, and send their kids to college.

6. Strong national defense: We need to ensure a strong national defense by restoring the essentials of our national security funding.

7. Raise the senior citizens' earning limit: We can put an end to government age discrimination that discourages seniors from working if they want.

8. Roll back government regulations: Let's slash regulations that strangle small business and let's make it easier for people to invest in order to create jobs and increase wages.

9. Common-sense legal reform: We can finally stop excessive legal claims, frivolous lawsuits, and overzealous lawyers.

10. Congressional term limits: Let's replace career politicians with citizen legislators. After all, politics shouldn't be a lifetime job.
(Please see reverse side to know if the candidate from your district has signed the Contract as of October 5, 1994.)

IF WE BREAK THIS CONTRACT, THROW US OUT, WE MEAN IT.

Figure 24-1

The Contract with America

24-1 Uncertainty and Policy

A blunt way of stating the first argument in favor of policy restraints is that those who know little should do little. The argument has two parts: Macroeconomists, and by implication the policy makers who rely on their advice, know little; and they should therefore do little. Let's look at each part separately.

How Much Do Macroeconomists Actually Know?

Macroeconomists are like doctors treating cancer. They know a lot, but there is also a lot they don't know.

Take an economy which suffers from high unemployment, and where the central bank is considering the use of monetary policy to increase economic activity. Think of the sequence of links between an increase in money and an increase in output—all the questions the central bank faces when deciding whether and by how much to increase the money supply:

- Is the current high rate of unemployment above the natural rate of unemployment, or has the natural rate of unemployment itself increased (Chapters 8 and 9)?
- If the unemployment rate is close to the natural rate of unemployment, isn't there a risk that a monetary expansion will lead to a decrease in unemployment below the natural rate of unemployment and an increase in inflation (Chapters 8 and 9)?

- By how much will the increase in the money supply decrease the short-term interest rate (Chapter 4)? What will be the effect of the decrease in the short-term interest rate on the long-term interest rate (Chapter 15)? By how much will stock prices increase (Chapter 15)? By how much will the currency depreciate (Chapters 20 and 21)?
- How long will it take for lower long-term interest rates and higher stock prices to affect investment and consumption spending (Chapter 16)? How long will it take for the J-curve effects to work themselves out and for the trade balance to improve (Chapter 19)? What is the danger that the effects come too late, when the economy has already recovered?

When assessing these questions, central banks—or macroeconomic policy makers in general—do not operate in a vacuum. They rely in particular on macroeconometric models. The equations in these models give estimates of how these individual links have looked in the past. But different models give different answers. This is because they have different structures, different lists of equations, and different lists of variables.

Figure 24-2 shows an example of this diversity. The example comes from a study commissioned in the late 1980s by the Brookings Institution—a research institute in Washington, D.C.—asking the builders of the 12 main macroeconometric models to answer a similar set of questions. (The models are described in the Focus box "Twelve Macroeconometric Models.") The goal was to see how the answers would differ across models. One question was:

> Consider a case where the U.S. economy is growing at its normal growth rate, and where unemployment is at its natural rate of unemployment; call this the *baseline* case. Suppose now that over the period of a year, the Fed increases money faster than in the baseline, so that after a year, nominal money is 4% higher than it would have been in the baseline case. From then on, nominal money grows at the

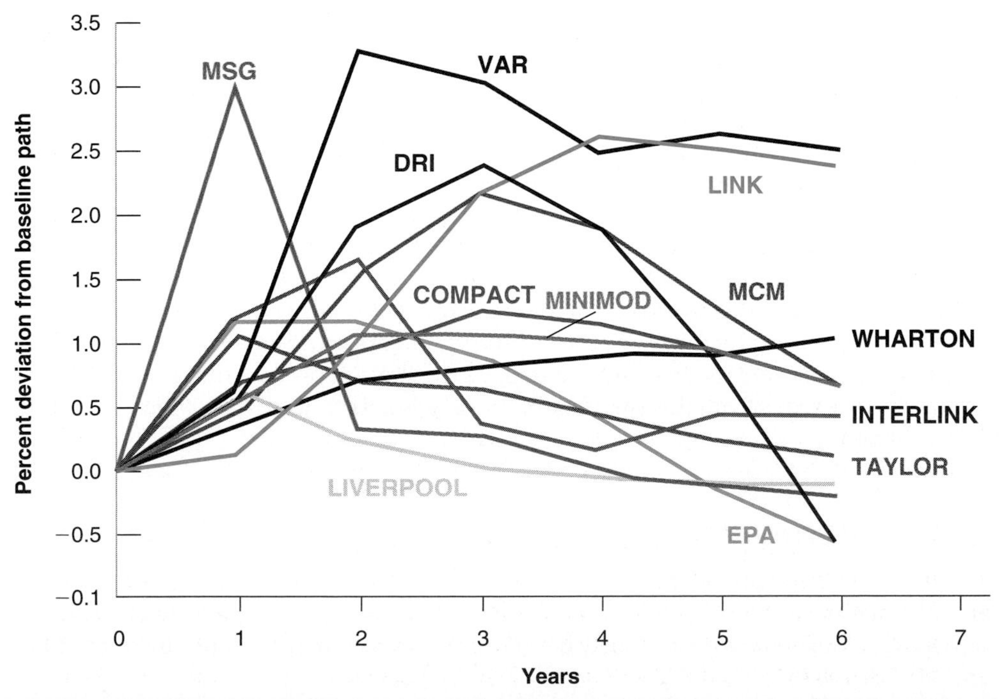

Figure 24-2

The Response of Output to a Monetary Expansion: Predictions from 12 Models

While all 12 models predict that output will increase for some time in response to a monetary expansion, the range of answers regarding the size and the length of the output response is large.

Twelve Macroeconometric Models

FOCUS

Together, the set of models used in the Brookings project is representative of the different types of macroeconomic models used for forecasting and policy in the world today:

- Two models, DRI (Data Resources Incorporated) and WHARTON, are commercial models. They are used regularly to generate and sell economic forecasts to firms and financial institutions.
- Five are used for forecasting and help in the design of policy. MCM (MultiCountry Model) is used by the Federal Reserve Board in Washington for the conduct of monetary policy; INTERLINK is used by the OECD in Paris; COMPACT is used by the Commission of the European Union in Brussels; EPA is used by the Japanese Planning Agency. Each of these four models was constructed by one team of researchers doing all the work, that is, building submodels for countries or groups of countries and linking them through trade and financial flows. In contrast, the fifth, LINK, is composed of individual country models—models constructed in each country by researchers from that country and then linked together by trade and financial relations. The advantage of this approach is that researchers from a particular country are likely to understand that country very well; the disadvantage is that different country models may have quite different structures, and be hard to link to each other.
- Four models incorporate rational expectations explicitly: the LIVERPOOL model, based in England; MINIMOD, used at the International Monetary Fund; MSG, developed by Warwick McKibbin and Jeffrey Sachs at Harvard University; and the TAYLOR model—which we saw in Section 7-4—developed by John Taylor of Stanford University. Because it is technically difficult to solve for large models under rational expectations, these models are typically smaller models, with less detail than those listed above. But they are better at capturing the expectation effects of various policies.
- The last one, VAR (for Vector AutoRegression, the technique of estimation used to build the model), developed by Christopher Sims and Robert Litterman at Minnesota, is very different from the others. It is not a structural model but rather a statistical summary of the relations between the different variables, without an explicit economic interpretation. Its strength is in its fit of the data, with a minimum of restrictions. Its weakness is that it is, essentially, a (very big) black box.

same rate as in the baseline case, so the level of nominal money remains 4% higher than it would have been without the change in monetary policy. Suppose further that interest rates in the rest of the world remain unchanged. What will happen to U.S. output?

A description of the models and of the study is given in Ralph Bryant et al., *Empirical Macroeconomics for Interdependent Economies* (Washington, DC: Brookings Institution, 1988). The study shows the effects not only of monetary policy, but also of fiscal policy. (The simulation described in the text is simulation E in the supplemental volume.)

Figure 24-2 shows the deviation of output from the baseline predicted by each of the 12 models. All 12 models predict that output will increase for some time after the increase in money. After one year, the average deviation of output from the baseline is positive. But the range of answers is large, from nearly no change to close to an increase of 3%; even leaving out the most extreme prediction, the range is still more than 1%. Two years out, the average deviation is 1.2%; again leaving out the most extreme prediction, the range is still 2%. And six years out, the average deviation is 0.6%, and the answers range from –0.3 to 2.5%. In short, if we measure uncertainty by the range of answers from this set of models, there is substantial uncertainty about the effects of policy.

Should Uncertainty Lead Policy Makers to Do Less?

Should uncertainty about the effects of policy lead policy makers to do less? In general, the answer is: Yes. Consider the following example, which builds on the simulation we just looked at (and is loosely based on the situation in the United States at the end of 2001.)

Suppose the U.S. economy is in recession. The unemployment rate is 7% and the Fed is considering using monetary policy to expand output. To concentrate on uncertainty about the effects of policy, let's assume the Fed knows everything else for sure. Based on its forecasts, it knows that, absent changes in monetary policy, unemployment will still be 7% next year. It *knows* that the natural rate of unemployment is 5%, and therefore the unemployment rate is 2% above the natural rate. And it knows, from Okun's law, that 1% more output growth for a year leads to a reduction in the unemployment rate of 0.4%.

In the real world, of course, the Fed does not know any of these things with certainty. It can only make forecasts. It does not know the exact value of the natural rate of unemployment, or the exact coefficient in Okun's law. Introducing these sources of uncertainty would reinforce our basic conclusion.

Under these assumptions, the Fed knows that if it could use monetary policy to achieve 5% more output growth over the coming year, the unemployment rate a year from now would be lower by $0.4 \times 5\% = 2\%$, so it would be down to the natural rate of unemployment, 5%. By how much should the Fed increase the money supply?

Taking the average of the responses from the different models in Figure 24-2, an increase in the money supply of 4% leads to a 0.85% increase in output in the first year. Equivalently, a 1% increase in the money supply leads to a $0.85/4 = 0.21\%$ increase in output.

Suppose the Fed takes this average relation as holding with *certainty*. What it should then do is straightforward. To return the unemployment rate to the natural rate in one year requires 5% more output growth. And 5% output growth requires the Fed to increase money by $5\%/0.21 = 23.8\%$. The Fed should therefore increase the money supply by 23.8%. If the economy's response is equal to the average response from the 12 models, this increase in money will return the economy to the natural rate of unemployment at the end of the year.

Suppose the Fed actually increases money by 23.8%. But let's now take into account uncertainty, as measured by the range of responses of the different models in Figure 24-2. Recall that the range of responses of output to a 4% increase in money after one year varies from 0 to 3%; equivalently, a 1% increase in money leads to a range of increases in output from 0 to 0.75%. These ranges imply that an increase in money of 23.8% leads, across models, to an output response anywhere between 0 and 17.9% ($23.8\% \times 0.75$). These output numbers imply in turn a decrease in unemployment anywhere between 0 and 7%, or values of the unemployment rate a year hence anywhere between 7 and 0%!

The conclusion is clear: Given the range of uncertainty about the effects of monetary policy on output, increasing money by 23.8% would be irresponsible. If the effects of money on output are as strong as suggested by one of the 12 models, unemployment by the end of the year could be 5% below the natural rate of unemployment, leading to enormous inflationary pressures. Given this uncertainty, the Fed should increase money by much less than 23.8%. For example, increasing money by 10% leads to a range for unemployment a year hence of 7 to 4%, clearly a safer range of outcomes.

This example relies on the notion of *multiplicative uncertainty*—that because the effects of policy are uncertain, more active policies lead to more uncertainty. See William Brainard, "Uncertainty and the Effectiveness of Policy," *American Economic Review*, May 1967, 411–425.

Uncertainty and Restraints on Policy Makers

Let's summarize: There is substantial uncertainty about the effects of macroeconomic policies. This uncertainty should lead policy makers to be more cautious, to use less active policies. Policies should be broadly aimed at avoiding prolonged recessions, slowing down booms, and avoiding inflationary pressure. The higher unemployment or inflation is, the more active the policies should be. But they should stop well short of **fine-tuning**, of trying to achieve constant unemployment or constant output growth.

These conclusions would have been controversial 20 years ago. Back then, there was a heated debate between two groups of economists. One group, headed by Milton

Friedman and Modigliani are the same two economists who independently developed the modern theory of consumption we saw in Chapter 16.

Friedman from Chicago, argued that because of long and variable lags, activist policy is likely to do more harm than good. The other group, headed by Franco Modigliani from MIT, had just built the first generation of large macroeconometric models and believed that the economists' knowledge was becoming good enough to allow for increasing fine-tuning of the economy. Today, most economists recognize there is substantial uncertainty about the effects of policy. They also accept the implication that this uncertainty should lead to less active policies.

Note that what we have developed so far is an argument for *self-restraint* by policy makers, not for *restraints on* policy makers. If policy makers understand the implications of uncertainty—and there is no reason to think they don't—they will, on their own, follow less active policies. There is no reason to impose further restraints, such as the requirement that money growth be constant or that the budget be balanced. Let's now turn to arguments for restraints *on* policy makers.

24-2 Expectations and Policy

One reason the effects of macroeconomic policy are uncertain is the interaction of policy and expectations. How a policy works, and sometimes whether it works at all, depends not only on how it affects current variables but also on how it affects expectations about the future (the main theme of Chapter 17). The importance of expectations for policy goes, however, beyond uncertainty about the effects of policy. This brings us to a discussion of *games.*

Until 20 years ago, macroeconomic policy was seen in the same way as the control of a complicated machine. Methods of **optimal control**, initially developed to control and guide rockets, were being increasingly used to design macroeconomic policy. Economists no longer think this way. It has become clear that the economy is fundamentally different from a machine, even from a very complicated one. Unlike a machine, the economy is composed of people and firms who try to anticipate what policy makers will do, who react not only to current policy but also to expectations of future policy. Hence, macroeconomic policy must be thought of as a **game** between the policy makers and "the economy"—more concretely, the people and the firms in the economy. So, when thinking about policy, what we need is not **optimal control theory** but rather **game theory**.

Even machines are becoming smarter: HAL (the robot in the 1968 movie *2001: A Space Odyssey*) starts anticipating what humans in the spaceship will do. The result is not a happy one. (See the movie.)

Warning: When economists say "game," they do not mean "entertainment," they mean **strategic interactions** between **players**. In the context of macroeconomic policy, the players are the policy makers and the economy—people and firms. The strategic interactions are clear: What people and firms do depends on what they expect policy makers to do. In turn, what policy makers do depends on what is happening in the economy.

Game theory has given economists many insights, often explaining how some apparently strange behavior makes sense when one understands the nature of the game being played. One of these insights is particularly important for our discussion of restraints here: Sometimes you can do better in a game by giving up some of your options. To see why, let's start with an example from outside economics—governments' policies toward hijackers.

Game theory is becoming an important tool in all branches of economics. The 1994 Nobel Prize in economics was awarded to three game theorists, John Nash from Princeton, John Harsanyi from Berkeley, and Reinhard Selten from Germany.

Hijackings and Negotiations

Most governments have a stated policy that they will not negotiate with plane hijackers. The reason for this stated policy is clear: to deter hijacking by making it unattractive to hijack planes.

Suppose that, despite the stated policy, a hijacking takes place. Now that the hijacking has taken place anyway, why not negotiate? Whatever compensation the hijackers demand is likely to be less costly than the alternative—the likelihood that lives will be lost if the plane has to be taken by force. So, the best policy would appear to be: Announce that you will not negotiate, but if a hijacking happens, negotiate.

Upon reflection, it is clear this would in fact be a very bad policy. Hijackers' decisions do not depend on the stated policy, but on what they expect will actually happen if they hijack a plane. If they know that negotiations will actually take place, they will rightly consider the stated policy as irrelevant. And hijackings will take place.

So, what is the best policy? Despite the fact that once hijackings have taken place, negotiations typically lead to a better outcome, the best policy is for governments to commit *not* to negotiate. By giving up the option to negotiate, they are likely to prevent hijackings in the first place.

Let's now turn to a macroeconomic example, based on the relation between inflation and unemployment. As you will see, exactly the same logic is involved.

This example was developed by Finn Kydland, from Carnegie Mellon, and Edward Prescott, from the University of Minnesota, in "Rules Rather than Discretion: The Inconsistency of Optimal Plans," *Journal of Political Economy*, 85-3, June 1977, 473–492.

Inflation and Unemployment Revisited

Recall the relation between inflation and unemployment we derived in Chapter 8 (equation [8.9], with the time indexes omitted for simplicity)

$$\pi = \pi^e - \alpha(u - u_n) \qquad (24.1)$$

Inflation, π, depends on expected inflation, π^e, as embodied in wages set in labor contracts, and on the difference between the actual unemployment rate, u, and the natural rate of unemployment, u_n. The coefficient α captures the effect of unemployment on inflation, given expected inflation: When unemployment is above the natural rate, inflation is lower than expected; when unemployment is below the natural rate, inflation is higher than expected.

A refresher: Given labor market conditions, and given their expectations of what prices will be, firms and workers set nominal wages. Given the nominal wages firms have to pay, the firms then set prices. So, prices depend on expected prices and labor market conditions. Equivalently, price inflation depends on expected price inflation and labor market conditions. This is what is captured in equation (24.1).

Suppose the Fed announces it will follow a monetary policy consistent with zero inflation. On the assumption that wage setters believe the announcement, expected inflation, π^e, as embodied in wage contracts is equal to zero, and the Fed faces the following relation between inflation and unemployment:

$$\pi = -\alpha(u - u_n) \qquad (24.2)$$

If the Fed follows through on its announced policy of zero inflation, expected inflation and actual inflation will both be equal to zero, and unemployment will be equal to the natural rate of unemployment.

For simplicity, I assume the Fed can choose the rate of inflation exactly. In doing so, I ignore uncertainty about the effects of policy (the topic of Section 24-1, but not central here).

Zero inflation and unemployment equal to the natural rate of unemployment is not a bad outcome. But it would seem the Fed can actually do even better:

- Recall from Chapter 8 that in the United States, α is roughly equal to 1. So equation (24.2) implies that by accepting just 1% inflation, the Fed can achieve an unemployment rate of 1% below the natural rate of unemployment.

  Suppose the Fed—and everybody else in the economy—finds the trade-off attractive, and decides to decrease unemployment by 1% in exchange for an inflation rate of 1%. This incentive to deviate from the announced policy once the other player has made his move—in this case, once wage setters have set the wage—is known in game theory as the **time inconsistency** of optimal policy. In our example, the Fed can improve the outcome this period by deviating from its

If $\alpha = 1$, equation (24.2) becomes $\pi = -(u - u_n)$. If $\pi =$ 1%, then $(u - u_n) = -1\%$.

Remember that the natural rate of unemployment is neither natural nor best in any sense (see Chapters 6 and 8). It may be reasonable for the Fed and everyone else in the economy to prefer an unemployment rate lower than the natural rate of unemployment.

announced policy of zero inflation: By accepting some inflation, it can achieve a substantial reduction in unemployment.

- Unfortunately, this is not the end of the story. If the Fed has increased money by more than it announced it would, wage setters are likely to wise up and begin to expect positive inflation of 1%. If the Fed still wants to achieve an unemployment rate 1% below the natural rate, it will have to achieve 2% inflation. However, if it does achieve 2% inflation, wage setters are likely to increase their expectations of inflation further, and so on.
- The eventual outcome is likely to be high inflation. Because wage setters understand the Fed's motives, expected inflation catches up with actual inflation, and the Fed must eventually be unsuccessful in its attempt to achieve unemployment below the natural rate of unemployment. In short, attempts by the Fed to make things better lead in the end to things being worse. The economy ends up with the *same unemployment rate* as would have prevailed if the Fed had followed its announced policy, but with *much higher inflation.*

How relevant is this example? Very relevant. Reread Chapter 8. We can read the history of the Phillips curve and the increase in inflation in the 1970s as coming precisely from the Fed's attempts to maintain unemployment below the natural rate of unemployment, leading to higher and higher expected inflation, and higher and higher actual inflation. In that light, the shift of the original Phillips curve can be seen as the adjustment of wage setters' expectations to the behavior of the central bank.

So what is the best policy for the Fed to follow in this case? It is to make a credible commitment that it will not try to decrease unemployment below the natural rate. By giving up the option of deviating from its announced policy, the Fed can achieve unemployment equal to the natural rate of unemployment and zero inflation. The hijacking analogy is clear: By credibly committing not to do something that would appear desirable at the time, policy makers can achieve a better outcome: no hijackings in our earlier example, no inflation here.

Establishing Credibility

How can a central bank credibly commit not to deviate from its announced policy?

One way to establish its credibility is for the central bank to give up—or to be stripped by law of—its policy-making power. For example, the mandate of the bank can be defined by law in terms of a simple rule, such as setting money growth at 0% forever. (An alternative, which we discussed in Chapter 21, is to adopt a hard peg, such as a currency board or even dollarization: In that case, instead of giving up its ability to use money growth, the central bank gives up its ability to use the exchange rate and the interest rate.)

Such a law surely takes care of the problem of time inconsistency. But such a tight restraint comes close to throwing the baby out with the bathwater. We want to prevent the central bank from pursuing too high a rate of money growth in an attempt to lower unemployment below the natural unemployment rate. But—subject to the restrictions discussed in Section 24-1—we still want the central bank to be able to expand the money supply when unemployment is far above the natural rate, and contract the money supply when unemployment is far below the natural rate. Such actions become impossible under a constant money growth rule. There are indeed better ways to deal with time inconsistency. In the case of monetary policy, our discussion suggests a way this can be done:

1. First, make the central bank independent. Appointing central bankers for longer terms and making it harder to fire them will make them more likely to resist political pressure to decrease unemployment below the natural rate of unemployment.

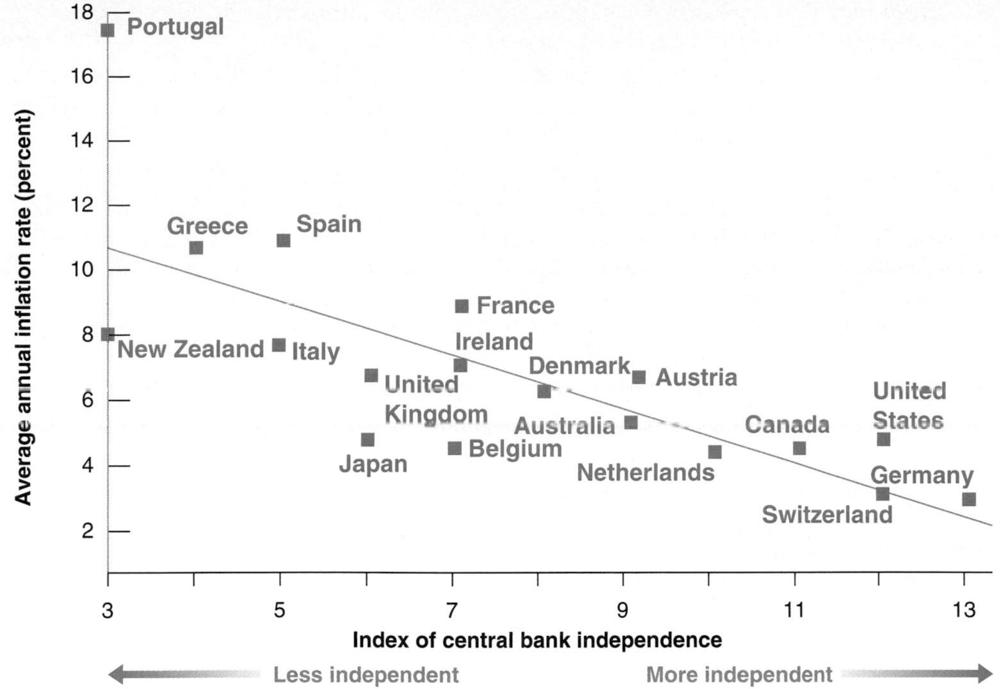

Figure 24-3

Inflation and Central Bank Independence

Across OECD countries, the higher the degree of central bank independence, the lower the rate of inflation.

Source: Vittorio Grilli, Donato Masciandaro, and Guido Tabellini, "Political and Monetary Institutions and Public Financial Policies in the Industrial Countries," Economic Policy, October 1991, 341–392.

2. Then, choose a "conservative" central banker, somebody who dislikes inflation and is unwilling to accept more inflation in exchange for less unemployment when unemployment is at the natural rate. When the economy is at the natural rate, such a central banker will not be tempted to embark on a monetary expansion. Thus, the problem of time inconsistency will disappear altogether.

Appointing as the head of the central bank somebody who does not have the same preferences as the people as a whole might seem like a solution that only game theorists would concoct. But this is actually the way many countries have been responding to the problem of time consistency in monetary policy. In many countries in the last two decades, central banks have been given more independence. And governments typically have appointed central bankers who are more "conservative" than the governments themselves—central bankers who appear to care more about inflation and less about unemployment than the government. (See the Focus box "Was Alan Blinder Wrong in Speaking the Truth?")

Figure 24-3 suggests that this approach has been successful. The vertical axis gives the average annual inflation rate in 18 OECD countries for the period 1960–1990. The horizontal axis gives the value of an index of "central bank independence," constructed by looking at several legal provisions in the bank's charter—for example, whether and how the government can remove the head of the bank. There is a striking inverse relation between the two variables, as summarized by the regression line: More central bank independence appears to be systematically associated with lower inflation.

It is reasonable to argue this does not prove that central bank independence leads to lower inflation. It may be that countries that dislike inflation tend both to give more independence to their central bankers and have lower inflation. (Another example of the difference between correlation and causality is discussed in Appendix 3 at the end of the book.)

Time Consistency and Restraints on Policy Makers

Let's summarize what we have learned in this section:

We have examined arguments for putting restraints on policy makers, based on the issue of time inconsistency.

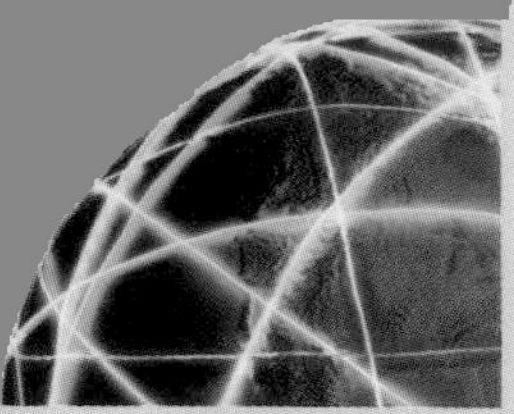

FOCUS

Was Alan Blinder Wrong in Speaking the Truth?

In the summer of 1994, President Clinton appointed Alan Blinder, an economist from Princeton, vice-chairman (in effect, second in command) of the Federal Reserve Board. A few weeks later Blinder, speaking at an economic conference, indicated his belief that the Fed has both the responsibility and the ability, when unemployment is high, to use monetary policy to help the economy recover. This statement was badly received. Bond prices decreased, and most newspapers ran editorials critical of Blinder.

Why was the reaction of markets and newspapers so negative? It was surely not that Blinder was wrong. There is no doubt that monetary policy can and should help the economy out of a recession. Indeed, the Federal Reserve Bank Act of 1978 requires the Fed to pursue full employment as well as low inflation.

The reaction was negative because, in terms of the argument we developed in the text, Blinder revealed by his words that he was not a conservative central banker, that he cared about unemployment as well as about inflation. With the unemployment rate at the time equal to 6.1%, close to what was thought to be the natural rate of unemployment at the time, markets interpreted Blinder's statements as suggesting that he might want to decrease unemployment below the natural rate. Interest rates increased because of higher expected inflation—bond prices decreased.

The moral of the story: Whatever views central bankers may hold, they should try to look and sound conservative. . . . This is why many heads of central banks are reluctant to admit, at least in public, the existence of any trade-off between unemployment and inflation, even in the short run.

We have looked at the case of monetary policy. But similar issues arise in the context of fiscal policy: In Chapter 26, we shall discuss for example the issue of debt repudiation—the option for the government to cancel its debt obligations—and see the conclusions are very similar to the case of monetary policy.

When issues of time inconsistency are relevant, tight restraints on policy makers—such as a fixed money growth rule in the case of monetary policy—can provide a rough solution. But the solution may have large costs if it prevents the use of macroeconomic policy altogether. Better ways typically involve designing better institutions (such as an independent central bank) that can reduce the problem of time inconsistency without eliminating monetary policy as a macroeconomic policy tool.

24-3 Politics and Policy

We have assumed so far that policy makers were *benevolent*—they tried to do what was best for the country. However, much public discussion challenges that assumption: Politicians or policy makers, the argument goes, do what is best for themselves, and this is not always what is best for the country.

You have heard the arguments: Politicians avoid the hard decisions, they pander to the electorate, partisan politics leads to gridlock, and nothing ever gets done. Discussing the flaws of democracy goes far beyond the scope of this book. What we can do here is to briefly review how these arguments apply to macroeconomic policy, then look at the empirical evidence, and see what light it sheds on the issue of policy restraints.

Games Between Policy Makers and Voters

Many macroeconomic measures involve trading off short-run losses against long-run gains—or, symmetrically, short-run gains against long-run losses.

Take, for example, tax cuts. By definition, tax cuts lead to lower taxes today. They are also likely to lead to an increase in output, and so an increase in pretax income, for some time. But unless they are matched by equal decreases in government spending, they lead to a larger budget deficit and to the need for an increase in taxes in the future. If voters are shortsighted, the temptation for politicians to cut taxes may prove irresistible. Politics may lead to systematic deficits, at least until the level of government debt has become so high that politicians are scared into action.

The Reagan tax cuts both decreased tax rates and increased activity in the early 1980s (see the Focus box in Chapter 20). But the cuts also led to a long sequence of deficits, which took nearly two decades to eliminate. We shall look at the relation between current and future taxes more closely when we examine the implications of the government budget constraint in Chapter 26.

Now move from taxes to macroeconomic policy in general. Again suppose that voters are shortsighted. If the politicians' main goal is to please voters and get reelected, what better policy than to expand aggregate demand before an election, leading to higher growth and lower unemployment? True, growth in excess of the normal growth rate cannot be sustained, and eventually the economy must return to the natural level of output: Higher growth must be followed later by lower growth. But with the right timing and shortsighted voters, higher growth can win the elections. Thus, we might expect a clear **political business cycle**, with higher growth on average before elections than after elections.

From Okun's law, output growth in excess of normal growth leads to a decline in the unemployment rate below the natural rate of unemployment. In the medium run, we know that the unemployment rate must increase back to the natural rate of unemployment. This, in turn, requires output growth below normal output growth for some time. See Chapter 9 (in particular, Table 9-1).

The arguments I have just laid out are familiar; in one form or another, you have heard them before. And their logic is convincing. So it may come as a surprise that they do not fit the facts very well.

For example, our discussion of taxes would lead you to expect that budget deficits and high government debt have always been and will always be with us. Figure 24-4, which gives the evolution of the ratio of government debt to GDP in the United States since 1900, shows this is not the case. Note how the first three buildups in debt all

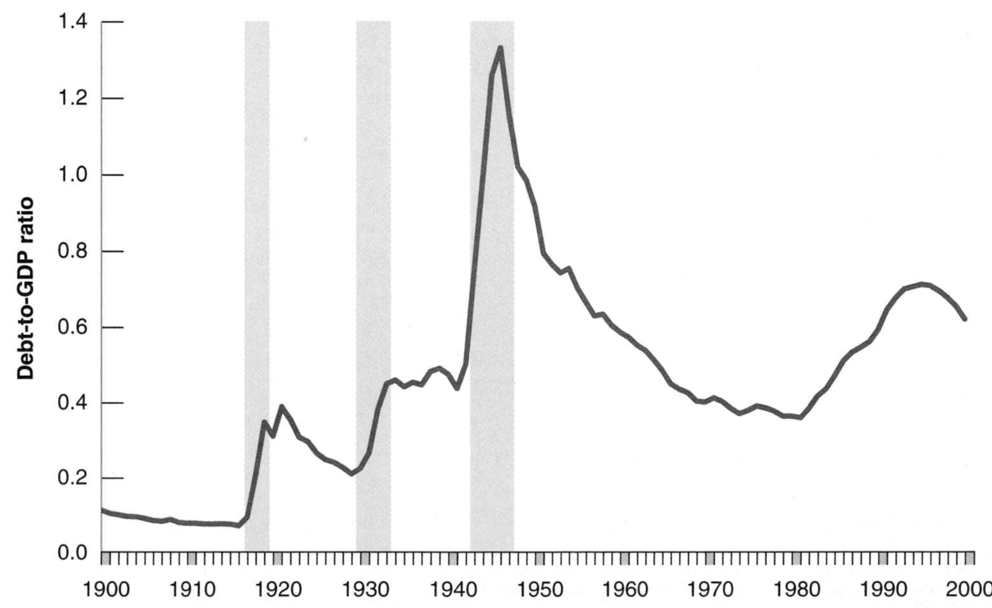

Figure 24-4

The Evolution of the Ratio of Debt to GDP in the United States, 1900–2000

The three major buildups of debt since 1900 have been associated with World War I, the Great Depression, and World War II.

Source: Historical Statistics of the United States, *Department of Commerce; and* Economic Report of the President.

happened in very special circumstances: World War I, the Great Depression, and World War II—periods of unusual declines in output or unusually high military spending. Note also how from the end of the World War II to the end of the 1970s, the ratio of debt to GDP steadily *decreased*. By 1979, the ratio of debt to GDP was 33%, down from 130% in 1946.

True, the steady increase in debt from the early 1980s to the mid-1990s fits the argument of shortsighted politicians quite well. During that time, the ratio of debt to GDP steadily increased, from a low of 31.6% in 1981 to a high of 68.2% in 1995. But since then, the deficit has steadily decreased, turning into a surplus in 1998, so the ratio of debt to GDP is again falling. Explaining the behavior of debt over a period of 15 years through the behavior of shortsighted politicians raises the issue of why things were different before 1981, and also after 1995. The broader historical record suggests that by itself, shortsightedness does not explain much of the past evolution of deficits and debt.

The relation between the deficit, debt, and GDP is explored in detail in Chapter 26.

Chapter 26 will examine alternative—and, empirically, more successful—explanations for the evolution of government debt, both over time and across countries.

Return to the *political business cycle* argument in which policy makers try to get high output growth before the elections so they will be reelected. If the political business cycle were important, we would expect to see faster growth before elections than after. Table 24-1 gives GDP growth rates for each of the four years of each U.S. administration since President Truman in 1948. Growth has indeed been highest on average in

Table 24-1 Growth During Democratic and Republican Administrations (percent per year)

	Year			
	First	Second	Third	Fourth
Democratic				
Truman	0.0	8.5	10.3	3.9
Kennedy/Johnson	2.6	5.3	4.1	5.3
Johnson	5.8	5.8	2.9	4.1
Carter	4.7	5.3	2.5	–0.2
Clinton I	2.7	4.0	2.7	3.6
Clinton II	4.4	4.3	4.1	4.1
Average: Democratic	3.4	5.5	4.4	3.5
Republican				
Eisenhower	4.0	–1.3	5.6	2.1
Nixon	2.4	–0.3	2.8	5.0
Nixon/Ford	5.2	–0.5	–1.3	4.9
Reagan I	1.9	–2.5	3.6	6.4
Reagan II	3.6	3.0	2.7	3.0
Bush	2.5	1.2	–0.7	2.6
Bush (George W)	1.1			
Average: Republican	3.3	–0.1	2.1	4.0
Average	3.3	2.6	3.2	3.7

Source: Alberto Alesina, "Macroeconomics and Politics," NBER Macroeconomics Annual, 1988, 13–61, Table 4. Updated.

the last year of an administration. But the average difference across years is small: 3.7% in the last year of an administration versus 3.3% in the first year. (There are other interesting features in the table, such as the difference between Republican and Democratic administrations; we return to these shortly.) There is little evidence of manipulation—or at least of successful manipulation—of the macroeconomy to win elections.

Games Between Policy Makers

Another line of argument focuses not on games between politicians and voters, but rather on games between political parties. For example, take the issue of budget deficit reduction in the United States. Despite the fact that by the mid-1980s large budget deficits were widely perceived to be one of the main macroeconomic problems facing the United States, it took another 15 years before the deficit was eliminated. Some of the delays are part of the normal democratic process: Deficit reductions involve making painful decisions, and forging a consensus takes time. But other factors seem to be at work as well. While agreeing on the need for deficit reduction, the two political parties differ on how it should be done. Because they believe in a smaller role for government, Republicans focus on decreases in spending. In contrast, Democrats are more open to increases in taxes. Each side holds out, hoping the other side will give in.

Game theorists refer to these situations as **wars of attrition**. The hope that the other side will give in leads to long and often costly delays. Such wars of attrition happen often in the context of fiscal policy. Deficit reduction often occurs long after it should. This is particularly visible during episodes of hyperinflation. As you saw in Chapter 23, hyperinflations arise from the use of money creation to finance large budget deficits. While the need to reduce those deficits is usually recognized early on, support for stabilization programs—which include the elimination of those deficits—typically comes about only when inflation has reached such high levels that economic activity is severely affected.

◀ Wars of attrition are not limited to fiscal policy: Think of the 1998 NBA strike in the United States, where more than half of the season was cancelled because owners and players could not reach an agreement.

Another example of games between political parties is movements in economic activity brought about by the alternation of parties in power. Republicans typically worry more than Democrats about inflation. They worry less than Democrats about unemployment. So, we would expect Democratic administrations to show stronger growth—and thus less unemployment and more inflation—than Republican administrations. This prediction appears to fit the facts quite well. Look at Table 24-1 again. The most striking contrast in growth rates is in the second year of each administration. During the second year of each Democratic administration since Truman, growth has been very high. During the second year of each Republican administration, growth has been very low. In four out of six Republican administrations, growth in the second year has been negative.

An intriguing question: Why is the effect so much stronger in the administration's *second* year? The theory of unemployment and inflation we developed in Chapter 9 suggests a plausible answer. There are lags in the effects of policy, so it takes about a year for a new administration to affect the economy. And sustaining higher growth than normal for too long would lead to increasing inflation, so even a Democratic administration would not want to sustain higher growth throughout its term. Thus, growth rates tend to be much closer to each other during the second halves of Democratic and Republican administrations, more so than during first halves.

Back to the Balanced-Budget Amendment

Let's end this chapter with one of the issues we started with, the case for and against a balanced-budget amendment. What have we learned?

- Despite common beliefs, the picture of politicians pandering to shortsighted voters does not fit the broad evidence on the evolution of deficits and debt. The large peacetime U.S. budget deficits of the 1980s and 1990s are the exception rather than the rule. Fiscal policy is not typically characterized by chronic deficits.

- This is not to say that all is well, or that the political process always delivers the best macroeconomic policy decisions. Hard decisions are often delayed. Deficit reductions often come late, only after debt has increased to high levels.

Do these problems justify the addition of a balanced-budget amendment to the U.S. Constitution? Let's look at both sides of the case.

The Case Against a Balanced-Budget Amendment

A balanced-budget amendment would eliminate the problem of deficits. But it would also eliminate the use of fiscal policy as a macroeconomic policy instrument, a very high price to pay.

The evidence suggests the problem is not that politicians systematically want deficits. Rather, it appears to be that politicians find it difficult to agree on and implement a deficit-reduction plan when it is needed. Deficit control and reduction can be achieved with looser constraints and mechanisms than a constitutional amendment.

Consider, for example, the case for a mechanism that triggers automatic spending cuts when the deficit gets too large (this is clearly a looser constraint on fiscal policy than a balanced-budget amendment). Suppose, for example, that the budget deficit is too large, and it is desirable to cut spending across-the-board by 5%. Members of Congress may find it difficult to explain to their constituency why their favorite spending program was cut by 5%. Now suppose the deficit triggers automatic across-the-board spending cuts of 5% without any congressional action. Knowing that other programs will be cut, members of Congress may accept cuts in their favorite programs more easily. They may also be better able to deflect the blame for the cuts: Members of Congress who succeed in limiting the cuts to their favorite program to, say, 4% (by convincing Congress to make deeper cuts in some other programs, to maintain the lower overall level of spending) can then return to their constituents and claim success in having avoided even larger cuts.

The Case for a Balanced-Budget Amendment

To some economists, however, the answer is yes, a balanced-budget amendment is necessary. These economists are typically more skeptical of the usefulness of macroeconomic policy in general, and of fiscal policy in particular. They worry that running deficits during recessions may have adverse effects on financial markets, hindering rather than helping the recovery (a potentially perverse effect of fiscal policy we discussed in Chapter 17). Because of the lags involved in the legislative process, they are also skeptical of the ability of Congress to change fiscal policy in time to stabilize the economy. So, they are willing to give up fiscal policy as a macroeconomic instrument.

These economists are also skeptical of any rule that Congress may impose upon itself, but can undo by a vote later on. And so they conclude that nothing short of a constitutional amendment can do the job of ending deficits forever.

In the light of this debate, the decrease in the budget deficit in the 1990s is particularly interesting. Is it due, as the opponents of a strict balanced-budget amendment argue, to the use of cleverly designed but flexible rules to decrease the deficit? Or is it due, as proponents of a strict balanced-budget amendment argue, to luck, namely, to unusually strong growth of output, resulting in high government revenues, in the United States in the 1990s? I explore the issue in the Focus box "Did Rules Help Reduce the U.S. Budget Deficit?" below. My reading of the evidence is that growth explains much of the reduction in the deficit, but that rules have helped. At least for the United States, a balanced-budget amendment is not needed; more flexible rules can do the job.

Two related Focus boxes are "Monetary Contraction and Fiscal Expansion: The United States in the Early 1980s" in Chapter 20, and "The Clinton-Greenspan Policy Mix" in Chapter 5. ▶

Did Rules Help Reduce the U.S. Budget Deficit?

The figure below shows the evolution of the budget deficit as a ratio to GDP in the United States since 1980. (Because this is the way the budget numbers are constructed and presented, the years in the figure and in the rest of the box are fiscal rather than calendar years. The fiscal year runs from October 1 of the preceding calendar year to September 30 of the current calendar year. For example, fiscal year 1990 runs from October 1989 to September 1990.) Deficits increased sharply in the early 1980s, reaching 6.1% of GDP in 1983. They then went down and up again, reaching 4.7% in 1992. Since 1992, however, they have decreased steadily, and in 1998, the U.S. budget was in surplus, for the first time in 30 years.

You saw in Chapter 20 how the deficits were triggered by the large tax cuts under the Reagan administration. The question we focus on here is how the deficits were reduced and, eventually, eliminated.

1. *The Gramm-Rudman-Hollings bill*

The first serious attempt to reduce the deficit took place in 1985. Frustrated by the inability of Congress to achieve deficit reduction, two Republican senators, Gramm and Rudman, and one Democratic senator, Hollings, jointly introduced a bill aimed at forcing deficit reduction through restraints on the budget process.

The bill easily passed the Senate and the House. Its principle was simple: The bill set ceilings for the deficit in each fiscal year, with the goal of eliminating the deficit by 1991. If the budget proposed by Congress implied a deficit above the ceiling, a procedure known as sequestration automatically went into effect, with spending on all programs cut by the same percentage so as to achieve the target deficit (*sequester* means remove).

A number of spending programs were excluded from the cuts, mainly interest payments on the debt, Social Security benefits, and some low-income transfer programs. There were also escape clauses to prevent deficit reduction from standing in the way of macroeconomic stabilization. For example, if projected growth was below 3%, the deficit ceiling was relaxed in proportion to the difference between projected growth and 3%.

How did Gramm-Rudman-Hollings (GRH) work in practice? It had a short and checkered history.

The first obstacle was a constitutional challenge on the grounds that GRH took too much power away from the legislative bodies. The bill was indeed declared unconstitutional by the Supreme Court in 1986. But the ruling was based largely on technicalities, and a second GRH bill, which avoided the problems mentioned by the Court, was passed in 1987. The occasion was used, however, to increase the ceilings, and move the target date for zero deficit from 1991 to 1993!

The later history of GRH was full of loopholes, optimistic forecasts, and other gimmicks:

- Because the GRH ceiling applied only to the coming year's budget, Congress systematically shifted spending to the previous year's budget. This creative

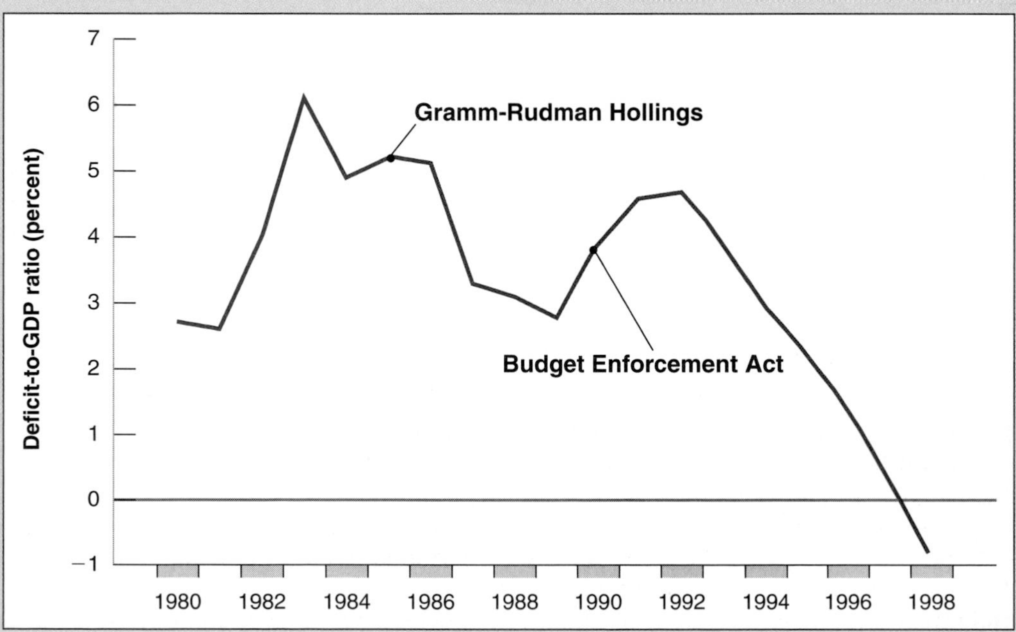

Figure 1 *U.S. Deficit, 1980–1998 (percent of GDP)*

Continued

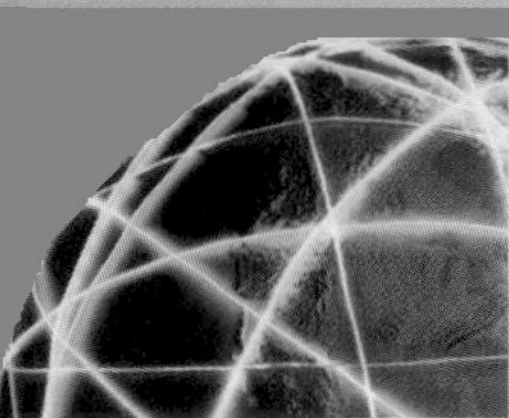

accounting made the deficit in the previous fiscal year look worse. But it allowed the current year's budget to satisfy the GRH ceilings more easily.

- Public assets were sold, and proceeds from sales counted as revenues, reducing the measured deficit but doing little to reduce the true deficit. (We discuss the role of asset sales further in Chapter 26.)
- Optimistic projections for economic activity were used. The result was optimistic projections for revenues and optimistically low projections for deficits.

In view of all these gimmicks, how effective was GRH in reducing deficits? Table 1 gives the initial ceilings (GRH I), the revised ceilings (GRH II), and the actual deficits—both in current dollars and in ratio to GDP—for each fiscal year from 1986 to 1990, the year in which GRH was replaced by another set of rules (more on this shortly).

In each of the fiscal years 1987 to 1989, the budget adopted by Congress satisfied the GRH ceiling. In each of those years, however, the realized deficit was larger than the GRH ceiling, by anywhere between $6 billion in 1987 to $16 billion in 1989. Nevertheless, the period was characterized by a steady decrease in the ratio of the deficit to GDP, from 5.1% in 1986 to 2.8% in 1989.

In 1990, however, the actual deficit was $121 billion above the GRH ceiling. There were two main reasons: (1) Economic activity was lower than forecast when the budget had been passed; GDP growth was only 1.2% in 1990. And (2), the government was faced with a savings-and-loan crisis: Many S&L institutions had become insolvent, and the government had to make good on its promise to insure depositors against losses.

Both phenomena—unusually low growth and the S&L crisis—were temporary and justified a higher deficit. Nevertheless, because the actual deficit was so much higher than the ceiling, GRH had lost its credibility. A new system of rules, known as the Budget Enforcement Act of 1990, was introduced.

2. *The Budget Enforcement Act of 1990*

This new set of rules differed from GRH in several ways:

- First, it imposed constraints only on spending. Spending was divided into two categories, discretionary spending (roughly, spending on goods and services, including defense) and mandatory spending (roughly, transfer payments to individuals). Constraints, called caps, were set on discretionary spending for the following five years. These caps were set in such a way as to require a small but steady decrease in real terms in discretionary spending. Explicit provisions were made for emergencies. For example, spending on Operation Desert Storm during the Gulf War in 1991 was not subject to the caps.
- Second, any new transfer program could be adopted only if it could be shown not to increase deficits in the future (either by raising new revenues, or by decreasing spending on some other existing program). This rule is known as the pay-as-you-go or PAYGO rule.

By focusing on spending rather than on the deficit itself, this set of rules had one important implication. If there was a recession, hence a decrease in revenues, the deficit could increase without triggering a decrease in spending. This happened in 1991 and 1992 when, because of the recession, the deficit increased—despite the fact that spending satisfied the constraints imposed by the caps. The shift in focus had two desirable effects: (1) allowing for a larger fiscal deficit during a recession—a good thing from the point of view of macroeconomic policy—and (2) decreasing the pressure to break the rules during a recession—a good thing from a political point of view.

On the surface, it would appear that the Budget Enforcement Act of 1990 (extended by new legislation in 1993 and 1997) was a great success: By 1998, the deficit

Table 1 Gramm-Rudman-Hollings Ceilings and Actual Deficits

	Deficit Ceiling under:		*Actual Deficit*	*Actual Deficit*
	GRH I	GRH II		
Fiscal Year	(billions of current dollars)			ratio to GDP (%)
1986	172		221	5.1
1987	144		150	3.3
1988	108	144	155	3.1
1989	72	136	152	2.8
1990	36	100	221	3.9

was gone. Looking more closely however, the answer is more ambiguous. Table 2 gives the evolution of total spending, of total revenues, and of the deficit, for each fiscal year from 1990 to 1998, together with the decomposition of spending between discretionary spending (itself decomposed into defense spending and nondefense spending) and mandatory spending.

Looking first at total spending, revenues, and the deficit in columns (4) to (6), it is clear that the reduction in the deficit from 1990 to 1998 was due in nearly equal parts to a decrease in spending and to an increase in tax revenues (relative to GDP). The increase in tax revenues can be attributed mostly to growth. Because the income tax is progressive—the tax rate increases with the level of income—steady growth increases tax revenues as a proportion of GDP; this is what happened in the 1990s. Turning to the decrease in spending, a comparison of columns (4) (total spending) and (3) (discretionary spending) shows that the decrease in spending, from 21.8% in 1990 to 19.1% in 1998 is largely accounted for by the decrease in discretionary spending, from 8.7% in 1990 to 6.4% in 1998. This would appear to be good news for rules, as discretionary spending is the part of spending that was subject to caps. But a look at column (1) suggests that another factor must get most of the credit: the end of the Cold War, and the resulting decrease in defense spending, from 5.2 to 3.1%.

Does this mean the budget enforcement act had no effect? Probably not. In its absence, judging from past trends, both the nondefense part of spending and mandatory spending would probably have risen substantially as a proportion of GDP. They did not.

What lessons should we draw from the U.S. experience? That restraints can help, but that good design of these restraints is essential. It is important both to limit loopholes and to allow for realistic escape clauses (cases where the rules are suspended). But some loopholes may actually make restraints more flexible and therefore more acceptable. The outcomes from 1986 to 1989 can be read in that light: Despite the use of creative accounting and optimistic forecasts, the ratio of the deficit to GDP was steadily reduced. Realistic escape clauses or exceptions are also important. In view of low growth and the S&L crisis, the deficit of 1990 was largely justified. But because it was so much larger than the GRH ceiling, GRH's credibility was destroyed, and another system had to be put in place. This new system was more flexible and, combined with growth, eventually achieved its goal.

How long will this goal be maintained? At the time of this writing, there are worries that the very presence of surpluses since 1998 has led policy makers to relax and abandon restraint, and that the United States may be on verge of a new sequence of sustained deficits. . . . This may be, but it is too early to tell.

Table 2 Federal Spending, Revenues, and Deficit, as a Percent of GDP, 1990–1998

	Discretionary Expenditures			***Expenditures***	***Revenues***	***Deficit***
	Defense	Nondefense	Total	Total	Total	
Year	(1)	(2)	(3)	(4)	(5)	(6)
1990	5.2	3.5	8.7	21.8	18.0	3.8
1991	5.4	3.6	9.0	22.3	17.8	4.5
1992	4.9	3.7	8.6	22.2	17.5	4.7
1993	4.5	3.8	8.2	21.5	17.6	3.9
1994	4.1	3.7	7.8	21.1	18.1	2.9
1995	3.7	3.7	7.4	20.7	18.5	2.2
1996	3.5	3.5	7.0	20.3	18.9	1.4
1997	3.3	3.4	6.7	19.6	19.3	0.3
1998	3.1	3.2	6.4	19.1	19.9	–0.8

Source: Historical Tables, Budget of the United States Government, Fiscal Year 2002.

Summary

- The effects of macroeconomic policies are always uncertain. This uncertainty should lead policy makers to be more cautious, to use less active policies. Policies must be broadly aimed at avoiding prolonged recessions, slowing down booms, and avoiding inflationary pressure. The higher the level of unemployment or inflation, the more active the policies should be. But they should stop short of fine-tuning, of trying to maintain constant unemployment or constant output growth.
- Using macroeconomic policy to control the economy is fundamentally different from controlling a machine. Unlike a machine, the economy is composed of people and firms who try to anticipate what policy makers will do, who react not only to current policy but also to expectations of future policy. In this sense, macroeconomic policy can be thought of as a game between policy makers and the economy.
- When playing a game, it is sometimes better for a player to give up some options. For example, when a hijacking occurs, it is best to negotiate with hijackers. But a government that credibly commits not to negotiate with hijackers—that gives up the option of negotiation—is actually more likely to deter hijackings from occurring.
- The same argument applies to various aspects of macroeconomic policy. By credibly committing not to use monetary policy to decrease unemployment below the natural rate of unemployment, a central bank can alleviate fears that money growth will be high, and decrease both expected and actual inflation. When issues of time inconsistency are relevant, tight restraints on policy makers—such as a fixed money growth rule in the case of monetary policy—can provide a rough solution. But the solution may have large costs if it prevents the use of macroeconomic policy altogether. Better methods typically involve designing better institutions (such as an independent central bank) that can reduce the problem of time inconsistency without eliminating monetary policy as a macroeconomic policy tool.
- Another argument for putting restraints on policy makers is that policy makers may play games either with the public or among themselves, and these games may lead to undesirable outcomes. Politicians may try to fool a shortsighted electorate by choosing policies with short-run benefits but large long-term costs—for example, large budget deficits. Political parties may delay painful decisions, hoping that the other party will make the adjustment and take the blame. These problems exist, although they are less prevalent than is often perceived. In such cases, tight restraints on policy, such as a constitutional amendment to balance the budget, can, again, provide a rough solution. Better ways typically involve better institutions and better ways of designing the process through which policy and decisions are made.

Key Terms

- fine-tuning, 513
- optimal control, 514
- game, 514
- optimal control theory, 514
- game theory, 514
- strategic interactions, 514
- players, 514
- time inconsistency, 515
- political business cycle, 519
- wars of attrition, 521

Questions and Problems

Quick Check

1. *Using the information in this chapter, label each of the following statements* true, false, *or* uncertain. *Explain briefly.*
   a. There is so much uncertainty about the effects of monetary policy that we would be better off not using it.
   b. Elect a Democrat as president if you want low unemployment.
   c. There is clear evidence of political business cycles in the United States: low unemployment around elections, higher unemployment the rest of the time.
   d. Rules are ineffective in reducing budget deficits.
   e. Governments would be wise to announce a no-negotiation policy with hostage takers.
   f. Under no circumstances should governments ever negotiate with hostage takers.
   g. Under rational expectations, people expect policy makers to do whatever it is they do, and so macroeconomic policy cannot have any effect on the economy.

2. *Has the problem of "time consistency" ever arisen in your personal life? Who were the players in that "game"?*

3. *You are the economic adviser to a newly elected president. In four years' time she will face another election. Inflation last year was 3%, and the unemployment rate was equal to the natural rate. The Philips curve is given by*

$$\pi_t = \pi_{t-1} - \alpha(u_t - u_n)$$

   a. Assume you can use fiscal and monetary policy to achieve any unemployment rate you want for each of the next four years. Write a short memo to the president indicating what unemployment and inflation rates she should try to achieve.

b. If the Philips curve is given by

$$\pi_t = \pi_t^e - \alpha(u_t - u_n)$$

how would you change the content of your memo? (The evidence is that people form rational expectations.)

4. *What measures (constitutional amendments, legal procedures, technological devices) would you put in place to deal with hostage taking by terrorists?*

5. *New Zealand rewrote the charter of its central bank in the early 1990s to make steady low inflation its only goal. Why would New Zealand want do this?*

Dig Deeper

6. *There are two parties: the Democrats, who care a lot more about unemployment than inflation and the Republicans, who care a lot more about inflation than unemployment.*

The Philips curve is given by

$$\pi_t = \pi_t^e - \alpha(u_t - u_n)$$

where π_t^e *denotes expectations held in year* t – 1 *for inflation in year* t.

There are elections at the end of this year. Democrats and Republicans have an equal chance of winning and being in power next year.

a. Describe how people will form expectations of inflation for next year.
b. Given these expectations, describe what happens to inflation and unemployment next year if the Democrats win.
c. Given these expectations, describe what happens to inflation and unemployment next year if the Republicans win.
d. Do these results fit the evidence in Table 25-1? Why or why not?
e. Now suppose that everybody expects Democrats to win the elections. Suppose the Democrats indeed win. What happens to inflation and unemployment next year? Explain.

7. *Suppose there is a budget deficit. It can be reduced by cutting military spending, or by cutting welfare programs, or by cutting both.*

The Democrats have to decide whether to support cuts in welfare programs. The Republicans have to decide whether to support cuts in military spending. Each party has to decide what to do, without knowing the decision of the other party.

The possible outcomes can be represented in a table:

		Welfare cuts: Yes	Welfare cuts: No
Defense cuts	Yes	(R = 1, D = 1)	(R = –2, D = 3)
	No	(R = 3, D = –2)	(R = –1, D = –1)

To read this table, look, for example, at the box in the bottom left corner. If Democrats vote for welfare cuts, and Republicans vote against cuts in military spending, the outcome is such that the Republicans are very happy, the Democrats unhappy. The Republicans get 3 (a high positive number) and the Democrats get –2. Make sure you understand each of the four boxes.

a. If the Republicans decide to cut military spending, what is the Democrats' best response? Given this response, how much will the Republicans get?
b. If the Republicans decide not to cut military spending, what is the Democrats' best response? Given this response, how much will the Republicans get?
c. What will the Republicans do? What will the Democrats do? Will the budget deficit be reduced? Why or why not? (This is an example of a game known as the prisoner's dilemma in game theory.) Is there a way to improve the outcome?

We invite you to visit the Blanchard page on the Prentice Hall Web site at:
www.prenhall.com/blanchard
for this chapter's World Wide Web exercises

Further Readings

A leading proponent of the view that governments misbehave and should be tightly restrained is James Buchanan, from George Mason University. Buchanan received the Nobel Prize in 1986 for his work on public choice. Read his book, written with Richard Wagner, *Democracy in Deficit: The Political Legacy of Lord Keynes* (New York, NY: Academic Press, 1977).

For a survey of the politics of fiscal policy, read Alberto Alesina and Roberto Perotti, "The Political Economy of Budget Deficits," IMF Staff Papers, 1995. Also look at James Poterba, "Do Budget Rules Work?" in Alan Auerbach, ed., *Fiscal Policy. Lessons from Economic Research* (Cambridge, MA: MIT Press, 1997).

For more on the politics of monetary policy, read Alberto Alesina and Lawrence Summers, "Central Bank Independence and Macroeconomic Performance: Some Comparative Evidence," *Journal of Money, Credit and Banking*, May 1993, 289–297.

Monetary Policy: A Summing Up

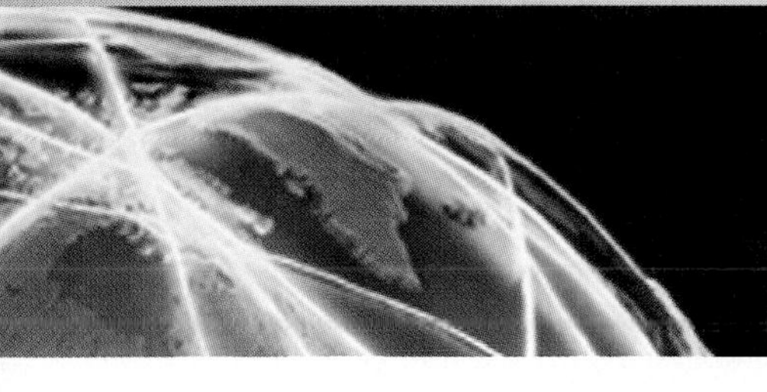

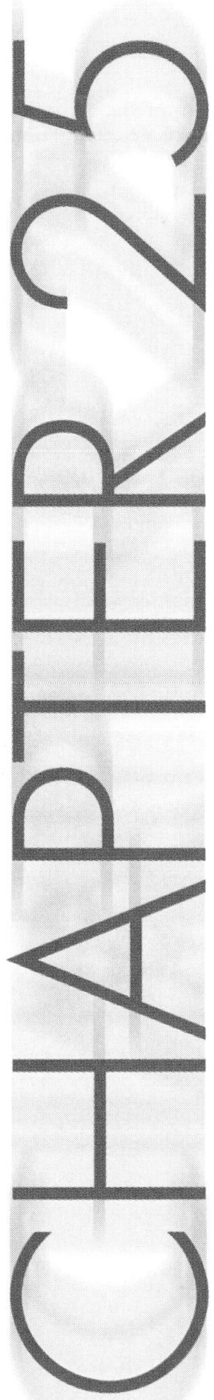

Nearly every chapter of this book has touched upon an aspect of monetary policy. This chapter puts it all together and ties up the remaining loose ends.

Let's first briefly review what you have learned (the Focus box "Monetary Policy: What You Have Learned and Where" gives a more detailed summary):

- **In the short run, monetary policy affects the level of output as well as its composition:**

  An increase in money leads to a decrease in interest rates and a depreciation of the currency.

  These lead to an increase in the demand for goods and an increase in output.

- **In the medium run and the long run, monetary policy is neutral:**

  Changes in either the level or the rate of growth of money have no effect on output or unemployment.

  Changes in the level of money lead to proportional increases in prices.

  Changes in the rate of nominal money growth lead to corresponding changes in the inflation rate.

With these conclusions in mind, this chapter explores three issues:

- Section 25-1 discusses what inflation rate central banks should try to achieve in the medium and long run.
- Section 25-2 discusses how monetary policy should be designed both to achieve this inflation rate in the medium and long run, as well as to reduce output fluctuations in the short run.
- Section 25-3 describes how monetary policy is actually carried out in the United States today. ■

Monetary Policy: What You Have Learned and Where

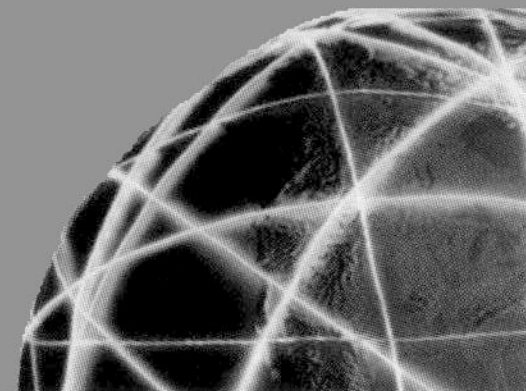

FOCUS

- In Chapter 4, we looked at the determination of money demand, of money supply, and the effects of monetary policy on the interest rate.

  You saw how an increase in the money supply, achieved through an open-market operation, leads to a decrease in the interest rate.
- In Chapter 5, we looked at the short-run effects of monetary policy on output.

  You saw how an increase in money leads, through a decrease in the interest rate, to an increase in spending and to an increase in output.
- In Chapter 7, we looked at the effects of changes in money on output and prices, not only in the short run but also in the medium run.

  You saw that in the medium run, money is neutral: Changes in money are fully reflected in changes in the price level.
- In Chapter 9, we looked at the relation between nominal money growth, inflation, and unemployment.

  You saw that in the medium run, nominal money growth is reflected one for one in inflation, leaving the unemployment rate unaffected. You saw that in the short run however, decreases in nominal money growth lead to lower output and higher unemployment for some time.
- In Chapter 14, we introduced a distinction between the nominal interest rate and the real interest rate.

  You saw how higher nominal money growth leads to a lower nominal interest rate and a lower real interest rate in the short run, but to a higher nominal interest rate and an unchanged real interest rate in the medium run.
- In Chapter 17, we returned to the short-run effects of monetary policy on output, taking into account the effects of monetary policy on expectations.

  You saw that monetary policy affects the short-term nominal interest rate, but that spending depends primarily on both current and expected future short-term real interest rates. You saw how the effects of monetary policy on output depend on how expectations respond to monetary policy.
- In Chapter 20, we looked at the effects of monetary policy in an economy open both in goods markets and financial markets.

  You saw how, in an open economy, monetary policy affects spending and output not only through the interest rate, but also through the exchange rate. An increase in money leads both to a decrease in the interest rate and a depreciation, both of which increase spending and output.
- In Chapter 21, we discussed the pros and cons of different monetary policy regimes, flexible exchange rates versus fixed exchange rates.

  We discussed the pros and cons of adopting a common currency such as the Euro, or even giving up monetary policy altogether, through the adoption of a currency board or dollarization.
- In Chapter 22, we looked at the implications of the liquidity trap, the fact that monetary policy cannot decrease the nominal interest rate below zero. You saw how the liquidity trap and deflation can combine to turn a recession into a slump or a depression.
- In Chapter 23, we studied hyperinflations and looked at the conditions under which such episodes arise, and eventually end.

  We focused on the relation between the budget deficit, nominal money growth, and inflation. You saw how a large budget deficit can lead to high nominal money growth, and, in turn, to hyperinflation.
- In Chapter 24, we looked at the problems facing macroeconomic policy in general, and monetary policy in particular.

  You saw that uncertainty about the effects of policy should lead to more cautious policies. You saw that even well-intentioned policy makers may sometimes not do what is best, and that there is a case for restraints on policy makers. We also looked at the case for giving independence to the central bank, and appointing a conservative central banker.
- In this chapter, we discuss the issues of the optimal inflation rate, the design of monetary policy, and how the Fed actually conducts monetary policy in the United States today.

25-1 The Optimal Inflation Rate

Table 25-1 shows how inflation has steadily gone down in rich countries since the early 1980s. In 1981, average inflation in the OECD was 10.5%; in 2000, it was down to 2.5%. In 1981, two countries (out of 30) had an inflation rate below 5%; in 2000, the number of countries had increased to 24.

Does this imply most central banks have now achieved their goal? Or should they aim for an even lower inflation rate, perhaps 0%? The answer depends on the costs and benefits of inflation.

Table 25-1 Inflation Rates in the OECD, 1981–2000

Year	1981	1985	1990	1995	2000
OECD average (%)*	10.5	6.6	6.2	5.2	2.5
Number of countries with inflation below 5%**	2	10	15	21	24

*Average of inflation rates, using the GDP deflator, and relative GDPs at PPP prices as weights.
**Out of 30 countries.

The Costs of Inflation

We saw in Chapter 23 how very high inflation, say, 30% a month or more, can disrupt economic activity. The debate in OECD countries today, however, is not about the costs of inflation rates of 30% a month or more. Rather, it centers on the advantages of, say, 0% versus 4% inflation a year. Within that range, economists identify four main costs of inflation: (1) shoe-leather costs, (2) tax distortions, (3) money illusion, and (4) inflation variability.

Shoe-Leather Costs

In the medium run, a higher inflation rate leads to a higher nominal interest rate, and so to a higher opportunity cost of holding money. As a result, people decrease their money balances by making more trips to the bank—thus the expression **shoe-leather costs**. These trips would be avoided if inflation were lower, and people could be doing other things instead, such as working more or enjoying leisure.

From Chapter 14: In the medium run, the real interest rate is not affected by inflation. Thus, an increase in inflation is reflected one for one in an increase in the nominal interest rate (this is called the Fisher effect).

During hyperinflations, shoe-leather costs can become quite large. But their importance in times of moderate inflation is limited. If an inflation rate of 4% leads people to go the bank say, one more time every month, or to do one more transaction between their money market fund and their checking account every month, this hardly qualifies as a major cost of inflation.

Tax Distortions

The second cost of inflation comes from the interaction between the tax system and inflation.

Consider, for example, the taxation of capital gains. Taxes on capital gains are typically based on the change in the dollar price of the asset between the time it was purchased and the time it is sold. This implies that the higher the rate of inflation, the higher the tax. An example will make this clear:

- Suppose inflation has been running at $\pi\%$ a year for the last 10 years.
- Suppose you bought your house for \$50,000 10 years ago, and you are selling it today for $\$50{,}000 \times (1 + \pi\%)^{10}$—so its real value is unchanged.
- If the capital-gains tax is 30%, the *effective tax rate* on the sale of your house—defined as the ratio of the tax you pay to the price for which you sell your house—is equal to:

The numerator of the fraction equals the sale price minus the purchase price. The denominator is the sale price.

$$(30\%)\ \frac{50{,}000(1+\pi\%)^{10} - 50{,}000}{50{,}000(1+\pi\%)^{10}}$$

- Because you are selling your house for the same real price for which you bought it, your real capital gain is zero and you should not be paying any tax. Indeed, if $\pi = 0$—if there has been no inflation—then the effective tax rate is 0. But if $\pi = 4\%$, then the effective tax rate is 9.7%: Despite the fact that your real capital gain is zero, you end up paying a high tax.

The problems created by the interactions between taxation and inflation extend beyond capital-gains taxes. Although we know that the real rate of return on an asset is the real interest rate, not the nominal interest rate, income for the purpose of income taxation includes nominal interest payments, not real interest payments. Or, to take yet another example: Until the early 1980s in the United States, the income levels corresponding to different income-tax rates were not increased automatically with inflation. As a result, people were pushed into higher tax brackets as their nominal income—but not necessarily their real income—increased over time, an effect known as *bracket creep*.

Some economists argue the costs of bracket creep were much larger. As tax revenues steadily increased, there was little pressure on the government to control spending. The result, they argue, was an increase in the size of the government in the 1960s and 1970s far beyond what would have been desirable.

You may argue this cost is not a cost of inflation per se, but rather the result of a badly designed tax system. In the house example we just discussed, the government could eliminate the problem if it *indexed* the purchase price to the price level—that is, it adjusted the purchase price for inflation since the time of purchase—and computed the tax on the difference between the sale price and the adjusted purchase price. Under that computation, in our example there would be no capital gains and therefore no capital-gains tax to pay. But because tax codes rarely allow for such systematic adjustment, the inflation rate matters and leads to distortions.

Money Illusion

The third cost comes from **money illusion**—the notion that people appear to make systematic mistakes in assessing nominal versus real changes. A number of computations that would be simple under price stability become more complicated when there is inflation. In comparing their income this year to their income in the past, people have to keep track of the history of inflation. In choosing between different assets or deciding how much to consume or save, they have to keep track of the difference between the real interest rate and the nominal interest rate. Casual evidence suggests that many people find these computations difficult and often fail to make the relevant distinctions. Economists and psychologists have gathered more formal evidence, and it suggests that inflation often leads people and firms to take incorrect decisions (see the Focus box "Money Illusion"). If this is the case, then a simple solution is to have no inflation.

Inflation Variability

This cost comes from the fact that higher inflation is typically associated with *more variable inflation*. And more variable inflation means financial assets such as bonds, which promise fixed nominal payments in the future, become riskier.

Take a bond that pays $1,000 in 10 years. With constant inflation over the next 10 years, not only the nominal value, but also the real value of the bond in 10 years is known with certainty—we can compute exactly how much a dollar will be worth in 10 years. But with variable inflation, the real value of $1,000 in 10 years becomes uncertain. The more variability, the more uncertainty. Saving for retirement becomes more difficult. For those who have invested in bonds, lower inflation than expected means a better retirement; but higher inflation may mean poverty. This is one of the reasons retirees, for whom part of income is fixed in dollar terms, typically worry more about inflation than other groups in the population.

A good, but sad movie about surviving on a fixed pension in post–World War II Italy is *Umberto D* by Vittorio de Sica, made in 1952.

You may argue, as in the case of taxes, that these costs are not due to inflation per se, but rather to the financial markets' inability to provide assets that protect their holders against inflation. Rather than issuing only nominal bonds (bonds that promise a fixed nominal amount in the future), governments or firms could also issue *indexed bonds*, bonds that promise a nominal amount adjusted for inflation, so people do not have to worry about the real value of the bond when they retire. Indeed, as we saw in Chapter 15, a number of countries, including the United States, have now

Money Illusion

There is a lot of anecdotal evidence that many people fail to adjust properly for inflation in financial computations. Recently, economists and psychologists have started looking at money illusion more closely. In a recent study, two psychologists, Eldar Shafir from Princeton and Amos Tversky from Stanford, and one economist, Peter Diamond from MIT, designed a survey aimed at finding the presence and the determinants of money illusion. Among the many questions they asked of people in various groups (people at Newark International Airport, people at two New Jersey shopping malls, and a group of Princeton undergraduates) is the following:

> Suppose Adam, Ben, and Carl each received an inheritance of $200,000 and each used it immediately to purchase a house. Suppose each sold his house one year after buying it. Economic conditions were, however, different in each case:
>
> - During the time Adam owned the house, there was a 25% deflation—the prices of all goods and services decreased by approximately 25%. A year after Adam bought the house, he sold it for $154,000 (23% less than he had paid.)
> - During the time Ben owned the house, there was no inflation or deflation—the prices of all goods and services did not change significantly during the year. A year after Ben bought the house, he sold it for $198,000 (1% less than he had paid.)
> - During the time Carl owned the house, there was a 25% inflation—the prices of all goods and services increased by approximately 25%. A year after Carl bought the house, he sold it for $246,000 (23% more than he had paid.)
>
> Please rank Adam, Ben, and Carl in terms of the success of their house transactions. Assign 1 to the person who made the best deal, and 3 to the person who made the worst deal.

In nominal terms, Carl clearly made the best deal, followed by Ben, followed by Adam. But what is relevant is how they did in real terms—adjusting for inflation. In real terms, the ranking is reversed: Adam, with a 2% real gain, made the best deal, followed by Ben (with a 1% loss), followed by Carl (with a 2% loss).

The survey's answers are summarized in the table.

Rank	Adam (%)	Ben (%)	Carl (%)
1st	37	15	48
2nd	10	74	16
3rd	53	11	36

Carl was ranked first by 48% of the respondents, and Adam was ranked third by 53% of the respondents. These answers are very suggestive of money illusion. In other words, people (even Princeton undergraduates . . .) have a hard time adjusting for inflation.

introduced such bonds, so people can better protect themselves against movements in inflation.

The Benefits of Inflation

Inflation is actually not all bad. One can identify three benefits of inflation: (1) seignorage, (2) the option of negative real interest rates for macroeconomic policy, and (3) (somewhat paradoxically) the use of the interaction between money illusion and inflation in facilitating real wage adjustments.

Seignorage

Money creation—the ultimate source of inflation—is one of the ways in which the government can finance its spending. Put another way, money creation is an alternative to borrowing from the public or raising taxes.

As you saw in Chapter 23, the government typically does not "create" money to pay for its spending. Rather, the government issues and sells bonds, and spends the proceeds. But if the bonds are bought by the central bank, which then creates money to pay for them, the result is the same: Other things equal, the revenues from money creation—that is, *seignorage*—allow the government to borrow less from the public or to lower taxes.

How large is seignorage in practice? When looking at hyperinflations in Chapter 23, you saw that seignorage is often an important source of government finance in countries with very high inflation rates. But its importance in OECD economies today, and for the range of inflation rates we are considering, is much more limited. Take the case of the United States. The ratio of the monetary base—the money issued by the Fed (see Chapter 4)—to GDP is about 6%. An increase in nominal money growth of 4% per year (which eventually leads to a 4% increase in inflation) would lead therefore to an increase in seignorage of 4% × 6%, or 0.24% of GDP. This is a small amount of revenues to get in exchange for 4% more inflation.

Let H denote the monetary base—the money issued by the central bank. Then

$$\frac{\text{Seignorage}}{Y} = \frac{\Delta H}{PY} = \frac{\Delta H}{H}\frac{H}{PY}$$

where $\Delta H/H$ is the rate of growth of the monetary base, and H/PY is the ratio of the monetary base to nominal GDP.

Therefore, while the seignorage argument is sometimes relevant (for example, in economies that do not yet have a good fiscal system in place), it seems hardly relevant in the discussion of whether OECD countries today should have, say, 0% versus 4% inflation.

The Option of Negative Real Interest Rates

This argument follows from our discussion of the liquidity trap and its macroeconomic implications in Chapter 22. A numerical example will help here.

- Consider two economies, both with a real interest rate equal to 2%. In the first economy, the central bank maintains an average inflation rate of 4%, so the nominal interest rate is on average equal to 2% + 4% = 6%. In the second economy, the central bank maintains an average inflation rate of 0%, so the nominal interest rate is on average equal to 2% + 0% = 2%.
- Suppose both economies are hit by a similar adverse shock, which leads, at a given interest rate, to a decrease in spending and a decrease in output in the short run. In the first economy, the central bank can decrease the nominal interest rate from 6 to 0%, a decrease of 6%. Under the assumption that expected inflation does not change immediately, and remains equal to 4%, the real interest rate decreases from 2 to –4%. This is likely to have a strong positive effect on spending, and help the economy recover. In the second economy, the central bank can only decrease the nominal interest rate from 2 to 0%, a decrease of 2%. Under the assumption that expected inflation does not change right away, and remains equal to 0%, the real interest rate decreases only by 2%, from 2 to 0%. This small decrease in the real interest rate may not increase spending by very much.

In short, an economy with a higher average inflation rate has more scope to use monetary policy to fight a recession. An economy with a low average inflation rate may find itself unable to use monetary policy to return output to the natural level of output. As you saw in Chapter 22, this is far from being just a theoretical possibility. Japan is precisely faced with such a limit on monetary policy, and the recession has turned into a slump. Some economists worry that other countries may also be at risk. Many countries, including the United States, have low inflation and low nominal interest rates. If, for any reason, some of these countries were to be faced with further adverse shocks to spending, the room for monetary policy to help avoid a decline in output would clearly be limited.

At the time of writing, the three-month nominal interest rate in the United States is 2% and the inflation rate is 2.6%. The three-month nominal interest rate in the Euro zone is 3.3%; the inflation rate is 2.5%.

In the early 1990s, the Fed decreased the nominal interest rate by 7%. This was still not enough to avoid a recession.

Money Illusion Revisited

Paradoxically, the presence of money illusion provides at least one argument *for* having a positive inflation rate.

To see why, consider two scenarios. In the first, inflation is 4% and your wage goes up by 1% in nominal terms—in dollars. In the second, inflation is 0% and your wage goes down by 3% in nominal terms. Both lead to the same 3% decrease in your real wage, so you should be indifferent. The evidence, however, is that many people will accept the real wage cut more easily in the first case than in the second case.

Why is this example relevant to our discussion? Because, as you saw in Chapter 13, the constant process of change that characterizes modern economies means some workers must sometimes take a real pay cut. Thus, the argument goes, the presence of inflation allows for these downward real-wage adjustments more easily than when there is no inflation. This argument is plausible. Economists have not established its importance; but, because so many economies now have very low inflation, we may soon be in a position to test it.

◀ **See, for example, the results of a survey of managers by Alan Blinder and Don Choi, in "A Shred of Evidence on Theories of Wage Rigidity," *Quarterly Journal of Economics*, 1990, 1003–1016.**

◀ **A conflict of metaphors:**

Because inflation makes these real-wage adjustments easier to achieve, some economists say inflation "greases the wheels" of the economy.

Others, emphasizing the adverse effects of inflation on relative prices, say that inflation "puts sand" in the economy.

The Optimal Inflation Rate: The Current Debate

At this stage, the debate in OECD countries is between those who think some inflation (say, up to 4%) is fine and those who want to achieve price stability—that is, 0% inflation.

Those who want an inflation rate around 4% emphasize that the costs of 4% versus 0% inflation are small and that the benefits of inflation are worth keeping. They argue some of the costs of inflation could be avoided by indexing the tax system and issuing more indexed bonds. They also say that going from current rates of inflation to 0% would require some increase in unemployment for some time, and that this transition cost may well exceed the eventual benefits.

Those who want to aim for 0% make the point that 0% is a very different target rate from any other: It corresponds to price stability. This is desirable in itself. Knowing the price level will be roughly the same in 10 or 20 years as it is today simplifies many decisions, and eliminates the scope for money illusion. Also, given the time consistency problem facing central banks (discussed in Chapter 24), credibility and simplicity of the target inflation rate are important. Price stability may achieve these goals better than a target inflation rate of 4%.

The debate is not settled. For the time being, most central banks appear to be aiming for low but positive inflation—that is, inflation rates between 2 and 4%.

25-2 The Design of Monetary Policy

Until the 1990s the design of monetary policy focused on nominal money growth, from the choice of a nominal money growth target to rules for the adjustment of nominal money growth in response to short-run fluctuations in output. In the past decade, however, this design has evolved. Increasingly, central banks focus on an *inflation rate target* rather than a nominal money growth rate target. And, increasingly, central banks think about monetary policy in terms of the *determination of the nominal interest rate* rather than in terms of the rate of nominal money growth.

Money Growth Targets and Target Ranges

Consider the following propositions:

- The choice by the central bank of an optimal inflation rate determines the rate of nominal money growth it should achieve in the medium run.

  This rate of nominal money growth should be equal to the desired inflation rate plus the normal growth rate of output (the rate implied by the rate of technological progress and the rate of population growth). For example, if the desired rate of inflation is 4%, and the normal rate of growth of output is 3%, then the central bank should try to achieve a rate of nominal money growth of 7%.

- Because monetary policy can and should be used to respond to short-run fluctuations, the central bank may want to allow for deviations of nominal money growth from its desired medium-run rate of growth. If, for example, the economy is in a recession, the central bank may want to increase nominal money growth above its medium-run value, to allow for a decrease in the interest rate and a faster recovery of output.
- To communicate its intentions to the public, the central bank may want to announce *a target* for nominal money growth, making clear both what it wants to achieve in the medium run and why it may want to deviate from this value in the short run. Or, given the need to adjust to unexpected developments in the economy, the central bank may want to announce a *target range* rather than a *target point*—a range within which it intends to keep nominal money growth in the short run.

Until recently, these propositions were the basis for the design of monetary policy in most countries. Details of implementation differed across countries. Some central banks announced a target point for nominal money growth. Some announced instead a target range, an upper and a lower band for nominal money growth. Some took these bands as best guesses, and were willing to step out of the bands if economic conditions required it. Some took these bands as constraints, to be broken only in exceptional circumstances. In the past decade, however, most central banks have become disenchanted and have moved away from this approach. Let's now see why.

Money Growth and Inflation Revisited

Recall how inflation and nominal money growth move together during episodes of hyperinflation (Chapter 23).

The design of monetary policy around nominal money growth is based on the assumption of a close relation between inflation and nominal money growth in the medium run. The problem is that this relation is in fact not very tight. If nominal money growth is high, inflation will also be high; and if nominal money growth is low, inflation will be low. But the relation is not tight enough that, by choosing a rate of nominal money growth, the central bank can achieve precisely its desired rate of inflation, not even in the medium run.

*M*1 Growth and Inflation

From Chapter 4: *M*1 measures the amount of money in the economy, and is constructed as the sum of currency and checkable deposits. The Fed does not directly control *M*1. What it controls is *H*, the monetary base; but it can choose *H* to achieve any value of *M*1 it wants. So, it is reasonable to think of the Fed as controlling *M*1.

The relation between inflation and nominal money growth is shown in Figure 25-1, which plots 10-year averages of the inflation rate (using the CPI as the price index) against 10-year averages of the growth rate of the money stock (*M*1) from 1970 to 2000. The reason for using 10-year averages should be clear: In the short run, changes in nominal money growth affect mostly output, not inflation. It is only in the medium run that a relation between nominal money growth and inflation should emerge. Taking 10-year averages of both nominal money growth and inflation is a way of detecting such a medium-run relation.

Figure 25-1 shows that for the United States since 1970, the relation between *M*1 growth and inflation has not been very tight. True, both went up at the beginning of the period, and both have come down since. But note how inflation started declining in the early 1980s, while nominal money growth remained high for another decade, and has only come down in the 1990s.

From *M*1 to *M*2, *M*3, and Other Monetary Aggregates

Why is the relation between *M*1 growth and inflation not tighter? Answer: Because of *shifts in the demand for money*. An example will help. Suppose that, as the result of the

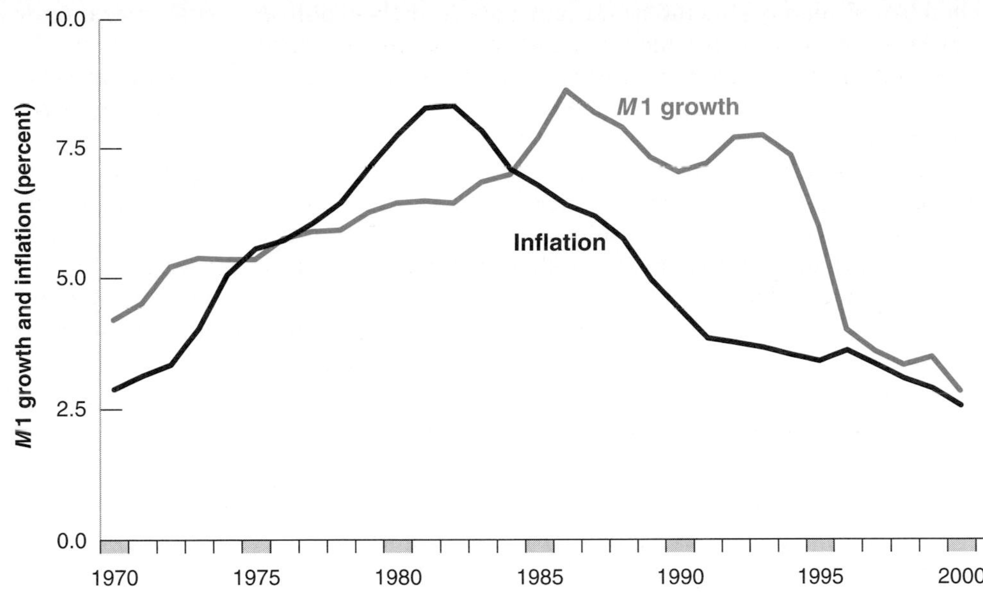

Figure 25-1

M1 Growth and Inflation: 10-year Averages, 1970–2000

There is no tight relation between M1 growth and inflation, not even in the medium run.

introduction of credit cards, people decide to hold only half the amount of money they held before; in other words, the real demand for money decreases by half. In the medium run, the real money stock must also decrease by half. For a given nominal money stock, the price level must double. Even if the nominal money stock is constant, there will be a period of inflation as the price level doubles. During this period, there will be no tight relation between nominal money growth (which is zero) and inflation (which is positive).

From equation (5.3) (the *LM* equation): The real money supply (the left side) must be equal to the real demand for money (the right side)

$$\frac{M}{P} = Y\,L(i)$$

If, as a result of the introduction of credit cards, the real demand for money halves, then

$$\frac{M}{P} = \frac{1}{2}Y\,L(i)$$

For a given level of output and a given interest rate, M/P must also halve. Given M, this implies P must double.

The reason why the demand for money shifts over time goes beyond the introduction of credit cards. To understand why, we must challenge an assumption we have maintained until now, namely, that there is a sharp distinction between money and other assets. In fact, there are many financial assets that are close to money. They cannot be used for transactions—at least not without restrictions—but they can be exchanged for money at little cost. In other words, they are very **liquid**; this makes them attractive substitutes for money. Shifts between money and these assets are the main factor behind shifts in the demand for money.

Take, for example, *money market fund shares.* Money market funds are financial intermediaries that hold as assets short-maturity securities (typically, Treasury bills) and have deposits (or shares, as they are called) as liabilities. The funds pay depositors an interest rate close to the T-bill rate minus the administrative costs of running the fund. Deposits can be exchanged for money on notice and at little cost. Most money market funds allow depositors to write checks but only above a certain amount, typically $500. Because of this restriction, money market funds are not included in *M*1. When these funds were introduced in the mid-1970s, people were able for the first time to hold a very liquid asset while receiving an interest rate close to that on T-bills. Money market funds quickly became very attractive, increasing from nothing in 1973 to $321 billion in 1989. Many people reduced their bank account balances and moved to money market funds. In other words, there was a large negative shift in the demand for money.

For comparison: Checkable deposits were equal to $280 billion in 1989.

The presence of shifts between money and other liquid assets have led central banks to construct and report measures that include not only money, but also other liquid assets. These measures are called **monetary aggregates**, and typically come under the names of *M*2, *M*3, and so on. In the United States, ***M*2**—which is also sometimes

In 2000, $M2$ was equal to \$4.7 trillion, compared to \$1.1 trillion for $M1$.

called **broad money**—includes $M1$ (currency and checkable deposits), plus money market mutual fund shares, money market deposit accounts (the same as money market shares, but issued by banks rather than money market funds), and time deposits (deposits with an explicit maturity of a few months to a few years, and with a penalty for early withdrawal).

The construction of $M2$ and other monetary aggregates would appear to offer a solution to our earlier problem: If most of the shifts in the demand for money are between $M1$ and other assets within $M2$, the demand for $M2$ should be more stable than the demand for $M1$, and so there should be a tighter relation between $M2$ growth and inflation than between $M1$ growth and inflation. If so, the central bank could choose targets for $M2$ growth rather than for $M1$ growth. This is indeed the solution that many central banks adopted. But it has not worked well either, for two reasons:

- While the relation between $M2$ growth and inflation is tighter than the relation between $M1$ growth and inflation, it is still not very tight. This is shown in Figure 25-2 which plots 10-year averages of the inflation rate and of the rate of growth of $M2$. The evolution of $M2$ growth is closer to the evolution of inflation than was the case for $M1$ growth. But the fit is still not tight. Note, for example, how $M2$ growth was nearly 5% above inflation in the 1970s, and how this difference has disappeared over time. Put another way, a given rate of $M2$ growth is associated with 5% more inflation than it was in the 1970s.
- More importantly, while the central bank controls $M1$, it does not control $M2$. If people shift from T-bills to money market funds, this will increase $M2$—which includes money market funds, but does not include T-bills. There is little the central bank can do about this increase in $M2$. Thus, $M2$ is a strange target: It is neither under the direct control of the central bank, nor is it what the central bank ultimately cares about.

M2 Growth: Target Range and Realizations

The combination of large shifts in the demand for money (be it demand for $M1$ or for $M2$), the resulting lack of a tight relation between $M2$ growth and inflation, combined

Figure 25-2

***M2* Growth and Inflation: 10-year Averages, 1970–2000**

While the relation between $M2$ growth and inflation is tighter than the relation between $M1$ growth and inflation, it is still not very tight.

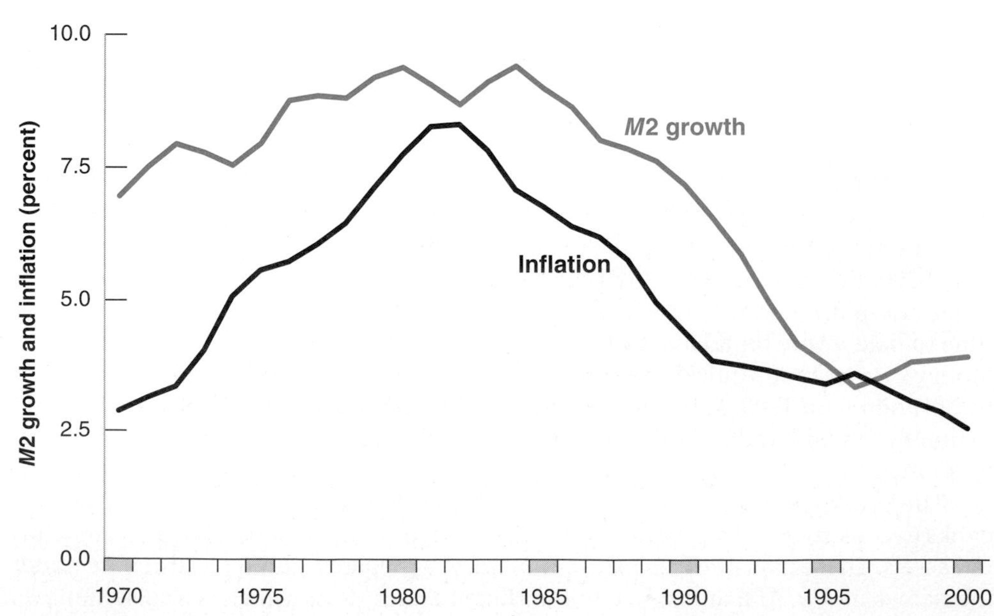

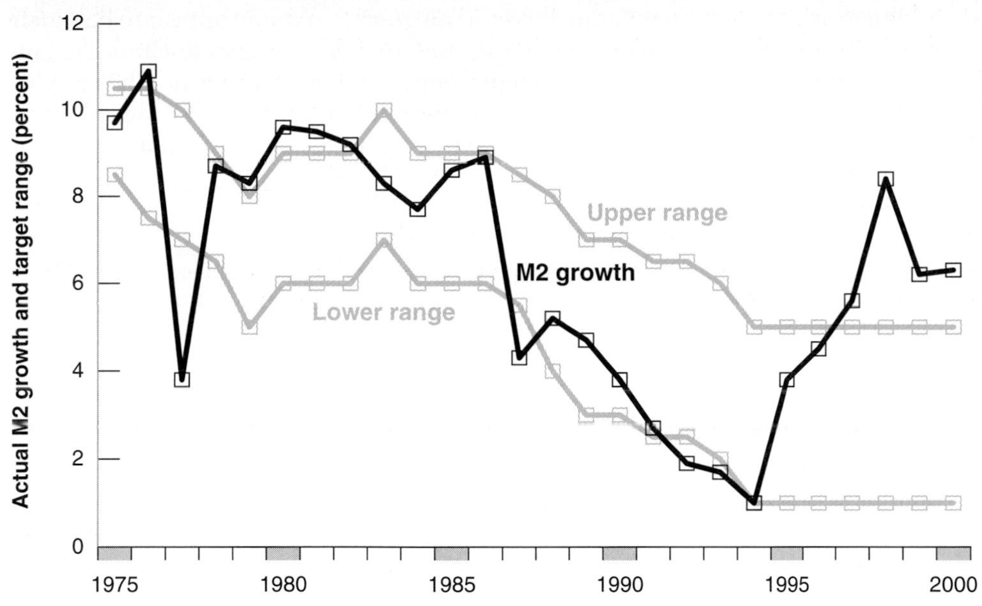

Figure 25-3

M2 Growth, 1975–2000: Actual Growth Rate and Target Growth Range

Actual *M2* growth has ended out of the target range for 11 out of the last 26 years.

with the difficulty for the central bank to control *M*2 in the first place, has had a predictable effect: *M*2 growth has often ended up far from the target announced by the central bank.

Figure 25-3 shows what has happened in the United States. It plots, for each year from 1975 to 2000, the actual value of *M*2 growth for the year, as well as the upper band and the lower band of the range announced by the Fed for *M*2 growth at the beginning of the year. Clearly, the Fed has not always hit its target range: Actual *M*2 growth has ended out of the range for 11 out of the last 26 years! Note in particular how, in the late 1990s, *M*2 growth has increased from the bottom of the target range to far above the top of the target range. Given that inflation has remained very low, the overshooting of the target has not worried financial market participants, who attribute the high growth in *M*2 to shifts in the demand for *M*2. But these sharp swings in *M*2 growth, and the frequent misses of the target range, raise an obvious question: What is the point of announcing a range for *M*2 if you miss the range so often? This is indeed the conclusion the Fed reached in 2000. As a result, it no longer announces a target range for *M*2.

Inflation Targeting and Interest Rate Rules

The Fed is not the only central bank to have changed the way it conducts monetary policy. Most central banks have been looking for a better design for monetary policy. In the last decade, a new design has indeed emerged, based on *inflation targeting,* and on *interest rate rules.* Let me discuss both aspects in turn.

Inflation Targeting

In many countries, central banks have defined as their primary, and sometimes their exclusive goal, the achievement of a low inflation rate, both in the short run and in the medium run. This is known as **inflation targeting**.

First to adopt inflation targeting was New Zealand in 1990, which set a target range for inflation of 0 to 2%, later extended to 0 to 3%. Next was Canada in 1991, setting a target range for inflation of 0 to 2%. Since then, some form of inflation targeting has been adopted by, among others, the United Kingdom, Sweden, Israel, and Spain.

- Trying to achieve a given inflation target *in the medium run* would seem, and indeed is, a clear improvement over trying to achieve a nominal money growth target. After all, in the medium run, the primary goal of monetary policy is to achieve a given rate of inflation. Better then to have the inflation rate as the target than a nominal money growth target, which, as you have seen, may not lead to the desired rate of inflation.

- Trying to achieve a given inflation target *in the short run* would appear to be much more controversial. An exclusive focus on inflation would seem to eliminate any role for monetary policy to reduce fluctuations. But, in fact, this is not the case. To see why, return to the Phillips curve relation between inflation, π_t, lagged inflation, π_{t-1}, and the deviation of the unemployment rate, u_t from the natural rate of unemployment, u_n (equation [8.10]):

$$\pi_t = \pi_{t-1} - \alpha(u_t - u_n)$$

Let the inflation rate target be π^*. Suppose the central bank could achieve its inflation target exactly in every period. Then, the relation would become

$$\pi^* = \pi^* - \alpha(u_t - u_n)$$

$0 = -\alpha(u_t - u_n) \Rightarrow u_t = u_n$ ▶

The unemployment rate, u_t, would always equal u_n, the natural rate of unemployment; by implication, output would always be equal to its natural level of output. In effect, inflation targeting would lead the central bank to act in such a way as to eliminate all deviations of output from its natural level of output.

The intuition: If the central bank saw that an adverse demand shock was going to lead to a recession, it would know, that, absent a monetary expansion, the economy would experience a decline in inflation below the target rate of inflation. To maintain stable inflation, the central bank would then rely on a monetary expansion to avoid the recession. The same would apply to a favorable demand shock: Fearing an increase in inflation above the target rate, the central bank would rely on a monetary contraction to slow down the economy, and keep output at the natural level of output. In short: As a result of this active monetary policy, output would remain at the natural level of output all the time.

The result we have just derived—that inflation targeting eliminates deviations of output from its natural level—is striking. But it is too strong, for two reasons:

- The central bank cannot always achieve the rate of inflation it wants in the short run. So suppose that, for example, the central bank was not able to achieve its desired rate of inflation last year, so π_{t-1} is higher than π^*. Then it is not clear that the central bank should try to hit its target this year, and achieve $\pi_t = \pi^*$: The Phillips curve relation implies that such a decrease in inflation would require a potentially large increase in unemployment. We return to this issue below.
- Like all other macroeconomic relations, the Phillips curve relation above does not hold exactly. It will happen that, for example, inflation increases even when the unemployment is at the natural rate of unemployment. In this case, the central bank will face a more difficult choice: Whether to keep unemployment at the natural rate and allow inflation to increase, or to increase unemployment above the natural rate, to keep inflation in check.

These qualifications are important, but the general point remains: Inflation targeting makes good sense in the *medium run,* and allows for monetary policy to stabilize output around its natural level in the *short run.*

Taylor's Rule

The next question is how to achieve the inflation target. Inflation is clearly not under the direct control of the central bank. In answer to this question, John Taylor, from Stanford University, argued that, since it is the interest rate that directly affects spending, the central bank should think in terms of the choice of an interest rate rather than a rate of nominal money growth. He then suggested a rule that the central bank may want to follow. **Taylor's rule** goes as follows:

Let π_t be the rate of inflation, and π^* be the target rate of inflation.

Let i_t be the nominal interest rate, and i^* be the target nominal interest rate—the nominal interest rate associated with the target rate of inflation π^* in the medium run.

From Chapter 14: In the medium run, the real interest rate is given, equal to r_n, so the nominal interest rate moves one for one with the inflation rate: If r_n = 2% and the target inflation rate π^* = 2%, then the target nominal interest rate i^* = 2% + 2% = 4%. If the target inflation rate π^* is 0%, then i^* = 2% + 0% = 2%.

Let u_t be the unemployment rate, and u_n be the natural unemployment rate.

Think of the central bank as choosing the nominal interest rate, i (recall, from Chapter 4, that, through open-market operations, the central bank can achieve any short-term nominal interest rate it wants). Then, Taylor argued, the central bank should follow the following rule:

$$i_t = i^* + a(\pi_t - \pi^*) - b(u_t - u_n)$$

where a and b are positive coefficients. Let's look at what the rule says:

- If inflation is equal to target inflation ($\pi_t = \pi^*$), and the unemployment rate is equal to the natural rate of unemployment ($u_t = u_n$), then the central bank should set the nominal interest rate, i_t, equal to its target value, i^*. This way, the economy can stay on the same path, with inflation equal to the target inflation rate, and unemployment equal to the natural rate of unemployment.
- If inflation is higher than the target ($\pi_t > \pi^*$), the central bank should increase the nominal interest rate, i_t, above i^*. This higher interest rate will increase unemployment, and this increase in unemployment will lead to a decrease in inflation.

  The coefficient a should therefore reflect how much the central bank cares about unemployment versus inflation. The higher a, the more the central bank will increase the interest rate in response to inflation, the more the economy will slow down, the more unemployment will increase, and the faster inflation will return to the target inflation rate.

  In any case, Taylor pointed out, a should be larger than one. Why? Because what matters for spending is the real interest rate, not the nominal interest rate. When inflation increases, the central bank, if it wants to decrease spending and output, must increase the *real* interest rate. In other words, *it must increase the nominal interest rate more than one for one with inflation.*
- If unemployment is higher than the natural rate of unemployment ($u > u_n$), the central bank should decrease the nominal interest rate. The lower nominal interest rate will increase output, leading to a decrease in unemployment. Like the coefficient a, the coefficient b should reflect how much the central bank cares about unemployment relative to inflation. The higher b, the more the central bank will be willing to deviate from target inflation to keep unemployment close to the natural rate of unemployment.

In stating this rule, Taylor did not argue that it should be followed blindly: Many other events, such as an exchange rate crisis, or the need to change the composition of spending on goods, and thus the mix between monetary policy and fiscal policy, justify changing the nominal interest rate for other reasons than those included in the rule. But, he argued, the rule provided a useful way of thinking about monetary policy: Once the central bank has chosen a target rate of inflation, it should try to achieve it by adjusting the nominal interest rate. The rule it should follow should take into account not only current inflation but also current unemployment.

Since it was first introduced, the Taylor rule has generated a lot of interest, both from researchers and from central banks:

- Interestingly, researchers looking at the behavior of both the Fed in the United States and the Bundesbank in Germany, have found that, although these two central banks surely did not think of themselves as following a Taylor rule, this rule actually described their behavior over the last 15–20 years quite well.

- Other researchers have explored whether it is possible to improve on this simple rule: for example, whether the nominal interest rate should be allowed to respond not only to current inflation, but also to expected future inflation.
- Yet other researchers have discussed whether central banks should adopt an explicit interest rate rule and follow it closely, or whether they should use the rule more informally, and feel free to deviate from the rule when appropriate. We shall return to this issue in discussing the behavior of the Fed in the next section.

In general, it appears that most central banks have now shifted from thinking in terms of nominal money growth to thinking in terms of an interest rate rule. Whatever the implications for nominal money growth of following such a nominal interest rate rule, these are increasingly seen as unimportant, both by the central bank and by financial markets. To take an example, the large rates of growth of $M2$ observed in the United States since 1997 do not seem to trouble either the Fed or financial markets. They are seen as shifts in the demand for $M2$, shifts that the Fed can accommodate without running the risk of higher inflation.

25-3 The Fed in Action

Having discussed the design of monetary policy in general, let me end this chapter by looking at how the Fed actually carries out monetary policy in the United States.

The Fed's Web site (www.federalreserve.gov/) gives a lot of information about how the Fed is organized, and what it does.

The Mandate of the Fed

The mandate of the Federal Reserve System was most recently defined in the **Humphrey-Hawkins Act**, passed by Congress in 1978. The act requires the Fed to

The Humphrey-Hawkins Act expired in mid-2000. Congress does not appear to be in a big hurry to renew it.

> maintain long-run growth of the monetary and credit aggregates commensurate with the economy's long-run potential to increase production, so as to promote effectively the goals of maximum employment, stable prices, and moderate long-term interest rates.

There is one important point behind the heavy official language: The Fed has a mandate not only to achieve low inflation in the medium and long run but also to stabilize economic activity in the short run.

The Organization of the Fed

The Federal Reserve System is composed of three parts:

- A set of 12 **Federal Reserve Districts**, each with a Federal Reserve District Bank. The main functions of these regional banks are to manage check clearing and to supervise banking and financial activities in the district.
- The **Board of Governors**, located in Washington, D.C. The board has seven members, including the chairman of the Fed. Each governor is appointed by the president for a nonrenewable term of 14 years and must be confirmed by the U.S. Senate. The chairman is appointed by the president for a renewable term of four years. The Board of Governors is in charge of the design of monetary policy.
- The **Federal Open-Market Committee (FOMC)** is also located in Washington. The committee has 12 members. Five are Federal Reserve District Bank presidents, and the other seven are the governors. The principle behind this composition is that Federal Reserve Bank presidents are more likely to be attuned to the economic situation in their districts, the governors more attuned to national trends and evolutions. The main function of the committee is to give instructions to the

Open-Market Desk, the desk in charge of open-market operations—the purchase and sale of bonds by the Fed—in New York City.

This description might suggest that the Fed is a complex organization with many centers of power. The reality is simpler: The chairman is typically very powerful. And the most important decisions are made by the Federal Open Market Committee.

We discussed in Chapter 24 the importance of central bank independence. The Fed is one of the most independent central banks in the world. The main control lever available to the president and Congress is the nomination and confirmation of the chairman every four years. But during his four-year tenure, the chairman is largely free to choose monetary policy as he thinks best. The Fed's budget is not subject to congressional oversight, so Congress cannot put pressure on the Fed by threatening to cut its funding. The chairman of the Fed testifies twice a year in front of Congress to explain the stance of monetary policy. Members of Congress often complain and grumble about the Fed's decisions, but there is not much they can actually do about it.

Note in Figure 24-3 that the United States has the second highest index of central bank independence.

Under the Humphrey-Hawkins Act, the chairman had the obligation to testify. Although the Act expired in 2000, the tradition continues.

The Instruments of Monetary Policy

You saw in Chapter 4 that we can think of the interest rate as being determined by the demand for and the supply of central bank money. Recall the equilibrium condition (equation [4.11]) is given by

Recall—from Chapter 4—we can think of the determination of the interest rate in three equivalent ways:

- **The supply of central bank money must be equal to the demand for central bank money.**
- **The supply of reserves, equal to central bank money minus the currency held by people, must be equal to the demand for reserves by banks.**
- **The supply of money (currency and demand deposits) must be equal to the demand for money.**

$$H = [c + \theta(1 - c)]\,\$YL(i) \qquad (25.1)$$

On the left side is H, the supply of central bank money—equivalently, the monetary base. On the right side is the demand for central bank money—the sum of the demand for currency by people $c\,\$YL(i)$, and the demand for reserves by banks $\theta(1 - c)\$YL(i)$. A quick refresher:

- Start with $\$YL(i)$, the overall demand for money (currency and checkable deposits, $M1$). This demand depends on income and the opportunity cost of holding money—the interest rate on bonds.
- The parameter c is the proportion of money people want to hold in the form of currency. So $c\,\$YL(i)$ is the demand for currency by people.
- What people do not hold in currency, they hold in the form of checkable deposits. Checkable deposits are therefore a fraction $(1 - c)$ of the overall demand for money, so checkable deposits are equal to $(1 - c)\,\$YL(i)$. The parameter θ denotes the ratio of reserves held by banks to checkable deposits. So the demand for reserves by banks is $\theta(1 - c)\,\$YL(i)$.
- Adding the demand for currency, $c\,\$YL(i)$, and the demand for reserves by banks, $\theta(1 - c)\,\$YL(i)$, gives the total demand for central bank money— the right side of the equation.

See Chapter 4 for a review.

The equilibrium interest rate is then the interest rate at which the supply and the demand for central bank money are equal. The Fed has three instruments at its disposal to affect this interest rate. The first, *reserve requirements,* affects the demand for reserves, and so affects the demand for central bank money. The other two, *lending to banks* and *open-market operations,* affect the supply of central bank money.

Reserve Requirements

The Fed determines **reserve requirements**, the minimum amount of reserves that banks must hold in proportion to checkable deposits. Even without such requirements, banks would want to hold some reserves to be able to satisfy their depositors' demand for cash. But the Fed typically sets reserve requirements above the level that banks would choose. The current requirement is that banks hold reserves equal to 10% of their checkable deposits.

An increase in θ increases the demand for reserves by banks, increasing the demand for central bank money. Given an unchanged supply, the interest rate must increase.

By changing reserve requirements, the Fed changes the amount of reserves banks must hold for a given amount of demand deposits, and so changes the demand for central bank money. An increase in reserve requirements leads to an increase in the demand for central bank money, leading in turn to an increase in the equilibrium interest rate. It works in the other direction as well: A decrease in the reserve requirement leads to a decrease in the interest rate.

An increase in reserve requirements by the Fed can force banks to take drastic actions to increase their reserves, such as recalling some of the loans they have made. For this reason, the Fed has become increasingly reluctant to use reserve requirements as an instrument of macroeconomic policy, preferring to rely on its other instruments instead.

Lending to Banks

The Fed can also lend to banks (an instrument we ignored in Chapter 4). How much it lends and under what conditions is called the Fed's **discount policy**. The rate at which it lends to banks is called the **discount rate**. When the Fed lends to banks, it is said to lend through the **discount window**.

Once upon a time, there must have been an actual window at the central bank where banks would come and borrow funds. This is no longer the case.

From the point of view of the Fed, lending to banks is very similar to buying bonds in an open-market operation. In both cases, the Fed creates money and so increases H, the monetary base. In lending to banks, the Fed receives in exchange a claim on the bank. In open-market operations, the Fed acquires a government bond, a claim on the government.

Until the introduction of open-market operations in the 1930s, the discount policy was the Fed's main instrument for changing the money supply. But its role has steadily declined in favor of open-market operations. The Fed typically discourages banks from borrowing at the discount window except for short-run or seasonal reasons.

Changes in the discount rate still play a role, but mostly as a signal of the Fed's intentions. Financial markets often interpret a decrease in the discount rate as a signal that the Fed is going to follow a more expansionary policy—that it is going to decrease interest rates in the future. Through its effect on expectations of future interest rates, a decrease in the discount rate often leads to a decrease in medium-term and long-term interest rates.

From Chapter 15: Medium-term and long-term interest rates are weighted averages of expected short-term interest rates. A decrease in the discount rate, which leads participants in financial markets to expect lower short-term interest rates in the future, leads to a decline in medium-term and long-term interest rates.

Open-Market Operations

The Fed's third and main tool is *open-market operations*, in which the Fed buys and sells bonds in the bonds market. Open-market operations are carried out by the Open-Market Desk in New York and are typically conducted in markets for short-term Treasury bills.

When the Fed buys bonds, it pays for them by creating money, increasing H; when it sells bonds, it decreases H. Over the years, the Fed has found open-market operations to be the most convenient and flexible way of changing the supply of central bank money, and thus of changing the interest rate. Open-market operations are the main instrument of U.S. monetary policy today.

For more on open-market operations, review Chapter 4.

The Practice of Monetary Policy

Most important monetary policy decisions are taken at the meetings of the FOMC, which take place about every six weeks. For these meetings, the Fed staff prepares forecasts and simulations of the effects of different monetary policies. The forecasts show what is likely to happen to the economy under unchanged monetary policy and what the major sources of uncertainty appear to be. The simulations show the evolution of the economy under alternative assumptions about monetary policy.

The FOMC then decides on the course of monetary policy. At the end of each meeting, it issues a general directive to the Open-Market Desk about what to do during the following six weeks. The conduct of open-market operations between FOMC meetings is left to the manager of the Open-Market Desk. The manager focuses on the interest rate in the market for central bank money, the *federal funds market*. In that market, banks that have excess reserves (reserves in excess of what they are required to hold) lend overnight to banks that have insufficient reserves. The rate in that market is called the *federal funds rate*. As new information comes in, indicating, for example, that the economy is stronger or weaker than expected, the manager (in consultation with the FOMC members) intervenes to change the federal funds rate as he or she sees best, until the next FOMC meeting.

We have looked so far at the organization and the instruments of the Fed. This does not tell us however what monetary policy the Fed actually follows. Does the Fed have an inflation target, and, if so, what is it? Does the Fed follow an interest rate rule, and, if so what is the rule?

- One answer to these two questions is: We do not know. Alan Greenspan, the chairman of the Fed since 1987, has never specifically stated an inflation target. Nor has he ever described the decisions of the Fed in terms of an interest rate rule, or in terms of any rule for that matter. Indeed, his testimonies to Congress are renowned for their lack of transparency. They typically state something to the effect that after carefully weighing the many aspects of the current economic situation, the Fed is doing what it deems appropriate in the context of present circumstances—or some equally bland statement . . .
- Another answer, however, is that, just from observing the behavior of the Fed, we actually know a lot. The evidence strongly suggests that the Fed has in fact an implicit inflation target of about 3%. And it is also clear that the Fed adjusts the federal funds rate in response both to the inflation rate and to deviations of unemployment from the natural rate. Indeed, recall from our earlier discussion that the Taylor rule appears to give a good description of the behavior of the Fed over the last 15–20 years.

Does it matter that the Fed does not have an *explicit* inflation target, that it does not have an *explicit* interest rate rule? On this question as well, economists disagree:

- Many economists say: Do not to argue with success. And, at the time of this writing, nearly all economists agree that the record of monetary policy under Greenspan has been outstanding:

  Without an explicit inflation target, he has convinced financial markets that the Fed was committed to low inflation, and inflation has indeed remained low.

  At the same time, he has shown a willingness to use interest rates to stabilize activity when it was needed. Figure 25-4 shows the evolution of the federal funds rate since 1987—the year in which he became chairman of the Fed. Most macroeconomists agree that while the sharp decline in the federal funds rate in the early 1990s, from close to 10% in 1989 to around 3% in 1992, was not enough to avoid a recession, it decreased its depth and its length. The years 2001 and 2002 appear in many ways to be a repeat of the early 1990s. In 2001, the Fed aggressively cut the federal funds rate, from 7 down to 2% at the end of the year. Again, it appears these cuts were not enough to avoid a slowdown. But most observers expect that they have limited its depth, and, thanks to low interest rates, most expect output growth to be positive in 2002.

Figure 25-4

The Federal Funds Rate, 1987–2001

In 1990–1992, and again in 2001, the Fed dramatically decreased the federal funds rate to try to avoid a recession.

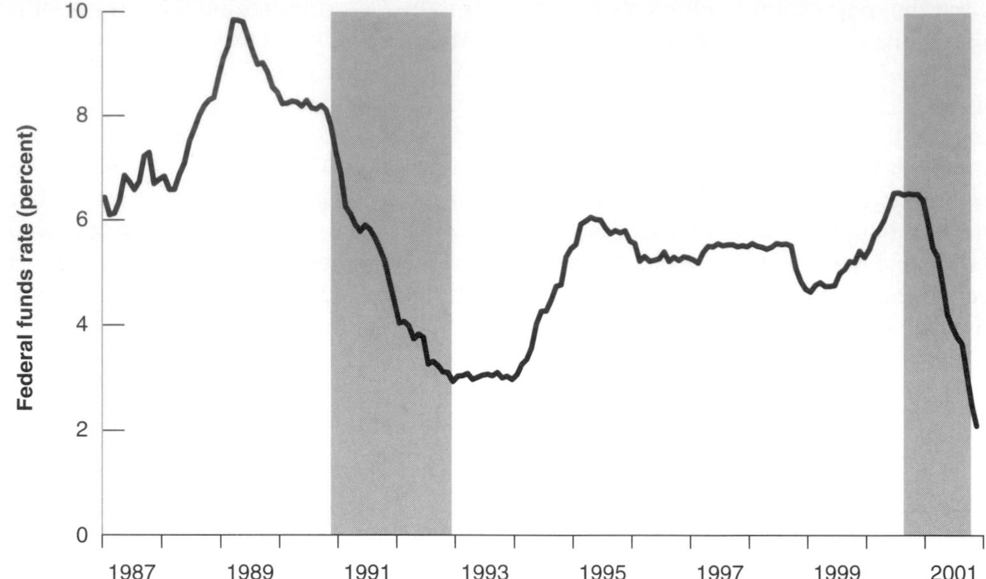

- Other economists are more skeptical. They argue it is unwise to have monetary policy depend so much on one individual, that the next chairman of the Fed may not be able to achieve the same mix of credibility and flexibility. They argue that improvements in the design of policy, such as the shift to explicit inflation targeting, and a more explicit discussion of interest rules can and should be made. This debate is likely to be with us for a long time to come.

Summary

On the optimal rate of inflation

- Inflation is down to very low levels in most OECD countries. One question facing central banks is whether they should try to achieve price stability—that is, zero inflation.
- The main arguments for zero inflation are:
  Inflation, together with an imperfectly indexed tax system, leads to tax distortions.
  Because of money illusion, inflation leads people and firms to make incorrect decisions.
  Higher inflation typically comes with higher inflation variability, creating more uncertainty and making it more difficult for people and firms to make decisions.
  As a target, price stability has a simplicity and a credibility that a positive inflation target does not have.
- There are also arguments for maintaining low but positive inflation:
  Positive revenues from nominal money growth—seignorage—allow for decreases in taxes elsewhere in the budget. However, this argument is quantitatively unimportant when comparing inflation rates of 0% versus, say, 4%.
  Positive actual and expected inflation allow the central bank to achieve negative real interest rates, an option that can be useful when fighting a recession.
  Positive inflation allows firms to achieve real wage cuts when needed without requiring nominal wage cuts.
  A further decrease from the current positive rate of inflation to zero inflation would imply an increase in unemployment for some time, and this transition cost may exceed whatever benefits come from zero inflation.

On the design of monetary policy

- Traditionally, the design of monetary policy was focused on nominal money growth. Central banks would determine the rate of nominal money growth consistent with the optimal rate of inflation. They would then announce a nominal money growth target or nominal money growth target bands.
- Because of the poor relation between inflation and nominal money growth, whether it is *M*1 growth or the growth of other monetary aggregates such

 Back to Policy

as $M2$, this approach has been abandoned by most central banks.

- Increasingly, central banks focus on an inflation rate target rather than a nominal money growth rate target. And, increasingly, they think about monetary policy in terms of the determination of the nominal interest rate rather than in terms of the rate of nominal money growth.
- The Taylor rule gives a useful way of thinking about the choice of the nominal interest rate. The rule states that the central bank should move its interest rate in response to two main factors: the deviation of the inflation rate from the inflation target, and the deviation of the unemployment rate from the natural rate of unemployment. A central bank that follows this rule will stabilize activity and achieve its target inflation rate in the medium run.

On the Fed

- The Federal Reserve System is composed of three parts: 12 Federal Reserve Districts; a Board of Governors, with seven members including the Chairman; and the Federal Open-Market Committee, composed of the seven members of the Board of Governors and five Federal Reserve District Bank presidents.
- Open-market operations are the main instrument of monetary policy. The other two, reserve requirements and discount policy, are used infrequently.
- Decisions about the course of monetary policy are made every six weeks by the Federal Open-Market Committee. Daily decisions about open-market operations are left to the manager of the Open-Market Desk in New York City, in consultation with members of the Federal Open-Market Committee.
- The Fed has neither an explicit inflation target nor an explicit interest rate rule. But, in fact, it appears to have an inflation target around 3%, and to change the nominal interest rate in a manner well described by the Taylor rule.
- Monetary policy has been very successful in the last 15–20 years. Inflation has remained low. At the same time, the Fed has used monetary policy to stabilize output.

Key Terms

- shoe-leather costs, 531
- money illusion, 532
- liquid asset, 537
- monetary aggregates, 537
- broad money ($M2$), 537, 538
- inflation targeting, 539
- Taylor's rule, 540
- Humphrey-Hawkins Act, 542
- Federal Reserve Districts, 542
- Board of Governors, 542
- Federal Open-Market Committee (FOMC), 542
- Open-Market Desk, 543
- reserve requirements, 543
- discount policy, 544
- discount rate, 544
- discount window, 544

Questions and Problems

Quick Check

1. *Using the information in this chapter, label each of the following statements* true, false, *or* uncertain. *Explain briefly.*
   a. The most important argument in favor of a positive rate of inflation in OECD countries is seignorage.
   b. The Fed should target $M2$ growth because it moves quite closely with inflation.
   c. Fighting inflation should be the Fed's only purpose.
   d. Announcing target ranges for money growth would limit the flexibility and therefore the usefulness of monetary policy.
   e. We would do just as well if we replaced the chairman of the Fed by a Taylor rule.
   f. The higher the inflation rate, the higher the effective tax rate on income.
   g. U.S. monetary policy has been outstanding since the early 1980s.

2. *Explain how each of the following would affect the demand for M1 and M2:*
   a. Banks reduce penalties on early withdrawal from time deposits.
   b. The government forbids the use of money market funds for check-writing purposes.
   c. The U.S. government legislates a tax on all ATM transactions.
   d. Congress decides to impose a tax on all transactions in short-term government securities.

3. *Suppose you have a mortgage of $50,000. Consider two cases:*

   1. Expected inflation is 0%, the nominal interest rate on your mortgage is 4%.

   2. Expected inflation is 10%, the nominal interest rate on your mortgage is 14%.

   a. What is the real interest rate you are paying on your mortgage in each case?
   b. Suppose you can deduct nominal mortgage interest payments from your income before paying income tax (as is the case in the United States). Assume the tax rate is 25%. So, for each dollar you pay in mortgage interest, you pay 25 cents less in taxes, in effect getting a subsidy from the government for your mortgage costs. Compute, in each case, the real

interest rate you are paying on your mortgage, taking into account this subsidy.

c. "In the United States, inflation is good for homeowners." Discuss.

4. Suppose that M1 growth is very high, but M2 growth is equal to zero. Should you worry about inflation?

5. Using the equation

$$H = [c + \theta(1 - c)]\ \$YL(i)$$

show three ways in which monetary policy can decrease the equilibrium interest rate, given the level of output. In each case, explain how it works.

Dig Deeper

6. "The worry that with deflation, real interest rates cannot be negative, is misplaced. Fiscal policy can decrease the cost of borrowing as much as it wants, by offering subsidies to borrowers." Discuss.

7. Many countries around the world have set explicit inflation targets for the central bank. Suppose the inflation target is π^* and the Phillips curve looks like the one described in the chapter:

$$\pi_t = \pi_{t-1} + \alpha(u_t - u_n)$$

a. If the central bank is able to keep the inflation rate equal to the target inflation rate every period, does this imply that there will be dramatic fluctuations in unemployment?

b. Given your answer to (a), should all countries adopt inflation targets?

Explore Further

8. Go the Web site of the Board of Governors of the Federal Reserve at **www.federalreserve.gov/** *and read the most recent minutes of the Federal Open-Market Committee.*

a. What has happened to the growth rate of money since the last meeting?

b. Does the FOMC seem to be more worried about a slowdown in growth or an increase in inflation?

c. What is happening to the benchmark federal funds rate?

d. Was the committee's action unanimously approved by all of its members? If not, why did some members disagree?

We invite you to visit the Blanchard page on the Prentice Hall Web site at:
www.prenhall.com/blanchard
for this chapter's World Wide Web exercises

Further Readings

"Modern Central Banking," written by Stanley Fischer for the 300th anniversary of the Bank of England (published in Forrest Capie, Stanley Fischer, Charles Goodhart, and Norbert Schnadt, eds, *The Future of Central Banking* [Cambridge, London: Cambridge University Press, 1995]), provides a very nice discussion of the current issues in central banking. Read also "What Central Bankers Could Learn from Academics—and Vice Versa," by Alan Blinder, *Journal of Economic Perspectives,* Spring 1997, 3–19.

On inflation targeting, read "Inflation Targeting: A New Framework for Monetary Policy?" by Ben Bernanke and Frederic Mishkin, *Journal of Economic Perspectives,* Spring 1997, 97–116.

For more detail on how the Fed operates, read Glenn Hubbard, *Money, the Financial System, and the Economy* (Reading, MA: Addison-Wesley, 2001).

For more on monetary policy under Alan Greenspan, read N. Gregory Mankiw, "U.S. Monetary Policy During the 1990s," 2001 (**post.economics. harvard.edu/faculty/mankiw/papers.html**)

For a more relaxing read, read *Maestro; Greenspan's Fed and the American Boom,* a biography of Greenspan by Bob Woodward (New York, NY: Simon & Schuster, 2001).

Fiscal Policy: A Summing Up

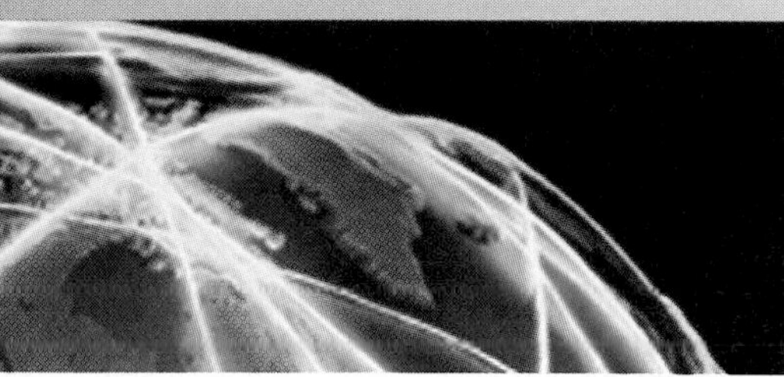

CHAPTER 26

In this chapter, we do for fiscal policy what we did for monetary policy in Chapter 25—review what we have learned and tie up the remaining loose ends.

Let's first review what you have learned (the Focus box "Fiscal Policy: What You Have Learned and Where" gives a more detailed summary).

- In the short run, a budget deficit (triggered, say, by a decrease in taxes) increases demand and output. What happens to investment spending is ambiguous.
- In the medium run, output returns to the natural level of output. The interest rate and the composition of spending are different, however. The interest rate is higher, investment spending is lower.
- In the long run, lower investment implies a lower capital stock, and therefore a lower level of output.

In deriving these conclusions, we did not pay close attention to the government budget constraint, that is, to the relation between debt, deficits, government spending, and taxes. Nevertheless, as our discussion of fiscal policy in Japan in Chapter 22 made clear, this relation is important: After a decade of large budget deficits, government debt in Japan has become very high, and this in turn very much restricts the scope for further use of fiscal policy. So, our main task in this chapter is to look at the government's budget constraint and its implications.

- Section 26-1 derives the government budget constraint, and examines its implications for the relation between budget deficits, the interest rate, the growth rate, and government debt.
- Section 26-2 examines a number of fiscal policy issues where this constraint plays a central role, from the proposition that deficits do not really matter, to the dangers of accumulating very high levels of public debt.
- Section 26-3 looks at the current U.S. budget and the issues on the horizon, from the effects of the tax cuts passed by the Bush administration, to the implications of the aging of America. ■

Fiscal Policy: What You Have Learned and Where

FOCUS

- In Chapter 3, we looked at the role of government spending and taxes in determining demand and output in the short run.

  You saw how, in the short run, a fiscal expansion—that is, increases in government spending or decreases in taxes—increases output.
- In Chapter 5, we looked at the short-run effects of fiscal policy on output and on the interest rate.

  You saw how a fiscal expansion leads to an increase in output and an increase in the interest rate. You also saw how fiscal policy and monetary policy can be used to affect both the level and the composition of output.
- In Chapter 7, we looked at the effects of fiscal policy in the short run and in the medium run.

  You saw that in the medium run (taking the capital stock as given), a fiscal expansion has no effect on output, but is reflected in a different composition of spending. The interest rate is higher, and investment spending is lower.
- In Chapter 11, we looked at how saving and thus the budget deficit affect the level of capital accumulation and the level of output in the long run.

  You saw how once capital accumulation is taken into account, a larger budget deficit, and, by implication, a lower national saving rate, decreases capital accumulation, leading to a lower level of output in the long run.
- In Chapter 17, we returned to the short-run effects of fiscal policy, taking into account not only its direct effects through taxes and government spending, but also its effects on expectations.

  You saw how the effects of fiscal policy depend on expectations of future fiscal policy and future monetary policy. In particular, you saw how a deficit reduction may, in some circumstances, lead to an increase in output, even in the short run.
- In Chapter 19, we looked at the effects of fiscal policy when the economy is open in the goods market.

  You saw how fiscal policy affects both output and the trade balance, and examined the relation between the budget deficit and the trade deficit. You saw how fiscal policy and exchange-rate adjustments can be used to affect both the level of output and its composition.
- In Chapter 20, we looked at the role of fiscal policy in an economy open in both goods markets and financial markets.

  You saw how in the presence of international capital mobility, the effects of fiscal policy depend on the exchange-rate regime. Fiscal policy has a much stronger effect on output under fixed exchange rates than under flexible exchange rates.
- In Chapter 23, we looked at the relation between fiscal policy, money growth, and inflation.

  You saw how budget deficits must be financed either by borrowing or by money creation. When money creation becomes the main source of finance, the result of large budget deficits is high money growth and high inflation.
- In Chapter 24, we looked at the problems facing fiscal policy makers, from uncertainty about the effects of policy to issues of time consistency and credibility.

  You saw the pros and cons of restraints on the conduct of fiscal policy, such as a constitutional amendment to balance the budget.
- In this chapter, we look further at the implications of the budget constraint facing the government and discuss current issues of fiscal policy in the United States.

26-1 The Government Budget Constraint

Suppose that starting from a balanced budget, the government cuts taxes, creating a budget deficit. What will happen to debt over time? Will the government need to increase taxes later? If so, by how much?

The Arithmetic of Deficits and Debt

To answer these questions, we must start with a definition of the budget deficit. We can write the budget deficit in year *t* as

$$\text{deficit}_t = rB_{t-1} + G_t - T_t \qquad (26.1)$$

All variables are in real terms:

- B_{t-1} is government debt at the end of year $t - 1$, or, equivalently, at the beginning of year t; r is the real interest rate, which we shall take to be constant here. Thus, rB_{t-1} equals the real interest payments on the government debt in year t.

- G_t is government spending on goods and services during year t.
- T_t is taxes minus transfers during year t.

In words: The budget deficit equals spending, including interest payments on the debt, minus taxes net of transfers.

Note two characteristics of equation (26.1):

- We measure interest payments as real interest payments—that is, the product of the *real* interest rate times existing debt—rather than as actual interest payments—that is, the product of the nominal interest rate times existing debt. As I show in the Focus box "Inflation Accounting and the Measurement of Deficits," this is the correct way of measuring interest payments. Official measures of the deficit, however, include actual (nominal) interest payments and are therefore incorrect. When inflation is high, official measures can be seriously misleading. The correct measure of the deficit is sometimes called the **inflation-adjusted deficit**.
- For consistency with our earlier definition of G as spending on goods and services, G does not include transfer payments. Transfers are instead subtracted from T, so that T stands for *taxes minus transfers*. Official measures of government spending

◀ Do not confuse the words *deficit* and *debt*. (Many journalists and politicians do.) Debt is a *stock*, what the government owes as a result of past deficits. The deficit is a *flow*, how much the government borrows during a given year.

Transfer payments are government transfers to individuals, such as unemployment benefits or Medicare. ◀

Inflation Accounting and the Measurement of Deficits

Official measures of the budget deficit are constructed as (dropping the time indexes, which are not needed here) nominal interest payments, iB, plus spending on goods and services, G, minus taxes net of transfers, T:

$$\text{official measure of the deficit} = iB + G - T$$

This is an accurate measure of the cash flow position of the government. If it is positive, the government is spending more than it receives, and must therefore issue new debt. If it is negative, the government buys back previously issued debt.

But it is not an accurate measure of the change in real debt—that is, the change in how much the government owes, expressed in terms of goods rather than dollars.

To see why, consider the following example: Suppose the official measure of the deficit is equal to zero, so the government neither issues nor buys back debt. Suppose inflation is positive and equal to 10%. Then, at the end of the year, the real value of the debt has decreased by 10%. If we define—as we should—the deficit as the change in the real value of government debt, the government has decreased its real debt by 10% over year. In other words, it has in fact run a budget surplus equal to 10% times the initial level of debt.

More generally, if B is debt and π is inflation, the official measure of the deficit overstates the correct measure by an amount equal to πB. Put another way, the correct measure of the deficit is obtained by subtracting πB from the official measure:

$$\begin{aligned}\text{correct measure of the deficit} &= iB + G - T - \pi B \\ &= (i - \pi)B + G - T \\ &= rB + G - T\end{aligned}$$

where $r = i - \pi$ is the real interest rate. The correct measure of the deficit is then equal to real interest payments plus government spending minus taxes net of transfers—this is the measure we have used in the text. (Note that, here, r is equal to the nominal interest rate minus actual inflation. It would be more accurate to call it the "realized real interest rate," to distinguish it from the real interest rate, which is equal to the nominal interest rate minus expected inflation.)

The difference between the official and the correct measures of the deficit equals πB. So, the higher the rate of inflation, π, or the higher the level of debt, B, the more inaccurate the official measure is. In countries in which both inflation and debt are high, the official measure may record a very large budget deficit, when in fact real government debt is actually decreasing. This is why you should always do the inflation adjustment before deriving conclusions about the position of fiscal policy.

Figure 1 plots the official measure and the inflation-adjusted measure of the (federal) budget deficit for the United States for fiscal years 1968 to 2001 (recall that the fiscal year runs from October 1 of the preceding calendar year to September 30 of the current calendar year).

Continued

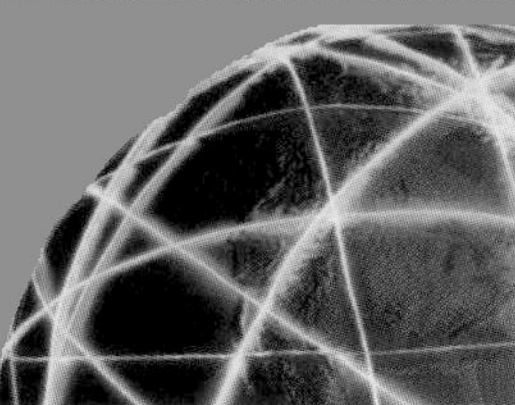

The official measure shows a deficit in every year from 1970 to 1997 (a negative value corresponds to a deficit). The inflation-adjusted measure shows, instead, alternating deficits and surpluses until the late 1970s. However, both measures show how much worse the deficit became after 1980, and how things have improved in the 1990s. Today, with inflation running at about 2.5% a year, and the ratio of debt to GDP equal to roughly 30%, the difference between the two measures is roughly equal to 2.5% times 30%, or 0.7% of GDP. Put another way, an official budget deficit of 0.0% of GDP corresponds to an actual budget surplus of about 0.7%.

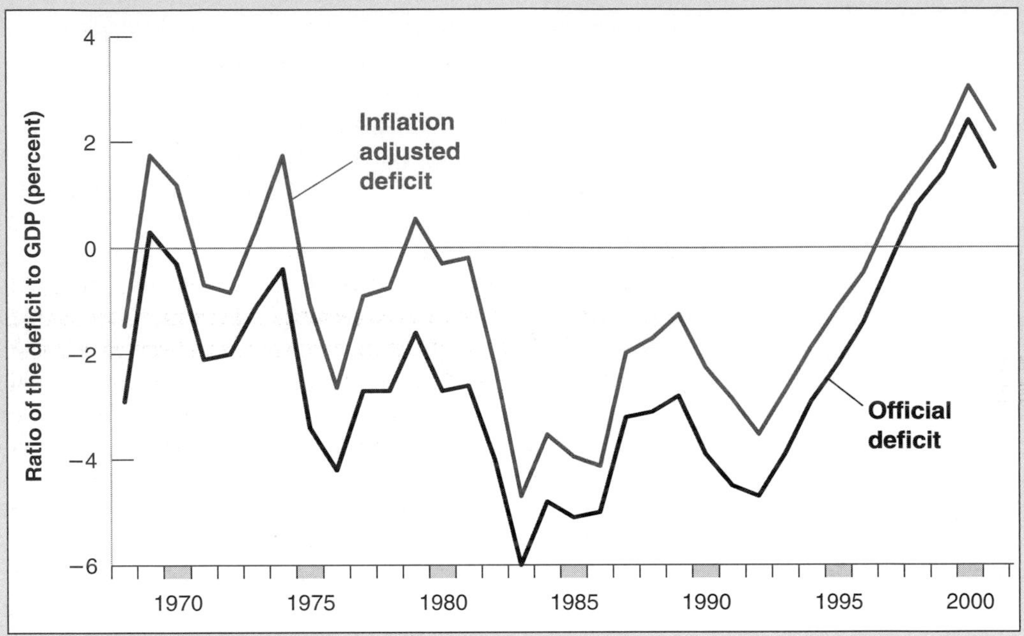

Figure 1 *Official Budget Deficit and Inflation-Adjusted Budget Deficit for the United States, 1968–2001*

add transfers to spending on goods and services, and define revenues as taxes, not taxes net of transfers.

These are only accounting conventions. Whether transfers are added to spending or subtracted from taxes makes a difference to the measurement of G and T, but clearly does not affect $G - T$, and thus does not affect the measure of the deficit.

The **government budget constraint** then simply states that the *change in government debt during year t* is equal to the *deficit during year t*

$$B_t - B_{t-1} = \text{deficit}_t$$

If the government runs a deficit, government debt increases. If the government runs a surplus, government debt decreases.

Using the definition of the deficit (equation [26.1]), we can rewrite the government budget constraint as

$$B_t - B_{t-1} = rB_{t-1} + G_t - T_t \tag{26.2}$$

The government budget constraint links the change in government debt to the initial level of debt (which affects interest payments) and to current government spending and taxes. It is often convenient to decompose the deficit into the sum of two terms:

- Interest payments on the debt, rB_{t-1}.
- The difference between spending and taxes, $G_t - T_t$. This term is called the **primary deficit** (equivalently, $T_t - G_t$ is called the **primary surplus**).

Using this decomposition, we can rewrite equation (26.2) as

$$\overbrace{B_t - B_{t-1}}^{\text{Change in the debt}} = \overbrace{rB_{t-1}}^{\text{Interest payments}} + \overbrace{(G_t - T_t)}^{\text{Primary deficit}}$$

Or, moving B_{t-1} to the right and reorganizing

$$\overbrace{B_t}^{\text{Debt at end of } t} = \overbrace{(1+r)B_{t-1}}^{(1+r)B_{t-1} \text{ at end of } (t-1)} + \overbrace{G_t - T_t}^{\text{Primary deficit}} \quad (26.3)$$

Debt at the end of year t, B_t, equals $(1 + r)$ times debt at the end of year $t - 1$, B_{t-1}, plus the primary deficit during year t, $(G_t - T_t)$. This relation will prove very useful in what follows.

Current Versus Future Taxes

Let's look at the implications of a one-year decrease in taxes for the path of debt and future taxes. Start from a situation where, until year 1, the government has balanced its budget, so that initial debt is equal to zero. During year 1, the government decreases taxes by 1 (think 1 billion dollars, for example) for one year. Thus, debt at the end of year 1, B_1, is equal to 1. The question we take up: What happens thereafter?

Full Repayment in Year 2

Suppose the government decides to fully repay the debt during year 2. From equation (26.3), the budget constraint for year 2 is given by

$$B_2 = (1 + r)B_1 + (G_2 - T_2)$$

If debt is fully repaid during year 2, then debt at the end of year 2 is equal to zero: $B_2 = 0$. Replacing B_1 by 1 and B_2 by 0 and transposing terms gives

$$T_2 - G_2 = (1 + r)1 = (1 + r)$$

To repay the debt fully during year 2, the government must run a primary surplus equal to $(1 + r)$. It can do so in one of two ways: a decrease in spending or an increase in taxes. I shall assume here and in what follows that the adjustment comes through taxes, so that the path of spending is unaffected. It follows that the decrease in taxes by 1 during year 1 must be offset by an increase in taxes by $(1 + r)$ during year 2.

The path of taxes and debt corresponding to this case is given in Figure 26-1, panel (a): If debt is fully repaid during year 2, the decrease in taxes of 1 in year 1 requires an increase in taxes equal to $(1 + r)$ in year 2.

◄ **Full repayment in year 2: $T_1 \downarrow$ by 1 $\Rightarrow T_2 \uparrow$ by $(1 + r)$**

Full Repayment in Year *t*

Now suppose the government decides to wait until year t to repay the debt. So, from year 2 to year $t - 1$, the primary deficit is equal to zero—taxes are equal to spending, not including interest payments on the debt.

During year 2, the primary deficit is zero. So, from equation (26.3), debt at the end of year 2 is

$$B_2 = (1 + r)B_1 + 0 = (1 + r)1 = (1 + r)$$

where the second equality uses the fact that $B_1 = 1$.

Figure 26-1

Tax Cuts, Debt Repayment, and Debt Stabilization

(a): If debt is fully repaid during year 2, the decrease in taxes of 1 in year 1 requires an increase in taxes equal to $(1 + r)$ in year 2. (b): If debt is fully repaid during year 5, the decrease in taxes of 1 in year 1 requires an increase in taxes equal to $(1 + r)^4$ during year 4. (c): If debt is stabilized from year 2 on, then taxes must be permanently higher by r from year 2 on.

(a) **Debt Reimbursement in Year 2**

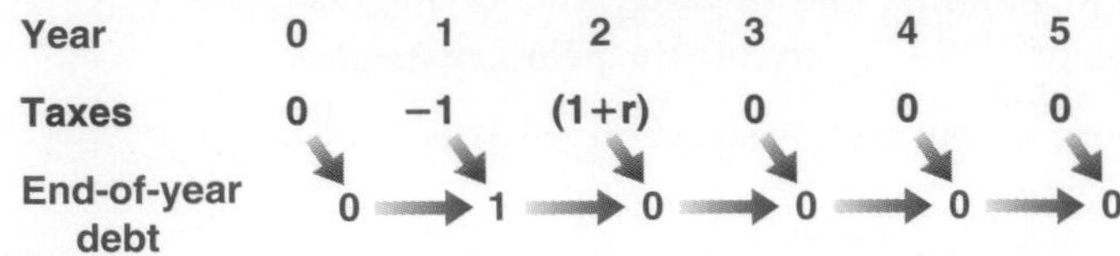

(b) **Debt Reimbursement in Year 5**

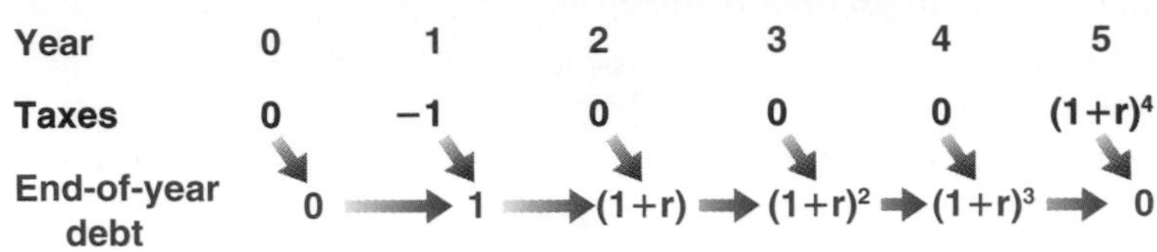

(c) **Debt Stabilization in Year 2**

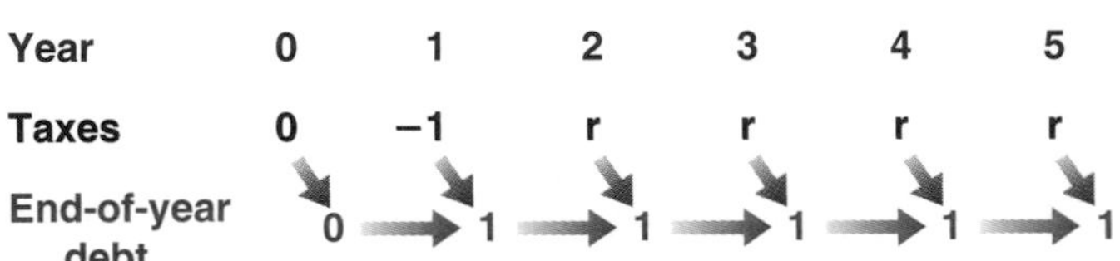

With the primary deficit still equal to zero during year 3, debt at the end of year 3 is

$$B_3 = (1 + r)B_2 + 0 = (1 + r)(1 + r)1 = (1 + r)^2$$

Solving for debt at the end of year 4 and so on, it is clear that as long as the government keeps a primary deficit equal to zero, debt grows at a rate equal to the interest rate, and thus debt at the end of year $t - 1$ is given by

$$B_{t-1} = (1 + r)^{t-2} \quad (26.4)$$

Despite the fact that taxes are cut only in year 1, debt keeps increasing over time, at a rate equal to the interest rate. The reason is simple: While the primary deficit is equal to zero, debt is now positive, and so are interest payments on the debt. Each year, the government must issue more debt to pay the interest on existing debt.

In year t, the year in which the government decides to repay the debt, the budget constraint is

$$B_t = (1 + r)B_{t-1} + (G_t - T_t)$$

If debt is fully repaid during year t, then B_t (debt at the end of year t) is zero. Replacing B_t by zero, and B_{t-1} by its expression from equation (26.4), gives

$$0 = (1 + r)(1 + r)^{t-2} + (G_t - T_t)$$

Add exponents: $(1 + r)(1 + r)^{t-2} = (1 + r)^{t-1}$ See Appendix 2 at the end of this book.

Reorganizing and bringing $(G_t - T_t)$ to the left implies

$$T_t - G_t = (1 + r)^{t-1}$$

To repay the debt, the government must run a primary surplus equal to $(1 + r)^{t-1}$ during year t. If the adjustment is done through taxes, the initial decrease in taxes of 1 during year 1 leads to an increase in taxes of $(1 + r)^{t-1}$ during year t. The path of taxes and debt corresponding to the case where debt is repaid in year 5 is given in Figure 26-1, panel (b).

Full repayment in year 5: $T_1 \downarrow$ by 1 $\Rightarrow T_5 \uparrow$ by $(1 + r)^4$

This example yields our first set of conclusions:

- If government spending is unchanged, a decrease in taxes must eventually be offset by an increase in taxes in the future.
- The longer the government waits to increase taxes or the higher the real interest rate, the higher the eventual increase in taxes.

Debt Stabilization in Year *t*

We have assumed so far that the government fully repays the debt. Let's now look at what happens to taxes if the government only stabilizes the debt. (Stabilizing the debt means changing taxes or spending so that debt remains constant.)

Suppose the government decides to stabilize the debt from year 2 on. Stabilizing the debt from year 2 on means the debt at the end of year 2 and thereafter remains at the same level as at the end of year 1.

From equation (26.3), the budget constraint for year 2 is

$$B_2 = (1 + r)B_1 + (G_2 - T_2)$$

Under our assumption that debt is stabilized in year 2, $B_2 = B_1 = 1$. Replacing in the preceding equation:

$$1 = (1 + r) + (G_2 - T_2)$$

Reorganizing, and bringing $(G_2 - T_2)$ to the left side:

$$T_2 - G_2 = (1 + r) - 1 = r$$

To avoid a further increase in debt during year 1, the government must run a primary surplus equal to real interest payments on the existing debt. It must do so in following years as well: Each year, the primary surplus must be sufficient to cover interest payments, leaving the debt level unchanged. The path of taxes and debt is shown in Figure 26-1, panel (c): Debt remains equal to 1 from year 1 on. Taxes are permanently higher from year 1 on, by an amount equal to r; equivalently, from year 1 on, the government runs a primary surplus equal to r.

◀ **Stabilizing the debt from year 2 on:**
$T_1 \downarrow$ by 1 $\Rightarrow T_2, T_3, \ldots \uparrow$ by r

The logic of this argument extends directly to the case where the government waits until year *t* to stabilize. Whenever the government stabilizes, it must from then on run a primary surplus sufficient to pay interest on the debt.

This example yields our second set of conclusions:

- The legacy of past deficits is higher government debt.
- To stabilize the debt, the government must eliminate the deficit.
- To eliminate the deficit, the government must run a primary surplus equal to the interest payments on the existing debt.

The Evolution of the Debt-to-GDP Ratio

We have focused so far on the evolution of the *level* of debt. But in an economy in which output grows over time, it makes more sense to focus instead on the *ratio of debt to output*. To see how this change in focus modifies our conclusions, we need to go from equation (26.3) to an equation that gives the evolution of the **debt-to-GDP ratio**—the **debt ratio** for short.

The Arithmetic of the Debt Ratio

To derive the evolution of the debt ratio takes a few steps. Do not worry: The final equation is easy to understand.

First divide both sides of equation (26.3) by real output, Y_t, to get

$$\frac{B_t}{Y_t} = (1+r)\frac{B_{t-1}}{Y_t} + \frac{G_t - T_t}{Y_t}$$

Next rewrite B_{t-1}/Y_t, as $(B_t/Y_{t-1})(Y_{t-1}/Y_t)$ (in other words, multiply the numerator and the denominator by Y_{t-1}):

$$\frac{B_t}{Y_t} = (1+r)\left(\frac{Y_{t-1}}{Y_t}\right)\frac{B_{t-1}}{Y_{t-1}} + \frac{G_t - T_t}{Y_t}$$

Start from $Y_t = (1 + g)\, Y_{t-1}$. Divide both sides by Y_t; so: $1 = (1 + g)Y_{t-1}/Y_t$ Reorganize to get: $Y_{t-1}/Y_t = 1/(1 + g)$

This approximation is derived as proposition 6 in Appendix 2 at the end of this book.

To simplify this equation, assume that output growth is constant and denote the growth rate of output by g, so Y_{t-1}/Y_t can be written as $1/(1 + g)$. And use the approximation $(1 + r)/(1 + g) = 1 + r - g$. Using these two assumptions, rewrite the preceding equation as

$$\frac{B_t}{Y_t} = (1+r-g)\frac{B_{t-1}}{Y_{t-1}} + \frac{G_t - T_t}{Y_t}$$

Finally, reorganize to get

$$\frac{B_t}{Y_t} - \frac{B_{t-1}}{Y_{t-1}} = (r-g)\frac{B_{t-1}}{Y_{t-1}} + \frac{G_t - T_t}{Y_t} \qquad (26.5)$$

It took a few steps, but this final relation has a simple interpretation. The change in the debt ratio over time (the left side of the equation) is equal to the sum of two terms:

- The first term is the difference between the real interest rate and the growth rate times the initial debt ratio.
- The second term is the ratio of the primary deficit to GDP.

If two variables (here debt and GDP) grow at rates r and g respectively, then their ratio (here the ratio of debt to GDP) will grow at rate $(r - g)$. See proposition 8 in Appendix 2 at the end of this book.

Compare equation (26.5), which gives the evolution of the ratio of debt to GDP, to equation (26.2), which gives the evolution of the level of debt itself. The difference is the presence of $(r - g)$ in equation (26.5) compared to r in equation (26.2). The reason for the difference is simple: Suppose the primary deficit is zero. Debt will then increase at a rate equal to the real interest rate, r. But if GDP is growing as well, the ratio of debt to GDP will grow more slowly; it will grow at a rate equal to the real interest rate minus the growth rate of output, $(r - g)$.

The Evolution of the Debt Ratio in OECD Countries

Equation (26.5) implies that the increase in the ratio of debt to GDP will be larger:

the higher the real interest rate,
the lower the growth rate of output,
the higher the initial debt ratio,
the higher the ratio of the primary deficit to GDP.

The OECD includes most of the rich countries in the world. (See Chapter 1 for a description and a list of countries).

This list provides a useful guide to the evolution of the debt-to-GDP ratio over the last four decades in the OECD countries.

1960s: high g, low $r \Rightarrow B/Y \downarrow$

- The 1960s was a decade of strong growth, so strong that the average growth rate exceeded the average real interest rate in most countries. As a result, $(r - g)$ was negative, and most countries were able to decrease their debt ratios without having to run large primary surpluses.

1970s: lower g, very low $r \Rightarrow B/Y \downarrow$

- The 1970s was a period of lower growth, but of very low real interest rates (nominal interest rates were high, but expected inflation was high as well). Thus, $(r - g)$

Table 26-1 Debt and Primary Surpluses for the United States, the European Union, and Selected Countries, 1981–2000 (percent of GDP)

	Debt/GDP (%)			Primary Surplus/GDP (%)
Country	1981	1995	2000	2000
United States	25.8	49.2	34.7	4.8
European Union	24.0	53.5	47.7	4.1
Italy	56.4	108.7	98.7	6.0
Belgium	82.2	125.2	103.0	6.6
Greece	26.1	108.7	103.8	7.4

Source: *OECD Economic Outlook*, June 2001. Tables 32, 34, 35.

U.S. debt numbers come from "The Budget for Fiscal Year 2002. Historical Tables," 2001. Except for Greece, "Debt" is net debt—that is, financial liabilities of the government minus financial assets held by the government.

was again negative on average, and the result was a further decrease in the debt ratio in most OECD countries.

- The situation changed dramatically in the early 1980s. Real interest rates increased at the same time as growth rates decreased. To avoid an increase in their debt ratios, OECD countries would have had to run large primary surpluses. They did not, and their debt ratios increased rapidly.

1980s:
low g, high $r \Rightarrow B/Y \uparrow$

- In the 1990s, real interest rates remained high and growth rates remained low. It became increasingly clear that most countries had no alternative to stabilize their debt ratios other than to run larger primary surpluses. Most OECD countries have now done so. At the end of the 1990s, most countries are now running a primary surplus sufficient to imply a steady decline in their debt ratios.

1990s:
low g, high r,
primary surplus > 0 $\Rightarrow$
B/Y ›

Table 26-1 gives the evolution of debt ratios for the United States and the European Union, as well as for three individual countries, Italy, Belgium, and Greece, from 1981 to 2000.

Note how much the debt ratio has increased in both the United States and the European Union since the early 1980s. Since the mid-1990s, things have turned around however, and the debt ratio is now slowly declining. As shown in the last column, the reason for the turnaround is that both the United States and the European Union are now running primary surpluses.

For more on the reduction of deficits in Europe, see the discussion of the Maastricht Treaty—which put a ceiling on deficits in Euro area countries—in Chapter 21. For more on the reduction of deficits in the United States, see Chapter 24.

Note also how steep the increase in the debt ratio has been in Italy, Belgium, and Greece. All three countries have debt ratios around 100% of GDP. Even in these countries, however, things have now turned around, and large primary surpluses are also leading to a steady decline in the debt ratio.

To summarize what you have learned in this section. We have looked at the government budget constraint. You have seen that the change in the ratio of debt to GDP can be expressed as the sum of the ratio of the primary deficit to GDP plus the ratio of debt to GDP times the real interest rate minus the growth rate.

In the 1980s, high interest rates, low growth, and primary deficits all contributed to an increase in debt in most OECD countries.

In the 1990s, countries have reacted by running large primary surpluses, and the debt to GDP ratio is now falling in most OECD countries.

26-2 Four Issues in Fiscal Policy

Having looked at the mechanics of the government budget constraint, we can now take up four issues in which this constraint plays a central role.

Ricardian Equivalence

How does taking into account the government budget constraint affect the way we should think of the effects of deficits on output?

One extreme view is that once the government budget constraint is taken into account, neither deficit nor debt has an effect on economic activity! This argument is known as the **Ricardian equivalence** proposition. David Ricardo, a nineteenth-century English economist, was the first to articulate its logic. His argument was further developed and given prominence in the 1970s by Robert Barro, then at the University of Chicago, now at Harvard University. For this reason, the argument is also known as the **Ricardo-Barro proposition**.

While Ricardo stated the logic of the argument, he also argued there were many reasons why it would not hold in practice. In contrast, Barro argues that the argument is not only logically correct, but is a good description of reality.

The best way to understand the logic of the proposition is to use the example of tax changes from Section 26-1:

- Suppose that the government decreases taxes by 1 (again, think 1 billion dollars) this year. And as it does so, it announces that to repay the debt, it will increase taxes by $(1 + r)$ next year. What will be the effect of the initial tax cut on consumption?
- One answer: No effect at all. Why? Because consumers realize that the tax cut is not much of a gift: Lower taxes this year are exactly offset, in present value, by higher taxes next year. Put another way, their human wealth—the present value of after-tax labor income—is unaffected. Current taxes go down by 1, but the present value of next year's taxes goes up by $(1 + r)/(1 + r) = 1$, and the net effect of the two changes is exactly equal to zero.
- Another way of coming to the same answer, this time looking at saving rather than at consumption: To say that consumers do not change consumption in response to the tax cut is the same as saying that *private saving increases one for one with the deficit.* So the Ricardian equivalence proposition says that if a government finances a given path of spending through deficits, private saving will increase one for one with the decrease in public saving, leaving total saving unchanged. The total amount left for investment will not be affected. Over time, the mechanics of the government budget constraint imply that government debt will increase. But this increase will not come at the expense of capital accumulation.

See Chapter 16 for a definition of human wealth and a discussion of its role in consumption.

Under the Ricardian equivalence proposition, the long sequence of deficits and the increase in government debt that characterized the OECD for most of the last 20 years are no cause for worry. As governments were dissaving, the argument goes, people were saving more in anticipation of the higher taxes to come. The decrease in public saving was offset by an equal increase in private saving. Total saving was therefore unaffected, and so was investment. OECD economies have the same capital stock today that they would have had if there had been no increase in debt. High debt is no cause for concern.

How seriously should you take the Ricardian equivalence proposition? Most economists would answer: "Seriously, but not seriously enough to think that deficits and debt are irrelevant." A major theme of this book has been that expectations matter, that consumption decisions depend not only on current income but also on future income. If it were widely believed that a tax cut this year is going to be followed by an offsetting increase in taxes *next year*, the effect on consumption would probably be small. Many consumers would save most or all of the tax cut in anticipation of higher taxes next year. (Replace "year" by "month" or "week" and the argument becomes even more convincing.)

Of course, tax cuts rarely come with the announcement of corresponding tax increases a year later. Consumers have to guess when and how taxes will eventually be increased. This fact does not by itself invalidate the Ricardian equivalence argument: No matter when taxes will be increased, the government budget constraint still implies that the present value of future tax increases must always be equal to the decrease in taxes today. Take the second example we looked at in Section 26-1—drawn in Figure 26-1, panel (b)—in which the government waits t years to increase taxes, and so increases taxes by $(1 + r)^{t-1}$. The present value in year 0 of this expected tax increase is $(1 + r)^{t-1}/(1 + r)^{t-1} = 1$—exactly equal to the original tax cut. The change in human wealth from the tax cut is still zero.

The increase in taxes in t years is $(1 + r)^{t-1}$. The discount factor for a dollar t years from now is $1/(1 + r)^{t-1}$. So, the value of the increase in taxes t years from now as of today is $(1 + r)^{t-1}/(1 + r)^{t-1} = 1$.

But insofar as future tax increases appear more distant and their timing more uncertain, consumers are in fact more likely to ignore them. This may be the case because they expect to die before taxes go up, or, more likely, because they just do not think that far into the future. In either case, Ricardian equivalence is likely to fail.

So, it is safe to conclude that budget deficits have an important effect on activity—although perhaps a smaller effect than we thought before going through the Ricardian equivalence argument. In the short run, larger deficits are likely to lead to higher demand and to higher output. In the long run, higher government debt lowers capital accumulation and, as a result, lowers output.

Deficits, Output Stabilization, and the Cyclically Adjusted Deficit

The fact that budget deficits have long-run adverse effects on capital accumulation and, in turn, on output, does not imply fiscal policy should not be used to reduce output fluctuations. Rather, it implies that deficits during recessions should be offset by surpluses during booms, so as not to lead to a steady increase in debt.

Note the analogy with monetary policy: The fact that higher money growth leads in the long run to more inflation does not imply higher money growth should never be used for output stabilization.

To help assess whether fiscal policy is on track, economists have constructed deficit measures that tell them what the deficit would be, under existing tax and spending rules, if output were at the natural level of output. Such measures come under many names, from **full-employment deficit**, to **mid-cyle deficit**, to **standardized employment deficit**, to **structural deficit** (the term used by the OECD). I shall use **cyclically adjusted deficit**, the term I find the most intuitive.

Such a measure gives a simple benchmark by which to judge the direction of fiscal policy: If the actual deficit is large but the cyclically adjusted deficit is zero, then current fiscal policy is consistent with no systematic increase in debt over time. Debt will increase as long as output is below the natural level of output; but as output returns to its natural level, the deficit will disappear and the debt will stabilize.

Ignore output growth in this section, and so ignore the distinction between stabilizing the debt and stabilizing the debt-to-GDP ratio. (Verify that the arguments here extend to the case where output is growing.)

It does not follow that the goal of fiscal policy should be to maintain a cyclically adjusted deficit equal to zero at all times. In a recession, the government may want to run a deficit large enough that even the cyclically adjusted deficit is positive. In that case, the fact that the cyclically adjusted deficit is positive provides a useful warning. A warning that the return of output to its natural level will not be enough to stabilize the debt: The government will have to take specific measures, from tax increases to cuts in spending, to decrease the deficit at some point in the future.

The *theory* underlying the cyclically adjusted deficit is simple. The *practice* has proven tricky. To see why, we need to look at how measures of the cyclically adjusted deficit are constructed. Construction requires two steps. First, establish how much lower the deficit would be if output were, say, 1% higher. Second, assess how far output is from its natural level.

- The first step is straightforward. A reliable rule of thumb is that a 1% decrease in output leads automatically to an increase in the deficit of 0.5% of GDP. This increase occurs because most taxes are proportional to output, while most government spending does not depend on the level of output. That means a decrease in output, which leads to a decrease in revenues and not much change in spending, naturally leads to a larger deficit.

  If output is, say, 5% below its natural level, the deficit as a ratio to GDP will therefore be about 2.5% larger than it would be if output were at the natural level of output. (This effect of activity on the deficit has been called an **automatic stabilizer**: A recession naturally generates a deficit, and therefore a fiscal expansion, which partly counteracts the recession.)
- The second step is more difficult. Recall from Chapter 6 that the natural level of output is the output level that would be achieved if the economy were operating at the natural rate of unemployment. Too low an estimate of the natural rate of unemployment will lead to too high an estimate of the natural level of output, therefore to too optimistic a measure of the cyclically adjusted deficit.

  Look at our earlier discussion of the evolution of the debt ratio in the OECD. ▶

  This difficulty explains in part what happened in Europe in the 1980s. Based on the assumption of an unchanged natural unemployment rate, the cyclically adjusted deficits of the 1980s did not look that bad: If European unemployment had returned to its level of the 1970s, the associated increase in output would have been sufficient to reestablish budget balance in most countries. But, it turned out, much of the increase in unemployment reflected an increase in the natural unemployment rate, and unemployment remained very high during the 1980s. As a result, the decade was characterized by high deficits and a large increase in debt-to-GDP ratios.

  Return to the discussion of high European unemployment in Chapters 1, 9, and 13. ▶

Wars and Deficits

Wars typically bring about large budget deficits. As you saw in Chapter 24, the two largest increases in U.S. government debt in the twentieth century were during World War I and World War II. We examine the case of World War II further in the Focus box "Deficits, Consumption, and Investment in the United States During World War II."

Look at the two peaks associated with World War I and World War II in Figure 24-4. ▶

Is it right for governments to rely so much on deficits to finance wars? After all, war economies are usually operating at low unemployment, so the output stabilization reasons for running deficits we examined earlier are irrelevant. The answer, nevertheless, is yes. In fact, there are two good reasons to run deficits during wars:

- The first is distributional: Deficit finance is a way to pass some of the burden of the war to those alive after the war, and it seems only fair for future generations to share in the sacrifices the war requires.
- The second is more narrowly economic: Deficit spending helps reduce tax distortions.

Let's look at each reason in turn.

Passing on the Burden of the War

Wars lead to large increases in government spending. Consider the implications of financing this increased spending either through increased taxes or through debt. To distinguish this case from our earlier discussion of output stabilization, let's also assume that output is fixed at the natural level of output.

Deficits, Consumption, and Investment in the United States During World War II

In 1939, the share of U.S. government spending on goods and services in GDP was 15%. By 1944, it was 45%! The increase was due to increased spending on national defense, which went from 1% of GDP in 1939 to 36% in 1944.

Faced with such a massive increase in spending, the U.S. government reacted with large tax increases. For the first time in U.S. history, the individual income tax became a major source of revenues; individual income tax revenues, which were 1% of GDP in 1939, increased to 8.5% in 1944. But the tax increases were still far less than the increase in expenditures. The increase in federal revenues, from 7.2% of GDP in 1939 to 22.7% in 1944, was only a little more than half the increase in expenditures.

The result was a sequence of large budget deficits. By 1944, the federal deficit reached 22% of GDP. The ratio of debt to GDP, already high at 53% in 1939 because of the deficits the government had run during the Great Depression, was 110%!

Was the increase in government spending achieved at the expense of consumption or private investment? (As you saw in Chapter 18, it could in principle have come from higher imports and a current account deficit. But the United States had nobody to borrow from during the war. Rather, it was lending to some of its allies: Transfers from the U.S. government to foreign countries were 6% of U.S. GDP in 1944.)

The answer: It was achieved by a decrease in both. The share of consumption in GDP decreased by 23%, from 74 to 51%. Part of the decrease in consumption may have been due to anticipations of higher taxes after the war; part was also the result of the unavailability of many consumer durables; and patriotism probably also played a role in leading people to save more and buy the war bonds issued by the government to finance the war. But the increase in government purchases was also met by a 6% decrease in the share of (private) investment in GDP—from 10 to 4%. Part of the burden of the war was therefore passed on in the form of lower capital accumulation to those living after the war.

FOCUS

- Suppose the government relies on deficit finance. With government spending sharply up, there will be a very large increase in the demand for goods. Given our assumption that output stays the same, the interest rate will have to increase enough to maintain equilibrium. Investment, which depends on the interest rate, will decrease sharply.
- Suppose instead that the government finances the spending increase through an increase in taxes—say, income taxes. Consumption will decline sharply. Exactly how much depends on consumers' expectations: The longer they expect the war to last, then the longer they will expect higher taxes to last, and the more they will decrease consumption. In any case, the increase in government spending will be partly offset by a decrease in consumption. Interest rates will increase by less than they would have increased under deficit spending. Investment will decrease by less.

In short, for a given output, the increase in government spending requires either a decrease in consumption or a decrease in investment. Whether the government relies on tax increases or deficits determines whether consumption or investment does more of the adjustment when government spending goes up.

Assume that the economy is closed, so that $Y = C + I + G$. Suppose that G goes up, and Y remains the same. Then, $C + I$ must go down.

If taxes are not increased, most of the decrease comes from a decrease in I. If taxes are increased, most of the decrease comes from a decrease in C.

How does all this affect who bears the burden of the war? The more the government relies on deficits, the smaller the decrease in consumption during the war and the larger the decrease in investment. Lower investment means a lower capital stock after the war, and so lower output after the war. By reducing capital accumulation, deficits become a way of passing some of the burden of the war onto future generations.

Reducing Tax Distortions

There is another argument for running deficits, not only during wars but, more generally, in times when government spending is exceptionally high. Think, for example, of reconstruction after an earthquake or the costs involved in the reunification of Germany in the early 1990s.

See the Focus box "German Unification and the German Monetary Fiscal Tug of War" in Chapter 5.

The argument is as follows: If the government were to increase taxes to finance the increase in spending, tax rates would have to be very high. Very high tax rates can lead to very high economic distortions: Faced with very high income tax rates, people work less or engage in illegal, untaxed activities. Rather than moving the tax rate up and down to maintain a balanced budget, it is better (from the point of view of reducing distortions) to maintain a relatively constant tax rate, to *smooth taxes.* **Tax smoothing** implies running large deficits when government spending is exceptionally high and small surpluses the rest of the time.

The Dangers of Very High Debt

You have now seen two costs of high government debt—lower capital accumulation, and higher tax rates and higher distortions. The recent experience of several countries with high debt ratios points to yet another cost: High debt can lead to vicious cycles and make the conduct of fiscal policy extremely difficult.

To see why this is so, return to equation (26.5), which gave the evolution of the debt ratio:

$$\frac{B_t}{Y_t} - \frac{B_{t-1}}{Y_{t-1}} = (r - g)\frac{B_{t-1}}{Y_{t-1}} + \frac{(G_t - T_t)}{Y_t}$$

Take a country with a high debt ratio, say, 100%. Suppose the real interest rate is 3% and the growth rate is 2%. The first term on the right is (3% − 2%) × 100% = 1% of GDP. Suppose further that the government is running a primary surplus of 1%, thus just enough to keep the debt ratio constant [the entire right side of the equation equals 1% + (− 1%) = 0%].

Now suppose financial investors start requiring a higher interest rate to hold government bonds. This higher interest rate may come from the fact that investors worry the government will not be able to keep the deficit under control, and so may not be able to repay the bonds in the future. The specific reason does not matter here. For concreteness, suppose the domestic real interest rate increases from 3 to, say, 12%.

Now assess the fiscal situation: $(r - g)$ is now 12% − 2% = 10%. With the increase in $(r - g)$ from 1 to 10%, the government must increase its primary surplus from 1 to 10% of GDP *just to keep the debt-to-GDP ratio constant.* This opens the scope for potential vicious cycles.

Suppose the government takes steps to avoid an increase in the debt ratio. The spending cuts or tax increases are likely to prove politically costly, generating even more political uncertainty and the need for an even higher interest rate. Also, the sharp fiscal contraction is likely to lead to a recession, decreasing the growth rate. Both the increase in the real interest rate and the decrease in growth further increase $(r - g)$, making it even harder to stabilize the debt ratio.

Alternatively, suppose the government proves unable or unwilling to increase the primary budget surplus by 9% of GDP. Debt then starts increasing, leading financial markets to become even more worried and require an even higher interest rate. The higher interest rate leads to even larger deficits, an even faster increase in the debt ratio, and so on. At some point, the government has no other option than to default.

In short, the higher the ratio of debt to GDP, the larger the potential for catastrophic debt dynamics. Even initially unfounded fears that the government may not fully repay the debt can easily become self-fulfilling. By increasing the interest rate the government must pay on its debt, those increased interest payments can lead the government to lose control of its budget, and lead to an increase in debt to a level so that the government is unable to repay the debt, validating initial fears.

◀ See the Focus box on Argentina in Chapter 21.

If this reminds you of our discussion of exchange rate crises, and the possibility of self-fulfilling crises, you are right. Very much the same mechanisms are at work: Expectations that a problem may arise lead to the emergence of the problem, validating initial expectations. Indeed, in some crises, both mechanisms are at work. In the Brazilian crisis of 1998, fears of a devaluation of the *real* (the Brazilian currency) forced Brazil to increase interest rates to very high levels. These high interest rates led to much larger budget deficits, raising questions about whether the Brazilian government could repay its debt, further increasing interest rates. Eventually, Brazil had no choice but to devalue. It did so in early 1999.

◀ Exchange rate crises were studied in Chapter 21.

If a government decides that its debt ratio is too high, how and how fast should it reduce it? Answer: through many years, even many decades, of surpluses. The historical reference here is that of England in the nineteenth century. By the end of its wars against Napoleon in the early 1800s, England had run up a debt ratio in excess of 200% of GDP. It spent most of the nineteenth century reducing the ratio, so that by 1900 the ratio stood at only 30% of GDP.

The prospect of many decades of fiscal austerity is unpleasant. Thus, when debt ratios are very high, an alternative solution keeps coming up—**debt repudiation**. The argument is simple: Repudiating the debt—canceling it in part or in full—is good for the economy. It allows for a decrease in taxes and thus a decrease in distortions. It decreases the risk of vicious cycles. The problem with this argument is the problem of time inconsistency we studied in Chapter 24. If the government reneges on its promises to repay its debt, it may have great difficulty trying to borrow again for a long time in the future; financial markets will remember what happened and be reluctant to lend again. What seems best today may be unappealing in the long run. Debt repudiation is very much a last resort, to be used when everything else has failed.

26-3 The U.S. Budget

We conclude this chapter by looking at the U.S. budget. Table 26-2 gives the basic budget numbers for fiscal year 2001.

You may notice that some of the numbers are not the same as the numbers you have read in the press. The reason is that there are many different definitions of *expenditures, revenues,* and *deficit.*

Sometimes, numbers refer to the budget of the federal government only. Sometimes, numbers consolidate the accounts of the federal, state, and local governments. State and local governments typically run surpluses: In fiscal year 2001, the combined surplus of state and local governments was about 0.2% of GDP. The surplus for the government as a whole—federal, state, and local—was therefore equal to the surplus of the federal government, 1.5% of GDP, plus the surplus of state and local governments, 0.2%, so 1.7% of GDP.

◀ Many states operate under rules that prevent them from running deficits.

I shall focus here only on the *federal budget.* Even there, there exists two sets of numbers:

Table 26-2 U.S. Federal Budget Revenues and Expenditures, Fiscal Year 2001 (percent of GDP)

Revenues	20.1		
Personal taxes		10.0	
Corporate profit taxes		2.0	
Indirect taxes		1.0	
Social insurance contributions		7.0	
Expenditures, excluding interest payments	16.2		
Consumption expenditures		5.0	
Defense			3.3
Nondefense			1.7
Transfers		8.1	
Grants to state/local governments		2.6	
Other spending		0.5	
Primary surplus (1) (+ sign: surplus)	3.9		
Net interest payments (2)	2.4		
Real interest payments (3)		1.7	
Inflation component		0.7	
Official surplus: (1) minus (2)	1.5		
Inflation adjusted surplus: (1) minus (3)	2.2		
Memo item. Debt-to-GDP ratio	31.0		

Source: Survey of Current Business, December 2001, Tables 3-2 and 3-7.

- The government uses its own accounting system and, because this is the system used to present and discuss the budget in Congress, these are the numbers you are most likely to encounter when reading newspapers.
- An alternative accounting system is provided in the national income and product accounts (NIPA). It provides a more economically meaningful set of budget numbers. The numbers in Table 26-2 are NIPA numbers.

Here are the main differences between the government numbers and the NIPA numbers:

For more details on the differences, read *The Economic and Budget Outlook: Fiscal Years 2000–2009*, Appendix D (Washington, D.C.: Congressional Budget Office, January 1999). (www.cbo.gov/)

- The government budget numbers are presented by *fiscal year* (again, from October 1 of the preceding calendar year to September 31 of the current calendar year). The NIPA numbers are typically reported for the calendar year, not the fiscal year. (Given that the NIPA numbers are available for each quarter, it is easy to construct NIPA numbers for each fiscal year. The numbers in Table 26-2 are reported for the fiscal year 2001, to facilitate comparisons with other numbers in this section.)
- The government budget numbers are presented in two categories: *on budget* and *off budget*. The most important off-budget item is Social Security. In fiscal year 2001 the on-budget deficit was $34 billion. This deficit was more than offset by an off-budget surplus of $161 billion, leading to a combined surplus of $161 – $34 = $127 billion; the main source of the off-budget surplus was an excess of Social Security taxes over Social Security benefits.

By separating the Social Security system from the rest of the budget (by putting it in a "lockbox," the expression coined by the Clinton administration), the on-budget/off-budget distinction serves a useful political purpose; namely, it makes it harder for Congress and the president to use the Social Security surplus to finance the rest of the budget. It is, however, a meaningless distinction from an economic viewpoint. The NIPA measure makes no such distinction; the NIPA deficit corresponds most closely to the sum of the on-budget and off-budget deficits.

- The two accounting systems differ in how they treat the sale of government assets. Government accounts treat asset sales as revenues. The NIPA accounts correctly recognize that asset sales bring revenues today, but reduce revenues in the future (as the government no longer receives the revenues from these assets); thus, asset sales are not included in revenues in the NIPA accounts.
- The two accounting systems differ in the way they treat government investment. Government accounts count all expenditures, including investment purchases such as aircraft carriers. The NIPA accounts, which measure current expenditures rather than capital expenditures, exclude investment but include depreciation on existing government owned capital.

◀ We saw in Chapter 24 that such sales were used to make the deficit numbers consistent with the Gramm-Rudman-Hollings restrictions in the late 1980s.

◀ When you hear a deficit number, ask

- **Federal? or federal, state, and local?**
- **Fiscal year? or calendar year?**
- **Government? or NIPA accounts?**
- **If government accounts, on budget? off budget? or the sum of the two?**

Finally, you are likely to encounter two numbers for (federal) government debt.

One is *gross debt*, the sum of the federal government's financial liabilities. When Congress votes to increase the debt ceiling, this is the number to which the ceiling applies. At the end of 2001, gross debt was equal to $5.6 trillion, or 55% of GDP.

The other, more relevant number, is *net debt*, or, equivalently, *debt held by the public*. At the end of 2001, net debt was only $3.1 trillion, or 31% of GDP. Where did the difference between gross debt and net debt come from? $2.5 trillion of government debt was held not by the public but by government agencies; for example, about $1.1 trillion was held by the Social Security Trust Fund (more on this Trust Fund later in the section).

Now look at the numbers in Table 26-2. In 2001, federal revenues were 20.1% of GDP. Expenditures excluding interest payments were 16.2% of GDP, so the federal government was running a primary surplus of 3.9% of GDP.

Interest payments on the debt held by the public were 2.4%. The official surplus was therefore equal to 3.9% − 2.4% = 1.5%. We know, however, that this measure is incorrect (see the Focus box in Section 26-1). The correct measure, the sum of the primary surplus minus *real* interest payments, was 3.9% − 1.7% = 2.2%. The government was running a surplus of 2.2%.

Will the U.S. government continue to run such surpluses in the future? At the end of 2000, most projections were for very large surpluses as far as the eye could see. Since then, three things have happened, all leading to a more pessimistic budget outlook:

- First—and largely as a result of the large projected surpluses—there was considerable pressure on politicians to cut taxes and increase spending. Tax cuts were one of the major promises of George Bush's presidential campaign. And, in early 2001, the new Bush administration and Congress passed a large package of tax cuts (called the Economic Growth and Tax Relief Reconciliation Act).
- Second, in the spring of 2001, the U.S. economy slowed down much more than had been expected, leading to lower tax revenues than had been projected.
- Third, the events of September 11, 2001, have led to an increase in government spending—on defense (the war in Afghanistan), homeland security, and so on.

At the time of this writing, it is very difficult to predict what will happen to the budget in the future. Current forecasts are for small federal budget deficits at least for fiscal years 2002 and 2003, and then for small surpluses for the rest of the decade. Many economists believe that larger surpluses would be desirable. They rely on two separate arguments:

- The U.S. saving rate is still very low and should be increased. One way to increase it is to increase public saving—equivalently, run larger budget surpluses.
- Looking far into the future, changes in demographics imply large increases in spending in several government programs, increases to which the government should start responding now, by raising revenues and running budget surpluses now.

Let me discuss both arguments in turn.

Surpluses and the Low U.S. Saving Rate

The U.S. saving rate is one of the lowest among OECD countries: In the 1990s, the average U.S. saving rate was 16.5% of GDP, about 4.5% below the OECD average. Should this low saving rate be a matter of concern? We discussed the issue in general in Chapter 11. The saving rate does affect the level of capital and the level of output in the long run. A higher saving rate would lead over time to a higher standard of living in the future.

For the effects of the saving rate on output in the long run, review Chapter 11.

If we believe that the United States, as a nation, is not saving enough for the future, there is a strong argument for taking measures to increase private saving, or offsetting low private saving by higher public saving. This is the first argument for running large budget surpluses.

This advice raises an intriguing issue. Under current projections, the ratio of debt to GDP is projected to decline to less than 10% by the end of this decade. If the government ran even larger surpluses than those currently projected, the government net debt position would decrease faster, and could become negative. Is this feasible? Could the government have a negative net debt position? The answer is yes. As the government ran surpluses, it could first buy back all of its debt, and when this was done, start buying private bonds or stocks. Or—and this would more likely be the case—it could do both at the same time, i.e., leave some amount of government debt in the economy, and use the surpluses to buy private bonds or equities. In any case, the government would turn from being a net debtor to being a net creditor. This would be historically unusual, but is perfectly feasible.

There are OECD countries where the government is a net creditor: Net debt to GDP is −36% in Finland, −35% in Korea, and −61% in Norway.

Surpluses and the Aging of America

About half of U.S. federal spending is on **entitlement programs**. These are programs that require the payment of benefits to all who meet the eligibility requirements established by the law. The three largest programs are Social Security (which provides benefits to retirees), Medicare (which provides health care to retirees), and Medicaid (which provides health care to the poor).

Table 26-3 shows actual and projected spending on each of these three programs, as a percent of GDP, from 1998 to 2060. The projections are from the Congressional Budget Office (CBO), and are constructed using economic forecasts and current rules (including future changes in rules if these changes have already been incorporated in the law) for each program.

The numbers are striking: Under existing rules, Social Security benefits are projected to increase from 4% of GDP in 1998 to 7% in 2060. Medicare benefits are projected to increase from 2 to 7%, Medicaid benefits from 1 to 3%. If nothing is done, the

Table 26-3 Projected Spending on Social Security, Medicare, and Medicaid, 1998–2060 (percent of GDP)

	1998	2010	2040	2060
Social Security	4.0	5.0	7.0	7.0
Medicare	2.0	3.0	6.0	7.0
Medicaid	1.0	2.0	3.0	3.0
Total	7.0	10.0	16.0	17.0

Source: "The Economic and Budget Outlook: Fiscal Years 1998–2060," Congressional Budget Office, January 1999, Table 2-5.

ratio of entitlement spending to GDP is projected to increase by 10% of GDP over the next 60 years.

These projected increases have two sources:

- The first and main one is the *aging of America*, the rapid increase in the proportion of people over 65 that will take place as the Baby Boom generation begins reaching retirement age, from year 2010 on. The *old age dependency ratio*—the ratio of the population 65 years old or more to the population between 20 and 64 years old—is projected to increase from about 20% in 1998 to above 40% in 2060. This evolution explains the projected growth of Social Security benefits, and a good part of the increase in Medicare.
- The second, which explains the rest of the growth of Medicare and the growth in Medicaid, is the steadily increasing cost of health care.

◀ See the Focus box "Social Security, Social Security Reform, and Capital Accumulation in the United States" in Chapter 11.

Can these increases in entitlement spending be offset by decreases in other government expenditures? The answer is no. From Table 26-2, you can see that even if *all* expenditures other than transfers were eliminated, there would still not be enough to cover the projected increase in entitlement spending: In 2001, total expenditures excluding interest payments and transfers, were equal to 16.2% − 8.1% = 8.1% of GDP, less than the 10% projected increase in entitlement spending.

It is therefore clear that major changes in entitlement programs will have to take place. Social Security benefits may have to be reduced (relative to projections), the provision of medical care will have to be limited (again, relative to projections). There is also little doubt that taxes, such as the payroll taxes used to finance Social Security, will have to be increased.

It is also clear that waiting to act until spending starts increasing would be waiting too long. The cut in benefits or the increase in tax rates needed to finance entitlement programs would be too large. To finance just projected Social Security benefits, the payroll tax rate would have to increase from approximately 12% today to about 20% in 2060. Financing Medicare and Medicaid increases would require further and even larger increases in the tax rate. There is a general agreement that the government should not wait, but should start taking measures now.

What should these measures do? They have to combine tax increases and benefit reductions to increase surpluses now and accumulate assets in anticipation of future spending. This is the approach that has been taken in dealing with Social Security. Since 1983, Social Security contributions have exceeded Social Security benefits, leading to surpluses and the accumulation of assets in a **Social Security Trust Fund**. Assets in this trust fund are now equal to about 12% of GDP.

How does such accumulation help in dealing with future increases in spending? First, decumulation of these assets later on can delay the date at which taxes have to be increased or benefits decreased. And if accumulation in the fund is large enough, this can avoid the need for tax increases or benefit cuts altogether. An example will help here. Suppose the real interest rate is 3%. Then, if the trust fund accumulated assets in an amount equal to 100% of GDP, real interest payments from the fund would be equal to 3% of GDP, an amount sufficient to cover the whole projected increase in Social Security benefits as a percentage of GDP from 1998 to 2060.

Under current assumptions, however, the trust fund does not come close to reaching such a level. It is projected to reach about 20% of GDP in 2020, then to decline and be equal to zero by 2030. So, there is a need to do more, not only for Social Security but, as we have seen, for Medicare and Medicaid programs as well. What to do and how to do it are likely to remain the main items on the budget agenda for the foreseeable future.

This section has concentrated on the United States. But similar problems, namely, the aging of population and the increase in medical costs, are affecting all OECD countries.

Summary

- The government budget constraint gives the evolution of government debt as a function of spending and taxes. One way of expressing the constraint is that the change in debt (the deficit) is equal to the primary deficit plus interest payments on the debt. The primary deficit is the difference between government spending on goods and services, G, and taxes net of transfers, T.
- If government spending is unchanged, a decrease in taxes must eventually be offset by an increase in taxes in the future. The longer the government waits to increase taxes or the higher the real interest rate, the higher the eventual increase in taxes.
- The legacy of past deficits is higher debt. To stabilize the debt, the government must eliminate the deficit. To eliminate the deficit, it must run a primary surplus equal to the interest payments on the existing debt.
- Under the Ricardian equivalence proposition, a larger deficit is offset by an equal increase in private saving. Deficits have no effect on demand and on output. The accumulation of debt does not affect capital accumulation. In practice, Ricardian equivalence fails. Larger deficits lead to higher demand and higher output in the short run. The accumulation of debt leads to lower capital accumulation, and thus to lower output in the long run.
- To stabilize the economy, the government should run deficits during recessions, and surpluses during booms. The cyclically adjusted deficit shows what the deficit would be, under existing tax and spending rules, if output were at the natural level of output.
- Deficits are justified in times of high spending, such as wars. Relative to an increase in taxes, deficits lead to higher consumption and lower investment during wars. They therefore shift some of the burden of the war from people living during the war to those living after the war. Deficits also help smooth taxes and reduce tax distortions.
- Several European countries have very high debt-to-GDP ratios. In addition to reducing capital and requiring higher taxes and thus creating tax distortions, high debt ratios increase the risk of fiscal crises.
- In 2001, the U.S. budget showed a surplus. Whether there will be deficits or surpluses in the future is unclear. Several economists believe that large surpluses are very much needed. They rely on two arguments:

  The U.S. saving rate is low. Larger public saving (larger surpluses) would increase national saving, increase capital accumulation, and increase output in the long run.

  America is aging. The proportion of retirees will increase steadily over the next 70 years in the United States. This implies that spending on several entitlement programs will greatly increase in the future, and that we should prepare for it today.

Key Terms

- inflation-adjusted deficit, 551
- government budget constraint, 552
- primary deficit (primary surplus), 553
- debt-to-GDP ratio, debt ratio, 555
- Ricardian equivalence, Ricardo-Barro proposition, 558
- full-employment deficit, 559
- midcycle deficit, 559
- standardized employment deficit, 559

- structural deficit, 559
- cyclically adjusted deficit, 559
- automatic stabilizer, 560
- tax smoothing, 562
- debt repudiation, 563
- entitlement programs, 566
- Social Security Trust Fund, 567

Questions and Problems

Quick Check

1. *Using the tables and graphs in this chapter, label each of the following statements* true, false, *or* uncertain. *Explain briefly.*
   a. Tax smoothing and deficit finance help spread the burden of war across generations.
   b. The government can never have a negative debt position.
   c. The prudent course of action at this stage for the United States would be to run large budget surpluses.
   d. If Ricardian equivalence holds, then an increase in income taxes will affect neither consumption nor saving.
   e. If Ricardian equivalence holds, then government bonds are worthless.
   f. If Ricardian equivalence holds, then government spending has no effect on activity.
   g. The ratio of debt to GDP cannot exceed 100%. If it did, more than GDP would be needed to pay interest on the debt.

2. *Consider an economy where*
   The official budget deficit is 4% of GDP.
   The debt-to-GDP ratio is 100%.
   The nominal interest rate is 10%.
   The inflation rate is 7%.
   a. What is the primary deficit/surplus?
   b. What is the inflation-adjusted deficit/surplus?
   c. Suppose the unemployment rate is 2% above the natural rate. What is the cyclically adjusted, inflation-adjusted deficit/surplus?
   d. Suppose the unemployment rate is equal to the natural rate. Suppose that the normal growth rate is 2%. Is the debt-to-GDP ratio going up or down?
   e. If things continue as in (d), what will be the debt-to-GDP ratio in 10 years?

3. *Suppose that in the economy described in the previous problem, financial investors worry that the level of debt is too high, and that a devaluation may result. They start expecting a devaluation of 20% with probability 0.5 within a year.*
   a. If the foreign interest rate is and remains equal to 10%, what happens to the domestic interest rate?
   b. Suppose that inflation remains the same. What happens to the domestic real interest rate? What is likely to happen to the growth rate?
   c. What happens to the official budget deficit? To the inflation adjusted deficit?
   d. Suppose the growth rate decreases from 2 to –2%. What happens to the change in the debt ratio?
   e. Were the investors right to worry?

4. *"A deficit during a war can be a good thing. First, the deficit is temporary, so after it is over, the government can go right back to its old level of spending and taxes. Second, given that the evidence supports Ricardian equivalence proposition, the deficit will stimulate the economy during wartime, helping to keep the unemployment rate low." Identify three distinct mistakes in this statement. Is anything in this statement correct?*

Dig Deeper

5. *"It may have made sense in the 1930s to force people to save to make sure they would have enough to live on in their old age. But now, people are much more aware of the need to save for retirement. It does not make sense for the government to continue to act as big brother. So the solution to the Social Security problem is in fact quite simple. Allow young people, say, everybody under the age of 25 today, to save what they want and how they want; in other words, let them out of the Social Security system. Then, what happens to them is their problem. And there is no longer a problem of financing Social Security." Discuss.*

6. *Ricardian equivalence*
   *Suppose that the only tax the government can use is a tax on dividends from stocks. And suppose that consumption is a function of the value of the stock market. Will this economy exhibit Ricardian equivalence? (*Hint: *Think of the government increasing the tax this year, and decreasing it in the future to satisfy its budget constraint. What will happen to stock prices today? What will happen to consumption?)*

We invite you to visit the Blanchard page on the Prentice Hall Web site at:
www.prenhall.com/blanchard
for this chapter's World Wide Web exercises

Further Readings

The modern statement of the Ricardian equivalence proposition is by Robert Barro, "Are Government Bonds Net Wealth?" *Journal of Political Economy*, December 1974, 1095–1117.

The *Guide to the Federal Budget*, by Stanley Collender, published every year by the Brookings Institution Press in Washington, D.C., is one of the most useful descriptions of the budget process and the budget numbers.

Each year, the Congressional Budget Office, an office of the U.S. Congress, publishes *The Economic and Budget Outlook* for the current and future fiscal years (the January 2002 edition gives the outlook for fiscal years 2002 to 2012). The document provides a clear and unbiased presentation of the current budget, of current budget issues, and of budget trends (it is available at **www.cbo.gov/**).

A good introduction to the issues of Social Security reform is given in *Social Security: A Primer*, Congressional Budget Office, September 2001. Visit the CBO site: **www.cbo.gov/**. Then go to Publications, and then to Social Security.

Epilogue: The Story of Macroeconomics

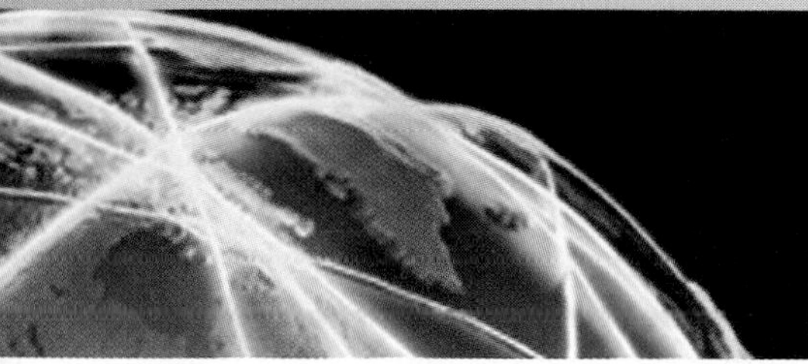

CHAPTER 27

I have spent 26 chapters presenting the framework that most economists use to think about macroeconomic issues and the major conclusions they draw, as well as the issues on which they disagree. How this framework has been built over time is a fascinating story. It is the story I want to tell in this chapter.

- Section 27-1 starts at the beginning of modern macroeconomics—with Keynes and the Great Depression.
- Section 27-2 turns to the *neoclassical synthesis*, a synthesis of Keynes's ideas with the ideas of earlier economists—a synthesis that dominated macroeconomics until the early 1970s.
- Section 27-3 describes the *rational expectations critique*, the strong attack on the neoclassical synthesis that led to a complete overhaul of macroeconomics in the 1970s and the 1980s.
- Section 27-4 describes current research developments.
- Section 27-5 concludes by restating common beliefs, the set of central propositions on which most macroeconomists agree. ■

27-1 Keynes and the Great Depression

John Maynard Keynes

The history of modern macroeconomics starts in 1936, with the publication of Keynes's *General Theory of Employment, Interest, and Money*. As he was writing the *General Theory*, Keynes confided to a friend: "I believe myself to be writing a book on economic theory which will largely revolutionize—not, I suppose at once but in the course of the next ten years, the way the world thinks about economic problems."

Keynes was right. The book's timing was one of the reasons for its immediate success. The Great Depression was not only an economic catastrophe, but also an intellectual failure for the economists working on **business cycle theory**—as macroeconomics was then called. Few economists had a coherent explanation for the Depression, either for its depth or for its length. The economic measures taken by the Roosevelt administration in the New Deal had been based on instinct rather than on economic theory. The *General Theory* offered an interpretation of events, an intellectual framework, and a clear argument for government intervention.

The *General Theory* emphasized **effective demand**—what we now call *aggregate demand*. In the short run, Keynes argued, effective demand determines output. Even if output eventually returns to its natural level, the process is slow at best. One of Keynes's most famous quotes is: "In the long run, we are all dead."

In the process of deriving effective demand, Keynes introduced many of the building blocks of modern macroeconomics:

- The multiplier, which explains how shocks to demand can be amplified and lead to larger shifts in output.
- **Liquidity preference** (the term Keynes gave to the demand for money), which explains how monetary policy can affect interest rates and aggregate demand.
- The importance of expectations in affecting consumption and investment; and the idea that *animal spirits* (shifts in expectations) are a major factor behind shifts in demand and output.

The *General Theory* was more than a treatise for economists. It offered clear policy implications, and they were in tune with the times. Waiting for the economy to recover by itself was irresponsible. In the midst of a depression, trying to balance the budget was not only stupid, it was dangerous. Active use of fiscal policy was essential to returning the country to high employment.

27-2 The Neoclassical Synthesis

Within a few years, the *General Theory* had transformed macroeconomics. Not everybody was converted, and few agreed with it all. But most discussions became organized around it.

By the early 1950s a large consensus had emerged, based on an integration of many of Keynes's ideas and the ideas of earlier economists. This consensus was called the **neoclassical synthesis**. To quote from Paul Samuelson, in the 1955 edition of his textbook, *Economics*—the first modern economics textbook:

> In recent years, 90 per cent of American economists have stopped being "Keynesian economists" or "Anti-Keynesian economists." Instead, they have worked toward a synthesis of whatever is valuable in older economics and in modern theories of income determination. The result might be called neo-classical

economics and is accepted, in its broad outlines, by all but about five per cent of extreme left-wing and right-wing writers.

The neoclassical synthesis was to remain the dominant view for another 20 years. Progress was astonishing, leading many to call the period from the early 1940s to the early 1970s the golden age of macroeconomics.

Progress on All Fronts

The first order of business after publication of the *General Theory* was to formalize mathematically what Keynes meant. While Keynes knew mathematics, he had avoided using it in the *General Theory.* One result was endless controversies about what Keynes meant and whether there were logical flaws in some of his arguments.

The *IS-LM* Model

A number of formalizations of Keynes's ideas were offered. The most influential was the *IS-LM* model, developed by John Hicks and Alvin Hansen in the 1930s and early 1940s. The initial version of the *IS-LM* model—which was actually very close to the version presented in Chapter 5 of this book—was criticized for emasculating many of Keynes's insights: Expectations played no role, and the adjustment of prices and wages was altogether absent. Yet the *IS-LM* model provided a basis from which to start building, and as such it was immensely successful. Discussions became organized around the slopes of the *IS* and *LM* curves, what variables were missing from the two relations, what equations for prices and wages should be added to the model, and so on.

Franco Modigliani

Theories of Consumption, Investment, and Money Demand

Keynes had emphasized the importance of consumption and investment behavior, and of the choice between money and other financial assets. Major progress was soon made along all three fronts.

In the 1950s, Franco Modigliani (then at Carnegie Mellon and now at MIT) and Milton Friedman (then at the University of Chicago, now at the Hoover Institution at Stanford) independently developed the theory of consumption you saw in Chapter 16. Both insisted on the importance of expectations in determining current consumption decisions.

James Tobin, from Yale, developed the theory of investment based on the relation between the present value of profits and investment. The theory was further developed and tested by Dale Jorgenson, from Harvard. You saw this theory in Chapter 16.

Tobin also developed the theory of the demand for money, and more generally, the theory of the choice between different assets based on liquidity, return, and risk. His work has become the basis not only for an improved treatment of financial markets in macroeconomics, but also for the theory of finance in general.

James Tobin

Growth Theory

In parallel with the work on fluctuations, there was a renewed focus on growth. In contrast to the stagnation in the pre–World War II era, most countries were growing fast in the 1950s and 1960s. Even if they experienced fluctuations, their standard of living was rising rapidly. The growth model developed by MIT's Robert Solow in 1956, which you saw in Chapters 11 and 12, provided a framework to think about the determinants of

Robert Solow

growth. It was followed by an explosion of work on the roles of saving and technological progress in growth.

Macroeconometric Models

All these contributions were integrated in larger and larger macroeconometric models. The first U.S. macroeconometric model, developed by Lawrence Klein at the University of Pennsylvania in the early 1950s, was an extended *IS* relation, with 16 equations. With the development of the National Income and Product Accounts (making available better data) and the development of econometrics and of computers, the models quickly grew in size. The most impressive effort was the construction of the MPS model (MPS stands for MIT-Penn-SSRC, for the two universities and the research institution—the Social Science Research Council—involved in its construction), developed during the 1960s by a group led by Franco Modigliani. Its structure was an expanded version of the *IS-LM* model, plus a Phillips curve mechanism. But its components—consumption, investment, and money demand—all reflected the tremendous theoretical and empirical progress made since Keynes.

Lawrence Klein

Keynesians Versus Monetarists

With such rapid progress, many macroeconomists, who defined themselves as **Keynesians**, came to believe that the future was bright. The nature of fluctuations was increasingly well understood; the development of models allowed for a better use of policy. The time when the economy could be fine-tuned, and recessions all but eliminated, seemed not far in the future.

This optimism was met with skepticism by a small but influential minority, the **monetarists**. Their intellectual leader was Milton Friedman. While Friedman saw much progress being made—and was himself the father of one of the major contributions, the theory of consumption—he did not share in the general enthusiasm. He believed that the understanding of the economy remained very limited. He questioned the motives of governments as well as the notion that they actually knew enough to improve macroeconomic outcomes.

In the 1960s, debates between *Keynesians* and *monetarists* dominated the economic headlines. The debates centered around three issues, (1) the effectiveness of monetary policy versus fiscal policy, (2) the Phillips curve, and (3) the role of policy:

Milton Friedman

Monetary Policy Versus Fiscal Policy

Keynes had emphasized *fiscal* rather than *monetary* policy as the key to fighting recessions. And this had remained the prevailing wisdom. The *IS* curve, many argued, was quite steep: Changes in the interest rate had little effect on demand and output. Thus, monetary policy did not work very well. Fiscal policy, which affects demand directly, could affect output faster and more reliably.

Friedman strongly challenged this conclusion. In a 1963 book, *A Monetary History of the United States, 1867–1960,* Friedman and Anna Schwartz painstakingly reviewed the evidence on monetary policy and the relation between money and output in the United States over a century. Their conclusion was not only that monetary policy was very powerful, but that movements in money did explain most of the fluctuations in output. They interpreted the Great Depression as the result of a major mistake in monetary policy, a decrease in the money supply due to bank failures—a decrease that the Fed could have avoided by increasing the monetary base, but had not. (We discussed this interpretation in Chapter 22.)

Friedman and Schwartz's challenge was followed by a vigorous debate and by intense research on the respective effects of fiscal policy and monetary policy. In the end, a consensus was in effect reached. Both fiscal policy and monetary policy clearly had effects. And if policy makers cared about not only the level but also the composition of output, the best policy was typically a mix of the two.

Edmund Phelps

The Phillips Curve

The second debate focused on the Phillips curve. The Phillips curve was not part of the initial Keynesian model. But because it provided such a convenient (and apparently reliable) way of explaining the movement of wages and prices over time, it had become part of the neoclassical synthesis. In the 1960s, based on the empirical evidence up to then, many Keynesian economists believed that there was a reliable trade-off between unemployment and inflation, even in the long run.

Milton Friedman and Edmund Phelps (from Columbia University) strongly disagreed. They argued that the existence of such a long-run trade-off flew in the face of basic economic theory. They argued that the apparent trade-off would quickly vanish if policy makers actually tried to exploit it—that is, if they tried to achieve low unemployment by accepting higher inflation. As you saw in Chapter 8 when we studied the evolution of the Phillips curve, Friedman and Phelps were definitely right. By the mid-1970s, the consensus was indeed that there was no long-run trade-off between inflation and unemployment.

The Role of Policy

The third debate centered on the role of policy. Skeptical that economists knew enough to stabilize output and that policy makers could be trusted to do the right thing, Friedman argued for the use of simple rules, such as steady money growth (a rule we discussed in Chapter 25). Here is what he said in a testimony to Congress in 1958:

> A steady rate of growth in the money supply will not mean perfect stability even though it would prevent the kind of wide fluctuations that we have experienced from time to time in the past. It is tempting to try to go farther and to use monetary changes to offset other factors making for expansion and contraction [. . .] The available evidence casts grave doubts on the possibility of producing any fine adjustments in economic activity by fine adjustments in monetary policy—at least in the present state of knowledge. There are thus serious limitations to the possibility of a discretionary monetary policy and much danger that such a policy may make matters worse rather than better.
>
> Political pressures to "do something" in the face of either relatively mild price rises or relatively mild price and employment declines are clearly very strong indeed in the existing state of public attitudes. The main moral to be drawn from the two preceding points is that yielding to these pressures may frequently do more harm than good.

As you saw in Chapter 24, this debate on the role of macroeconomic policy has not been settled. The nature of the arguments has changed a bit, but they are still with us today.

27-3 The Rational Expectations Critique

Despite the battles between Keynesians and monetarists, macroeconomics around 1970 looked like a successful and mature field. It appeared successful at explaining events, at guiding policy choices. Most debates were framed within a common intellectual framework. But, within a few years the field was in crisis. The crisis had two sources.

Robert Lucas

Thomas Sargent

Robert Barro

One was *events*. By the mid-1970s, most countries were experiencing *stagflation*, a word coined at that time to denote the simultaneous existence of high unemployment and high inflation. Macroeconomists had not predicted stagflation. After the fact and after a few years of research, a convincing explanation was provided, based on the effects of adverse supply shocks on both prices and output. (We discussed the effects of such shocks in Chapter 7.) But it was too late to undo the damage to the discipline's image.

The other was *ideas*. In the early 1970s, a small group of economists—Robert Lucas from the University of Chicago; Thomas Sargent, then from the University of Minnesota and now at Stanford; and Robert Barro, then from Chicago and now at Harvard—led a strong attack against mainstream macroeconomics. They did not mince words. In a 1978 paper, Lucas and Sargent stated

> That the predictions [of Keynesian economics] were wildly incorrect, and that the doctrine on which they were based was fundamentally flawed, are now simple matters of fact, involving no subtleties in economic theory. The task which faces contemporary students of the business cycle is that of sorting through the wreckage, determining what features of that remarkable intellectual event called the Keynesian Revolution can be salvaged and put to good use, and which others must be discarded.

The Three Implications of Rational Expectations

Lucas and Sargent's main argument was that Keynesian economics had ignored the full implications of the effect of expectations on behavior. The way to proceed, they argued, was to assume that people formed expectations as rationally as they could, based on the information they had. Thinking of people as having *rational expectations* had three major implications, all highly damaging to Keynesian macroeconomics.

The Lucas Critique

The first implication was that existing macroeconomic models could not be used to help design policy. While these models recognized that expectations affect behavior, they did not incorporate expectations explicitly. All variables were assumed to depend on current and past values of other variables, including policy variables. Thus, what the models captured was the set of relations between economic variables as they had held in the past, under past policies. Were these policies to change, Lucas argued, the way people formed expectations would change as well, making estimated relations—and, by implication, simulations generated using existing macroeconometric models—poor guides to what would happen under these new policies. This critique of macroeconometric models became known as the **Lucas critique**. To take again the history of the Phillips curve as an example, the data up to the early 1970s had suggested a trade-off between unemployment and inflation. As policy makers tried to exploit that trade-off, it disappeared.

Rational Expectations and the Phillips Curve

The second implication was that when rational expectations were introduced in Keynesian models, these models actually delivered very un-Keynesian conclusions. For example, the models implied that deviations of output from its natural level were short-lived, much more so than Keynesian economists claimed. This argument was based on a re-examination of the aggregate supply relation.

In Keynesian models, the slow return of output to its natural level came from the slow adjustment of prices and wages through the Phillips curve mechanism. An increase in money, for example, led first to higher output and to lower unemployment. Lower unemployment then led to higher nominal wages and to higher prices. The adjustment continued until wages and prices had increased in the same proportion as nominal money, until unemployment and output each returned to their natural levels.

This adjustment, Lucas pointed out, was highly dependent on wage setters' backward-looking expectations of inflation. In the MPS model, for example, wages responded only to current and past inflation, and to current unemployment. But once the assumption was made that wage setters had rational expectations, the adjustment was likely to be much faster. Changes in money, to the extent that they were anticipated, might have no effect on output: For example, anticipating an increase in money of 5% over the coming year, wage setters would increase the nominal wages set in contracts for the coming year by 5%. Firms would, in turn, increase prices by 5%. The result would be no change in the real money stock, and no change in demand or output.

Within the logic of the Keynesian models, Lucas therefore argued, only *unanticipated changes in money* should affect output. Predictable movements in money should have no effect on activity. More generally, if wage setters had rational expectations, shifts in demand were likely to have effects on output for only as long as wages were set in nominal terms, a year or so. Even on its own terms, the Keynesian model did not deliver a convincing theory of the long-lasting effects of demand on output.

Optimal Control Versus Game Theory

The third implication was, if people and firms had rational expectations, it was wrong to think of policy as the control of a complicated but passive system. Rather, the right way was to think of policy as a game between policy makers and the economy. The right tool was not *optimal control*, but *game theory*. And game theory led to a different vision of policy. A striking example was the issue of *time inconsistency* discussed by Finn Kydland and Edward Prescott (then at Carnegie Mellon, now at the University of Minnesota), an issue that we discussed in Chapter 24: Good intentions on the part of policy makers could actually lead to disaster.

To summarize, when rational expectations were introduced, Keynesian models could not be used to determine policy, Keynesian models could not explain long-lasting deviations of output from the natural level of output, and the theory of policy needed to be redesigned, using the tools of game theory.

The Integration of Rational Expectations

As you might guess from the tone of Lucas and Sargent's quote, the intellectual atmosphere in macroeconomics was tense in the early 1970s. But, within a few years, a process of integration (of ideas, not people, because tempers remained high) had started, and it was to dominate the 1970s and the 1980s.

Fairly quickly, the idea that rational expectations was the right working assumption gained wide acceptance. This was not because macroeconomists believe that people, firms, and participants in financial markets always form expectations rationally. But rational expectations appears to be a natural benchmark, at least until economists have made more progress in understanding whether and how actual expectations systematically differ from rational expectations.

Work then started on the challenges raised by Lucas and Sargent.

The Implications of Rational Expectations

First, there was a systematic exploration of the role and the implications of rational expectations in goods markets, in financial markets, and in labor markets. Much of what was discovered has been presented in this book already. For example:

Robert Hall

- Robert Hall, then from MIT and now at Stanford, showed that if consumers are very foresighted (in the sense defined in Chapter 16), then changes in

Rudiger Dornbusch

Stanley Fischer

John Taylor

consumption should be unpredictable: The best forecast of consumption next year would be consumption this year! Put another way, changes in consumption should be very hard to predict. This result came as a surprise to most macroeconomists at the time, but it is in fact based on a simple intuition: If consumers are very foresighted, they will change their consumption only when they learn something new about the future. But by definition, such news cannot be predicted. This consumption behavior, known as the **random walk of consumption**, has served as a benchmark in consumption research ever since.

- Rudiger Dornbusch, from MIT, showed that the large swings in exchange rates under flexible exchange rates, which had previously been thought of as the result of speculation by irrational investors, were fully consistent with rationality. His argument, which we saw in Chapter 21: Changes in monetary policy can lead to long-lasting changes in nominal interest rates; changes in current and expected nominal interest rates lead in turn to large changes in the exchange rate. Dornbusch's model, known as the *overshooting* model of exchange rates, has become the benchmark in discussions of exchange-rate movements.

Wage and Price Setting

Second, there was a systematic exploration of the determination of wages and prices, going far beyond the Phillips curve relation. Two important contributions were made by MIT's Stanley Fischer and John Taylor, then from Columbia University and now at Stanford. Both showed that the adjustment of prices and wages in response to changes in unemployment can be *slow even under rational expectations.*

They pointed to an important characteristic of both wage and price setting, the **staggering** of wage and price decisions. In contrast to the simple story we told earlier, where all wages and prices increased simultaneously in anticipation of an increase in money, actual wage and price decisions are staggered over time. So there is not one sudden synchronized adjustment of all wages and prices to an increase in money. Rather, the adjustment is likely to be slow, with wages and prices adjusting to the new level of money through a process of leapfrogging over time. Fischer and Taylor thus showed that the second issue raised by the rational expectations critique could be resolved, that a slow return of output to the natural level of output can be consistent with rational expectations in the labor market.

The Theory of Policy

Third, thinking about policy in terms of game theory led to an explosion of research on the nature of the games being played, not only between policy makers and the economy but also between policy makers—between political parties, or between the central bank and the government, or between governments of different countries. One of the major achievements of this research has been the development of a way of thinking more rigorously about such fuzzy notions as "credibility," "reputation," and "commitment." At the same time, there has been a distinct shift in focus from "what governments should do" to "what governments actually do," and so an increasing awareness of the political constraints that economists should take into account when advising policy makers.

To summarize, by the end of the 1980s, the challenges raised by the rational expectations critique had led to a complete overhaul of macroeconomics. The basic structure had been extended to take into account the implications of rational expectations, or more generally, of forward-looking behavior by people and firms. Indeed, what I have presented in this book is what I see as the synthesis that has emerged, and that now constitutes the core of macroeconomics.

Before I summarize what I see as the core of macroeconomics—something I shall do in the last section, let me turn briefly to current research. Much of it is still too speculative to have made it into the core, but no doubt some of it will do so soon.

27-4 Current Developments

Since the late 1980s, three groups have dominated the research headlines: the *new classicals*, the *new Keynesians*, and the *new growth theorists*. (Note the generous use of the word *new*. Unlike producers of laundry detergents, economists stop short of using *new and improved*. But the subliminal message is the same.)

New Classical Economics and Real Business Cycle Theory

Edward Prescott

The rational expectations critique was more than just a critique of Keynesian economics. It also offered its own interpretation of fluctuations. Instead of relying on imperfections in labor markets, on the slow adjustment of wages and prices, and so on to explain fluctuations, Lucas argued, macroeconomists should see how far they could go in explaining fluctuations as the effects of shocks in competitive markets with fully flexible prices and wages.

This is the research agenda that has been pursued by the **new classicals**. The intellectual leader is Edward Prescott, and the models he and his followers have developed are known as **real business cycle (RBC) models**. These models assume that output is always at its natural level. That means all fluctuations in output are movements of the natural level of output, as opposed to movements of output away from the natural level of output.

Where do these movements come from? The answer proposed by Prescott is technological progress. As new discoveries are made, productivity increases, leading to an increase in output. The increase in productivity leads to an increase in the wage, which makes it more attractive to work, leading workers to work more. Productivity increases therefore lead to increases in both output and employment, just as we observe in the real world.

The RBC approach has been criticized on many fronts. As we discussed in Chapter 12, technological progress is the result of very many innovations, each taking a long time to diffuse throughout the economy. It is hard to see how this process could generate anything like the large short-run fluctuations in output that we observe in practice. It is also hard to think of recessions as times of technological *regress*, times in which productivity and output both go down. Finally, as we have seen, there is very strong evidence that changes in money, which have no effect on output in RBC models, in fact have strong effects on output in the real world.

At this point, most economists do not believe that the RBC approach provides a convincing explanation of major fluctuations in output. But the approach has proved useful. It has reinforced the important point that not all fluctuations in output are deviations of output from its natural level. At a more technical level, the RBC approach has provided several new techniques for solving complex models, which are widely used in research today. It is likely to evolve rather than disappear. Some RBC models have started introducing nominal rigidities along the lines of Fischer and Taylor. These models imply that output fluctuations come not only from productivity shocks, but also from changes in nominal money.

New Keynesian Economics

The term **new Keynesians** denotes a loosely connected group of researchers who share a common belief that the synthesis that has emerged in response to the rational

George Akerlof

expectations critique is basically correct. But they also share the belief that much remains to be learned about the nature of imperfections in different markets, and about the implications of those imperfections for macroeconomics.

One line of research has focused on the determination of wages in the labor market. We discussed in Chapter 6 the notion of *efficiency wages*—the idea that wages, if perceived by workers as being too low, may lead to shirking by workers on the job, to problems of morale within the firm, to difficulties in recruiting or keeping good workers, and so on. One influential researcher in this area has been George Akerlof from the University of California at Berkeley, who has explored the role of "norms," the rules that develop in any organization—in this case, the firm—to assess what is fair or unfair (Akerlof received the Nobel Prize in 2001). This research has led him and others to explore issues previously left to research in sociology and psychology, and to examine their macroeconomic implications.

Another line of new Keynesian research has explored the role of imperfections in credit markets. Except for a discussion of the role of banks in the Great Depression and in the current Japanese recession, I have typically assumed in this book that the effects of monetary policy worked through interest rates, and that firms and people could borrow as much as they wanted at the market interest rate. In practice, most people and many firms can borrow only from banks. And banks often turn down potential borrowers, despite the willingness of these borrowers to pay the interest rate charged by the bank. Why this happens, and how it affects our view of how monetary policy works, has been the subject of much research, in particular by Ben Bernanke of Princeton.

Yet another direction of research is **nominal rigidities**. As we saw earlier in this chapter, Fischer and Taylor have shown that with staggering of wage or price decisions, output can deviate from its natural level for a long time. This conclusion raises a number of questions. If staggering of decisions is responsible, at least in part, for fluctuations, why don't both wage setters and price setters synchronize decisions? Why aren't prices and wages adjusted more often? Why aren't all prices and all wages changed, say, on the first day of each week? In tackling these issues, Akerlof and N. Gregory Mankiw (from Harvard University) have derived a surprising and important result, often referred to as the **menu cost** explanation of output fluctuations:

Each wage setter or price setter is largely indifferent about when and how often he changes his own wage or price (for a retailer, changing the prices on the shelf every day or every week does not make much difference to profits). Even small costs of changing prices—such as those costs involved in printing a new menu, for example—may lead to infrequent and staggered price adjustment. This staggering leads to slow adjustment of the price level, and to large aggregate output fluctuations in response to movements in aggregate demand. In short, decisions that do not matter much at the individual level (how often to change prices or wages) lead to large aggregate effects (slow adjustment of the price level, and large effects of shifts in aggregate demand on output).

Paul Romer

New Growth Theory

After being one of the most active topics of research in the 1960s, growth theory went into an intellectual slump. Since the late 1980s, however, growth theory has made a strong comeback. The set of new contributions goes under the name of **new growth theory**.

Two economists, Robert Lucas (the same Lucas who spearheaded the rational expectations critique) and Paul Romer, then from the University of California at Berkeley, now at Stanford, have played an important role in defining the issues. When growth theory faded in the late 1960s, two issues were left largely unresolved. One issue was the determinants of technological progress. The other was the role of increasing returns to scale—whether, say, doubling capital and labor may actually lead to more than a doubling of output. These are the two major issues on which new growth theory has concentrated. The discussions of technological progress in Chapter 12, and of the interaction between technological progress and unemployment in Chapter 13, reflect some of the advances economists have made on this front. One example is the work of Philippe Aghion (from Harvard University) and Peter Howitt (from Brown University) who have developed a theme first explored by Joseph Schumpeter in the 1930s, the notion that growth is a process of *creative destruction*, in which new products are constantly introduced, making old ones obsolete. Another example is the work of Alwyn Young (from the University of Chicago) on growth in fast-growing Asian countries, which we discussed in Chapter 12.

To summarize, current research is proceeding mainly on three fronts:

1. The new classical approach: Identifying how much of the fluctuations can be thought of as movements in the natural level of output and in the natural unemployment rate.

2. The new Keynesian approach: Identifying the precise nature of market imperfections and nominal rigidities that give rise to deviations of output from its natural level.

3. The new growth theory: Identifying the factors responsible for technological progress and growth in the long run.

Increasingly, these three fronts overlap. Some models use the techniques developed by the new classical approach, but allow for some of the imperfections emphasized by the new Keynesian approach. Other models focus on the short-run effects on output of the process of creative destruction emphasized by new growth models, thus integrating the new growth and the new classical approaches. For the time being, exploration and synthesis rather than major intellectual battles dominate the field.

27-5 Common Beliefs

As we come to the end of this brief history of macroeconomics, and to the end of the book, let me restate the basic set of propositions on which most macroeconomists agree:

- In the *short run*, shifts in aggregate demand affect output. Higher consumer confidence, a larger budget deficit, and faster growth of money are all likely to increase output, and to decrease unemployment.
- In the *medium run*, output returns to the natural level of output. This natural level depends on the natural rate of unemployment (which, together with the size of the labor force, determines the level of employment), on the capital stock, and on the state of technology.
- In the *long run*, two main factors determine the evolution of the level of output. One is capital accumulation, the other is the rate of technological progress.
- *Monetary policy* affects output in the short run, but not in the medium run or the long run. A higher rate of money growth eventually translates one for one into a higher rate of inflation.
- *Fiscal policy* has short-run, medium–run, and long-run effects on output. Higher budget deficits are likely to increase output in the short run. They leave output unaffected in the medium run. And they are likely to decrease capital accumulation and output in the long run.

These propositions leave room for disagreements:

- One is about the length of the "short run," the period of time over which aggregate demand affects output. At one extreme, real business cycle theorists start from the assumption that output is always at the natural level of output: The "short run" is very short! At the other extreme, the study of slumps and depressions (which we explored in Chapter 22) imply that the effects of demand may be extremely long-lasting, that the "short run" may be very long.
- Another is about the role for policy. While conceptually distinct, it is largely related to the first. Those who believe that output returns quickly to the natural level of output are typically willing to impose tight rules on both monetary and fiscal policy, from constant money growth to the requirement of a balanced budget. Those who believe the adjustment is slow typically believe in the need for more flexible stabilization policies.

But, behind these disagreements, there is a largely common framework in which most research is conducted and organized. The framework gives us a way of interpreting events and discussing policy. This is what I have done in this book.

Summary

- The history of modern macroeconomics starts in 1936, with the publication of Keynes's *General Theory of Employment, Interest and Money*. Keynes's contribution was formalized in the *IS-LM* model by John Hicks and Alvin Hansen in the 1930s and early 1940s.
- The period from the early 1940s to the early 1970s can be called the golden age of macroeconomics. Among the major developments were the development of the theories of consumption, investment, money demand, and portfolio choice; the development of growth theory; and the development of large macroeconometric models.
- The main debate during the 1960s was between Keynesians and monetarists. Keynesians believed developments in macroeconomic theory allowed for better control of the economy. Monetarists, led by Milton Friedman, were more skeptical of the ability of governments to help stabilize the economy.
- In the 1970s, macroeconomics experienced a crisis. For two reasons: One was the appearance of stagflation, which came as a surprise to most economists. The other was a theoretical attack led by Robert Lucas. Lucas and his followers showed that when rational expectations were introduced, (1) Keynesian models could not be used to determine policy, (2) Keynesian models could not explain long-lasting deviations of output from its natural level, and (3) the theory of policy needed to be redesigned, using the tools of game theory.
- Much of the 1970s and 1980s was spent integrating rational expectations into macroeconomics. As is reflected in this book, macroeconomists are now much more aware of the role of expectations in determining the effects of shocks and policy, and of the complexity of policy, than they were two decades ago.
- Current research in macroeconomic theory is proceeding along three lines: New classical economists are exploring the extent to which fluctuations can be explained as movements in the natural level of output, as opposed to movements away from the natural level of output. New Keynesian economists are exploring more formally the role of market imperfections in fluctuations. New growth theorists are exploring the role of R&D and of increasing returns to scale in growth.
- Despite the differences, there exists a set of propositions on which most macroeconomists agree. Two of these propositions are (1) in the short run, shifts in aggregate demand affect output; (2) in the medium run, output returns to its natural level.

Key Terms

- business cycle theory, 572
- effective demand, 572
- liquidity preference, 572
- neoclassical synthesis, 572
- Keynesians, 574
- monetarists, 574
- Lucas critique, 576
- random walk of consumption, 578
- staggering (of wage and price decisions), 578
- new classicals, 579
- real business cycle (RBC) models, 579
- new Keynesians, 579
- nominal rigidities, 580
- menu costs, 580
- new growth theory, 580

Further Readings

Two classics are J. M. Keynes, *The General Theory of Employment, Money and Interest* (London: Macmillan Press, 1936), and Milton Friedman and Anna Schwartz, *A Monetary History of the United States, 1867–1960* (Princeton, NJ: Princeton University Press, 1963). *Warning*: The first makes for hard reading, and the second is a heavy volume.

For an account of macroeconomics in textbooks since the 1940s, read Paul Samuelson's, "Credo of a Lucky Textbook Author," *Journal of Economic Perspectives*, Spring 1997, 153–160.

In the introduction to *Studies in Business Cycle Theory* (Cambridge, MA: MIT Press, 1981), Robert Lucas develops his approach to macroeconomics, and gives a guide to his contributions.

The paper that launched real business cycle theory is Edward Prescott, "Theory Ahead of Business Cycle Measurement," *Federal Reserve Bank of Minneapolis Review*, Fall 1986, 9–22. It is not easy reading.

For more on new Keynesian economics, read David Romer, "The New Keynesian Synthesis," *Journal of Economic Perspectives*, Winter 1993, 5–22.

For more on new growth theory, read Paul Romer, "The Origins of Endogenous Growth," *Journal of Economic Perspectives*, Winter 1994, 3–22. A more complete treatment is given in Charles Jones *An Introduction to Economic Growth*, 2nd ed., (New York, NY: W.W. Norton, 2002).

In a lighter mode, for a well-written set of essays on many economists and their ideas, read David Warsh, *Economic Principals: Masters and Mavericks of Modern Economics* (New York, NY: Free Press, 1993).

Most economics journals are heavy on mathematics and are hard to read. But a few make an effort to be more friendly. The *Journal of Economic Perspectives* in particular has nontechnical articles on current economic research and issues. The *Brookings Papers on Economic Activity*, published twice a year, analyze current macroeconomic problems, as does *Economic Policy*, published in Europe, which focuses more on European issues.

Most regional Federal Reserve Banks also publish reviews with easy-to-read articles; these reviews are available free of charge. Among these are the *Economic Review* published by the Cleveland Fed, the *Economic Review* published by the Kansas City Fed, the *New England Economic Review* published by the Boston Fed, and the *Review* published by the Minneapolis Fed.

More advanced treatments of current macroeconomic theory—roughly at the level of a first graduate course in macroeconomics—are given by David Romer, *Advanced Macroeconomics*, 2nd ed., (New York: McGraw-Hill, 2001) and by Olivier Blanchard and Stanley Fischer, *Lectures on Macroeconomics* (Cambridge, MA: MIT Press, 1989).

Appendices

APPENDIX 1 An Introduction to National Income and Product Accounts

This appendix introduces the basic structure and the terms used in the national income and product accounts. The basic measure of aggregate activity is gross domestic product, or GDP. The **national income and product accounts (NIPA** or, simply, **national accounts**) are organized around two disaggregations of GDP. The first looks at *income*: Who receives what? The other looks at *product*: What is produced, and who buys it?

The Income Side

Table A1-1 looks at the income side of GDP—who receives what.

The top part of the table (lines 1–9) goes from GDP to national income, the sum of the incomes received by the different factors of production.

- The starting point, in line 1, is **gross domestic product**, or **GDP**. It is defined as *the market value of the goods and services produced by labor and property located in the United States.*

  The next three lines take us from GDP to **GNP, the gross national product** (line 4). GNP is an alternative measure of aggregate output. It is defined as *the market value of the goods and services produced by labor and property supplied by U.S. residents.*

  Until recently, most countries used GNP rather than GDP as the main measure of aggregate activity. The emphasis in the U.S. national accounts shifted from GNP to GDP in 1991. The difference between the two comes from the distinction between "located in the United States" (used to define GDP) and "supplied by U.S. residents" (used to define GNP). For example, profit from a U.S.-owned plant in Japan is not included in U.S. GDP, but *is* included in U.S. GNP.

  Thus, to go from GDP to GNP, we must first add **receipts of factor income from the rest of the world**, which is income from U.S. capital or U.S. residents abroad (line 2), and then subtract **payments of factor income to the rest of the world**, which is income received by foreign capital and foreign residents in the United States (line 3). In 2001, payments to the rest of the world exceeded receipts from the rest of the world by $6 billion, so GNP was smaller than GDP by $6 billion.
- The next step takes us from GNP to **NNP, the net national product** (line 6). The difference between GNP and NNP is the depreciation of capital, which is called **consumption of fixed capital** in the national accounts.
- Finally, lines 7 to 9 take us from NNP to **national income** (line 9), defined as the *income that originates in the production of goods and services supplied by residents of the United States.*

  The main step in going from NNP to national income is to subtract **indirect taxes** (line 7) (sales taxes) that decrease the amount left for factor income—the payments going to the various factors of production. There are also a few other corrections, which sum to $160 billion in line 8. Most of them you can safely ignore. One, called the *statistical discrepancy* however, deserves a short discussion.

  National income is actually constructed in two independent ways. One is from the top down, starting from GDP constructed from the product side and going through the steps we have just gone through in Table A1-1. The other is from the bottom up, by adding the different components of factor income (compensation of employees, corporate profits, and so on). The two measures typically differ, and the difference is called the "statistical discrepancy." In 2001, national income computed from the top down (the number in line 9) was less than national income computed from the bottom up by

Table A1-1 GDP: The Income Side, 2001 (billions of dollars)

From gross domestic product to national income:		
1 **Gross domestic product** (GDP)	10,208	
2 Plus: receipts of factor income from the rest of the world		335
3 Minus: payments of factor income to the rest of the world		−341
4 Equals: **Gross national product**	10,202	
5 Minus: consumption of fixed capital		−1,351
6 Equals: **Net national product**	8,851	
7 Minus: indirect taxes		−794
8 Minus: other, including statistical discrepancy		160
9 Equals: **National income**	8217	
The decomposition of national income:		
10 Compensation of employees	6010	
11 Wages and salaries		5098
12 Supplements to wages and salaries		912
13 Corporate profits	767	
14 Net interest	554	
15 Proprietors' income	743	
16 Rental income of persons	143	

Source: Survey of Current Business, April 2002, Tables 1-9 and 1-14.

$149 billion. The statistical discrepancy is a reminder of the statistical problems involved in constructing the national income accounts.

The bottom part of the table (lines 10–16) disaggregates national income into different types of income.

- **Compensation of employees** (line 10), or labor income, is by far the largest component, accounting for 73.1% of national income. It is the sum of wages and salaries (line 11) and of supplements to wages and salaries (line 12). These range from employer contributions for social insurance (by far the largest item) to exotic items such as employer contributions to marriage fees to justices of the peace.
- **Corporate profits** (line 13). Profits are revenues minus costs (including interest payments) and minus depreciation.
- **Net interest** (line 14) is the interest paid by firms minus the interest received by firms, plus interest received from the rest of the world minus interest paid to the rest of the world.

  In 2001, most of net interest represented net interest paid by firms: The United States received about as much in interest from the rest of the world as it paid to the rest to the world. So the sum of corporate profits plus net interest paid by firms was approximately \$767 billion + \$554 billion = \$1321 billion, or about 16.1% of national income.
- **Proprietors' income** (line 15) is the income received by persons who are self-employed. It is defined as *the income of sole proprietorships, partnerships, and tax-exempt cooperatives.*
- **Rental income of persons** (line 16) is equal to the income from the rental of real property, minus depreciation on this real property. Houses produce housing services; rental income measures the income received for these services.

  If the national accounts counted only actual rents, rental income would depend on the proportion of apartments and houses that were rented versus owner occupied. For example, if everybody became the owner of the apartment or the house in which they lived, rental income would go to zero, and thus measured GDP would drop. To avoid this problem, national accounts treat houses and apartments as if they were all rented out. Thus, rental income is constructed as actual rents plus *imputed* rents on those houses and apartments that are owner occupied.

Table A1-2	From National Income to Personal Disposable Income, 2001 (billions of dollars)		
1	**National income**	8217	
2	Minus: corporate profits		−767
3	Plus: personal dividend income		+416
4	Minus: net interest		−554
5	Plus: personal interest income		+993
6	Plus: government and business transfers		+1149
7	Minus: contributions for social insurance		−731
8	Equals: **Personal income**	8723	
9	Minus: personal tax and nontax payments		−1306
10	Equals: **Personal disposable income**	7417	

Source: Survey of Current Business, April 2001, Tables 1-9 and 2-1.

Before we move to the product side, Table A1-2 shows how we can go from national income to personal disposable income—the income available to consumers after they have received transfers and paid taxes.

- Not all national income (line 1) is distributed to persons. Some of the corporate profits are retained by firms. So, the first step is to subtract all corporate profits (line 2, also line 13 in Table A1-1), and add back that part of profits that is distributed to persons, *personal dividend income* (line 3).
- Similarly, not all interest payments paid by firms go to persons. Some go to banks, some go abroad. So the next step is to subtract all net interest payments by firms and by the rest of the world (line 4, also line 14 in Table A1-1), and add back all interest payments received by persons (line 5).
- Finally, people receive income not only from production, but also from transfers (line 6). Transfers accounted for $1149 billion in 2001, of which all but $35 billion came from the government. From these transfers must be subtracted contributions for social insurance paid by workers, $731 billion (line 7).
- The net result of these adjustments is **personal income**, the income actually received by persons (line 8). **Personal disposable income** (line 10) is then equal to personal income minus personal tax and nontax payments (line 9). In 2001, personal disposable income was equal to $7417 billion, or about 72.6% of GDP.

The Product Side

Table A1-3 looks at the product side of the national accounts, at who buys what.

Let us start with the three components of domestic demand: consumption, investment, and government spending.

- Consumption, called **personal consumption expenditures** (line 2), is by far the largest component of demand, accounting for 69% of GDP. It is defined as *the sum of goods and services purchased by persons resident in the United States.*

  In the same way that they include imputed rental income on the income side, national accounts include imputed housing services as part of consumption. Owners of a house are assumed to consume housing services, for a price equal to the imputed rental income of that house.

  Consumption is disaggregated into three components, purchases of **durable goods** (line 3), **nondurable goods** (line 4), and **services** (line 5). Durable goods are commodities that can be stored and have an average life of at least three years; automobile purchases are the largest item here. Nondurable goods are commodities that can be stored but have a life of less than three years. Services are commodities that cannot be stored, so must be consumed at the place and time of purchase.
- Investment is called **gross private domestic fixed investment** (line 6). It is the sum of two very different components:

  Nonresidential investment (line 7) is the purchase of new capital goods by firms. These may be either **structures** (line 8)—mostly new plants—or **equipment and software** (line 9), such as machines, computers, or office equipment.

Table A1-3 GDP: The Product Side, 2001 (billions of dollars)

1	**Gross domestic product**	10208		
2	Personal consumption expenditures	7064		
3	Durable goods		858	
4	Nondurable goods		2055	
5	Services		4151	
6	Gross private domestic fixed investment	1692		
7	Nonresidential		1246	
8	Structures			330
9	Equipment and Software			916
10	Residential		446	
11	Government purchases	1839		
12	Federal		616	
13	National Defense			399
14	Nondefense			217
15	State and local		1223	
16	Net exports	−330		
17	Exports		1050	
18	Imports		−1380	
19	Changes in business inventories	−58		

Source: *Survey of Current Business,* April 2002, Table 1-1.

Residential investment (line 10) is the purchase of new houses or apartments by persons.

- **Government purchases** (line 11) are equal to purchases of goods by the government plus compensation of government employees. (Government employees are thought of as selling their services to the government.)

  Government purchases are the sum of purchases by the federal government (line 12) (which themselves can be disaggregated between spending on national defense [line 13] and nondefense spending [line 14]) and purchases by state and local governments (line 15).

  Note that government purchases do not include transfers from the government, or interest payments on government debt. These do not correspond to purchases of either goods or services, and so are not included here. This means that the number for government purchases you see in Table A1-3 is substantially smaller than the number you typically hear for government spending—which includes transfers and interest payments.

- The sum of consumption, investment, and government purchases gives the demand for goods by U.S. firms, U.S. persons, and the U.S. government. If the United States were a closed economy, this would be the same as the demand for U.S. goods. But because the U.S. economy is open, the two numbers are different. To get to the demand for U.S. goods, we must make two adjustments. First, we must add the foreign purchases of U.S. goods, **exports** (line 17). Second, we must subtract U.S. purchases of foreign goods, **imports** (line 18). In 2001, exports were less than imports by $330 billion. Thus, **net exports** (or, equivalently, the **trade balance**) was equal to minus $330 billion (line 16).
- Adding consumption, investment, government purchases, and net exports gives the total purchases of U.S. goods. Production may, however, be less than those purchases if firms satisfy the difference by decreasing inventories. Or production may be greater than purchases, in which case firms accumulate inventories. The last line of Table A1-3 gives **changes in business inventories** (line 19), also sometimes

called (rather misleadingly) "inventory investment." It is defined as the *change in the physical volume of inventories held by business.* The change in business inventories can be positive or negative. In 2001, it was negative: U.S. production was lower than total purchases of U.S. goods by $58 billion.

Warning

National accounts give an internally consistent description of aggregate activity. But underlying these accounts are many choices of what to include and what not to include, where to put some types of income or spending, and so on. Here are three examples:

- Work within the home is not counted in GDP. If, for example, two women decide to babysit each other's child rather than take care of their own child and pay each other for the babysitting services, measured GDP will go up, while true GDP clearly does not change. The solution would be to count work within the home in GDP, the same way that we impute rents for owner-occupied housing. But, so far, this has not been done.
- The purchase of a house is treated as an investment, and housing services are then treated as part of consumption. Contrast this with the treatment of automobiles. Despite the fact that they provide services for a long time—although not as long a time as houses do—purchases of automobiles are not treated as investment. They are treated as consumption and appear in the national accounts only in the year in which they are bought.
- Firms' purchases of machines are treated as investment. The purchase of education is treated as consumption of education services. But education is clearly in part an investment: People acquire it in part to increase their future income.

The list could go on. However, the purpose of these examples is not to make you conclude that national accounts are wrong. Most of the accounting decisions we just saw were made for good reasons, often because of data availability or for simplicity of treatment. Rather, the point is that to use national accounts best, you should understand their logic, but also understand the choices that have been made and thus their limitations.

Key Terms

- national income and product accounts (NIPA), national accounts, A-1
- gross domestic product (GDP), A-1
- gross national product (GNP), A-1
- receipts of factor income from the rest of the world, payments of factor income to the rest of the world, A-1
- net national product (NNP), A-1
- consumption of fixed capital, A-1
- national income, A-1
- indirect taxes, A-1
- compensation of employees, A-2
- corporate profits, A-2
- net interest, A-2
- proprietors' income, A-2
- rental income of persons, A-2
- personal income, A-3
- personal disposable income, A-3
- personal consumption expenditures, A-3
- durable goods, nondurable goods, and services, A-3
- gross private domestic fixed investment, A-3
- nonresidential investment, structures, equipment and software, A-3
- residential investment, A-4
- government purchases, A-4
- exports, imports, A-4
- net exports, trade balance, A-4
- changes in business inventories, A-4

Further Reading

For more details, read "A Guide to the NIPAs," *Survey of Current Business,* Bureau of Economic Analysis, June 2001 (**www.bea.doc.gov/bea/an/nipaguid.htm**).

APPENDIX 2 A Math Refresher

This appendix presents the mathematical tools and the mathematical results that are used in this book.

Geometric Series

Definition. A geometric series is a sum of numbers of the form

$$1 + x + x^2 + \ldots + x^n$$

where x is a number that may be greater or smaller than one, and x^n denotes x to the power n, that is, x times itself n times.

Examples of such series are:

- The sum of spending in each round of the multiplier (Chapter 3). If c is the marginal propensity to consume, then the sum of increases in spending after n rounds is given by

$$1 + c + c^2 + \ldots + c^{n-1}$$

- The present discounted value of a sequence of payments of one dollar each year for n years (Chapter 14), when the interest rate is equal to i

$$1+\frac{1}{1+i}+\frac{1}{(1+i)^2}+\ldots+\frac{1}{(1+i)^{n-1}}$$

We usually have two questions we want to answer when encountering such a series: What is the sum? Does the sum explode as we let n increase, or does it reach a finite limit; if so, what is that limit?

The following propositions tell you what you need to know to answer these questions.

Proposition 1 tells you how to compute the sum:

Proposition 1.

$$1+x+x^2+\ldots+x^n=\frac{1-x^{n+1}}{1-x} \qquad (A2.1)$$

Here is the proof: Multiply the sum by $(1 - x)$, and use the fact that $x^a x^b = x^{a+b}$ (that is, one has to add exponents when multiplying):

$$\begin{aligned}(1+x+x^2+\ldots+x^n)(1-x) &= 1+x+x^2+\ldots+x^n \\ &\quad -x-x^2-\ldots-x^n-x^{n+1} \\ &= 1-x^{n+1}\end{aligned}$$

All the terms on the right except for the first and the last cancel. Dividing both sides by $(1 - x)$ gives equation (A2.1).

This formula can be used for any x and any n. If, for example, x is 0.9 and n is 10, then the sum is equal to 6.86. If x is 1.2 and n is 10, then the sum is 32.15.

Proposition 2 tells you what happens as n gets large:

Proposition 2. If x is less than one, the sum goes to $1/(1 - x)$ as n gets large. If x is equal to or greater than one, the sum explodes as n gets large.

Here is the proof: If x is less than one, then x^n goes to zero as n gets large. Thus, from equation (A2.1), the sum goes to $1/(1 - x)$. If x is greater than one, then x^n becomes larger and larger as n increases, $1 - x^n$ becomes a larger and larger negative number, and the ratio $(1 - x^n)/(1 - x)$ becomes a larger and larger positive number. Thus, the sum explodes as n gets large.

Application from Chapter 14: Consider the present value of a payment of $1 forever, starting next year, when the interest rate is i. The present value is given by

$$\frac{1}{(1+i)}+\frac{1}{(1+i)^2}+\ldots \qquad (A2.2)$$

Factoring out $1/(1 + i)$, rewrite this present value as

$$\frac{1}{(1+i)}\left[1+\frac{1}{(1+i)}+\ldots\right]$$

The term in brackets is a geometric series, with $x = 1/(1 + i)$. As the interest rate i is positive, x is less than one. Applying Proposition 2, when n gets large, the term in brackets equals

$$\frac{1}{1-\frac{1}{(1+i)}}=\frac{(1+i)}{(1+i-1)}=\frac{(1+i)}{i}$$

Replacing the term in brackets in the previous equation by $(1 + i)/i$ gives

$$\frac{1}{(1+i)}\left[\frac{(1+i)}{i}\right]=\frac{1}{i}$$

The present value of a sequence of payments of one dollar a year forever, starting next year, is equal to $1 divided by the interest rate. If i is equal to 5% per year, the present value equals $1/0.05 = $20.

Useful Approximations

Throughout this book, we use several approximations that make computations easier. These approximations are most reliable when the variables x, y, and z below are small, say, between 0 and 10%. The numerical examples in Propositions 3 through 10 below are based on the values $x = .05$ and $y = .03$.

Proposition 3.

$$(1 + x)(1 + y) \approx (1 + x + y) \qquad (A2.3)$$

Here is the proof. Expanding $(1 + x)(1 + y)$ gives $(1 + x)(1 + y) = 1 + x + y + xy$. If x and y are small, then the product xy is very small and can be ignored as an approximation (for example, if $x = .05$ and $y = .03$, then $xy = .0015$). So $(1 + x)(1 + y)$ is approximately equal to $(1 + x + y)$.

For the values x and y above, for example, the approximation gives 1.08 compared to an exact value of 1.0815.

Application from Chapter 18: Arbitrage between domestic bonds and foreign bonds leads to the following relation:

$$(1+i_t)=(1+i_t^*)\left(1+\frac{(E_{t+1}^e-E_t)}{E_t}\right)$$

Using Proposition 3 on the right-hand side of the equation gives

$$(1+i_t^*)\left(1+\frac{(E_{t+1}^e-E_t)}{E_t}\right)\approx\left(1+i_t^*+\frac{(E_{t+1}^e-E_t)}{E_t}\right)$$

Using this expression to replace the term on the left side of the arbitrage equation gives

$$(1+i_t)\approx\left(1+i_t^*+\frac{(E_{t+1}^e-E_t)}{E_t}\right)$$

Subtracting 1 from both sides gives

$$i_t\approx i_t^*+\frac{(E_{t+1}^e-E_t)}{E_t}$$

The domestic interest rate is approximately equal to the foreign interest rate plus the expected rate of depreciation of the domestic currency.

Proposition 4.

$$(1 + x)^2 \approx 1 + 2x \qquad (A2.4)$$

The proof follows directly from Proposition 3, with $y = x$. For the value of $x = .05$, the approximation gives 1.10, compared to an exact value of 1.1025.

Application from Chapter 15: From arbitrage, the relation between the two-year interest rate and the current and the expected one-year interest rates is given by

$$(1 + i_{2t})^2 = (1 + i_{1t})(1 + i_{1t+1}^e)$$

Using Proposition 4 for the left side of the equation gives

$$(1 + i_{2t})^2 \approx 1 + 2i_{2t}$$

Using Proposition 3 for the right side of the equation gives

$$(1 + i_{1t})(1 + i_{1t+1}^e) \approx 1 + i_{1t} + i_{1t+1}^e$$

Replacing in the original arbitrage relation gives

$$1 + 2i_{2t} = 1 + i_{1t} + i_{1t+1}^e$$

Or, reorganizing:

$$i_{2t}=\frac{(i_{1t}+i_{1t+1}^e)}{2}$$

The two-year interest rate is approximately equal to the average of the current and the expected one-year interest rates.

Proposition 5.

$$(1 + x)^n \approx 1 + nx \qquad (A2.5)$$

The proof follows by repeated application of Propositions 3 and 4. For example, $(1 + x)^3 = (1 + x)^2 (1 + x) \approx (1 + 2x)(1 + x)$ by Proposition 4, $\approx (1 + 2x + x) = 1 + 3x$ by Proposition 3.

The approximation becomes worse as n increases, however. For example, for $x = .05$ and $n = 5$, the approximation gives 1.25, compared to an exact value of 1.2763. For $n = 10$, the approximation gives 1.50, compared to an exact value of 1.63.

Proposition 6.

$$\frac{(1+x)}{(1+y)}\approx(1+x-y) \qquad (A2.6)$$

Here is the proof: Consider the product of $(1 + x - y)(1 + y)$. Expanding this product gives $(1 + x - y)(1 + y) = 1 + x + xy - y^2$. If both x and y are small, then xy and y^2 are very small, so $(1 + x - y)(1 + y) \approx (1 + x)$. Dividing both sides of this approximation by $(1 + y)$ gives the proposition above.

For the values of $x + .05$ and $y = .03$, the approximation gives 1.02, while the correct value is 1.019.

Application from Chapter 14: The real interest rate is defined by

$$(1+r_t)=\frac{(1+i_t)}{(1+\pi_t^e)}$$

Using Proposition 6 gives

$$(1+r_t)\approx(1+i_t-\pi_t^e)$$

Simplifying:

$$r_t\approx i_t-\pi_t^e$$

This gives us the approximation we use at many points in this book: The real interest rate is approximately equal to the nominal interest rate minus expected inflation.

These approximations are also very convenient when dealing with growth rates. Define the rate of growth of x by $g_x \equiv \Delta x/x$, and similarly for z, g_z and y, g_y. The numerical examples below are based on the values $g_x = .05$ and $g_y = .03$.

Proposition 7. If $z = xy$, then

$$g_z \approx g_x + g_y \tag{A2.7}$$

Here is the proof: Let Δz be the increase in z when x increases by Δx and y increases by Δy. Then, by definition,

$$z+\Delta z=(x+\Delta x)(y+\Delta y)$$

Divide both sides by z.
The left side becomes

$$\frac{(z+\Delta z)}{z}=\left(1+\frac{\Delta z}{z}\right)$$

The right side becomes

$$\frac{(x+\Delta x)(y+\Delta y)}{z}=\frac{(x+\Delta x)}{x}\frac{(y+\Delta y)}{y}=\left(1+\frac{\Delta x}{x}\right)\left(1+\frac{\Delta y}{y}\right)$$

where the first equality follows from the fact that $z = xy$, the second equality from simplifying each of the two fractions.

Using the expressions for the left and right sides gives

$$\left(1+\frac{\Delta z}{z}\right)=\left(1+\frac{\Delta x}{x}\right)\left(1+\frac{\Delta y}{y}\right)$$

Or, equivalently,

$$(1+g_z)=(1+g_x)(1+g_y)$$

From Proposition 3, $(1+g_z)\approx(1+g_x+g_y)$, or, equivalently,

$$g_z \approx g_x + g_y$$

For $g_x = 0.05$ and $g_y = 0.03$, the approximation gives $g_z = 8\%$, while the correct value is 8.15%.

Application from Chapter 13: Let the production function be of the form $Y = NA$, where Y is production, N is employment, and A is productivity. Denoting the growth rates of Y, N, and A by g_Y, g_N, and g_A, respectively, Proposition 7 implies

$$g_Y \approx g_N + g_A$$

The rate of output growth is approximately equal to the rate of employment growth plus the rate of productivity growth.

Proposition 8. If $z = x/y$, then

$$g_z \approx g_x - g_y \tag{A2.8}$$

Here is the proof: Let Δz be the increase in z, when x increases by Δx and y increases by Δy. Then, by definition,

$$z+\Delta z=\frac{x+\Delta x}{y+\Delta y}$$

Divide both sides by z
The left side becomes

$$\frac{(z+\Delta z)}{z}=\left(1+\frac{\Delta z}{z}\right)$$

The right side becomes

$$\frac{(x+\Delta x)}{(y+\Delta y)}\frac{1}{z}=\frac{(x+\Delta x)}{(y+\Delta y)}\frac{y}{x}=\frac{(x+\Delta x)/x}{(y+\Delta y)/y}=\frac{1+(\Delta x/x)}{1+(\Delta y/y)}$$

where the first equality comes from the fact that $z = x/y$, the second equality comes from rearranging terms, and the third equality comes from simplifying.

Using the expressions for the left and right sides gives

$$1+\Delta z/z=\frac{1+(\Delta x/x)}{1+(\Delta y/y)}$$

Or, substituting:

$$1+g_z=\frac{1+g_x}{1+g_y}$$

From Proposition 6, $(1+g_z)\approx(1+g_x-g_y)$, or equivalently,

$$g_z \approx g_x - g_y$$

For $g_x = .05$ and $g_y = .03$, the approximation gives $g_z = 2\%$, while the correct value is 1.9%.

Application from Chapter 9: Let aggregate demand be given by $Y = \gamma M/P$, where Y is output, M is nominal money, P is the price level, and γ is a constant. It fol lows from Propositions 7 and 8 that

$$g_Y \approx g_\gamma + g_M - \pi$$

where π is the rate of growth of prices, equivalently the rate of inflation. As γ is constant, g_γ is equal to zero. Thus,

$$g_Y \approx g_M - \pi$$

The rate of output growth is approximately equal to the rate of growth of nominal money minus the rate of inflation.

Functions

I use functions informally in this book, as a way of denoting how a variable depends on one or more other variables.

In some cases, I look at how a variable Y moves with a variable X. I write this relation as

$$\underset{(+)}{Y = f(X)}$$

A plus sign below X indicates a positive relation: An increase in X leads to an increase in Y. A minus sign below X indicates a negative relation: An increase in X leads to a decrease in Y.

In some cases, I allow the variable Y to depend on more than one variable. For example, I allow Y to depend on X and Z:

$$\underset{(+,\ -)}{Y = f(X, Z)}$$

The signs indicate that an increase in X leads to an increase in Y, and that an increase in Z leads to a decrease in Y.

An example of such a function is the investment function (5.1) in Chapter 5:

$$\underset{(+,-)}{I = I(Y, i)}$$

This equation says that investment, I, increases with production, Y, and decreases with the interest rate, i.

In some cases, it is reasonable to assume that the relation between two or more variables is **linear**. A given increase in X always leads to the same increase in Y. In that case, the function is given by

$$Y = a + bX$$

This relation can be represented by a line giving Y for any value of X.

The parameter a gives the value of Y when X is equal to zero. It is called the **intercept** because it gives the value of Y when the line representing the relation "intercepts" (crosses) the vertical axis.

The parameter b tells us by how much Y increases when X increases by 1. It is called the **slope** because it is equal to the slope of the line representing the relation.

A simple linear relation is the relation $Y = X$, which is represented by the 45-degree line and has a slope of one. Another example of a linear relation is the consumption function (3.2) in Chapter 3:

$$C = c_0 + c_1 Y_D$$

where C is consumption and Y_D is disposable income. The parameter c_0 tells us what consumption would be if disposable income were equal to zero. The parameter c_1 tells us by how much consumption increases when income increases by 1 unit; c_1 is called the marginal propensity to consume.

Logarithmic Scales

A variable that grows at a constant growth rate increases by larger and larger increments over time. Take a variable, X, that grows over time at a constant growth rate, say, at 3% per year.

- Start in year 0 and assume $X = 2$. So, a 3% increase in X represents an increase of 0.06 (0.03 times 2).
- Go to year 20. X is now equal to $2(1.03)^{20} = 3.61$. A 3% increase now represents an increase of 0.11 (0.03 times 3.61).
- Go to year 100. X is equal to $2(1.03)^{100} = 38.4$. A 3% increase represents an increase of 1.15 (0.03 times 38.4), so an increase about 20 times larger than in year 0.

If we plot X against time using a standard (linear) vertical scale, the plot looks like Figure A2-1, panel (a). The increases in X are larger and larger over time (0.06 in year 0, 0.11 in year 20, 1.15 in year 100). The curve representing X against time becomes steeper and steeper.

Another way of representing the evolution of X is to use a *logarithmic scale* to measure X on the vertical axis. The property of a logarithmic scale is that the same *proportional* increase in this variable is

Figure A2-1

(a) The Evolution of X (using a linear scale)
(b) The Evolution of X (using a logarithmic scale)

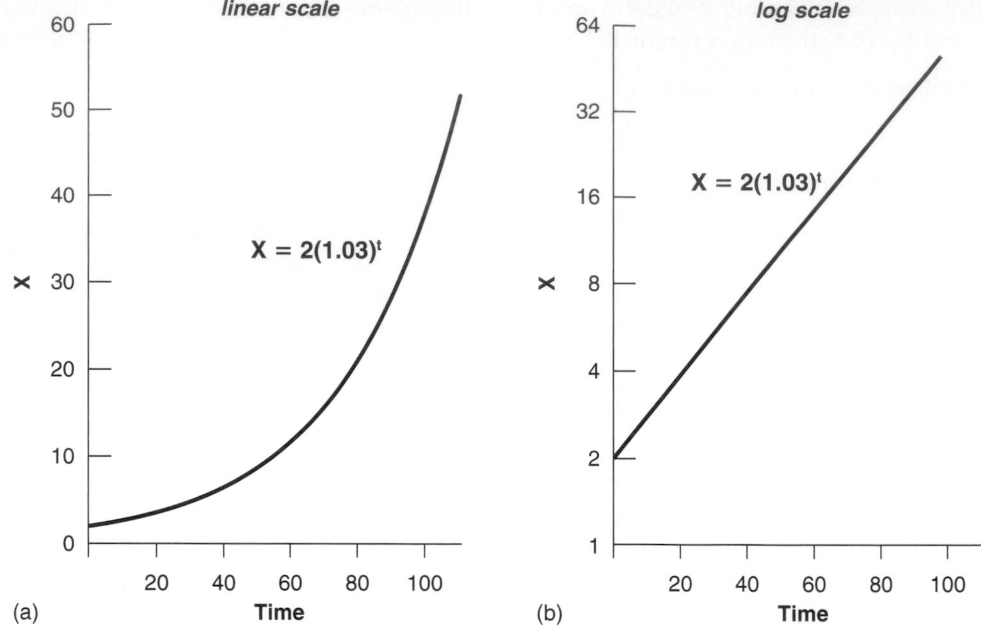

represented by the same vertical distance on the scale. So, the behavior of a variable such as X which increases by the same proportional increase (3%) each year—is now represented by a straight line. Figure A2-1, panel (b) represents the behavior of X, this time using a logarithmic scale on the vertical axis. The fact that the relation is represented by a line indicates that X is growing at a constant growth rate over time. The higher the rate of growth, the steeper the line.

In contrast to X, economic variables such as GDP do not grow at a constant growth rate every year. Their growth rate may be higher in some decades, lower in others. A recession may lead to a few years of negative growth. Yet, when looking at their evolution over time, it is often more informative to use a logarithmic scale rather than a linear scale. Let's see why.

Figure A2-2, panel (a) plots real U.S. GDP from 1890 to 2000 using a standard (linear) scale. Because

Figure A2-2

(a) The Evolution of U.S. GDP (using a linear scale)
(b) The Evolution of U.S. GDP (using a logarithmic scale) from 1890–2000

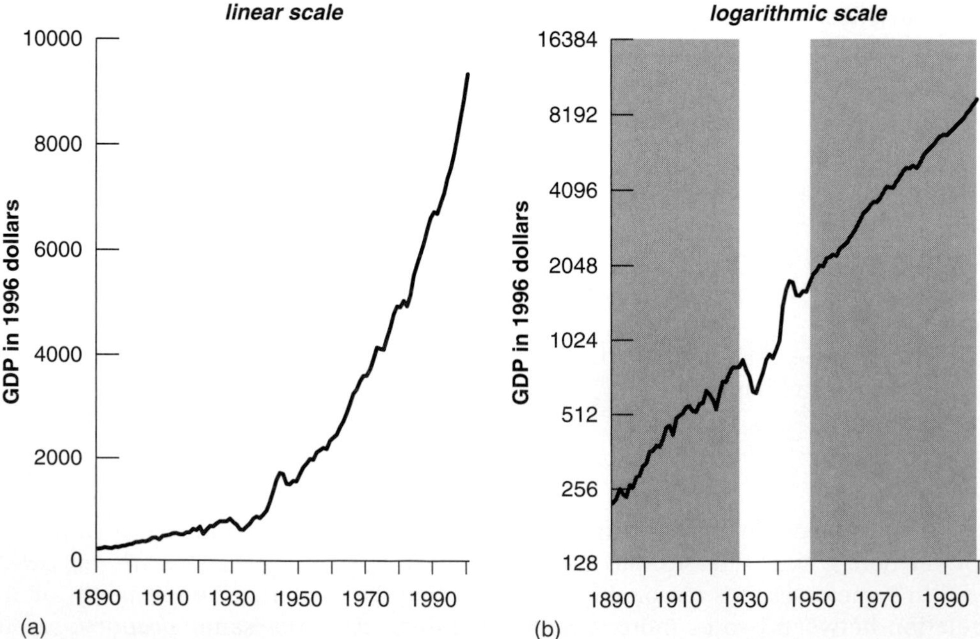

real U.S. GDP is about 43 times bigger in 2000 than in 1890, the same proportional increase in GDP is 43 times bigger in 2000 than in 1890. So the curve representing the evolution of GDP becomes steeper and steeper over time. It is very difficult to see from the figure whether the U.S. economy is growing faster or slower than it was 50 years or 100 years ago.

Figure A2-2, panel (b) plots U.S. GDP from 1890 to 2000, now using a logarithmic scale. If the growth rate of GDP was the same every year—so the proportional increase in GDP was the same every year—the evolution of GDP would be represented by a line—the same way as the evolution of X was represented by a straight line in Figure A2-1, panel (b). Because the growth rate of GDP is not constant from year to year—so the proportional increase in GDP is not the same every year—the evolution of GDP is no longer represented by a line. But it does not explode over time the way it did in Figure A2-2, panel (a). And it is very informative:

- If, in Figure A2-2, panel (b), we were to draw a line to fit the curve from 1890 to 1929, and another line to fit the curve from 1950 to 2000 (the two periods are represented by the shaded areas in Figure A2-2, panel [b]), the two lines would have roughly the same slope. What this tells us is that the average growth rate was roughly the same during the two periods.
- The decline in output from 1929 to 1933 is very visible in Figure A2-2, panel (b). So is the strong recovery of output which follows. By the 1950s, output appears to be back to its old trend line. This suggests that the Great Depression was not associated with a permanently lower level of output.

Note, in both cases, that you could not have derived these conclusions by looking at Figure A2-2, panel (a), but you can derive them by looking at Figure A2-2, panel (b). This shows the usefulness of using a logarithmic scale.

Key Terms

- linear relation, A-9
- intercept, A-9
- slope, A-9

APPENDIX 3 An Introduction to Econometrics

How do we know that consumption depends on disposable income?

How do we know the value of the propensity to consume?

To answer these questions, and, more generally, to estimate behavioral relations and find out the values of the relevant parameters, economists use *econometrics*—the set of statistical techniques designed for use in economics. Econometrics can get very mathematical, but the basic principles behind econometric techniques are simple.

My purpose in this appendix is to show you these basic principles. I shall use as an example the consumption function introduced in Chapter 3, and I shall concentrate on estimating c_1, the propensity to consume out of disposable income.

Changes in Consumption and Changes in Disposable Income

The propensity to consume tells us by how much consumption changes for a given change in disposable income. A natural first step is simply to plot changes in consumption versus changes in disposable income and see how the relation between the two looks. You can see this in Figure A3-1.

The vertical axis in Figure A3-1 measures the annual change in consumption minus the average annual change in consumption for each year from 1960 to 2000. More precisely, let C_t denote consumption in year t. Let ΔC_t denote $C_t - C_{t-1}$, the change in consumption from year $t-1$ to year t. Let $\overline{\Delta C}$ denote the average annual change in consumption since 1960. The variable measured on the vertical axis is constructed as $\Delta C_t - \overline{\Delta C}$. A positive value of the variable represents an increase in consumption larger than average, a negative value an increase in consumption smaller than average.

Similarly, the horizontal axis measures the annual change in disposable income, minus the average annual change in disposable income since 1960, $\Delta Y_{Dt} - \overline{\Delta Y_D}$.

A particular square in the figure gives the deviations of the change in consumption and disposable income from their respective means for a particular year between 1960 and 2000. In 2000, for example, the change in consumption was higher than average by \$174 billion, the change in disposable income was higher than average by \$126 billion. (For our purposes, it is not important to know to which year each square refers, just what the set of points in the diagram looks like. So, except for 2000, the years are not indicated in Figure A3-1.)

Figure A3-1 suggests two main conclusions:

1 There is a clear positive relation between changes in consumption and changes in disposable income. Most of the points lie in the upper-right and lower-left quadrants of the figure: When disposable

Figure A3-1

Changes in Consumption Versus Changes in Disposable Income, 1960–2000

There is a clear positive relation between changes in consumption and changes in disposable income.

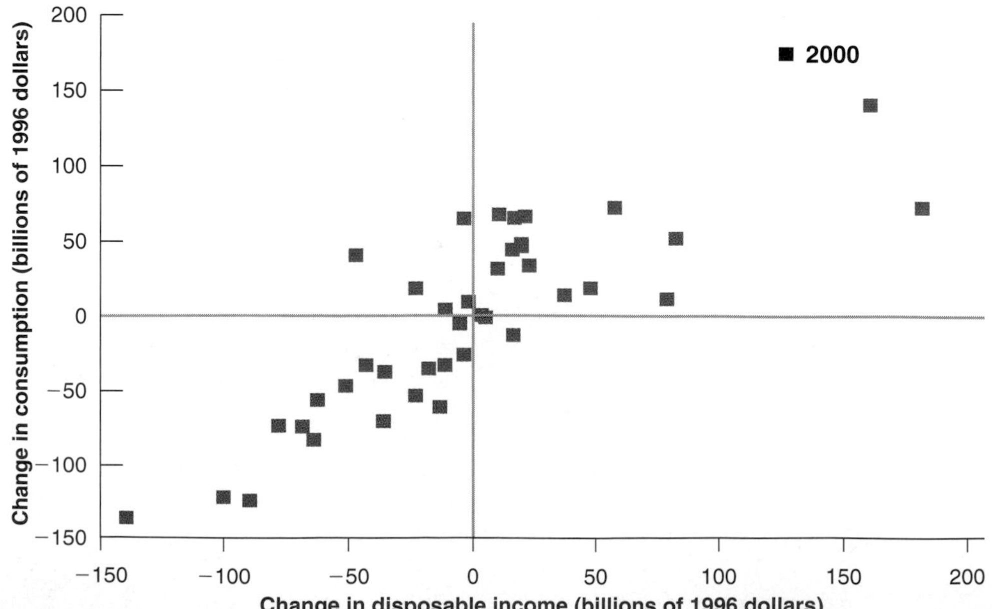

income increases by more than average, consumption also typically increases by more than average; when disposable income increases by less than average, so typically does consumption.

2 The relation between the two variables is good but not perfect. In particular, some points lie in the upper-left quadrant: These points correspond to years when smaller-than-average changes in disposable income were associated with higher-than-average changes in consumption.

Econometrics allows us to state these two conclusions more precisely and to get an estimate of the propensity to consume. Using an econometrics software package, we can find the line that fits the cloud of points in Figure A3-1 best. This line-fitting process is called **ordinary least squares (OLS)**. The term *least squares* comes from the fact that the line has the property of minimizing the sum of the squared distances of the points to the line—thus gives the "least squares" The word *ordinary* comes from the fact that this is the simplest method used in econometrics. The estimated equation corresponding to the line is called a **regression**, and the line itself is called the **regression line**.

In our case, the estimated equation is given by

$$(\Delta C_t - \overline{\Delta C}) = 0.88(\Delta Y_{Dt} - \overline{\Delta Y_D}) + \text{residual} \qquad \bar{R}^2 = 0.70 \tag{A3.1}$$

The regression line corresponding to this estimated equation is drawn in Figure A3-2. Equation (A3.1) reports two important numbers (econometrics packages give more information than reported here; a typical printout, together with further explanations, is given in the Focus box "A Guide to Understanding Econometric Results"):

- The first important number is the estimated propensity to consume. The equation tells us that an increase in disposable income of \$1 billion above normal is typically associated with an increase in consumption of \$0.88 billion above normal. In other words, the estimated propensity to consume is 0.88. It is positive but smaller than 1.
- The second important number is $\bar{R}^2$, which is a measure of how well the regression line fits.

Having estimated the effect of disposable income on consumption, we can decompose the change in consumption for each year into that part which is due to the change in disposable income—the first term on the right in equation (A3.1)—and the rest, which is called the **residual**. For example, the residual for 2000 is indicated in Figure A3-2 by the vertical distance from the point representing 2000 to the regression line.

If all the points in Figure A3-2 were exactly on the estimated line, all residuals would be zero; all changes in consumption would be explained by changes in disposable income. As you can see, however, this is not the case. $\bar{R}^2$ is the statistic that tells us how well the line fits. $\bar{R}^2$ is always between 0 and 1. A value of 1 would imply that the relation

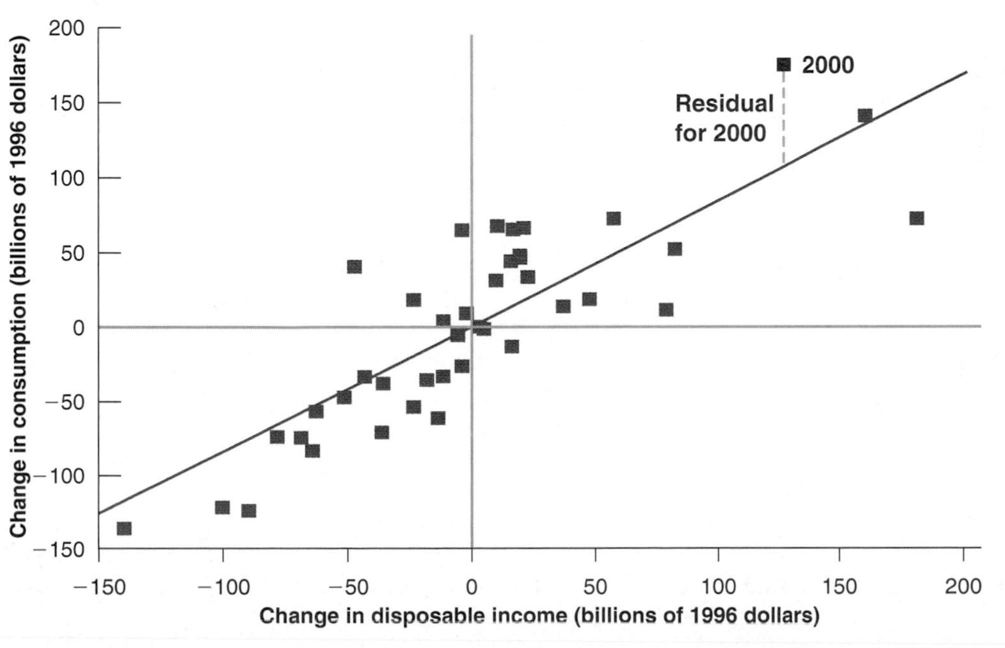

Figure A3-2

Changes in Consumption and Changes in Disposable Income: The Regression Line

The regression line is the line that fits the scatter of points best.

A Guide to Understanding Econometric Results

In your readings, you may run across results of estimation using econometrics. Here is a guide, which uses the slightly simplified, but otherwise untouched, computer output for the equation (A3.1):

① The variable we are trying to explain is called the **dependent variable**. Here the dependent variable is DC—the annual change in consumption minus its mean.

② The period of estimation includes all years from 1960 to 2000. There are therefore 41 **usable observations** used in the regression. **Degrees of freedom** is the number of observations minus the number of parameters to be estimated. There is one estimated parameter here: the coefficient on DYD. Thus, there are $41-1=40$ degrees of freedom. A simple rule is that one needs at least as many observations as parameters to be estimated, and preferably much more; put another way, degrees of freedom must be positive, and the larger the better.

③ $\bar{R}^2$ is a measure of fit. The closer to 1, the better the fit of the regression line. A value of 0.70 indicates that much but not all of the movement in the dependent variable can be explained by movements in the independent variables.

Dependent Variable DC—Estimation by Least Squares
Annual Data From 1960 To 2000
Usable Observations: 41
Degrees of Freedom: 40
$\bar{R}^2$: 0.70

Variable	Coefficient	t-statistic
DYD	0.88	9.71

④ The variables that we use to explain the dependent variable are called the **independent variables**. Here there is only one independent variable, DYD—the annual change in disposable income minus its mean.

⑤ For each independent variable, the computer then gives the estimated coefficient, as well as a **t-statistic**. The t-statistic associated with each estimated coefficient tells us how confident we can be that the true coefficient is different from zero. A t-statistic above 2 indicates that we can be at least 95% sure that the true coefficient is different from zero. A t-statistic of 9.71, as on the coefficient associated with disposable income, is so high that we can be nearly completely sure (more than 99.99% sure) that the true coefficient is different from zero, or, in other words, that changes in disposable income lead to changes in consumption.

FOCUS

between the two variables is perfect, that all points are exactly on the regression line. A value of zero would imply that the computer can see no relation between the two variables. The value of $\bar{R}^2$ of 0.70 in equation (A3.1) is high, but not very high. It confirms the message from Figure A3-2: Movements in disposable income clearly affect consumption, but there is still quite a bit of movement in consumption that cannot be explained by movements in disposable income.

Correlation Versus Causality

What we have established so far is that consumption and disposable income typically move together. More formally, we have seen that there is a positive **correlation**—the technical term for *co-relation*—between annual changes in consumption and annual changes in disposable income. And we have interpreted this relation as showing **causality**—that an increase in disposable income causes an increase in consumption.

We need to think again about this interpretation. A positive relation between consumption and disposable income may reflect the effect of disposable income on consumption. But it may also reflect the effect of consumption on disposable income. Indeed, the model we developed in Chapter 3 tells us that if, for any reason, consumers decide to spend more, then output, and, therefore, income and, in turn, disposable income will increase. If part of the relation between consumption and disposable income comes from the effect of consumption on disposable income, interpreting equation (A3.1) as telling us about the effect of disposable income on consumption is not right.

An example will help here: Suppose consumption *does not depend on disposable income,* so that the true value of c_1 is zero. (This is not very realistic, but it will make the point most clearly.) So, draw the consumption function as a horizontal line (a line with a zero slope) in Figure A3-3. Next, suppose disposable income equals Y_D, so that the initial combination of consumption and disposable income is given by point *A*.

Now suppose that because of improved confidence, consumers increase their consumption, so the consumption line shifts up. If demand affects output, then income and, in turn, disposable income increase, so that the new combination of consumption and disposable income will be given by, say, point *B*. If, instead, consumers become more pessimistic, the consumption line shifts down, and so does output, leading to a combination of consumption and disposable income given by point *D*.

If we look at that economy, we observe points *A*, *B*, and *D*. If, as we did earlier in Figure A3-2, we draw the best-fitting line through these points, we estimate an upward-sloping line, such as *CC′*, and so estimate a positive value for propensity to consume, c_1. Remember, however, that the true value of c_1 is zero. Why do we get the wrong answer—a positive value for c_1 when the true value is zero? Because we interpret the positive relation between disposable income and consumption as showing the effect of disposable income on consumption, where, in fact, the relation reflects the effect of consumption on disposable income: Higher consumption leads to higher demand, higher output, and so higher disposable income.

There is an important lesson here, *the difference between correlation and causality.* The fact that two variables move together does not imply that movements in

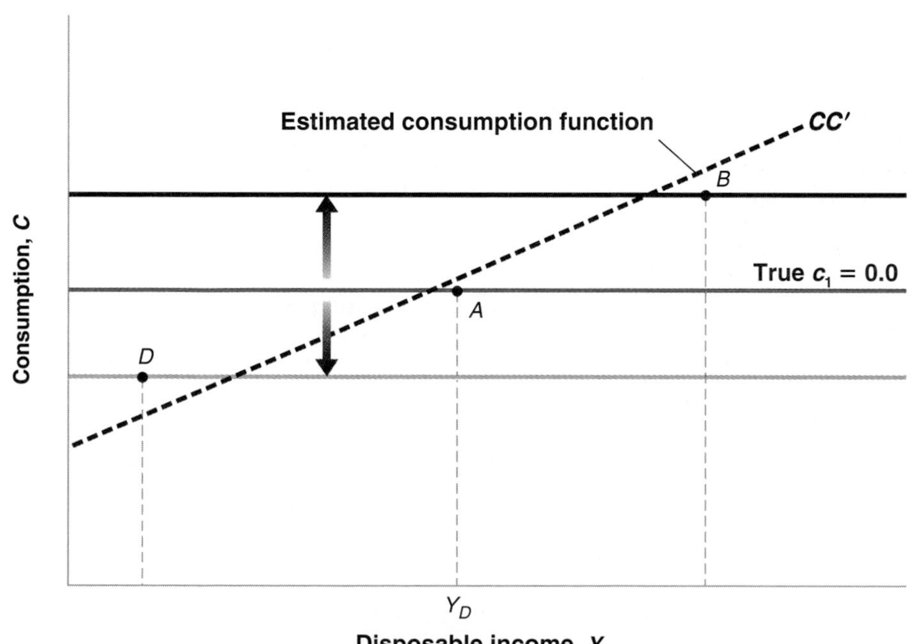

Figure A3-3

A Misleading Regression

The relation between disposable income and consumption comes from the effect of consumption on income rather than from the effect of income on consumption.

the first variable cause movements in the second variable. Perhaps the causality runs the other way: Movements in the second variable cause movements in the first variable. Or perhaps, as is likely to be the case here, the causality runs both ways: Disposable income affects consumption, *and* consumption affects disposable income.

Is there a way out of the correlation versus causality problem? If we are interested—and we are—in the effect of disposable income on consumption, can we still learn that from the data? The answer: Yes, but only by using more information.

Suppose we *knew* that a specific change in disposable income was not caused by a change in consumption. Then, by looking at the reaction of consumption to *this* change in disposable income, we could learn how consumption responds to disposable income; we could estimate the propensity to consume.

This answer would seem to assume away the problem: How can we tell that a change in disposable income is not due to a change in consumption? In fact, sometimes we can tell. Suppose, for example, that the government embarks on a major increase in defense spending, leading to an increase in demand and, in turn, an increase in output. In that case, if we see both disposable income and consumption increase, we can safely assume that the movement in consumption reflects the effect of disposable income on consumption, and thus estimate the propensity to consume.

This example suggests a general strategy:

- Find exogenous variables—that is, variables that affect disposable income but are not in turn affected by it.
- Look at the change in consumption in response not to all changes in disposable income—as we did in our earlier regression—but in response to those changes in disposable income that can be explained by changes in these exogenous variables.

By following this strategy, we can be confident that what we are estimating is the effect of disposable income on consumption, and not the other way around.

The problem of finding such exogenous variables is known as the **identification problem** in econometrics. These exogenous variables, when they can be found, are called **instruments**. Methods of estimation that rely on the use of such instruments are called **instrumental variable methods**.

When equation (A3.1) is estimated using an instrumental variable method—using current and past changes in government defense spending as the instruments—rather than ordinary least squares as we did earlier, the estimated equation becomes

$$(\Delta C_t - \overline{\Delta C}) = 0.47(\Delta Y_{Dt} - \overline{\Delta Y_D})$$

Note that the coefficient on disposable income, 0.47, is smaller than 0.88 in equation (A3.1). This decrease in the estimated propensity to consume is exactly what we would expect: Our earlier estimate in equation (A3.1) reflected not only the effect of disposable income on consumption, but also the effect of consumption back on disposable income. The use of instruments eliminates this second effect, which is why we find a smaller estimated effect of disposable income on consumption.

This short introduction to econometrics is no substitute for a course in econometrics. But it gives you a sense of how economists use data to estimate relations and parameters, and to identify causal relations between economic variables.

Key Terms

- ordinary least squares (OLS), A-13
- regression, regression line, A-13
- residual, $\bar{R}^2$, A-13
- dependent, independent variables, A-14
- usable observations, degrees of freedom, A-14
- t-statistic, A-14
- correlation, causality, A-15
- identification problem, A-16
- instruments, instrumental variable methods, A-16

Glossary

above the line, below the line In the balance of payments, the items in the *current account* are above the line drawn to divide them from the items in the *capital account*, which appear below the line.

accelerationist Phillips curve See *modified Phillips curve*.

adaptive expectations A backward-looking method of forming expectations by adjusting for past mistakes.

adjusted nominal money growth Nominal money growth minus normal output growth.

aggregate demand relation The demand for output at a given price level. It is derived from equilibrium in goods and financial markets.

aggregate output Total amount of output produced in the economy.

aggregate private spending The sum of all nongovernment spending. Also called *private spending*.

aggregate production function The relation between the quantity of aggregate output produced and the quantities of inputs used in production.

aggregate supply relation The price level at which firms are willing to supply a given level of output. It is derived from equilibrium in the labor market.

animal spirits A term introduced by Keynes to refer to movements in investment that could not be explained by movements in current variables.

anticipated money Movements in nominal money that could have been predicted based on the information available at some time in the past.

appreciation (nominal) An increase in the price of the domestic currency in terms of a foreign currency. Corresponds to a decrease in the exchange rate.

appropriability (of research results) The extent to which firms benefit from the results of their research and development efforts.

arbitrage The proposition that the expected rates of return on two financial assets must be equal. Also called *risky arbitrage* to distinguish it from *riskless arbitrage*, the proposition that the actual rates of return on two financial assets must be the same.

Asian crisis The financial and economic crisis in Asia that started in 1997.

Asian miracle The fast growth in many Asian countries over the last 20 to 30 years.

automatic stabilizer The fact that a decrease in output leads, under given tax and spending rules, to an increase in the budget deficit. This increase in the budget deficit in turn increases demand and thus stabilizes output.

autonomous spending That component of the demand for goods that does not depend on the level of output.

balance of payments A set of accounts that summarize a country's transactions with the rest of the world.

balanced budget A budget in which taxes are equal to government spending.

balanced growth The situation in which output, capital, and effective labor all grow at the same rate.

band (for exchange rates) The limits within which the exchange rate is allowed to move under a fixed exchange rate system.

bank reserves Holdings of central bank money by banks. The difference between what banks receive from depositors and what they lend to firms or hold as bonds.

bank run Simultaneous attempts by depositors to withdraw their funds from a bank.

bargaining power The relative strength of each side in a negotiation or a dispute.

barter The exchange of goods for other goods rather than for money.

base year When constructing real GDP by evaluating quantities in different years using a given set of prices, the year to which this given set of prices corresponds.

behavioral equation An equation that captures some aspect of behavior.

big bang The simultaneous implementation of many reforms at once.

bilateral exchange rate The real exchange rate between two countries.

Board of Governors The group of seven members that governs the Federal Reserve System and is in charge of the design of monetary policy.

bond A financial asset that promises a stream of known payments over some period of time.

bond rating The assessment of a bond based on its default risk.

broad money See *M2*.

budget deficit The excess of government expenditures over government revenues.

business cycle theory The study of macroeconomic fluctuations.

business cycles See *output fluctuations*.

capital account In the balance of payments, a summary of a country's asset transactions with the rest of the world.

capital accumulation Increase in the capital stock.

capital controls Restrictions on the foreign assets domestic residents can hold and on the domestic assets foreigners can hold.

cash flow The net flow of cash a firm is receiving.

causality A relation between cause and effect.

central bank money Money issued by the central bank. Also known as the *monetary base* and *high-powered money*.

central parity The reference value of the exchange rate around which the exchange rate is allowed to move under a fixed exchange rate system. The center of the *band*.

changes in business inventories In the national income and product accounts, the change in the physical volume of inventories held by businesses.

checkable deposits Deposits at banks and other financial institutions against which checks can be written.

churning The concept that new goods make old goods obsolete, that new production techniques make older techniques and worker skills obsolete, and so on.

collective bargaining Bargaining about wages between firms and unions.

compensation of employees In the national income and product accounts, the sum of wages and salaries and of supplements to wages and salaries.

confidence band When estimating the dynamic effect of one variable on another, the range of values where we can be confident the true dynamic effect lies.

Congressional Budget Office (CBO) An office of Congress in charge of constructing and publishing budget projections.

constant returns to scale The proposition that a proportional increase (or decrease) of all inputs leads to the same proportional increase (or decrease) in output.

consumer confidence index An index computed monthly that estimates consumer confidence regarding current and future economic conditions.

Consumer Price Index (CPI) The cost of a given list of goods and services consumed by a typical urban dweller.

consumption (C) Goods and services purchased by consumers.

consumption function A function that relates consumption to its determinants.

consumption of fixed capital Depreciation of capital.

contractionary open-market operation An open-market operation in which the central bank sells bonds to decrease the money supply.

controlled experiment A set of test conditions in which one variable is altered while the others are kept constant.

convergence The tendency for countries with lower output per capita to grow faster, leading to convergence of output per capita across countries.

coordination (of macroeconomic policies between two countries) The joint design of macroeconomic policies to improve the economic situation in the two countries.

corporate bond A bond issued by a corporation.

corporate profits In the national income and product accounts, firms' revenues minus costs (including interest payments) and minus depreciation.

correlation A measure of the way two variables move together. A positive correlation indicates that the two variables tend to move in the same direction. A negative correlation indicates that the two variables tend to move in opposite directions. A correlation of zero indicates that there is no apparent relation between the two variables.

cost of living index The average price of a consumption bundle.

coupon bond A bond that promises multiple payments before maturity and one payment at maturity.

coupon payments The payments before maturity on a coupon bond.

coupon rate The ratio of the coupon payment to the face value of a coupon bond.

crawling peg An exchange rate mechanism in which the exchange rate is allowed to move over time according to a prespecified formula.

creative destruction The proposition that growth simultaneously creates and destroys jobs.

credibility The degree to which people and markets believe that a policy announcement will actually be implemented and followed through.

credit channel The channel through which monetary policy works by affecting the amount of loans made by banks to firms.

currency Coins and bills.

currency board An exchange rate system in which: (i) the central bank stands ready to buy or sell foreign currency at the official exchange rate; (ii) it cannot engage in open-market operations, that is buy or sell government bonds.

current account In the balance of payments, the summary of a country's payments to and from the rest of the world.

Current Population Survey (CPS) A large monthly survey of U.S. households used in particular to compute the unemployment rate.

current yield The ratio of the coupon payment to the price of a coupon bond.

cyclically adjusted deficit A measure of what the government deficit would be under existing tax and spending rules, if output were at its natural level. Also called a *full-employment deficit, midcycle deficit, standardized employment deficit*, or *structural deficit*.

debt finance Financing based on loans or the issuance of bonds.

debt monetization The printing of money to finance a deficit.

debt ratio See *debt-to-GDP ratio*.

debt repudiation A unilateral decision by a debtor not to repay its debt.

debt-to-GDP ratio The ratio of debt to gross domestic product. Also called simply the *debt ratio*.

decreasing returns to capital The property that increases in capital lead to smaller and smaller increases in output as the level of capital increases.

decreasing returns to labor The property that increases in labor lead to smaller and smaller increases in output as the level of labor increases.

default risk The risk that the issuer of a bond will not pay back the full amount promised by the bond.

deflation Negative inflation.

degrees of freedom The number of usable observations in a *regression* minus the number of parameters to be estimated.

demand deposit A bank account that allows depositors to write checks or get cash on demand, up to an amount equal to the account balance.

demand for domestic goods The demand for domestic goods by people, firms, and governments, both domestic and foreign. Equal to the domestic demand for goods plus net exports.

dependent variable A variable whose value is determined by one or more other variables.

depreciation (nominal) A decrease in the price of the domestic currency in terms of a foreign currency. Corresponds to an increase in the exchange rate.

depreciation rate A measure of how much usefulness a piece of capital loses from one period to the next.

depression A deep and long-lasting recession.

devaluation An increase in the exchange rate in a fixed exchange-rate system.

discount bond A bond that promises a single payment at maturity.

discount factor The value today of a dollar (or other national currency unit) at some time in the future.

discount policy The conditions under which the Fed lends to banks.

discount rate (i) The interest rate used to discount a sequence of future payments. Equal to the nominal interest rate when discounting future nominal payments, to the real interest rate when discounting future real payments. (ii) The interest rate at which the Fed lends to banks.

discount window Metaphorically, the window where the Fed lends to banks. More generally, the means by which the Federal Reserve Bank lends to banks.

discouraged worker A person who has given up looking for employment.

disinflation A decrease in inflation.

disposable income The income that remains once consumers have received transfers from the government and paid their taxes.

dividends The portion of a corporation's profits that the firm pays out each period to shareholders.

dollar GDP See *nominal GDP.*

dollarization The use of dollars in domestic transactions in a country other than the United States.

domestic demand for goods The sum of consumption, investment, and government spending.

dual labor market A labor market that combines a *primary labor market* and a *secondary labor market.*

durable goods Commodities that can be stored and have an average life of at least three years.

duration of unemployment The period of time during which a worker is unemployed.

dynamics Movements of one or more economic variables over time.

econometrics Statistical methods applied to economics.

effective demand Synonym for *aggregate demand.*

effective labor The number of workers in an economy times the state of technology.

effective real exchange rate See *multilateral exchange rate.*

efficiency wage The wage at which a worker is performing a job most efficiently or productively.

endogenous variable A variable that depends on other variables in a model and is thus explained within the model.

entitlement programs Programs that require the payment of benefits to all who meet the eligibility requirements established by law.

equilibrium The equality between demand and supply.

equilibrium condition The condition that supply be equal to demand.

equilibrium equation An equation that represents an equilibrium condition.

equilibrium in the goods market The condition that the supply of goods be equal to the demand for goods.

equity finance Financing based on the issuance of shares.

equity premium Risk premium required by investors to hold stocks rather than short-term bonds.

Euro The new European currency, which replaced national currencies in 11 countries in 2002.

European central bank (ECB) The central bank, located in Frankfurt, in charge of determining monetary policy in the Euro zone.

European Monetary System (EMS) A fixed exchange rate system in place in most of the countries of the European Union, from 1978 to 1999.

European Union A political and economic organization of 15 European nations. Formerly called the European Community.

Eurosclerosis A term coined to reflect the belief that Europe suffers from excessive rigidities, especially in the labor market.

exchange rate mechanism (ERM) The rules that determined the bands within which the member countries of the European Monetary System had to maintain their bilateral exchange rate.

exogenous variable A variable that is not explained within a model but rather is taken as given.

expansion A period of positive GDP growth.

expansionary open-market operation An open-market operation in which the central bank buys bonds to increase the money supply.

expectations hypothesis The hypothesis that financial investors are risk neutral, which implies expected returns on all financial assets have to be equal.

expectations-augmented Phillips curve See *modified Phillips curve.*

expected present discounted value The value today of an expected sequence of future payments. Also called *present discounted value* or *present value.*

experiment A test carried out under controlled conditions to assess the validity of a model or hypothesis.

exports (X) The purchases of domestic goods and services by foreigners.

face value (on a bond) The single payment at maturity promised by a discount bond.

fad A period of time during which, for reasons of fashion or overoptimism, financial investors are willing to pay more than the fundamental value of a stock.

Fed accommodation A change in the money supply by the Fed to maintain a constant interest rate in the face of changes in money demand or in spending.

federal deposit insurance Insurance provided by the U.S. government that protects each bank depositor up to $100,000 per account.

federal funds market The market where banks that have excess reserves at the end of the day lend them to banks that have insufficient reserves.

federal funds rate The interest rate determined by equilibrium in the federal funds market. The interest rate affected most directly by changes in monetary policy.

Federal Open Market Committee (FOMC) A committee composed of the seven governors of the Fed, plus five District

Bank presidents. The FOMC directs the activities of the *Open Market Desk*.

Federal Reserve Bank (Fed) The U.S. central bank.

Federal Reserve Districts The 12 regional districts that constitute the Federal Reserve System.

fertility of research The degree to which spending on research and development translates into new ideas and new products.

financial intermediary A financial institution that receives funds from people or firms, and uses these funds to make loans or buy financial assets.

financial investment The purchase of financial assets.

financial markets The markets in which financial assets are bought and sold.

financial wealth The value of all of one's financial assets minus all financial liabilities. Sometimes called *wealth*, for short.

fine-tuning A macroeconomic policy aimed at precisely hitting a given target, such as constant unemployment or constant output growth.

fiscal consolidation See *fiscal contraction*.

fiscal contraction A policy aimed at reducing the budget deficit through a decrease in government spending or an increase in taxation. Also called *fiscal consolidation*.

fiscal expansion An increase in government spending or a decrease in taxation, which leads to an increase in the budget deficit.

fiscal policy A government's choice of taxes and spending.

fiscal year An accounting period of 12 months. In the United States, the period from October 1 of the previous calendar year through September 30 of the current calendar year.

Fisher effect or **Fisher hypothesis** The proposition that in the long run an increase in nominal money growth is reflected in an identical increase in both the nominal interest rate and the inflation rate, leaving the real interest rate unchanged.

Fisher hypothesis See *Fisher effect*.

fixed exchange rate An exchange rate between the currencies of two or more countries that is fixed at some level and adjusted only infrequently.

fixed investment See *investment (I)*.

float The exchange rate is said to float when it is determined in the foreign exchange market, without central bank intervention.

floating exchange rate An exchange rate determined in the foreign-exchange market without central bank intervention.

flow A variable that can be expressed as a quantity per unit of time (such as income).

forecast error The difference between the actual value of a variable and a forecast of that variable.

foreign direct investment The purchase of existing firms or the development of new firms by foreign investors.

foreign exchange Foreign currency; all currencies other than the domestic currency of a given country.

foreign-exchange reserves Foreign assets held by the central bank.

four tigers The four Asian economies of Singapore, Taiwan, Hong Kong, and South Korea.

full-employment deficit See *cyclically adjusted deficit*.

fully funded social security system Retirement system in which the contributions of current workers are invested in financial assets, with the proceeds (principal and interest) given back to the workers when they retire.

fundamental value (of a stock) The present value of expected dividends.

G-7 The seven major economic powers in the world: the United States, Japan, France, Germany, the United Kingdom, Italy, and Canada.

game *Strategic interactions* between *players*.

game theory The prediction of outcomes from *games*.

GDP deflator The ratio of nominal GDP to real GDP; a measure of the overall price level. Gives the average price of the final goods produced in the economy.

GDP in current dollars See *nominal GDP*.

GDP in terms of goods See *real GDP*.

GDP in constant dollars See *real GDP*.

GDP adjusted for inflation See *real GDP*.

GDP in chained (1992) dollars See *real GDP*.

GDP growth The growth rate of real GDP in year *t*; equal to $(Y_t - Y_{t-1})/Y_{t-1}$.

general equilibrium A situation in which there is equilibrium in all markets (goods, financial, and labor).

geometric series A mathematical sequence in which the ratio of one term to the preceding term remains the same. A sequence of the form $1 + c + c^2 + \cdots + c^n$.

gold standard A system in which a country fixed the price of its currency in terms of gold and stood ready to exchange gold for currency at the stated parity.

golden-rule level of capital The level of capital at which long-run consumption is maximized.

government bond A bond issued by a government or a government agency.

government budget constraint The budget constraint faced by the government. The constraint implies that an excess of spending over revenues must be financed by borrowing, and thus leads to an increase in debt.

government purchases In the national income and product accounts, the sum of the purchases of goods by the government plus compensation of government employees.

government spending (G) The goods and services purchased by federal, state, and local governments.

government transfers Payments made by the government to individuals that are not in exchange for goods or services. Example: Social Security payments.

Great Depression The severe worldwide depression of the 1930s.

gross domestic product (GDP) A measure of aggregate output in the national income accounts. (The market value of the goods and services produced by labor and property located in the United States.)

gross national product (GNP) A measure of aggregate output in the national income accounts. (The market value of the goods and services produced by labor and property supplied by U.S. residents.)

gross private domestic fixed investment In the national income and product accounts, the sum of nonresidential investment and residential investment.

growth The steady increase in aggregate output over time.

hedonic pricing An approach to calculating real GDP that treats goods as providing a collection of characteristics, each with an implicit price.

heterodox stabilization program A stabilization program that includes incomes policies.

high-powered money See *central bank money*.

hires Workers newly employed by firms.

housing wealth The value of the housing stock.

human capital The set of skills possessed by the workers in an economy.

human wealth The labor-income component of wealth.

Humphrey-Hawkins Act A 1978 act of the U.S. Congress defining the goals of monetary policy.

hyperinflation Very high inflation.

hysteresis In general, the proposition that the equilibrium value of a variable depends on its history. With respect to unemployment, the proposition that a long period of sustained actual unemployment leads to an increase in the equilibrium rate of unemployment.

identification problem In econometrics, the problem of finding whether correlation between variables *X* and *Y* indicates a causal relation from *X* to *Y*, or from *Y* to *X*, or both. This problem is solved by finding exogenous variables, called *instruments*, that affect *X* and do not affect *Y* directly, or affect *Y* and do not affect *X* directly.

identity An equation that holds by definition, denoted by the sign ≡.

imports (Q) The purchases of foreign goods and services by domestic consumers, firms, and the government.

income The flow of revenue from work, rental income, interest, and dividends.

incomes policies Government policies that set up wage and/or price guidelines or controls.

independent variable A variable that is taken as given in a relation or in a model.

index number A number, such as the GDP deflator, that has no natural level and is thus set to equal some value (typically 1 or 100) in a given period.

indexed bond A bond that promises payments adjusted for inflation.

indirect taxes Taxes on goods and services. In the United States, primarily sales taxes.

industrial policy A policy aimed at helping specific sectors of an economy.

inflation A sustained rise in the general level of prices.

inflation rate The rate at which the price level increases over time.

inflation targeting The conduct of monetary policy to achieve a given inflation rate over time.

inflation tax The product of the rate of inflation and real money balances.

inflation-adjusted deficit The correct economic measure of the budget deficit: The sum of the *primary deficit* and real interest payments.

instrumental variable methods In econometrics, methods of estimation that use *instruments* to estimate causal relations between different variables.

instruments In econometrics, the exogenous variables that allow the identification problem to be solved.

intercept In a linear relation between two variables, the value of the first variable when the second variable is equal to zero.

interest parity condition See *uncovered interest parity relation*.

intermediate good A good used in the production of a final good.

International Monetary Fund (IMF) The principal international economic organization. Publishes the *World Economic Outlook* annually and the *International Financial Statistics (IFS)* monthly.

inventory investment (I_s) The difference between production and sales.

investment (I) Purchases of new houses and apartments by people, and purchases of new capital goods (machines and plants) by firms.

investment income In the current account, income received by domestic residents from their holdings of foreign assets.

***IS* curve** A downward-sloping curve relating output to the interest rate. The curve corresponding to the *IS relation*, the equilibrium condition for the goods market.

***IS* relation** An equilibrium condition stating that the demand for goods must be equal to the supply of goods, or equivalently that investment must be equal to saving. The equilibrium condition for the goods market.

J-curve A curve depicting the initial deterioration in the trade balance caused by a real depreciation, followed by an improvement in the trade balance.

junk bond A bond with a high risk of default.

labor force The sum of those employed and those unemployed.

labor hoarding The practice of retaining workers during a period of low product demand rather than laying them off.

labor in efficiency units See *effective labor*.

labor market rigidities Restrictions on firms' ability to adjust their level of employment.

labor productivity The ratio of output to the number of workers.

Laffer curve A curve showing the relation between tax revenues and the tax rate.

lagged value The value of a variable in the preceding time period.

layoffs Workers who lose their jobs either temporarily or permanently.

leapfrogging Advancing on and then overtaking the leader. Used to describe the process by which economic leadership passes from country to country.

life cycle theory of consumption The theory of consumption, developed initially by Franco Modigliani, which emphasizes that the planning horizon of consumers is their lifetime.

linear relation A relation between two variables such that a one-unit increase in one variable always leads to an increase of *n* units in the other variable.

liquid asset An asset that can be sold easily and at little cost.

liquidity preference The term introduced by Keynes to denote the demand for money.

liquidity trap The case where nominal interest rates are equal to zero, and monetary policy cannot therefore decrease them further.

***LM* curve** An upward-sloping curve relating the interest rate to output. The curve corresponding to the *LM relation*, the equilibrium condition for financial markets.

***LM* relation** An equilibrium condition stating that the demand for money must be equal to the supply of money. The equilibrium condition for financial markets.

logarithmic scale A scale in which the same proportional increase is represented by the same distance on the scale, so that a variable that grows at a constant rate is represented by a straight line.

long run A period of time extending over decades.

long-term bond A bond with maturity of 10 years or more.

Lucas critique The proposition, put forth by Robert Lucas, that existing relations between economic variables may change when policy changes. An example is the apparent trade-off between inflation and unemployment, which may disappear if policy makers try to exploit it.

M1 The sum of currency, traveler's checks, and checkable deposits—assets that can be used directly in transactions. Also called *narrow money*.

M2 *M1* plus money market mutual fund shares, money market and savings deposits, and time deposits. Also called *broad money*.

M3 A *monetary aggregate* constructed by the Fed and broader than *M2*.

macroeconomics The study of aggregate economic variables, such as production for the economy as a whole, or the average price of goods.

Maastricht Treaty A treaty signed in 1991 that defined the steps involved in the transition to a common currency for the European Union.

marginal propensity to consume (*mpc* or c_1) The effect on consumption of an additional dollar of disposable income.

marginal propensity to import The effect on imports from an additional dollar in income.

marginal propensity to save The effect on saving of an additional dollar of disposable income. (Equal to one minus the marginal propensity to consume.)

Marshall-Lerner condition The condition under which a real depreciation leads to an increase in net exports.

maturity The length of time over which a financial asset (typically a bond) promises to make payments to the holder.

medium run A period of time between the *short run* and the *long run*.

medium-term bond A bond with maturity of one to 10 years.

menu cost The cost of changing a price.

merchandise trade Exports and imports of goods.

microeconomics The study of production and prices in specific markets.

midcycle deficit See *cyclically adjusted deficit*.

model A conceptual structure used to think about and interpret an economic phenomenon.

models of endogenous growth Models in which accumulation of physical and human capital can sustain growth even in the absence of technological progress.

modified Phillips curve The curve that plots the change in the inflation rate against the unemployment rate. Also called an *expectations-augmented Phillips curve* or an *accelerationist Phillips curve*.

monetarism, monetarists A group of economists in the 1960s, led by Milton Friedman, who argued that monetary policy had powerful effects on activity.

monetary aggregate The market value of a sum of liquid assets. *M1* is a monetary aggregate that includes only the most liquid assets.

monetary base See *central bank money*.

monetary contraction A change in monetary policy, which leads to an increase in the interest rate. Also called *monetary tightening*.

monetary expansion A change in monetary policy, which leads to a decrease in the interest rate.

monetary-fiscal policy mix The combination of monetary and fiscal policies in effect at a given time.

monetary tightening See *monetary contraction*.

money Those financial assets that can be used directly to buy goods.

money illusion The notion that people appear to make systematic mistakes in assessing nominal versus real changes.

money market funds Financial institutions that receive funds from people and use them to buy short-term bonds.

money multiplier The increase in the money supply resulting from a one-dollar increase in central bank money.

multilateral exchange rate (multilateral real exchange rate) The real exchange rate between a country and its trading partners, computed as a weighted average of bilateral real exchange rates. Also called the *trade-weighted real exchange rate* or *effective real exchange rate*.

multiplier The ratio of the change in an *endogenous variable* to the change in an *exogenous variable* (for example, the ratio of the change in output to a change in autonomous spending).

Mundell-Fleming model A model of simultaneous equilibrium in both goods and financial markets for an open economy.

narrow banking Restrictions on banks that would require them to hold only short-term government bonds.

narrow money See *M1*.

national accounts See *national income and product accounts*.

national income In the United States, the income that originates in the production of goods and services supplied by residents of the United States.

national income and product accounts The system of accounts used to describe the evolution of the sum, the composition, and the distribution of aggregate output.

National Industrial Recovery Act (NIRA) A New Deal program that asked industries to sign codes of behavior, to establish minimum wages, and not to impose further wage cuts.

National Recovery Administration (NRA) The administration in charge of the set of programs designed to help the U.S. economy recover from the Great Depression.

natural experiment A real-world event that can be used to test an economic theory.

natural level of employment The level of employment that prevails when unemployment is equal to its natural rate.

natural level of output The level of production that prevails when employment is equal to its natural level.

natural rate of unemployment The unemployment rate at which price and wage decisions are consistent.

neoclassical synthesis A consensus in macroeconomics, developed in the early 1950s, based on an integration of Keynes's ideas and the ideas of earlier economists.

net capital flows Capital flows from the rest of the world to the domestic economy minus capital flows to the rest of the world from the domestic economy.

net exports The difference between exports and imports. Also called the *trade balance*.

net interest In the national income and product accounts, the interest paid by firms minus the interest received by firms, plus interest received from the rest of the world minus interest paid to the rest of the world.

net national product (NNP) Gross national product minus capital depreciation.

net transfers received In the current account, the net value of foreign aid received minus foreign aid given.

neutrality of money The proposition that an increase in nominal money has no effect on output or the interest rate but is reflected entirely in a proportional increase in the price level.

new classicals A group of economists who interpret fluctuations as the effects of shocks in competitive markets with fully flexible prices and wages.

New Deal The set of programs put in place by the Roosevelt administration to get the U.S. economy out of the Great Depression.

New Economy The proposition that rapid technological progress in the information technology sector is fundamentally changing the nature of the U.S. economy.

new growth theory Recent developments in growth theory that explore the determinants of technological progress and the role of increasing returns to scale in growth.

new Keynesians A group of economists who believe in the importance of nominal rigidities in fluctuations, and who are exploring the role of market imperfections in explaining fluctuations.

nominal exchange rate The price of foreign currency in terms of domestic currency. The number of units of domestic currency you can get for one unit of foreign currency.

nominal GDP The sum of the quantities of final goods produced in an economy times their current price. Also known as *dollar GDP* and *GDP in current dollars*.

nominal interest rate Interest rate in terms of the national currency (in terms of dollars in the United States). Tells us how many dollars one has to repay in the future in exchange for one dollar today.

nominal rigidities The slow adjustment of nominal wages and prices to changes in economic activity.

nonaccelerating inflation rate of unemployment (NAIRU) The unemployment rate at which inflation neither decreases nor increases. See *natural rate of unemployment.*

nondurable goods Commodities that can be stored but have an average life of less than three years.

nonemployment rate The ratio of population minus employment, to population.

nonhuman wealth The financial and housing component of wealth.

noninstitutional civilian population The number of people potentially available for civilian employment.

nonresidential investment The purchase of new capital goods by firms: *structures* and *producer durable equipment.*

normal growth rate The rate of output growth needed to maintain a constant unemployment rate.

North American Free Trade Agreement (NAFTA) An agreement signed by the United States, Canada, and Mexico in which the three countries agreed to establish all of North America as a free-trade zone.

not in the labor force Number of people who are neither employed nor looking for employment.

***n*-year interest rate** See *yield to maturity.*

Okun's law The relation between GDP growth and the change in the unemployment rate.

Open Market Desk The Federal Reserve agency in charge of open-market operations. Located in New York City.

open-market operation The purchase or sale of government bonds by the central bank for the purpose of increasing or decreasing the money supply.

openness in factor markets The opportunity for firms to choose where to locate production and for workers to choose where to work and whether or not to migrate.

openness in financial markets The opportunity for financial investors to choose between domestic and foreign financial assets.

openness in goods markets The opportunity for consumers and firms to choose between domestic and foreign goods.

optimal control The control of a system (a machine, a rocket, an economy) by means of mathematical methods.

optimal control theory The set of mathematical methods used for *optimal control.*

ordinary least squares A statistical method to find the best fitting relation between two or more variables.

Organization for Economic Cooperation and Development (OECD) An international organization that collects and studies economic data for many countries. Most of the world's rich countries belong to the OECD.

orthodox stabilization program A stabilization program that does not include incomes policies.

output fluctuations Movements in output around its trend. Also called *business cycles.*

output per capita A country's gross domestic product divided by its population.

overnight interest rate The interest rate charged in the *federal funds market* for lending and borrowing overnight.

overshooting The large movement in the exchange rate triggered by a monetary expansion or contraction.

panel data set A data set that gives the values of one or more variables for many individuals or many firms over some period of time.

paradox of saving The result that an attempt by people to save more may lead both to a decline in output and to unchanged saving.

parameter A coefficient in a behavioral equation.

participation rate The ratio of the labor force to the noninstitutional civilian population.

patent The legal right granted to a person or firm to exclude anyone else from the production or use of a new product or technique for a certain period of time.

pay-as-you-go social security system Retirement system in which the contributions of current workers are used to pay benefits to retirees.

payments of factor income to the rest of the world In the United States, income received by foreign capital and foreign residents.

peg The exchange rate to which a country commits under a fixed exchange rate system.

permanent income theory of consumption The theory of consumption, developed by Milton Friedman, that emphasizes that people make consumption decisions based not on current income, but on their notion of permanent income.

personal consumption expenditures In the national income and product accounts, the sum of goods and services purchased by persons resident in the United States.

personal disposable income *Personal income* minus personal tax and non-tax payments. The income available to consumers after they have received transfers and paid taxes.

personal income The income actually received by persons.

Phillips curve The curve that plots the relation between (i) movements in inflation and (ii) unemployment. The original Phillips curve captured the relation between the inflation rate and the unemployment rate. The *modified Phillips curve* captures the relation between (i) the change in the inflation rate and (ii) the unemployment rate.

players The participants in a *game*. Depending on the context, players may be people, firms, governments, and so on.

point-year of excess employment A difference between the actual unemployment rate and the natural unemployment rate of one percentage point for one year.

policy mix See *monetary-fiscal policy mix.*

political business cycle Fluctuations in economic activity caused by the manipulation of the economy for electoral gain.

post-industrial economies Economies in which the manufacturing sector's share of gross domestic product is small.

present value See *expected present discounted value.*

price level The general level of prices in an economy.

price liberalization The process of eliminating subsidies, decontrolling prices, and allowing them to clear markets.

price-setting relation The relation between the price chosen by firms, the nominal wage, and the markup.

primary deficit Government spending, excluding interest payments on the debt, minus government revenues. (The negative of the *primary surplus.*)

primary labor market A labor market where jobs are good, wages are high, and turnover is low. Contrast to the *secondary labor market.*

primary surplus Government revenues minus government spending, excluding interest payments on the debt.

private saving (S) Saving by the private sector. The value of consumers' disposable income minus their consumption.

private spending See *aggregate private spending.*

privatization The transfer of state-owned firms to private ownership.

producer durable equipment Durable goods such as machines, computers, and office equipment purchased by firms for production purposes.

producer price index (PPI) A price index of domestically produced goods in manufacturing, mining, agricultural, fishing, forestry, and electric utility industries.

production function The relation between the quantity of output and the quantities of inputs used in production.

profitability The expected present discounted value of profits.

propagation mechanism The dynamic effects of a *shock* on output and its components.

proprietors' income In the national income and product accounts, the income of sole proprietorships, partnerships, and tax-exempt cooperatives.

propensity to consume (c_1) The effect of an additional dollar of disposable income on consumption.

propensity to save The effect of an additional dollar of disposable income on saving (equal to one minus the propensity to consume).

public saving Saving by the government; equal to government revenues minus government spending. Also called the *budget surplus.* (A *budget deficit* represents public dissaving.)

purchasing power Income in terms of goods.

purchasing power parity (PPP) A method of adjustment used to allow for international comparisons of GDP.

quits Workers who leave their jobs in search of better alternatives.

quotas Restrictions on the quantities of goods that can be imported.

$\bar{R}^2$ A measure of fit, between zero and one, from a *regression*. An $\bar{R}^2$ of zero implies that there is no apparent relation between the variables under consideration. An $\bar{R}^2$ of 1 implies a perfect fit: all the *residuals* are equal to zero.

random walk The path of a variable whose changes over time are unpredictable.

random walk of consumption The proposition that, if consumers are foresighted, changes in their consumption should be unpredictable.

rate of growth of multifactor productivity See *Solow residual.*

rational expectations The formation of expectations based on rational forecasts, rather than on simple extrapolations of the past.

rational speculative bubble An increase in stock prices based on the rational expectation of further increases in prices in the future.

real appreciation An increase in the relative price of domestic goods in terms of foreign goods. A decrease in the real exchange rate.

real business cycle (RBC) models Economic models that assume that output is always at its natural level. Thus, all output fluctuations are movements of the natural level of output, as opposed to movements away form the natural level of output.

real depreciation A decrease in the relative price of domestic goods in terms of foreign goods. An increase in the real exchange rate.

real exchange rate The relative price of foreign goods in terms of domestic goods.

real GDP A measure of aggregate output. The sum of quantities produced in an economy times their price in a base year. Also known as *GDP in terms of goods, GDP in constant dollars, GDP adjusted for inflation.* The current measure of real GDP in the United States is called *GDP in (chained) 1996 dollars.*

real GDP in chained (1996) dollars See *real GDP.*

real interest rate Interest rate in terms of goods. Tells us how many goods one has to repay in the future in exchange for one good today.

realignment Adjustment of parities in a fixed exchange-rate system.

receipts of factor income from the rest of the world In the United States, income received by U.S. capital or U.S. residents abroad.

recession A period of negative GDP-growth. Usually refers to at least two consecutive quarters of negative GDP growth.

regression The output of *ordinary least squares.* Gives the equation corresponding to the estimated relation between variables, together with information about the degree of fit and the relative importance of the different variables.

regression line The best-fitting line corresponding to the equation obtained by using *ordinary least squares.*

rental cost of capital See *user cost.*

rental income of persons In the national income and product accounts, the income from the rental of real property, minus depreciation on this property.

research and development (R&D) Spending aimed at discovering and developing new ideas and products.

reservation wage The wage that would make a worker indifferent to working or becoming unemployed.

reserve ratio The ratio of bank reserves to checkable deposits.

reserve requirements The minimum amount of reserves that banks must hold in proportion to checkable deposits.

residential investment The purchase of new homes and apartments by people.

residual The difference between the actual value of a variable and the value implied by the *regression line*. Small residuals indicate a good fit.

revaluation A decrease in the exchange rate in a fixed exchange-rate system.

Ricardian equivalence The proposition that neither government deficits nor government debt has an effect on economic activity. Also called the *Ricardo-Barro proposition.*

Ricardo-Barro proposition See *Ricardian equivalence.*

risk averse A person is risk averse if he/she prefers to receive a given amount for sure to an uncertain amount with the same expected value.

risk neutral A person is risk neutral if he/she is indifferent between receiving a given amount for sure or an uncertain amount with the same expected value.

risk premium The difference between the interest rate paid on a given bond and the interest rate paid on a bond with the highest rating.

riskless arbitrage See *arbitrage.*

risky arbitrage See *arbitrage.*

sacrifice ratio The number or point-years of excess unemployment needed to achieve a decrease in inflation of 1%.

saving The sum of private and public saving, denoted by S.

saving rate The proportion of income that is saved.

savings The accumulated value of past saving. Also called *wealth.*

scatter diagram A graphic presentation that plots the value of one variable against the value of another variable.

secondary labor market A labor market where jobs are poor, wages are low, and turnover is high. Contrast to the *primary labor market.*

seignorage The revenues from the creation of money.

separations Workers who are leaving or losing their jobs.

services Commodities that cannot be stored and thus must be consumed at the place and time of purchase.

severance payments Payments made by firms to laid-off workers.

share A financial asset issued by a firm that promises to pay a sequence of payments, called dividends, in the future. Also called *stock.*

shocks Movements in the factors that affect aggregate demand and/or aggregate supply.

shoe leather costs The costs of going to the bank to take money out of a checking account.

short run A period of time extending over a few years at most.

short-term bond A bond with maturity of one year or less.

simulation The use of a model to look at the effects of a change in an exogenous variable on the variables in the model.

skill-biased technological progress The proposition that new machines and new methods of production require skilled workers to a greater degree than in the past.

Social Security Trust Fund The funds accumulated by the U.S. Social Security system as a result of surpluses in the past.

slope In a linear relation between two variables, the amount by which the first variable increases when the second increases by one unit.

soft budget constraint The granting of subsidies to firms that make losses, thus decreasing the incentives for these firms to take the measures needed to generate profits.

Solow residual The excess of actual output growth over what can be accounted for by the growth in capital and labor.

stabilization program A government program aimed at stabilizing the economy (typically stopping high inflation).

stagflation The combination of stagnation and inflation.

staggering of wage decisions The fact that different wages are adjusted at different times, making it impossible to achieve a synchronized decrease in nominal wage inflation.

standardized employment deficit See *cyclically adjusted deficit.*

state of technology The degree of technological development in a country or industry.

statistical discrepancy A difference between two numbers that should be equal, coming from differences in sources or methods of construction for the two numbers.

steady state In an economy without technological progress, the state of the economy where output and capital per worker are no longer changing. In an economy with technological progress, the state of the economy where output and capital per effective worker are no longer changing.

stock A variable that can be expressed as a quantity at a point in time (such as wealth). Also a synonym for *share.*

stocks An alternative term for *inventories.*

strategic interactions An environment in which the actions of one player depend on and affect the actions of another player.

structural deficit See *cyclically adjusted deficit.*

structural rate of unemployment See *natural rate of unemployment.*

structures In the national income and product accounts: plants, factories, office buildings, and hotels.

supply siders A group of economists in the 1980s who believed that tax cuts would increase activity by enough to increase tax revenues.

Tanzi-Olivera effect The adverse effect of inflation on tax revenues and in turn on the budget deficit.

tariffs Taxes on imported goods.

Taylor's rule A rule, suggested by John Taylor, telling a central bank how to adjust the nominal interest rate in response to deviations of inflation from its target, and of the unemployment rate from the natural rate.

tax smoothing The principle of keeping tax rates roughly constant, so that the government runs large deficits when government spending is exceptionally high and small surpluses the rest of the time.

technological progress An improvement in the state of technology.

technological unemployment Unemployment brought about by technological progress.

technology gap The differences between states of technology across countries.

term structure of interest rates See *yield curve.*

time inconsistency In game theory, the incentive for one player to deviate from his previously announced course of action once the other player has moved.

Tobin's q The ratio of the value of the capital stock, computed by adding the stock market value of firms and the debt of firms, to the replacement cost of capital.

total wealth The sum of human wealth and nonhuman wealth.

tradable goods Goods that compete with foreign goods in domestic or foreign markets.

trade balance The difference between exports and imports. Also called *net exports.*

trade deficit A negative trade balance, that is, imports exceed exports.

trade surplus A positive trade balance, that is, exports exceed imports.

trade-weighted real exchange rate See *multilateral exchange rate.*

transfers See *government transfers.*

Treasury bill (T-bill) A U.S. government bond with a maturity of up to one year.

Treasury bond A U.S. government bond with a maturity of 10 years or more.

Treasury note A U.S. government bond with a maturity of one to 10 years.

t-statistic A statistic associated with an estimated coefficient in a regression that indicates how confident one can be that the true coefficient differs from zero.

twin deficits The budget and trade deficits that have characterized the United States since the early 1980s.

unanticipated money Movements in nominal money that could not have been predicted based on the information available at some time in the past.

uncovered interest parity relation An arbitrage relation stating that domestic and foreign bonds must have the same expected rate of return, expressed in terms of the domestic currency.

underground economy That part of a nation's economic activity that is not measured in official statistics, either because the activity is illegal or because people and firms are seeking to avoid taxes.

unemployment rate The ratio of the number of unemployed to the labor force.

union density The proportion of the work force that is unionized.

usable observation An observation for which the values of all the variables under consideration are available for *regression* purposes.

user cost of capital The cost of using capital over a year, or a given period of time. The sum of the real interest rate and the depreciation rate. Also called the *rental cost of capital.*

value added The value a firm adds in the production process, equal to the value of its production minus the value of the intermediate inputs it uses in production.

velocity The ratio of nominal income to money; the number of transactions for a given quantity of money, or the rate at which money changes hands.

voucher privatization A method of privatization in which the government grants vouchers to private citizens allowing them to bid for shares in state-owned firms.

wage indexation A rule that automatically increases wages in response to an increase in prices.

wage-price spiral The mechanism by which increases in wages lead to increases in prices, which lead in turn to further increases in wages, and so on.

wage-setting relation The relation between the wage chosen by wage setters, the price level, and the unemployment rate.

war of attrition When both parties to an argument hold their grounds, hoping that the other party will give in.

wealth See *financial wealth.*

yield curve The relation between yield and maturity for bonds of different maturities. Also called the *term structure of interest rates.*

yield to maturity The constant interest rate that makes the price of an *n*-year bond today equal to the present value of future payments. Also called the *n-year interest rate.*

Index

P

R

S

T

U

V

W

Y

Z

Symbols Used in This Book

Symbol	Term	Introduced in Chapter
$(\ )^d$	Superscript ^{d} means demanded	
$(\ )^e$	Superscript ^{e} means expected	
A	Aggregate private spending	17
	Also: Labor productivity/States of technology	6, 12
α	Effect on the inflation rate of the unemployment rate, given expected inflation	8
B	Goverment debt	26
β	Effect of an increase in output growth on the unemployment rate	9
C	Consumption	3
CU	Currency	4
c	Proportion of money held as currency	4
c_0	Consumption when disposable income equals zero	3
c_1	Propensity to consume	3
D	Checkable deposits	4
	Also: Real dividend on a stock	15
$\$D$	Nominal dividend on a stock	15
δ	Depreciation rate	11
E	Nominal exchange rate (price of foreign currency in terms of domestic currency)	18
$\bar{E}$	Fixed nominal exchange rate	20
E^e	Expected future exchange rate	18
ε	Real exchange rate	18
G	Government spending	3
g_A	Growth rate of technological progress	12
g_K	Growth rate of capital	12
g_m	Growth rate of nominal money	9
g_N	Growth rate of population	12
g, g_y	Growth rate of output	9
$\bar{g}_y$	Normal rate of growth of output	9
H	High powered money/monetary base/ central bank money	4
	Also: Human capital	11
I	Fixed investment	3
$\bar{I}$	Investment, taken as exogenous	3
I_S	Inventory investment	3
IM	Imports	3
i	Nominal interest rate	4
i_1	One-year nominal interest rate	15
i_2	Two-year nominal interest rate	15
i^*	Foreign nominal interest rate	18
K	Capital stock	10

Symbol	Term	Introduced in Chapter
L	Labor force	2
M	Money stock (nominal)	4
M^d	Money demand (nominal)	4
M^s	Money supply (nominal)	4
μ	Markup of prices over wages	6
N	Employment	2
N_n	Natural level of employment	6
NX	Net exports	19
P	GDP deflator/CPI/price level	2
P^*	Foreign price level	18
π	Inflation	2
Π	Profit per unit of capital	16
Q	Real stock price	15
$\$Q$	Nominal stock price	15
R	Bank reserves	4
r	Real interest rate	14
S	Private saving	3
s	Private saving rate	11
T	Net taxes (taxes paid by consumers minus transfers)	3
Tr	Government transfers	26
θ	Reserve ratio of banks	4
U	Unemployment	2
u	Unemployment rate	2
u_n	Natural rate of unemployment	6
V	Present value of a sequence of real payments z	14
$\$V$	Present value of a sequence of nominal payments $\$z$	14
W	Nominal wage	6
Y	Real GDP/output/supply of goods	2
$\$Y$	Nominal GDP	2
Y_D	Disposable income	3
Y_L	Labor income	16
Y_n	Natural level of output	6
Y^*	Foreign output	19
X	Exports	3
Z	Demand for goods	3
z	Factors that affect the wage, given unemployment	6
z	Real payment	14
$\$Z$	Nominal payment	14

READ THIS LABEL AND THE AGREEMENT PRINTED ON THE LAST PAGE OF THE BOOK BEFORE OPENING THIS PACKAGE.

By opening this Software package, you accept the terms and conditions on this label and in the agreement. If you do not agree, DO NOT OPEN THE SOFTWARE PACKAGE. Return the sealed package to us within thirty (30) days [[for a full refund of any amount you paid for the software.]]

WARRANTY DISCLAIMERS AND REMEDY LIMITS

The enclosed software is distributed on an "AS IS" basis, WITH NO warranties. NEITHER THE COMPANY NOR ITS LICENSORS MAKE ANY REPRESENTATION, EITHER EXPRESS OR IMPLIED, WITH RESPECT TO THE SOFTWARE, ITS QUALITY, ACCURACY, OR FITNESS FOR A SPECIFIC PURPOSE. THE COMPANY AND ITS LICENSORS SHALL HAVE NO LIABILITY WITH RESPECT TO ANY LOSS OR DAMAGE CAUSED OR ALLEGED TO HAVE BEEN CAUSED DIRECTLY OR INDIRECTLY BY THE SOFTWARE. THIS INCLUDES, BUT IS NOT LIMITED TO, INTERRRUPTION OF SERVICE, LOSS OF DATA, LOSS OF CLASSROOM TIME, LOSS OF CONSULTING OR ANTICIPATORY PROFITS, OR CONSEQUENTIAL DAMAGES FROM USE OF THE SOFTWARE. If the disk medium is defective in materials or workmanship, you may return it for replacement within 30 days.